A HISTORY OF WESTERN MUSIC

Sixth Edition

A HISTORY OF WESTERN MUSIC

Sixth Edition

DONALD JAY GROUT
Late of Cornell University

CLAUDE V. PALISCA
Yale University

W. W. NORTON & COMPANY · NEW YORK · LONDON

Printed in the United States of America

The text of this book is composed in Minion
with the display set in Gill Sans
Composition by UG / GGS Information Services, Inc.
Manufacturing by Quebecor World
Book design by Mary McDonnell
Cover illustration: Georges Braque. *Musical Instruments* (detail). 1908. Private collection.

Sixth Edition

Library of Congress Cataloging-in-Publication Data
Grout, Donald Jay.
A history of western music/Donald Jay Grout, Claude V. Palisca—6th ed.
p. cm.
Includes bibliographical references and index.
ISBN 0-393-97527-4
1. Music—History and criticism. I. Palisca, Claude V.

ML160.G872 2001
780′.9—dc21

00-058411

W. W. Norton & Company, Inc., 500 Fifth Avenue, New York, N.Y. 10110
www.wwnorton.com

W. W. Norton & Company Ltd., Castle House, 75/76 Wells Street, London W1T 3QT

4 5 6 7 8 9 0

CONTENTS

MAPS

COLOR PLATES

EDITORIAL ADVISORY BOARD

PREFACE TO THE SIXTH EDITION

A new edition of a venerable text is an opportunity to make it worthy of continued veneration in a changing world. In 1980, we turned the Third Edition of Donald Jay Grout's *A History of Western Music* (HWM) from a one-volume history of music to a package of resources for teaching and learning that included a two-volume anthology and accompanying recordings. In my limited participation in that edition, I mainly contributed the brief analytical and contextual comments on the music of my then new *Norton Anthology of Western Music* (NAWM). The early music movement of the time, which gave birth to numerous professional and semi-professional ensembles, made hearing its varied and comprehensive repertory possible—even though we succeeded in obtaining only some licenses to the best performances for the accompanying recordings. But with each successive edition of NAWM the industry has responded more positively to our demands, and we now have some of the finest representative performances.

For the Fourth Edition (1988) of HWM I wrote extended commentaries on the *Anthology* selections and sequestered them in boxes where they would not interrupt the historical narrative. Donald J. Grout having sadly passed away in 1987 after a long illness, I thoroughly revised the first half of the book, profiting from the great progress made since 1960 in the study of medieval, Renaissance, and Baroque music. I integrated the bibliographies and the chronologies, previously located at the back of the book, with the content of the chapters. I also added "vignettes," in which composers, musicians, and observers comment characteristically and pointedly about the music of their time.

In the Fifth Edition (1996) the commentaries on the anthology selections migrated to NAWM. The convenience for those studying the scores and listening to the recordings made it a popular move. I rewrote much of the second half of HWM, taking advantage of the thriving scholarship of the 1980s and 1990s on the Classic and Romantic periods, and amplified coverage of the twentieth century. Altogether three chapters and part of a fourth now covered the last century, one of them, partly retrospective, devoted to American music. I restored the glossary, freshly rewritten, and indicated where the terms were used in the text. We added twelve color plates, illustrating parallel developments in the visual arts or showing music-making in its social context. The designer also introduced color in the body of the text, particularly for the new marginal headings that steer the browser to information in the text.

This present edition not only looks different but is improved in content and presentation. The entire book underwent critical review by a panel of experts. For the Sixth Edition of this text and the Fourth of the *Anthology*, the publisher accepted my suggestion of appointing an editorial advisory to appraise specific chapters. The names of the advisers are listed on page x. I am profoundly grateful to them for their conscientious critiques and recommendations on both the Fifth Edition and my draft of the sixth. I also received advice on Italian opera from James Hepokoski, to whom I owe special thanks. Much that is new in this edition was stimulated by this process, but they share no responsibility for any shortcomings that may still exist.

I continued in this edition to rewrite many passages and entire sections, taking recent research into account, striving for direct communication and a consistent style, toning down personal attitudes toward music and history, and curtailing discussions of peripheral problems. New illustrations and color plates have been added, and though a picture may be worth a thousand words, it usually takes a substantial caption to tell why it's worth so much. Timelines replace the chronologies; there are new vignettes; and historical maps, newly drawn, locate the important places that made music history. I am indebted to Kathryn Talalay, Norton's staff editor, for contributing to these improvements, and to Jan Hoeper for her organizational skills.

Recent recognition of the important roles that women have played in the history of music led me to give greater attention to their many accomplishments and contributions as both composers and performers. Their music is discussed here and also represented in NAWM.

A valuable enhancement begun with the Fifth Edition of HWM and the Third Edition of NAWM, J. Peter Burkholder's *Study and Listening Guide,* offers suggestions for study, outlines of chapter objectives and content, questions to ponder, review of terminology, exercises in analysis, and self-tests. A new ancillary publication, the *Instructor's Manual* compiled by Amy Edmonds, builds on the experience of a dedicated and innovative teacher.

Finally, a wealth of unique interactive materials designed specifically for use with HWM and NAWM is available through Norton's Web site, **www.wwnorton.com/grout.** The site is divided into two parts. The first, a download site, includes about seventy brief listening guides synchronized to the recordings. The second site, the *History of Western Music* webBOOK, offers students open access to chapter outlines, review quizzes, and a glossary that is linked to pictures and music. In addition, Peter Burkholder has designed a Web-based set of interactive listening exercises.

In fundamental ways, HWM remains the scholarly and comprehensive history of music that Donald Jay Grout set out to write in the 1950s. To be sure, the scope of what we teach and study under the heading of music history has broadened since Professor Grout wrote the first version of this book. The limits of Western music were generally agreed upon then, and hardly anyone doubted the value of studying its history. As populations everywhere have become more diverse, the relevance of the Western art tradition to the music that is practiced and heard daily has understandably been questioned. *Western Music* in our title, which motivated an Internet retailer to award it the distinction of "best-seller" in the category Country and Western Music, really acknowledges that the musical culture of Europe and the Americas is but one of several cultures whose distinguished histories deserve study. Teachers of music history have also recognized this and, sensitive to local interests and preferences, have stretched the horizons of their courses, particularly to embrace traditional ethnic musics, popular music, and jazz. Laudable as this practice is in the classroom, to follow their example and convert this book into a universal history of music would not only have been impractical, but would have robbed the text of the authority it has earned over the years. A book cannot take the place of a resourceful teacher facing a particular class. In this edition I continue to respect the limits set by the original author and editors and within these limits to aim for an honest and readable survey of the musical tradition we have known best.

We now have more reason than ever to address this tradition. The music discussed in *A History of Western Music* continues to engage new adherents in every corner of the globe, and some of its best interpreters are from non-Western countries. The range of music played and sung in concerts and heard in recordings throughout the world embraces much of the repertory considered here, from the first chapters to the last. That was not true in 1960, when very little early music was performed, and twentieth-century works were less accessible.

What radio stations call "classical music" is truly a global pursuit. This book, in one edition or other, has been or is being translated into Chinese, Dutch, French, Italian, Japanese, Korean, Latvian, Portuguese, Spanish, and Welsh. Its international English edition is widely read in the United Kingdom, Australia, and New Zealand. We have an obligation to inform this great diversity of readers about the best of this music.

Our title silently passes over the fact that in the past this book was concerned only with "art" music, admittedly a loose concept. Traditional or folk music, popular and entertainment music, jazz, rock, rap, and comparable manifestations are often artful, but we cannot do justice in these pages to this extended repertory, which deserves serious study in its own right. But the vernacular music of the United States, insofar as it has influenced and become a part of its concert music, receives attention in the final chapter, "The American Twentieth Century."

A reader who finds some of the earliest chapters an uphill battle should not hesitate to skip them until a later time, for example, to answer questions about the origin of the modes or to fill in the background on Renaissance humanism. The most technical discussions here and elsewhere in the book have been distinguished typographically, and they too may be safely skipped until a pertinent question arises.

Although I have purged the book of much unwanted detail, the abundance of information still overwhelms some undergraduates. How much they need to learn, they say, is not always clear. Certainly, they do not need to know many of the names, works, and facts. Teachers must guide their students' study and emphasize what is important. Marginal headings help the reader to skim and scan for topics. Although this volume is widely used as a textbook, it remains a viable history that reflects the richness and complexity of its subject. Facts that may not seem relevant at first reading or for a particular course or purpose may answer a question at another time. We want those who lack a library of reference books to keep it as a resource for years to come, long after a course is over.

Although the *Anthology* can stand alone, it preserves a close link to this book, since nearly every selection is discussed, often at some length, in HWM, and all are mentioned. Occasionally, when a musical example from NAWM appears in this text, the commentary in HWM may overlap or repeat what has been said in NAWM. The additional examples and their integration into the historical survey make HWM, too, more self-sufficient. The redundancy serves the pedagogical ends of reinforcement and review.

The entire musical content of the two volumes of NAWM is available in recorded form, on two sets of six compact disks each. A good number of selections and performances are new to this edition. They represent some of the best performers and ensembles working today. A core set of four compact disks is also available.

Norton's music editor, Michael Ochs, and his staff have been a constant source of ideas and support; I cannot thank them enough for their dedication.

I owe loving thanks to my wife, Elizabeth A. Keitel, for affectionately sharing our life and home with the inevitable physical and mental clutter of a compulsive author.

CLAUDE V. PALISCA
Hamden, Connecticut

ABBREVIATIONS

AIM	American Institute of Musicology; publications include CEKM, CMM, CSM, MD, MSD. For lists, see MD 42 (1988): 217–56.
AM	*Acta Musicologica,* 1929–.
AMM	Richard H. Hoppin, ed., *Anthology of Medieval Music* (New York: Norton, 1978).
CDMI	I *Classici della Musica Italiana,* 36 vols. (Milan: Istituto Editoriale Italiano, 1918–20; Società Anonima Notari la Santa, 1919–21).
CEKM	*Corpus of Early Keyboard Music,* AIM. 1963–.
CM	*Collegium Musicum* (New Haven, 1955–; second series, Madison, A-R Editions, 1969–).
CMI	I *Classici Musicali Italiani,* 15 vols. (Milan, 1941–43, 1956).
CMM	*Corpus mensurabilis musicae,* AIM, 1948–.
CSM	*Corpus scriptorum de musica,* AIM, 1950–.
DdT	*Denkmäler deutscher Tonkunst,* 65 vols. (Leipzig: Breitkopf & Härtel, 1892–1931; repr., Wiesbaden, 1957–61).
DTB	*Denkmäler deutscher Tonkunst, 2. Folge: Denkmäler der Tonkunst in Bayem,* 38 vols. (Braunschweig, 1900–38).
DTOe	*Denkmäler der Tonkunst in Oesterreich* (Vienna: Artaria, 1894–1904; Leipzig: Breitkopf & Härtel, 1905–13; Vienna: Universal, 1919–38; Graz: Akademische Druck- und Verlagsanstalt, 1966–).
EM	*Early Music,* 1973–.
EMH	*Early Music History,* 1981–.
EP	R. Eitner, ed., *Publikationen älterer praktischer und theoretischer Musikwerke, vorzugsweise des XV. und XVI. Jahrhunderts,* 29 vols. in 33 Jahrgänge (Berlin: Bahn & Liepmannssohn; Leipzig: Breitkopf & Härtel, 1873–1905; repr., 1967).
GLHWM	*Garland Library of the History of Western Music.*
GMB	Arnold Schering, ed., *Geschichte der Musik in Beispielen* (History of Music in Examples) (Leipzig: Breitkopf & Härtel, 1931).
HAM	Archibald T. Davison and Willi Apel, eds. *Historical Anthology of Music* (Cambridge, Mass.: Harvard University Press, 1950). Vol. 1: Oriental, Medieval, and Renaissance Music; Vol 2: Baroque, Rococo, and Pre-Classical Music.
HAMW	*Historical Anthology of Music by Women,* ed. James R. Briscoe (Bloomington: Indiana University Press, 1987).
JAMS	*Journal of the American Musicological Society,* 1948–.
JM	*Journal of Musicology,* 1982.
JMT	*Journal of Music Theory,* 1957–.
MB	*Musica Brittanica* (London: Stainer & Bell, 1951–).
MD	*Musica Disciplina,* 1946–.
MGG	*Die Musik in Geschichte und Gegenwart* (Kassel: Bärenreiter, 1949–86).
MM	Carl Parrish and John F. Ohl, eds., *Masterpieces of Music Before 1750* (New York: Norton, 1951).
ML	*Music and Letters,* 1920–.
MQ	*The Musical Quarterly,* 1915–.

MR	Gustave Reese, *Music in the Renaissance,* rev. ed. (New York: Norton, 1959).
MRM	Edward Lowinsky, ed., *Monuments of Renaissance Music* (Chicago: University of Chicago Press, 1964–).
MSD	*Musicological Studies and Documents,* AIM, 1951–.
NAWM	Claude V. Palisca, ed. *Norton Anthology of Western Music,* 3rd ed., 2 vols. (New York: Norton, 1996).
NG	*New Grove Dictionary of Music and Musicians,* ed. Stanley Sadie (London: Macmillan, 1980).
NOHM	*New Oxford History of Music* (London: Oxford University Press, 1954–).
OMM	Thomas Marrocco and Nicholas Sandon, eds., *Oxford Anthology of Medieval Music* (New York: Oxford University Press, 1977).
PAM	*Publikationen älterer Musik . . . bei der deutschen Musikgesellschaft* (Leipzig: Breitkopf & Härtel, 1926–40).
PMFC	*Polyphonic Music of the Fourteenth Century* (Monaco: Édition de l'Oiseau-Lyre, 1956–; repr. 1975).
PMMM	*Publications of Medieval Music, Manuscripts* (Brooklyn: Institute of Medieval Music, 1957–).
SR	Oliver Strunk, *Source Readings in Music History* (New York: Norton, 1950).
SRrev	Revised edition of Strunk, *Source Readings in Music History,* Leo Treitler, gen. ed. (New York: Norton, 1998). Also published as separate paperbacks, Vols. 1–7.
TEM	Carl Parrish, ed., *A Treasury of Early Music* (New York: Norton, 1958).

Pitch Designations

In this book, a note referred to without regard to its octave register is designated by a capital letter in italics *(A)*. A note in particular octave is designated in the following way:

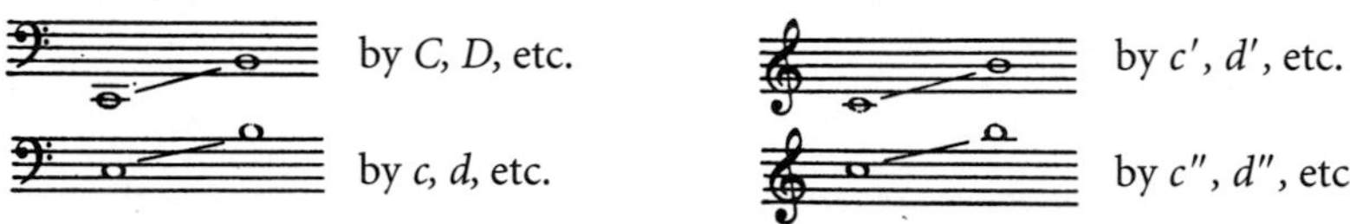

A HISTORY OF WESTERN MUSIC

Sixth Edition

CHAPTER 1

MUSICAL LIFE AND THOUGHT IN ANCIENT GREECE AND ROME

THE GREEK AND ROMAN HERITAGE

Western culture has undeniable ties to ancient Greece and Rome. Its ideals of beauty and art were rooted there. Its philosophy was founded on the precepts of Plato and Aristotle. And its literature, particularly European poetry and drama, was built on ancient Greek and Latin traditions. Since the Middle Ages, Europe (and later America) has turned to Greece and Rome for instruction and inspiration.

Western music has also drawn on the same sources, though not in such obvious ways as the visual arts, literature, history, philosophy, and government have, in part because very little of the music survived. Roman literature—Vergil, Ovid, Horace, Cicero—could be studied and read throughout the Middle Ages. In the fourteenth and fifteenth centuries, more Roman works came to light, and the surviving literature of Greece was gradually recovered. Medieval or Renaissance artists could study ancient sculpture and architecture and even imitate it; they had the actual statues and buildings or ruins to look at. But musicians of the Middle Ages did not have a single example of Greek or Roman music, and only a few ancient songs and hymns were identified during the Renaissance. We are somewhat better off today: about forty-five complete pieces or fragments of ancient music ranging from the third century B.C.E. to the fourth century C.E. have been recovered, all of them employing a system of ancient Greek musical notation. Some of these were composed during the period of Roman dominance but used Greek texts. Although no authentic settings of Latin texts survive, we know from written accounts, bas-reliefs, mosaics, paintings, and sculptures that music occupied an important place in Roman life.

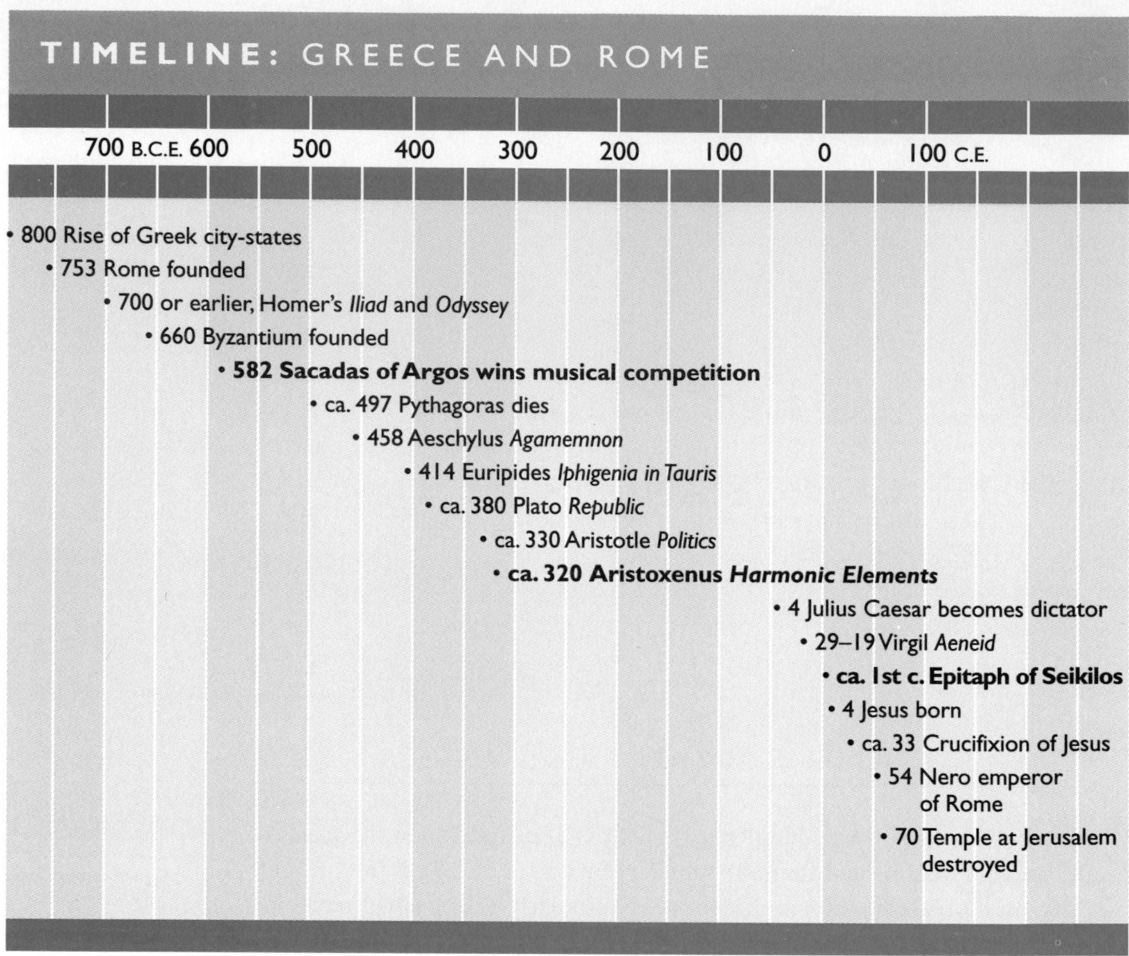

The music of the later Roman Empire left few traces, partly because the music itself was deliberately suppressed. Leaders of the early Christian church looked with horror on the theater, secular festivals, and pagan religious exercises in which music flourished. The church fathers wanted to blot out from memory the revels and rituals associated with Roman music.

Yet some features of ancient musical practice lived on in the Middle Ages, if only because banning them would have meant abolishing music itself. Furthermore, ancient music theory was the foundation of medieval theory and was part of most philosophical systems. So in order to understand medieval music, we must know something about the music of ancient peoples, and in particular about the musical practice and theory of the Greeks.

MUSIC IN ANCIENT GREEK LIFE AND THOUGHT

Music's power

In Greek mythology, music had a divine origin: its inventors and earliest practitioners were gods and demigods, such as Apollo, Amphion, and Orpheus. In this dim, prehistoric world, music had magic powers. People thought it could heal sickness, purify the body and mind, and work miracles in the realm of nature. Similar powers are attributed to music in the Hebrew Scriptures: we need only recall the stories of David curing Saul's madness by playing the harp (1 Samuel 16:14–23), or of the trumpet blasts and shouting that toppled the walls of Jericho (Joshua 6:12–20). At banquets in the Homeric age, bards sang long poems in praise of heroes (*Odyssey* 8.62–82).

Music in religion

From earliest times music was an inseparable part of religious ceremonies. In the cult of Apollo the lyre was the characteristic instrument; for followers of Dionysus it was the aulos. Both instruments probably came from Asia Minor. The lyre and its larger counterpart, the kithara, had five to seven strings (later as many as eleven). The instruments were played alone and to accompany the singing or recitation of epic poems. The aulos (sometimes incorrectly identified as a flute) was a single- or double-reed instrument, normally played with twin pipes. It was used in the worship of Dionysus to accompany the singing of poems called *dithyrambs*, forerunners of the Greek drama. The great tragedies of the classical age by Aeschylus, Sophocles, Euripides, and others have choruses and other musical portions that were accompanied by—or alternated with—the sounds of the aulos. The Greeks also had a wide array of percussion instruments and *psalteria*, string instruments plucked with the fingers rather than strummed with the plectrum, as were the lyre and kithara.

Lyre and kithara

Aulos

Pythic *nomos*

From the sixth century B.C.E. or even earlier, both the lyre and the aulos were independent solo instruments. An account of a musical competition held at the Pythian games in 582 B.C.E. tells of someone playing the *Nomos Pythicos*, a composition for the aulos that musically portrays the combat between Apollo and the serpent Python. Contests of kithara and aulos players, as well as festivals of instrumental and vocal music, became increasingly popular after the fifth century B.C.E. As instrumental music grew more independent, the number of virtuosos increased and the music itself became more complex and

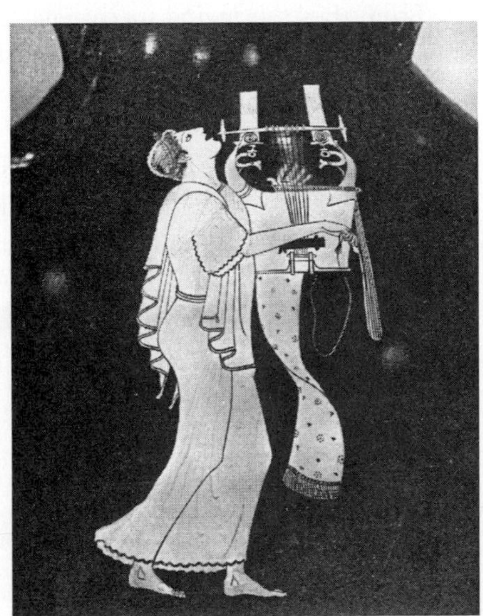

Kitharode singing to his own accompaniment on the kithara. His left hand, which supports the instrument with a sling (not visible), is damping some of the strings, while the right hand has apparently just swept over all the strings with the plectrum. A professional musician like this one wore a long, flowing robe (chiton) *and a mantle* (himation). *Detail of an Attic red-figured amphora from the fourth century* B.C.E., *attributed to the Berlin Painter.* (COURTESY, THE METROPOLITAN MUSEUM OF ART, FLETCHER FUND, 1956.)

showy. Whenever famous artists appeared thousands gathered to listen. The kitharodes (singers who accompanied themselves on the kithara) accumulated great wealth through their concert tours, particularly after they won fame by winning competitions. Among the musicians acclaimed for their recitals were a number of women, who were excluded by law from competing in the games, but special decrees gave exceptional performers the chance to be heard outside the framework of the contests. Women were limited to playing stringed instruments, since the aulos was considered suitable only to slaves, courtesans, and entertainers.

Aristotle on music education

Sons of leading citizens, taught to play the aulos or kithara as part of their upbringing, sometimes aspired to reach the level of the virtuosos, as Nero later did in Rome. But Aristotle warned against too much professional training in general music education:

> The right measure will be attained if students of music stop short of the arts which are practiced in professional contests, and do not seek to acquire those fantastic marvels of execution which are now the fashion in such contests, and from these have passed into education. Let the young practice even such music as we have prescribed, only until they are able to feel delight in noble melodies and rhythms, and not merely in that common part of music in which every slave or child and even some animals find pleasure.[1]

Surviving music

Most surviving Greek music comes from relatively late periods. The chief examples are a fragment of a chorus from Euripides' *Orestes* (lines 338–44) from a papyrus of about 200 B.C.E., the music possibly by Euripides himself (NAWM 2[2]; CD 1 [2]); a fragment from Euripides' *Iphigenia in Aulis* (lines 783–93); two Delphic hymns to Apollo, fairly complete, the second of which is from 128–27 B.C.E.; an epigram on a tombstone from around the first century C.E. (NAWM 1; CD 1 [1] ◇1◇); and the *Hymn to Nemesis*, *Hymn to the Sun*, and *Hymn to the Muse Calliope* by Mesomedes of Crete from the second century C.E.

Characteristics

From these surviving specimens and from what was written about Greek music, we may gather that it resembled the music of the early Middle Ages. It was primarily *monophonic*—that is, melody without harmony or counterpoint—but instruments often embellished the melody while a soloist or an ensemble sang it, thus creating *heterophony*. Yet neither heterophony nor the inevitable singing in octaves, as when men and boys took part, could be termed polyphony of independent parts, which would develop later. The melody and rhythm of Greek music were too intimately bound up with the melody and rhythm of poetry, and there is no evidence of any continuity in practice from the Greeks to the early Christians.

1. Aristotle *Politics* 8.6 (1341a), trans. B. Jowett, in R. McKeon, ed., *The Basic Works of Aristotle* (New York, 1941), p. 1313. Cf. also Plato *Laws* 2 (669e and 670a).
2. The acronym NAWM, which is used throughout this edition, refers to the *Norton Anthology of Western Music*, 4th edition, ed. Claude V. Palisca (New York: Norton, 2001).

■ *A woman playing the double-aulos in a drinking scene. Usually a single-reed but sometimes a double-reed instrument, the aulos was typically played in pairs. Red-figured drinking cup ascribed to the Attic vase painter Oltos, 525–500* B.C.E. *(MADRID, MUSEO ARQUEOLOGICO NACIONAL)*

Greek Musical Thought

Greek theory, on the other hand, did affect the music of western Europe in the Middle Ages. We know much more about Greek musical thought than about the music itself. There were two kinds of theoretical writings: (1) doctrines on the nature of music, its place in the cosmos, its effects, and its proper uses in human society; and (2) systematic descriptions of the materials and patterns of musical composition. In both the philosophy and the science of music, the Greeks achieved insights and formulated principles that have survived to this day. Of course, Greek music theory continued to evolve from the time of its legendary founder, Pythagoras (ca. 500 B.C.E.), to Aristides Quintilianus (fourth century C.E.), its last important writer. The following, necessarily simplified, emphasizes the features that were most characteristic and important for the later history of Western music.

Music and number

The word *music* had a much wider meaning to the Greeks than it has to us. In the teachings of Pythagoras and his followers, music was inseparable from numbers, which were thought to be the key to the entire spiritual and physical universe. So the system of musical sounds and rhythms, being ordered by numbers, exemplified the harmony of the cosmos and corresponded to it. This doctrine was thoroughly and systematically explained by Plato in the *Timaeus*, the most widely known of his dialogues in the Middle Ages, and in his *Republic*. Plato's views on the nature and uses of music profoundly influenced medieval and Renaissance speculations about music and its place in education.

Plato

Ptolemy

For some Greek thinkers, music also had a close connection with astronomy. Indeed, Claudius Ptolemy (second century C.E.), the most systematic of the ancient music theorists, was also the leading astronomer of antiquity. Mathematical laws were thought to underlie the systems both of musical intervals and of the heavenly bodies, and certain modes and even certain notes were believed to correspond with particular planets, their distances from each other, and their movements. The idea was given poetic form by Plato[3] in the myth of

3. Plato *Republic* 10 (617).

the "music of the spheres," the unheard music produced by the revolutions of the planets; the notion was invoked by writers on music throughout the Middle Ages and later, including Shakespeare and Milton.

Union of music and poetry

The close union of music and poetry is another measure of the Greeks' broad conception of music. For them the two were practically synonymous. Plato defined song (*melos*) as a blend of speech, rhythm, and "harmony" (a complex of relationships of pitches in a melody).[4] "Lyric" poetry meant poetry sung to the lyre; "tragedy" incorporates the noun *ōdē*, "the art of singing."

Many other Greek words that indicated the different kinds of poetry, such as *hymn*, were musical terms. In his *Poetics*, Aristotle, after enumerating, melody, rhythm, and language as the elements of poetry, goes on to say: "There is another art which imitates by means of language alone, and that either in prose or verse . . . but this has hitherto been without a name."[5] The Greeks did not have a word for artful speech that did not include music.

The Doctrine of *Ethos*

Greek writers believed that music possessed moral qualities and could affect character and behavior. This idea fit into the Pythagorean view of music as a system of pitch and rhythm ruled by the same mathematical laws that operated in the visible and invisible world. The human soul was seen as a composite that was kept in harmony by numerical relationships. Music not only reflected this orderly system but also penetrated the soul, and, indeed, the inanimate world. From this it followed that the legendary musicians of mythology could perform miracles.

Theory of imitation

Aristotle explained through his doctrine of imitation how music could affect behavior.[6] Music, he wrote, imitates the passions or states of the soul, such as gentleness, anger, courage, temperance, and their opposites. Music that imitates a certain passion arouses that same passion in the listener. Habitual listening to music that rouses ignoble passions distorts a person's character. In short, the wrong kind of music makes the wrong kind of person, and the right kind tends to make the right kind of person.[7]

Music in education

Plato and Aristotle agreed that the "right" kind of person could be molded through a system of public education that stressed gymnastics to discipline the body and music to discipline the mind. In his *Republic*, written about 380 B.C.E., Plato insists that these two educational components must be balanced, for too much music makes a man effeminate or neurotic while too much gymnastics makes him uncivilized, violent, and ignorant. "He who mingles music with gymnastics in the fairest proportions, and best accommodates them to the soul, may be rightly called the true musician."[8] But only certain music is

4. Plato *Republic* 3 (398c).
5. Aristotle *Poetics* 1 (1447a–b), trans. S. H. Butcher, in *Aristotle's Theory of Poetry and Fine Art* (New York: Dover, 1951), p. 9.
6. Aristotle *Politics* 8 (1340a–b); cf. Plato *Laws* 2 (665–70c).
7. Also see Plato *Republic* 3 (401d–e).
8. Plato *Republic* 3 (412a).

BOETHIUS TELLS HOW PYTHAGORAS DISCOVERED THE RATIOS OF THE CONSONANCES

For some time Pythagoras was seeking a way to acquire, through reason, full and accurate knowledge of the criteria for consonances. In the meantime, by a kind of divine will, while passing the workshop of blacksmiths, he overheard the beating of hammers somehow emit a single consonance from differing sounds. Thus in the presence of what he had long sought, he approached the activity spellbound. Reflecting for a time, he decided that the strength of the men hammering caused the diversity of sounds, and in order to prove this more clearly, he commanded them to exchange hammers among themselves. But the property of sounds did not rest in the muscles of the men; rather, it followed the exchanged hammers. When he observed this, he examined the weight of the hammers. There happened to be five hammers, and those that sounded together the consonance of the octave were found to be double in weight. Pythagoras determined further that the one which weighed twice the second was in the ratio 4:3 with another, with which it sounded a diatessaron (fourth). Then he found that the same double of the second formed the ratio 3:2 with still another, and that it joined with it in the consonance of the diapente (fifth).

Adapted from Boethius, *The Fundamentals of Music*, trans. with intro. and notes by Calvin M. Bower (New Haven: Yale University Press, 1989), Book 1, Chapter 10, p. 18.

deemed suitable. Those being trained to govern should avoid melodies expressing softness and indolence. He recommended two modes, or styles of song, the Dorian and Phrygian, because they fostered the virtues of temperance and courage. He excluded other modes and deplored current styles that resorted to a multiplicity of notes, complex scales, and the mixing of incompatible genres, rhythms, and instruments.[9] Musical conventions, once established, must not be changed, for lawlessness in art and education inevitably leads to license in manners and anarchy in society.[10] The political maxim "Let me make the songs of a nation and I care not who makes its laws" was a pun on the word *nomos*, which meant "custom" or "law" but also designated the melodic scheme of a piece.[11] Aristotle, in his *Politics* (about 330 B.C.E.), was less restrictive than Plato about particular rhythms and modes. He held that music could be used for amusement and intellectual enjoyment as well as for education. He also believed that emotions like pity and fear could be purged by inducing them in people through music and drama.[12]

9. Plato *Republic* 3 (398c–399e); also *Laws* 7 (812c–813a).
10. Plato *Republic* 4 (424c); also *Laws* 3 (700b–e).
11. Plato *Laws* 7 (799e–800b).
12. Aristotle *Politics* 8 (1339b–1340a).

THE GREEK MUSICAL SYSTEM

Harmonics

Harmonics, or the study of matters concerning pitch, traditionally consisted of seven topics: notes, intervals, genera, scale systems, tonoi, modulation, and melodic composition. They are listed by Cleonides (author of uncertain date, between the second and fourth centuries C.E.)[13] in his treatise on the theory of Aristoxenus and his school. Aristoxenus himself, in his *Harmonic Elements*

13. His *Harmonic Introduction* is translated in Oliver Strunk and Leo Treitler, gen. eds., *Source Readings*, rev. ed. (hereafter abbreviated SRrev; New York: Norton, 1998) 1, *Greek Views of Music*, ed. Thomas J. Mathiesen, pp. 35–46.

GREEK MUSIC THEORY IN DEPTH

Genera

Greek music theory described three *genera* (classes) of tetrachord: the *diatonic, chromatic,* and *enharmonic.* The bounding notes of the tetrachord were considered stable in pitch, whereas the two middle notes could be located at suitable points within the continuum between the outer pitches. The lowest interval was normally the smallest, the highest interval the largest (Examples 1.1a, b, c). In the diatonic, the two top intervals were whole tones and the bottom one a semitone. In the chromatic the top interval was a semiditone (minor third) and the two lower intervals, making up a *pyknon* (dense region), were semitones. In the enharmonic, the top interval was a ditone (major third) and the lower two intervals of the *pyknon* were smaller than semitones, possibly quarter tones. All these components of the tetrachord could vary slightly in size, and this variety gave rise to "shades" within the genera.

Example 1.1 *Tetrachords*

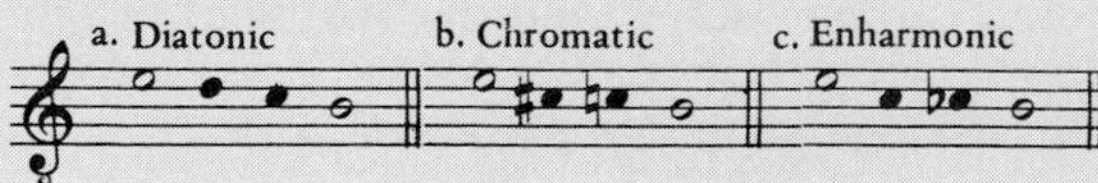

Aristoxenus

Aristoxenus maintained that the true way to determine the size of intervals was by ear, not by numerical ratio, as the followers of Pythagoras taught. We can infer from Aristoxenus' descriptions and from accounts by later theorists that the ancient Greeks, like most Eastern peoples to the present day, commonly made use of intervals smaller than the semitone.

Tetrachord names

Four tetrachords were named according to their position. *Hyperbolaion,* literally "of the extremes," is the tetrachord encompassing the highest notes. The name of the next tetrachord, *diezeugmenon,* comes from the fact that a whole-tone interval separates it from the middle tetrachord, the *meson,* and for that reason is called disjunct (in Greek, *diazeuxis* with respect to the *mese*). Below the *meson* were the tetrachords *hypaton,* the "first" tetrachord, and the *proslambanomenos,* an "added" note that completed the

Tetrachord	Note	Position	Tetrachord
	a′	Nete	
Hyperbolaion	*g′*	Paranete	
	f′	Trite	
	e′	Nete	
	d′	Paranete	
	c′	Trite	Diezeugmenon
	b	Paramese	
		Disjunction	
	a	Mese	
Meson	*g*	Lichanos	
	f	Parhypate	
	e	Hypate	
	d	Lichanos	
	c	Parhypate	Hypaton
	B	Hypate	
		Disjunction	
	A	Proslambanomenos	

two octaves. (The pitches in the chart above are purely conventional. The Greeks were not concerned with any absolute pitch in their theory.)

This system came to be called the Greater Perfect System. (See Example 1.2.) The theorists also recognized a *synemmenon* (conjunct) tetrachord that could take the place of the *diezeugmenon* and *hyperbolaion* tetrachords. In this case, the *mese* served as a common note, and the *synemmenon* tetrachord added the trite (b♭), paranete (c′), and nete (d′). All five tetrachords considered together comprised an "Immutable System."

Note names

Each of the notes had a double name, in which the first word gave the position of the note in its tetrachord, and the second word was the name of the tetrachord itself. (For example, *a″*,[14] the highest note in the Hyperbolaion tetrachord, was called *nete hyperbolaion.*) Some of the notes were named from the position of the hand and fingers when playing the lyre, others from their place in the system. *Lichanos* means "index finger" or "forefinger." *Hypate* was named from being the first in the hypaton and meson tetrachords. *Nete* was so named from *neatos,* "the last."

Example 1.2 *The Greater Perfect System*

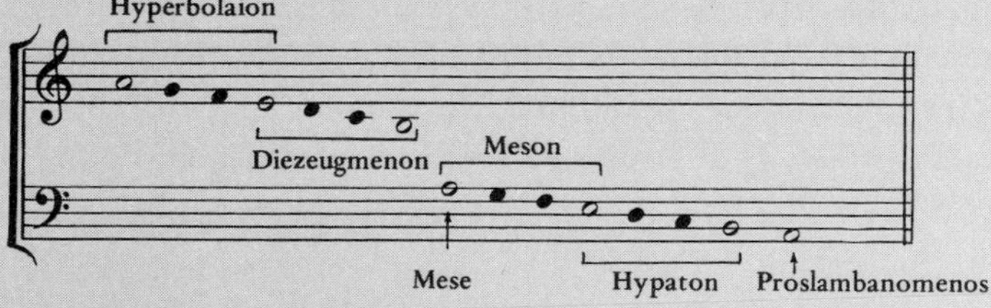

14. See *Pitch designations,* p. xvi

Shades

In Example 1.2 the outer or fixed tones of the tetrachords have been rendered in modern notation with open (white) notes. The two inner tones of each tetrachord (shown in black notes) could, as was explained above, be altered in pitch to produce the various shades and the enharmonic and chromatic genera. But regardless of pitch modification, these notes retained the same names they had in the diatonic genus (for example, *mese*, *lichanos*, *parhypate*, and *hypate*).

Tonoi

The topic of *tonoi* generated disagreement among the ancient writers. This is not surprising, because the tonoi (plural of *tonos*) were not theoretical pre-compositional constructions but a means of organizing melody, and melodic practices differed widely over the geographical and chronological range of Greek culture. Names such as Dorian, Ionian, and Aeolian given to the tonoi referred originally to the styles of music practiced in different regions. As one historian of Greek music has summarized:

> Ancient Greek music included the Ionian (that is, Asian) epic chants of Homer and the rhapsodes, the Aeolic (Greek islander) songs of Sappho and Alcaeus, the Dorian (Southern Greek) lyrics of Pindar (epinician poet [maker of triumphal or victory songs]), the plays of Aeschylus, Sophocles, Euripides (the tragic poets), and Aristophanes (the comic poet), the Hellenistic Delphic (Northern Greek) paeans to Apollo, the funerary, pagan, Seikilos inscription from the first century, a "Christian hymn" from the fourth, and the rest of an entire corpus, almost all of it lost, of Greek music composed without, and then with, the aid of notation and technical schooling throughout the period of some 1,200 years from Homer to Boethius.[15]

Aristoxenus compared the disagreements about the number and pitch of the tonoi to the disparities between the calendars of Corinth and Athens.

Cleonides on tonoi

His own view has not survived, but Cleonides' exposition is perhaps derived from it. The word *tonos* (tone), he wrote, has four meanings: note, interval, region of the voice, and pitch. *Tonos* is used to describe the region of the voice—that is, its overall height or depth of pitch—when the word is combined with an ethnic name, as in "Dorian tonos" or "Phrygian tonos." Cleonides adds that Aristoxenus recognized thirteen tonoi; he then names them, showing that there is one starting on each semitone of an octave, including the boundary notes, adding up to thirteen.

Species of consonances

Cleonides also discusses the species of consonances, observing that there are three species of the fourth, four species of the fifth, and seven of the octave. That is to say, the tones and semitones (or lesser intervals) could be arranged in one way fewer than the number of steps contained in the interval. (T = whole tone and s = semitone.) The diatonic fourth could ascend s–T–T (as *B–c–d–e*), T–T–s (as *c–d–e–f*), and T–s–T (as *d–e–f–g*).

15. Jon Solomon, "Towards a History of Tonoi," JM 3 (1984):242–51. See also the other papers in this symposium, "The Ancient Harmoniai, Tonoi, and Octave Species in Theory and Practice," ibid., pp. 221–86.

There were similar species of the chromatic and enharmonic fourth, and of the fifth and octave. To the species of octave he gave the ethnic names such as Dorian and Phrygian, and showed that they could be represented as segments of the Greater Perfect System in its natural form. So the Mixolydian octave species may be represented by *B–b′*, the Lydian by *c–c′*, the Phrygian by *d–d′*, the Dorian by *e–e′*, up to the Hypodorian by *a–a′*. Thus represented, the octave species look and sound like an ascending series of modes.

Names of octave species

Later authors state that two higher tonoi were added by the "younger musicians," and in fact Alypius (ca. fourth or fifth century C.E.) gave tables of notation for fifteen tonoi. The tables show that each tonos had the structure of the Immutable System, with each (except for the first, of course) higher than its lower neighbor by a semitone. Such a system leads to an overall range of more than three octaves between the bottom note of the lowest tonos and the uppermost note of the highest tonos. Ptolemy, however, believed only seven tonoi were needed, because he speculated that the purpose of the tonoi was to permit music to be sung or played within the limited range of a voice or instrument. As there were only seven species of the octave, the complicated system of tonoi could be reduced to seven. In fact, Cleonides' names for the seven octave species coincide with Ptolemy's names for the tonoi that produce them in his system (see Example 1.3).

Ptolemy's Dorian tonos falls in the middle of the system. It was a natural scale, which we would notate without accidentals. The Dorian mese was in the middle of the two-octave system; a whole tone above that was the Phrygian mese, a whole tone above that the Lydian's, and a semitone higher the Mixolydian's. A half step down from the Dorian mese was the Hypolydian's, a whole step down from that was the Hypophrygian's, a whole step from it the Hypodorian's. Whereas Alypius represented in letter notation the entire constitution of fifteen notes transposed up and down, Ptolemy regarded the bounds of the voice as confined to two octaves, so that the only tonos that could fit within the space of the complete Greater Perfect System in its normal order was the Dorian (see Example 1.3). Tonoi higher than the Dorian were missing notes at the top and had superfluous notes at the bottom, while the contrary was true of those lower than Dorian. The central octave contained the *mesai* (plural of mese) of all the tonoi. Thus *d* was the mese of the Mixolydian, *c♯* the mese of the Lydian, and so on. These were mesai by virtue of their function in the transposition of the Greater Perfect System, whereas the *thetic*, or fixed, mese remained always in the central position. Imagine a harp of fifteen strings, each string with its proper name and thetic position, such as mese or paramese diezeugmenon, which retains its name even if a different function is assigned to it or if it is slightly retuned. Thus the Phrygian functional mese may be placed on *b*, or thetic paramese, a whole step above the natural, thetic, or Dorian mese *a*.

Ptolemy's seven tonoi

Ptolemy's argument for replacing the system of fifteen tonoi with his system of seven tonoi rested on the belief that height of pitch (or what we call register) was not the only important source of variety and expression in music. Rather, the arrangement of intervals within a vocal register was

Example 1.3 *Cleonides' System of Octave-Species and Ptolemy's System of Tonoi*

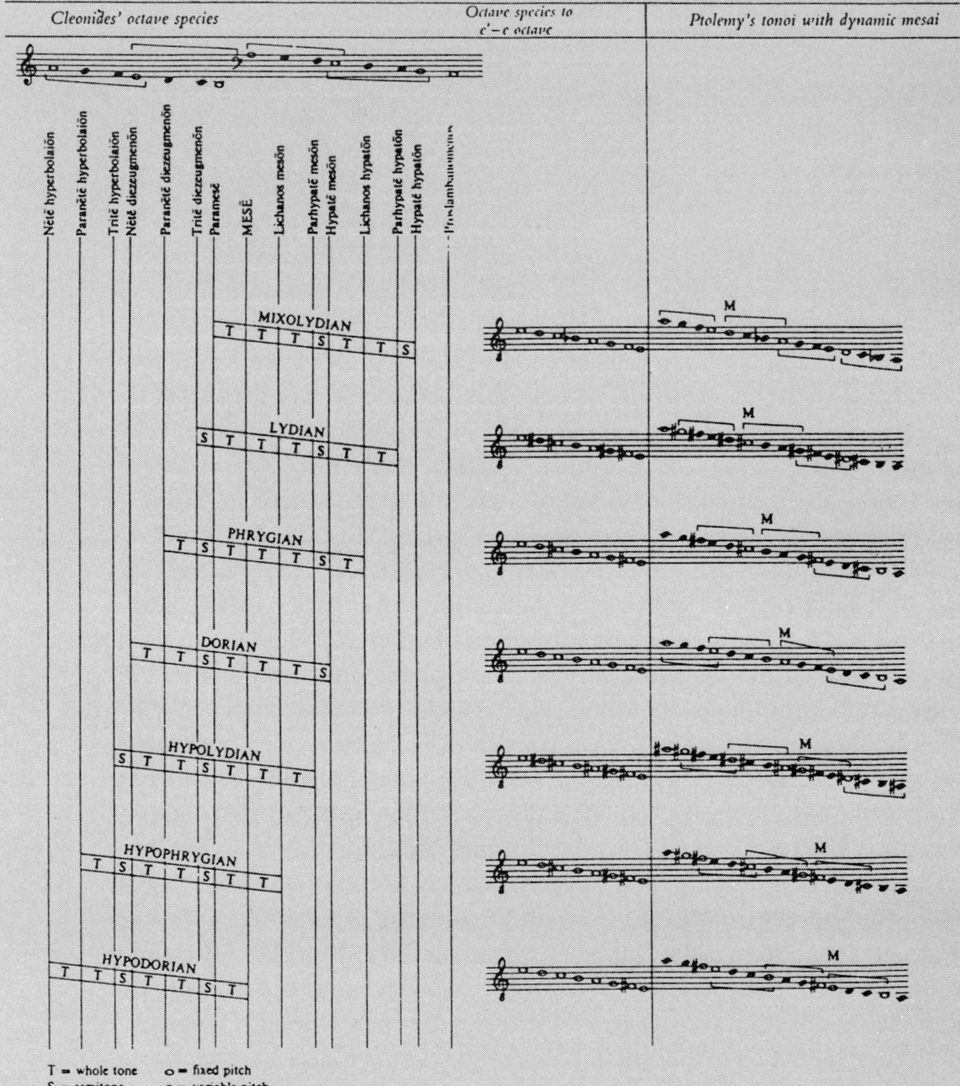

From C. Palisca, "Theory and Theorists," *The New Grove Dictionary of Music and Musicians,* 1980; reprinted with the kind permission of Stanley Sadie, ed.

much more important. In fact, he disparaged the system of fifteen tonoi, because a shift from one tonos to another in this system left the melody unchanged and merely moved it up or down in register. In his system, however, a shift from one tonos to another could actually alter the intervallic structure of the melody and the functional meaning of each note. These changes could also change the character (*ethos*) of the melody. While

Ptolemy's system is ingenious, there is little evidence in the surviving fragments that it reflects actual practice.

Aristotle on harmoniai

We may now consider what Plato and Aristotle meant by a *harmonia*, which is usually translated "mode." It must be remembered that they were writing about the music of a period much earlier than the theoretical expositions utilized above. Aristotle stated:

> The musical modes differ essentially from one another, and those who hear them are differently affected by each. Some of them make men sad and grave, like the so-called Mixolydian; others enfeeble the mind, like the relaxed modes; another, again, produces a moderate and settled temper, which appears to be the peculiar effect of the Dorian; the Phrygian inspires enthusiasm.[16]

Emotional character

Does the settled pattern of tones and semitones of the Dorian octave species or harmonia have the moderating effect Aristotle describes? Or is it the centrality of the Dorian octave *e–e'* in the Greater Perfect System, which locates melodies in this tonos in the middle of the masculine pitch range? It may be a little of each, but rather than anything so technical and specific, Aristotle probably had in mind the general expressive quality of the melodies and melodic turns characteristic of a certain mode; and he clearly connects with these the particular rhythms and poetic genres associated with that mode.

There may have been other associations, neither poetic nor musical, such as traditions, customs, and acquired attitudes toward different types of melody. It is also possible that originally the names "Dorian," "Phrygian," and the others may have referred to particular styles of music or manners of performance characteristic of various ethnic groups.

Despite the contradictions and vagueness of the ancient writings about music, there are striking consistencies between the theoretical precepts from Aristoxenus to Alypius and the musical examples that survive. Let us look at two of them: the Seikilos song (NAWM 1; CD 1 [1] ⟨1⟩) and a chorus from the *Orestes* of Euripides (NAWM 2; CD 1 [2]).

Seikilos song

The song inscribed in a tomb stele, or tombstone, probably set up by Seikilos and dating from around the first century C.E., is of particular interest because of its clear rhythmic notation. Marks above the alphabetical signs for the notes indicate whether the normal duration of a syllable is to be doubled or tripled. Every note of the octave *e–e'*, with *f* and *c'* sharped (see Example 1.4), is in the song, so that the octave species is unambiguously identifiable as that called Phrygian by Cleonides, equivalent to the D-octave on the white keys of a piano.

16. *Politics* 8 (1340a). Compare Plato *Republic* 3 (398ff).

Example 1.4 *Seikilos Song, Transcription*

As long as you live, be lighthearted
Let nothing trouble you. Life is only too short, and time takes its toll.

Source: From Thomas J. Mathiesen, *Apollo's Lyre: Greek Music and Music Theory in Antiquity and the Middle Ages* (Lincoln: University of Nebraska Press, 1999), p. 149.

Euripides fragment

The fragment of the chorus from Euripides' *Orestes* (NAWM 2) is written on a papyrus from the third to the second century B.C.E. The tragedy has been dated 408 B.C.E. It is possible that the music was composed by Euripides himself, who was renowned for his musical settings. The example is particularly interesting because the notation calls for either the enharmonic or chromatic genus along with the diatonic. Some instrumental notes punctu-

■ *Tomb stele from Aiden, near Tralles, Asia Minor. It bears an epitaph with pitch and rhythm notation, probably first century C.E. See the transcription in NAWM 1.* *(COPENHAGEN, NATIONAL MUSEUM, INVENTORY NO. 14897)*

ate the lines of the melody. This chorus is a *stasimon*, an ode sung while the chorus remained fixed in the *orchestra*, a semicircular rim between the stage and the benches of the spectators. The papyrus contains seven lines with musical notation, but only the middle of each of the seven lines survives.

Stasimon

In this stasimon, the chorus of women of Argos implore the gods to have mercy for Orestes, who, six days before the play began, murdered his mother, Clytemnestra. He had plotted with his sister Electra to punish their mother for infidelity to their father, Agamemnon. The chorus begs that Orestes be released from the madness that has overwhelmed him since the murder. The rhythm of the poetry, and therefore of the music, is dominated by the dochmiac foot, which was used in Greek tragedy in passages of intense agitation and grief. The dochmiac combines three long with two short syllables, and often, as here, a long syllable is resolved into two short ones.

Orestes

(ca. 330 B.C.E.), discussed each of these topics at length. He distinguished between two kinds of movement of the human voice: the *continuous*, in which the voice glides up and down as it does in speech, without lingering on a pitch; and the *diastematic*, in which pitches are sustained and discrete intervals are perceptible between them. Intervals, such as tones, semitones, and ditones (thirds), were combined into systems or scales. The principal building block of the octave or double-octave scales was the tetrachord, made up of four notes spanning a diatessaron (fourth). The fourth, fifth, and octave were recognized early as consonances. Legend tells us that Pythagoras discovered their ratios when he heard hammers of different sizes pounding on an anvil at a blacksmith shop (see vignette). More likely, he observed that when a string was divided, segments whose lengths were in the simple ratios of 2:1 sound an octave, 3:2 a fifth, and 4:3 a fourth.

MUSIC IN ANCIENT ROME

We do not know whether the Romans made any significant contributions to the theory or practice of music. They took their art music from Greece, especially after the Greek islands became a Roman province in 146 B.C.E. It is possible that the imported Greek culture replaced an unknown Etruscan or Italian music. The *tibia* (the Roman version of the aulos) and its players, called *tibicines*, occupied an important place in religious rites, military music, and theatrical performances. Several brass instruments were also prominent. The *tuba*, a long straight trumpet derived from the Etruscans, was also used in religious, state, and military ceremonies. The most characteristic instruments were a large G-shaped circular horn called the *cornu* and a smaller version, the *buccina*. Music must have been part of almost all public manifestations. But it also had a place in private entertainment and education. Cicero, Quintilian,

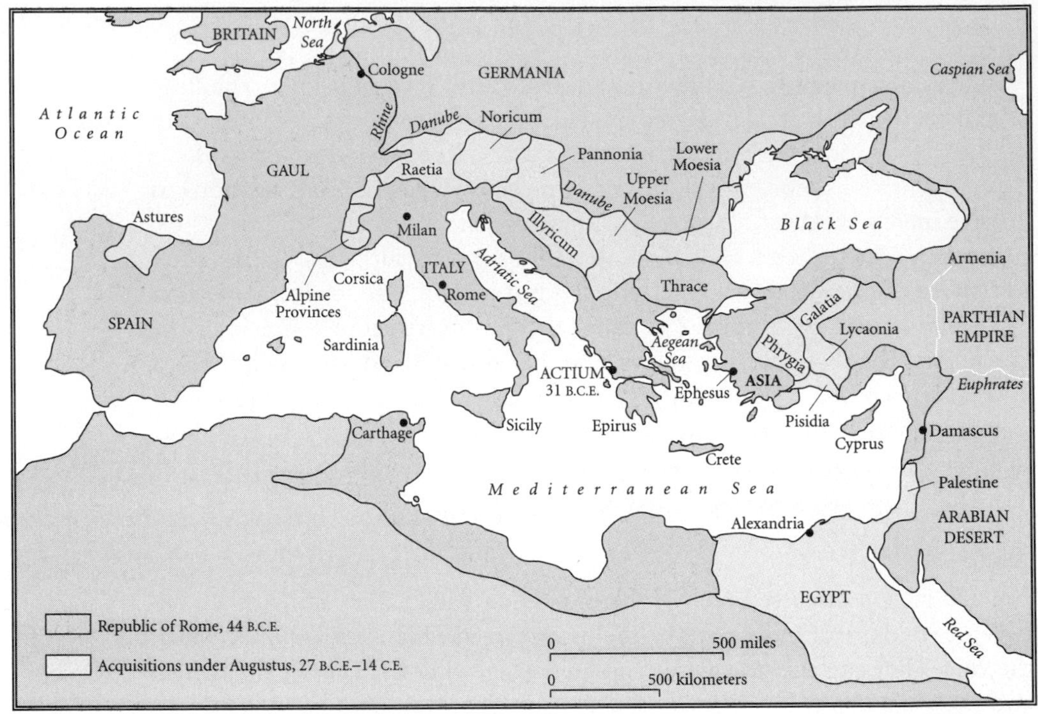

■ *The Roman Empire at the death of Augustus in 14* C.E.

and other writers make it clear that cultivated people were supposed to be educated in music, just as they were expected to know Greek.

During the great days of the Roman Empire (the first and second centuries), art, architecture, music, philosophy, new religious rites, and many other aspects of Greek culture were imported from the Hellenistic world. Ancient writers tell of famous virtuosos, large choruses and orchestras, and grandiose musical festivals and competitions. Many of the emperors supported and cultivated music; Nero even aspired to personal fame as a musician. But with the economic decline of the empire in the third and fourth centuries, the production of music on the large and expensive scale of earlier days ceased.

The ancient heritage

To summarize: although many details are uncertain, we know that in the ancient world (1) music consisted essentially of pure, unencumbered melodic lines; (2) melody was intimately linked with the rhythm and meter of words; (3) musicians did not read from notation; performers relied on their memories and knowledge of traditional musical formulas and conventions; (4) philosophers conceived of music as an orderly system interlocked with the system of nature and as a force in human thought and conduct; (5) a scientifically founded acoustical theory developed; (6) scales were built up from tetrachords; and (7) theorists developed sophisticated musical terminology.

The last three elements of this heritage (Nos. 5, 6, and 7) were specifically Greek; the others were common in the ancient world. The West absorbed it, if

■ *Roman funeral procession on a sarcophagus relief from Amiternum, end of first century* B.C.E. *In the top row are two players of the cornu and one of the lituus, both Etruscan-Roman brass instruments. Before them are four players of the tibia, which was similar to the Greek aulos.* (AQUILA, MUSEO CIVICO)

incompletely and imperfectly, through the Christian Church, the writings of the church fathers, and early medieval scholarly treatises that dealt with music along with a multitude of other subjects.

THE EARLY CHRISTIAN CHURCH

Rome's decline

Anyone living in a fifth-century province of the Roman Empire might have seen roads fallen into disuse, ruined temples and arenas that had once held throngs, and life becoming poorer, more insecure, and more brutish. Rome, which had in the time of its greatness imposed peace on most of western Europe and on large parts of Africa and Asia as well, had grown weak and unable to defend itself. Invaders poured in from the north and east, and the common civilization of Europe was splintering into fragments that would take many centuries to reform gradually into our modern nations.

While Rome declined as an empire, the Christian Church quietly moved forward. Until the tenth century it was the main—and often the only—unifying force and channel of culture in Europe. Despite three hundred years of sporadic persecution, the earliest Christian communities grew steadily and spread their faith to all parts of the empire. Emperor Constantine converted to Christianity in 312 and made it the religion of the imperial family. In 395 the political unity of the ancient world was formally broken up by the division into Eastern and Western Empires, with capitals at Byzantium (modern-day Istanbul) and Rome. When the last Western emperor finally stepped down from his throne in 476 after a terrible century of wars and invasions, the papal power was already firmly enough established for the church to take over Rome's mission of civilizing and unifying the people under its sway.

Constantine

During its first two or three centuries, the Christian Church must have absorbed some features from the music of Greece and from the mixed Oriental-

Hellenistic societies around the eastern Mediterranean. But the church definitely rejected the idea of cultivating music purely for enjoyment, and it disdained the forms and types of music connected with great public spectacles such as festivals, competitions, and dramatic performances, as well as the music of more intimate convivial occasions. It was not that leaders of the church disliked the music itself, but that they wanted to wean converts away from everything associated with their pagan past, even banning, for a time, all instrumental music.

The Judaic Heritage

Music historians long held that the ancient Christians modeled their worship services on those of the Jewish synagogue. Scholars now believe that church and synagogue liturgies developed independently. Indeed, the early Christians may have deliberately avoided imitating Jewish services so as to highlight the distinct character of their beliefs and rituals. The religious functions of the early synagogue differed greatly from those of the Jewish Temple. The second Temple of Jerusalem, which existed on the site of the original Temple of Solomon from 539 B.C.E. until its destruction by the Romans in 70 C.E., was a place for public worship. The service consisted mainly of a sacrifice, usually of a lamb; the ritual was performed by priests, assisted by Levites—including musicians—and witnessed by lay Israelite citizens. Depending on the occasion, priests, and even lay worshipers, ate some of the "burned" animal. These sacrifices were celebrated twice daily, with additional services on Sabbaths and festivals. In the course of the ritual, a choir of at least twelve Levites sang a psalm specific for each day of the week, accompanied by stringed instruments. On important festivals, such as the eve of Passover, Psalms 113 to 118, which have Alleluia refrains, were sung while people offered their personal sacrifices; a wind instrument resembling an aulos joined the string accompaniment. Individuals also prayed at the Temple, but most prayer was done at home or outdoors while facing in the direction of the Temple.

The Temple

Sacrifice

There are obvious parallels between the Temple sacrifice and the Christian Mass, which takes the form of a symbolic sacrifice. The priest partook of the blood of Christ in the form of wine, and the worshipers joined in partaking of his body in the form of bread that was shared. But insofar as the Mass also commemorates the Last Supper, it imitates the festive Jewish meal, in particular the ceremonial Passover meal, which was accompanied by music in the form of psalm singing.

Christian sacrifice

The synagogue was a center for readings and homilies rather than sacrifice or prayer. There, at meetings or services, the Hebrew Scriptures were read and discussed. Certain readings were assigned to ordinary Sabbath mornings and to market days of Monday and Thursday, while readings proper to the occasion were required on pilgrimage festivals, minor festivals, fast days, and days of the new moon. After the destruction of the Temple, the synagogue service incorporated elements that substituted for the Temple sacrifices, but these developments probably occurred too late in the first and second centuries to

Synagogue

serve as models for the Christians. What the Christian liturgy does owe to the synagogue is the practice of readings specific to a calendar and public commentary upon them in a meeting house.

The Spread of Christianity

As the early church spread from Jerusalem through Asia Minor and westward into Africa and Europe, it continued to pick up musical elements from diverse areas. For example, the monasteries and churches of Syria were important in the development of psalm singing and the use of hymns. Both of these types of church song spread from Syria by way of Byzantium to Milan (Italy) and other Western centers. Hymn singing is the earliest recorded musical activity of the Christian Church (Matt. 26:30; Mark 14:26). Pliny the Younger, about the year 112, reported the Christian custom of singing "a song to Christ as if to a god" in Bithynia, the Asia Minor province he governed.[17] He associated the Christians' singing with the act of binding themselves to their faith by an oath.

Psalms and hymns

Byzantium

The Eastern churches, in the absence of a strong central authority, developed different liturgies throughout their various regions. Although we have no manuscripts older than the ninth century of the music used in these Eastern rites, we can still make inferences about early Eastern church music.

The city of Byzantium (later Constantinople) was rebuilt by Constantine and designated in 330 as the capital of his reunited Roman Empire. In 395, after the permanent division into Eastern and Western Empires, the city remained the capital of the Eastern Empire for more than a thousand years, until its capture by the Turks in 1453. During much of this time, Byzantium was the seat of the most powerful government of its day and the center of a flourishing culture that blended Hellenistic and Oriental elements. Byzantine musical practices left their mark on Western chant, particularly in the classification of that repertory into eight modes and in various chants borrowed by the West between the sixth and ninth centuries.

Western Liturgies

In the West, as in the East, local churches were relatively independent at first. Although they shared a large area of common practice, each region of the West probably received the Eastern heritage in a slightly different form. These original differences, combined with varying local conditions, produced several distinct liturgies and bodies of liturgical music between the fifth and eighth centuries. Eventually most of the local versions either disappeared or were absorbed into a single uniform practice with authority emanating from Rome. From the ninth to the sixteenth centuries, in theory and in practice, the liturgy of the Western church was increasingly Romanized.

17. Pliny *Letters* 10.96.

Hymns

The finest and most characteristic examples of medieval Byzantine music were the hymns. One important type is the strophic *kontakion*, a poetic elaboration on a biblical text. The foremost exponent of *kontakia* was St. Romanus the Melode, a converted Syrian Jew active at Constantinople in the first half of the sixth century. Other types of hymns originated when *troparia*, the short responses between verses of the psalms, were furnished with melodies or melody types possibly borrowed from Syria or Palestine. These insertions gradually increased in importance, and some of them eventually developed into independent hymns, of which there are two principal kinds: the *stichera* and the *kanones*. The stichera were sung between the verses of the ordinary Psalms of the Office. A *kanon* was a nine-section elaboration on the nine biblical canticles or odes.[18]

Each section corresponded to one of the odes, and each contained several stanzas sung to the same melody. The first stanza of each ode was its *heirmos*, or model stanza, whose melodies were collected in books called *heirmologia*. By the tenth century, the second ode was usually omitted.

Kanones

The texts of the Byzantine *kanones* were not wholly original creations but patchworks of stereotyped phrases. Likewise, their melodies were constructed according to a principle, common in all Eastern music, called *centonization*, which was used in some Western chants as well. Melodies were created out of standard motives or formulas used as building blocks. Some of the motives suited the beginning, some the middle, and some the end of a melody, while others made good connecting links. Standard ornamental formulas (*melismas*) were also used. It is not clear to what extent the individual singer could choose the formulas, or how much a "composer" fixed them in advance. By the time the melodies came to be written down in manuscripts, however, the selection of formulas was relatively fixed.

Melody types

Melody types or modes have different names in different musical cultures—*rāga* in Hindu music, *maqām* in Arabic, *echos* in Byzantine Greek. They are known by various terms translatable as "mode" in Hebrew. A *rāga*, *maqām*, *echos*, or *mode* is at once a vocabulary of available pitches and a store of melodic motives. The choice of a particular rāga or mode may depend on the nature of the text to be sung, the particular occasion, the season of the year, or sometimes (as in Hindu music) the hour of the day. Byzantine music had a system of eight *echoi*, which served to classify the melodies in the collections for the *kanones*. The eight Byzantine echoi were grouped

Echoi

18. The nine biblical canticles, lyrical texts similar to psalms but occurring outside the Psalms, are: (1) Canticle of Moses after passing through the Red Sea, Exodus 15–19; (2) Canticle of Moses before dying, Deuteronomy 32–43; (3) Canticle of Hannah, 1 Samuel 2–10; (4) Canticle of Habakkuk, Habakkuk 3–19; (5) Canticle of Isaiah, Isaiah 26:9–19; (6) Canticle of Jonah, Jonah 2–9; (7) Canticle of the Three Children, first part, Apocrypha, Daniel 3:6–45, 52–56; (8) second part of same, 3:7–88; (9) Canticle of the Blessed Virgin Mary, Magnificat, Luke 1:6–55; and Canticle of Zechariah, *Benedictus Dominus*, Luke 1:8–79. In the Byzantine Church all nine canticles were sung in the morning Office, except in Lent, when only three were used. The Roman Church had one Old Testament canticle per day at Lauds, and all three New Testament canticles (Luke 1:46–55, 1:68–74, and 2:24–32) at Lauds, Vespers, and Compline every day.

in four pairs, which had as their final tones respectively *D*, *E*, *F*, and *G*. Similarly, four pairs of modes with these same finals became the basis for classifying Western chant during the eighth or ninth century. Thus the foundation of the Western system of modes seems to have been imported from the East, but the theoretical elaboration of the system was strongly influenced by Greek musical theory as transmitted by a fifth-century writer named Boethius.

Chant dialects

During the seventh and early eighth centuries, control of western Europe was distributed among the Lombards, Franks, and Goths, and each of these political divisions had its own repertory of melodies for singing sacred texts. We call these melodies *chants*, and the different regional styles may be called *dialects* by analogy to language. In Gaul—approximately modern-day France—there was the *Gallican* chant; in Ireland and parts of the British isles, *Celtic* chant; in southern Italy, the *Beneventan*; in Rome, the *Old Roman* chant; in Spain, the *Visigothic* or *Mozarabic*; around Milan, the *Ambrosian*. Later, England developed its own dialect of chant, called the *Sarum* (Salisbury) *use*, which persisted from the late Middle Ages to the Reformation.

Gallican chant

The Franks retained the Gallican liturgy, which included both Celtic and Byzantine elements. Near the end of the eighth century, Pepin and his son Charlemagne imposed the Roman chant on their domains and suppressed the Gallican so successfully that little is known about it today.

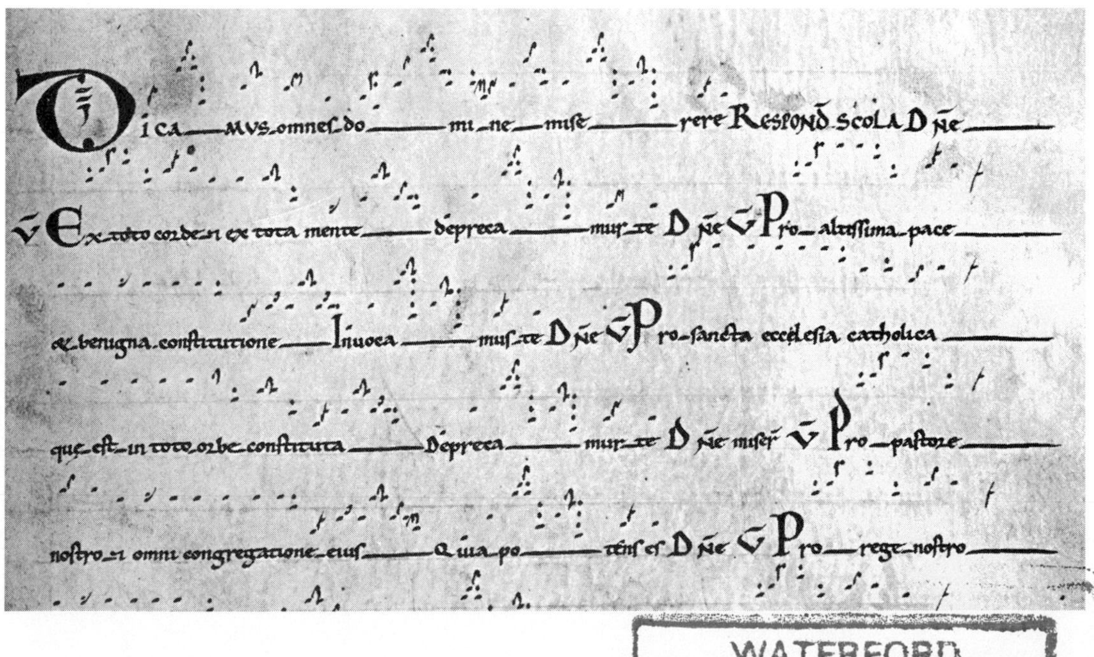

■ *Gallican chant. A folio from the eleventh-century Gradual of St. Yrieux, containing prayers of the Gallican liturgy. The music on this page is a litany for the Feast of St. Mark the Evangelist.* (PARIS, BIBLIOTHÈQUE NATIONALE, MS LAT. 903, FOL. 136)

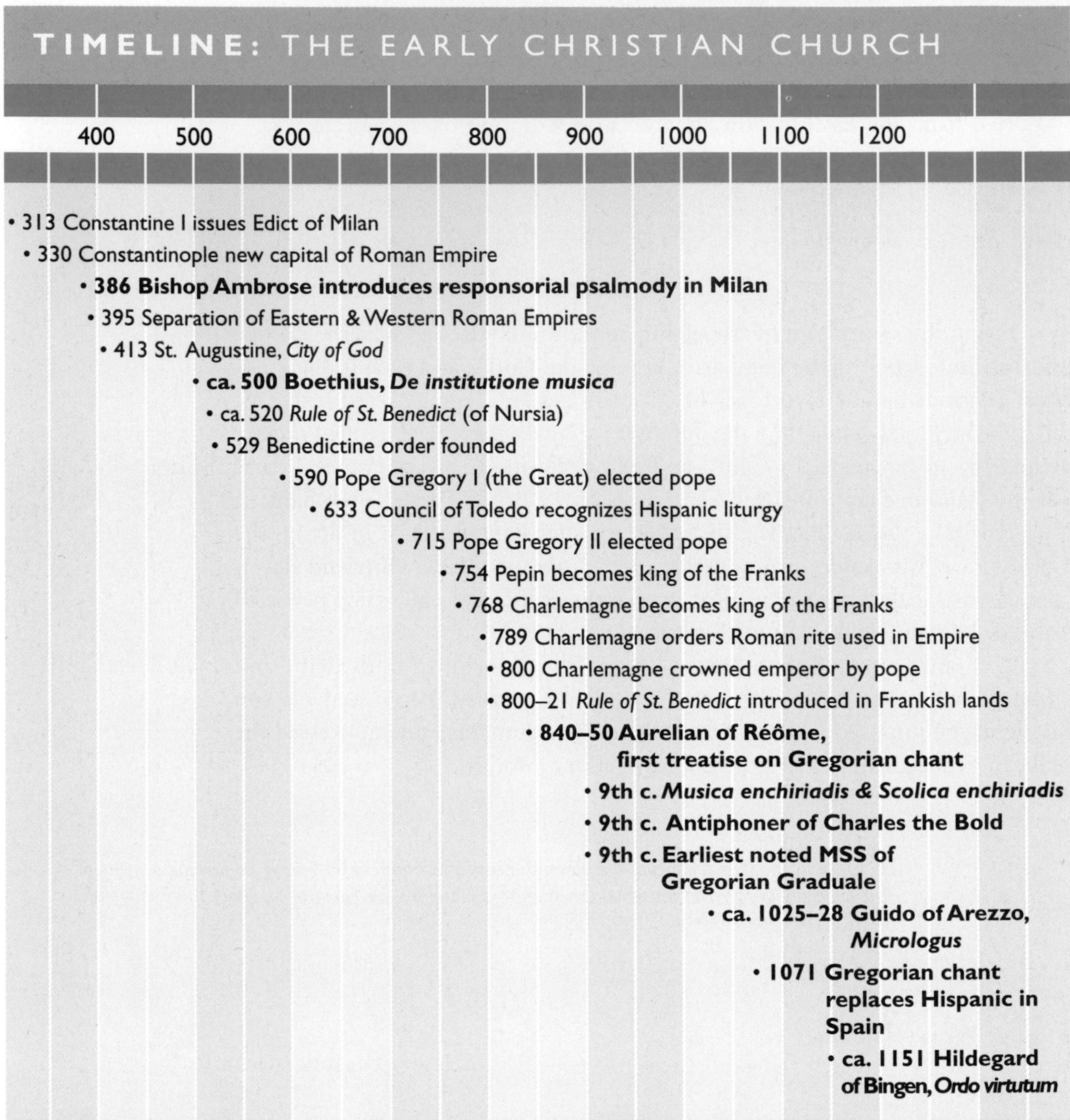

Mozarabic chant

On the other hand, nearly all the ancient Spanish texts and their melodies are preserved, but in a notation that has defied transcription because it was obsolete by the time chants were noted on staff lines. The Hispanic uses were recognized by the Council of Toledo in 633, and after the Muslim conquest in the eighth century, this liturgy acquired the name *Mozarabic* (although there is no evidence of any Arab influence on the music). The Hispanic chant was not officially replaced by the Roman rite until 1071, and even today some traces of it remain in a few churches in Toledo, Salamanca, and Valladolid.

■ *Mozarabic chant, from a Missal of the Mozarabic rite containing Masses for saints' feasts. This page has parts of the Office for the Feast of St. Servandus and St. Germanus. The melodies are indecipherable.* (BY PERMISSION OF THE BRITISH LIBRARY)

Old Roman chant

The Old Roman chant repertory found in manuscripts from Rome dating between the eleventh and twelfth centuries can be traced back to the eighth. This group of chants probably represents an older usage that continued to be developed in Rome even after the repertory later called *Gregorian,* heavily penetrated by northern, Frankish styles, spread across Europe. The Frankish kingdom, established by Charlemagne (742–814), occupied modern-day France, Switzerland, and western Germany.

No one can say for sure which melodies were brought from Rome to the Frankish lands. The formulas used to recite psalms and other simple types of chant were very ancient and may have been preserved practically intact. Some thirty or forty elaborate melodies called antiphons may also belong to a very old layer of chant. A great many of the more complex melodies must have been in use (perhaps in simpler versions) at Rome before spreading north. Some of the early melodies may be preserved in the manuscripts of the Old Roman chant. In any case, most or all of the music transmitted north was probably altered before finally being written down. Furthermore, a great many new melodies and new types of chant grew up in the north after the ninth century. In sum: practically the whole body of the chant as we now know it comes from Frankish sources that are probably based on Roman versions, with additions and changes by local scribes and musicians.

Since most of the manuscripts transmit a repertory that was compiled and edited in the Frankish kingdom, the chants were once thought to have originated there. However, recent comparisons of the Frankish and Old Roman versions suggest that the Old Roman represents the original fund of chants, which were only slightly modified after they reached Gaul. The Frankish manuscripts, then, are thought to transmit the repertory as it was reorganized under papal direction, perhaps beginning under Pope Vitalian (657–72).

Gregorian chant

This reorganization, long attributed to Pope Gregory I (the Great; 590–604), was more likely named for Pope Gregory II (715–31). After Charlemagne was crowned in 800 as the head of the Holy Roman Empire, he and his successors tried to promulgate this Gregorian repertory and suppress the various chant dialects, such as the Celtic, Gallican, Mozarabic, and Ambrosian, but they did not succeed in eliminating all local usages.

Modern editions

Over one thousand years later, in the 1880s, monks at the Benedictine Abbey of Solesmes in France began publishing facsimile editions with commentaries on the sources of Gregorian chant. They also issued modern editions in separate volumes for various categories of chant, which Pope Pius X proclaimed in 1903 were the official Vatican editions. But with the encouragement of the vernacular Mass by the Second Vatican Council (1962–65), these books, including the *Liber usualis*, are seldom used in modern services and rarely reprinted.

Ambrosian chant

The most important Western church center outside Rome was Milan, a thriving city with close cultural ties to Byzantium and the East. It was the chief residence for the Western emperors in the fourth century, and later became the capital for the Lombard kingdom in northern Italy, which flourished from 568 to 744. St. Ambrose, the bishop of Milan from 374 to 397, is responsible for introducing responsorial psalmody to the West. In this manner of singing the psalms, a soloist or reader sang the first half of a psalm verse and the congregation responded by singing the second half. Because of Milan's importance and St. Ambrose's energy and personal reputation, the Milanese liturgy and music exerted a strong influence not only in France and Spain but also in Rome, and, as a result, responsorial psalmody was incorporated into the Roman Mass. The songs of the Milanese rite later became known as Ambrosian chant, though it is doubtful that any of the music dates from the time of St. Ambrose. Some of the Ambrosian liturgy and its chants survive in present-day Milan despite vari-

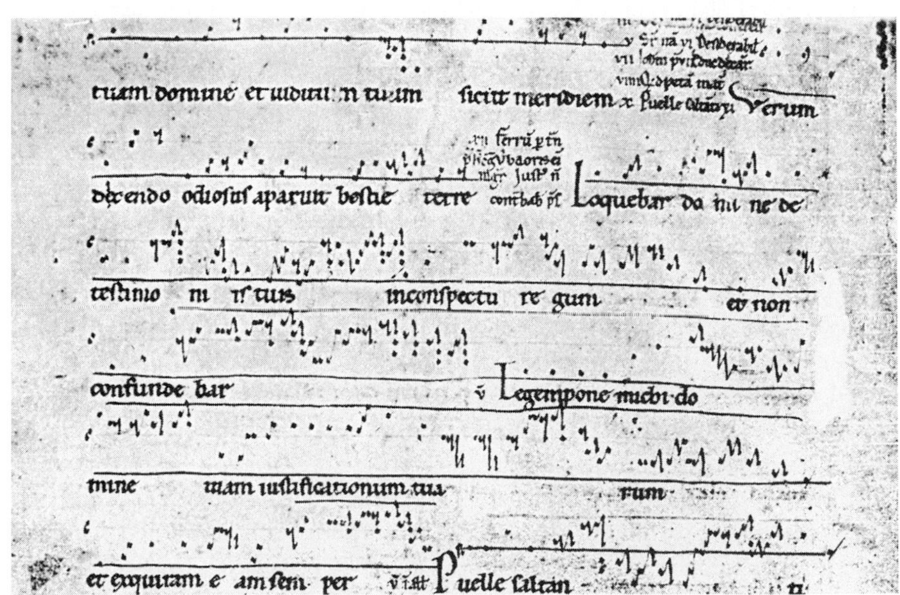

■ *Ambrosian chant, from a twelfth-century* Manuale ambrosiano. *This folio contains portions of the Office and Mass of the Feast of the Beheading of St. John the Baptist.* (VATICAN LIBRARY, MS. 10645, FOL. 58V.)

ous attempts to suppress them. Many of these chants are similar to those of the Roman Church, indicating either an interchange or a derivation from a common source. Where there are two versions of the same melody, if it is of an ornate type (such as an alleluia), the Ambrosian is usually more elaborate than the Roman; if a plain type (such as a psalm tone), the Ambrosian is simpler than the Roman.

The Dominance of Rome

Rome recognizes Christianity

During the first centuries of the modern era, Rome was home to a large number of Christians who met and carried on their rites in secret. In 313 Emperor Constantine finally recognized the Christians as a group entitled to equal rights and protection in the empire. The church emerged from its underground life and later in the fourth century replaced Greek with Latin as the official language of the liturgy in Rome. As the prestige of the Roman emperor declined, that of the Roman bishop increased, and Christians began to acknowledge the bishop's authority in matters of faith and discipline.

The *Rule of St. Benedict*

With more and more converts, services could no longer be conducted in the informal manner typical of the early days. The church started building monasteries and large oblong structures, called basilicas, for public services. From the fifth to the seventh centuries many popes were concerned with revising the liturgy and music. The *Rule of St. Benedict* (ca. 520), a set of instructions on how to run a monastery, mentions a cantor but does not specify his duties. But in the next few centuries, the monastic cantor became a key person in the musical program: he maintained the library and scriptorium (copying shop for the scribes) and directed the performance of the liturgy. By the eighth century the city of Rome had a *Schola cantorum*, a specific group of singers and teachers responsible for training boys and men as church musicians. A papal choir existed in the sixth century, and Gregory I was said to have tried regulating and standardizing the liturgical chants (see page 37). Whether this reorganization was undertaken by Gregory himself or by another pope (or popes) remains unclear. In any case, particular items of the liturgy and their music were assigned to the various services throughout the year in an order that remained essentially unchanged until the sixteenth century.

The Church Fathers

The church fathers, highly influential Christian writers and scholars, interpreted the Bible and set down some principles to guide the early church. Some—Clement of Alexandria, Origen, St. Basil, and St. John Chrysostom—wrote in Greek; others—St. Ambrose, St. Augustine, and St. Jerome—wrote in Latin. Like the Greeks, they believed the value of music lay in its power not only to inspire divine thoughts but also to influence—for good or evil—the character of its listeners. Philosophers and church leaders of the early Middle Ages did not dwell on the idea—which we take for granted today—that music might be heard solely for sheer delight in the play of sounds. While they did not deny that the sound of music was pleasurable, they held to the Platonic principle that beautiful things existed to remind us of divine and perfect beauty. Apparent worldly beauties that inspire only self-centered enjoyment, or desire of possession, were to be rejected. This view formed the basis for many of the pronouncements about music made by the church fathers and, later, by some theologians of the Protestant Reformation.

Music a servant of religion

Music, then, was the servant of religion, and only music that opened the mind to Christian teachings and disposed it to holy thoughts was deemed worthy of hearing in church. On these grounds, instrumental music was initially excluded from public worship, though the faithful were allowed to use a lyre for accompanying hymns and psalms in their homes and on informal occasions. The fathers ran into difficulty over their ban on instrumental music, since the Hebrew Scriptures (the Old Testament), and especially the Psalms, are full of references to the psaltery, harp, organ, and other musical instruments.

Excluding certain kinds of music from early church worship also had practical motives. Through long habit, the first converts associated elaborate singing, large choruses, instruments, and dancing with pagan spectacles. Until the pleasure attached to such music could somehow be transferred from the theater and the marketplace to the church, the music was distrusted.

Defense of church music

"Some claim that I have ensnared the people by the melodies of my hymns," said St. Ambrose, adding proudly, "I do not deny it."[19] Some church leaders undoubtedly despised music and tended to regard all art and culture as hostile to religion. Others, however, not only defended pagan art and literature but found themselves so deeply touched by them that they actually feared the pleasure they experienced in listening to music, even in church. The well-known words of St. Augustine express this dilemma (see vignette).

Augustine's *De musica*

Music was more than a passing fancy for St. Augustine, who in 387 began a treatise, *On Music*, completing six books during his lifetime. The first five, after a brief introductory definition of music, deal with the principles of meter and rhythm. The sixth, revised around 409, discusses psychology, ethics, and esthetics of music and rhythm. Augustine originally projected six more books on melody.

Transmission of Greek music theory

The music theory and philosophy of the ancient world—or whatever was still accessible after the breakdown of the Roman Empire and the invasions from the north—was gathered up, summarized, modified, and transmitted to the West during the early centuries of the Christian era. Most notable in this process were Martianus Capella and Boethius.

Martianus Capella

Martianus produced an appealing textbook on the seven liberal arts in his encyclopedic treatise *The Marriage of Mercury and Philology* (early fifth century). It covered grammar, dialectic, rhetoric, geometry, arithmetic, astronomy, and harmonics, respectively. The first three—the verbal arts—came to be called the *trivium* (three paths), while the last four were called the *quadrivium* (four paths) by Boethius and consisted of the mathematical disciplines.

19. Migne, *Patrologiae* 1 16:1017.

SAINT AUGUSTINE, FROM *CONFESSIONS*, ON THE PLEASURES AND DANGERS OF MUSIC

When I remember the tears I shed at the psalmody of Thy church, when I first recovered my faith, and how even now I am moved not by the singing but by what is sung, when it is sung with a clear voice and apt melody, I then acknowledge the great usefulness of this custom. Thus I hesitate between dangerous pleasure and approved wholesomeness, though I am inclined to approve of the use of singing in the church (yet I would not pronounce an irrevocable opinion upon the subject), so that the weaker minds may be stimulated to devout thoughts by the delights of the ear. Yet when I happen to be moved more by the singing than by what is sung, I confess to have sinned grievously, and then I wish I had not heard the singing. See the state I am in! Weep with me, and weep for me, you who can control your inward feelings to good effect. As for those of you who do not react this way, this is not a concern of yours. But Thou, O Lord my God, listen, behold and see, and have mercy upon me, and heal me—Thou, in whose sight I have become a problem to myself; and this is my weakness.

Saint Augustine, *Confessions* 10:33.

Martianus charmingly disguised introductions to these subjects as speeches made by bridesmaids at the wedding of Mercury and Philology.

Boethius

Anicius Manlius Severinus Boethius (ca. 480–524/26) was the most revered and influential authority on music in the Middle Ages. His *De institutione musica* (The Fundamentals of Music), written in the first years of the sixth century when Boethius was a young man, is a compendium of music within the scheme of the quadrivium. Together with similar texts on geometry, arithmetic, and astronomy, it prepared students for further studies in philosophy. There is little that is original in the music treatise: Boethius compiled it from Greek sources that he had at hand, mainly a lengthy treatise by Nicomachus that has not survived, and the first book of Ptolemy's *Harmonics*. Although medieval readers may not have realized how much Boethius depended on other authors, they understood that his statements rested on Greek mathematics and music theory. They were not bothered by the contradictions in *De institutione musica*, in which the first three books were heavily Pythagorean, the fourth contained elements derived from Euclid and Aristoxenus, and the fifth, based on Ptolemy, was partly anti-Pythagorean. Most readers came away with the message that music was a science of numbers and that numerical ratios determined the melodic intervals, the consonances, the composition of scales, and the tuning of instruments and voices.

His compendium of Greek music theory

■ *Fanciful portrayals of Boethius and Pythagoras, above, and Plato and Nicomachus, below. Boethius measures out notes on a monochord. Pythagoras strikes the bells with hammers. The others were revered as authorities on music. An early twelfth-century drawing.* (BY PERMISSION OF THE SYNDICS OF CAMBRIDGE UNIVERSITY LIBRARY, ENGLAND)

Musica mundana, humana, and *instrumentalis*

In what is the most original part of the book, the opening chapters, Boethius divides music into three kinds. The first is *musica mundana* (cosmic music), the orderly numerical relations seen in the movements of the planets, the changing of the seasons, and the elements. The second is *musica humana,* which controls the union of the body and soul and their parts. Last is *musica instrumentalis,* audible music produced by instruments, including the human voice, which exemplifies the same principles of order, especially in the numerical ratios of musical intervals. Boethius emphasized the influence of music on character and morals. As a consequence, music occupied an important place in the education of the young, both in its own right and as an introduction to more advanced philosophical studies. Boethius, who became a consul and minister to Theodoric, ruler of Italy, later wrote a philosophical treatise in poetic form, *The Consolation of Philosophy*, while imprisoned as a victim of political intrigue.

In placing *musica instrumentalis*—the art of music as we understand it now—in the third and presumably lowest category, Boethius showed that he and his mentors saw music as an object of knowledge. Music, he wrote, is the discipline of examining the diversity of high and low sounds by means of reason and the senses. Therefore, the true musician is not the singer or someone who makes up songs by instinct without understanding the nature of the medium, but the philosopher, the critic, "who exhibits the faculty of forming judgments according to speculation or reason relative and appropriate to music."[20]

Bibliography

Sources

Transcriptions of many but not all extant Greek melodies and fragments are given in Egert Pöhlmann, *Denkmäler altgriechischer Musik: Fragmente und Fälschungen* (Nuremberg: Carl, 1970).

Most of the Greek writings referred to in this chapter are available in English translation. Relevant selections of Aristotle, Plato, and Cleonides appear in Oliver Strunk and Leo Treitler, gen. eds., *Source Readings in Music History*, rev. ed., Vol. 1, *Greek Views of Music*, ed. Thomas J. Mathiesen (New York: Norton, 1998).

Andrew Barker, ed., *Greek Musical Writings* (Cambridge: Cambridge University Press). Vol. 1 , *The Musician and His Art* (1984), contains English translations of writings by poets, dramatists, and philosophers, including a new translation of pseudo-Plutarch, *On Music*. Vol. 2, *Harmonic and Acoustic Theory* (1989), contains writings on these subjects by early Pythagoreans, Plato, Aristotle and his school, Theophrastus, Aristoxenus, Nicomachus, Ptolemy, Aristides Quintilianus, and the Euclidian *Division of the Canon.*

The following translations of individual treatises are also available:

Aristoxenus, *The Harmonics of Aristoxenus*, ed. with trans., notes, and intro. by Henry S. Macran (Oxford: Clarendon Press, 1902).

The Euclidian Division of the Canon, ed. and trans. André Barbera (Lincoln: University of Nebraska Press, 1991).

Sextus Empiricus, *Against the Musicians*, ed. and trans. Denise Davidson Greaves (Lincoln: University of Nebraska Press, 1986).

Aristides Quintilianus, *On Music in Three Books*, trans. with intro., commentary, and annotations by Thomas J. Mathiesen (New Haven: Yale University Press, 1983).

Bacchius Senior, trans. in Otto Steinmayer, "Bacchius Geron's *Introduction to the Art of Music*," JMT 29 (1985):271–98.

Martianus Capella, *De nuptiis Philologiae et Mercurii*, trans. in William Harris Stahl et al., *Martianus Capella and the Seven Liberal Arts* (New York: Columbia University Press, 1971).

---

20. Boethius, *De institutione musica* 1.34, trans. Calvin M. Bower, p. 51.

Boethius, *Fundamentals of Music (De institutione musica libri quinque)*, trans. with intro. and notes by Calvin M. Bower, ed. Claude V. Palisca (New Haven: Yale University Press, 1989).

For Further Reading

Greek

The most comprehensive survey of Greek music, its history, instruments, practice and theory is Thomas J. Mathiesen, *Apollo's Lyre: Greek Music and Music Theory in Antiquity and the Early Middle Ages* (Lincoln: University of Nebraska Press, 1999). See also his "Greece, I," in NG, rev. ed.

For a discussion of ethos, see Warren De Witt Anderson, *Ethos and Education in Greek Music* (Cambridge, Mass.: Harvard University Press, 1966).

On the *Oresteia* and its dramatic and musical structure, see William C. Scott, *Musical Design in Aeschylean Theater* (Hanover, N.H.: University Press of New England, 1984).

Hebrew

On Hebrew music, see A. Z. ldelsohn, *Jewish Music in Its Historical Development* (New York, 1929; repr. New York: Schocken, 1967).

For a summary of the scholarship and the latest views on the connections between Jewish music and the music of the early Christian Church, see James W. McKinnon, "The Question of Psalmody in the Ancient Synagogue," EMH 6 (1986):159–91; and Peter Jeffery, *Re-Envisioning Past Musical Cultures: Ethnomusicology in the Study of Gregorian Chant* (Chicago: University of Chicago Press, 1992).

Byzantine

See Oliver Strunk, *Essays on Music in the Byzantine World* (New York: Norton, 1977); Egon Wellesz, *A History of Byzantine Music and Hymnody*, 2nd ed. (Oxford: Clarendon Press, 1971); Wellesz, *Eastern Elements in Western Chant* (Oxford: Byzantine Institute, 1947).

Western Liturgy

For the study of the Mass and Office, see Cheslyn Jones, Geoffrey Wainwright, and Edward Yarnold, SJ, *The Study of Liturgy* (New York: Oxford University Press, 1978).

On the origins of Gregorian Chant, see Kenneth Levy, *Gregorian Chant and the Carolingians* (Princeton: Princeton University Press, 1998); Leo Treitler, "Homer and Gregory: The Transmission of Epic Poetry and Plainchant," MQ 55 (1974):333–72, and GLHWM 1; Helmut Hucke, "Toward a New Historical View of Gregorian Chant," JAMS 33 (1980):437–67; and Jeffery, *Re-Envisioning Past Musical Cultures.* The controversy over the origins of Gregorian Chant is also summarized in Andrew Hughes, *Medieval Music: The Sixth Liberal Art* (Toronto: University of Toronto Press, 1980), section 605ff.

On Boethius's sources: Calvin M. Bower, "Boethius and Nicomachus: An Essay Concerning the Sources of *De institutione musica*," *Vivarium* 16 (1978):1–45. On music in the trivium and quadrivium: E. A. Lippman, "The Place of Music in the System of Liberal Arts," in Jan LaRue, ed., *Aspects of Medieval and Renaissance Music: A Birthday Offering to Gustave Reese* (New York: Norton, 1966), pp. 545–59; and David L. Wagner, ed., *The Seven Liberal Arts in the Middle Ages* (Bloomington: Indiana University Press, 1983).

See also J. W. McKinnon, ed. *Music in Early Christian Literature* (Cambridge: Cambridge University Press, 1987); and McKinnon, ed., *Antiquity and the Middle Ages: From Ancient Greece to the 15th Century* (Englewood Cliffs, N.J.: Prentice-Hall, 1991), a collection of chapters by various authorities.

CHAPTER 2

CHANT AND SECULAR SONG IN THE MIDDLE AGES

ROMAN CHANT AND LITURGY

The chants of the Roman Church are one of the great treasures of Western civilization. Like Romanesque architecture, they stand as a memorial to religious faith in the Middle Ages, embodying the sense of community and esthetic sensibility of the time. Not only does this body of plainchant include some of the oldest and noblest melodies ever created, it also served as the source and inspiration for much Western art music up to the sixteenth century. As beautiful as the chants are to listen to, it would be misleading to treat them purely as music, for they cannot be separated from their ceremonial context and purpose.

Plainchant is musical prayer, heightened speech that unites the faithful through melody and rhythm in the articulation of devout thoughts. But it is the text—its phraseology, punctuation, and syntax—that gives form to the songful delivery. Chant can be as simple as recitation on a single pitch, heard in the Gospel reading at Mass. A slight fall in pitch from the reciting tone may mark the end of a thought. A rise to the reciting tone calls attention to the beginning of a reading or to a major section of the text. The formulas for chanting the Psalms elaborate on this simple recitation by offering a variety of pitch patterns for beginnings, endings, half-endings, and resumptions of the recitation. More melodious chants, although they expand on this basic structure, still cling to the form of the verbal message. How elaborate the melody is depends on how weighty or solemn the occasion, how the text functions in the ritual, and who is performing the chant—a soloist, a choir, or the congregation. In short, it is determined by the liturgy.

Liturgy

Liturgy is the body of texts and rites that make up a sacred service. Over time, certain texts and rituals have been added or deleted. The readings, prayers, and songs mark or commemorate special individuals, events, days, or times of the year. In the early Christian church, the liturgy centered on a ritual recalling the Last Supper of Jesus and his disciples as recounted in the New Testament. This liturgy developed into the Mass. From the collective praying and singing of psalms, which was adapted from Jewish practice, grew the liturgy of the Divine Office, or the Canonical Hours.

History of chant

The liturgy and, with it, the chant developed over many centuries. The repertory changed and expanded, even as certain rituals remained stable. Written descriptions, called ceremonials, preserved the formal order of ceremonies, while manuscript books recorded the prayers and readings themselves. Eventually signs inserted above the words indicated patterns of chanting. The oldest manuscripts we have that preserve musical signs date from the ninth century, but the indication of pitch in these documents is only approximate, a memory aid rather than a record or prescription of what was to be sung. Notation of pitch intervals became more precise only a century or two later. Some of the chants preserved in these later manuscripts probably reflect melodies sung to their texts in earlier centuries. Before melodies were written down, singers memorized them or recreated them by improvising on formulas handed down from older singers, that is, by oral tradition. Ultimately, some of the traditional chants were written down, especially those that were hardest to remember or least often sung.

Most Christian chant originated in the Middle Ages, but it has been kept alive and continuously sung since, although often in corrupt versions. The Second Vatican Council of 1962–65, in an effort to engage congregations more directly in worship, replaced the Latin language of the rituals with the local vernacular, and today chant has virtually disappeared from regular services of the Catholic Church. In Europe, chant survives in some monasteries and for certain services of larger parochial churches. In America, it is cultivated even less. Although Latin remains the official language and plainchant the official music of the church, the traditional chants have been mostly replaced by music considered more suitable for an entire congregation to sing: simplified versions with vernacular translations of the familiar chant melodies, newly composed tunes, and music in popular styles.

Today, chant is ceremonial music that may still be in use, as well as a historical repertory that can be heard in concerts and recordings. The music historian who wants to represent chant in versions that are true to medieval practices faces a problem because recent editions reflect current interpretations. Many recordings are based on the Vatican's officially approved publications, edited by the monks of the Benedictine Abbey of Solesmes in the late nineteenth and early twentieth centuries. For practical reasons, then, we must consider the chant repertory as reflected in recent times, even if this obscures the chronological succession of styles and practices.

The Roman Liturgy

The two principal classes of services are the *Office* and the *Mass.*

The Office

The *Offices,* or *Canonical Hours,* first codified in the *Rule of St. Benedict* (ca. 520) consists of a series of eight prayer services celebrated daily at specified times by the clergy and members of religious orders; public recitation takes place only in monasteries and certain cathedral churches. *Matins* is sung before daybreak, *Lauds* at sunrise, *Prime, Terce, Sext, Nones* respectively at about 6 A.M., 9 A.M., noon, and 3 P.M. *Vespers* is sung at sunset, and *Compline* usually right after Vespers. The Office consists of prayers, psalms, canticles, antiphons, responses, hymns, and readings. The music for the Offices is collected in a liturgical book called an *Antiphoner* (in Latin *Antiphonale*), which gets its name from the antiphon, a chant that varies with the calendar and is sung before or in association with a psalm. The chief musical features of the Offices are the chanting of psalms with their antiphons, the singing of hymns and canticles, and the chanting of lessons (passages of Scripture) with their musical responses, called responsories.

Chants of the Office

From a musical standpoint, the most important Offices are Matins, Lauds, and Vespers. Matins includes some of the most ancient chants of the church. Vespers incorporates the canticle *Magnificat anima mea Dominum* (My soul doth magnify the Lord; Luke 1:46–55). Because it is the only Office that admitted polyphonic singing from early times, Vespers is especially important to the history of sacred music. At Compline celebrants sing the four antiphons of the Blessed Virgin Mary—the so-called Marian antiphons, one for each of the main divisions of the church year:[1] *Alma Redemptoris Mater* (Sweet mother of the Redeemer) from Advent to February 1; *Ave Regina caelorum* (Hail, queen of the heavens) from February 2 to Wednesday of Holy Week; *Regina caeli laetare* (Rejoice, queen of heaven) from Easter to Trinity Sunday; and *Salve Regina* (Hail, queen) from Trinity until Advent. (See illustration on page 38 and Example 2.1, page 39).

The Mass

The *Mass* remains the most important service of the Catholic Church. (For a description of a typical complete Mass, see the discussion accompanying NAWM 3.) The core of the Mass is the Eucharist. The early Christians gathered together to give thanks (*eucharistein*, in Greek) and praise to God. Prayers of thanksgiving, the presenting of offerings, and the breaking of bread were eventually combined into the Liturgy of the Eucharist, in which the sacrifice of Christ and the Last Supper were remembered, and the worshipers received, in communion, bread and wine that the church fathers designated as the body and blood of Christ. In other Christian churches the service is also known as the Eucharist, the Liturgy, Holy Communion, or the Lord's Supper, but all of them culminate in a symbolic reenactment of the Last Supper (Luke 22:19–20; 1 Cor. 11:23–26) in which the celebrant consecrates bread and wine and offers them to the faithful. The word "Mass" (Latin *Missa*) comes from the service's closing phrase: *Ite, missa est* (Go, the congregation is dismissed).

1. The principal seasons of the liturgical year in the Roman calendar are:
Advent, starting with the fourth Sunday before Christmas.
Christmas (December 25), including the following twelve days to
Epiphany (January 6) and the following weeks.
Pre-Lenten season, beginning nine weeks before Easter (date is movable)
Lent, the forty days from Ash Wednesday to Easter.
Eastertide, including Ascension (forty days after Easter) and continuing to
Pentecost or *Whitsunday* (seven weeks after Easter).
Trinity, from the first Sunday after Pentecost to the beginning of Advent.
Advent and Lent are sometimes called the "penitential" seasons.

EGERIA'S EYEWITNESS REPORT OF AN EARLY OFFICE IN JERUSALEM

As soon as the first cock crows, straightway the bishop comes down and enters the cave in the Anastasis. All the gates are opened, and the entire throng enters the Anastasis, where already countless lamps are burning, and when the people are within, one of the priests sings a psalm and all respond, after which there is a prayer. Then one of the deacons sings a psalm, similarly followed by a prayer, and a third psalm is sung by some cleric, followed by a third prayer and the commemoration of all. When these three psalms have been sung and the three prayers said, behond censers (*thiamataria*) are brought into the cave of the Anastasis, so that the entire Anastasis basilica is filled with the smell. And then as the bishop stands behind the railings, he takes the Gospel book and goes to the gate and the bishop himself reads the Resurrection of the Lord. When the reading of it has begun, there is such moaning and groaning among everybody and such crying, that even the hardest of hearts could be moved to tears because the Lord has suffered so much for us. When the Gospel has been read, the bishop leaves and is led with hymns to the Cross, accompanied by all the people. There, again, one psalm is sung and a prayer said. Then he blesses the people, and the dismissal takes place. And as the bishop goes out, all approach to kiss his hand.

From *Itinerarium Egeriae* xxiv, 9–11, in *Music in Early Christian Literature*, ed. James W. McKinnon (Cambridge: Cambridge University Press, 1987), p. 115.

The order and components of the Mass varied according to time and place. The earliest writings describing the celebration of the Last Supper, or Eucharist, already mention two parts: the Liturgy of the Word and the Liturgy of the Eucharist. Around 381–84, Egeria, a pilgrim from Spain or Gaul, gave an account of the liturgy at Jerusalem in which she speaks of the prayers, readings, and chanting in various parts of the services (see vignette). The Roman rite, however, eventually became dominant. The *Ordo romanus primus*, a late seventh-century instruction by the bishop of Rome for performing the liturgy, tells us that the Introit, Kyrie, Gloria, and Collect precede the readings from the Bible (such as the Gospel) and the prayers of the faithful gathered for the Eucharist.

By the end of the sixth century, the Canon of the Mass (the part between the Sanctus and the Communion) was fairly well established. It began with a dialogue in which the celebrant asked the people to lift up their hearts, and it ended with the communion and a post-communion prayer. If we look at sacramentaries—books of instruction for celebrants of the Eucharist, baptism, and other rites—dating from around 600 and later, we find considerable uniformity in the practice of this central part of the Mass. In 1570 Pope Pius V issued a Missal that fixed the texts and rites of the Mass to reflect decisions of the Council of Trent. This Tridentine liturgy (Tridentum was the Latin name for Trent) remained in force until it was modified by the Second Vatican Council in the 1960s. The Mass, as it was practiced from the late Middle Ages and codified in the 1570 Missal, is outlined below.

The Mass liturgy

In its Tridentine form, the liturgy of the Mass begins with the *Introit.* Originally this was an entire psalm with its antiphon, chanted during the entrance of the priest (the *antiphona ad introitum,* or antiphon for the entrance), but later it was shortened to a single verse of the psalm preceded by an antiphon. Next the choir sings the *Kyrie,* to the Greek words *Kyrie eleison* (Lord have mercy upon us), *Christe eleison* (Christ have mercy upon us), *Kyrie eleison,* each invocation being sung three times. The *Gloria* (omitted in the penitential seasons of Advent and Lent) is intoned by the priest with the words *Gloria in excelsis Deo* (Glory be to God on high) and continued by the choir from *Et in terra pax* (And on earth peace). Then come the prayers (*Collects*) and the reading of the *Epistle* for the day (from the letters of Paul and other apostles in the New Testament), followed by the *Gradual* and *Alleluia,* both sung by a soloist or soloists with responses by the choir. In penitential seasons and at a *Requiem* Mass (Mass for the Dead), the Alleluia is replaced by the more solemn *Tract,* and at a Requiem and on certain feasts, including Easter, Whitsunday, and Corpus Christi, a Sequence is added. After the reading of the *Gospel* and the sermon (if any) comes the *Credo,* begun by the priest with the words *Credo in unum Deum* (I believe in one God) and continued by the choir from *Patrem omnipotentem* (the Father Almighty), bringing to a close the Liturgy of the Word, the first main division of the Mass.

THE HIGH MASS

	Proper	Ordinary
Introductory	Introit	
		Kyrie
		Gloria
Liturgy of the Word	Collects	
	Epistle	
	Gradual	
	Alleluia/Tract	
	Sequence (rare now, common in the Middle Ages)	
	Gospel	
	[Sermon]	
		Credo
Liturgy of the Eucharist	Offertory	
	Secret	
	Preface	
		Sanctus
	Canon	
		Agnus Dei
	Communion	
	Post-Communion	
		Ite, missa est

The Offertory, which opens the Eucharist proper, is sung while the bread and wine are prepared. The *Secret* and the *Preface* lead into the *Sanctus* (Holy, holy, holy) and *Benedictus* (Blessed is He that cometh), both sung by the choir. Then comes the *Canon*, or prayer of consecration, followed by the *Pater noster* (the Lord's Prayer) and the *Agnus Dei* (Lamb of God). After the bread and wine have been consumed, the choir sings the *Communion*, which is followed by the chanting of the priest's *Post-Communion* prayers. The service then concludes with *Ite, missa est* or *Benedicamus Domino* (Let us bless the Lord), sung responsively by the priest and choir.

Proper

The texts of certain parts of the Mass are fixed; others change according to the season or the dates of particular feasts or commemorations. The variable portions are called the *Proper of the Mass* (*Proprium missae*). The Collects, Epistle, Gospel, Preface, and the Post-Communion and other prayers are all part of the Proper. The principal musical portions of the Proper are the Introit, Gradual, Alleluia, Tract, Offertory, and Communion. The fixed parts of the service are called the *Ordinary of the Mass* (*Ordinarium missae*), and include the Kyrie, Gloria, Credo, Sanctus, Benedictus, and Agnus Dei. These parts are sung by the choir, though in early Christian times they were also sung by the congregation. Since the fourteenth century, almost all polyphonic compositions called Mass are settings of the Ordinary only.

Ordinary

Chant and service books

The music for the Mass, both Proper and Ordinary, is published in a liturgical book called the *Graduale.* The *Liber usualis,* another book of music, contains a selection of the most frequently used chants from both the *Graduale* and *Antiphonale.* Texts of the Mass without the music are published in the *Missale* (Missal); texts of the Offices are collected in the *Breviarium* (Breviary).

Modern Plainchant Notation

The staff in modern plainsong notation (see page 38; transcription opposite) has four lines, one of which is designated by a clef as either *c′* (𝄡) or the *f* immediately below it (𝄢). These clefs do not indicate absolute pitches; pitch is relative. Although chant in the early Middle Ages was probably sung rhythmically, with notes of varying durations, today it is usual to interpret all the notes (which are called *neumes*) as having essentially the same duration, regardless of shape; a dot after a neume doubles its value. A neume may carry only one syllable of text. Two or more neumes in succession on the same line or space, if on the same syllable, are sung as though tied. A horizontal dash above a neume means the note should be slightly lengthened. *Composite* neumes (single signs representing two or more notes) are read from left to right, except for the *podatus* or *pes* ( ), in which the lower note is sung first. An oblique neume ( ) indicates two different notes (not a *portamento*). Flat signs, except in a signature at the beginning of a line, are valid only until the next vertical division line or until the beginning of the next word. The *custos* (sentinel) at the end of a line heralds the first note in the following line. An asterisk in the text shows where the chorus takes over from the soloist, and the signs *ij* and *iij* indicate that the preceding phrase is to be sung twice or three times.

Transmission of chant

Chant melodies are preserved in hundreds of manuscripts dating from the ninth century and later. These manuscripts were written at different times and in widely disparate areas. Very often the same melody appears in many different manuscripts, in almost identical form. How should we interpret this remarkable fact? One possibility, of course, is that the melodies came from one source and were transmitted with great accuracy and fidelity, either by purely oral means or with the help of some early notation of which no specimens have survived. Such an interpretation was advanced by writers of the eighth and ninth centuries, coupled with statements that the "one source" was St. Gregory himself.

A large body of chant already existed when notation was first introduced; how it was transmitted has been a subject of much study. One theory holds that the chant was reconstructed partly from memory and partly through improvisation at the moment of rehearsal (of a group) or performance by a soloist. The performers were guided by a set of conventions tied to a particular liturgical function or occasion, and they relied on their memory of previous renditions.

This theory of oral composition arose partly through observation of singers from the area known until recently as Yugoslavia. They could recite long epic poems, thousands of lines long, seemingly by memory but actually following precise formulas associating themes, sound patterns, syntax patterns, meters, caesuras, line ends, and so on.[2] Evidence for this formulary approach also exists in the chant literature. Its application in the Gregorian and Old Roman traditions may be compared in Example 2.2 (page 40)[3], the second phrase of the first half of several verses of the Tract *Deus, Deus meus*—an example of solo psalmody. Whether this is how the melodies were handed down and became settled into their fairly consistent written versions continues to be questioned and investigated.[4]

Systematic notation of the chant melodies coincided with a determined campaign by the Frankish monarchs to consolidate their polyglot kingdom. They needed a uniform liturgy and body of music to bind their entire population of worshipers. Numerous liturgical-musical "missionaries" traveled between Rome and the north in the late eighth and ninth centuries, and a potent weapon in their propaganda was the legend that St. Gregory wrote down the chant melodies, guided by divine inspiration (in the form of a dove singing in his ear). Naturally, their efforts met with resistance, and there was much confusion before uniformity was finally achieved. Notating the melodies helped

2. See *The Making of Homeric Verse: The Collected Papers of Milman Parry*, ed. Adam Parry (Oxford, 1971), and Albert Lord, *The Singer of Tales* (Cambridge, Mass., 1960; New York, 1968). Also Leo Treitler "Homer and Gregory: The Transmission of *Epic* Poetry and Plainchant," MQ 60 (1974): 333–72; " 'Centonate' Chant: *übles Flickwerk* or *E pluribus unus*," JAMS 28 (1975):123; and "The 'Unwritten' and 'Written Transmission' of Medieval Chant and the Start-up of Musical Notation," JM 10 (1992):131–91. See also Helmut Hucke, "Towards a New Historical View of Gregorian Chant," JAMS 33 (1980):437–67. For a somewhat different view, see Kenneth Levy, *Gregorian Chant and the Carolingians* (Princeton: Princeton University Press, 1998).
3. From Leo Treitler, "Homer and Gregory," p. 361.
4. A constructive critique of Treitler's theory of transmission, pointing out the many problems it raises, is Peter Jeffery, *Re-Envisioning Past Musical Cultures: Ethnomusicology in the Study of Gregorian Chant* (Chicago: University of Chicago Press, 1992).

■ *The Antiphon to the Blessed Virgin Mary,* Salve Regina mater misericordiae *(Hail, O Queen, Mother of mercy) as notated in a modern book of the once most frequently used chant of the Mass and Offices, the* Liber usualis.

assure that from then on the chants would be sung the same way everywhere. Thus notation was both a result of the striving for uniformity and a means of perpetuating that uniformity.

CLASSES, FORMS, AND TYPES OF CHANT

Classes

All chants may be divided into those with *biblical* and those with *nonbiblical* texts, and both categories may be subdivided into chants with *prose* texts and those with *poetical* texts. Examples of biblical prose texts are the lessons of the Office and the Epistle and Gospel of the Mass. Poetic biblical texts include the Psalms and canticles. Among nonbiblical prose texts are the Te Deum, many antiphons, and three of the four Marian antiphons. The hymns and sequences (see pages 47f) are chants with nonbiblical poetical texts.

Chants may also be classified according to the manner in which they were sung in earlier times. *Antiphonal* chants were sung by alternating choirs, *responsorial* by a soloist alternating with a choir, *direct* without alternation.

Example 2.1 *Antiphon*: Salve Regina

Hail, O Queen, Mother of mercy, our life, our sweetness and our hope! To thee we cry, banished children of Eve; to thee we send up our sighs, mourning and weeping in this vale of tears. Turn then, our Advocate, thine eyes of mercy toward us; and after this our exile, show unto us the blessed fruit of thy womb, Jesus. O clement, O loving, O sweet Virgin Mary.

This modern transcription reproduces certain signs that accompany the neumes in the manuscript. The asterisk indicates where the chant alternates between soloist and choir, or between the two halves of the choir. The straight lines under some pairs of notes are extensions of the sign for a slight lengthening of the notes. The small notes correspond to a sign probably indicating a light vocalization of the first ("voiced") consonant in such combinations as ergo *and* ventris*. The wavy line represents assign that probably called for a slight ornamenting of the note, perhaps something like a short trill or mordent.*

Example 2.2 *Tract* Deus, Deus meus *in Gregorian and Old Roman Traditions*

Still another classification is based on the relation of notes to syllables. Chants in which almost each syllable has a single note are called *syllabic.* Those characterized by long melodic passages on a single syllable are called *melismatic.* This distinction is not always clear-cut, since chants that are prevailingly melismatic usually include some syllabic sections or phrases, and many otherwise syllabic chants have occasional short melismas of four or five notes on some syllables, passages that are sometimes called *neumatic.*

Melody

In general, the melodic outline of a chant reflects the way the Latin words were pronounced, with prominent syllables set to higher notes or to more notes. This procedure, called *tonic* accent, has many exceptions. It cannot be fully applied in recitative-like chants, where many successive syllables are sung to the same note, or in hymns, where every strophe has to be sung to the same melody. In florid chants, the melodic curve is often given greater importance than the word accent, resulting in long melismas on final, weak syllables, as on the final "a" of "alleluia," or the "us" of "Dominus" and "exultemus," or the "e" of "Kyrie." In such cases, the important words and syllables of a phrase are emphasized by simple settings, which stand in contrast to the rich ornamentation of the unstressed syllables. In plainchant there is seldom any repetition of single words or word groups. The melody is adapted to the rhythm of the text, to its general mood, and to the liturgical function of the chant. Only rarely does the melody attempt to express emotional or pictorial effects. This is not to say that chant is inexpressive; its purpose is to proclaim the text, sometimes in straightforward, other times in highly ornamented ways.

■ *Gregory the Great (ca. 540–604) alternately listens to the dove (symbolizing the Holy Spirit) revealing the chants to him and dictates them to a scribe. The scribe, puzzled by the intermittent pauses in the pope's dictation, has lowered his slate and is peeking from behind the screen.*

Every chant melody is divided into phrases and periods corresponding to the phrases and periods of the text (see vignette, a quotation by the twelfth-century theorist John "Cotton," or "of Afflighem"). These sections are marked in modern chant books by a vertical line in the staff, shorter or longer accord-

JOHN "COTTON" ON MUSICAL SYNTAX

Just as in prose, three kinds of *distinctiones* are recognized, which can also be called "pauses"—namely, the colon, that is, "member"; the comma, or *incisio*; and the period, *clausula* or *circuitus*—so also it is in chant. In prose, where one makes a pause in reading aloud, this is called a colon; when the sentence is divided by an appropriate punctuation mark, it is called a comma; when the sentence is brought to an end, it is a period. For example, "In the fifteenth year of the reign of Tiberius Caesar:"—here and at all such points there is a colon. Later, where it continues "in the high-priesthood of Annas and Caiaphas," a comma follows; but at the end of the verse, after "the son of Zacharias in the wilderness" [Luke 3:1–2], there is a period.

From John "Cotton," also known as John "of Afflighem," *On Music*, in *Hucbald, Guido, and John on Music: Three Medieval Treatises*, trans. Warren Babb, ed. with intros. by Claude V. Palisca (New Haven and London: Yale University Press, 1978), p. 116. The entire biblical passage in the revised standard English version, but punctuated as in John's treatise, reads as follows: "In the fifteenth year of the reign of Tiberius Caesar: Pontius Pilate being governor of Judea: and Herod being tetrarch of Galilee: and his brother Philip tetrarch of the region of Ituraea and Trachonitis: and Lysanias tetrarch of Abilene: in the high-priesthood of Annas and Caiaphas, the word of God came to John the son of Zechariah in the wilderness."

ing to the importance of the subdivision. Most often the melodic curve takes the form of an arch; it begins low, rises to a higher pitch, where it remains for some time, then descends at the end of the phrase.

Recitation Formulas

We shall now examine some of the more important categories of chants used in the Mass and Office, beginning with syllabic and proceeding to melismatic kinds. The formulas for chanting the Psalms and reading the Epistle and Gospel are among the oldest chants of the liturgy, as are the slightly more ornate tones for the Preface and Lord's Prayer. The chants for reciting prayers and readings from the Bible lie on the border between speech and song. They consist of a single *reciting note* or *tenor* (usually *a* or *c'*), on which each verse or period of the text is rapidly chanted. Occasionally, the upper or lower neighboring note brings out an important accent. The reciting note may be preceded by a two- or three-note introductory formula called the *initium.* The end of each verse or period is marked by a short melodic cadence.

Tenor

Similar to these recitation formulas, but slightly more complex, are the formulas called *psalm tones.* There is one tone for each of the eight church modes (concerning which, see below, pages 52–54) and an extra one called the *Tonus peregrinus,* or "wandering tone." In the office a psalm may be sung to any one of the tones. (See, for example, Psalm 109, *Dixit Dominus* in NAWM 4c [CD 1 15 ⟨5⟩]; Psalm 110, *Confitebor tibi Domine,* NAWM 4e; Psalm 111, *Beatus vir qui timet Dominum,* NAWM 4g; Psalm 129, *De profundis clamavi ad te,* NAWM 4i, all part of the Office of Second Vespers on Christmas Day.) This type of melodic formula also occurs in many other chants.

Psalm tones

A psalm tone consists of the *initium* (used only in the first verse of the psalm), *tenor, mediatio* (semicadence in the middle of the verse), and *terminatio,* or final cadence (see Example 2.3). Usually the last verse of a psalm is followed by the *Lesser Doxology,* that is, the formula "Gloria Patri, et Filio, et Spiritui Sancto. Sicut erat in principio, et nunc, et semper, et in saecula saecu-

Example 2.3 *Outline of the Psalmody of the Office*

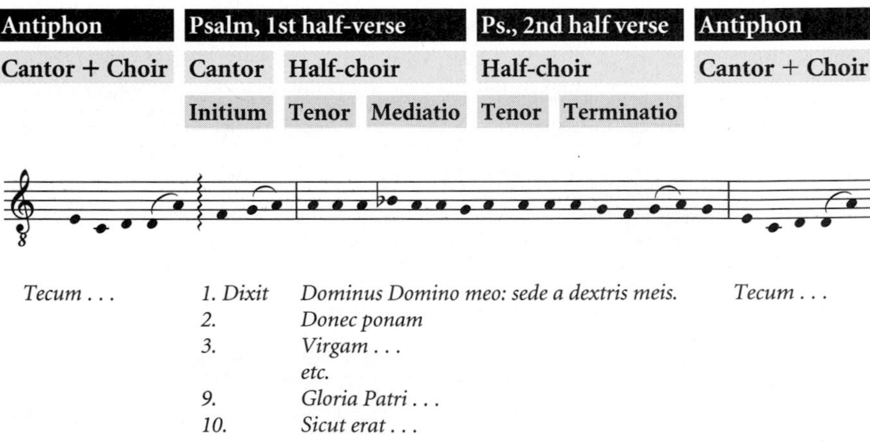

lorum. Amen." (Glory be to the Father, and to the Son, and to the Holy Ghost. As it was in the beginning, is now, and ever shall be, world without end. Amen.) In the chant books the closing words of the Doxology (praise to God) are indicated by the vowels *e u o u a e* below the last notes of the music. These vowels are an abbreviation for the last six syllables of the phrase *et in secula saEcUlOrUm, AmEn.* The chanting of a psalm in an Office is preceded and followed by the antiphon prescribed for the particular day of the calendar. The chanting of the Antiphon and Psalm, as performed in an Office, may be outlined as in Example 2.3 (the full text of the antiphon *Tecum principium* and Psalm 109 may be found in NAWM 4b and 4c).

This kind of psalmodic singing is called *antiphonal,* because the singing alternates either between the full choir and a half-choir, or between two half-choirs. The practice, believed to imitate ancient Syrian models, was adopted early in the history of the Christian Church, but it is not known precisely how the choirs alternated. In one possible model (Example 2.3), the cantor sings the first words of the antiphon and the full choir sings the rest of it. Then the cantor sings the first words of the psalm as an intonation, a half-choir completes the half-verse, and the other half-choir sings the second half-verse. The rest of the psalm is sung in alternation, but the intonation is not repeated. Finally, the Doxology, "Gloria Patri . . . ," is sung by the half-choirs in alternation. The full choir then repeats the antiphon.

Antiphons

Antiphons are more numerous than any other type of chant; about 1,250 are found in the modern *Antiphonale.* (See, for example, in NAWM 4 the antiphons for Second Vespers for the Nativity: 4b, *Tecum principium* [CD 1 14 ◇4]; 4d, *Redemptionem*; 4f, *Exortum est in tenebris*; 4h, *Apud Dominum*). However, many antiphons employ the same melody, using only slight variations to accommodate the text. Since antiphons were originally intended to be sung by a group rather than a soloist, the older ones are usually syllabic or only slightly florid, with stepwise melodic movement, limited range, and comparatively simple rhythm. The antiphons of the canticles are somewhat more elaborate than those of the psalms (for example, *Hodie Christus natus est,* the antiphon to the Magnificat, NAWM 4m).

In earliest times, the antiphon, a verse or sentence with its own melody, was probably repeated after every verse of a psalm or canticle, like the phrase "quoniam in aeternum misericordia ejus" (for His mercy endureth forever)—in Latin Psalm 135 (English 136). Eventually, only the intonation or opening phrase of the antiphon was sung before the psalm, with the entire antiphon performed after the psalm.

Most antiphons, such as *Redemptionem* and *Exortum est in tenebris* of the Christmas Second Vespers (NAWM 4d and 4f), are set in a fairly simple style, reflecting their origin as congregational or choral responsive songs. Some more elaborate pieces, originally antiphons, developed into independent chants—for example, the Introit, Offertory, and Communion of the Mass, retaining only a single psalm verse (see the Introit, *Puer natus est nobis,* NAWM

3a; CD 1 [3]) or none at all (the Offertory, *Tui sunt caeli*, NAWM 3g; CD 1 [10], or the Communion, *Viderunt omnes*, NAWM 3j; CD 1 [13]). Many antiphons were composed for additional feasts introduced between the ninth and the thirteenth centuries. This same period produced a number of independent antiphons—that is, not attached to particular psalms—for use in processions and for other special occasions. The four *Marian antiphons*—liturgically speaking, not antiphons at all but independent compositions—are of comparatively late date (see Example 2.1)

Responsory or Respond

Akin to the antiphon is the *responsory* or *respond*, a short verse that is sung by the soloist, repeated by the choir before a prayer or a short sentence of Scripture, and repeated again by the choir at the end of the reading. The responsory, in full or in part, was originally sung by the choir, in the manner of the antiphon, after each verse of the reading. This early practice survives in a few present-day responsories containing several verses that are sung at Matins or Nocturns of high feasts. For lesser feasts, such *responsoria prolixa*, or Long Responsories, are sung only before and after the soloist's single short reading. The Short Responsory, on the other hand, is sung after the biblical reading known as the Chapter, as in *Verbum caro* during Christmas Second Vespers (NAWM 4j; CD 1 [16]).

Antiphonal Psalmody

Moderately ornate antiphonal psalmody appears in the Introit and Communion of the Mass. The Introit (e.g., NAWM 3a; CD 1 [3]), as noted above, was originally a complete psalm with its antiphon. In the course of time, this part of the service was very much shortened, so that today the Introit consists only of the original antiphon, a single psalm verse with the customary *Gloria Patri*, and a repetition of the antiphon. The Communion (NAWM 3j; CD 1 [13]), coming near the end of the Mass as a counterpart to the Introit at the beginning, is a short chant, often consisting of only one scriptural verse.

Proper Chants of the Mass

Musically, the most highly developed chants of the Mass are the Graduals, Alleluias, Tracts, and Offertories. The Tract was originally a solo song. The Gradual and Alleluia are responsorial. The Offertory probably began as an antiphonal chant, but today no trace of the original psalm remains, and what must have been the original antiphon is performed as a responsorial chant by soloist and choir.

Tracts

The Tracts are the longest chants in the liturgy, both because they have long texts and because their melodies are extended by melismatic figures. The first half of a typical verse begins with a recitation embellished by melismas and is rounded off by a florid mediation (the end of a half-verse; see Example 2.2). The second half of the verse proceeds in a similar way and ends with a melisma. The final verse may end with a particularly extended melisma. Certain recurring melodic formulas are found in the same place in many different Tracts, and regularly in the same place—for example, at the mediation and at the beginning of the second half of the verse.

Graduals

Graduals came to the Frankish churches from Rome in a form that was already highly developed (see NAWM 3d; CD 1 [6]). Their melodies are more florid than those of Tracts, and their structure is different. A Gradual in a modern chant book is a shortened responsory—that is, it has an introductory *respond,* or refrain, that is followed by a single verse of a psalm. A soloist begins the refrain and the choir continues; the verse is then sung by a soloist and the choir joins in on the last phrase. Certain melismatic formulas recur in different Graduals at similar points in the chant—intonations, internal cadences, or terminating melismas. Some melodies are made up almost entirely of such formulas joined together, a process called *centonization.*

Alleluias

Alleluias consist of a refrain, on the single word "alleluia," and a psalm verse, followed by a repetition of the refrain (see NAWM 3e; CD 1 [8]). The final "ia" receives an effusive melisma called a *jubilus.* The Alleluia proceeds as follows: the soloist (or solo group) sings the word "alleluia"; the chorus repeats it and continues with the jubilus; the soloist then sings the psalm verse, with the chorus joining on the last phrase; after that the entire "alleluia" is sung by the soloist, and the chorus joins at the jubilus, as in the following scheme:

Soloist	**Chorus**	**Soloist**	**Chorus**	**Soloist**	**Chorus**
Alleluia	**Allelu-ia* . . . (jubilus) . . .	*Ps. Verse* . . .	* . . .	*Allelu-ia*	(jubilus)

The "alleluia" is moderately florid, while the jubilus is, of course, melismatic. The verse usually combines shorter and longer melismas. Very often the last part of the verse repeats part or all of the refrain melody.

Offertories

Offertories are similar in melodic style to Graduals (see NAWM 3g; CD 1 [10]). They began as very long chants sung by both congregation and clergy during the donation of bread and wine. When this ceremony was curtailed, the Offertory was shortened, but traces of its original use are evident in occasional text repetitions.

Chants of the Ordinary

Kyrie

The chants for the Ordinary of the Mass probably started out as simple syllabic melodies sung by the congregation. After the ninth century, these were replaced by more ornate settings. The syllabic style is retained only in the Gloria and Credo. The Kyrie, Sanctus, and Agnus Dei, by the nature of their texts, have three-part sectional arrangements. The Kyrie, for example, suggests the following setting:

A *Kyrie eleison*
B *Christe eleison*
A *Kyrie eleison*

Since each exclamation is uttered three times, there may be an aaa, aab, aba, or aba′ form within each of the three principal sections. More sophisticated versions of the Kyrie may have the pattern ABC, with motivic interconnections.

Agnus Dei

In an analogous fashion, the Agnus Dei may take the form ABA, though nearly the same music is sometimes used for all sections (as in NAWM 3i; CD 1 [12] ⟨3⟩):

A *Agnus Dei . . . miserere nobis* (Lamb of God . . . have mercy upon us)
A′ *Agnus Dei . . . miserere nobis*
A *Agnus Dei . . . dona nobis pacem* (Lamb of God . . . grant us peace)

Sanctus

The Sanctus is likewise divided into three sections; a possible distribution of musical materials is as follows:

A *Sanctus, sanctus, sanctus . . .* (Holy, holy, holy)
B *Pleni sunt caeli et terra . . .* (Heaven and earth are full)
B′ *Benedictus qui venit . . .* (Blessed is He that cometh)

LATER DEVELOPMENTS OF THE CHANT

Between the fifth and the ninth centuries, the peoples of western and northern Europe converted to Christianity and adopted the doctrines and rites of the Roman Church. The official "Gregorian" chant was established in the Frankish Empire before the middle of the ninth century, and from then until near the close of the Middle Ages, all important developments in European music took place north of the Alps. This shift of musical center occurred in part because of political conditions. The Muslim conquests of Syria, North Africa, and Spain,

Holy Roman Empire under Charlemagne around 800

completed by 719, left the southern Christian regions either in the hands of the Islamic rulers or under a constant threat of attack. Meanwhile, various cultural centers were arising in western and central Europe. Between the sixth and eighth centuries, missionaries from Irish and Scottish monasteries established schools in their own lands and abroad, especially in what is now Germany and Switzerland. A resurgence of Latin culture in England early in the eighth century produced scholars whose reputation extended to continental Europe. An English monk, Alcuin, helped Charlemagne in his project to revive education throughout the Frankish Empire. One result of this eighth- and ninth-century Carolingian renaissance was the development of important musical centers, the most famous of which was the Monastery of St. Gall in Switzerland.

This northern influence on plainchant may be seen in melodic lines with greater use of skips, especially thirds, and the introduction of both new melodies and new forms of chant. The same period saw the rise of secular monodic song and the earliest experiments in polyphony, developments to be taken up shortly.

Tropes

Tropes originated as newly composed additions, usually in neumatic style and with poetic texts, to antiphonal chants of the Proper of the Mass (most often to the Introit [see NAWM 7; CD 1 [20]], less often to the Offertory and Communion). Later, such additions were fitted also to chants of the Ordinary (especially the Gloria). We find three kinds of tropes: new words and music added to a regular chant; music only, extending melismas or adding new ones; and text only, added to existing melismas. Many fine tropes were written by Tuotilo (d. 915), a monk at the Monastery of St. Gall, an important center of troping. Trope composition flourished especially in monastic churches in the tenth and eleventh centuries; in the twelfth century it fell out of favor, although tropes continued to be used until the Council of Trent banned them from the liturgy four hundred years later. The so-called Kyrie tropes survive today only in titles of certain Masses (for example, Kyrie *Cunctipotens Genitor Deus* of Mass IV).

The terms *trope* and *troping* have often been extended to designate all additions and interpolations to a chant, making the *sequence* a subclass of trope. However, it is better to consider it separately, since sequences were often independent compositions.

Sequences

Some tenth-century manuscripts contain long melodies without text or with one or more texts. When these melodies are melismas, the word "alleluia" usually appears at the beginning of the music. Long melismas of this sort are also found attached to the Alleluia of the Mass, either as amplifications or as elaborate new compositions. Such extensions and additions were given the name *sequentia* or "sequence" (from the Latin *sequor*, to follow). When provided with a "text to the sequence," or *prosa ad sequentiam* (diminutive, *prosula*), the extension became a "sequence" in the fuller sense, a texted melody. Most of these

NOTKER BALBULUS ON THE GENESIS OF HIS PROSES

To Liutward, who for his great sanctity has been raised in honor to be a high priest, a most worthy successor to that incomparable man, Eusebius, Bishop of Vercelli; abbot of the monastery of the most holy Columbanus, and defender of the cell of his disciple, the most gentle Gallus; and also the arch-chaplain of the most glorious emperor Charles, from Notker, the least of the monks of St. Gall.

When I was still young, and very long melodies—repeatedly entrusted to memory—escaped from my poor little head, I began to reason with myself how I could bind them fast.

In the meantime it happened that a certain priest from Jumièges (recently laid waste by the Normans) came to us, bringing with him his antiphonary, in which some verses had been set to sequences; but they were in a very corrupt state. Upon closer inspection I was as bitterly disappointed in them as I had been delighted at first glance.

Nevertheless, in imitation of them I began to write *Laudes Deo concinat orbis universus, qui gratis est redemptus*, and further on *Coluber adae deceptor.* When I took these lines to my teacher Iso, he, commending my industry while taking pity on my lack of experience, praised what was pleasing, and what was not he set about to improve, saying, "The individual motions of the melody should receive separate syllables." Hearing that, I immediately corrected those which fell under *ia*; those under *le* or *lu*, however, I left as too difficult; but later, with practice, I managed it easily—for example in "Dominus in Sina" and "Mater." Instructed in this manner, I soon composed my second piece, *Psallat ecclesia mater illibata*.

When I showed these little verses to my teacher Marcellus, he, filled with joy, had them copied as a group on a roll; and he gave out different pieces to different boys to be sung. And when he told me that I should collect them in a book and offer them as a gift to some eminent person, I shrank back in shame, thinking I would never be able to do that.

Notker Balbulus, Preface to *Liber hymnorum* (Book of Hymns), trans. in Richard Crocker, *The Early Medieval Sequence* (Berkeley, Los Angeles, and London: University of California Press, 1977), p. 1.

early long melismas and sequences, however, are independent of any parent Alleluia. Notker Balbulus (his name means "the stammerer"; ca. 840–912), another Frankish monk of St. Gall, describes how he learned to write words syllabically under long melismas to help him memorize the notes. (See his account in the vignette.)

Notker Balbulus

Sequence settings began with a phrase of music set to a single text, followed by two phrases of music each set to two different texts. The two texts had the same number of syllables and pattern of accents, like a poetic couplet. The final phrase of music also had a single text. The number of syllables varied from phrase to phrase. The typical sequence pattern *a bb cc dd . . . . n* (where *a* and *n* represent the unpaired verses) is plainly evident in the celebrated *Victi-*

mae paschali laudes (Praises to the paschal Victim, NAWM 5; CD 1 17 ⟨6⟩), ascribed to Wipo, chaplain to Emperor Conrad and Henry III in the first half of the eleventh century. This sequence also employs the common device of unifying the different melodic segments by similar cadential phrases.

The sequence was an important creative outlet from the tenth to the thirteenth centuries and later. Popular sequences were imitated and adapted for secular genres, and in the late Middle Ages there was considerable mutual influence between sequences and contemporary types of semi-sacred and secular music, both vocal and instrumental.

Prosa

In the twelfth century, the term *prosa,* originally applied to prose texts set to Alleluia melismas, also embraced poetic sequence texts. Adam of St. Victor is credited with a large number of *prosae* (the texts only, not their melodies) that have uniform line lengths and well-defined patterns of accents and rhyme. Some later rhymed sequences approach the form of the hymn—*Dies irae,* for example, attributed to Thomas of Celano (early thirteenth century). In this famous work, which is included in the Requiem Mass, a melody with the pattern AA BB CC is invoked three times (though with a modified ending the third time), just as a hymn melody is repeated for successive stanzas.

Hildegard of Bingen

Hildegard of Bingen (1098–1179) stands out among the authors of poetic sequences because she composed the melodies as well as the verse. Founder and abbess of the convent at Rupertsberg in Germany, she was famous for her prophetic powers and revelations. Her most remarkable literary work, *Scivias* (Know the Ways), is an account of twenty-six visions. Hildegard's sequences *Columba aspexit* and *O virga ac diadema* differ from those of St. Victor in that they have lines of varying length and no regular meter. She preserved the sequence form of double versicles but varied the second versicle to accommodate the shorter or longer line.

Most sequences were banned from the Catholic service by the liturgical reforms of the Council of Trent (1545–63). Only four were retained: *Victimae paschali laudes,* at Easter; *Veni Sancte Spiritus* (Come, Holy Ghost), on Whitsunday; *Lauda Sion* (Zion, praise), attributed to St. Thomas Aquinas, for the festival of Corpus Christi; and the *Dies irae* (Days of rage). A fifth sequence, the *Stabat Mater* (By the cross the Mother standing), ascribed to Jacopo da Todi, a Franciscan monk of the thirteenth century, was reintroduced to the liturgy in 1727.

Liturgical Drama

One of the earliest of the liturgical dramas, *Quem quaeritis in sepulchro,* was based on a tenth-century dialogue or trope preceding the Introit of the Mass for Easter. The Easter dialogue represents the three Marys coming to the tomb of Jesus. The angel asks them, "Whom do you seek in the sepulcher?" They reply, "Jesus of Nazareth," to which the angel answers, "He is not here, He is risen as He said; go and proclaim that He has risen from the grave" (Mark 16:5–7). Accounts from the period indicate that not only was this dialogue sung responsively but also that it was accompanied by appropriate dramatic

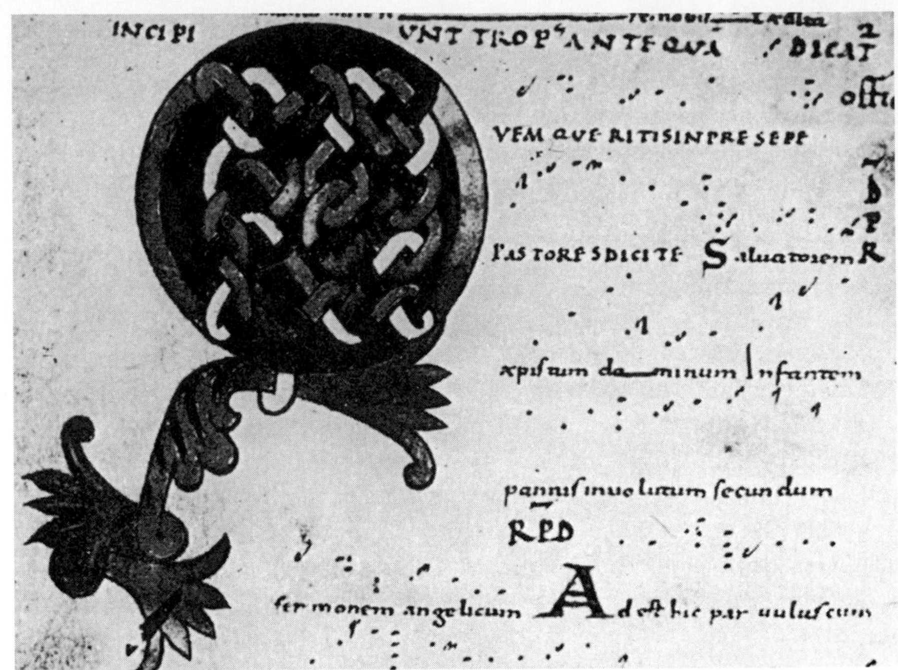

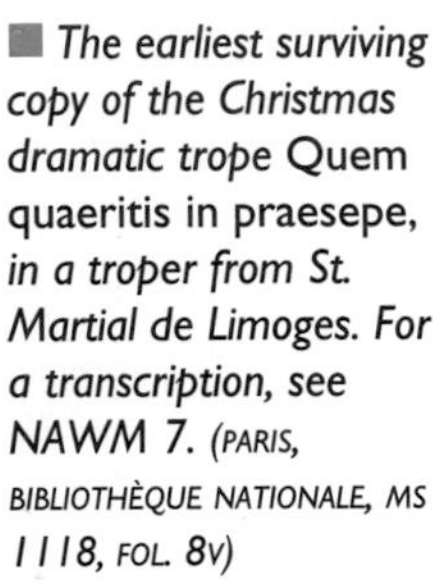

■ *The earliest surviving copy of the Christmas dramatic trope* Quem quaeritis in praesepe, *in a troper from St. Martial de Limoges. For a transcription, see NAWM 7.* (PARIS, BIBLIOTHÈQUE NATIONALE, MS 1118, FOL. 8V)

action. The trope *Quem quaeritis in praesepe* (Whom do you seek in the manger? NAWM 7; CD 1 [20]) to the Introit for the Third Mass of Christmas Day, *Puer natus est nobis* (A son is born unto us, NAWM 3a; CD 1 [3]), functions in a similar way. The midwives at Christ's birth question the shepherds who come to admire the child. The shepherds answer that they are looking for their Savior, the infant Christ.

The Easter and Christmas plays were the most common and were performed all over Europe. Certain other plays survive from the twelfth century and later. Among them the early thirteenth-century *Play of Daniel* from Beauvais and *The Play of Herod*, concerning the slaughter of the innocents, from Fleury, have now become (rather overelaborated) staples in the repertories of early-music ensembles. The music for these plays consists of a number of chants strung together, with processions and actions that approach theater. A few manuscripts contain evidence that a stage, scenery, costumes, and actors drawn from the clergy were sometimes used.

Hildegard of Bingen's *Ordo Virtutum* (The Virtues, ca. 1151), a nonliturgical sacred music drama, is a morality play in which all the parts—such as the Prophets, the Virtues, the Happy Soul, the Unhappy Soul, and the Penitent Soul—except the Devil's are sung in plainchant. The final chorus of the Virtues (NAWM 6; CD 1 [18] ⟨7⟩) is typical of her expansive melodies.

MEDIEVAL MUSIC THEORY AND PRACTICE

Treatises in the Carolingian era and in the later Middle Ages were much more oriented toward practice than earlier writings were. Boethius was regularly mentioned with reverence, and the mathematical fundamentals of music that he transmitted remained at the root of scale building and speculation about intervals and consonances. But reading Boethius did not help solve the immediate problems of notating, reading, classifying, and singing plainchant and of improvising or composing early polyphony. These topics now dominated the treatises. In his *Micrologus* (ca. 1025–28), for example, Guido of Arezzo (ca. 991–after 1033) credits Boethius with explaining the numerical ratios of the intervals. Guido recounts the story that Pythagoras discovered these relationships while hearing the hammers in a blacksmith shop. Guido then takes these ratios and divides a monochord in the manner of Boethius. (The monochord was a string stretched over a long wooden resonator, with a movable bridge to vary the sounding length of the string.) However, after reporting Boethius's scheme, Guido presents a simpler method that yields the same diatonic scale, tuned to produce pure fourths and fifths as well as octaves and a single size of whole tone, in the ratio 9:8. Guido also departs from Greek theory by constructing a scale that is not based on the tetrachord and by demonstrating a set of modes that have no connection with the tonoi or harmoniai of the ancients. He takes great pains to instruct the student in the characteristics and power of the modes and shows how to invent melodies based on them and how to combine two or more voices in simultaneous chanting. Guido found some models for this *diaphony* or *organum* in an anonymous ninth-century treatise known as *Musica enchiriadis.* (See below, page 72.)

Treatises such as *Musica enchiriadis*—and even more the accompanying *Scolica enchiriadis*, a dialogue between teacher and pupil—were directed at students who aspired to enter clerical orders. The monasteries and the schools

■ *Guido of Arezzo (left) with his sponsor, Bishop Theodaldus, calculating the string lengths of the scale steps (starting on gamma-ut). Guido dedicated to the bishop his* Micrologus, *a treatise in which he proposed a division of the monochord that is simpler than that transmitted by Boethius. Twelfth-century manuscript of German origin.* (VIENNA, OESTERREICHISCHE NATIONALBIBLIOTHEK)

attached to cathedral churches were educational as well as religious institutions. In the monasteries, musical instruction was practical, with a scattering of nonmusical subjects at an elementary level. The cathedral schools gave more attention to speculative studies, and, from the beginning of the thirteenth century, it was chiefly these schools that prepared students for the universities. But formal education in medieval times was mainly oriented toward practical matters, and the musical treatises reflect this attitude. Their authors pay their respects to Boethius in an introductory chapter or two and then turn, with evident relief, to more pressing topics. Some of the instruction books are in verse; others are written as dialogues between an eager student and an omniscient master, reflecting the customary oral method of teaching with great emphasis on memorization.[5] Visual aids appeared in the shape of diagrams and tables. Students were taught to sing intervals, to memorize chants, and, later, to read notes at sight. Toward these ends, one of the most essential components of the curriculum was the system of eight modes, or *toni* (tones), as medieval writers called them.

The Church Modes

The medieval modal system developed gradually, and not all stages of the process can be clearly traced. In its complete form, achieved by the eleventh century, the system encompassed eight modes, differentiated according to the position of the whole tones and semitones in a diatonic octave built on the *finalis*, or *final*. In practice, this note was usually the last note in the melody. The modes were identified by numbers and grouped in pairs; the odd-numbered modes were called *authentic*, and the even-numbered modes *plagal* (collateral). A plagal mode always had the same final as its corresponding authentic mode. The authentic modal scales may be thought of as analogous to white-key octave scales on a modern keyboard rising from the notes *D* (mode 1), *E* (mode 3), *F* (mode 5), and *G* (mode 7), with their corresponding plagals (modes 2, 4, 6, and 8) a fourth lower (Example 2.4). These notes, of course, do not stand for a specific "absolute" pitch—a concept foreign to plainchant and to the Middle Ages in general; they are simply a convenient way to distinguish the interval patterns of the modes.

The finals of each mode are shown in Example 2.4 as 𝅜. In addition to the final, each mode has a second characteristic note, called the *tenor* (as in the psalm tones; see above, page 42), *repercussio*, or *reciting tone* (shown in Example 2.4 as 𝅝). The finals of the corresponding plagal and authentic modes are the same, but the tenors differ. A handy way to identify the tenors using the scheme of Example 2.4 is to remember that (1) in the authentic modes the tenor is a fifth above the final; (2) in the plagal modes the tenor is a third below the tenor of the corresponding authentic mode, except (3) whenever a tenor would fall on the note *B*, it is moved up to *C*.

5. The dialogue form was still used in Renaissance treatises, such as Morley's *Plaine and Easie Introduction* of 1597, and even as late as Fux's *Gradus ad Parnassum* of 1725.

Example 2.4 *The Medieval Church Modes*

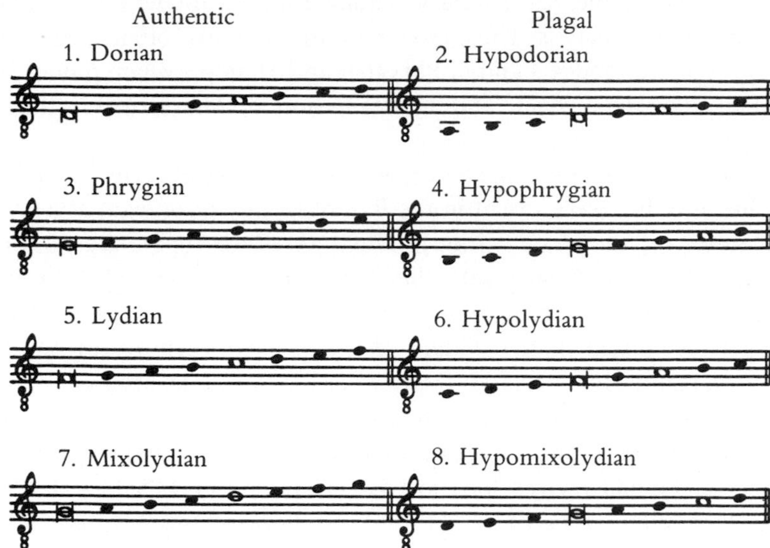

The final, tenor, contour, and range all contribute to characterizing a mode. In the authentic modes, the range of a chant lies above the final, with the possibility of one note below the final. Chants in the plagal modes, by contrast, have their final in the middle of the plagal octave, and their range may extend beyond this octave. Thus modes 1 and 8 have the same range, different finals and tenors, and distinct contours.

Accidentals

The only accidental properly used in notating plainchants is a flat, and only with the note *B*. Under certain conditions, the *B* was flatted in modes 1 and 2, making their octave scales analogous to the modern natural minor; modes 5 and 6 could similarly be made to resemble the modern major. Accidentals were necessary, of course, when a modal melody was transposed; if a chant in mode 1, for example, were written on *G*, a flat would be required in the signature.

The modes became a means for classifying chants and arranging them in books for liturgical use. Many of the chants existed before the theory of modes evolved. Some chants remain entirely within the range of a fifth above the final and one note below; others use the entire octave range with perhaps one note beyond in either direction; still others, such as the sequence *Victimae paschali laudes* (NAWM 5; CD 1 17 ◇6◇), cover the entire combined range of the authentic mode and its corresponding plagal. Some chants which combine the characteristics of two modes that have different finals cannot be definitely assigned to either mode. In short, the modality of actual chant melodies does not entirely conform to modal theory.

Application of Greek names

In the tenth century, a few authors applied the names of the Greek tonoi and harmoniai to the church modes. Misreading Boethius, they named the *A*-octave the Hypodorian, the *B*-octave Hypophrygian, and so forth. The two systems are not at all parallel, however. Although neither medieval treatises nor modern liturgical books refer to the modes by the Greek names (preferring numerals), the ethnic names are generally used in modern textbooks on counterpoint and analysis. Thus, modes 1 and 2 are now often called Dorian and Hypodorian; modes 3 and 4, Phrygian and Hypophrygian; modes 5 and 6, Lydian and Hypolydian; and modes 7 and 8, Mixolydian and Hypomixolydian.

Modes with finals on *a*, *b*, and *c'*; were not recognized in medieval theory, partly because they were absent in the Byzantine system of eight *echoi*, which was a model for the western modes. They were also superfluous, since the modes on *d*, *e*, and *f*, sung with the flatted *b* (which was available in the system), are equivalent to the modes on *a*, *b*, and *c'*. The modes on *a* and *c'* were first recognized in the middle of the sixteenth century by the Swiss theorist Glareanus. In his treatise *Dodekachordon* (1547), he proposed a system of twelve modes in which the authentic and plagal modes on *a* became modes 9 and 10, and those on *c'* became modes 11 and 12. Laboring under the illusion that he had revived long-lost Greek modes, he called modes 9 and 10, Aeolian and Hypoaeolian, 11 and 12, Ionian and Hypoionian. He rejected the final on *b*, because it lacked a perfect fifth above and a perfect fourth below.

Solmization

For teaching sight singing, the eleventh-century monk Guido of Arezzo proposed a set of syllables, *ut*, *re*, *mi*, *fa*, *sol*, *la*, to help singers remember the pattern of whole tones and semitones in the six steps that begin on *G* or *C*. In this pattern, (for example, *C–D–E–F–G–A*), a semitone falls between the third and fourth steps, and all other steps are whole tones. The syllables were derived from a hymn text (dating from at least the year 800) that Guido may have set to music to illustrate the pattern: *Ut queant laxis*. Each of the six phrases of the hymn begins with one of the notes of the pattern in regular ascending order—the first phrase on *C*, the second on *D*, and so on. (See Example 2.5.) The initial syllables of these six phrases became the names of the steps. These solmization syllables (so called from *sol–mi*) are still employed in teaching, except some teachers say *do* for *ut* and add a *ti* above *la*. The advantage of the six-note pattern is that there is only one semitone, always between *mi* and *fa*.

Example 2.5 *Hymn*: Ut queant laxis

That thy servants may freely sing forth the wonders of thy deeds, remove all stain of guilt from their unclean lips, O Saint John.

Example 2.6 *The System of Hexachords*

The hexachord system

After Guido, the six-step solmization pattern developed into a system of hexachords. The *hexachord*, or interval pattern of the six notes from *ut* to *la*, could be found at different places in the scale: beginning on *C*, on *G*, and (by flatting the *B*) on *F*. The hexachord on *G* used the *B*-natural, for which the sign was ♮ "square b" (*b quadrum*); the *F* hexachord used the *B*-flat, which had the sign ♭ "round b" (*b rotundum*). Although these signs are obviously the models for our ♮, ♯, and ♭, their original purpose was not the same as that of the modern accidentals; originally they served to indicate the syllables *mi* and *fa*. The hexachord on *G* with the square *B* was called "hard" (*durum*), and that on *F* with the round *B* was called "soft" (*molle*); the one on *C* was called the "natural" hexachord. The entire musical space used by medieval composers and considered by medieval theorists extended from *G* (which was written as the Greek letter Γ, and called *gamma*) to *e″*. Within this range, every note was named not only by its letter but also according to the position it occupied within the hexachord or hexachords to which it belonged. Thus *gamma*, which was the first note of its hexachord, was called *gamma ut* (from which our word *gamut*); *e″*, as the top note of its hexachord, was *e la*. Middle *c′*, which belonged to three different hexachords, was *c sol fa ut* (see Example 2.6). Both the Greek and the medieval note names were retained by theorists until well into the sixteenth century, but only the medieval names were in practical use.

Using the syllables to learn a melody that exceeded a six-note range required changing from one hexachord to another. This was done by a process called *mutation*, whereby a note was begun as if it were in one hexachord and quitted as if it were in another, the way a pivot chord is used in modern harmony. For instance, in the Kyrie *Cunctipotens Genitor Deus* (Example 2.7), the fifth note *a* is begun as *la* in the *C* hexachord and quitted as *re* in the *G* hexachord; the reverse mutation occurs on the third note *a* of the following phrase.

Followers of Guido developed a pedagogical aid called the "Guidonian hand." Pupils were taught to sing intervals as the teacher pointed with the

Example 2.7 *Kyrie*: Cunctipotens Genitor Deus

index finger of the right hand to the different joints of the open left hand. Each joint stood for one of the twenty notes of the system; any other note, such as F♯ or E♭, was considered to be "outside the hand." No late medieval or Renaissance music textbook was complete without a drawing of this hand.

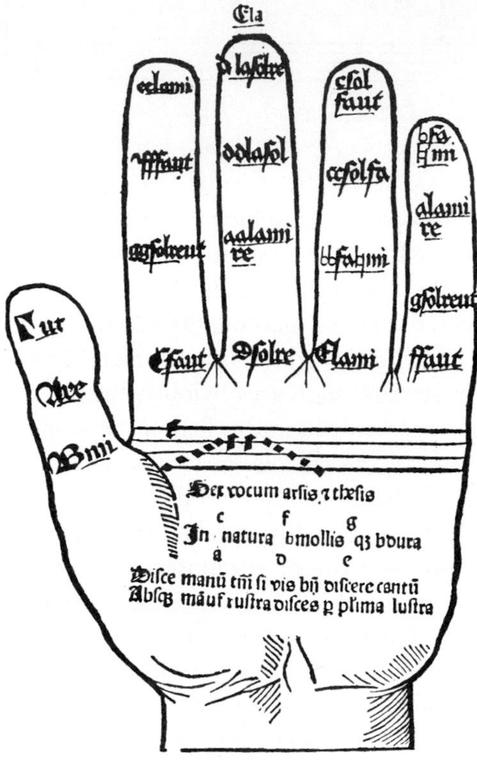

■ *The "Guidonian hand," a mnemonic device used for locating the pitches of the diatonic scale, particularly the semitones mi-fa, which occupy the four corners of the polygon containing the four fingers. Although credited to Guido, the hand was probably a later application of his solmization syllables.*

Notation

Theorists of the Middle Ages also worked on developing an adequate musical notation. As long as the chants were transmitted orally and texts could be fitted loosely to the traditional melodies, all that was needed was an occasional reminder of the tune's general outline. Beginning sometime before the middle of the ninth century, signs called *neumes* were placed above the words to indicate an ascending melodic line (/), a descending one (\), or a combination of the two (/\). These neumes were probably derived from grammatical accent marks such as those still used in modern French. By the tenth century, scribes were placing neumes at varying heights above the text to indicate the course of the melody more precisely; these are called *heighted* or *diastematic* neumes. Sometimes dots were added to the solid lines to indicate the relationship between the individual notes of a neume, making it clearer what intervals the neume represented. A decisive change occurred when a scribe drew a horizontal red line to represent the pitch *f* and grouped the neumes about this line; in time, a second line, usually yellow, was drawn for *c′*. By the eleventh century

Guido of Arezzo was describing a staff then in use, on which letters indicated the lines for *f*, *c′* and sometimes *g′* (these eventually became our modern clef signs).

The invention of the staff not only enabled scribes to notate (relative) pitches precisely, but also freed music from its dependence on oral transmission. This achievement was as crucial for the history of Western music as the invention of writing was for the history of language. The staff notation with neumes was still imperfect, however: it conveyed the pitch of the notes but not their relative durations. Some medieval chant manuscripts contain signs indicating rhythm, but modern scholars have not agreed on their meaning. There is evidence that different note shapes once indicated different durations, and that from the ninth to the twelfth centuries chant singers used definite long and short time values. But this manner of singing seems to have gone out of use after the twelfth century. One modern practice is to treat the notes of a chant as if they all had the same basic value; notes are grouped rhythmically in twos or threes, and these groups are flexibly combined into larger rhythmic units. This interpretation, worked out in the early twentieth century by the Benedictine monks of the Abbey of Solesmes under the leadership of Dom André Mocquereau, was approved by the Catholic Church as conforming with the spirit of the liturgy. The Solesmes editions of the liturgical books, intended for practical use rather than historical study, include some interpretive signs that are not in the manuscripts. Plainchant specialists doubt that the Solesmes interpretations reflect medieval practice.

NONLITURGICAL AND SECULAR MONODY

Early Secular Genres

The oldest written specimens of secular music are songs with Latin texts. The earliest of these form the repertory of *Goliard songs* from the eleventh and twelfth centuries. The Goliards—named after a probably mythical patron, Bishop Golias—were students or footloose clerics who migrated from one school to another in the days before the great universities were founded. Their vagabond way of life, scorned by respectable people, was celebrated in their songs, which were gathered in numerous manuscript collections. The texts are drawn largely from three topics of interest to young men of the time: wine, women, and satire. The treatment is sometimes delicate, sometimes ribald, as we may readily sense when listening to the modern musical settings in Carl Orff's *Carmina burana.* Only a little of the Goliard music is notated in the manuscripts, and that bit is in staffless neumes; therefore, modern transcriptions are conjectural unless a melody is preserved in a source with more precise notation.

Another kind of monophonic song from the same period—the eleventh, twelfth, and thirteenth centuries—is the *conductus* (plural also *conductus*). Conductus straddle the vague dividing line between sacred and secular music.

Conductus

Originally they may have been sung when a cleric in a liturgical drama or a celebrant in a liturgical service was formally "conducted" from one place to another. Their texts were metrical verses in Latin, like those of sequences from the same period. But their connection with the liturgy was so tenuous that by the end of the twelfth century, the term *conductus* applied to any serious, nonliturgical Latin song with a metrical text on any sacred or secular subject. An important feature of the conductus was that, as a rule, its melody was newly composed, not borrowed or adapted from plainchant.

Chanson de geste

The secular spirit of the Middle Ages comes through clearly in the songs with vernacular texts. One of the earliest known types was the *chanson de geste*, or "song of deeds," an epic narrative poem recounting the deeds of national heroes, sung to simple melodic formulas. A single formula serves unchanged for each line throughout long sections of the poem. The poems, transmitted orally, were not reduced to writing until comparatively late; virtually none of the music has been preserved. The most famous *chanson de geste* is the *Song of Roland*, the national epic of France, which dates from about the second half of the eleventh century, though its story belongs to the age of Charlemagne.

Jongleurs

The people who sang the *chansons de geste* and other secular songs in the Middle Ages were the *jongleurs* or *ménestrels* (minstrels), a class of professional musicians who first appear about the tenth century. These men and women wandered singly or in small groups from village to village and castle to castle, earning a precarious living by singing, playing, performing tricks, and exhibiting trained animals. They were social outcasts, often denied the protection of the laws and the sacraments of the church. With the economic recovery of Europe in the eleventh and twelfth centuries, society became more stably organized on a feudal basis and towns sprang up. The condition of the minstrels improved, though for a long time people continued to regard them with a mixture of fascination and revulsion. In the eleventh century, they organized themselves into brotherhoods, which later developed into guilds of musicians offering professional training, much as a modern conservatory does.

The minstrels were not poets or composers in the usual sense. They sang, played, and danced to songs composed by others or taken from the popular repertory, no doubt altering them or making up their own versions as they went along. Their professional traditions and skill played a role in an important development of secular music in western Europe—the body of song known today as the music of the troubadours and the trouvères.

Troubadours and Trouvères

Troubadours (feminine singular and plural, *trobairitz*) were poet-composers who flourished in what is now the south of France and spoke Provençal, the *langue d'oc* (also called *Occitan*). *Trouvères* were their equivalent in northern France. (The verb *trobar* in the southern dialect and its corresponding *trouver* in the north meant "to find"; thus troubadours and trouvères were finders or inventors of songs.) Their art, taking its inspiration from the neighboring culture of Moorish Spain, spread quickly northward, especially to the provinces of Champagne and Artois. There the trouvères, active throughout the thirteenth century, spoke the *langue d'oïl*, the medieval French dialect that became modern French.

Neither troubadours nor trouvères constituted a well-defined group. They flourished in generally aristocratic circles (there were even kings among their number), but artists of lower birth might be accepted into a higher social class on the grounds of their talent. Many of the poet-composers not only created their songs but sang them as well; when they did not they could entrust the performance to a minstrel. Versions of the same song often differ from one manuscript to another, perhaps because the documents were written by different scribes at different times. More likely, however, different minstrels who had learned the song by rote modified it to suit themselves, which is what happens when music is transmitted orally for a time before being written down. The songs are preserved in collections called *chansonniers*, some of which have

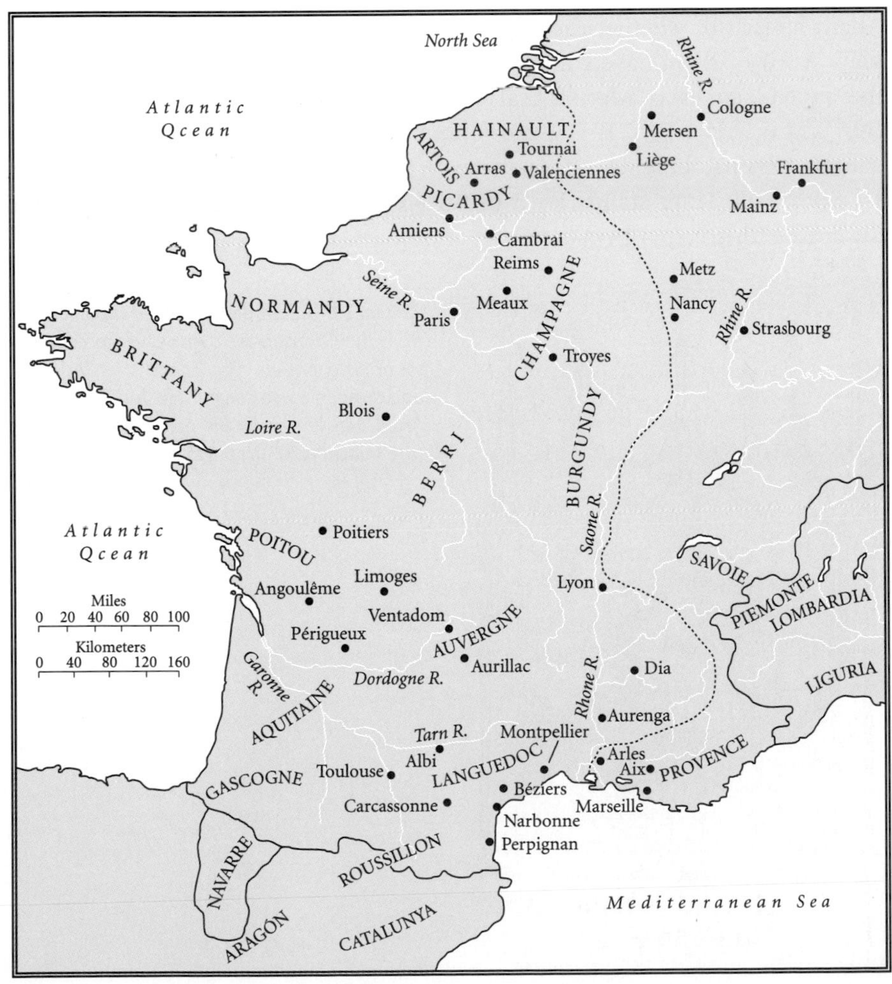

■ *French kingdom, duchies, and regions in the fifteenth century*

been published in modern editions or facsimiles. About 2,600 troubadour poems and about one-tenth as many melodies have been preserved. By contrast, we have some 2,130 trouvère poems, but at least two-thirds of their melodies are known.

The poetic and musical structures of the songs show great variety and ingenuity. Some ballads are simple, others dramatic, suggesting two or more characters. Some of the dramatic ballads were probably intended to be mimed; many obviously called for dancing. The dance songs may include a refrain sung by a chorus of dancers. The troubadours, especially, wrote love songs, the subject par excellence for their poetry. There are songs on political and moral topics, and songs whose texts debate or argue abstruse points of chivalric or courtly love. Religious songs, characteristically northern, appear only late in the thirteenth century. Each type of song included many subtypes that followed certain conventions about subject matter, form, and treatment.

Robin et Marion

Musical plays were built around some of the narrative pastoral songs or *pastourelles.* The most famous of such musical plays was *Jeu de Robin et de Marion* (about 1284) by Adam de la Halle (dates uncertain), the last of the trouvères. We do not know whether the songs in this work were written by Adam himself or whether they were all popular chansons incorporated in the play. A few of them have come down to us in polyphonic settings. Typical of the tuneful songs is Marion's at the opening of the play, *Robins m'aime* (NAWM 8; CD 1 [21]). It is a monophonic *rondeau,* a form that has unison choral refrains, here in the pattern ABaabAB. (In representing formal schemes, each letter stands for a distinct musical phrase: capitals for choral, lower case for solo performance.)

Image of Adam de la Halle in a miniature from the Chansonnier d'Arras, which contains six of his chansons. The legend says "Adans li bocus made these songs." His family, from Arras, was known by the name "le Bossu" (the hunchback). (ARRAS, BIBLIOTHÈQUE MUNICIPALE)

The pastoral and other narrative songs adapted folk material. The Provencal love songs, on the other hand, were aristocratic creations. Many were openly sensual; others hid sensuality under the veil of courtly love. The object of the passion expressed was a real woman—usually another man's wife—but she was adored from a distance, with such discretion, respect, and humility that the lover is made to seem more like a worshiper content to suffer in the service of his ideal Love. The lady herself is depicted as so remote, calm, lofty, and unattainable that she would be stepping out of character if she condescended to reward her faithful lover. It is significant that trouvère songs praising the Virgin Mary have the same style, the same vocabulary, and sometimes the same melodies that were used to celebrate earthly love.

Among the best preserved songs is *Can vei la lauzeta mover* (NAWM 9; CD 1 22 ⑨) by the troubadour Bernart de Ventadorn (ca. 1150–ca. 1180). The second of its eight stanzas typifies the lover's complaints that are the main subject of this repertory.[6]

Ai, las! tan cuidava saber	Alas! I thought I knew so much
d'amor, e tan petit en sai,	of love, and I know so little;
car eu d'amar no·m posc tener	for I cannot help loving
celeis don ia pro non aura.	a lady from whom I shall never obtain any favor.
Tout m'a mo cor, e tout m'a me,	She has taken away my heart and my self
e se mezeis e tot lo mon;	and herself and the whole world;
e can se·m tolc, no·m laisset re	and when she left me, I had nothing left
mas dezirer e cor volon.	but desire and a yearning heart.

All the stanzas are sung to the same through-composed melody, which is conceived in the first church mode.

Troubadour and Trouvère Melodies

The melodic settings of both troubadour and trouvère songs were generally syllabic with occasional short melismatic figures, mostly on the penultimate syllable of a line. Such a simple melody invited improvised ornaments and other variants as the singer passed from one stanza to the next. The range is narrow, frequently no more than a sixth and hardly ever more than an octave. Because the songs are chiefly written in the first and seventh church modes and their plagals, the entire body of works displays a certain coherence. The notation yields no clue to the rhythm of the songs. Some scholars maintain that they were sung in a free, unmeasured style, as the notation implies. Others contend that they were measured by long and short notes corresponding to the accented and unaccented syllables of the words. This divergence of opinion is shown in Example 2.8 by the five different transcriptions of the

6. Text and translation are from Hendrik van der Werf, *The Chansons of the Troubadours and Trouvères* (Utrecht: A. Oosthoek, 1972), pp. 91–95, which presents versions of the melody from five different sources, showing surprising consistency of readings. The dot splitting two letters of a word, as in no·m, stands for contraction.

Example 2.8 *Troubadour melody*: Reis glorios, *Guirault de Bornelh (1173–1220)*

Glorious King, true light and clarity.

same phrase. Most scholars now prefer transcription in even notes without measure bars.

Each poetic line of this song gets its own melodic setting. Two poetic lines of the same length may be set to phrases of different lengths because some of the syllables are treated melismatically. Through variation, contrast, and the repetition of short, distinctive musical phrases, a variety of formal patterns emerges. But these patterns do not fall neatly into categories such as those to come in the fourteenth century. Many of the troubadour and trouvère melodies repeat the opening phrase or section before proceeding in a free style. Phrases are modified on repetition, and elusive echoes of earlier phrases are heard; but the main impression is one of freedom, spontaneity, and apparent artlessness.

Some of these features are illustrated in *A chantar* by the twelfth-century troubadour Comtessa Beatriz de Dia (NAWM 10; CD 1 [23]). In this strophic song, or *canso*, there are four distinct melodic components, arranged in the form a b a b c d b. The setting is syllabic, except that some syllables, particularly accented ones, receive two or three notes. The music for each poetic line comes to a distinct stop in nearly every line in a strong-weak pattern. An important structural feature of some trouvère songs is the *refrain*, a recurring line (or pair of lines) in the text, usually with a recurring musical setting.

Refrain

Minnesinger

The troubadours served as the model for a German school of knightly poet-musicians, the *Minnesinger*, who flourished between the twelfth and fourteenth centuries. The love (*Minne*) of which they sang in their *Minnelieder* (love songs) was even more abstract than troubadour love and sometimes had a distinctly religious tinge. The music is correspondingly more sober. Some of the melodies are written in the church modes, while others veer toward major tonality. Relying on the rhythm of the texts, scholars think that the majority of the tunes were sung in triple meter. As in France, strophic songs were also very common. Their melodies, however, were more tightly organized through melodic phrase repetition.

Meistersinger

The Minnesinger were succeeded by the *Meistersinger*, staunch tradesmen and artisans of German cities, whose lives and activities were portrayed centuries later by Richard Wagner in his opera *Die Meistersinger von Nürnberg.* Toward the end of the thirteenth century, the art of the trouvères in France passed from the nobility to cultured middle-class citizens. A similar change took place in Germany during the course of the fourteenth, fifteenth, and sixteenth centuries. Hans Sachs, the hero of Wagner's opera, is a typical figure—a sixteenth-century shoemaker in Nuremberg who composed thousands of poems and tunes for singing them. Some fine examples of Sachs's art have survived, one of the most beautiful being a commentary on the strife between David and Saul (1 Samuel 17), *Nachdem David war redlich* (NAWM 11; CD 1 [24]). It is composed in a German poetic form called *Bar,* which was adopted by the Meistersinger from the Minnelied. In bar form—a a b—a melodic phrase, *a,* is sung twice for a stanza's first two units of text (called *Stollen*), and the remainder, *b* (called *Abgesang*), generally longer and sung only once, contains new melodic material.

The Guild of the Meistersinger of Memmingen auditioning a prize singer. Miniature from Stamung Meisterbuch der Memminger Meistersinger (1626). *(MEMMINGEN, STADTARCHIV)*

Although the repertory includes some masterpieces, the art of the Meistersinger was so hedged in by rigid rules that their music seems stiff in comparison to the Minnelieder. The Meistersingers' guild had a long life, and was finally dissolved only in the nineteenth century.

Sacred songs

In addition to secular songs, there were also many monophonic religious songs in the Middle Ages that were not intended for use in church. Expressions of individual piety, they were composed to vernacular texts in a melodic idiom that was derived about equally from chant and from popular song.

Songs of Other Countries

The few surviving English songs of the thirteenth century show a variety of moods and suggest a much more extensive musical life than we can now reconstruct. From Spain, a beautifully illuminated manuscript collection prepared under the direction of King Alfonso el Sabio (the Wise) between about 1250 and 1280 preserves more than four hundred monophonic *cantigas*, songs of praise to the Virgin; they resemble in many ways the music of the troubadours.

Laude

Laude are Italian monophonic songs of a vigorous, popular character that were sung in lay confraternities and in processions by religious penitents. The lauda was still cultivated in Italy after the penitential craze of the thirteenth and fourteenth centuries—largely inspired by the ravages of the Black Death—and the texts were eventually given polyphonic settings. Related to the laude are the *Geisslerlieder*, flagellants' songs of fourteenth-century Germany.

MEDIEVAL INSTRUMENTAL MUSIC AND INSTRUMENTS

Estampie

Dances in the Middle Ages were accompanied both by songs and by instrumental music, such as the *estampie*, a dance piece for which we have several English and Continental examples from the thirteenth and fourteenth centuries. Sometimes monophonic and sometimes polyphonic, each of its several sections (*puncta*, or *partes*) was repeated, as in the plainchant sequence. The first statement ended with an "open" (*ouvert*), or incomplete, cadence. The repetition ended with a "closed" (*clos*), or full, cadence. The same open and closed endings were usually employed throughout an estampie, and the music preceding the endings was also similar. Derived from the French estampie, the *istampite* in a fourteenth-century Italian manuscript are a somewhat more complex variant of the same form. The *Istampita Palamento* (NAWM 12; CD 1 [25]) has five *partes*, each constructed in the way described above, with open and closed endings marking the two halves of each *pars*.

Estampies are the earliest known examples of an instrumental repertory that surely reaches back far beyond the thirteenth century. Probably all the instrumental music of the early Middle Ages was associated with singing or dancing.

Illuminations from the Cantigas de Santa Maria, *a collection of more than 400 songs—mostly narrating the miracles of the Virgin Mary or praising her—made between about 1250 and 1280 under the direction of Alfonso el Sabio, king of Castile and León. Against the background of a Moorish décor, musicians are shown playing the bagpipe, double shawms, organistrum (hurdy-gurdy), and transverse flute.* (EL ESCORIAL, REAL BIBLIOTECA DE SAN LORENZO)

Musical Instruments

Harp

Vielle

The Roman lyre survived into the Middle Ages, but the oldest characteristically medieval instrument was the harp, which was imported to the Continent from Ireland and Britain some time before the ninth century. The principal bowed instrument of medieval times was the *vielle* (in French) or *Fiedel* (in German), which had many different names and a great variety of shapes and sizes; it is the prototype of the Renaissance viol and the modern violin. The thirteenth-century vielle had five strings, one of them usually a drone. It is most often depicted in the hands of jongleurs, who are probably playing it to accompany their singing and recitations. Another stringed instrument, the organistrum, is described in a tenth-century treatise as a three-stringed vielle played by a revolving wheel turned by a crank, the strings being stopped by a set of rods instead of the player's fingers. In the early Middle Ages, the organistrum was a large instrument that required two players and was used in churches; after the thirteenth century it turned up in a smaller form, from which the modern hurdy-gurdy descended.

Organistrum

Psaltery and lute

The psaltery appears frequently in medieval art; it is a type of zither played by plucking or, more often, by striking the strings—a remote ancestor of the harpsichord and clavichord. The lute, known as early as the ninth century, was brought into Spain by the Arab conquerors, but it did not become common elsewhere much before the Renaissance. There were flutes, both the recorder and the transverse types, and shawms, reed instruments of the oboe variety. Trumpets were played by wandering musicians and later by tower watchmen. Another reed instrument, the bagpipe, was the universal folk instrument.

Wind instruments

Organs

In addition to the great organs in churches, the Middle Ages saw two smaller types, the portative and the positive. The portative organ was small enough to be carried (*portatum*), sometimes suspended by a strap around the neck of the player; it had a single rank of pipes, and the keys or "slides" were played by the right hand while the left worked the bellows. The positive organ could also be carried but had to be placed (*positum*) on a table to be played and required an assistant to pump the bellows.

Most of these instruments came into Europe from Asia, either by way of Byzantium or through the Arabs in North Africa and Spain. Their early history is obscure and their nomenclature often inconsistent and confusing. We can be sure, however, that music in the Middle Ages was much brighter and had a more varied instrumental color than the manuscripts alone suggest.

Bibliography

Sources: Music Facsimiles and Editions

Chant

Facsimiles of many of the earliest manuscripts of plainchant are published in *Paléographie musicale: les principaux manuscrits de chant Grégorien, Ambrosien, Mozarabe, Gallican*

(Solesmes: Imprimerie St-Pierre; and Tournai: Desclée, Lefebure, 1889–), two series. For a complete description of the volumes, refer to "Sources, MS, II," in NG.

Color reproductions from various manuscripts appear in Bruno Stäblein, ed., *Schriftbild der einstimmigen Musik*, Musikgeschichte in Bildern 3/4 (Leipzig: Deutscher Verlag für Musik, 1975).

The Liber Usualis with Introduction and Rubrics in English (New York: Desclée Co., 1961) is the practical reference for chant use in the modern Catholic liturgy. It has been obsolete since Vatican II and is therefore out of print. *LU* presents an idealized version that attempts to account for diverse sources and changes over the centuries. The chants of the Mass in plainsong notation with facsimiles of original neumes above and below are in *Graduale triplex* (Solesmes: Abbaye Saint-Pierre de Solesmes, 1979).

Liturgical Drama

The music is collected in Susan Rankin, *The Music of the Medieval Liturgical Drama in France and England*, 2 vols. (New York: Garland, 1989); Edmond de Coussemaker, ed., *Drames liturgiques du moyen age* (1860; New York: Broude Bros., 1964). Individual liturgical dramas: Noah Greenberg, ed., *The Play of Daniel* (New York: Oxford University Press, 1959); *The Play of Herod* (New York: Oxford University Press, 1965): both have literal transcriptions by William L. Smoldon. *The Play of Herod* also appears in *Medieval Music: The Oxford Anthology of Music*, ed. W. Thomas Marrocco and Nicholas Sandon (London: Oxford University Press, 1977). Editions of texts are found in Karl Young, *The Drama of the Medieval Church* (Oxford: Clarendon Press, 1933) and David Bevington, *Medieval Drama* (Boston: Houghton Mifflin, 1975); and the complete texts of all versions of the Easter plays have been compiled by Walther Lipphardt in *Lateinische Osterfeiern und Osterspiele*, 9 vols. (Berlin: DeGruyter, 1975–90).

Secular Monody, Nonliturgical Songs, Chansonniers

A color facsimile of the *Carmina burana* appears in Vol. 9 of PMMM, ed. B. Bischoff (Brooklyn: Institute of Medieval Music, 1967). Troubadour songs are ed. Hendrik van der Werf (texts ed. Gerald A. Bond), in *The Chansons of the Troubadors and Trouvères* (Utrecht: A. Oosthoek, 1972) and in *The Extant Troubadour Melodies: Transcriptions and Essays for Performers and Scholars* (Rochester, N.Y.: Author, 1984). Trouvère songs are in van der Werf, ed., *Trouvères-Melodies*, in Monumenta musicae medii aevi, 11–12 (Kassel: Bärenreiter, 1977–79).

For the lauda repertory: Fernando Liuzzi, ed., *La lauda e i primordi della melodia italiana*, 2 vols. (Rome: Libreria dello Stato, 1935). For the cantigas: Higini Anglès, *La música de las cantigas de Santa Maria del Rey Alfonso el Sabio* (Barcelona: Biblioteca Central. Sección de Musica, 1943–64), 15, 18–19; 3 vols. in 4 (Vols. 1 and 2 contain a facsimile and a complete transcription of the Escorial MS; Vol. 3 includes facsimiles and transcriptions of other music).

Chansonniers in facsimile: Pierre Aubry, *Le Chansonnier de l'Arsenal* (Paris: P. Geuthner, 1909), facs. and partial transcription; Jean Beck, *Le Chansonnier Cangé*, 2 vols. (Philadelphia: University of Pennsylvania Press, 1927) (Vol. 2 has transcriptions); Beck, *Le Manuscrit du Roi*, 2 vols. (Philadelphia: University of Pennsylvania Press, 1938); Alfred Jeanroy, *Le Chansonnier d'Arras* (Paris, 1925; repr. New York: Johnson, 1968).

Sources: Theoretical Treatises

Most of the treatises cited in the text have been translated into English; for Boethius, see Bibliography to Chapter 1.

Hucbald, *De institutione musica*, Guido of Arezzo, *Micrologus*, and Johannes "Cotto" or "Affligemensis," *De musica cum tonario*, trans. Warren Babb, in Claude Palisca, ed., *Hucbald, Guido and John on Music* (New Haven: Yale University Press, 1978). Hermannus Contractus, *Musica*, ed. with Eng. trans. by Leonard Ellinwood (Rochester: Eastman School of Music, 1952). *Musica enchiriadis and Scolica enchiriadis*, trans. with intro. and notes by Raymond Erickson, ed. Claude V. Palisca (New Haven: Yale University Press, 1995). A partial translation of *Scolica enchiriadis* is in SRrev, pp. 189–96; 2:79–86.

For Further Reading and Reference

For a history of Gregorian chant, see Kenneth Levy, *Gregorian Chant and the Carolingians* (Princeton: Princeton University Press, 1998). On the psalms: *The Place of the Psalms in the Intellectual Culture in the Middle Ages* (Albany: State University of New York, 1999). An annotated bibliography on medieval musical scholarship is Andrew Hughes, *Medieval Music: The Sixth Liberal Art* (Toronto: University of Toronto Press, 1980). Replacing an older volume of the New Oxford History of Music is *The Early Middle Ages to 1300*, ed. Richard Crocker and David Hiley (Oxford: Oxford University Press, 1990).

John R. Bryden and David Hughes, *An Index of Gregorian Chant* (Cambridge, Mass.: Harvard University Press, 1969), 2 vols.

On the structure of the liturgy and the types of chant, see Richard H. Hoppin, *Medieval Music* (New York: Norton, 1978); and, for a more concise treatment, Giulio Cattin, *Music of the Middle Ages* 1, trans. Steven Botterill (Cambridge: Cambridge University Press, 1984). Also John Harper, *The Forms and Orders of Western Liturgy from the Tenth to the Eighteenth Century* (Oxford: Clarendon Press, 1991); David Hiley, *Western Plainchant* (Oxford: Clarendon Press, 1993). For a study in depth of one of the chant dialects, see Thomas F. Kelly, *The Beneventan Chant* (Cambridge: Cambridge University Press, 1989). For a broad view of music in the culture of late antiquity and the Middle Ages, read the essays by expert authors in *Antiquity and the Middle Ages: From Ancient Greece to the 15th Century*, ed. James McKinnon (Englewood Cliffs, N.J.: Prentice Hall, 1990), or Christopher Page, *Discarding Images: Reflections on Music and Culture in Medieval France* (Oxford: Clarendon Press, 1993).

On later developments of chant, see Richard Crocker, "The Troping Hypothesis," MQ 52 (1966):183–203, and GLHWM 1; and his *The Early Medieval Sequence* (Berkeley: University of California Press, 1977); Margot Fassler, *Gothic Song: Victorine Sequences and Augustinian Reform in Twelfth-Century Paris* (Cambridge: Cambridge University Press, 1993).

On Hildegard of Bingen: *Voice of the Living Light: Hildegard of Bingen and Her World*, ed. Barbara Newman (Berkeley: University of California Press, 1998).

For general discussions of liturgical drama, see NG: "Medieval Drama"; Karl Young, *The Drama of the Medieval Church*; O. B. Hardison, *Christian Rite and Christian Drama in the Middle Ages* (Baltimore: Johns Hopkins Press, 1965); and W. L. Smoldon, "Liturgical Drama," NOHM 2:175–219. An overview of monastic life may be gained in James C. King and Werner Vogler, *The Culture of the Abbey of St. Gall* (Stuttgart: Belser, 1991).

An excellent study of monophonic setting of various kinds of texts, both sacred and secular, is John Stevens, *Words and Music in the Middle Ages: Song, Narrative, Dance and Drama, 1050–1350* (Cambridge: Cambridge University Press, 1986).

On notation, see "Notation" and "Neumatic Notation" in NG. Some new theories are presented by Treitler in "Early History of Music Writing in the West," JAMS 35 (1982):237–79.

For transcriptions of all the extant dances, see Timothy McGee, *Medieval Instrumental Dances* (Bloomington: Indiana University Press, 1989).

On secular monophony, see Margaret Switten, *The Medieval Lyric* (South Hadley, Mass.: Mount Holyoke College 1987–) and accompanying cassettes. Robert S. Briffault, *The Troubadours* (Bloomington: Indiana University Press, 1965) is a history of the troubadours.

F. Alberto Gallo, *Music in the Castle: Troubadours, Books, and Orators in Italian Courts of the Thirteenth, Fourteenth, and Fifteenth Centuries*, trans. Anna Herklotz (Chicago: University of Chicago Press, 1996). On Spanish secular monophony, see Robert Stevenson, *Spanish Music in the Age of Columbus* (The Hague: M. Nijhoff, 1960), pp. 1–49.

For texts of original sources of theoretical treatises, both manuscript and printed, connect to Thesaurus Musicarum Latinarum at http://www.music.indiana.edu/tml

CHAPTER 3

THE BEGINNINGS OF POLYPHONY AND THE MUSIC OF THE THIRTEENTH CENTURY

HISTORICAL BACKGROUND OF EARLY POLYPHONY

The years 1000–1100 witnessed a revival of economic life throughout western Europe, an increase in population, the reclamation of wastelands, and the beginning of modern cities. The Normans conquered England, while Spain was seeking to liberate itself from Muslim conquerors. The First Crusade united Christian ruling families from all over Europe in a campaign to drive the Turks from Jerusalem, which the Crusaders eventually took in 1099. Europe enjoyed a cultural revival. Important books were translated from Greek and Arabic into Latin. Institutions that later became universities sprang up in Paris, Oxford, and Bologna. Large Romanesque churches, built on the architectural principle of the round arch of the Roman basilica, began to dominate the landscape. Latin and vernacular literature and philosophy asserted their independence from pagan antiquity. The rivalry between the Western and Eastern churches reached a crisis in 1054, when the Roman pope excommunicated the patriarch of Constantinople after Norman invaders captured Byzantine-held territory in southern Italy. The patriarch of Constantinople reciprocated the discourtesy, splitting the Christian Church in two.

Polyphony

Meanwhile polyphony made its way slowly into church music. By polyphony we mean music in which separate voices sing together, not in unison or octaves but as diverging parts. When, in the eleventh century, singers improvising under the constraints of certain rules departed from simple parallel motion to give these parts some independence, a development unique in music history began. The kind of notation achieved during this century finally allowed scribes and composers to write down combinations of parts, and the

Notation

Composition

music could now be performed consistently and repeatedly. Notation could aid and replace memory as a means of preserving new and previously unwritten music. It also allowed and induced composers to structure their music more deliberately and follow certain precepts, such as the theory of the eight modes and rules governing rhythm and consonance. Such precepts were eventually set down in treatises.

These changes came about gradually; there was no sudden, sharp break with the past. Monophony remained the principal medium of both performance and new composition. Indeed, some of the finest monophonic chants, including antiphons, hymns, and sequences, were produced as late as the twelfth and thirteenth centuries. Musicians also continued to improvise during the eleventh century and beyond, and many stylistic details of the new composed music most probably grew out of improvisational practice.

By about 600 C.E., the Western church had absorbed and adapted almost all that it could from the music of antiquity and the East. During the next four hundred years, the material was systematized, codified, and disseminated throughout western Europe. On this heritage, musicians of the later Middle Ages built their monophonic and polyphonic creations.

EARLY ORGANUM

Heterophony

We have good reason to believe that polyphony existed in Europe long before it was first unmistakably described. Melodic doubling at the third, fourth, or fifth, along with *heterophony* is found in many cultures and probably existed also in Europe. Heterophony essentially consists of performing two or more simultaneous lines of music coordinated, if at all, on only the most elementary level. Needless to say, no documents of such early European polyphony survive. But the first clear description of music for more than one vocal part, written in the ninth century, definitely refers to a practice already in use, not a new

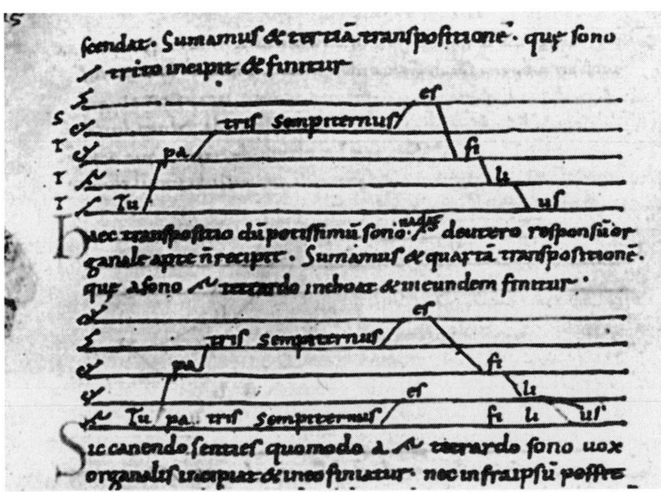

Two transpositions of the same fragment of chant from the Te Deum, in daseian notation, from Musica enchiriadis *(ca. 900), Chapter 18. The signs at the left identify the pitches of the syllables placed in the spaces. In the lower example, the reader is shown how to avoid the tritone when improvising an organal voice below the chant. Eleventh-century manuscript.* (EINSIEDELN, STIFTS-BIBLIOTHEK, COD. 79)

Musica and *Scolica enchiriadis*

one being proposed. Passages in an anonymous treatise, *Musica enchiriadis* (Music Handbook), and in a dialogue associated with it, *Scolica enchiriadis* (Excerpts from Handbooks), describe and illustrate two distinct kinds of "singing together," or diaphony, both designated by the name *organum* (pronounced órga-num). In one species of this early organum (Example 3.1), a plainsong melody in the "principal voice" (*vox principalis*) is duplicated at a fifth or a fourth below by an "organal voice" (*vox organalis*). Either voice or both may be further duplicated at the octave (Example 3.2). Singing in parallel fourths sometimes results in a tritone. For example, if the *vox organalis* sang D D E F in parallel fourths under the *vox principalis* on the words "Te humiles" in Example 3.3, a tritone would result. To avoid this disagreeable clash, a rule prohibited the organal voice from going below *G* or *C* in these situations; it was expected instead to remain on one note until it was safe once again to proceed in parallel fourths without meeting another tritone. Under this procedure, the organal part became differentiated from the plainchant and a greater variety of simultaneous intervals came into use, not all of them recognized consonances.

Example 3.1 *Parallel Organum*

You of the father are the everlasting son (from the *Te Deum*).

Example 3.2 *Modified Parallel Organum in Four Voices*

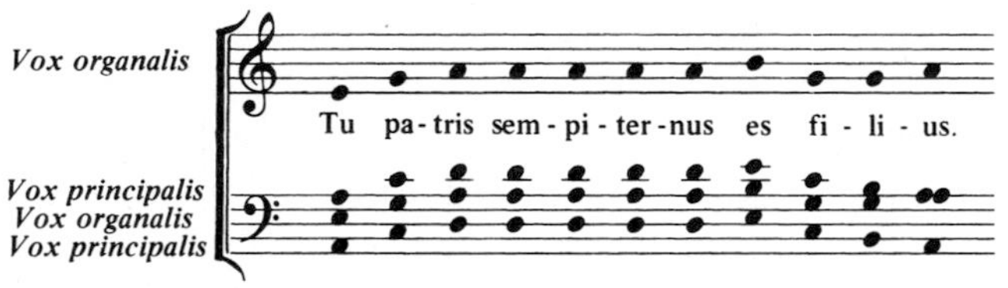

Example 3.3 *Organum with Oblique Motion*

[*Your*] *humble servants, worshipping with pious melodies, beseech you, as you command to free them from diverse ills* (from the sequence *Rex coeli*).

After the *enchiriadis* treatises, the next author to describe and illustrate organum was Guido in his *Micrologus* (ca. 1025–28). His examples show very little new except that two voices sometimes converge at the end of a phrase from a third to a unison. Meanwhile, organum was undoubtedly being sung, and musical examples of the eleventh century show greater melodic independence and more equal importance of the two voices, as contrary and oblique motion become regular features. By this time, the *vox organalis* usually sings above the *vox principalis* (though the parts often cross), and occasionally sings two notes

Example 3.4 *Eleventh-Century Organum*

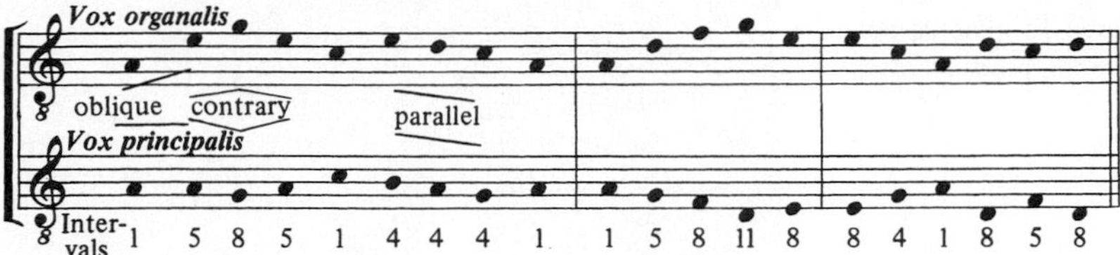

against one of the *vox principalis* (Example 3.4). The consonant intervals remain the unison, octave, fourth, and fifth; all others occur only incidentally and infrequently. The rhythm is that of plainsong, which forms the basis of these pieces.

Winchester Troper

The Winchester Troper, the oldest large collection of organum-style pieces consists of two eleventh-century manuscripts used at Winchester Cathedral. The "troping" appears mainly as an additional organal voice. Unfortunately, the two voices are notated in heighted neumes without staff lines, so the precise intervals can only be approximated, though in some cases the existence of a later manuscript with more exact notation has allowed us to reconstruct some melodies.

In the eleventh century, polyphonic setting was applied chiefly in the troped sections (such as in the Kyrie, Gloria, or *Benedicamus Domino*) of the Ordinary, in certain parts of the Proper (especially Graduals, Alleluias, Tracts, and Sequences), and in responsories of the Office. Even then, only the soloists' portions of the original chant were embellished polyphonically. In performance, therefore, polyphonic sections alternated with sections of monophonic chant. Whereas the full choir sang chant in unison, polyphony demanded trained soloists who could follow rules of consonance while improvising or reading the approximate notation. The solo sections from an Alleluia, the *Alleluia Justus ut palma* (NAWM 13; CD 1 30 10), are preserved in a set of instructions headed *Ad organum faciendum* (To make organum), known as the "Milan treatise" and dating from around 1100. The added voice proceeds mostly note-against-note above the chant but occasionally crosses below. At the end of the opening "Alleluia," the organal voice has a melismatic passage against the penultimate note of the chant (Example 3.5).

Example 3.5 *Organum*: Alleluia Justus ut palma

FLORID ORGANUM

A new type of organum, more florid in style, appeared early in the twelfth century. Examples are preserved in one manuscript at the Cathedral of Santiago de Compostela in northwestern Spain and in three manuscripts once thought

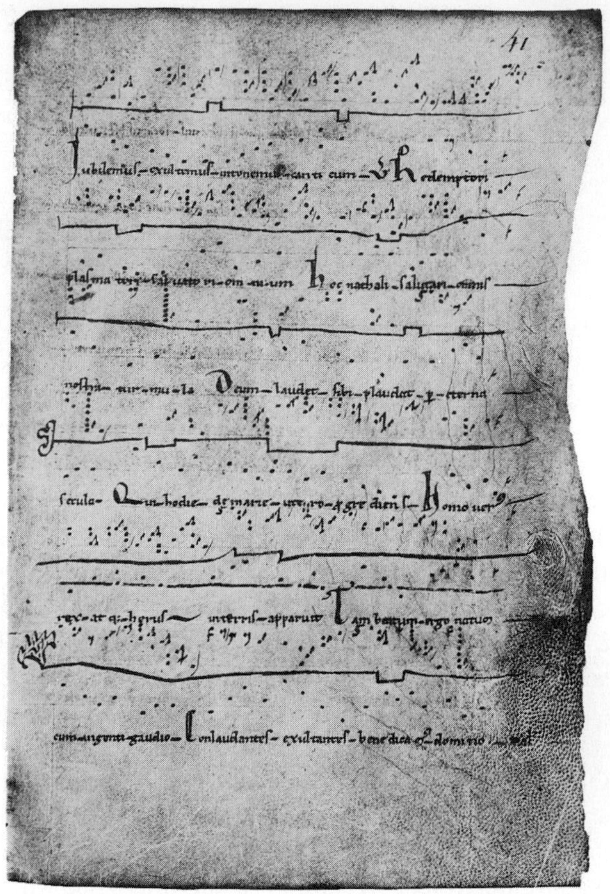

■ *A two-voice* Benedicamus Domino *trope, which may have been written as early as 1100. For a transcription see facing page and NAWM 14. (Photograph Bibliothèque Nationale de France, Paris, fonds latin, MS 1139, fol. 41)*

to have come from the Abbey of St. Martial at Limoges. All are now believed to have originated in southwestern France (which includes Limoges), then the duchy of Aquitaine, and so the music is referred to as Aquitanian polyphony. The lower voice, sometimes a recognizable plainchant melody, has long-held notes, allowing the upper (solo) voice to sing phrases of varying length against it. Most of the chants in the lower voice and their texts were probably composed anew. This new kind of organum resulted in much longer pieces than before; at the same time, the lower voice lost its original character as a definite tune, becoming instead a series of single-note "drones," with melodic elaborations above. The lower voice, because it held the principal melody, was called the *tenor*, from the Latin *tenere* (to hold). This word was used to designate the lowest part of a polyphonic composition until the middle of the fifteenth century.

Organum purum

Discant

Writers in the early twelfth century began distinguishing between two kinds of organum. The style just described, in which the lower voice holds long notes, they termed simply *organum*, *organum duplum*, or *organum purum* ("double" or "pure" organum). When both parts moved more or less note-against-note, they called it *discantus* (discant). When a contemporary praised Léonin as the *optimus organista*, they were calling him not an excellent organist but an excellent composer of organa—that is, of compositions of the kind now being discussed (see vignette, page 83). In the same passage, Pérotin was described as the best *discantor*, or maker of discants.

The texts

The texts of the Aquitanian organa included *Benedicamus Domino* tropes and sequences, and rhyming, scanning, accentual Latin poems called *versus* (singular and plural). As a rule, the two voices sang the same words; occasionally the lower voice carried the original plainsong text, while the upper voice sang the melody to the words of a trope. The versus, on the other hand, were newly composed texts, making some of this polyphony the earliest that was not based on chant.

Some of the pieces appear in "score" format, as in the two-part *Jubilemus, exultemus* (see facsimile on page 74, transcribed in NAWM 14; CD 1 [31]). Here, the voices line up one above the other, on a rhymed metrical text that ends with the words "benedicamus Domino." The two voices sing the same text, the tenor, one note per syllable, the upper part, typically three to six notes to each of the tenor's notes. The upper voice usually has longer melismas on the penultimate syllable (see Example 3.6). The upper voice often meets the syllabic lower voice at the beginning of a melisma, most frequently in perfect consonances—octaves, fifths, and fourths—but also thirds and sixths. Occasionally the composer seems to have purposely chosen a dissonance for variety and spice (for example, on "xul" of "exultemus" and "to" of "intonemus" in Example 3.6), and dissonances generously pepper the melismas. Octaves or unisons between the parts mark the ends of lines.

Example 3.6 *Jubilemus, exultemus*

Let us rejoice, let us exult, let us all sing.

Source: Paris, Bibliothèque Nationale, fonds latin, MS 1139, fol. 41.

Notation of organum purum

When organum purum was written down, one part sat over the other, fairly well aligned vertically, with the phrase marked off by short vertical strokes on the staff. Two singers, or one soloist and a small group, could not easily go astray. But when the rhythmic relation between the parts was complex, singers had to know exactly how long to hold each note. The late medieval notations of plainchant did not indicate duration. Indeed, no one felt a need to specify it, for the rhythm was evidently free or was tied to that of speech. The troubadour and trouvère melodies could also be written down in this notation, because the meter of the poetry guided the performer to sing some notes long and others short. Uncertainties about note duration did not seriously hinder solo or monophonic singing but could cause chaos when two or more melodies were sung simultaneously. Composers in northern France found a solution for this problem by devising a system of rhythmic modes.

NOTRE DAME ORGANUM

The Rhythmic Modes

The system that twelfth-century composers devised to notate rhythm proved adequate for all polyphonic music until well into the thirteenth century. It was based on a principle that differs fundamentally from that of modern notation. Instead of showing fixed relative durations by means of different note symbols, it indicated different rhythmic patterns by means of certain combinations of single notes and especially of note groups. By about 1250, these patterns were codified as the six rhythmic modes, identified simply by number:

I.	♩ ♪	IV.	♪ ♩ ♩.
II.	♪ ♩	V.	♩. ♩.
III.	♩. ♪ ♩	VI.	♪ ♪ ♪

The patterns correspond roughly to the metrical feet of French and Latin verse. Mode I, for example, corresponds to the trochee, II to the iamb, III to the dactyl, and IV to the anapest. Modes I and V were the most frequently used in practice, while Modes II and III were also common. Mode VI often served as a variant of I or II. Mode IV was rarely employed.

Theoretically, according to the system, a Mode I melody should consist of continued repetitions of the pattern, each phrase ending with a rest that replaced the shorter note:

But a melody following such a pattern would soon become monotonous, and in practice the rhythm was flexible. Either of the notes could be broken into shorter units, or the two notes of the pattern could be combined into one, and various other means for variety were available. Also, a melody in Mode I might be sung over a tenor holding long notes that were not strictly measured, or one organized in the pattern of Mode V:

An actual melody read as in Mode I may be seen in the upper voice of Example 3.9 at "nostrum."

Perfection

The basis of the system of rhythmic modes was a threefold unit of measure called by theorists a *perfectio*—a "perfection." This uniform measure permitted any mode to be combined with any other. The ternary division of the "beat" produced an effect somewhat like a modern $^6_8$ or $^9_8$ meter.

To let the singer know which rhythmic mode was in force, the notators used the ligatures in a novel way. Ligatures were signs derived from the compound neumes of plainchant notation that denoted groups of two, three, or more tones sung to one syllable. In melismatic chant, a number of such groups could be sung to a syllable. When a melody in a rhythmic mode appeared as in Example 3.7a—a single three-note ligature followed by a series of two-note ligatures—a singer would perform it in a rhythm that can be expressed in the modern notation of Example 3.7b. In other words, the particular series of ligatures in Example 3.7a signaled to the singer to choose the first rhythmic mode. The other rhythmic modes could be invoked in similar ways. Departures from the prevailing rhythmic pattern, changes of mode, or repeated tones (which could not be indicated in ligatures) called for modifications of the notation that are too complex to be described here.

Example 3.7 *Use of Ligatures to Indicate a Rhythmic Mode*

Polyphonic Composition

The art of polyphonic composition from the twelfth to the middle of the fourteenth centuries developed primarily in northern France and radiated from there to other parts of Europe. The highest achievements in organum came out of the Cathedral of Paris, Notre Dame. Organum was also sung in other regions of France and England, Spain, and Italy, though less extensively. We know the names of two early composers of polyphony associated with Notre Dame: the poet-musician Léonin, who lived in the third quarter of the twelfth century, and Pérotin, who worked there perhaps in the last decades of the twelfth century and the first part of the thirteenth.

Léonin

Magnus liber organi

Léonin is believed to have compiled the *Magnus liber organi* (The Great Book of Organum), a cycle of two-part Graduals, Alleluias, and responsories for the entire church year. The *Magnus liber* no longer exists in its original form, but its contents have survived in various manuscripts preserved in libraries at

TIMELINE: EARLY POLYPHONY

- **ca. 1140–ca. 1190 Bernart de Ventadorn**
- 1163 Cornerstone of Notre Dame of Paris laid
- **1163–90 Léonin at Notre Dame**
- **1180–ca. 1238 Pérotin at Notre Dame**
- 1189 Richard Coeur de Lion, king of England
- **12th c. Beatriz de Dia**
- 1209 St. Francis of Assisi founds Franciscan order
- 1215 Magna Carta signed
- **ca. 1280 Franco of Cologne, *Ars cantus mensurabilis***
- **ca. 1284 Adam de la Halle, *Robin et Marion***

Florence, Wolfenbüttel, Madrid, and elsewhere; some of them are available in modern editions or facsimiles. We do not know how much of the music Léonin composed. The organa of the "Great Book" are set to the solo portions of the responsorial chants in the Masses and Offices for certain major feasts. The Alleluia is such a chant, and the one for Easter Mass—*Alleluia Pascha nostrum*—was elaborated not only by Léonin but also by later composers, making it ideal for tracing the layers of polyphonic embellishment bestowed on this category of chant. A sampling of these layers is presented and discussed in detail in NAWM 15.

If we compare a setting of the Alleluia in the organum manuscripts (15b; CD 1 [32]) with the original chant (15a), we see that the "Great Book" provided music only for the traditionally solo portions of the chant, while the choir was expected to sing the rest of the chant in unison, either from memory or from another book. The plan of Léonin's organum may be diagrammed as follows:

Soloists	**Chorus**	**Soloists**		
Organum duplum	**Plainchant**	**Organum duplum**	**Discant**	**Organum duplum**
Alleluia ________	*Alleluia*___	*Pascha* ________	*no-strum* (melisma)	*immo-la-*

Soloists (cont.)	**Chorus**	**Soloists**	**Chorus**
Discant	**Plainchant**	_____**Discant**	**Plainchant**
(melisma) *-tus* (melisma) *est*	*Christus.*	*Alle- lu- ia.*	__________

The responsorial Alleluia chant by itself already displays contrasts in form and sound that are highlighted when we go from plainchant to organum to discant. The different styles of polyphonic composition, then, build even more contrast into the new sections. The opening intonation "Alleluia" (Example 3.8) resembles the older melismatic or florid organum: the plainsong melody is

Organum duplum by Léonin of the Alleluia verse Pascha nostrum. *It includes an ambiguously notated—probably rhythmically free—organum purum on* Pascha *and a clausula on* nostrum, *in which both parts are in modal rhythm. For one possible transcription, see* NAWM 15. (FLORENCE, BIBLIOTECA MEDICEA-LAURENZIANA, MS PLUTEUS 29.1)

stretched out into unmeasured long notes to form the tenor, against which a solo voice sings melismatic phrases, broken at irregular intervals by cadences and rests. The original notation (see illustration above) suggests a free, unmeasured rhythm. The succession of unequal phrases of fluid melody smacks of improvisatory practice. Nevertheless, some scholars have applied modal rhythm to such passages of organum purum, and their transcriptions are seen in many editions and heard in some recordings.

After the choir responds "Alleluia" in unison, the two-voice solo texture in organum purum resumes with the psalm verse on "Pascha." But beginning

Example 3.8 *Léonin,* Organum duplum: *First section of* Alleluia Pascha nostrum

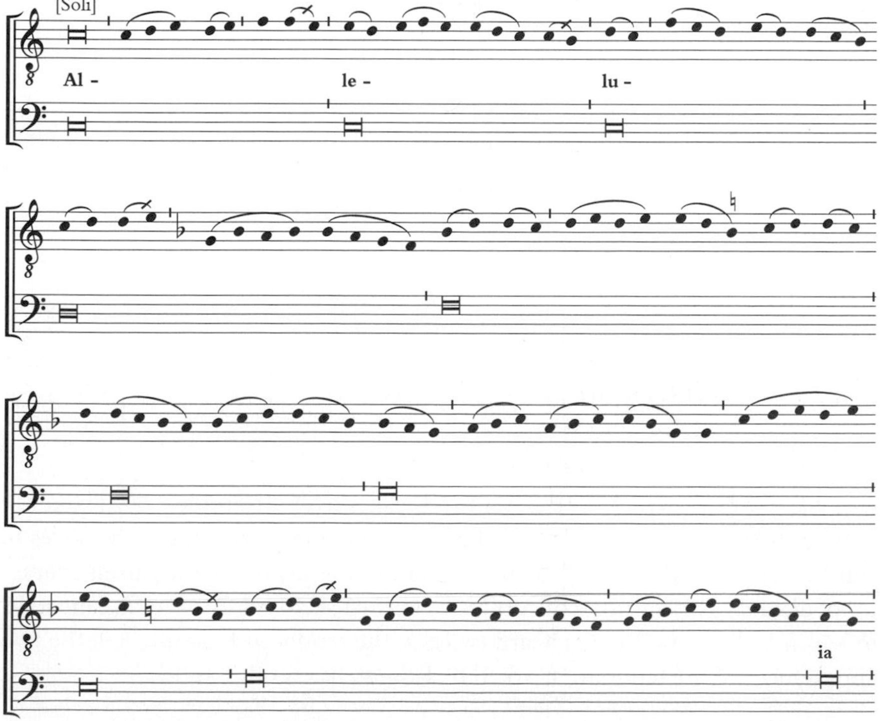

Example 3.9 *Léonin, Beginning of Verse from* Alleluia Pascha nostrum, *with Anonymous Clausula on "nostrum"*

with the word "nostrum," a different style takes over (Example 3.9). The tenor now sings in strictly measured rhythm while the upper voice, which moves in still faster notes (in Mode I), likewise assumes the distinctly measured character of discant. This section constitutes a *clausula*, a closed form in discant style, in which a chant melisma is heard twice in the tenor (in Example 3.9, the two appearances of the tenor are marked by Roman numerals I and II).

Clausula

Clausula features

The term *clausula* (plural, *clausulae*) means a grammatical close, but, like the English "period" and the Latin *punctus*, it also stands for the section of prose or music falling between two marks of punctuation—what we would call a clause, period, or phrase. Each clausula was kept distinct, terminated by a definite cadence. In the Florentine source from which Examples 3.8 and 3.9 are taken, the *Alleluia Pascha nostrum* has three clausulae: on *nostrum*, on *latus* of the word "immolatus," and on *lu* of the final "Alleluia." Between these clausulae there are contrasting sections in organum purum style. Since it was common to substitute new clausulae for old ones, these examples were probably not written by Léonin but by a later composer, particularly since at these points the other manuscripts containing this organum betray an older style. After the final discant section, the piece concludes with the chorus singing the last few phrases of the plainsong Alleluia on which the composition is based.

Léonin's generation liked to juxtapose old and new elements, passages of florid organum with the livelier rhythmic discant clausulae. But in the course of the thirteenth century, singers gradually abandoned organum purum in favor of discant. Clausulae became quasi-independent pieces and eventually evolved into a new form, the motet.

Pérotin Organum

Pérotin and his contemporaries continued the work of Léonin's generation. The basic formal structure of the organum—alternating unison chant and polyphonic sections—remained unchanged, but Pérotin's generation preferred to combine measured rhythm with the long-held tenor notes. The older florid organa were often replaced with discant clausulae, and many of the older clausulae were replaced with other, so-called substitute clausulae in definite and stylized rhythmic patterns. The tenors of Pérotin's organa were characteristically laid out in a series of repeated rhythmic motives, corresponding usually to the fifth or third rhythmic mode. (Modern transcriptions exhibit distinct groupings of two measures or multiples of two, as in Example 3.10, page 82). Moreover, Pérotin's tenor melodies, typically using shorter notes than Léonin's, often had to be repeated, at least in part, to make a section long enough to suit the composer. These two kinds of repetition—of rhythmic motive and of melody—also characterized the formal structure of the later thirteenth-century motet. In Example 3.10c the tenor is laid out in identical repeated rhythmic patterns that foreshadow the fourteenth-century isorhythmic motet (see Chapter 4, pages 100–01).

Substitute clausulae

Pérotin and his contemporaries expanded organum by increasing the number of voice parts, first to three and then to four. Since the second voice was called the duplum, by analogy the third was called the *triplum* and the fourth the *quadruplum*. These same terms also designated the composition as a whole, a three-voice organum being called an *organum triplum*, or simply *triplum*, and a four-voice organum a *quadruplum*. The triplum became the standard in the Pérotin period and remained in favor for a long time; examples are found in manuscripts dating from the second half of the thirteenth cen-

Triple and quadruple organum

Example 3.10 *Tenors on "Domino" from* Haec dies

tury. Most tripla begin with long-held notes of the chant in the tenor and two voices moving above in measured phrases. This style resembles the sustained-note portions of Léonin's organum, that is organum purum, but they use the rhythmic precision of discant in the upper voices.

Sederunt

One of Pérotin's most impressive works is his organum quaduplum *Sederunt* (see NAWM 16 [CD 1 42 ⟨11⟩] and facsimile on facing page) on the intonation of the Respond of the Gradual for St. Stephen's Day. It is part of a very long composition that must have taken about twenty minutes to perform. Since the composer could not be guided by a text to organize the music, he resorted to abstract, purely musical devices, such as voice exchange. In *Sederunt*, two voices exchange motives as short as two measures and as long as ten or more. The interchange made the music more interesting to the singers, although listeners would simply have heard a section repeated. Particularly notable is the coupling of nearly identical phrases, such as those at the end of NAWM 16 (measures 131–34 and 135–38).

In a typical Pérotin organum, an opening section of this sort is followed by one or more discant sections in which the tenor is also measured, though it moves less rapidly than the upper voices. As the composition proceeds, sections in sustained-tone style elaborate the more syllabic parts of the chant. These blend and alternate with sections in discant style, which usually correspond to the melismatic parts of the original chant. The tripla and quadrupla of Pérotin and his generation are the summit of ecclesiastical polyphony in the early thirteenth century.

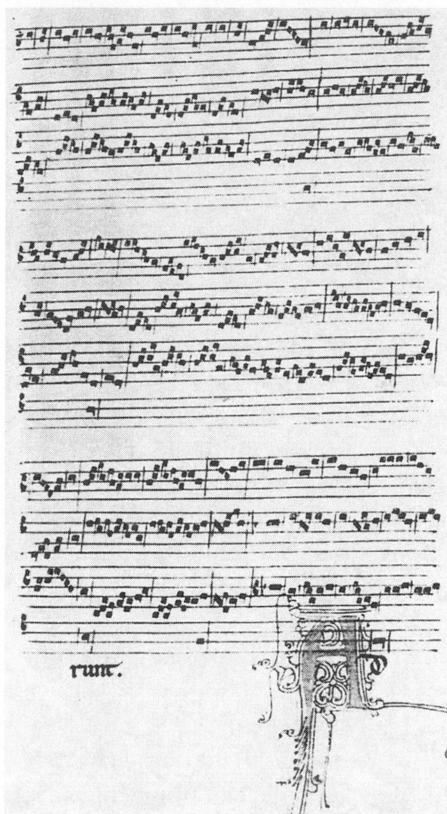

The end of the passage from Pérotin's organum quadruplum Sederunt principes, *culminating in the syllable* runt. *The upper three parts are in modal rhythm over a sustained tenor note. For a transcription, see NAWM 16.* (FLORENCE, BIBLIOTECA MEDICEA-LAURENZIANA, MS PLUTEUS 29.1, FOL. 6R.)

ANONYMOUS IV COMPARES THE ACHIEVEMENTS OF LÉONIN AND PÉROTIN

Note that Master Leonin, according to what was said, was the best composer of *organa*, who made the great book of *organum* from the gradual and antiphonary to elaborate the divine service. And it was in use up to the time of Perotin the Great, who edited it and made very many better *clausulae* or *puncta*, since he was the best composer of discant, and better than Leonin. But this is not to be said about the subtlety of the *organum*, etc.

But Master Perotin himself made excellent *quadrupla*, like "Viderunt" and "Sederunt," with an abundance of colors of the harmonic art; and also several very noble *tripla*, like "Alleluia posui adiutorium," "Nativitas," etc. He also composed three-part conductus, like "Salvatoris hodie," and two-part conductus, like "Dum sigillum summi patris," and even monophonic conductus [*simplices conductus*] with several others, like "Beata viscera," etc.

Jeremy Yudkin, *The Music Treatise of Anonymous IV: A New Translation*, MSD 41 (Neuhausen-Stuttgart: AIM/Hänssler-Verlag, 1985), p. 39. The author of the treatise, a pupil of Johannes de Garlandia, is the fourth anonymous in C.-E.-H. de Coussemaker's collection of medieval treatises (Paris, 1864–76).

POLYPHONIC CONDUCTUS

The conductus grew out of quasi-liturgical genres such as the hymn and the sequence but later admitted secular words. In a polyphonic conductus, two or more voices sing the same text in essentially the same rhythm. Its texts, like those of the earlier monophonic conductus and the Aquitanian versus, consist of metrical Latin poems, rarely liturgical though often on sacred themes. When secular, the text deals seriously with current or historical events or moral and ecclesiastical issues.

Characteristics

The polyphonic conductus by Pérotin and other composers of the Notre Dame era are written for two, three, or four voices. As in organum, the entire vocal range is narrow and the voices cross and recross. The basic sonorities are octaves, fourths, and fifths, but thirds are prominent in some conductus. Voice interchange is fairly frequent.

Besides homorhythmic texture, two other features distinguished the polyphonic conductus of the early thirteenth century. First, the words were set syllabically, for the most part. An exception occurs in conductus that introduced fairly untexted passages, called *caudae* (literally, tails), at the beginning, at the end, and before important cadences, among other places. These caudae sometimes incorporated previously composed clausulae, so that a mixture of conductus and organum styles resulted. The caudae may have been played by instruments.

A second distinguishing characteristic of these conductus was that the tenor, instead of being taken from a plainchant or some other preexisting source, was often newly composed. The conductus and its antecedent, the versus, were thus the first completely original polyphonic works that were independent of borrowed melodic material, even though the new melody was used as if it were itself a borrowed melody. In the manuscripts, the conductus, like the organa, are notated in score arrangement, with corresponding notes of the voice parts aligning vertically and the text written only under the lowest (tenor) part.

The conductus *Ave virgo virginum* (NAWM 17 [CD 1 [45]] and Example 3.11), from one of the manuscripts that contain the Notre Dame repertory, is addressed to the Virgin Mary and was probably used in special devotions and processions. Three strophes are served by the same music, and, besides, the first two couplets have identical music in all voices.

The nearly homorhythmic writing displayed in this example is often called "conductus style." Two- or three-part settings of hymns, sequences, ballades, and rondeaux were written in this style throughout the twelfth and thirteenth centuries, as were some early thirteenth-century motets. Both organum and conductus gradually dropped out of favor after 1250, leaving the polyphonic field to the motet.

THE MOTET

Clausulae, cut loose from the larger organa, often enjoyed a second life as separate compositions when Latin or French words were added to the upper voice. This new work was called a *motet* (a diminutive form of the French *mot*, mean-

Example 3.11 *Early Thirteenth-Century Conductus:* Ave virgo virginum

Hail, virgin of virgins, shrine of the word made flesh, who for men's salvation pours out milk and honey. You have borne the Lord; you were a rush-basket to Moses.

Source: Florence, Biblioteca Medicea-Laurenziana, MS Pluteus 29.1, fols. 240-240v.

ing "word"), a term soon applied to the work as a whole. The Latin form, *motetus,* also designates the second voice—the original duplum—in three- and four-part motets, while the third and fourth voices carry the same names—triplum and quadruplum—they had in organum.

Origins and General Features

Léonin, as we have seen, introduced discrete sections—clausulae in discant style—into his organa. Pérotin and others produced hundreds of such clausulae, many of them designed as alternates or substitutes for those of Léonin and the earlier composers. These substitute clausulae were interchangeable: as many as ten might be written using the same tenor, and a choirmaster could select any one of them for a particular occasion. Sometime before the middle of the century, words began to be fitted to them—usually tropes or paraphrases of the tenor text in rhymed Latin verse. Later, light French verse was substituted, and many new melodies with French texts were composed for favorite tenor melodies. Since most of these motets have a different text in each voice, they are identified by a compound title made up of the first word or words of each of the voice parts in turn, beginning with the highest, as in Examples 3.12 and 3.13. Composers and performers freely used and altered a common stock of motet melodies, both tenors and upper parts, indeed any music known to them, without acknowledgment.

The earliest type of motet, based on the substitute clausula with Latin texts supplied for the upper voices, was soon modified in various ways. (1) Composers discarded the original upper voices, and wrote one or more new melodies to go with the existing tenor. It is significant that in the process the plainsong tenor lost its connection with a specific function in the service and became raw material for composition. (2) Composers wrote motets to be sung outside the church services, with vernacular texts in the upper voices. Since there was no point in singing the original cantus firmus text, the tenor was probably played on instruments. (3) By 1250 it was customary to use different but topically related texts in the two upper voices. Both texts could be in Latin or in French; only rarely were the two languages combined.

Sources of tenors

In the first half of the thirteenth century nearly all motet tenors had Latin texts drawn from the repertory of clausula tenors in the *Magnus liber* (see above, page 77). Since these clausulae had originally been written over melismatic portions of the chant, the texts consisted of a few words at most, and sometimes only of a single word or even part of a word. Consequently, the motet tenors had very short texts—one or two syllables, a word, or a phrase such as *-latus* (from *immolatus*), *nostrum* (from *Alleluia Pascha nostrum*), or *Haec dies*, *Domino*, *Quoniam*, or *In seculum* (from the Easter Gradual *Haec dies*). Even when the actual text was longer than a phrase, the motet manuscripts provided only the incipit under the tenor line, probably on the assumption that the church singers would know the rest of the words, and outside the church the words were not needed. Tenors were usually laid out in repetitive rhythmic patterns, such as those shown in Example 3.10 and the tenor of Example 3.11.

Both the original and the substitute clausulae of the organum *Alleluia Pascha nostrum* (NAWM 15b; CD 1 [32]) in the *Magnus liber* were reworked as motets by adding Latin or French texts. For example, the duplum voice of the clausula on *nostrum* (NAWM 15c) received a Latin text, *Gaudeat devotio fidelium*, that expands on the meaning of Christ's sacrifice and turns it into a motet (15d; CD 1 [35]). Similarly, the duplum of the clausula on *la* of *immolatus* (NAWM 15e) received a Latin text, *Ave Maria, Fons letitie*, in praise of the mother of the sacrificed "lamb" celebrated in the Alleluia (15f; CD 1 [37]).

After the middle of the thirteenth century, and particularly after 1275, motet tenors were taken from sources other than the Notre Dame books, such as Kyries, hymns, and antiphons. Composers also began to use tenors from contemporary secular songs and from instrumental estampies. The application of the rhythmic modes became more flexible, and greater continuity was achieved by having the phrase endings of the three voices fall in different places (as in Example 3.12).

Motet Texts

On the surface, the poems used as texts for motets may not seem particularly noteworthy. They abound in alliteration, stereotyped images and expressions, and various schemes of rhyme and stanza. Nevertheless, the interrelationship of the multiple texts in a single composition is often quite clever, and the best motets represent highly complex intertextual creations. Certain vowels or syllables are emphasized in all the voices, so that a similarity of ideas in the texts is reinforced by a similarity of vowel sounds. The upper voices of many French motets incorporated a refrain, a line or two of poetry (usually at the end of the stanza) that appeared in identical form in other songs of the thirteenth century.

Example 3.12 *Motet*: Amours mi font souffrir—En mai, quant rose est florie—Flos filius

Triplum: *Love wrongly makes me suffer pain,*
because my lady, who is killing me
Duplum: *In May, when the rose blooms,*
and I hear the birds sing
Tenor: [*The Virgin, Mother of God, is the branch,*] *the son its flower.*

The Franconian Motet

In the earlier motets, all the upper parts were written in one melodic style. Later composers sought to distinguish the upper voices from each other as well as from the tenor. This new kind of motet is sometimes called *Franconian*, after Franco of Cologne, a composer and theorist who was active from about 1250 to 1280. The triplum had a longer text than the motetus and had a fast-moving melody with many short notes in short phrases of narrow range. Against this, the motetus sang a comparatively broad, long-breathed, lyrical melody. Toward the end of the thirteenth century even the tenor's rigid rhythmic scheme was relaxed in favor of a flexible style approaching that of the other two parts.

Amours mi font souffrir—En mai, quant rose est florie—Flos filius (Example 3.12 and NAWM 18; CD 1 46 ⟨14⟩) is a charming Franconian motet. All the voices are based on the first rhythmic mode, consisting of a long followed by a breve. In the upper parts both the long and the breve are frequently broken up into shorter notes, a device theorists called *fractio modi* (breaking up of the mode). The chant melody in the tenor, *Flos filius eius*, is from a melismatic passage in the Responsory, *Stirps Jesse*. The tenor performs the chant melody twice, repeating throughout a rhythmic pattern that occupies two measures of the transcription. Since the music of the motetus was first a clausula duplum, the French text was composed after the music. This accounts for the uneven lengths of poetic lines and the irregular rhyme scheme. The triplum's text and melody are more independent, and its textual-musical lines do not match those of the motetus but sometimes overlap. This feature, together with the breaking up of the mode, assures constant animation, and it averts the stops and starts of many motets of this period.

Petronian motet

In the late thirteenth century, a type of motet emerged in which the triplum had a lively, free, speechlike rhythm, while the motetus proceeded more slowly, and only the plainchant tenor had a uniform rhythmic pattern. This type is often called *Petronian*, after Petrus de Cruce (Pierre de la Croix), one of the few identifiable thirteenth-century composers, who was active from about 1270 to 1300. *Aucun vont—Amor qui cor—Kyrie* (Example 3.13) may be by Petrus. The tenor is laid out in uniform perfect longs (dotted half notes of the transcription), while the duplum has no more than two semibreves (transcribed as eighth notes) per breve. The triplum, however, breaks away from the limited subdivision of note values allowed by the rhythmic modes and has two to six semibreves per breve. The duplum, as in many earlier motets, is organized in four-measure phrases, but the triplum's cadences never coincide with the duplum's endings, giving the music a breathless continuity. In character with the music, the duplum's Latin text ascetically tempers the effusive praise of love in the French triplum text.

Example 3.13 *Motet*: Aucun vont—Amor qui cor—Kyrie

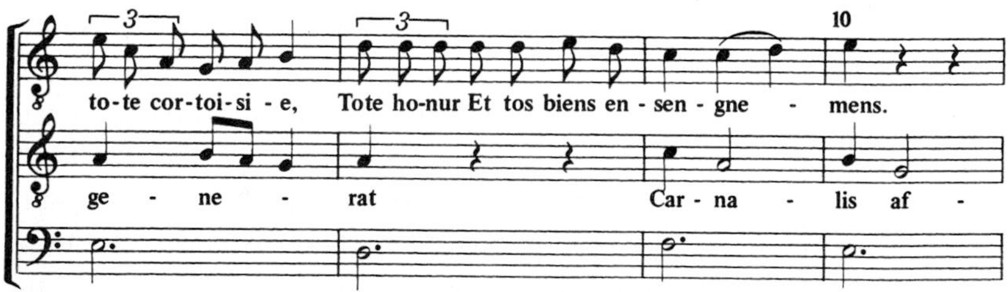

Triplum: Some, through envy, often speak ill of love; but there is no life so good as loving loyally. For from loving comes all courtesy, all honor . . .
Duplum: Love that wounds the human heart, that carnal affection generates [can never, or rarely, be without vice] . . .

Source: Richard Hoppin, *Anthology of Medieval Music* (New York: Norton, 1978), No. 54.

Harmonic vocabulary

The harmonic vocabulary of the motet changed less during the thirteenth century than did the rhythmic structure. In 1300, as in 1200, the fifth and octave were expected on strong beats. Composers treated the fourth more and more as a dissonance, and thirds continued to be favored over other "dissonant" intervals. Changes of consonance followed the rhythm of the tenor part—that is, each new tenor note brought a new set of consonances above it. Between these notes, however, the parts were free to make dissonances. Cadences acquired profiles that remained standard for the next two centuries (see Example 3.14).

Example 3.14 *Cadence Forms*

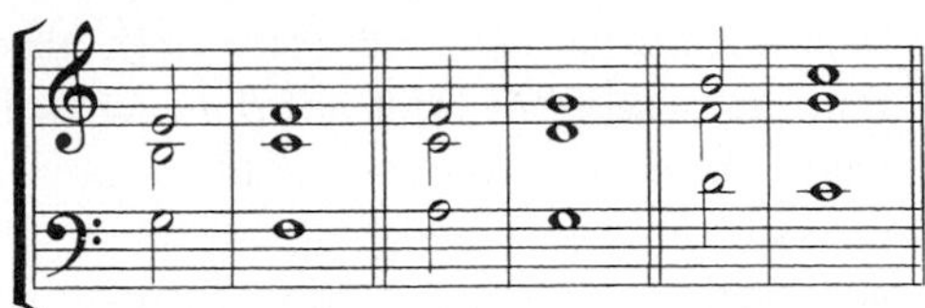

Tempo

Theorists distinguished three tempos for motets: slow, when the breve in the triplum was subdivided into many shorter notes (motets in Petronian style); moderate, for those motets that had no more than three semibreves to a breve (motets in Franconian style); and fast, for hockets.

Hocket

Composers in the thirteenth and fourteenth century cleverly used a technique called *hocket* to animate and aerate the polyphonic texture. In hocket (French *hoquet*, "hiccup"), rests interrupt the flow of melody in such a way that another voice supplies the notes that would have been sung by the resting voice. Thus the melody is divided between the voices. Passages in hocket are occasionally found in secular conductus and motets of the late thirteenth century and, more frequently, in the early fourteenth century. Pieces in which hocketing was used extensively were themselves called hockets. Such compositions might be either vocal or instrumental, but they were always fast, particularly those for instruments.

Notation in the Thirteenth Century

A notation based on the conventions of ligatures and rhythmic modes suited music that was either melismatic or had metrical texts. But once composers started setting prose texts syllabically and wanted greater rhythmic variety, a new system had to be devised. Ligatures continued to serve for the textless tenors in modal rhythm, but the upper parts required that the time values of each note be fixed precisely.

Franco of Cologne codified a usable system of notation in his *Ars cantus mensurabilis* (The Art of Measurable Music), written probably about 1280. In this system, the relative time values of notes, ligatures, and rests are clearly laid out. The system remained in use through the first quarter of the fourteenth century, and many of its features survived until the middle of the sixteenth.

The Franconian system allowed the breve to be divided into either two or three semibreves. When Petrus de Cruce began writing music that had four or

FRANCO OF COLOGNE ON MEASURED MUSIC

Mensurable music is song measured by long and short units of time. To understand this definition, let us consider what measure is and what time is. Measure is a quantitative attribute showing the length and brevity of any mensurable melody. I say mensurable, because in plainsong this kind of measure is not present. Time is the measure of a sound's duration as well as of the opposite, the omission of sound, commonly called a rest. I say rest is measured by time, because if this were not the case two different melodies—one with rests, the other without—could not be proportionately accommodated to one another.

Mensurable music is divided into wholly and partly mensurable. Music wholly mensurable is discant, because discant is measured by time in all its voice parts. Music partly mensurable is organum, because organum is not measured in all its voice parts. The word organum, be it known, is used in two senses—in its proper sense and in the sense commonly accepted. For organum in its proper sense is organum duplum, also called organum purum. But in the sense commonly accepted, organum is any ecclesiastical chant measured by time.

From *Ars cantus mensurabilis*, ca. 1280, trans. Oliver Strunk, rev. James McKinnon, in *Source Readings in Music History*, rev. ed., Oliver Strunk and Leo Treitler, gen. eds. (New York: Norton, 1996), pp. 226–27; 2:117–18.

more notes to a breve, he simply used as many semibreves as he needed for the syllables of the text, sometimes indicating their grouping by dots. Although values shorter than a lesser semibreve were already being used by the end of the thirteenth century, there were no specific notational symbols to represent them. Eventually, of course, the notation was modified to accommodate shorter note values.

The evolution of thirteenth-century motet style brought about one further notational change. The earliest motets were written in score, like the clausulae from which they were derived. As the upper voices acquired longer texts and as each syllable had to have a separate note-symbol, composers and scribes soon found these voices taking much more room on the page than the tenor, a part that had fewer notes and, being melismatic, could be written in the compressed modal notation of ligatures. In a score, there would be long vacant stretches on the tenor staff, a waste of space and costly parchment (see Example 3.13). And since the upper voices sang different texts, it seemed natural to separate them. So, in a three-voice motet, the triplum and the motetus came to be written either on facing pages or in separate columns on the same page, with the tenor on a single staff extending across the bottom. This pattern, known as *choirbook* format, remained the usual way of notating polyphonic compositions from 1280 until the sixteenth century.

THIRTEENTH-CENTURY NOTATION IN DEPTH

Franconian Notation

Franconian notation, like the rhythmic modes, was based on the principle of ternary grouping. There were four signs for single notes: the double long: ▀▌; the long: ▪▌; the breve: ■; and the semibreve: ◆. The basic time unit, the *tempus* (plural, *tempora*), was the breve. A double long always had the value of two longs; a long might be perfect (three tempora) or imperfect (two tempora). A breve normally was worth one tempus, but might under certain conditions be worth two tempora, in which case it was called an "altered" breve. Similarly, the semibreve might be either lesser (1/3 of a tempus) or greater (2/3 of a tempus). Three tempora constituted a "perfection," equivalent to a modern measure of three beats. The system does not provide for what we call ties across a barline; a pattern must be completed within a perfection.

The main principles governing the relationships of the long and the breve are indicated in the following table, where the perfect long is transcribed as a dotted half note:

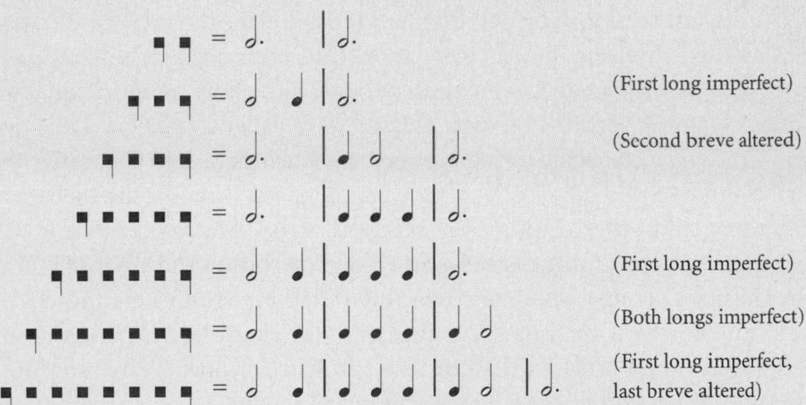

Any of these relationships could be changed by introducing a dot, which indicated a division between two perfections, for example:

Similar principles regulated the relations of the semibreve to the breve. In addition, signs were established for rests, and rules were given on how to recognize notes in ligatures as longs, breves, or semibreves.

SUMMARY

After tentative beginnings in the eleventh century, two types of polyphonic composition gained a secure place by 1250 among a core of musicians in France: organum and conductus. Later in the thirteenth century, the motet emerged as the dominant medium for polyphonic composition in both the sacred and secular spheres.

These new genres arose from the process of elaborating on existing pieces. Composers continued to trope plainchant by furnishing texts for melismas or by adding new texts and music to the traditional liturgy. But now the process of elaboration took a new turn, as particular chants were embellished and expanded by adding a voice to the portions formerly sung alone by the cantor. At first, the second voice sang at consonant intervals, note-against-note, with the voice carrying the chant. This was the earliest kind of organum. Then the second voice indulged in florid runs between its consonant meetings with the chant voice. But where the chant was melismatic, the second voice tended to bond with the first voice, note-against-note or nearly so, a process called *discant*, while the florid style was still called *organum* or *organum purum*.

The discant sections enjoyed further kinds of elaboration. The durational patterns called rhythmic modes were applied to both parts of discant so that the two voices performed combinations of long and short notes in equal units of time. Extended sections of such discant were called *clausulae*. Later composers wrote new clausulae to replace the old. Since clausulae decorated chant melismas sung to a single syllable, they were untexted, but, like the melismas of the Alleluias and other chants, they received verbal troping. Words in Latin and French were set to the discant part in meters suiting the rhythmic modes of the music. The new composite was the motet, and soon new motets were written on the chant melismas independently of clausulae. Composers often added a third voice with a different text and its own modal rhythm. Similar compositions based on an original tenor and having a single nonliturgical Latin text for all parts were called *conductus*. Meanwhile, the organal sections were also subjected to the rhythmic modes, allowing for much more complex relationships between the parts, and as many as three parts were layered against chant.

The principal technical achievements of these years were the codification of the rhythmic modal system and the invention of a new kind of notation for measured rhythm, which gave the composer more control over performances.

At the beginning of the thirteenth century, nearly all polyphonic music was sacred; by the end of the century, although no clear distinction between sacred and secular musical styles had yet developed, both sacred and secular texts were receiving polyphonic settings. One genre in particular, the late thirteenth-century motet, reflected the medieval intellectual delight in complicated patterns and multiple layers of meaning, discovered through music, literature, and other arts.

By the end of the thirteenth century, the structure of the motet was beginning to expand. The authority of the rhythmic modes gradually weakened, and the chant tenor was relegated to a purely formal function, elevating the triplum to the status of a solo voice against the accompanying lower parts. The road was open to a new musical style, a new way of composing, in an age that would look back on the music of the latter half of the thirteenth century as the antique, outdated way.

Bibliography

Sources: Music Facsimiles and Editions

Organum and Conductus

Winchester Troper: W. H. Frère, *The Winchester Troper* (London: Henry Bradshaw Society, 1894), partial facs. and edition of texts; Andreas Holschneider, *Die Organa von Winchester* (Hildesheim: G. Olms, 1968), music and facs.; Alejandro Planchart, *The Repertory of Tropes at Winchester*, 2 vols. (Princeton: Princeton University Press, 1977), music edition.

Compostela: W. M. Whitehill and German Prado, *Liber Sancti Jacobi, Codex Calixtinus*, 3 vols. (Santiago de Compostela, 1944), facs., transcriptions, commentary.

Theodore Karp, *The Polyphony of St. Martial and Santiago de Compostela* (Oxford: Clarendon Press, 1992), Vol. 1, introduction; Vol. 2, transcriptions.

Notre Dame: The three major sources believed to be the most complete descendants of the *Magnus liber organi* are the manuscripts Wolfenbüttel, Helmstedt 628 (formerly 677), called W1; Wolfenbüttel, Helmstedt 1099 (1206), called W2; and Florence, Bibl. Medicea-Laurenziana, pluteo 29.1 (called F). All three are published in facs.: W1 in J. H. Baxter, ed., *An Old St. Andrews Music Book* (London: St. Andrews University Publications, 1931); W2 in Luther A. Dittmer, ed., *Wolfenbüttel 1099*, PMMM 2 (Brooklyn: Institute of Medieval Music, 1960); and F in Dittmer, ed., *Firenze, Biblioteca Mediceo-Laurenziana, pluteo 29.1*, 2 vols., PMMM 10–11 (Brooklyn: Institute of Medieval Music, 1966–67).

Heinrich Husmann, ed., *Die drei- und vierstimmige Notre-Dame Organa* (Leipzig: Breitkopf & Härtel, 1940; repr. Hildesheim: G. Olms, 1967) includes all three- and four-part organa by Pérotin. Ethel Thurston, *The Works of Perotin* (New York: Kalmus, 1970), is a performing edition of all the works attributed to him by Anonymous IV. Recent editions of conductus are Janet Knapp, ed., *Thirty-five Conductus for Two and Three Voices* (New Haven: Yale University Press, 1965); Thurston, ed., *The Conductus Collection of MS Wolfenbüttel 1099*, 3 vols. (Madison, Wisc.: A-R Editions, 1980); and Gordon Anderson, ed., *Notre-Dame and Related Conductus. Opera omnia* (Henryville, Penn.: Institute of Medieval Music, 1979–).

Motets

The most complete edition of motets, which presents each motet in several versions from various manuscripts, is Hans Tischler, ed., *The Earliest Motets (to circa 1270): A Complete Comparative Edition* (New Haven: Yale University Press, 1982), 3 vols.: 1–2, Modern Edition; 3, Index, notes, bibliography.

W2: Gordon Anderson, ed., *The Latin Compositions of Fascicules VII and VIII of the Notre Dame Manuscript Wolfenbüttel Helmstedt 1099 (1206)*, 2 vols. (Brooklyn: Institute of Medieval Music, 1968). Includes commentary and translation of texts of primarily Latin motets.

The Montpellier Codex: Yvonne Rokseth, *Polyphonies du xiii*[e] *siècle; le manuscript H 196 de la Faculté de Médecine de Montpellier* (Paris: Éditions de l'Oiseau-Lyre, 1935–39), 4 vols.: 1, Facsimiles; 2, 3, Transcriptions; 4, Commentary; Hans Tischler, ed., *The Montpel-*

lier Codex, Recent Researches in the Music of the Middle Ages and Early Renaissance, Vols. 2–8 (Madison, Wisc.: A-R Editions, 1978–85).

The Bamberg Codex: Pierre Aubrey, *Cent motets du xiii*[e] *siècle: publiés d'après le manuscript Ed.IV.6 de Bamberg* (Paris: A. Rouart, Lerolle & Co., P. Geuthner, 1908), 3 vols.: 1, Facsimiles; 2, Transcriptions; 3, Commentary; Gordon Anderson, ed., *Compositions of the Bamberg Manuscript*, CMM 75 (Neuhausen-Stuttgart: Hänssler, 1977).

The Las Huelgas Codex: Higini Anglès, *El codex musical de Las Huelgas* (Barcelona: Institut d'estudis catalans, Biblioteca de Catalunya, 1931), 3 vols.: 1, Commentary; 2, Facsimiles; 3, Transcriptions.

English motets: *Motets of English Provenance*, ed. Frank Ll. Harrison (Monaco: Éditions de l'Oiseau-Lyre, 1979).

See also the series published by L'Oiseau Lyre in the Bibliography for Chapter 4

Sources: Theorists

For translations of *Musica Enchiriadis, Scolica Enchiriadis*, and Guido, see Bibliography for Chapter 2.

Joannes de Garlandia, *Concerning Measured Music (De mensurabili musica)*, trans. Stanley H. Birnbaum (Colorado Springs: Colorado College Music Press, 1978); the section on modes and notation is in SRrev, pp. 223–26; 2:113–16.

Anonymous IV, *De mensuris et discantu*, trans. Jeremy Yudkin, MSD 41 (Neuhausen-Stuttgart: AIM/Hänssler, 1985).

De musica mensurata: The Anonymous of St. Emmeram, ed. Jeremy Yudkin (Bloomington: Indiana University Press, 1990), presents a critical ed. and trans. of a treatise from 1279.

Franco of Cologne's *Ars cantus mensurabilis* is trans. in SRrev, pp. 226–45; 2:116–35.

Johannes de Grocheo's music treatise is unique in emphasizing secular genres such as the motet, conductus, and estampie: Albert Seay, trans., *Concerning Music (De musica)*, 2nd ed. (Colorado Springs: Colorado Music Press, 1973).

All of these Latin treatises and many others, whether in manuscript or early printed editions, are in TML (see the Bibliography for Chapter 2).

For Further Reading

General Issues

Cultural and Social Background For a view of how music fit into the life of the monastery, church, and city, read Marion S. Gushee, "The Polyphonic Music of the Medieval Monastery, Cathedral and University," and Christopher Page, "Court and City in France, 1100–1300," both in *Antiquity and the Middle Ages*, ed. James McKinnon (Englewood Cliffs, N.J.: Prentice Hall, 1991), pp. 143–69; 197–217. In *Discarding Images: Reflections on Music and Culture in Medieval France* (Oxford: Clarendon Press, 1993), Page challenges conventional views of the thirteenth century as rationalistic, Pythagorean, constructive, and ascetic, and pleads for a more intuitive understanding of its human qualities. For scholarly surveys of the early Middle Ages, consult David Hiley and Richard L. Crocker, *The Early Middle Ages to 1300*, New Oxford History of Music, rev. ed. (London and New York: Oxford University Press, 1990).

Rhythm A comprehensive work on rhythm is William G. Waite, *The Rhythm of Twelfth-Century Polyphony* (New Haven: Yale University Press, 1954). Many of Waite's conclusions have been challenged: Leo Treitler, "Meter and Rhythm in the Ars Antiqua," MQ 65 (1979):524–58, argues that rhythm was accentual rather than quantitative. One of the keenest controversies revolves around the rhythm of organum purum—Jeremy Yudkin, "The

Rhythms of Organum Purum," JM 2 (1983–84):335–76, summarizes the differing views and offers his own challenge to Waite and others.

Regarding sources for meter and rhythm before Notre Dame, see Margot E. Fassler, "Accent, Meter and Rhythm in Medieval Treatises 'De rithmis'," JM 5 (1987):164–90.

Consonance Richard Crocker, "Discant, Counterpoint, and Harmony," JAMS 15 (1962):1–21, and GLHWM 2, shows how the later rules of counterpoint and harmony evolved from the rules of discant. Ernest Sanders, "Tonal Aspects of 13th-century English Polyphony," AM 37 (1965):19–34, discusses the importance of tonal unity in English as opposed to French 13th-century composition. Sanders, "Consonance and Rhythm in the Organum of the 12th and 13th Centuries," JAMS 33 (1980):264–86, and Sarah Fuller, "Theoretical Foundations of Early Organum Theory," AM 53 (1981):52–84, confront the relationship of rhythm and consonance by citing contemporary theorists.

Notation For details of the notation of twelfth- and thirteenth-century polyphonic music, consult Willi Apel, *The Notation of Polyphonic Music*, 5th ed. (Cambridge, Mass.: Medieval Academy of America, 1961); Carl Parrish, *The Notation of Medieval Music* (New York: Norton, 1978); and W. Waite, *The Rhythm of Twelfth-Century Polyphony.*

Specific Repertories

St. Martial Leo Treitler, "The Polyphony of St. Martial," JAMS 17 (1964):29–42, and GLHWM 2. Sarah Fuller, "The Myth of 'Saint Martial' Polyphony," MD 33 (1979):5–26, refutes the idea that this repertory emanated from a single center.

Notre Dame Craig Wright reviews the history of music at Notre Dame during the Middle Ages and early Renaissance with fascinating detail in *Music and Ceremony at Notre Dame of Paris: 500–1500* (Cambridge: Cambridge University Press, 1989). The standard index of the Notre Dame repertory is Friedrich Ludwig, *Repertorium organorum recentioris et motetorum vetustissimi stili* (Brooklyn: Institute of Medieval Music, 1964–78).

Concerning the origin and manuscripts of the *Magnus liber organi*, see Wright, *Music and Ceremony*; Edward Roesner, "The Origins of W1," JAMS 29 (1976):337–80 and GLHWM 2; and Rebecca Baltzer, "Thirteenth-Century Illuminated Miniatures and the Date of the Florence Manuscript," JAMS 25 (1972):1–18, which uses iconographical evidence to determine the date and provenance of F.

Motet Friedrich Gennrich, ed., *Bibliographie der ältesten französischen und lateinischen Motetten* (Darmstadt: Author, 1957) catalogues the motets and provides information on concordance, related clausulae, origins of tenors, and bibliography.

CHAPTER 4

FRENCH AND ITALIAN MUSIC IN THE FOURTEENTH CENTURY

GENERAL BACKGROUND

After the comparative stability of the thirteenth century, the fourteenth saw change and disruption. The state of the papacy exemplified this difference. In the earlier century people looked up to the church, which was centered in the papacy in Rome, as the supreme authority not only in matters of faith and morals but also, to a large extent, in intellectual and political affairs. In the fourteenth century this authority, and especially the supremacy of the pope, was widely questioned. For most of the century—from 1305 to 1378—the popes had their seat in Avignon in southeastern France. King Philip IV (the Fair) of France had engineered the election of a French pope, Bertrand de Got as Clement V (1305–14), who never went to Rome because of the hostility there to foreigners. For the next thirty-nine years, until 1417, there were two and even three rival claimants to the papacy. This state of affairs, as well as the often scandalous and corrupt life of the higher clergy, drew increasingly sharp criticism, expressed both in writings and the rise of divisive and heretical movements that foreshadowed the Protestant Reformation.

Europeans in the thirteenth century could generally reconcile revelation and reason, the divine and the human, the claims of the kingdom of God and those of political states. In the fourteenth century, on the other hand, the separation between religion and science and between the church and the state emerged as doctrines that are held today. Philosophers drew a distinction between divine revelation and human reason, each prevailing only in its own sphere. The church cared for people's souls, while the state looked out for their earthly concerns.

Social Conditions

The growth of cities in the previous two hundred years had brought increased political power to the middle classes and a corresponding decline of the old feudal aristocracy. But the terrible plague of the Black Death (1348–50) and the Hundred Years' War (1338–1453) led to urban discontent and peasant insurrections. By the fourteenth century, chivalry had become a mere form, a code of manners and ceremonies rather than a vital force. The medieval ideal of European political unity gave way to the reality of separate, independent powers. France was moving toward a centralized absolute monarchy, while the Italian peninsula was divided into many little states, whose rulers often rivaled one another in their patronage of art and letters.

Vernacular literature

A healthy growth of literature in the spoken languages testifies to the new importance of secular pursuits. Dante's *Divine Comedy* (1307), Boccaccio's *Decameron* (1353), and Chaucer's *Canterbury Tales* (1386) remain some of the great literary landmarks of the fourteenth century. The same period saw a renewed interest in classical Latin and Greek literature, an important force in the culture of the Renaissance. In painting, Giotto (ca. 1266–1337) broke away from the formalized Byzantine style toward more naturalistic representation (see Plate I, facing page 110). Literature, education, and the arts all turned from the relatively stable, unified, religiously centered viewpoint of the thirteenth century toward worldly human concerns.

Painting

Secular arts

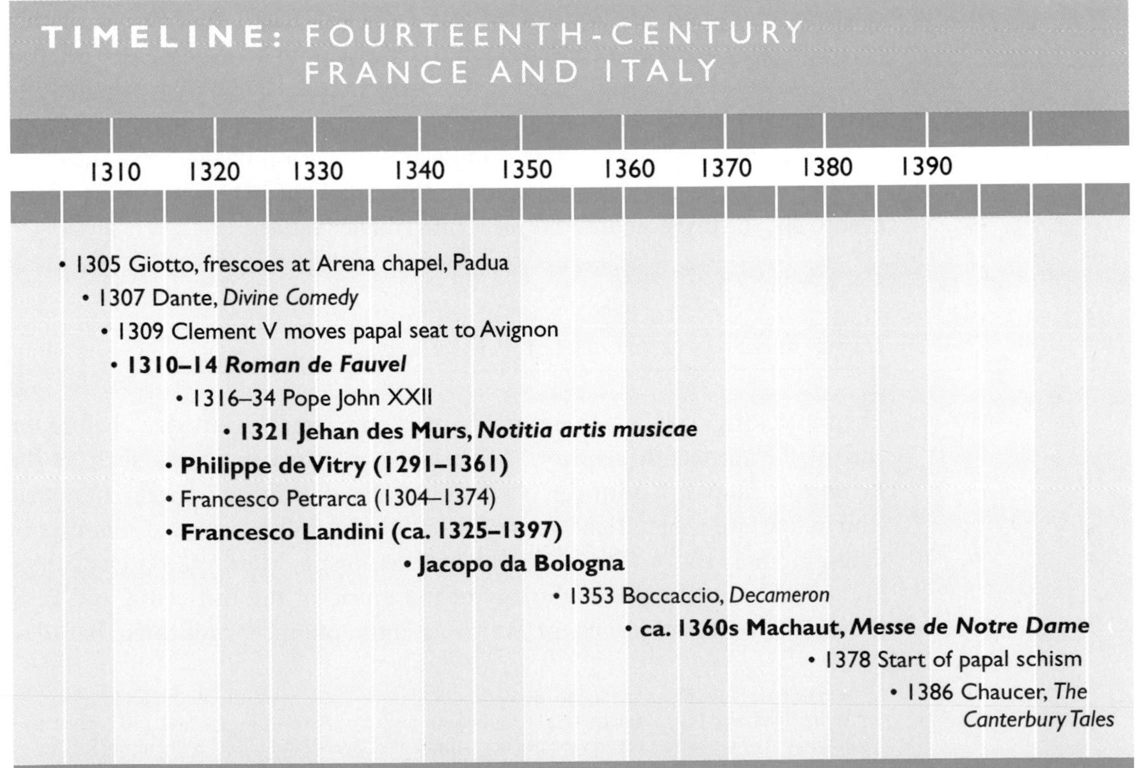

The change came as a gradual shift in emphasis, not a sudden reversal of values. Many tendencies and traits that were characteristic of the fourteenth century had appeared before 1300, and many features of the thirteenth century persisted long after its close.

Musical Background

de Vitry

Musicians consciously struck out in a new direction. The French composer, poet, and bishop of Meaux, Philippe de Vitry (1291–1361), is named by one author (Anonymous III) as the "inventor of a new art"—an *ars nova.* Several manuscripts of a treatise from about 1322–23 end with the words "this completes the *Ars nova* of Magister Philippe de Vitry."[1] The term *ars nova* fit so well that it came to denote the French musical style during the first half of the fourteenth century. Opponents as well as supporters acknowledged the change. The Flemish theorist Jacques de Liège vigorously defended the "old art" of the late thirteenth century against the innovations of the "moderns" in his encyclopedic *Speculum musicae* (The Mirror of Music, ca. 1325; see vignette, page 101).

Advocates of the new and old arts disagreed on two technical issues. One was whether the duple division of note values should be allowed along with the traditional triple division. The long and breve (and, eventually, semibreve) were normally thought to be "perfect"—that is, divisible only into three equal (or two unequal) units of the next smaller value. Now an "imperfect" division of these values into two equal units was proposed. Jehan des Murs, a mathematician and astronomer as well as a music theorist, in his *Notitia artis musicae* (1321), after a long disquisition on the perfection of the ternary number, defends the viability of the imperfect division of note values.[2] The other innovation resisted by the conservative camp was the division of the breve into four or more semibreves—already begun in the motets of Petrus de Cruce—and, eventually, the division of semibreves into smaller values.

des Murs

THE *ARS NOVA* IN FRANCE

Motet

The motet, originally a sacred form, had become largely secularized before the end of the thirteenth century. This trend continued in works such as the *Roman de Fauvel,* a satirical poem interpolated with 167 pieces of music (thirty-four are motets) and preserved in a beautifully decorated manuscript dating from 1310–14 (Paris, Bibliothèque nationale, MS fr. 146). The collection provides a veritable anthology of the music of the thirteenth and early fourteenth centuries much of which is monophonic—rondeaux, ballades,

1. "Explicit Ars Nova Magistri Philippi de Vetri": Philippe de Vitry, *Ars nova,* ed. Gilbert Reaney, André Gilles, and Jean Maillard, CSM 8 (American Institute of Musicology, 1964), p. 31. The attribution and originality of the treatise has been questioned. See Sarah Fuller, "A Phantom Treatise of the Fourteenth Century? The *Ars nova,*" JM 4 (1985–86):23–50.
2. See Book 2 from this treatise, trans. in SRrev, pp. 261–69; 2:152–59.

■ *A charivari, or noisy serenade, awakens Fauvel and Vaine Gloire after their wedding in the* Roman de Fauvel *(1310–14), a poem by Gervais du Bus with many musical interpolations. Fauvel is an allegorical horse or ass that incarnates the sins represented by the letters of his name: flatterie, avarice, vilainie, variété (fickleness), envie, and lâcheté (cowardice).* (PARIS, BIBLIOTHÈQUE NATIONALE, MS FR. 146)

chanson-refrains, and a variety of plainsong. Many of the motet texts denounce the lax morals of the clergy, while others refer to political events. Such allusions came to characterize the fourteenth-century motet, as they earlier had the conductus. Indeed, the motet in the 1300s often celebrated ecclesiastical or secular occasions, and it continued to do so through the first half of the following century.

de Vitry's motets

Petrarch praised de Vitry as "the one real poet of France."[3] Five of the three-part motets in the *Roman de Fauvel* are believed to be by Philippe de Vitry; nine other motets probably by him are in a manuscript copied about 1360 (the Ivrea Codex). De Vitry's motet tenors provide the earliest examples of a unifying device called *isorhythm.* These tenors are laid out in segments of identical rhythm, on the same principle we have already encountered in some late thirteenth-century motets (see Example 3.10c). As in some earlier motets, the rhythmic formula may be varied after a certain number of repetitions. But now, all this takes place on a much larger scale. The tenor is longer, the rhythms are more complex, and the whole line moves so ponderously against the faster notes of the upper voices that it can no longer be recognized as a melody. Rather, the tenor functions as a foundation for the entire polyphonic structure.

3. *Letters from Petrarch,* trans. Morris Bishop (Bloomington: Indiana University Press, 1966), p. 87.

The Isorhythmic Motet

Under the influence of de Vitry, composers and theorists recognized two recurring elements in the motet tenors, one melodic and the other rhythmic. They called the repeating series of pitches the *color*, and the long recurring rhythmic unit the *talea* (a "cutting" or segment). Color and talea could coincide, beginning and ending together over the course of the piece. Or the color could extend over two, three, or more taleae, with the two factors still coordinated. But if the endings of color and talea did not coincide, then repetitions of the color began in the middle of a talea. Motets that have tenors built up of colores and taleae are termed *isorhythmic* (same rhythm) motets. Upper voices could also be organized isorhythmically, and the technique was occasionally applied to compositions in other genres.

de Vitry's *In arboris*

The motet *In arboris—Tuba sacre fidei—Virgo sum*, attributed to Philippe de Vitry in the *Ars nova* treatise from around 1322–23, shows the isorhythmic method applied to a work primarily in duple meter (see NAWM 19 [CD 1 47] and Example 4.1). The composer divided the melody on *Virgo sum* into three equal parts to fit three statements of the rhythmic unit, or talea. He then repeated the melody again for a second color, using the same rhythmic scheme but reducing the note values by half. *In arboris* displays yet another level of complexity. The tenor in the original notation is written partly in red notes to warn the singer that the segment in this "colored" notation (denoted in the transcription by half-brackets) is in triple meter as opposed to the duple meter of black notation. Such mixing of duple and triple groupings is one of the novel techniques of the *ars nova*. Another distinctive feature of the colored segments in this motet is that all the parts are isorhythmic and feature a hocketing in which the upper voices alternate singing and resting to project a single melodic line.

Example 4.1 *Philippe de Vitry, Tenor of the Motet* In arboris—Tuba sacre fidei—Virgo sum

JACQUES DE LIÈGE RAILS AGAINST THE *ARS NOVA*

In a certain company in which some able singers and judicious laymen were assembled, and where new motets in the modern manner and some old ones were sung, I observed that even the laymen were better pleased with the ancient motets and the ancient manner than with the new. And even if the new manner pleased when it was a novelty, it does so no longer, but begins to displease many. So let the ancient music and the ancient manner of singing be brought back to their native land; let them come back into use; let the rational art flourish once more. It has been in exile, along with its manner of singing; they have been cast out from the fellowship of singers with near violence, but violence should not be perpetual.

Wherein does this lasciviousness in singing so greatly please, this excessive refinement, by which, as some think, the words are lost, the harmony of consonances is diminished, the value of the notes is changed, perfection is brought low, imperfection is exalted, and measure is confused?

From *Speculum musicae*, ca. 1325, Book 7, Chapter 46, trans. James McKinnon in SRrev, p. 278; 2:168.

The basic idea of isorhythm—arranging time values in a pattern that repeats—was not new in the fourteenth century, but it came to be applied in ever more extended and complex ways. Isorhythm gave coherence to long compositions that had no other formal organization. True, the interlocked repetitions of color and talea, extending over long stretches of the music, might hardly be noticed by the listener. Yet the isorhythmic structure does impose a certain unity on the entire piece that is felt at some level of consciousness.

Guillaume de Machaut

The leading composer of the *ars nova* in France was Guillaume de Machaut (ca. 1300–1377). Born in the province of Champagne in northern France, he was educated as a cleric and took Holy Orders. In his early twenties he became secretary to King John of Bohemia, whom he accompanied on military campaigns over many parts of Europe. After King John died in the battle of Crécy in 1346, Machaut entered the service of the French court and eventually ended his days as a canon at Rheims. Machaut was famous not only as a musician but also as a poet. His musical works, written in most of the genres then current, reveal a composer of mingled conservative and progressive tendencies.

Motets

Most of Machaut's twenty-three motets followed the traditional texture in which an instrumental liturgical tenor supports two upper voices with different texts. Like other motets of the time, Machaut's were longer, more secular, and more rhythmically complex than earlier examples. Some are pan-isorhythmic—that is, the isorhythmic structure involves all three voices. Considerable use is made of hocket in these motets, and there is one motetlike work specifically called a "hocket"; it is apparently instrumental and has an isorhythmic tenor from the melisma on the word "David" in an Alleluia verse.

Machaut's monophonic songs continued the trouvère tradition. They comprise nineteen *lais*, a twelfth-century form similar to the sequence, and about twenty-five *chansons balladées*, more commonly called *virelais*. Characteristic of the virelai is the form A b b a . . . A in which A stands for the refrain, b the first part of the stanza (which is repeated), and a the last part of the stanza (which uses the same melody as the refrain). There are usually three stanzas, the refrain A being repeated after each.

Virelais

A typical virelai strophe is represented below:

	Refrain		Stanza				Refrain	
Lines of poetry:	1	2	3	4	5	6	1	2
Sections of music:	A		b	b	a		A	

Machaut also wrote seven polyphonic virelais. The vocal solo is accompanied by an instrumental tenor part below, and there is an occasional musical rhyme between the endings of the two melodic sections.

Ars nova traits

Ars nova tendencies show up most clearly in Machaut's polyphonic virelais, rondeaux, and ballades—the so-called *formes fixes* (fixed forms), in which the text and music have particular patterns of repetition that are determined by the poetic structure. Machaut exploited the possibilities of the new duple division of time. For example, he subdivided into two each beat of a large triple in the Agnus Dei from the Mass (NAWM 21; CD 2 [4] / 1 ⟨18⟩) and plainly organized the rhythm in the more prominently heard duple (with triple subdivision) in the rondeau *Rose, liz* (NAWM 20; CD 2 [1] / 1 ⟨15⟩).

In another innovation, Machaut made the top part, or cantus, the principal voice, supporting it with the tenor and the triplum (or contratenor) and, rarely, a fourth voice. Although we still hear parallel fifths and many pungent dissonances in Machaut's works, the pervading milder sonorities of the third and sixth and their orderly succession distinguish his music from that of his predecessors. A new lyricism speaks through the finely wrought, flexible, melodic line in the solo voice, which has an accent of sincerity that imparts warmth even to the stylized language of chivalric verse. Machaut himself declared that true song and poetry could come only from the heart: "Car qui de sentiment non fait son oeuvre et son chant contrefait" (For whoever does not compose from feeling counterfeits his work and song).[4]

Ballade style

One of Machaut's most important achievements was the development of the ballade or cantilena style, in which the treble voice carrying the text dominates the three-part texture, while the two lower voices are most often performed instrumentally. His polyphonic virelais and rondeaux, as well as the forty-one *ballades notées*—so called to distinguish them from his poetic ballades without music—exhibit this hierarchy of parts. The form of Machaut's ballades, inherited in part from the trouvères, consisted of three or four stanzas, each sung to the same music and each ending with a refrain. Machaut wrote ballades with two, three, and four parts and for various combinations of voices with instruments, but his typical settings were for high tenor solo or

4. Machaut, *Remède de fortune*, lines 407–08, in *Oeuvres*, ed. Ernest Hoeppfner (Paris: Firmin Didot, 1811), 2:15.

duet with two lower parts. Those for two voices, each with its own text, are called *double ballades.*

Rondeau

The rondeau form captivated poets and musicians of the late Middle Ages. Like the virelai (see above), it consisted of only two musical phrases, and the refrain, which is heard at the beginning and the end, contains all the music. In *Rose, liz* (NAWM 20), the first part of the refrain has two phrases and closes without finality on *D*, while the second part has one line and closes on the key tone, *C*. The first couplet, of two lines, is set to the music of the first part of the refrain; the second couplet, of three lines, uses all of the music. The form is ABaAabAB (capital letters signify the refrain text) and is represented below:

	Refrain					Half-Refrain					Refrain		
Lines of poetry:	1	2	3	4	5	6(1)	7(2)	8	9	10	11(1)	12(2)	13(3)
Sections of music:	A		B	a		A		a		b	A		B

As in most of Machaut's secular songs, the music is constructed around a two-voice framework in which the tenor serves as a slower-moving support to the cantus, the only voice provided with a text (although all the parts may sometimes have been sung). The contratenor, in the same range as the tenor, reinforces or complements it, while the triplum shares the upper octave and exchanges motives with the cantus. Characteristic of French fourteenth-century secular music are the long melismas, as on "liz" (lily) and "fleur" (flower). These melismas occupy as much as four measures at the beginning,

Guillaume de Machaut in his study is visited by Amour, who introduces his three children, Doux Penser (Sweet Thoughts), Plaisance (Pleasure), and Espérance (Hope). Miniature from the atelier of Jean Bondol in a manuscript of Machaut's works. (PARIS, BIBLIOTHÈQUE NATIONALE, MS FR. 1584)

or sometimes in the middle, of lines. Although they may fall on unimportant words and even on unaccented syllables, they have a formal and decorative function and in a general way convey the mood of the text.

Among Machaut's highly sophisticated rondeaux, one in particular is cited for its ingenuity: *Ma fin est mon commencement et mon commencement ma fin* (My end is my beginning and my beginning my end). The melody of the tenor is that of the topmost voice sung backward, and the second half of the contratenor's melody is the reverse of its first half.

Mass

Machaut's *Messe de Notre Dame* was one of the earliest polyphonic settings of the Ordinary. It was preceded by at least four anonymous cycles that are more or less complete, but Machaut's stands out for its spacious dimensions, its control of consonance and dissonance in a four-part texture, and its carefully planned isorhythmic structures. Although it is not, like some later Masses, unified by a single cantus firmus—each movement is based on a different one—there is a unity of approach and style, as well as a tonal focus on *D* and *F*, that holds the movements together.

In the twelfth and thirteenth centuries, composers did not write many polyphonic settings of Ordinary texts, and when such settings were performed together in one service, the combination was completely fortuitous. No one seemed to care whether the Kyrie, Gloria, Credo, Sanctus, and Agnus Dei were in the same mode or were musically unified. In the manuscripts, the different parts of the Mass were usually separated out—all the Glorias placed together, followed by all the Credos, and so on. A choirmaster could choose appropriate items from these collections to form a complete Ordinary. This practice prevailed until about the second quarter of the fifteenth century.

In the *Messe de Notre Dame*, Machaut clearly regarded the five divisions of the Ordinary as one musical composition rather than separate pieces. How musical unity is achieved in this work is not immediately obvious. Some motives recur, and a decorative diminution appears throughout the work:

Example 4.2 *A Frequently Occurring Diminution in Machaut's Mass*

Isorythm

The Kyrie, Sanctus, Agnus Dei, and *Ite, missa est* are isorhythmically organized. The Gloria and Credo, having longer texts, are essentially syllabic and note-against-note, and end with elaborate Amens. The Agnus Dei (NAWM 21) is typical of the isorhythmic movements. The tenor melody uses the Agnus Dei setting of the plainchant Mass numbered XVII in modern chant books (*Liber usualis*, page 61), though in a slightly different version. The isorhythmic structure begins at the words "qui tollis"—that is, after the intonation of each Agnus (Agnus III repeats Agnus I). Since the "qui tollis" section of the chant is identical in Agnus I and II, the two statements of this constitute the two colores. The first color (Agnus I) has two taleae (measures 7–13 and 14–20); the second color (Agnus II) has six taleae, each of four notes. The more frequent cadences at the end of the short taleae of Agnus II set it apart and provide contrast with the longer spans of Agnus I (and its repetition in Agnus III). In addition to the tenor, the triplum and contratenor are also wholly or partly isorhythmic. The two upper parts enliven the rhythm with almost constant syncopation.

For the most part, the music of Machaut's Mass remains on a lofty, impersonal plane, and does not reflect the emotion expressed in the text. One striking exception occurs in the Credo: the words "ex Maria Virgine" (of the Virgin Mary) are set in strong relief by sudden, long-held chords. Later composers established the custom of emphasizing this entire portion of the Credo, "Et incarnatus est de spiritu sancto ex Maria Virgine et homo factus est" (And he was incarnate by the Holy Ghost of the Virgin Mary and was made man) through similar means, using a slower rhythm and more forceful declamation.

We cannot be certain just how Machaut's Mass was meant to be performed. All the voice parts may have been doubled by instruments. The contratenor part was probably played rather than sung, given its general melodic style and the lack in some of the manuscript sources of any accompanying text. In the isorhythmic movements, at least, the tenor part may also have been played or doubled by an instrument. In the Gloria and Credo there are numerous short interludes for tenor and contratenor that have an instrumental character, but what instruments were used and to what extent, we cannot say. Nor do we know for what occasion the work was written, but it must have been one of unusual solemnity and magnificence. On the basis of comparison with datable songs, the Mass dates from the early 1360s.

Summary

Machaut was typical of fourteenth-century composers in that his sacred compositions represented only a small portion of his total output. The production of sacred music declined in this period as the prestige of the church weakened and the arts were becoming more secularized. In addition, the church itself had second thoughts about using elaborate musical settings in its services. From the twelfth century on, numerous ecclesiastical pronouncements railed against complicated music and against displays of virtuosity by singers. These practices were thought to distract the minds of the worshipers and to turn the Mass into a form of entertainment, obscure the words, and make the liturgical melodies unrecognizable.

In Italy, to which we shall turn next, this official attitude apparently discouraged composers altogether from writing polyphonic church music. However, a kind of polyphony resulted from *alternatim* performance of the Mass Ordinary, in which the choir sang one phrase in plainsong and the organist played the next phrase, adding a line of florid counterpoint above the notes of the chant. On occasion, choirs improvised simple polyphony in discant style over the written notes of a chant. This practice conformed literally to a decree of Pope John XXII, issued from Avignon in 1324:

> On festal days or in solemn Masses and in the Divine Office, some concords (such as the octave, fifth, and fourth) that enrich the melody may be sung above the simple ecclesiastical chant, in such manner however that the integrity of the chant itself remains undisturbed.

ITALIAN *TRECENTO* MUSIC

Italian music in the fourteenth century, or *trecento* (short for *mille trecento*—that is, the 1300s), developed differently from French music because of Italy's social and political climate. Where France had a monarchy with increasing power and stability, Italy was a collection of city-states, each with its own political, cultural, and linguistic traditions and alliances. Composers associated with the church who were trained in notation and counterpoint wrote polyphony as a refined secular entertainment for elite circles. Most other music remained unwritten. At the courts, Italian *trovatori* of the thirteenth century followed in the footsteps of the troubadours, singing their songs from memory. The only music of the people to have come down to us in manuscripts are the monophonic laude, the processional songs already mentioned (page 64). Polyphony in fourteenth-century Italian church music was largely improvised.

Florence

The principal centers of Italian *trecento* music were in the central and northern part of the peninsula, notably Bologna, Padua, Modena, Milan, Perugia, and above all Florence, a particularly important cultural center from the fourteenth through the sixteenth centuries. Florence is the birthplace of two celebrated works of literature, the *Decameron* of Giovanni Boccaccio (1313–1375) and the *Paradiso degli Alberti* of Giovanni Gherardi da Prato (ca. 1367–ca. 1444). From these writings and others of the time, we learn how music, both vocal and instrumental, accompanied nearly every aspect of Italian social life. In the *Decameron*, for example, each of the company mingles the day's round of stories with singing and dancing (see vignette).

Squarcialupi Codex

It is possible that some of the music described by Boccaccio would have been polyphonic, but if so, the polyphony would probably have been improvised or performed from memory. Very few examples of Italian polyphony from before 1330 have survived, but after that date, we find several fourteenth-century manuscripts written either in Italy or southern France. The most copious source—though unfortunately late and not altogether reliable—is the magnificent Squarcialupi Codex, named for its former owner, the Florentine organist Antonio Squarcialupi (1416–1480). This codex, probably copied about 1420, is now in the Biblioteca Medicea-Laurenziana in Florence. Written on vellum and richly ornamented in bright colors, it contains 354 pieces, mostly for two and three voices, by twelve composers of the *trecento* and early *quattrocento*. A miniature portrait of each composer appears at the beginning of the section containing his works (see Plate II, facing page 111). Three types of secular Italian pieces appear in this and other manuscripts: *madrigal, caccia*, and *ballata*.

The Madrigal

Madrigals were idyllic, pastoral, satirical, or love poems usually written for two voices. The poems consist of several three-line stanzas, followed by a closing pair of lines. All the stanzas are set to the same music; the additional pair of

GIOVANNI BOCCACCIO, FROM THE *DECAMERON*

The tables having been cleared away, the queen commanded that instruments be brought in, for all the ladies knew how to do the round dance, and the young men too, and some of them could play and sing very well. Upon her request, Dioneo took a lute and Fiammetta a viol and began sweetly to play a dance. Then the queen together with other ladies and two young men chose a carol and struck up a round dance with a slow pace—while the servants were sent out to eat. When this was finished, they began to sing charming and merry songs. They continued in this way for a long time, until the queen thought it was time to go to sleep.

Giovanni Boccaccio, *Decameron*, Day One, Introduction.

lines, called the *ritornello*, are set to different music with a different meter. Melismatic passages decorate the ends (and sometimes beginnings) of lines:

	Stanza			Stanza			Ritornello	
Lines of poetry:	1	2	3	4	5	6	7	8
Sections of music:	a			a			b	

In Jacopo da Bologna's *Fenice fù* (NAWM 22; CD 2 [7]), as in most madrigals of this period, the two voices have the same text, and both parts were meant to be sung. The more florid upper voice has long, flowing runs on the last accented syllable of each line. In two short passages the voices indulge in a hocketlike alternation, and elsewhere they are in imitation, a technique Jacopo may have picked up from the caccia.

The Caccia

The caccia parallels the French *chace*, in which a popular-style melody was set in strict canon to lively, graphically descriptive words. The Italian caccia, which flourished chiefly from 1345 to 1370, was written for two equal voices in canon at the unison. Unlike its French and Spanish counterparts, it usually had an additional free instrumental part in slower motion below. Its poetic form was irregular, although, like madrigals, many cacce had ritornellos, which were not always in canonic style. The French and Italian words both mean "hunt," or "chase." In the case of the caccia, the name refers not only to the pursuit of one voice after the other but also to the subject matter of the text. A typical caccia described a hunt or some other animated scene, such as a fishing party, a bustling marketplace, a party of girls gathering flowers, a fire, or a battle. The music adds vivid details with spirit and humor—shouts, bird songs, horn calls, exclamations, dialogue—often with the aid of hocket and echo effects. Similar realistic touches were sometimes incorporated into the Italian madrigal and ballata, as they had been into the French virelai.

GIOVANNI DA PRATO, FROM *PARADISO DEGLI ALBERTI*, CA. 1425

Now the sun rose higher and the heat of the day increased. The whole company remained in the pleasant shade, as a thousand birds sang among the verdant branches. Someone asked Francesco [Landini] to play the organ a little, to see whether the sound would make the birds increase or diminish their song. He did so at once, and a great wonder followed. When the sound began many of the birds fell silent and gathered around as if in amazement, listening for a long time. Then they resumed their song and redoubled it, showing inconceivable delight, and especially one nightingale, who came and perched above the organ on a branch over Francesco's head.

Il Paradiso degli Alberti, ed. A. Wesselofsky (Bologna, 1867), pp. 111–13, trans. D. J. Grout.

The Ballata

The polyphonic ballata, which flourished later than the madrigal and caccia, showed some influence of the French ballade style. The word "ballata" originally signified a song to accompany dancing (from the Italian *ballare*, to dance). Thirteenth-century ballate (of which no musical examples are known today) were monophonic dance songs with choral refrains, and in Boccaccio's *Decameron* the ballata was still associated with dancing. Although a few early fourteenth-century monophonic ballate have survived, most of the examples found in the manuscripts are for two or three voices and date from after 1365. In form, these purely lyrical, stylized, polyphonic ballate resemble the French virelai.

Landini

Francesco Landini (ca. 1325–1397) was the leading composer of ballate and the foremost Italian musician of the *trecento*. Blind from boyhood as a result of smallpox, Landini nevertheless became an esteemed, well-educated poet and a master of the theory and practice of music. A virtuoso on many instruments, he was especially known for his skill at the organetto, a small portative organ, which he played "as readily as though he had the use of his eyes, with a touch of such rapidity (yet always observing the measure), with such skill and sweetness, that beyond all doubt he excelled all organists within memory."[5]

Landini is a principal character in Giovanni da Prato's *Paradiso degli Alberti*. This book, though written around 1425, supposedly records scenes and conversations from the year 1389. Among the short stories (*novelle*) contained in it—set in a framework similar to that of Boccaccio's *Decameron* and Chaucer's *Canterbury Tales*—is one supposed to have been told by Landini himself (see vignette).

Landini wrote no sacred music. His extant works comprise 90 two-part and 42 three-part ballate, and some others that survive in both two- and three-

5. From an account by a fourteenth-century Florentine chronicler, Filippo Villani, *Le Vite d'uomini illustri fiorentini*, ed. G. Mazzuchelli (Florence, 1847), p. 46.

part versions. There are, besides, a caccia and ten madrigals. The two-part ballate are evidently early works; in style they resemble the madrigals, except that the melodic line is more ornate. Like French ballades, many of the three-part ballate are for solo voice with two accompanying parts.

Landini's ballata, *Non avrà ma' pietà* (NAWM 23; CD 2 [8]/ 1 ⟨21⟩), is in a form typical of his work in this genre. A three-line refrain (*ripresa*) is sung both before and after a seven-line stanza. The first two pairs of lines in the stanza, which were called *piedi*, have their own musical phrase, while the last three lines, the *volta*, use the same music as the refrain. The form may be represented as follows:

	Ripresa	Stanza	(2 piedi)	Volta	Ripresa
Lines of poetry:	1 2 3	4 5	6 7	8 9 10	1 2 3
Sections of music:	A	b	b	a	A

Having a melisma on the first and penultimate syllables of a line is characteristic of the Italian style. The end of every line, and often the first word and the midpoint or caesura of a line, is marked by a cadence. It is usually of the type that has become known as the "Landini" cadence, in which the passage from the major sixth to the octave is ornamented by a lower neighbor leaping up a third in the upper part (see measures 3–4, 5–6, 10–11 of Example 4.3, which shows the first line of the ripresa). Sometimes, both the voices that rise

Example 4.3 *Francesco Landini, Ballata:* Non avrà ma' pietà

She will never have pity, this lady of mine . . . Perhaps by her will be extinguished [*the flames*] . . .

Source: *Polyphonic Music of the Fourteenth Century*, IV, p. 144 (Monaco: Éditions de l'Oiseau-Lyre, 1958).

Double leading-tone cadence

to the final chord do so by semitone motion, creating a *double leading-tone cadence* (measures 3–4). One of the charms of Landini's music, in addition to its graceful vocal melody, is the sweetness of its harmonies. Gone are the parallel seconds and sevenths that abounded in the thirteenth century, and there are few parallel fifths and octaves. Sonorities containing both the intervals of the third and fifth or of the third and sixth are plentiful, though they are never used to start or end a section or piece.

French influence

Toward the end of the fourteenth century, the music of Italian composers began losing its specific national characteristics and absorbing the contemporary French style. The trend was noticeable especially after the papal court returned from Avignon to Rome in 1377. Italians wrote songs to French texts and in French genres, and their works recorded in late fourteenth-century manuscripts often appear in French notation. Toward the end of the century, northern composers began to settle in Italy. In about 1390, or possibly earlier, the Liègois composer and theorist Johannes Ciconia (ca. 1370–1412) established himself in Padua. There and in the neighboring city of Venice he pursued a successful musical career. As it turned out, Ciconia was the first in a long line of Flemish, Netherlandish, French, English, and (later) Spanish musicians who flocked to Italy during the fifteenth century. They were welcomed—so warmly, indeed, that for many years nearly every important musical post in that country was filled by a foreigner. Unquestionably, the music these composers wrote was influenced by what they heard and learned in Italy.

Performance

There was no uniform way of performing music in the fourteenth century. That a part lacks a text does not make it instrumental, since another manuscript may supply words for the same part. Conversely, the presence of a text does not mean that the part was always sung. A purely vocal performance of a piece for two, three, or four parts was likely in certain settings, particularly in a chapel that lacked an organ. The tenor parts of Landini's ballate and Machaut's ballades, with their long notes, frequent wide skips, and notation using many ligatures, were probably written for instruments. The contratenor parts were evidently composed after the superius (the highest part) and tenor, with the aim of completing the consonant sonorities. The contratenor lines were certainly played in some cases, but many are equally suited for singing, and many of those have texts. The superius, which is often quite florid, always has a vocal character. Of course, instruments might have doubled a vocal line (perhaps with added embellishments) or played in alternation with the voice. Finally, we have evidence of vocal pieces that were played instrumentally throughout, with added embellishments in the melodic line. Instrumental embellishments were largely improvised, but sometimes such pieces were written down. The Robertsbridge Codex (British Library, MS Add. 28550) from about 1325 includes organ arrangements of three motets, and the Faenza Codex (Faenza, Biblioteca comunale, MS 117) from the first quarter of the fifteenth century contains—in addition to keyboard pieces based on plainchant Mass sections—

I. *Giotto (1266–1337),* Wedding procession. *This fresco is one of a series on the life of the Virgin painted around 1305 in the Chapel of the Madonna della Carità de Arena, the so-called Scrovegni Chapel, named after the banker Enrico Scrovegni, who built the chapel on the site of a Roman amphitheater. Mary (with the halo) leads the virgins, while a vielle player and two pipers provide music. Marchetto da Padua's* Ave Regina celorum *may have been performed at the chapel's dedication. The large-leaf branch jutting from the window is a sign of the Virgin's pregnancy. Giotto distinguished himself from his predecessors in the naturalness of facial expressions and posture. He achieved depth by placing figures and objects on different planes of the pictorial space.* (CAMERAPHOTO / ART RESOURCE, NEW YORK)

II. *Anonymous portrait of Francesco Landini playing a portative organ, which is set inside the initial letter* M *of the madrigal* Musica son *(I am music). From the "Squarcialupi Codex," an early fifteenth-century manuscript named for its fifteenth-century owner Antonio Squarcialupi.* (FLORENCE, BIBLIOTECA MEDICEA-LAURENZIANA, MS PALATINO 87, FOL. 121V)

ornate keyboard versions of ballades by Machaut as well as keyboard versions of madrigals and ballate by other Italian *trecento* composers, including Landini.

FRENCH MUSIC OF THE LATE FOURTEENTH CENTURY

In a paradox typical of the later fourteenth century, the papal court at Avignon stood out more for its secular music than for its sacred composition. There and at other courts across southern France, a brilliant chivalric society allowed many French and Italian composers to flourish. Their music consisted chiefly of ballades, virelais, and rondeaux for solo voice with supporting instrumental tenor and contratenor parts. Composers probably wrote most of the texts themselves. Some of the ballades include references to people and events of the time, but the majority of the pieces are love songs. They are examples of aristocratic art in the best sense of the word —works of refined beauty, with sensitive melodies and delicately colored harmonies. Their elevated musical style is matched by their sumptuous appearances, some teeming with fanciful decorations, intermingled red and black notes, ingenious notation, and occasional caprices that include a love song written in the shape of a heart (see illustration, page 114) or a canon in the shape of a circle.

Rhythm

French secular music of this period has remarkable rhythmic flexibility. The solo melody exhibits subtle nuances that capture in notation the free, rubato-like delivery of a singer. Beats are subdivided in many different ways, and the phrase lines are broken by pauses in hocket, or held in suspense through chains of syncopations. Rhythmic complexities abound, as voices move in contrasting meters and in contrasted groupings within the beat. Harmonies are purposely blurred through suspensions and syncopations. Sometimes composers carried their fascination with technique to extremes that degenerated into a kind of ultra-sophistication that musicologists have termed *ars subtilior* (the subtler manner).

Example 4.4 (page 113) shows a typical phrase from a rondeau by Anthonello da Caserta, a late fourteenth-century Italian composer who beat the French at their own game (the two lowest staves are merely a reduction of the parts, not an accompaniment). Here the syncopation gives the effect of a delayed entrance by the soloist. The rhythmic subtlety of the passage is of an order not to be matched before the twentieth century, yet everything falls logically into place. The delightful effect of the sixth at measure 2 is noteworthy, as is the coquettish hesitation between *B*♭ and *B* after the first rest in the solo part. Anthonello allows the contratenor to sound now above, now below the tenor, so that the real bass of the harmony alternates between the two voices and is sometimes revealed in one when the other pauses. Playing these two lower

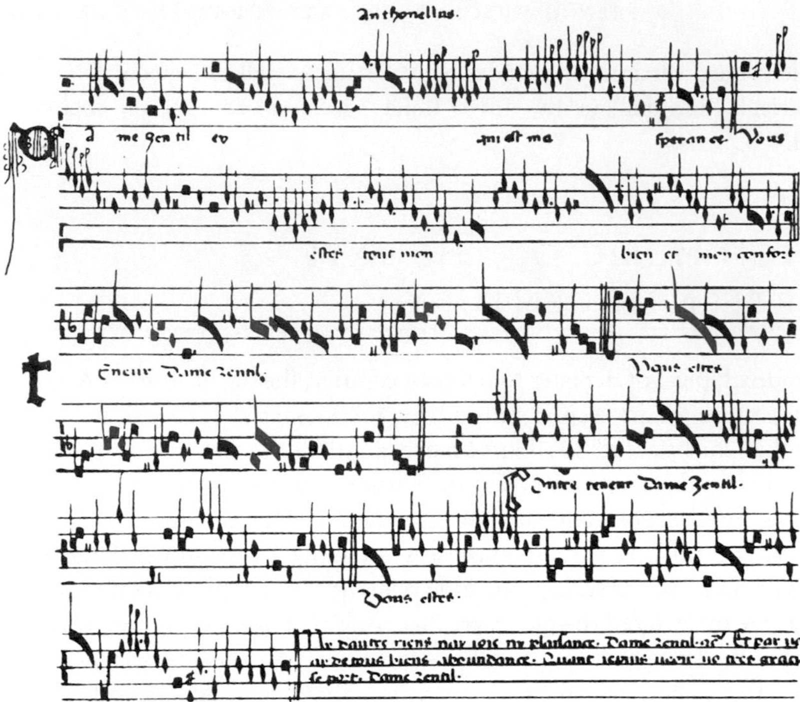

■ *The rondeau* Dame zentil *by Anthonello da Caserta in the Modena manuscript, ca. 1410. The sharp near the end of the first staff belongs with the B, not the C.* (MODENA, BIBLIOTECA ESTENSE, MS α. M. 24)

parts on instruments of contrasting timbres yields an ever-changing palette of sonorities.

Since most of the passage quoted in Example 4.4 is a melisma, the text has been omitted.[6] Accidentals below or above the notes do not appear in the original. The so-called partial signatures—different signatures in different voices—were common in the fourteenth and fifteenth centuries.

Baude Cordier's rondeau, *Belle, bonne, sage* (NAWM 24; CD 2 [11]), participates half-seriously in the intellectual play of the late fourteenth century in both the music and its graphic presentation (see illustration, page 114). The complication in the music results from three levels of hemiola. Two of these may be seen in Example 4.5. At measure 9 of the cantus part, each of the quarter notes of the $\frac{3}{4}$ measure is subdivided into three eighth notes, converting it to a $\frac{9}{8}$ measure. Meanwhile the contratenor in measures 8–11 has one measure of $\frac{3}{2}$ against two measures of $\frac{2}{4}$. These shifts of mensuration are notated by means of red notes in the manuscript. Adding further color and visual interest, the word "heart" in the text is replaced with a red heart, and, of course, the entire piece is notated in the shape of a heart.

A striking feature of this chanson is the anticipation of the opening vocal line by the contratenor and tenor. The conservative use of rhythmic complication, the fluid setting of the text, and the fullness of the harmony foreshadow fifteenth-century practices.

The sophisticated music of the southern French courts was intended for professional performers and highly cultivated listeners. Its formidable rhythmic and notational complexities were going out of fashion toward the end of

6. The entire composition may be found in Willi Apel, ed., *French Secular Music of the Late Fourteenth Century* (Cambridge, Mass., 1950).

Example 4.4 *Anthonello da Caserta, Rondeau: Portion of* Dame Zentil

the fourteenth century. At the same time, northern France saw a simpler type of secular polyphony being developed by guilds of musicians who were, in a sense, heirs to the trouvère tradition. Their poems had a popular character: instead of the polished sentiments of courtly love, they offered realistic scenes of the hunt and the marketplace. The music was lively and fresh, imitating the vigorous straightforward rhythms of folksong. Although few examples are preserved, this simpler art must have flourished widely.

MUSICA FICTA

The practice of raising or lowering certain notes by a half step gave a special flavor to much fourteenth-century French and Italian music. Such alterations resulted in flatted or sharped notes that were outside the standard gamut, therefore *musica ficta*—"false," or "feigned" music. Implied or indicated in manuscripts by accidentals, they were common at cadences in which a minor sixth called for by the mode was raised to a major sixth before a cadential octave, as at the cadence on *D* in Example 4.6a and b. Composers, singers, and theorists apparently also agreed that a third contracting to a unison should be made minor, and a sixth expanding to an octave be changed to major. Actually, cadences of the type shown in Example 4.6b would have *both* upper notes

Example 4.5 *Baude Cordier, Rondeau*: Belle, bonne, sage

of the penultimate chord raised to avoid the tritone, or augmented fourth, resulting in a double leading-tone cadence (Example 4.6c). Cadences on *G* and *C* were altered similarly. In cadences on *E*, however, the penultimate outer interval already formed a major sixth, so no alteration was required (see Example 4.6d). This succession of chords, in which the lower voice descends by semitone, has come to be called a *Phrygian cadence*.

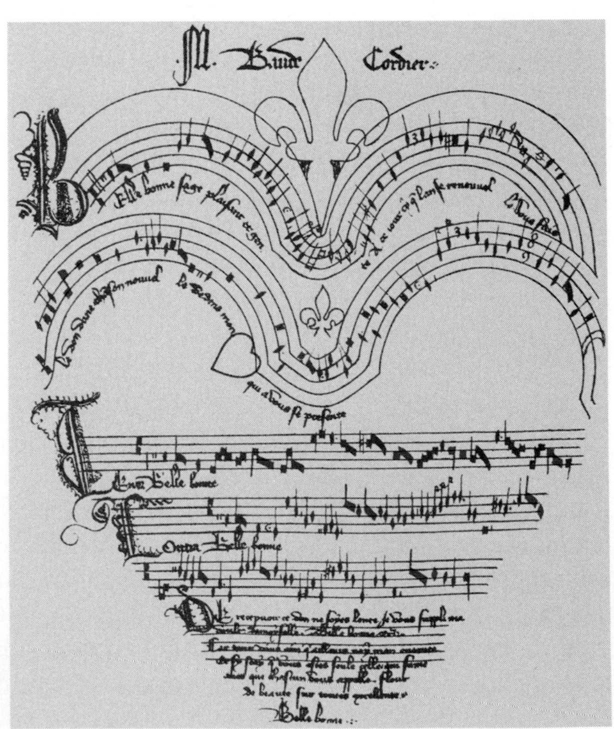

■ *The rondeau* Belle, bonne, sage *by Baude Cordier (after 1400) in a supplement to the Chantilly manuscript. The texted cantus is accompanied by textless tenor and contratenor lines. The shape of the notation is a pun on the composer's name (cor is Latin for heart).* (MUSÉE CONDÉ, MS. 564)

PROSDOCIMO DE' BELDOMANDI, FROM *CONTRAPUNCTUS*, 1412, BOOK 5, CHAPTERS 1–6

. . . . Musica ficta is the feigning of syllables or the placement of syllables in a location where they do not seem to be—to apply *mi* where there is no *mi* and *fa* where there is no *fa*, and so forth. Concerning musica ficta, it is necessary to know first of all that it is never to be applied except where necessary, because in art nothing is to be applied without necessity.

2. It must be known, too, that musica ficta was invented exclusively for the sake of coloring some consonance that could not be colored except by musica ficta. . . .

3. It must be known, too, that the signs of musica ficta are two, round or soft ♭ and square or hard ♮ [modern ♮ or ♯]. These two signs show us the feigning of syllables in a location where such syllables cannot be. . . .

6. Last, for understanding the placement of these two signs, round ♭ and square ♮, it must be known that these signs are to be applied to octaves, fifths, and similar intervals as it is necessary to enlarge or diminish them in order to make them good consonances if they earlier were dissonant, because such intervals ought always to be major or consonant in counterpoint. But these signs are to be applied to imperfectly consonant intervals—the third, the sixth, the tenth, and the like—as is necessary to enlarge or diminish them to give them major or minor inflections as appropriate, because such intervals ought sometimes to be major and sometimes minor in counterpoint; . . . for you should always choose that form, whether major or minor, that is less distant from that location which you intend immediately to reach. . . . There is no other reason for this than a sweeter-sounding harmony. . . . This is because the closer the imperfect consonance approaches the perfect one it intends to reach, the more perfect it becomes, and the sweeter the resulting harmony.

Prosdocimo de' Beldomandi, *Contrapunctus (Counterpoint)*, trans. Jan Herlinger (Lincoln: University of Nebraska Press, 1984), pp. 71–85.

Example 4.6 *Alterations at Cadences*

a. Strict modal forms

b. Chromatically altered forms

c. Form with double leading tones

d. Modal (Phrygian) cadence on *E*

Pitches were also raised or lowered to avoid sounding an augmented fourth against the lowest note of a texture, to avoid the tritone interval *F–B* in a melody, or simply to make a smoother-sounding melodic line. As Prosdocimo de' Beldomandi observed (see vignette), sometimes notes were

FOURTEENTH-CENTURY NOTATION IN DEPTH

A detailed description of fourteenth-century notation is beyond the scope of this book. We shall indicate here only some of the principles that guided Italian and French musicians in working out a notation allowing for both triple and duple subdivision of longer notes, the introduction of many new short note values, and the greater rhythmic flexibility that marked the music of the latter part of the century.

Italian notation

The basis of the Italian system was described by Marchetto of Padua in his *Pomerium* of 1318.[7] Briefly, the method consisted of dividing semibreves into groups set off by dots; adding certain letter signs to indicate the various combinations possible in triple and duple subdivisions; and adding newly invented note forms to mark exceptions to the general rules of rhythmic grouping and to express shorter note values. This kind of notation, particularly convenient for florid melodic lines, served Italian music well until the later part of the century; by then it was supplemented and eventually replaced by the French system, which had proved itself better adapted to the musical style of the time.

French notation

The French system of notation expanded on Franconian principles. The long, (▪) the breve, (▪) and the semibreve (◆) could each be divided into either three or two notes of the next smaller value. The division of the long was called *mode* (*modus*), that of the breve *time* (*tempus*), and that of the semibreve *prolation* (*prolatio*). Division was *perfect* or *major* if it was triple, *imperfect* or *minor* if duple. Two new note forms were introduced to indicate values shorter than the semibreve: the *minim* ♦, one-half or one-third of a semibreve; and the *semiminim* ♦, one-half of a minim. The system may be plotted as follows:

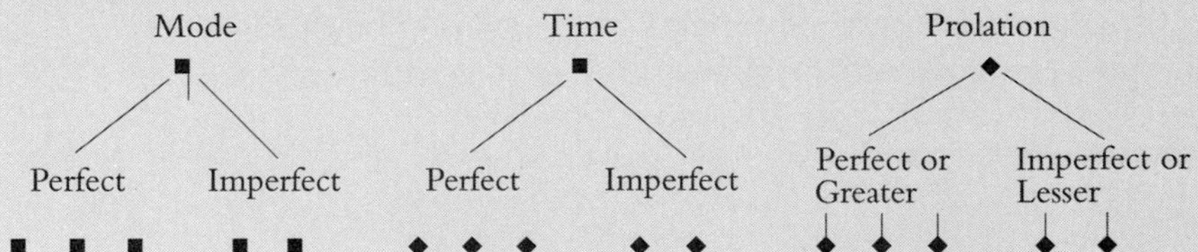

Time signatures

Eventually, the original signs for perfect and imperfect mode were dropped, and simplified signs for time and prolation were combined. A circle indicated perfect time and a half-circle imperfect time; a dot inside the circle or half-circle indicated major prolation, and the absence of a dot, minor prolation. Thus four "prolations" were recognized, and they were represented as follows:

perfect time and major prolation

7. This section is translated in SRrev, pp. 251–61; 2:141–51.

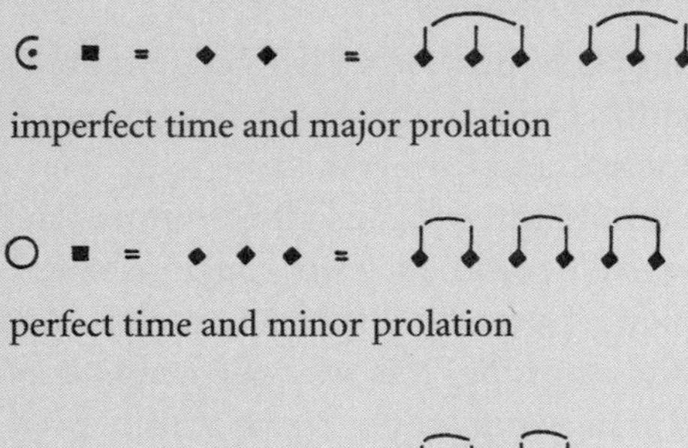

imperfect time and major prolation

perfect time and minor prolation

imperfect time and minor prolation

Proportions

The half-circle C, has come down to us as the modern sign for $\frac{4}{4}$ time. Our ¢, with its corresponding designation *alla breve*, is a relic of the late medieval and Renaissance system of "proportions." By means of this system, the unit of movement (the "beat") could be changed from one note value to another according to a specified ratio. In the case of ¢ or $\frac{2}{2}$, the beat was shifted from the usual semibreve to the breve—that is, the beating of breves was now as fast as the beating of semibreves had been before the sign. Or, if the beat was thought of as constant, a note worth two beats before was now worth one.

"Black" and "white" notations

About 1425, scribes began writing all the forms pictured above as "white" notes—that is, with black outlines unfilled (ᒣ □ ◇ ◇)[8] the semiminim became ◆, and shorter notes were devised by adding flags to the semiminim ♪ ♬ ♬. The change from diamond-shaped notes to the rounded heads we use today took place toward the end of the sixteenth century.

"Colored" notation

In addition to the signs shown above, the French employed other notational devices. They used dots—though not always in the same way as the Italians did—and colored notes. Red notes served a multitude of purposes, among them to show perfection or imperfection where the normal reading would indicate the opposite interpretation, and to show that the notes were to be sung at half (or some other fraction) of their normal value. "White" note forms replaced "black," and black notation was used to signify special meanings. Different voices in one piece might be notated with different prolational signatures, and signatures in one voice-line could frequently change. Occasionally, the different prolation signs were used as a shorthand notation for canons in which the imitating voice or voices proceeded at a different rate from that of the leading voice. The melody in such a canon was written only once but was provided with two or more different time signatures. Such "mensuration canons" became more common in the fifteenth and sixteenth centuries. Fourteenth-century composers also worked out ingenious ways to indicate syncopation, which was a prominent feature in some melodic lines in the latter part of the century (see Example 4.4).

Mensuration canons

8. This change may have come at that time because scribes shifted from writing on parchment to paper. Filling in black notes on rough-surfaced paper with the crude pens then common would have increased the chance of spattered ink and a ruined page.

sharped or flatted simply to provide a "sweeter-sounding" harmony. Such alterations in fourteenth-century music would present no difficulty to modern performers if composers and scribes had been in the habit of writing the sharps, flats, and naturals in the manuscript. Unfortunately for us, they often did not, and even when they did, they were inconsistent: the same passage appears in different manuscripts with different written accidentals.

If accidentals were missing, this was not mere carelessness; it accorded with the theoretical framework within which music was set down in writing. The system of hard, soft, and natural hexachords permitted semitones (pronounced in solmization *mi–fa*) between *B* and *C*, *E* and *F*, and *A* and *B*♭. This was the realm of *musica vera* (true music) or *musica recta* (correct music)—that is, the gamut of notes located in the Guidonian hand. A note outside this realm was considered "outside the hand," "false" (*falsa*), or "feigned" (*ficta*). Composers and scribes were reluctant to commit unsanctioned pitches to paper. Singers, meanwhile, were trained to recognize situations in which a note should be altered to produce a smoother melody or progression of intervals (see the statement by Prosdocimo de' Beldomandi in the vignette). After a while, it became almost an insult to specify a flat or sharp where a professional musician would have known to sing or play them; indeed, the criteria for making such judgments became something of an insider's art.

Accidentals

Manuscripts of the fourteenth and early fifteenth centuries, especially those from Italy, are relatively well supplied with accidentals, but after 1450 until about 1550 accidentals were scorned except for transpositions of mode. We are still not sure whether this reflected a real change in the sound—a reversion to the purity of the diatonic modes—or whether (as is more likely) it was simply a matter of notation, and the performers continued to apply alterations as before. In view of these uncertain factors, conscientious modern editors of this music include only those accidentals found in the original sources and indicate in some way (usually above or below the staff) those they believe the performers should supply.

INSTRUMENTS

A full and accurate account of instrumental music in the fourteenth and fifteenth centuries is impossible, for the simple reason that the music manuscripts rarely tell us whether a given part is instrumental or vocal, let alone specify the instruments. Composers were content to rely on musicians' habits and on tradition.

We know from pictorial and literary sources of the fourteenth and early fifteenth centuries that polyphonic music was usually performed by a small vocal or instrumental ensemble or a combination of the two, with only one voice or instrument to a part. Evidence also suggests that an instrument doubled the solo voice part of pieces in cantilena style and added embellishments, thereby producing heterophony. The Latin tenors in isorhythmic motets and

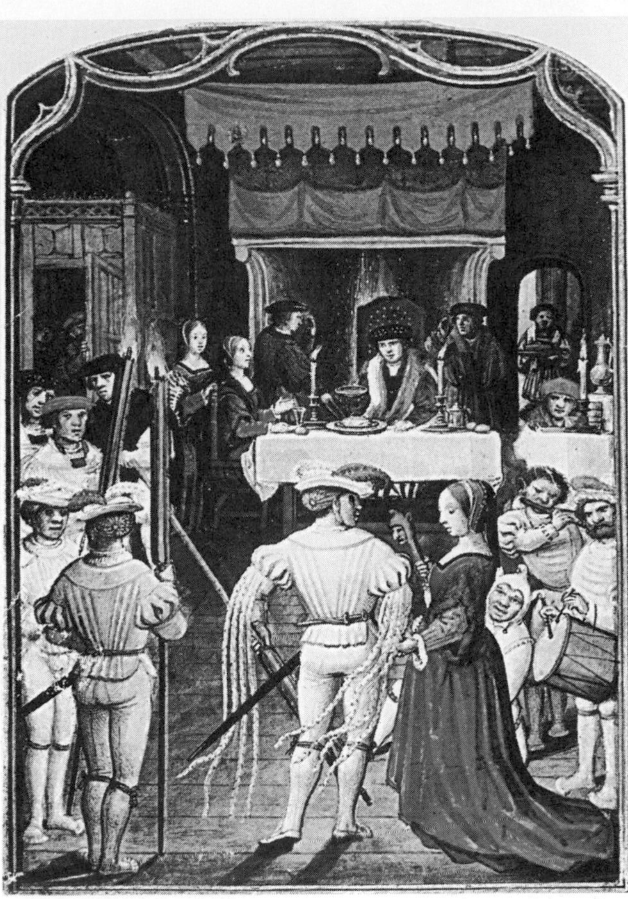

■ *Dancers in costume, some bearing torches, performing at a feast to the accompaniment of a flute, drum, and a partly visible string instrument. Book of Hours, Flemish, ca. 1500.* (BRITISH LIBRARY, MS ADD. 24098, FOL. 19V.)

the textless tenors in Landini's three-part ballate were almost surely instrumental rather than vocal. But beyond making a few suppositions like these, we can say only that performances probably varied according to circumstances, depending on their tastes and on the singers or players who happened to be at hand.

High and low instruments

Out-of-doors music, dancing, and especially festive or solemn ceremonies called for relatively larger ensembles and louder instruments. The fourteenth-century distinction betwen "high" (*haut*) and "low" (*bas*) instruments referred to loudness, not pitch. The most common low instruments were harps, vielles, lutes, psalteries, portative organs, transverse flutes, and recorders. Among the high instruments were shawms (double-reed woodwind), cornetts (hollowed-out wood, with finger holes and a brass-type mouthpiece), slide trumpets, and sackbuts (early trombones). Percussion instruments, including kettledrums, small bells, and cymbals, were common in ensembles of all kinds. The prevailing tone quality was clear, bright, or shrill. To judge from the representations in the art of the time, instruments of contrasting timbres were grouped together: viol, lute, harp, and sackbut, for example, or viol, lute, psaltery, recorder, and drum. Motets and other vocal pieces were sometimes performed by instruments alone. There was also, of course, a large repertory of instrumental dance music, but as these pieces were generally either improvised or played from memory, few written examples have been preserved.

Keyboard instruments

Although the earliest keyboard instruments of the clavichord and harpsichord type were invented in the fourteenth century, they were not commonly used until the fifteenth. In addition to the portative organ, or organetto, positive organs were frequently employed, and large organs installed in churches. Pedal keyboards were added to organs in Germany during the late 1300s. A mechanism of stops enabling the player to select different ranks of pipes at will and the addition of a second keyboard were both achievements of the early fifteenth century.

SUMMARY

Fourteenth-century composers made use of a greatly increased variety of musical resources. New forms and practices came about because of a pronounced shift of interest from sacred music to secular composition. Some composers late in the century carried the new rhythmic freedom to almost unperformable extremes. In planning counterpoint around definite tonal areas, composers exhibited a growing sense of organization. The imperfect consonances—thirds and (to a lesser degree) sixths—were favored on strong as well as weak beats, though the final sonority remained a unison, octave, or fifth. Passages of parallel thirds and sixths appeared, while parallel fifths and octaves became rarer. Musica ficta made cadential points more emphatic and melodic lines more flexible. The range of voices extended upward. The abstract structure of the thirteenth-century motet gave way to the more melodic-harmonic idiom of cantilena texture, as composers aimed for a sensuously attractive sound. In France, the motet continued to be a special genre of composition, less liturgical and more political and ceremonial in function as well as more intricate in structure.

New genres of composition emerged. Some, like the caccia and the madrigal, probably derived from popular musical practice. The ballata and other songs with refrains, inherited from the thirteenth century, can also be traced back—though more remotely—to popular models. The *formes fixes*, sophisticated genres that likewise continued an earlier tradition, were literary as well as musical forms: the virelai; the ballade; and the rondeau, which was increasingly favored toward the end of the century and was branching out into more complex types.

By the year 1400, the French and Italian musical styles, formerly distinct, began to merge, moving toward a pan-European style. As we shall see in the next chapter, this new style was influenced by various sources, chiefly from England and the Low Countries, and it began to diversify in the fifteenth century.

Bibliography

Music Collections: Facsimiles and Editions

Facsimiles

Black-and-white facsimile of the *Roman de Fauvel,* with extensive introductory comments: François Avril, Nancy Regaldo, and Edward Roesner, *Le Roman de Fauvel and Other Works: Facsimile with Introductory Essay* (New York: Broude Bros., 1986). Facsimiles from various manuscripts of polyphonic music: Heinrich Besseler and Peter Gülke, *Schriftbild der mehrstimmigen Musik.* Musikgeschichte in Bildern 3/5 (Leipzig: VEB Deutscher Verlag für Musik, 1973).

Editions

Polyphonic Music of the Fourteenth Century (Monaco: Éditions de l'Oiseau-Lyre, 1956–58; repr. 1975), various editors, is the most comprehensive series of fourteenth-century music: Vol. 1, *Roman de Fauvel*; 2–3, Machaut; 4, Landini; 5, Ivrea MS; 6–11, Italian secular music; 12–13, Italian sacred and ceremonial music; 14, English 13th–14th century music; 15, English motets; 16–17, English Mass, Office and ceremonial music; 18–22, French secular music (Chantilly, Musée Condé); 23, French sacred music.

In the Corpus Mensurabilis Musicae series, Italian music is represented in CMM 8, *Music of Fourteenth-Century Italy,* ed. Nino Pirrotta; CMM 2, Machaut, Mass; 13, Mass of Tournai; 29, fourteenth-century Mass music in France; 36–37 Codex Reina; 39, Mss. of Chantilly, Musée Condé, and Modena; and 53, *French Secular Compositions of the Fourteenth Century,* 3 vols, ed. Willi Apel.

Johannes Wolf, *Der Squarcialupi Codex* (Lippstadt: Kistner & Siegel, 1955).

CEKM No. 1, *Keyboard Music of the Fourteenth and Fifteenth Centuries,* ed. W. Apel.

Keyboard music from the Codex Faenza in MSD 10 (facs.) and CMM 57 (transcribed and ed. Dragan Plamenac).

Machaut editions: ed. Leo Schrade in PMFC, 2–3 (see above). A new edition is in progress by Sylvette Leguy, ed., *Guillaume de Machaut 1300–1377: Oeuvres complètes* (Paris: Le Droict Chemin de Musique, 1977–). Vol. 1, Les virelais; 2, Les rondeaux; 3, Les ballades; 4, Les lais; 5, Les motets; 6, La messe de Notre Dame; 7, Le remède de fortune. An older edition is Friedrich Ludwig, ed., *Guillaume de Machaut: Musikalische Werke* (Leipzig: Breitkopf & Härtel, 1926; repr. 1968)

W. Thomas Marrocco, ed., *Fourteenth-Century Italian Cacce,* 2nd rev. ed. (Cambridge, Mass.: Medieval Academy of America, 1942, 1961); and idem, *The Music of Jacopo da Bologna* (Berkeley: University of California Press, 1954).

For Further Reading

French *Ars Nova*

Selections from fourteenth-century treatises in SRrev: Jean de Murs, *Notitia artis musicae,* pp. 261–68/2:151–59; and Jacques de Liège, *Speculum musicae,* pp. 269–80/2:159–68.

Philippe de Vitry A translation by Leon Plantinga of the *Ars nova* attributed to Philippe de Vitry is in JMT 5 (1961):204–23. Concerning the authorship of the treatise, see Sarah Fuller, "A Phantom Treatise of the Fourteenth Century? The *Ars nova,*" JM 4 (1985–86):23–50. See also Ernest Sanders, "The Early Motets of Philippe de Vitry," JAMS 28 (1975):24–45.

Guillaume de Machaut For a short but excellent survey, see Gilbert Reaney, *Guillaume de Machaut* (London: Oxford University Press, 1971). On the Mass, see Daniel Leech-Wilkinson, *Machaut's Mass: An Introduction* (Oxford: Clarendon Press, 1990). Articles dealing with various aspects of Machaut's work: Gilbert Reaney, "Fourteenth-Century Harmony and the Ballades, Rondeaux and Virelais of Guillaume de Machaut," MD 7 (1953):129–46; Vol. 5, no. 4 of EM (1977) is devoted almost entirely to this composer.

Italian *Trecento*

A good account of the musical scene is Michael Long, "Trecento Italy," in *Antiquity and the Middle Ages*, ed. James McKinnon (Englewood Cliffs, N.J.: Prentice Hall, 1991), pp. 241–68. Several important articles by Nino Pirrotta on the unwritten tradition are collected in his *Music and Culture in Italy from the Middle Ages to the Baroque: A Collection of Essays* (Cambridge, Mass.: Harvard University Press, 1984). Further references in Viola L. Hagopian, *Italian Ars Nova Music: A Bibliographic Guide to Modern Editions and Related Literature* (Berkeley: University of California Press, 1964; rev. and enl., 1973).

Landini Michael Long, "Francesco Landini and the Florentine Cultural Elite," EMH 3 (1983):83–99.

Prosdocimo Prosdocimo de' Beldomandi, *Contrapunctus (Counterpoint)*, trans. Jan Herlinger (Lincoln: University of Nebraska Press, 1984).

Marchetto of Padua Part of Marchetto's *Pomerium* is translated in SRrev, pp. 251–61; 2:141–51. His *Lucidarium* is ed. and trans. in Jan Herlinger, *The Lucidarium of Marchetto of Padua* (Chicago: University of Chicago Press, 1985). See also N. Pirrotta, "Marchettus di Padua and the Italian *Ars Nova*," MD 9 (1955):57–73.

General

Margaret Bent, "Musica Recta and Musica Ficta," MD 26 (1972):73–100, and GLHWM 2:163.

Sarah Fuller, "Discant and the Theory of Fifthing," AM 50 (1978):217–41.

On instruments in the music of this period, see essays by Edmund A. Bowles, Frank Ll. Harrison, and G. Reaney in *Aspects of Medieval and Renaissance Music: A Birthday Offering to Gustave Reese*, ed. Jan LaRue (New York: Norton, 1966).

CHAPTER 5

ENGLAND AND THE BURGUNDIAN LANDS IN THE FIFTEENTH CENTURY

Music in the fifteenth century continued to move toward an international style. Composers from England, France, and Italy contributed to its formation. Secular genres still dominated, as did their treble-dominated texture, which even affected settings of the Mass and the motet, itself now a quasi-secular and ceremonial genre.

ENGLISH MUSIC

General Features

From the earliest times, English sacred and secular art music, like that of northern Europe generally, kept close connections with folk style. Unlike their Continental peers, English composers cared little for abstract theories as a guide to practice. They leaned toward major tonality as opposed to the modal system, wrote homophony rather than independent lines with divergent texts, and preferred consonances to the dissonances of the French motet. English music also exhibited a fuller sound than the music of the Continent and a freer use of thirds and sixths. Parallel thirds had already occurred in the twelfth-century *Hymn to St. Magnus*, patron saint of the Orkney Islands, and written and improvised parallel thirds and sixths were common in English thirteenth-century practice.

Fourteenth Century

As we saw earlier, the basic chant repertory in England was that of the Sarum rite (of the Cathedral Church of Salisbury), whose melodies differed somewhat from those of the Roman rite that appeared in the *Liber usualis* and other modern chant books. Fifteenth-century English composers and many on the Continent used the Sarum rather than the Roman versions of plainchant as a starting point for polyphonic composition.

Worcester fragments

Our knowledge of fourteenth-century English music comes primarily from a group of manuscripts known collectively as the Worcester fragments. Their content, chiefly motets, conductus, tropes of various sections of the Mass Ordinary, and selections from the Proper, suggests that a school of composition was centered at Worcester Cathedral.

Rondellus

The *rondellus*, an English type of motet, characteristically uses voice exchange (sometimes referred to as *Stimmtausch*), as in the three-voice motet *Fulget coelestis curia—O Petre flos—Roma gaudet* (Example 5.1) from one of the Worcester fragments. The rondellus itself is framed by an introduction, prominently using sequences and canonic imitation in two of the voices, and a coda that draws from the music of the rondellus. The central part of the piece is in two halves, each of which has three simultaneous melodies taken up in turn by each of the voices or players, as in the following:

Triplum	a b c	d e f
Duplum	c a b	f d e
Tenor	b c a	e f d

Example 5.1 shows the original statement and one of the interchanges in the first half (the first two columns in the table, above). Normally in a rondellus all the voices exchange texts along with the music, but in this motet only the outer voices do so. Since the three voices are in the same range, the listener hears a threefold repetition of each half. The fresh, folklike quality of all the melodic lines and the harmonious blending of the voices characterize English music of this time.

■ Sumer is icumen in *(ca. 1250). A rota or infinite canon for four voices, sung against a two-part* pes, *in which the voices exchange a short phrase. The upper parts have a secondary Latin text.* (LONDON, BRITISH LIBRARY, MS HARLEIAN 978, FOL. 11. BY PERMISSION OF THE BRITISH LIBRARY)

Example 5.1 *Rondellus:* Fulget coelestis curia—O Petre flos—Roma gaudet

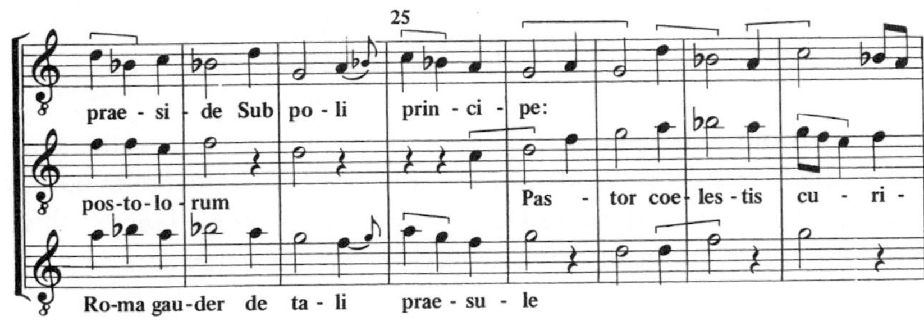

Heaven's court shines forth, with Peter sitting as guard under the Prince of Heaven.
Rome delights in such a bishop.
O Peter, flower of the apostles, shepherd of the heavenly court, nourish your sheep sweetly, leading them to higher things.
Rome delights in such a bishop, granted by divine gift.

Source: Luther Dittmer, ed., *The Worcester Fragments.*

Conductus

The conductus and some of the conductus-like tropes of the Ordinary reveal a new stylistic feature: successions of simultaneous thirds and sixths in parallel motion. Such writing reflected the English preference for full, harmonious sounds.

Fauxbourdon

Continental composers of the early to mid-fifteenth century became fascinated with successions of thirds and sixths, perhaps through hearing music imported from England (see Example 5.2, page 125, measures 18–19). From about 1420 to 1450, this manner of writing, called *fauxbourdon*, affected every genre of composition. As written, a fauxbourdon consisted of a chant accompanied by a lower voice in parallel sixths, each phrase ending with an octave. Against these written parts, a third voice improvised a fourth below the treble.

Example 5.2 *Burden from Carol*: Salve, Sancta parens

Hail, holy parent . . .

Source: John Stevens, ed. *Mediaeval Carols*, Musica Britannica, 4 (London, 1952), p. 71.

The fauxbourdon technique was used chiefly for settings of the simpler Office chants—hymns and antiphons—and of psalms and psalmlike texts, such as the Magnificat and the Te Deum. However, the importance of this device was not in the production of these pieces but in the emergence around the 1450s of a new way of writing for three parts. In it the upper voice has the principal melodic line, as it does in the fourteenth-century cantilena. But in the older cantilena style, the two lower voices stood apart, holding to a slower rhythm and serving as a more or less neutral background for the melody. Now, by contrast, the top voice and the tenor are coupled as if in a duet, and the two parts—and eventually the contratenor as well—are more nearly equal in importance, in melodic quality, and in rhythm. All three voices join in a euphonious progression of sonorities. This new sound strongly influenced all types of composition; it steered composers to write homophonic or homorhythmic textures, and helped win acceptance for the conspicuous third and sixth sonorities in the harmonic vocabulary.

The Old Hall Manuscript

The chief collection of early fifteenth-century English music is in the Old Hall manuscript (now in the British Library, formerly at the College of St. Edmund in Old Hall, near Ware). A great number of the repertory are settings of sections from the Mass Ordinary, and the remainder are motets, hymns, and sequences.

Use of plainchant

Most of the Mass settings show greater melodic activity in the top voice, and many incorporate plainchant melodies in one of the inner voices, notably the next-to-the lowest. Putting the plainsong melody in the next-to-lowest voice of a four-part texture not only allows the composer greater harmonic freedom; historically it foreshadows the way composers used plainsong tenors in the Masses of the late fifteenth and early sixteenth centuries. Other Mass sections in the Old Hall manuscript are in cantilena style, with the principal melody in the treble. In still others, a plainsong melody appears—now in one voice, now in another—as a "migrant" cantus firmus. A small proportion of the compositions in this collection, including both Masses and settings of other texts, are isorhythmic.

English music became known on the Continent not through the Old Hall mansucript but through the large number of works copied into Continental manuscripts during the first half of the fifteenth century. A French poem of about 1440–42 by Martin Le Franc describes the *contenance angloise* (English guise or quality), which made music so joyous and brilliantly consonant with "marvelous pleasingness" (see vignette, page 128). In the poem, Le Franc alludes specifically to the leading English composer of the time, John Dunstable.

Dunstable

John Dunstable (ca. 1390–1453) may have worked much of his life in France, large portions of which came under English rule after Henry V's victory at the famous battle of Agincourt in 1415. It was only in 1451 that the English were driven out of France. This may explain why Dunstable's compositions are preserved mainly in continental manuscripts and why his style had such an influence on European music.

Among Dunstable's seventy or so known compositions, we find examples of all the principal types and styles of polyphony that existed in his lifetime: isorhythmic motets, Ordinary Mass sections, secular songs, and three-part settings of miscellaneous liturgical texts. His twelve isorhythmic motets show that this older form was still in fashion. His most celebrated motet, a four-part setting that combines the hymn *Veni creator spiritus* and the sequence *Veni sancte spiritus,* is both a splendid example of isorhythmic structure and a thoroughly impressive piece of music, embodying the English preference for the full sonority of thirds together with fifths or sixths. A liturgical melody set forth isorhythmically in the tenor also underlies some of the Mass sections, which comprise about one-third of Dunstable's known works.

Dunstable's Three-Part Sacred Works

Dunstable's most numerous and historically important works are his three-part sacred pieces—settings of antiphons, hymns, and other liturgical or biblical texts; some have a cantus firmus in the tenor part or an ornamented chant melody in the treble (as in Example 5.3). Others, with a florid treble line and a

Example 5.3 *John Dunstable, Treble of Motet:* Regina Caeli laetare

MARTIN LE FRANC DESCRIBES THE MUSIC OF HIS TIME IN *LE CHAMPION DES DAMES*, 1440–42

Tapissier, Carmen, Cesaris	Tapissier, Carmen, Cesaris
Na pas longtemps si bien chanterrent	not long ago sang so well
Quilz esbahirent tout paris	that they astonished all Paris
Et tous ceulx qui les frequenterrent;	and all who came to hear them.
Mais oncques jour ne deschanterrent	But the day came when they did not discant
En melodie de tels chois	such finely wrought melody—
Ce mont dit qui les hanterrent	so those who heard them told me—
Que G. Du Fay et Binchois.	as G. Du Fay or Binchois.
Car ilz ont nouvelle pratique	For they have a new practice
De faire frisque concordance	of making lively consonance
En haulte et en basse musique	both in loud and soft music,
En fainte, en pause, et en muance	in feigning, in rests, and in mutations.
Et ont prins de la contenance	They took on the guise
Angloise et ensuy Dunstable	of the English and follow Dunstable
Pour quoy merveilleuse plaisance	and thereby a marvelous pleasingness
Rend leur chant joyeux et notable.	makes their music joyous and remarkable.

French text in C. Van den Borren, *Guillaume Du Fay: son importance dans l'évolution de la musique au xve siècle* (Brussels, 1926), pp. 53–54.

borrowed melody in the middle voice, have a tenor moving mostly in thirds and sixths below. Still others, like the antiphon *Quam pulchra es* (NAWM 25; CD 2 [12] / 1 ⟨24⟩), do not borrow thematic material.

The three voices of *Quam pulchra es*, each similar in character and nearly equal in importance, move mostly homorhythmically and usually pronounce the same syllables together. In musical texture it resembles a conductus, and the short melisma at the end of the word "alleluia" conforms with the ornamented conductus style. The composer, unfettered by a cantus firmus or an isorhythmic scheme, freely determined the form of the music, guided only by the text.

The Fifteenth-Century Motet

Quam pulchra es is classified as a motet. This term, previously used to denote both a thirteenth-century French genre and later isorhythmic pieces, had begun to take on a broader meaning in the fourteenth century. Originally, a motet was a composition on a liturgical text for use in church. By the later thirteenth century, the term was applied to works with secular texts as well, even those with a secular melody as a cantus firmus. The isorhythmic motet was a conservative form, retaining older characteristics such as tenors formed from chant melodies, multiple texts, and strongly contrapuntal texture. It participated only slightly in the general evolution of musical style during the late fourteenth and early fifteenth centuries; by 1450 it had become an anachronism and disappeared. A few later motets with plainsong tenors did not much resemble the older medieval types.

Meanwhile, the first half of the fifteenth century saw the term *motet* applied to settings of liturgical or even secular texts in the newer musical style of the time. This broader meaning of the word is still in use today: a motet is now almost any polyphonic composition on a Latin text other than the Ordinary of the Mass, including settings of antiphons, responsories, and other texts from the Proper and the Office. Since the sixteenth century, the term has been applied also to sacred compositions in languages other than Latin.

The Carol

The *carol*, originally a monophonic dance song with alternating solo and choral portions, had by the fifteenth century become stylized as a two- or three-part setting of a religious poem in popular style, sometimes in a quaint mixture of English and Latin rhyming verses. The carol consisted of a number of stanzas, all sung to the same music, and a *burden*, or refrain, with its own musical phrase, sung at the beginning and then repeated after each stanza. Carols were not folksongs, but their fresh, angular melodies and lively triple rhythms give them a distinctly popular character and an unmistakably English quality. The carol *Salve, sancta parens* (NAWM 26; CD 2 [13]), written in the style of improvised English discant (Example 5.2), is a typical burden. The outer voices move mostly in parallel sixths, while the middle part fills in a third above the bottom, making a fourth against the top voice. Measures 16 to 19 illustrate the cadence reached by moving out from one of the parallel sixths and thirds to the octave and fifth.

Burden

MUSIC IN THE BURGUNDIAN LANDS

The dukes of Burgundy, although feudal vassals of the kings of France, virtually equaled them in power. During the second half of the fourteenth century and the early years of the fifteenth, they acquired vast territories, partly through a series of political marriages and partly through diplomacy that took full advantage of their kings' distress in the Hundred Years' War. Thus to their original fiefs, the medieval duchy and county of Burgundy in east-central France, they added most of what are today Holland, Belgium, northeastern France, Luxembourg, and Lorraine. The dukes of Burgundy ruled over the whole as virtually independent sovereigns until 1477. Though their nominal capital was Dijon, the dukes had no fixed city of residence but sojourned from time to time at various places in their dominions. The main orbit of the peripatetic Burgundian court after the middle of the century was around Lille, Bruges, Ghent, and especially Brussels, an area comprising modern Belgium and the northeastern corner of France. Most of the leading northern composers of the late fifteenth century came from this general region, and many of them were connected in one way or another with the Burgundian court.

Duchy of Burgundy

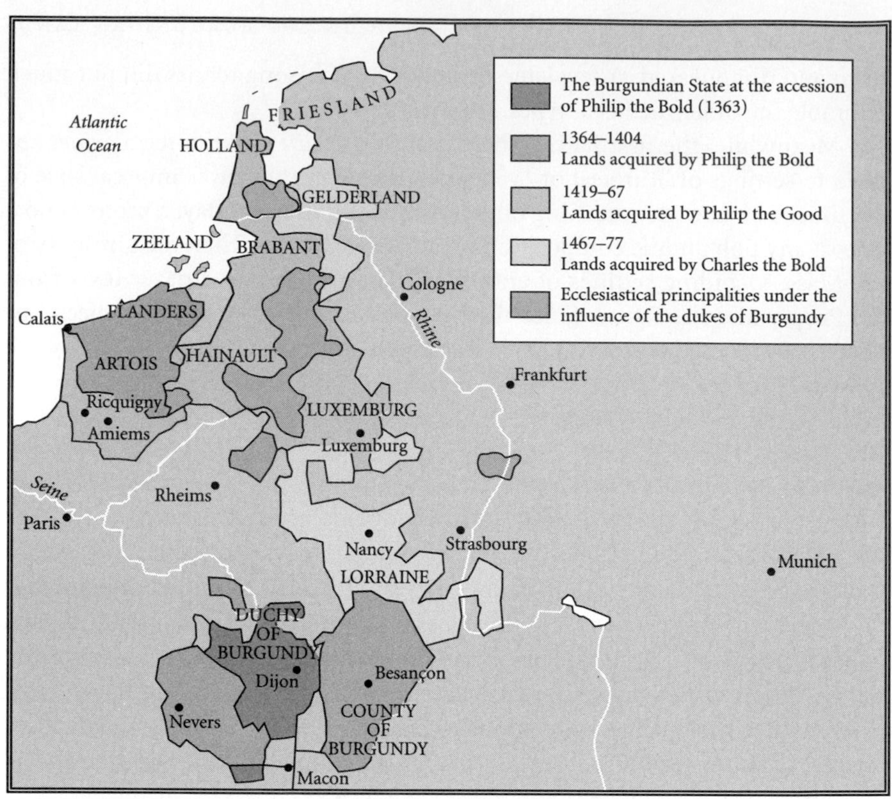

■ *Growth of Burgundian possessions, 1363–1477*

Court chapels

Chapels with elaborate musical resources—institutions that were not necessarily associated with a particular building—were springing up all over Europe in the late fourteenth and early fifteenth centuries. Popes, emperors, kings, and princes competed for the services of eminent composers and singers. The Burgundian dukes maintained a chapel with a corps of salaried composers, singers, and instrumentalists who furnished music for church services. These musicians probably contributed to the secular entertainment of the court as well and accompanied their ruler on journeys. The court and chapel of Philip the Good, duke of Burgundy from 1419 to 1467, were the most resplendent in Europe. At the death of his predecessor Philip the Bold, in 1404, the Burgundian chapel had twenty-eight musicians. Its ranks thinned for a while, then grew again to seventeen by 1445. In the early part of the century, musicians were recruited chiefly from northern France. But because Philip the Good and his successor, Charles the Bold (1467–77), resided in the north rather than in Dijon, most of their musicians came from Flanders and the Low Countries.

Training musicians

Church musicians received their training principally as choir boys. In some cathedrals and chapels, choir schools systematically taught not only singing but also music theory, grammar, mathematics, and other primary and advanced subjects. Antwerp, Bruges, Cambrai, Paris, Lyons, and later Rome, Venice, and other Italian cities were the centers most renowned for their musical training. Most of the composers whose names are remembered were hired as singers, though their reputations rested on their compositions. Because only male children were admitted into choirs, women did not have this educational opportunity or the chance to make careers in the public churches and princely courts. Nuns and novices did receive musical instruction, and a few distinguished themselves as composers.

In addition to his chapel, Philip the Good maintained a band of minstrels—trumpeters, drummers, viellists, lutenists, harpists, organists, and players of bagpipes and shawms—which included musicians from France, Italy, Germany, and Portugal. Charles the Bold was particularly keen on music, being an amateur instrumentalist and composer, and issued detailed regulations for his chapel (see vignette, page 133).

Pan-European Style

The cosmopolitan atmosphere of such a fifteenth-century court was constantly renewed by visits from foreign musicians; in addition, members of the chapel themselves were continually changing, moving from one court to another in response to better opportunities. These circumstances could not help but produce a common musical style. The prestige of the Burgundian court was such that the music cultivated there influenced other European musical centers: the chapels of the pope at Rome, of the emperor in Germany, of the French and English kings, and of the various Italian courts, as well as cathedral choirs—the more so because many of their musicians either had once been or

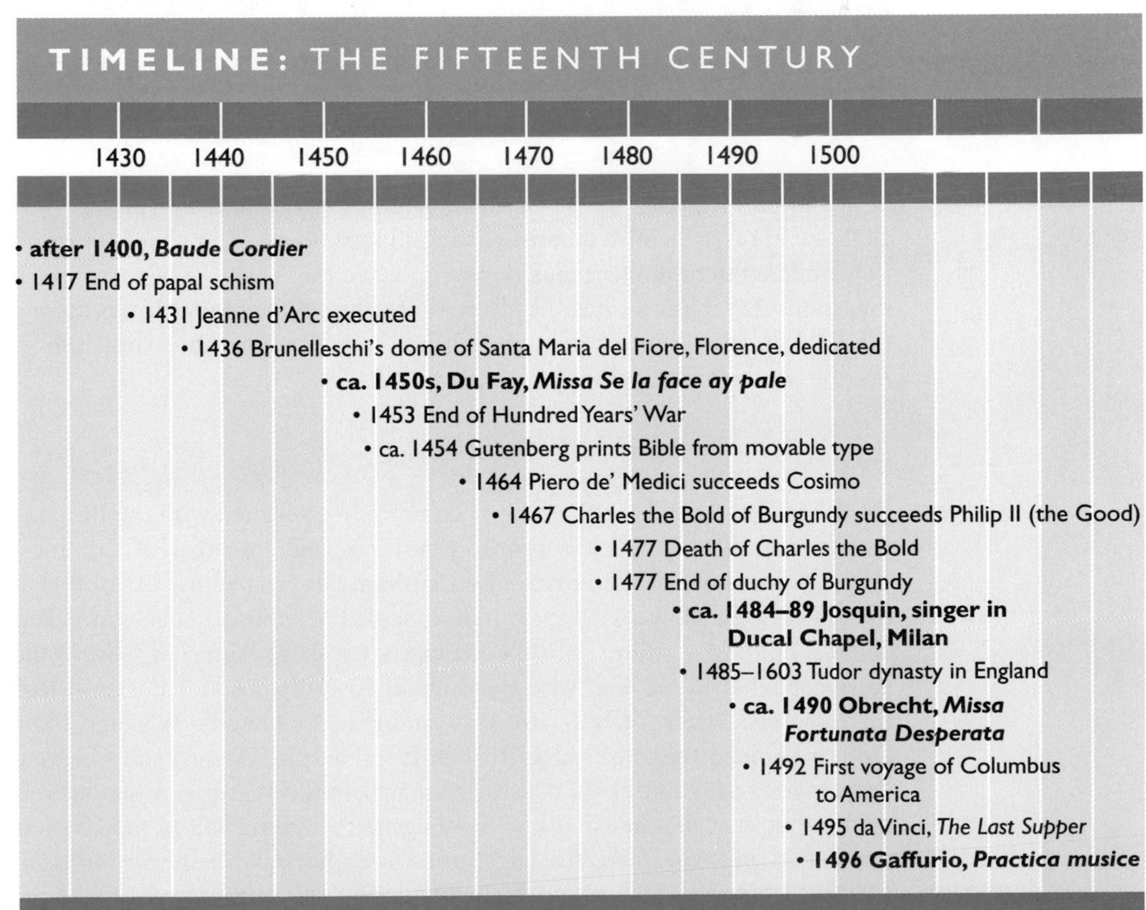

An outdoor entertainment at the court of Duke Philip the Good (1396–1467) of Burgundy. Musicians play for the duke (center) and his company, while in the background hunters are chasing game. Detail from a sixteenth-century copy of an anonymous fifteenth-century painting. (MUSÉE NATIONAL DU CHÂTEAU DE VERSAILLES)

hoped to be in the service of the duke of Burgundy. Johannes Tinctoris (ca. 1435–ca. 1511), a Flemish theorist writing about 1475, tells how the honor and riches offered to prominent musicians stimulated the growth of talent so much that in his day music seemed like "a new art, the source of which was among the English, with Dunstable at their head, and, contemporary with him in France, Du Fay and Binchois."

Du Fay

Career

Guillaume Du Fay (ca. 1397–1474) is commonly associated with the Burgundian court, although he was probably not a regular member of the ducal chapel. Born about 1397 in or around Cambrai, Du Fay became a choirboy at the cathedral in 1409. As a young man he served at various Italian courts and chapels, holding positions with the Malatesta family of Pesaro in Italy, at the papal chapel at Rome, and with the duke of Savoy (whose territories at that time included parts of Italy, Switzerland, and France). Between 1435 and 1437, Du Fay rejoined the pope's chapel when it resided in Florence and Bologna. From at least 1439 until 1450, Du Fay's home base was Cambrai, where he was made a canon at the cathedral by Pope Eugene IV. From 1452 to 1458 he was mostly back in Savoy; thereafter he returned to Cambrai, where he died in 1474.

Manuscript sources

The works of Du Fay and his contemporaries are preserved in a large number of manuscripts, mostly of Italian origin. The two most important are a

THE ORGANIZATION OF THE CHAPEL OF CHARLES THE BOLD IN 1469

Ordinances of the House of My Lord Duke of Burgundy

. . . that henceforth his domestic chapel in his house be maintained and governed by 25 persons named below, that is, 13 chaplains, 6 clerks,[1] 5 *sommeliers*,[2] and 1 *fourrier*,[3] who shall be salaried and shall perform daily the divine service. . . .

My Lord shall have: five battle trumpets . . . six minstrel trumpets . . . three players of soft instruments. . . .

My Lord intends that among the twelve chaplains some may not be priests yet shall have all the wages of a chaplain . . . and according to the merit of their voices and good services, clerks and *sommeliers* may rise from one rank to another, that is, from *sommelier* to clerk and from clerk to chaplain . . .

My Lord wishes and orders that all the said twelve chaplains, clerks, *sommeliers*, and *fourrier*, be obedient to the first chaplain . . .

Item: each day of the year at a suitable hour an ordinary high mass shall be celebrated by the said chapel by these chaplains, clerks, and other servants in chant and discant . . .

Item: for singing [polyphony] from the book there will be at least 6 trebles, 3 tenors, 3 bass contras and 2 middle contras without counting the 4 chaplains of the high masses or the *sommeliers*, who, if they are not occupied at the altar or otherwise will be expected within reason to serve with the others.

. . . [members of the chapel] should avoid all company of dissolute persons, or those suspected of vice, all card and dice games, and others prohibited by holy decrees . . . going around at night making noise and tumult, or singing and shouting in the streets night or day. . . .

Item: they shall expressly avoid all concubinage and not keep with or near them nor bring or have brought to them suspicious women . . .

Trans. from David Fallows, "Specific Information on the Ensembles for Composed Polyphony, 1400–1474," in *Studies in the Performance of Late Mediaeval Music*, ed. Stanley Boorman (Cambridge: Cambridge University Press, 1983), pp. 146–51. The document is in Oxford, Bodleian Library, MS Hatton 13.

1. A clerk (*clerc*) was a singer of rank immediately below that of chaplain (*chapelain*).
2. *Sommeliers*, besides singing, read the Epistle at certain High Masses and assisted at the altar and at Offices of the hours, prepared the altar, guarded the jewels and wine, and performed other duties.
3. A *fourrier* arranged lodgings, guarded the door, provided seating, candles, etc.

manuscript now in the Bodleian Library at Oxford (Canonici misc. 213), copied in northern Italy about 1460 and containing 325 works dating from about 1400 to 1440; and the Trent Codices, seven volumes now in the library of the National Museum in the Castello del Buonconsiglio in Trent, containing more than 1,600 compositions written between 1400 and 1475. Transcriptions

■ *Guillaume Du Fay, next to a portative organ, and Gilles Binchois, holding a harp, in a miniature from Martin Le Franc's poem* Le Champion des dames *(1440–42; see vignette, p. 128).* (PARIS, BIBLIOTHÈQUE NATIONALE, MS FR. 12476)

from these and other manuscripts of the period are available in modern editions.

Genres and style

The Burgundian period produced four principal types of composition: Masses, Magnificats, motets, and secular chansons with French texts. Voice combinations were the same as in the French ballade and the Italian ballata: tenor and contratenor both moving within the narrow range *c* to g', and a treble or discantus spanning about a tenth—*a* to c'' or c' to e''. As in fourteenth-century music, each line has a distinct timbre, with the principal melody in the discantus. The homophonic texture of fauxbourdon still allows for a certain amount of melodic freedom and contrapuntal independence, including occasional imitation. The typical discantus line flows in warmly expressive lyrical phrases, breaking into graceful melismas when it approaches important cadences.

Cadences

The preferred cadence formula was still a major sixth expanding to an octave (Example 3.14, page 89), often with the "Landini" embellishment figure (Example 4.3, page 109). In a newer version of this cadence, found in three-part writing, the lowest voice under the sixth-to-octave progression skips up an octave, so that the ear hears the effect of a bass rising a fourth (as in the modern dominant-tonic cadence; see Example 5.4a–d).

The great majority of Burgundian compositions were in some form of triple meter, with frequent cross-rhythms resulting from the combination of the patterns ♩ ♩ ♩ and ♩♩♩ ♩♩♩ which we recognize as *hemiola*; see Example 5.4b and d. Duple meter was used mainly in subdivisions of longer works, to provide contrast.

Example 5.4a–d *Cadential Formulas*

a. Du Fay, *Motet* b. Binchois, *Rondeau*

c. Du Fay, *Mass* d. Du Fay, *Mass*

The Burgundian Chanson

In the fifteenth century, the term *chanson* stood for any polyphonic setting of a French secular poem. Burgundian chansons were, in effect, accompanied solo songs, though some scholars believe that all parts were sung. They were nearly always love poems and most often took the form of the rondeau with its traditional two-line refrain, although there was also the *rondeau quatrain*, which had stanzas and refrains of four lines each, and the *cinquain*, with five lines. Meanwhile ballades in the traditional *aabC* form went out of fashion and were relegated to ceremonial occasions. In keeping with the ballade's refined tradition, the vocal part is much more florid than in the rondeau. In Du Fay's ballade *Resvellies vous et faites chiere lye* (NAWM 27; CD 2 [14]), for example, each line ends with a melisma that occupies eight or ten bars of the transcription. An unusual feature of this chanson is the acclamation in long-held block chords, "Charle gentil" (noble Charles), addressed to Carlo Malatesta, for whose wedding to Vittoria Colonna (niece of Pope Martin V) it was written in 1423.

Binchois

Gilles Binchois (ca. 1400–1460), who stood at the center of musical life in the Burgundian court, was a master of the chanson, especially of the rondeau. Born probably near Mons in the province of Hainaut, he served in the chapel of Duke Philip the Good from the 1420s until his retirement in Soignies in 1453. Binchois's chansons excel in expressing tender melancholy, touched with sensuous longing. He continued the treble-dominated style of the fourteenth century, but his fluid, gently arching melodies avoided rhythmic complications. Other composers frequently used his songs as subjects for Masses. Ockeghem's *Missa De plus en plus* (NAWM 31; CD 2 [28]) is based on and named for Binchois's best-known rondeau (NAWM 30; CD 2 [26] / 1 [32]), and John

■ *The Cathedral of Santa Maria del Fiore, in Florence. Du Fay wrote the isorhythmic motet* Nuper rosarum flores *for the consecration of the dome in 1436.*

Bedingham's *Missa Dueil angouisseus* is based on a Binchois ballade with a text by Christine de Pisan. Binchois left numerous Mass movements, Magnificats, and motets, but no cyclical Mass.

Burgundian Motets

The Burgundian musical style cast such a spell that it lingered in Europe long after the duchy of Burgundy had ceased to exist as an independent political power (1477). At first no distinctive sacred style emerged; both motets and Masses were written in the manner of the chanson. A freely melodic treble held sway, supported by a tenor and contratenor in the usual three-voice texture. The treble might be newly composed, but in many cases it was an embellished version of a chant. For example, Du Fay's *Alma Redemptoris Mater* (Gracious mother of the Redeemer) has such an embellished chant melody in the treble. In Burgundian motets, the Gregorian melody begged to be recognized as an expressive musical line, no longer appearing in a distorted and unrecognizable form as a symbolic link to tradition, merely to anchor the structure.

Du Fay's hymns

Du Fay's hymn settings, such as *Conditor alme siderum* (Bountiful creator of the stars, NAWM 28; CD 2 [17]), also have the chant in the treble. As in the fauxbourdon tradition, the two outer voices were written down, and the middle voice improvised to fill out the harmony. Only the even-numbered stanzas were sung polyphonically; the others were performed as plainchant.

Isorhythmic motets

In addition to motets in the modern chanson style and fauxbourdons, Du Fay and his contemporaries still wrote occasional isorhythmic motets for solemn public ceremonies, following the convention that an archaic musical style, like an archaic literary style, was more fitting for ceremonial and state occasions. Du Fay's *Nuper rosarum flores* (Recently roses) was such a work; it was performed in 1436 at the dedication of Filippo Brunelleschi's magnificent dome for the Church of Santa Maria del Fiore (the *Duomo*) in Florence. Pope Eugene IV officiated in person. A writer who attended the ceremony (see vignette) described the bright-robed company of trumpeters, viellists, and other instrumentalists, and the singing choirs that struck the listeners with awe, so that the sound of music, the aroma of incense, and the sight of the beautiful decorations filled the spectators with ecstasy.

Masses

It was for the Mass that Burgundian composers developed a specifically sacred musical style. As we have noted, the number of polyphonic settings of the Mass increased in the late fourteenth and early fifteenth centuries. Until about 1420, the various sections of the Ordinary were nearly always composed as separate pieces (Machaut's Mass and a few others excepted), though occasionally a compiler would group such separate items together. In the course of the fifteenth century, it became standard practice for composers to set the Ordinary as a musically unified whole. At first only a pair of sections (for example, the Gloria and Credo) were wedded together in a perceptible musical relationship; gradually the practice widened to cover all five divisions of the Ordinary. In order to give Mass settings a single thread, composers developed cyclical forms, that is, they based the movements on a single melodic subject. To write a cohesive Mass became the supreme challenge to a musician's creative ingenuity.

Some musical unity resulted simply from composing all five parts of the Ordinary in the same general style, such as in a ballade or a chanson style. This impression of unity was strengthened even more when each movement used a separate chant (which usually appeared in ornamented form in the treble) as a starting point for the composition. When a chant or secular melody was adapted for this purpose, we call the melody a *cantus firmus* (one of the Latin terms for "plainchant," along with *cantus planus*). When the composer used a different chant as the basis for each movement, unity resided in the liturgical association rather than in the musical resemblance, since the plainsong melodies were not necessarily related to one another. A Mass using Gregorian themes in this way is called a *missa choralis* or *plainsong Mass.*

Cantus firmus

Plainsong Mass

GIANOZZO MANETTI, AN EYEWITNESS OF THE SERVICE DEDICATING THE DUOMO, WRITES ABOUT THE MUSIC

The senses of all began to be uplifted. . . . But at the elevation of the Most Sacred Host, the whole space of the temple was filled with such choruses of harmony and such a concert of divers instruments that it seemed (not without reason) as though the symphonies and songs of the angels and of divine paradise had been sent forth from Heaven to whisper in our ears an unbelievable celestial sweetness. Therefore, in that moment, I was so possessed by ecstasy that I seemed to enjoy the life of the blessed here on earth; whether it happened so to others present I know not, but concerning myself I can bear witness.

Quoted in Dufay, *Opera omnia*, ed. Guillaume de Van, CMM 1 (Rome, 1947–49), 2:xxvii.

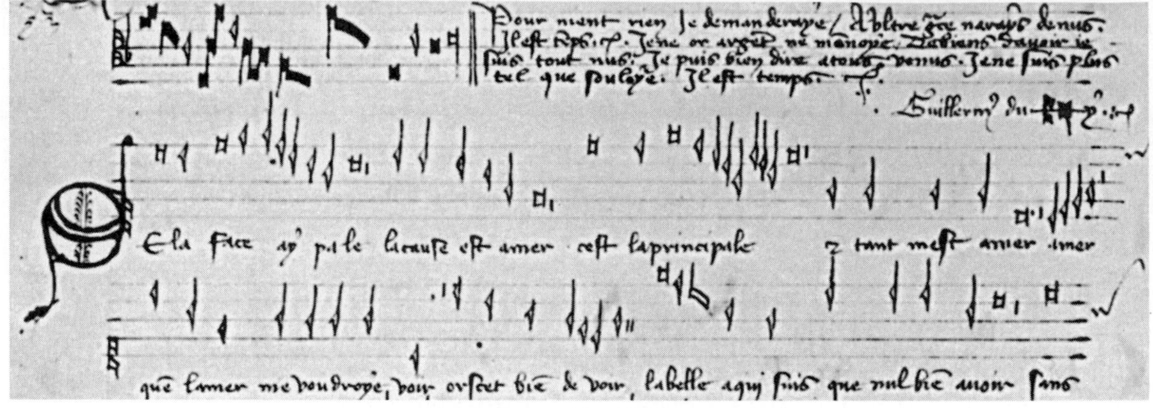

■ *The cantus part of the three-part ballade* Se la face ay pale, *by Du Fay (for a transcription see NAWM 29a). The second stanza is given after the cantus part.* (OXFORD, BODLEIAN LIBRARY, MS CANONICI MISC. 213, FOL. 53V)

Motto Mass

Cantus firmus Mass

Composers could achieve a more noticeable and effective musical interconnection by using the same thematic material in all sections of the Mass. At first, the connection consisted only in beginning each movement with the same melodic motive, usually in the treble; a Mass that uses such a "head motive" is sometimes called a *motto Mass.* But this technique was soon superseded by (or combined with) another, that of constructing every movement around the same cantus firmus, which was placed in the tenor. The resulting cyclical form is known as a *cantus-firmus Mass* or *tenor Mass.* English composers wrote the earliest such Masses, but the practice was quickly adopted on the Continent, and by the second half of the fifteenth century it became customary.

Placing the borrowed melody in the tenor followed the medieval motet tradition but created compositional problems. The sound-ideal of the fifteenth century needed the lowest voice to function as a harmonic foundation, particularly at cadences. Letting the lowest voice carry a chant melody that could not be altered would have limited the composer's ability to provide such a foundation. The solution was to add a part below the tenor, called at first *contratenor bassus* (low contratenor) and later simply *bassus.* Above the tenor sounded a second contratenor called *contratenor altus* (high contratenor), later *altus.* The highest part was the treble. called variously the *cantus* (melody), *discantus* (discant), or *superius* (highest part). These four voice parts became standard by the middle of the fifteenth century and remain so today.

The Mass inherited from the medieval motet the practice of writing the tenor cantus firmus in long notes and in an isorhythmic pattern. When this melody was a plainchant, a rhythmic pattern was imposed on it and repeated if the melody was repeated. When the borrowed melody was a secular tune, the song's original rhythm was retained, but in successive appearances the pattern could be made faster or slower in relation to the other voices. This procedure obscured the identity of the borrowed tune even more than in the isorhythmic motet, because now it lay in an inner voice. This did not diminish its power to unify the five divisions of the Mass. Plainsong cantus firmi came from the

Example 5.5 L'homme armé

The armed man is to be feared; everywhere it has been proclaimed that everyone should arm himself with an iron coat of mail.

Proper or the Office, secular ones most often from the tenors of chansons. In neither case did they have any liturgical connection with the Ordinary, but the Mass usually owed its name to the borrowed melody, as in *Missa L'homme armé*. Nearly every composer for more than a century—from Du Fay and Ockeghem to Palestrina—wrote at least one Mass on the chanson *L'homme armé* (The armed man; see Example 5.5).

Missa Se la face ay pale

One of the most beautifully integrated Masses is Du Fay's *Missa Se la face ay pale* (If my face is pale; based on the tenor of his own ballade, NAWM 29a; CD 2 [19] / 1 ◊25◊; see the Gloria of the Mass in NAWM 29b; CD 2 [20] / 2 ◊26◊). In the Kyrie, Sanctus, and Agnus Dei, the value of each note of the ballade is doubled. In the Gloria and Credo, the cantus firmus is heard three times, first in triple the normal note values, then in doubled note values, and finally at normal note values, so that the melody becomes easily recognizable only at the third hearing. Du Fay thus applied the method of the isorhythmic motet on a larger scale. In Example 5.6a, we see the first phrase of the song in very long notes in the tenor at "Adoramus te," its first appearance in the Gloria. The next time this opening phrase occurs, at "Qui tollis peccata mundi" (6b), the original note values are doubled. The third time, at "Cum sancto spiritu" (6c), the song is heard at its normal tempo. The speeding up of the tenor's cantus firmus and the imitation of some of its motives in the other parts contribute to the excitement of the closing Amen.

Layered texture

More immediately obvious to the listener than the unity achieved by the threefold statement of the chanson melody in the tenor is the diverse character of the voices. Each is an independent layer having its own melodic and rhythmic logic and function. The top two voices—the superius and the contratenor altus—maintain soft melodious contours and occasionally exchange motives, while the contratenor bassus, more angular though still vocal, provides a harmonic foundation. The most obvious level of temporal organization in this piece is the perfect tempus, represented in the transcription by the $\frac{3}{2}$ measures. Each of the three beats within this tempus is divided into two (minor prolation). A broader triple organization is evident in the tenor's perfect modus

Modus, tempus, prolation

Example 5.6 *Guillaume Du Fay*, Missa Se la face ay pale: Gloria

consisting of three tempora, or three of the modern measures (as in Example 5.6a). A complication appears in the use of hemiola between the superius and the altus (measures 19–20), and in the altus, where the meter shifts to a compound duple $\frac{6}{4}$ from the normal $\frac{3}{2}$ (measures 26 and 34).

Consonance and dissonance

Consonance and dissonance are also carefully controlled. The stronger lingering dissonances are properly resolved suspensions, as at measure 33, while other dissonances, mainly between beats, pass quickly. Otherwise Du Fay favored thirds and sixths sounding with octaves, fifths, and fourths, producing many combinations of triads (as they were later called) on the beats of the tempus.

Du Fay's four-part cantus-firmus Masses are late works, dating for the most part after the middle of the century. Their constructive methods distinguish them from the earlier chansons and chansonlike motets and Masses. Some of their new features reflect a "learned" musical style that rose to dominance after the middle of the century. In any case, composers writing after about 1430 emphasized aspects that were to differentiate the musical style of the Renaissance from that of the late Middle Ages: control of dissonance, predominantly consonant sonorities including sixth–third successions, equal importance of the voices, melodic and rhythmic identity of lines, four-part texture, and occasional use of imitation.

Bibliography

Music Collections: Facsimiles and Editions

English

The Worcester fragments: PMMM 5; Luther A. Dittmer, ed., *The Worcester Fragments: A Catalogue Raisonné and Transcription,* MSD 2.

The Old Hall Manuscript, ed. Andrew Hughes and Margaret Bent, CMM 46, 4 vols.

The Eton Choirbook, transcribed by Frank Ll. Harrison, is in MB 10–12; description and catalogue in *Annales musicologiques* 1 (1953):151–75.

English medieval carols are in MB 4.

H. E. Wooldridge, ed., *Early English Harmony from the 10th to the 15th Century*, 2 vols. Vol. 1, Facsimiles; 2, Transcriptions and notes (London: B. Quaritch, 1897–1913).

See also CMM 9, 19, 21, 50; *Early English Church Music*, ed. F. Ll. Harrison (London: Stainer & Bell, 1963–), vol. 8.

Continental, Masses

Trent Codices: facsimile, *Codex Tridentinus 87–93* (Rome: Bibliopola, 1969–70); partial transcription in the following volumes of DTOe: 14/15 (Year 7); 22 (Year 11, Pt. 1); 38 (Year 19, Pt. 1); 53 (Year 27, Pt. 1); 61 (Year 31); and 76 (Year 40). Canons from the Trent Codices, ed. Richard Loyan, in CMM 38.

A new edition of the Chansonnier El Escorial, which contains pieces attributed to Dunstable, Du Fay, Binchois, et al., is Martha K. Hanen, *The Chansonnier El Escorial*, 3 vols. Vol. 1, Commentary; Vols. 2–3, Transcriptions (Henryville, Penn.: Institute of Medieval Music, 1983).

Laurence Feininger, ed., *Monumenta polyphoniae liturgicae* (Rome, 1947–) Series I, Ordinary of the Mass; Vol. I of this series contains ten early Masses on *L'homme armé*; Series II, Proper of the Mass: scholarly editions preserving all features of the original manuscripts.

Oxford, Bodleian library, MS. Canon. Misc. 213, with intro. and inventory by David Fallows (Chicago: University of Chicago Press, 1995).

Individual Composers

Modern editions of music by the composers mentioned in this chapter include:

Dunstable, *Complete Works*, ed. Manfred F. Bukofzer, MB 8.

Du Fay, *Opera omnia*, ed. Heinrich Besseler, CMM 1. Vol. 6 (Chansons), rev. David Fallows, 1994. Hymns for three and four voices, ed. Rudolf Gerber in *Das Chorwerk* 49 (1937).

Binchois, *Die Chansons von Gilles Binchois (1400–1460)*, ed. Wolfgang Rehm (Mainz: B. Schott, 1957)

For Further Reading

General

Excellent surveys of the music of this period are Reinhard Strohm, *The Rise of European Music, 1380–1500* (Cambridge: Cambridge University Press, 1993); Howard M. Brown and Louise Stein, *Music in the Renaissance* (rev. ed.; Upper Saddle River, NJ: Prentice Hall, 1999); Allan Atlas, *Renaissance Music* (New York: Norton, 1998); and Iain Fenlon, ed., *Music in Medieval and Early Modern Europe: Patronage, Sources, and Texts* (Cambridge: Cambridge University Press, 1981). A more detailed study is Leeman Perkins, *Music in the Age of the Renaissance* (New York: Norton, 1998).

For historical and social background for music making, see Iain Fenlon, ed., *The Renaissance* (Englewood Cliffs, NJ: Prentice-Hall, 1989).

English Music

For a concise survey of Dunstable's music, see Margaret Bent, *Dunstaple* (London: Oxford University Press, 1980); and for a description of English musical traits, see Sylvia W. Kenney, *Walter Frye and the Contenance angloise* (New Haven: Yale University Press, 1964).

Burgundy

Craig Wright, *Music at the Court of Burgundy, 1364–1419* (Henryville, Penn.: Institute of Mediaeval Music, 1979).

Guillaume Du Fay

An up-to-date work on Du Fay is David Fallows, *Du Fay* (New York: Vintage Books, 1987). Important findings are reported in Charles Hamm, *A Chronology of the Works of Guillaume Du Fay* (Princeton: Princeton University Press, 1964). Craig Wright, "Du Fay at Cambrai: Discoveries and Revisions," JAMS 28 (1975):175–229, repr. GLHWM 4, gives a glimpse of the activities of the composer in the last thirty-five years of his life in an important religious center and its social context; includes many documents in Latin and in translation.

Motet

Dolores Pesce, ed., *Hearing the Motet of the Middle Ages and Renaissance* (New York: Oxford University Press, 1997).

Musica Ficta

Karol Berger, *Musica Ficta: Theories of Accidental Inflections in Vocal Polyphony from Marchetto da Padova to Gioseffo Zarlino* (Cambridge: Cambridge University Press, 1987).

Music in Convents

Anne Bagnall Yardley, " 'Ful weel she soong the service dyvyne': *The Cloistered Musician in the Middle Ages,*" in *Women Making Music: The Western Art Tradition, 1150–1940,* ed. Jane Bowers and Judith Tick (Urbana: University of Illinois Press, 1986): 15–38.

Secular Music

Howard M. Brown, *Music in the French Secular Theatre, 1400–1550,* and the companion volume, *Theatrical Chansons of the Fifteenth and Early Sixteenth Centuries* (Cambridge, Mass.: Harvard University Press, 1963).

Sacred Music (Mass, Motet, Hymn)

Philip Gossett, "Techniques of Unification in Early Cyclic Masses and Mass Pairs," JAMS 19 (1966):205–31; Edgar H. Sparks, *Cantus Firmus in Mass and Motet, 1420–1520* (Berkeley: University of California Press, 1963).

CHAPTER 6

THE AGE OF THE RENAISSANCE: MUSIC OF THE LOW COUNTRIES

GENERAL CHARACTERISTICS

Revival of ancient ideals

The great renewal of European interest in ancient Greek and Roman culture during the fifteenth and sixteenth centuries deeply affected how people thought about music. To be sure, they could not experience ancient music itself as they could architectural monuments, sculptures, and poems. But they could read the writings of classical philosophers, poets, essayists, and music theorists that were being newly translated. They learned about the power of music to move the listener and wondered why modern music did not have the same effect. One influential religious leader, Bernardino Cirillo, expressed disappointment with the learned music of his time and yearned for the greatness of the past (see vignette). He urged musicians to follow the example of the sculptors, painters, and architects who had rediscovered ancient art, and the scholars who had restored Greek and Roman literature, and reclaim the power of the classical styles and modes.

Humanism

This interest in the culture of antiquity was quite common among laypersons. Yet at the same time, musicians like Gioseffo Zarlino (1517–1590) were pointing with pride toward the achievements of modern contrapuntal techniques. Both the critics and the defenders of modern music were reacting to *humanism,* a movement that revived ancient learning, particularly grammar, rhetoric, poetry, history, and moral philosophy. People were asked to judge their lives, artworks, customs, and social and political structures by the standards of antiquity. Although Cirillo and Zarlino disagreed on other fronts, they both

A CRITICAL VIEW OF POLYPHONIC MUSIC IS EXPRESSED BY BERNARDINO CIRILLO IN A LETTER OF 1549

You know how much music was valued among those good ancients as the finest of the fine arts. With it they worked great effects that today we do not, either with rhetoric or oratory, in controlling the passions and affections of the soul. With the power of song it was easy for them to move any sage mind from the use of reason and drive it to fury and rage. . . . With the efficacy of song the lazy and lax would become agressive and quick, the angry peaceful, the dissolute modest, the afflicted consoled, the joyful sad. . . . I see and hear the music of today, which is said to have arrived at an ultimate refinement and perfection such as never was or could be known before. Yet I do not hear or see any part of those ancient modes. . . . Kyrie eleison means "Lord, have mercy upon us." An ancient musician would have expressed this affection of asking God's pardon in the Mixolydian mode, which would have crushed as well as made contrite a heart and soul and moved every stony disposition if not to tears at least to a pious affection. Thus he would have adapted similar modes in keeping with the texts and made the Kyrie different from the Agnus Dei, and the Gloria from the Credo, or the Sanctus from the Pleni, and these from the psalms and motets. Today all such things are sung in a promiscuous and uncertain genus. . . . In short, when a Mass is sung in church, I should like the music to consist of certain harmonies and rhythms apt at moving our sentiments to religion and piety according to the meaning of the words. . . . Today every effort and diligence is bent on making a work in strict fugue so that when one says "Sanctus," another pronounces "Sabaoth," while a third sings "Gloria tua," with certain wails, bellows, and bleating that at times they sound like cats in January. . . .

Letter of February 16, 1549, to Ugolino Gualteruzzi, from *Lettere volgari di diversi nobilissimi huomini*, ed. Aldo Manuzio, Vol. 3 (Venice, 1564), fols. 114^r–115^r. Cirillo was the head or archpriest of the famous shrine and destination for pilgrimages, the Santa Casa of Loreto.

lamented the decline of music after the classical age and wanted to see the ancient heights scaled again. The polyphonic Masses Cirillo heard in church were inadequate because they did not move him and did not come up to classical standards. Zarlino, however, believed that the music of one composer, Adrian Willaert (ca. 1490–1562), reached a height parallel to that of antiquity (see vignette). He credited Willaert, who became a leader of a movement in the 1540s toward emotional expression in music, with ushering in a new golden age. Zarlino devoted an entire chapter of his book *Le istitutioni harmoniche* (The Harmonic Foundations) of 1558 on how to express and set the words of a text to music effectively and faithfully.[1]

1. Gioseffo Zarlino, *On the Modes*, Part 4 of *Le istitutioni harmoniche*, 1558, trans. Vered Cohen, ed. with an intro. By Claude V. Palisca (New Haven: Yale University Press, 1983), chs. 32–33, pp. 94–99.

Humanism was the most characteristic intellectual movement of the Renaissance. It touched music later than poetry and literary textual criticism, but the delay was not so great as writers have claimed. In Vittorino da Feltre's school for noble and talented youth founded in 1424 in the court of Mantua, students read the music treatise of Boethius as a classical text rather than as a basis for professional training. This change in approach marked a rebirth of interest in music theory's Greek past. Over the next half century, Greeks emigrating from Byzantium and Italian manuscript hunters brought the principal Greek music treatises to the West. Among these were the musical treatises of Bacchius Senior, Aristides Quintilianus, Claudius Ptolemy, Cleonides, Euclid, and one attributed to Plutarch. Also newly available was the section on music in the pseudo-Aristotle *Problems*, the *Deipnosophists* of Athenaeus (which contained a long section on music), the eighth book of Aristotle's *Politics*, and passages concerning music in Plato's dialogues, particularly the *Republic* and the *Laws*.[2] By the end of the fifteenth century, all of these were translated into Latin, although some of the translations were commissioned for the private use of scholars and were not in general circulation.

Rediscovery of the Greek treatises

Gaffurio

Franchino Gaffurio (1451–1522), a musician-scholar who owned some of these translations, incorporated much Greek learning and theory into his major writings, *Theorica musice* (Theory of Music, 1492), *Practica musice* (The Practice of Music, 1496), and *De harmonia musicorum intrumentorum opus* (A Work concerning the Harmony of Musical Instruments, 1518). Gaffurio's treatises were the most influential of his time. Along with published translations and commentaries in some of the works mentioned above, his writings stimulated new thought on matters such as the modes, consonance and dissonance, the elements and scope of the tonal system, tuning, word-music relations, and the harmony of music, of the human body and mind, and of the cosmos.

Power of the modes

The ancient philosophers believed that composers could tap a listener's emotions by their choice of mode. Both Plato and Aristotle insisted that the various modes had different ethical effects, although it is not clear what they meant by modes. The story that Pythagoras was able to calm an agitated youth bent on violence by having the piper change from one mode to another, and the account of Alexander the Great suddenly getting up from the banquet table and arming himself for battle when he heard a Phrygian tune, were told countless times. Theorists and composers assumed that these Greek modes were identical to the similarly named church modes and that the emotional powers of the former could be attributed to the latter. The Swiss theorist Heinrich Glareanus (1488–1563) in his famous book *Dodekachordon* (The Twelve-String Lyre, 1547) added four new modes to the traditional eight: the Aeolian and Hypoaeolian with the final on *A*, and the Ionian and Hypoionian with the final on *C*. With these additions, he made the theory of the modes more consistent with the current practice of composers, who had frequently employed

Glareanus

2. Selections from these texts may be found in SRrev, pp. 3–94; 1:9–94, and in Andrew Barker, ed., *Greek Musical Writings*: Vol. 1, *The Musician and His Art*, and Vol. 2, *Harmonic and Acoustic Theory* (Cambridge: Cambridge University Press, 1984–89).

GIOSEFFO ZARLINO RECOGNIZES A REBIRTH OF MUSIC IN HIS TIME, 1558

Whether because of the unfavorable time or the negligence of those who had little esteem not only for music but other studies as well, music fell from that supreme height in which it was once held to the vilest depths. Whereas incredible honor was once bestowed on it, later it was reputed to be so base and despicable and so little valued that learned men barely acknowledged its existence. This happened, it seems to me, because it retained neither a part nor a vestige of that honored severity it used to have. Therefore everyone gleefully tore it apart and treated it badly with many unworthy manners. Nevertheless it is agreeable to the almighty God that his infinite power, wisdom, and goodness be magnified and manifested to men through hymns accompanied by gracious and sweet accents. He seemingly could not tolerate that the art that serves in his worship be held as vile, for here below we acknowledge how much sweetness can reside in the song of the angels who in the heavens praise his majesty. Therefore he conceded to grace our times with the birth of Adrian Willaert, truly one of the rarest intellects that ever practiced music. In the guise of a new Pythagoras, examining minutely what music needed and finding an inifinity of errors, he began to remove them and to restore music to that honor and dignity it once had and that it reasonably ought to have. He demonstrated a rational order of composing every musical piece with elegant manner, clear models of which he gave us in his own compositions.

From *Le istitutioni harmoniche* (Venice, 1558), Part 1, Chapter 1, pp. 1–2.

the modes on *A* and *C*. For example, by analyzing a number of motets by Josquin des Prez, Glareanus demonstrated how his music utilized the power of the twelve modes (although Josquin knew only eight). But Glareanus's claim of having reestablished Aristoxenus's tonal system was unfounded.

Consonances and dissonances

As thirds and sixths became theoretically as well as practically accepted, a sharper distinction was drawn between consonance and dissonance, and masters of counterpoint devised new rules for controlling dissonance. The outstanding instruction book on counterpoint in the fifteenth century was the *Liber de arte contrapuncti* (A Book on the Art of Counterpoint, 1477) by Johannes Tinctoris (ca. 1435–ca. 1511), a Flemish composer who settled in Naples at the court of King Ferrante I in the early 1470s. He deplored the works of the "older composers in which there were more dissonances than consonances" (Book 2, Chapter 23) and proclaimed in his preface that nothing written more than forty years earlier was worth hearing. Tinctoris devised very strict rules for introducing dissonances, limiting them to unstressed beats and to syncopated passages (or what we call suspensions) at cadences. These rules were further refined in later treatises by Italian authors and finally synthesized in Zarlino's great work, *Le istitutioni harmoniche.*

Tinctoris

TIMELINE: THE SIXTEENTH CENTURY

1515 1530 1545 1560 1575 1590 1605

- **ca. 1500 Isaac, *Innsbruck, ich muss dich lassen***
- **1501 Petrucci publishes *Odhecaton***
- 1503 Leonardo da Vinci, *Mona Lisa*
- 1504 Michelangelo, *David*
- 1514 Machiavelli, *The Prince*
- 1516 Ariosto, *Orlando furioso*
- 1517 Martin Luther, ninety-five theses
- 1519–56 Charles V, Holy Roman Emperor
- **1521 Death of Josquin**
- **1526 Gombert joins chapel of Charles V**
- 1527 Sack of Rome
- 1528 Castiglione, *The Courtier*
- **1539 Arcadelt, first book of five-part madrigals**
- **ca. 1540 Willaert, *Musica nova***
- 1543 Copernicus, *De revolutionibus orbium coelestium*
- 1545–1563 Council of Trent
- **1547 Attaingnant, Danseries a 4 Parties**
- **1558 Zarlino, *Le istitutioni harmoniche***
- **1565 Lasso, *Penitential Psalms***
- **1566 Rore, *Da le belle contrade d'oriente***
- **ca. 1567 Palestrina, *Pope Marcellus* Mass**
- 1572 Massacre of Protestants in Paris
- **1575 Byrd and Tallis, *Cantiones sacrae***
- **1581 V. Galilei, *Dialogo della musica***
- **1588 N. Yonge, *Musica transalpina***
- 1590 Spenser, *The Faerie Queene*, Books 1–3
- 1594 Shakespeare, *Romeo and Juliet*
- **1594 Death of Palestrina**

Tuning Systems

Pythagorean tuning

Despite the constant use of thirds and sixths, Pythagorean tuning, in which these intervals sounded rough, prevailed in the mid-fifteenth century. This tuning, which yielded perfectly tuned fourths and fifths, resulted from dividing the monochord according to the instructions of Boethius, Guido, and others writing from the Middle Ages. Only in 1482 did Bartolomé Ramos de Pareja, a Spanish mathematician and music theorist residing in Italy, propose that this division be modified to produce more pleasing thirds and sixths. The idea was slowly accepted both in theory and practice, though not without opposition from conservatives like Gaffurio. By the beginning of the sixteenth century, instruments were tuned to make the imperfect consonances (thirds and sixths) sound quite acceptable. Until that time only perfect consonances (fourths, fifths, and octaves), which in the Pythagorean system were in their purest intonation, were allowed on the final beat of a cadence.

Just intonation

A tuning system devised by Ptolemy, which was first revealed in the Renaissance by Gaffurio, allowed for both perfect and imperfect consonances that were pure—that is, in the simple ratios, 3:2 and 4:3 for the fifths and fourths, and 5:4 and 6:5 for the major and minor thirds. This system, known as *just intonation* and called by Ptolemy the "syntonic diatonic" (sharp diatonic) tuning, was championed as the ideal solution by a number of theorists, most notably Lodovico Fogliano in 1529 and Zarlino in 1558. But it later was shown to have disadvantages for polyphonic music, and various compromises, such as mean-tone tuning and equal temperament, gained favor.

Musica ficta

Musicians experimented with new tuning systems because they wanted consonances to sound sweeter and because they were expanding their tonal vocabulary to include the notes of the chromatic scale. Improvised musica ficta called for a limited number of accidentals—mainly *F*♯, *C*♯, *G*♯, *B*♭, and *E*♭—but as composers sought to achieve new expressive effects, they began exploring cycles of fifths, which led them to recognize notes as remote from the diatonic scales as *C*♭ and *B*♭♭. Composers contrived "ficta" scales patterned on the conventional gamut to accommodate these notes. In the Pythagorean tuning system in use in the fifteenth century, however, a sharped note and its corresponding flatted note, such as *G*♯ and *A*♭, were different pitches. This led to the development of organs and harpsichords with separate keys for such pairs of tones. The composer Nicola Vicentino (1511–ca. 1576) gained notoriety for inventing a harpsichord with three keyboards that could play in the chromatic and enharmonic genera as well as the diatonic. He claimed thereby to have recaptured the powers of the ancient Greek scales.

Words and Music

Humanism succeeded in bringing music into closer alliance with the literary arts. The image of the ancient poet and musician united in a single person inspired both poets and composers to seek a common expressive goal. Authors became more concerned with the sound of their verses, and composers with imitating that sound. The punctuation and syntax of a text guided the composer in shaping the structure of the musical setting and in marking pauses in the text with cadences of different degrees of finality. The poet's message and images inspired the composer's melodies, rhythms, and textures, as well as the mixture of consonances and dissonances. Composers sought new ways to dramatize the content of the text. It became the rule to follow the rhythm of speech and not to violate the natural accentuation of syllables, whether in Latin or the vernacular. Where previously singers had to match syllables with the notated pitches and rhythms, composers now took charge.

These changes in outlook, which made music more directly appealing and meaningful to listeners, did not occur suddenly but evolved during the entire

Renaissance (roughly 1450 to 1600). Because of the rapid changes that music underwent during this century and a half—at different rates in different countries, to be sure—it is not possible to define a Renaissance musical style. The Renaissance was more a general cultural movement and state of mind than a specific set of musical techniques.

The term *Renaissance*

Renaissance means "rebirth" in French, a term first used in 1855 by Jules Michelet in his *Histoire de France.* It was adopted by historians of culture, particularly of art and eventually of music, to designate a period of history. The idea of rebirth was, of course, not foreign in an age whose scholars and artists aimed to restore the learning and ideals of ancient Greece and Rome. But there was another side to the idea of rebirth: a rededication to human as opposed to spiritual values. Besides salvation after death, fulfillment in life was now a desirable goal. It was no longer considered evil to express the full range of human emotions and to enjoy the pleasures of the senses. Artists and writers now turned to secular as well as religious subject matter and sought to make their works not only acceptable to God but understandable and delightful to people.

Human goals

Why Italy?

Why the Renaissance movement should have begun in Italy is a question that has aroused much discussion. The Italian peninsula in the fifteenth century was made up of a collection of city-states and small principalities that were often at war with each other. The rulers, many of whom had gained their positions by force, sought to glorify themselves and magnify their cities' reputations. They did so by erecting impressive palaces and country houses decorated with new artworks and newly unearthed artifacts from ancient civilizations; by maintaining chapels of talented singers and ensembles of gifted instrumentalists; and by lavishly entertaining neighboring potentates. Meanwhile the citizenry, no longer in feudal service to a lord and free of military duties (which were usually relegated to mercenaries), accumulated wealth through commerce, banking, and crafts. Although they prayed and attended church, these people gave priority to worldly matters. They wanted prosperity for their families, property and beautiful objects for themselves, and education for their children along classical rather than religious lines. Personal fulfillment through learning, public service, and accomplishment motivated their individual lives and their social contacts and institutions.

Prelates as patrons

Once the seat of the church returned from Avignon to Rome, popes and cardinals were as committed as the secular princes to a high standard of cultural activity and patronage. Some of the best musicians, artists, and scholars of the Renaissance were sponsored by cardinals from the Medici family in Florence, the Estes in Ferrara, the Sforzas in Milan, and the Gonzagas in Mantua.

Importation of Flemish musicians

The ruling princes and oligarchies in Italy were generous sponsors of music. They brought the most talented composers and musicians from France, Flanders, and the Netherlands to the Italian cities. Lorenzo de' Medici in the 1480s reorganized the cathedral chapel and recruited the Flemish singer-composers Heinrich Isaac (ca. 1450–1517) and Alexander Agricola (ca. 1446–1506). Music and the arts were suppressed for a time during the dominance of the charismatic preacher Girolamo Savonarola and the popular revolt ousting the Medici from power in 1494. But by 1511, the Medici were re-installed, patronage was renewed, and Philippe Verdelot (active ca. 1500–1550) and Jacques Arcadelt founded a tradition of madrigal composition in Florence. Milan, ruled from the 1450s by the Sforza family, had eighteen chamber singers and twenty-two chapel singers by 1474. Among them at various times was Josquin des Prez. The court of Ferrara under the Este dukes played host to Jacob Obrecht (ca. 1457/58–1505), Antoine Brumel (ca. 1460–ca. 1515), and Willaert. Mantua, ruled by the Gonzaga family, was another center of patronage, thanks to the presence of Isabella d'Este (wife of Marchese Francesco II Gonzaga), who had studied music seriously. Some of the singers from these courts, including Josquin, served in the papal chapel in Rome for periods of time. The republic of Venice cultivated Italian talent until, in 1527, current fashion led to the appointment of Willaert as choirmaster of St. Mark's and after his death the Netherlander Cipriano de Rore (ca. 1515–1565), but their successors were again Italians.

Italian musicians also worked in the princely courts, but until around 1550 those from France, Flanders, and the Netherlands dominated. They brought their music, their methods of singing and composition, and their vernacular songs with them. At the same time they absorbed the less complicated, chordal, treble-dominated, often danceable manner of the improvised and popular music they encountered in Italy. This combination of northern and Italian elements accounted for many characteristics of the prevailing style in the sixteenth century.

Italian influence on northerners

Music Printing

All this activity created a demand for music. Every chapel or court compiled music manuscripts to suit the local repertory. Sumptuously decorated and illuminated manuscripts were also copied and presented as gifts at weddings, anniversaries, and other occasions. This process, although slow and expensive, did not always transmit the composer's music accurately. The growth of printing made much wider dissemination of written music possible.

Printing from movable type, known in China for centuries and perfected in Europe by Johann Gutenberg around 1450, was first used for liturgical books with plainchant notation about 1473. This method proved much more practical than printing music from wood blocks, as was done in a few theory or instruction books in the late fifteenth century. The first collection of polyphonic music printed entirely from movable type, the *Harmonice musices odhecaton* (see below, page163), containing mainly chansons, was brought out in 1501 by Ottaviano Petrucci (1466–1539) in Venice. By 1523 Petrucci had published fifty-nine volumes (including reprints) of vocal and instrumental music. His publications, especially the earliest ones, are models of clarity and accuracy. Petrucci used a triple impression—that is, each sheet went through the press three times: once to print the staff lines, another time to print the words, and a third to print the notes. The process was long, difficult, and expensive, and some printers soon reduced it to two impressions, one for the words and one for the music. Printing from a single impression—using pieces

Petrucci

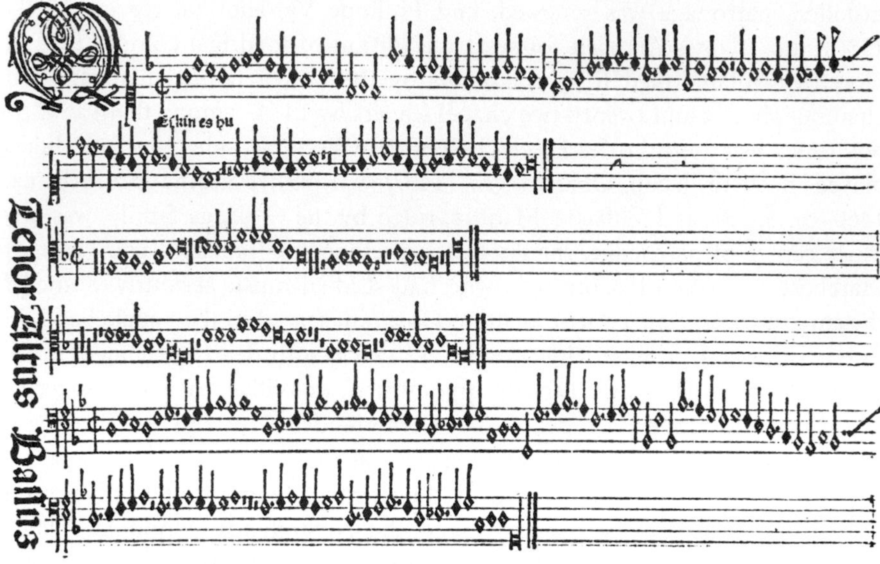

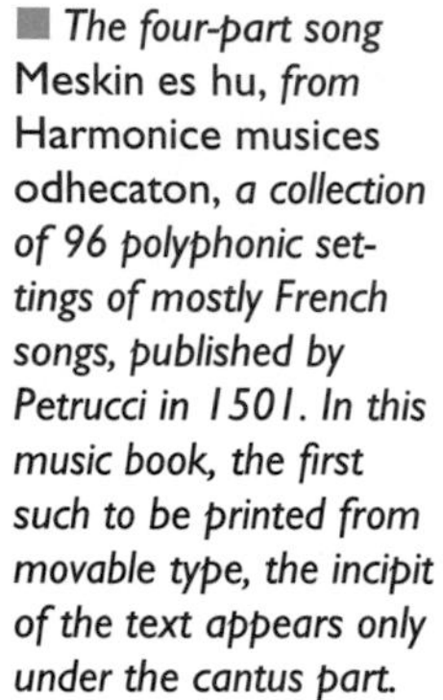
■ *The four-part song* Meskin es hu, *from* Harmonice musices odhecaton, *a collection of 96 polyphonic settings of mostly French songs, published by Petrucci in 1501. In this music book, the first such to be printed from movable type, the incipit of the text appears only under the cantus part.*

of type that printed staff, notes, and text in one operation—was apparently first practiced by John Rastell in London about 1520 and first applied systematically on a large scale by Pierre Attaingnant in Paris in 1528. Music printing began in Germany about 1534 and in the Netherlands in 1538. Venice, Rome, Nuremberg, Paris, Lyons, Louvain, and Antwerp were the principal centers in the sixteenth century.

Most ensemble music published in the sixteenth century was printed in the form of oblong part-books—one small volume for each voice, so that a complete set was needed to perform any piece. Part-books were intended to be used at home or in social gatherings (see illustration below). Most church

■ *Title page of Silvestro Ganassi's instruction book in recorder playing,* Opera intitulata Fontegara. *A recorder consort and two singers perform from printed part-books. In the foreground are two cornetti and on the wall three viols and a lute.*

PIETRO ARON ON COMPOSING ALL THE PARTS AT ONCE

Many composers contended that first the cantus should be devised, then the tenor, and after the tenor the contrabass. They practiced this method, because they lacked the order and knowledge of what was required for creating the contralto. Thus they made many awkward passages in their compositions, and because of them had to have unisons, rests, and ascending and descending skips difficult for the singer or performer. Such compositions were bereft of sweetness and harmony, because when you write the cantus or soprano first and then the tenor, once this tenor is done, there is no place for the contrabass, and once the contrabass is done, there is often no note for the contralto. If you consider only one part at a time, that is, when you write the tenor and take care only to make this tenor consonant [with the soprano], and similarly the contrabass, the consonance of every other part will suffer.

Therefore the moderns have considered this matter better, as is evident in their compositions for four, five, six, and more parts. Every one of the parts occupies a comfortable, easy, and acceptable place, because composers consider them all together and not according to what is described above. But if you feel like composing the cantus, tenor, or contrabass first, you are free to choose this method and rule. It may be observed that some do this at present, for often they begin with the contrabass, sometimes with the tenor, and at other times with the contralto.

You may find [the method of composing all the parts at once] difficult and awkward at first; so you will begin part by part. When you have become somewhat experienced in the practice, you will follow the order and method previously explained.

Pietro Aron, *Toscanello in musica* (Venice, 1524), Book II, Chapter 16.

choirs continued to use the large handwritten choirbooks, and new ones were still being hand-copied in the sixteenth century, even as printed versions began appearing.

Compositional method

Composers' concern for filling out harmonies and writing imitative passages led them to make constant adjustment to one part or another while drafting a piece. The method taught in earlier manuals—to begin with a two-part framework, usually tenor and soprano, and then add a third part, and finally a fourth—was now considered inadequate. Pietro Aron (or Aaron, ca. 1480–ca. 1550), writing in 1524, counseled composers to write all the parts simultaneously rather than one at a time, although he admitted that beginners would be well advised to follow the old layered method (see vignette). As a guide to attaining full harmony at every point by joining both the fifth and third or both the sixth and third to the bottom voice, Aron and other theorists published "consonance tables." These listed the bass and alto options for any interval between the soprano and tenor. This concern for simultaneous sonorities and the coordination of the independent voices encouraged the use of scores for study and for sketching and drafting music. Composers sometimes drafted scores on erasable slates or on cheap paper before transferring the individual voices to part-books. The earliest printed ensemble score appeared in 1577.

Effects of music printing

The application of movable type to printing of music had far-reaching consequences. Instead of a few precious manuscripts laboriously copied by hand and liable to all kinds of errors and variants, a plentiful supply of new music in copies of uniform accuracy was now available—not exactly at a low price, but still less costly than equivalent manuscripts. Printed music spread throughout the world, including North and South America, the works of composers who otherwise would have been known by only a small circle. It encouraged both amateurs and professionals to form vocal, instrumental, and mixed ensembles to perform the available repertory. Moreover, the existence of printed copies meant that many more works would be preserved for performance and study by later generations.

NORTHERN COMPOSERS AND THEIR MUSIC

The dominance of the Franco-Flemish and Netherlandish composers, which had begun early in the fifteenth century, is vividly illustrated in the careers of leading composers and performers between 1450 and 1550. Most of them passed a large part of their lives in the service of the king of France, the pope, or the Holy Roman Emperor (for whom one might be called to Spain, Germany, Bohemia, or Austria). Many also worked in Italy, in the courts or cities of Naples, Florence, Ferrara, Modena, Mantua, Milan, and Venice, which were the chief centers for spreading the art of the French, Flemish, and Netherlandish composers.

Johannes Ockeghem

"I know well that Ockeghem was, so to speak, the first who in these times rediscovered music, which had almost entirely died out—not in other wise than Donatello, who in his time rediscovered sculpture." Cosimo Bartoli paid this tribute in his *Ragionamenti accademici* (1567) a half century after Johannes Ockeghem (ca. 1420–1497) had died. Closer to his own time was a poetic eulogy, the *Déploration sur le trépas de Jean Ockeghem* (see vignette), written in the composer's memory and set to music by Josquin des Prez in 1497. It was customary in the fifteenth century to compose laments—*dèplorations*—on the death of famous musicians. In Josquin's setting, four voices lament in mostly chordal texture, with occasional imitation, while the tenor intones the Introit from the Requiem Mass ("Requiem aeternam"—Grant them eternal rest). Where the poet implores the composers Josquin, Pierson, Brumel, and Compère to mourn, the cantus firmus drops out, to return when all join together at "Requiem, Amen." This motet, reprinted in Antwerp many decades later, is one of several that memorialized Ockeghem.

DEPLORATION SUR LE TREPAS DE JEAN OCKEGHEM

Nymphes de bois, deesses des fontaines,	Nymphs of the woods, goddesses of the fountains,
Chantres experts de toutes nations,	skilled singers of all nations,
Changez vos voix tant cleres et haultaines	change your voices so clear and proud
En cris tranchants et lamentations.	to sharp cries and lamentations.
Car Atropos, tres terrible satrappe,	For Death, terrible satrap,
A vostre Ockeghem attrappe en sa trappe,	has trapped your Ockeghem in his trap,
Vray tresorier de musique et chief d'oeuvre,	true treasurer of music and chef d'oeuvre,
Doct, elegant de corps et non point trappe;	learned, handsome in appearance, and not stout.
Grant dommaige est que la terre le coeuvre.	Great pity that the earth should cover him.
Acoutrez vous d'habits de deuil:	Clothe yourselves in mourning,
Josquin, Piersson, Brumel, Compère,	Josquin, Piersson, Brumel, Compère,
Et plourez grosses larmes d'oeil:	and weep great tears from your eyes,
Perdu avez vostre bon pere.	for you have lost your good father.
Requiescant in pace. Amen.	May they rest in peace. Amen.

This poem was set to music by Josquin des Prez. For a facsimile of the music, commentary, and transcription, see Edward E. Lowinsky, ed., *The Medici Codex of 1518*, in MRM (Chicago: University of Chicago Press, 1968), III, pp. 8–9, 213–17; IV, 338–46. Line 7 of the poem alludes to Ockeghem's position as treasurer of the Abbey of St. Martin in Tours. The four names in line 11 are those of famous composers of the time ("Piersson" is Pierre de La Rue).

Career

Ockeghem sang in the choir of the cathedral at Antwerp in 1443. Several years later we find him in France, serving Charles I, duke of Bourbon. He entered the royal chapel of the king of France in 1452 and is referred to in a document of 1454 as *premier chapelain.* He probably retained that position until he retired, having served three kings: Charles VII, Louis IX, and Charles VIII. In view of his preference for low sonorities, he must have been a bass singer. Although Ockeghem was celebrated both as a composer and as the teacher of many leading composers of the next generation, his primary occupation was that of singer.

Ockeghem's compositions

Ockeghem's known output was relatively small for a composer of his renown: thirteen Masses, ten motets, and some twenty chansons. Most of his Masses resemble Du Fay's in their general sonority. Four voices of essentially like character interact in a contrapuntal texture of independent melodic lines. The bass, which before 1450 was rarely notated below *c*, is now extended downward to *G* or *F*, and sometimes as much as a fourth lower in special combinations of low voices. Otherwise the ranges are about the same as they had been in the early part of the century (see Example 6.1). In compass, the su-

Example 6.1 *Normal Range of Voice Parts in the Late Fifteenth Century*

perius corresponds to the modern alto, and the tenor and contratenor (the "tenor altus") are nearly equal and frequently cross each other. Ockeghem achieved a fuller, thicker texture, a sonority that is both darker and more homogeneous than we find earlier.

Some of Ockeghem's Masses, like Du Fay's *Se la face ay pale*, are based on a cantus firmus, using a single given melody as the framework for every movement. For example, the Mass *De plus en plus* (Kyrie and Agnus Dei in NAWM 31; CD 2 [28]) takes as its cantus firmus the tenor part of a chanson by Binchois (NAWM 30; CD 2 [26] / 1 ⟨32⟩), with whom Ockeghem may have studied. This type of Mass is called a "cyclical mass" because the Kyrie, Gloria, Credo, Sanctus, and Agnus Dei are all based on the same cantus firmus, the tenor part of the chanson by Binchois, which, though not as attractive and recognizable as the top voice, makes an excellent foundation for a composition. (See Example 6.2, giving the first phrase of Binchois's chanson and the beginning of Ockeghem's Agnus Dei; the notes of the chanson are numbered in the tenor.) As customary, Ockeghem assigns the cantus firmus to the tenor part, though it occasionally invades the other voices. Most of the time the other parts weave free counterpoints around the tenor, with only occasional moments of imitation, as at measures 9–10 of Example 6.2b.

The composer achieves a full harmonic sound by including three different consonant pitches in the simultaneous sonorities (forming what we call triads), except in the last chord of an important cadence, which admits only perfect consonances. Where the tenor or the lowest voice descends at a cadence, one or more voices syncopate to cause a suspension, as in measure 8 of Example 6.2b. Otherwise, dissonances occur at the semiminim level, while minims, with a few exceptions, are consonant. This gives the work an overwhelmingly consonant sound. Despite the continuous flow of the meandering voices, the graceful contour of the discantus and the strategically placed cadences provide a clear structure for the listener.

To vary the sonority, Ockeghem followed the example of earlier fifteenth-century composers and wrote whole sections as trios or duets. Sometimes he set one pair of voices against another pair, a device that occurs often in early sixteenth-century music, both sacred and secular. In general, he did not rely heavily on imitation in his Masses, and the occasional imitative passage seldom involves all the voices.

Naming Masses

In the fifteenth and sixteenth centuries, Masses without a cantus firmus sometimes took their titles from the mode in which they were written (for example, *Missa quinti toni*—"Mass in Mode 5"). Ockeghem's *Missa mi-mi* derives its name from the first two notes of the bass voice, *e–A*, both of which in solmization were sung to the syllable *mi*. Some Masses, including Ockeghem's

Example 6.2 **a.** *Gilles Binchois,* De plus en plus, *Tenor*

b. *Johannes Ockeghem, Agnus Dei from* Missa De plus en plus

Discantus: A - gnus de - - - - i qui tol - - - - - lis
Contratenor: A - gnus de - - - - i qui tol - - - - - lis
Tenor: A - gnus de - - - - i ...pec - - - - - ca -
Contratenor 2: A - gnus de - i qui tol - lis

Missa prolationum and *Missa cuiusvis toni* (both discussed below), were named for a structural feature, in these cases a canon. A Mass having neither a cantus firmus nor any other identifying peculiarity, or one whose source the composer did not wish to reveal, was often called a *Missa sine nomine* (without a name).

Canon

The device of canon is a conspicuous exception to Ockeghem's sparing use of imitation. In the prevailing method, the composer wrote out a single voice part and left instructions explaining how the singers should derive the additional voices from that part. The instruction or rule by which these further parts were derived was called a *canon*, which means "rule" in Greek and Latin. For example, the rule might instruct the second voice to sing the same melody starting a certain number of beats or measures after the original; the second voice might be an inversion of the first—that is, moving by the same intervals but in the opposite direction—or it might be the original voice in reverse, a type called a *retrograde* or *cancrizans* (crab) canon. What we now call canon was then called *fuga*, the strict form of which was a species of canon. The term *fuga* (fugue), was also used more loosely for a point of imitation—a series of entries of the same subject—whether imitated strictly in terms of intervals and durations or not.

Mensuration canon

Another possibility was to make the two voices move at different rates of speed. Canons of this sort, sometimes called *mensuration* canons, could be notated by prefixing two or more different mensuration signs (see pages 116–17) to a single written melody. In a mensuration canon the ratio between the time values of two voices might be simple augmentation or diminution (the second voice moving in note values twice or half as long as the first), or some more complex ratio. Furthermore, the derived voice could start on a different pitch and, of course, any of the devices just described might be used in combination.

Double canon

A composition could also involve *double canon*—that is, two canons (or even

This miniature from a French manuscript of about 1530 shows Ockeghem and eight musicians of his chapel singing a Gloria in the usual fashion of the time, from a large manuscript choirbook on a lectern. (PARIS, BIBLIOTHÈQUE NATIONALE, MS FR. 1587, FOL. 58V)

Example 6.3 *Ockeghem, Kyrie II from* Missa prolationum

more) sung or played simultaneously. Finally, two or more voices might proceed in canon while other voices moved in independent lines.

Missa prolationum

Ockeghem's *Missa prolationum* is a technical tour de force in which every movement is a double mensuration canon. For example, the second Kyrie is notated in two parts, superius and contra, as in Example 6.3a. Each singer observes the pertinent clef and mensuration sign placed at the beginning of one of the two written parts. A soprano reads the notes of the superius part in the soprano clef (the *C*-clef on the lowest staff-line) in the mensuration C, an alto according to the mezzo-soprano *C*-clef on the second line in the mensuration O; tenors and basses similarly read the contra part. Example 6.3b shows the results in modern notation.

Missa cuiusvis toni

Another display of compositional skill and challenge to singers is Ockeghem's *Missa cuiusvis toni*, a Mass that can be sung "in any mode" by reading the music according to one or another of four different clef combinations and making the necessary adjustments to avoid the interval *F–B♮* either melodically or harmonically with the bass (see Example 6.4). The resulting music can be heard in any of four different modes.

The importance of these and similar flights of virtuosity can easily be exaggerated. They hold a fascination for everyone who enjoys puzzles, musical or otherwise. In the comparatively few compositions where Ockeghem used such constructions, they were most artfully hidden. They did not affect his ability to communicate through the music, even to listeners with no background in musical composition. Ockeghem and his contemporaries believed that as far as the ordinary listener was concerned, the perfect canon, like the perfect crime, must not even be suspected, much less detected.

Puzzle canons

Composers took a sly pleasure in concealed ingenuity, occasionally forcing performers into a kind of guessing game. The directions for deriving the second voice (or even for singing the written one) are sometimes only hinted at in an intentionally obscure or jocular fashion. Thus "Clama ne cesses" (Shout without ceasing) means that the musicians must ignore the rests. When music printing took hold in the sixteenth century, publishers were often careful to furnish solutions to such riddles.

Example 6.4 *Ockeghem, Qui tollis from* Missa cuiusvis toni

Thou that takest away the sins of the world, receive our prayer.

The Generation after Ockeghem

Many of the next generation of Franco-Flemish composers were directly or indirectly pupils of Ockeghem. The three most eminent figures were Jacob Obrecht, Heinrich Isaac, and Josquin des Prez, all born around the middle of the century—Obrecht probably in Bergen op Zoom, Isaac perhaps in Bruges, and Josquin somewhere in the territory of Hainaut. All received their earliest musical training and experience in the Low Countries. All traveled widely, working in various courts and churches in different parts of Europe, including Italy. Their careers, like those of most of their contemporaries, illustrate the lively interchange in musical matters between northern and southern Europe, that is, between the Franco-Flemish centers and those of Italy and, later, Spain. It is no surprise, then, that their music mixes and even combines northern and southern elements: the serious tone, the leaning toward rigid structure, the intricate polyphony, the smoothly flowing rhythms of the north; the more spontaneous mood, simpler homophonic texture, more distinct rhythms, and more clearly articulated phrases of the Italians.

Jacob Obrecht

Career

Jacob Obrecht was born in 1457/58, son of a professional trumpeter for the city of Ghent. He trained for the priesthood, and in 1480 or 1481 was choirmaster for the Guild of Our Lady in Bergen op Zoom. In 1484, his appointment as master of choristers at Cambrai Cathedral describes him as "magister," indicating that he had a university degree. From 1485 to 1491 he was *succentor* (supervisor of the singers and trainer of the boys) at St. Donatian in Bruges. From 1487 to 1488, he was in the service of Duke Ercole I, in Ferrara. During the rest of his career he shuttled between short-term jobs as either choirmaster or singer within a small circle of cities—Antwerp, Bergen op Zoom, and Bruges. He returned to the service of Duke Ercole in 1504–05 and died there the following year, of the plague.

Masses

Obrecht's surviving works include the unusually large number of twenty-nine Masses, twenty-eight motets, chansons, songs in Dutch, and instrumental pieces. He built most of his Masses on cantus firmi—either secular songs or Gregorian melodies—but there is much variety in the way he treated them. In some Masses the entire borrowed melody is used in every movement; in others the first phrase is used in the Kyrie, the second in the Gloria, and so on. Still others have two or more cantus firmi in combination: the *Missa carminum* introduces about twenty different secular tunes.

Missa Caput

The Agnus Dei of Obrecht's *Missa Caput* (Example 6.5) begins with a pair of voices in a way that makes the relationship between them immediately apparent to the listener: the second voice imitates the first at the interval of a fifth. Although the imitation proceeds like a canon throughout the duet, it is not exact. For example, a rising fifth may be answered by a rising fourth. The

Example 6.5 *Jacob Obrecht, Agnus Dei from* Missa Caput

lead melody, a long arching curve over ten measures, is made up of little motives, often subtly related. In the opening motive, a rising fourth is expanded to a fifth in the next two statements, leading to a cadence that neatly closes off this melisma on the syllable "A." Later Renaissance composers would have considered it faulty to have a cadence before a thought was complete or a rest in the middle of a word, but this kind of literalness did not bother Obrecht. He achieved motivic unity in another way, as seen in the altus part, measures 7–9, where the rhythm on *D–E–G–F–D* is repeated in the notes that follow. These relationships between parts and in the melodic continuity make the structure of the music coherent to the listener.

The *Odhecaton*

Petrucci's first publication, the *Odhecaton*, contained chansons written between about 1470 and 1500 by composers ranging from the late Burgundian era to the generation of Obrecht, Isaac, and Josquin. It appeared in Venice in 1501 under the title *Harmonices musices odhecaton A* (One Hundred Polyphonic Songs) [actually there are only ninety-six]; see facsimile, page 152). The letter *A* indicates that this is the first of a series; Petrucci issued two sequels: *Canti B* in 1502 and *Canti C* in 1504. More than half of the chansons in the *Odhecaton* are for three voices, which are written primarily in the older styles. Over the next half century Petrucci and other Italian music printers issued a great number of such anthologies of chansons by French or Franco-Flemish composers.

In the four-voice chansons of the *Odhecaton*, we see the genre developing toward a fuller texture, a more completely imitative counterpoint, clearer harmonic structure, and greater equality of voices, duple meter replacing the more common triple meter of the Burgundian period. Many of these chansons, like contemporary Masses, were based either on a popular tune or on a single voice from some earlier chanson.

Ockeghem's chansons

By contrast with Ockeghem, Josquin virtually abandoned the formes fixes, choosing instead many strophic texts and simple four- or five-line poems. The polyphonic fabric of his chansons is not layered, like Ockeghem's, but is interlaced with imitation. Instead of the tenor-cantus pair serving as the skeleton of the music with the other voices filling in, all the parts are now equal.

Josquin's chansons

Josquin and his contemporaries often arranged popular songs, as he did in *Faulte d'argent.*[3] Josquin set the melody in strict canon at the lower fifth between the contratenor and the *quinta pars* (fifth part). Around this the other three voices weave a web of close imitation. Another procedure Josquin favored places the original melody in the tenor and encloses it with two outer voices that echo motives from the tune in lighthearted imitative play. Still another method arranges separate motives from a given melody in a free four-part polyphonic texture. Again, the tune, or a paraphrased version of it, may be heard in the highest voice. In these and other ways, composers in the period 1500 to 1520 blended popular elements with the courtly and contrapuntal tradition of the chanson.

3. Ed. in HAM No. 91.

■ *Woodcut purported to be a portrait of Josquin des Prez, from Petrus Opmeer,* Opus chronographicum, *1611.*

JOSQUIN DES PREZ

Out of the large number of first-rank composers active around 1500, few musicians have enjoyed higher renown while they lived or exercised more profound and lasting influence than Josquin des Prez (ca. 1450s–1521). Contemporaries hailed him as "the best of the composers of our time," the "father of musicians." "He is the master of the notes," said Martin Luther. "They must do as he wills; as for the other composers, they have to do as the notes will." Cosimo Bartoli wrote in 1567 that Josquin was without peer in music—on a par with Michelangelo in architecture, painting, and sculpture: "Both opened the eyes of all those who now take pleasure in these arts and shall find delight in the future."

Career

Josquin was born probably in France across the border from Hainaut, which belonged to the Holy Roman Empire. Between 1477 and 1478 he was in the chapel of René of Anjou in Aix en Provence. His whereabouts are unknown between then and 1483, when he stopped in Condé-sur-l'Escaut to receive an inheritance. He sang in the ducal chapel of Milan beginning around 1484 until 1489. During this period he may have traveled with Cardinal Ascanio Sforza (d. 1505), younger brother of the former Duke. From 1489 to 1494 or 1495 he was at the Sistine Chapel in Rome. Josquin was in France from 1501 to 1503, perhaps at the court of Louis XII. He was appointed *maestro di cappella* at the court of Ercole I d'Este in Ferrara in 1503 at the highest salary in the history of that chapel but left Italy for France the following year, escaping the plague that took Obrecht's life. From 1504 until his death on August 27, 1521, Josquin resided at Condé-sur-l'Escaut, where he was provost at the church of Notre Dame. A large number of sixteenth-century printed and manuscript anthologies contain his compositions, which include some eighteen Masses, one hundred motets, and seventy secular vocal works.

The Chanson

Ockeghem's chansons

Secular composition did not lag far behind Mass composition in prestige and craft. Composers expanded the miniature proportions typical of the early Burgundian chanson into larger musical forms. Chansons of 1460–80 show more and more use of imitative counterpoint, at first between the superius and tenor voices, later among all three parts. Most of Ockeghem's chansons, as well as those of his equally famous contemporary Antoine Busnois (d. 1492), made use of the traditional formes fixes of courtly poetry. The chansons of Ockeghem, Busnois, and their successors were immensely popular. Certain favorites, such as Ockeghem's *Ma bouche rit* and Josquin's *Adieu mes amours*, appear again and again in manuscripts and prints from many different countries. Chansons were freely altered, rearranged, and transcribed for instruments. Above all, they provided an inexhaustible supply of cantus firmi for Masses, which might be based on the superius or tenor of the chanson. Thus, Ockeghem used the superius of his *Ma maitresse* complete and unchanged for the Gloria of a Mass, the first section in the contratenor and the second section later in the tenor, so that the same melody which served once for "My mistress and my own dear love" is sung to the words "And on earth, peace to men of good will." Examples of putting secular melodies to religious use were extremely common in this period. Obrecht's Mass *Je ne demande* takes over not only the tenor but also material from the other voices of a four-part chanson by Busnois.

Masses

Josquin's work straddles the Middle Ages and the modern world. Conservative features, as we might expect, are most conspicuous in the Masses, which abound in technical ingenuity. Most use a secular tune as a cantus firmus. In the *Missa L'homme armé super voces musicales*, Josquin transposed the familiar fifteenth-century tune to successive degrees or syllables of the hexachord—*voces musicales*—beginning on *C* for the Kyrie, *D* for the Gloria, and so on. This Mass also includes a mensuration canon.[4]

Josquin's Masses employ many of the techniques commonly used in the sixteenth century. The theme of the *Missa Hercules dux Ferrariae* offers an example of a *soggetto cavato dalle vocali*, a "subject [theme] drawn from the vowels" of a word or sentence by letting each vowel indicate a corresponding syllable of the hexachord, thus:

4. See the Agnus Dei in HAM No. 89.

The subject honored Hercules, or Ercole I, duke of Ferrara from 1471 to 1505.

Imitation Masses

Josquin's *Missa Malheur me bat* illustrates a procedure that became more common later in the sixteenth century. Instead of basing the Mass on a single voice of a chanson, the composer subjects all its voices to free fantasy and expansion. In the process, such a Mass can take over many attributes of the model, including its characteristic motives, fugal statements and answers, and even its general structure. The resulting composition is best termed *imitation Mass*, though it has also been called *parody Mass*. In Josquin's time, his Mass would have been called "Mass in imitation of the music of *Malheur me bat*."

Around 1520 the imitation Mass began to replace the cantus firmus Mass. In it the composer reworked the model's initial and subsequent points of imitation in each movement of the Mass. Thus the motives and the imitative texture of the model—most often a motet or madrigal—permeate the music of the Mass, endowing it with a discernible individuality. At best, the new composition's set of artful glosses paid a creative tribute to the borrowed original.

Missa Pange lingua

The *Pange lingua* Mass, one of the last Josquin des Prez composed, is based on the melody of the hymn *Pange lingua gloriosi* (text by St. Thomas Aquinas). Josquin paraphrased the hymn melody in all the movements of the Mass—though not all the subdivisions—(see Kyrie and excerpt from the Credo in NAWM 32; CD 2 [33] / 1 ⟨34⟩). Rather than rigidly placing the chant in a single voice, he had all the voices sharing it. Individual phrases of the hymn melody serve as material for motives and subjects that are developed by polyphonic imitation.

The "Et incarnatus est" and "Crucifixus" of the Credo demonstrate Josquin's attention to text-expression. The solemn proclamation "Et incarnatus est"—"And he was made incarnate by the Holy Ghost of the Virgin Mary, and was made man"—is declaimed in block chords, with the soprano paraphrasing the opening line of the hymn. Josquin took advantage of the plaintive semitone motion of the hym's opening to express the word "crucifixus." He broke into the imitative texture with block chords in a somber tempo at the mention of Christ's trial and burial "[sub Pontio Pilato] passus, et sepultus est." Lively triple time in minims and close imitations mark the words "Et resurrexit tertia die" (And he rose again on the third day).

Text Setting

In keeping with humanist ideals, Josquin and his contemporaries strove to make the music better communicate the meaning of the texts. They carefully fitted the musical stress to the accentuation of the words, whether Latin or vernacular, and wanted the words to be heard and understood. This meant that the task of matching the words to the music could no longer be left to singers during a performance, and that parts had to have the text underlaid (positioned under the music) clearly and completely. The highly florid lines of Ockeghem and other Franco-Flemish composers gave way to more direct syllabic settings in which a phrase of text could be grasped as an uninterrupted thought. Composers turned to the chanson and the Italian popular genres as models for their vocal writing.

Musica Reservata

"Suiting the music to the meaning of the words, expressing the power of each different affection, placing the object as if actually before our eyes . . ."—these words are from a famous description of music written by a later Franco-Flemish composer,[5] but they apply equally well to Josquin. The author adds: "This kind of music is called *musica reservata*" (literally, reserved music). The term came into use shortly after the middle of the sixteenth century to denote the "new" style of music by composers who introduced chromaticism, modal variety, ornaments, and extreme contrasts of rhythm and texture into their music in order to project the words forcefully and graphically. It may also be that such music was "reserved" for a particular patron's chambers, and that its beginnings were connected with Josquin. His pupil Adrian Petit Coclicus claimed in the preface of his *Compendium musices* (Nuremberg, 1552) that his primary purpose in writing the treatise was "to restore to light that music which is commonly called *reservata*," an art he says he learned from Josquin des Prez. Despite some concrete usages, the meaning of the term remains clouded.

Motets

The high proportion of motets in Josquin's output is noteworthy. In his day the Mass was still the traditional vehicle by which composers demonstrated mastery of their craft. But the Mass's liturgical formality, unvarying text, and established musical conventions left little room for experimentation. Motets, on the other hand, could be written on a wide range of relatively unfamiliar texts that offered interesting new possibilities for word-music relationships. This made the motet the most inviting genre for sacred composition.

It is easy to see why his contemporaries believed that Josquin brought the musical and verbal messages closer together when we study one of his finest motets, *De profundis clamavi ad te* (Psalm 129, English 130: Out of the depths I cried to thee, NAWM 33; CD 2 [39] / 1 ⟨37⟩). The music is deeply expressive of its text and is wedded to it on several levels. The composer appropriately scored it for low voices and shaped the music throughout to the form, rhythm, accentuation, and meaning of the text. Josquin captured the spirit of the whole psalm in the opening line of the superius (Example 6.6, page 168). It traces the "Dorian" species of fifth (like our A minor), leaping down a fifth for the word "profundis" and reaching up to the minor sixth above for "clamavi," a perfect image of a soul in despair crying for help and straining to be heard. The other voices imitate the first five pitches and durations exactly. This motet was probably composed during the last twenty years of Josquin's life.

We can see Josquin's typical approach to motet writing in another work, *Ave Maria . . . virgo serena*,[6] one of his most widely copied compositions. It is

5. Trans. from the Latin of Samuel Quickelberg, quoted in Wolfgang Boetticher, *Orlando di Lasso und seine Zeit* (Kassel: Bärenreiter, 1958), 1:250. The passage refers to the *Penitential Psalms* of Lasso, which were written about 1560 and published in 1584. Quickelberg, a Dutch scholar and physician residing at the court of Munich, wrote this description in 1565.

6. *The Norton Scores: A Study Anthology*, Vol. 1, 8th edition, ed. Kristine Forney (New York: Norton, 1999), pp. 25–32.

Example 6.6 *Josquin des Prez, Motet:* De profundis clamavi ad te

Fugal imitation

found in a manuscript that dates from around 1476 and thus represents an earlier style than that of *De profundis.* Its main constructive method is fugal imitation, in which each phrase of text is assigned a musical subject that is then taken up in turn by each of the voices. The subject is usually imitated exactly at the unison, octave, fifth, or fourth. The first voices to enter either drop out after stating the subject, as in the opening of this motet, or continue with free counterpoint until a cadence is reached. Before the last voice has finished its phrase, a different voice begins the next phrase of text with a new subject. Josquin avoided a cadence and thus preserved the continuity of the text in the music. For example, the phrase "Ave Maria" progresses to "gratia plena" without a cadence, then "plena" is linked to "Dominus tecum" through a weak cadence at measure 16, where the two phrases overlap. At "virgo serena," the final phrase of the sentence, all the voices sing together for the first time in a "drive to the cadence" in which the rhythmic activity accelerates to the semiminim level (eighth notes of the transcription).

The text of this motet consists of a four-line quotation from a sequence framing a metrical rhymed poem of five strophes. Two of the quoted lines precede the poem as a prologue (see Example 6.7, measures 1–31), and two follow it as an epilogue. The strophes are each of four octosyllabic lines in iambic meter. The form of the poem determines the form of the music. There is an evaded cadence at the end of the prologue (measure 31), and a full cadence at the end of each strophe on the central tonality of C. Although Josquin ostensibly followed the custom of inventing a new melodic subject for each phrase of text, subtle motivic resemblances link them together.

Example 6.7 *Josquin des Prez, Motet:* Ave Maria . . . virgo serena

Hail Mary, full of grace, the Lord be with you, serene maiden.

SOME CONTEMPORARIES OF OBRECHT AND JOSQUIN

Heinrich Isaac

Heinrich Isaac (ca. 1450–1517) absorbed musical influences from Italy, France, Germany, Flanders, and the Netherlands, so that his output and style are more pan-European in character than those of his contemporaries. Flemish by birth, he served the Medici under Lorenzo the Magnificent in Florence from about 1484 to 1492. In 1497 he became court composer to Emperor Maximilian I at Vienna and Innsbruck, but seems to have spent most of the years from 1501 until his death in 1517 in Florence.

Isaac wrote a large number of songs with French, German, and Italian texts, and many other short, chansonlike pieces that, since they appear without words in the sources, are usually regarded as instrumental ensemble works. During his first sojourn in Florence, Isaac undoubtedly composed some of the *canti carnascialeschi* (carnival songs) for the festive processions and pageants that marked the Florentine holiday seasons.

Trade guilds promoted their products in tuneful verses sung from elaborate floats. In an early example of the singing commercial, the scribes of Florence

Example 6.8 *Canto carnascial esco:* Orsu car' Signori

Or-su, or-su, car' Si-gno - ri, Chi soe bol-le vol
Or-su, or-su, car' Si-gno - ri, Chi soe bol-le vol
Or-su, or-su, car' Si-gno - ri, Chi soe bol - le
Or-su, or-su, car' Si - gno - ri, Chi soe bol - le
spe-di - re, Ven-ga ad nui che siam scri - ptu - ri.
spe-di - re, Ven-ga ad nui che siam scri-ptu - ri.
vol spe-dir Ven-ga ad nui che siam scri-ptu - ri.
vol spe - di - re, Ven-ga ad nui che siam scri-ptu - ri.

Step up, dear sirs, if you wish your bulls [decrees] quickly certified. Come to us, for we are scribes.

Example 6.9 *Heinrich Isaac,* Innsbruck, ich muss dich lassen

Innsbruck, I must leave you, I am going on my way.

boasted of the quality of their services in the anonymous *Orsu car' Signori* (Example 6.8). The voices sing the syllables together, except for one moment of imitation, involving three parts (measures 5–6). The harmony almost always contains the third and fifth or sixth to the bass, with dissonance by syncopation at the cadences, which neatly mark the lines of poetry. The simultaneous *B–D–F* combination in measure 6 is not corrected by musica ficta but treated as a consonance.

The simple chordal declamatory style of the mainly anonymous carnival songs influenced Isaac's settings of German popular songs such as *Innsbruck, ich muss dich lassen* (Example 6.9 and NAWM 34; CD 2 [43]). The melody is in the soprano, and, except for some pseudo-imitative entries at the beginning, the other parts harmonize, with clear rests separating each phrase, as in the Italian part-songs.

Isaac's sacred compositions include some thirty Mass Ordinary settings and a cycle of motets based on the texts and melodies of the Proper (including many sequences) for a large portion of the church year. Although this monumental three-volume cycle of motets—comparable to the *Magnus liber* of Léonin and Pérotin—is known as the *Choralis Constantinus,* only the second volume was commissioned by the church at Constance, while the first and third were destined for the Habsburg court chapel.

Other composers

Other important contemporaries include Pierre de La Rue (ca. 1460–1518), a Flemish composer of numerous Masses and motets, and the Frenchman Jean Mouton (1459–1522). Mouton held several positions in France before beginning a long period of service in the royal chapel under two kings, Louis XII and Francis I. Described by the theorist Glareanus as one of the "emulators" of Josquin, Mouton wrote Masses and motets that are remarkable for their smooth-flowing melodic lines and skillful use of various unifying devices. He was highly esteemed in Italy, where he spent some time in 1515, and he was the teacher of Adrian Willaert, who became the leading figure in the rise of the Venetian school (see pages 178ff).

SUMMARY

Style

Around 1500 a prevailing style emerged out of the variety of compositional techniques practiced in England and on the Continent during the previous century. The structure of the text now largely determined that of the music. Composers wrote polyphonic parts that were singable—even if they ended up being played—and nearly equal in importance. The quest for fullness of harmony, vocality of melody, and motivic relationships between the voices made the layering method of composition impractical, and composers worked out the parts more or less simultaneously. Although the tenor remained a key voice in the structure, the bass took over the foundation of the harmony. Cadences continued to close in perfect consonances, but between them composers aimed for full triadic sonorities. Simplification and standardization of rhythm favored the alla breve duple measure. Borrowed melodies, whether sacred or secular, were still being used to unify large compositions, but the borrowed material was distributed among the voices rather than confined to the tenor or superius. The cyclical Mass and the motet were the preferred sacred genres. The chanson, breaking out of its formes fixes, was cast in new shapes pervaded by imitation. Hidden and esoteric structural devices gave way to transparent forms, principally that of overlapping fugal or imitative sections, relieved occasionally by homophonic textures. These trends gave composers greater flexibility than they had had before and more opportunity to communicate with a wider audience.

Genres

BIBLIOGRAPHY

Music Collections

INDIVIDUAL COMPOSERS

Modern editions of music by the composers mentioned in this chapter include:

Isaac: *Opera Omnia*, ed. Edward R. Lerner, CMM 65, 7 vols. (1974–84). See also *Choralis Constantinus*, Books I and II, in DTOe, Vols. 10 and 32; Book III, ed. Louise Cuyler

(Ann Arbor: University of Michigan Press, 1950); *Five Polyphonic Masses,* ed. L. Cuyler (Ann Arbor: University of Michigan Press, 1956); *Messen,* ed. Martin Staehelin, Musikalische Denkmäler, 7–8 (Mainz: B. Schott, 1971–73).

Josquin des Prez: *Werken,* ed. Albert Smijers, 13 vols. (Amsterdam: Vereeniging voor nederlandse muziekgeschiedenis, 1921–69). *New Josquin Edition,* ed. Willem Elders et al. (Utrecht: Vereniging voor Nederlandse Muziekgeschiedenis, 1987–), in progress.

La Rue: *Liber missarum P. de la Rue,* ed. A. Tirabassi (Malines: Maison Dessain, 1941).

Mouton: *Opera omnia,* ed. Andrew C. Minor, 4 vols., CMM 43.

Obrecht: *Werken,* ed. Johannes Wolf, 8 vols. (Amsterdam: G. Alsbach; Leipzig: Breitkopf & Härtel, 1912–21; repr. 1968). *Opera Omnia,* ed. Marcus van Crevel, 5 vols. (Amsterdam: G. Alsbach, 1953–); *New Obrecht Edition,* Chris Maas, gen. ed. (Amsterdam: Vereeniging voor Nederlandse Muziekgeschiedenis, 1983–)

Ockeghem: *Collected Works,* ed. Dragan Plamenac, Vols. 1 and 2, 2nd ed. (New York: American Musicological Society, 1959–66); Vol. 3, Motets and Chansons, ed. Richard Wexler and D. Plamenac, 1992).

Manuscripts and Early Music Printing

Howard M. Brown, *A Florentine Chansonnier from the Time of Lorenzo the Magnificent,* 2 vols., MRM 7 (Chicago: University of Chicago Press, 1983).

The Medici Codex of 1518, ed. Edward E. Lowinsky, MRM 3 (Chicago: University of Chicago Press, 1968).

The Chanson Albums of Marguerite of Austria, ed. Martin Picker (Berkeley: University of California Press, 1965).

The Mellon Chansonnier, ed. Leeman Perkins and Howard Garey, 2 vols. (New Haven: Yale University Press, 1979), complete facs. and edition.

Ottaviano Petrucci, *Harmonice Musices Odhecaton A* (Venice: Petrucci, 1504; repr. New York: Broude Brothers, 1973). Edition by Helen Hewitt with literary texts ed. by Isabel Pope (Cambridge, Mass.: Medieval Academy of America, 1946).

Petrucci, *Canti B numero cinquanta* (Venice: Petrucci, 1502; repr. New York: Broude Brothers, 1975). Edition by Helen Hewitt, MRM 2 (Chicago: University of Chicago Press, 1967).

Petrucci, *Canti C numero cinquanta* (Venice: Petrucci, 1504; repr. New York: Broude Brothers, 1978).

For a complete list, with descriptions, of the publications of Petrucci, see Claudio Sartori, *Bibliografia delle opere musicali stampate da Ottaviano Petrucci,* Biblioteca di Bibliografia Italiana 18 (Florence: L. Olschki, 1948).

For Further Reading

General

See the bibliography for Chapter 5.

For biographies and summaries of works and style of the major composers: Gustave Reese et al., *The New Grove High Renaissance Masters: Josquin, Palestrina, Lassus, Byrd, Victoria* (New York: Norton, 1984).

Special Topics

On the practice of composition: Jessie Ann Owens, *Composers at Work: The Craft of Musical Composition, 1450–1600* (New York: Oxford University Press, 1997); Bonnie J. Blackburn, "On Compositional Process in the Fifteenth Century," JAMS 40 (1987):210–84.

On humanism: Claude V. Palisca, *Humanism in Italian Renaissance Musical Thought* (New Haven: Yale University Press, 1985); Palisca, "Humanism and Music," in Albert

Rabil, Jr., *Renaissance Humanism: Foundations, Forms, and Legacy,* Vol. 3: Humanism and the Disciplines (Philadelphia: University of Pennsylvania Press, 1988), pp. 450–85; D. P. Walker, "Musical Humanism in the 16th and Early 17th Centuries," *The Music Review* 2 (1941):1–13, 111–21, 220–27, 288–308; 3 (1942):55–71, and GLHWM 4.

On patronage: several studies, listed below, examine musical activities in the context of Renaissance culture and society and the relationship between patronage and musical production in specific geographic locations.

Reinhard Strohm, *Music in Late Medieval Bruges,* rev. ed. (Oxford: Clarendon Press, 1990). A vivid picture of musical life in a Flemish community of the fifteenth century, particularly strong in documenting the role of the churches and confraternities as patrons of music.

William Prizer, "Music and Ceremonial in the Low Countries: Philip the Fair and the Order of the Golden Fleece," EMH 5 (1985):113–35.

Lewis Lockwood, *Music in Renaissance Ferrara, 1400–1505: The Creation of a Musical Center in the Italian Renaissance* (Cambridge, Mass.: Harvard University Press, 1987).

Allan Atlas, *Music at the Aragonese Court of Naples* (Cambridge: Cambridge University Press, 1985).

Frank A. D'Accone, *The Civic Muse: Music and Musicians in Siena during the Middle Ages and the Renaissance* (Chicago: University of Chicago Press, 1997).

Christopher A. Reynolds, *Papal Patronage and the Music of St. Peter's, 1380–1513* (Berkeley: University of California Press, 1995).

Iain Fenlon, *Music Patronage in Sixteenth-Century Mantua,* 2 vols. (Cambridge: Cambridge University Press, 1980 and 1984).

Iain Fenlon, ed., *Music in Medieval and Early Modern Europe: Patronage, Sources, and Texts* (Cambridge: Cambridge University Press, 1981).

Frank D'Accone, "The Singers of San Giovanni in Florence during the 15th Century," JAMS 14 (1961):307–58, and GLHWM 3; his "The Musical Chapels at the Florentine Cathedral and Baptistry during the First Half of the Sixteenth Century," JAMS 24 (1974):1–50.

Nino Pirrotta, "Music and Cultural Tendencies in 15th-Century Italy," JAMS 19 (1966):127–61, and GLHWM 4; and Carl Anthon, "Some Aspects of the Status of Musicians during the Sixteenth Century," MD 1 (1946):111–23, 222–34, and GLHWM 3.

Denis Arnold, "Music at a Venetian Confraternity in the Renaissance," AM 38 (1965):62–67. Frank Ll. Harrison, *Music in Medieval Britain* (London: Routledge & Kegan Paul, 1958), studies the period from the eleventh century to the Reformation, and deals with musical style and the institutions under whose patronage the music was composed and performed. David Price, *Patrons and Musicians of the English Renaissance* (Cambridge: Cambridge University Press, 1981).

Howard M. Brown, *Instrumental Music Printed before 1600* (Cambridge, Mass.: Harvard University Press, 1965).

Accounts of the earliest music printers in France are in Daniel Heartz, *Pierre Attaingnant, Royal Printer of Music* (Berkeley: University of California Press, 1968).

On the imitation, or "parody," technique of Mass writing: Lewis Lockwood, "On 'Parody' as a Term and Concept," in Jan LaRue, ed., *Aspects of Medieval and Renaissance Music: A Birthday Offering to Gustave Reese* (New York: Norton, 1966), 560–75, and GLHWM 4.

On text underlay: see the discussion in Lowinsky's edition of the *Medici Codex,* pp. 90–107. For theories of text underlay as discussed in contemporary treatises, see Don Harrán, *Word-Tone Relations in Musical Thought from Antiquity to the Seventeenth Century,* MSD 40 (American Institute of Musicology, 1986).

On *musica reservata:* Claude Palisca, "A Clarification of 'Musica Reservata,'" AM 31 (1959):133–61.

INDIVIDUAL COMPOSERS

Antoine Busnois Paula Higgins, *Antoine Busnoys: Method, Meaning, and Context in Late Medieval Music* (Oxford: Clarendon Press, 1997).

Heinrich Isaac For bibliography, see Martin Picker, *Heinrich Isaac: A Guide to Research* (New York: Garland, 1991).

Josquin des Prez Edward E. Lowinsky, with Bonnie J. Blackburn, eds., *Josquin des Prez, Proceedings of the International Josquin Festival-Conference, New York, 1971* (London: Oxford University Press, 1976); Leeman Perkins, "Mode and Structure in the Masses of Josquin," JAMS 26 (1973):189–239. For bibliography, see Sydney Robinson Charles, *Josquin des Prez: A Guide to Research* (New York: Garland, 1983). Recent archival discoveries have considerably altered the chronicle of his life. See particularly Lora Matthews and Paul Merkley, *Music and Patronage in the Sforza Court* (Turnhout: Brepols, 1999); and Pamela Starr, "Josquin, Rome, and a Case of Mistaken Identity," JM 15 (1997):43–65.

Obrecht Rob C. Wegman, *Born for the Muses: The Life and Masses of Jacob Obrecht* (Oxford: Clarendon Press, 1994). For further bibliography, see Martin Picker, *Johannes Ockeghem and Jacob Obrecht: A Guide to Research* (New York: Garland, 1988).

Ockeghem Philippe Vendrix, ed., *Johannes Ockeghem: Actes du xl*[e] colloque international d'études humanistes, Tours, 2–8 febrier 1997 (Paris: Klincksieck, 1998). Special issue of *Tijdschrift van de Vereniging voor Nederlandse Muziekgeschidenis.* For further bibliography, see under Obrecht.

Mouton Lewis Lockwood, "Jean Mouton and Jean Michel: New Evidence on French Music and Musicians in Italy," JAMS 32 (1979): 191–246.

THEORISTS

Several of the treatises mentioned or quoted in this chapter have been translated into English:

Aron *Toscanello in musica*, trans. Peter Bergquist (Colorado Springs: Colorado College Music Press, 1970). *Treatise on the Nature and Recognition of All the Tones of Figured Song*, excerpts in SRrev, pp. 415–28; 3:137–50.

Gaffurio *Theorica musice*, trans. with intro. and notes by Walter K. Kreyszig, ed. Claude V. Palisca, as *The Theory of Music* (New Haven: Yale University Press, 1993); *De Harmonia musicorum instrumentorum opus*, trans. Clement A. Miller, MSD 33 (Stuttgart: American Institute of Musicology/Hänssler, 1977); *Practica musice*, trans. C. A. Miller, MSD 20 (American Institute of Musicology, 1968), also trans. Irwin Young in *The Practica musicae of Franchinus Gaffurius* (Madison: University of Wisconsin Press, 1969). An extensive commentary on the *Theorica musice* is W. Kreyszig, *Franchino Gaffurio's Theorica musice (1492): A Study of the Sources* (Vienna: W. Braumüller Universitäts-Verlagsbuchhandlung, forthcoming).

Glareanus *Dodekachordon*, trans. Clement A. Miller, MSD 6 (American Institute of Musicology, 1965). Excerpts in SRrev, pp. 428–35; 3:150–57.

Ramos de Pareja *Musica practica,* trans. Clement A. Miller (American Institute of Musicology, 1993). Excerpts in SRrev, pp. 407–14; 3:129–36.

Tinctoris *Liber de arte contrapuncti,* trans. Albert Seay, *The Art of Counterpoint,* MSD 5 (American Institute of Musicology, 1961). Extracts in SRrev, pp. 401–07; 3:123–29. A recent investigation of the life of Tinctoris is Ronald Woodley, "Iohannes Tinctoris: A Review of the Biographical Evidence," JAMS 34 (1981): 217–48.

Zarlino *Le istitutioni harmoniche,* Part 3, in *The Art of Counterpoint,* trans. Guy A. Marco and Claude V. Palisca (New Haven: Yale University Press, 1968; New York: Da Capo, 1983); Part 4, in *On the Modes,* trans. Vered Cohen, ed. C. V. Palisca (New Haven: Yale University Press, 1983); excerpts in SRrev, pp. 436–62; 3:158–84.

CHAPTER 7

NEW CURRENTS IN THE SIXTEENTH CENTURY

THE FRANCO-FLEMISH GENERATION (1520–50)

Between 1520 and 1550 the dominant Franco-Flemish style underwent a transformation, partly because northerners working in Italy and southern Germany assimilated the musical idioms of their adopted homes. Instrumental music increased in both importance and production, and it too was affected by musicians' migrations as well as by the changing character of vocal music.

Church music changed more gradually than secular music. Indeed, some church composers returned to the continuous contrapuntal style of Ockeghem, as though reacting against the highly personal and adventurous experiments of Obrecht and Josquin. Even those conservative composers, however, almost completely abandoned the canons and similar devices of the older school. The imitation Mass gradually replaced the older technique of basing a Mass on a single cantus firmus. Chant melodies, more freely treated, still served as subjects for Masses and motets, both of which were now being written for five or six voices rather than four.

Nicolas Gombert

The northern motet style of the period 1520–50 is exemplified in works by Nicolas Gombert, thought to have been a pupil of Josquin. As an official of the chapel of Emperor Charles V, Gombert accompanied the court on numerous voyages and worked in Vienna, Madrid, and Brussels. We can see his approach to the motet in *Super flumina Babilonis*[1] (one of more than 160 motets that

1. Ed. in HAM No. 114.

survive). Gombert breaks a continuous series of imitative sections with interlocking cadences by inserting a single short contrasting section in triple meter and fauxbourdon harmony. This use of an archaic style is apparently prompted by the words "Quomodo cantabimus canticum Domini in terra aliena" (How shall we sing the Lord's song in a strange land?). Because of its generally smooth and uniformly dense texture, with few rests and most dissonances carefully prepared and resolved, Gombert's music seems undramatic compared to many of Josquin's works.

Jacobus Clemens

Another important Flemish composer of this period, Jacobus Clemens (ca. 1510–ca. 1556, also known as "Clemens non Papa") worked in Bruges and various Netherlands churches. His compositions include chansons, fifteen Masses, more than two hundred motets, and four books of psalms (*Souterliedeken*) with Dutch texts, in which tunes of popular origin are set in simple three-part polyphony. He based all but one of his Masses on polyphonic models. His motets are similar in style to Gombert's, but Clemens tidily delineated phrases, crafting them to the sense of the words, and he clearly defined the modes through cadences and melodic profile.

Adrian Willaert

Adrian Willaert (ca. 1490–1562) was a pioneer in bringing text and music into closer rapport, and his experiments in chromaticism and rhythm were on the cutting edge of new developments. Born in Flanders, Willaert studied composition in Paris with Jean Mouton. Account books show him working in Rome for Cardinal Ippolito I d'Este in 1515. After holding various positions in Ferrara and Milan, Willaert became director of music at Venice's St. Mark's Church in 1527. He remained here until his death thirty-five years later and was a leading spirit in Venetian musical life, composing both sacred and secular music. Among all the Franco-Flemish composers of his generation, he was most deeply affected by the humanist movement and by Italian musical practices. He trained many eminent musicians, who spread his fame and influence all over Italy. Among his pupils were Zarlino, Rore, Nicola Vicentino (1511–1576), Andrea Gabrieli (ca. 1510–1586), and Costanzo Porta (ca. 1528–1601).

Music and words

In Willaert's sacred compositions, which comprise the bulk of his work, the text determines every dimension of the musical form. Willaert was one of the first composers to insist that syllables be printed under their notes and that scrupulous attention be paid to the stresses of Latin pronunciation. We may assume that the rules for underlaying text set forth by his pupil Zarlino were based on Willaert's practices and teachings.[2] He carefully planned his compo-

2. Zarlino, *Le istitutioni harmoniche*, Venice, 1558, Book IV, Chapters 32–33, trans. in SRrev, pp. 436–61; 3:179–84, and in Zarlino, *On the Modes*, trans. Vered Cohen, ed. Claude V. Palisca (New Haven: Yale University Press, 1983), pp. 94–99.

sitions to suit the accentuation, rhetoric, and punctuation of the text. He never allowed a rest to interrupt a word or thought within a vocal line, and he postponed the cadence in a voice until a unit of text was completed. Willaert put in a strong cadence only when a principal period in the text ended, and he avoided full cadences—in which the major sixth proceeds to the octave and the bass rises a fourth or descends a fifth—except at significant textual breaks. Lesser points of rest might receive weaker cadences, such as the "Phrygian cadence," in which the bass descends a semitone and the top voice rises a tone (Example 7.1b, page 180, measures 79–80).

Evading the cadence

As Zarlino described it, evading the cadence occurs "when the voices give the impression of leading to a perfect cadence, and turn instead in a different direction."[3] This pattern of preparation, almost always taking the form of a suspension followed by evasion, contributes to the clarity of the counterpoint while maintaining continuity. The technique bypasses the constant resting points characteristic of earlier imitative pieces while still avoiding the long-winded seamlessness of music such as Gombert's. The evaded cadence also permits some voices to continue an imitative texture after others have come to a close, so that each voice can have a long arching line with a beginning, middle, and an end. Example 7.1a shows evaded cadences from the motet *O crux, splendidior cunctis astris* (O cross, shining more brightly than all stars; published 1539). The framework of the polyphonic cadence—the major sixth moving to the octave—underlies most of these evaded cadences, but other voices proceed in a way that minimizes the finality of the cadential formula. Where Willaert wanted to mark an important close, he did so with a deliberate accumulation of close imitations, multiple suspensions, and strategically placed dissonances, as in the end of the *prima pars* (first part) of this motet (Example 7.1b).

Use of chant

Although *O crux* is based throughout on the plainchant antiphon (see *Liber usualis,* page 1453), no one voice monopolizes the borrowed melody, as in the older cantus-firmus procedure; the melody is not treated in canon in two voices, as in some of Willaert's earlier motets, and it is not tied to formal fugal procedures, as in Josquin's *Ave Maria.* Instead, the chant fragments are subjects for an extremely free imitative development. In Example 7.2 (page 181), the Tenor (at measure 1), Altus (measure 2), Quintus (measure 7), and Bassus (measure 7) all paraphrase the chant melody, but each does so in a different way.

Modality

How to preserve modality, which was being undermined by musica ficta, was a problem faced by early Renaissance composers, who saw the modes as a link between the Christian tradition and the emotional effects of ancient music. But few succeeded in capturing the essence of a mode as Willaert did. In *O crux* he adopted the chant's Mode I but transposed it up a fourth by means of one flat (see Example 7.2). In the initial melodies of all the voices he gave prominence to the "species" characteristic of Mode I: the rising fifth, *G–D* (which in this key has the interval-species tone–semitone–tone–tone), and the

3. Book III, Chapter 54, in Zarlino, *The Art of Counterpoint,* trans. Guy A. Marco and Claude V. Palisca (New Haven: Yale University Press, 1968; repr. Da Capo Press, 1983), pp. 151–53.

Example 7.1 *Adrian Willaert,* O crux, splendidior

a. *Evaded cadences*

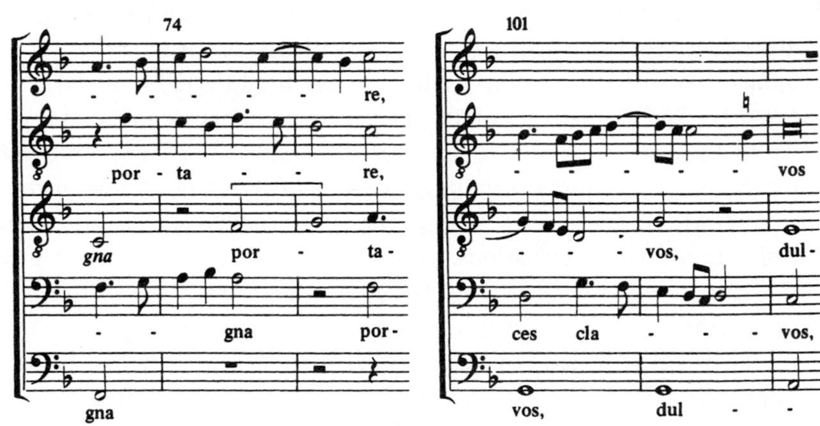

b. *Close of* prima pars

Example 7.2 *Willaert, Opening of Motet* O crux, splendidior

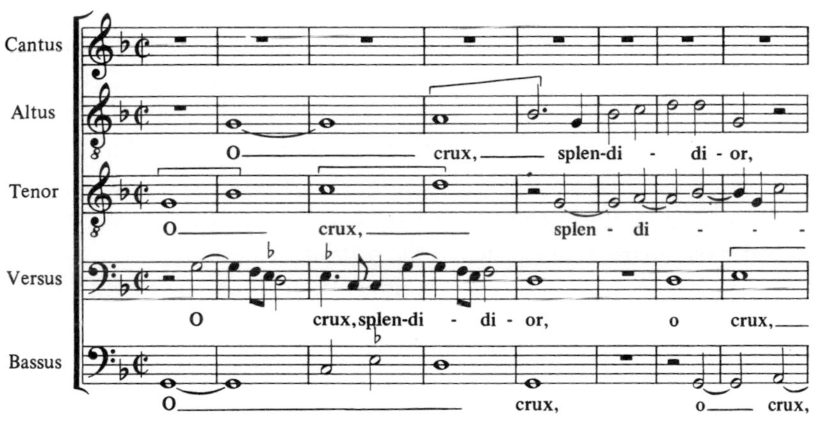

O cross, shining more brightly than all the stars, renowned throughout the world

fourth, *D–G* (tone–semitone–tone). He also made sure that each of the perfect cadences—those marking major points of punctuation—closed on *G*. With good reason, Zarlino believed that Willaert had reached technical perfection in his sacred music.

THE RISE OF NATIONAL STYLES

Italy

Franco-Flemish composers settled all over western Europe in the early sixteenth century, taking with them their musical idiom. But each country also had its own distinctive music that was surely better known and more popular locally than the learned art of the northerners. These national idioms would gradually rise to prominence and eventually transform the prevailing style. This process occurred most markedly in Italy, where the formidable influence of native music is vividly illustrated in the careers of Willaert and his disciples. As director of music at St. Mark's in Venice—the most prestigious musical post in Italy—he taught numerous Italians, including Andrea Gabrieli (ca. 1533–1586), whose own pupil and nephew, Giovanni Gabrieli (ca. 1553–1612), became the most celebrated Venetian composer of his generation. In 1609 a promising young German composer, Heinrich Schütz (1585–1672), came to Venice to study with Giovanni Gabrieli. In fact, Italy had by then supplanted France and the Low Countries as the center of European musical life, a primacy that endured for two hundred years. Europeans who had spent the 1500s looking to Flanders and the Netherlands for musical leadership now turned toward Italy; but in the meantime each country had also developed a national style of its own.

Venice

The Frottola

Petrucci's earliest music collections, printed in Venice beginning in 1501, contained chansons, Masses, and motets. But between 1504 and 1514, he published no fewer than eleven collections of *frottole* (singular, *frottola*), four-part strophic songs that were set syllabically and homophonically, with the melody in the upper voice, marked rhythmic patterns, and simple diatonic harmonies. Some *frottola* sub-types, such as the *barzelletta, capitolo, terza rima*, and *strambotto*, had fixed forms; others, such as the *canzone*, were free.

The frottola flourished in the late fifteenth and early sixteenth centuries. Usually the top voice was sung, while the other parts were played. Beginning in 1509, Francisco Bossinensis published a large number of frottole by various composers in arrangements for lute and voice. Since the lute part preserved the vocal parts of the original, the solo singer could deal freely with the written notes, introducing improvised melismatic flourishes at principal cadences.

Cara

The frottola *Io non compro più speranza* (NAWM 35; CD 2 [44]) by Marco Cara (ca. 1470–ca. 1525) is the lighthearted complaint of a disappointed lover; it appeared in Petrucci's first book. The six beats to the measure are organized now in duple groups, now in triple, producing the hemiola that was so characteristic of the canzonets—light dance-songs popular throughout the century—and was later adopted in seventeenth-century monody. The harmonization consists almost entirely of root chords, a style that had a far-reaching effect on music produced in Italy in the sixteenth century by both natives and foreigners.

Despite the frottole's simple music and their earthy and satirical texts, they were neither popular nor "folk" music. They flourished in Italian princely courts such as Ferrara and Urbino, and especially at Mantua, where Cara and Bartolomeo Tromboncino (ca. 1470–after 1535) worked. Most frottola composers were Italian, though northerners living in Italy also wrote a few. This song type is historically important as a forerunner of the Italian madrigal. It may also have had a subtle influence on the style of the French chansons that began to appear in the 1520s.

The Lauda

The religious counterpart of the frottola was the polyphonic *lauda* (pl. *laude*), a popular nonliturgical devotional song. (See discussion of monophonic laude, page 64.) The texts, in Italian or Latin, were set in four parts, the melodies often taken from secular songs. Petrucci published two books of laude, in 1507 and 1508. Laude were commonly sung in semi-public devotional gatherings, either a cappella or possibly with instruments playing the three lower voices. Like frottole, laude were typically syllabic and homophonic, with regular rhythm and with the melody in the highest voice. In their simple harmonic settings they were often remarkably expressive. Although related in mood and purpose to liturgical music, laude seldom incorporated Gregorian themes and showed little resemblance to the Franco-Flemish church idiom. On the contrary, Netherlanders in Italy must have admired the homophonic writing and simple syllabic text setting of the lauda and frottola. Declamatory passages in the music of many late sixteenth-century composers, including Palestrina and Victoria, seem inspired by the lauda tradition.

THE ITALIAN MADRIGAL

The madrigal, the most important genre of Italian secular music in the sixteenth century, made Italy the leader in European music for the first time in its history. The sixteenth-century madrigal resembled the *trecento* madrigal—a strophic song with a ritornello—in name only. The early sixteenth-century madrigal had no refrains or any other features of the old formes fixes, with their patterned repetitions of musical and textual phrases. In the typical sixteenth-century madrigal, the composer made up new music suited to the rhythm and sense of the words for every line of poetry, that is, it was "through-composed."

Madrigal texts

In contrast with the poetry of the frottola, madrigal poetry was more elevated and serious. Many of the texts were written by major poets, including Francesco Petrarca (1304–1374), Pietro Bembo, Jacopo Sannazaro (1457–1530), Ludovico Ariosto (1474–1533), Torquato Tasso (1544–1595), and Giovanni Battista Guarini (1538–1612). The music of the frottola was essentially a tune for singing the poetry, marking the end of each line with a cadence and usually two long notes, with the lower parts providing a harmonic foundation. The madrigal dealt much more freely with the verses, using a variety of homophonic and contrapuntal textures in a series of overlapping sections, each based on a single phrase of the text. Most important, madrigal composers aimed both to match the seriousness, nobility, and artfulness of the poetry and to convey its ideas, images, and passions to their performers and audience.

Text forms and subjects

Madrigal, like *frottola*, was a generic term that included a variety of poetic types: sonnet, ballata, canzone, ottava rima, and poems written expressly to be set as madrigals. Most madrigal texts consisted of a single stanza with a free rhyme scheme and a moderate number of seven- and eleven-syllable (hendecasyllabic) lines. The subject matter was sentimental or erotic, with scenes and allusions borrowed from pastoral poetry. The text usually had an epigrammatic ending that served as a climax in the last line or two.

Social setting

Madrigals were sung in all sorts of aristocratic social gatherings (see, for example, Plate III, facing page 206). In Italy they were often heard at meetings of academies—societies organized to study and discuss literary, scientific, or artistic matters. In these circles the performers were mainly amateurs, but around 1570 princes and other patrons began to employ professional groups of virtuoso singers. Madrigals also appeared in plays and other theatrical productions. The demand for this music was great: counting reprints and new editions, some two thousand collections were published between 1530 and 1600, and its popularity continued well into the seventeenth century.

Voices

Most of the early madrigals, dating from about 1520 to 1550, were set for four voices; after the middle of the century five voices became the rule, and settings for six or more parts were not unusual. The word "voices" should be taken literally: the madrigal was a piece of vocal chamber music intended for performance with one singer to a part. As always in the sixteenth century, however, instruments often doubled the voices or took their place.

Early Madrigal Composers

The leading Italian madrigal composers in the early period were the Franco-Fleming Philippe Verdelot (ca. 1480–1545) and the Italians Bernardo Pisano (1490–1548) and Francesco de Layolle (1492–ca. 1540), all active in Florence, and Verdelot, Pisano, and Costanzo Festa (ca. 1490–1545) in Rome. Festa was one of the few Italian members of the papal chapel in the early sixteenth century and one of the first Italian composers to compete seriously with the emigrants from the north. Venice, another early center, boasted Adrian Willaert and Jacques Arcadelt (ca. 1505–ca. 1568), a northerner who for a time was head of the pope's chapel and after his sojourn in Venice joined the royal chapel in Paris. The earliest madrigals, such as those of Pisano and Festa and the four-voice pieces by Verdelot, resemble the frottola in texture: they are mostly homophonic, with leisurely cadences at line endings. In Verdelot's madrigals we see a transition to the motetlike texture of frequent imitation, varying voice-groupings, and overlapping parts at cadences.

Festa

Verdelot

Arcadelt

Arcadelt's compositions were changing similarly; his *Il bianco e dolce cigno* (The white and sweet swan, NAWM 36; CD 2 [51] / 1 ⟨41⟩), from the mid-1530s, illustrates a transitional style. Its mainly homophonic motion and square rhythms ally it to the chanson and frottola. But the first three lines do not follow the structure of the poem, as was customary in those genres. The first cadence falls in the middle of the second line, and the end of that line runs into the third, observing the verse's enjambment (Example 7.3). Thus the composer not only preserves the syntax and meaning but underscores the word "more" (dies) with a dissonant suspension. At "Et io piangendo" (And I, weeping), he marks the sharp contrast between the swan's song and the lover's tears with an excursion into the E♭-harmony. The juxtaposition of the major triads on *F* and *E*♭, causing a false relation between *A* and *E*♭ (measure 6), be-

Example 7.3 *Jacob Arcadelt, Madrigal:* Il bianco e dolce cigno

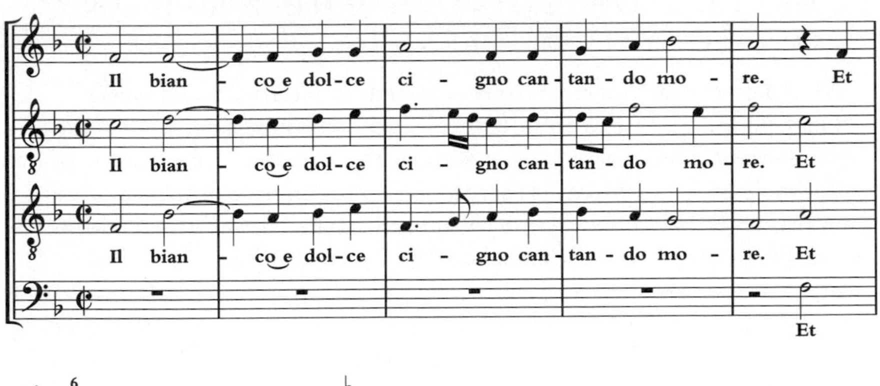

The white and sweet swan
dies singing. And I,
weeping, come to the end of my life.

comes a metaphor for death; this same relation exists in transposition later in the madrigal, between the triads on B♭ and C.

The Petrarchan Movement

Pietro Bembo

The rise of the madrigal was inseparably bound up with the currents of taste in Italian poetry. Led by Cardinal Pietro Bembo (1470–1547), poets, readers, and musicians returned to the sonnets and canzoni of Petrarch (1304–1374) and the ideals embodied in his works. Bembo, himself a poet and critic, was largely responsible for the renewed veneration of this fourteenth-century poet. In editing Petrarch's *Canzoniere* in 1501, Bembo discovered a music of vowels, consonants, and sounding syllables that could inspire composers to imitate these effects in their counterpoint. He noted that Petrarch would often revise the sound of the words without changing the imagery or meaning. Bembo identified two opposing qualities that Petrarch, more interested than other poets in variety of feeling, sought in his verses: *piacevolezza* (pleasingness) and *gravità* (severity). In the pleasing category Bembo included grace, sweetness, charm, smoothness, playfulness, and wit, while in the severe he comprehended modesty, dignity, majesty, magnificence, and grandeur. Rhythm, distance of rhyme, number of syllables per line, patterns of accents, lengths of syllables,

ZARLINO ON SUITING THE HARMONY TO THE WORDS, 1558

When a composer wishes to express harshness, bitterness, and similar things, he will do best to arrange the parts of the composition so that they proceed with movements that are without the semitone, such as those of the whole tone and ditone. He should allow the major sixth and major thirteenth, which by nature are somewhat harsh, to be heard above the lowest note of the concentus, and should use the suspension [*sincopa*] of the fourth or the eleventh above the lowest part, along with somewhat slow movements, among which the suspension of the seventh may also be used. But when a composer wishes to express effects of grief and sorrow, he should (observing the rules given) use movements which proceed through the semitone, the semiditone, and similar intervals, often using minor sixths or minor thirteenths above the lowest note of the composition, these being by nature sweet and soft, especially when combined in the right way and with discretion and judgment.

It should be noted, however, that the cause of the various effects is attributed not only to the consonances named, used in the ways described above, but also the movements which the parts make in singing. These are two sorts, namely, natural and accidental. Natural movements are those made between the natural notes of a composition, where no sign or accidental note intervenes. Accidental movements are those made by means of the accidental notes, which are indicated by the signs ♯ and ♭. The natural movements have more virility than the accidental movements, which are somewhat languid. . . . For this reason the former movements can serve to express effects of harshness and bitterness, and the latter movements can serve for effects of grief and sorrow.

Gioseffo Zarlino, *Le istitutioni harmoniche*, Book III, Chapter 31, trans. Vered Cohen in Zarlino, *On the Modes*, p. 95.

and the sound qualities of the vowels and consonants all contributed to making a verse either pleasing or severe. Composers became sensitive to these sonic values. Many of the early madrigalists turned to Petrarch for their texts; later composers preferred his imitators and other modern poets, almost all of whom worked under Petrarch's shadow.

Madrigal composers favored the sonnet among poetic genres. It suited their objectives because it contained no internal repetition and progressed toward a climax and resolution. Often the first eight lines (the *ottava* or octave) set up a situation, sometimes a conflict, while the last six (the *sestina* or sestet) offered a solution.

Willaert

Willaert's sonnet *Aspro core e selvaggio* (NAWM 37 [CD 2 [53]] and Example 7.4) seemingly grows out of Bembo's theory. Petrarch expressed his beloved Madonna Laura's "harsh and savage heart" in a *grave* line, filled with double consonants and clipped, harsh sounds; he then described her "sweet, humble, angelic face" in a contrasting *piacevole* line made up of liquid, resonant, and sweet sounds. For the first line of his remarkable setting (Example 7.4a), Willaert lingered on the rawer consonances with parallel major thirds and major sixths, favoring melodic motion in whole steps and major thirds. For the second line (Example 7.4b), he chose the sweeter consonances of minor thirds and minor sixths (realized through accidental flats), melodic motion by semitones and minor thirds, and simulated triple time to match Petrarch's deliberate arrangement of accented syllables.

Example 7.4 *Adrian Willaert, Madrigal*: Aspro core e selvaggio

Harsh and savage heart, and a cruel will in a sweet, humble, angelic face

Cipriano de Rore

Cipriano de Rore (1516–1565) was also devoted to the poetry of Petrarch, whose verses he matched with great refinement in imagery, expression, and technique. Flemish by birth, Rore worked in Italy, chiefly in Ferrara and Parma, and briefly succeeded Willaert as music director at St. Mark's in Venice. He became the leading madrigalist of his generation and set the trends that madrigal composers would follow during the second half of the century.

In his madrigal *Da le belle contrade d'oriente* (1566; NAWM 38; CD 2 [58] / 1 ⟨43⟩), Rore imbued every detail of the music with the sense and feeling of Petrarch's sonnet. The texture shifts between homophony and imitation, the temporal organization between triple and duple, the note values between long and short, depending on the immediate text. The expanded range of five voices suits this sonnet particularly well, since it allowed Rore to divide the ensemble into two personae in the second quatrain, when the woman's speech is distinguished from the narrating poet's (Example 7.5). Rore has the two sopranos form a duet, while the other voices accompany or echo them. The woman's first phrase, "Speranza del mio cor" (Hope of my heart), brightly climbs the circle of fifths in major triads; then the line ominously descends in minor chords to a deceptive cadence, after which she exclaims, "T'en vai, haimè! Adio!" (You're leaving me, alas! Farewell!), interrupted by sighs marked by rests and a plaintive chromatic inflection on "lasci!"

Chromaticism

Just as artists of the time were stretching the limits of realistic depiction (see, for example, Plate IV, facing page 207), composers began exploring the chromatic scale—through both half-step motion and excursions out of the mode—partly in order to revive the chromatic and enharmonic genera of Greek music.

Vicentino

The most influential experimenter, Nicola Vicentino, proposed such a revival in his treatise, *L'antica musica ridotta alla moderna prattica* (Ancient Music Adapted to the Modern Practice, 1555). He designed an *arcicembalo* and *arciorgano* to perform music containing half-step and microtonal progressions that were impossible to play on normal keyboard instruments. Many of his contemporaries scoffed at his ideas and his music; nevertheless, a number of his madrigals reach a high level of artistry, among them *L'aura ch'el verde lauro* on a Petrarch sonnet, published in 1572 in his fifth book of madrigals. At one point he incorporated the Greek chromatic tetrachord, descending a minor third and two semitones, as a motive for imitation (see Example 7.6, page 190, at "soavemente").

Chromatic notation

Chromaticism of this kind has nothing to do with "chromatic notation," which came into fashion around the middle of the sixteenth century and was simply writing music in $\frac{4}{4}$ time (signature C), instead of in the older ¢ *alla breve* or one breve to the measure. The change resulted in the use of shorter notes (for example, ♩ to signify about the same duration that the 𝅗𝅥 had formerly signified). The large number of black notes appearing on the page gave the notation its

Example 7.5 *Cipriano de Rore, Madrigal*: Da le belle contrade d'oriente

When I heard after a burning sigh:
"Hope of my heart, sweet desire,
you're leaving me, alas, all alone! Farewell!"

Example 7.6 *Nicola Vicentino, Madrigal*: L'aura ch'el verde lauro

[*The breeze, which the green laurel and the aurous hair*] *softly sighing moves.*

name "chromatic"—that is, "colored," or "*a note nere*" (in black notes). The possibility of using black note heads allowed composers to set words such as "dark," "night," and "blind" in blackened note forms. Often this practice made no difference in the actual sound but was merely a bit of "eye music" to be appreciated by the singers looking at the page. As this point illustrates, madrigals of the period were written and sung mostly for the enjoyment of the performers rather than for an audience: they were, in a word, social music and not concert pieces.

Later Madrigalists

Among the many northern composers who wrote madrigals after the middle of the century, Orlando di Lasso, Philippe de Monte, and Giaches de Wert made important contributions to the genre. Orlando di Lasso (1532–1594) is most important as a church composer, but his was a universal genius equally at

Lasso

Monte

home with the madrigal, the chanson, and the lied. Like Lasso, Philippe de Monte (1521–1603) was enormously productive in both sacred and secular domains. He began writing madrigals while a young man in Italy and continued uninterrupted through his many years of service under the Habsburg emperors in Vienna and Prague, publishing thirty-two collections of secular madrigals and several books of *madrigali spirituali.* Giaches de Wert (1535–1596), although born near Antwerp, spent nearly his entire life in Italy; he continued to develop the kind of madrigal composition begun by Rore. His late style, full of bold leaps, recitative-like declamation, and extravagant contrasts, exercised marked influence on Monteverdi. The leading madrigalists toward the end of the century were native Italians.

Wert

Marenzio

Luca Marenzio (1553–1599) depicted contrasting feelings and visual details with the utmost artistry and virtuosity. Like other madrigal composers of the late sixteenth century, Marenzio favored pastoral poetry. One of his most celebrated madrigals is *Solo e pensoso* on Petrarch's sonnet (NAWM 39; CD 3 [1]). The image of the pensive poet measuring his steps in a deserted field is rendered by a slow chromatic scale in the topmost voice rising an octave, half-step per measure, while the other parts form a background of expressively drooping figures.

Women's vocal ensembles

The formation of chamber concerti or ensembles of professional or semiprofessional singers encouraged composers to write music that demanded accurate delivery of florid runs, trills, and turns, and a variety of attacks, dynamics, and vocal color. In 1580 Duke Alfonso d'Este of Ferrara established the most famous of these ensembles—the *concerto delle donne* (women's ensemble)—a group of trained singers (Laura Peverara, Anna Guarini, and Livia d'Arco) who were appointed as ladies-in-waiting to his music-loving wife, Margherita Gonzaga. Their performances at court, frequently together with professional male singers, attracted so much attention and praise that the Gonzagas of Mantua and the Medici of Florence formed ensembles to rival that of Ferrara (see vignette, page 192). Ferrara had a tradition of women's singing groups before 1580, but the groups' members were, rather than trained singers, daughters and wives of the nobility, among them Lucrezia and Isabella Bendidio, Leonora Sanvitale di Scandiano, and Vittoria Bentivoglio. Giaches de Wert and Claudio Monteverdi destined many of their madrigals, especially those with florid upper parts, for the ensembles of Mantua, and Luzzasco Luzzaschi and Carlo Gesualdo, for those of Ferrara.

Carlo Gesualdo

Carlo Gesualdo, prince of Venosa (ca. 1561–1613), was a picturesque character whose fame as a murderer preceded his reputation as a composer. In 1586 he married his cousin Maria d'Avalos, who soon took a lover, the duke of Andria. Discovered *in flagrante delicto* by her husband, she and the duke were murdered on the spot. Gesualdo survived the scandal to marry Leonora d'Este, the niece of Duke Alfonso II of Ferrara, in 1593. In Ferrara, Gesualdo came under the influence of the madrigalist Luzzasco Luzzaschi (1545–1607), who was accus-

VINCENZO GIUSTINIANI ON THE WOMEN'S VOCAL ENSEMBLES OF FERRARA AND MANTUA

The dukes of Ferrara and Mantua took extreme delight in music, especially in having numerous women and the leading ladies [of the court] appear singing and playing excellently. They spent sometimes entire days in little sitting rooms elegantly decorated for this purpose with pictures and art works. There was much rivalry between the women of Mantua and of Ferrara, who competed not only in the timbre and natural quality of their voices but in aptly introducing exquisite runs [*passaggi*], yet not excessively (as the falsetto Giovanni Luca [Conforti?] of Rome, who also served in Ferrara, was guilty of doing). They moderated or increased the voice—forte or piano—making it thinner or ampler, and, as the occasion demanded, sustaining the voice, cutting it off with a gentle sigh, or drawing out long, smoothly flowing, clearly articulated passages of embellishment, turns [*groppi*] and trills [*trilli*], both long and short. Sometimes they sang the passages sweetly and softly, at other times echoes were suddenly heard answering. They accompanied the music and the text with appropriate glances and gestures, though without unbecoming movements of the body, lips, or hands that did not contribute to the success of the performance. They articulated the words in such a way that you could hear the very last syllable of every word when it was not interrupted or smothered by passages of embellishment or other ornaments. They sang with many other artful manners and subtleties that would be detected by those more experienced than I.

Vincenzo Giustiniani, *Discorso sopra la musica de' suoi tempi* (Discourse Concerning the Music of His Time), ed. in Angelo Solerti, *Le origini del melodramma* (Turin: Fratelli Bocca, 1903), pp. 107–08.

tomed to improvising on Vicentino's chromatic-enharmonic arcicembalo and on a specially built enharmonic organ. Gesualdo's chromaticism was no mere affectation of antiquity but a deeply moving response to the text, as we may observe in the madrigal *"Io parto" e non più dissi* (NAWM 40; CD 3 [6]). For the lover's exclamation "Dunque ai dolori resto" (Hence I remain in suffering; Example 7.7), Gesualdo combined melodic half-step motion with ambiguous successions of chords whose roots are a third apart. He fragmented the poetic line, yet achieved continuity by avoiding conventional cadences. Despite the departures from the diatonic system, he emphasized the main steps of the mode on *E* at key points, such as rhythmic breaks and beginnings and ends of lines.

Gesualdo's chromaticism

Claudio Monteverdi

The madrigal had a special place in the career of Claudio Monteverdi, whose compositions made the crucial stylistic transition in this genre—from the polyphonic vocal ensemble to the instrumentally accompanied solo and duet.

Example 7.7 *Carlo Gesualdo, Madrigal*: "Io parto" e non più dissi

Hence I remain in suffering. May I not cease [to languish in painful laments.]

Born in Cremona in 1567, Monteverdi received his earliest training there from Marc' Antonio Ingegneri, who directed the music in the cathedral. In 1590, Monteverdi entered the service of Vincenzo Gonzaga, duke of Mantua, and twelve years later rose to master of the ducal chapel. From 1613 until his death in 1643, he was choirmaster at St. Mark's in Venice.

Madrigals

Monteverdi's first five books of madrigals, published between 1587 and 1605, are monuments in the history of the polyphonic madrigal. Without going to such extremes as Gesualdo, Monteverdi demonstrated remarkable expressive power through his smooth combination of homophonic and contrapuntal part-writing, his faithful reflection of the text, and his free use of chromaticism and dissonances. But certain features—hinted at in the music of his contemporaries—indicate that Monteverdi was moving swiftly and with remarkable assurance toward a new idiom. For example, many of the musical motives are not melodic but declamatory, in the manner of the later recitative; the texture often departs from the medium of equal voices and becomes a duet over a harmonically supporting bass; and ornamental dissonances and embellishments that previously would have occurred only in improvisation are written into the score.

Cruda Amarilli

Cruda Amarilli (NAWM 53; CD 3 [59] / 2 ⟨13⟩) exemplifies the flexible, animated, evocative, and variegated style of Monteverdi's polyphonic madrigals. It is rich in musical invention, humorous yet sensitive, and audacious yet perfectly logical in its harmonic progress. (See more detailed discussion below, pages 254–55).

Other Italian Secular Vocal Genres

Villanella

Lighter kinds of part-song were also cultivated in Italy during the sixteenth century. The most important, the *canzon villanesca* (peasant song), or *villanella,* first appeared in the 1540s and flourished chiefly in the Neapolitan area. Composers often deliberately used parallel fifths in the three-voice villanella, a lively little strophic piece in homophonic style. Such harmonic crudities emphasized its rustic character and sometimes deliberately mocked the correct, more sophisticated madrigals. The same Italians and northerners who composed serious madrigals entertained sophisticated audiences with these trifling songs. In the course of time, the villanella grew to resemble the madrigal so much that it lost its identity.

Canzonetta and balletto

Toward the end of the sixteenth century, two other light genres gained prominence: the *canzonetta* (little song) and the *balletto.* They were written in a neat, vivacious, homophonic style, with clear and distinct harmonies and evenly phrased sections that were often repeated. Balletti, as the name suggests, were intended for dancing as well as singing or playing and are identifiable by their "fa–la–la" refrains. The leading composer of canzonette and balletti was Giacomo Gastoldi (d. 1622). Both genres—and even individual works—were imitated by German and English composers.

SECULAR SONG OUTSIDE ITALY

France

French composers of the early sixteenth century continued to write Masses and motets in a modified version of the prevailing style. But during the long reign of Francis I (1515–47), composers working in and around Paris developed a type of chanson, often called the "Parisian chanson," that was more distinctively national in both poetry and music. Between 1528 and 1552, Pierre Attaingnant (ca. 1494–ca. 1551), the first French music printer, brought out more than fifty collections of such chansons, about 1,500 pieces altogether, and other publishers soon followed his lead. Hundreds of transcriptions for the lute and arrangements for voice and lute published during the sixteenth century in both France and Italy attest to the popularity of the chanson.

Attaingnant

"Parisian chanson"

The typical Parisian chanson of the earliest Attaingnant collections resembled the Italian frottola, *canto carnascialesco,* and early madrigal. It was a light,

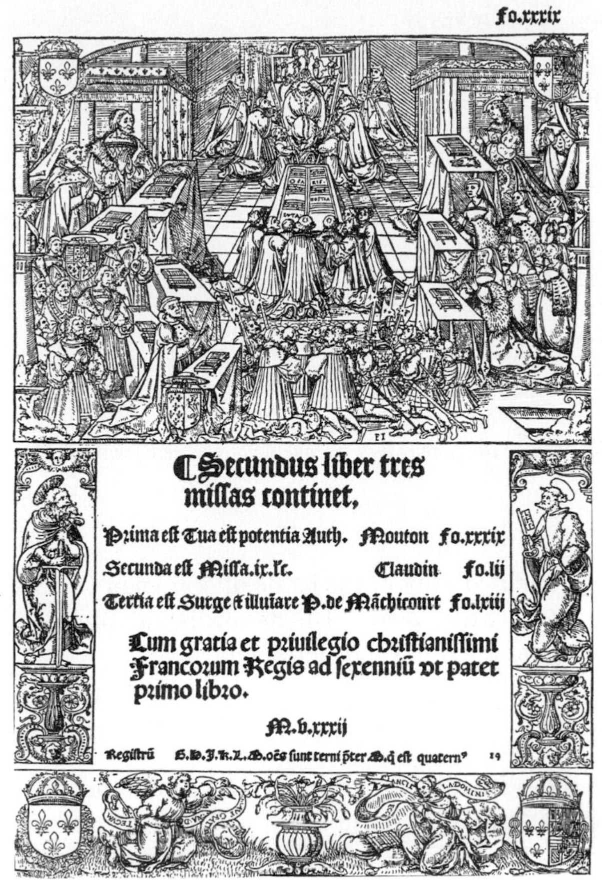

■ *Title page of the second of seven volumes of Masses published by Pierre Attaingnant (Paris, 1532). This volume contained Masses by Mouton, Claudin de Sermisy, and Pierre de Manchicourt. The singers (center) are reading plainchant from a large choirbook.*

fast, strongly rhythmic song for four voices. The text, in any number of verse forms, was set syllabically with many repeated notes, mostly in duple meter. Favored subjects were situations that allowed for double meanings, although serious texts were occasionally chosen. The texture of the music, largely homophonic with short points of imitation, had the principal melody in the highest voice. The piece was divided into distinct short sections, repeated to form an easily grasped pattern, such as a a b c or a b c a.

Sermisy

Tant que vivray by Claudin de Sermisy (ca. 1490–1562) illustrates some of these traits (see Example 7.8; for the entire song, see NAWM 41; CD 3 [9] / 1 ⟨46⟩). As in a frottola, the melody is in the top voice, and the harmony consists of thirds and fifths with only an occasional sixth. Instead of syncopation at the cadence, the note that becomes a dissonance—for example, the *c′* in measure 3—coincides with the downbeat, giving an "appoggiatura" effect. The end of each line of text corresponds with a relatively long note or with repeated notes, thereby emphasizing the form of the poetry.

Janequin

The two principal chanson composers represented in the first Attaingnant collections were Sermisy and Clément Janequin (ca. 1485–ca. 1560). Janequin was particularly celebrated for his descriptive chansons, which featured imitations of bird calls, hunting calls, street cries, and sounds of war. His most

Example 7.8 *Claudin de Sermisy,* Tant que vivray

As long as I am able bodied, I shall serve the potent king of love through deeds, words, songs, and harmonies.

famous chanson, *La Guerre,* supposedly about the battle of Marignan (1515), foreshadowed innumerable later "battle" pieces. The decidedly humorous *Le Chant des oiseaux*[4] is filled with vocal warbles and chirping.

The Later Franco-Flemish Chanson

Besides Attaingnant and his colleagues in Paris, the principal chanson publishers of the 1530s to 1550s were Jacques Moderne in Lyons and Tilman Susato in Antwerp. Susato focused on Franco-Flemish composers, such as Gombert, Clemens, Pierre de Manchicourt (d. 1564), and Thomas Crecquillon (d. 1557). Their chansons were more contrapuntal than their Parisian counterparts, and had fuller texture, more melismatic lines, and a less marked rhythmic beat. While these composers were influenced by the French trend toward homophony, they were, in fact, maintaining the older chanson tradition.

As the chanson continued to flourish in the second half of the sixteenth century, the polyphonic tradition remained alive longest in the north, as reflected in the 1594 and 1612 chanson collections by the Dutch composer Jan Pieterszoon Sweelinck (1562–1621). In France, however, the tradition was modified by a lively interest in the Italian madrigal, whose influence appears in the works of Orlando di Lasso. Lasso's powerful musical personality impressed itself on the chanson as it did on every other type of vocal composition. Many of Lasso's chansons with French texts are written in a tight polyphonic texture with close imitations and sudden changes of pace in tense but humorous settings. Others are in the homophonic style of the Parisian chanson, with varied rhythms that seem to spring spontaneously from each nuance and accent in the text.

Lasso

4. Ed. in Clément Janequin, *Chansons polyphoniques,* ed. A. Tillman Merritt and François Lesure, 1 (Monaco: Éditions de l'Oiseau-Lyre, 1965):5–22.

Musique mesurée

The treatment of rhythm in a number of the homophonic chansons reflects the ideas of a group of poets and composers who formed an Académie de Poésie et de Musique (Academy of Poetry and Music) in 1570. The poet Jean-Antoine de Baïf wrote strophic French verses in ancient Greek and Latin meters (*vers mesurés à l'antique*), using the classical long and short syllables instead of the modern stress accent. Since French lacked any consistent distinction between long and short vowels, the theorists of *vers mesuré* assigned them durations, and composers set them accordingly. Claude Le Jeune (1528–1600), who was the leading exponent of this genre, gave a long note to each long syllable and a note half as long to each short syllable. The variety of verse patterns produce a corresponding variety of musical rhythms in which duple and triple groupings alternate freely, as in Le Jeune's *Revecy venir du printans* (NAWM 42; CD 3 [11]).

Le Jeune

This *musique mesurée* (measured music), as it was called, was too artificial to endure for long, but it did introduce irregular meters into the *air de cour*, the dominant French vocal music after about 1580.

Germany

Secular polyphony developed later in Germany than in the rest of Europe. The monophonic art of the Minnesinger flourished at German courts through the 1300s and that of the Meistersinger in cities and towns from about 1450 and throughout the 1500s. Franco-Flemish music made its appearance in Germany about 1530.

The Lied

With the rise of a prosperous merchant class in the cities came a distinctive type of German polyphonic *Lied* (song). The *Lochamer Liederbuch* (Locheim Songbook) of 1455–60, one of the earliest collections of German polyphonic songs, contains both monophonic melodies and three-part settings in which the tenor has the leading melody. Similar three-part settings appear in the *Glogauer Liederbuch* (Glogau [now Glogáw] Songbook) from around 1480, but with the melody sometimes in the highest voice.

Lied composers skillfully blended traditional German songs with Franco-Flemish contrapuntal technique. The first true masters of the polyphonic lied were Isaac and his contemporaries Heinrich Finck (1445–1527) and Paul Hofhaimer (1459–1537), court organist of Emperor Maximilian. With Ludwig Senfl (ca. 1486–1542 or 43), who served chiefly at the Bavarian court of Munich, the lied became a highly artful genre. Their German text notwithstanding, his lieder are not only full-fledged motets of the northern type but exquisite examples of that genre.[5] Senfl also wrote many shorter songs on folk-

Senfl

5. See, for example, Nos. 32 and 48 in his *Sämtliche Werke*, Bd. 2 (ed. A. Geering and A. Altwegg).

like tenor tunes; though filled with picturesque or witty touches, they exhibit a certain earthy, serious quality.

Collections of German lieder continued to be published during the first half of the sixteenth century, chiefly at Nuremberg, a leading center of German culture at this time. After 1550, when German taste veered toward Italian madrigals and villanelle, the lied declined in importance or took on Italianate characteristics. Until then, however, it had provided a musical model and a great deal of musical material for Lutheran church chorales.

Major Composers

Lasso

Chief among the Franco-Flemish composers in Germany was Orlando di Lasso (1532–1594), who entered the service of Duke Albrecht V of Bavaria in 1556 or 1557 (see Plate V, facing page 238). He became head of the ducal chapel in Munich and remained in that post from 1560 until his death in 1594. Among the vast number of Lasso's compositions were seven collections of German lieder. *Ich armer Mann* has somewhat uncouth verses that Lasso matched with suitably raucous music (see Example 7.9). Instead of surrounding a familiar tune in the tenor with a web of counterpoint, he set the text in the manner of a madrigal, with all parts equally important in the interplay of motives and with bits of imitation, echoes, and mock-pathetic melismas at the phrase "muss ich im hader stahn" (I must always be bickering).

Hassler

Hans Leo Hassler (1564–1612), the greatest German composer of the late sixteenth century, united Italian suavity with German seriousness. Born in Nuremberg, Hassler studied in 1584 with Andrea Gabrieli in Venice. From 1585 until his death he held various positions at Augsburg, Nuremberg, Ulm, and Dresden. His works include pieces for instrumental ensemble and keyboard, canzonets and madrigals with Italian texts, German lieder, Latin motets and Masses, and settings of Lutheran chorales. In his lieder *Ach Schatz* and *Ach, süsse Seel'*,[6] we can see his polished melodic lines, sure harmonic structure, and clearly articulated form with its varied repetitions and balanced echoing of motives.

Spain

By the late fifteenth century, the works of Burgundian and Franco-Flemish composers were known and sung in Spain, while a national school of polyphonic composition was also growing. Like their German counterparts, Spanish composers incorporated some popular elements and held out for a long time against foreign influences. The principal genre of secular polyphony, the

Villancico

villancico, may be regarded as the Spanish equivalent of the Italian frottola. A short strophic song with a refrain, typically in the pattern aBccaB, the villancico had the principal melody in the top voice, which was probably performed by a soloist accompanied by two or three instruments. Villancicos were col-

6. See HAM No. 165 for *Ach Schatz*, and GMB No. 152 for *Ach, süsse Seel'*.

Example 7.9 *Orlando di Lasso, Lied*: Ich armer Mann

I, poor man, what have I done? I have taken a wife. [*It would be better if I had never done it; how often I have rued it you may well imagine:*] *all day long I am being scolded and nagged* [*at bedtime and at table*].

lected in *cancioneros* (songbooks) and many were also published for solo voice with lute. The principal poet and composer of the early sixteenth century was Juan del Encina (1469–1529), whose pastoral plays usually ended with a villancico.

Eastern Europe

Late medieval and Renaissance music in the eastern countries reflected musical developments in western Europe. The Catholic church music of the two areas had a common basis in Western chant, examples of which appear in eastern European manuscripts from the eleventh century on. Foreign elements mixed with native popular traditions; for example, composers adapted vernacular texts to melodies of sequences, tropes, and liturgical dramas. Influences came from western European composers serving at eastern European royal courts, and from local musicians trained in Germany, France, or Italy. Franco-Flemish music was known in Bohemia during the reign of the Holy Roman Emperor Charles IV (1347–78), and the earliest examples of Polish polyphony date from the thirteenth century. Nicholas of Radom (Mikołaj z Radomia; fl. 1420–40), motet composer and court harpsichordist at Cracow, was among the first to use the term "faux bourdon" (actually, the Latin *per bordunum*) as an instruction to singers. By the sixteenth century, Polish and Bohemian composers were writing chansons, Masses, and motets as well as music for lute, organ, and instrumental ensembles. Polish organ tablatures are particularly important during this period. The leading eastern European composers of Catholic church music were Wacław of Szamotuł (ca. 1520–ca. 1567) in Poland and the Slovenian Jacob Handl (1550–1591), also known as Jacobus Gallus, in Bohemia.

Bohemia and Poland

The English Madrigal

Musica transalpina

The golden age of secular part-song came to England later than it did in the Continental countries. In 1588, Nicholas Yonge published *Musica transalpina*, a collection of Italian madrigals translated into English. According to Yonge's preface, many of these works were already part of the singing repertory of gentlemen and merchants who met daily at his home. This anthology and others that appeared in the next decade gave impetus to a period of English madrigal composition that flourished from the 1590s to the 1630s. Leading figures were Thomas Morley (1557–1602), Thomas Weelkes (ca. 1575–1623), and John Wilbye (1574—1638).

Morley

Morley, the earliest and most prolific of the three, wrote light madrigals as well as *balletts* and *canzonets*. His balletts were modeled on the Italian balletti, especially those by Gastoldi. Mainly homophonic with the tune in the topmost voice, they are written in dancelike meters (as the name suggests). Full cadences mark off distinct sections, which repeat in formal patterns such as AABB or the like. A refrain was often sung to the syllables *fa–la*, so the pieces were sometimes called *fa–las*.

Weelkes

The presence of the syllables "fa–la" in a madrigal sometimes disguises its serious message, as in *O Care, thou wilt despatch me* (NAWM 43; CD 3 [20] / 1 ⟨48⟩) by Weelkes. Particularly notable is the opening (Example 7.10), with its learned imitations in direct and contrary motion, and a chain of suspensions (including a diminished seventh in measure 3) to convey the poet's complaint. Weelkes evaded a resolution of this series of dissonances by turning away from the major triad on *G* (measure 7): the soprano moves to make a minor sixth

Example 7.10 *Thomas Weelkes, Madrigal*: O Care, thou wilt despatch me

with the bass, causing a diminished fourth with the tenor. He intensified the subsequent chain of suspensions by preparing two dissonances with a fourth. Weelkes's harmony is as intense and wry as Marenzio's or Gesualdo's, but its overall effect is one of liquid vocality and broadly sweeping momentum. He achieved a smooth progression to the gleeful fa–las by introducing their music as early as the second line, producing the pattern ABBCDD.

Triumphes of Oriana

In 1601, Thomas Morley published a collection of twenty-five madrigals by different composers modeled after a similar Italian anthology called *Il trionfo di Dori* (1592). He called his *The Triumphes of Oriana* in honor of Queen Elizabeth I (reigned 1558–1603). Each madrigal in Morley's collection ends with the words "Long live fair Oriana," a name from the conventional vocabulary of pastoral poetry often applied to Elizabeth. These works combine expressive and pictorial traits in the music with accurate, nimble declamation of the English texts. The accents of the words are maintained independently in each voice (the original had no barlines), so that the ensembles produce sparkling counterpoints of continuous rhythmic vitality. But even with great sharpness of detail, the long line of the music is never obscured. The collection highlights one of the important ways in which the English madrigal

THOMAS MORLEY ON THE MADRIGAL AS A GENRE

The light music hath been of late more deeply dived into so that there is no vanity which in it hath not been followed to the full; but the best kind of it is termed Madrigal, a word for the etymology of which I can give no reason; yet use showeth that it is a kind of music made upon songs and sonnets such as Petrarch and many poets of our time have excelled in. This kind of music were not so much disallowable if the poets who compose the ditties would abstain from some obscenities which all honest ears abhor, and sometime from blasphemies to such as this, "ch'altro di te iddio non voglio" [I wish no other god but thee], which no man (at least who hath any hope of salvation) can sing without trembling. As for the music it is, next unto the Motet, the most artificial and, to men of understanding, most delightful. If therefore you will compose in this kind you must possess yourself with an amorous humour (for in no composition shall you prove admirable except you put on and possess yourself wholly with that vein wherein you compose), so that you must in your music be wavering like the wind, sometime wanton, sometime drooping, sometime grave and staid, otherwhile effeminate; you may maintain points and revert them, use Triplas, and show the very uttermost of your variety, and the more variety you show the better shall you please. In this kind our age excelleth, so that if you would imitate any I would appoint you these for guides: Alfonso Ferrabosco for deep skill, Luca Marenzio for good air and fine invention, Horatio Vecchi, Stephano Venturi, Ruggiero Giovanelli, and John Croce, with divers others who are very good but not generally good as these.

From *A Plain and Easy Introduction to Practical Music*, ed. R. Alec Harman (New York: Norton, 1973), p. 294.

differed from its Italian prototype: the overall musical structure received greater attention.

Madrigals, balletts, and canzonets were all written primarily for ensembles of unaccompanied solo voices, though many of the printed collections of partbooks indicate on the title page that the music is "apt for voices and viols," presumably in any available combination. This flexibility made these publications ideal for amateurs. Ability to read a vocal or instrumental part in such pieces was expected of educated persons in Elizabethan England.

English Lute Songs

The solo song with lute and viol accompaniment, which had flourished on the Continent for nearly a century, became popular in England with the decline of the madrigal during the early 1600s. The leading composers of lute songs were John Dowland (1562–1626) and Thomas Campion (1567–1620). The poetry of the English airs is considerably better than that of the madrigals. The

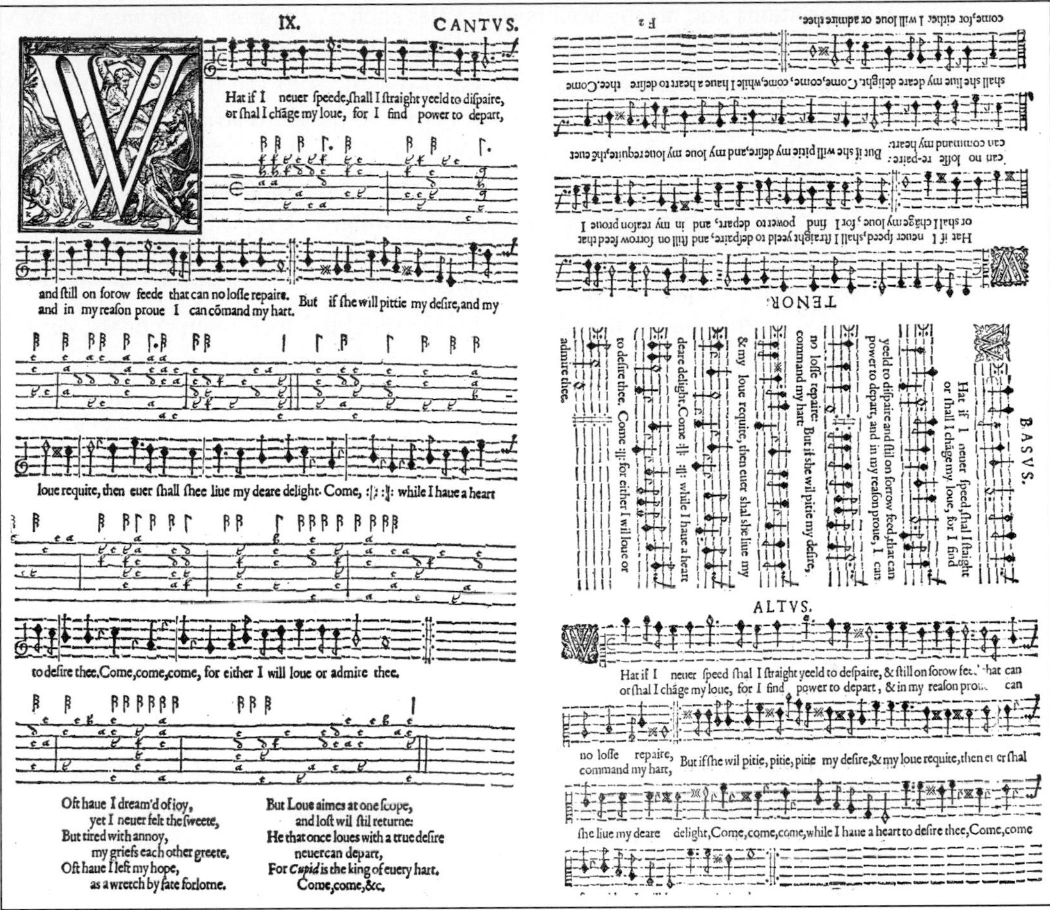

■ *John Dowland's song* What if I never speede, *as printed in his* Third and Last Book of Songs or Aires . . . *(London, 1603), may be performed either as a soprano solo with lute accompaniment or as a four-part arrangement, with or without lute accompaniment. The parts are so arranged that singers around a table can read from a single book.* (LONDON, BRITISH LIBRARY. BY PERMISSION OF THE BRITISH LIBRARY)

melodies, especially those of Dowland, are remarkable for their subtlety and their sensitive text declamation. The lute accompaniments, always carefully subordinated to the voice, have a certain rhythmic and melodic independence. The voice and lute parts are usually printed on the same page in vertical alignment, allowing singers to accompany themselves. In some collections the songs are also printed in an alternative version, with the lute part written out for three voices so arranged on the page that performers sitting around a table could all read their parts from the same book (see illustration above). These vocal and instrumental versions rarely differ except in slight details. The alternative four-part version, which sometimes resembled a madrigal, could be performed with either voices or instruments or both.

Dowland

The Dowland air best known to Elizabethans, *Flow, my tears* (NAWM 44; CD 3 [24] / 1 ⟨52⟩) from his *Second Booke of Ayres* of 1600, spawned a whole series of variations and arrangements with titles such as *Pavana Lachrymae* (NAWM 46; CD 3 [29] / 2 ⟨1⟩). Its form is a compromise between strophic and through-composed: a performer sang the first two stanzas to the first strain, the next two to the second, and the final stanza twice to the third strain, resulting in the musical pattern aabbCC. This duplicates the pattern of the *pavane*, a sixteenth-century Italian processional dance, which suggests that Dowland's piece may have been conceived as a dance-song. The repeats prevent any concrete expression of individual words and phrases, but Dowland captured the dark mood that pervades all five stanzas.

While the madrigal and the air were indebted to foreign models, *consort songs* came out of a native English tradition of singing solos or duets to a consort (ensemble) of viols. William Byrd (1543–1623) raised the technical level of this medium with skillful imitative counterpoint in his collection *Psalmes, Sonets and Songs* (1588).

Summary

Vocal polyphony

The generation of Heinrich Isaac and Josquin des Prez reached a height of technical perfection in the a cappella medium. Glareanus called Josquin's music an *ars perfecta*, "a perfect art, to which nothing can be added, so that nothing can be expected after it but the deterioration of old age."[7] Northern composers, such as Gombert, Clemens, Mouton, and Senfl, consolidated that technique. Two other northerners, Willaert and Arcadelt in Italy, did likewise, but the spirit of humanism drove them to seek a closer rapport between music and text. In both his sacred and secular compositions, Willaert made the music follow the syntax and rhythms of the Latin and Italian language and in his secular works went beyond this to represent musically the essence of a text's message. Still he remained faithful to the inherited ideal of modal, diatonic counterpoint, equality and independence of voices, full harmony, controlled dissonance, and clarity of form.

Music and text

Willaert's pupils and their contemporaries—Vicentino, Rore, and Lasso, for example—continued to seek a close bond between music and text, but they tilted the balance, at least in the madrigal, toward the expression of a poem's varied feelings and images, losing a certain cohesion and homogeneity of style. The homophony of Italian popular songs and of the courtly frottola invaded the imitative texture, making the text ever more declamatory. During the last decades of the century, composers found new ways to express intense passions and the conceits of modern poetry. Gesualdo explored chromaticism, while Monteverdi experimented with dissonance and with new textures and rhythms. A number of English composers enthusiastically took up the new Italian trends, but the most characteristic genre to emerge from the widespread cultivation of vocal chamber music in the British Isles was the lute song and consort song.

The chanson

The societal and cultural changes that led to the development of the madrigal in Italy transformed the French chanson and the German part-song.

7. Glareanus, *Dodekachordon* (Basel, 1547), p. 241.

In Paris, composers turned from serious, motetlike polyphony to a light, tuneful, treble-dominated song. Elsewhere they mostly preferred the older type of chanson. Toward the end of the century, humanism reshaped the chanson, but not in the same way it had changed the madrigal. The promoters of the *vers mesurés á l'antique* thought they could recover the fabled powers of ancient Greek music by wedding the neglected classical quantitative meters to the French language. Composers, notably Le Jeune, realized some success in setting these meters to a *musique mesurée* according to the strict rules of syllabic quantity.

INSTRUMENTAL MUSIC OF THE SIXTEENTH CENTURY

The Rise of Instrumental Music

During the hundred years between 1450 and 1550, distinct styles, genres, and forms of instrumental music emerged. Independent instrumental music existed earlier, of course, in the form of dances, fanfares, and the like, but since performers played from memory or improvised, the music has not survived. Much of the early written instrumental music that is extant consists of transcriptions for keyboard. Medieval manuscripts, such as the Robertsbridge and

Holy Roman Emperor Maximilian I (reigned 1486–1519), surrounded by his musicians. Among the instruments are pipe organ, harp, spinet, drums, kettledrum, lute, sackbut, flute, cromorne, recorders, viol, and marine trumpet. Woodcut by Hans Burkmair (1473–1531).

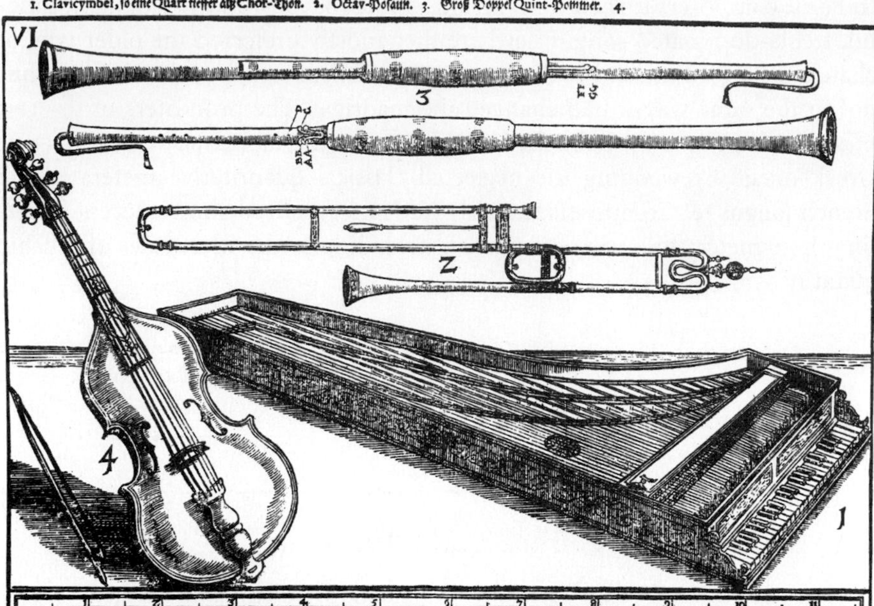

■ *Instruments illustrated in Michael Praetorius,* Syntagma musicum, *Vol. 2 (Wolfenbüttel, 1620): 1) harpsichord, 2) trombone, 3) pommer, 4) bass viola da gamba.*

Faenza codices, which include keyboard arrangements and elaborations of cantilenas and motets, undoubtedly represent only a fraction of the music that was transcribed in this way. Moreover, a great deal of music written for voices was often performed instrumentally, and instruments had participated with voices in the performance of polyphonic music since the Middle Ages.

So the seeming increase in instrumental music after 1450 is an illusion: it simply means that more of it was being written down. Even so, the manuscripts and prints preserve only a small portion of the instrumental music of the Renaissance, and at that, only approximately because performers usually elaborated by improvising embellishments.

Books on Instruments

Publications that describe instruments or give instructions for playing them manifest the sixteenth century's growing regard for instrumental music. From these books we learn about the problems of pitch, temperament, and tuning, and about the art of embellishing a melodic line. The first such publication was Sebastian Virdung's *Musica getutscht und ausgezogen* (A Summary of the Science of Music in German, 1511). Others followed in increasing numbers throughout the century. Most of these books addressed the practicing musician, so they were written in the vernacular instead of Latin. One of the richest, the second volume of *Syntagma musicum* (A Systematic Treatise of Music, 1618) by Michael Praetorius (ca. 1571–1621), contains descriptions and woodcuts of the instruments then in use. From the illustrations of an extraordinary

Praetorius's *Syntagma musicum*

III. *A vocal quartet reading from partbooks. The rich costumes suggest that these are aristocratic amateurs performing for their own pleasure in the privacy of an idyllic island. Detail from an anonymous sixteenth-century painting.* (BOURGES, MUSÉE DE BERRY)

IV. *Iacopo Carrucci, called Pontormo (1494–1557), painted this altarpiece in the 1520s for the chapel of Lodovico Capponi in the Church of S. Felicità in Florence. The subject is the entombment of Christ after his deposition from the cross. There is no trace of the cross or any objects to situate the scene in real space except the hard ground and one cloud. Even identifiable characters are lacking. The sweeping curves guide the viewer to the individual faces, red-eyed from crying, expressing inconsolable desolation, except for the face of Christ, at peace with heaven and earth. Pontormo has been called a mannerist because the convoluted patterns of energetic gestures sacrificed Renaissance realism and equilibrium for exaggeration and dynamism, here restrained by grief.* (FLORENCE, S. FELICITÀ CAPPONI CHAPEL / ART RESOURCE, NEW YORK)

number and variety of wind instruments we learn that instruments were built in sets or families, so that one uniform timbre was available throughout the entire range from soprano to bass. A complete set, usually called a "chest" or "consort"—of viols or recorders, for example—consisted of four to seven instruments.

Wind instruments

Besides recorders, the principal wind instruments were shawms (double-reed forerunners of the oboe); the capped-reed instruments, such as the krummhorn, kortholt, and rauschpfeife; transverse flutes, and cornetts (made of wood or ivory, with cup-shaped mouthpieces); trumpets; and sackbuts (ancestors of the modern trombones). Most of the winds had a softer sound than their modern counterparts.

Viols

The viols differed in many details of construction from the present-day violin family of bowed instruments: the neck was fretted, there were six strings tuned a fourth apart with a major third in the middle (as *A–d–g–b–e′–a′*), and the tone, played without vibrato, was more delicate, finer, and less taut. The player held the instrument on or between the legs, so it was called a *viola da gamba* (leg viol). Another type of viol, the *viola da braccio* (arm viol), was used for accompanying and was played on the arm.

Organ

The organ had a full-bodied sound that covered a broad range with a uniform sonority. The tone of the organ changed over time with the addition of solo and other stops that could be combined with the principals and mixtures of the medieval instrument. By about 1500, the large church organ was similar in essentials to the instrument we know today, although the pedal keyboard was employed in Germany and the Low Countries long before it was adopted elsewhere. The medieval portative organ had gone out of fashion, but small positive organs (without pedals), including the regal, had reed pipes of a quietly strident tone.

Clavichord and harpsichord

Two types of stringed keyboard instruments held sway, the clavichord and the harpsichord. In the clavichord, a metal tangent struck the string and remained in contact with it; the tone was very soft, but within narrow limits the performer could control the volume and could even effect a vibrato. Instruments of the harpsichord type used a quill to pluck the string. They came in different shapes and sizes and had various names—virginal, spinet, clavecin, and clavicembalo, among others. Its tone, more robust than the clavichord's, could not be shaded by varying the pressure on the key. A builder could achieve different timbres and degrees of loudness by adding a second manual or a stop mechanism, which allowed coupling with another string, usually tuned an octave higher. The clavichord was essentially a solo instrument suitable for small rooms. The harpsichord served both solo and ensemble playing in spaces of moderate size.

The Lute

By far the most popular household solo instrument of the Renaissance was the lute. Lutes had been known in Europe for more than five hundred years.

Before the end of the sixteenth century they were being built in various sizes, often made of costly materials and with exquisite workmanship. Except for the *vihuela de mano*, a Spanish type of lute with a guitarlike body, the standard instrument was pear-shaped. It had one single and five double strings, tuned *G–c–f–a–d′–g′*, which were plucked with the fingers. Frets—strips of leather wound around the neck—marked where the player stopped the string. The pegbox was turned back at a right angle. Chords, melodies, runs, and ornaments of all kinds, eventually even contrapuntal pieces, were performed on the lute, and a skilled player could produce a great variety of effects. Lutenists performed solos, accompanied singing, and played in ensembles. *Tablature*, a special kind of notation developed for the lute, showed not the pitch of each sound but the fret at which the finger stopped the string to produce the required pitch (see illustrations, pages 203 and 303). Tablatures were also devised for viols and keyboard instruments.

Tablature

Relation of Instrumental to Vocal Music

At the opening of the sixteenth century, instrumental music was still closely associated, both in style and performance, with vocal music. Instruments doubled or replaced some of the voices in secular and sacred polyphonic compositions. A large proportion of the repertory of solo and ensemble intrumental music derived from vocal music. But increasingly composers wrote directly for instruments, if not always for specific instruments. This repertory, therefore, will be discussed under the following categories, which reflect their relationship (dependence or independence) to the vocal repertory: (1) arrangements of vocal compositions; (2) polyphonic elaborations of chant or secular melodies; (3) instrumental compositions modeled on vocal genres; (4) preludes and other introductory pieces; (5) dance music; (6) sets of variations on sacred or secular melodies.

Instrumental Arrangements

Ensembles of instrumentalists reading from vocal parts performed the entire work polyphonically, often adding their own embellishments. These arrangements of madrigals, chansons, or motets, decorated by turns, trills, and runs, were written out by editors and printed. Lutenists and keyboard players also made impromptu arrangements of vocal pieces, some of which they wrote down and preserved. This music, printed in great quantities in the sixteenth century, often characterized as "for singing and playing" (*per cantar et sonar*), represented the bulk of what musicians played when they were not improvising or accompanying singers. Polyphonic vocal pieces were also intabulated, that is, transcribed for players who did not read staff notation or found the tablature more convenient.

Polyphonic Elaborations of Chant or Secular Melodies

In nomine

When John Taverner (ca. 1490–1545) made an instrumental arrangement of the passage, "in nomine Domini," from the Benedictus of his Mass *Gloria tibi Trinitas*, he started a trend. Taverner's own arrangement follows the vocal parts note for note. Others used the "in nomine" cantus firmus as a theme for creative elaboration. Organ pieces on liturgical or other cantus firmi were also written as independent works; these instrumental compositions were analogous to vocal cantus-firmus motets or mass movements. Short organ pieces based on chant melodies were called *verses* or *versets* and sometimes replaced portions of a religious service that were normally sung.

Organ versets

Compositions Modeled on Vocal Genres: The Canzona

The Italian *canzona* or *canzona da sonar* (chanson to be played) is an example of a newly composed piece modeled on a genre of vocal music. Also called *canzone alla francese* (chansons in the French manner), they were written for both ensembles and solo instruments. The canzona began as an instrumental composition in the style of a French chanson: it was light, fast-moving, strongly rhythmic, with a fairly simple contrapuntal texture. From the chanson, composers also adopted the typical opening rhythmic figure that occurs in nearly all canzonas—a single note followed by two notes each half the value of the first (such as a half note followed by two quarters). The canzona became the leading genre of contrapuntal instrumental music in the late sixteenth century. The earliest Italian examples (apart from mere transcriptions) were for organ. Ensemble canzonas made their appearance about 1580 and eventually developed into the *sonata da chiesa* (church sonata) of the seventeenth century.

Division into sections

The essential step in this development was the division of the canzona into more or less distinct sections. Many of the earliest canzonas had a single theme, or perhaps several themes very similar in character, treated contrapuntally in one continuous and unchanging movement. Others, however, introduced themes of contrasting character, each theme worked out in turn. Since the themes themselves were noticeably different from one another in melodic outline and rhythm, the piece as a whole began to take on the aspect of a series of contrasting sections, even though the divisions between sections were usually concealed by overlapping at cadences. In Example 7.11 (page 210) we see the four contrasting themes in a canzona of this type written by the Flemish composer Jean (or Giovanni) de Macque (ca. 1550–1614).

A. Gabrieli

A further step toward independent sections is illustrated in Example 7.12 (page 210), which reproduces themes from an instrumental piece by the Venetian composer Andrea Gabrieli (ca. 1510–1586). Although called a ricercare, the work is of the canzona type (the terminology had not yet become fixed). The themes display greater contrast than those in de Macque's canzona,

Example 7.11 *Jean de Macque, Themes from a Canzona*

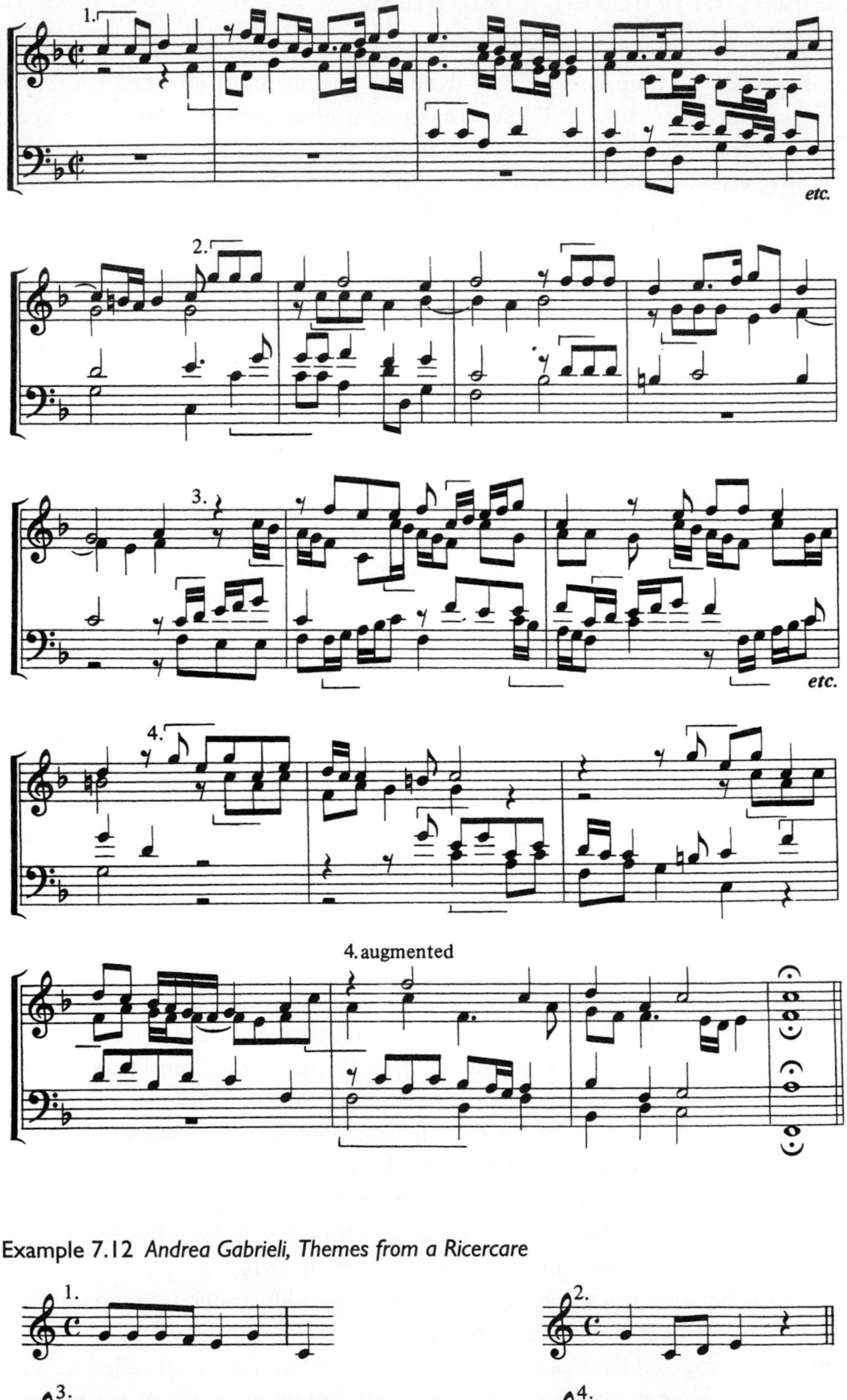
1.
etc.
2.
3.
etc.
4.
4. augmented

Example 7.12 *Andrea Gabrieli, Themes from a Ricercare*

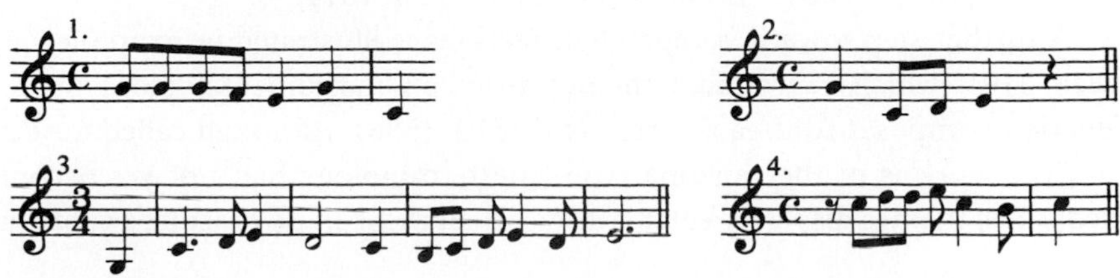

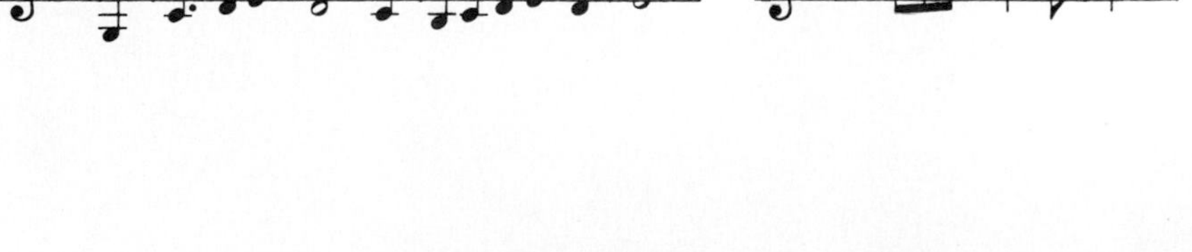
1.
2.
3.
4.

■ *At a party in the court of Duke Albrecht IV in Munich, three couples dance a stately pavane, accompanied by a flute and drum visible in the left balcony, while the right balcony holds a kettledrum player and two trumpeters, whose instruments are hung up. In the background the duke and a lady play cards. Engraving by Matthäus Zasinger, ca. 1500.* (DRESDEN, KUPFERSTICHKABINETT)

and the second section of the piece is set off from the others by its predominantly homophonic texture. The opening section is repeated in its entirety after section four.

Sonata

The Venetian sonata of the late 1500s—the sacred version of the canzona—consisted of a series of sections each based on a different subject or on variants of a single subject. This sectional character links it to the later sonata da chiesa, which in the seventeenth century consisted of movements in different tempos, meters, and moods. Giovanni Gabrieli (ca. 1557–1612), nephew of Andrea Gabrieli and, like him, organist at St. Mark's in Venice, left seven sonatas in addition to some thirty-six canzonas.

G. Gabrieli

One Venetian innovation was the application of the polychoral medium to instruments. (For a discussion of G. Gabrieli's vocal polychoral music, see Chapter 9.) The famous *Sonata pian' e forte*[8] from G. Gabrieli's *Sacrae symphoniae* (1597) is essentially a double-chorus motet for instruments. This composition has earned a prominent place in music history because it is among the first instrumental ensemble pieces to designate specific instruments in the printed parts. The first choir names a cornett and three sackbuts, the second, a violin and three sackbuts. The mild tone of the cornett blended well in an ensemble. Sackbuts, which came in five sizes from soprano to bass, also had a relatively mild tone. Another innovation in the printed music was the indication *pian* (piano), or *forte* (loud) appearing either when each choir was playing alone or when both were playing together—one of the earliest instances of dynamic markings in music.

Cornetts and sackbuts

8. Ed. in HAM No. 173.

Preludes and Other Introductory Pieces

Compositions that resemble improvisations are among the earliest specimens of music for solo players. They appeared under various names: *prelude* or *preambulum, fantasia,* or *ricercare.* Not based on any preexisting melody, they unfold freely, often in a rambling fashion, with varying textures and without adhering to a definite meter or form. The fantasias of Luis Milán (ca. 1500–ca. 1561), recorded in his *Libro de musica de vihuela de mano intitulado El Maestro* (Valencia, 1536), give us an idea of the improvisations that lutenists played before accompanying themselves or a singer in a song, such as a *villancico, soneto,* or *romance.* Each of the fantasias is in the same mode as the vocal piece that follows it. Fantasia XI, for example, sets the tonality of Modes I and II for the subsequent vocal piece by moving repeatedly toward a cadence on the final. Brilliant rapid scale passages add tension and suspense before the final chord.

Milán

The *toccata* was the chief form of keyboard music in improvisatory style during the second half of the century. This name, from the Italian verb *toccare* (to touch), carries the suggestion of a lutenist exercising on the fingerboard. The toccatas by the Venetian organist Claudio Merulo (1533–1604) exemplify the transfer of the genre to the keyboard (Example 7.13).[9]

Toccata

Merulo

Example 7.13 *Claudio Merulo, Toccata Sections*

9. Ed. in HAM No. 153, it was published in Merulo's *Toccate, Libro secondo* (1604).

etc.
b.
etc.
c.

In the opening succession of broadly conceived harmonies centered on *F* (Example 7.13a), Merulo took advantage of the organ's power to sustain tones, closing first on the final and then moving to a half cadence on the fifth degree. The numerous suspensions and other prolonged and repeated dissonances are idiomatic to the organ. Embellishments and scale passages in freely varied rhythms animate the texture. A contrasting middle section takes up four short subjects, each developed successively by imitation (the first of these is shown in Example 7.13b). The passage that follows resembles the opening but with more spacious harmonies and with even more fantastic play of brilliant running passages. The majestic slowing down of the chordal changes, or harmonic rhythm, in this last free section, coupled with the increasing liveliness and ever wider sweep of the runs, makes an impressive climax (Example 7.13c). Pieces of this sort did not necessarily contain fugal sections, nor were they uniformly labeled toccatas; they were also called *fantasia*, *intonazione*, and *prelude*.

Ricercare

One type of prelude, the *ricercare* or *ricercar*, evolved into a motetlike succession of fugal sections. The term *ricercare*—an Italian verb meaning both "to seek out" and "to attempt"—probably comes from lutenists' jargon for picking out (*ricercare*) notes on the instrument and testing the tuning. The earliest ricercari, for lute, were brief and improvisatory; when transferred to the keyboard, the genre acquired occasional bits of imitation. Later its form became clearer as composers introduced repeated phrases and passages of paired imitation. By 1540, the ricercare consisted of successive themes without marked individuality or contrast, each developed in imitation and overlapping with the next at the cadence—in effect, a textless imitative motet. Compared with their vocal counterparts, these ricercari displayed freer voice leading and had embellishments that were more typically instrumental. Most ricercari were intended for ensemble playing, but some were still written for keyboard instruments and for lute.

Dance Music

Social dancing

Social dancing was widespread and highly regarded in the Renaissance, and people of breeding were expected to be expert dancers. A considerable portion of sixteenth-century instrumental music consisted of dance pieces for lute, keyboard, or ensembles. Much of it was still improvised, as it had been in the late Middle Ages, but many pieces written out in tablatures or part-books appeared in printed collections issued by Petrucci, Attaingnant, and other publishers. As befits their purpose, these pieces are divided into distinct sections and usually have rhythmic patterns that are clearly marked and quite regular. There is little or no contrapuntal interplay of lines. The principal melody may be highly ornamented. In writing dance pieces, which owed little to vocal models, early sixteenth-century composers developed a characteristic instrumental style. Eventually they also wrote stylized pieces that retained the rhythms and outlines of dance music but were not intended for dancing.

In the late 1500s, publishers issued more and more collections of dance music for lute, keyboard instruments, and ensembles. Some of the dances were simple arrangements of tunes for popular use, but the majority seem to have been written for social occasions at the homes of the bourgeoisie or the courts

Example 7.14 Czayner Thancz *from the Tablature of John of Lublin*

of the aristocracy. The ballet, which had flourished earlier in the Burgundian and Italian courts, now reached France. The earliest surviving French ballet music was composed for the *Ballet comique de la reine* (The Queen's Dramatic Ballet), performed in Paris in 1581.

Ballet

Dances were commonly grouped in pairs or threes, and these sets, precursors of the later dance suites, consisted of stylized dances rather than music for dancing. A favorite combination was a slow dance in duple meter followed by a fast one in triple meter on the same tune, the second dance being a variation of the first. One such pair, the *pavane* (*pavana, paduana*) and *galliard*, was a favorite in sixteenth-century France. The English excelled in writing artful pavanes and galliards not intended for dancing. A popular pair in Italy was the *passamezzo* and *saltarello*. In both combinations, the first dance was slow and stately and in duple time, and the second dance, a more lively movement in triple time, was usually based on the same melody. The label *proportio* or *proportz* on the second dance in German sources indicated that some form of triple ratio was applied to the durations of the first dance to determine the values of the second. Similarly paired dances occur in Polish tablatures of the same period (see Example 7.14).

Dance medleys

Pavane and galliard

Allemande

Courante

The *allemande* or *alman*, a dance in moderate duple meter, came into favor about the middle of the sixteenth century; it was retained in stylized form as a regular component of the later dance suites. The *courante*, in a fast, flowing triple meter, another regular constituent of the later suites, also made its appearance in the sixteenth century.

Basse danse

Written dance music tells us much about improvisatory practice. It gives evidence of two ways in which sixteenth-century performers improvised: they ornamented a given melodic line, or they added one or more contrapuntal parts to a given melody. Improvisation was an important aspect of a musician's training. In fact, instrumentalists performed the favorite courtly dance of the late fifteenth and early sixteenth centuries, the *basse danse*, by improvising over a borrowed tenor. Later basses danses, however, such as those published by Attaingnant in the 1530s, have the melody in the top line, as in NAWM 45 (CD 3 [27] / 1 ⟨55⟩). Attaingnant notated the basses danses in duple time, but the choreography often called for a mixture of duple and triple to form twelve-beat units, named *quaternions* by the dancing master Thoinot Arbeau (1520–1595) in his *Orchésographie* (1588).[10] A basse danse in triple time (see NAWM 45b) was called *branle gay*.

Variations

Improvising on a tune to accompany dancing has ancient roots. Actual written-out variations on Venetian and Ferrarese pavane tunes appeared in 1508 in the lute tablatures of Joan Ambrosio Dalza (fl. early 1500s) published in *Intabulatura di lauto*. In a related practice, composers and performers wrote and improvised variations on *ostinato* patterns—short bass lines repeated over and over—such as the *passamezzo antico* and *moderno*, both deriving from the pavane. (These were prototypes of the later chaconne and passacaglia.) They also created sets of variations on standard treble airs for singing verses, such as the *Romanesca*, *Ruggiero*, and *Guardame las vacas*. Spanish lute and keyboard composers carried the art of making variations on popular tunes to a level of great refinement. The works in this genre of the great Spanish organist and composer Antonio de Cabezón (1510–1566) and the lutenist Enriquez de Valderrábano[11] (fl. mid-1500s) particularly stand out.

Virginalists

The variation enjoyed an extraordinary flowering in the late sixteenth century among a group of English keyboard composers called the *virginalists*, from the name applied at the time to all plucked keyboard instruments. The leading composer of this group was William Byrd (1543–1623). Important colleagues were John Bull (ca. 1562–1628), Orlando Gibbons (1583–1625), and Thomas Tomkins (1572–1656). Of the many English manuscript collections of keyboard music dating from this period, beginning with the *Mulliner Book* (ca. 1540–85), the most comprehensive is the *Fitzwilliam Virginal Book* (Cambridge, Fitzwilliam Museum, MS 32.g.29). Copied by Francis Tregian between 1609 and 1619, its pages contain nearly three hundred compositions from the

10. Thoinot Arbeau, *Orchesography*, trans. Mary Stewart Evans (New York: Dover, 1967), p. 57.
11. See his *Diferencias sobre Guardame las vacas* in HAM No. 124.

■ *Title page of* Parthenia, *a collection of music for virginals by William Byrd, John Bull, and Orlando Gibbons presented to Princess Elizabeth and Prince Frederick on their wedding in 1613. The title—parthenia were Greek maidens' choral dance-songs—alludes whimsically to the bride, the instrument's name, and the fact that this is the first such collection ever printed.*

late sixteenth and early seventeenth centuries. Among them are transcriptions of madrigals, contrapuntal fantasias, dances, preludes, descriptive pieces, and many sets of variations. Most of the variations in the *Fitzwilliam Virginal Book* are on slow dance tunes (as Bull's *Spanish Paven*) or familiar songs (as John Mundy's *Goe from my window*).[12] Many folk tunes of the time also served as subjects for variation.

Themes

The melodies used as a basis for the variations were generally short, simple, songlike, and regular in their phrasing, with a clear binary or ternary pattern marked by distinct cadences. A set consisted of an uninterrupted sequence of variations, numbering from a half dozen to more than twenty. Each variation preserves the phrase structure, harmonic plan, and cadences of the theme. The melody may be presented intact throughout an entire set of variations, passing occasionally from one voice to another; more often, it is broken up by decorative figuration, so that its original profile is only suggested. Some of the passage work, particularly in the variations by Bull, demands a high order of virtuosity.

Fancy

Another favorite subject for keyboard and ensemble consisted of the six notes of the hexachord (*ut, re, mi, fa, sol, la*), around which English composers wrote many ingenious counterpoints. One celebrated "hexachord fancy" by John Bull (ca. 1562–1628) takes the hexachord through all twelve keys in turn. This extraordinary composition was most likely modeled on a sinfonia by Alfonso della Viola (d. ca. 1570), one of several Italian composers who experi-

12. Ed. in HAM No. 177.

mented with radical chromaticism. Since Bull's "fancy" appears also as a keyboard piece, it has been suggested that some approximation to equal temperament (see discussion of tuning, page 349) must have been known in England by the end of the sixteenth century; however, the keyboard version we have may be only a condensed score of a fantasy for four viols.

Figuration

In most English virginal music, technical display is not a prominent feature. Each variation typically makes use of one type of figuration. Sometimes the two halves of a variation or two successive variations are paired by the use of the same figure in the right hand for one and in the left hand for the other, as in the third and fourth variations of Bull's *Spanish Paven* in the Fitzwilliam book. Apart from such pairing, the only comprehensive plan in most sets of variations was to increase the animation as the work progressed, though with intermittent quieter interludes. Changes of meter may be introduced, and composers sometimes showed off their skill by writing variations that used two or three different meters simultaneously. The final variation is often slower, a broadened restatement of the theme but with fuller sonority and richer harmonization.

Byrd

We can study variation technique in the pavan for keyboard (NAWM 46; CD 3 [29] / 2 ⟨1⟩) that Byrd wrote on Dowland's air *Flow, my tears* (NAWM 44; CD 3 [24] / 1 ⟨52⟩). The air itself has the typical form of a pavane, that is, three strains, each immediately repeated. Byrd added a variation after each strain; he retained the outline of the tune in the right hand while adding short accompanying motives or decorative turns, figurations, and scale patterns that are imitated between the hands.

English Composers on the Continent

English musicians in the early seventeenth century were in demand abroad and influential in the northern countries of Europe. The *Fitzwilliam Virginal Book* and other contemporary collections are eloquent witnesses to their accomplishments. John Dowland served from 1598 to 1607 as lutenist to the king of Denmark. Peter Philips (1561–1628) and Richard Dering (ca. 1580–1630) were among the English Catholics who emigrated to the Continent; their music was published chiefly in the Netherlands. William Brade (1560–1630) held various positions in Denmark and in Germany, where he published a number of suites for viols. John Bull went to Brussels in 1613, and from 1617 until his death served as organist at the cathedral in Antwerp. Whether Sweelinck knew him personally or not, he certainly knew the music of Bull and his English contemporaries; the influence is evident in Sweelinck's Keyboard works, which include several excellent sets of variations.

Summary

During this period, instrumental music came out of the shadows cast by the oral tradition. Dance music dominated the field as before, but by the end of the century, many other independent genres of written instrumental music could be distinguished by their functions and procedures. First identified with a particular instrument, most of these genres spread to other instruments and to ensembles—for example, the toccata, ricercare, prelude, fantasia, canzona, sonata, and sets of variations. Around 1600 English lute and keyboard composers took the lead in instrumental writing.

Bibliography

Music Collections

Modern collected editions of the works of composers mentioned in this chapter:

Arcadelt: CMM 31, ed. Albert Seay.
Clemens: CMM 4, ed. K. Ph. Bernet Kempers.
Giovanni Contino: MMI, ed. Ottavio Beretta
Crecquillon: CMM 63, ed. Barton Hudson, Mary Tiffany Ferer, and Laura Youens.
Fayrfax: CMM 17, ed. Edwin B. Warren.
Festa: CMM 25, ed. Alexander Main.
A. Gabrieli: *Complete Madrigals*, ed. A. Tillman Merritt (Madison, Wis.: A-R Editions, 1981).
G. Gabrieli: CMM 12, ed. Denis Arnold; continued by Richard Charteris.
Gesualdo: *Sämtliche Werke*, ed. Glenn Watkins and Wilhelm Weismann (Hamburg: Ugrino, 1957–67).
Gombert: CMM 6, ed. Joseph Schmidt-Görg.
Hassler: *Sämtliche Werke*, ed C. Russell Crosby (Wiesbaden: Breitkopf & Härtel, 1961–).
Isaac: CMM 65, ed. Edward Lerner.
Janequin: *Chansons polyphoniques: oeuvres complètes*, ed. A. Tillman Merritt and François Lesure (Monaco: Éditions de l'Oiseau-Lyre, 1965–71).
Lasso: *Sämtliche Werke*, ed. Franz X. Haberl and Adolf Sandberger (Leipzig: Breitkopf & Härtel, 1894–1927; repr. 1974); *Sämtliche Werke, neue Reihe*, ed. Siegfried Hermelink et al. (Kassel: Bärenreiter, 1956–).
Layolle: CMM 32/3–6, ed. Frank D'Accone.
Le Jeune: *Airs*, ed. David Percival Walker (AIM, Miscellanea 1).
Manchicourt: CMM 55, ed. John D. Wicks and Lavern Wagner.
Marenzio: CMM 72, ed. Bernhard Meier and Roland Jackson; PAM 4, 6, ed. A. Einstein; *The Secular Works*, ed. Steven Ledbetter and Patricia Myers (New York: Broude Bros., 1977–).
Monte: *Opera*, ed. Charles Van den Borren and Julius van Nuffel (Bruges and Düsseldorf: Schwann, 1927–39; repr. New York, 1965); *Opera, New Complete Edition*, ed. René B. Lenaerts (Louvain: University Press, 1975–).
Monteverdi: *Tutte le opere*, ed. Gian Francesco Malipiero (Asola, 1926–42; repr. Vienna: Universal, 1967); *Opera omnia*, Fondazione Claudio Monteverdi (1970–); *New Monteverdi Edition*, ed. Bernard Bailly de Surcy (Paris: Editions Renaissantes, 1972–).
Morales: *Monumentos de la musica española*, ed. Higini Anglès, Vols. 11, 13, 15, 17, 20, 21, 24, 34 (1952–).
Nicolaus of Radom: *Les oeuvres complètes*, ed. Adam Sutkowski (Brooklyn: Institute of Medieval Music, 1969).
Pisano: CMM 32/1, ed. Frank D'Accone.
Rore: CMM 14, ed. Bernhard Meier.
Senfl: *Sämtliche Werke* (Basel: Hug; Wolfenbüttel: Möseler, 1937–).
Sermisy: CMM 52, ed. Gaston Allaire and Isabelle Cazeaux.

Titelouze: *Oeuvres complètes d'orgue*, ed. Alexandre Guilmant and André Pirro (Paris: Durand, 1898; repr. 1972).
Verdelot: CMM 28, ed. Anne-Marie Bragard.
Vicentino: CMM 26, ed. Henry W. Kaufmann.
Wert: CMM 24, ed. Carol MacClintock and Melvin Bernstein.
Willaert: CMM 3, ed. Hermann Zenck, Walter Gerstenberg, and Bernhard Meier.

Selected Collections

H. Colin Slim, *A Gift of Madrigals and Motets* (Chicago: University of Chicago Press, 1972), 2 vols. (edition and commentary).

Motets by French and Franco-Flemish composers of the first half of the sixteenth century are published in Albert Smijers, ed., *Treize livres de motets paru chez Pierre Attaingnant en 1534 et 1535* (Paris: Éditions de l'Oiseau-Lyre, 1934–36), 3 vols.; see also Henry Expert, ed., *Monuments de la musique française au temps de la Renaissance*, Vol. 2 (Paris: Senart, 1925); and CMM 48 (works of Lhéritier, ed. Leeman Perkins, with extensive introduction and commentary).

Examples of the frottola and related forms are in Alfred Einstein's *The Italian Madrigal* (Princeton: Princeton University Press, 1949), Vol. 3, Nos. 1–14. See also Rudolf Schwarz's edition of Petrucci's first and fourth books of frottole in PAM 8; and Raffaello Monterosso, ed., *Frottole nell'edizione principe di O. Petrucci* (Cremona: Athenaeum Cremonense, 1954). Otto Gombosi, ed., *Compositione di Meser Vincenzo Capirola* (The Capirola Lute Book; Neuilly-sur-Seine: Société de Musique d'Autrefois, 1955), contains lute transcriptions of frottole.

Knud Jeppesen's *Der mehrstimmige italienische Laude um 1500* (Leipzig: Breitkopf & Härtel, 1935) contains 98 laude in transcription, as well as detailed analysis of the poetry and music.

Other collections of early sixteenth-century Italian music: Frank D'Accone, ed., *Music of the Florentine Renaissance*, 4 vols. (CMM 32); Claudio Gallico, ed., *Un canzoniero musicale italiano del cinquecento* (Florence: L. Olschki, 1961). New anthologies of madrigals are *The Oxford Book of Italian Madrigals*, ed. R. Alec Harman (London: Oxford University Press, 1983); and *20 Italienske Madrigaler (1605–1606)* (Copenhagen: Edition Egtved, 1983).

For examples of the French chanson from the first half of the sixteenth century see François Lesure, ed., *Anthologie de la chanson parisienne au xvie siècle* (Monaco: Éditions de l'Oiseau-Lyre, 1953); Martin Picker, ed., *Chanson Albums of Marguerite of Austria* (Berkeley: University of California Press, 1965); see also Daniel Heartz, ed., *Preludes, Chansons and Dances for Lute published in Paris [Attaingnant] 1529–30* (Neuilly-sur-Seine: Société de Musique d'Autrefois, 1964).

See also François Lesure and Geneviève Thibault, *Bibliographie des éditions d'Adrien Le Roy et Robert Ballard* (Paris: Société française de musicologie, 1955); Daniel Heartz, *Pierre Attaingnant, Royal Printer of Music* (Berkeley: University of California Press, 1970); Samuel Pogue, *Jacques Moderne: Lyons Music Printer of the 16th Century* (Geneva: Librairie Droz, 1969).

The Lochamer *Liederbuch* was published in facsimile edition by Konrad Ameln (Kassel: Bärenreiter, 1972) and in modern transcription by Konrad Escher and Walter Lott (Berlin: Wölbig, 1926; repr. Wiesbaden, 1969); the polyphonic compositions from this book were published in transcription by K. Ameln (Augsburg: Bärenreiter, 1926). A modern edition of the Glogauer *Liederbuch* by Heribert Ringmann and Christian Väterlein is in *Das Erbe deutscher Musik*, Series I, Vols. 4, 8, 85 and 86 (Leipzig, 1936–81), and a facsimile was published by Garland in 1987.

German lieder of the first half of the sixteenth century are in EP, Years 1–4, 7–8, 33; other late sixteenth-century lieder are in EP, Years 23 (Regnart) and 25 (Eccard).

For modern editions of Spanish music of the sixteenth century, see the various volumes of the series *Monumentos de la musica española*, Higini Anglès, gen. ed., 1941–; also the series *Hispaniae schola musica sacra*, ed. Felipe Pedrell (Barcelona: J. B. Pujol; Leipzig: Breitkopf & Härtel, 1894–98); also the edition by Jesus Bal y Gay of the *Cancionero de Upsala* (Mexico: El Colegio de México, 1944), with a historical essay on the polyphonic villancico by Isabel Pope. See also *Madrigales españoles ineditos del siglo xvi*, ed. Miguel Querol Gavalda (Barcelona: Instituto Español de Musicologia, 1981).

One of the English manuscripts containing secular music from the time of Henry VIII is edited by John Stevens in MB 18; also from this period is the *Early Tudor Songs and Carols*, MB 36, ed. J. Stevens. See also Philip Ledger, ed., *The Oxford Book of English Madrigals* (London: Oxford University Press, 1979).

Organ pieces based on *cantus firmi* are contained in Yvonne Rokseth, ed., *Deux Livres d'orgue parus chez Pierre Attaingnant* (Paris: E. Droz, 1925); and Denis Stevens, ed., *The Mulliner Book*, MB 1. Transcriptions of vocal pieces for organ are found in Knud Jeppesen, ed., *Die italienische Orgelmusik am Anfang des Cinquecento* (Copenhagen: E. Munksgaard, 1943; 2nd ed., 1960). Luis Milan's *Libro de musica de vihuela de mano intitulado El Maestro*, ed. Leo Schrade, is in PAM, Year 2, Part 1 (repr. Hildesheim, 1967). Examples of Italian lute music are found in Arthur J. Ness, ed., *The Lute Music of Francesco Canova da Milano*, Harvard Publications in Music 3–4 (Cambridge, Mass.: Harvard University Press, 1970).

English madrigals are published in Edmund H. Fellowes, ed., *The English Madrigal School*, 36 vols. (London: Stainer & Bell, 1913–24); and ayres in Fellowes, ed., *The English School of Lutenist Song Writers*, 16 vols. (London: Winthrop Rogers, 1920–32); second series, 16 vols. (1925–27). Refer also to Allison Hall, *E. H. Fellowes, An Index to the English Madrigalists and the English School of Lutenist Song Writers* (Boston: Music Library Association, 1984).

For examples of Italian keyboard music from the sixteenth to the early eighteenth centuries see vol. 3 in Luigi Torchi, ed., *L'arte musicale in Italia*, 7 vols. (Milan, 1897–1908). Italian and other keyboard music of the sixteenth century in CEKM 2, 6, 9, 12, 14, 33, 34, 35, 37, 38, 41, 47.

English keyboard music in MB: 1, *The Mulliner Book*; 5, Tomkins; 14, 19, Bull; 20, O. Gibbons; 24, Farnaby; 27, 28, Byrd. Other editions: John M. Ward, ed., *The Dublin Virginal Manuscript* [ca. 1570] (Wellesley, 1954); a facs. ed. by Otto Erich Deutsch of *Parthenia* (the first printed collection [1611] of virginal music) (London: Chiswick, 1942); *The Fitzwilliam Virginal Book*, ed. J. A. Fuller Maitland and W. Barclay Squire, 2 vols. (New York: Dover, 1963); Byrd's *My Ladye Nevells Booke*, ed. Hilda Andrews (New York: Dover, 1969); Byrd, *Forty-five Pieces for Keyboard Instruments*, ed. Stephen D. Tuttle (Paris: Éditions de l'Oiseau-Lyre, 1939); Gibbons, *Complete Keyboard Works*, ed. Margaret Glyn, 5 vols. (London: Stainer & Bell, 1922–25).

For Further Reading

For translations of Zarlino, see Bibliography for Chapter 6.

On modality in polyphonic music, read Bernhard Meier, *The Modes of Classical Vocal Polyphony*, trans. Ellen S. Beebe (New York: Broude Bros., 1988). Also see Harold Powers, "Tonal Types and Modal Categories in Renaissance Polyphony," JAMS 34 (1981):428–70, and GLHWM 3; Powers, "Mode," in NG.

Individual Composers

Arcadelt James Haar, "Toward a Chronology of the Madrigals of Arcadelt," JM 5 (1987): 28–54, discusses his musical style.

Cara William Prizer, "Marchetto Cara at Mantua: New Documents on the Life and Duties of a Renaissance Court Musician," MD 32 (1978):87–110; idem., *Courtly Pastimes: The Frottole of Marchetto Cara* (Ann Arbor: UMI Research Press, 1981).

Festa James Haar, "The *Libro primo* of Costanzo Festa," AM 52 (1980):147–55; Richard Agee, "Filippo Strozzi and the Early Madrigal," JAMS 38 (1985):230–36.

A. Gabrieli Denis Arnold, *Giovanni Gabrieli* and *Giovanni Gabrieli and the Music of the Venetian High Renaissance* (Oxford: Oxford University Press, 1974 and 1979); Martin Morell, "New Evidence for the Biographies of Andrea and Giovanni Gabrieli," EMH 3 (1983):101–22; Richard Charteris, *Giovanni Gabrieli: A Thematic Catalogue of His Music* (Stuyvesant, NY: Pendragon Press, 1996).

Gesualdo Glenn Watkins, *Gesualdo, The Man and His Music*, 2nd. ed. (Oxford: Clarendon Press, 1991).

Lasso James Erb, *Orlando di Lasso: A Guide to Research* (New York: Garland, 1990).

Marenzio Denis Arnold, *Marenzio* (London: Oxford University Press, 1965); James Chater, *Luca Marenzio and the Italian Madrigal, 1577–1593* (Ann Arbor: UMI Research Press, 1981).

Monte Brian Mann, *The Secular Madrigals of Filippo di Monte, 1521–1603* (Ann Arbor: UMI Research Press, 1983).

Monteverdi For basic works on Monteverdi, see Bibliography for Chapter 9.

Vicentino Henry W. Kaufmann, *Nicola Vicentino (1511–ca. 1576), The Life and Works*, MSD 11, AIM, 1966.

Weelkes David Brown, *Thomas Weelkes* (London: Faber & Faber, 1969).

Wert Carol MacClintock, *Giaches de Wert, Life and Works*, AIM, 1966.

Willaert Armen Carpetyan, "The *Musica Nova* of Adrian Willaert," MD 1 (1946):200–21, and GLHWM 3. Lewis Lockwood, "Adrian Willaert and Cardinal Ippolito d'Este," EMH 5 (1985): 85–112.

National Styles

On the frottola, see William Prizer, *Courtly Pastimes: The Frottole of Marchetto Cara* (Ann Arbor: UMI Research Press, 1981); and Prizer, "Isabella d'Este and Lucretia Borgia as Patrons of Music: The Frottola at Mantua and Ferrara," JAMS 38 (1985):1–33.

On the sixteenth-century French chanson, see the essays in James Haar, ed., *Chanson and Madrigal, 1480–1530* (Cambridge, Mass.: Harvard University Press, 1961); Lawrence Bernstein, "The 'Parisian Chanson': Problems of Style and Terminology," JAMS 31 (1978): 193–240, and GLHWM 3; and idem, "Notes on the Origin of the Parisian Chanson," JM 1 (1982):275–326.

On music at the court of Maximilian, see Louise Cuyler, *The Emperor Maximilian and Music* (London: Oxford University Press, 1973).

On musique mesurée: David Percival Walker, "The Influence of *Musique mesurée à l'antique*, Particularly on the *Airs de cour* of the Early Seventeenth Century," MD 2 (1948): 141–63, and GLHWM 5.

Surveys of English music of this period include Denis Stevens, *Tudor Church Music* (London: Faber & Faber, 1966); and Peter LeHuray, *Music of the Reformation in England, 1549–1660* (New York: Oxford University Press, 1967). On secular music, see John Stevens, *Music & Poetry in the Early Tudor Court* (London: Methuen, 1961); Philip Brett, "The English Consort Song," *Proceedings of the Royal Musical Association* 88 (1961–62):73–88.

Madrigal

On Italian madrigal poetry, see Walter Rubsamen, *Literary Sources of Secular Music in Italy (ca. 1500)* (Berkeley: University of California Press, 1943); and Dean T. Mace, "Pietro Bembo and the Literary Origins of the Italian Madrigal," MQ 55 (1969):65–86, and GLHWM 4.

Alfred Einstein, *The Italian Madrigal* (Princeton: Princeton University Press, 1949; repr., with additions, 1971) is the definitive work on this subject. On the interrelationship of various forms of secular vocal music in this period, see James Haar, ed., *Chanson and Madrigal, 1480–1530*; see also the survey by Jerome Roche, *The Madrigal*, 2nd ed. (New York: Oxford University Press, 1990). Major studies of the madrigal since Einstein's work are Martha Feldman, *City Culture and the Madrigal in Venice* (Berkeley: University of California Press, 1995); Iain Fenlon and J. Haar, *The Italian Madrigal in the Early Sixteenth Century* (Cambridge: Cambridge University Press, 1988); J. Haar, *Essays on Italian Poetry and Music in the Renaissance, 1350–1600* (Berkeley: University of California Press, 1986); and Anthony Newcomb, *The Madrigal at Ferrara, 1579–1597* (Princeton: Princeton University Press, 1980).

On the other Italian genres (villanella, villanesca, canzone, and canzonetta) and their relationship to the madrigal, see Ruth I. DeFord, "Musical Relationships between the Italian Madrigal and Light Italian Genres," MD 39 (1985):107–68.

On the English madrigal, see Edmund H. Fellowes, *The English Madrigal Composers*, 2nd ed. (New York: Oxford University Press, 1948); Joseph Kerman, *The Elizabethan Madrigal* (New York: American Musicological Society, 1962). On the song, see Ian Spink, *English Song: Dowland to Purcell* (London: Batsford, 1974; rev. 1986).

Morley's *A Plaine and Easie Introduction to Practicall Musicke (1597)* has been published in a modern edition by R. Alec Harman (London: Dent, 1952).

Instrumental Music

Willi Apel, *The History of Keyboard Music to 1700*, trans. Hans Tischler (Bloomington: Indiana University Press, 1972); idem, *Early European Keyboard Music* (Stuttgart: F. Steiner, 1989), a collection of older articles; John Caldwell, *English Keyboard Music before the Nineteenth Century* (New York: Praeger, 1979); Virginia Brookes, *British Keyboard Music to c. 1660: Sources and Thematic Index* (London: Oxford University Press, 1996).

John M. Ward, "Parody Technique in 16th-Century Instrumental Music," in *The Commonwealth of Music*, ed. Gustave Reese and Rose Brandel (New York: Free Press, 1965), and GLHWM 4.

CHAPTER 8

CHURCH MUSIC OF THE LATE RENAISSANCE AND REFORMATION

THE MUSIC OF THE REFORMATION IN GERMANY

When Martin Luther nailed his ninety-five theses to the door of the Schlosskirche at Wittenberg in 1517, he had no intention of initiating a movement toward a Protestant church completely separate from Rome. Even after the break, the Lutheran Church retained much of the traditional Catholic liturgy, along with a considerable use of Latin in the services. Similarly, it continued to employ a good deal of Catholic music, both plainsong and polyphony. In some cases the original Latin text was retained, in others it was translated into German, and in still others, new German texts were fitted to the old melodies.

Lutheran liturgy

Lutheran church music

The central position of music in the Lutheran Church, especially in the sixteenth century, reflected Luther's own convictions. He was a singer, a composer of some skill, and a great admirer of Franco-Flemish polyphony, especially the works of Josquin des Prez. He believed strongly in the educational and ethical power of music and wanted the entire congregation to participate in the music of the services. Although he altered the words of the liturgy to conform to his own views on certain theological points, Luther also wished to retain Latin in the service, partly because he thought it was valuable for educating the young.

In applying Luther's beliefs to their own local conditions, congregations developed a number of different usages. Large churches with trained choirs generally kept much of the Latin liturgy and its polyphonic music. Smaller congregations adopted a German Mass (*Deudsche Messe*), first published by Luther in 1526, that followed the main outlines of the Roman Mass but dif-

German Mass

fered from it in many details: the Gloria was omitted; the recitation tones were adapted to the natural cadence of the German language; several parts of the Proper were condensed or omitted; and German hymns replaced the remaining items of the Proper and most of the Ordinary. But Luther never intended either this German Mass or any other formula to prevail uniformly in Lutheran churches; indeed, almost every imaginable compromise between the Roman usage and the new practices could be found somewhere in sixteenth-century Germany. Latin Masses and motets continued to be sung, and Latin remained in the liturgy at some places well into the eighteenth century. In the Leipzig of Bach's time, for example, some portions of the services were still sung in Latin.

The Lutheran Chorale

The most distinctive and important musical innovation of the Lutheran Church was the strophic congregational hymn called a *Choral* or *Kirchenlied* (church song) in German and a *chorale* in English. Most people today know these hymns in four-part harmonized settings, but the chorale, like plainsong, consisted essentially of only two elements, a text and a tune. Of course, the chorale, like plainsong, lent itself to enrichment through harmony and counterpoint and could be reworked into large musical forms. Just as most Catholic church music in the sixteenth century grew out of plainsong, so Lutheran church music of the seventeenth and eighteenth centuries largely grew out of the chorale.

Four collections of chorales were published in 1524, and others followed at frequent intervals. From the outset, these songs were intended for congregational singing in unison, without harmonization or accompaniment. The chorales were probably sung with notes of fairly uniform length, with modifications suggested by the natural flow of the words, and with a pause of indefinite length on the final note of each phrase.

Sources of tunes

For a long time the demand for suitable songs in the Lutheran Church far exceeded the supply. Luther himself wrote many chorale texts and some of the melodies. For example, he wrote the words to the well-known *Ein' feste Burg ist unser Gott* (A mighty fortress is our God, 1529), and probably the melody as well. Many chorale tunes were newly composed, but even more were derived from secular and sacred songs or Latin chants. Thus the Gregorian hymn *Veni Redemptor gentium* became *Nun komm' der Heiden Heiland* (Come, Savior of the Gentiles), and the Easter sequence *Victimae paschali laudes* (NAWM 5) was the model for *Christ lag in Todesbanden* (Christ lay in the bonds of death).

Contrafacta

The *contrafacta*—extant melodies, with new or spiritualized texts—were an important class of chorales. The most famous of the contrafacta and one of the most beautiful, *O Welt, ich muss dich lassen* (O world, I must leave you), adapted Isaac's lied *Innsbruck, ich muss dich lassen* (NAWM 34). In a later and

Example 8.1

a. *Hans Leo Hassler,* Mein G'müth ist mir verwirret

My peace of mind is shattered by a tender maiden's charms, I've lost my way completely, my heart is deeply sore.

b. *J. S. Bach,* Passion according to St. Matthew

Entrust your ways and whatever grieves your heart to the most faithful care, to the One who rules heaven.

c. *J. S. Bach,* Passion according to St. Matthew

If someday I must depart, then do not part from me! If I must bear death, then step forth!

somewhat startling example, Bach set the tune from Hassler's lied *Mein Gmüth ist mir verwirret* (My peace of mind is shattered [by a tender maiden's charms]) to the sacred words *Herzlich thut mich verlangen* (My heart is filled with longing) and later to *O Haupt voll Blut und Wunden* (O head, all bloody and wounded). Example 8.1 shows the transformation of Hassler's original version into two of the settings in Bach's *Passion according to St. Matthew.*

Polyphonic Chorale Settings

Lutheran composers soon began to write polyphonic settings for chorales. Some composers used the older lied technique, with the plain chorale tune in long notes in the tenor, surrounded by three or more free-flowing parts. Others developed each phrase of the chorale imitatively in all the voices in the manner of Franco-Flemish motets. The preferred arrangement during the last third of the century, called *cantional* style, had the tune in the highest voice, accompanied by block chords with a minimum of contrapuntal figuration.

Cantional style

In 1524 Luther's principal musical collaborator, Johann Walter (1496–1570), published a volume of thirty-eight German chorale settings together with five Latin motets. Later editions had a larger proportion of Latin motets. Georg Rhau (1488–1548), the leading music publisher of Lutheran Germany, issued an important collection of 123 polyphonic chorale arrangements and motets in 1544 that included pieces by all the leading German and Swiss-German composers of the first half of the sixteenth century. Lucas Osiander (1534–1604) published the first collection in cantional style, *Fünfzig Lieder und Psalmen* (Fifty Chorales and Psalms), in 1586. The most important collections of cantional settings in the early seventeenth century were by Hans Leo Hassler (1562–1612)—*Kirchengesänge* (1608); Michael Praetorius—*Musae Sioniae* (1607–10); and Johann Hermann Schein (1586–1630)—*Leipziger Kantional* (1627).

Chorale publications

Rhau

The choir, sometimes doubled by instruments, generally alternated stanzas with the congregation singing in unison without accompaniment. After 1600, it became customary to have all the parts played on the organ while the congregation sang the tune.

Performance of chorales

The Chorale Motet

By the end of the sixteenth century, many German congregations had returned to the Catholic faith, and the line that marked the boundary between the Protestant northeast and the Catholic southwest has remained substantially the same to this day. The separation encouraged a new and distinctive kind of Lutheran polyphonic church music. Composers of chorale settings during the early Reformation had aimed at preserving the words and melody of the chorale intact. They treated the chorale the way medieval composers of organa had treated the chant: as something established and not to be altered, to be adorned but not interpreted in any personal sense. By the end of the sixteenth century this attitude changed. Led by the example of Lasso, Protestant German composers freely created polyphonic compositions around the traditional melodies, incorporating personal interpretations and pictorial details. These new settings were called *chorale motets*. An example of the Lutheran chorale motet is the *bicinium* (two-part song) based on the chorale *Vater unser* (Our Father), by Michael Praetorius (Example 8.2, page 228).

Composers of German motets could—and did—break away altogether from the traditional chorale tunes, though they still used melodic material in the style of the chorale or lied. These motets widened the division between simple congregational hymns and more elaborate music for a trained choir.

Example 8.2 *Michael Praetorius, Bicinium*: Vater unser

Our Father in Heaven, who dost bid us all alike to be brothers and to call upon Thee, and desirest prayers from us.

The leading composers of German motets at the turn of the sixteenth century—Hassler, Johannes Eccard (1553–1611), Leonhard Lechner (ca. 1553–1606), and Praetorius—established the Lutheran church music style in Germany that culminated more than a hundred years later in the works of J. S. Bach.

REFORMATION CHURCH MUSIC OUTSIDE GERMANY

The Psalter

Calvinist churches

The Reformation influenced musical developments in France, the Low Countries, and Switzerland quite differently from Germany. John Calvin (1509–1564) and other leaders of the Protestant sects opposed certain elements of Catholic liturgy and ceremonial much more strongly than Luther had. They distrusted the allure of art in worship services and prohibited singing of texts not found in the Bible. As a result, the only notable contributions to music that emerged from the Calvinist churches were their Psalters—rhymed metrical translations of the Book of Psalms that were set to newly composed melodies or, in many cases, to tunes that were of popular origin or adapted from plainchant.

French Psalter

The principal French Psalter was published in 1562, with psalm texts translated by Clément Marot and Théodore de Bèze and set to melodies selected or composed by Loys Bourgeois (ca. 1510–ca. 1561). Calvinists originally sang the psalms in unaccompanied unison at church services. For devotional use at home, settings were made in four and more parts, with the tune in either the tenor or the soprano, sometimes in simple chordal style and sometimes in fairly elaborate motetlike arrangements. Eventually some of the simpler four-part settings were also used in public worship.

The most important French composers of psalm settings were Claude Goudimel (ca. 1505–1572) and Claude Le Jeune; the most important Netherlands composer was Sweelinck. Translations of the French Psalter appeared in Germany, Holland, England, and Scotland, and the Reformed churches in those countries took over many of the French tunes. In Germany, many Psalter melodies were adapted as chorales. In Holland, the translation of 1566 replaced an earlier Dutch Psalter, the *Souterliedekens* of 1540, whose melodies had been taken from popular songs and were later set in three parts by Clemens.

The French model also influenced the most important English Psalter of the sixteenth century, that of Thomas Sternhold and John Hopkins (1562), and influenced the Scottish Psalter of 1564 even more. In 1620, the Pilgrims came to New England with a combination of English and French-Dutch traditions, embodied in the Psalter issued by Henry Ainsworth in Amsterdam in 1612 for English Separatists in Holland. This collection remained in use for many years after the appearance of the first American Psalter, the *Bay Psalm Book* of 1640.

The French Psalter melodies are on the whole suave, intimate, and somewhat austere in comparison with the forthright, vigorous quality of the German chorales. Since the Calvinist churches discouraged musical elaboration, the Psalter tunes were seldom expanded into larger forms of vocal and instrumental music, as the Lutheran chorales were, so they figure less conspicuously in the history of music. Their melodic lines, which move mostly by step, have a plainsong quality, and the phrases are organized in a rich variety of rhythmic patterns. It is surprising that so few of the melodies from the French Psalter of 1562 are found in modern hymnals. The best-known example is the tune sung originally to Psalm 134, used in the English Psalters for Psalm 100 and known as "Old Hundredth" (Example 8.3, page 230).

Bohemia

A pre-Reformation movement in Bohemia led by Jan Hus (1373–1415) resulted in the virtual banishment there of polyphonic music and instruments from the church until the middle of the sixteenth century. The Hussites sang simple hymns of folklike character that were usually monophonic. As the earlier strictures gradually relaxed, part-music, though still in note-against-note

Example 8.3

a. *Original Melody from French Psalter of 1562*

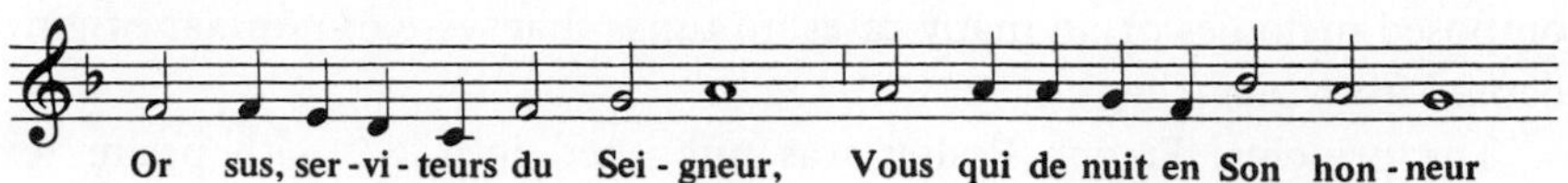

Arise ye servants of the Lord, which by night [stand] in the house of the Lord.

b. *Presbyterian Hymnal*

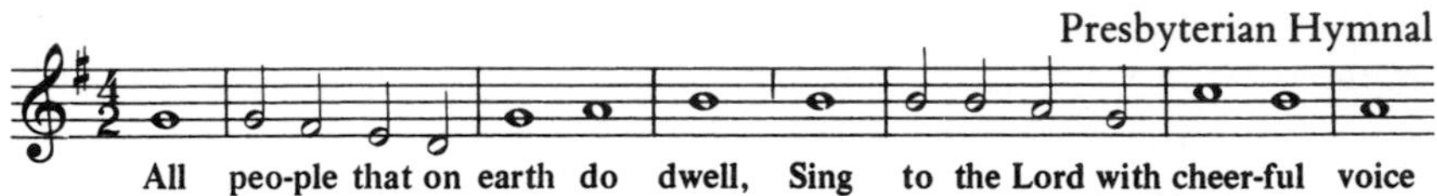

style, was permitted. In 1561, a group known as the Czech Brethren published a hymnbook with texts in Czech and melodies borrowed from Gregorian chant, secular songs, and French Calvinist Psalm settings. The Czech Brethren, later called the Moravian Brethren, emigrated to America in the early eighteenth century, and their settlements—especially the one at Bethlehem, Pennsylvania—became important centers of music.

Pre-Reformation Music in England

Production of music in England had declined during the Wars of the Roses (1455–85). When a revival began during the reign of Henry VII (1485–1509), English composers, though aware of developments on the Continent, worked in relative isolation. No Franco-Flemish musicians came to England until after 1510, and the method of prevailingly imitative counterpoint was adopted only gradually. Apart from isolated earlier examples, this style was first applied systematically in psalm settings and motets around 1540. Meanwhile, native production of secular music continued. Manuscripts from the time of Henry VII and Henry VIII (reigned 1509–47) contain a variety of songs and instrumental pieces in three and four parts that reflect many facets of court life, including popular elements.

Most of the surviving English polyphonic music of the late fifteenth and early sixteenth centuries is sacred—Masses, Magnificats, and votive antiphons (the four antiphons for the Blessed Virgin Mary that are sung at Compline: *Alma Redemptoris Mater, Ave Regina caelorum, Regina caeli,* and *Salve Regina*). Many of these works illustrate the English preference for a fuller sonority of five or six voices instead of the more common four-part imitative texture of Continental music. Accordingly, the music displays a strong feeling for the harmonic dimension of music and for achieving textural variety through the use of contrasting voice groups. Long melismas on a single syllable of text often resulted in passages of extraordinary beauty and expressiveness.

William Cornysh the younger (1465–1523), distinguished for both secular songs and motets, and Robert Fayrfax (ca. 1464–1521), who wrote Masses and other sacred works, were two leading English composers at the beginning of the sixteenth century. Their works are included in the Eton Choirbook, which some consider the most beautiful surviving English musical manuscript. The Choirbook, compiled for Eton College between about 1490 and 1502, originally contained sixty-seven antiphons in honor of the Virgin used in a daily special service at the college.

Eton Choirbook

The greatest English musician of this period was John Taverner (ca. 1490–1545), whose career included four years as director of a large choir of forty at Oxford. Taverner's festal Masses and Magnificats, mostly written in the full, florid English style of the early part of the century, have occasional sequential passages and some imitation. His *Western Wynde* Mass, one of three on this tune by sixteenth-century English composers, treats the cantus firmus as a series of variations, a form also favored by later English keyboard composers. A similar technique is used in the Mass *Gloria tibi trinitas*, said to have been performed at the Field of the Cloth of Gold, near Calais, where Henry VIII of England and Francis I of France met in 1520.

Taverner

Toward the middle of the century, the leading English composers were Christopher Tye (ca. 1505–ca. 1572), Thomas Tallis (ca. 1505–1585), and Robert Whyte (ca. 1538–1574). The most important was Tallis, whose musical production bridges early and late sixteenth-century English styles and whose career reflects the religious upheavals and bewildering political changes that influenced English church music in this period. Under Henry VIII, Tallis wrote Masses (including one imitation Mass) and votive antiphons. Under Edward VI (reigned 1547–53), after the break with the pope, Tallis composed music for the English service and anthems to English texts. During the reign of Queen Mary, who restored the Roman rite, he wrote a number of Latin hymns, and his large seven-voice Mass *Puer nobis* probably dates to her reign. Under Queen Elizabeth, Tallis set music to both Latin and English words. His late works include two sets of *Lamentations* that are among the most eloquent of all settings of these verses from the Hebrew Scriptures. One remarkable feature of his compositions and of much sixteenth-century English music is the vocal quality of the melodies. They strike the listener as an interplay not of abstract musical lines but of voices—so closely is the melodic curve wedded to the natural inflection of speech, so imaginatively does it project their content, and so naturally does it lie for the singer.

Tallis

Anglican Church Music

The Church in England formally separated from the Roman Catholic communion in 1534 under Henry VIII. Since the grounds for this action were political rather than doctrinal, no immediate changes in liturgy or music were involved. However, English gradually replaced Latin in the church service, and in 1549 the Act of Uniformity made the English Book of Common Prayer the only prayerbook permitted for public use. Roman Catholicism returned briefly under Queen Mary (reigned 1553–58), but Elizabeth I restored the English rites, and during her reign (1558–1603) the Church of England was established essentially in its present-day form.

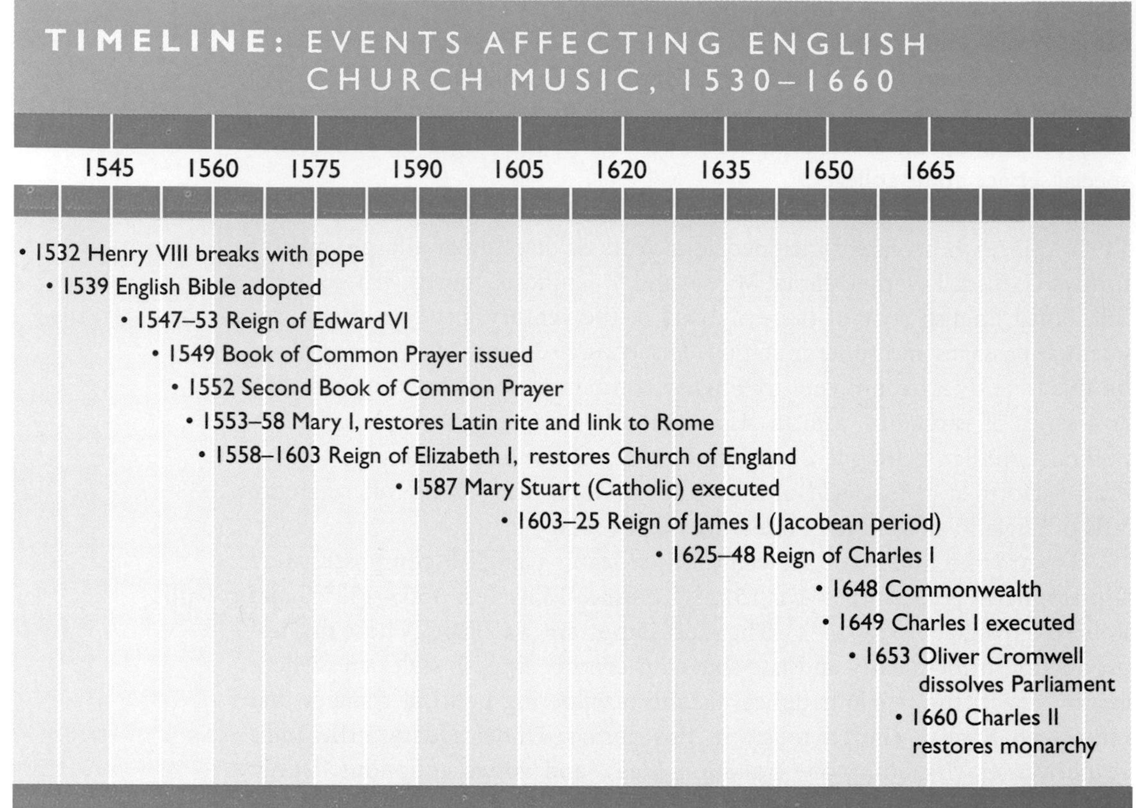

Syllabic setting

All these events, of course, had repercussions for church music. In 1548, Edward VI admonished the dean and chapter of Lincoln Minster to sing only English, "settyng thereunto a playn and distincte note, for every sillable one"[1]—in other words, a plain, syllabic, homophonic style. Such a drastic change from the massive, highly ornate, florid Catholic music of the early part of the century must have struck English composers as catastrophic. Fortunately, the more extreme demands were later relaxed to allow for some counterpoint. Latin motets of Tallis and Byrd remained favorites in English translation. Also, Queen Elizabeth specifically provided for the continued use of Latin in certain collegiate chapels and churches where it would have been familiar to the congregations.

The changes in language and liturgy finally gave rise to a new body of English church music. Tye and Tallis, whose major efforts went into Latin church composition, both contributed some English works. William Byrd, a Roman Catholic composer of Latin motets and Masses, nevertheless wrote five Services and about sixty anthems for Anglican use. Orlando Gibbons is often called the father of Anglican church music; his works are thoroughly English in spirit, even though their technique derives from the Latin tradition.

Service

The principal forms of Anglican music are the *Service* and the *anthem.* A complete Service consists of the music for fixed portions of Morning and

1. Quoted in Gustave Reese, *Music in the Renaissance* (New York: Norton, 1954), p. 796.

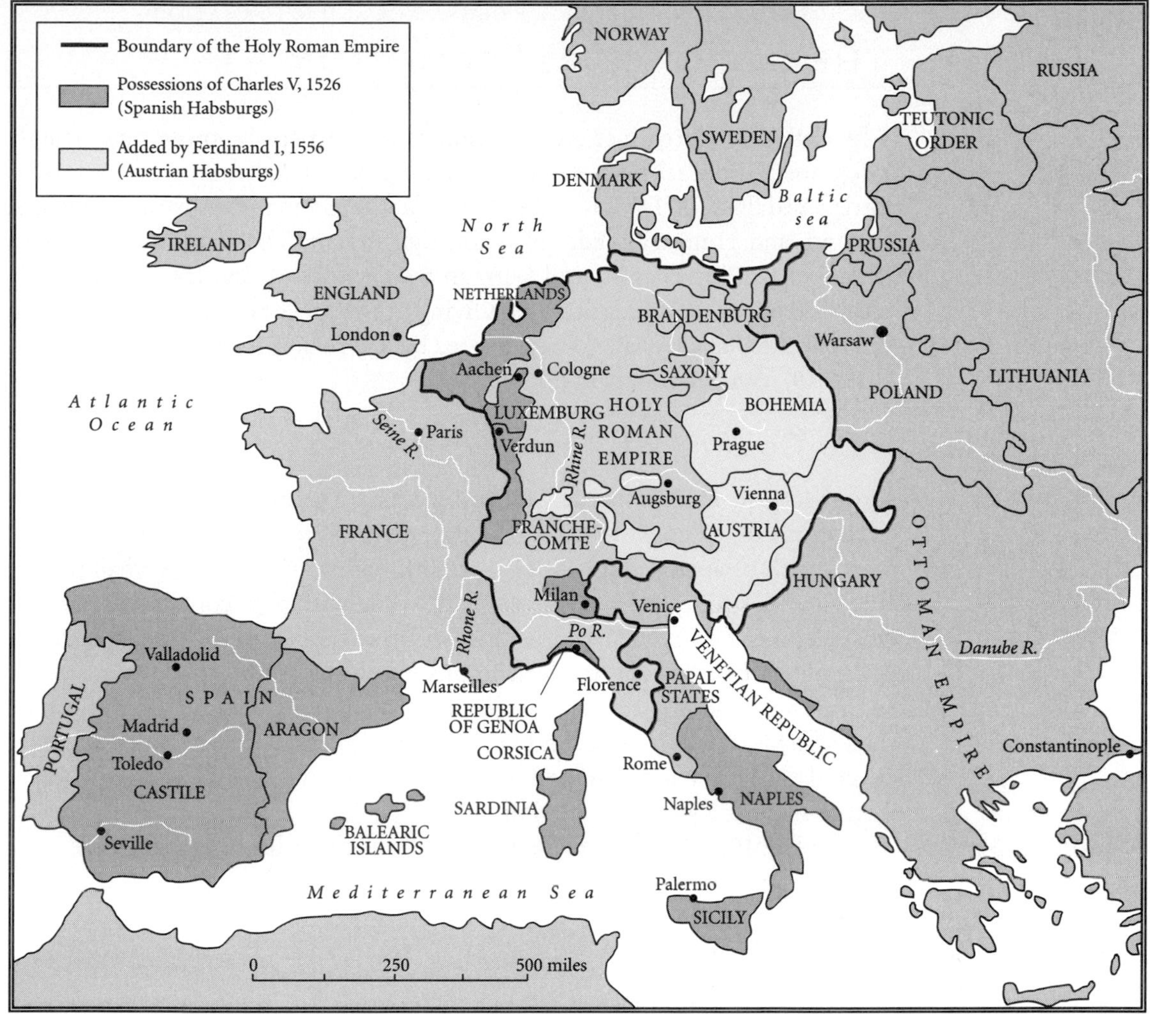

■ *Europe around 1560*

Evening Prayer (corresponding to the Catholic Matins and Vespers) and for Holy Communion (which corresponds to the Roman Mass). Often only the Kyrie and the Creed were composed, for Communion held a less important place in the Anglican musical scheme than it did in the Roman. The music of a *Great Service* is contrapuntal and melismatic; that of a *Short Service* is chordal and syllabic, with no difference in content between the two.

Full anthem

The English anthem corresponds to the Latin motet. One type, which came to be called a *full anthem*, was usually written in contrapuntal style for unaccompanied chorus throughout. Fine examples are Tomkins's *When David heard*[2] and Byrd's energetic and vivid *Sing joyfully unto God* (NAWM 50; CD 3 [47] / 2 ⟨9⟩). The *verse anthem* employed one or more solo voices with organ or viol accompaniment and had brief alternating passages for chorus. This type, which developed from the consort song, was most popular in England during the seventeenth century.

Verse anthem

2. Ed. in HAM No. 169.

THE COUNTER-REFORMATION

The Catholic Church met the defection of its northern brethren by starting a program of internal reform known as the *Counter-Reformation.* The loss or threatened loss of England, the Netherlands, Germany, Austria, Bohemia, Poland, and Hungary made this campaign urgent. The capture and sack of Rome in 1527 by Spanish and German mercenaries of Charles V had already dealt a blow to the secularized high living of the prelates in that city. It was in this climate that advocates of reform, led by Pope Paul III (Alessandro Farnese, 1534–49), came to power in the church.

The Council of Trent

From 1545 to 1563, a special Council, meeting intermittently in the northern Italian city of Trent, worked to formulate and pass measures aimed at purging the church of abuses and laxities. Church music took up only a small part of the Council's time, but it heard serious complaints. Some contended that basing the music on secular cantus firmi such as chansons, profaned the Mass. Complicated polyphony made it impossible to understand the words, even when pronounced correctly. Musicians were accused of using inappropriate instruments, being careless, and having irreverent attitudes; the pope even delivered a memorable reprimand on this subject to the choir of St. Peter's. Nevertheless, after a week's discussion of a draft submitted by the papal legates on September 10, 1562 (see vignette), the Council issued a very general pronouncement. Neither polyphony nor imitation of secular models was specifi-

Pronouncement

COUNCIL OF TRENT, RECOMMENDATION ON CHURCH MUSIC

Draft: All things should indeed be so ordered that the Masses, whether they be celebrated with or without singing, may reach tranquilly into the ears and hearts of those who hear them, when everything is executed clearly and at the right speed. In the case of those Masses which are celebrated with singing and with organ, let nothing profane be intermingled, but only hymns and divine praises. The whole plan of singing in musical modes should be constituted not to give empty pleasure to the ear, but in such a way that the words be clearly understood by all, and thus the hearts of the listeners be drawn to desire of heavenly harmonies, in the contemplation of the joys of the blessed.

Final version: They shall also banish from church all music that contains, whether in the singing or in the organ playing, things that are lascivious or impure.

From A. Theiner, *Acta . . . Concilii tridentini . . .*, 2 (1874):122, trans. in Gustave Reese, *Music in the Renaissance*, p. 449. Thanks to Craig A. Monson for clarifying the Council's final statement.

cally forbidden. The Council merely banished from the church everything "lascivious or impure." It left the task of implementing the directive to the diocesan bishops.

Palestrina legend

According to a legend from the late 1590s, Palestrina saved polyphony from the Council's condemnation by composing a six-voice Mass that was reverent in spirit and did not obscure the text. The work in question was the *Missa Papae Marcelli*, published in 1567 (see the Credo and Agnus I, NAWM 47; CD 3 [32] / 2 ⟨4⟩). Legend or not, the Council was almost certainly influenced by the music of a Flemish composer, Jacobus de Kerle (ca. 1532–1591), whose *preces speciales* (special prayers, 1561) were sung at one of its sittings. The transparent part-writing, frequent use of homophonic idiom, and sober, devotional spirit of these pieces must have convinced many Council members of the value of polyphonic music and silenced its opponents.

Palestrina

Career

Giovanni Pierluigi da Palestrina (1525 or 1526–1594), born in the small town of Palestrina, served as a choirboy and received his musical education in nearby Rome. After seven years there as a church musician, he became choirmaster of the Cappella Giulia at St. Peter's in 1551. He dedicated his first book of Masses (1554) to his patron, Pope Julius III. In 1555 he served briefly as a singer in the Cappella Sistina, the pope's official chapel, but had to relinquish the honor because he was married. He spent the remaining forty years of his career in Rome as choirmaster at two important churches, St. John Lateran and Santa Maria Maggiore, as teacher at a newly founded Jesuit Seminary, and once again as choirmaster of the Cappella Giulia, from 1571 until his death in 1594.

Palestrina refused two offers which would have taken him away from Rome: one from Emperor Maximilian II in 1568 (Philippe de Monte eventually took this position) and another in 1583 from Duke Guglielmo Gonzaga in Mantua, for whom he later wrote nine Masses.

Editing of chant books

During the latter part of his life, Palestrina supervised the revision of the official chant books to accord with the changes ordered by the Council of Trent. His task was to purge the chants of "barbarisms, obscurities, contrarieties, and superfluities" acquired, according to Pope Gregory XIII, "as a result of the clumsiness or negligence or even wickedness of the composers, scribes, and printers."[3] This work, not completed during Palestrina's lifetime, was completed by others, and the Medicean edition of the Gradual was published in 1614. It remained in use until the Vatican Edition, published by the monks of Solesmes, appeared in 1908.

By far the greatest part of Palestrina's work was sacred. He wrote 104 Masses, about 250 motets, many other liturgical compositions, and some 50 spiritual madrigals with Italian texts. His secular madrigals (approximately 100) are technically polished but conservative; even so, Palestrina later confessed that he "blushed and grieved" to have written music for love poems.

3. *Brief on the Reform of the Chant*, in SRrev, pp. 374–76; 3:96-98.

The Palestrina Style

Palestrina has been called "the Prince of Music" and his works the "absolute perfection" of church style. Better than any other composer, he captured the essence of the sober, conservative aspect of the Counter-Reformation. Not long after he died it was common to speak of the "stile da Palestrina," the Palestrina style, as a standard for polyphonic church music. Indeed, counterpoint instruction books, from Johann Joseph Fux's *Gradus ad Parnassum* (1725) to more recent texts, have aimed at guiding young composers to re-create this style.

Palestrina studied the works of outstanding Franco-Flemish composers and completely mastered their craft. Half of his Masses are based on polyphonic models, many of them by leading contrapuntists of previous generations. Eleven of these models are found in *Motetti del fiore*, two collections published by Jacques Moderne in 1532 and 1538.

Masses

Palestrina used the old-fashioned cantus firmus method for a few of his Masses (including the first of two he wrote on the traditional *L'homme armé* melody), but he generally preferred to paraphrase the chant in all the parts rather than confine it to the tenor voice. Other works reminiscent of the older

IOANNIS PETRI
Loysij Praenestini in basilica
S. Petri de vrbe capellae
Magistri.
MISSARVM LIBER PRIMVS.

■ *Title page of the first published collection of works by Palestrina. (Rome: Valerio and Luigi Dorico, 1554). The composer is shown presenting the music to Pope Julius III.* (STAATS-BIBLIOTHEK ZU BERLIN, PREUSSISCHER KULTURBESITZ, MUSIK-ABTEILUNG)

Flemish tradition are his early *Missa ad fugam*, written throughout in double canon, and his Mass *Repleatur os meum* of 1570, which systematically introduces canons at every interval from the octave down to the unison, ending with a double canon in the last Agnus Dei. Canons also occur in Palestrina's later Masses, though seldom carried through so rigorously as in these two works. The largest group of Palestrina's Masses are imitation masses, many derived from polyphonic compositions by other composers, a smaller number on his own motets and madrigals.

Melody

Palestrina's individual voice parts have an almost plainsong-like quality; their curve often describes an arch, and the motion is mostly stepwise, with short, infrequent leaps. In the first Agnus Dei from the famous *Pope Marcellus Mass* (Example 8.4, page 238; the entire Agnus I is in NAWM 47b; CD 3 37 / 2 ⟨4⟩),[4] for example, we observe long-breathed, flexibly articulated, easily singable lines, staying for the most part within the range of a ninth. The few leaps greater than a third are smoothed over by a return to a note within the interval of the skip. There are few repeated notes, and the rhythmic units vary in length.

Fluency of line is matched by fidelity to the diatonic modes. Palestrina studiously avoided chromaticism even in his secular madrigals, the more so in his sacred works, and above all in the Masses. He admitted only the essential alterations demanded by the conventions of musica ficta.

Counterpoint

Palestrina's counterpoint conforms in most details with the teachings of Willaert's school as transmitted by Zarlino in his *Le istitutioni harmoniche.*[5] The music is written almost entirely in the alla breve measure of ¢, which in the original editions (as in Example 8.5, page 239) consists of a downbeat and upbeat of one semibreve each (a half note in the transcription of Example 8.4).

Control of dissonance

The independent lines are expected to meet in a full triad on each beat. This convention is broken for suspensions, in which a voice is consonant with the other parts on the upbeat, but one or more of the other parts makes a dissonance against it on the downbeat, and the suspended voice resolves a step down. This alternation of tension and relaxation—strong dissonance on the downbeat and sweet consonance on the upbeat—more than the recurrence of accented syllables, endows this music with a pendulum-like pulse. Dissonances between beats may occur if the voice that is moving does so in a stepwise fashion. Palestrina's only exception to this rule is the *cambiata*, as it was later called,[6] in which a voice leaps a third down from a dissonance to a consonance instead of approaching it by step.

4. The Credo of this work appears in NAWM 49a. The entire Mass may be found in the Norton Critical Scores, ed. Lewis Lockwood.
5. See particularly Chapter 42 of Part 3: "Diminished Counterpoint for Two Voices: How Dissonances May Be Used," in Zarlino, *The Art of Counterpoint*, trans. Guy A. Marco and Claude V. Palisca (New Haven: Yale University Press, 1968; repr. New York: Da Capo Press, 1983), pp. 92–102.
6. The term means "exchanged"—that is, a dissonance is exchanged for a consonance, as would happen in Example 8.5, m. 14, if in the top voice two eighth notes *F–E*, instead of *F*, sounded against *G* in the bass. This pattern of dissonance-consonance is the reverse of the normal consonance-dissonance pattern on relatively prominent beats, and, thus, a dissonance is "exchanged" for a consonance. The Palestrina *cambiata*, found also in earlier sixteenth-century music, omits the intervening consonant note (*E* in this example).

Example 8.4 *Giovanni Pierluigi da Palestrina*, Pope Marcellus Mass: *Agnus Dei I*

V. *Orlando di Lasso at the virginal leading his chamber ensemble in St. George's Hall at the court of Duke Albrecht V in Munich. Shown are three choirboys, about twenty singers, and fifteen instrumentalists. Miniature by Hans Mielich (1516–1573) in a manuscript of Lasso's Penitential Psalms.* (MUNICH, BAYERISCHE STAATS-BIBLIOTHEK)

VI. *Michelangelo Merisi da Caravaggio (1571–1610),* The Lute Player, *painted 1595–96 for Vincenzo Giustiniani, the Roman nobleman who wrote an important* Discorso sopra la musica *(1628). The young man appears to be singing while accompanying himself on the lute. The bass partbook is open to madrigals by Arcadelt. The decorated initial "V" begins the text, "Voi sapete," from his first book of madrigals (known in editions of 1539 and later). As was a common practice, the boy must be singing either the bass or another part and improvising an accompaniment from what he remembers of the other parts. The painting is a study of sensation: the lute and violin evoke the sense of hearing; the partbook, sight; the player's fingers, touch; the flowers and fruit, the senses of smell and taste.* (PRIVATE COLLECTION. PHOTOGRAPH COURTESY THE METROPOLITAN MUSEUM OF ART, NEW YORK)

Example 8.5 *Contrapuntal Analysis of Example 8.4, measures 10–15, Tenors I, II, Basses I, II*

The alternation of consonance and dissonance is clearly evident in Example 8.5. In the lowest four voices of measures 10–15, notated in their original values, P stands for passing note, S for suspension, C for cambiata; numbers indicate the dissonant intervals and their resolutions; and arrows mark the down- and upbeats.

The smooth diatonic lines and the discreet handling of dissonance give Palestrina's music a consistent serenity and clarity. Another positive quality of his counterpoint lies in the vertical combination of the voices. By varying the voice grouping and spacing, the same harmony produces a large number of subtly different shadings and sonorities.

Rhythm

The rhythm of Palestrina's music—and that of sixteenth-century polyphony in general—is a mixture of the rhythms of the individual voices plus a collective rhythm resulting from the harmonies on the beats. When each voice is barred according to its own natural rhythm (as in Example 8.6, which reproduces the first seven measures of Example 8.4), we can see graphically how independent the individual lines are. But when the piece is performed and all the voices are sounding together, we perceive a fairly regular succession of $\frac{2}{2}$ or $\frac{4}{4}$ "measures" that are set off mostly by the harmonic changes and the sus-

Example 8.6 *Palestrina,* Pope Marcellus Mass: *Agnus Dei I, Rhythms*

pensions on strong beats. This gently marked regularity of rhythm characterizes the Palestrina style.

Form

This same Agnus Dei also illustrates how Palestrina unifies a composition by purely musical means. Each phrase of the text has its own musical motive, and the contrapuntal development of each motive overlaps at a cadence with that of the next. But there Palestrina achieved organic unity by systematically repeating motives and by limiting the main cadences to scale degrees that define the mode.

Text comprehension

All these traits are evident in the *Pope Marcellus Mass*, as is Palestrina's conscious striving to make the text intelligible. He wrote the work in 1562–63, precisely when the Council of Trent was issuing the *Canon on Music to be Used in the Mass*, in which it is urged that "the words be clearly understood by all" (see vignette, page 234). His attention to text setting is particularly evident in the Credo (NAWM 47a; CD 3 [32]), where the voices pronounce a given phrase simultaneously rather than in the staggered manner of imitative polyphony.

Texture

To achieve variety, Palestrina divided the six-voice choir into various smaller groups, each with its particular tone color, and reserved the full six voices for climactic or particularly significant words, such as "per quem omnia facta sunt" (through whom all things were made) or "Et incarnatus est" (and He was made flesh).

In Example 8.7, we can see this flexible approach to musical textures. The group C–A–TII–BI is answered by the group C–TI–TII–BII singing the same words, "Et in unum Dominum." Each group pronounces a segment of text in speech rhythm and arrives at its own cadence, in both cases one now considered weak based on the major sixth–to–octave succession. The "Filium Dei unigenitum" is sung by a trio, symbolizing the three-in-one essence of the Trinity, moving in parallel sixths and thirds—fauxbourdon resurrected.

Palestrina also avoided monotony by rhythmic means. Just as in the Agnus Dei discussed above, the accents in each voice fall on different beats of the measure. Accented syllables may occur on any of the beats, and only after a cadence is the normal alternation of down- and upbeat restored. For example, in the section "Et in unum Dominum" the listener hears the following sequence of triple, duple, and single beat rhythms: 3 2 2 3 3 3 3 1 3 2 2.

Severe style

Palestrina's style was the first in the history of Western music to be consciously preserved, isolated, and imitated as a model in later ages. It is this style that seventeenth-century musicians had in mind when they spoke of *stile antico* (old style) or *stile grave* (severe style).

Palestrina's Contemporaries

Animuccia

Giovanni Animuccia (ca. 1500–1571), Palestrina's predecessor at St. Peter's, is noted chiefly for the laude he wrote for the Congregation of the Oratory, a Roman group founded by the Florentine priest Filippo Neri. There, members heard religious lectures, prayed, and sang laude. The Congregation's name came from the original place of meeting, the "oratory" (prayer chapel) of one of the Roman churches. In later times, the laude and similar devotional songs were occasionally given dialogue form or otherwise dramatized.

Example 8.7 *Palestrina*, Pope Marcellus Mass: *Credo*

And in one Lord Jesus Christ, the only-begotten Son of God, born of the Father before all ages.

Spain

Like all of continental Europe in the late fifteenth and early sixteenth centuries, Spain fell under the spell of Franco-Flemish polyphony. Spanish manuscripts of the period include many works by masters such as Gombert, Manchicourt, Crecquillon, and others who worked in Spain from time to time. The expression of religious feelings achieved a passionate intensity in Spanish sacred music through expansive melodies, moderate, selective use of fugal procedures, and adventurous harmonic progressions not limited by modal constraints. These qualities are heard in the motet *Emendemus in melius* (Let us make amends)[7] by Cristobal de Morales (ca. 1500–1553), the most eminent Spanish composer of his time, who acquired fame in Italy as a member of the papal chapel between 1535 and 1545.

Morales

Victoria

Tomás Luis de Victoria (1548–1611) was, after Palestrina, the most illustrious exponent of the Roman polyphonic style. A close connection existed between Spanish and Roman composers throughout the sixteenth century. In 1565 Victoria enrolled in the Jesuit German College in Rome and may have studied at the nearby Roman Seminary with Palestrina. Victoria took a teaching post at the College in 1571, and in 1573 became the Seminary's choir director. He left that position in 1577 to join a community of lay priests. Returning to Spain about 1587, he became chaplain to the Empress Maria, for whose funeral services he wrote a famous *Officium defunctorum* (Office for the Dead) in 1603. Although his style resembles Palestrina's, Victoria infused his music, which was exclusively sacred, with greater expressive intensity, and, like Morales, he took more advantage of notes outside the diatonic modes. For example, in his Mass *O magnum mysterium* (see NAWM 48; CD 3 [38]), which is in transposed first mode, the sixth degree is often lowered and the seventh raised as in the later minor mode. On the other hand, Victoria tended to limit his internal cadences to the final of the mode.

Mass *O magnum mysterium*

Like most of Victoria's Masses, *O magnum mysterium* is an imitation Mass based on one of his own motets (NAWM 48a). The motet exploits a variety of textures and motives to express successively the mystery, wonder, and joy of the Christmas season. In the Kyrie (NAWM 48b), Victoria converted the opening of the motet (Example 8.8a) into a fugue on two similar subjects (Example 8.8b) derived from the motet's single subject. The Mass does, however, preserve the motet's paired entrances. The Christe, as in other imitation Masses, utilizes a freely invented subject. On its return, the Kyrie borrows the music of the motet's "iacentem in praesepio" almost literally. Like Palestrina, Victoria aimed for complete triadic harmony, except that he preferred to end the Kyrie sections with the pure sound of perfect consonances.

Other notable Spanish composers of church music include Francisco Guerrero (1528–1599), who worked in various Spanish cities and went to

Guerrero

7. Ed. in HAM No. 128.

Example 8.8 Tomás Luis de Victoria

a. *Motet:* O magnum mysterium

1

Cantus: O ma - gnum my - ste - ri - um, et ad - mi - ra - bi-

Altus: O ma - gnum my - ste - ri - um,

Tenor

Bassus

6

le sa - cra - men - - - tum, o

et ad - mi - ra - bi - le sa - cra - men - tum, o

O ma - gnum my -

O

11

ma - gnum my - ste -

ma - gnum my - ste - ri - um,

ste - ri - um, et ad - mi - ra - bi - le

ma - gnum, my - ste - ri - um,

b. *Mass,* O magnum mysterium: *Kyrie*

Pujol

Rome in 1574, and the Catalan Juan Pujol (ca. 1573–1626), who belongs to a later era but whose style resembles Palestrina's and Victoria's.

Philippe de Monte and Orlando di Lasso were the last in the illustrious line of sixteenth-century Franco-Flemish composers. Unlike Palestrina and Victoria, they wrote many secular works. Monte nevertheless produced thirty-eight Masses and more than three hundred motets in which he demonstrated his mastery of the old contrapuntal technique, with some modern touches.

Lasso

Orlando di Lasso (1532–1594) ranks with Palestrina among the great composers of sacred music in the late sixteenth century. If Palestrina was above all a master of the Mass, Lasso's chief glory is his motets. In both his career and his compositions, Lasso was one of the most cosmopolitan figures in the history of music. By the age of twenty-four he had already published books of madrigals, chansons, and motets, and his total production eventually amounted to more than two thousand works. The principal collection of his

Motets

motets, the *Magnum opus musicum* (Great Work of Music), was published by his sons in 1604, ten years after his death. Lasso had an impulsive, emotional, and dynamic temperament. In his motets, the rhetorical, pictorial, and dramatic interpretation of the text determines the overall form and the details.

Tristis est anima mea

Lasso's *Tristis est anima mea* (published 1565; NAWM 49; CD 3 [43] / 2 ⟨5⟩), one of his most deeply moving and vivid settings, illustrates this approach. The text, a Respond for Maundy Thursday, is based on the words of Jesus before he was crucified as reported by Matthew (26:38) and Mark (14:34). The motet's opening (Example 8.9) is a masterful sound-image of sadness, depicted through a descending-semitone motive sung to the word "Tristis," which dominates the first nine measures, along with carefully wrought, drawn-out suspensions. The consonant suspension in the first two measures prepares the more pungent dissonant suspension in the alto and the unusual suspension in the soprano, which resolves on the downbeat instead of the upbeat. This use of the suspension to achieve emotional tension rather than to prepare a cadence was common in the madrigal but still rare in sacred music. Later in the motet Lasso wrote a lively contrapuntal section to represent the watchful vigilance Jesus demanded of his disciples. Lasso also depicted the flight of the eleven disciples (as Jesus is attacked by the twelfth disciple, Judas, and the mob) with eleven stretto-entrances of a running subject. The words of the text simulated not only the rhythms, accents, and contours of the musical motives but the music's every gesture: harmonic effects, textures, constructive devices such as suspensions and fugal imitation, and the weight and placement of cadences.

Under the influence of the Counter-Reformation, Lasso devoted the latter years of his life to setting sacred texts, particularly spiritual madrigals, renouncing the "merry" and "festive" songs of his youth for music of "more substance

Example 8.9 *Orlando di Lasso, Motet:* Tristis est anima mea

[Note values halved]

and energy." We cannot properly speak of a Lasso style; he was too versatile for that. Franco-Flemish counterpoint, Italian harmony, Venetian opulence, French vivacity, German severity—all abound in his work. More fully than any other sixteenth-century composer, he synthesized the achievements of an epoch.

Byrd

William Byrd (1543–1623) was the last of the great Catholic church composers of the sixteenth century. He studied music as a boy probably under Thomas Tallis and was appointed organist of Lincoln Cathedral in 1563. About ten years later he moved to London to take up duties as a member of the royal chapel, a post he held for the rest of his life even though he remained a Roman Catholic, a sign of the respect shown him by Queen and court. In 1575 he and Tallis were granted a monopoly for the printing of music in England, which he continued to control after Tallis's death in 1585.

Byrd's works include English polyphonic songs, keyboard pieces (see Chapter 5), and music for the Anglican Church. His Latin Masses and motets may be his best vocal compositions. Given the religious situation in England at the time, it is not surprising that Byrd wrote only three Masses (one each for three, four, and five voices); these are beyond doubt the finest Masses written by an English composer.

Motets

Byrd probably intended his earlier motets for private devotional gatherings, but he designed the two books of *Gradualia* (1605, 1607) for liturgical use by Catholic recusants who worshipped secretly. The dedication for the first collection paid tribute to the power of scriptural texts to inspire a composer's imagination:

> I have found there is such a power hidden away and stored up in those words [of Scripture] that—I know not how—to one who meditates on divine things, pondering them with detailed concentration, all the most fitting melodies come as it were of themselves, and freely present themselves when the mind is alert and eager.

Byrd was the first English composer to absorb Continental imitative techniques so thoroughly that he could apply them imaginatively and without constraint. In the motet *Tu es Petrus*, at the words "aedificabo Ecclesiam meam" (I will build my church), Byrd musically portrayed the erection of the church by a theme that rises an octave, first through a minor third, then through stepwise motion (see Example 8.10). More than twenty imitations of this motive, with only rare alteration of the intervals, are heard in the various parts. A long pedal point on the word "petram" (rock) makes a musical pun on the name of the apostle Petrus (Peter), upon whom, like a rock, Christ would build his church. Byrd avoided cadence during this fourteen-measure section, and he occasionally suggested fauxbourdon in the closing Alleluia, as a Continental composer of the early part of the century might have done. But Byrd's grand metaphor on the building of a church allies this motet more with the late sixteenth-century madrigal.

Example 8.10 *William Byrd, Motet:* Tu es Petrus

. . . and on this rock I will build my church.

SUMMARY

Changes in musical style occur gradually, in complex ways, and at different times in different places. Late Renaissance practices persisted well into the seventeenth century, and many features of early Baroque music made their appearance long before the end of the sixteenth. That is why the discussion in the last few chapters has at times overstepped the arbitrary boundary of the year 1600, which we set as the limit of the Renaissance period.

Texture

Let us now consider how the changes that took place between 1450 and 1600 affected some general features of musical style. Writing for contrapuntal voice parts that are similar and of equal importance remained the rule for Palestrina, Lasso, and Byrd, as it had been for Ockeghem and Josquin. This texture and the coordination of parts through free and fugal imitation, more than any other features, characterized Renaissance music. Even so, homophony had begun to intrude in all forms of polyphonic writing.

Rhythm

Rhythm, supported by the alternation of consonance and dissonance, had become comparatively steady and predictable by the end of the century, whether in the contrapuntal style of Palestrina or in such apparently free compositions as the Venetian organ toccatas. The basic rhythmic medium of vocal music was the alla breve duple measure, sometimes alternating with a triple proportion or with hidden triple groupings within the duple.

Melody and harmony

The prevailing style of sacred music revealed smooth vocal parts joining in a succession of full triadic harmonies. The plainchant modes, reinterpreted in terms of polyphony, guided the composer's large-scale structures. The range of the individual voices, the avoidance of chromatic excursions, the choice of notes on which to build cadences, and the pitches of fugal entrances all helped to maintain modal unity and character. Only a few church composers in the last decades of the sixteenth century indulged in the pictorial and expressive touches that had become common in the madrigal.

BIBLIOGRAPHY

Music Collections

For editions of Clemens non Papa, Hassler, Lasso, Le Jeune, Monte, and Senfl, see also the Bibliography for Chapter 7.

Modern collected editions of the composers mentioned in this chapter:

Byrd: *The Collected Vocal Works of William Byrd*, ed. Edmund H. Fellowes (London: Stainer & Bell, 1937–50), 20 vols., with Vols. 18–20 devoted to keyboard music. Rev. ed. by Thurston Dart (1970–) as *The Collected Works*. A new edition in progress: *The Byrd Edition*, Philip Brett, gen. ed. (London: Stainer & Bell; New York: Galaxy, 1976–)

G. Gabrieli: CM 12, ed. Denis Arnold.

Goudimel: *Oeuvres complètes*, ed. Pierre Pidoux, Henri Gagnebin, Rudolf Häusler, Eleanor Lawry, Gesamtausgaben 3 (Brooklyn: Institute of Medieval Music, 1967–83); also Henry Expert, ed., *Maîtres musiciens de la Renaissance française*, Vols. 2, 4, 6.

Guerrero: *Monumentos de la música española* 16 and 19, ed. Miguel Querol Gavaldá.
Handl: Collected Edition, ed. Dragotin Cvetko (Ljubljana, 1966–); DTOe, Vols. 12, 14, 30, 40, 48, 51, 52, 78, 94, 95, 118, 119.
Lechner: *Werke*, ed. Konrad Ameln (Kassel: Bärenreiter, 1954–)
Lasso: Besides the complete-works editions listed in the Bibliography for Chapter 7, Peter Bergquist is editing a series of works for A-R Editions, Madison, Wisconsin. So far published: *Lectiones sacrae novem, ex libris Hiob excerptae (ca. 1582)* (1983); *The Seven Penitential Psalms and Laudate Dominum de caelis* (1990); and *The Complete Motets* (1995–).
Le Jeune: *Maîtres musiciens de la Renaissance française* 11, 21, 22, 23 , ed. H. Expert.
Merulo: CMM 51; *Canzoni d'intavolatura d'organo*, ed. Walker Cunningham and Charles McDermott (Madison, Wis.: A-R, 1992).
Palestrina: *Opera omnia*, ed. Theodor de Witt, F. X. Haberl, et al. (Leipzig: Breitkopf & Härtel, 1862–1903); DdT 1, ed. Heinrich Bellermann (1896); *Le opere complete*, ed. Raffaele Casimiri and Lavinio Virgili (Rome: Fratelli Scalera, 1939–). The *Pope Marcellus Mass* is published in the Norton Critical Scores, ed. Lewis Lockwood.
H. Praetorius: DdT 23.
M. Praetorius: *Gesamtausgabe der musikalischen Werke*, ed. Friedrich Blume, Arnold Mendelssohn, Wilibald Gurlitt (Wolfenbüttel: Kallmeyer, 1928–60).
Pujol: *Opera omnia*, ed. Higini Anglès (Barcelona, Biblioteca de Catalunya, 1926–32).
Schein: *Sämtliche Werke*, ed. Arthur Prüfer (Leipzig: Breitkopf & Härtel, 1901–23), incomplete; *Neue Ausgabe sämtlicher Werke*, ed. Adam Adrio (Kassel: Bärenreiter, 1963–).
Schütz: see Bibliography for Chapter 9.
Senfl: *Sämtliche Werke* (Basel: Hug; Wolfenbüttel: Möseler, 1937–).
Sweelinck: *Werken*, ed. Max Seiffert, Hermann Gehrmann (The Hague: M. Nijhof; Leipzig: Breitkopf & Härtel, 1894–1901; repr. 1968); rev. and enl., 1943 (Amsterdam: Alsbach); *Opera omnia, editio altera*, ed. R. Lagas et al. (Amsterdam: Alsbach, 1957–90).
Victoria: *Opera omnia*, ed. Felipe Pedrell (Leipzig: Breitkopf & Härtel, 1902–13; repr. 1965); *Opera omnia*, corrected and augmented, H. Anglès, ed., *Monumentos de la música española* 25, 26, 30, 31.
Walther: *Sämtliche Werke*, ed. Otto Schröder (Kassel: Bärenreiter, 1953–73). Johann Walther's *Geystliche gesangk Buchleyn* of 1524 is published in EP, Vol. 7 (Year 6).
Zieleński: *Opera omnia*, ed. W. Malinowski and Zdzisław Jachimecki, *Monumenta musicae in Polonia*, Series A (Krakow: Polskie Wydawn. Muzyczne, 1966–71).

Luther's *Deudsche Messe* (1526) is published in facsimile by Bärenreiter (Kassel, 1934).
Rhau's collection of 1544, *Newe deudsche geistliche Gesenge CXXIII* is Vol. 34 of DdT.

For church music of the Reformation in France and in the Netherlands see Pierre Pidoux, *Le Psautier huguenot du xvie siècle* (Basel: Bärenreiter, 1962); Waldo Selden Pratt, *The Music of the French Psalter of 1562* (New York: Columbia University Press, 1939).

A facsimile reprint of the *Bay Psalm Book* has been published by the Chicago University Press, 1956. See also Richard G. Appel, *Music of the Bay Psalm Book*, 9th ed. (Brooklyn: Institute for Studies in American Music, 1975).

Compositions by Andrea and Giovanni Gabrieli are published in the first two volumes of *Istituzioni e monumenti dell'arte musicale italiana* (Milan: Ricordi, 1931–41).

For Further Reading

The basic work on Lutheran church music is Friedrich Blume, *Protestant Church Music* (New York: Norton, 1974).

On English music of the late sixteenth and early seventeenth centuries: Peter LeHuray, *Music and the Reformation in England, 1549–1660* (New York: Oxford University Press, 1967); and E. H. Fellowes, *English Cathedral Music*, 5th ed., rev. J. A. Westrup (London: Methuen, 1969); Richard Turbet, *Tudor Music: A Research and Information Guide, with an Appendix Updating William Byrd* (New York: Garland, 1994).

On Spanish music of the period covered in this chapter, see Robert Stevenson, *Spanish Cathedral Music in the Golden Age* (Berkeley: University of California Press, 1961).

On Italian church music, see Jerome Roche, *North Italian Church Music in the Age of Monteverdi* (Oxford: Clarendon Press, 1984).

Waldo S. Pratt, *The Music of the Pilgrims* (Boston: O. Ditson, 1921), contains a description of the Ainsworth Psalter.

The NG articles on Palestrina, Lasso, Byrd, and Victoria have been published together with updated bibliographies as *The New Grove High Renaissance Masters* (New York: Norton, 1984).

Individual Composers

Byrd Major works on Byrd are the three volumes of the new series, The Music of William Byrd: 1, Joseph Kerman, *The Masses and Motets of William Byrd* (Berkeley: University of California Press, 1980); 2, Philip Brett, *The Songs, Services and Anthems of William Byrd* (in preparation); and 3, Oliver W. Neighbor, *The Consort and Keyboard Music of William Byrd* (1978). See also John Harley, *William Byrd: Gentleman of the Chapel Royal* (Aldershot, Hants, England: Scolar Press, 1997); *Byrd Studies*, ed. Alan Brown and Richard Turbet (Cambridge: Cambridge University Press, 1992).

G. Gabrieli Denis Arnold, *Giovanni Gabrieli and the Music of the Venetian High Renaissance* (London: Oxford University Press, 1979); Egon Kenton, *Life and Work of Giovanni Gabrieli*, AIM, 1967.

Lasso Jerome Roche, *Lassus*, Oxford Studies of Composers (London: Oxford University Press, 1982), is the only monograph in English devoted to this composer. For bibliography, see James Erb, *Orlando di Lasso: A Guide to Research* (New York: Garland, 1990).

Palestrina Knud Jeppesen's *The Style of Palestrina and the Dissonance*, 2nd ed., trans. Edward J. Dent (London: Oxford University Press, 1946) subjects Palestrina's music to detailed analysis. Quentin W. Quereau, "Aspects of Palestrina's Parody Procedure," JM 1 (1982):198–216. On the legend surrounding the *Pope Marcellus Mass*, see the studies in the Norton Critical Scores, ed. Lewis Lockwood (New York: Norton, 1975).

Tallis Paul Doe, *Tallis* (London: Oxford University Press, 1968).

Taverner Colin Hand, *John Taverner: His Life and Music* (London: Eulenburg, 1978).

CHAPTER 9

MUSIC OF THE EARLY BAROQUE PERIOD

GENERAL CHARACTERISTICS

The term *baroque*

Around 1750 the well-traveled Charles de Brosses complained that the façade of the Pamphili Palace in Rome (see illustration) was being made over with a kind of filigree ornamentation more suitable to tableware than to architecture. Addicted to colorful language, he called this decorative style *baroque*[1] (from the Portuguese *barroco*, describing a deformed pearl). Thus was launched the career of a term that art historians in the late nineteenth century embraced to characterize a whole period of art and architecture. Years earlier, an anonymous music critic called the music of Jean-Philippe Rameau's *Hippolyte et Aricie* (1733) "barocque," complaining that it was noisy and unmelodious, with capricious and extravagant modulations, repetitions, and metrical changes.[2] Before the term was ever used by art or music critics, *baroque* meant abnormal, bizarre, exaggerated, grotesque, or in bad taste, and it retains that sense today.

It took the art criticism of Jacob Burckhardt and Karl Baedeker in the nineteenth century to overcome these derogatory aspects of the term and bring out its positive side. For them *baroque* summed up the admirably flamboyant, decorative, and expressionistic tendencies of seventeenth-century painting and architecture. In the 1920s, music historians followed suit and applied the term back to music from the late sixteenth century until about the mid-eighteenth. *Baroque* came to represent a particular style of music from an entire era, but it

1. Charles de Brosses, *L'Italie il y a cent ans ou Lettres écrites d'Italie à quelques amis en 1739 et 1740*, ed. M. R. Colomb (Paris, 1836), 2:117f. The letters from Rome were not drafted until after his return to France between 1745 and 1755.
2. *Lettre de M *** à Mlle *** sur l'origine de la musique* in *Mercure de France*, May 1734, pp. 861ff.

■ *Detail of the Pamphili Palace (now Doria-Pamphili) in Rome, from the façade on Via del Corso, designed by Gabriele Valvassori and completed ca. 1739. Charles de Brosses, writing about it in his* Lettres familières écrites d'Italie *around 1755, criticized as "baroque" the delicate, detailed decoration of the sort that he deemed more suitable for silverware and gold cases than for a building. His is thought to be the first use of the word in relation to one of the visual arts.*

was soon recognized that this century and a half encompassed a diversity of styles too great to be embraced by one word. In this book, *baroque* will rarely be used to designate a style. Nevertheless, because it evokes the artistic and literary culture of an entire era, we will use the term to identify the period.

The period

Historians chose the term *baroque* to cover the music of 1600–1750 because they thought that the music shared certain qualities with the architecture, painting, literature—perhaps even the science and philosophy—of the time. General labels like *Baroque* (or *Gothic* or *Romantic*) are sometimes preferable to a designation such as "thoroughbass period," which may seem more precise—although it doesn't fit many compositions—but fails to acknowledge the relationship between music and other cultural branches.

As with other epochs, boundary dates are only approximations. Many characteristics of the period appeared before 1600 and many were declining by the 1730s. But within the chronological limits of 1600–1750, composers accepted a set of conventions for organizing music and shared ideals of how it should sound. Most important, they believed that music's principal goal was to move the affections.

Geographical and Cultural Background

Italian attitudes dominated the musical thinking of this period. By the end of the Baroque era, in fact, the music of Europe had become a single language with Italian roots.

Italy

From the mid-sixteenth to the mid-eighteenth centuries, Italy remained Europe's most influential musical region. The Italian peninsula during that time was split into areas ruled by Spain and Austria, the Papal States, and a half-dozen smaller independent states that heartily distrusted one another and allied themselves from time to time with larger European powers. Several Italian cities loomed large on the musical map—out of proportion to their real size or political power. Florence, for example, hosted a brilliant period of musico-theatrical innovation at the dawn of the seventeenth century. Rome exerted a steady influence on sacred music and for a time was an important center of opera, cantata, and instrumental music. Venice, a leading musical city throughout the seventeenth century, became a center of opera, as did Naples during most of the eighteenth. Meanwhile, Bologna and other northern cities witnessed important developments in instrumental music.

France

Even France, a country that developed and maintained its own distinctive national idiom, could not entirely escape the Italian influence, which was particularly strong throughout the first half of the seventeenth century. Its own national style of music emerged in the 1630s and held sway for more than a hundred years. Ironically, the composer whose works did most to establish this national style, Jean-Baptiste Lully, was a Florentine brought to France at age thirteen to help a noblewoman practice speaking Italian.

Germany

In Germany, the calamity of the Thirty Years' war (1618–48) overwhelmed an already weakened musical culture. In the second half of the century, German composers built their music on an Italian style. Despite political disunity, the subsequent generations enjoyed a resurgence, most notably through the music of Johann Sebastian Bach. But the art of Bach also owed much to Italy, and Handel's work was as much Italian as German.

England

The musical glories of the Elizabethan and Jacobean ages in England faded with the period of the Civil War and the Commonwealth (1642–60); a brilliant revival toward the end of the century gave way to a nearly complete surrender to the Italian style.

Patronage

Wealthy absolute governments ruled Europe between 1600 and 1750—the time of American colonization—and their patronage helped cultivate new genres of music. Many of the European courts maintained important centers of musical culture. The most imposing of these, and the model for all lesser establishments in the late seventeenth and early eighteenth centuries, was the court of Louis XIV of France (reigned 1643–1715). Other patrons of music included popes, emperors, kings of England and of Spain, and rulers of smaller Italian and German entities. City-states, such as Venice and many of the northern German towns, also maintained musical establishments, both ecclesiastical and secular. The church itself, of course, continued to support music, but its role was less important in the Baroque era than it had been. Along with aristocratic, civic, and ecclesiastical patronage, many cities had "academies"—private associations that sponsored musical activities. Public concerts to which one subscribed or paid admission were still rare. The first such undertaking occurred in England in 1672; others followed in Germany (1722) and France (1725), but the practice did not become widespread until the later 1700s.

Literature, the arts, and sciences

The arts and sciences flourished along with music in the Baroque era. To realize how magnificent this age was in the history of Western civilization, we need only recall the names of a few great writers and artists of the seventeenth century: in England, John Donne and Milton; in Spain, Cervantes; in France,

Corneille, Racine, and Molière; the Netherlands, its musical golden age past, produced the painters Rubens and Rembrandt; Spain, somewhat isolated and of secondary importance in music, could boast the painters Velázquez and Murillo. Italy had the sculptor Bernini and the architect Borromini. In the seventeenth century, one of the great ages in the history of philosophy and science, Bacon, Descartes, Leibniz, Galileo, Kepler, and Newton established the foundations of modern science, mathematics, and rational thought.

New Musical Idiom

Music was profoundly influenced by the changes taking place in the intellectual and artistic realms. Just as seventeenth-century philosophers left behind outmoded ways of thinking about the world and proposed new explanations, musicians expanded their vocabulary to meet new expressive needs. As philosophers developed new ideas within the frame of older methods, so musicians—such as Gesualdo in his madrigals and Giovanni Gabrieli in his motets—poured more intense and more varied emotions into the musical genres they inherited from the Renaissance. Much early seventeenth-century music was truly experimental or, at least, displayed a gap between intention and realization. By the middle of the century, the new resources of harmony, color, and form coalesced into a common language with a firm vocabulary, grammar, and syntax.

The Two Practices

Although Claudio Monteverdi must have known that he was breaking new ground, he could not have anticipated that his madrigal *Cruda Amarilli* would ignite a controversy that would smolder for thirty years. The text of Monteverdi's *Cruda Amarilli* (NAWM 53; CD 3 [59] / CD 2 ⟨13⟩) is a speech from Giovanni Battista Guarini's pastoral play *Il pastor fido*, a favorite source for Marenzio and other composers as well. Although Monteverdi's setting was first published in the fifth book of 1605, the work must have circulated before the turn of the century, since its contrapuntal licenses were criticized in Giovanni Maria Artusi's dialogue of 1600, *L'Artusi overo delle imperfettioni della moderna musica* (The Artusi, or Imperfections of Modern Music; see vignette, page 256). One interlocutor in the dialogue objected in particular to measures 12–14 of Example 9.1, which he quotes, pointing out that the soprano part in measure 13 fails to agree with the bass.[3] The other interlocutor, however, defends the passage, arguing that if one assumes a *G* on the first beat of the soprano part, the figure resembles an *accento*—an improvised embellishment common at this time—replacing the stepwise motion *G–F–E* with *G–A–F–E*. Such written-out embellishments, then called *diminutions*, also season the harmony with runs in measure 12 and especially in measure 2. Here the diminution of the skip *D–B* and *B–G* in the upper parts causes the grating dissonances that aptly express the complaint "Cruda Amarilli" (Cruel Amaryllis). Although some of Monteverdi's dissonances may be rationalized as embellishments, his

3. SRrev 4:19–22.

Example 9.1 *Claudio Monteverdi, Madrigal:* Cruda Amarilli

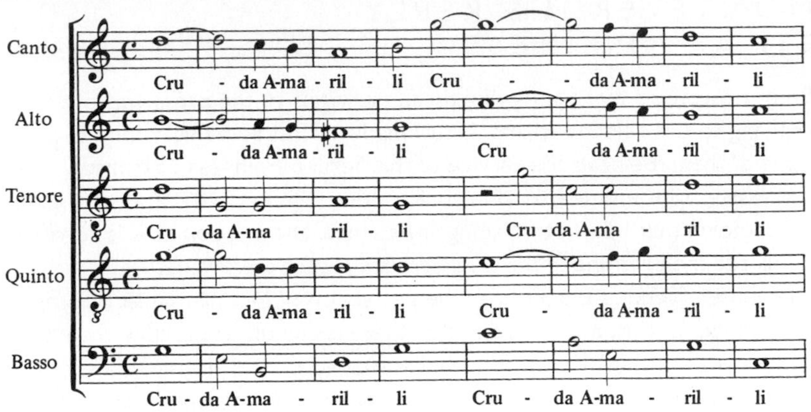

Cruel Amaryllis, who with your name, to love, alas, [*bitterly you teach . . .*]

real motivation in writing them was to convey through harmony, rather than through graphic images, the meaning and feeling of the poet's message.

Monteverdi defended himself against Artusi's criticism in a concise credo printed in the fifth book of madrigals (see vignette, page 256). He promised to deal with the matter more extensively in a book, which never appeared.

Composers and observers recognized that they had inherited a plurality of styles from the previous century. Monteverdi in 1605 distinguished between a *prima pratica* and a *seconda pratica*, or first and second "practices." By the first, he meant the style of vocal polyphony codified by Zarlino. By the second, Monteverdi meant the adventurous style of the modern Italians such as Rore, Marenzio, and himself. According to Monteverdi, in the first practice music dominated the verbal text, while in the second practice the text dominated the music. In the new style, the old rules could be broken and dissonances used more freely to express the feelings evoked in the text. Others called the two practices *stile antico* and *stile moderno* (old and modern style), or *stylus gravis* and *stylus luxurians* (severe and embellished style).

MONTEVERDI'S REPLY TO ARTUSI, 1605

Be not surprised that I am giving these madrigals to the press without first replying to the objections that Artusi made against some very minute portions of them. Being in the service of this Serene Highness of Mantua, I am not master of the time I would require. Nevertheless I wrote a reply to let it be known that I do not do things by chance, and as soon as it is rewritten it will see the light under the title, *Seconda pratica overo Perfettione della moderna musica* [Second Practice, or the Perfection of Modern Music]. Some will wonder at this, not believing that there is any other practice than that taught by Zerlino [*sic*]. But let them be assured concerning consonances and dissonances that there is a different way of considering them from that already determined, which defends the modern manner of composition with the assent of the reason and the senses. I wanted to say this both so that the expression *seconda pratica* would not be appropriated by others and so that men of intellect might meanwhile consider other second thoughts concerning harmony. And have faith that the modern composer builds on foundations of truth.
Live happily.

From C. V. Palisca, "The Artusi-Monteverdi Controversy," in *The New Monteverdi Companion*, ed. Denis Arnold and Nigel Fortune (London and Boston: Faber & Faber, 1985), pp. 151–52.

By the middle of the century, theorists had proposed more complex and comprehensive systems of style classification; the most widely accepted was a threefold division into church, chamber, and theater music. Each of these distinct styles had a particular social function and certain technical traits. But by the end of the century, composers were glossing over these distinctions and writing in nearly the same way for the three categories.

Idiomatic Writing

Polyphony tended to homogenize instrumental and vocal writing. Much of it could be sung or played by almost any combination of voices and instruments. But even the earliest music for solo lute, organ, or harpsichord had a signature that was peculiar to the instrument. The prominent role of the soloist—whether singer, violinist, or trumpeter—invited composers to address their thoughts to a particular medium, such as the violin or the solo voice. The development of the violin family was especially important, because the forceful overhand bowing, in contrast to the gentle underhand bowing on viols, produced an unvocal and idiosyncratic sound. While violins were replacing viols in Italy, composers in France developed a virtuosic viol idiom that transcended the formerly ideal vocal sound. Technical improvements in wind instruments made them suitable for exposed solo performance. Famous teachers and practitioners of the art of singing promoted new standards of virtuosity, color, and vocal projection. Instrumental and vocal styles began to diverge, eventually becoming so distinct that composers could consciously borrow vocal idioms in instrumental writing, and vice versa.

The Affections

Vocal and instrumental composition were united in a common goal—to express or represent a wide range of feelings vividly and vigorously—continuing efforts begun in the late sixteenth-century madrigal. Composers sought musical means to express or arouse the *affections* such as rage, excitement, grandeur, heroism, lofty contemplation, wonder, or mystic exaltation—then thought of as relatively stable states of the soul. Composers were not trying to express their personal feelings; rather, they wanted to represent the affections in a generic sense. In fact, they deliberately distanced themselves from feelings so they could endow them with a more objective reality. In Baroque architecture, sculpture, and painting, the normal forms of objects were sometimes distorted, so that the images would embody the passionate intensity of the artist's vision. Similarly in music, composers breached the limits of the old order of consonance and dissonance, of regular and equable rhythmic flow. But, unlike sculpture and painting, music did not have to represent natural objects, nor was music bound, like architecture, by any unyielding physical demands of medium and function. Music was free to expand its expressive field in whatever directions a composer's imagination led. This freedom stimulated the development of music's emotional power and elevated its standing among the arts.

Rhythm

In contrast with the even, rhythmic flow of Renaissance polyphony, music in the Baroque period was either very regular or very free. Regular dance rhythms were characteristic of much earlier instrumental music, but not until the seventeenth century was most music written in *measures* marked by barlines, implying patterns of strong and weak beats. At first these patterns were not recurrent: time signatures corresponding to a varying succession of harmonic and accentual patterns, set off by barlines at regular intervals, became common only after mid-century. Composers used irregular, flexible rhythms when writing vocal recitative and improvisatory solo instrumental pieces such as toccatas and preludes. The two types of rhythms—the regular and the irregular—could not, of course, occur simultaneously, but in succession they provided deliberate contrast, as in the customary pairing of recitative and aria and of toccata or prelude and fugue.

The Basso Continuo

Texture

The typical texture of Renaissance music was a polyphony of independent voices; the typical texture of the Baroque period was a firm bass and a florid treble, held together by unobtrusive harmony. A single melody supported by accompanying parts was not in itself new: something like it had been used in the cantilena style of the fourteenth century, in the Burgundian chanson, in the early frottola, in the sixteenth-century lute song, and in the Elizabethan air. New was the emphasis on the bass and the highlighting of the treble—the two essential lines of the texture. One result of this polarity, a seeming indifference to the inner parts as lines, was evident in the system of notation called *thoroughbass* or *basso continuo.*

Notation

In this system, the composer wrote out only the melody and the bass. The bass was played on one or more *continuo* instruments—for example, harpsichord, organ, or lute—usually reinforced by a sustaining instrument such as a bass viola da gamba, violoncello, or bassoon. Above the bass notes, the keyboard or lute player filled in the required chords, which were not otherwise written out. If these chords were other than common triads in root position, or if chord tones (such as suspensions) or accidentals beyond those in the key signature were required, the composer added numbers (*figures*) or flat or sharp signs above or below the bass notes.

Realization

The *realization*—the actual playing—of such a *figured bass* varied according to the type of piece and the skill and taste of the player, who had a good deal of room for improvisation within the framework set by the composer. The performer might play only simple chords, or introduce passing tones, or incorporate melodic motives that imitated the treble or bass parts. To realize the basso continuo was not always essential: many pieces with a continuo already provided the full harmony in the notated melodic parts. In motets and madrigals for four or five voices, for example, the continuo instrument merely doubled or supported the voices. But for solos and duets, the continuo was usually necessary to complete the harmonies as well as to produce a fuller sonority. This filling was sometimes called *ripieno,* a term used in Italian cooking to mean "stuffing." (A modern edition of a composition with a figured bass usually prints the editor's realization in smaller notes: see the facsimile above and its realization in NAWM 51.)

The New Counterpoint

Use of continuo

It might seem as if the development of basso continuo meant a total rejection of sixteenth-century counterpoint. This was true when the continuo was used alone to accompany a solo, unless the composer chose to give the bass line itself some melodic significance. But a firm bass supporting a florid treble was not the only musical texture in use. Composers continued to write unaccompanied motets and madrigals (though they sometimes conformed with current practice by adding a basso continuo). Some instrumental ensemble pieces, as well as all solo keyboard and lute music, had no basso continuo. Most important, even for ensembles where the continuo was used, counterpoint remained the basis of composition, but a new kind of counterpoint. The different melodic lines now had to fit into the pattern of chords set up by the continuo. This type of harmonically driven counterpoint, in which individual lines were

■ Giulio Caccini's madrigal *Vedrò 'l mio sol,* as printed in *Le nuove musiche* (Florence: Marescotti, 1601/2). In this early example of thoroughbass notation, the bass is figured with the exact intervals to be sounded in the chords above it—for example, the dissonant eleventh resolving to the tenth in the first measure.

subordinated to a succession of chords, held sway throughout the remainder of the Baroque era.

Dissonance

With the chordal structure articulated so clearly, dissonance was recognized less as an interval between two voices than as an individual tone that did not fit into a chord. As a result, greater variety of dissonances was tolerated, though by the middle of the century certain conventions governed when and how they could be introduced and resolved. Dissonance helped define the tonal direction of a piece, particularly in the instrumental music of Arcangelo Corelli (1653–1713) and others, in which chains of dissonant suspensions led inexorably to a cadence establishing a keynote or tonic.

Chromaticism

Chromaticism followed a similar development, from experimental forays on the one hand, to freedom within an orderly scheme on the other. Gesualdo's chromatic harmonies in the early 1600s were expressionistic digressions within a loose structure that respected the confines of a mode. Throughout the seventeenth century, composers used chromaticism in improvisatory instrumental pieces, such as the toccatas of Girolamo Frescobaldi (1583–1643) and Johann

Jakob Froberger (1616–1667), and in vocal works to express intense passions of a text. But later composers submitted chromaticism, as they did dissonance, to the control of tonal harmony.

Major-Minor Tonalities

Tonal harmony operated within the system of major-minor tonalities familiar to us from music of the eighteenth and nineteenth centuries. In a tonal composition, harmonies are organized around a triad on the tonic supported primarily by triads on its dominant and subdominant, with other chords secondary to these. Temporary modulations to other keys do not diminish the supremacy of the principal key. Music of the late Renaissance foreshadowed this kind of tonal organization. Rameau's *Treatise on Harmony* in 1722 completed the theoretical formulation of the system, which by then had existed in practice for at least a half century.

Rameau's *Treatise on Harmony*

Evolution of tonality

Like the medieval modal system, the major-minor system evolved gradually through musical practice. The habitual, long-standing use of certain techniques—bass movement by a fourth or fifth, successions of secondary chords culminating in a cadential progression, modulations to the most nearly related keys—eventually bred a consistent theory. Just as the repeated use in the early Middle Ages of certain melodic formulas led to the theory of the modes, so the constant use in the seventeenth century of particular harmonic and melodic successions led to the theory of major-minor tonality. The figured basso continuo, which drew attention to the succession of chords, contributed to this theoretical development. The figured bass bridged counterpoint to homophony and linear-melodic to a chordal-harmonic structure.

EARLY OPERA

Forerunners

An opera is a drama that combines soliloquy, dialogue, scenery, action, and continuous (or nearly continuous) music. Although the earliest works in this genre date only from the very end of the sixteenth century, the association of music with drama goes back to ancient times. The choruses and some lyric speeches in the plays of Euripides and Sophocles were sung. The medieval liturgical dramas were sung, and music figured—albeit incidentally—in the religious mystery and miracle plays of the late Middle Ages. In the Renaissance theater, where so many tragedies and comedies imitated Greek models, choruses were sometimes sung, especially at the opening or the ending of an act. Moreover, between acts of a comedy or tragedy, *intermedi* or *intermezzi*—pastoral, allegorical, or mythological interludes—occupied the stage. On important state occasions, such as princely weddings, these intermedi offered spectacular and elaborate musical productions, with choruses, soloists, and large instrumental ensembles.

Intermedi

The most costly and spectacular of the intermedi, for the 1589 wedding in Florence of Grand Duke Ferdinand de' Medici of Tuscany and Christine of Lorraine, were produced by the Roman nobleman Emilio de' Cavalieri (ca. 1550–1602) and directed by the Florentine Count Giovanni Bardi (1534–1612). The opening solo madrigal, *Dalle più alte sfere* (From the highest spheres, Example 9.2), from the first of the five intermedi, typifies the solo songs of this period. The singer doubles and ornaments the highest of the four instrumental parts. The simple homophonic texture and cadences at the end of each line resemble a frottola, but this song makes an altogether different impression because of its virtuoso runs and cadenzas, which capture the brilliant improvisation that a well-trained singer could carry off. It was sung by the most famous soprano of that time, Vittoria Archilei, who was a member of the duke's musical staff (see illustration, page 263).

Cavalieri

Example 9.2 *Emilio de' Cavalieri, Madrigal*: Dalle più alte sfere

From the highest spheres

Costume designs by Bernardo Buontalenti for Necessity and the three Fates, who turn the spindle of the cosmos, according to the account in Plato's Republic. *These designs are for the first* intermedio*—on the subject of the harmony of the spheres—before the comedy* La Pellegrina *by Girolamo Bargagli, performed in Florence in 1589 at the wedding of Grand Duke Ferdinand de' Medici and Christine of Lorraine. The text was by Giovanni Bardi and Ottavio Rinuccini, the music by Emilio de' Cavalieri and Christofano Malvezzi.* (FLORENCE, BIBLIOTECA NAZIONALE CENTRALE)

Madrigal Cycles

Some madrigals in the sixteenth century were miniature dramas. *Madrigal cycles* represented a series of scenes or moods or wove a simple comic plot in dialogue. Contrasting groups of voices and short solos set off the characters. These works are now usually called *madrigal comedies*, a rather unfortunate designation since they were not intended for stage performance but only for private concerts. Their music—for the most part light, lively, and humorous—had little contrapuntal interest but captured the spirit of the words. The most famous madrigal comedy was *L'Amfiparnaso* (The Slopes of Parnassus, 1597), by Orazio Vecchi (1550–1605). Adriano Banchieri (1568–1634) wrote cycles around the end of the century, but the genre was short-lived.

Vecchi's *L'Amfiparnaso*

The Pastoral

The pastoral poem, the predominant genre of Italian verse composition in the Renaissance, provided one model for the early musical plays. Pastorals told of idyllic love in loosely dramatic form. The genre demanded the poet's skill for conveying the atmosphere of a remote, fairy-tale world of nature, refined and civilized. Their stories were peopled by simple rustic youths and maidens and the ancient deities of the fields, woods, and fountains. Uncomplicated subject matter, bucolic landscape, and a nostalgic mood of yearning for an unattainable earthly paradise made pastoral poetry attractive to composers. In this imaginary world, music seemed not only the natural mode of communication but the missing link to the poets' visions and longings. Pastoral poetry was at once the last stage of the madrigal and the first stage of the opera libretto.

Vittoria Archilei in the role of the Dorian harmonia in the first intermedio *of 1589. Costume design by Bernardo Buontalenti. In the preface to his* Euridice, *Jacopo Peri called her "the Euterpe of our age who has always found my music worthy of her performance, adorning it with those ornaments and long vocal runs, both simple and double, which her lively genius invents at every moment, more to go along with the custom of our time than because she thinks that in them resides the beauty and power of our singing. She adds also those charms and graces that cannot be written and, if written, cannot be learned from the notation."* (FLORENCE, BIBLIOTECA NAZIONALE CENTRALE)

Greek Tragedy as a Model

Greek tragedy served as a distant model for the Renaissance theater, although scholars disagreed on how centrally music figured in Greek drama. One view, that only the choruses were sung, was put into practice in a performance of Sophocles' *Oedipus rex.* For that production of 1585, mounted in Vicenza in an Italian translation as *Edippo Tiranno*, Andrea Gabrieli cast the choruses in a completely homophonic declamatory style that emphasized the rhythm of the spoken word.[4]

Edippo Tiranno

Another view was that the entire text of a Greek tragedy was sung, including the actors' parts, an opinion authoritatively expressed by Girolamo Mei (1519–1594), a Florentine scholar who had edited a number of the Greek tragedies. While working in Rome as a cardinal's secretary, he embarked on a thorough investigation of Greek music, particularly its role in the theater. Between 1562 and 1573 he read in Greek almost every ancient work on music that had survived. He reported on his research in a treatise in four books, *De modis* (Concerning the Modes), parts of which were communicated to his colleagues in Florence.

Mei

The Florentine Camerata

Two of Mei's most frequent correspondents were Giovanni Bardi and Vincenzo Galilei (d. 1591). From the early 1570s, Count Bardi hosted an informal academy at his palace in Florence, where scholars discussed literature, science,

Bardi

4. The choruses are published in Leo Schrade, *La représentation d'Edipo Tiranno au Teatro Olimpico (Vicence, 1585)* (Paris: CNRS, 1960).

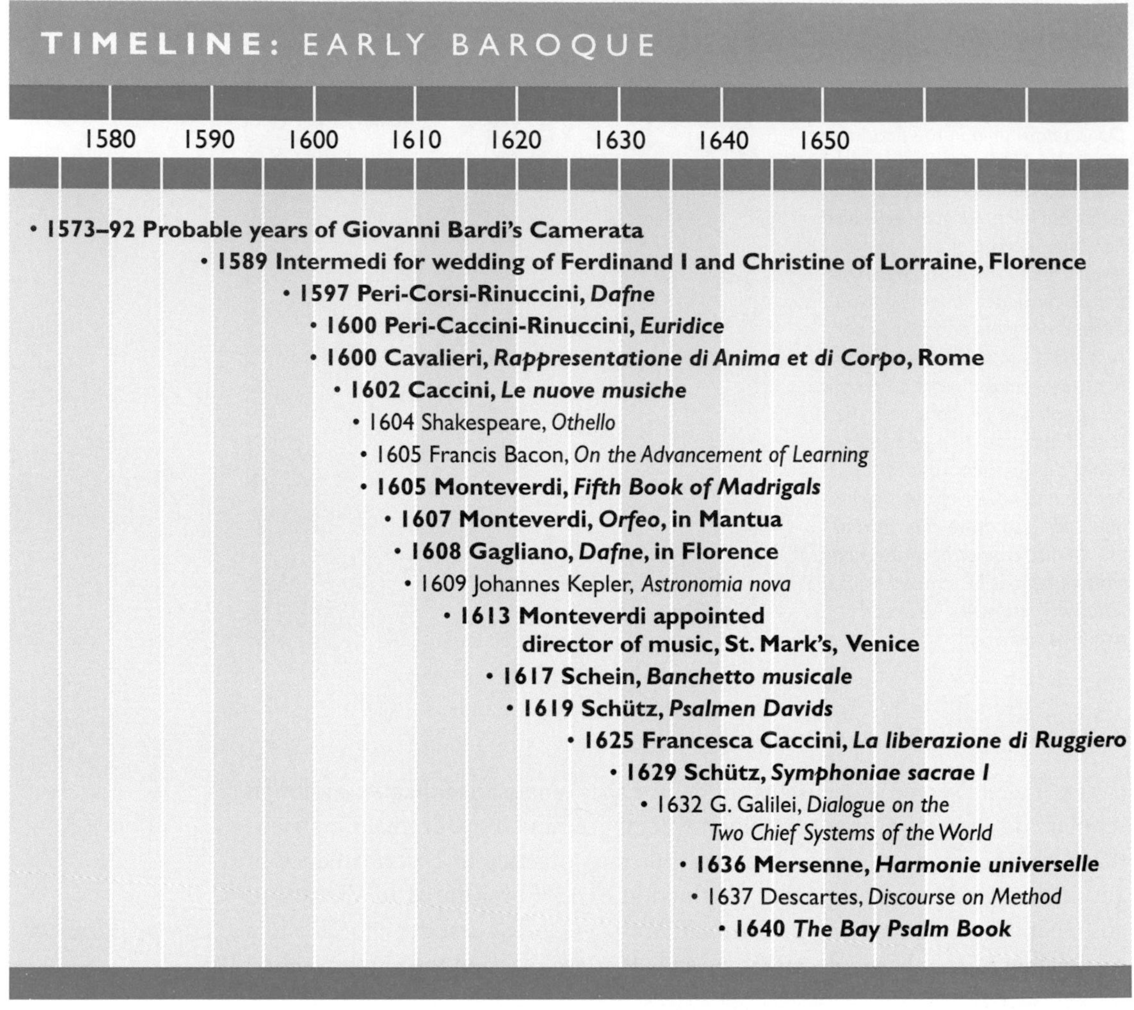

and the arts, and musicians performed new music. Bardi's protégé, the singer-composer Giulio Caccini (1551–1618), later referred to this gathering as the *Camerata* (circle or coterie) of Bardi. Around 1577, Mei's letters about Greek music often appeared on the agenda. Mei had concluded that the Greeks obtained powerful effects with their music because it consisted of a single melody, whether sung by a soloist with or without accompaniment, or by a chorus. This melody could move the listener through the natural expressiveness of vocal registers, rises and falls in pitch, and changing rhythms and tempo.

Galilei

In his *Dialogo della musica antica et della moderna* (Dialogue concerning Ancient and Modern Music, 1581), Vincenzo Galilei, father of the famous astronomer and physicist Galileo, used the doctrines of Mei to attack the theory and practice of vocal counterpoint as exemplified in the Italian madrigal. His argument, in brief, held that only a single line of melody, with pitches and rhythms appropriate to the text could express a given line of poetry. Therefore, when several voices simultaneously sang different melodies and words, in different rhythms and registers, music could never deliver the emotional message of the text. If some voices were low and others high, some rising and others descending, some moving in slow notes and others in fast, then the resulting chaos of contradictory impressions served only to show off the cleverness of the composer and the ability of the performers. If it had any value at all, he wrote, this kind of music was suitable only for an ensemble of instruments. Word-painting, imitations of sighing, and the like, so common in the sixteenth-century madrigal, he dismissed as childish. Only a solo melody could enhance the natural speech inflections of a good orator or actor. Galilei tried his hand at monodies of this sort, setting some verses from Dante's *Divina commedia* for a solo voice with accompaniment of viols, but the music has not survived.

The Earliest Operas

Rinuccini

It was through such discussions that the poet Ottavio Rinuccini (1562–1621) and the composer Jacopo Peri (1561–1633) became convinced—as they wrote in their prefaces to *L'Euridice*—that the ancient tragedies were sung in their entirety. They first experimented with Rinuccini's poem *Dafne* under the sponsorship of another nobleman, Jacopo Corsi, who also held meetings and musicales at his palace. Only fragments of *Dafne*, produced in Florence in 1598, survive. Peri and Giulio Caccini each set to music a second more ambitious poem, Rinuccini's *L'Euridice*, and both scores were published. Meanwhile, Emilio de' Cavalieri, who was in charge of theater, art, and music at the Florentine ducal court, mounted some smaller scenes in Florence that contained his own music written in a similar style (he later claimed to have been the first to do so). In February 1600 he produced in Rome his sacred musical play representing the rivalry between the Soul and the Body, *Rappresentatione di Anima et di Corpo*, at that time the longest entirely musical stage work (see page 289).

Peri, Caccini, and Cavalieri had similar approaches to theatrical music. Both Peri and Caccini were singers by profession, and Cavalieri—diplomat, choreographer, composer, and administrator—taught singing. They all aimed for a kind of song that was halfway between spoken recitation and singing. Caccini and Cavalieri wrote in a style based on the madrigal and on the airs that poets and singers improvised upon when singing or reciting poetry (see page 279 for a description of a popular air called the romanesca). Peri modeled his prologue (NAWM 52a; CD 3 [54]) on the air for singing poetry. But for dialogue he invented a new idiom, which was soon known as *stile recitativo* or *recitative style*. This should not be confused with the term *monody* (*monodia*: from the Greek *monos*, alone, and *aidein*, to sing), a term that embraces all the styles of solo singing practiced in the early years of the seventeenth century, including recitative, arias, and madrigals.

Monody

Solo singing was certainly not new: performers commonly improvised on melodic formulas to recite epic and other strophic poems. Many songs were composed for solo voice and lute, and it was common in the sixteenth century to sing one part of a polyphonic madrigal while instruments played the other parts, a practice often followed in the intermedio (see Example 9.2; see also Plate VI, facing page 239, depicting a lutenist reading from a bass partbook of Arcadelt madrigals.). Moreover, many late sixteenth-century madrigals seem written for a soprano solo with chordal accompaniment. In the 1580s, Luzzasco Luzzaschi composed "solo madrigals," songs for one, two, or three sopranos with harpsichord accompaniment. All these pieces had a solidly harmonic and polyphonic texture. One or more soloists sang upper voices decorated with coloratura passages, while instruments played the lower parts.

Caccini

Caccini developed a songful yet mainly syllabic style of solo writing. He aimed at clear and flexible declamation of the words but embellished the melodic line at appropriate places. Monody thus received a patina of vocal virtuosity. In performing polyphonic music in the sixteenth century, singers commonly introduced ornaments—scalar figures, turns, runs, passing notes, and the like. They embellished any long note of a written line, usually without regard to the character of the text. Caccini, on the other hand, chose and placed his ornaments carefully to enhance the message of the text. He wrote two types of songs—airs, which were strophic, and madrigals, which were through-composed—some of which go back to the 1590s but were not published until 1602 under the title *Le nuove musiche* (The New Music). Caccini boasted in his foreword that the madrigal *Vedrò 'l mio sol* (NAWM 51; CD 3 [51]; see also facsimile, page 259) was greeted in Bardi's Camerata around 1590 "with affectionate applause." Each line of poetry is set as a separate phrase, ending either in a cadence or a sustained note or pair of notes. Repeated notes in speech rhythm abounded particularly in the arias, as they did in improvised airs throughout the sixteenth century. At a number of the cadences, Caccini wrote into the score the kind of embellishments that singers would usually have added, because he did not trust singers to invent appropriate ones on their own. Other refinements and ornaments that Caccini considered essential were crescendos and decrescendos, trills (called *gruppi*), rapid repetitions of the same pitch (called *trilli*), "exclamations"—a sforzando at the point of releasing a tone—and departures from strict observance of the printed note values, or what we call *tempo rubato.*

Le nuove musiche

The Recitative Style

Peri's and Caccini's *Euridice*

In 1600, Peri set to music the pastoral-mythological verse play *Euridice*, by Ottavio Rinuccini, which was publicly performed in Florence that year at the marriage of Henry IV of France and Maria de' Medici, niece of the reigning grand duke. But Caccini would not allow his singers to perform music composed by others, so a portion of his setting was incorporated into the production. Both versions were published in the following year, and these two scores remain the earliest complete operas that survive.

Euridice elaborated the well-known myth of Orpheus and Eurydice, treated in the then-fashionable manner of the pastoral. In deference to the joyful occasion, it was provided with a happy ending. Of the two settings, Caccini's is more melodious and lyrical, resembling the madrigals and airs of his *Nuove musiche.* Peri's is more dramatic; he not only realized a style that lies between speech and song, but he varied his approach according to the dramatic situation.

Peri

While Caccini built his solo vocal idiom on the improvised air and the polyphonic madrigal, Peri reached for a new solution to the needs of the stage. In his preface to *Euridice* (see vignette), Peri recalled the distinction made in ancient Greek theory between the "continuous" change of pitch in speech and the intervallic, or "diastematic," motion in song. He wanted to find a kind of speech-song that was halfway between them, similar to the style scholars thought ancient Greeks used for reciting heroic poems. By holding steady the

PERI'S DESCRIPTION OF HIS RECITATIVE STYLE

Putting aside every other manner of singing heard up to now, I dedicated myself wholly to searching out the imitation that is owed to these poems. And I reflected that the sort of voice assigned by the ancients to song, which they called diastematic (as if to say sustained and suspended), could at times be hurried and take a moderate course between the slow sustained movements of song and the fluent and rapid ones of speech, and thus suit my purpose (just as the ancients, too, adapted the voice to reading poetry and heroic verses), approaching that other [voice] of conversation, which they called continuous and which our moderns (though perhaps for another purpose) also used in their music.

I recognized likewise that in our speech certain sounds are intoned in such a way that a harmony can be built upon them, and in the course of speaking we pass through many that are not so intoned, until we reach another that permits a movement to a new consonance.

Keeping in mind those manners and accents that serve us in our grief and joy and similar states, I made the bass move in time with these, faster or slower according to the affections. I held the bass fixed through both dissonances and consonances until the voice of the speaker, having run through various notes, arrived at a syllable that, being intoned in ordinary speech, opened the way to a new harmony. I did this not only so that the flow of the speech would not offend the ear (almost tumbling upon the repeated notes with more frequent consonant chords), but also so that the voice would not seem to dance to the movement of the bass, particularly in sad or severe subjects, granted that other more joyful subjects would require more frequent movements. Moreover, the use of dissonances lessened or masked the advantage gained from the necessity of intoning every note, which perhaps for this purpose was less needed in ancient music.

From Peri, *Le musiche sopra l'Euridice* (Florence, 1600), trans. in Palisca, *Humanism in Italian Renaissance Musical Thought* (New Haven: Yale University Press, 1985), pp. 428–32.

notes of the basso continuo while the voice moved through both consonances and dissonances—thereby simulating the continuous motion of speech—he liberated the voice from the harmony enough so that it seemed like free, pitchless declamation. When a syllable arrived that would be emphasized in speech—in his words, "intoned"—he formed a consonance with the bass and its harmony.

Example 9.3 shows how Peri followed his own prescription for the new style (see vignette, page 267). The vertical boxes identify the syllables that are sustained or accented in speech and support a consonant harmony; the horizontal boxes contain the syllables that are passed over quickly in speech and may be set by either dissonances (marked by asterisks) or consonances against the bass and its implied chords. The manner in which the dissonances are in-

Example 9.3 *Jacopo Peri,* L'Euridice

Ma la bel-la Eu-ri - di - ce Mo-ea dan-zan-do il piè sul ver - de pra -

to Quand' ahi ria sor - te a - cer - ba An-gue cru-do, e spie-

ta - to Che ce-la - to gia - cea tra fio-ri e l'er - ba Pun - se-le il piè

But the lovely Eurydice
dancingly moved her feet on the green grass
when—o bitter, angry fate—
a snake, cruel and merciless,
that lay hidden in the grass
bit her foot . . .

■ *Jacopo Peri as the legendary singer Arion in the fifth intermedio of 1589 (see captions for illustrations on pages 262 and 263). Arion, returning from concerts in Corinth, sings an echo aria just before he plunges into the sea to escape his mutinous crew. The music was by Jacopo Peri and Christofano Malvezzi, the costume by Bernardo Buontalenti.*

troduced and then left often violates the rules of counterpoint, as in measures 3, 4, and 5; the effort to imitate speech exempts these notes from normal musical conventions. This combination of speechlike freedom and sustained harmonized accented syllables realized Peri's idea of a medium halfway between speech and song.

Peri's *Euridice*

Three excerpts from Peri's *Euridice*—the Prologue, Tirsi's song, and Dafne's speech—illustrate three types of monody employed in this work (NAWM 52; CD 3 [54]), only one of which is truly new. The Prologue (52a) is modeled on the strophic aria for singing verses as practiced throughout the sixteenth century. Each line of verse is sung to a melodic scheme that consists of a repeated pitch and a cadential pattern ending in two sustained notes. A ritornello separates the strophes. Tirsi's song (52b) is a canzonet, or dance-song, markedly rhythmic and tuneful, with harmonically strong (mostly dominant-tonic) cadences at the ends of lines. It is framed by a short "symphony" that is the longest purely instrumental interlude in the score. Finally, the speech in which Dafne tells of Euridice's death (NAWM 52c and Example 9.3) is a true example of the new recitative. The chords specified by the basso continuo and its figures have no rhythmic profile or formal plan and are there only to support the voice's recitation, which is free to imitate the inflections and rhythms of speech.

In his *Euridice*, Peri devised an idiom that met the demands of dramatic poetry. Although he and his associates knew that they had not brought back Greek music, they claimed to have realized a speech-song that was not only

■ *Orfeo's aria* Possente spirto *from Monteverdi's* Orfeo, *in the score printed in Venice in 1609, two years after the first performance in Mantua. Two versions of the vocal part are given, one simple, the other ornamented. Two violins interpolate runs and other figures between the lines of the poem.*

close to what had been used in the ancient theater but was also compatible with modern musical practice.

The various styles of monody—recitative, aria, and madrigal—quickly made their way into all kinds of music, both secular and sacred, in the first decades of the seventeenth century. Monody made musical theater possible, because it could convey in music both dialogue and narrative clearly, quickly, and with the flexibility needed for truly dramatic expression.

Claudio Monteverdi

Monteverdi's *L'Orfeo*, produced in Mantua in 1607, was patterned both in its subject matter and its mixture of styles on the *Euridice* operas. Rinuccini's little pastoral was expanded by the poet Alessandro Striggio into a five-act drama, and Monteverdi, already an experienced composer of madrigals and church music, drew on a rich palette of vocal and instrumental resources. His recitative achieves more continuity and a longer line through careful tonal organization, and, at significant key moments, it becomes songful and lyrical. In addition, Monteverdi introduced many solo airs, duets, madrigalesque ensembles, and dances, which, taken together, make up a large proportion of the work and furnish a welcome contrast to the recitative. The ritornellos and choruses help organize the scenes into schemes of almost ceremonial formality.

L'Orfeo

Three sections from *Orfeo* are more or less analogous to those from *Euridice* discussed above—the Prologue, Orfeo's song, and the messenger's narration of Euridice's death (NAWM 54a, b, c; CD 4 [1]/ 2 ⟨18⟩)—but it is immediately obvious that the proportions are very much expanded. The ritornello to the Prologue is carefully scored, and although the Prologue itself is patterned on the air for singing poetry, Monteverdi wrote out each strophe, varying the melody while leaving the harmony intact. Orfeo's famous aria in Act III, *Possente spirto* (Powerful spirit), follows the same procedure, but the composer furnished a different ornamentation for each of the first four strophes, which he wrote on an extra staff under the melodic formula (see facsimile above). The fifth strophe he set as a solo madrigal, while the sixth strophe he left unornamented.

Ornamentation

Orfeo's strophic canzonet, *Vi ricorda, o boschi ombrosi* (Do you recall, o shady woods, NAWM 54b), resembles Peri's aria for Tirsi in spirit, but the ritornello is worked out in five-part counterpoint. Again the idiom is a traditional one: the hemiola rhythm is the same as that in Cara's frottola *Io non compro più speranza* (NAWM 35), and the harmonization with root-position chords is also similar.

Like Peri, Monteverdi reserves the most modern style for dramatic dialogue and impassioned speeches. The Messenger's narrative, *In un fiorito prato* (In a flowered meadow, NAWM 54c), imitates the recitative style developed by Peri, but the harmonic movement and melodic contour are more broadly conceived. Orfeo's lament, which follows (Example 9.4), attains a new height of lyricism that leaves the first monodic experiments far behind. In the passage

Example 9.4 *Claudio Monteverdi*, Orfeo: Tu se' morta

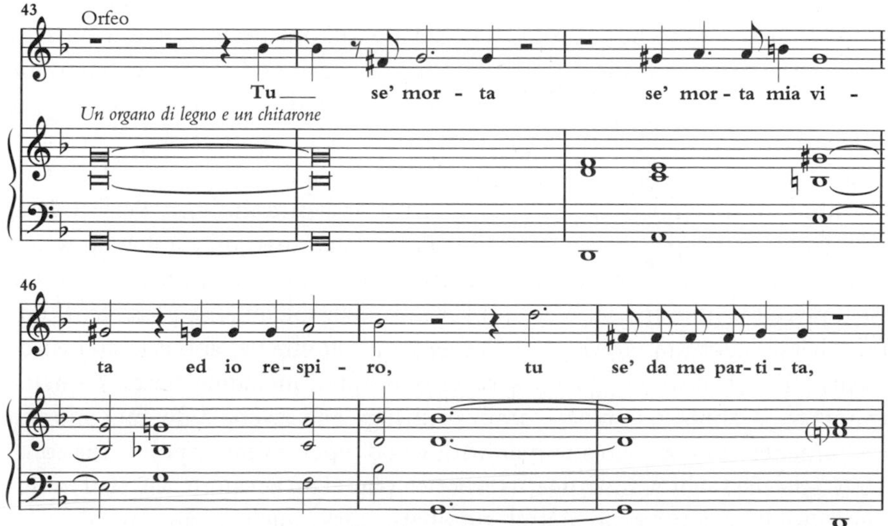

You are dead, my life, and I still breathe? You have departed from me, never to return, and I remain? No, for if verses have any power I shall go safely to the most profound abyss. . . .

that begins "Tu se' morta," each phrase of music, like each phrase of text, builds on the preceding one, intensifying it through pitch and rhythm. The dissonances against the sustained chords not only enhance the illusion of speech but also echo in the void of Orfeo's bleak prospects. The raw passage from an E-major chord to a G-minor chord (measures 3–4) drives home the irony of his question: why must he continue to live, when his bride—his "life"—is dead? The melody conveys Orfeo's resolve to make a desperate expedition to the depths of the underworld.

Orchestra

Monteverdi employed a large and varied orchestra in *Orfeo.* Peri's opera, performed in an apartment of the Pitti Palace, had used only a few lutes and similar instruments, together with a harpsichord for accompaniment; these were placed behind the scenery and kept as inconspicuous as possible. Monteverdi's orchestra in *Orfeo*, on the other hand, numbered about forty instruments (though they never all played at one time), including flutes, cornetts, trumpets, sackbuts, a complete family of strings, and several different continuo instruments, among them an organ with wood pipes. At many points the composer specified which instruments were to play. Furthermore, the score contains twenty-six brief orchestral numbers; these include an introductory "toccata" (a short fanfare-like movement played three times) and several ritornellos.

Only one extended scene, Arianna's lament *Lasciatemi morire*, survives from Monteverdi's next opera, *Arianna* (1608). This famous piece in an enhanced recitative style was widely admired as a supreme example of expressive monody that always moved audiences to tears. Monteverdi later arranged it as a five-part madrigal and then reset the original version to a sacred text.

Francesca Caccini

Despite the stir aroused by the early musical pastorals, the Florentine court continued to prefer ballets, masques, and intermedi to glamorize state weddings and other events. Only a few more such operas were written and performed during the next thirty years: *Dafne* (1608) and *Il Medoro* (1619; the music is lost) by Marco da Gagliano (1582–1643), and *La Flora* (1628) by Gagliano and Peri. For the visit of the Prince Ładisław Sigismund of Poland in 1625, the court staged a performance, in the courtyard of the grand duchess's villa in Poggio Imperiale, that was a combination of ballet and musical scenes resembling the intermedi (see illustration, below). The work, *La liberazione di Ruggiero dall'isola d'Alcina* (The Freeing of Ruggiero from the Island of Alcina), was composed by Francesca Caccini (1587–ca. 1640), daughter of Giulio. Known as "La Cecchina," Francesca had performed frequently both as a solo singer and with her sister Settimia and her stepmother Margherita (Giulio's wife) in a trio, sometimes joined by Vittoria Archilei, to form a con-

Stage design by Giulio Parigi for the second change of scene in La liberazione di Ruggiero, *produced (1625) at the Medici Villa of Poggio Imperiale, with music by Francesca Caccini. The setting is the enchanted island of the sorceress Alcina, who holds the crusader Ruggiero captive there (based on an episode in Ariosto's* Orlando furioso*). In the next scene, Ruggiero succeeds in breaking her spell, burning down her castle, and escaping. Engraving by Alfonso Parigi.*

certo delle donne to rival that of Ferrara. The group performed at secular entertainments but also sang sacred music, as when the court was in Pisa during Holy Week. Francesca Caccini composed music for ballets as early as 1607 (*La Stiava*), and *La liberazione* climaxed her brilliant career: she became the highest-paid musician in the duke's service.

Although billed as a ballet, the work had all the trappings of an opera—an opening sinfonia, a prologue, recitatives, arias, choruses, and instrumental ritornellos. It also had dances, some of which may have been performed while the chorus sang, but the purely instrumental dance music is not included in the published score, even though the dancers' names—eight ladies and eight gentlemen of the court—are listed. Most of the choruses are homophonic and suitable for dancing, but a few are madrigals. The *Coro delle Piante incantate* (Example 9.5) is an appeal by the people who have been turned into plants to be relieved of their pain.

Rome

For a variety of reasons, opera did not take root in Rome until the 1620s, even though the city was teeming with wealthy prelates who vied with each other in offering lavish entertainment to their guests. When Maffeo Barberini was elected Pope Urban VIII in 1623, his nephews were put in an advantageous position, and they became ardent sponsors of opera.

Librettos Some opera librettos were based on the lives of saints, but most treated mythological subjects or episodes from the epic poems of Tasso, Ariosto, and Marino. The most prolific librettist of sacred, serious, and comic operas was Giulio Rospigliosi, who in 1667 was elected pope as Clement IX. The most famous of his librettos, *Sant' Alessio* (1632), based on the life of the fifth-century Saint Alexis, was set to music by Stefano Landi (ca. 1590–ca. 1655). Roman composers also produced a number of pastoral operas and, oddly enough, it was in Rome that the comic opera began its independent career.

Music In the music of the Roman operas, solo singing fell more and more into two clearly defined types, recitative and aria. The recitative was more speech-like than Peri's or Monteverdi's, while the arias were melodious and mainly strophic. Domenico Mazzocchi (1592–1665), composer of *La catena d'Adone* (1626), found a middle ground in half-arias (*mezz'arie*), short tuneful interludes in the midst of recitative. The many concerted vocal pieces in the Roman operas developed from the madrigal tradition, modified by the presence of a continuo and by more regular rhythm.

Prophetic of later developments, the prelude to Landi's *Sant' Alessio* consists of a slow chordal introduction followed by a livelier contrapuntal canzona. A two-movement form of this kind later became the accepted pattern for the seventeenth-century opera overture; it was sometimes followed by a closing reminiscence of the slow introduction.

L. Rossi The last Roman opera composer of the early Baroque was Luigi Rossi (1597–1653). His *Orfeo* of 1647, on a libretto by Francesco Buti, treats the same subject as the earlier operas of Peri, Caccini, and Monteverdi but epitomizes the change that had come over the opera libretto during the previous

O, how much merit, how much praise you will have if you appease our weeping!

Source: Francesca Caccini, *La liberazione di Ruggiero,* ed. Doris Silbert (Northampton, Mass.: Smith College, 1945), p. 73.

half century. The antique simplicity of the myth is almost buried under a mass of incidents and characters, spectacular scenic effects, and comic episodes. Italian librettists of the seventeenth century typically allowed the comic, the grotesque, and the merely sensational to intrude into a serious drama. The practice suggests that composers no longer put the integrity of the drama first, as Monteverdi and the early Florentines had done. The ancient Greek and Roman myths now served merely as conventional material to be elaborated in any way that provided good entertainment to the audience and promised opportunities to the composer and singers. Rossi's *Orfeo* is a succession of beautiful arias and ensembles that make the hearer forgive its dramatic faults.

Venetian Opera

Andromeda

A troupe from Rome brought opera to Venice. The librettist, composer, and theorbist Benedetto Ferrari (ca. 1603–1681) and the composer Francesco Manelli (after 1594–1667) inaugurated opera in Venice with a 1637 production of *Andromeda* in the Teatro San Cassiano. This theater admitted the paying public, a decisive step in the history of opera, since until then musical theater depended on wealthy or aristocratic patrons. The production was a low-budget operation, with the librettist Ferrari doubling as musician. Among the six singers were the composer and his wife and three castrati. The twelve instruments included two harpsichords, two trumpets, and strings. In this opera and others mounted later in Venice, producers tried to duplicate on a small scale the stage marvels of the intermedi and the Roman operas.

Audience

Venice was an ideal place for opera to flourish. Its reputation for freedom from religious and social restraints made it a Mecca for revelers who wanted to lose themselves during Carnival in masked balls and other delights denied them most of the year. The population of Venice swelled with visitors for the six to ten weeks from the day after Christmas, when Carnival officially began, to Shrove Tuesday, the day before Lent, which began a penitential period of forty days when public entertainments were discouraged. The Venetian Carnival brought together a diverse audience, and producers sought to lure them to the opera.

Rich merchants built and supported theaters. Less wealthy families could lease boxes, and anyone could rent a seat in the ground-level stalls for a single performance. Everyone, including box holders, had to buy admission tickets. With steady financing and a guaranteed audience for at least part of the year, librettists, composers, producers, designers, and companies of singers and musicians could count on multiple performances of a work during a season. Between 1637, when San Cassiano opened, and 1678, when San Giovanni Grisostomo, the last new theater of the century, was completed, more than 150 operas were produced in nine Venetian theaters.

Mythological themes

Mythological themes continued to inspire the librettos, populated by figures such as Venus, Adonis, Apollo, Orpheus, Daphne, Jason, Bellerephon, Andromeda, Hercules, and Narcissus. Around the middle of the century, librettists drew on episodes concerning the heroes of the Crusades from the epic poems of Tasso and Ariosto. Similarly, the Trojan Wars provided adventurous tales of Ulysses, Paris, Helen, Dido, Aeneas, Aegisthus, and Achilles. The poets and librettists eventually mined Roman history for its military heroes—Alexander, Scipio, Pompey, Hannibal—and its rulers. The plots, chosen with an eye for striking stage effects, called for clouds bearing flocks of singers, enchanted gardens, magical transformations, as well as dramatic personal relationships and conflicts.

L'incoronazione di Poppea

Monteverdi composed his two last operas for Venice: *Il ritorno d'Ulisse* (The Return of Ulysses, 1641) and *L'incoronazione di Poppea* (The Coronation of Poppea, 1642). *Poppea*, Monteverdi's operatic masterpiece, lacks the varied orchestral colors and large instrumental and scenic apparatus of *Orfeo* but surpasses the earlier work in its musical depiction of human character and passions.

Despite the trend toward separating recitative and aria, Monteverdi continued to write in a fluid mixture of speechlike recitative and more lyrical and formal monody. For example, the love scene between Nero and Poppea in Act I, Scene 3 (NAWM 55; CD 4 [16]) passes through various levels of recitative: unmeasured, speechlike passages with few cadences; airs for singing poetry, as in the Prologue of *Orfeo*; and measured arioso. The aria passages are similarly varied in their degrees of formal organization and lyricism. Even when the poet, Giovanni Francesco Busenello, did not provide strophic or other aria-like verse, the composer sometimes turned to aria style. Content more than poetic form and heightened emotional expression rather than the wish to charm and dazzle determined the shifts from recitative to aria and back, and from one level of speech-song to another.

Cavalli

Monteverdi's pupil Pier Francesco Cavalli (1602–1676), who was one of the leading Venetian opera composers, helped meet the steady demand by the Venetian theaters for new works. Among his forty-one operas, the most celebrated, *Giasone* (1649), had a full-blown score in which arias and recitatives alternate, the two styles being always clearly differentiated. Among Cavalli's other operas, *Egisto* (1643), *Ormindo* (1644), and *Calisto* (1651) have been revived in recent decades, with alterations and additions that would have astonished the composer. Cavalli's recitative lacks the variety and psychological shadings of Monteverdi's, but it is still rich in dramatic and pathetic touches. The arias, much more developed than Monteverdi's, are true solo numbers.

Cesti

The operas of Antonio Cesti (1623–1669) are more polished but less forceful in style than Cavalli's. Cesti excelled in lyrical arias and duets. His most famous opera, *Il pomo d'oro* (The Golden Apple, 1667), was performed in Vienna to celebrate the wedding of Emperor Leopold I. With no expense spared, the opera abounded in features not common in Venice, such as an unusually large orchestra and many choruses. Elaborate machinery allowed for the staging of naval battles, sieges, storms, shipwrecks, descents of gods from the sky, and miraculous sudden transformations of all kinds, surpassing any spectacle attempted in Venetian opera.

More typical is Cesti's *Orontea* (ca. 1649), one of the operas most frequently performed in the seventeenth century, not only in Venice but in Rome, Florence, Milan, Naples, Innsbruck, and elsewhere. Orontea's Act II aria, *Intorno all'idol mio* (NAWM 56), shows how elaborate the aria had become by mid-century. The form is strophic, with some musical adjustments to the new text of the second stanza. The dimensions are generous, and a new

■ *One of twenty-four elaborate sets designed by Ludovico Burnacini for the sumptuous production of Antonio Cesti's* Il pomo d'oro *(The Golden Apple) at the Habsburg court in Vienna in 1668. The scene represents the palace of Paris, where he is to choose the most beautiful among Pallas Athena, Juno, and Venus. Engraving by Matthaeus Küsel.*

vocal idiom reigns throughout, one that became known as *bel canto*—smooth, mainly diatonic lines and easy rhythm gratifying to the singer. The two violins, no longer restricted to ritornellos before and after the singer's strophes, play throughout the aria.

Features

By the middle of the seventeenth century, Italian opera had acquired the main features it would maintain without essential change for the next two hundred years: (1) concentration on solo singing to the detriment of ensembles and instrumental music; (2) the separation of recitative and aria; and (3) the introduction of distinctive styles and patterns for the arias. One additional feature concerned the relation of text and music. The Florentines had considered music accessory to poetry; the Venetians treated the libretto as hardly more than a scaffolding for the musical structure.

VOCAL CHAMBER MUSIC

Except in Venice, where it became the focus of musical life, opera was an extraordinary event. The bulk of secular music produced in Italy for amateur and professional performance was chamber music, most of it involving voices. The new monodic idioms and the basso-continuo texture permeated this genre as well. But since dramatic dialogue and the representation of actions were outside the scope of chamber music, composers felt free—indeed compelled—to find new ways of organizing their musical thoughts.

Strophic method

The strophic aria, neglected in the polyphonic madrigal but kept alive in the canzonet and other popular forms, now offered the best framework for setting poems without interfering with their continuity. Using the strophic method, the composer could repeat the same melody, perhaps with minor rhythmic modifications, for each stanza of poetry (as Caccini did in *Udite, udite, amanti* and a number of other arias in *Le nuove musiche*); write new music for each strophe; or keep the same harmonic and melodic plan for all the strophes—the favored technique, known as *strophic variation.*

Example 9.6 *Outline of the Romanesca Aria*

A popular way to compose a strophic song was to base it on a standard formula, such as the *romanesca*, which was an air for singing *ottave rime* (poems having a stanza of eight eleven-syllable lines, the eighth rhyming with the seventh). The romanesca consisted of a treble formula with a standard harmonization and bass. The formula, reduced to its essentials, is given in Example 9.6. In some compositions based on the romanesca, only the bass is recognizable, so it is often referred to as a *ground bass*, or *basso ostinato*, a bass that is repeated intact while the melody above it changes. Monteverdi based his setting of the ottava rima *Ohimè dov'è il mio ben* (Alas, where is my love) as a strophic duet on the romanesca air.

Most composers invented their own music for the first strophe of an aria and then reworked it for subsequent stanzas to make it reflect the changing stresses and emphases of the text and, even more important, to have the melody and harmonic elaboration express the sense and feeling of the separate lines of the poem.

Chaconne and passacaglia

Some short ground-bass patterns, such as the *chaconne* (Spanish: *chacona*; Italian: *ciaccona*) and *passacaglia* (Spanish: *passecalle*; French: *passecaille*) were not associated with any particular poetic form. The chacona, a dance-song with a refrain that followed a simple pattern of guitar chords, was probably imported into Spain from Latin America. The Italian ciaccona variations reduced the harmonic pattern into a bass line. The passacaglia originated in Spain as a ritornello—that is, music having a certain pattern of guitar chords, played before and between the strophes of a song. It too evolved into a variety of bass formulas, usually in triple meter and minor mode, that were suitable for supporting instrumental or vocal variations. Characteristic of both the chaconne and passacaglia in the seventeenth century is the continuous repetition of a four-bar formula in triple meter and slow tempo. In the eighteenth century the two terms became confused, as shown in Example 9.7, where what Buxtehude called a "ciacona," J. S. Bach called a "passsacaglia."

Example 9.7 *Bass Patterns*

a. Buxtehude (ca. 1637–1707), *Ciacona*

b. Bach, *Passacaglia* (ca. 1717)

Example 9.8 *Descending Tetrachord Figures*

a. Major diatonic form

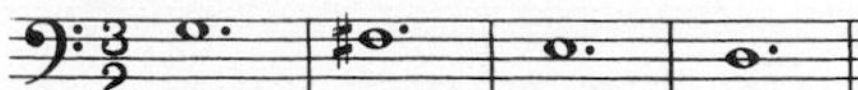

b. Minor diatonic form

c. Chromatic form

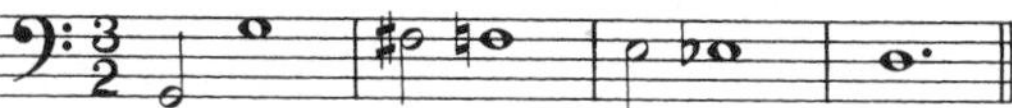

d. Chromatic form extended (Purcell *Dido and Aeneas,* 1689)

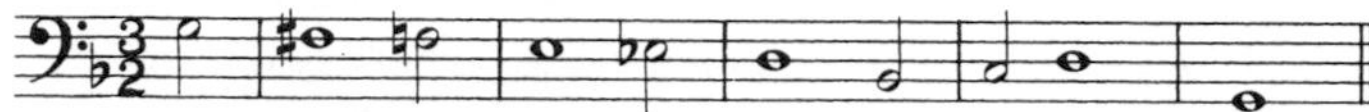

Another four-bar ostinato, a stepwise descent spanning a fourth, or tetrachord, was also frequently used (see Example 9.8).

The Concertato Medium

The practice of writing out separate parts for voices and instruments, or different groups of voices and instruments, gave rise to the *concertato* medium. (The adjective *concertato* comes from the Italian verb *concertare,* meaning to reach agreement; the English *consort* and the verb *concert* are derived from the same root.) In a musical *concerto,* diverse and sometimes contrasting forces are brought together in a harmonious ensemble. *Concertato madrigal* describes a work in which instruments join with voices on an equal footing. *Sacred concerto* means a sacred vocal work with instruments. *Instrumental concerto* is a piece for various instruments, sometimes including one or more soloists and an orchestra with several players to a part. Today we think of a concerto mainly as a piece for soloists and orchestra, but the older sense was more inclusive. The seventeenth-century concertato medium, then, is not a style but a mingling of voices with instruments that are playing independent parts.

We can trace the changing patterns of instrumental participation, strophic variation, and other novel devices in Monteverdi's fifth through eighth books of madrigals (1605, 1614, 1619, 1638). Beginning with the last six madrigals of Book 5, all include a basso continuo, and many call for other instruments as well. Solos, duets, and trios are set off against the vocal ensemble, and there are instrumental introductions and recurring instrumental interludes (ritornellos). The seventh book, titled *Concerto,* is described as consisting of "madrigals and other kinds of songs."

Ohimè dov'è il mio ben

One of the most beautiful compositions in the seventh book is the romanesca for two sopranos, *Ohimè dov'è il mio ben,* (Alas, where is my treasure?) in which the composer applied both concertato method and the organizing force of the strophic variation. The two often dissonant solo voices are brought into harmonious agreement through the ostinato pattern and its basso continuo. Each note of the ostinato pattern (shown in Example 9.6) usually occupies three measures, while the treble parts preserve the outline of the melody for singing ottave rime, of which this poem is an example. This strong structural scaffolding freed Monteverdi to indulge in a variety of artful and expressive devices—canonlike imitation between the voices, moments of recitative, word-descriptive madrigalisms, striking dissonant clashes, and passages of runs, turns, and other figures such as a singer would ordinarily improvise.

Book 8, *Madrigali guerrieri et amorosi* (Madrigals of War and Love), is especially noteworthy for its variety of forms and types, including madrigals for five voices; solos, duets, and trios with continuo; and large works for chorus, soloists, and orchestra. Among the finest compositions in this volume is the madrigal *Hor che'l ciel e la terra e'l vento tace* (Now that heaven and earth and the wind are silent) for six voices, two violins, and continuo, a composite of moods, sonorities, abundantly varied harmonies, and vivid dramatic contrasts. The eighth book also contains two *balli* (semi-dramatic ballets) and the *Combattimento di Tancredi e Clorinda* (The Combat of Tancred and Clorinda), a work in the *genere rappresentativo* (theatrical medium), first performed in 1624. Here Monteverdi set a portion of the twelfth canto of Tasso's *Jerusalem Delivered* describing the combat between the crusader knight Tancred and the armed pagan heroine Clorinda, ending with her death. The bulk of Tasso's text is straight narrative, which Monteverdi assigned to a tenor soloist in recitative. The few short speeches of Tancred and Clorinda are sung by a tenor and soprano, who also mime the actions while the narrative is sung. The instruments (string quartet with bass gamba and continuo), in addition to accompanying the voices, play interludes that suggest the action—the galloping of horses, the clash of swords, the excitement of combat. For such purposes, Monteverdi used what he called the *stile concitato* (excited style). One striking device for this mode of expression is the prolonged rapid reiteration of a single note or series of them, either with quickly spoken syllables in the voice or instrumentally as a measured string tremolo. It was used for warlike sentiments and actions.

Stile concitato

Points of style

The musical style of Monteverdi and his contemporaries contained diverse elements, some dating back to the sixteenth century, others new. Monody and madrigal were combined; formal articulation was achieved through the organization of the bass and the harmonies it supported and through the systematic introduction of ritornellos; and the texture was varied by the use of the concertato medium. Through these means, composers enlarged and enriched the representational and pictorial resources of music.

■ *The scene from Torquato Tasso's epic poem* Gierusalemme liberata, *in which Tancredi, after mortally wounding an enemy warrior in the Crusades, discovers on removing the Saracen's armor that it is his beloved Clorinda. At her request he baptizes her. Monteverdi set their speeches (Canto 12, 408–544) to music in his* Combattimento di Tancredi e Clorinda. *Accompanied by two violins, a viola da braccio, and basso continuo, she sings, "The heavens open; I go in peace." From Tasso,* La Giervsalemme Liberata con le figure di Bernardo Castello *(Genoa, 1590).* (BEINECKE RARE BOOK AND MANUSCRIPT LIBRARY, YALE UNIVERSITY)

Aria

The gradual separation of recitative and aria left the composer free to write melodious arias without having to follow every nuance of the text. Arias began to unfold in graceful, smoothly flowing phrases supported by simple harmonies, most often in slow triple meter with a single persistent rhythmic motive (Example 9.9; see also Cesti's *Intorno all'idol mio*, NAWM 56; CD 4 [21]). This bel canto style of vocal writing, a creation of Italian composers, was imitated all over Europe and influenced both vocal and instrumental music throughout the Baroque period and beyond.

Example 9.9 *Pier Francesco Cavalli, Aria from* Giasone

Delightful pleasures that bless the soul, remain in my heart; delay no more the joys of love. O my dear pleasures, remain.

Genres of Vocal Solo Music

From the beginning of the century, Italian composers turned out thousands of monodies—solo madrigals, strophic arias, and canzonets. These pieces were far more widely known than any of the operas, which were performed only a few times for restricted audiences. Monodies and music for small ensembles were sung everywhere and were published in copious collections of madrigals, arias, dialogues, duets, and the like. Caccini's *Nuove musiche* was the first important collection of monodies. The solo songs of Sigismondo d'India (ca. 1582–before 1629), as well as his polyphonic madrigals and motets, marked him as an outstanding musical personality of his time.

Cantata

The *cantata* (literally, a piece "to be sung") eventually engaged most Italian composers. The term was applied before 1620 to a published collection of arias in the form of strophic variations. Neither that form nor any other was consistently called by that name until the middle of the century. By then, *cantata* had come to mean a composition with continuo, usually for solo voice, on a lyrical or quasi-dramatic text; it consisted of several sections that included both recitatives and arias. The Roman Luigi Rossi, the first eminent master of this type of cantata, also wrote others in simpler forms—either plain strophic songs, strophic variations, arias with ostinato bass, or arias in an ABA pattern. Among leading Italian cantata composers of the mid-seventeenth century were Giacomo Carissimi (1605–1674), who is remembered chiefly for his sacred oratorios; the opera composer Antonio Cesti; and the singer Barbara Strozzi (1619–1677), composer of eight published collections of motets, madrigals, arias, and cantatas.

Barbara Strozzi

Barbara Strozzi's *Lagrime mie* (NAWM 57; CD 4 [23]), with its successive sections of recitative, arioso, and aria, is representative of the solo cantatas. The poet is unknown, but, like many of the verses Barbara Strozzi set, it may be by Giulio Strozzi (of a Florentine noble family but residing in Venice), who is believed to be her father. (He founded an academy, the Unisoni, partly to provide an outlet for her performances and compositions.) In the opening recitative (Example 9.10), Barbara Strozzi artfully exploits rhetorical devices that the Roman composers had introduced into the cantata. The hesitations on the dissonant *D♯*, *A*, and *F♯* over the opening E-minor harmony, together with

Example 9.10 *Barbara Strozzi, Cantata:* Lagrime mie

My tears, [*what holds you back*] *. . . ?*

the C♮ of the harmonic-minor scale, make this one of the most moving and vivid projections of the weeping and sobbing lamenting lover. In the Arioso that follows, tasteful word-inspired runs at "adoro" (adore), "pietoso" (pitying), and "rigor" (severity), the delicate chromaticism at "tormenti," and the compelling seventh chords and suspensions—particularly over the descending basses—show a mastery of the expressive vocabulary of this genre.

Beyond Italy

Although often strongly influenced by Italian models, composers in other countries produced songs of distinctively national character. Among the Germans were Heinrich Albert (1604–1651) and Andreas Hammerschmidt (1612–1675). In France, the *air de cour* flourished in the form of charming solos and duets, some of them independent vocal chamber music and others written for court ballets. English composers of the early and middle seventeenth century—Nicholas Lanier (1588–1666), John Wilson (1595–1674), Henry Lawes (1596–1662), and others—likewise wrote many songs with continuo accompaniment for court masques and as independent solos, some in a declamatory, recitative style, others purely tuneful in dancelike rhythms. Vocal chamber music in the early seventeenth century appeared in many forms and styles, and combined elements of the madrigal, the concerto, monody, dance songs, national idioms, dramatic recitative, and the bel canto aria.

Influences on Church Music

The innovations of the late sixteenth and early seventeenth centuries strongly affected the normally conservative category of sacred music. Monody, the basso continuo, and the concertato medium were all soon applied to sacred texts. Opposition to the new styles did arise in the Roman Catholic Church, which never completely abandoned polyphony, Indeed, Palestrina's style, called *stile antico,* became the supreme model for church music. Composers were routinely trained to write in this style of counterpoint, which throughout the seventeenth century coexisted with the *stile moderno.* A composer might utilize both styles, sometimes in a single piece; Monteverdi, for example, wrote with equal mastery in both. In the course of time, the old style was modernized: a basso continuo was often added, rhythms became more regular, and the older modes gave way to the major-minor system. Johann Joseph Fux (1660–1741) codified this quasi-Palestrinian counterpoint in his famous treatise *Gradus ad Parnassum* (Steps to Parnassus, 1725), which remained the most influential textbook on the subject for the next two centuries.

Fux

VENICE

Social Conditions in Venice

Venice was, next to Rome, the most important city of the Italian peninsula. Geographically secure and isolated on its lagoons (though it held some colonies on the mainland), it tried to stay out of the quarrels of its neighbors. It was nominally a republic but actually a tightly knit oligarchy. As the chief port for

European trade with the East, Venice had reached the summit of its power, wealth, and splendor in the fifteenth century. Wars and other misfortunes reduced its position in the sixteenth century, but the flourishing community that was the outgrowth of past prosperity continued without obvious abatement.

Church of St. Mark

The heart and center of Venetian musical culture was the great eleventh-century Church of St. Mark, with its Byzantine domes, bright gold mosaics, and spacious interior suffused with dim greenish-golden light. Like Venice itself, St. Mark's was independent. Its clergy and musicians were responsible more directly to the reigning doge than to any outside ecclesiastical authority. Most of the civic ceremonies took place in this church and in its vast piazza. Venetian music glorified the majesty of state and church on solemn and festive occasions in magnificent displays of sound and pageantry. Life in Venice had little of the ascetic, devotionally centered quality associated with Rome. Venetians took their religion more easily. The city's wide commercial interests, especially the centuries-old trade with the East, had given it a peculiarly cosmopolitan, flamboyant atmosphere.

Music in St. Mark's was supervised by officials of the state, which spared no pains or expense. The position of choirmaster, the most coveted musical post in all Italy, had been held in the sixteenth century by Willaert, Rore, and Zarlino and by Monteverdi in the early seventeenth. Renowned artists, who were chosen after stringent examination, played the two organs; they included Jacques Buus, Annibale Padovano, Claudio Merulo, Andrea Gabrieli, and his nephew, Giovanni Gabrieli (ca. 1557–1612).

Many Venetian sixteenth-century composers had contributed notably to the madrigal, and Venice produced the best Italian organ music. Venetian music was characteristically full and rich in texture, homophonic rather than contrapuntal, varied and colorful in sonority. Massive chordal harmonies replaced the intricate polyphonic lines of the Franco-Flemish composers.

Venetian Polychoral Motets

From before the time of Willaert, composers in the Venetian region had often written for double chorus. Psalms lent themselves especially well to antiphonal performance. A set of five *laudate* psalms (each begins with a form of the verb *laudare*—to praise) was sung for First Vespers in this split-choir technique at many feasts during the year. This method of performance added luster to these occasions, when the normal painted altarpiece was moved out of the way to reveal one of sculptured gold. The medium of divided choirs (*cori spezzati*), which encouraged homophonic choral writing and broad rhythmic organization, did not originate in Venice but found a congenial home there. In the polychoral music of Giovanni Gabrieli, the performance forces grew to unheard-of proportions. Two, three, four, even five choruses, each with a different combination of high and low voices, mingled with instruments of diverse timbres, answered one another antiphonally, alternated with solo voices, and joined together in massive sonorous climaxes. Gabrieli's motet *In ecclesiis* (NAWM 58; CD 4 28) explored these new resources.

G. Gabrieli

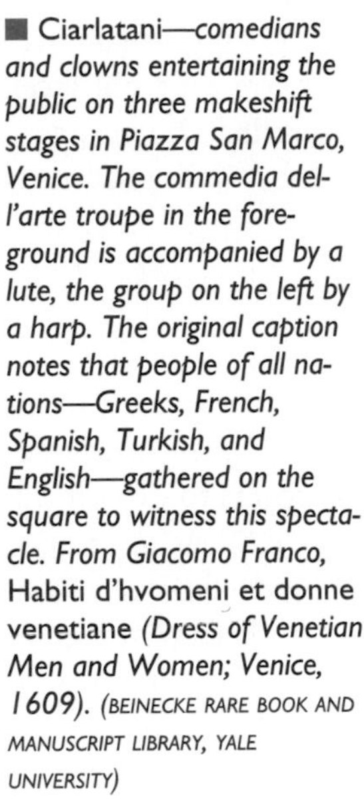

■ Ciarlatani—*comedians and clowns entertaining the public on three makeshift stages in Piazza San Marco, Venice. The commedia dell'arte troupe in the foreground is accompanied by a lute, the group on the left by a harp. The original caption notes that people of all nations—Greeks, French, Spanish, Turkish, and English—gathered on the square to witness this spectacle. From Giacomo Franco,* Habiti d'hvomeni et donne venetiane *(Dress of Venetian Men and Women; Venice, 1609).* (BEINECKE RARE BOOK AND MANUSCRIPT LIBRARY, YALE UNIVERSITY)

Venetian Influence

Venctian choirmasters and composers through their teaching, writing, and composing, exercised broad influence in the late sixteenth and early seventeenth centuries. Gabrieli's students and admirers spread his style throughout northern Italy, Germany, Austria, and Scandinavia. His most famous pupil was the German Heinrich Schütz (1585–1672). In northern Germany, Hieronymus Praetorius (1560–1629) of Hamburg promoted the Venetian style. Most of the works of Jacob Handl (Jacobus Gallus, 1550–1591), a Slovenian by birth who was active at Olmütz and Prague, show a close affinity with that style, particularly his motets for double chorus. The motets of Hans Leo Hassler, a German pupil of Andrea Gabrieli, are prevailingly polychoral, with typical Venetian fullness of sound and richness of harmony. In Poland, the polychoral style was cultivated by Mikołaj Zieleński (d. 1615).

GENRES OF CATHOLIC CHURCH MUSIC

The Grand Concerto

Roman counterpoint, although invaluable for study and discipline, played a less important role in early seventeenth-century composition than the medium of the *grand concerto.* Exemplified by the large-scale motets of

Gabrieli, these sacred works, for huge aggregations of singers and players, sometimes reached colossal proportions. The master of this medium and one of the major figures in seventeenth-century Catholic church music was Orazio Benevoli (1605–1672). Written mostly for St. Peter's in Rome during the 1640s, his works include Psalms, motets, and Masses for three, four, or more choruses with a figured bass for the organ, but they could be sung equally well unaccompanied. The choruses, stationed at separate places on different levels within the ample basilica of St. Peter's, literally surrounded the listeners. Benevoli combined and controlled the sonorities with utmost skill, producing antiphonal effects alternating with massive climaxes.

Benevoli

The Concerto for Few Voices

Viadana

The concerto for few voices, in which one, two, or three solo voices sang to the accompaniment of an organ continuo, was much more familiar to the average parishioner than the grand concerto. One of the first composers to exploit this medium for church music was Lodovico Viadana (1560–1627), who in 1602 published a collection, *Cento concerti ecclesiastici* (One Hundred Sacred Concertos), in 1602. In *O Domine, Jesu Christe* (Example 9.11 and NAWM 59; CD 4 [34]) from this publication, Viadana feigned polyphony in a single voice by having it imitate itself at a different pitch level. This reduction of a complex texture to a few voices meant that a work could be performed by a small number of singers, making it unnecessary to double or replace any vocal parts with instruments.

Where resources permitted, the grand concerto was combined with the concerto for few voices, as in Monteverdi's pioneering *Vespers* of 1610. In these

Example 9.11 *Lodovico Viadana, Sacred Concerto*: O Domine, Jesu Christe

Have mercy on all faithful.

settings for the liturgical Office, Monteverdi incorporated the traditional psalm tones while exploiting all the new musical resources of the time—recitative, aria, and all varieties of solo, choral, and instrumental groupings, large and small.

Grandi

Alessandro Grandi (ca. 1575/80–1630), who greatly impressed the German composer Heinrich Schütz, was particularly noted for his sacred compositions in the new style. His solo motet *O quam tu pulchra es* (NAWM 60; CD 4 [35]) on a text from the *Song of Songs*, a favorite source for musical setting at the time, shows a composer incorporating elements from theatrical recitative, solo madrigal, and bel canto aria into a single composition.

Monody, the concertato medium, and even the apparatus of the theater were all turned to sacred uses. In February 1600, even before the first surviving opera was performed in Florence, Emilio de' Cavalieri (see page 265) produced a morality play with music on a stage in Rome. Titled *Rappresentatione di Anima et di Corpo* (Representation of the Soul and Body), it was, in effect, a sacred opera with allegorical characters. It incorporated verses from an earlier lauda and, like the lauda, was intended for an informal devotional service. This work did not establish a genre, but it must have whetted the appetite of the Roman curia for its rich mixture of monody, choral declamation, dancelike instrumental music, and tuneful airs.

Oratorio

The dramatic impulse in Rome found an outlet in the sacred dialogues, which combined elements of narrative, dialogue, and meditation or exhortation, but were not usually intended for stage performance. Toward the middle of the century, works of this kind began to be called *oratorios*, because they were most often performed in the oratory, the part of a church where lay societies met to hear sermons and sing devotional songs. The libretto of an oratorio might be in Latin (*oratorio latino*) or Italian (*oratorio volgare* [vernacular]). The principal master of the Latin oratorio at this time was Giacomo Carissimi.

Carissimi's *Jephte*

A synopsis of Carissimi's *Jephte* exemplifies a mid-century oratorio. The Latin libretto is based on the Book of Judges 11:29–40, with some paraphrasing and added material. The narrator, called the *storicus* or *testo*, introduces the story. Jephtha (tenor solo) vows that if the Lord gives him victory in the impending battle, he will sacrifice the first person to greet him on his return home. This much is in recitative. Jephtha's victory over the Ammonites is then recounted, with appropriate imitative effects and much stile concitato, by the chorus and soloists. The next scene, narrated by the storicus in recitative, relates how Jephtha returns to his home in triumph. But the first to greet him is his daughter, so, alas, he must sacrifice her. The daughter's companions follow with songs of rejoicing (solo arias, duets, choruses). After a section of dialogue, in recitative, between Jephtha and his daughter, the chorus tells how the daughter, still a virgin, goes away to the mountains with her companions to bewail her approaching untimely death. She then sings a lament, to which the chorus responds, as in the *kommos* of the Greek tragedy (this final scene is in NAWM 61; CD 4 [38]). The lament is a long, affecting recitative, sweetened, as was customary in sacred music, with moments of florid song and with arioso passages built on sequences. Two sopranos, representing the daughter's companions, echo some of her cadential flourishes. The choral response, a magnificent six-voice lamentation, employs both polychoral and madrigalistic effects.

Oratorio vs. opera

Both oratorios and operas used recitative, arias, duets and instrumental preludes and ritornellos, but oratorios differed from operas in numerous ways: their subject matter was sacred; narration was included; the chorus was used for dramatic, narrative, and meditative purposes; and they were seldom if ever meant to be staged. Action was described or suggested, not played out.

Private Music of the Convent

Invisible and mostly unheard by the public was the music-making in the convents. Church administrators in Rome and in the cities put many obstacles in the way of convents trying to develop a full musical life for its nuns and novices. These administrators would not allow experienced male music directors, composers, or outside musicians to enter the convents for the purpose of instructing the young singers or joining them in rehearsals. A lively musical culture developed in the convent of Santa Cristina della Fondazza in Bologna in the sixteenth and seventeenth centuries, despite the many regulations that made serious musical activity a clandestine operation.[5] Lucrezia Vizzani, who became an accomplished composer of sacred music in the monodic style and concerted media, entered Santa Cristina as a child, and received the necessary training only because an aunt at the same convent could teach her. The nuns aggressively fought for a level of music-making that came up to the standards and styles outside the walls of the institution. Vizzani's *Componimenti musicali* (Musical Compositions, published in 1623 by Bartholomeo Magni in Venice, but printed, apparently privately, by the Gardano firm) contained twenty motets, most of them for one or two soprano voices accompanied by a basso continuo.

Lucrezia Vizzani

LUTHERAN CHURCH MUSIC

The New Styles

In the German-speaking regions, both the Catholic and Lutheran churches took up the new monodic and concertato techniques. Sacred music in Austria and the Catholic southern cities of Germany remained wholly under Italian influence, with Italian composers particularly active in Munich, Salzburg,

5. Craig A. Monson, *Disembodied Voices: Music and Culture in an Early Modern Italian Convent* (Berkeley: University of California Press, 1995).

Prague, and Vienna. Composers in the Lutheran central and northern regions began, early in the seventeenth century, to employ the new media, sometimes using chorale tunes as melodic material. Along with these compositions in stile moderno, the Lutheran composers continued to write polyphonic chorale motets as well as biblical motets that did not use chorale melodies. Many of the latter type by Hassler, Praetorius, and other early seventeenth-century composers were in the grand concerto medium, testifying to German musicians' admiration for the Venetian fashion.

The concerto for few voices also attracted German composers. Johann Hermann Schein (1586–1630) published an important collection of such pieces in 1618 and 1626 at Leipzig titled *Opella nova* (New Little Works) and subtitled *Geistliche Konzerte . . . auff ietzo gebräuchliche italiänische Invention* (Sacred Concertos in the Nowadays Customary Italian Manner). In many respects the pieces are Lutheran counterparts of some of Monteverdi's concertato madrigals. The collection consists chiefly of duets and a few solos on chorale texts. Schein sometimes dispensed with chorale melodies, but when he did use them he treated them freely, inserting vocal embellishments, breaking up the phrases and dividing them among the voices. He included a continuo and sometimes one or two solo instruments, and occasionally an orchestral sinfonia or an ensemble for chorus and instruments. These sacred concertos of Schein set a precedent for a long series of similar works by Lutheran composers of the seventeenth century.

Sacred concerto in Germany

Heinrich Schütz

Career

The greatest German composer of the mid-seventeenth century, Heinrich Schütz (1585–1672), spanned the musical styles of the north and south. He studied in Venice with Giovanni Gabrieli from 1609 to 1612 and there brought out his first published work, a collection of five-part Italian madrigals. From 1617 to the end of his life, Schütz was master of the chapel of the elector of Saxony at Dresden, although during the Thirty Years' War he spent several years as court conductor in Copenhagen. Schütz renewed his acquaintance with Italian music on a trip to Venice in 1628. As far as we know, Schütz did not write any strictly independent instrumental music. He is reputed to have composed the first German opera, as well as several ballets and other stage works, but no such music survives. What remains is a great quantity and variety of church music dating from 1619 to his final years.

Psalm settings

The simplest of these works are plain four-part harmonic settings of a German Psalter (1628). Contrasting with the Calvinist plainness of these Psalm settings are the Latin motets of the *Cantiones sacrae* (1625). Here, a Roman contrapuntal style is enlivened by harmonic novelties and by madrigalian traits, such as the musical representation of sleep and waking at the beginning of *Ego dormio et cor meum vigilat* (I sleep, and my heart wakes; Example 9.12).

Venetian magnificence and color appear frequently in Schütz's music. The *Psalmen Davids* (1619) for multiple choruses, soloists, and concertato instru-

Example 9.12 *Heinrich Schütz,* Ego dormio

I sleep, and my heart wakes.

ments, combines the massive colorful sonority of the grand concerto with sensitive treatment of the German text. Indeed, Schütz completed the fusion of Italian and German styles begun by Hassler and others toward the end of the sixteenth century. His works lack only one significant element of the fully developed Lutheran style: he seldom made use of traditional chorale melodies, although he set many chorale texts.

Concertato motets

In 1636 and 1639, when war had sadly reduced the electoral chapel, Schütz published his *Kleine geistliche Konzerte* (Little Sacred Concertos), motets for one to five solo voices with organ accompaniment. The year 1636 also saw the publication of the *Musikalische Exequien* (funeral music for Schütz's friend and patron Prince Heinrich Posthumus von Reuss), for soloists and choruses in various combinations with accompaniment of basso continuo. Another collection of German motets, written in a severe contrapuntal style, was the *Geistliche Chormusik* (Spiritual Choral Music, 1648). Most important of Schütz's concertato motets are the *Symphoniae sacrae* (Sacred Symphonies), published in three series (1629, 1647, and 1650). The first two use various small combinations of voices and instruments, up to a total of five or six parts with continuo. The *Symphoniae sacrae* (1629) betray the strong influence of Monteverdi and Grandi.

O quam tu pulchra es

O quam tu pulchra es from that collection has approximately the same text as Grandi's (NAWM 60), but though it consists of the same ingredients—

Example 9.13 *Schütz,* O quam tu pulchra es

Your hair is like a flock of goats. How fair you are.

recitative, aria, and solo madrigal styles—it deploys them quite differently. Schütz sets the phrase addressed to the beloved, "O how fair you are . . . ," as a refrain—supplying a kind of ritornello, with two violins, in triple-time aria style—while praises to the individual parts of her body are sung in recitative, arioso, or madrigal style. The madrigalistic sections abound in word-painting, and the recitative shows how well Schütz had assimilated the bold dissonance practices of his Venetian colleagues.

Example 9.13 illustrates some of these points: (a) anticipation and trill on a dissonant accented passing note, (b) a suspension left by upward movement, leading through (c) an auxiliary note left by a skip to the (d) normal note resolving the suspension, and (e) the refrain section with its characteristic downward leap of the diminished fourth B♭–F♯. Licenses such as these were described as musico-rhetorical figures in the *Tractatus compositionis augmentatus,* a treatise by the composer and theorist Christoph Bernhard (1627–1692), a member of Schütz's choir in Dresden.[6]

6. Translated by Walter Hilse in "The Treatises of Christoph Bernhard," *The Music Forum* 3 (1973):31–179.

The last installment of the *Symphoniae sacrae* (1650), published after the end of the Thirty Years' War, called on the full musical resources of the Dresden chapel, now again available. It calls for as many as six solo voices and two solo instrumental parts with continuo, supplemented by a full choral and instrumental ensemble. Many of these works are laid out as dramatically conceived "scenes," sometimes with a closing chorus of pious reflection or exhortation, in a plan approaching that of the later church cantata.

Saul, was verfolgst du mich

One of the most dramatic scenes brings to life the moment when Saul, a Jew on the way to Damascus to fetch Christian prisoners, is stopped in his tracks by a blinding flash of light and the voice of Christ calling to him: "Saul, why do you persecute me?" (Acts 26:12–18, *Saul, was verfolgst du mich*, NAWM 62; CD 4 [40] / 2 ⟨27⟩). The experience led him to convert to Christianity and devote himself under the name Paul to spreading the Gospel. The concerto is set for six solo voices (the ensemble Schütz called *favoriti*), two violins, two four-voice choirs, and, it may be assumed, an orchestra that doubles the choral parts. Paired solo voices rising from the depths of the basses through the tenors to the sopranos and violins represent the light and the voice leaping from the desert. Christ's question, "Why do you persecute me?" is a mesh of dissonant anticipations and suspensions. Then the grand concerto takes over as the choruses and soloists together reverberate with echoes, suggesting the effect of Christ's voice bouncing off rocky projections in the desert.

Oratorios

Schütz's oratorio compositions include his most famous work, *The Seven Last Words* (1645?). Here he set the narrative portions mostly as solo recitative (in two instances, for chorus) over a basso continuo, while the words of Jesus, in free and highly expressive monody, are always accompanied by continuo and strings. There is a short introductory chorus and sinfonia. After the setting of the seventh and final word, the sinfonia is repeated, followed by another short closing chorus.

The *Christmas Oratorio* (1664) is on a larger scale. Rapid recitative takes over the narrative portions, while the concertato medium dominates the "scenes," treated separately with arias, choruses, and instrumental accompaniment. Schütz's three Passions, written toward the end of his life, by comparison austere, go back in spirit to a chantlike projection of the narrative. Unaccompanied ensembles represent the *turba* (crowd), that is, the disciples, the priests, and other groups.

INSTRUMENTAL MUSIC

Compositional categories

Instrumental music did not escape the spell of the recitative and aria styles, although these had less impact than the basso continuo. The sonata for solo instruments, especially, surrendered to vocal influences. The violin, which rose to prominence in the seventeenth century, emulated the solo singing voice, absorbing many of the vocal techniques into its vocabulary. (For a 1535 depiction of violin-family instruments, see Plate VII, facing page 366.)

Instrumental music in the first half of the seventeenth century gradually became the equal, both in quantity and content, of vocal music. Certain basic ways of proceeding resulted in these broad categories of composition:

1. Fugal pieces in continuous (nonsectional) imitative counterpoint, which bore a variety of names, including *ricercare, fantasia, fancy, capriccio, fuga, verset.*

2. Canzona-type pieces in discontinuous (sectional) imitative counterpoint, sometimes with an admixture of other styles, replaced in mid-century by the *sonata da chiesa.*

3. Pieces that vary a given melody or bass, including *partita, passacaglia, chaconne, chorale partita,* and *chorale prelude.*

4. Dances and other pieces in more or less stylized dance rhythms, either strung loosely together or more closely integrated in the *suite.*

5. Pieces in improvisatory style for solo keyboard instrument or lute, called *toccata, fantasia,* or *prelude.*

These classifications are useful as an introduction to a complex field, but the categories are neither exhaustive nor mutually exclusive. For example, the procedure of varying a given theme is found not only in the variations but often in ricercari, canzonas, dance pairs, and dance suites. Toccatas may include fugal sections; canzonas may have interludes in improvisatory style. In short, the various types may be intertwined in many ways.

Ricercare

The seventeenth-century ricercare is typically a brief, serious, composition for organ or clavier in which one theme is continuously developed in imitation. One example is the *Ricercar dopo il Credo*[7] (after the Credo) by Girolamo Frescobaldi (1583–1643), who was organist of St. Peter's in Rome from 1608 until his death. It appeared in *Fiori musicali* (Musical Flowers, 1635), a collection of organ pieces intended for use in the church service. This ricercare, part of the music for the *Missa della Madonna* (Mass for feasts of the Blessed Virgin; No. IX in the *Liber usualis*, page 40), is remarkable for the skillful handling of chromatic lines and the subtle use of shifting harmonies and dissonances, exuding a quiet intensity that characterizes much of Frescobaldi's organ music (see Example 9.14, page 296).

Frescobaldi

7. MM No. 34.

Example 9.14 *Girolamo Frescobaldi*, Ricercar dopo il Credo

Fantasia, Fancy

The keyboard *fantasia* is constructed on a larger scale than the simple ricercare and has a more complex formal organization. The leading fantasia composers in this period were the Amsterdam organist Jan Pieterszoon Sweelinck (1562–1621) and his German pupils Samuel Scheidt (1587–1654) of Halle and Heinrich Scheidemann (ca. 1596–1663) of Hamburg. In Sweelinck's fantasias, a fugal exposition usually leads to successive sections with different countersubjects and toccata-like figurations. Such pieces must have been intended to set and explore a mode or key in preparation for some other music.

Sweelinck

Genres

Although titles such as ricercare, fantasia, fancy, capriccio, sonata, sinfonia, and canzona may seem to have been applied rather indiscriminately, each represented a tradition and a set of precedents that composers of the time generally respected. A sense of genre was very strong in the early seventeenth century, as the writings of Athanasius Kircher (*Musurgia universalis*, 1650) and Michael Praetorius (*Syntagma musicum*, Part III, 1618) attest. In general the ricercare and fantasia were built on a theme or themes of sustained legato character, the fantasia using borrowed themes and learned devices more frequently to develop the themes as a series of fugues. Indeed, *fuga* was the name used in Germany for pieces of this sort from the earliest years of the seventeenth century. The canzona, on the other hand, had livelier, more markedly rhythmic melodic material, with emphasis on the division of the piece into sections, betraying its origin from the French chanson.

English consort music

Consort (ensemble) music for viols flourished in England beginning in the early decades of the seventeenth century, when the works of Alfonso Ferrabosco the Younger (before 1578–1628) and John Coprario (Cooper; d. 1626) were popular. The fancies of John Jenkins (1592–1678), the leading composer of viol consort music in the mid-seventeenth century, exhibit a variety of procedures. His early five-part contrapuntal fancies for viols and organ have ricercare-like melodic subjects, though often more than one theme is presented, and a suggestion of sectional division, as in the canzona is evident. His later three-part fancies for two violins and bass resemble Italian trio sonatas in their light texture, tuneful themes, and their division into sections of contrasting styles. In still other works, Jenkins used the term *fancy* for an introductory movement in imitative counterpoint followed by one or more dances or "ayres."

The contrapuntal fantasia for strings without basso continuo, the leading form of early seventeenth-century English chamber music, was cultivated even after the Restoration (1660). The principal later composers were Matthew Locke (1621–1677) and Henry Purcell (1659–1695), whose fantasias for viols, written about 1680, are the last important examples of the species.

Canzona

Composers approached the canzona in a variety of ways. One was to build several contrasting sections, each on a different theme in fugal imitation (much like a vocal chanson), rounding off the whole with a cadenza-like flourish. In another type, called the *variation canzona,* the composer used transformations of a single theme in successive sections, as in the keyboard canzona of Giovanni Maria Trabaci (ca. 1575–1647) illustrated in Example 9.15. A similar structure appealed to Frescobaldi and his most distinguished German pupil, the Viennese organist Johann Jakob Froberger (1616–1667). Some keyboard canzonas, however, and most ensemble canzonas are a patchwork of short thematically unrelated sections that might be repeated literally or in varied form later in the work. Tarquinio Merula (ca. 1594–1665) wrote ensemble canzonas of this kind.

Example 9.15 *G. M. Trabaci, Keyboard Canzona*

Sonata

Merula himself called such a piece a *canzona*, but a later composer would probably have called it a *sonata*. This term, the vaguest of all designations for instrumental pieces in the early 1600s, gradually came to mean a composition that resembled a canzona in form but that also had special features. Early seventeenth-century sonatas were often scored for one or two melody instruments, usually violins, with a basso continuo, while the ensemble canzona was traditionally written in four parts that could be played just as well without a continuo. Moreover, sonatas often took advantage of the idiomatic possibilities offered by a particular instrument. They had a somewhat free and expressive character, while the typical canzona displayed more of the formal, abstract quality of instrumental polyphony in the Renaissance tradition.

Biagio Marini

The differences, as well as the similarities, will be most evident if we compare one of the earliest sonatas for solo violin and continuo, by Biagio Marini (ca. 1587–1663), with contemporary canzonas. Marini's *Sonata per il violino per sonar con due corde*, Op. 8, published in 1629, is an early example of what may be called "instrumental monody." Like the canzona, it has contrasting sections, the last of which is particularly in the canzona spirit. It opens with a sentimental melody reminiscent of a Caccini solo madrigal, but it turns almost immediately to violinistic sequential figures (see Example 9.16). There are no literal repetitions, although the recurring cadences on *A* and the alternation of rhapsodic with regularly metrical sections give coherence to the piece. Most notable is the idiomatic violin style, which makes use of sustained tones, runs, trills, double stops, and improvised embellishments called *affetti*.

By the middle of the seventeenth century the canzona and the sonata had thoroughly merged, and the term *sonata* came to stand for both. Sometimes the name was qualified, as *sonata da chiesa*, since many such pieces were intended for use "in church." Sonatas were written for many different combinations of instruments, a common medium being two violins with continuo. The texture of two treble melodic parts, vocal or instrumental, above a basso continuo attracted composers throughout the seventeenth century. Sonatas of this type were usually called *trio sonatas.*

Sonata da chiesa

Variations

The variation principle permeates many of the instrumental genres of the seventeenth century as it does the strophic vocal airs. The theme and variations form itself, a favorite type of late Renaissance keyboard composition, underwent further development. Pieces using this method were called "Aria con variazioni," "Variationes super . . . ," or "Veränderungen über . . ." and "Diferencias" (German and Spanish for "variations"). But just as often, *variation* did not appear in the title. The term *partite* (divisions or parts) was often

Variation techniques

Example 9.16 *Biagio Marini, Sonata*

used in the early seventeenth century for sets of variations; only later was it applied to sets, or suites, of dances. Of the techniques used in such pieces, the most common were the following:

1. The melody could be repeated with little or no change, although it might wander from one voice to another amid different contrapuntal material in each variation. This type is sometimes called the *cantus firmus variation*, whose leading seventeenth-century composers were Sweelinck, Scheidt, and the English virginalists.

2. The melody itself could receive different embellishment in each variation. Most often it was in the topmost voice, with the underlying harmonies remaining essentially unchanged. One of the leading composers of this type of variation was the Hamburg organist Johann Adam Reincken (1623–1722).

3. The bass or the harmonic structure, rather than the melody, could supply the constant factor. Often, as in the case of the romanesca, a treble tune is associated with the bass, but it is usually obscured by figuration.

Example 9.17

a. *The Ruggiero theme*

b. *Frescobaldi,* Partite 12 sopra l'Aria di Ruggiero, Decima parte

The set of partite by Frescobaldi on the *Aria di Ruggiero*[8] (Example 9.17a) represents an early example of the third type. Like the romanesca, *Ruggiero* was an air or tune for singing ottave rime.[9] The bass and harmony of the air are clearly the fixed elements in Frescobaldi's twelve partite, and only in the sixth *parte* or variation is the melody at all prominent. Perhaps recalling the *Ruggiero*'s original function as a poetic recitation formula, Frescobaldi made the first variation very rhapsodic and free, like a recitative. The tenth *parte* falls into a syncopated mode similar to that used later by Buxtehude and Bach in their passacaglias (Example 9.17b).

An important class of organ compositions from middle and northern Germany comprised works based on chorale melodies. These pieces were produced in large numbers and in a great variety of forms after the middle of the seventeenth century, but examples already appear in the works of Sweelinck and Scheidt. In 1624, Scheidt published a large collection of compositions for the organ under the title *Tabulatura nova.* He called it new, because instead of the old-fashioned German organ tablature, Scheidt adopted the modern Italian practice of writing out each voice on a separate staff. Notable among the

Scheidt

8. Ed. Pierre Pidoux in Frescobaldi, *Orgel- und Klavierwerke* 3 (Kassel, 1954):60–66.
9. Indeed it may have received its name from the stanza in Ariosto's *Orlando furioso* once sung to it, Bradamante's vow of loyalty to Ruggiero: "Ruggier, qual sempre fui, tal sempre voglio / Fin alla morte, e più, se più si puote" (Canto 44, stanza 61: Ruggiero, what I always was, I want to remain / Until death and beyond, if that is possible).

collection's chorale pieces are a fantasia on the melody *Ich ruf' zu dir* (I call to you) and several sets of variations on other chorale tunes. There are also shorter organ settings of plainsong melodies, many variations on secular songs, and several monumental fantasias. The works of Scheidt, and his influence as a teacher, were the foundation of a remarkable development of North German organ music in the Baroque era.

Dance Music

Dance music was important not only for its own sake but also because its rhythms permeated vocal and instrumental music, both sacred and secular. The characteristic rhythm of the sarabande, for example, and the lively movement of the gigue appear in many compositions that are not called dances at all. German collections from this time contain numerous pieces called *Polnischer Tanz* (Polish Dance), *Polacca*, and the like, evidence that folk-based music of Poland was becoming well known in western Europe.

Suites

The suite, as a composition in several movements rather than a mere succession of short pieces each in a certain mood and rhythm, was a German phenomenon. The technique of thematic variation—already established in the pavane-galliard, Tanz-Nachtanz, and passamezzo-saltarello combinations of the sixteenth century—was now extended to all the dances of a suite.

Schein

This organic musical connection exists among dances in all the suites of Johann Hermann Schein's *Banchetto musicale* (Musical Banquet, 1617). The movements "finely correspond both in key and invention," Schein claimed in his foreword. Some of the suites build on one melodic idea that recurs in varied form in every dance. In other suites, subtle melodic reminiscence rather than outright variation provides the connection. The *Banchetto* contains twenty suites in five parts, each suite having the sequence paduana, gagliarda, courante, and allemande with a *tripla* (a variation in triple meter of the allemande). The music is dignified, aristocratic, vigorously rhythmic, and melodically inventive, with that union of richness and decorum, of Italianate charm and Teutonic gravity, so characteristic of this moment in Germany.

Among the dances sometimes included in a suite and sometimes published separately was the *intrada*, a piece usually of festive, marchlike character (though often written in triple meter); as the name suggests, it might serve as the opening movement of a suite.

French Lute and Keyboard Music

Composers in France established a characteristic idiom for the individual dances through their arrangements of actual ballet music. These arrangements were written not for an ensemble but for a solo instrument: first the lute and later the *clavecin* (the French term for harpsichord) or the *viole* (the French term for viola da gamba). Such a version for lute is *La Poste* (NAWM 63a;

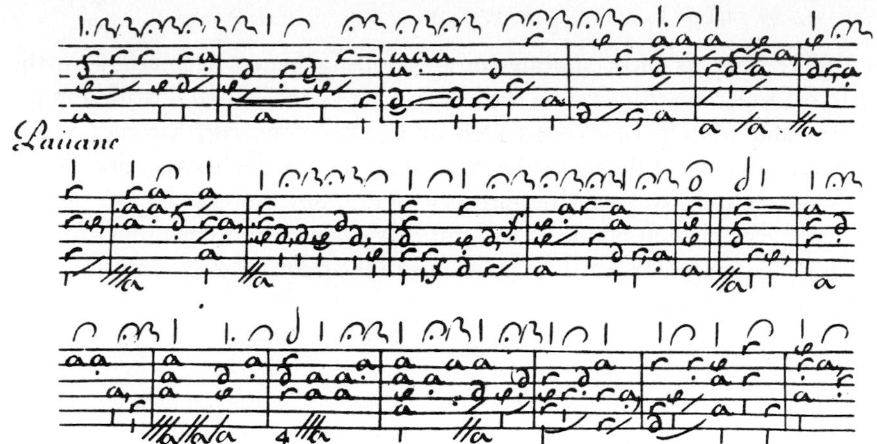

■ *A pavane in Denis Gaultier's collection of lute pieces* La Rhétorique des dieux *(Paris, ca. 1652), arranged according to mode. The horizontal lines in this French tablature represent the strings, with the lowest at the bottom; the frets are indicated by letters, a, b, c, etc.*

CD 4 [42]) by Ennemond Gaultier (1575–1651). Lute arrangements were sometimes transcribed for the harpsichord, as in the gigue drawn from this piece (NAWM 63b; [43]), in the process transferring ornaments and textures that are peculiar to the lute.

Since lutenists normally struck only one note at a time, it was necessary to sketch in the melody, bass, and harmony by sounding the appropriate tones—now in one register, now in another—relying on the listener's imagination to supply the continuity of the various lines. This technique, the *style brisé* (broken-chord style), was adapted by other French composers to the harpsichord. Lutenists also developed systematically the use of little ornaments (*agréments*), either indicated on the page or left to the discretion of the player. The French lute style was the basis for important developments in keyboard music and, indeed, for the entire French style of composition in the late 1600s and early 1700s.

Denis Gaultier

Lute music flourished in France during the early seventeenth century, culminating in the work of Denis Gaultier (1603–1672). A manuscript collection of Gaultier's compositions titled *La Rhétorique des dieux* (The Rhetoric of the Gods) contains twelve sets (one in each mode) of highly stylized dances. Each set includes an allemande, a courante, and a sarabande, with other dances added apparently at random. Each suite is thus actually a little anthology of short character pieces, many of which were given fanciful titles.

The earliest important composer in the new keyboard idiom was Jacques Champion de Chambonnières (1601 or 1602–72), the first of a long and brilliant line of French clavecinists that included Louis Couperin (1626–1661), Jean Henri d'Anglebert (1635–1691), Elisabeth-Claude Jacquet de La Guerre, and François Couperin. (Concerning the the last two composers, see Chapter 11.)

Froberger

The French style was carried to Germany by Froberger, who established the allemande, courante, sarabande, and gigue as standard components of dance suites. In Froberger's manuscripts the suites end with a slow dance, the sarabande. In a later, posthumous publication of the suites in 1693, they were revised so as to end with a lively gigue. The fusion of genre pieces and dance rhythms in the mid-seventeenth-century keyboard suite is well illustrated in one of Froberger's most famous compositions, a lament (*tombeau*) on the death of Emperor Ferdinand III in 1657 (NAWM 64 ; CD 4 [44]), written in the pattern and rhythm of a slow allemande. The *style brisé*, through which Froberger was one of the first to imitate lute music on the harpsichord, dominates the texture. Not only the rare key of F minor but also the prominent threefold *F* at the end allude to the emperor's name. Another programmatic touch is the arpeggio from deep in the bass to the treble to represent the ascent of the emperor's soul.

Improvisatory Compositions

Frescobaldi's toccatas

The toccatas of Girolamo Frescobaldi sacrifice virtuosity in favor of quiet contemplation, an unusual trait for this genre. In contrast to the imposing extroverted grandeur and virtuosity of Merulo and other Venetians, Frescobaldi's toccatas are often reserved, subjective, and mystical, with sustained harmonies and extraordinary original chord progressions. Others of his keyboard toccatas are related to the Venetian type. Long series of loosely connected sections with a great luxuriance of musical ideas allow for virtuosity, as in the third toccata of Book One (1637; NAWM 65; CD 4 [45] / 2 ⟨29⟩). Like so many others of Frescobaldi, this toccata has a restless character. The music constantly approaches a cadence on either the dominant or tonic, but until the very end the goal is always evaded or weakened harmonically, rhythmically, or through continued voice movement. According to the composer's preface, the various sections of these toccatas may be played separately and the player may end the piece at any appropriate cadence. Frescobaldi indicated that the tempo is not subject to a regular beat but may be modified according to the sense of the music, especially by retarding at cadences.

Froberger's toccatas

Froberger wrote more solidly constructed though less exuberant toccatas. His free improvisatory passages provide a framework for systematically developed sections in the contrapuntal style of the fantasia. Froberger's pieces were the model for the later merging of toccata and fugue, as in the works of Buxtehude, or their coupling, as in the familiar Toccata and Fugue in D minor of Bach.

Bibliography

Music Collections

Vocal Music

Facsimiles of Italian operas from the mid-seventeenth century are found in *Italian Opera, 1640–1770*, gen. ed. Howard M. Brown (New York: Garland, 1978–). Composers include Cavalli and Cesti. See also *The Italian Cantata in the Seventeenth Century*, gen. ed. Carolyn Gianturco (New York: Garland, 1986–), for facs. of cantatas by Carissimi, Cesti, Legrenzi, Stradella, Barbara Strozzi, and others.

Intermedi David Percival Walker, ed., *Les fêtes du mariage de Ferdinand de Médicis et de Christine de Lorraine, Florence, 1589*, 1: Musique des intermèdes de "la Pellegrina" (Paris: Éditions du Centre national de la recherche scientifique, 1963).

Benevoli *Opera Omnia* (Rome: Societas Universalis Sanctae Ceciliae, 1966–); the Salzburg Festival Mass is in DTOe, Vol. 20 (Year 11/1).

Caccini *Le nuove musiche, 1600,* ed. H. Wiley Hitchcock (Madison, Wis.: A-R Editions, 1970); *Nuove musiche e nuova maniera di scriverle, 1614,* ed. H. W. Hitchcock (Madison, Wis.: A-R Editions, 1978). Modern editions of *Euridice* include an incomplete setting in EP, Vol. 20 (Year 9) and a critical edition, ed. Angelo Coan (Florence: Edizioni Musicali OTOS, 1980); facs. ed. (Bologna: Forni, 1976).

Carissimi The oratorios are published by the Istituto Italiano per la Storia della Musica, ed. Lino Bianchi (Rome, 1951–). See also *Jephte* with basso continuo realization, ed. Gottfried Wolters (Wolfenbüttel and Zurich: Möseler, 1969); *Six Solo Cantatas,* ed. Gloria Rose (London: Faber & Faber, 1969).

Cavalieri *Rappresentatione di Anima et di Corpo,* facs. ed. (Farnborough, Eng.: Gregg International, 1967); transcription, ed. Eike Funck (Wolfenbüttel: Möseler, 1979); selections in CDMI, Vol. 10.

Cavalli *Giasone* (Prologue and Act I only) in EP, Vol. 12. Performing editions prepared by Raymond Leppard (London: Faber Music; New York: G. Schirmer) are available for *La Calisto* (1975), *Egisto* (1977), and *Ormindo* (1969).

Cesti *Orontea,* ed. William C. Holmes, in The Wellesley Edition, No. 11 (Wellesley College, 1973); *Il pomo d'oro,* ed. Guido Adler, in DTOe,Vols. 3/2 and 4/2 (1896), and a new edition of Acts 3 and 5 by Carl B. Schmidt in *Recent Researches in the Music of the Baroque Era,* Vol. 42 (Madison, Wis.: A-R Editions, 1982).

Landi *Il Sant'Alessio,* facs. ed. (Bologna: Forni, 1967).

Mazzocchi *La Catena d'Adone,* facs. ed. (Bologna: Forni, 1969).

Monteverdi *Tutte le opere,* 16 vols., ed. Gian Francesco Malipiero (Asolo: G. F. Malipiero, 1926–42; rev. and repr. Vienna: Universal Edition, 1968). A new critical edition is in progress under Raffaello Monterosso, ed. (Cremona: Athenaeum cremonense, 1970–). Good editions of *Orfeo* have been prepared by Denis Stevens (London: Novello, 1967), Gregg International, 1972 (with intro. by Stevens), and a critical edition by Edward H. Tarr (Paris: Éditions Costallat, 1974).

Peri Facsimile editions of *Euridice* have been published by Broude Brothers (New York, 1973) and Edizioni Musicali OTOS (Florence, 1970); modern performing edition by Howard M. Brown in *Recent Researches in the Music of the Baroque Era,* Vol. 36/37 (Madison, Wis.: A-R Editions, 1981); *Le varie musiche and Other Songs,* ed. Tim Carter (Madison, Wis.: A-R Editions, 1986).

Schütz Sámtliche Werke, 18 vols., ed. Philipp Spitta and Arnold Schering (Leipzig: Breitkopf & Härtel, 1885–1927); *Neue Ausgabe sämtlicher Werke* (Kassel: Bärenreiter, 1955–). Consult also D. Douglas Miller and Anne L. Highsmith, comps., *Heinrich Schütz: A Bibliography of the Collected Works and Performing Editions* (New York: Garland, 1986).

Instrumental Music

D'Anglebert *Pièces de clavecin,* ed. M. Roesgen-Champion, Publications de la Société française de musicologie, Vol. 8 (Paris: Librairie E. Droz, 1934); newer edition by Kenneth Gilbert, Le Pupitre, No. 54 (Paris: Heugel, 1975).

Chambonnières *Oeuvres complètes*, ed. Paul Brunold and André Tessier (Paris: Éditions Maurice Senart, 1925); repr. with Eng. trans. by Denise Restout (New York: Broude Brothers, 1967).

Couperin, L *Oeuvres complètes*, ed. P. Brunold (Paris: Éditions de l'Oiseau-Lyre, 1936); *Pièces de clavecin*, ed. Alan Curtis, Le Pupitre, No. 18 (Paris: Heugel, 1970).

Frescobaldi *Opere complete* (Milan: Edizioni Suvini Zerboni, 1976–); keyboard works, ed. Pierre Pidoux, 5 vols. (Kassel: Bärenreiter, 1949–54).

Froberger Keyboard pieces have been edited by G. Adler in DTOe, Vols. 8, 13, and 21 (Years 4/1, 6/2, 10/2); organ works in *Süddeutsche Orgelmeister des Barock* 5, ed. Rudolf Walter (Altötting: A. Coppenrath, 1968); new critical edition of the suites by Howard Schott, Le Pupitre, No. 57 (Paris: Heugel, 1979).

Gaultier, D. *La Rhétorique des dieux* (facs. and transcription), Publications de la Société française de musicologie, Vols. 6 and 7 (Paris: Librairie E. Droz, 1932–33).

Jacquet de la Guerre *Pièces de clavecin*, ed. Carol H. Bates (Paris: Heugel, 1986). Selected clavecin pieces and the cantata *Semelé* in *Historical Anthology of Music by Women*, ed. James R. Briscoe (Bloomington: Indiana University Press, 1987), pp. 57–76.

Jenkins Consort music in MB 26 and 39. Consult other MB volumes for more consort and viol music by English composers of this period.

Scheidt Collected works, ed. Gottlieb Harms and Christhard Mahrenholz, 13 vols. (Klecken and Hamburg: Ugrino; Leipzig: VEB Deutsche Verlag für Musik, 1923–); the *Tabulatura nova*, DdT, Vol. 1.

Schein Collected works, ed. Arthur Prüfer et al., 7 vols. (Leipzig: Breitkopf & Härtel, 1901–23; repr. 1970). New edition by Adam Adrio and Siegmund Helms (Kassel: Bärenreiter, 1963–).

Sweelinck *Opera omnia*, Vol. 1: *The Instrumental Works*, ed. Gustav Leonhardt et al. (Amsterdam: Vereeniging voor Nederlandse Muziekgeschiedenis, 1968; 2nd rev. ed., 1974).

Viadana A modern edition of *Cento concerti ecclesiastici* is in Viadana, *Opere*, Series 1, no. 1 (Kassel: Bärenreiter, 1964).

For Further Reading

General

Manfred F. Bukofzer, *Music in the Baroque Era* (New York: Norton, 1947), is a comprehensive survey of the entire Baroque, though no longer current, with music examples and bibliographies; Claude V. Palisca, *Baroque Music*, 3rd ed. (Englewood Cliffs, N. J.: Prentice Hall, 1991), is a selective introduction to the principal styles and genres, with music examples and annotated bibliographies; Tim Carter, *Music in Late Renaissance and Early Baroque Italy* (London: Batsford, 1992). Consult also the revised articles in The New Grove Composer Biography Series (New York: Norton): *The New Grove Italian Baroque Masters* (Monteverdi, Frescobaldi, Cavalli, Corelli, A. Scarlatti, Vivaldi, D. Scarlatti), by Denis Arnold et al., 1984; *The New Grove North European Baroque Masters* (Schütz, Froberger, Buxtehude, Purcell, Telemann), by Joshua Rifkin et al., 1985; and *The New Grove French Baroque Masters* (Lully, Charpentier, Lalande, Couperin, Rameau), by James Anthony et al., 1986. Further bibliography in John Baron, *Baroque Music: A Research and Information Guide* (New

York: Garland, 1993); and Julie Anne Sadie, *Companion to Baroque Music* (London: Dent, 1990).

Basso Continuo

Frank Arnold's *The Art of Accompaniment from a Thorough-Bass as Practiced in the XVIIth and XVIIIth Centuries*, 2 vols. (New York: Dover, 1965), is the basic work on this subject, with copious quotations and examples from the sources. A very useful introduction, both scholarly and practical, is Peter F. Williams, *Figured Bass Accompaniment*, 2 vols. (Edinburgh and Chicago: Edinburgh University Press, 1970).

Early Opera

For a survey on opera, see Donald J. Grout, *A Short History of Opera*, 3rd ed. with Hermine Weigel Williams (New York: Columbia University Press, 1988); and on opera from the beginning to Lully, Robert Donington, *The Rise of Opera* (London and Boston: Faber & Faber, 1981); on early opera, Frederick W. Sternfeld, *The Birth of Opera* (Oxford: Clarendon Press, 1993). On early Italian opera, see Howard M. Brown, "How Opera Began: An Introduction to Jacopo Peri's *Euridice* (1600)," in *The Late Italian Renaissance, 1525–1630*, ed. Eric Cochrane (New York: Harper & Row, 1970), pp. 401–43, and in GLHWM 5:1–43.

For a comprehensive history of Venetian opera, read Ellen Rosand, *Opera in Seventeenth-Century Venice: The Creation of a Genre* (Berkeley: University of California Press, 1991). For a discussion of early Roman opera, see Margaret Murata, *Operas for the Papal Court, 1631–1668* (Ann Arbor: UMI Research Press, 1981). A useful bibliography is Guy A. Marco's *Opera: A Research and Information Guide* (New York: Garland, 1984).

The Florentine Camerata

Background literature on the Florentine Camerata includes Claude V. Palisca, *The Florentine Camerata: Documentary Studies and Translations* (New Haven: Yale University Press, 1988); idem, "The 'Florentine Camerata': A Reappraisal," in *Studi musicali* 1 (1972):203–36, and GLHWM 11:45–79; Nino Pirrotta, "Temperaments and Tendencies in the Florentine Camerata," MQ 40 (1954):169–89. Also see C. V. Palisca, *Girolamo Mei, Letters on Ancient and Modern Music to Vincenzo Galilei and Giovanni Bardi*, 2nd ed. (Stuttgart: Hänssler/AIM, 1977).

Italian Vocal Chamber Music

For an informative survey on solo song, see Nigel Fortune, "Italian Secular Monody from 1600 to 1635: An Introductory Survey," in MQ 39 (1953):171–95, and in GLHWM 5:47–71; and on cantata, Gloria Rose, "The Italian Cantata of the Baroque Period," in *Gattungen der Musik in Einzeldarstellungen: Gedenkschrift Leo Schrade*, ed. Wulf Arlt et al. (Bern: Francke, 1973), 1:655–77, and in GLHWM 5:241–63.

Monteverdi

Two of the most readable introductions are Denis Arnold, *Monteverdi*, rev. Tim Carter (London: J. M. Dent, 1990), and Gary Tomlinson, *Monteverdi and the End of the Renaissance* (Berkeley: University of California Press, 1987). An older survey is Leo Schrade, *Monteverdi: Creator of Modern Music* (New York: Norton, 1950; repr. 1964). For an extensive bibliography and detailed studies, see *The New Monteverdi Companion*, ed. Denis Arnold and Nigel Fortune (London: Faber & Faber, 1985); Jeffrey Kurtzman, *Essays on the Monteverdi Mass and Vespers of 1610*, Rice University Studies, Vol. 64, no. 4, Houston, 1979; John Whenham, ed., *Monteverdi, 'Orfeo'* (Cambridge: Cambridge University Press, 1986), an opera handbook. A well-researched and fascinating compilation is *The Letters of Claudio Monteverdi*, trans. with intro. by Denis Stevens (London: Faber & Faber, 1980).

Peri

Tim Carter, *Jacopo Peri, 1561-1633: His Life and Works* (New York: Garland, 1989).

Venice

Giovanni d'Alessi, "Precursors of Adriano Willaert in the Practice of *Coro spezzato*," JAMS 5 (1952):187–210, and GLHWM 3; James H. Moore, "The *Vespro delle Cinque Laudate* and the Role of *Salmi spezzati* at St. Mark's," JAMS 34 (1981):249–78; on the relationship between the architecture and the musical style, David Bryant, "The 'Cori Spezzati' of St. Mark's: Myth and Reality," EMH 1 (1981):165–86; on Gabrieli, Egon Kenton, *The Life and Works of Giovanni Gabrieli*, MSD 16 (Rome, 1967), and Denis Arnold, *Giovanni Gabrieli and the Music of the Venetian High Renaissance* (London: Oxford University Press, 1979).

Oratorio

An excellent comprehensive study of this genre is Howard E. Smither, *A History of the Oratorio*, 3 vols. (Chapel Hill: University of North Carolina Press, 1977–87); see also his "The Baroque Oratorio: A Report on Research since 1945," in AM 48 (1976):50–76.

Schütz

The standard work on this composer is Hans Joachim Moser, *Heinrich Schütz*, trans. Carl F. Pfatteicher (St. Louis: Concordia Publishing House, 1959). On the influence of Monteverdi and the "new style" on Schütz, see Denis Arnold, "The Second Venetian Visit of Heinrich Schütz," MQ 71 (1985):359–74. Allen Skei's *Heinrich Schütz: A Guide to Research* (New York: Garland, 1981) is an indispensable reference tool.

Instrumental Music

David D. Boyden, *The History of Violin Playing from Its Origins to 1761* (London: Oxford University Press, 1965); William S. Newman, *The Sonata in the Baroque Era*, 4th ed. (New York: Norton, 1983); Peter Allsop, *The Italian "Trio" Sonata from Its Origins until Corelli* (Oxford: Clarendon Press, 1992); Willi Apel, *The History of Keyboard Music to 1700*, trans. and rev. Hans Tischler (Bloomington: Indiana University Press, 1972); Frank E. Kirby, *A Short History of Keyboard Music* (New York: Free Press, 1966); Alan Curtis, *Sweelinck's Keyboard Music* (Leiden: University Press; London: Oxford University Press, 1969). On Frescobaldi's life and works, see Frederick Hammond, *Girolamo Frescobaldi* (Cambridge, Mass.: Harvard University Press, 1983), and Alexander Silbiger, "The Roman Frescobaldi Tradition, c. 1640–1670," JAMS 33 (1980):42–87, on the impact of Frescobaldi in Rome, his pupils and followers. For a discussion on the history of the chaconne and passacaglia, see Thomas Walker, "Ciaccona and Passacaglia: Remarks on their Origin and Early History," JAMS 21 (1968):300–20; and Richard Hudson, *The Folia, the Saraband, the Passacaglia, and the Chaconne*, MSD 35, 4 vols. (Neuhausen-Stuttgart: Hänssler, 1982). Bruce Gustafson and David Fuller, *A Catalogue of French Harpsichord Music, 1699–1780* (Oxford: Clarendon Press, 1990).

CHAPTER 10

OPERA AND VOCAL MUSIC IN THE LATE SEVENTEENTH CENTURY

OPERA

Venice

As opera spread throughout Italy and outward to other countries, the principal Italian center remained Venice, whose opera houses were famous all over Europe. More than the drama or spectacle attracting a cosmopolitan public, it was the singers and arias. Impresarios competed for the most popular singers by paying high fees. The singers Signora Girolama and Giulia Masotti earned twice to six times as much for an opera's run as Cavalli, the best-paid composer, received for writing it. The librettist Giulio Strozzi published a book glorifying Anna Renzi (see illustration, page 312), who created the roles of Ottavia in Monteverdi's *Poppea* and Deidamia in Francesco Sacrati's *La finta pazza* (1640). She inaugurated the vogue of the operatic diva, and composers wrote parts expressly for her special talents.

Singers

Librettists responded to the demand for arias by writing more of their verses in meters and forms suitable for arias, and composers outdid them by indulging in aria-like lyrical expansions whenever a few lines of dialogue or a situation provided an opportunity. It was common in mid-century to have two dozen arias in an opera; by the 1670s, sixty arias were the norm. The favorite form was the strophic song, in which several stanzas were sung to the same music. Other favorites were short two-part arias in AB form, and three-part, ABB′ and ABA or ABA′ forms. Many arias had refrains, a few lines of text that recurred with the same music.

Librettists

Arias

Typical arias used characteristic rhythms from the march, gigue, sarabande, or minuet. Others relied on ostinato basses, sometimes in combination

Aria types

Example 10.1 *Antonio Sartorio, Aria:* Vittrici Schieri, *from* L'Adelaide

Victorious ranks, martial trumpets

with dance rhythms. Musical motives in both the vocal part and the accompaniment reflected the content of the text. For example, a composer might imitate trumpet figures to portray martial or vehement moods, as in the aria *Vittrici schieri* (Example 10.1)[1] in the opera *L'Adelaide* (1672) by Antonio Sartorio (1630–1680).

Composers in the last quarter of the century often used the quasi-ostinato *running bass* accompaniment (a steadily flowing pattern of eighth notes) illustrated in *Crudo mostro è gelosia* (Example 10.2) from *Totila* (1677) by Giovanni Legrenzi (1626–1690). The ostinato pattern modulates first to the dominant, then to the dominant of that dominant.

1. Ed. in GMB No. 223 and in Ellen Rosand, *Opera in Seventeenth-Century Venice* (Berkeley and Los Angeles: University of California Press, 1991), pp. 370–73. The entire opera is in the Garland Series, Vol. 8, where this aria is on p. 4.

Example 10.2 *Giovanni Legrenzi, Aria:* Crudo mostro è gelosia, *from* Totila

A cruel monster is jealousy. It has entrapped Ceraste's hair. Born from the depths of the Styx, its armaments are sprinkled with poison.

Some arias consciously parodied the heroic opera for comic effect. *Tra cruci funesti*[2] (Amidst fatal tortures), from *Corispero* by Alessandro Stradella (1644–1682), with its vigorous gigue-like rhythm, is a mock "fury-revenge" aria. It is also a *continuo aria*—that is, its accompaniment consists only of harpsichord and bass—although it is framed by orchestral ritornellos.

Venetian Opera Exported

Carlo Pallavicino (1630–1688), one of the many Italian composers who in the late seventeenth and early eighteenth centuries brought Italian opera to the eagerly receptive German courts, worked chiefly in Dresden. Another was Agostino Steffani (1654–1728), active in Munich and Hanover. His later works include amply proportioned arias and accompaniments of rich concertato texture. He always managed to maintain an equal balance between form and emotional content in his music. One of the best Italian opera composers of his time, Steffani left works that are important both in themselves and for their decisive influence on eighteenth-century composers, especially Keiser and Handel.

Steffani

2. Ed. in HAM No. 241.

■ *The famous opera singer Anna Renzi, about whom Giulio Strozzi wrote in* Le glorie della signora Anna Renzi romana *(Venice, 1644): "Our Signora Anna is endowed with such lifelike expression that her responses and speeches seem not memorized but born at the very moment. In sum, she transforms herself completely into the person she represents, and seems now a Thalia full of gaiety, now a Melpomene rich in tragic majesty."* (QUOTED FROM ELLEN ROSAND, OPERA IN SEVENTEENTH-CENTURY VENICE, *p. 232)*

Steffani's aria *Un balen d'incerta speme*[3] (A flash of uncertain hope), from the opera *Enrico detto il Leone* (Henry the Lion; Hanover, 1689), illustrates his early style. The dimensions of the aria, in ABA form, are modest. The prominent though not excessive coloratura passages occur on pictorial words such as *raggio* (ray), while the passage on *dolor* (pain) expresses the thought with melodic and harmonic chromaticism (Example 10.3). Two features of this aria occur often in other examples from the period: (1) a *motto beginning,* in which the voice announces a short musical subject developed later in the aria, but which continues only after an instrumental interruption; and (2) a running-bass accompaniment.

Naples

Italian opera in the late seventeenth century tended toward stylized musical language and simple musical texture, concentrating on the melodic line of the solo voice, supported by ingratiating harmonies. From this, an operatic style developed that was more concerned with musical elegance and intrinsic effect than with dramatic force and truth, but the beauty of the music redeemed the new approach. Developed principally in Naples, it dominated the eighteenth century.

The recitatives, though short, support the quick changes of feeling and ideas in the text with their striking harmonic progressions. Two distinct types

3. Ed. in HAM No. 244.

Example 10.3 *Agostino Steffani, Aria:* Un balen, *from* Enrico detto il Leone

. . . is the only ray [of hope] that sustains me amidst the clouds of pain.

of recitative emerged. One type, accompanied by a basso continuo, traversed stretches of dialogue or monologue in as speechlike a fashion as possible. It would later be called *recitativo semplice* (simple recitative) and eventually *recitativo secco* (dry recitative). The other type, called *recitativo obbligato* and later *recitativo accompagnato* or *strumentato,* used stirring and impressive orchestral outbursts to dramatize tense situations. These interjections reinforced the rapid changes of emotion in the dialogue and punctuated the singer's phrases. Meanwhile, a further category of sung monody evolved: the *recitativo arioso* (aria-like recitative), or *arioso,* which stood somewhere between the free recitative and the rhythmically regular aria.

Recitativo semplice

Recitativo obbligato

Arioso

Alessandro Scarlatti (1660–1725) made the transition from the older seventeenth-century opera to the newer style just described. In many of his later works, notably *Mitridate* (Venice, 1707), *Tigrane* (Naples, 1715), and *Griselda* (Rome, 1721), the shrewdly dramatic conception of the arias and the detailed working out of the orchestral parts demonstrated his devotion to serious artistic goals. For the arias, Scarlatti favored the *da capo* form.

A. Scarlatti

The *da capo aria* takes its name from the words "Da capo" (from the head) inserted at the close of the second section of a two-section form; these words instruct the performers to return to the beginning of the aria and to repeat the first section. In Scarlatti's hands, it was the perfect vehicle for sustaining a lyrical moment through a musical design that expressed a single sentiment, sometimes joined with an opposing or related one. Thus *Mi rivedi, o selva ombrosa* (You see me again, O shady wood, NAWM 66; CD 4 46), the aria that opens Act II of Scarlatti's *Griselda,* exemplifies the use of the da capo aria to portray conflicting reactions. A queen for fifteen years, Griselda has been repudiated

Da capo aria

by her husband, King Gualtiero of Sicily, and must return to her humble origins. The mood of subjection is summed up in the melody of the first line (Example 10.4a), out of which the rest of the main A section develops through extension, sequence, and combinatorial methods. The subordinate B section, linked to the A section rhythmically, presents the bright side for a moment—her pleasure at being home (Example 10.4b).

Having completed the B section, the singer follows the direction "Dal segno," to return to her first entrance, skipping the opening ritornello. The abbreviated scheme is

		𝄋		Fine			Dal segno
Section:	**Ritornello**	***A***	**Transitional Rit.**		***B***		
Key:	**C minor**				**Modulation to E♭**		
Measure:	*1*	*4*	*16*	*18*	*19*	*26*	*(27=)4–18*

The opening ritornello and the A section, in C minor, occupy eighteen measures; the B section, 8 measures long, modulates from the C-minor cadence at the end of A to E♭. Then the A section follows immediately, in C minor, closing the aria on the fermata at the end of the transitional ritornello. This contracted form of the da capo aria was popular in the 1720s.

Example 10.4 *Alessandro Scarlatti,* Griselda, *Aria:* Mi rivedi, o selva ombrosa

You see me again, o shady forest, but no longer queen and bride; unfortunate, disdained, a shepherdess.

France

By around 1700, Italian opera flourished in every corner of western Europe except France. Parisians saw a few Italian operas in the mid-seventeenth century, but the genre did not catch on. Under the patronage of Louis XIV (reigned 1643–1715), the French achieved a distinctive kind of opera in the 1670s, which persisted for a century. Two powerful traditions influenced French opera: the sumptuous and colorful ballet, which had flourished at the royal court ever since the *Ballet comique de la reine* of 1581; and the classical French tragedy, represented best by the works of Pierre Corneille (1606–1684) and Jean Racine (1639–1699). France's literary and theatrical culture demanded that poetry and drama be given priority on the stage. After tentative experiments by Robert Cambert (ca. 1627–1677), Jean-Baptiste Lully succeeded in reconciling the demands of drama, music, and ballet in a new genre of theatrical work, *tragédie en musique*, later named *tragédie lyrique.*

National traditions

Tragédie lyrique

The court ballet was a substantial musical work, some of which was danced. At the beginning of each act, non-dancers sang solo *récits* in a style similar to the air de cour. There were polyphonic choruses as well. The costumed and masked dancers appeared at the *entrées*, music that reinforced the dancers' characterizations. The evening ended with a *grand ballet*, in which the leading nobility and the king himself took part. Lully, even before he wrote music for these ballets, danced in them.

Court ballet

Louis XIV

As unusual as it may seem, Louis XIV fully participated in the art form he patronized, the ballet. Eventually earning a reputation as one of the most brilliant dancers of his time, he first appeared on the stage of the Palais-Royal Theatre for five performances of the *Ballet de Cassandre* (music is lost) in February 1651 at the age of thirteen. The following year he played six different roles in the *Ballet des fêtes de Bacchus*, for which the music survives. His most famous part was the Rising Sun in the *Ballet de la Nuit* (1653). By the time he took the reins of state on the death of Cardinal Mazarin in 1661, he had represented, alongside the best professional dancers, a bacchante, a Fury, a dryad, a Moor, a Spaniard, Jupiter dressed as Diane, a rake, the spirit of dance, and in one role he serenaded a beautiful woman (played by a famous Italian danseuse) while playing the guitar, his favorite instrument. Soon after he took over the government of France, he danced publicly at Versailles, as Ruggiero in the *Ballet d'Alcidiane*, based on incidents in Ariosto's *Orlando furioso.* The king's diversion became an institution when he created the Royal Academy of Dance in 1661. He justified his decree by saying that the art of dance "has been recognized as one of the most honest and necessary in forming the body and giving it its first and most natural movements for all sorts of exercises, among them those of arms"[4] (see vignette, page 316). Some years later he also established the Academy of Sciences (1669) and the Academy of Music (1671).

4. Quoted in Philippe Beaussant, *Louis XIV artiste* (Paris: Payot, 1999), p. 51.

LOUIS XIV ON THE IMPORTANCE OF PUBLIC ENTERTAINMENTS

A prince and a king of France may place special value on public entertainments, for they are not as much ours as of our court and of all our people. There are nations where the majesty of kings consists in great part of not letting themselves be seen, which may seem reasonable to minds accustomed to servitude and rule by fear and terror. This is not in the French character, for, as far back as our history can teach us, if there is something unique about our monarchy, it is the free and easy access to the prince by his subjects. It is a balanced justice between him and them that holds them so to speak in a sweet and honest association, despite the almost infinite differences of birth, rank, and power. . . . This association of pleasures, which gives persons of the court an honest familiarity with us, touches and charms them more than one can say. The people, on their part, take pleasure in the spectacle, which fundamentally always aims at pleasing them, and all our subjects, in general, rejoice to see that we love what they love, the things at which they are most successful. Through this we hold their mind and heart, sometimes more forcefully, perhaps, than with rewards and benefits. As for foreigners, when they see a state flourishing and well governed spending on what may pass as superfluous, it makes a very advantageous impression of magnificence, power, wealth, and grandeur. . . .

Translated from Louis XIV, *Mémoires & réflexions* (Paris: Communication & Tradition, 1995), pp. 74–75.

Jean-Baptiste Lully

Jean-Baptiste Lully (1632–1687), an Italian musician, came to Paris when he was fourteen years of age. From 1653, as a member of King Louis XIV's twenty-four-piece string orchestra, the *vingt-quatre violons du roy,* he composed instrumental dance pieces that were added to productions of Italian operas. He also provided overtures, dances, and vocal numbers in both the Italian and French styles for court ballets. Dramatic contrasts and ethnic characterizations abound in the *Ballet des nations,* appended to the *Bourgeois gentilhomme* (1670), a product of his collaboration with the playwright Jean-Baptiste Molière. Among the exotic figures represented are the stock characters of the *commedia dell'arte,* Scaramouche and Harlequin (See NAWM 67; CD 4 [49]).

Quinault

Lully became the virtual musical dictator of France when a royal privilege of 1672 gave his Académie Royale de Musique a monopoly in the medium of sung drama. His librettist, the esteemed playwright Jean-Philippe Quinault, provided Lully with texts that combined serious mythological plots with frequent long interludes (called *divertissements*) of dancing and choral singing. Quinault's texts cleverly intermingled episodes of romance and adventure with adulation of the king, glorification of the French nation, and moral reflections. As Charles Perrault summed up the genre in 1692, the librettos, though grounded in the probable and common actions of real life, escaped to the mythologically miraculous and fabulous (see vignette, page 318).

For these librettos Lully composed music that was appropriately pompous or gracious. It also projected the highly formal splendor of the French royal court and the conventions of courtly love and knightly conduct. The public found Lully's spectacular choruses and lively ballet scenes especially appealing. Dances from Lully's ballets and operas became so widely popular that they were arranged in independent instrumental suites; many new suites were composed in imitation of Lully's divertissements.

Lully adopted the style of Italian recitative to the French language and French poetry—no simple task, since neither the rapid recitativo secco nor the quasi-melodic arioso of Italian opera suited the rhythms and accents of the French language. Lully is said to have solved the problem by listening to celebrated French actors and actresses and closely imitating their declamation, but this idea has not been substantiated. Certainly the timing, pauses, and inflections often resemble stage speech, but the rhythmic bass and the often songful melody do not attain the illusion of speech of Italian recitative.

Récitatif simple

In what would later be called *récitatif simple*, Lully in the dialogue of the characters shifted the meter, or grouping of note values, between duple and triple. This recitative was frequently interrupted by a more songlike, uniformly measured style, *récitatif mesuré*, which had more deliberate motion in the accompaniment. Discrete sections of *recitatif mesuré* are sometimes marked

Récitatif mesuré

■ *The burning of Armide's palace, which she ordered in a fury over her failure to murder Renaud (see her monologue in NAWM 68b) and over his escape from her power. In the foreground Renaud, in armor, bids goodbye to Armide. Ink-wash by Jean Bérain.* (PARIS, BIBLIOTHÈQUE NATIONALE)

CHARLES PERRAULT ON THE LIBRETTOS FOR FRENCH OPERA

The probable (*vraisemblable*) and the marvelous are the two pivots of this poetry [of opera]. Comedy revolves entirely around the probable and does not at all admit the marvelous. Tragedy blends the marvelous and probable. As dramatic poetry is entirely confined to the probable, is it not necessary that there must be another opposite kind—opera—confined to the marvelous, while tragedy holds the middle between the two, a blend of the marvelous and the probable? You will find proof of this in that whatever makes a comedy beautiful is a fault in an opera, and what charms in an opera would be ludicrous in a comedy. In a comedy all must take place in one same location. In an opera nothing is more pleasing than change of scene, not only from one place on earth to another but from earth to heaven and the opposite, from heaven to earth. In a comedy everything must be ordinary and natural; in an opera everything must be extraordinary and supernatural. Nothing can be too fanciful in this genre of poetry. The tales of old or those of Psyche [the soul-goddess] furnish the best subjects and give more pleasure than the best laid out and regular plot. . . . They have the gift of pleasing all sorts of minds—great geniuses as well as common people, the elderly as well as children. These well managed fantasies amuse and put reason to sleep—although opposed to reason itself—and charms it altogether more than all the probable that can be imagined. Thus we can say that the ingenious invention of opera is not a negligible addition to beautiful and great poetry.

Charles Perrault, *Paralelle des anciens et des modernes en ce qui regarde la poesie*, 3 (Paris: Coignard, 1692), pp. 282–84.

"Air" in the scores, but they lack the closed form or the rhyme schemes of the true air, which most often has the meter and form of a dance.

Armide's monologue in *Armide* (1686; NAWM 68b; CD 5 [4]) illustrates this mixture of styles (Example 10.5). It begins in the unmeasured idiom. Armide, dagger in hand, stands over her captive warrior, the sleeping Renaud, but because of her deep love for him, she cannot bring herself to kill him. She sings in an unmetrical rhythm: measures of four and of two quarters are interspersed with measures of three, permitting the two accented syllables of each poetic line to fall on downbeats. Rests follow each line and are also used dramatically, as when Armide hesitates between uncertainty and resolve (Example 10.5). A six-measure transition in the measured style leads to an air in minuet meter.

Another type of air, less rooted in dramatic action, is exemplified by *Bois épais*, from the opera *Amadis* (1684; Example 10.6). Here, the poet captures a quiet scene and the contemplative feelings it aroused. Musical mood paintings of this kind—serious, restrained, elegantly proportioned, full of aristocratic yet sensuous charm—were much admired and often imitated by later composers.

Example 10.5 *Jean-Baptiste Lully, Monologue:* Enfin il est en ma puissance, *from* Armide

What in his favor does pity want to tell me? Let us strike. . . . Heavens! Who can stop me? Let us get on with it. . . . I tremble! . . . let us avenge. . . . I sigh!

Example 10.6 *Jean-Baptiste Lully, Air,* Bois épais, *from* Amadis

Thick forest, redouble your shadows: you cannot be dark enough, you cannot sufficiently conceal my unhappy love.

The *Ouverture*

Even before he began to write operas, Lully had established a two-part form of *ouverture*—the "French overture" for the ballets. The first section is homophonic, slow, and majestic, marked by persistent dotted rhythms and by figures rushing toward the downbeats. The second section begins with a semblance of fugal imitation and is comparatively fast-moving without sacrificing a certain grave and serious character. The slow section, or one like it, sometimes returns at the end. Throughout the remainder of the Baroque era, *ouvertures* were used to introduce ballets, operas, oratorios, and instrumental works such as suites, sonatas, and concertos; they also appeared as independent pieces. The overture to *Armide* (NAWM 68a) typifies the genre. The *ouverture* was originally intended to create a festive atmosphere for the ballet or opera that followed; its function, among others, was to welcome the king to a dance or performance. Venetian overtures of the early seventeenth century had served some of the same purposes. But by the end of the century, Italian opera composers were introducing curtain raisers of a different type (see page 276), called *sinfonie* (singular, *sinfonia*). Meanwhile, the French remained faithful to their traditional form.

Orchestra

Lully's influence extended beyond the fields of opera and ballet. The discipline with which he directed his orchestra and his methods of scoring elicited admiration and imitation elsewhere in France and in Germany. The core of his orchestra, the *vingt-quatre violons du roy* (the king's twenty-four "violins"), comprised six soprano violins, tuned like the modern violin; twelve alto and tenor violins of various sizes tuned like the modern viola but playing three separate parts; and six bass violins, tuned like the modern cello but a tone lower. Lully also directed the *petits violons*, a select group also of twenty-four strings, used for the king's private chamber music. The two groups were often combined for ballet and opera. The rich, five-part texture of these string bands was augmented by woodwinds, which both supported the strings and played contrasting passages, often for a trio of solo wind instruments (usually two oboes and bassoon). Georg Muffat (1653–1740), an Alsatian strongly influenced by Lully, adopted the French manner of composition and of orchestral playing in Germany.

Lully's followers

Followers of Lully in France continued to write the type of opera that he had founded, introducing, however, an occasional aria in Italian style and da capo form (which they called *ariette*) and expanding the scenes of *divertissement* still further. An outgrowth of this expansion, the *opéra-ballet*, was a mixed form, initiated by André Campra (1660–1744) with *L'Europe galante* (1697). Meanwhile Lully's music continued to be performed into the eighteenth century, even outside France, such as in Holland.

England

Masque

Opera in England—or what was known there as opera—had a short career in the second half of the seventeenth century. The *masque*, an aristocratic entertainment similar to the French court ballet, had flourished in England for

■ *An English masque. It was customary for ladies of the court in England to perform in masques, as the French did in the* ballet de cour. *Painting by Marcus Gheerhardts, Woburn Abbey.*

years. Milton's *Comus*, produced in 1634 with music by Henry Lawes (1596–1662), is the best known. The most elaborate of these private entertainments, *Cupid and Death* (1653), with music by Matthew Locke (ca. 1621–1677) and Christopher Gibbons (1615–1676), included many dances and other instrumental pieces, songs of various types, recitatives, and choruses.

Meanwhile, English opera had a modest beginning under the Commonwealth (1649–60), although the English composers and public did not especially like it. Stage plays were prohibited, but a play set to music could be called a concert and so avoid the ban. Beginning with the Restoration (1660–85), this pretext was no longer necessary. Thus nearly all the English "semi-operas" of the seventeenth century were really plays with a large proportion of vocal solos and ensembles, choruses, and instrumental music. The only important exceptions were John Blow's *Venus and Adonis* (1684 or 1685) and Henry Purcell's *Dido and Aeneas* (1689), both of which were sung throughout.

John Blow

John Blow (1649–1708) served two terms as organist of Westminster Abbey and also held the official positions of organist and composer in the Chapel Royal. *Venus and Adonis*, though titled a "masque," is really an unpretentious pastoral opera that contains some charming and moving music. It combines elements of the Italian cantata with the native English and fashionable French styles of the period. The overture and prologue were obviously modeled on those of French operas; many of the airs and recitatives adopted the emotionally expressive contours of Italian bel canto; and other songs have more purely English rhythms and melodic outlines. The final chorus, *Mourn for thy servant,* is typically English in its simple, direct interpretation of the text, its grave rhythms, flawless declamation, lucid part writing, and frequent harmonic audacities.

Henry Purcell

Henry Purcell (1659–1695), a pupil of Blow, also served as organist of Westminster Abbey and held other musical posts in London. In addition to his many odes for chorus and orchestra, cantatas, songs, catches, anthems, Services, fancies, chamber sonatas, and keyboard works, he wrote incidental music for forty-nine plays, mostly during the last five years of his life.

Dido and Aeneas

Purcell composed *Dido and Aeneas* (1689) for a girls' boarding school at Chelsea. The libretto by Nahum Tate dramatized the familiar story from Vergil's *Aeneid* in a way that proved conducive to musical setting. Purcell's score is a masterpiece of opera in miniature: there are only four principal roles, the orchestra consists of strings and continuo, and the three acts, including dances and choruses, take only about an hour to perform. Purcell's style incorporated both the achievements of earlier English theater music and its Continental influences. The French overture and the homophonic choruses in dance rhythms resemble those of Lully, as in the minuet rhythm of the chorus *Fear no danger to ensue,* alternating iambs and trochees.

Thoroughly English, on the other hand, is the tune *Pursue thy conquest, Love* as well as the melody of the chorus *Come away, fellow sailors,* with its fascinating phrasing of 3 + 5, 4 + 4 + 4, and 4 + 5 measures, and the sly mock-pathetic chromatics at the words "silence their mourning." The choruses, which are freely intermingled with the solos, are an important part of the work. The recitatives are neither the rapid chatter of the Italian recitativo secco nor the stylized rhythms of French operatic recitative, but free, plastic melodies flexibly molded to the accents, pace, and emotions of the English text. Three of the arias are built entirely over a ground bass; the last of these—and one of the most moving in all opera—is Dido's lament *When I am laid in earth* (NAWM 69; CD 5 [7] / 2 ⟨30⟩). It is preceded by a recitative that does more than serve as a vehicle for the text: by its slow stepwise descent of a seventh, it portrays the dying Dido and thus prepares for what is to come. The lament follows a tradition in Italian opera of setting such scenes over a ground bass. The bass itself grows out of the descending fourth, common in such pieces, but it is extended by a two-measure cadence formula, adding up to a five-measure pattern, which is repeated nine times. Purcell creates great tension and forward thrust by re-attacking suspended notes on the strong beat, intensifying the dissonance.

The closing chorus, *With drooping wings* (NAWM 69; CD 5 [10]), was surely suggested to Purcell by the final chorus of Blow's *Venus and Adonis.* Equally perfect in workmanship, it is on a larger scale and conveys a more profound depth of sorrow. Descending minor-scale figures portray the cupids' "drooping wings," and arresting pauses mark the words "never part."

Incidental music

The rest of Purcell's output of dramatic music was all incidental music for plays, mostly consisting of a few short pieces. There are a few plays, however, in which the musical portions are so extensive as to make them operas within the seventeenth-century English meaning of the word—that is, dramas in spoken dialogue with overtures, entr'actes, and long ballets or other musical scenes. Purcell's principal "operas" of this sort were *Dioclesian* (1690), *King Arthur* (1691), *The Fairy Queen* (1692; an adaptation of Shakespeare's *A Midsummer Night's Dream*), *The Indian Queen* (1695), and *The Tempest* (1695). In *The Fairy Queen*, Purcell assimilated several Italian aria types. In *Hark: the ech'ing air a triumph sings* (NAWM 70; CD 5 [11]), for example, the voice and trumpet exchange fanfares and turns (we may compare it to Sartorio's aria in Example 10.1, page 310)

Unfortunately for English music, no composer during the next two centuries would develop and maintain a national tradition in the face of Italian opera's popularity. Instead, English audiences lavished their enthusiasm on the productions of Italian, French, or German composers.

Germany

The most important center for opera in Germany was the northern free city of Hamburg, where the first public opera house outside Venice opened in 1678 and a national opera emerged. The Hamburg opera existed until 1738, when German opera lost favor. During those sixty years, to be sure, many German librettos were translations or imitations of those by Venetian poets, and the music betrayed the influence of both Venetian and French models.

The principal native streams in the formation of German opera were the *school drama* and the German solo song. School dramas, performed by students, were little plays of a pious, moral, or didactic character with inserted musical numbers. They were fairly numerous in the sixteenth and early seventeenth centuries but died out during the Thirty Years' War. The serious religious tone of *Seelewig* (1644), an early allegorical pastorale by the Nuremberg organist Sigmund Theophil Staden (1607–1655), runs through the earliest Hamburg operas, many of which were on biblical subjects.

Singspiel

The German version of opera was the *Singspiel* ("sing-play"), a play that interspersed songs with spoken dialogue. When German composers replaced the spoken dialogue with recitative, they adopted wholesale the recitative style of Italian opera. In their arias, however, they were both more eclectic and more independent, occasionally writing airs in the French style and in the rhythms of French dances. Other arias, such as *Schöne Wiesen* (Lovely meadows) in *Erindo* (Hamburg, 1693) by Johann Sigismund Kusser (1660–1727),[5] a composer who otherwise assimilated the French style, combine German gravity

5. Arias from this opera are ed. by Helmuth Osthoff in *Das Erbe deutscher Musik*, Series 2, *Schleswig-Holstein und Hansestädte* 3 (1938).

with Italian elegance. More common in early German opera are short strophic songs of native origin displaying brisk, forthright melodies and rhythms. These airs, so different in both form and spirit from the da capo arias of Italian opera, owe much to the popular musical style that flourished especially in northern Germany.

Reinhard Keiser

Reinhard Keiser (1674–1739), the foremost and most prolific of the early German opera composers, wrote more than a hundred works for the Hamburg stage between 1696 and 1734. At their best, Keiser's operas bring together Italian and German qualities. The subject matter and general plan of the librettos follow those of Venetian opera, and the virtuoso arias even surpass their Italian counterparts in vigor and brilliance. The slower melodies, though lacking the suave flow of the Italian bel canto, can be profoundly expressive, and the harmonies are well organized in broad, clear structures. Keiser was no slave to the Italian fashion of casting nearly every aria in da capo form. When he did use this pattern, he often modified it. He also introduced songs of a purely German flavor and arioso melodies that were not bound to any rhythmic or formal scheme. Keiser's accompaniments, like those of other German Baroque composers, have a full polyphonic texture with interesting bass lines. Varied combinations of orchestral instruments concertize or compete with the voice in independent melodic figures.

Keiser's feeling for nature imbues his pastoral scenes with freshness and naturalism. In his famous opera *Croesus* (Hamburg, 1710), for example, he combined the effect of rustic instruments with a melodic line that realistically mimics bird songs (Act II, Scene 1). Late in his life Keiser set many farces to music; these are historically interesting because they show the beginnings of German comic opera.

VOCAL CHAMBER MUSIC

The Cantata in Italy

The cantata in Italy evolved from the early seventeenth-century monodic strophic variations and developed into a genre consisting of many short, contrasting sections. By the second half of the century, it had settled into a more clearly defined pattern of alternating recitatives and arias—normally two or three of each—for solo voice with continuo accompaniment. The text, usually love-poetry, took the form of a dramatic narrative or soliloquy. The whole performance lasted ten to fifteen minutes. So in both its literary and musical aspects, the cantata resembled a scene detached from an opera, although its poetry and music were on a more intimate scale. Also because the cantata was designed for performance before a small discriminating audience in a room without a stage, scenery, or costumes, it attained an elegance and refinement of workmanship that would have been lost in the amplitude of an opera house. Thus, more than opera, it offered the composer opportunity to experiment. Great quantities of cantatas were produced by Italian composers, notably Carissimi (see page 289), Luigi Rossi (see pages 274–76), Cesti (see page 277), Legrenzi (see page 310), Stradella (see page 310), and Alessandro Scarlatti.

Alessandro Scarlatti

The more than six hundred cantatas of Alessandro Scarlatti mark a high point in this repertory. His *Lascia, deh lascia* (Cease, O cease) is typical of the genre. It begins with a short section of arioso (Example 10.7a). The recitative that follows (Example 10.7b) exemplifies Scarlatti's mature style in its wide harmonic range: there is a noteworthy modulation to the remote key of E♭ minor at the words "inganni mortali." The next movement, a full da capo aria (Example 10.7c) with long, supple melodic phrases over a bass in stately eighth-note rhythm, displays unusual harmonic progressions and chromatics underscoring the word "tormentar."

Example 10.7 *Alessandro Scarlatti, Cantata:* Lascia, deh lascia

Cease, O cease to torment me.

[. . . bitterness] of an adored one too ungrateful, among the deceptions of mortal life; if it is the purpose of the wrath of adverse fate [only to make me die . . .]

Enough, cruel love; torment me no more, because I want to die.

In many of Scarlatti's modulations, the unprepared diminished-seventh chord—rare for the time—serves as a pivot chord. Scarlatti sometimes exploited the enharmonic ambiguity of this chord, but more often he used it to add bite to a cadence. Numerous instances of this chord, in both melodic and harmonic form, occur in the brief passage reproduced in Example 10.7c.

Other Vocal Chamber Music

Although most seventeenth-century cantatas were written for a solo soprano with continuo, some vocal chamber works were provided with ensemble accompaniments and ritornellos, and many were scored for more than one voice. The vocal chamber duet, with two equal high voices over a figured bass—a very popular medium—corresponded to the instrumental trio sonata. Steffani was especially renowned for this combination, and his duets were imitated by Bach, Handel, and many other composers.

Serenata

Midway between cantata and opera was the *serenata*, a semidramatic piece usually written for some special occasion to be performed by a small orchestra and several singers. Stradella, one of the first to write serenatas, was followed by Scarlatti, Handel, and most other composers of the late seventeenth and eighteenth centuries.

Song in Other Countries

Throughout the seventeenth century, France and Germany saw a modest but steady production of airs, some in the older tradition in courtly vocal music and others in a more popular cast. Meanwhile, composers across Europe imitated or adapted the Italian chamber cantata, though to a lesser extent than they did Italian opera. In France, Marc-Antoine Charpentier (1634–1704), a

France

pupil of Carissimi, composed both secular cantatas and sacred oratorios in the Italian style. Throughout the early eighteenth century, Italian influence remained strong on most of the French cantata composers. Thus, Louis Nicolas Clérambault (1676–1749), who published five books of cantatas between 1710 and 1726, alternated recitatives in the manner of Lully with Italianate arias, sometimes even with Italian words.

Germany

Keiser and his German contemporaries wrote songs and arias on sacred texts as well as cantatas in Italian and in German. The most notable of these composers was Adam Krieger (1634–1666) of Dresden, a pupil of Scheidt. His *Neue Arien* (New Airs, 1667 and 1676) were for the most part strophic melodies in a charmingly simple popular style with short five-part orchestral ritornellos. He also wrote cantatas with through-composed texts set in contrasting movements. Orchestral accompaniments and ritornellos were more common in German solo songs than in those of other countries. Toward the end of the seventeenth century, the German song had been absorbed into composite forms—the opera or the cantata—and had almost disappeared as an independent composition.

England

The songs of Henry Purcell and John Blow owed little to foreign models. In addition to many theater songs, Purcell wrote a large number of vocal solos, duets, and trios, many of which were published in *Orpheus Britannicus* (Vol. 1, 1698). John Blow issued a similar collection of songs under the title *Amphion Anglicus* (1700). A specialty of English composers in this period was the *catch*, a round or canon with often humorous, ribald texts to be sung unaccompanied by a convivial group.

The restoration of the English monarchy in 1660 encouraged the creation of large works for chorus, soloists, and orchestra for ceremonial or state occasions, such as royal birthdays, the king's return to London, or holidays. Purcell's magnificent *Ode for St. Cecilia's Day* (1692) was a direct ancestor of Handel's English oratorios.

CHURCH MUSIC

The strict contrapuntal style found continued life throughout the Baroque era in the music of the Roman Catholic Church. We find works in the old, strict style; in the modern, free style; and in a style that mingled the two. Composers produced hundreds of liturgical compositions that emulated Palestrina-style counterpoint, for example, anachronisms such as imitation Masses and Masses based on cantus firmi, for unaccompanied voices or with instruments merely doubling the vocal parts. These works frequently included canons and other learned contrapuntal devices. Meanwhile, some church composers eagerly took up the new musical resources of solo singing, the basso continuo, and the concertato medium of multiple choirs and groups of solo voices and instruments. The sacred works of Monteverdi, Carissimi, and Schütz, among others, furnished models for these new resources.

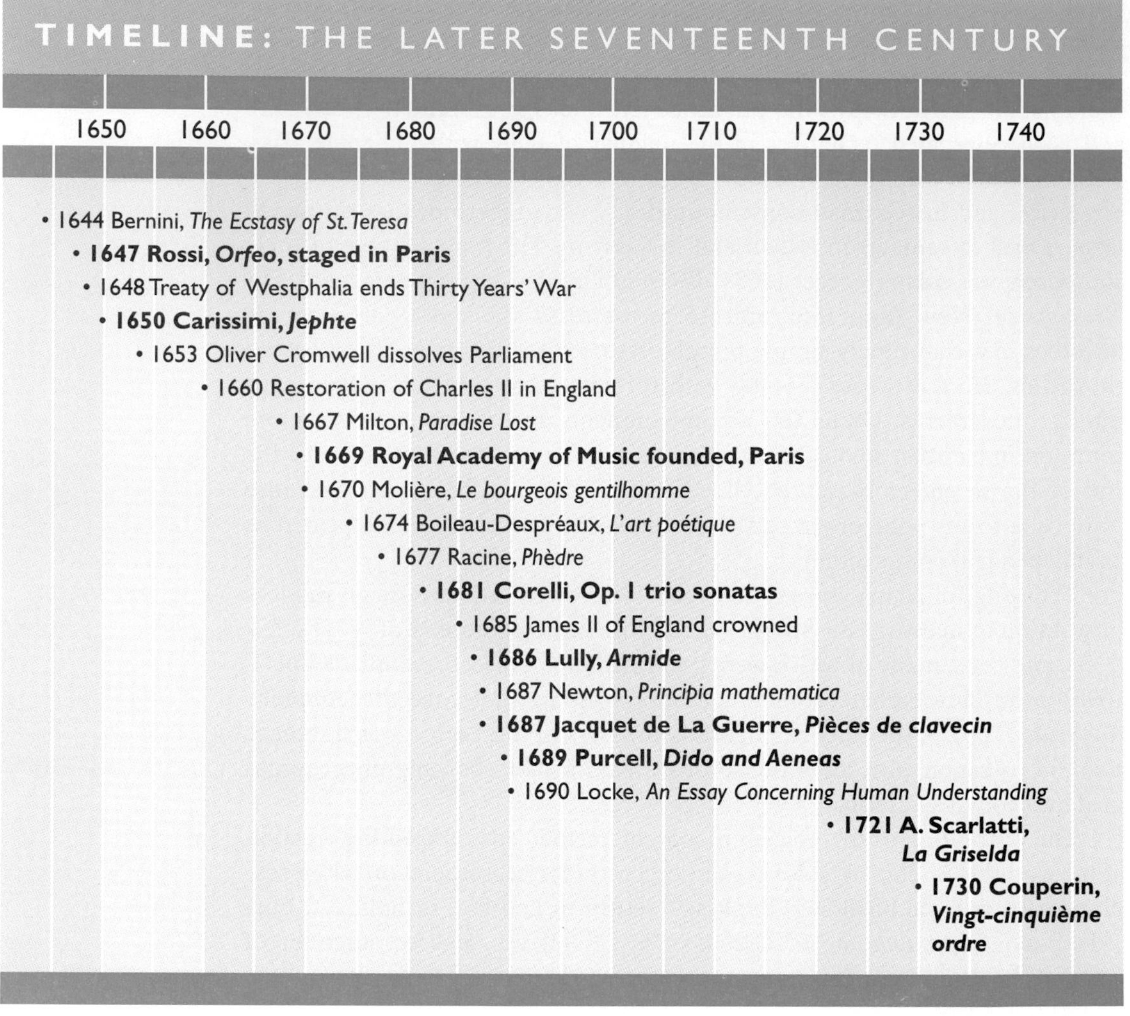

Italy

Cazzati

Bologna and its basilica of San Petronio was a thriving center of church music in both the old and concerted forms. One of its music directors, Maurizio Cazzati (ca. 1620–1677), published nearly fifty collections of sacred vocal music between 1641 and 1678. At one end of the spectrum, his *Messa a cappella* of 1670 is in a slightly modernized *stile antico.* His *Magnificat a 4* of the same year, however, consists of florid duets in the modern style alternating with choruses in the older style. In other works he plays his soloists against a full choir, like a *concertino* against the *ripieno* in the later instrumental concerto.

Colonna

Giovanni Paolo Colonna (1637–1695), who succeeded Cazzati in 1674, went beyond the customary doubling of voices by the strings and assigned them independent parts. His *Messa a nove voci concertata con stromenti*[6] from

6. Anne Schnoebelen in *Recent Researches in the Music of the Baroque Era,* Vol 17 (Madison, Wis.: A-R Editions, 1974).

the mid-1680s is one of the grand works written to celebrate the feast of San Petronio. Like Masses of other Bolognese composers, it consists of only the Kyrie and Gloria, preceded by a sinfonia. Most of the movements, such as the opening of the Gloria, employ two choirs and a five-part instrumental ensemble. In the Kyrie, for example, there are separate fugal entries for the five instrumental parts as well as the nine voices. The specific instruments are not designated, but it was common to use as many as a hundred musicians and singers on the patron saint's day, including trumpets and trombones, and a large string section.

Sentimental style

The northern Italian composers Legrenzi and Lotti, and the Neapolitans Alessandro Scarlatti and Giovanni Battista Pergolesi (1710–1736), went in another direction—toward the fragile texture, the admirably balanced phrasing,

ANDRÉ MAUGARS ON THE ITALIAN ORATORIO, 1639

There is another kind of music that is not used at all in France and for that reason merits separate treatment. It is called *recitative style*. The best that I have heard was in the Oratory of San Marcello, where there is a Congregation of the Brothers of the Holy Crucifix, made up of the grandest lords of Rome, who consequently have the power to assemble all the rarest resources that Italy produces. In fact, the most excellent musicians compete to appear, and the most consummate composers covet the honor of having their compositions heard there and strive to exhibit all the learning that they possess.

They do this admirable and ravishing music only on Fridays of Lent, from three to six. The church is not as big as the Sainte-Chapelle of Paris. At its end there is a spacious jube [a gallery between the nave and the choir] with a modest organ that is very sweet and suits voices very well. On the sides of the church there are two other little galleries, in which some of the most excellent instrumentalists were placed. The voices would begin with a psalm in the form of a motet, and then all the instruments would play a very good symphony. The voices would then sing a story from the Old Testament in the form of a spiritual play, for example that of Susanna, of Judith and Holofernes, or of David and Goliath. Each singer represented one person in the story and expressed the force of the words perfectly. Then one of the most famous preachers made the exhortation. When this was done, the choir recited the Gospel of the day, such as the history of the good Samaritan, of Canaan, of Lazarus, or of Magdalen, and the Passion of our Lord, the singers imitating perfectly well the different characters that the evangelist spoke about. I cannot praise this recitative music enough; you have to hear it on the spot to judge its merits.

Maugars, *Response faite à un curieux sur le sentiment de la musique d'Italie, escrite à Rome le premier octobre 1639*, ed. Ernest Thoinan (pseud. for Antoine Ernest Roquet), in *Maugars, sa biographie* (Paris: A. Claudin, 1865; facs. London: H. Baron, 1965), p. 29.

■ *Interior of the cathedral of Salzburg.* Grands motets *in the polychoral concerato medium were performed there in the seventeenth century. Engraving by Melchior Küssel, from around 1680.*

the lyrically sentimental tone, and the plaintive chromaticism that Italian religious composers adopted in the eighteenth century. German writers used the term *Empfindsamkeit* (sentimentality) to describe this style.

South Germany

A mixture of the old and new styles was also common in the Catholic centers of southern Germany—Munich, Salzburg, and especially Vienna, the seat of the imperial chapel. The four emperors who reigned there from 1637 to 1740 not only financially supported music but further encouraged it by their interest and actual participation as composers. A late example of church music in the conservative style is the *Missa di San Carlo* (1716),[7] or *Missa canonica*, of Johann Josef Fux. Every movement of this work is an elaborate, strictly canonic development of original themes. Fux's dedicatory letter states that he composed this Mass particularly in order to revive the "taste and dignity of ancient music."

The modern church music in southern Germany united Italian and German characteristics. In their Masses and other liturgical compositions, composers freely intermingled orchestral preludes and ritornellos, magnificent choruses, and festive solo ensemble sections, all supported by full orchestral

7. Ed. J. E. Habert and G. A. Glossner in DTOe I/1 (1894):63–88.

accompaniment. The Amen sections of the Gloria and Credo received especially elaborate treatment. Sequential repetitions, clearly oriented in the major-minor system, became a common constructive device.

Vienna

Caldara

Antonio Caldara (ca. 1670–1736), a native of Venice, worked in Rome from 1709 to 1715, before becoming Vice-Kapellmeister of the imperial court in Vienna. His Masses contain solo or ensemble sections within choral movements, as well as independent, self-contained arias and duets with concertizing instruments and orchestral ritornellos. In their succession of separate musical numbers, these Masses resemble operas, but they lack operatic recitative and only rarely include a full da capo aria.

In Caldara's *Stabat Mater* (Example 10.8), scored for four-voice choir, strings, two trombones, organ, and basso continuo, the mournful message

Example 10.8 *Antonio Caldara,* Sabat Mater

The sorrowful Mother stood weeping [at the Cross]. . . who grieved and suffered.

"The mother [of Jesus] remained grieving . . ."[8] is conveyed by a stunning array of augmented and diminished melodic intervals, diminished seventh and augmented fifth chords, and bold chromaticism.

Oratorio

Although oratorios were still performed in churches, they were also presented in the palaces of princes and cardinals, in academies, and in other institutions as a substitute for opera during Lent or at other seasons when the theaters were closed. Most oratorios were in two parts, usually divided by a sermon, or, in private entertainments, by an intermission with refreshments. Since the oratorio, whether on biblical subjects or not, had a verse libretto, it followed the conventions of opera rather than those of liturgical music.

Oratorio volgare

Hasse

After Carissimi's time, the Latin oratorio with choruses gave way to the *oratorio volgare* ("vernacular," that is, with Italian words), even in the Catholic centers of Germany. Adolph Hasse's *La conversione di Sant' Agostino* (The Conversion of St. Augustine, 1750), first performed in Taschenberg Palace in Dresden, consists of an overture, recitatives, da capo arias with coloratura and cadenzas, and short choruses.

French Church Music

Like French opera, church music in France went its own way. Carissimi's disciple Marc-Antoine Charpentier introduced the Latin oratorio into France, combining Italian and French recitative and air styles. He usually assigned a prominent role to the chorus, often a double chorus, in his thirty-four works in this genre. Charpentier loved dramatic contrasts, and his music brought details of the text to life.

Motet

Grands motets

Motets on biblical texts were principally cultivated in the royal chapel of Louis XIV, where composers produced a large number of motets for solo voices with continuo, much in the style of the currently fashionable secular cantata, as well as more elaborate motets and similar works for soloists, double choruses, and full orchestra. The latter were known as *grands motets* because the forces assembled to perform them were truly grand: the royal chapel in 1712 had a chorus of eighty-eight and a five-part string orchestra, to which were added harpsichord, organ, three oboes, two transverse flutes, a bassoon, two serpents, viole da gamba, solo violins, archlutes, crumhorns, and theorbos. The *grands motets* were multisectional pieces made up of preludes, vocal solos (called *récits*), ensembles, and choruses; frequent changes of tempo and meter were indicated by proportional signs.

Lalande

Henri Dumont (1610–1684), Lully, and Charpentier had written outstanding *grands motets.* Louis XIV's favorite composer of sacred music was Michel-Richard de Lalande (1657–1726), whose more than seventy motets re-

8. The entire work ed. Eusebius Mandyczewski in DTOe 25 (13/1):34–60.

veal a masterly command of the resources of the *grand motet*: syllabic *récits*, sweeping homophonic choruses, double fugues, and florid, opera-like airs and duets. Their rich harmony—spiced, when expression demanded, with dissonances—had surprising contrasts of texture and mood.

The French version of the sacred concerto for few voices was the *petit motet*. François Couperin (1668–1733) made an important contribution in this arena with his *Leçons de ténèbres* (1714), on texts from the Matins and Lauds for Holy Week, for one or two solo voices with a spare concertato accompaniment.

F. Couperin

Anglican Church Music

Anthems and Services remained the principal genres of Anglican church music after the Restoration. Since Charles II favored solo singing and orchestral accompaniments, Blow, Purcell, and their contemporaries, such as Pelham Humfrey (1647–1674), produced many anthems of the verse type.

■ *A singer rehearsing to the accompaniment of a positive organ. Engraving by Martin Englebrecht (1684–1765). "The Organ," a poem inscribed below the illustration, reads in translation: "The organ may be called the foundation of music, because through its ranks of pipes much wisdom may be imparted. All voices must conform to its sound and cadence. One need only pull the stops, and it resonates strong, dulcet, low, or mild. It leads a variety of instruments in sweet harmonies and lets itself be heard most delightfully in churches to praise the Supreme One."*

Coronation ceremonies inspired especially elaborate works, such as Purcell's *My heart is inditing*[9] and the splendid coronation anthems of Blow.[10] Less pretentious occasions demanded "cathedral" or "full" anthems for chorus without soloists, of which Purcell's earlier four-part *Thou knowest, Lord, the secrets of our hearts*[11] is a beautiful example. Purcell also set nonliturgical texts, pieces for one or more solo voices usually in a rhapsodic arioso style with continuo accompaniment, evidently designed for private devotional use.

Lutheran Church Music

Lutheran music enjoyed a golden age between 1650 and 1750. After the ravages of the Thirty Years' War, churches in the Lutheran territories of Germany quickly restored their musical forces. However, two conflicting tendencies had arisen within the church, and they inevitably affected musical composition. The Orthodox party, holding to established dogma and public institutional forms of worship, favored using all available resources of choral and instrumental music in the services. Opposed to Orthodoxy, the widespread movement known as Pietism emphasized the freedom of the individual believer. Pietists distrusted formality and high art in worship and preferred music of simpler character that expressed personal feelings of devotion.

Chorales

Crüger

Lutheran composers possessed as a common musical heritage the chorale, the congregational hymn cultivated in the earliest days of the Reformation. Toward the middle of the seventeenth century, Paul Gerhardt (1607–1676) made notable additions to the repertory of hymn texts. Johann Crüger of Berlin (1598–1662) set many of them to music. In 1647, Crüger edited and published *Praxis pietatis melica* (Practice of Piety in Song), a collection that became the most influential Lutheran songbook of the next half century. He and his many successors intended such songs not for congregational singing but rather for use in the home. Only gradually did these new melodies make their way into the official hymnbooks. Meanwhile, the growing practice of congregational chorale singing with organ accompaniment encouraged settings that smoothed out the older metrical irregularities. This type of chorale, in which melodies moved in equal notes and a fermata marked the close of each phrase, became known as *cantional style*, and is familiar from the arrangements of J. S. Bach.

Concerted Church Music

Sacred concerto

The Orthodox centers provided a favorable environment and material resources for the development of the sacred concerto. Several musical and textual components of diverse origin went into its music. The backbone was the

9. Ed. H. E. Wooldridge and G. E. P. Arkwright in Purcell, *Works*, Vol. 17 (London, 1907):69–118.
10. Ed. in MB 7.
11. Ed. Anthony Lewis and Nigel Fortune in Purcell, *Works*, Vol. 29 (1960):46–50.

concerted chorus on a biblical text, as established by Schein, Scheidt, Schütz, and other composers of the early and mid-seventeenth century. Of more recent vintage was the solo aria on a strophic, non-biblical text. The chorale was the most characteristic and traditional ingredient. From these elements composers fashioned three types of sacred concerto consisting of (1) arias only or arias and choruses in the concertato medium; (2) chorales only, in the concertato medium; and (3) both arias and chorales, the latter either in simple harmonic settings or in the concertato medium. Although these combinations are now often referred to as cantatas, we may more properly call them, as their composers did, sacred concertos.

The type of sacred concerto in the manner of Schütz, for chorus, solo voices, and orchestra without any use of chorale melodies, may be illustrated by a chorus, *Die mit Tränen säen* (Example 10.9, page 336), from a larger work by Schütz's pupil, the Hamburg organist Matthias Weckmann (1619–1674). Weckmann's treatment of the words "They that sow in tears shall reap in joy" juxtaposes two contrasting musical ideas within the same metrical scheme, the first made tearful by suspensions and dissonances, the second made joyful by dotted rhythms and a rising florid line.[12]

A setting of *Wachet auf, ruft uns die Stimme* for solo voice, strings, and continuo by Franz Tunder (1614–1667) of Lübeck (Example 10.10, page 337) provides an example of a sacred concerto on a chorale text and melody for a smaller performing group. (For the chorale melody, see NAWM 81, no. 7, page 544.) The chorale, only slightly decorated at the cadence, is set against a simple string accompaniment, which competes for attention by imitating the rising triadic motive.[13]

More subjective in mood and showing some influence of Pietist sentiment were the influential *Gespräche zwischen Gott und einer Gläubigen Seelen* (Dialogues between God and a Believing Soul, 1645) by Andreas Hammerschmidt (ca. 1611–1675).[14] In the duet *Wende dich, Herr* (Example 10.11, page 338) a trombone obbligato joins as the tenor in the alto-bass dialogue.

Buxtehude

Composers frequently applied the variation technique to chorale-based concertato compositions. Dieterich Buxtehude (ca. 1637–1707), Tunder's son-in-law and his successor at the Marienkirche in Lübeck, wrote variations on *Wachet auf*[15] in which each stanza of the chorale serves in turn as the basis for elaboration by voices and instruments. A short festive instrumental prelude, or *sinfonia*, is derived from the first two phrases of the chorale melody. The first stanza of the chorale is set for soprano voice and orchestra (strings, bassoon, continuo), the second for bass voice with orchestra, and the third for two sopranos and bass. All the movements are in the same key, D major, so that contrast is achieved mainly through changes in texture and rhythm.

Abendmusiken

Buxtehude composed much of his church music for the *Abendmusiken*, public concerts following the afternoon church services in Lübeck during the

12. The entire concerto ed. Max Seiffert in Ddt 6 (1901):79–100.
13. The entire concerto ed. Max Seiffert in Ddt 3 (1900):107–09.
14. Ed. A. W. Schmidt in DTOe 15 (1901):131–36.
15. Ed. Gottlieb Harms and Hilmart Rede in *Dietrich Buxtehudes Werke* 6 (Hamburg, 1935):60–79.

Example 10.9 *Matthias Weckmann, Chorus from Cantata:* Wenn der Herr die Gefangenen zu Zion

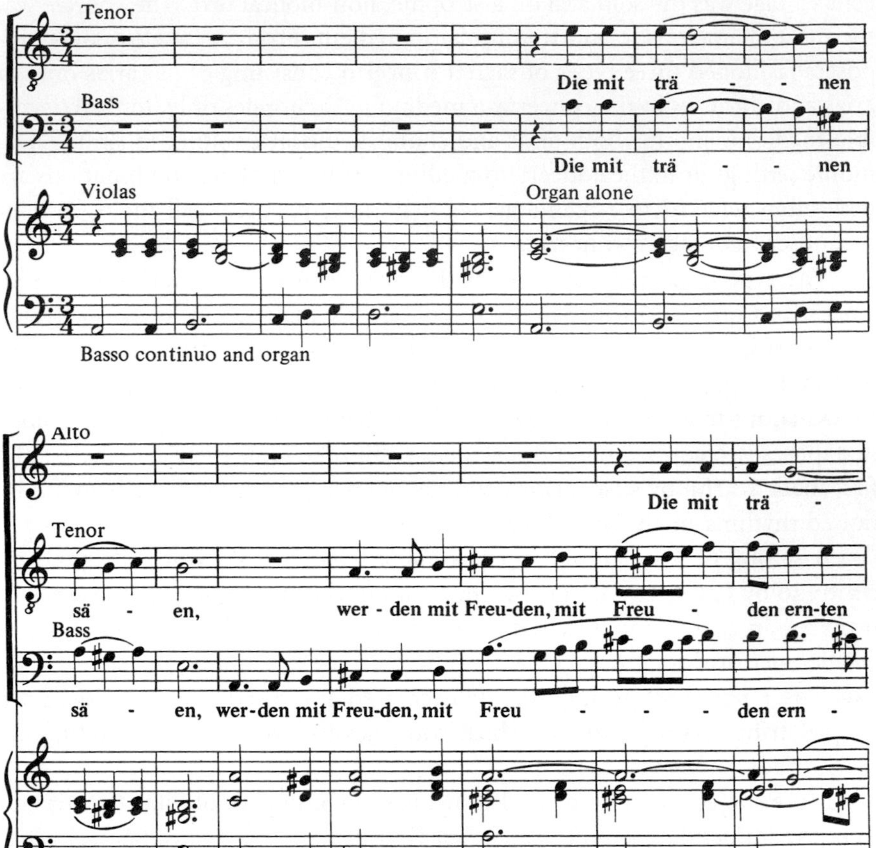
Tenor
Die mit trä - - nen
Bass
Die mit trä - - - nen
Violas
Organ alone
Basso continuo and organ
Alto
Die mit trä -
Tenor
sä - en, wer - den mit Freu-den, mit Freu - den ern-ten
Bass
sä - en, wer-den mit Freu-den, mit Freu - - - - den ern -
Soprano
Wer-den mit
Alto
- nen sä - en.
Bass
ten,
Vln. II
Vln. I
Vla. II
Vla. I
etc.

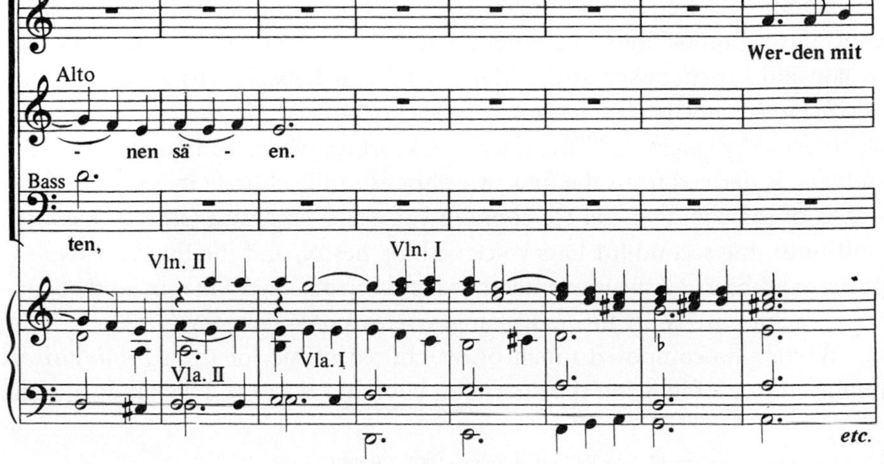

They that sow in tears shall reap in joy.

Example 10.10 *Franz Tunder, Chorale:* Wachet auf, ruft uns die Stimme

"Wake up," call the voices of the watchmen, high up in the tower; "Wake up, O town of Jerusalem!" Midnight is this hour; they call us with loud voices: "Where are you, wise virgins?"

Example 10.11 *Andreas Hammerschmidt, Dialogue:* Wende dich, Herr

Bass: *Is not Ephraim my dear son and my beloved child? Because I remember well* [*what I have said to him . . .*]
Alto: *Turn thee, O Lord, and be merciful unto me.*

Advent season. These were quite long, varied, quasi-dramatic affairs, on the order of loosely organized oratorios, incorporating recitatives, strophic arias, chorale settings, and polyphonic choruses, as well as organ and orchestral music. The *Abendmusiken* attracted musicians from all over Germany; the twenty-year-old J. S. Bach heard them in the autumn of 1705.

When not using a chorale melody, composers felt free to employ a more flexible arrangement, alternating short solo arioso sections with ensemble and choral parts. Toward the end of the century a somewhat standardized pattern of concerted church music developed. It consisted of a motetlike opening chorus on a Bible verse, a solo movement or movements, either aria or arioso, and finally a choral setting of a chorale verse. Free writing in the concertato medium without chorale prevails in the vocal works of Johann Pachelbel (1653–1706), the most famous of a long line of composers working in or near Nuremberg. Like many composers in southern Germany, where Venetian influence persisted, Pachelbel frequently wrote for double chorus.

The Lutheran Church Cantata

Neumeister

In 1700, Erdmann Neumeister (1671–1756) of Hamburg, an Orthodox theologian but a poet of decidedly Pietist leanings, introduced a new kind of sacred poetry for musical setting, which he called by the Italian term "cantata" (see vignette). Throughout the seventeenth century, composers drew chiefly from the Bible or the church liturgy, together with verses taken from or modeled on chorales. Neumeister added poetry that brought the meaning of the day's scriptural reading home to the individual worshiper through devout meditations. He intended these poetic texts to be set as ariosos or arias, the latter usually in da capo form and often including an introductory recitative. Neumeister and his imitators invited the composer's imagination by writing their poetry in the so-called madrigal style, that is, in lines of unequal length with irregularly placed rhymes; many of Bach's cantata texts and the arias in

ERDMANN NEUMEISTER ON THE SACRED CANTATA, 1704

If I may express myself succinctly, a cantata appears to be nothing but a piece out of an opera, put together from recitative style and arias. Whoever understands what these two demand will find this genre of song not difficult to work with. Just the same, let me say a little about each of them as a service to beginners in poetry. For a recitative choose an iambic verse. The shorter it is, the more pleasing and comfortable will it be to compose, although in an affective period now and then one or a pair of trochaic lines—and no less a dactylic—may be inserted nicely and expressively. As far as arias are concerned, they may consist mainly of two, seldom three, strophes and always contain some affection or moral or something special. You should choose a suitable genre according to your pleasure. In an aria the so-called *capo*, or beginning, may be repeated at the end in its entirety, which in music is altogether welcome.

Erdmann Neumeister, *Geistliche Cantaten statt einer Kirchen-Musik*, 1704, quoted in Max Seiffert, ed., J. P. Krieger, *21 Ausgewählte Kirchen Kompositionen*, DdT 52/53 (Leipzig, 1916), p. lxxvii.

his *St. Matthew Passion* take this form. Neumeister—and several later Lutheran poets—wrote cycles of cantata texts, intended to fit each slot in the church calendar.

The widespread acceptance by Lutherans of this new type of cantata brought the Orthodox and Pietistic tendencies together. Its poetry blended objective and subjective, formal and emotional elements. Its musical scheme incorporated all the great traditions of the past—the chorale, the solo song, the concerted medium—and added to these the dramatically powerful elements of operatic recitative and aria. Strictly speaking, the designation "cantata" applies only to compositions of this type. Concerted church works lacked any generic name and were variously called *Kantate, Konzert, Geistliches Konzert,* or simply *die Musik.*

J. S. Bach would become the greatest master of the church cantata, but several composers preceded him in defining its form: Johann Philipp Krieger of Weissenfels (1649–1725), who also composed operas; Johann Kuhnau (1660–1722), Bach's predecessor at Leipzig; and Friedrich Wilhelm Zachow (1663–1712) of Halle. In Zachow's cantatas,[16] recitatives and da capo arias are intermingled with choruses, which sometimes make use of chorale melodies. The writing for both solo and chorus is brilliant in sonority and strong in rhythm, and instruments are prominently used in concertato fashion. His works point directly and unmistakably to the cantatas of Bach.

Zachow

The cantata was central to the sacred output of many of Bach's contemporaries, among whom Georg Philipp Telemann (1681–1767) stands out. In Bach's time, Telemann and Handel were regarded as the greatest living composers. Telemann was particularly influential because his works were so widely known; among his publications were four complete annual cycles of cantatas (1725–26, 1731–32, 1744, and 1748). His immense production included some thirty operas, twelve cantata cycles (more than a thousand cantatas altogether), forty-six Passions, and a large number of oratorios and other church compositions, as well as hundreds of overtures, concertos, and chamber works. He was renowned for his vivid interpretations of the images and affections suggested by his texts. Johann Adolph Scheibe (1708–1776), who criticized Bach for being excessively clever in his music and overelaborating inner parts, found Telemann's tunefulness, harmonic directness, and simpler accompaniments more natural and appealing.

Telemann

The Passion

In Lutheran Germany, the *historia,* a musical setting based on some biblical narrative such as the Christmas story, was favored over the oratorio, and the most important type of *historia* was the *Passion.* Plainsong settings of the suffering and death of Christ according to the Gospel accounts had existed since early medieval times. After the twelfth century it was customary to recite the

16. Ed. Max Seiffert in *Gesammelte Werke von Friedr. Wilh. Zachow,* Ddt 21–22 (Leipzig, 1905).

story in a semidramatic mode, one priest singing the narrative portions, another the words of Christ, and a third the words of the crowd or *turba*, all with appropriate contrasts of range and tempo. After the late fifteenth century, composers wrote polyphonic settings of the *turba* portions in motet style, contrasting with the plainsong solo parts; this type of setting was known as the *dramatic* or *scenic Passion*. Johann Walter adapted the dramatic Passion with a German text to Lutheran use in his *St. Matthew Passion* of 1550, and many Lutheran composers, including Heinrich Schütz, followed his example. Catholic composers beginning in the mid-fifteenth century wrote *Motet Passions*, in which the entire text was set as a series of polyphonic motets, and some Lutheran composers took this up in the sixteenth century.

Dramatic Passion

The rise of the concerted medium led, in the late seventeenth century, to a new type of Passion derived from the oratorio. Called the *oratorio Passion*, this setting employs recitatives, arias, ensembles, choruses, and instrumental pieces, all of which lend themselves to a dramatic, almost operatic presentation. Schütz approached this kind of musical treatment in his *Seven Last Words*, although his text is a composite of all four Gospels instead of being taken exclusively from one.

Oratorio Passion

Poetic meditations on the Gospel story were inserted at appropriate points in the Passion text and were typically set as solo arias, sometimes with preceding recitatives. At appropriate points in the historia, the choir or congregation sang chorales traditionally associated with the Passion story.

Under the influence of Pietism, a new kind of Passion text appeared in 1706 with Christian Friedrich Hunold ("Menantes"), *Der blutige und sterbende Jesus* (The Bleeding and Dying Jesus, 1704). This author freely paraphrased the biblical narrative and added crude realistic details and tortured symbolic interpretations in the fashion of the time. A popular Passion text in a similar vein, by Barthold H. Brockes (1712), was set to music by Keiser, Telemann, Handel, Mattheson, and some fifteen other composers in the eighteenth century. J. S. Bach drew from it some aria texts in his *St. John Passion*.

Bibliography

Music Collections

Opera

Facsimiles of late seventeenth-century operas are in Howard M. Brown, gen. ed., *Italian Opera, 1640–1770* (New York: Garland, 1978–), which includes operas by Legrenzi, Lotti, Steffani, and others. Some of Keiser's operas are also in facsimilies. in *Handel Sources: Material for the Study of Handel's Borrowing*, ed. John H. Roberts (New York: Garland, 1986–).

Modern editions of late seventeenth-century Italian operas include Steffani, *Alarico*, 1687, in DTB, Vol. 11/2, and *Enrico detto il Leone*, ed. Theodor Werner, in *Musikalische Denkwürdigkeiten*, Vol. 1 (Hannover, 1926). For A. Scarlatti, consult the 8-vol. edition, *The Operas of Alessandro Scarlatti*, gen. ed. D. J. Grout (Cambridge, Mass.: Harvard University Press, 1974–83).

There is a collected edition (incomplete) of the works of Lully, ed. Henry Pruniäres, 10 vols. (Paris: Éditions de *La Revue musicale*, 1930–39; rep. New York: Broude Brothers, 1966). Thematic catalogue: Herbert Schneider, *Chronologisches-thematisches Katalog sämtlicher Werke von Jean-Baptiste Lully* (Tutzing: Hans Schneider, 1981). Vocal scores of operas by Lully and other composers, mostly French, of the seventeenth and eighteenth centuries are in the series *Les Chefs d'oeuvres classiques de l'opéra français*, 40 vols. (Paris: T. Michaelis, ca. 1880; rep. New York: Broude Bros., 1972).

Excerpts from incidental music for English plays and masques (1616–1641) are in J. P. Cutts, ed., *La musique de scène de la troupe de Shakespeare, The King's Men, sous le règne de Jacques I*, 2nd rev. ed. (Paris: Éditions du Centre national de la recherche scientifique, 1971). Three masques by Shirley and Davenant with music by Lawes are in *Trois masques à la cour de Charles 1er d'Angleterre*, ed. Murray Lefkowitz (Paris: CNRS, 1970). A modern edition of John Blow's *Venus and Adonis* is by Anthony Lewis (Monaco: Éditions de l'Oiseau-Lyre, 1949).

The works of Purcell are in the complete edition of 32 volumes (London: Novello, 1878–; rev. 1957–).

A modern edition of Keiser's *Octavia*, 1705, is in Vol. 6 of the supplement to the Deutsche Händelgesellschaft edition of Handel's works, ed. Friedrich Chrysander (Leipzig: Breitkopf & Härtel, 1858–94). DdT, Vol. 37/38, contains *Croesus* (1710 and 1730) and *L'inganno fedele* (1714), incomplete. EP, Vol. 18, Year 21/22, has *Der lächerliche Prinz Jodelet*, 1726.

Cantata and Song

For facsimiles of cantata manuscripts and prints by Legrenzi, Cazzati, A. Scarlatti, et al., see *The Italian Cantata in the Seventeenth Century*, gen. ed. Carolyn Gianturco (New York: Garland, 1986–). Concerning Stradella's works, see C. Gianturco and Eleanor McCrickard, *Alessandro Stradella (1639–1682): A Thematic Catalogue of His Compositions* (Stuyvesant, N.Y.: Pendragon Press, 1991).

Some modern editions of Italian vocal chamber music of the seventeenth and eighteenth centuries are CDMI, Vols. 2 (G. B. Bassani), 17 (Marcello), 30 (A. Scarlatti); CMI, Vol. 2 (Marcello). A. Scarlatti's *Lascia, deh lascia* is edited by R. Jakoby (Cologne: Arno Volk Verlag, 1968).

Two cantatas for soprano and chamber ensemble by Clérambault, *L'Ile de Délos* and *La Muse de l'opéra*, are edited by Donald H. Foster in *Recent Researches in Music of the Baroque Era*, Vol. 27 (Madison, Wis.: A-R Editions, 1979).

Krieger's *Neue Arien* are in DdT, Vol. 19.

A good selection of catches may be found in *The Catch Club; or Merry Companions*, 1733, facs. (New York: Da Capo Press, 1965); or 1762, facs., consisting of pieces by Purcell, Blow, et al. (Farnborough, Eng.: Gregg International, 1965).

Church Music and Oratorio

Facsimiles of Italian oratorios by Colonna, Caldara, Marcello, et al. are found in *The Italian Oratorio: 1650–1800*, ed. Joyce Johnson and Howard Smither (New York: Garland, 1986–); facsimilies. of solo motets by Cazzati are in *Solo Motets from the Seventeenth Century*, Vols. 6 and 7, ed. Anne Schnoebelen (New York: Garland, 1986–).

Some modern editions of seventeenth-century Italian church works: Caldara, in DTOe 26 (Year 13/1); Colonna, *Messa a nove voci concertate con stromenti*, ed. A. Schnoebelen in *Recent Researches in the Music of the Baroque Era*, Vol. 17 (Madison, Wis.: A-R Editions, 1974); Fux, *Sämtliche Werke*, ed. H. Federhofer (Kassel and New York: Bärenreiter, 1959–); Hasse, *La conversione di Sant'Agostino* in DdT 20; Marcello, *Gioaz*, in CMI, Vol. 8.

Pergolesi's collected works are found in *Opera omnia*, 26 vols., ed. Francesco Caffarelli (Rome: Gli Amici della Musica da Camera, 1939–42; rep. 1943 in 5 vols.). Vocal works have accompaniments in piano score with instrumental cues. The edition contains many works that have since been rejected as spurious, and omits a number of authentic works; sources are not named and the editing is questionable. See Marvin E. Paymer, *A Thematic Catalogue of the Opera Omnia, with an Appendix Listing Omitted Compositions* (New York: Pendragon Press, 1977). A New Pergolesi Edition is in progress: *Complete Works*, gen. eds., Barry S. Brook, Francesco Degrada, Helmut Hucke (New York: Pendragon Press; Milan: G. Ricordi, 1986–).

Charpentier, *Oeuvres*, 15 vols. (incomplete), ed. Guy Lambert (Paris, 1948–53).

John Blow's Coronation Anthems are in MB 7; Pelham Humfrey's church music in MB 34–35. Anthologies of English church music are Peter Le Huray, ed., *The Treasury of English Church Music II, 1545–1650* (London: Blandford Press, 1965; Cambridge: Cambridge University Press, 1982); and Christopher Dearnley, *The Treasury of English Church Music III, 1650–1760* (London: Blandford Press, 1965).

The eight volumes of *Dietrich Buxtehudes Werke* (Klecken-Ugrino Abtlg. Verlag, 1925–37; rep. New York: Broude Brothers, 1977–) contain only vocal works. The cantata *Wachet auf* is in Vol. 6 of this edition. (There is a different setting by Buxtehude of these words in DdT, Vol. 14, 139.) A new *Collected Works* is being published by the Broude Trust, New York. So far issued is Vol. 9: *Sacred Works for 4 Voices and Instruments*, Part 2, ed. Kerala J. Snyder (1987). Georg Karstädt, *Thematisch-systematisches Verzeichnis der musikalischen Werke von Dietrich Buxtehude* (Wiesbaden: Breitkopf & Härtel, 1974).

Selected works of Hammerschmidt are in DdT, Vol. 40; Pachelbel, DTB, Vol. 6/i; Tunder in DdT, Vol. 3; Weckmann, solo cantatas and accompanied choral works, in DdT, Vol. 6; Zachow, cantatas, in DdT, Vols. 21/22.

Telemann's *Der harmonische Gottesdienst* (cycle of solo cantatas, 1725–26) is in Vols. 2–5 of his *Musikalische Werke* (Kassel: Bärenreiter, 1950–); the *Lukas Passion*, 1728, is in Vol. 15. *Thematisches Verzeichnis der Vokalwerke*, Vol. 1, ed. Werner Menke (Frankfurt am Main: Vittorio Klostermann, 1982).

For Further Reading (see also Chapter 9: General)

Opera, Cantata, and Song

For a survey of Italian opera in the second half of the seventeenth century, consult Grout, Donington, and Rosand listed under "Early Opera" in Chapter 9.

On A. Scarlatti and his music, see Edward J. Dent, *Alessandro Scarlatti* (second impression, London: E. Arnold, 1960), and Donald J. Grout, *Alessandro Scarlatti: An Introduction to His Operas* (Berkeley: University of California Press, 1979).

The seventeenth-century Italian cantata is discussed by Gloria Rose in her article cited under "Italian Vocal Chamber Music" in Chapter 9.

For an invaluable overview on French music of this period, see James R. Anthony, *French Baroque Music from Beaujoyeulx to Rameau*, rev. ed. (Portland, Ore.: Amadeus Press, 1997). On Lully: Philippe Beaussant, *Lully, ou, Le musicien du soleil* (Paris: Gallimard, 1992). On the relationship of music and monarchy from the Valois to Louis XIV, see R. M. Isherwood, *Music in the Service of the King: France in the Seventeenth Century* (Ithaca, N. Y.: Cornell University Press, 1973).

On Baroque English opera, refer to Edward J. Dent, *Foundations of English Opera* (Cambridge: Cambridge University Press, 1928; rep. New York: Da Capo Press, 1965), which contains synopses of plots; Eric W. White, *A History of English Opera* (London: Faber & Faber, 1983).

Recommended books on Purcell are J. A. Westrup, *Purcell* (New York: Collier Books, 1962); Franklin B. Zimmerman, *Henry Purcell, His Life and Times* (London: Macmillan, 1967; 2nd rev. ed., Philadelphia: University of Pennsylvania Press, 1983); idem, *Henry Purcell, An Analytical Catalogue of His Music* (New York: St. Martin's Press, 1963); Curtis Price, ed., *Purcell, Dido and Aeneas*, Norton Critical Scores (New York: Norton, 1987).

Church Music and Oratorio

H. Wiley Hitchcock, "The Latin Oratorios of Marc-Antoine Charpentier," MQ 41 (1955):41–65, surveys the historical background and style of Charpentier's work and gives a catalogue of his oratorios, as well as his table of the "key-feelings" of eighteen major and minor keys. See also Hitchcock's catalogue, *Les oeuvres de Marc-Antoine Charpentier* (Paris: Picard, 1982), and his *Marc-Antoine Charpentier* (Oxford: Oxford University Press, 1990).

An exemplary study of Buxtehude and his environment in Lübeck is Kerala J. Snyder, *D. Buxtehude* (New York: Schirmer Books, 1987).

For a brief overview of Anglican church music, read Edmund Fellowes, *English Cathedral Music* (London: Methuen, 1941; rev. J. A. Westrup, 1969). More detailed accounts are Peter Le Huray, *Music and the Reformation in England, 1549–1660* (New York: Oxford University Press, 1967); and Christopher Dearnley, *English Church Music, 1650–1750* (London: Barrie & Jenkins, 1970).

On the chorale and the cantata, see Friedrich Blume et al., *Protestant Church Music* (New York: Norton, 1974). For printed sources and translations of individual chorales, consult John Julian, ed., *Dictionary of Hymnology*, 2 vols. (Grand Rapids, Mich.: Kregel Publications, 1985).

On the history of the Passion, see F. Blume, *Protestant Church Music*, and Basil Smallman, *The Background of Passion Music: J. S. Bach and His Predecessors* (London: SCM Press, 1957; rev. 1970).

CHAPTER 11

INSTRUMENTAL MUSIC IN THE LATE BAROQUE PERIOD

In the second half of the seventeenth century composers no longer wrote for a certain number of parts, leaving decisions about instrumentation to the performer. Having to write for specific instruments both inspired and challenged a composer's imagination. The possibilities offered by the modern organs, the two-manual harpsichord, and the violin family elicited new idioms, genres, and formal structures.

The principal types of compositions associated with each of the two major instrumental categories are

Keyboard: toccata (or prelude, fantasia) and fugue; arrangements of Lutheran chorales or other liturgical material (chorale prelude, verset, etc.); variations; passacaglia and chaconne; suite; and sonata (after 1700).

Ensemble: sonata (sonata da chiesa), sinfonia, and related genres; suite (sonata da camera) and related genres; and concerto.

ORGAN MUSIC

The Baroque Organ

The so-called Baroque organ is familiar to us from the many modern copies of early-eighteenth-century instruments, especially those built by Arp Schnitger (1648–1718) and Gottfried Silbermann (1683–1753; see illustration, page 351). Silbermann was trained in France and Alsace, and, like other German organ builders, was influenced by the French full organ, or *plein jeu*, and by the colors of the stops used in France to play solos and contrapuntal lines. The German builders also learned from the highly developed instruments constructed in Antwerp and Amsterdam. These organs provided a great variety of registration, including principals, or flue pipes, mixtures—in which pitches representing the upper partials added brilliance to the fundamental—and reeds.

Werke

German organ builders adopted the Dutch practice of dividing the pipes into a number of *Werke*. These functioned like separate organs, each with its own set of pipes having a certain character and function. The *Werke* included the *Brustwerk* (in front of the player), *Hauptwerk* (great organ, immediately above the player), *Oberwerk* (the upper chest over the great organ), and the pedal organ, usually arranged symmetrically in the center and at the sides of the great organ. Only the largest German organs had all of these, and some had, in addition, a *Rückpositiv* (chair organ, behind the player). The rich combinations that players created required a higher wind pressure than was customary in the sweeter Italian organs. Still, this wind pressure was only a fraction of that used in some of the huge instruments of the nineteenth and twentieth centuries.

North Germany

Organ music reached a golden age in Germany between about 1650 and 1750. In the north, Georg Böhm (1661–1733) at Lüneburg, and Buxtehude at Lübeck continued the tradition established by Sweelinck and Scheidt. A central group in Saxony and Thuringia (the Bach region) included Zachow and Kuhnau, as well as Johann Christoph Bach (1642–1703) of Eisenach. One of the most notable of the German organ composers was Johann Pachelbel of Nuremberg (the composer of the famous canon).

Much of the organ music written for Protestant churches served as a prelude to something else—a hymn, a scriptural reading, or a larger work. In northern Germany these preludes were often organ chorales, or toccatas or praeludia that either contained fugues or culminated in them.

The Toccata

The typical German toccata consists of a succession of fugal and nonfugal sections. The latter simulate improvisation in a number of ways: by contrasting irregular or free rhythm with an unceasing drive of sixteenth notes; by using phrases that are deliberately irregular or have inconclusive endings; and by abrupt changes of texture. The improvisatory effect is maintained most often through a contrived uncertainty in the harmonic flow and through quick, erratic shifts of direction. At the opposite extreme a slow-paced section might consist of long, harmonically static stretches that usually include extended pedal points. The capricious, exuberant character of toccatas made them ideal vehicles for virtuosic display at the keyboard and on the pedals.

Fugal sections

Toccatas began early to incorporate well-defined sections of imitative counterpoint. Out of these sections emerged the fugue, which was later conceived as a separate piece that followed the toccata proper. Buxtehude's toccatas, for example, are made up of shorter sections in free style that alternate with longer ones in imitative counterpoint. They are filled with movement and climaxes, display a great variety of figuration, and take full advantage of the idiomatic qualities of the organ. The opening, a free improvisatory section end-

Example 11.1 *Varied Forms of a Fugal Subject in Dieterich Buxtehude, Praeludium in E, BuxWV 141.*

ing with a solid cadence, is followed by a fugue on a catchy subject with well-marked rhythm. The fugue merges at length into a second toccata section, shorter than the first, again leading to a cadence. At this point the composition may close, but as a rule Buxtehude continued to a second and sometimes a third fugue, with brief interludes and a closing climactic section in toccata style. When there is more than one fugue, the subjects are usually variants of one musical idea (see Example 11.1). The keyboard fantasies of Sweelinck and Scheidt, the variation canzonas of Frescobaldi and Weckmann, and the toccatas of Froberger all apply variation in their fugal subjects as well.

Buxtehude's Praeludium in E, BuxWV 141 (NAWM 71; CD 5 [12]), which is designated in the manuscripts simply as "Praeludium," has all the earmarks of a toccata. It contains four fugal sections, each preceded by free figurative preambles or transitions. The longest free section is the first; the internal ones are transitional. The first fugue, on the subject given in Example 11.1, has two full expositions in the four voices, arranged in Buxtehude's favorite order of soprano, alto, tenor, bass. After we hear an episode modulating to the dominant built on the tail of the subject, there is another, incomplete exposition. The free section that follows has exuberant runs, which climb to the highest pitch in the piece and feature two "long trills"—so marked in the score—in the pedal part. The second fugal section comes from a subject in the first section, as shown in Example 11.1. After only two entrances the fugue breaks up into imitations of a short figure. By means of a brief suspenseful transition, the tonic is reaffirmed for an informal three-voice fugue without pedal in $^{12}_{8}$ gigue time. A transitional Adagio leads to the final, quite formal exposition of the subject, marked "Second variation" in Example 11.1. The form of the piece may be summarized as follows:

4/4				12/8	4/4		
Free	**Fugue**	**Free**	**Fugal/Figurative**	**Fugal**	**Trans.**	**Fugue + Coda**	
1	*13*	*47*	*60*	*75*	*87*	*91*	*110*

In the seventeenth century, such keyboard pieces were called "toccata," "prelude," "praeludium," "preambulum," or by some similar name, even though they included fugal sections. The simple coupling of two contrasted movements—a prelude in free or homophonic style and a fugue in contrapuntal style—is found only in the eighteenth century. Most seventeenth-century compositions that were later called "Prelude and Fugue" show a relationship to those Buxtehude toccatas that have a long fugal section in the middle.

The Fugue

Composers wrote fugues both as independent pieces and as sections within preludes. By the end of the seventeenth century, the fugue had almost entirely replaced the ricercare. Fugue subjects have a more sharply chiseled melodic character and a livelier rhythm than ricercare themes. As in the ricercare, independent voices enter with the theme in turn. In a fugue a set of these entries is called an exposition. Normally the subject, or *dux* (leader), is stated in the tonic and receives an *answer* or *comes* (companion) in the dominant. The other voices then alternate subject and answer. Short *episodes*, passages in which the subject does not appear, characterized by lighter texture or sequences, usually separate the first exposition from the subsequent full or partial expositions. These episodes may modulate to various keys, before the final statement of the subject returns to the tonic. The return is often intensified by devices such as pedal point, *stretto*—in which statements of the subject pile up in quick succession—or *augmentation*, in which the note-values of the subject are doubled.

Sets of preludes and fugues

Although preludes and fugues served important functions in the church service, they were also useful for training students in composition and performance. To this end, J. K. F. Fischer (ca. 1665–1746) compiled a collection of keyboard preludes and fugues, *Ariadne musica* (1715), written in nineteen different major and minor keys. This was neither the first nor the most complete tour of the chromatic octave. As early as 1567 the lutenist Giacomo Gorzanis had published a cycle of twenty-four passamezzo-saltarello pairs, and Vincenzo Galilei left a manuscript dated 1584, also for lute of twenty-four passamezzo antico–romanesca–saltarello sets. The lute was a natural instrument for such cycles because its frets marked off twelve equal semitones in the octave.

Temperament

Keyboard players were reluctant to give up the sweeter imperfect consonances and truer perfect consonances possible in nonequal divisions of the octave. Keyboard composers of the early fifteenth century exploited the pure fifths and fourths of the Pythagorean tuning, in which the major thirds were uncomfortably large and the minor thirds excessively small. When simultaneities combining fifths and thirds, and thirds and sixths, became common in the later fifteenth century, keyboard players began to compromise the tuning of the fifths and fourths to get better-sounding thirds and sixths. This was usually accomplished through *meantone* temperament, in which major thirds were either pure or slightly larger than pure, and fifths were slightly smaller than perfect. However, meantone temperament resulted in one "wolf" or very rough fifth, usually between *C*♯ and *A*♭ or between *G*♯ and *E*♭. Playing in every possible key or modulating through the entire cycle of fifths risked unpleasant results.

Meantone temperament

Equal temperament, in which all semitones are equal and all intervals except the octave are less than true but acceptable, offered a solution proposed as early as the sixteenth century and eventually embraced by many keyboard players, composers, and organ builders of the Baroque era. The title J. S. Bach gave to his first set of preludes and fugues in all twenty-four keys, *Das wohltemperirte Clavier* (The Well-Tempered Keyboard, Book I, 1722), suggests that he had equal temperament in mind. On the other hand, it has been pointed out that "well tempered" can mean good or nearly equal temperament as well as truly equal temperament. Fischer's set of preludes and fugues clearly did not imply equal temperament, since he omitted certain keys.

Equal temperament

The Well Tempered Keyboard

Chorale Compositions

While toccatas, preludes, and fugues remained independent of vocal music, organ compositions based on chorales used the melodies of the Lutheran hymns in four ways: as separate presentations of the chorale melody enhanced by harmony and counterpoint; as themes for variations; as subjects for fantasias; and as melodies to embellish and accompany.

The simplest organ chorales were essentially harmonizations with contrapuntal activity in the accompanying parts. The congregation, singing in unaccompanied unison, would alternate strophes with the organ. Sometimes each melodic phrase of the chorale was a subject for imitation, which resulted in a more contrapuntally elaborate setting resembling the motet.

Organ chorales

In the *chorale variation*, sometimes called *chorale partita*, the chorale tune served as the subject for a set of variations. This genre emerged early in the seventeenth century in the works of Sweelinck and Scheidt. Sweelinck usually stated the chorale as a cantus firmus in long notes, introducing different figurations in the other parts against each presentation of the whole chorale. Buxtehude's *Danket dem Herrn, denn er ist sehr freundlich* (Thank the Lord, for He is very kind; NAWM 72; CD 5 17) is such a set of variations. Buxtehude treated the chorale as

Chorale variation

a cantus firmus, putting it in a different voice in each variation. For each statement of the chorale, Buxtehude invented a new, highly individualized subject that he developed first by imitation, then through free counterpoint.

Chorale fantasia

In a *chorale fantasia* the composer fragments the chorale melody and develops the resultant motives through virtuoso fingerwork, echoes, imitative counterpoint, and ornamentation. The severe contrapuntal style of Scheidt's fantasias gradually gave way to the free, loquacious compositions of Reincken, Buxtehude, and other North German composers.

The Chorale Prelude

Chorale prelude, a term often applied to any chorale-based organ work, will be used here to denote a short piece in which the entire melody is presented just once in readily recognizable form. This form of the chorale prelude did not appear until the middle of the seventeenth century. The name suggests an earlier liturgical practice in which the organist played through the tune, with improvised accompaniment and ornaments, as a prelude to the congregation's or choir's singing of the chorale. Later (when they were written down) these pieces were called "chorale preludes" even if they did not serve the original purpose. In effect, the chorale prelude is a single variation on a chorale, which may be constructed in one of the following ways:

Compositional types

(1) Each phrase of the melody serves in turn as the subject of a short fugue, the piece as a whole adding up to a chain of them. This form resembles the chorale fantasia but is more concise and more consistent in style.

(2) In this type, chiefly associated with Pachelbel, the phrases appear in turn, usually in the top voice, in long notes with relatively little ornamentation. Each appearance is preceded by a brief imitative development in the other voices as a *diminution* (a version in shorter notes) of the motive that follows. Normally an introductory section develops the first phrase in a fairly extended fugue.

(3) The melody begins without any introduction, ornamented in an imaginative manner, sometimes with a long melismatic phrase at the final cadence. The accompaniment borrows many of its motives from the chorale tune and proceeds freely with great variety from phrase to phrase. Buxtehude and Georg Böhm excelled in this subjective and often highly poetic form of the chorale prelude.

(4) The melody, usually unadorned, is accompanied in one or more of the lower voices by a continuous rhythmic figure not related motivically to the melody itself. This type, not common in the seventeenth century, is often found in the work of J. S. Bach.

Organ Music in the Catholic Countries

South German and Italian organists shunned the austere mystic grandeur of the northern toccatas and fugues. They preferred the ricercare, the variation canzona, pieces based on Catholic liturgical cantus firmi, and the early type of

■ *The organ built by Andreas Silbermann (1678–1734) at the Abbey Church in Marmoutier (Alsace), France, 1708–10, and enlarged by his son Johann Andreas in 1746. In the foreground is the* Rückpositiv, *above the hidden console the* Hauptwerk. *The tall pipes are for the pedals.*

toccata that included incidental episodes of counterpoint. In general, the organ music of the southern countries, whether for church service or other purposes, tended toward the light and graceful. For example, the works by Spanish organist Juan Bautista José Cabanilles (1644–1712)—his many *tientos* (that is, imitative ricercari), passacaglias, toccatas, and other pieces—ranged from the severe, sometimes chromatic, style of Frescobaldi's sectional pieces to the light texture and lilting rhythms of the eighteenth-century keyboard sonata.

France

A distinctive French school of organ music produced attractive settings of popular airs and pieces resembling the overtures and expressive recitatives of French opera. We also find more learned, contrapuntal works and antiphonal "dialogues" for the three or four divisions of a large organ. This music has the typically French ornaments (*agréments*). Many pieces show off particular color possibilities of specified stops. Among the finest French organ music are the "Masses" (versets and interludes to be played in the Mass) of François Couperin.

HARPSICHORD AND CLAVICHORD MUSIC

In the Baroque period, especially in Germany, it is not always clear whether a given piece was intended for the harpsichord or clavichord or if, indeed, for the organ. The most important secular genres were the *theme and variations* and the *suite.*

Theme and Variations

The statement of a theme (a song, dance, or the like) followed by a series of variations goes back to the early history of instrumental music. Composers after 1650 preferred to write an original songlike theme (often called an *aria*) rather than follow the earlier practice of borrowing a familiar tune.

Suite

Suites made up a large proportion of later Baroque keyboard music. Two distinct kinds existed: the amorphous collections produced by the French clavecinists, and the German variety clustered around four standard dances. By 1700, the keyboard suite (or *partita*) in Germany assumes a definite order of four dances: allemande, courante, sarabande, and gigue. To these might be added an introductory movement or one or more optional dances placed either after the gigue or before or after the sarabande. The suite has a striking international character: the allemande is probably of German origin, the courante French, the sarabande Spanish (imported from Mexico), and the gigue Anglo-Irish. The four standard dance movements have different meters.

Jacquet de La Guerre and Couperin

Two representative composers of suites in France were Elisabeth-Claude Jacquet de La Guerre (1665–1729) and François Couperin (1668–1733). Jacquet de La Guerre earned an enviable reputation as a singer and harpsichordist and as a composer of cantatas, church music, and works for harpsichord and chamber ensembles. The *Mercure galant* hailed her musicianship as "the marvel of our century." Couperin, who wrote in all of these media and for the organ as well, published twenty-seven groups of clavecin pieces, which he called *ordres*, between 1713 and 1730.

Allemande

The allemande is usually in a moderately fast duple meter; it begins with a short upbeat, and all the voices participate in a smooth, continuous movement of eighth notes and/or sixteenth notes (see Froberger's *Lamentation*, NAWM 64).

Courante

The typical courante is in a moderate compound duple or compound triple meter ($\frac{6}{4}$ or $\frac{3}{2}$) or shifts between the two (see Example 11.2). The hemiola resulting from such shifting is particularly effective at cadences. Sometimes the French courante is replaced in suites by the Italian corrente, a faster dance in $\frac{3}{4}$ time with more homophonic texture.

Sarabande

The sarabande is a slow movement in $\frac{3}{2}$ or $\frac{6}{4}$ meter, often with the rhythmic pattern 𝅗𝅥 𝅗𝅥. ♩ | 𝅗𝅥 𝅝 or ♩ ♩ ♩ | ♩. ♪ ♩, with emphasis on the second beat (Example 11.3). It is generally more homophonic than the allemande and courante. The sarabande is sometimes followed by a *double*, that is, an ornamented variation of the original dance.

Gigue

The gigue, usually the final number of the suite, may be in $\frac{12}{8}$, $\frac{6}{8}$, or $\frac{6}{4}$ (sometimes, $\frac{3}{8}$, $\frac{3}{4}$, or even $\frac{4}{4}$), with wide melodic skips and continuous lively triplets. Quite often the style is fugal or quasi-fugal (Example 11.4, page 354). The second section may invert the subject of the first.

Couperin: *ordres*

The *ordres* of François Couperin each comprised a loose aggregation of as many as twenty or more miniature pieces, most in dance rhythms of the

Example 11.2 *Elisabeth-Claude Jacquet de La Guerre, Courante, from* Pièces de clavecin, *1687*

Source of Examples 11.2, 11.3, 11.4: *Pièces de clavecin,* ed. Carol Henry Bates (Paris: Heugel, HE 32629), pp. 32, 34, 35.

courante, sarabande, gigue, and the like, highly stylized and refined. Their transparent texture, delicate melodic lines decorated with many embellishments, conciseness, and humor are typical of French music from the Regency period. Most of them carry fanciful titles, as in François Couperin's *Vingt-cinquième ordre* (NAWM 73; CD 5 [20]). *La Visionaire* (The Dreamer), *La Misterieuse* (The Mysterious One), *La Monflambert* (probably named after Anne Darboulin, who married Monflambert, the king's wine merchant; CD 2 ⟨33⟩), *La Muse victorieuse* (The Victorious Muse; CD 2 ⟨34⟩), and *Les Ombres errantes*

Example 11.3 *Jacquet de La Guerre, Sarabande, from* Pièces de clavecin, *1687*

Example 11.4 *Jacquet de La Guerre, Gigue, from* Pièces de clavecin, *1687*

(The Roving Shadows) are the suggestive titles found in the Twenty-fifth Ordre of Couperin's fourth book for clavecin (1730). *La Visionaire,* the first movement of this ordre, is a French overture, but a rather whimsical one. *La Misterieuse* is a more proper allemande in $\frac{4}{4}$, with mainly steady sixteenth-note motion. It takes the typical binary dance form, the first half modulating to the dominant. *La Monflambert* is a gigue in $\frac{6}{8}$, perhaps a favorite of Darboulin's; these pieces were intended as recreation for amateurs. *La Muse victorieuse* displays a formal device that is characteristic of binary movements by Couperin and later Domenico Scarlatti: the last eleven measures of the first half, which progresses to the dominant, are paralleled in the tonic close of the second half. *Les Ombres errantes* may owe its title to the syncopated middle voice, which erratically shadows the top voice forming chains of suspensions, some of which resolve upward.

Chaconne and passacaglia

The chaconne, a stately movement in triple rhythm made popular by Lully's stage music (see page 279), often served as a movement of a suite. All sorts of alterations could be made to the basic harmonic scheme, as in the *Passacaille ou Chaconne* from Couperin's first Suite for Viols (1728), which makes no distinction between chaconne and passacaglia. It maintains regular phrasing of 4 + 4 measures for 199 measures, but neither the bass nor the chord patterns are consistent, as we see in Example 11.5. The characteristic ornaments or agréments of both the keyboard and ensemble music of Couperin are indicated in the score by certain signs that the performer must interpret. Example 11.5 illustrates some of these signs and their resolution. In his *L'Art de toucher le clavecin* (The Art of Playing the Clavecin, 1716), one of the most important practical musical treatises of the eighteenth century, Couperin gave precise and detailed instructions for fingering and executing the agréments and discussed other aspects of clavecin performance as well.

The Keyboard Sonata

Kuhnau

Most early sonatas were written for instrumental ensemble. Johann Kuhnau first transferred the genre to the keyboard in 1692. His *Frische Klavierfrüchte* (Fresh Keyboard Fruits, 1696) consists entirely of sonatas. More interesting than these

In his suites for viol, Couperin used the agrément *signs that were normally applied to harpsichord music instead of those for viols. Acording to his* Explication, *they are to be interpreted as follows:*

Since each ornament begins on the beat and takes its time value from the note to which it is attached, the upper line of parts a and b of this example would be played approximately as follows:

■ *Double-manual harpsichord built by Michel Richard, Paris, 1688.* (NEW HAVEN, YALE UNIVERSITY, COLLECTION OF MUSICAL INSTRUMENTS, THE ALBERT STEINERT COLLECTION. PHOTO COPYRIGHT 1995 BY THOMAS A. BROWN)

somewhat experimental pieces are his six "biblical" sonatas published in 1700. Bearing titles such as *Saul's Madness Cured by Music, The Combat between David and Goliath*, and *Hezekiah's Illness and Recovery*, they represent stories from the Old Testament cleverly and sometimes humorously told in music.

ENSEMBLE MUSIC

By around 1700, the French clavecinists and the North German organists had established distinct styles. But in the realm of instrumental chamber music, as in the opera and cantata, Italians remained the undisputed masters and teachers. The late seventeenth and early eighteenth centuries were the age of the great violin makers of Cremona—Nicolò Amati (1596–1684), Antonio Stradivari (1644–1737), and Giuseppe Bartolomeo Guarneri (1698–1744). It was also the age of great string music in Italy.

Violin makers

The Ensemble Sonata

The word *sonata* appears regularly on Italian title pages throughout the seventeenth century. In the earlier decades the term (like the parallel word, *sinfonia*) chiefly denoted a prelude or interlude in a predominantly vocal work. After 1630 the two terms were used more and more often to designate separate instrumental compositions. The early stages of the sonata's emergence from the canzona have been sketched in Chapter 9.

The typical instrumental sonata has several sections or movements in contrasting tempos and textures and is scored for two to four solo instruments with basso continuo. Within this general scheme, we can distinguish two main

■ *Cities in Italy that were centers of violin making, playing, and composition, around 1650*

types after about 1660. The *sonata da chiesa*, or church sonata, had a mixture of abstract movements and others that were essentially dance movements. The *sonata da camera*, or chamber sonata, was a suite of stylized dances, though the opening movement was not always a dance. The most common instrumentation after 1670 for both church and chamber sonatas was two treble instruments (usually violins) and bass. Although called a *trio sonata*, such a work required four players, because, while a cello or other bass instrument played the basso continuo line, the harpsichordist or organist doubled the line, filling in the chords implied or indicated in that bass part. The texture exemplified in the trio sonata—two high melody lines over a bass—was fundamental to many other types of solo music, both vocal and instrumental.

Trio sonata

Solo sonatas, for solo violin (or flute or viola da gamba) with continuo, were at first less numerous than trio sonatas but gained in popularity after 1700. Com-

Solo sonata

posers also began writing sonatas for larger groups, up to eight instrumental parts with continuo, as well as a few for unaccompanied stringed or wind instruments.

Nomenclature

Chamber sonatas were called by fancifully diverse names. The general title of a collection might simply list the dances included, followed by the words "da camera." "trattenimento," "divertimento," "concertino," "concerto," "ballo," and "balletto" were some of the designations used. These different titles implied no particular musical forms or types.

Canzona-sonata

Seventeenth-century canzona-sonata movements increased in length and diminished in number, although the order of the movements did not become standardized until the end of the century. Traces of the old cyclical variation-canzona survived for many years; thematic similarity between movements survives in many sonatas of Giovanni Battista Vitali (ca. 1644–1692) and in some by his son Tommaso Antonio Vitali (ca. 1665–1747). On the other hand, complete thematic independence of the various movements became the rule in the late seventeenth century, as illustrated in the sonata *La Raspona* by Giovanni Legrenzi (NAWM 74; CD 5 [26]). It consists of two movements, Allegro and Adaggio [*sic*], each of which has a canzona-like structure and a combination of fugal and nonfugal textures.

Italian Chamber Music

Cazzati

The most important center of chamber music was the Church of San Petronio in Bologna, where Maurizio Cazzati (ca. 1620–1677) directed the music. His sonata *La Pellicana* (1670) for solo violin and continuo[1] is representative of the music that was often played during church services. It is in four movements: (1) Allegro, $\frac{12}{8}$, *alla giga*, in imitative style, with the strange tempo mark *Largo e vivace*; (2) Grave, $\frac{4}{4}$ which unfolds through close canonic imitation at the fifth and fourth; (3) Presto, $\frac{4}{4}$ which treats a strongly rhythmic theme imitatively; and (4) Prestissimo, $\frac{3}{8}$ which is likewise imitative and is looser in texture than the preceding movements. The themes of the four movements vaguely resemble each other. Unlike German and earlier Italian composers, Cazzati shunned technical display and special effects. This restraint and serious approach characterized the Bologna school.

Arcangelo Corelli

The violin sonatas of Arcangelo Corelli (1653–1713) are perfect examples of the serene, classical phase of seventeenth-century musical art. Corelli, a well-known performer as well as composer, studied for four years at Bologna and thoroughly assimilated the craft of the Bolognese masters. After 1671 he passed most of his life tranquilly in Rome, publishing the following works:

Opus 1. Twelve trio sonatas (sonate da chiesa), 1681.
Opus 2. Eleven trio sonate da camera and a chaconne, 1685.
Opus 3. Twelve trio sonate da chiesa, 1689.
Opus 4. Twelve trio sonate da camera, 1695.

1. Ed. in HAM No. 219.

Opus 5. Twelve solo sonatas (six da chiesa, five da camera, and one set of variations), 1700.

Opus 6. Twelve concerti grossi, 1714 (composed before 1700, some probably as early as 1682).

Trio sonatas

Corelli's trio sonatas were the crowning achievement of Italian chamber music in the late seventeenth century. His solo sonatas and concertos served as models that composers followed for the next half century. Unlike his compatriots, he apparently wrote no vocal music at all but sang through the violin, the instrument that most nearly approaches the lyric quality of the human voice. As if acknowledging this kinship, Corelli deliberately shunned virtuosic display by the two violins of his trio sonatas. He never required a player to reach beyond the third position and seldom called for extremely low notes, fast runs, or difficult double stops. The two violins, treated exactly alike, constantly cross and exchange music, interlocking in suspensions that give his works a decisive forward momentum.

Tonal organization

Corelli relied on sequences to achieve clear tonal organization. Whether constructed diatonically within one key or modulating downward in the circle of fifths, the sequence is a powerful agent for establishing tonality. Corelli's modulations within a movement—most often to the dominant and (in minor keys) the relative major—are always logical and straightforward. The principles of tonal architecture that he developed were further elaborated and extended by Handel, Vivaldi, Bach, and other composers of the next generation. Corelli's music is almost completely diatonic: chromaticism is limited virtually to the rare diminished seventh or the occasional flatted (Neapolitan) sixth at a cadence.

Church sonatas

Many of Corelli's church trio sonatas consist of four movements in the same slow–fast–slow–fast order favored by other composers of the late Baroque. But this pattern has many exceptions and should not be taken as a standard. The first slow movement of a typical church sonata has a contrapuntal texture and a majestic, solemn character. The Allegro that follows is usually a fugue. This movement is the musical center of gravity for the church sonata, and it most obviously retains traits of the canzona—in its use of imitative style, in the rhythmic character of the subject, and in the modification of the subject after the exposition. (In some of Purcell's sonatas, for instance, a movement like this is actually called "canzona.") The middle slow movement most often resembles a triple-time operatic aria or duet. The last movement is likely to be a carefree dance in binary form.

Chamber sonatas

Corelli's chamber sonatas, both trio and solo, usually begin with a *preludio*, after which two or three dances follow in the normal suite order, with a gavotte sometimes replacing the final gigue. In many of Corelli's chamber sonatas, the first two movements retain the serious character of the church sonata as well as its outward forms. The chamber sonatas remind us of the French overture: a slow introduction with persistent dotted rhythms, followed by an imitative, canzona-like Allegro. This combination of slow introduction and fugal Allegro preceding a series of dances was common in this genre. The dance movements are almost always in binary form, the first section (played twice) closing on the dominant or relative major and the second section (also repeated) making its way back to the tonic.

Unity of key

Like his contemporaries, Corelli kept all the movements of a trio sonata in the same key, but in all his later major-key solo sonatas, he cast one slow movement in the relative minor. Every concerto grosso has a slow movement in a contrasting key.

Unity of theme

In general, movements are thematically independent, although there are rare instances of thematic similarity (such as the two slow movements of the Trio Sonata Op. 3, No. 7). There are no contrasting or "secondary" themes within a movement. The subject of the whole musical discourse is stated at the outset in a complete sentence with a definite—often Phrygian—cadence. From then on the music unfolds in a continuous expansion of this subject, with sequential treatment, brief modulations closing in nearby keys, and fascinating subtleties of phrasing. This steady spinning out of a single theme is highly characteristic of the late Baroque. Unlike the procedures used by later composers for developing motives from a theme, the original idea seems to generate a spontaneous flow of musical thoughts. Corelli sometimes combined this method with a repetition of preceding material, but his movements never display anything like the full recapitulation found in the Classic sonata. He often stated the last phrase of a movement twice, as though to avoid too abrupt a leavetaking, and at cadences in triple meter he favored the hemiola.

Corelli's Trio Sonata Op. 3, No. 2 (NAWM 75; CD 5 [28] / 2 ◊35◊), illustrates some of these points. In the first movement, marked Grave, the two violins imitate each other, meet in chains of suspensions, cross, and separate over a walking bass. The following Allegro has a lively fugue subject that after the first expositions tends to drop its opening notes. The middle slow movement is like a sarabande in which the two violins hold an intense dialogue. The final movement, simply labeled Allegro, is a gigue in binary form. Like the first Allegro, it is fugal in conception, and the subject of the second half is an inversion of the subject of the first half.

Solo sonatas

The movements of Corelli's solo sonatas correspond to those of the church and chamber sonatas. In the first Allegro, the solo violin employs double and triple stops to simulate the rich three-part sonority of the trio sonata. In general, the violin part demands some virtuosity to execute fast runs, arpeggios, cadenzas, and extended perpetual-motion passages.

Corelli as teacher

The solo sonatas give us a comprehensive idea of what Corelli expected from his students. His teaching was the foundation of most eighteenth-century violin schools and influenced later generations of players as well as composers. Others may have surpassed him in bravura, but he had the good taste to avoid empty displays of virtuosity, and no one understood the cantabile qualities of the violin better than he did. His most technically difficult and, at the same time, most enduringly popular composition is the masterly set of twenty-four variations that concludes his Opus 5. The theme is the *Folia* (or *les Folies d'Espagne*), a well-known tune from the early sixteenth century. Its bass resembles that of the romanesca (see Example 9.3); like the romanesca, the *Folia* was a favorite subject for variations in the seventeenth century.

Improvisation in Musical Performance

Performers in the Baroque era were always expected to add to what the composer had written. For example, keyboard players realized figured basses by improvising chords, arpeggios, and even counterpoints. Vocal and instrumental solo performers applied skill, taste, and experience to realize the full effect of the music by means of ornaments and embellishments. Such impromptu complements varied from country to country and from one generation to another. Modern scholars, conductors, and performers who have tried to reconstruct these performance practices have found the task to be complex, delicate, and controversial.

Ornaments

Ornaments usually originated in improvisation. Even though they might be written out later or at least indicated by special symbols (as in Example 11.5), they still retained a certain spontaneity. For us the word *ornamentation* may suggest an unessential or superfluous process, but Baroque musicians saw it differently. In their view, ornaments were not merely decorative, they were a means for moving the affections. Also some of the more common ornaments—especially the trill and the appoggiatura—added a spice of dissonance that the notated music lacked.

Musicians recognized two principal ways of ornamenting a given melodic line: (1) Small melodic formulas, such as trills, turns, appoggiaturas, and mor-

■ *The Adagio of Corelli's Sonata Opus 5, No. 3, in the edition printed about 1711 for John Walsh, London, and based on a 1710 edition by Estienne Roger, Amsterdam. The violin part is given both as originally published and in an embellished version said to represent the way Corelli himself performed it.* (NEW HAVEN, YALE UNIVERSITY MUSIC LIBRARY)

dents, were attached to one or two written notes. Special signs sometimes, though not always, indicated their placement. (2) More extended embellishments, such as scales, runs, leaps, arpeggios, and the like, were added to make up a free and elaborate paraphrase of the written line. This process, sometimes called *division, diminution*, or *figuration*, was most appropriate for melodies in slow tempo. Embellished versions of slow movements from Corelli's solo sonatas have been preserved in an edition of 1710 by Estienne Roger of Amsterdam (see the facsimile of a later London print, above). Roger claimed that his edition represented the way the composer played the sonatas. Whether or not these ornamented versions were Corelli's own, they surely reflected embellishment practices of his time.

Cadenza

The *cadenza* was still another species of embellishment. Commonly found in opera and in some of the instrumental music of Corelli and his contemporaries, it was usually an elaborate extension of the six-four chord at a final cadence. The second-movement cadenza of Corelli's Violin Sonata Op. 5, No. 3, foreshadows the long concerto cadenzas of the Classic and Romantic periods.

Performers thus had the liberty to add to the composer's written score; they were equally free to subtract from it or change it in various other ways. Arias were omitted from operas, or different arias were substituted, almost at the whim of the singers. Frescobaldi let organists end his toccatas at any appropriate point they pleased. Composers of variations, suites, and sonatas took it for granted that movements would be omitted *ad libitum*. Title pages of ensemble collections encouraged players to choose which instruments and even how many to use for a performance. For example, sonatas were issued for violin and basso continuo with an additional violin or two "if desired," and string concertos could be played as trio sonatas.

Ensemble Sonatas outside Italy

Italian trio sonatas were imitated or adapted by composers all over Europe. Their influence on the English composer John Jenkins has already been noted. Purcell "endeavor'd a just imitation of the most fam'd Italian masters" in his two sets of trio sonatas published in 1683 and 1697, although some traces of French influence may also be discerned in his rhythms and melodies. Another English composer, John Ravenscroft, published a set of twelve trio sonatas (Rome, 1695) in a style nearly indistinguishable from Corelli's. Handel's trio sonatas resemble Corelli's as well in their four-movement form and compositional approach.

Germany

In Germany, sonatas for trio or larger combinations were written by Georg Muffat (*Armonico tributo*—A Harmonic Tribute, 1682), Reincken (*Hortus musicus*—The Garden of Music, 1687), Buxtehude (1696), Fux, Caldara, Christoph Graupner, and others. The sonatas of Fux and Graupner contain some remarkable examples of intricate fugal writing.

The earliest and the most important trio sonatas in France were by François Couperin. Some of them probably date back to 1692, although they were not published until many years later. His collection *Les Nations: Sonades et suites de simphonies en trio* (1726) contains four ordres, each consisting of a sonata da chiesa (the *sonade*) in several movements followed by a suite of dances (the *suite de simphonies*). The style, though obviously influenced by Corelli and other Italians, is distinguished throughout by the refined melody and exquisite taste in ornaments that mark Couperin's clavecin pieces.

France: Couperin

Couperin admired the works of both Lully and Corelli, and he maintained a neutral position in the raging controversy over the respective merits of French and Italian music. Through the titles, prefaces, and choice of contents for his published collections he proclaimed that the perfect music would be a union of the two national styles (see vignette). Two other trio suites hold to this ideal: *Parnassus, or the Apotheosis of Corelli* and *The Apotheosis of Lully.* In the second, Lully is represented as joining Corelli on Parnassus to play the first and second violins in a French overture and in the trio sonata that follows. The rest of Couperin's chamber music comprises a series of twelve *concerts*, or harmonious ensembles; they are not concertos but suites. Intended for harpsichord and various combinations of instruments, each consists of a prelude and a number of dance movements. The first four are generally known as the *Concerts royaux* (having been played before Louis XIV in 1714 and 1715). To the last eight (1724) Couperin gave the collective title *Les goûts-réünis* (The Reunited Tastes), signifying that they joined the two principal styles, French and Italian.

COUPERIN ON THE UNION OF THE ITALIAN AND FRENCH STYLES

The Italian and French styles have long divided up the Republic of Music in France. As for me, I have always esteemed the things that deserved to be, without regard to the composer or nation. The first Italian sonatas that appeared in Paris more than thirty years ago and encouraged me to start composing some myself, to my mind wronged neither the works of Monsieur de Lully nor those of my ancestors, who will always be more admirable than imitable. Thus, by a right that my neutrality confers upon me, I sail under the happy star that has guided me until now.

Since Italian music has the right of seniority over ours, at the end of this volume you will find a grand trio sonata titled *L'Apothéose de Corelli.* A feeble spark of self-love persuaded me to present it in score. If some day my muse outdoes itself, I shall dare to undertake likewise something in the style of the incomparable Lully, although his works alone ought to suffice to immortalize him.

From François Couperin, Preface, *Les goûts-réünis* (Paris, 1724). The original French is in *Oeuvres complètes*, Vol. 8, ed. André Schaeffner.

The Solo Sonata after Corelli

Although composers after Corelli continued to write trio sonatas, they were increasingly attracted to the solo sonata. The solo violin sonata had always been a prime vehicle for experiments in special bowings, multiple stops, and all kinds of difficult passage work. Twelve sonatas by Johann Jakob Walther (1650–1717?), published in 1676 under the title *Scherzi*, surpassed all other works in technical brilliance. Likewise a virtuoso player, Heinrich Ignaz Franz von Biber (1644–1704) was a composer of broader interests. Although Biber composed church music and instrumental ensemble works, he is remembered chiefly for his fifteen Mystery (Rosary) Sonatas for Violin (ca. 1675), which represent meditations on episodes in the life of Christ.[2] These clever examples of program music make considerable use of *scordatura*, unusual tunings of the violin strings to facilitate the playing of particular notes or chords.

Walther

Biber

Both Walther and Biber often interspersed rhapsodic movements or toccata-like sections in their sonatas, and both wrote many of their longer movements in the form of a passacaglia or a theme and variations. Biber's Passacaglia for unaccompanied solo violin, which is appended to the collection of Mystery Sonatas, is perhaps the most important precursor of Bach's great Chaconne in D minor. Most German violin composers after Biber and Walther came under the influence of the Italian schools and developed a style based on that foundation.

Geminiani

One of Corelli's most influential pupils was Francesco Geminiani (1687–1762), who had a long career as virtuoso and composer in London. His method, *The Art of Playing on the Violin* (1751), undoubtedly embodies the principles of technique and interpretation taught by Corelli and the other Italian masters. Geminiani's solo sonatas and concerti grossi are founded on the style of Corelli, intermingled with traits that betray their late date. Handel's concerti grossi also lean on Corelli's approach to the medium. The Corelli tradition lived on as well in the compositions of two other famous violinists, Francesco Maria Veracini (1690–ca. 1750) and Pietro Locatelli (1695–1764), the latter also a Corelli pupil. Most celebrated of all the Italian virtuosos was Giuseppe Tartini (1692–1770). His solo sonatas and concertos are mainly in the early Classic style of the mid-eighteenth century.

Corelli pupils

Leclair

The principal French composer of violin sonatas was Jean-Marie Leclair (1697–1764). His music combines the classic purity of Corelli with a peculiarly French grace and sweetness of melody, perfect clarity of texture and form, and abundant tasteful decoration.

Works for Larger Ensembles

From the days of Giovanni Gabrieli through the first half of the seventeenth century, Italy produced a steady flow of canzonas, dance suites, sonatas, and sinfonias for groups of three or more melody instruments, in addition to a basso continuo. Many Venetian sonatas of this period resemble the contempo-

2. Heinrich Franz Biber, *Sechzehn Violinsonaten*, ed. Erwin Luntz in DTOe 25 (Year 12/2; Graz, 1959).

■ *Outdoor concert by the* collegium musicum *of the University of Jena in the 1740s. Bach led a similar group in Leipzig.* (HAMBURG, MUSEUM FÜR KUNST UND GEWERBE)

rary Venetian opera overtures. The Bolognese composers in the late seventeenth century also wrote many works for larger groups, which in form and style resembled either the trio sonata or the concerto.

Suite

The instrumental ensemble sonata and, more especially, the suite had a particularly long life in Germany. The most notable (though atypical) works in this genre after Schein's *Banchetto musicale* were eleven chamber sonatas for five strings ("or other instruments") and continuo by Johann Rosenmüller (ca. 1620–1684), published in 1670.[3] Each sonata consists of a sinfonia followed by an allemande, a courante, a ballo (a short, light-humored, sharply rhythmic movement in $\frac{4}{4}$, and a sarabande, sometimes interspersed with an intrada or other dance. The remarkable sinfonias, inspired by the opera overtures heard in Venice (where Rosenmüller lived for twenty-six years), alternate solemn majestic sections in moderate or slow triple meter with contrasting faster sections.

The German musical tradition had a familiar, direct quality; composers preferred relatively large ensembles and liked the sound of wind instruments as well as strings. *Collegia musica* (associations of performers) in many German towns offered citizens the opportunity to play and sing together for their own pleasure. Town bands (*Stadtpfeifer*) and, in Lutheran regions, church musicians enriched the daily lives of the people. In some places, chorales or

3. Ed. Karl Nef in DdT, Vol. 18 (Leipzig, 1904).

sonatas called *Turmsonaten* (tower sonatas) were played daily on wind instruments from the tower of the Rathaus (town hall) or a church.

Orchestral Music

Compared to chamber music

Toward the end of the seventeenth century, a generally recognized distinction arose between *chamber* music—ensemble music with only one instrument to a part—and *orchestral* music. Prior to that composers did not express their preferences, and the choice depended on circumstances. For instance, an orchestral ensemble might play a trio sonata da chiesa that was scored for two solo violins if the size of the auditorium made it desirable or if the occasion were festive. But neither the designation "sinfonia" or "concerto" nor the presence of three, four, or more melodic parts above the bass necessarily called for an orchestra rather than a chamber group of players. Beyond the use of basso continuo and the predominance of stringed instruments, no common standard regulated either the makeup of an ensemble or the number of instruments to a part.

Opera houses, of course, maintained orchestras, so opera overtures in both Italy and France, as well as the numerous dances that formed an indispensable part of French opera, were always written specifically for orchestral performance. Lully brought the Paris orchestra, the most famous in Europe, to a height of technical perfection that was previously unheard of for so large a group of instrumental performers.

The Orchestral Suite

Lully's German disciples introduced French standards of playing, along with the French musical style, into their own country. One result was a new type of *orchestral suite* that flourished in Germany from about 1690 to 1740. The dances of these suites, patterned after those of Lully's ballets and operas, did not appear in any standard number or order. Because they were always introduced by a pair of movements in the form of a French overture, the word *ouverture* soon came to designate the suite itself. Among the early collections of orchestral suites was Georg Muffat's *Florilegium* (1695 and 1698), which includes an essay with musical examples about the French system of bowing, the playing of the agréments, and similar matters.[4] Another important collection was J. K. F. Fischer's *Journal de Printemps* (1695).[5] Fux, Telemann, and a host of other German composers, including J. S. Bach, wrote overture suites.

The Concerto

The concerto, a new kind of orchestral composition that appeared in the 1680s and 1690s, soon became the most important type of Baroque orchestral music.

4. *Florilegium secundum*, ed. Heinrich Rietsch in DTOe 2/2 (Vienna, 1895).
5. Ernst von Werra in DdT, Vol. 10 (Leipzig, 1902).

VII. *The emergence of the violin family of string instruments in the early sixteenth century is documented in this fresco (1535–36) by Gaudenzio Ferrari on the cupola of the Church of Santa Maria delle Grazie, Saronno (Piedmont), Italy. The cello and the viola are being bowed overhand; above and to the left of the cellist, a violin is played pizzicato. The shape and the S-holes are those of the modern violin. Saronno is not far from Milan and the early centers of violin making, Brescia and Verona.* (SARONNO, SANTA MARIA DELLE GRAZIE / ART RESOURCE, NEW YORK)

VIII. *Women singers and string players (upper left), thought to be from the Pio Ospedale della Pietà, give a concert in Venice honoring Archduke Paul and Mary Fedorov of Russia. Painting by Francesco Guardi (1712–1793).* (MUNICH, ALTE PINAKOTHEK / PHOTOGRAPH BY JOACHIM BAUEL-ARTOTHEK)

It afforded composers the chance to combine in one work several favorite traits: the contrasts of the *concertato* medium; the texture of a firm bass and a florid treble; the musical organization based on the major-minor key system; and the construction of a longer work out of separate and autonomous movements.

Concerto types

Three kinds of orchestral concertos were being written around 1700. One of these, the *orchestral concerto* (also called *concerto-sinfonia, concerto-ripieno,* or *concerto a quattro*), was a work in several movements that emphasized the first violin and the bass and that usually avoided the more complex contrapuntal texture characteristic of the sonata and sinfonia. The *concerto grosso* and the *solo concerto,* more numerous and in retrospect more important, systematically played on the contrast in sonority between many instruments and one or only a few. The concerto grosso set a small ensemble of solo instruments, the *concertino,* against a large ensemble, the *concerto grosso.* In the solo concerto a single instrument contrasted with the large ensemble. The large group was almost always a string orchestra, usually divided into first and second violins, violas, cellos, and bass viols, with basso continuo. The solo instruments were also usually strings: in the solo concerto, a violin; in the concerto grosso, most often two violins and continuo, though other solo string or wind instruments might be added or substituted. In both the solo concerto and the concerto grosso, the full orchestra was designated *tutti* (all) or *ripieno* (full).

Origins of the concerto

The practice of contrasting solo instruments against a full orchestra preceded the earliest instrumental concertos. Concerto-like instrumentation animated canzonas and other instrumental ensemble works. Lully inserted episodes for a solo wind trio in some of the dances in his operas. Solo instruments and tutti tossed short phrases back and forth in orchestral suites, church cantatas, chamber sonatas, and sinfonias. Sinfonias and sonatas for one or two solo trumpets with string orchestra were especially popular in Venice and Bologna. Various elements of the concerto are also found in Venetian opera overtures, which were occasionally played as independent instrumental sonatas. Oratorio and opera arias sometimes featured a concertino that accompanied and interacted with the solo singer, while the ripieno orchestra played mainly in the ritornellos. Stradella in Rome liked to use this combination in both the opening sinfonias and in arias of his oratorios.

Concertos, like sonatas and sinfonias, functioned as "overtures" to a Mass or as instrumental Offertories. For use at a Christmas Mass, composers often added an optional movement in pastoral style. Corelli's *Christmas* Concerto (Op. 6, No. 8) contains the best known as well as one of the most beautiful of these pastorales. Other pastorale movements in the late Baroque period include the *Sinfonia* that opens the second part of Bach's *Christmas* Oratorio and the *Sinfonia pastorale* in Handel's *Messiah.*

Corelli's concertos

Corelli's concerti grossi, among the earliest examples of the genre, employ soli-tutti contrasts in a special way. Corelli did not usually distinguish the solo portions from the tutti by musical material or manner of playing. Much of the time his concertos are in effect church sonatas or chamber sonatas divided between soli and tutti, in which the larger group echoes the smaller, fortifies ca-

GEORG MUFFAT ON CONVERTING SONATAS INTO CONCERTOS

Friendly reader:

It is very true that the beautiful concertos of a new kind that I enjoyed in Rome gave me great courage and reawakened in me some ideas that perhaps will not displease you. If nothing else, at least I tried to serve your convenience, since you may concert these sonatas in various manners with the following conditions:

1. They may be played with only three instruments, namely two violins and a cello or bass viol as a foundation. . . .

2. They may be played by four or five instruments. . . .

3. If, further, you wish to hear them as full concertos [*concerti pieni*] with some novelty or variety of sonority, you may form two choirs in this way. Make a small ensemble [*concertino*] of three or two violins and a cello [*violoncino*] or viola da gamba, which three solo parts, not doubled, will play throughout. From these parts you will draw the two [solo] violins as well as the violins to be doubled for the large ensemble [*concerto grosso*] when you find the letter *T*, which signifies "tutti." You will have these rest at the letter *S*, when the small ensemble will play solo. The middle violas will be doubled in proportion to the other parts of the large ensemble with which they will play, except when you find the letter *S*, when it will be enough that this part be played solo and not doubled. I went to all this trouble to achieve this opportune variety.

Trans. from the Italian in *Armonico tributo* (Salzburg, 1682), DTOe XI/2, Vol. 22 (Vienna, 1904), p. 118.

dential passages, or otherwise punctuates the structure. The relative prominence of the first violin part occasionally suggests the texture of the later solo concerto.

Concerto in Germany

German composers similarly adopted the form and style of the sonata in their earliest concerti grossi. Georg Muffat wrote in 1701 that he first encountered this new genre in Rome and decided to try his hand at it (see vignette). Well into the eighteenth century, many concertos continued to exhibit at least one characteristic trait of the sonata, the fugal or quasi-fugal Allegro. Because most composers (Geminiani, for example) shared Corelli's conception that concerti grossi were sonatas with the musical substance divided between concertino (soli) and ripieno (tutti), these works tended to be conservative. But in the solo concerto, composers experimented with new rhythmic ideas, textures, and formal schemes.

Torelli

Giuseppe Torelli (1658–1709), a leading figure in the Bologna school, contributed most to the development of the concerto around the turn of the century. The six violin concertos of Torelli's Opus 8 (1709), which also includes six concerti grossi, represent a significant stage in the evolution of a new type of concerto that departs from Corelli's model. Most of Torelli's are in three movements in the order fast–slow–fast, a succession adopted by later concerto composers. Each of the Allegro movements begins with a ritornello that develops one or more motives in the full orchestra. This leads to a solo episode that presents entirely new material, after which the tutti recalls some part of the ritornello in a different key. This alternation may recur several times before the movement is rounded off and brought to a close with a final tutti in the tonic that is almost identical with the opening ritornello.

Ritornello

The term *ritornello* is derived from vocal music, where it meant refrain. Indeed, Torelli's scheme is something like that of the rondeau, with the important exception that in a concerto all the ritornellos except the first and last are customarily in different keys. This ritornello structure is typical for first and last movements of the concertos of Torelli, Vivaldi, and some of their contemporaries. Thus the concerto combines recurrence of familiar music with the variety and stability of key relationship. A typical scheme is illustrated by the final Allegro of Opus 8, No. 8.[6] The movement consists of an opening ritornello, two modulating solo sections separated by an abbreviated statement of the ritornello in the relative major, and a repetition of the opening ritornello to close the movement as diagramed below:

	Tutti		Soli	Tutti		Soli		Tutti		
	Ritornello I		**Solo I**	**Ritornello II**		**Solo II**		**Ritornello III**		
Motives:	a	b		a	b			a	b	
Measures:	*1*	*11*	*17*	*26*	*30*	*34*	*43*	*47*	*57*	*66*
Keys:	c	c	g	E♭		f	cV_7	c		

Other composers of concertos

The achievements of Torelli in the realm of the concerto were matched and extended by other Italian composers, especially the Venetian Tomaso Albinoni (1671–1750) and the Italian-German Evaristo Felice dall'Abaco (1675–1742). The concerti grossi of Geminiani and Locatelli are generally conservative, but Locatelli's solo concertos introduced virtuoso passages that foreshadowed the importance of this element in the concertos of the Classic period. The greatest master of the Italian concerto of the late Baroque period was Antonio Vivaldi, whose works we shall study in the following chapter.

Bibliography

Music Collections

Böhm *Klavier- und Orgelwerke,* 2 vols., ed. Gesa Wolgast (Wiesbaden: Breitkopf & Härtel, 1952?)

Buxtehude *Sämtliche Orgelwerke,* 4 vols., ed. Josef Hedar (Copenhagen: Hansen, 1952); *Sämtliche Orgelwerke,* ed. Klaus Beckmann (Wiesbaden: Breitkopf & Härtel, 1971–72). See also the Bibliography in Chapter 10.

6. Ed. in HAM No. 246 and NAWM, 2nd ed., No. 94.

Cabanilles *Opera omnia,* ed. Higini Anglès in Biblioteca Central Sección de Música, *Publicaciones,* Vols. 4, 8, 13, and 17 (Barcelona, 1927–56).

Pachelbel *Orgelwerke,* 4 vols., ed. Traugott Fedtke (Frankfurt: Litolff; New York: C. F. Peters, 1972–73).

French composers of organ music are represented in Alexandre Guilmant, ed., *Archives des maîtres de l'orgue,* 10 vols. (Paris: A. Durand & fils, 1898–1910). F. Couperin's organ works are published in Vol. 3 of his *Oeuvres complètes,* revised critical ed. by Kenneth Gilbert and Davitt Moroney (Monaco: Éditions de l'Oiseau-Lyre, 1982).

A selection of chorale preludes by contemporaries of J. S. Bach is given in Vol. 9 of *Das Erbe deutscher Musik,* Series 1. See also: Karl Straube, ed., *Choralvorspiele alter Meister,* Edition Peters No. 3048, and *Alte Meister des Orgelspiels,* Edition Peters No. 4301a–b (2 vols.); for other collections, see the list in Bukofzer, *Music in the Baroque Era* (New York: Norton, 1947), pp. 463–64.

Music for Harpsichord, Clavichord, and Lute (See also Chapter 9: Instrumental Music)

Couperin, F. *Oeuvres complètes,* 12 vols. (Paris: Éditions de l'Oiseau-Lyre, 1932–33); new critical edition by Kenneth Gilbert et al. (Monaco: Éditions de l'Oiseau-Lyre, 1980–); K. Gilbert, ed., *Pièces de clavecin,* in Le Pupitre, Nos. 21–24 (Paris: Heugel, 1969–72).

Couperin, L. *Pièces de clavecin,* ed. Paul Brunold, rev. Davitt Moroney (Monaco: Éditions de l'Oiseau-Lyre, 1985).

Fischer, J. K. F. *Sämtliche Werke für Klavier und Orgel,* ed. Ernst von Werra (Leipzig: Breitkopf & Härtel, 1901; repr. New York: Broude Brothers, 1965).

Kuhnau, J. Klavierwerke, ed. Karl Päsler, in DdT, Vol. 4.

Suites by Pachelbel are in DTB, Vol. 2/i; Poglietti, in DTOe 27 (Year 13/2).

Compositions for lute by E. Reusner and S. L. Weiss are published in *Das Erbe deutscher Musik,* Series I, Vol. 12; see also DTOe, Vols. 50 (Year 25/2) and 84.

Solo Violin and Ensemble Music

Biber Some of Biber's works are published in DTOe: the violin sonatas of 1681 (Vol. 2, Year 5/2), and the "Mystery" violin sonatas (Vol. 25, Year 12/2); the first printing was faulty because the composer's *scordatura* was misread; separate sheets were issued later to correct the mistakes, but not all libraries have these.

Corelli *Oeuvres,* 5 vols., Joseph Joachim and Friedrich Chrysander, eds. (London: Augener, 1888–91; repr. 1952; solo and trio sonatas repr. New York: Dover, 1992). There is a new critical edition of the complete works under the general editorship of Hans Oesch, *Historisch-kritische Gesamtausgabe der musikalischen Werke* (Cologne: A. Volk, 1976–).

Geminiani The twelve sonatas of Geminiani's Op. 1 (1716), ed. Ross L. Finney, are in Vol. 1 of the Smith College Music Archives (Northampton, Mass., 1935).

Legrenzi Sonatas, Op. 2, Op. 10, ed. Stephen Bonta (Cambridge, Mass.: Harvard University Press, 1984, 1992).

Leclair Violin sonatas are in EP, Vol. 27 (Year 31); six sonatas were published by l'Oiseau-Lyre, 1952; complete edition of four books of sonatas for violin and basso continuo are in

Recent Researches in the Music of the Baroque Era, Vols. 4–5, 10–11, ed. Robert E. Preston (New Haven: A-R Editions, 1969–95).

Rosenmüller The sonate da camera are in DdT, Vol. 18.

Telemann A selection of sonatas and suites can be found in Telemann's *Musikalische Werke* (Kassel: Bärenreiter, 1950–). *Telemann, Thematisch-systematisches Verzeichnis seiner Werke*, Vols. 1–2: Instrumental Works, ed. Martin Ruhnke (Kassel: Bärenreiter, 1984); *Thematisches Verzeichnis der Vokalwerke*, ed. Werner Menke (Frankfurt: Klostermann, 1982), Vol. 1, Cantatas.

Walther, J. J. The *Scherzi* are published in Vol. 17 of *Das Erbe deutscher Musik*, Series I.

Instrumental ensemble works by G. B. Vitali, G. B. Bassani, and other Italian composers can be found in J. W. von Wasielewski, ed., *Anthology of Instrumental Music from the End of the Sixteenth to the End of the Seventeenth Century* (New York: Da Capo Press, 1974); see also three books by Erich Schenk, ed.: *The Italian Trio Sonata*, *The Solo Sonata*, and *The Trio Sonata Outside Italy* (Cologne: A. Volk, 1955, 1960, 1970).

The Orchestral Suite Georg Muffat's *Florilegium* is published in DTOe, Vols. 2 and 4 (Years 1/2 and 2/2); J. K. F. Fischer's *Journal de Printemps* is in DdT, Vol. 10, together with another collection of orchestral suites, the *Zodiacus musicus*, Part 1 (1698) of J. A. Schmicorer. Suites by Fux (called *Ouverture*, *Sinfonia*, or *Serenada*) are found in his *Concentus musico-instrumentalis* (1701), in DTOe, Vol. 47 (Year 23/2); suites by Telemann (*Tafelmusik*, 1733), in DdT, Vol. 61/62 and in his *Musikalische Werke* (see under Telemann).

The Concerto Concertos and other instrumental ensemble pieces by Georg Muffat are in DTOe, Vols. 1, 2, 4, 23, and 89 (Years 1/2, 2/2, 9/2, and 11/2). There are several editions of concertos by Torelli, such as those published by Doblinger in Vienna, and H. Sikorski in Hamburg; concertos by Albinoni have been edited by Walter Kolneder (Adliswil-Zurich: A. J. Kunzelmann, 1980–). Dall'Abaco's concertos and sonatas are published in DTB, Years 1 and 9/1, and in DTOe, Vols. 23 (Year 11/2) and 89. See also DdT, Vol. 29/30; and the anthologies *Das Concerto Grosso* and *Das Solokonzert*, ed. Hans Engel (Cologne: A. Volk, 1962, 1964).

For Further Reading (see also Chapter 9: General)

Published collections of Italian instrumental music up to 1700 are listed in Claudio Sartori's *Bibliografia della musica strumentale italiana stampata in Italia fino al 1700*, 2 vols. (Florence: Leo S. Olschki, 1952).

On fugue and counterpoint, see J. J. Fux, *Gradus ad Parnassum*, facs. in *Monuments of Music and Music Literature in Facsimile*, Series 2, No. 24 (New York, 1966); *The Study of Counterpoint from Johann Joseph Fux's 'Gradus ad Parnassum'*, rev. ed., trans. and ed. A. Mann and J. Edmunds (New York: Norton, 1965); Imogene Horsley, *Fugue: History and Practice* (New York: Free Press, 1966).

Recommended studies on Baroque ornamentation are Robert Donington, *A Performer's Guide to Baroque Music* (New York: Scribner's Sons, 1973); and Frederick Neumann, *Ornamentation in Baroque and Post-Baroque Music, with Special Emphasis on J. S. Bach* (Princeton: Princeton University Press, 1978).

Organ Music

Friedrich Blume et al., *Protestant Church Music* (New York: Norton, 1974). A useful catalogue listing organ preludes and composers has been compiled by J. E. Edson, *Organ Pre-*

ludes: An Index to Compositions on Hymn Tunes, Chorales, Plainsong Melodies, Gregorian Tunes, and Carols (Metuchen, N.J.: Scarecrow Press, 1970).

Buxtehude The definitive study of the composer's life and works is Kerala J. Snyder, *Dieterich Buxtehude: Organist in Lübeck* (New York: Schirmer Books, 1987).

Couperin, F. Wilfrid Mellers, *François Couperin and the French Classical Tradition* (London: Denis Dobson, 1950; New York: Dover, 1968); David Tunley, *Couperin* (London: BBC, 1982); *L'Art de toucher le clavecin*, 1716, ed. and trans. Anna Linde and Mevanwy Roberts (Leipzig: Breitkopf & Härtel, 1933).

Geminiani *Art of Playing on the Violin* (facsimile), ed. David Boyden (London and New York: Oxford University Press, 1952).

Ensemble Music

Ernst H. Meyer, *Early English Chamber Music from the Middle Ages to Purcell*, 2nd ed., with Diana Poulton (London: Lawrence & Wishart, 1982); Eleanor Selfridge-Field, *Venetian Instrumental Music from Gabrieli to Vivaldi* (Oxford: Blackwell, 1975), which considers the history of instrumental genres in addition to music performance in Venice; William Klenz, *Giovanni Maria Bononcini: A Chapter in Baroque Instrumental Music* (Durham, N.C.: Duke University Press, 1962); David Boyden, *The History of Violin Playing from its Origins to 1761* (London: Oxford University Press, 1965).

On the sonata in particular, see William S. Newman, *The Sonata in the Baroque Era*, 3rd ed. (New York: Norton, 1983), which is the best comprehensive study of the genre; Peter Allsop, *The Italian 'Trio' Sonata from its Origins until Corelli* (Oxford: Clarendon Press, 1992); Henry Mishkin, "The Solo Violin Sonata of the Bologna School," MQ 29 (1943):92–112; Stephen Bonta, "The Uses of the Sonata da Chiesa," in JAMS 22 (1969):54–84, and in GLHWM 5:54–84. Bonta's article discusses the specific employment of the sonata da chiesa in the Roman rite of the seventeenth and eighteenth centuries.

For a detailed study of the concerto, see Arthur Hutchings, *The Baroque Concerto*, 3rd ed. (London: Faber & Faber, 1973).

Corelli Marc Pincherle, *Corelli: His Life, His Music*, trans. H. E. M. Russell (New York: Norton, 1968).

CHAPTER 12

MUSIC IN THE EARLY EIGHTEENTH CENTURY

The term *baroque*

The French philosopher Noël Antoine Pluche described two kinds of music that he had heard in Paris around 1740: *la musique barroque* (baroque music) and *la musique chantante* (songful music)[1] His was one of the earliest applications of the word "baroque" to music (see also page 251). Because of the term's association with misshapen pearls, it became fashionable to dismiss as baroque objects of nature or art that were deviant or bizarre. To Pluche the instrumental music that shocked the listener with its unusual boldness and speed—the Italian sonatas and concertos that could be heard in Paris at the *Concert spirituel*—was baroque. But Pluche greatly admired the songful music, which sounded natural in the human voice and moved people, without having to resort to excessive artfulness.

Paris

Paris at this time was a musical crossroads where the public could enjoy the latest from Italian as well as native composers. Parisians heard the sentimental, neatly phrased, flowing, simply accompanied vocal melodies of Giovanni Battista Pergolesi (1710–1736)—Pluche's *musique chantante.* Listeners also savored the highly charged, virtuosic, difficult, brilliant music of Vivaldi, and the intense, restless music of Rameau, with its wry dissonances, rich harmonies, and complex rhythms—Pluche's *musique barroque.* And they knew the music of Pluche's favorite composer, Jean-Joseph Cassanéa de Mondonville (1711–1772), who combined a little of both styles. These contrasts are typical of the decades between 1720 and 1750, when Bach and Handel were writing their most important works and, like Vivaldi or Rameau, were touched by the stylistic turmoil of the time. In their late works, particularly, these

1. Noël Antoine Pluche, *Spectacle de la nature* (Paris: Veuve Estienne, 1732–50). Vol. 7, in which this occurred, was first published in 1746.

■ *Drawing by Antonio Canal, known as Canaletto, of singers crammed into a pulpit at St. Mark's in Venice, reading from a large choirbook; a similar pulpit is seen at the opposite side of the transept.*
(HAMBURG, KUNSTHALLE)

composers vacillated between the more natural and melodious *galant* style (see pages 427–28) and the older, grander, variegated, and richer idiom.

Venice

At the beginning of the eighteenth century, Venice, though declining in political power and headed for economic ruin, still remained the most glamorous city in Europe. It was full of travelers, especially musicians, attracted to its colorful, exuberant life—life set to music, like a perpetual opera. People sang on the streets and on the lagoons; gondoliers had their own repertory of songs (among them verses of Tasso declaimed to traditional melodies); patrician families who owned opera theaters recognized and rewarded fine musicians and composers (see vignette), and they themselves played and sang.

Public festivals, more numerous in Venice than elsewhere, remained occasions of musical splendor. The city had always taken pride in its church music (exemplified by the choir of St. Mark's), its instrumental works, and its opera. Even in the eighteenth century, Venice never had fewer than six opera compa-

BURNEY REPORTS ON VENETIAN OPERA

In 1720, there were ten new operas at the different theatres of Venice, set by Buini, Orlandini, Vivaldi, and Porta. The author of *Notitia di Teatri di Venezia*, complains this year of the enormous salaries of the first singers; and says, that more was then given to a single voice than need to be expended on the whole exhibition. Formerly, says he, the sum of a hundred crowns was thought a great price for a fine voice, and the first time it amounted to one hundred and twenty, the exorbitance became proverbial. But what proportion does this bear, continues he, with the present salaries, which generally exceed a hundred sequins [Italian gold zecchini]; and which has such an effect upon the rest of the troop, that the demands of every one go on increasing, in the ratio of the first singer's vanity and over-rated importance. The consequences, indeed, are fatal, when the performers combine, as often happens, in a resolution to extort from the managers a contract for *certain* sums, of which the *uncertainty* of success in public exhibitions, renders the payment so precarious.

Charles Burney, *A General History of Music*, Vol. 4 (London: Author, 1789), pp. 536–37.

nies, which together played a total of thirty-four weeks a year. Between 1700 and 1750 the Venetian public heard ten new operas annually, and the count was even higher in the second half century. Outside the theaters musical programs were frequently sponsored by private individuals, religious confraternities called *scuole*, and academies. Services in the churches on festival days resembled great instrumental and vocal concerts.

ANTONIO VIVALDI

Career

Antonio Vivaldi (1678–1741), son of one of the leading violinists of St. Mark's chapel, was educated both for the priesthood and for music (under Legrenzi), not an unusual combination in those days. He was known as *il prete rosso* (the red-headed priest), the sort of nickname that the Italian public loved to bestow on its favorite artists. From 1703 to 1740, Vivaldi worked as conductor, composer, teacher, and general superintendent of music at the Pio Ospedale della Pietà in Venice (see Plate VIII, facing page 367). He traveled extensively, composing and conducting operas and concerts throughout Italy and Europe.

The Pietà

The Pietà was one of many pious conservatories founded in Venice and Naples to shelter orphans and illegitimate children.[2] Run like a convent, it provided excellent musical training for its young students and a highly favorable

2. Edward Wright, *Some Observations Made in Travelling through Italy* [etc.] (London, 1730), 1:79, reports that the Pietà sometimes held as many as six thousand girls.

environment for Vivaldi. Such institutions, through their teaching, had a notable impact on the musical life of the entire country: these enthusiastic young amateurs were given special privileges and were stimulated by the presence of outstandingly gifted individuals.

The concerts at the Pietà and at other places of worship in Venice attracted large audiences. Travelers wrote of these occasions with enthusiasm mixed with amusement at the spectacle of a choir and orchestra composed mainly of teenage girls (see vignette).

The eighteenth-century public constantly demanded new music. There were no "classics," and few works of any kind survived more than two or three seasons. Vivaldi was expected to furnish new oratorios and concertos for every recurring festival at the Pietà. Such unceasing pressure accounts both for the vast output of many eighteenth-century composers and for the phenomenal speed at which they worked. Vivaldi may hold the record with his opera *Tito Manlio,* which he is said to have completed in only five days. He prided himself on being able to compose a concerto faster than a copyist could write out the parts.

Vivaldi's output

Like his contemporaries, Vivaldi composed every work for a definite occasion and for a particular company of performers. He fulfilled forty-nine opera commissions, most of them for Venice, and a few also for Florence, Ferrara, Verona, Rome, Vienna, and elsewhere. He composed many of his concertos, a genre commonly used at church festival services, for the Pietà, but he dedicated a large number of those published to foreign patrons. In addition to his operas, five hundred concertos and sinfonias survive, as well as ninety solo and trio sonatas, and many cantatas, motets, and oratorios.

The Vocal Works

Vivaldi is known today mainly for his orchestral music; the only works printed during his lifetime (mostly at Amsterdam) were about forty sonatas and a hundred concertos. It would be a mistake, however, to ignore his achievements in opera, cantata, motet, and oratorio. Between 1713 and 1719, the theaters of Venice staged more works of his than of any other composer, and his fame was by no means limited to his own city and country. Among the compositions that demonstrate Vivaldi's artistry in choral writing are the Gloria in D major (RV 588)[3] and a polychoral psalm-setting, Dixit Dominus (RV 594).

The Concertos

Vivaldi's instrumental works, and especially the concertos, have a freshness of melody, rhythmic verve, skillful treatment of solo and orchestral color, and clarity of form that have made them perennial favorites. Many of the sonatas, as well as some of the early concertos, betray their debt to Corelli. However, in

3. There are several catalogues of Vivaldi's works, the most recent and reliable of which, known as "RV," is Peter Ryom, *Verzeichnis der Werke Antonio Vivaldis: kleine Ausgabe* (Leipzig, 1974; suppl., Poitiers, 1979).

CHARLES DE BROSSES ON THE CONCERTS IN VENICE

A transcending music here is that of the hospitals [orphanages]. There are four, all made up of bastard or orphaned girls or whose parents are not in a condition to raise them. They are reared at public expense and trained solely to excel in music. So they sing like angels and play the violin, the flute, the organ, the violoncello, the bassoon. In short no instrument is large enough to frighten them. They are cloistered in the manner of nuns. They alone perform, and each concert is given by about forty girls. I swear to you that there is nothing so charming as to see a young and pretty nun in her white robe, with a bouquet of pomegranate flowers over her ear, leading the orchestra and beating time with all the grace and precision imaginable. Their voices are adorable for their quality and lightness, because here they don't know about roundness or a sound drawn out like a thread in the French manner. . . .

The hospital I go to most often is that of the Pietà, where one is best entertained. It is also first for the perfection of the symphonies. What an upright performance! It is only there that you hear the first stroke of the bow (*le premier coup d'archet*)—the first chord of a piece attacked as one by the strings, of which the Opéra in Paris falsely boasts.

Charles de Brosses, *L'Italie il y a cent ans ou Lettres écrites d'Italie à quelques amis en 1739 et 1740*, ed. M. R. Colomb (Paris: Alphonse Levavasseur, 1836), 1:213–14.

his first published collection of concertos (Opus 3, ca. 1712) Vivaldi already showed that he was fully aware of the modern preference for the distinct musical form, vigorous rhythm, and idiomatic solo writing that characterized the music of Torelli and Albinoni.

Solo concertos

About two-thirds of Vivaldi's concertos are scored for one solo instrument with orchestra—most for violin, but a considerable number also for cello, flute, or bassoon. The concertos for two violins give the soloists equal prominence, producing the texture of a duet for two high voices. But many works that call for several solo instruments are, in effect, solo or duo concertos rather than genuine concerti grossi: the first violin or the first and second violins, the wind instruments, and even the mandolin are treated in a virtuoso manner that sets them apart from the rest of the concertino. There are also a few important concertos for solo instruments with continuo, but without the usual ripieno strings.

Instrumentation

Vivaldi's orchestra at the Pietà probably consisted of twenty to twenty-five stringed instruments, with harpsichord or organ for the continuo. This was always the basic group, though in many concertos he also called for flutes, oboes, bassoons, or horns, any of which might be used either as solo instruments or in ensemble combinations. The exact size and makeup of the orchestra depended on what players were available for a particular occasion. Vivaldi achieved a remarkable variety of color with different groupings of solo and orchestral strings. The familiar *Primavera* (Spring) concerto—the first of a group of four concertos in Opus 8 (1725) representing the four seasons—displays his instinct for sonorities.

Form of the concertos

Most of Vivaldi's concertos follow the usual pattern of three movements: an Allegro; a slow movement in the same key or a closely related one (relative minor, dominant, or subdominant); and a final Allegro somewhat shorter and sprightlier than the first. Vivaldi abandoned the older fugal style in favor of a texture more homophonic than contrapuntal, emphasizing the two outer voices. In the fast movements, as in Torelli's, ritornellos for the full orchestra alternate with episodes for the soloist or soloists. Vivaldi distinguished himself in the spontaneity of his musical ideas, his clear, formal structures, assured harmonies, varied textures, and forceful rhythms. He established a certain dramatic tension between solo and tutti, not only giving the soloist contrasting figuration, as Torelli had already done, but letting the soloist stand out as a dominating musical personality.

Form of the Allegro

Vivaldi's approach to the first Allegro is illustrated in the second movement (the first is an introductory Adagio) of the Concerto grosso in G minor, Op. 3, No. 2, RV 578 (NAWM 76b; CD 5 [34] / 2 ⟨38⟩). The concertino consists of two violins and a cello. The opening ritornello has three motivic sections (marked a, b, and c in Example 12.1), the last of which is an inverted counterpoint of the second. The solo sections contain mostly figurative work, but the second solo section makes a veiled reference to the opening tutti motive. An unusual feature is that the closing ritornello reverses the order of the themes, the concertino playing the opening one. This movement is also unusual because only one of the four main tutti is in a foreign key, D minor. Far from

Example 12.1 *Antonio Vivaldi, Concerto grosso Op. 3, No. 2, RV 578, Allegro (inner parts omitted)*

■ *Ritornello from the aria* Soffrin pur rabbiosi fremiti *in Alessandro Stradella's oratorio* San Giovanni Battista *(1675). The performers are divided, as in the later concerto grosso, into a concertino of two (solo) violins and bass and (under the double slash) a "concerto grosso delle viole," calling for the normal string orchestra.* (MODENA, BIBLIOTECA ESTENSE, MS MUS. F. 1129)

following a textbook plan, Vivaldi's Allegro structures show almost infinite variety.

Slow movements

Vivaldi was the first composer to make the slow movement as important as the two Allegros. His slow movement is typically a long-breathed expressive cantabile melody, like an adagio operatic aria or arioso, to which the performer was expected to add embellishments. The slow movements of the later concertos are particularly forward-looking. The Largo (NAWM 77; CD 5 [41]) from the Concerto for Violin Op. 9, No. 2 (1728), exhibits many features of the early Classic style: balanced phrases, frequent half cadences clarifying the structure, trills, triplets, and cadences softened by appoggiaturas.

Changing style

Vivaldi's music parallels the stylistic changes of the first half of the eighteenth century. At the conservative extreme are some of the sonatas and concertos in the style of Corelli. At the progressive extreme are the solo concerto finales, the orchestral concertos (those without solo instruments), and most of the twenty-three *sinfonias*—works that establish Vivaldi as a founder of the Classic symphony. The concise form, the markedly homophonic texture, the melodically neutral themes, the minuet finale, even many of the little mannerisms of style that were thought to have been invented by German composers of the Mannheim school—these had already appeared in Vivaldi's works.

Program music

In his program music, such as the widely admired *Seasons* and some dozen similar pieces, Vivaldi shared with his contemporaries the half-serious, half-playful attitude toward the imitation of nature. Although he chose certain instrumental colors or modified the normal order of movements with pictorial effects in mind, he never allowed the external program to upset the musical structure of the concerto.

TIMELINE: THE EARLY EIGHTEENTH CENTURY

1700 1710 1720 1730 1740 1750

- **1700 J. S. Bach in Lüneburg**
- **1703 Handel in Hamburg**
- **1708 J. S. Bach in Weimar**
- **1710 Campra, *Fêtes Vénitiennes***
- **1711 Handel, *Rinaldo* in London**
- 1711 Charles VI crowned Holy Roman Emperor
- **1712 Vivaldi, Concertos, Op. 3**
- 1714 Elector of Hanover crowned George I of England
- **1717 J. S. Bach in Cöthen**
- 1717 Watteau, *Embarkation for Cythera*
- **1722 Rameau, *Traité de l'harmonie***
- **1722 J. S. Bach *The Well-Tempered Keyboard I***
- **1723 J. S. Bach in Leipzig**
- **1725 Fux, *Gradus ad Parnassum***
- **1725 Vivaldi, *The Seasons***
- 1726 Swift, *Gulliver's Travels*
- 1727 George II of England crowned
- **1728 Gay, *Beggar's Opera***
- **1729 J. S. Bach, *St. Matthew Passion***
- **1733 Pergolesi, *La serva padrona***
- **1733 Rameau, *Hippolyte et Aricie***
- 1740 Frederick the Great of Prussia crowned
- **1742 Handel, *Messiah***
- **1749 J. S. Bach, *The Art of Fugue***

Vivaldi's Influence

Vivaldi's influence on instrumental music in the middle and later eighteenth century equaled that of Corelli a generation earlier. Composers of the Classic concerto adopted and developed Vivaldi's dramatic conception of the soloist's role. His successors admired and emulated his concise themes, clarity of form, rhythmic vitality, and logical flow of musical ideas. These qualities, so characteristic of Vivaldi's music, directly influenced J. S. Bach, who made keyboard arrangements of at least nine Vivaldi concertos.

JEAN-PHILIPPE RAMEAU

Career

Practically unknown before the age of forty, Jean-Philippe Rameau (1683–1764) was the foremost French musician of the eighteenth century. He first attracted attention as a theorist and only afterward as a composer. He wrote most of the musical works for which he became famous between the ages of fifty and fifty-six. Attacked then as a radical, he was assailed twenty years later even more severely as a reactionary. He enjoyed the favor of the French court and prospered during the later years of his life, always remaining a solitary, argumentative, and unsociable person but a conscientious and intelligent artist.

From his father, an organist in Dijon, Rameau received his first and, as far as we know, only formal musical instruction. After holding provincial posts for two decades, he published his famous *Traité de l'harmonie* (Treatise on Harmony) in 1722. He moved to Paris in 1723, the cultural as well as national capital. Only there could a composer achieve true success and reputation, and the high road for a composer—indeed the only road to real fame—was the opera. Rameau's prospects were poor: he had neither money nor influential friends, nor the disposition of a good courtier. Worse still, his reputation as a theorist had preceded him, and people would not believe that someone who discoursed so learnedly on intervals, scales, and chords—a *savant*, a *philosophe*—could write music that they would want to hear. Aware of this handicap, Rameau tried to combat it by emphasizing in a letter of 1727 that he had "studied nature" and learned to reproduce its "colors and nuances" in appropriate musical language. Seeking better opportunities, he wrote airs and dances for three or four little musical comedies, pieces with spoken dialogue performed at the popular theaters of Paris. He published some cantatas (1728) and three more books of clavecin pieces (1724, ca. 1728, and 1741); meanwhile, his reputation as a teacher and organist began to attract students. Finally, Rameau's luck turned when in 1731 he was taken under the protection of La Pouplinière, the leading patron of music in France.

La Pouplinière

Alexandre-Jean-Joseph Le Riche de la Pouplinière (1693–1762), descendant of an ancient and noble French family, had inherited an immense fortune that he increased by speculation. He maintained several residences in Paris as well as houses in the country nearby. His salon attracted a motley company of aristocrats, literati (Voltaire and J.-J. Rousseau), painters (Van Loo and La Tour), adventurers (Casanova), and above all, musicians.

Eager for novelty, La Pouplinière sought out promising but obscure musicians and took pleasure in promoting their careers. At his château in Passy near Paris he maintained an orchestra of fourteen players, augmented by outside artists as needed. The weekly schedule included a concert on Saturday, Mass in the private chapel with orchestra on Sunday morning, a large concert in the gallery of the château on Sunday afternoon, and a more intimate concert in the evening after supper—all this in addition to two or more concerts during the rest of the week. A select audience at the château heard many of the operas and most of the orchestral concerts before they were presented to the public. Rameau was La Pouplinière's organist, conductor, and composer-in-residence from 1731 to 1753. He had to compose or prepare music not only for concerts and church but also for balls, plays, festivals, dinners, ballets, and

■ *Prison scene in Rameau's* Dardanus, *design (1760) by Machy, a pupil of Piranesi. Jean-Nicholas Servandoni had pioneered the perspective from a side angle at the Paris Opéra between 1726 and 1746. Engraving by Daumont.* (PARIS, BIBLIOTHÈQUE DE L'OPÉRA)

all sorts of special occasions. He gave lessons on the clavecin to Marie-Thérèse Deshayes, La Pouplinière's wife, who became his ardent admirer. Marie-Louise Mangot, an accomplished clavecinist from a Lyons family of musicians and Rameau's own wife, frequently played his compositions at the château.

Rameau's operas

La Pouplinière helped Rameau make his name as an opera composer. Rameau composed *Hippolyte et Aricie* to a poem by the Abbé Simon-Joseph Pellegrin, a popular librettist he met through his patron, and it was performed privately in 1733 before being produced in Paris later the same year. A more distinct success came in 1735 with his opera-ballet *Les Indes galantes* (The Gallant Indies). Two years later he composed *Castor et Pollux*, the opera that is usually regarded as his masterpiece. It was followed by the opera-ballet *Les Fêtes d'Hébé ou Les Talents lyriques* and the opera *Dardanus* (both 1739). From the first, Rameau's operas stirred up a storm of critical controversy. The Paris intelligentsia, always eager for a battle of words, divided into two noisy camps, one supporting Rameau and the other attacking him as a subverter of the good old French opera tradition of Lully. The Lullists found Rameau's music difficult, forced, grotesque, thick, mechanical, and unnatural—in a word, baroque.

Rameau protested, in a foreword to *Les Indes galantes*, that he had "sought to imitate Lully, not as a servile copyist but in taking, like him, nature herself—so beautiful and so simple—as a model." As the quarrel of the Lullists and Ramists raged on, Rameau's increasing popularity sparked many parodies of his operas—lighthanded, familiar imitations or adaptations of the originals.

Rameau's later stage works were lighter and less significant than the operas and opera-ballets of the 1730s. Exceptions were the comedy-ballet *Platée* (1745) and the serious opera *Zoroastre* (1749), the most important of Rameau's later works. In the 1750s Rameau became embroiled, through no fault of his own, in another critical battle, this one on the relative merits of French and Italian music. The famous War of the Buffonists (*Guerre des bouffons*), as this quarrel was called, will be discussed more fully in the next chapter. For now it is enough to note that Rameau, the most eminent living French composer, was exalted by one side as the champion of French music and thus became the idol of the very faction that twenty years earlier castigated him for not writing like Lully. The celebrated Jean-Jacques Rousseau (1712–1778) led the Italian supporters, joined by some of the other *philosophes* who wrote articles on music in Diderot's *Encyclopédie.*

Polemical writings and further theoretical essays occupied Rameau's closing years. He died in Paris in 1764; feisty to the end, he found strength even on his deathbed to reproach the priest administering the last rites for bad chanting.

Rameau's Theoretical Works

Theory or, as it was called at the time, the "science" of music, engaged Rameau throughout his life. In his numerous writings he sought to derive the basic principles of harmony from the laws of acoustics. He not only clarified the musical practice of his time but also influenced music theory for the next two hundred years. Rameau considered the chord the primal element in music and held that the major triad was generated naturally when a string was divided into two, three, four, and five equal parts, which yields the octave, the fifth above it, the double-octave and the major third above that. (He later became aware that the overtone series supported his beliefs.) He had more difficulty using "natural principles" to account for the minor triad, though he did establish the so-called melodic minor scale. He theorized that chords were built up by thirds within the octave—so that triads could be expanded to seventh chords—and downward beyond the octave to ninth and eleventh chords. Rameau recognized the identity of a chord through all its inversions. This was a most important insight, as was his corollary idea of the *basse fondamentale*—root progressions in a succession of harmonies. Moreover, Rameau established the tonic, dominant, and subdominant chords as the pillars of tonality, and he related other chords to these, formulating the hierarchies of functional harmony. He also stated the idea that modulation might result from the change of function of a chord (in modern terminology, a pivot chord). Less significant were his theory deriving all melody from harmony (expressed or implied) and his views on the particular character of specific keys. His numerical specula-

The chord

Functional harmony

tions and analogies, which he thought mathematically legitimized his theory of harmony, were discredited by scientists. In *Eléments de musique théorique et pratique suivant les principes de M. Rameau* (Paris, 1752), the encyclopedist and mathematician Jean Le Rond d'Alembert (1717–1783) published a compendium of Rameau's theory that purged the numerical and geometric rationalizations and reduced it to its essentials.

Musical Style

French opera after Lully acquired an ever larger proportion of decorative elements: scenic spectacle, descriptive orchestral music, dances, choruses, and songs. More and more the drama, even in works called *tragédies lyriques*, had deteriorated in both importance and quality, and eventually opera-ballet lost all but the thinnest thread of continuity between dramatic scenes. For example, Rameau's *Les Indes galantes*, one of his most frequently performed works in modern times, had four *entrées* or acts, each with a self-contained plot located in a different quarter of the globe. It presented a variety of decorations and dances that gratified the early eighteenth-century French public's interest in exotic scenes and peoples. The *entrée*, "The Generous Turk," set in "an island of the Indian Ocean," has a plot outline later used by Mozart for his *Abduction from the Seraglio*. The other *entrées* were "The Incas of Peru," "The Flowers, a Persian Festival," and "The Savages," which takes place in "a forest of America" and introduces Spanish and French characters as well as Indians. Rameau's music, especially in the *entrée* of the Incas, is far more dramatic than the libretto would suggest.

The musical features of Rameau's theater works resemble Lully's in several ways: both composers exhibit realistic declamation and precise rhythmic notation in the recitatives; both mix recitative with more tuneful, formally organized airs, choruses, and instrumental interludes; and both include frequent long scenes of *divertissement*. In addition, the form of the overture in Rameau's early operas is the same as Lully's. But within this general framework, Rameau introduced many changes, so that the resemblance between his music and Lully's is largely superficial.

Melodic style

Perhaps the melodic lines, by their nature, offer the most notable contrast. Rameau the composer constantly practiced the doctrine of Rameau the theorist—that all melody is rooted in harmony. Many of his melodic phrases are plainly triadic and leave no uncertainty as to the harmonic progressions that must support them. Also, orderly relationships within the major-minor tonal system of dominants, subdominants, and secondary chords and modulations govern the harmony. Rameau drew from a rich palette of both consonant and dissonant chords, direct and strained progressions, and modulation for expressive purposes, diversifying his style much more than Lully's. Rameau's harmonies are for the most part diatonic, but on occasion he uses chromatic and enharmonic modulations most effectively. In the trio of the Fates in Act II of *Hippolyte et Aricie* (Example 12.2), a descending chromatic sequence modulates rapidly through five keys in as many measures, underlining the words "Où cours-tu, malheureux? Tremble, frémis d'effroi!" (Where do you flee, wretch? Tremble, shudder with terror!).

Harmonic style

Example 12.2 *Jean-Philippe Rameau, Modulations in* Hippolyte et Aricie

Overture form

Rameau experimented with different formal plans for the overtures. Even when he maintained Lully's pattern of the French *ouverture*, as he did in *Castor et Pollux* and *Les Indes galantes*, Rameau expanded and deepened the second movement. In his last works, he freely adapted the three-movement form of the Italian sinfonia. Quite often he introduced a theme in the overture that reappeared later in the opera, and occasionally, as in *Zoroastre*, the overture became a kind of symphonic poem, predicting the course of the drama to follow.

Compared to Italian opera composers, Rameau, like Lully and other French composers, minimized the contrast between recitative and air. Rameau's vocal airs, in all their variety of dimensions and types, fall into two basic patterns: the relatively short two-part form AB, and the longer form with repetition after contrast, either ABA or a rondo-like pattern. Their outstanding traits are elegance, a picturesque quality, piquant rhythms, fullness of harmony, and melodic ornamentation by means of agréments.

Rameau's harmony achieved dramatic force in the monologues. The opening scenes of *Castor et Pollux* and the monologue *Ah! faut-il* in Act IV of *Hippolyte et Aricie* (NAWM 78; CD 5 [42] /2 ⟨45⟩) have a grandeur that is unsurpassed in eighteenth-century French opera. Hippolyte's anguish is expressed with highly charged dissonances that propel the harmony forward, as we see from the number of sevenths, ninths, diminished fifths, and augmented fourths called for by the figured bass, and the obligatory appoggiaturas and other notated ornaments. But the most powerful effects are achieved by the joint use of solo and chorus. Choruses, which remained prominent in French opera long after they were no longer used in Italy, are numerous throughout Rameau's works. The invocation to the sun (*Brilliant soleil*) in Act II of *Les Indes galantes* exhibits highly effective homophonic choral writing.

Instrumental music

Rameau made his most original contribution in the instrumental sections of his operas—the overtures, the dances, and the descriptive symphonies that accompany the stage action. In all of these his invention was inexhaustible. Themes, rhythms, and harmonies have a marked individuality and a decisive pictorial quality. The French valued music for its powers of depiction, and Rameau was their champion tone painter. His musical pictures range from graceful miniatures to broad representations of thunder (*Hippolyte*, Act I), tempest (*Les Surprises de l'Amour* [1757], Act III), or earthquake (*Les Indes galantes*, Act II). The pictorial quality is often enhanced by novel orchestration. Rameau's use of the bassoons and horns and the independence of the woodwinds in his later scores rivaled even the most advanced orchestral practices of his time.

Clavecin pieces

Rameau's clavecin pieces have the fine texture, rhythmic vivacity, elegance of detail, and humor that we associate with the works of Couperin. Rameau's only published instrumental ensemble music was a collection of trio sonatas, *Pièces de clavecin en concerts* (1741). In these the harpsichord shares equally with the other instruments in presenting and working out the thematic material.

Summary

Even in the heroic early operas and opera-ballets, the French traits of clarity, grace, moderation, and elegance, and a constant striving toward the picturesque, characterize Rameau's work. In these respects he may be compared to his contemporary, the painter Jean Watteau (see Plate IX, facing page 494). He was also a *philosophe* as well as a composer, an analyst as well as a creator; and in this respect he may be compared to another contemporary, Voltaire. Rameau was one of the most complex and productive musical personalities of the eighteenth century.

JOHANN SEBASTIAN BACH

Career

Posterity has raised Johann Sebastian Bach (1685–1750) to the very pinnacle of composers of all time. This contrasts with his reputation in his own day, when he was renowned in Protestant Germany as an organ virtuoso and writer of learned contrapuntal works, but at least a half-dozen composers were more widely performed in Europe. However, his final position as cantor of St. Thomas's School and music director in Leipzig (1723–50) had considerable prestige in the Lutheran world, and he regarded himself as a conscientious craftsman doing the job to the best of his ability. It was only in the nineteenth century that his Passions, cantatas, and instrumental music became known, performed, published, and greatly admired.

Johann Sebastian was one of a large family of Bachs that came from the German region of Thuringia. In the course of six generations, from around 1560 to the nineteenth century, the Bach family produced an extraordinary number of good musicians and several outstanding ones. J. S. Bach received his earliest training from his father, a town musician of Eisenach, and from his elder brother Johann Christoph, an organist who was a pupil of Pachelbel. He studied the music of other composers by copying or arranging their scores, a habit he retained throughout his life. In this way he became familiar with the methods of the foremost composers in France, Germany, Austria, and Italy, assimilating the characteristic excellences of each.

Before settling in Leipzig in 1723, Bach served as organist at Arnstadt (1703–7) and Mühlhausen (1707–8); as court organist and later concertmaster in the chapel of the duke of Weimar (1708–17); and as music director at the court of a prince in Cöthen (1717–23).

Bach composed in all the genres practiced in his time with the exception of opera. He wrote primarily to fulfill the needs of the positions he held; his works may be grouped accordingly. Thus at Arnstadt, Mühlhausen, and Weimar, where he was employed to play the organ, most of his compositions were for that instrument. At Cöthen, where he had nothing to do with church

Cities that figured in J. S. Bach's career are indicated in color on this map of modern Germany. In Bach's time, Germany comprised a number of duchies, bishoprics, principalities, and electorates of the Holy Roman Empire. For example, Leipzig and Dresden were in the Electorate of Saxony, Lüneburg in that of Hanover, Berlin in that of Brandenburg. Hamburg and Lübeck belonged to the Duchy of Holstein, and Anhalt-Cöthen and Weimar were themselves tiny dukedoms.

music, he composed mostly works for harpsichord, clavichord, or instrumental ensembles as well as music for instruction and for domestic or court entertainment. He produced most of his cantatas and other church music in his early years in Leipzig, although some of his most important mature compositions for organ and other keyboard instruments also date from the Leipzig period. Consequently, our survey of Bach's compositions follows the order that corresponds to his places of employment.

BACH'S INSTRUMENTAL MUSIC

The Organ Works

Bach was trained as a violinist and organist, but it was organ music that first attracted his interest as a composer. As a youth he visited Hamburg to hear the organists there, and while working in Arnstadt he made a journey on foot to Lübeck—a distance of about two hundred miles. There the music of Buxtehude so fascinated him that he overstayed his leave.

Early works

Bach's earliest organ compositions include chorale preludes, several sets of variations on chorales, and some toccatas and fantasias that in their length and exuberance of ideas recall the toccatas of Buxtehude. While at the court of Weimar, Bach became interested in the music of Italian composers, and with his usual diligence copied their scores and arranged their works. He reduced several of Vivaldi's string concertos to concertos for organ or harpsichord and orchestra, writing out the ornaments, occasionally reinforcing the counterpoint, and sometimes adding inner voices. He also wrote fugues on subjects by Corelli and Legrenzi. As a natural consequence of these studies, Bach's own style began to change. From the Italians, especially Vivaldi, he learned to write concise themes and to clarify and tighten the harmonic scheme. Above all, he learned to develop subjects into grandly proportioned formal structures, particularly concerto-ritornello movements. He imbued these qualities with his own prolific imagination and his profound mastery of contrapuntal technique. Merging characteristics of Italian, French, and German music, he forged a personalized and highly distinctive style of his own.

The Preludes and Fugues

One of the favorite larger musical structures in this period was the combination of prelude (or toccata or fantasia) and fugue. Most of Bach's important compositions in this form date from the Weimar period, though a few were written at Cöthen and Leipzig. While they are idiomatic for the organ and technically difficult, they never parade empty virtuosity.

Toccata

The Toccata in D minor, BWV 565[4] (before 1708?), exemplifies the form established by Buxtehude, in which the fugue is interspersed with sections of free fantasia. On the other hand, in the Passacaglia in C minor, BWV 582 (before 1708?), variations on a bass theme serve as an expansive prelude to a double fugue, one of whose subjects is the first half of the passacaglia theme. Some of the preludes are extended compositions in two or three movements: for example, the Fantasia and Fugue in G minor, BWV 542 (Fugue: Weimar; Fantasia: Cöthen), is a passionately expressive fantasia/toccata with contrapuntal interludes.

The well-defined melodic and rhythmic contours of Bach's fugue subjects display remarkable inventiveness (see Example 12.3). Elements of the Italian concerto are evident in a number of the toccatas and fugues, particularly in the Prelude and Fugue in A minor, BWV 543 (NAWM 79; CD 5 [43] / 2 ⟨46⟩). In the prelude, violinistic figuration resembling that of concerto solos alternates with toccata-like sections, including a pedal solo and chains of suspensions in the

4. BWV (abbreviation for "Bach-Werke-Verzeichnis") stands for *Thematisch-systematisches Verzeichnis der musikalischen Werke von Johann Sebastian Bach* (Thematic-Systematic Index of the Musical Works of J. S. Bach), ed. Wolfgang Schmieder (Leipzig, 1950). The abbreviation S. (for Schmieder) is sometimes used instead of BWV.

Example 12.3 *J. S. Bach, Organ Fugue Subjects*

manner of Corelli. The fugue's structure resembles a concerto Allegro: the expositions on the violinistic subject appear, like tutti, in related keys as well as the tonic, and the episodes have the character of solo sections.

Later works

From the later years of Bach's life come the gigantic Prelude and Fugue ("St. Anne's") in E♭ major, BWV 552, published in 1739. They appear as the opening and closing sections of Part III of the *Clavier-Übung* (literally, "Keyboard Practice," a catchall title that Bach used for four different collections of keyboard pieces). Part III comprises a series of chorale preludes on the hymns of the Lutheran Catechism and Mass (Kyrie and Gloria, the so-called *Missa brevis*). In symbolic recognition of the Trinity, the conclusion is a triple fugue in three sections with a key signature of three flats. Each section of the fugue has its own subject, and the first subject is combined contrapuntally with each of the other two.

Bach's Trio Sonatas

According to his biographer J. N. Forkel, Bach wrote the six Trio Sonatas, BWV 525–530, for organ solo, in Leipzig for his eldest son, Wilhelm Friedemann. These works reveal how Bach adapted the Italian trio sonata for a single performer. The contrapuntal texture of three independent voices is assigned to two manuals and the pedals. The fast–slow–fast order of movements and the character of the themes show the influence of their Italian models.

The Chorale Preludes

As an organist and a devout Lutheran, Bach cared deeply about the chorale. In writing some 170 organ chorales, he exhausted all the known types of setting in a constant search for artistic perfection. Bach's *Orgelbüchlein* (Little Organ Book), which Bach compiled at Weimar and Cöthen, contains short chorale preludes. He originally planned to include chorale settings for the entire church year, 164 in all. The undertaking was a typically ambitious one, but he completed only forty-five. Many of his mature compositions participated in some large, unified design—for example, the Preludes and Fugues in all the major and minor keys in *The Well-Tempered Keyboard*, the cycle of catechism chorales in the *Clavier-Übung*, the canons at increasing intervals in the *Goldberg* Variations, the exhaustive treatment of a single subject in *A Musical Offering*, and the comprehensive collection of fugue types in *The Art of Fugue*.

Pedagogic aims

It was also characteristic of Bach to plan a collection with his pupils in mind. Thus the title page of the *Orgelbüchlein* reads, "Little organ book, in which a beginning organist is given guidance in all sorts of ways of developing a chorale, and also for improving his pedal technique, since in these chorales the pedal is treated as completely *obbligato* [essential, not optional]." He added a rhymed couplet, "To honor the Most High God alone, and for the instruction of my fellow-men." It is understandable that Bach, who was always a humble and diligent student, should have been a wise and kindly teacher. He compiled two *Little Notebooks*—collections of short keyboard pieces—for Wilhelm

Friedemann and for his second wife, Anna Magdalena, that taught technique and musicianship. His two-part *Inventions* and three-part *Sinfonie* are pedagogical works, as is the first book of *The Well-Tempered Keyboard.*

Sacred and secular

Given his religious outlook, it is not surprising that Bach dedicated a book of church music—chorale preludes—to "the Most High God," or that he inscribed the scores of his cantatas and Passions with the letters J. J. (*Jesu, juva*—Jesus, help) at the beginning, and S. D. G. (*soli Deo gloria*—glory be to God alone) at the end. But Bach did not differentiate between sacred and secular art, both being "to the glory of God," and sometimes used the same music with sacred and secular words. The music for the Osanna in the B-minor Mass, for example, had previously been used in a cantata (BWV Anh. 11) honoring Friedrich August I, elector of Saxony and king of Poland (his title as king was August II), when he was on a state visit to Leipzig.

Orgelbüchlein

In each of the chorale preludes in the *Orgelbüchlein,* the tune is heard once through in a readily recognizable form. The melody is sometimes treated in canon and sometimes presented with fairly elaborate ornaments. The accompanying voices are not necessarily derived from the chorale melody and, in some places, may symbolize the visual images or underlying ideas of the chorale text through pictorial or graphic motives. One of Bach's most striking organ representations is *Durch Adams Fall ist ganz verderbt* (Through Adam's fall, all is spoiled; NAWM 80b; CD 5 [45]). A jagged series of dissonant leaps in the pedals depicts the idea of "fall," departing from a consonant chord and falling into a dissonant one—as if from innocence into sin—while the twisting chromatic lines in the inner voices suggest at once temptation, sorrow, and the sinuous writhing of the serpent (Example 12.4).

Bach compiled three collections of organ chorales during the Leipzig period. He transcribed the six *Schübler* chorales, BWV 645–50, from cantata movements.

Leipzig chorales

The *Eighteen Chorales,* BWV 651–68, which Bach collected and revised between 1747 and 1749, were composed at earlier periods of his life. They include all kinds of organ chorale settings: variations, fugues, fantasias, trios, and extended chorale preludes. In the catechism chorales in Part III of the *Clavier-Übung,* BWV 669–89, he coupled a longer setting requiring the organ pedals with a shorter one (usually fugal) for manuals only. Bach conceived the later organ chorales in grander proportions than those of the *Orgelbüchlein.* The works are less intimate and subjective, replacing the vivid expressive details of the earlier works with a purely musical development of ideas.

Example 12.4 *J. S. Bach, Chorale Prelude:* Durch Adams Fall

The Harpsichord and Clavichord Music

Bach's music for these two keyboard instruments includes masterpieces in every current genre: preludes, fantasies, and toccatas; fugues and other pieces in fugal style; dance suites; and sets of variations. In addition, there are early sonatas and capriccios, miscellaneous short works (including many teaching pieces), and concertos with orchestra. He wrote a large proportion of this music in Cöthen, although he composed many important works in the Leipzig period. The harpsichord compositions, which were not bound to a local German tradition or liturgy, as organ works were, reveal the international features of Bach's style—the intermingling of Italian, French, and German characteristics.

The Toccatas

Among the most notable toccatas are those in F♯ minor, BWV 910, and C minor, BWV 911 (both ca. 1717). Each begins with free running passages in improvisatory style. The C-minor Toccata leads into one of Bach's characteristic driving fugues on a triadic, concerto-like theme. The Chromatic Fantasia and Fugue in D minor, BWV 903 (ca. 1720, revised ca. 1730), is Bach's greatest work in this genre.

The Well-Tempered Keyboard

Undoubtedly the best known of Bach's works for harpsichord or clavichord is the double set of preludes and fugues that he titled *Das wohltemperirte Clavier* (The Well-Tempered Keyboard, 1722 and ca. 1740). Each of the two parts consists of twenty-four preludes and fugues, one set in each of the twelve major and minor keys. Part I is more unified in style and purpose than Part II, which includes compositions from many different periods of Bach's life. In addition to demonstrating the possibility of using all the keys, with the then still novel equal- or nearly equal-tempered tuning, Bach had particular pedagogic intentions in Part I.

In the typical prelude, Bach assigned the player a specific technical task, so that the piece functioned as an étude. Some of Bach's little preludes, such as BWV 933–43, as well as all of the two-part inventions and three-part sinfonias, may be regarded as preliminary studies for these exercises. But the teaching aims of *The Well-Tempered Keyboard* go beyond mere technique because the preludes illustrate different types of keyboard composition. For example, Nos. 2, 7, and 21 of Book I are toccatas, No. 8 is a trio-sonata Grave, and No. 17 a concerto Allegro.

Fugues

The fugues as a set constitute a compendium of monothematic fugal writing. Book I, No. 4 in C♯ minor represents the archaic ricercare; others illustrate the techniques of inversion, canon, and augmentation (No. 8, E♭ minor), a da capo ending (No. 3, C♯ major), and much more. In Part II, the Fugue in D major (No. 5) offers a superb example of a concentrated abstract musical structure using the simplest materials, while the Prelude and Fugue in F♯ minor (No. 14) stands out for the beauty of its themes and its proportions. As

Mm.21 (2nd half)–24 (1st half), in Bach's autograph

Mm.21–26, in Carl Czerny's edition

Mm.22–24, in Hans Bischoff's edition

■ *This passage from the first prelude in Part I of* The Well-Tempered Keyboard *is shown in Bach's autograph manuscript and in two publications. Carl Czerny's edition (first published in the 1830s), evidently based on a copy made after Bach's death, incorporates an inauthentic extra measure after measure 22; elsewhere, Czerny adds phrasings, tempo markings, and dynamics not present in Bach's manuscript (e.g., the* dimin. *in measure 21). In his edition of 1883, Hans Bischoff tries to present as accurate a reproduction of the source as possible. This aim, while not without its problems in practice, is generally adhered to by modern scholars.*

in the organ fugues, each subject has a clearly defined musical personality that unfolds throughout the entire fugue.

The Harpsichord Suites

Bach's harpsichord suites show the influence of French and Italian as well as German models. He wrote three sets of six: the English Suites, BWV 806–11 (1715); the French Suites, BWV 812–17 (original versions in the *Clavierbüchlein,* 1722–25); and the six Partitas, BWV 825–30, which were first published separately and then collected to form Part I of the *Clavier-Übung* (1731). Part II of this collection (1735) also contains a large Partita in B minor, BWV 831, entitled *Ouvertüre nach französischer Art* (Overture in the French Style) for two-manual harpsichord.

The designations "French" and "English" for the suites are not Bach's own, and both collections blend French and Italian qualities in a highly personal style. Each set consists of the standard four-dance movements—allemande, courante, sarabande, and gigue—with additional short movements following the sarabande; each of the English Suites opens with a prelude. In the preludes, Bach transferred Italian ensemble idioms to the keyboard. The prelude of the third suite, for example, simulates a concerto Allegro movement with alternating tutti and solo. An even more striking adaptation of the concerto form, the *Concerto nach italiänischen Gusto* (Concerto in the Italian Style, BWV 971, in *Clavier-Übung*, Part II), utilizes the harpsichord's two manuals to emphasize the tutti-solo contrasts. The dances in the English Suites, based on French models, include several examples of the *double* or ornamented repetition of a movement.

Goldberg Variations

Bach raised the keyboard theme-and-variations genre to a new level of complexity and artfulness in the *Aria mit verschiedenen Veraenderungen* (Aria with Sundry Variations, BWV 988; published in 1741 or 1742 as Part IV of the *Clavier-Übung*), generally known as the *Goldberg* Variations. All thirty variations preserve the bass and the harmonic structure of the theme, a sarabande in two balanced sections. Every third variation is a canon, the first at the interval of a unison, the second at a second, and so on through the ninth. For the thirtieth and last variation, Bach wrote a *quodlibet*, a mixture of two popular song melodies combined in counterpoint above the bass of the theme. The end work repeats the original theme. The noncanonic variations take many different forms: invention, fugue, French overture, ornamental slow aria, and, at regular intervals, a sparkling bravura piece for two manuals.

Works for Solo Violin and Cello

In his six sonatas and partitas for violin alone, BWV 1001–6 (1720), six suites for cello alone, BWV 1007–12 (ca. 1720), and partita for solo flute, BWV 1013, Bach created the illusion of a harmonic and contrapuntal texture. By requiring the player to stop several strings at once, he suggested an interplay of independent voices. The famous chaconne from Bach's solo violin Partita in D minor illustrates this technique.

Ensemble Sonatas

Bach's chief compositions for chamber ensemble are six sonatas for violin and harpsichord, BWV 1014–19 (1717–23), three for viola da gamba and harpsichord, BWV 1027–29 (ca. 1720), and six for flute and harpsichord, BWV 1030–35 (1717–23). Most of these works have four movements in slow–fast–slow–fast order, like the sonata da chiesa. Indeed, most of them are virtual trio sonatas, since often the right-hand harpsichord part is written as a melodic line in counterpoint with the other instrument.

Concertos

Brandenburg Concertos

In the six Brandenburg Concertos, BWV 1046–1051, composed in 1721 and dedicated to the Margrave of Brandenburg, Bach fully assimilated the Italian style while investing it with his own extensions and complications. He adopted the three-movement, fast–slow–fast order of the Italian concerto, as well as its triadic themes, steadily driving rhythms, and the ritornello form of the Allegro movements. At the same time, he introduced tutti material into the soli, and he expanded the form with devices such as the long cadenzas of the Fifth Brandenburg Concerto and elaborately developed fugues, as the one in da capo form of this same concerto. The Third and Sixth are ripieno concertos without featured solo instruments. The others are concerti grossi, pitting solo instruments in various combinations against the body of strings and continuo. Bach also wrote two concertos for solo violin and the Concerto in D minor for Two Violins, BWV 1043.

Harpsichord concertos

Bach was one of the first to write (or arrange) concertos for harpsichord. There are seven for solo harpsichord with orchestra, three for two harpsichords, two for three harpsichords, and one for four harpsichords and orchestra, this last an arrangement of a Vivaldi concerto for four violins. Most, and possibly all, of the harpsichord concertos are, in fact, arrangements of violin compositions by Bach or by other composers.

Arrangements

Bach worked several movements from his chamber and orchestral compositions into his Leipzig cantatas. The prelude from the E-major solo Violin Partita, BWV 1006, received a full orchestral setting as the sinfonia of the cantata *Wir danken Dir, Gott*, BWV 29. The first movement of the Third Brandenburg Concerto, with two horns and three oboes added to the orchestra, became the sinfonia of *Ich liebe den Höchsten*, BWV 174. No fewer than five movements from the solo harpsichord concertos found a niche in cantatas. The opening chorus of *Unser Mund sei voll Lachens*, BWV 110, is based on the first movement of the orchestral Suite in D major, BWV 1069.

The Orchestral Suites

The four *Ouvertures*, or orchestral suites, BWV 1066–69, contain some of Bach's most exuberant and attractive music. The Third and Fourth Suites (ca. 1729–31), which have trumpets and timpani added to the strings and winds, were undoubtedly intended for performance out-of-doors.

Other Works

Two of Bach's late instrumental works form a class in themselves. *Musikalisches Opfer* (A Musical Offering), BWV 1079, contains a three- and a six-part ricercare for keyboard and ten canons, all based on a theme proposed by Frederick the Great of Prussia (Example 12.5, page 396). Bach had improvised on the theme while visiting the monarch at Potsdam in 1747 and then had written out and revised his improvisations. He added a trio sonata in four movements for flute (King Frederick's instrument), violin, and continuo, in which the

Example 12.5 *J. S. Bach, Theme from* A Musical Offering

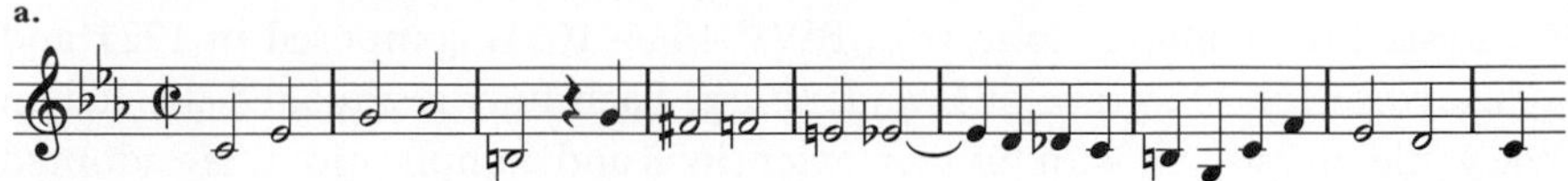

Example 12.6 *J. S. Bach, Theme from* The Art of Fugue

theme also appears, had the set printed, and dedicated it to the king. *Die Kunst der Fuge* (The Art of Fugue), BWV 1080, composed in 1749–50 and apparently left unfinished at Bach's death, systematically demonstrates all types of fugal writing. It consists of eighteen canons and fugues in the strictest style, all based on the same subject (Example 12.6) or one of its transformations, and arranged in a general order of increasing complexity.

BACH'S VOCAL MUSIC

Bach at Leipzig

Leipzig in 1723 was a flourishing commercial city with about 30,000 inhabitants. Noted as a center of printing and publishing, it was also the seat of one of Europe's oldest universities. It had a good theater and an opera house. (The opera house, which had irritated Bach's predecessor at St. Thomas's, Johann Kuhnau, for supposedly enticing away his best singers, closed in 1729.) There were five churches in Leipzig, as well as university chapels. Bach assumed responsibility for the music at the two most important churches, St. Nicholas and St. Thomas.

St. Thomas's School took in both day and boarding pupils. It provided fifty-five scholarships for boys and youths chosen on the basis of their musical and general scholastic ability. In return, they sang or played in the services of four Leipzig churches and fulfilled other musical duties.

Appointment and duties

Bach's appointment was the responsibility of the city council and subject to confirmation by the consistory, the governing body for churches and schools. Bach was not the council's first choice; the consistory wanted a more "modern" musician. Both Georg Philipp Telemann of Hamburg and Christoph Graupner of Darmstadt had been offered the position. Telemann used the offer to wangle a raise in salary in Hamburg, and Graupner withdrew after his resignation was turned down by the Landgrave of Darmstadt and his stipend was greatly increased. Bach, having passed the usual examination and satisfied the council about his theological soundness, was then unanimously elected, and he assumed the post in May of 1723. As "Cantor of St. Thomas and Director of Music of Leipzig" he was obliged to teach four hours each day (Latin as well as music) and to prepare music for the church services. He also had to pledge himself to lead an exemplary Christian life and not to leave town without permission from the mayor. He and his family lived in an apartment in one wing of the school, where his study was separated by a thin partition from the home room of the second-year schoolboys.

The citizens of Leipzig enjoyed abundant opportunities for public worship. Daily services were conducted in all the churches. The regular Sunday program at St. Nicholas's and St. Thomas's consisted of three short services in addition to the principal one, which began at seven in the morning and lasted until about noon. At this service the choir sang a motet, a Lutheran Mass (Kyrie and Gloria only), hymns, and a cantata on alternate Sundays. The cantor directed the first choir at the church whose turn it was to hear the cantata, while a deputy conducted the second choir in simpler music at the other important church. The third and fourth choirs, meanwhile, made up of the poorest singers, took care of the modest musical requirements in the two remaining churches. A note in Bach's hand (1730?) indicates the minimum requirements as twelve singers (three to each part) for each of the first three choirs and eight for the fourth choir.

Performing forces

The orchestra that accompanied the first choir was recruited partly from the school, partly from the town, partly from the *collegium musicum* of the university, an extracurricular musical society that performed contemporary music. Telemann had founded it in 1704, and Bach became its director in 1729. The church orchestra consisted of two flutes (when needed), two or three oboes, one or two bassoons, three trumpets, timpani, and strings with continuo—a total of eighteen to twenty-four players.

Working conditions in the Leipzig position may not have been ideal, but they served to stimulate a composer's creative power. New compositions were

The Thomaskirche in Leipzig, where J. S. Bach served as cantor and director musices *(1723–50). The building at the far end of the square, beyond the fountain, is the Thomasschule (after it was enlarged in 1732), where Bach taught.* (BERLIN, ARCHIV FÜR KUNST UND GESCHICHTE)

ORDER OF THE DIVINE SERVICE IN LEIPZIG ON THE FIRST SUNDAY IN ADVENT: MORNING

1) Preluding
2) Motet
3) Preluding on the Kyrie, which is performed throughout in concerted manner [*musiciret*]
4) Intoning before the altar
5) Reading of the Epistle
6) Singing of the Litany
7) Preluding on [and singing of] the Chorale
8) Reading of the Gospel
9) Preluding on and performance of] the principal composition [cantata]
10) Singing of the Creed [Luther's Credo hymn]
11) The Sermon
12) After the Sermon, as usual, singing of several verses of a hymn
13) Words of Institution [of the Sacrament]
14) Preluding on [and performance of] the composition probably the second part of the cantata]. After the same, alternate preluding and singing of chorales until the end of the Communion, *et sic porrò* [and so on].

From *The New Bach Reader: A Life of Johann Sebastian Bach in Letters and Documents*, ed. Hans T. David and Arthur Mendel, rev. and enl. by Christoph Wolff (New York: Norton, 1998), p. 113.

required at regular, frequent intervals. Singers and instrumentalists, however inadequate they may have been at times, were always on hand. And Bach's position, although a step lower than his earlier post of Kapellmeister and not without its petty annoyances, was secure and honorable, indeed, highly coveted.

The Church Cantatas

The sacred cantata figured prominently in the Lutheran liturgy of Leipzig. The subject matter was often linked to the content of the Gospel reading that immediately preceded the cantata. Bach sketched out the order of events, particularly the musical ones, on the back of the autograph score of Cantata 61 (see vignette) at the time of its performance on November 28, 1723.

Altogether, the Leipzig churches required fifty-eight cantatas each year, in addition to Passion music for Good Friday, Magnificats at Vespers for three festivals, an annual cantata for the installation of the city council, and occasional music such as funeral motets and wedding cantatas. Between 1723 and 1729 Bach composed four complete annual cycles of cantatas, each with about sixty cantatas. He apparently composed a fifth cycle during the 1730s and early 1740s, but many of these and of the fourth cycle do not survive.

Cantata cycles

Approximately two hundred of his cantatas have been preserved, some of them newly written for Leipzig, others refashioned from earlier works. In the early cantatas the composer responded to the changing affections and images of the text with music of intense dramatic expression and unexpectedly varied forms. By comparison, the later Leipzig cantatas are less subjective in feeling and more regular in structure. However, no generalized description can possibly suggest the infinite variety and the wealth of musical invention, technical mastery, and religious devotion in Bach's cantatas. Two or three examples will serve as an introduction to this vast treasure of music.

Neumeister Cantatas

Erdmann Neumeister's innovative idea—to introduce opera-like recitatives and arias into the cantata—deeply affected Bach, even though he set only five of the pastor's texts. In the text for *Nun komm', der Heiden Heiland* (Come, Gentiles' Savior, 1714), BWV 61,[5] Neumeister combined chorale verses, newly invented metrical poetry, and prose from the Bible. For the opening choral movement, based on the text and melody of the chorale *Nun komm, der Heiden Heiland*, Bach wrote an elaborate variation in the style and form of a French overture. The choice of this genre is significant, not only because Bach was preoccupied at the time with assimilating foreign styles but also because it was written for the opening (*ouverture*) of the church year, the first Sunday of Advent. The Cantata also includes other operatic movements: a simple recitative, an accompanied recitative, two da capo arias, one of which is a *siciliano* (based on a folk dance), and a final chorus on a different chorale. Thus Bach combined secular genres and Lutheran hymn settings in a work full of youthful ingenuity.

Chorale Cantatas

Christ lag in Todes Banden

Bach treated chorale texts and melodies in a multitude of different ways in his cantatas. In the well-known *Christ lag in Todes Banden* (Christ lay in the bonds of death), BWV 4, which dates from around 1708, the seven strophes of the chorale are set as variations on the hymn tune. Following the opening sinfonia, the performing resources are arranged symmetrically around the quartet of soloists in the center: Chorus—Duet—Solo—Quartet—Solo—Duet—Chorus. This order is thought to symbolize the cross.

Wachet auf

More typically, Bach based the opening chorus on a chorale melody and ended the work with a simple or embellished statement of the same chorale. The texts of the interior solos and duets often paraphrased strophes of the chorale, but the music referred back to the hymn tune only rarely. For example, in *Wachet auf, ruft uns die Stimme* ("Wake up," the voice calls to us; NAWM 81; CD 6 [1] / 2 ⟨48⟩), BWV 140, the middle movement is constructed like a chorale prelude. Each phrase of the chorale, sung plainly by the tenor, is

5. The haphazard order of the cantatas in BWV follows that of the nineteenth-century Bach-Gesellschaft edition of the complete works.

preceded and accompanied by a musical commentary in unison strings. (Bach, in fact, converted this composition into a chorale prelude as one of the Schübler chorales, BWV 645.) The opening chorus imaginatively combines concerto form with cantus-firmus technique. The sixteen-measure ritornello for orchestra is heard four times (once abbreviated), to frame the two *Stollen* and the *Abgesang* of the chorale melody. With its repeated dotted-note chords and halting syncopations, it sets a mood of apprehensive anticipation as the wise and foolish virgins wait for the bridegroom mentioned in the first stanza of the chorale. The parable is told in Matthew 25:1–23, the Gospel reading for the twenty-seventh Sunday after Trinity, the occasion for which Bach wrote the cantata in 1731. A violino piccolo and the first oboe, as if paired in a concertino, exchange running figures that elaborate upon motives from the chorale melody. The sopranos, supported by a "corno"—perhaps a hunting horn—sing the phrases of the hymn in long notes, while motives derived from the same phrases are developed imitatively in the three other parts (Example 12.7). Bach wrote "Aria" at the head of two of the other movements and introduced each with a recitative, one *secco* and one *accompagnato.* The arias are actually duets modeled on operatic love duets, but here the dialogues are between Jesus and an individual soul seeking salvation. In the first duet a violino piccolo weaves arabesques, as in an embellished Corelli adagio but with more structure. In the second duet an oboe develops figures borrowed from the voices.

Example 12.7 *J. S. Bach*, Wachet auf: *Chorus,* Wachet auf

Wake up, the voice calls to us

Secular Cantatas

Bach customarily gave the title "dramma per musica" to cantatas that he composed for secular occasions. He was not averse to reusing a secular cantata for church and vice versa. For example, eleven numbers of his *Christmas Oratorio* also appear in secular works, six of them in *Hercules auf dem Scheidewege* (Hercules at the Crossroads), BWV 213. Among the best of the "musical dramas" are *Der Streit zwischen Phoebus und Pan* (The Quarrel between Phoebus and Pan) BWV 201, and *Schleicht, spielende Wellen* (Glide gently, playful waves), BWV 206, written in October 1736 to celebrate the birthday of August III, king of Poland and elector of Saxony (his title as elector was Friedrich August II). The *Coffee* Cantata (ca. 1734–35), BWV 211, and the burlesque *Peasant* Cantata (1742), BWV 212, are delightful specimens of Bach's lighter music. In some of these cantatas of the 1730s Bach experimented with the new *galant* style by toning down his tendency to write elaborate accompaniments and letting the vocal line dominate. He also invented melodies that divide symmetrically into antecedent and consequent phrases, and indulged in other mannerisms of the new operatic style.

Galant style

Motets

In Bach's time, the term *motet* signified a composition for chorus, generally in contrapuntal style, on a biblical or chorale text. The motets sung in the Leipzig churches were relatively short and served to introduce the service. Apparently they were chosen from a traditional repertory of existing works, and the cantor was not expected to furnish new motets. Of the six surviving motets of Bach, BWV 225–230, three were written for memorial services, one for a funeral, and one, *Singet dem Herrn* (Sing to the Lord), BWV 225, for the birthday of August II, king of Poland (Friedrich August I as elector of Saxony). They are long works, and four of them are for double chorus. The voice parts, always complete in themselves, may have been sung during Bach's time with instrumental doubling, as were other works in motet style. The five-voice *Jesu meine Freude* (Jesus, my joy), BWV 227, uses the chorale melody in six of its eleven movements.

Magnificat and *Christmas Oratorio*

The great Magnificat (1723, revised ca. 1728–31), BWV 243, for five-part chorus and orchestra, is one of Bach's most melodious works, more Italian in style than his other church music. The *Christmas Oratorio*, BWV 248, produced at Leipzig in 1734–35, is actually a set of six cantatas for the festivals of the Christmas and Epiphany season. The biblical narratives (Luke 2:1–21; Matt. 2: 1–12) are presented in recitative; appropriate arias and chorales reflect or comment on the various episodes of the story. The narrative element, not usually present in the cantata, justifies the designation "oratorio."

Passions

St. John Passion

Bach's two surviving Passions, according to St. John and according to St. Matthew, follow the North German tradition of Passion settings in oratorio style. For the *St. John Passion*, BWV 245, Bach used the Gospel story from John 18 and 19, with interpolations from the Book of Matthew, and fourteen chorales. In addition, he adapted lines for lyrical numbers from the popular Passion poem of B. H. Brockes, writing in some verses of his own. The work was first heard in Leipzig on Good Friday in 1724; Bach revised it several times for performances in later years. The *St. Matthew Passion*, BWV 244, for double chorus, soloists, double orchestra, and two organs, is a drama of epic grandeur. It was first performed in an early version on Good Friday in 1727. A tenor narrates the text from Matthew, chapters 26 and 27, in recitative with the help of the chorus. Chorales, a duet, and numerous arias, most of which are preceded by arioso recitatives, complement the narration. The "Passion Chorale" (see Example 8.1) appears five times, in different keys and in four different four-part harmonizations. The author of the text for the added recitatives and arias, Christian Friedrich Henrici (1700–1764), a Leipzig poet who also provided many of Bach's cantata texts, wrote under the pseudonym Picander. As in the *St. John Passion*, the chorus sometimes participates in the action and sometimes, like the chorus in Greek drama, introduces or reflects on the narrative. The opening and closing choruses of Part I are huge chorale fantasias; in the first, the chorale melody is sung by a special choir of sopranos.

St. Matthew Passion

The *St. Matthew Passion* merges pictorial musical figures with expressive effects. We suggest studying five examples: the accompanied recitative for alto, *Ach Golgatha*; the alto aria *Erbarme dich, mein Gott* (Have pity, my God); the last setting of the Passion Chorale, after Jesus' death on the cross, *Wenn ich einmal soll scheiden* (When I must depart); the three measures of chorus on the words *Wahrlich, dieser ist Gottes Sohn gewesen* (Truly this was the Son of God), and the deeply moving closing chorus, *Wir setzen uns mit Tränen nieder* (We sit down with tears).

In the *St. Matthew Passion*, the chorale, the concertato medium, the recitative, the arioso, and the da capo aria join to develop a central religious theme. Except for the chorale, all of these elements are equally characteristic of late Baroque opera. Although Bach never wrote an opera, its language, forms, and spirit pervade the Passions.

Mass in B Minor

Borrowings from other works

Bach compiled the Mass in B minor between 1747 and 1749, mostly from music he had composed earlier. He had already presented the Kyrie and Gloria in 1733 to Friedrich August II, the Catholic elector of Saxony, in hopes of getting an honorary appointment to the electoral chapel, which he received three years later. The Sanctus was first performed on Christmas Day 1724. He adapted some of the other movements from choruses of cantatas, replacing the German text with the Latin words of the Mass and sometimes reworking the music. Among these borrowings are two sections of the Gloria, the Gratias agimus (whose music is repeated for Dona nobis pacem) from the Cantata BWV 29 (1731), and the Qui tollis from the Cantata BWV 46 (1723). In the *Symbolum nicenum*, as Bach entitled the Credo, the sections derived from previously composed music were the Crucifixus, from Cantata BWV 12 (1714); Et expecto (NAWM 82c; CD 6 [18]), from the Cantata BWV 120 (1728–29); Patrem omnipotentem, from Cantata BWV 171 (1729?); Osanna, from a lost cantata of 1732, reused in 1734 for the secular Cantata BWV 215; Agnus Dei from the Cantata BWV 11 (1735); and possibly Et resurrexit, which may be based on a lost concerto movement. Of the newly composed sections, the opening of the Credo and the Confiteor (NAWM 82b; CD 6 [15]), are in *stile antico*, while the Et in unum Dominum, Et in spiritum sanctum (NAWM 82a; CD 6 [13]), and Benedictus are in a modern style that contrasts sharply with all that surrounds them. Bach never heard the work performed as a whole, though parts were sung at Leipzig, where an abbreviated Latin Mass still had a place in the liturgy.

Bach usually reworked his earlier compositions for new situations because he was pressed for time. But here he wanted to make a universal religious statement in the traditional and solemn medium of the Catholic Mass and, in so doing, to give certain movements that had cost him much creative energy a permanence they surely deserved.

Summary

Burial and resurrection describe the history of Bach's music. Compositions published or prepared by Bach for publication during his lifetime include only the *Clavier-übung*, the Schübler chorales, the variations on *Vom Himmel hoch*, the *Musical Offering*, and *The Art of Fugue*. The rest remained in handwritten copies. Bach's work was quickly forgotten after his death, because musical taste changed radically in the middle of the eighteenth century. During the very decades that Bach composed his most important works, in the 1720s and 1730s, a new style emanating from the opera houses of Italy invaded Germany and the rest of Europe, making Bach's music seem old-fashioned. The composer and critic Johann Adolph Scheibe (1708–1776) considered Bach unsurpassable as an organist and keyboard composer. However, he found much of the rest of Bach's music overly elaborate and confused (see vignette), preferring the more tuneful and straightforward styles of Johann Gottlieb Graun (1703–1771) and Johann Adolph Hasse.

Reception history

Bach's eclipse in the mid-eighteenth century was not total. Although no complete large work of his was published between 1752 and 1800, some of the preludes and fugues from *The Well-Tempered Keyboard* appeared in print, and the whole collection circulated in innumerable manuscript copies. Haydn owned a copy of the Mass in B minor; Mozart knew *The Art of Fugue* and studied the motets on a visit to Leipzig in 1789. Citations from Bach's works appeared frequently in the musical literature of the time, and the important periodical, the *Allgemeine musikalische Zeitung*, opened its first issue (1798) with a Bach portrait. A fuller discovery of Bach finally began in the nineteenth century. The publication of the biography by Johann Nikolaus Forkel in 1802 marked an important step. The revival of the *St. Matthew Passion* by the composer and conductor Carl Friedrich Zelter (1758–1832) and its performance at Berlin under Felix Mendelssohn's direction in 1829 did much to inspire interest in Bach's music. Finally, the establishment in 1850 of the Bach Gesellschaft (Bach Society) led to the collected edition of Bach's works, completed by 1900.

JOHANN ADOLPH SCHEIBE'S CRITIQUE OF BACH'S STYLE, 1737

This great man would be the admiration of whole nations if he had more amenity (*Annehmlichkeit*), if he did not take away the natural element in his pieces by giving them a turgid (*schwülstig*) and confused style, and if he did not darken their beauty by an excess of art. Since he judges according to his own fingers, his pieces are extremely difficult to play; for he demands that singers and instrumentalists should be able to do with their throats and instruments whatever he can play on the clavier. But this is impossible. Every ornament, every little grace, and everything that one thinks of as belonging to the method of playing, he expresses completely in notes; and this not only takes away from his pieces the beauty of harmony but completely covers the melody throughout. All the voices must work with each other and be of equal difficulty, and none of them can be recognized as the principal voice. In short, he is in music what Mr. von Lohenstein was in poetry. Turgidity has led them both from the natural to the artificial, and from the lofty to the somber; and in both one admires the onerous labor and uncommon effort—which, however, are vainly employed, since they conflict with Nature.

From an anonymous letter by "an able traveling musician" published in Scheibe's periodical review, *Der critische Musikus*, May 14, 1737, translated in *The Bach Reader*, ed. Hans T. David and Arthur Mendel, rev. and enl. by Christoph Wolff (New York: Norton, 1998), p. 338.

We realize the central position Bach occupies in the history of music when we consider that he absorbed into his works all the genres, styles, and forms of his time and developed hitherto unsuspected potentialities in them. In his music the often conflicting demands of harmony and counterpoint, of melody and polyphony, reached a tense but satisfying equilibrium. Among the qualities that account for the continuing vitality of his music are his concentrated and distinctive themes, his copious musical invention, the balance he struck between harmonic and contrapuntal forces, the strong rhythmic drive, clarity of form, grand proportions, imaginative use of pictorial and symbolic figures, intensity of expression always controlled by a ruling architectural idea, and technical perfection of every detail.

GEORGE FRIDERIC HANDEL

Compared to Vivaldi, Rameau, and Bach, who rarely traveled outside their countries, George Frideric Handel (1685–1759) moved comfortably between German- , Italian- , and English-speaking cities. He matured as a composer in England, the country then most hospitable to foreign composers. Moreover, England provided the choral tradition that made Handel's oratorios possible.

Frontispiece of Handel's secular oratorio Alexander's Feast, *which is based on John Dryden's poem. Under the portrait of the composer by Jacob Houbraken is a scene that suggests the power of music and the legend that the kithara player Timotheus, with his music, stirred Alexander into going to battle. The work, of course, was not staged. Published in London by John Walsh, 1738.*

Vivaldi's influence on the musical world was immediate, although he died totally forgotten; Rameau's was felt more slowly, and then exclusively in the fields of opera and music theory; and Bach's work lay in comparative obscurity for half a century. But Handel won international renown during his lifetime and has continued to be revered, for his oratorios and more recently for his operas.

Handel's Career

There were no musicians in Handel's family, but his father grudgingly allowed the obviously talented boy to take lessons from the composer Friedrich Wilhelm Zachow, organist and church music director in Handel's native town of Halle. Under Zachow's teaching, Handel became an accomplished organist and harpsichordist, studied violin and oboe, received a thorough grounding in counterpoint, and became familiar with the music of German and Italian composers by copying their scores. He matriculated at the University of Halle in 1702 and at eighteen was appointed cathedral organist. But almost immediately he decided to give up the cantor's career (for which he had prepared

Halle

under Zachow) in favor of writing opera. In 1703 he moved to Hamburg—then the principal center of German opera—and remained there from 1703 to 1706, where his musical colleagues were opera composers Reinhard Keiser and Johann Mattheson. At the age of nineteen he composed his first opera, *Almira*, which was performed at the Hamburg opera house in 1705. Hamburg

From 1706 until the middle of 1710, Handel lived in Italy, where, soon recognized as one of the coming young composers, he associated with the leading patrons and musicians of Rome, Florence, Naples, and Venice. His chief patron during this period, Marquis Francesco Ruspoli, employed the young man as a musician-composer in Rome and at his country estates. Handel made the acquaintance of Corelli, Caldara, and the two Scarlattis; Domenico, the son, was exactly Handel's age, and the two became friends when they competed in a keyboard contest at Cardinal Pietro Ottoboni's palace. He also met Agostino Steffani, whose musical style, along with Corelli's and Alessandro Scarlatti's, exerted an important influence on him. Handel's chief compositions of the period were several Latin motets, an oratorio, a large number of Italian cantatas, and the opera *Agrippina*, successfully produced at Venice in 1709. Handel returned to Germany at the age of twenty-five to become music director at the electoral court of Hanover, but his years in Italy helped lay the foundations of his style. Italy

Handel in London

The appointment in Hanover turned out to be only an episode. Almost immediately Handel took a long leave of absence, visiting London in the season of 1710–11, when he enjoyed sensational success with his opera *Rinaldo*. In the autumn of 1712, again granted permission to go to London, he agreed to come back "within a reasonable time." He had still not returned two years later when his master, the elector of Hanover, was crowned King George I of England. For a while the truant music director hesitated to show his face at court. The legend is that Handel regained favor by composing and conducting a suite of pieces for wind instruments that were played as a surprise for the king during a boating party on the Thames. These pieces, or some like them, were published in 1740 under the title *Water Music*. Enjoying the patronage of the royal family, Lord Burlington, the duke of Chandos, and other influential personages, Handel settled down to a long and prosperous career in London.

Italian opera was in fashion. In 1718–19, about sixty wealthy gentlemen organized a joint stock company, called the Royal Academy of Music, to present operas to the London public. They engaged Handel and two Italian composers, Giovanni Bononcini (1670–1747) and Filippo Amadei (active 1690–1730). Bononcini, who had already produced many operas in Rome, Berlin, and Vienna, was for a time Handel's most serious rival in London. For the Royal Academy of Music, which flourished from 1720 to 1728, Handel composed some of his best operas, including *Radamisto* (1720), *Ottone* (1723), *Giulio Cesare* (1724), *Rodelinda* (1725), and *Admeto* (1727). Italian opera

The popular success of Gay's *The Beggar's Opera* in 1728 (see pages

444–45) proved that the English public was growing tired of Italian opera; in addition, the Academy began to have financial difficulties. In 1729, when it stopped producing operas, Handel and a partner took over the theater. However, a competing organization, the Opera of the Nobility, which featured the Neapolitan composer Nicola Porpora (1686–1768) and the highest-priced singers in Europe, so completely divided the London public that by 1737 both companies were nearly bankrupt. Handel's chief operas during this period were *Orlando* (1733) and *Alcina* (1735). The best of his later operas were the comic *Serse* (1738) and the satirical *Deidamia* (1741). In both he abandoned his weightier style for the melodious idiom newly popular in Italy. Neither was very successful at the time, but *Serse* became a favorite in modern theaters.

Oratorios

Despite repeated failures, Handel clung to the opera tradition. Only when subscriptions to the 1738–39 season were insufficient did he turn his attention elsewhere. He composed an oratorio, *Saul*, which had an English text and used a novel orchestra that included three trombones, a carillon, and double-bass timpani. The work was well received and given six performances during 1739. When invited to write *Messiah* for Dublin in 1741, Handel committed himself to the new genre of the oratorio in English. Oratorios, much less expensive to mount than operas, appealed to a potentially large middle-class public that had never felt at home with the aristocratic entertainment of opera in Italian. Handel was no stranger to dramatic music with English words, having composed the serenata *Acis and Galatea* (1718), the oratorio *Esther* (first performed as a masque about 1720, revised version in 1732), and a setting of Dryden's ode *Alexander's Feast* in 1736. By 1739, the Handelian oratorio on a biblical subject with choruses had taken shape with *Saul* and *Israel in Egypt*.

Public acclaim

After the success of *Messiah* in Dublin in 1742, Handel and John Rich, who had managed *The Beggar's Opera*, leased a theater to present oratorios every year during Lent. As an added attraction at these performances, the composer improvised at the organ during intermissions. The English public's enthusiastic response to these concerts laid the foundation for the immense popularity that made Handel's music the prevailing influence in British musical life for more than a century. The most notable of his twenty-six English oratorios beyond those already mentioned were *Semele*, on a mythological text by Congreve (originally written in 1709 as an opera libretto), and the biblical *Judas Maccabaeus* (1746) and *Jephtha* (1751).

The English came to regard Handel as a national institution, and with good reason. He passed all his mature life in London, becoming a naturalized British subject in 1726, and wrote all his major works for British audiences. He was the most imposing figure in English music during his lifetime, and the English public nourished his genius and remained loyal to his memory. His body was buried with public honors in Westminster Abbey. His imperious, independent nature made him a formidable presence—he was satirized as a glutton and a tyrant—but the rougher aspects of his personality were balanced by a sense of humor and redeemed by a generous, honorable, and fundamentally pious nature (see vignette).

CHARLES BURNEY ON HANDEL'S PERSONALITY

The figure of Handel was large, and he was somewhat corpulent, and unwieldy in his motions; but his countenance, which I remember as perfectly as that of any man I saw but yesterday, was full of fire and dignity; and such as impressed ideas of superiority and genius. He was impetuous, rough, and peremptory in his manners and conversation, but totally devoid of ill-nature or malevolence; indeed, there was an original humour and pleasantry in his most lively sallies of anger or impatience, which, with his broken English, were extremely risible. His natural propensity to wit and humour, and happy manner of relating common occurrences, in an uncommon way, enabled him to throw persons and things into very ridiculous attitudes. . . .

He knew the value of time too well to spend it in frivolous pursuits, or with futile companions, however high in rank. Fond of his art, and diligent in its cultivation, and the exercise of it, as a profession, he spent so studious and sedentary a life, as seldom allowed him to mix in society, or partake of public amusements. . . . Handel's general look was somewhat heavy and sour, but when he [*did*] smile, it was his sire the sun, bursting out of a black cloud. There was a sudden flash of intelligence, wit, and good humour, beaming in his countenance, which I hardly ever saw in any other.

From Charles Burney, *An Account of the Musical Performances in Westminster Abbey and the Pantheon. . . . 1784 in Commemoration of Handel* (London, 1785), pp. 31–37.

Suites and Sonatas

Handel's keyboard works include three sets of concertos for harpsichord or organ, two collections of suites for harpsichord (1720 and 1733), and a number of miscellaneous pieces. The suites contain not only the usual dance movements but also examples of most of the current keyboard genres of the time. The popular set of variations called *The Harmonious Blacksmith* (a title bestowed in the nineteenth century) appears in the fifth suite of the first collection. Handel composed some twenty solo sonatas and a smaller number of trio sonatas for various instruments. Corelli's influence can be heard in these works, but the sophisticated harmonies and the smooth, easy assurance, particularly in the Allegros, reflect a later Italian style.

The Concertos

Handel's most significant instrumental works are those for full orchestra, including the overtures to his operas and oratorios, the two suites known as *Water Music* (1717) and *Music for the Royal Fireworks* (1749), and, above all, the six concertos for woodwinds and strings (usually called the "Oboe Concertos") and twelve *Grand Concertos*, Opus 6, composed in 1739.

Opus 6 concertos

The concerti grossi of Opus 6 combine modern traits with retrospective elements, which predominate. Handel adopted Corelli's conception of a sonata da chiesa for full orchestra and the conventional slow–fast–slow–fast scheme of movements, including one fugal Allegro, but he often added a movement or two. The solo parts are not different in character from the tuttis; in fact, the concertino strings often play throughout in unison with the ripieno or else appear by themselves only for brief, trio-like interludes. The few extended passages for the solo violins retain the thematic material and style of the tutti passages. Only rarely does Handel imitate Vivaldi in giving decorative figuration to a solo violin (as he does in Concertos Nos. 3, 6, and 11). The serious, dignified bearing and the prevailing full contrapuntal texture of this music hark back to the earlier part of the century, when Handel was forming his style in Italy.

Concerto grosso No. 6 in G minor exemplifies the range of Handel's orchestral writing. An opening Larghetto e affettuoso is followed by a vigorous fugal Allegro, a fine example of a ripieno concerto movement. The second slow movement, in E♭, is a broad pastoral landscape in the form of a *musette en rondeau.* The next Allegro begins with a solidly constructed tutti and continues in the manner of Vivaldi with the first violin featured in independent solo figuration. The concerto closes with a short, minuetlike Allegro in the usual binary dance form, with a spare, three-voice homophonic texture. The variety in these concertos, the individual quality of the themes, the inexhaustible flow of invention, and the grand proportions of the works have assured the Opus 6 concertos a permanent place in the repertory.

The Operas

The English-speaking public has long thought of Handel almost exclusively as an oratorio composer. But he devoted thirty-five years to composing and directing operas, which contain as much memorable music as do his oratorios. In an age when opera was the main concern of ambitious musicians, Handel excelled among his contemporaries. During his lifetime, his operas were heard not only in London but in Germany and Italy as well.

Librettos

Handel's choice of librettos depended on many factors. Because his audience did not understand Italian, the cast he could assemble assumed greater importance, for Londoners cared more about hearing their favorite singers than about the subject matter. Still, the libretto had to inspire Handel's best musical inventions and expressions of feeling in the arias. He often chose a subject because he had seen another composer's setting and could envision ways of adapting it for a London production. Nicola Fago's *Radamisto,* which he saw in Florence in 1709, may have led him to adopt this subject in 1720, though with a different libretto; and Lotti's *Teofane,* performed in Dresden in 1719, may have inspired *Ottone* (1723). A patron's taste, such as Lord Burlington's classical bent, influenced the choice of *Teseo* (1713), a tragedy based on Quinault's *Thésée* set by Lully in 1675, or *Lucio Cornelio Silla* (1713), with its classical Roman plot, or *Amadigi di Gaula* (1715), another product of the French classical theater. A political motive can be detected in a few librettos. In

Muzio Scevola (1721) the defenders of Roman republicanism might represent the aristocratic supporters of the London Royal Academy. The title role of *Floridante* (1721) was identified with John Churchill, duke of Marlborough, and *Riccardo Primo* (1727) celebrated the coronation of George II by analogy to Richard the Lionhearted. These three texts were by Paolo Rolli, a London resident who was a protégé of the influential sponsors of opera.[6]

Subjects

The subjects of the operas are the usual ones of the time: tales of magic and marvelous adventure, such as those by Ariosto and Tasso revolving around the Crusades or, more often, episodes from the lives of Roman heroes freely adapted to include the maximum number of intense dramatic situations.

Musical organization

The action develops through dialogue set as *recitativo secco*, accompanied by harpsichord. Particularly stirring moments, such as soliloquies, are enhanced through *recitativo obbligato*, that is, accompanied by the orchestra. For these accompanied recitatives—as indeed for many other features of his operas—Handel found impressive models in the works of Alessandro Scarlatti and Francesco Gasparini. Solo da capo arias allow the characters to respond lyrically to their situations. Each aria represents a single specific mood or affection, or sometimes two contrasting but related affections. The two types of recitative are sometimes freely combined with short arias or ariosos to make large scene-complexes that recall the freedom of early seventeenth-century Venetian opera and at the same time foreshadow the methods of later composers, such as Gluck. Examples of such scene-complexes occur in *Orlando* (end of Act II) and, on a smaller scale, in *Giulio Cesare* (Act I, Scene 7, and Act III, Scene 4). Instrumental symphonies mark key moments in the plot, such as battles, ceremonies, or incantations, and a few operas include ballets. Ensembles larger than duets are rare, as are also choruses, and most of these are actually ensembles in choral style, with only one singer to a part.

Arias

The arias had to be allocated according to the importance of each member of the cast and had to display the scope of the singers' vocal and dramatic powers. These constraints still left the composer plenty of freedom. Like most of his contemporaries, Handel could easily turn out an opera that would enjoy the usual brief success, but he could also on occasion create a masterpiece like *Ottone* or *Giulio Cesare.* His scores are remarkable for the wide variety of aria types. They range from brilliant coloratura displays to sustained, sublimely expressive pathetic songs, such as the *Cara sposa* in *Rinaldo* or *Se pietà* in *Giulio Cesare.* Arias of regal grandeur with rich contrapuntal and concertato accompaniments alternate with simple, folklike melodies. The pastoral scenes are especially noteworthy examples of eighteenth-century nature painting. Not all of Handel's arias are in da capo form; those composed in the 1730s, particularly, utilize simpler, abbreviated forms.

Orchestral accompaniment

Some of Handel's arias are *all'unisono,* that is, the strings play in unison with the voice throughout. Others feature the tone-color of a particular instrument to set the mood, as the French horn does in Caesar's aria, "Va tacito e

6. For a consideration of these and other factors in Handel's choice of librettos, see Reinhard Strohm, *Essays on Handel and Italian Opera* (Cambridge, 1985), "Handel and His Italian Opera Texts," pp. 34–79.

Example 12.8 *Handel, Serse, Act I, Scene 3: Aria,* Và godendo vezzoso e bello

Happily flowing, graceful and pretty, the brook enjoys its liberty.

nascosto," in *Giulio Cesare,* in which both the instrument and voice imitate a hunting horn. In another aria from this opera, Cleopatra's "V'adoro pupille" (NAWM 83; CD 6 [22] / CD 2 ⟨55⟩), Handel divides the orchestra into soli and tutti in the manner of a concerto grosso, a technique Alessandro Stradella had pioneered in his oratorios performed in Rome. The concertino demands solo players: on oboe, two muted violins, viola, harp, viola da gamba, theorbo, bassoon, and cello. Handel scored the tutti orchestra for strings with oboes doubling muted violins. The concertino continually accompanies the voice, while the tutti orchestra punctuates and complements this accompaniment, except in the B-section of the aria, when it is silent.

Modern style

Toward the end of his operatic career, Handel turned more and more to the fashionable light melodic manner of the modern Italian composers, especially in *Serse* (1738) and *Deidamia* (1741). It is ironic that one of Handel's best-known pieces, the "Largo from Xerxes," made famous in instrumental transcriptions, is an aria in this atypical style. In Romilda's aria *Và godendo vezzoso e bello* (Example 12.8) in *Serse,* the clearly articulated two-measure phrases, simply accompanied, are worlds apart from the typical Baroque da capo aria. The flutes and violins echo the pretty tune but stay out of the way.

The Oratorios

Handel's English oratorios constituted a new genre that differs from the Italian oratorio and his own London operas. Hardly more than an opera on a sacred subject, the eighteenth-century Italian oratorio was presented in concert instead of on stage. Handel had written such a work, *La resurrezione* (1708), during his stay in Rome. In his English oratorios, he picked up some aspects of this tradition by setting dialogue as recitative and lyrical verses as arias. Most of these arias resemble his opera arias in form, musical style, the nature of musical ideas, and the technique of expressing the affections. As in the operas also, recitative prepares the mood of each aria. But Handel and his librettists brought elements into their oratorios that were foreign to Italian opera: from the English masque, the choral anthem, French classical drama, ancient Greek drama, and the German historia. Everything, of course, was adapted for the London environment with the result that Handel's oratorios are a genre in themselves.

Librettos

The Hebrew Scriptures and Apocryphal books were a storehouse of both history and mythology that was well known to middle-class Protestant England in the eighteenth century. All of Handel's biblical oratorios, and especially his most popular ones, were based on Old Testament stories (even *Messiah* has more text from the Old than from the New Testament). Moreover, such subjects as *Saul, Israel in Egypt, Judas Maccabaeus,* and *Joshua* had an appeal based on something besides familiarity with the ancient sacred narratives: in an era of prosperity and expanding empire, English audiences felt a kinship with the chosen people whose heroes triumphed with the special blessing of God.

Handel was selected to compose music for important state occasions. He wrote four anthems for the coronation of George II (1727), the Funeral Anthem for Queen Caroline (1737), the Te Deum in thanksgiving for an English military victory at Dettingen in 1743, and the *Fireworks Music* of 1749 celebrating the Peace of Aix-la-Chapelle. The oratorio *Judas Maccabaeus* (1747), like the *Occasional Oratorio* of the preceding year, honored the duke of Cumberland for his victory over the Jacobite rebels at Culloden. But even where there was no connection with a national occasion, many of Handel's oratorios struck a responsive patriotic note with the British public.

Oratorios were not church music; they were intended for the concert hall and were much closer to theatrical performances than to church services. Not all of Handel's oratorios dealt with sacred subjects. Some, such as *Semele* and *Hercules* (both 1744), are mythological; others, such as *Alexander's Feast* (1736), the *Ode for St. Cecilia's Day* (1739), and *The Triumph of Time and Truth* (1757)—Handel's last composition—are allegorical. The dramatic conception varies. *Susanna* (1748), *Theodora* (1749), and *Joseph and His Brethren* (1743) are virtual operas. Most of the biblical oratorios stayed close to the original narrative, but the biblical text was rewritten in recitatives (sometimes prose, sometimes rhymed verse), arias, and choruses—although *Israel in Egypt* (1739) tells the story of the Exodus entirely in the words of Scripture. *Messiah* (1742) also has a purely scriptural text but is the least typical of all Handel's oratorios. Instead of telling a story it unfolds as a series of contemplations on the Christian idea of redemption, beginning with Old Testament prophecies and going through the life of Christ to His final triumph over death.

Use of chorus

Beyond question Handel's most important innovation in the oratorios was his use of the chorus. To be sure, the chorus had its place in the Latin and Italian oratorios of Carissimi, but later oratorios had at most a few "madrigals" and ensembles sometimes marked "coro." Handel's early training had made him familiar with Lutheran choral music and with the south German combi-

■ *Autograph manuscript page from the chorus* How dark, O Lord, are Thy decrees, *from Handel's oratorio* Jeptha. *At the foot of the page Handel noted on February 13, 1751, that his weakening eyesight forced him to stop composing temporarily.* (LONDON, BRITISH LIBRARY. BY PERMISSION OF THE BRITISH LIBRARY)

nation of the chorus with orchestra and soloists. But the English choral tradition impressed him most profoundly. He fully captured this English musical idiom in the *Chandos* anthems, written for the duke of Chandos between 1718 and 1720—masterpieces of Anglican church music from which the composer frequently borrowed in his later works.

Choral Style

The monumental character of Handel's choral style fits the oratorio's emphasis on communal rather than individual expression. Where an opera had an aria, Handel often inserted a chorus to comment on the action, as in the choruses of Greek drama. The chorus in *Saul* (1739), "O fatal Consequence of Rage" (NAWM 84; CD 6 [27]), for example, reflects on the morality of the situation in a succession of three fugues, each ending with majestic homorhythmic passages. The first fugue is based on "Quos pretioso sanguine" from the Te Deum by Antonio Francesco Urio (ca. 1631–ca. 1719). Handel also borrowed from five other places in Urio's Te Deum for *Saul.*

Action choruses

Handel's oratorio choruses also participate in the action, as they do in *Judas Maccabaeus* and *Solomon.* The chorus may even narrate, as in *Israel in Egypt,* where the choral recitative *He sent a thick darkness* is remarkable for its unusual form, its strange modulations, and its pictorial writing.

Handel's borrowings

In borrowing thematic ideas or reworking pieces from other composers, living or dead, Handel followed a common practice of his day. Three duets and eleven of the twenty-eight choruses of *Israel in Egypt,* for example, were taken in whole or in part from the music of others, while four choruses were arrangements from earlier works by Handel himself. Other borrowings, although not on such an extensive scale, have been traced in many of Handel's compositions written after 1737. For his last oratorio, *Jephtha* (1752), he based several movements on subjects derived from a Mass by Franz Habermann (1706–1783). In the chorus *How dark, O Lord, are Thy decrees* in *Jephtha* (1752), which voices the sorrow and dismay of the Israelites—and by extension of the spectators—on Jephtha's forced sacrifice of his own daughter, one of the fugues is on a subject derived from Habermann's Mass. One moment midway in the fugue strikingly resembles the "Et in terra pax" of Habermann's Gloria (see Example 12.9a and b).

Example 12.9

a. *Handel,* Jephtha: *Act II,* How dark, O Lord

b. *Franz Habermann, Mass: Gloria*

c. *Handel,* Larghetto *from* How dark, O Lord

It has been conjectured that Handel resorted to borrowing as a means of overcoming the inertia that sometimes afflicted him when he was beginning a new work, especially after 1737, when he suffered a paralytic stroke and nervous collapse. However that may be, Handel cannot be charged with plagiarism because borrowing, transcribing, adapting, rearranging, and parodying were universal and accepted practices. When Handel borrowed, he more often than not repaid with interest, clothing the borrowed material with new beauty and preserving it for generations that would otherwise scarcely have known of its existence.

Musical symbolism

Musical symbolism is a conspicuous and endearing feature of Handel's choral writing. Word-painting and descriptive figures were universal at the time, but Handel often used these devices in especially felicitous ways. Many examples are found in *Israel in Egypt*: the somewhat literal representation of frogs, flies, lice, hail, and the other plagues in Egypt is amusing rather than impressive, but the profound and moving portrayal of *The people shall hear* lifts this chorus to a height hardly equaled elsewhere. One playful use of word-painting in *Messiah* is surprisingly apt, given that the music, up to the last few measures, was adapted from a frivolous Italian duet that Handel had recently composed. The chorus sings: "All we like sheep have gone astray [diverging melodic lines]; we have turned [a rapidly twisting, turning figure that never gets away from its starting point] every one to his own way" [stubborn insistence on a single repeated note]; but the point is revealed suddenly, with dramatic force, at the solemn coda, "And the Lord hath laid on Him the iniquity of us all." A parallel though less striking dramatic contrast is heard in the chorus *For unto us a child is born*. This music is taken from another part of the same Italian duet; the carefree roulades that celebrate the birth of the Redeemer lead up to the mighty Handelian hammerstrokes on the words "Wonderful, Counsellor, the Mighty God."

Compositional skill

Passages such as these reveal Handel the dramatist, the master of grandiose effects. He knew how to write effectively for a chorus in a style simpler than Bach's, less finely chiseled, less subjective, less consistently contrapuntal. He alternated passages in open fugal texture with solid blocks of harmony and set a melodic line in sustained notes against one in quicker rhythm. Everything lies well for the voices; at points where he demanded the maximum fullness of choral sound Handel brought the four parts tightly together, the basses and tenors high, the sopranos and altos in the middle register.

Summary

Handel's historical significance rests largely on his contribution to the living repertory of performed music. His music aged well because he adopted the devices that became important in the new style of the mid-eighteenth century. Handel's emphasis on melody and harmony, as compared to the more strictly contrapuntal procedures of Bach, allied him with the fashions of his time. As a choral composer in the grand style he had no peer. He was a consummate master of contrast, not only in choral music but in all types of compositions. In the oratorios he deliberately appealed to a middle-class audience, recognizing social changes that would have far-reaching effects on music.

Bibliography

Music Collections

Bach Johann Sebastian Bach, *Werke*, 61 vols. in 47 Jahrgänge (Leipzig: Bach-Gesellschaft, 1851–99; supp. 1926). Reprinted, except Jg. 47 (Ann Arbor: J. W. Edwards, 1947); in miniature format, 1969. *Neue Ausgabe sämtlicher Werke* (Kassel: Bärenreiter, 1954–). *Faksimile-Reihe Bachser Werke und Schriftstücke* (Leipzig: Deutscher Verlag für Musik, 1955–).

Christoph Wolff, ed., *J. S. Bach, Organ Chorales from the Neumeister Collection* (Yale University, MS. LM 4708), contains previously unknown organ chorales by Bach (Kassel: Bärenreiter; New Haven: Yale University Press, 1985).

Mass in B Minor, facs. and commentary, ed. Alfred Dürr (Kassel and New York: Bärenreiter, 1965). *Cantata No. 4, Christ lag in Todesbanden*, ed. Gerhard Herz (New York: Norton, 1967). *Cantata No. 140, Wachet auf*, ed. Gerhard Herz (New York: Norton, 1972), contains a table showing a revised chronology of Bach's vocal music; both are available in Norton Critical Scores. For translations of cantata texts, see Charles Sanford Terry, *J. S. Bach, Cantata Texts* (London: Constable & Co., 1926).

Wolfgang Schmieder, ed., *Thematisch-systematisches Verzeichnis der musikalischen Werke von Johann Sebastian Bach* (BWV), 2nd rev. and expanded ed. (Wiesbaden: Breitkopf & Härtel, 1990), is a complete systematic-thematic index of Bach's works, with references to the Bach Society edition and also to other standard modern editions. See also Hans-Joachim Schulze and Christoph Wolff, *Bach Compendium: Analytisch-bibliographisches Repertorium der Werke Johann Sebastian Bachs* (Leipzig and Dresden: Peters, 1985–), for source, bibliographic, and analytical information on Bach's entire output, supplementing the BWV.

May DeForest McAll, *Melodic Index to the Works of J. S. Bach* (New York: Peters, 1962) identifies BWV numbers of Bach's works if only the melody is known.

Handel Georg Friedrich Händel, *Werke*, ed. Friedrich Chrysander (Leipzig: Breitkopf & Härtel, 1858–1903; repr. Ridgewood, N.J.: Gregg International, 1965–66). This edition consists of Vols. 1–48, 50–94, and six vols. of supplements; Vols. 49 and 95–96 never appeared. *Hallische Händel-Ausgabe*, ed. Max Schneider and Rudolf Steglich (Kassel: Bärenreiter, 1955–). For a complete listing of Handel's compositions, see A. Craig Bell, *Chronological-Thematic Catalogue*, 2nd ed. (Darley, Eng.: The Grian-Aig Press, 1972); see also the thematic catalogue by Bernd Baselt in the *Händel-Handbuch*, Vols. 1–3 (Kassel: Bärenreiter, 1978–86).

Rameau *Rameau, Oeuvres complètes*, ed. Camille Saint-Saëns (Paris: A. Durand et fils, 1895–1924; repr. New York, 1968), 18 vols. in 20; incomplete. A new edition is projected.

Vivaldi A practical collected edition of his works is ed. Antonio Fanna (Rome: Edizioni Ricordi, 1947–); thematic catalogue of the instrumental works in this edition by A. Fanna, 2nd ed. (Milan: Edizioni Ricordi, 1986). There are several other thematic catalogues, including one which constitutes the second volume of Marc Pincherle, *Vivaldi* (Paris: Floury, 1948). The most definitive is Peter Ryom, *Verzeichnis der Werke Antonio Vivaldis*, 2nd ed. (Leipzig: VEB Deutscher Verlag für Musik, 1977). A new scholarly edition, which includes vocal works, is in preparation by the Istituto Italiano Antonio Vivaldi, ed. Paul Everett and Michael Talbott (Milan: Ricordi, 1982–).

For Further Reading

Bach A volume of bibliography from the Bach Yearbooks, 1905–84, has been compiled by Christoph Wolff, *Bach, Bibliographie: Nachdruck der Verzeichnisse des Schrifttums über Johann Sebastian Bach, Bach-Jahrbuch, 1905–84* (Kassel: Merseburger, 1985).

The older biographies of Bach, such as that by Spitta, are of limited use, since Bach research has progressed considerably from the time of their publication. See Friedrich Blume, "Outlines of a New Picture of Bach," in *Music and Letters* 44 (1963):214–27, and in GLHWM 6:28–41, which evaluates Bach research since 1950. Good general studies of Bach's life and works are Malcolm Boyd, *Bach* (New York: Schirmer Books, 1997), and Karl Geiringer, *Johann Sebastian Bach* (New York: Oxford University Press, 1966).

An invaluable documentary anthology is Hans David and Arthur Mendel, *The Bach Reader*, rev. and enl. by Christoph Wolff (New York: Norton, 1998); it contains in English translation important sources from which our knowledge of Bach's life and reputation is drawn, as well as essays on Bach's music and public reception.

On Bach and his family, see Karl Geiringer, *The Bach Family* (New York: Oxford University Press, 1954; repr. New York, 1971); Percy M. Young, *The Bachs, 1500–1850* (New York: Crowell, 1970); and C. Wolff et al., *The New Grove Bach Family* (New York: Norton, 1983).

Other books on Bach and his music: Barbara Schwendowius and Wolfgang Dömling, eds., *J. S. Bach, Life, Times, Influence* (Kassel: Bärenreiter, 1976); Laurence Dreyfus, *Bach and the Patterns of Invention* (Cambridge, Mass.: Harvard University Press, 1996); Robert L. Marshall, *The Compositional Process of J. S. Bach: A Study of the Autograph Scores of the Vocal Works* (Princeton: Princeton University Press, 1972); Frederick Neumann, *Ornamentation in Baroque and Post-Baroque Music, with Special Emphasis on J. S. Bach* (Princeton: Princeton University Press, 1978); Charles S. Terry, *Bach's Chorales*, 3 vols. (Cambridge: Cambridge University Press, 1917–21); Peter F. Williams, *The Organ Music of J. S. Bach*, 2 vols. (Cambridge: Cambridge University Press, 1980–84), which gives a piece-by-piece commentary; C. Wolff, *Bach: Essays on His Life and Music* (Cambridge, Mass.: Harvard University Press, 1991); R. L. Marshall, *The Music of Johann Sebastian Bach: The Sources, the Style, the Significance* (New York: Schirmer Books, 1989).

Articles of interest include R. L. Marshall, "Bach the Progressive," MQ 62 (1976): 313–57, and in GLHWM 6:149–93 which discusses the influence of Bach's Dresden contemporaries and the Italian early classic style; Frederick Neumann, "Bach: Progressive or Conservative, and the Authorship of the Goldberg Aria," MQ 71 (1985):281–94, in response to Marshall's article.

Handel Recommended books are Paul Henry Lang, *George Frideric Handel* (New York: Norton, 1966); Otto E. Deutsch, *Handel, a Documentary Biography* (New York and London: Adam and Charles Black, 1955), which also contains a large bibliography; H. C. Robbins Landon, *Handel and His World* (London: Weidenfeld & Nicolson, 1984); Gerald Abraham, ed., *Handel: A Symposium* (London: Oxford University Press, 1954), a collection of essays on Handel's life and music; *The New Grove Handel*, by Winton Dean and Anthony Hicks (New York: Norton, 1983).

On Handel's operas, see Winton Dean and J. Merrill Knapp, *Handel's Operas, 1704–1726* (Oxford and New York: Clarendon Press, 1987); W. Dean, *Handel and the Opera Seria* (Berkeley: University of California Press, 1969); Reinhard Strohm, *Essays on Handel and Italian Opera* (Cambridge: Cambridge University Press, 1985), which includes studies on A. Scarlatti and Vivaldi; Ellen Harris, *Handel and the Pastoral Tradition* (London: Oxford University Press, 1980); E. Harris, "The Italian in Handel," JAMS 33 (1980):468–500, which compares the musical styles of A. Scarlatti and Handel.

The long chapter, "Origin of the Italian Opera in England and Its Progress There during the Present Century," in Burney's *General History of Music* (Book 4, Chapter 6), includes a detailed account of Handel's operas in London and many observations on the music. This chapter is found in the second edition of Burney's work, Frank Mercer, ed., 2 vols. (London: G. T. Foulis, 1935), pp. 651–904.

On *Messiah,* see Robert Manson Myers, *Handel's 'Messiah,' a Touchstone of Taste* (New York: Macmillan, 1948); Jens Peter Larsen, *Handel's 'Messiah': Origins, Composition, Sources,* 2nd ed. (New York: Norton, 1972); W. Dean, *Handel's Dramatic Oratorios and Masques* (London: Oxford University Press, 1959).

Some detailed articles on Handel (e.g., Chandos Anthems, and Handel in Hanover) are in Peter Williams, ed., *Bach, Handel, Scarlatti: Tercentenary Essays* (Cambridge: Cambridge University Press, 1985).

A useful bibliographic guide is Mary Ann Parker-Hale, *George Frideric Handel* (New York: Garland, 1985).

Rameau *Complete Theoretical Writings,* ed. Erwin Jacobi, 6 vols. (AIM, Series Misc. 3); *Treatise on Harmony,* trans. with intro. and notes by Philip Gossett (New York: Dover, 1971). The best comprehensive study in English is Cuthbert Girdlestone, *Jean-Philippe Rameau, His Life and Work* (New York: Dover, 1969). See also Thomas Christensen, *Rameau and Musical Thought in the Enlightenment* (Cambridge: Cambridge University Press, 1993); James Anthony, *French Baroque Music from Beaujoyeulx to Rameau,* rev., expanded ed. (Portland, Ore.: Amadeus Press, 1997); and Norman Demuth, *French Opera: Its Development to the Revolution* (Sussex: Artemis Press, 1963).

Vivaldi Marc Pincherle, *Vivaldi, Genius of the Baroque,* trans. Christopher Hatch (New York: Norton, 1957); Michael Talbot, *Vivaldi* (London: Dent, 1978); H. C. Robbins Landon, *Vivaldi: Voice of the Baroque* (London: Thames and Hudson, 1993); *Opera and Vivaldi,* Michael Collins and Elise Kirk, eds. (Austin: University of Texas Press, 1984). The best comprehensive study is Walter Kolneder, *Vivaldi,* trans. Bill Hopkins (London: Faber & Faber, 1970; Berkeley: University of California Press, 1971); W. Kolneder, ed., Kurt Michaelis, trans., *Antonio Vivaldi, Documents of His Life and Works* (New York: Heinrichshofen/ C.F. Peters, 1982).

For an eighteenth-century view of the Vivaldi concerto, see J. J. Quantz, *Essay on a Method for Playing the Transverse Flute* (1752), trans. Edward R. Reilly (New York: Schirmer Books, 1966); (excerpts in SRrev, pp. 799–806/5:65–73).

CHAPTER 13

SONATA, SYMPHONY, AND OPERA IN THE EARLY CLASSIC PERIOD

THE ENLIGHTENMENT

The movement known as the Enlightenment challenged established systems of thought and behavior. In the sphere of religion, it valued individual faith and practical morality more than the church as an institution. In philosophy and science, the emphasis on reasoning from experience and from careful observation favored the study of the human mind, the emotions, social relations, and organizations. In social behavior, naturalness was preferred to artificiality and formality. The belief that individuals had rights challenged the authority of the state. With the recognition that all people were equal and with the adoption of universal education, many believed that class privilege would disappear. Most important, the Enlightenment stood for the conviction that reason and knowledge could solve social and practical problems.

Religion, philosophical systems, science, the arts, education, the social order, all were being judged by how they contributed to the well-being of the individual. Some declared that the highest good was the harmonious development of a person's inborn capacities. Francis Hutcheson (1694–1746), in his treatise *Concerning Moral Good and Evil*, defined the ethical ideal as "the greatest happiness for the greatest numbers."

The *philosophes*

The French *philosophes* (as they were called), such as Rousseau, Montesquieu, and Voltaire, were truly social reformers rather than philosophers. They reacted to the conditions they saw around them and promoted social change. They developed doctrines about individual rights—some of which are incorporated in the American Declaration of Independence and Constitution—in response to the terrible inequalities between the condition of the

TIMELINE: THE ENLIGHTENMENT AND THE EARLY CLASSIC PERIOD

1750 1760 1770 1780 1790 1800

- 1740 Maria Theresa crowned Holy Roman Empress
- **1742 C. P. E. Bach, *Prussian* Sonatas for keyboard**
- 1745 Francis Stephen of Lorraine elected Holy Roman Emperor
- **1750 Death of J. S. Bach**
- 1751 First volume of *Encyclopédie* published
- **1752 Pergolesi, *La serva padrona* in Paris**
- ***1752 Querelle des bouffons***
- **1755 Graun, *Der Tod Jesu***
- 1757 Burke, *A Philosophical Inquiry*
- 1759 Voltaire, *Candide*
- 1760–1820 Reign of George III of England
- **1762 Gluck, *Orfeo ed Euridice* in Vienna**
- 1762 Rousseau, *Le contrat social*
- 1764 Winckelmann, *Geschichte der Kunst des Altertums*
- 1765 Joseph II becomes Holy Roman Emperor and co-ruler with Maria Theresa
- 1770 Gainsborough, *The Blue Boy*
- **1774 Gluck, *Orphée et Euridice* in Paris**
- 1774 First Continental Congress in Philadelphia
- 1774–92 Reign of Louis XVI, king of France
- 1775–83 American Revolution
- **1776 Sir John Hawkins, *A General History of the Science and Practice of Music***
- **1776 Charles Burney, *A General History of Music***
- 1776 Declaration of Independence
- 1776 Smith, *The Wealth of Nations*
- **1778 La Scala opera house opens, Milan**
- 1780 Death of Maria Theresa; Joseph II sole Habsburg ruler
- 1781 Kant, *Critique of Pure Reason*
- **1785 Mozart, Haydn *Quartets***
- **1787 Mozart, *Don Giovanni***
- 1788 Gibbon, *Decline and Fall of the Roman Empire*
- 1789–94 French Revolution
- **1791 Death of Mozart**
- 1791 Boswell, *The Life of Samuel Johnson*
- **1791 Haydn, first *London* Symphonies**
- **1799 Beethoven, First Symphony**
- 1800 David, *Madame Récamier*

■ *While opera had found a home in public theaters, spectacular courtly productions continued for special occasions. One such celebration took place at Naples in 1749 on the birth of the first son to Don Carlos of Bourbon, king of the two Sicilies and later Charles III of Spain. A serenata—an elaborate cantata—was staged, bringing together some of the most famous singers of the time, including the contralto Vittoria Tesi (La Moretta) and the castrati Gaetano Majorano (Caffarelli) and Gioacchino Conti (Gizziello), whose duet was the hit of the evening. A hall in the royal palace was transformed into a theater, with a pit for a large orchestra. The serenata was* Il sogno di Olimpia *(The Dream of Olympia), music by Giuseppe di Majo, libretto by Raniero de Calzabigi. The engraving is from* Narrazione delle solenni reali feste *(Naples, 1799).*
(BEINECKE RARE BOOK AND MANUSCRIPT LIBRARY, YALE UNIVERSITY)

common people and that of the privileged classes in Europe. This social criticism was particularly sharp in France during the years before the Revolution.

Science

Advances in the application of scientific discoveries affected not only industry and commerce but the arts as well. Rameau, for example, had based his theories of harmony and tuning on observed natural phenomena. But he was not enough of a scientist or mathematician to see the flaws in some of his rationalizations. His theories were criticized on physical and mathematical grounds, by the geometrician Jean Le Rond d'Alembert (see page 384), the naturalist Benjamin Stillingfleet (1702–1771), and the mathematician Antonio Eximeno (1729–1808). Although Rameau's analyses of chordal structure and harmonic progression survived the challenge, their pseudo-scientific underpinning was generally repudiated.

Aspects of Eighteenth-Century Life

Cosmopolitanism

The eighteenth century was a cosmopolitan age. Partly because of marriages between powerful families, foreign-born rulers abounded—German kings in England, Sweden, and Poland; a Spanish king in Naples; a French duke in Tuscany; a German princess (Catherine the Great) as empress of Russia. Intellectuals and artists traveled freely: the Frenchman Voltaire sojourned at the French-speaking court of Frederick II (the Great) of Prussia, the Italian poet Metastasio worked at the German imperial court in Vienna, while the German writer F. M. von Grimm gained prominence in Parisian literary and musical circles. The humanity that all people shared mattered more than national and linguistic differences, at least for those who could travel beyond their native region. Musical life reflected this cosmopolitan culture. German symphony composers were active in Paris, and Italian opera composers and singers worked in what are now Austria and Germany, in Spain, England, Russia, and France. The flutist Johann Joachim Quantz, writing from Berlin in 1752, proposed that the ideal musical style was made up of the best features of the music of all nations (see vignette, page 424). "Today there is but one music in all of Europe . . . this universal language of our continent," declared the composer and critic Michel-Paul-Guy de Chabanon in 1785.[1]

Vienna, an international center

Eighteenth-century Vienna is a striking example of an international cultural center. Between 1745 and 1765, the emperor was a Frenchman, Francis Stephen of Lorraine. The imperial poet was the Italian Pietro Metastasio. A German, Johann Adolph Hasse, composed operas in Italian set to Metastasio's librettos, sometimes for state occasions. The manager of the court theaters was Count Giacomo Durazzo, a diplomat from Italy. An imported French company mounted a regular season of *opéra comique*. French-style ballets were also popular, though the music tended to be by local composers, among them Gluck, whose partner in operatic reform was Raniero de Calzabigi, another Italian. The composer Giuseppe Bonno, born in Vienna but trained in Naples, became imperial Kapellmeister in 1774. The weekly concerts he conducted at the Palais Rofrano featured as soloists the soprano Caterina Gabrielli and the violinist Gaetano Pugnani, both Italians, and the Belgian Pierre van Maldere. The most influential musician in Vienna during the last quarter of the century was Antonio Salieri, who had been brought there from Venice at the age of fifteen. He eventually succeeded Florian Gassmann (1729–1774) as imperial court composer and conductor of Italian opera, a post he then held for thirty-six years. A program of Germanization begun in 1776 was unpopular and failed, and Italian opera was restored in 1783 under the guise of *opera buffa*. This mix of cultures underlay the phenomenon that has been called, not altogether appropriately, the "Viennese" Classical style.

Humanitarianism

The age of Enlightenment was humanitarian as well as cosmopolitan. Rulers not only patronized arts and letters, they also promoted social reform. The eighteenth century was a time of enlightened despots: Frederick the Great of Prussia, Catherine the Great of Russia, Holy Roman Emperor Joseph II, and (in the early part of his reign) Louis XVI of France.

Freemasonry

Freemasonry, built on humanitarian ideals and a longing for universal brotherhood, spread rapidly throughout Europe and numbered among its adherents kings (Frederick the Great and Joseph II), poets (Goethe), and composers (Haydn and Mozart).

1. Michel-Paul-Guy de Chabanon, *De la musique considérée en elle-même et dans ses rapports avec la parole* . . . (Paris, 1785), p. 97.

J. J. QUANTZ ON THE SUPERIORITY OF A NATIONALLY MIXED STYLE

In a style that consists, like the present German one, of a mix of the styles of different peoples, every nation finds something familiar and unfailingly pleasing. Considering all that has been discussed about the differences among styles, we must vote for the pure Italian style over the pure French. The first is no longer as solidly grounded as it used to be, having become brash and bizarre, and the second has remained too simple. Everyone will therefore agree that a style blending the good elements of both will certainly be more universal and more pleasing. For a music that is accepted and favored by many peoples, and not just by a single land, a single province, or a particular nation, must be the very best, provided it is founded on sound judgment and a healthy attitude.

Johann Joachim Quantz, *Versuch einer Anweisung, die Flöte traversiere zu spielen* (Berlin: J. F. Voss, 1752), Chapter 18, § 89.

Mozart's *Die Zauberflöte* (The Magic Flute) and Schiller's *Ode to Joy* reflect the eighteenth-century humanitarian movement.

Public pursuit of learning

The pursuit of learning and the love of art became more widespread, particularly among the expanding middle class. This growing interest made new demands on writers and artists that affected both the subject matter and its manner of presentation. Philosophy, science, literature, and the fine arts all began to address a general public that went beyond a select group of experts and connoisseurs. Popular treatises were written with an eye to bringing culture within the reach of all, while novelists and playwrights began depicting everyday people with everyday emotions. Powerful support for this popularization came from the "back to nature" movement, which prized sentiment in literature and the arts.

Public concerts

As private patronage declined, a modern audience for music emerged. Public concerts competed with the older-style private concerts and academies. In Paris, the composer and oboist Anne Danican Philidor (1681–1728) founded the *Concert spirituel* series in 1725, which lasted until 1790; he also started the more secular but short-lived *Concerts français* in 1727. In 1763, J. A. Hiller began a concert series in Leipzig, which continued after 1781 as the famous Gewandhaus concerts. Similar concert organizations were founded in Vienna (1771) and in Berlin (1790). Concert societies had flourished in London sporadically since 1672. In Dublin a music hall that opened in 1741 saw the first performance of *Messiah* the following year. At Oxford an auditorium designed for concerts, the Holywell Music Room, opened in 1748.

Publishing for amateurs

As they had in the past, music publishers catered mainly to amateurs; in addition, much music was issued in periodicals. Amateur musicians naturally demanded and bought music that was easy to understand and to play, and they also became interested in reading about music and discussing it. After the middle of the century, magazines devoted to musical news, reviews, and criticism began to appear. Not all the writing was for popular consumption: the first universal histories of music were written then, and the first collection of medieval treatises on music was published.

Eighteenth-Century Musical Taste

What people in the mid- and later eighteenth century wanted, according to its leading critics, might be described as follows: the language of music should be universal, that is, not limited by national boundaries; music should be noble as well as entertaining; it should be expressive within the bounds of decorum; and it should be "natural"—free of needless technical complications and capable of immediately pleasing any sensitive listener.

Plurality of styles

Still, old styles yielded only gradually to new styles, and the old and the new existed side by side. Works typical of the new—Pergolesi's comic opera *La serva padrona* (see NAWM 85), Sammartini's symphonies, overtures, and concertos (see NAWM 90), and some sonatas of C. P. E. Bach (1714–1788; Examples 13.2 and 13.8 and NAWM 94)—were being written in the 1730s and 1740s at the same time as Bach's B-minor Mass and *Goldberg* Variations or Handel's *Messiah*. Another inconsistency of this age was that despite their cosmopolitanism, intellectuals loved to debate the relative merits of various national musical styles. In every country new national forms of opera sprouted that would later blossom in the Romantic era.

Terminology in the Classic Period

Several terms have been used to describe the styles that flourished in the early Classic period beginning around 1730: *classic*, *classical*, *rococo*, *galant*, and *empfindsam*. Of these, *rococo* has lost favor, and only *galant* and *empfindsam*

Concert at Vauxhall pleasure gardens, where for a fee the public could enjoy music and other entertainment outdoors. Here Mrs. Weischel sings from the "Moorish-Gothick" temple, accompanied by the orchestra behind her, while Dr. Johnson, Boswell, and others eat in the supper box below. Watercolor (ca. 1784) by Thomas Rowlandson. (PRINT COLLECTION, MIRIAM AND IRA D. WALLACH DIVISION OF ARTS, PRINTS & PHOTOGRAPHS. THE NEW YORK PUBLIC LIBRARY, ASTOR, LENOX AND TILDEN FOUNDATIONS)

■ *Engraving by Daniel Nikolaus Chodowiecki (1769) of a chamber ensemble consisting of a singer, two violins, viola, cello, and harpsichord. The presence of a woman among the performers and the similarity of dress and wigs worn by the musicians and listeners suggest a group of amateurs.* (KUNSTSAMMLUNG DER VESTE COBURG)

were current in the period itself. This, of course, does not preclude our adopting the others, if they can be shown to be useful or fitting.

Classic

Classic has been applied most narrowly to the mature styles of Haydn and Mozart and more broadly to music of a period that extends from the 1720s to around 1800. The term as applied to music came by way of analogy to Greek and Roman art: at its best, classic music reached a consistently high standard, possessing the qualities of noble simplicity, equilibrium, perfection of form, diversity within unity, seriousness, and freedom from excesses of ornamentation and frills. We find these qualities most evident in the music of Gluck, Haydn, and Mozart, but we should not make the mistake of viewing the mid-eighteenth century composers merely as their lesser forerunners.

A Viennese school?

Some authors have viewed these three composers as the core of a "Viennese school" and their manner a "Viennese Classical style." Neither the notion of a monolithic Classic style nor the existence of a Viennese school of the eighteenth century will withstand close scrutiny[2]—there was too great a variety of

2. See the critique of this terminology in the chapter "Haydn's Maturity and the 'Classical Style'" in James Webster, *Haydn's "Farewell" Symphony and the Idea of Classical Style* (Cambridge: Cambridge University Press, 1991).

personal and regional styles and too much stylistic diversity among the various musical genres, such as opera and church music. And what was produced around Vienna was not always distinguishable from what came out of other European centers. Yet it is convenient and appropriate to call those years—roughly 1730 to 1815—the Classic period, and the label has gained acceptance. To be sure, the boundaries of the Classic period overlap with the Baroque and Romantic periods. For, while in Italy the manners of writing characteristic of the Baroque were dying out in the 1720s, particularly in the opera, they were very much alive in France, England, and some parts of Germany.

Rococo

Rococo has been used for some music of the early decades of this period. The term originally described a style of architecture that softened the heavier, more monumental, more angular forms of the post-Renaissance period with curved arabesques (*rocaille* or "rockwork"), especially in France at the end of the seventeenth century. The character pieces of François Couperin, with their refined ornamentation, may be seen as counterparts to the movement in architecture.

Galant

The French term *galant* was widely used for the courtly manner in literature and in titles suggesting courtly flirtation, as in the opéra-ballet *L'Europe galante* (1697) by André Campra (1660–1744). It was a catchword for everything that was considered modern, smart, chic, smooth, easy, and sophisticated. In their writings, C. P. E. Bach, Marpurg, Quantz, and later Kirnberger distinguish between the learned or strict style of contrapuntal writing and the freer, more chordal *galant* style (see vignette). The latter was characterized by

JOHANN PHILIPP KIRNBERGER (1721–1783) ON THE *GALANT* AND *EMPFINDSAM* STYLES, CA. 1760

In the past century, through the introduction of the opera and the concerto, music has received a new impetus. The arts of harmony are beginning to be pushed forward, and more melismatic ornaments are being introduced into singing. Thereby the so-called *galant* or free and light style and a much greater variety of beat and movement have gradually appeared. It cannot be denied that the melodic language of the emotions has gained extraordinarily thereby. . . . Certainly much has been gained in fire and liveliness and other manifold shades of feeling through the multiplicity of the new melodic invention and even through clever transgressions of the strict harmonic rules. But only great masters know how to take advantage of them.

Doubtless the Italians must be thanked for the delicate and very supple genius and the fine sensibility (*Empfindsamkeit*) of the music of recent times. But most of what has corrupted good taste has also come out of Italy, particularly the dominance of melodies that say nothing and merely tickle the ear.

Johann Philipp Kirnberger, in J. G. Sulzer, *Allgemeine Theorie der Schönen Künste* (Biel, 1777), s.v. "Musik" 3:438–39.

an emphasis on melody made up of short-breathed, often repeated motives organized in two-, three-, and four-bar phrases. These combined into larger periods, lightly accompanied with simple harmony, and punctuated by frequent cadences. The *galant* style is found in the early operatic arias of Leonardo Vinci (ca. 1696–1730), Leonardo Leo (1694–1744), Pergolesi, and Hasse; the keyboard music of Baldassare Galuppi (1706–1785); and the chamber music of Giovanni Battista Sammartini (1701–1775).

Empfindsamkeit

Empfindsamkeit is another term associated with the music of the mid-eighteenth century (see vignette). This German noun and the adjective *empfindsam* derive from the verb *empfinden*, to feel. *Empfindsamkeit*, which translates as "sentimentality" or "sensibility," is a quality associated with the refined passion and melancholy that typifies some slow movements and obbligato recitatives in particular. Characterized by surprising turns of harmony, chromaticism, nervous rhythmic figures, and rhapsodically free speechlike melody, it is found, for example, in certain late concertos of Vivaldi (see NAWM 77), in such works as Pergolesi's *Stabat Mater*, Graun's *Der Tod Jesu*, and, allied with the *galant* idiom, in C. P. E. Bach's keyboard sonatas and fantasies (see NAWM 91).

New Concepts of Melody, Harmony, and Form

The focus on melody in the new eighteenth-century style led to a linear kind of syntax that contrasts sharply with the motivic variation and thorough-bass accompaniment characteristic of earlier styles. J. S. Bach, for example, would announce the musical idea of a movement—a melodic-rhythmic subject embodying the basic affection—at the outset. This material was then spun out, with relatively infrequent and usually inconspicuous cadences, and with sequential repetition of phrases as a principal constructive device. The result was either a highly integrated movement without sharp contrasts, or (as in many Vivaldi concertos) a formal pattern of contrasts between thematic tutti and nonthematic solo sections. In either case, the phrase structure was usually so irregular that there was no pronounced feeling of musical *periodicity*. Such periodicity characterizes the newer styles, in which the melodic flow is broken up by resting points that divide it into, for example, antecedent and consequent phrases. By analogy with verbal composition, a musical unit made up of shorter phrases was considered a period, and a composition as a succession of such periods.

Melodic periodicity

Harmonic periodicity

Thus musical ideas, rather than being persistently spun out, were articulated through distinct phrases, typically two or four measures in length (but also frequently three, five, or six measures). This technique creates a structure marked by frequent full and half cadences and integrated through motivic correspondences. It was natural, then, to compare a melody to a sentence or a paragraph and to think of a musical composition as equivalent to prose or speech. (See the revealing parallels between oratory and music drawn by Johann Nikolaus Forkel [1749–1818] in the vignette.)

As in the treatment of melody, the continuously driving harmonic motion typical of the older styles is divided into a series of stable or even static mo-

JOHANN NIKOLAUS FORKEL ON ORATORY AND MUSIC

An orator would behave unnaturally and contrary to the goals of edifying, persuading, and moving [an audience] by giving a speech without first determining what is to be the main idea [*Hauptsatz*], the secondary ideas [*Nebensätze*], the objections and refutations of the same, and the proofs. . . .

As musical works of any substantial length are nothing other than speeches by which one seeks to move the listener to a certain empathy and to certain emotions, the rules for the ordering and arrangement of ideas are the same as in an actual oration. And so one has, in both, a main idea, supporting secondary ideas, dissections of the main idea, refutations, doubts, proofs, and reiterations. Similar means to our end (in the musical sense) must be used. This order and sequence of the individual sections is called the aesthetic ordering of the ideas. A musical work in which this ordering is so arranged that all thoughts mutually support and reinforce one another in the most advantageous way possible, is well ordered.

From *Allgemeine Geschichte der Musik* (Leipzig: Schwickert, 1788–1801), I, 50, adapted from the translation in Mark Evan Bonds, *Wordless Rhetoric: Musical Form and the Metaphor of the Oration* (Cambridge, Mass.: Harvard University Press, 1991), p. 123.

ments. Consequently, harmonic change slows down and modulations are less adventuresome. However, a great deal of bustling activity occurs during these relatively slow-moving and conventional harmonies.

One of the most widely used devices of mid-eighteenth-century keyboard music, the *Alberti bass,* animated the simple harmonies that accompanied the new, *galant*-style melody. Named for the Italian composer Domenico Alberti (ca. 1710–1740), who used it frequently (see Example 13.1), this device broke each of the underlying chords into a simple repeating pattern of short notes that produced a discreet chordal background, setting off the melody to advantage. Even Haydn, Mozart, Beethoven, and others well into the nineteenth century favored the handy Alberti bass.

Alberti bass

Example 13.1 *Domenico Alberti,* VII sonate per cembalo, *Op. I (London, 1748), Sonata III, Allegro ma non tanto*

MUSICAL RHETORIC IN DEPTH

In the first decades of the eighteenth century, numerous authors—among them Johann Mattheson (1681–1764), who called music "an oration in tones" (*Klangrede*), and Johann David Heinichen (1683–1729)—taught the subtle art of melodic invention and elaboration through methods modeled on verbal rhetoric. The most thorough of the guides to melodic composition based on rhetorical principles is the section on the "mechanical rules of melody" in volume 2 of the *Versuch einer Anleitung zur Composition* (Introductory Essay on Composition, 1787) by Heinrich Christoph Koch (1749–1816). Here the student is shown how to construct a melody by joining short melodic thoughts or incises to form phrases, and phrases to form periods, separating these units with "resting points of the spirit" (*Ruhe-puncte des Geistes*). He states that this kind of organization is necessary to make a melody intelligible and capable of moving our feelings, just as the sentences and clauses that break up a speech make it easier to follow the train of thought.

Koch likened the components of a musical phrase to a subject and predicate. In Example 13.2, Koch's theory is applied to the opening of the third movement of the Sonata in B♭ by Carl Philipp Emanuel Bach (1714–1788) H. 32,[3] dating from 1742.

As in a sentence, the subject is completed by the predicate. The first incise (Koch: *Einschnitt*) closes weakly and is followed by a rest; the second incise completes the thought with a more secure ending on a note of the tonic triad, forming a "I-phrase" (called *Grundabsatz* to distinguish it from a "V-phrase" or *Quintabsatz* ending on the triad of the fifth degree).[4] The two incises are linked by the bass motion up a fourth and the melodic motion down a third plus a step, as well as by the motive labeled "x" in Example 13.2. Because of the hesitation after the first incise, what could have been a four-measure phrase is extended to five measures. The subject and predicate are then varied, elaborated, and intensified through higher pitch in measures 5 to 10, completing a second I-phrase.

Bach then constructs a new incise from motive "x" and borrows the left hand's rhythm from measures 4–5. This time the antecedent incise is answered without hesitation to make a four-measure phrase ending at measure 14 on C, a note in the dominant triad, making this a V-phrase. Repetition in a higher register intensifies this phrase, which closes on the dominant to complete the period.

Like a skilled orator, Bach held to his subject, reinforcing it with repetition and new arguments and carefully arranging his thoughts to make them intelligible and at the same time persuasive and moving.

3. C. P. E. Bach's sonatas are identified through the numbers in E. Eugene Helm, *Thematic Catalogue of the Works of Carl Philipp Emanuel Bach* (New Haven: Yale University Press, 1989) or, in older sources, by the numbers in Alfred Wotquenne, *Verzeichnis der Werke Ph. E. Bachs* (Leipzig, 1905).
4. This English terminology is based on the translation by Nancy Kovaleff Baker in Heinrich Christoph Koch, *Introductory Essay on Composition: The Mechanical Rules of Melody, Sections 3 and 4* (New Haven: Yale University Press, 1983).

Example 13.2 *Carl Philipp Emanuel Bach, Sonata in B♭,* Württemberg *Sonata No. 4, H. 32 (Wq. 48/4): Allegro (third movement)*

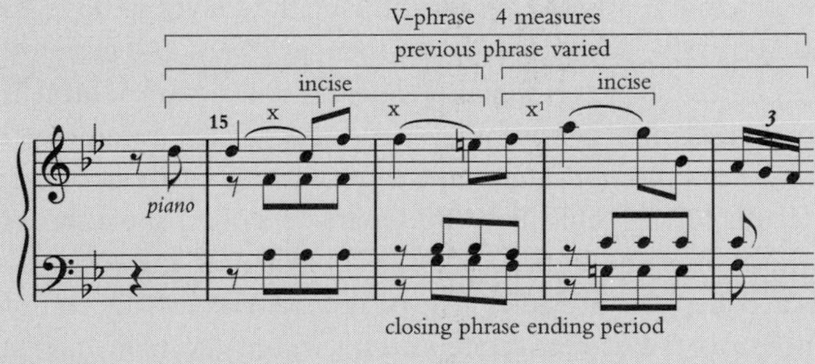

Emotional contrasts

Composers writing in the new manner of the eighteenth century still constructed movements based on related keys but abandoned the older idea of expressing one basic affection. Instead, they began to introduce contrasts between the various parts of a movement or even within the themes themselves, while retaining a certain unity of mood. Contemporaneously, natural philosophers also changed the way they conceived the emotional life of an individual. No longer believing that a person once aroused to, say, anger or fear remained in that affection until moved by some stimulus to a different state, they now observed that feelings were in a constant state of flux, jostled by associations that might take unpredictable turns. Daniel Webb spoke of the pleasure experienced "not, as some have imagined, the result of any fixed or permanent condition of the nerves and spirits, but from a succession of impressions, and greatly augmented by sudden or gradual transitions from one kind of strain of vibrations to another."[5] Composers stopped trying to sweep passive but willing listeners into a state of religious fervor or sympathetic identification with a character on stage. Instead, they now expected listeners to meet them halfway, to follow the musical thought, and to understand it as if it were a kind of verbal discourse. Listening to a piece of music could thus be a daring exploration of different related or even opposed feelings.

OPERA

Many of the stylistic traits associated with the Classic period had their origin in the Italian musical theater of the first decades of the eighteenth century. Because tradition weighed less heavily on comic opera, it was more hospitable to innovations than serious opera.

Early Italian Comic Opera

Opera buffa is one of the terms used in eighteenth-century Italy for comic opera; other terms were *dramma giocoso* (jocular drama), *dramma comico*, and *commedia in musica*. An *opera buffa* was a full-length work with six or more singing characters and, unlike comic opera in other countries, was sung throughout. It served a moral purpose by caricaturing the foibles of both aristocrats and commoners, vain ladies, miserly old men, awkward and clever servants, deceitful husbands and wives, pedantic lawyers and notaries, bungling physicians, and pompous military commanders. These often resemble the stock characters of the *commedia dell'arte*, the improvised comedy popular in Italy from the sixteenth century on. The comic characters often spoke or sang in a dialect, as they did in some of the Venetian comedies, or the entire play might be in the local dialect, as in Naples. The comic cast was usually complemented by a number of serious characters around whom the main plot revolved and who interacted with the comic characters, particularly in amorous intrigues. The dialogue was set in rapidly delivered recitative that was accompanied by the keyboard only.

Arias

The arias in the comic operas are made up of short tuneful phrases, often repeated, accompanied by simple harmonies, and organized into tidy periods. One of the pioneers of this style was Leonardo Vinci. His *Le zite 'ngalera* (The

5. Daniel Webb, *Observations on the Correspondence between Poetry and Music* (London: J. Dodsley, 1769), p. 47.

Spinsters in the Galley), with a libretto in Neapolitan dialect by Bernardo Saddumene, was premiered in Naples in 1722. It is one of the few early comic operas that survive complete. Many of Vinci's arias in this work are substantial—in da capo form, accompanied by a four-part string ensemble—while others are brief and supported only by continuo. An example of the latter type is the aria *T'aggio mmidea* (Example 13.3), which opens a scene between Belluccia, who is disguised as a man, and Ciommatella, a young woman who has fallen in love with "him." It is constructed of one-measure

Example 13.3 *Leonardo Vinci,* Le zite 'ngalera: *Act I, Scene 11,* T'aggio mmidea

Belluccia: I envy you, beautiful bird! You disport yourself among the branches, you sing, you want to hide. And I dress up in feathers, Ciommatella: Why in feathers? Belluccia: Ciomma, what's the use? I told you why, but you cast my words to the sea; you are truly hard-headed.

phrases in antecedent-consequent pairs (measures 4–5). But some of the phrases are extended (measures 6–7) or interrupted (measure 9), propelling the melody and its text directly into a recitative dialogue. The modulation to the dominant that ushers in the recitative is momentarily delayed by a deceptive cadence on the lowered sixth degree of the new key (measure 12). These techniques help to overcome the static effect of a series of balanced phrases with text repetitions and result in a dynamic melody that moves the drama forward.

Intermezzo

Another important type of Italian comic opera, the *intermezzo*, originated in the custom of presenting short comic musical interludes between the acts of a serious opera or play. These intermezzi contrasted sharply with the grand and heroic manners of the principal drama, sometimes even parodying its excesses. The plots were mostly situation comedies involving a few ordinary people, who sang, as in serious opera, recitatives and arias.

Pergolesi, *La serva padrona*

Giovanni Battista Pergolesi (1710–1736) was an early master of the intermezzo. One of the most original composers in the early Classic style, he also wrote important *opere serie.* Pergolesi wrote *La serva padrona* (The Maid as Mistress), for soprano, bass (a third character is mute), strings, and continuo, to be performed with his own *Il prigionier superbo* on September 5, 1733, in Naples. Its performance in Paris in 1752 set off the *Querelle des bouffons* (see page 442).

A scene in which Serpina, the maid, warns her boss and would-be lover, Uberto, that she is about to marry the mute character, Vespone, displays the extraordinary aptness and nimbleness of Pergolesi's music (see NAWM 85; CD 7 [1] / 3 ⟨1⟩). Serpina delivers the news in simple recitative, to which Uberto reacts first in an agitated *obbligato* recitative, then in a da capo aria. Neither the main nor the middle section develops a single musical motive; rather, there are as many melodic ideas as there are thoughts and moods in the text. The first line, in which Uberto exclaims, in a patter style, that he is confused, repeats the same music three times, reinforcing it for the listener but also suggesting

Example 13.4 *Giovanni Battista Pergolesi,* La serva padrona: Son imbrogliato io già

I am all mixed up. I have a certain something in my heart. Truly I cannot tell whether it's love or pity. I hear a voice that tells me: "Uberto, think of yourself."

Uberto's mental paralysis (Example 13.4a). Uberto then realizes that something mysterious is stirring in his heart (measure 15) and waxes lyrical as he asks himself whether it is love that he feels. But a sober voice within checks his ardor—he should think of himself, guard his independence and interests—and now the melody consists of deliberate, brooding, drawn-out notes (Example 13.4b). The middle section, rather than presenting contrasting music, develops earlier material by transmuting some of the musical motives of the first section into the minor mode.

Performance of an intermezzo, *a short comic work given between the acts of an* opera seria. *Painting, Venetian School, eighteenth century.* (MILAN, MUSEO TEATRALE ALLA SCALA)

Opera Seria

The light and charming style of arias such as those illustrated above by Vinci and Pergolesi soon invaded serious opera. The *opera seria* treated serious subjects, purged of comic scenes and characters. *Opera seria* received its standard form from the Italian poet Pietro Metastasio (1698–1782), whose dramas were set to music hundreds of times by many eighteenth-century composers (including Mozart). His success with librettos for Naples, Rome, and Venice, most notably *Didone abbandonata* in 1724, led to his appointment in 1729 as court poet in Vienna, succeeding Apostolo Zeno. He remained in Vienna for the rest of his life, turning out a profusion of Italian librettos and many occasional works for the imperial court. His heroic operas present a conflict of human passions, often pitting love against duty, in stories based on ancient Greek or Latin tales. His operas were intended to promote morality through entertainment and to present models of merciful and enlightened rulers. The magnanimous tyrant—for example, Alexander the Great in *Alessandro nell'Indie*, or Titus in *La clemenza di Tito*—is a favorite character. The librettos employ the conventional cast of two pairs of lovers and subordinate personages. The action provides opportunities for introducing varied scenes—pastoral or martial episodes, solemn ceremonies, and the like. The resolution of the drama, which rarely has a tragic ending, often turns on a deed of heroism or sublime renunciation by one of the principal characters.

Metastasio

Musical structure

The three acts consist almost unvaryingly of alternating recitatives and arias; recitatives develop the action through dialogue, while each aria is a virtual dramatic soliloquy in which a principal actor expresses feelings or reacts to the preceding scene. There are occasional duets, a few larger ensembles, and rare, simple choruses.

Instrumental accompaniment

Except in the overture, the orchestra serves mainly to accompany the singers. Composers differed in the attention they gave to *recitativo semplice* (recitative accompanied only by the harpsichord and usually a sustaining bass instrument), but at its best, lively, speechlike rhythms are propelled by quickly moving harmonic progressions. *Obbligato* (or orchestrally accompanied) recitatives, in which the voice and orchestra alternate freely, are reserved for the most important dramatic situations. With these exceptions, the musical interest of the Italian opera is centered in the arias, which were created by eighteenth-century composers in astounding profusion and variety.

The Aria

Da capo aria

The favored form in the first half of the century was the da capo aria, a basic scheme that permitted enormous variation in detail. Metastasio's two-stanza aria texts set the standard for the full blown da capo aria of the 1720s through the 1740s. The form may be represented by the following outline (in which the keys, indicated by Roman numerals, are hypothetical):

						Fine	Da capo al Fine
Music:	Ritornello	A1	Rit.	A2	Rit.	B	
Text:		lines 1–4		lines 1–4 developed		lines 5–8	
Key:	I	I → V	V	V → I	I	vi	

The opening ritornello generally announces the melodic material of the A section, sometimes simplified, at other times embellished. Normally the composer fit this music to the poetic text of the A section and then reworked and orchestrated it for the introductory music. The first A section presents the main melodic material in the tonic, then modulates to the dominant or related key. The ritornello that follows is usually short, transposing and contracting a passage from the opening. The second A section begins by restating the melody of the A1 section in the dominant or a related key but sometimes resets the text with a variation on the original melody. It often ends with a highly florid rendering of the last line or couplet. The B section, which is heard only once, is typically set quite syllabically with light accompaniment and may be in a different tempo and meter. Most often it states the text a single time, with repetition, perhaps, of only the final two lines. There is usually a fermata just before the end of both the A and B sections, inviting the singer to execute a cadenza. (See NAWM 86 for an example and discussion of an aria by Hasse that follows this form.)

Abbreviated da capo aria

After about the middle of the century, composers explored ways to shorten the repetitious and long-winded A sections with their full da capo reiteration. They invented various schemes that abbreviated the return of the ritornello and the primary section, often by altering the direction "da capo" (from the beginning) to "dal segno" (from the sign, indicating that only a portion of the A section is repeated), or writing out an abridged return. (See the aria by Pergolesi, NAWM 85, for an example.) It also became more common to write arias in a single movement—usually an expanded version of a da capo aria's A section.

The reign of the singers

Turning the aria into virtually the only significant musical ingredient in opera opened the way to abuses. The scheme of regularly alternating recitatives and arias came to be treated too rigidly. Singers, including the famed Italian *castrati* (male sopranos and altos who had been surgically castrated before their voices changed), made arbitrary demands on the poets and composers, compelling them to alter, add, and substitute arias without respect for dramatic or musical appropriateness. Moreover, the melodic embellishments and cadenzas that singers added at will were often mere displays of vocal acrobatics. Some of the excesses were enumerated in *Il teatro alla moda* (The Fashionable Theater), a famous satire on the opera and everything connected with it, published anonymously in 1720 (by the composer Benedetto Marcello).

New features of da capo arias

Despite these criticisms, the da capo aria continued to evolve. Arias written in the first decades of the century had usually projected a single affection through the development of a single motive. Now composers started to express a succession of moods, using a variety of musical material that ranged from lighthearted to tragic. Often two keys are contrasted in the first main period (the A1 section); then the material in the second key is recapitulated in the tonic at the close of the second main period (the A2 section). The aria's ritornello may introduce both the material sung later in the primary key and that in the secondary key, thus resembling the orchestral exposition of a concerto (see pages 457–58). In this way vocal music began incorporating structural methods of instrumental music—the sonata and concerto—something that remained true throughout the eighteenth century. But the vocal melody still dominated the music and carried it forward, and the orchestra provided harmonic support to the singer rather than adding independent contrapuntal lines. The melodies were usually made up of four-measure units, consisting of two-measure antecedent and consequent phrases. Deviating from this formula created a deliberately asymmetrical effect.

Handel employed this new idiom in his late operas, such as *Alcina* (1735) and *Serse* (1738), as did Pergolesi (see page 434), Giovanni Bononcini (see page 407), Carl Heinrich Graun (1704–1759), the Spaniard Domingo Terradellas (1713–1751)—who studied and worked in Naples—Nicola Porpora (1686–1768), who later taught Haydn in Vienna, and Johann Adolph Hasse (1699–1783).

Hasse

Hasse was acknowledged by most of his contemporaries as the great master of the *opera seria.* For most of his life he directed music and opera at the court of the elector of Saxony in Dresden, but he spent many years in Italy, married the celebrated Italian soprano Faustina Bordoni, and became so thoroughly Italian in his musical style that the Italians nicknamed him "il caro Sassone" (the dear Saxon). His music is the perfect complement to Metastasio's poetry; the great majority of his eighty operas use Metastasio librettos, some of which he set two and even three times. He was the most popular and successful opera composer in Europe around the middle of the century, and Burney's remarks about his music reveal the qualities that endeared him to connoisseurs:

Burney on Hasse

> . . . the most natural, elegant, and judicious composer of vocal music . . . now alive; equally a friend to poetry and the voice, he discovers as much judgment as genius, in expressing words, as well as in accompanying those sweet and tender melodies, which he gives to the singer. Always regarding the voice, as the first object of attention in a theatre, he never suffocates it, by the learned jargon of a multiplicity of instruments and subjects; but is as careful of preserving its importance as a painter, of throwing the strongest light upon the capital figure of his piece.[6]

6. Burney, *The Present State of Music in Germany,* 2nd ed., (London, 1775), 1:238–39.

The famous aria *Digli ch'io son fedele* (Tell him that I am faithful) from Hasse's *Cleofide* (1731), his first opera for Dresden (NAWM 86; CD 7 [7]), illustrates the qualities that Burney admired. The libretto had been adapted by Michelangelo Boccardi from Metastasio's *Alessandro nell'Indie*, but this aria, sung by Cleofide, is from Metastasio's original play.

Digli ch'io son fedele,	Tell him that I am faithful,
Digli ch'è il mio tesoro:	tell him that he's my darling;
Che m'ami, ch'io l'adoro,	to love me; that I adore him;
Che non disperi ancor.	that he not yet despair.
Digli che la mia stella	Tell him that my star
Spero placar col pianto;	I hope to placate with weeping;
Che lo consoli intanto	that meanwhile let him be consoled
L'immagine di quella	by the image of her
Che vive nel suo cor.	who lives in his heart.

The first four lines are set in the A section (Example 13.5), the next five in the B section, after which A is repeated da capo. The parallel rhythm of the first two lines allowed Hasse to construct parallel melodic phrases that capture both the natural rhythm of the poetry and the hopeful sentiment of Cleofide, queen of India. The endings on unstressed syllables at *fedele, tesoro,* and *adoro* result in the characteristic syncopated cadences. Even when a line ends on a stressed syllable, as at *ancor,* Hasse softened it with an appoggiatura. Further syncopations occur on the accented initial syllables of *m'a-mi, ch'i-o,* and *non* through the so-called Scotch snap or Lombardic rhythm (a short value followed by one three times as long). After the threefold repetition of the opening rhythm, these destabilizing events contribute to the excitement and suspense as the dominant is approached (measure 17).

Example 13.5 *J. A. Hasse,* Cleofide, *Act II, Scene 9:* Digli ch'io son fedele

Tell him that I am faithful, tell him that he's my darling; to love me: that I adore him; that he not yet despair.

Faustina Bordoni

The title role of Cleofide in 1731 was created by Hasse's bride, Faustina Bordoni (1700–1781). Bordoni, who established her reputation in Venice while still in her teens, made her German debut in Munich at the age of twenty-three. When she performed, she embellished the written vocal line.[7] An elaborated version of this aria survives in the hand of Frederick II, king of Prussia (reigned 1740–86), an amateur flutist and composer, as sung by the castrato Antonio Uberti, known as Porporino. This version, written out above Hasse's melody in Example 13.5,[8] is ablaze with trills, mordents, rapid turns, appoggiaturas, scales, triplets, and arpeggios. Scholars believe that such embellishments, were added particularly in the da capo repetition.

Vocal embellishment

COMIC OPERA

While *opera seria* maintained its character across national boundaries, comic opera took different forms in different countries. It usually represented everyday people in familiar situations and required relatively modest performing re-

7. An embellished version of the soprano line attributed to or composed for Faustina is published in Hellmuth Christian Wolff, *Original Vocal Improvisations from the 16th–18th Centuries* (Cologne: Arno Volk Verlag Hans Gerig, 1972), pp. 143–68.
8. This is published in a facsimile of the manuscript in Berlin, Deutsche Staatsbibliothek, Poelchau collection, in Friedrich II, *Auszierung zur Arie Digli ch'io son fedele aus der Oper Cleofide von Johann Adolf Hasse*, ed. Wolfgang Goldhan (Wiesbaden: Breitkopf & Härtel, 1991) and in MGG 5:1783, transcribed in Wolff, *Original Vocal Improvisations*, pp. 143–68. Both Hasse's original line and many of the embellishments notated by Frederick may be heard in the performance by Emma Kirkby in the recording of the opera by the Cappella Coloniensis, directed by William Christie in the Capriccio CD 10 193/96 (Königsdorf: Delta-Music, 1987).

■*Faustina Bordoni (1700–1781), universally admired as one of the great singer-actresses of her age. She married Johann Adolph Hasse in 1730 and enjoyed her first success in Germany in the title role of his* Cleofide *(Dresden, 1731; see NAWM 86). She created several roles in Handel's London operas in the 1720s. Burney praised her fluent articulation, trills, improvised embellishments, and expressive power. She is shown here as Attilia in Hasse's* Attilio Regolo *in a costume designed by Francesco Ponte for the original production at the Dresden Hoftheater, January 12, 1750.* (DRESDEN, DEUTSCHE FOTOTHEK, SÄCHSISCHE LANDESBIBLIOTHEK)

sources. Comic-opera librettos were always written in the national tongue, and the music itself tended to accentuate the national musical idiom. From humble beginnings the comic opera grew steadily in importance after 1760, and before the end of the century many of its characteristic features had been absorbed into the mainstream of operatic composition. Its historical significance was twofold: it responded to the widespread demand for naturalness in the latter half of the eighteenth century, and it represented the earliest passage toward musical nationalism, which became prominent in the Romantic period.

Italy

Librettos

Beginning about the middle of the century, the Italian dramatist Carlo Goldoni (1707–1793) introduced refinements in the comic-opera libretto. Serious, sentimental, or woeful plots began to appear alongside the traditional comic ones. Reflecting this change, the older designation *opera buffa* was replaced by *dramma giocoso*—literally a jocular but more accurately a pleasant or cheerful (nontragic, yet not farcical) drama. An example of this new type is *La buona figliuola* (The Good Girl, 1760) by Niccolò Piccinni (1728–1800), adapted by Goldoni from Richardson's popular novel *Pamela,* which had appeared twenty years earlier. Paisiello's *Barbiere di Siviglia* (The Barber of Seville, 1782), from Beaumarchais's drama, is a semi-serious treatment of current political issues, while his *Nina* (1789) has an out-and-out sentimental plot. Another famous work in this vein is *Il matrimonio segreto* (The Secret Marriage), by Domenico Cimarosa (1749–1801), premiered in Vienna in 1792.

Italian comic opera came a long way, both dramatically and musically, in the course of the century. Mozart would later make good use of its heritage of comic, serious, and sentimental drama mingled with a lively and flexible musical style.

Italian comic opera exploited the possibilities of the bass voice with particular success, both in straight comedy and in burlesque of other styles. Another development was the ensemble finale, which appeared in the comic operas of Nicola Logroscino (1698–ca. 1765) and Baldassare Galuppi. At the end of an act, all the characters were gradually brought on stage while the action continued with growing animation, until it reached a climax with all singers taking part. These ensemble finales were unlike anything in serious opera, and in writing them composers had to follow the rapidly changing action of the scene without losing coherence in the musical form.

Ensemble finale

France

The French version of light opera, known as *opéra comique*, began around 1710 as a lowly form of popular entertainment put on at parish fairs. Until the middle of the century, the music consisted almost entirely of popular tunes (*vaudevilles*) or simple melodies imitating such tunes. The visit of an Italian comic opera troupe to Paris in 1752, including a performance of Pergolesi's *La serva padrona*, stimulated the production of opéras comiques, in which original airs (called *ariettes*) in a mixed Italian-French style were introduced along with the old vaudevilles. The vaudevilles were gradually replaced by the ariettes until, by the end of the 1760s, all the music was freshly composed. One of the composers exposed to the French opéra comique during this transitional decade was Christoph Willibald Gluck, who arranged and composed a number of opéras comiques for the entertainment of the Vienna court.

The musical atmosphere in Paris was so charged that a production of Gluck's *Iphigénie en Aulide* (1774) awakened extraordinary interest. Long-simmering critical opposition to the old-fashioned, state-subsidized French opera had erupted in 1752 in a pamphlet war known as the *Querelle des bouffons* (Quarrel of the comic actors). The immediate occasion for the dispute was the presence in Paris of an Italian opera company that for two seasons had enjoyed sensational success with its performances of Italian comic operas (*opere buffe*) and intermezzi. Practically every intellectual and would-be intellectual in France had taken part in the quarrel—partisans of Italian opera on one side and friends of French opera on the other. Jean-Jacques Rousseau (1712–1778), one of the leaders of the "Italian" faction, published an article in which he argued that the French language was inherently unsuitable for singing and concluded "that the French have no music and cannot have any; or if they have, it will be so much the worse for them."[9] Rousseau and his friends, despite the foolish extremes to which they occasionally strayed in the heat of argument, represented enlightened opinion in Paris.

Querelle des bouffons

9. Jean-Jacques Rousseau, "Lettre sur la musique française" (1753), trans. in SRrev, p. 908; 5:174.

Example 13.6 *J.-J. Rousseau,* Le Devin du village: J'ai perdu tout mon bonheur

I have lost my servant,
I have lost all my joy.
Colin forsakes me.

Rousseau wrote a charming little opera in 1752 with airs and recitatives, *Le Devin du village* (The Village Soothsayer). The air *J'ai perdu tout mon bonheur* (I have lost all my joy, Example 13.6), inspired by the new Italian melodic style, is neatly phrased in groups of two measures, naively harmonized and simply accompanied. The air is interrupted by a passage that imitates Italian recitative in its speechlike delivery but somewhat incongruously introduces French-style ornaments. Rousseau

The French opéra comique, like all the national variants of light opera except the Italian, used spoken dialogue instead of recitative. Following the European trend in the second half of the century, the opéra comique dealt boldly with the social issues that were agitating France during the pre-Revolutionary years. The principal composers of the time were François André Danican Philidor (1726–1795; also a famous chess master), Pierre-Alexandre Monsigny (1729–1817), and above all the Belgian-born André Ernest Modeste Grétry Grétry

(1741–1813). His *Richard Coeur-de-Lion* (Richard the Lion-Hearted, 1784) was a forerunner of numerous "rescue" operas around the turn of the century—Beethoven's *Fidelio* was one—in which the hero, after trembling in imminent danger of death for two and a half acts, is finally saved through a friend's devoted heroism. The music in Grétry's fifty or more operas is never profound, but it is melodious, singable, and effective, with occasional moments of moving dramatic expression. The opéra comique, with its alternation of spoken dialogue and musical numbers, was extremely popular in France. It flourished throughout the Revolution and the Napoleonic era and took on even greater musical significance later in the nineteenth century.

England

The English *ballad opera* became popular after the extraordinary success of *The Beggar's Opera* in London in 1728. This piece broadly satirizes the fashionable Italian opera; its music, like that of the early opéra comique, consists for the most part of popular tunes, usually ballads, with a few numbers that parody familiar operatic airs (see the excerpts in NAWM 87; CD 7 [12]). One example, *My heart was so free,* parodies the simile aria of the Baroque operas (simile arias compare a character's situation with an image, like a ship in a storm). Another example, *O what pain it is to part,* is sung to the tune of the Scotch song *Gin thou wer't my e'ne thing.*

The immense popularity of ballad operas in the 1730s signaled a general reaction in England against foreign opera—that "exotic and irrational entertainment," as Dr. Samuel Johnson called it. As we have already seen, Handel

William Hogarth's satirical impression of the Beggar's Opera, *performed in a public square, portrays some of the actors with animal heads, suggesting that these actors bark, howl, and wail rather than sing. Harmony in the form of an angel flees on the wings of this song. An unlikely ensemble of bagpipe, xylophone, fife, and tromba marina accompany. The streamer urges "equals to sing and equals to respond."* (BETTMANN/CORBIS)

turned his energies from opera to oratorio in the latter part of his life (see page 408). The only notable composer of English opera in the eighteenth century was Thomas Augustine Arne (1710–1778).

Germany

Singspiel

Although *Singspiel* existed in Germany since the sixteenth century, the success of the ballad opera inspired its revival. At first librettists adapted English ballad operas, but they soon turned to translating or arranging French comic operas, for which the German composers provided new music in a familiar and appealing melodic vein. Many of the eighteenth-century Singspiel tunes found their way into German song collections and thus in the course of time have virtually become folksongs. The principal composer of Singspiel music during this period was Johann Adam Hiller (1728–1804) of Leipzig. In northern Germany, the Singspiel eventually merged with early nineteenth-century native opera. In the south, particularly in Vienna, farcical subjects and treatment became fashionable, with lively music in a popular vein influenced by Italian comic opera. *Doctor und Apotheker* (1786), the first Singspiel by the Viennese composer Carl Ditters von Dittersdorf (1739–1799), became a huge success and was followed by many more. The Singspiel was an important precursor of the German-language musical theater of composers such as Mozart and Weber.

BEGINNINGS OF OPERA REFORM

Certain Italian composers wanted to bring opera into harmony with changing ideals of music and drama. They sought to make the entire design more "natural"—that is, more flexible in structure, more deeply expressive, less laden with coloratura, and more varied in other musical resources. They did not abandon the da capo aria but modified it and introduced other forms as well; they alternated arias and recitatives more flexibly so as to move the action forward rapidly and realistically; they made greater use of obbligato recitative and ensembles, such as trios; they made the orchestra more important, both for its own sake and for adding harmonic depth to accompaniments; they reinstated choruses, long absent in Italian opera; and they stiffened their resistance to the arbitrary demands of the solo singers.

Jommelli and Traetta

Two of the most important figures in the movement of reform were Nicolò Jommelli (1714–1774) and Tommaso Traetta (1727–1779). That both of these Italian composers worked at courts where French taste predominated—Jommelli at Stuttgart and Traetta in Parma—naturally influenced them toward a cosmopolitan type of opera. Jomelli's popularity was such (he composed some one hundred stage works) that his arias permeate the many collections of Italian vocal music that circulated in manuscripts copied during the second half of the eighteenth century. Traetta aimed to combine the best of French *tragédie lyrique* and Italian *opera seria* in his *Ippolito ed Aricia* (1759), adapted by Carlo Frugoni from the libretto that Rameau had set. He even utilized some of Rameau's dance music and descriptive symphonies, and, unusual for this time in Italy, included a number of choruses. For the solo roles, Traetta relied on the conventional genres of recitative and aria. Thus Traetta in his own way reconciled the two types of music drama—French and Italian—years before Gluck set out to do so.

Gluck

Christoph Willibald Gluck (1714–1787) achieved a synthesis of French and Italian opera that made him the man of the hour. Born of Bohemian parents in what is now Bavaria, Gluck studied under Sammartini in Italy, visited London, toured in Germany as conductor of an opera troupe, became court composer to the Emperor Charles VI at Vienna, and triumphed in Paris under the patronage of Marie Antoinette. He began by writing operas in the conventional Italian style but was strongly affected by the reform movement in the 1750s. Spurred on by the forward-looking impresario Giacomo Durazzo, he collaborated with the poet Raniero de Calzabigi (1714–1795) to produce at Vienna *Orfeo ed Euridice* (1762) and *Alceste* (1767). In a dedicatory preface to *Alceste*, Gluck expressed his resolve to remove the abuses that had deformed Italian opera (see vignette) and to confine music to its proper function—to serve the poetry and advance the plot. This he wanted to accomplish without regard either to the outworn conventions of the da capo aria or the desire of singers to show off their skill in ornamental variation. He further aimed to make the overture an integral part of the opera, to adapt the orchestra to the dramatic requirements, and to lessen the contrast between aria and recitative.

As a composer, Gluck aspired to "a beautiful simplicity," which he realized in the celebrated aria *Che farò senza Euridice?* (What shall I do without Euridice?) from *Orfeo*, and in other airs, choruses, and dances from the same work. *Alceste* is more monumental, in contrast to the prevailingly pastoral and

GLUCK ON THE REFORM OF OPERA

I sought to confine music to its true function of serving the poetry by expressing feelings and the situations of the story without interrupting and cooling off the action through useless and superfluous ornaments. I believed that music should join to poetry what the vividness of colors and well disposed lights and shadows contribute to a correct and well composed design, animating the figures without altering their contours.

I further believed that the greater part of my task was to seek a beautiful simplicity, and I have avoided a display of difficulty at the expense of clarity. I assigned no value to the discovery of some novelty, unless it were naturally suggested by the situation and the expression. And there is no rule that I did not willingly consider sacrificing for the sake of an effect.

From Gluck's dedication, in Italian, to *Alceste* (Vienna, 1769). For a facsimile, see *New Grove Dictionary* 7:466.

elegiac tone of *Orfeo*. In both, the music is molded to the drama, with recitatives, arias, and choruses intermingled in large unified scenes. Gluck assigned an important role to the chorus. Compared to the final choruses Jommelli had employed in his Viennese operas in the early 1750s, Gluck's Chorus of Furies in Act II (NAWM 88; CD 7 [17]) is more integral to the action. In this scene Orfeo, accompanied by harp and strings to simulate a lyre, pleads for the liberation of Euridice, which the Furies resist, provoking and challenging Orfeo.

Gluck achieved his mature style in *Orfeo* and *Alceste*, amalgamating Italian melodic grace, German seriousness, and the stately magnificence of the French *tragédie lyrique*. He was now ready for the climax of his career, which was ushered in with the Paris production of *Iphigénie en Aulide* (Iphigenia in Aulis) in 1774.

Gluck cleverly represented himself—or was represented by his supporters—as wanting to prove that a good opera could be written to French words; he professed a desire for Rousseau's aid in creating "a noble, sensitive, and natural melody . . . music suited to all nations, so as to abolish these ridiculous distinctions of national styles."[10] He thus appealed at the same time to the patriotism and to the curiosity of the French public.

Gluck-Piccinni rivalry

Iphigénie en Aulide, with a libretto adapted from Racine's tragedy, was a tremendous success. Revised versions of *Orfeo* and *Alceste* (both with French texts) swiftly followed. In a mischievously instigated rivalry with the popular Neapolitan composer Niccolò Piccinni, Gluck and Piccinni were both induced to compose an opera on Quinault's *Roland*, but when Gluck heard that his rival was already at work on his version, Gluck set instead Quinault's *Armide* (1777), the same libretto that Lully had done in 1686. Gluck's next masterpiece, *Iphigénie en Tauride* (Iphigenia in Tauris, 1779), is a work of large proportions that displays an excellent balance of dramatic and musical interest and utilizes all the resources of opera—orchestra, ballet, solo and choral singing—to produce a total effect of classical tragic grandeur.

Gluck's operas became models for the works of his immediate followers in Paris. His influence on the form and spirit of opera was transmitted to the nineteenth century through composers such as his erstwhile rival Piccinni, Luigi Cherubini (1760–1842), Gasparo Spontini (1774–1851), and Hector Berlioz (1803–1869).

SONG AND CHURCH MUSIC

The Lied

While opera held sway in the larger public arena, solo songs, cantatas, and other types of secular vocal music entertained more intimate gatherings throughout Europe during the eighteenth century. The German song, or *Lied*,

10. Gluck, Letter to the Editor of *Mercure de France*, February 1773.

achieved a special artistic importance. The first significant collection of lieder was published at Leipzig in 1736 under the title *Die singende Muse an der Pleisse* (The Singing Muse on the Pleisse [River]). The songs in this collection are parodies, in the eighteenth-century sense of the term—that is, the words were written to fit existing melodies, mostly dances and marches. Subsequent collections included some parodied songs and some with original music. Song composition after the middle of the century centered in Berlin, where J. J. Quantz (1697–1773), C. H. Graun, and C. P. E. Bach were active. The Berlin composers favored lieder in strophic form, with melodies in a natural, expressive, folksong style: one note to a syllable with only the simplest possible accompaniments that were completely subordinate to the vocal line. These conventions, which reflected the taste of the time, were generally accepted in the eighteenth century. Eventually composers gradually transcended these artificial restrictions on the lied, primarily by making the structure more flexible and giving the accompaniment more independence. The leading Berlin composers toward the end of the century were Johann Abraham Peter Schulz (1747–1800) and the prolific Johann Friedrich Reichardt (1752–1814), whose seven hundred lieder included many on poems by Goethe (see Example 13.7). His daughter, Louise Reichardt (1779–1826), also made notable contributions to this repertory.

Berlin

Example 13.7 *J. F. Reichardt, Lied:* Erlkönig

Who rides so late through night and wind? It is a father with his child. He has the boy close in his arm, he holds him tight, he keeps him warm. "My son, why do you hide your face in fear? . . ."

"You dear child, come with me; I'll play very lovely games with you."

German publishers brought out more than 750 collections of lieder with keyboard accompaniment during the second half of the century, in addition to numerous Singspiele, which consist for the most part of songs similar to lieder. Nearly all Singspiel composers, in fact, also wrote lieder. The production continued steadily into the nineteenth century; when Schubert began composing songs in 1811 he was joining a long and rich tradition, which his own work carried to new heights.

Church Music

Sacred music, affected by the individualistic temperament of the late eighteenth century, conformed to the prevailing secular style, especially that of the theater. A few composers, such as the Barcelona master Francisco Valls (1665–1747) and the Roman, Giuseppe Ottavio Pitoni (1657–1743), ably carried on the *stile antico* tradition of Palestrina or the grand polychoral style of Benevoli. But for the most part, church music adopted the musical idioms and genres of opera, with orchestral accompaniment, da capo arias, and accompanied recitatives. A list of the leading eighteenth-century Italian church composers is almost identical with the list of leading opera composers of the period. Even more than the Mass and motet, the oratorio in Italy became almost indistinguishable from opera. At the same time some composers, particularly in northern Italy and what is now southern Germany and Austria, effected a compromise between conservative and modern elements. The resulting mixed style—influenced also by the instrumental symphonic forms of the Classic period—set the stage for the sacred compositions of Haydn and Mozart.

Stile antico and *moderno*

Germany

Lutheran church music rapidly declined in importance after the death of J. S. Bach. The half-sacred, half-secular genre of the oratorio became the principal medium of the North German composers. Those written after 1750 show some reaction against the excesses of operatic style. Nevertheless, Graun's *Der Tod Jesu* (The Death of Jesus; 1755), notable for its brilliant da capo arias, remained popular in Germany until the end of the nineteenth century.

England

In England, the enormous influence of Handel, together with the natural conservatism of the English, kept the Baroque styles of church music alive for a time. Moreover, the most gifted composers of sacred music, mainly cathedral organists, were a generation older than Haydn and more at home in the older style. Since the Anglican service did not require long musical settings, composers confined their writing to anthems and hymns. William Boyce (1710–1779), more famous for his theater music, served as the official composer for the Chapel Royal. Maurice Greene (1696–1755), John Stanley (1713–1786), and Charles Avison (1709–1770), all known for their orchestral and organ music, composed anthems of excellent quality. Stanley and Avison also added to the repertory of the oratorio and cantata. A generation later, Samuel Wesley (1766–1837) popularized Bach's music in England, and William Crotch (1775–1847) joined the ranks of Mozart and Mendelssohn as a famous musical prodigy.

INSTRUMENTAL MUSIC: SONATA, SYMPHONY, AND CONCERTO

Domenico Scarlatti

Career

Domenico Scarlatti (1685–1757), son of Alessandro Scarlatti and born the same year as Bach and Handel, was the chief Italian keyboard composer of the eighteenth century and a remarkably original creative artist. He left Italy in 1720 or 1721 to enter the service of the king of Portugal. When his pupil, the infanta of Portugal, was married to Prince Ferdinand of Spain in 1729, Scarlatti followed her to Madrid, where he remained for the rest of his life in the service of the Spanish court. He published his first collection of harpsichord sonatas (called on the title page *Essercizi*—exercises) in 1738, but most of his 555 sonatas are known to us through scribal copies from his time.

Forms of his sonatas

Scarlatti's sonatas are organized by means of tonal relationships into the standard late Baroque and early Classic binary pattern used for dance pieces and other types of composition. They have two sections, each repeated, the first closing in the dominant or relative major (rarely some other key), the second modulating further afield and then returning to the tonic. This basic scheme underlies much instrumental and solo vocal music in the eighteenth century. In Scarlatti's sonatas the closing part of the first section invariably returns at the end of the second section, but in the tonic key.

The one-movement sonata written around 1749 identified as K. 119 or Longo 415[11] (NAWM 89; CD 7 [22] / 3 ⟨7⟩) exhibits many of the genre's traits. It has two sections, each repeated. After a brilliant opening, several ideas are announced, each immediately restated. The ideas are not all of the same importance or function. The first, a broken-chord motive spanning two octaves, is introductory, but a fragment of it is superimposed on another idea to close each half of the sonata. The next bold theme (Example 13.8a), immediately repeated, never returns. The third (Example 13.8b) is purely cadential; the

11. The sonatas are identified by K. numbers in Ralph Kirkpatrick's index of the sonatas or by a different set of numbers in A. Longo's complete edition of the sonatas.

Example 13.8 *Domenico Scarlatti, Motives from Sonata K. 119*

fourth (Example 13.8c), imitating the rhythm and effect of castanets, has a modulatory function here but comes back again to close off both halves. Then the central idea arrives, in the dominant minor (Example 13.8d). It is inspired by Spanish guitar music, with an almost constant *a′* sounding like an open string being strummed along with those being fingered. This thematic element is most developed throughout the piece; in the second section it rises to a vigorous climax in which all the notes of the key but one are sounded together (Example 13.8e).

The majority of Scarlatti's sonatas after 1745 appear in the manuscripts in pairs, each pair comprising, in effect, a sonata of two movements, always in the same key (though one may be major and the other minor), sometimes similar in mood, sometimes contrasted. Many eighteenth-century composers, from Alberti to Mozart, wrote sonatas in two movements, possibly under Italian influence, although there is no evidence that they took the idea from Scarlatti. In fact, just as Scarlatti seems to have created his own keyboard idiom virtually without models, so too he had no successors, with the exception of a few Iberian composers, notably the Catalan Antonio Soler (1729–1783). The *Essercizi* of 1738 and a few other sonatas were known and admired in England in the eighteenth century, but very little of Scarlatti's music circulated in France and practically none of it was known in Germany or Italy.

Italian composers of the middle and late eighteenth century produced a large amount of music for harpsichord that remains less familiar than the works of C. P. E. Bach and other German composers. Yet Italians and Germans were equally active in experimenting with formal organization in the keyboard sonatas of the eighteenth century.

The Sonata

Most instrumental music of Haydn, Mozart, Beethoven, and their contemporaries, whether called sonata, trio, string quartet, or symphony, is written in three or four movements of contrasting mood and tempo. According to Koch's treatise of 1793, the form of the first movement, now known as *sonata form* or *first-movement form*, consists of two large divisions, each of which may be repeated.[12] The first has one main period, the second two, resulting in three periods within a binary form. In the first period the principal ideas are presented in the key of the movement, which prevails until a modulation to the dominant (or relative major in a minor key) leads to a resting point on the tonic of the new key. The remainder of the first period is in the new key. The second period often begins with the main theme on the dominant, occasionally with another idea or in another key, and modulates back to the tonic by means of still another melodic idea. The third period most frequently begins with the main theme in the key of the movement. Melodic ideas from the first period are reviewed, often shifting to the key of the subdominant without ever making a cadence. Finally the closing section of the first period, which had been presented in the dominant or relative key, is now repeated in the tonic.

Koch on sonata form

In symphonies, Koch remarks, the various melodic sections have a forceful and energetic character and tend to be more extended and flowing, with fewer perceptible phrase endings and cadences. In sonatas, on the other hand, fine nuances of feeling, more frequent phrase endings, and more developed melody signal the desire for more personal expression. Koch's description of a sonata Allegro does not coincide with the textbook definition of sonata form, but it is flexible enough not to exclude it. He was writing in the 1790s, when the form was not as settled as it seemed to the theorists and analysts of the 1830s who formulated what were later recognized as norms.

Sonata form—a modern view

This more recent view divides the movement also into three sections (see diagram below):

(1) An *exposition* (usually repeated), incorporating a first theme or group of themes in the tonic (P); a bridge passage (T) leading to a second, often more lyrical, theme or group (S) in the dominant or the relative major (if the movement is in a minor key); and a closing, frequently cadential, theme (K) also in the dominant or relative major—the different themes being connected by appropriate transitions. An introduction often precedes the exposition.

(2) A *development* section, which modulates to new keys, possibly even remote ones, and in which motives or themes from the exposition are presented in new aspects or combinations.

12. Heinrich Christoph Koch, *Introductory Essay on Composition: The Mechanical Rules of Melody*, Section 4, Chapter 4, trans. Baker, pp. 197–206. Koch describes this "sonata form" in the section on the symphony.

(3) A *recapitulation*, where the material of the exposition is restated in the original order but with all themes in the tonic; following the recapitulation there may be a *coda*.[13]

Section:	**(Intro)**	**‖: Exposition**			**:‖**
Key:	(I)	**‖: I**		**V or III**	**:‖**
Themes:		‖: P	T	S	K :‖

Development		
Foreign		**V**
P, S, other		

Recapitulation				**(Coda)**
I				
P	T	S	K	

This outline of sonata form is obviously an abstraction, dwelling particularly on the key scheme and the melodic-thematic ideas. So understood, it fits a good many sonata movements of the late Classic period and the nineteenth century, but many depart from it in creative ways.

Early Symphonies and Chamber Music

Keyboard sonatas and orchestral compositions of similar form in the early part of the eighteenth century were influenced by the Italian opera overture (*sinfonia*). About 1700, the overture assumed a three-movement structure in the order fast–slow–fast: an Allegro, a short lyrical Andante, and a finale in the rhythm of some dance, such as a minuet or a gigue. Such overtures, as a rule, have no musical connection with the opera they introduce and could be played as independent pieces in concerts. It was a natural step, then, for Italian composers to begin writing concert symphonies using the general plan of the opera overtures. The earliest of these, dating from around 1730, are equally indebted to the tradition of the late Baroque concerto and of the trio sonata in details of structure, texture, and thematic style. One of the early works in this genre, the Symphony in F major (ca. 1744) by Sammartini, is scored for two violins, viola, and bass. The opening Presto (NAWM 90; CD 7 [24])—its other two movements are Andante and Allegro assai—presents a variety of ideas in rapid succession, much like a Scarlatti sonata. The binary form, with full recapitulation of the opening tonic and closing dominant sections, fits Koch's description of a symphonic first movement (MT = Main theme, OI = Other ideas):

Music:	**Period 1: MT + OI**		**:‖**	**‖: Period 2: MT + OI**		**Period 3: MT + OI (from Period 1)**				**:‖**
Key:	**F**	**Modulation**	**C :‖**	**‖: C**	**Modulation**	**F**	**Mod. (B♭)**		**F**	**:‖**
Mm.:	*1*	*6*	*11*	*15*	*17*	*25*	*30*	*33*	*34*	*38*

13. In this diagram, P stands for primary-theme section, S for secondary-theme section, T for transitional material, and K for closing material.

The *Empfindsam* Style

German composers, though not the originators of the sentimental style (*empfindsamer Stil*, see page 428), began introducing it into their instrumental music toward the middle of the century. Two of J. S. Bach's sons made important contributions.

W. F. Bach

The eldest, Wilhelm Friedemann (1710–1784), was a gifted organist and composer whose life ended in disappointment and poverty because he could not adjust to the requirements for a successful musical career. Some of his works are conservative in style, like those of his great father and teacher, while others pay tribute to the fashionable *style galant.* His music exhibits a certain freedom, even capriciousness, in the details of harmony, melody, and rhythm; sudden contrasts of mood; and, on occasion, an intensely personal, almost Romantic emotion.

C. P. E. Bach

Carl Philipp Emanuel Bach was one of the most influential composers of his generation. Trained in music by his father, he served at the court of Frederick the Great in Berlin from 1740 to 1768 and then became music director of the five principal churches in Hamburg. His compositions include oratorios, songs, symphonies, concertos, and chamber music, but most numerous and important are his works for keyboard. In 1742 he published a set of six sonatas (the *Prussian* Sonatas) and in 1744 another set of six (the *Württemberg* Sonatas; see Example 13.2). These sonatas had a new style and exerted a strong influence on later composers. Bach's favorite keyboard instrument was not the harpsichord but the softer, more intimate clavichord, which had a capacity for delicate dynamic shadings. The clavichord enjoyed a spell of renewed popularity in Germany around the middle of the eighteenth century before both it and the harpsichord were gradually supplanted by the pianoforte. The last five sets of C. P. E. Bach's sonatas (1780–87) were evidently written with the pianoforte chiefly in mind, as were many of the later keyboard pieces of W. F. Bach. This instrument, ancestor of the modern piano and now commonly called the "fortepiano," permitted the player to vary the loudness from *piano* to *forte* by striking the keys with greater or lesser force.

Main characteristics

The main technical characteristics of the *empfindsam* style, of which C. P. E. Bach was a leading exponent, are apparent in the second movement, Poco Adagio (NAWM 91; CD 7 27 / 3 9), of the fourth of his *Sonaten für Kenner und Liebhaber* (Sonatas for Connoisseurs and Amateurs), composed in 1765 but not published until 1779. It begins with a kind of melodic sigh, a singing motive ending in an appoggiatura that resolves on a weak beat, followed by a rest. (See Example 13.9.) This opening is decorated with a turn, Scotch snaps, and a trill. The multiplicity of rhythmic patterns, nervously and constantly changing—short dotted figures, triplets, asymmetrical flourishes of five and thirteen notes—gives the music a restless, effervescent quality. Measures 6 to 10 make up the transition to the relative major tonal area, in which sequential repetition moves inevitably toward its tonal goal, while the nonharmonic tones, particularly appoggiaturas, assure that there is no letup of suspense and excitement. Here, ornamentation serves expression rather than being a mere accessory to melody.

Example 13.9 *C. P. E. Bach, Sonata, H. 186, Wq. 55/4: Poco Adagio*

The eighteenth-century ideal of simplicity or naturalness did not rule out ornamentation; indeed, composers looked upon it as a refined means of enhancing the expressive power of a composition. C. P. E. Bach also introduced in his instrumental works sections of musical dialogue and passages of recitative. Audiences were reportedly deeply stirred by his keyboard improvisations, whose character may well be preserved in his fantasias.

Bach's *Essay on the True Art of Playing Keyboard Instruments* (1753–62), a most important source of information on ornamentation during the mid-eighteenth century, reveals, like Quantz's essay on flute playing, much about the musical thought and practice of the period.

The expressive style of C. P. E. Bach and his contemporaries often exploited the element of surprise, with abrupt shifts of harmony, strange modulations, unusual turns of melody, suspenseful pauses, changes of texture, sudden *sforzando* accents, and the like. The subjective, emotional qualities of this *Empfindsamkeit* reached a climax during the 1760s and 1770s; the trend is sometimes described by the expression *Sturm und Drang* (storm and stress), a movement in German literature and art that relished tormented, gloomy, terrified, irrational feelings. Later, composers brought this emotionalism under control. This concept will be discussed further in the next chapter.

Sturm und Drang

German Symphonic Composers

Mannheim

Mannheim, Vienna, and Berlin were the principal German centers of symphonic composition after 1740. Under the leadership of Johann Stamitz (1717–1757), the Mannheim orchestra became renowned all over Europe for its virtuosity (Burney called it "an army of generals"), for its hitherto unknown dynamic range from the softest *pianissimo* to the loudest *fortissimo*, and for the thrilling sound of its crescendo, though many of the striking dynamic effects and the dramatic contrasts incorporated into the Mannheim symphonies were adapted from the Italian opera overture. The first movement (NAWM 92; CD 7 [29]) of Johann Stamitz's Sinfonia in E♭, the third in the collection *La melodia germanica*, from the mid-1750s, contrasts an energetic opening with variously lyrical, graceful, and playful ideas in the dominant section. The transition exploits the crescendo to build excitement by means of string tremolos that progress from *piano* to *fortissimo*.

Vienna

Another center of symphonic writing in the 1740s was Vienna, home to Georg Matthias Monn (1717–1750), an early composer of symphonies. Another Viennese composer was Fux's pupil Georg Christoph Wagenseil (1715–1777), in whose music, as also in that of the later Austrian composers Florian Leopold Gassmann (1729–1774) and Michael Haydn (1737–1806), we find the pleasant, typically Viennese lyricism and good humor that is such an important feature of Mozart's work. The Viennese composers for the most part favored contrasting theme groups in their sonata-form movements.

Berlin

The principal symphonists of the Berlin, or North German, school clustered around Frederick the Great, who was himself a composer; two of its chief members were Johann Gottlieb Graun (1702 or 1703–1771) and C. P. E. Bach. The North Germans were conservative in holding to the three-movement structure for the symphony and their reluctance to introduce sharp thematic contrasts within a movement. But their symphonies revealed thematic development within a dynamic, organically unified, serious, and quasi-dramatic style, enriching the symphonic texture with contrapuntal elements.

J. C. Bach

Career

Johann Christian Bach (1735–1782), J. S. Bach's youngest son, created a great stir in London with some of the earliest concertos for the pianoforte. He was an important composer of symphonies, as well as of chamber music, keyboard music, and operas. Trained in music by his father and his elder brother C. P. E. Bach, Johann Christian made his way to Milan at the age of twenty. He studied

■ *Frederick the Great playing the flute, accompanied by a small orchestra, with C. P. E. Bach at the harpsichord. Painting by Adolph von Menzel, 1852.* (STAATLICHE MUSEEN, PREUSSICHER KULTURBESITZ: NATIONALGALERIE)

with the celebrated theorist, teacher, and composer Padre Giovanni Battista Martini (1706–1784) of Bologna. Bach was appointed organist of the cathedral at Milan in 1760, by which time he had converted to the Roman Catholic faith. Two years later, after two of his operas had been successfully produced in Naples, he moved to London, where he enjoyed a long career as composer, performer, teacher, and impresario. He had great success there with some forty keyboard concertos, written between 1763 and 1777. The title of his Opus 7 (ca. 1770), *Sei concerti per il cembalo o piano e forte*, bears witness to his early adoption of the pianoforte for public performance. The eight-year-old Mozart spent a year in London (1764–65), during which he met Bach and was very much impressed with his music. Mozart converted three of Bach's keyboard sonatas into concertos (K. 107/21b) and must have had Bach's models in mind when he wrote his first complete piano concerto, K. 175, in 1773.

Concerto form

The first movement of J. C. Bach's Concerto for Harpsichord or Piano and Strings in E♭, Op. 7, No. 5 (NAWM 93; CD 7 [34]), exhibits many features typical of the concerto at this time. As in the violin concertos of Tartini and his contemporaries, the principal ideas are introduced in an orchestral exposition entirely in the tonic, then elaborated, expanded, and added to in a solo section. There, as in the sonata form, the secondary and closing themes appear in the dominant, and a modulatory or developmental section leads to a recapitulation in the tonic. Orchestral tutti, after the opening one, function either as transitions or to reinforce the conclusive effect of a passage toward a principal cadence. The parallel between this movement and Mozart's K. 488 (NAWM 99; CD 8 [12]) is striking though not surprising, since by 1770 the main outlines of the first-movement form for the solo concerto were well established.

The solo concerto of this period thus retains elements of the ritornello structure of the Baroque period but is imbued with the contrasts of key and thematic material characteristic of the sonata. The first movement usually exhibits the following succession of events:[14]

Section:	**Exposition**								
Key:	**Tonic**						**Dominant**		
Instruments:	***Orchestra***				***Solo with Orchestra***			***Orchestra***	
Themes:	P	TT	K	KT	P	TT	S	K	KT

Development		**Recapitulation**					
Foreign keys to dominant		**Tonic**					
Solo with Orchestra	***Solo***	***Solo with Orchestra***				***Solo***	***Orchestra***
Exposition or new material	Short cad.	P	TT	(S)	K	Cadenza	KT

The parallels to the Baroque concerto evident in this design will be discussed in relation to Mozart's K. 488, where they stand out even more in the context of his symphonic style.

Orchestral Music in France

Paris became an important center of composition and publication toward the middle of the eighteenth century. Symphonies and *symphonies concertantes* flowed from the presses of Parisian publishers in a steady stream, often as *symphonies périodiques* or "symphonies of the month." Among the many foreign composers who flocked there were the Austrians Wagenseil and Ignaz Holzbauer (1711–1783), and the Bavarian Anton Fils (1733–1760), as well as Sammartini, Stamitz, and many others. The Belgian François-Joseph Gossec (1734–1829) came to Paris in 1751 and eventually succeeded Rameau and

Gossec

Stamitz as conductor of La Pouplinière's orchestra. Gossec published his first symphonies in 1756 and his first string quartets in 1769. In the 1760s he turned to writing comic operas; he was one of the most popular composers of the Revolutionary period and one of the first directors of the Paris Conservatoire. Particularly important in his oeuvre were the marches and cantatas written for public ceremonies of the new republic. One such work, his *Marche lugubre*, must have been in Beethoven's mind when he composed the Funeral March

Saint-Georges

for his Third Symphony, the *Eroica*. Joseph Boulogne Saint-Georges (ca. 1739–1799), whose mother came from Guadeloupe, distinguished himself in the genre of the *symphonie concertante*, a concerto-like work employing two or more solo instruments in addition to the regular orchestra. Among the many composers of *symphonies concertantes* was Giovanni Giuseppe Cambini (1746–1825), an Italian living in Paris. A large number of native French composers also participated in the extraordinary flowering of this type of composition.

14. In this diagram, P stands for primary-theme section, S for secondary-theme section, K for closing-theme section, TT for transitional tutti, and KT for closing tutti.

The Symphony Orchestra

The eighteenth-century concert orchestra was much smaller than today's. Haydn's orchestra from 1760 to 1785 rarely had more than twenty-five players, comprising strings, flute, two oboes, two bassoons, two horns, and a harpsichord, with trumpets and kettledrums occasionally added. Even in the 1790s the Viennese orchestras did not usually number more than thirty-five players. In the last quarter of the eighteenth century the basso continuo was gradually abandoned in the symphony and in other forms of ensemble music, as all the essential voices were taken over by the melody instruments. The responsibility for conducting the group fell to the leader of the violins. The typical orchestration at midcentury gave all the essential musical material to the strings and used the winds only for doubling, reinforcing, and filling in the harmonies. Sometimes in performance woodwinds and brasses might be added to the orchestra even though the composer had written no parts specifically for them. Later in the century the wind instruments were entrusted with more important and more independent material.

Serenade

The Viennese serenade was designed primarily for out-of-doors or for informal occasions. Like the cassation and notturno, it was a hybrid, a cross

■ *Surrounding a harpsichord and a seated cellist is a chamber ensemble consisting of three violins, four woodwinds, two trumpets, and three singers. The instrumentalists read from music desks, while the singers hold their parts. The man at the end seems to be conducting with a scroll, but the folio in his left hand contains a Christian motto or perhaps the title of a cantata, rather than music notation. Anonymous eighteenth-century painting.* (GERMANISCHES NATIONAL-MUSEUM, NUREMBERG. COURTESY RCMI)

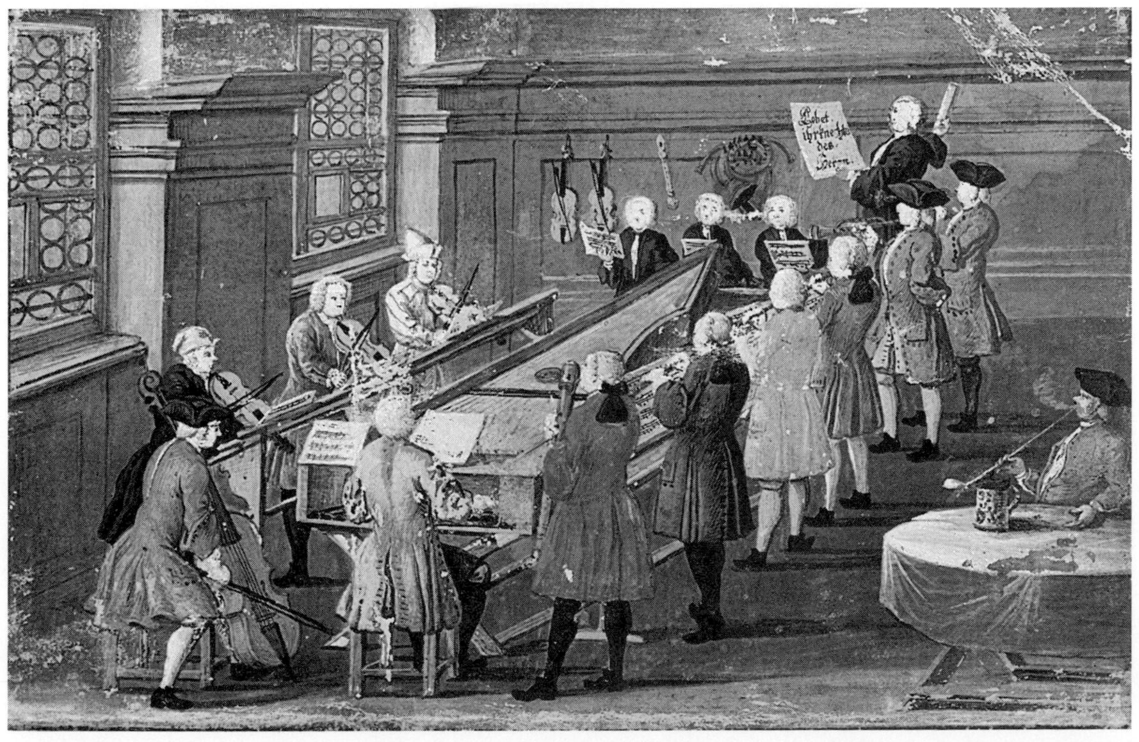

between symphony and concerto. Serenades were written for wind instruments alone, for strings alone, for full orchestra, or for as little as two violins. An outstanding example is Mozart's eight-movement *Haffner* Serenade, K. 250, in which a four-movement symphony encloses the slow movement and final rondo of a violin concerto, together with two extra Minuets.

Chamber Music

Wherever the keyboard has a fully written-out part in the chamber music of the 1770s and 1780s, it tends to dominate its one, two, or three partners. In chamber music for strings alone, the first violin carries most of the melodic substance, while the cello functions like a basso continuo and the viola like a filler. However, knowing that string-quartet players enjoyed hearing themselves in extended solos of several measures, composers wrote *concertante* quartets as well as quartets in which players exchanged shorter motives. One composer before Haydn who wrote such *concertante* quartets was the Mannheimer Franz Xaver Richter (1709–1789).

SUMMARY

The early Classic period explored a wealth of new genres, forms, and expressive means. Much of the innovation originated in opera, particularly comic opera. There, the urge to entertain and reach a diverse audience led to a simplification of means and a striving for naturalness of expression. From the Italian theaters the new styles spread through the cosmopolitan network of musicians, composers, and directors to centers such as Paris, Mannheim, and Vienna. Many practices broke out of the theater into the concert halls and private chambers. This movement purged the excesses of the Italian opera, and a spare, transparent, logical—almost proselike—flow of musical ideas ensued that could be grasped on first hearing. Instrumental music in particular profited from these developments, because it no longer needed a text or a title to render it intelligible. In this way this period laid the foundations for the triumph of instrumental music in the Classic period.

BIBLIOGRAPHY

Music Collections

COLLECTED WORKS OF INDIVIDUAL COMPOSERS

The collected works of J. C. Bach have been edited in facs. by E. Warburton et al.: *J. C. Bach: 1735–1782*, 48 vols. (New York: Garland, 1986–). An edition of the works of C. P. E. Bach is under way, ed. Rachel W. Wade and E. Eugene Helm (New York: Oxford University Press, 1989–). The *Opera omnia* of Pergolesi, ed. Francesco Caffarelli, 17 vols. (Rome,

1939–42), contains a large quantity of misattributed works, and numerous authentic works are missing. A new edition is in progress, ed. Barry S. Brook, Francesco Degrada, Helmut Hucke, Marvin Paymer, sponsored by the Pergolesi Research Center, City University of New York and the City of Jesi, Italy (New York: Pendragon Press, 1985–). For collected works of Domenico Scarlatti and Gluck, see below under "Keyboard Music" and "Opera."

Keyboard Music

A collected edition of Domenico Scarlatti's sonatas by Alessandro Longo (New York: G. Ricordi, 1947–51) consisted of 10 vols. and supplement. A representative selection, in a superior edition in 2 vols., is Ralph Kirkpatrick's *Sixty Sonatas* (New York: G. Schirmer, 1953); *Complete Keyboard Works*, ed. in facs. by R. Kirkpatrick, 18 vols. (New York: Johnson Reprint, 1972); another selection is ed. Eiji Hashimoto, *100 Sonatas* (New York: G. Schirmer, 1975). For a complete thematic catalogue with incipits and concordances, see the revised German translation of Kirkpatrick's *Domenico Scarlatti* (Munich: Heinrich Ellermann, 1972), Vol. 2.

A valuable selection of eighteenth- and early nineteenth-century compositions by Alberti, Platti, et al. can be found in *Thirteen Keyboard Sonatas*, ed. with critical commentaries by William S. Newman (Chapel Hill: University of North Carolina Press, 1947).

The collected works for solo keyboard by C. P. E. Bach have been edited in facs. by Darrell Berg, 6 vols. (New York: Garland, 1985); *Thematic Catalogue of the Works of C. P. E. Bach*, ed. E. E. Helm (New Haven: Yale University Press, 1989); an older thematic catalogue is by Alfred Wotquenne (Leipzig and New York: Breitkopf & Härtel, 1905; repr. Wiesbaden, 1964). See also Karl Geiringer, ed., *Music of the Bach Family* (Cambridge, Mass.: Harvard University Press, 1955).

Selections from the works of Schobert are published in DdT, Vol. 39.

Symphony and Chamber Music

A comprehensive collection of approximately 600 symphonies in full score begun under the editorship of Barry S. Brook, *The Symphony: 1720–1840* (New York and London: Garland, 1979–), consists of six series, A–F, each corresponding to a geographical region. Series C, Vol. 8, is C. P. E. Bach, *Six Symphonies*, ed. Charles C. Gallagher and E. E. Helm (1982).

Additional symphonies by Mannheim composers are found in DTB, Vols. 3/1, 7/2, and 8/2; a reprint of the music in 2 vols. is entitled *Mannheim Symphonists*, ed. Hugo Riemann (New York: Broude Brothers, 1956). Mannheim chamber music is in DTB, Vols. 15 and 16. Symphonies by Viennese composers are in DTOe, Vols. 31 and 39 (Years 5/2 and 19/2); North German symphonies, DdT, Vols. 51–52; symphonies by C. P. E. Bach, *Das Erbe deutscher Musik*, Series I, Vol. 18; chamber and symphonic music by Johann Christian Bach, ibid., Vols. 3, 30. Instrumental works of Michael Haydn in DTOe, Vol. 29 (Year 14/2); of Dittersdorf, in DTOe, Vol. 81 (Year 43/2). *The Symphonies of G. B. Sammartini*, ed. Bathia Churgin (Cambridge, Mass.: Harvard University Press, 1968–).

Opera, Song, and Church Music

A large number of operas from this period are published in facs. of manuscript copies in the series *Italian Opera 1640–1770*, ed. with intros. by Howard Mayer Brown (New York: Garland, 1977–84). Among the composers are J. C. Bach, G. Bonincini, Rinaldo di Capua, Galuppi, Gassmann, Gluck, Graun, Hasse, Jommelli, Leonardo Leo, Nicola Logroscino, G. M. Orlandini, David Perez, Pergolesi, Piccinni, Nicolo Porpora, Terradellas, Traetta, Leonardo Vinci, and Wagenseil. There are also companion volumes of librettos, *Italian Opera Librettos, 1640–1770*, with intros. by H. M. Brown (New York: Garland, 1978–).

Graun's *Montezuma* is published in DdT, Vol. 15; Jommelli's *Fetonte* in DdT, Vols.

32/33; selections from Traetta's operas in DTB, Vols. 14/1 and 17; Hasse's *Arminio* is in *Das Erbe deutscher Musik*, Series 1, Vols. 27/28.

Gluck's principal operas, beginning with *Orfeo*, were published in a sumptuous edition by J. Pelletan et al. (Leipzig, 1873–96), 7 vols.; a new edition of the complete works, ed. Rudolf Gerber et al., is in progress (Kassel: Bärenreiter, 1951–). See also DTB, Vol. 14/2; and DTOe, Vols. 44a, 60, 82 (Years 21/2, 30/2, 44); thematic catalogue by A. Wotquenne (Leipzig and New York: Breitkopf & Härtel, 1904; repr. Hildesheim, 1967).

Italian comic operas are published in CDMI, Vols. 13 (Galuppi) and 20 (Paisiello); and in CMI, Vol. 7 (Piccinni). For Pergolesi, see Chapter 10 under "Church Music and Oratorio."

A collected edition of the works of Grétry, in 49 vols., was published by the Belgian government (Leipzig: Breitkopf & Härtel, 1884–1936; repr. New York, 197–).

For ballad operas, see Walter H. Rubsamen, ed. *The Ballad Opera* (facs. of texts and music), 28 vols. (New York: Garland, 1974).

German Singspiele are available in these modern editions: Viennese: *Die Bergknappen* (The Miners), by Ignaz Umlauf (1746–1796), in DTOe, Vol. 36 (Year 18/1); *Der Dorfbarbier* (The Village Barber), by Johann Schenk (1753–1836), in DTOe, Vol. 48 (Year 24). See also the songs in DTOe, Vol. 64 (Year 33/1). North German: *Der Jahrmarkt* (The Fair), by Georg Benda (1722–1795), DdT, Vol. 64. Facsimiles of German and Austrian operas are found in *German Opera, 1770–1800*, ed. Thomas Bauman (New York: Garland, 1985–86). Composers include Hiller, Benda, Reichardt, Zumsteeg, Süssmayr, Salieri, and others.

The second part of Vol. 1 of Max Friedländer's *Das deutsche Lied im 18. Jahrhundert* (Stuttgart: J. G. Cotta, 1902) contains 236 songs, mostly from eighteenth-century collections. See also DTOe, Vols. 54 and 79 (Years 37/2 and 42/2); and DdT, Vols. 35/36 (Sperontes) and 57.

Viennese church music of the late eighteenth century is in DTOe, Vols. 62 and 83 (Years 33/1 and 45). Hasse's oratorio *La Conversione di S. Agostino* in DdT, Vol. 20; Jommelli's *Passione di Gesu Cristo* in CDMI, Vol. 15. Hasse's comic intermezzo *La contadina astuta* is published as a work of Pergolesi in the Caffarelli edition.

For Further Reading

A survey of music of the Classic period that is up-to-date in its research and methodology is Philip G. Downs, *Classical Music: The Era of Haydn, Mozart, and Beethoven* (New York: Norton, 1992), which is accompanied by the *Anthology of Classical Music*, ed. P. G. Downs (New York: Norton, 1992). Specialists in various aspects of this period are the authors of chapters in the volume of the New Oxford History of Music, *The Age of Enlightenment, 1745–1790*, ed. Egon Wellesz and Frederick W. Sternfeld (London and New York: Oxford University Press, 1973). A stimulating topical study based on the theorists of the time is Leonard G. Ratner, *Classic Music: Expression, Form, and Style* (New York: Schirmer Books, 1980). Important sources of information about eighteenth-century musical life are Charles Burney's *General History of Music* (1776), ed. F. Mercer (London: G. T. Foulis, 1935; repr. New York: Dover, 1957), and his two travel books: *The Present State of Music in France and Italy* (London, 1771) and *The Present State of Music in Germany, The Netherlands, and the United Provinces*, 2 vols. (London, 1775). Excerpts from *The Present State of Music in France and Italy* are in SRrev, pp. 989–99; 5:255–65); a new edition of the work appears under the title *Music, Men and Manners in France and Italy, 1770*, ed. Herbert E. Poole (London: Eulenburg Books, 1974). Percy Scholes also edited Burney's two travel books under the title *Dr. Burney's Musical Tours in Europe* (London and New York: Oxford University Press, 1959). For a modern historian's view, see William Weber, *The Rise of Musical Classics in Eighteenth-Century England: A Study in Canon, Ritual, and Ideology* (Oxford: Clarendon Press, 1992)

For readings on the general cultural scene in various countries and cities such as Vienna, Mannheim, London, etc., consult in the series Man and Music: *The Classical Era:*

From the 1740s to the End of the 18th Century, ed. Neal Zaslaw (Englewood Cliffs, N.J.: Prentice-Hall, 1989), in which each essay is written by a specialist. For comic opera in Vienna: Mary Hunter and James Webster, eds., *Opera buffa in Mozart's Vienna* (Cambridge: Cambridge University Press, 1998). Facsimiles of documents in the *Querelle des bouffons* originally printed in Paris and The Hague, 1752–54, are collected in Denise Launay, ed., *La Querelle des Bouffons* (Geneva: Minkoff, 1973).

On *galant*, see David A. Sheldon, "The Galant Style Revisited and Reevaluated," AM 47 (1975):240–70, which discusses the etymology and historical use of the word. C. P. E. Bach's *Versuch über die wahre Art, das Clavier zu spielen* was first published in 1753 (Pt. 1) and 1762 (Pt. 2); facs. ed. L. Hoffmann-Erbrecht (Leipzig: Breitkopf & Härtel, 1957); the trans. by William J. Mitchell as *Essay on the True Art of Playing Keyboard Instruments* (New York: Norton, 1949) combines the original and rev. editions of the eighteenth century. Excerpt in SRrev, pp. 851–56; 5:117–22. Bach's autobiography (1773) is available in facs. ed. with critical annotations by W. S. Newman in MQ 51 (1965):363–72.

The *Versuch einer Anweisung, die Flöte traversiere zu spielen* (Essay on Playing the Transverse Flute), by Johann Joachim Quantz (1697–1773), another important treatise of this period, was first published in 1752; facs. of 3rd ed., 1789 (Kassel: Bärenreiter, 1953); trans. Edward R. Reilly as *On Playing the Flute* (New York: Schirmer Books, 1966; rev. 1985). Excerpts in SRrev, pp. 799–807; 5:65–73.

A central work on the Italian opera of this period is Eric Weimer, *Opera seria and the Evolution of Classical Style, 1755–1772* (Ann Arbor, Mich.: UMI Research Press, 1984). Marcello's *Teatro alla moda*, in an annotated English translation by Reinhard G. Pauly, is in MQ 34 (1948):371–403, and 35 (1949):85–105. On the opéra comique, see David Charlton, *Grétry and the Growth of Opéra-comique* (Cambridge: Cambridge University Press, 1986); Edmond M. Gagey, *Ballad Opera* (New York: Columbia University Press, 1937); Thomas Bauman, *North German Opera in the Age of Goethe* (Cambridge: Cambridge University Press, 1985).

On the sonata, see W. S. Newman, *The Sonata in the Classic Era* (Chapel Hill: University of North Carolina Press, 1963); and Charles Rosen, *Sonata Forms* (New York: Norton, 1980; rev. ed., 1988).

Concerning the symphony in Mannheim in general and Johann Stamitz in particular, consult Eugene K. Wolf, *The Symphonies of Johann Stamitz: A Study in the Formation of the Classic Style* (Utrecht/Antwerp: Bohn, Scheltema & Holkema; The Hague: M. Nijhoff, 1981). On the symphonie concertante, see Barry S. Brook, *La Symphonie française dans la seconde moitié du xviiie siècle*, 3 vols. (Paris: Institut de musicologie de l'Université de Paris, 1962).

Bach Sons For books on the life and music of J. S. Bach's sons, see Chapter 12. See also David Schulenberg, *The Instrumental Music of C. P. E. Bach* (Ann Arbor, Mich.: UMI Research Press, 1984). The standard biography of Johann Christian Bach is by Charles Sanford Terry, 2nd rev. ed. (Westport, Conn.: Greenwood Press, 1980).

Gluck Patricia Howard, *Gluck: An Eighteenth-Century Portrait in Letters and Documents* (Oxford: Clarendon Press, 1995). Martin Cooper, *Gluck* (New York: Oxford University Press, 1935), and Alfred Einstein, *Gluck* (London: J. M. Dent, 1954), are comprehensive studies of the life, works, and musical environment; *Collected Correspondence*, ed. Hedwig and Erich H. Mueller von Asow, trans S. Thomson (London: Barrie & Rockliff, 1962). On Gluck's operas, see Ernest Newman, *Gluck and the Opera* (London: V. Gollancz, 1967); Bruce Alan Brown, *Gluck and the French Theatre in Vienna* (Oxford: Clarendon Press, 1991); F. W. Sternfeld, "Gluck's Operas and Italian Tradition," and J. Rushton, "From Vienna to Paris: Gluck and the French Opera," both in *Chigiana* 29–30 (1975):275–98; Daniel Heartz, "From Garrick to Gluck: The Reform of Theatre and Opera in the Mid-Eighteenth Century," *Proceedings of the Royal Musical Association* 94 (1967–68):111–27, and in GLHWM V 11:329–45. Patricia Howard, comp., *Gluck, Orfeo* (Cambridge: Cambridge

University Press, 1981), an opera handbook. Bibliography of Gluck's printed works by Cecil Hopkinson, 2nd ed. (New York: Broude Brothers, 1967). P. Howard, *C. W. Gluck: A Guide to Research* (New York: Garland, 1987).

Domenico Scarlatti The best book about D. Scarlatti is R. Kirkpatrick's *Domenico Scarlatti* (New York, 1968; new edition, Princeton University Press, 1983), a model of scholarly authority and musical insight. A more recent study is by Malcolm Boyd, *Domenico Scarlatti—Master of Music* (New York: Schirmer Books, 1986). On the state of Scarlatti research, see Joel Sheveloff, "D. Scarlatti: Tercentenary Frustrations," MQ 71 (1985):399–436, and 72 (1986):90–118; and Carole F. Vidali, *Alessandro and Domenico Scarlatti: A Guide to Research* (New York: Garland, 1993).

CHAPTER 14

THE LATE EIGHTEENTH CENTURY: HAYDN AND MOZART

Career

Haydn and Mozart, the two outstanding composers of the late eighteenth century, had a great deal in common: they were personal friends; each admired and was influenced by the music of the other; they were both practicing musicians—Mozart a virtuoso pianist, Haydn a fine violinist who also conducted from the harpsichord—and they both composed prolifically and with careful attention to detail.

Their lives and careers differed fundamentally, however. Haydn, born in 1732, was seventy-seven when he died in 1809. Mozart, born nearly a generation later in 1756, died in 1791 at the age of thirty-five. Haydn's growth to artistic maturity was much slower than that of Mozart, a child prodigy. Haydn worked contentedly during most of his career in the service of a noble Hungarian family. Mozart gave up a steady job in his hometown of Salzburg to become a free agent in Vienna. Most important, Mozart traveled a great deal in his early years—to England, Italy, Germany, and France—and absorbed the many styles and practices he found there, whereas Haydn took his models from local traditions around Vienna.

FRANZ JOSEPH HAYDN

Franz Joseph Haydn was born in Rohrau, a little town near the Hungarian border in what is now Austria. He received his first musical training from an uncle with whom he went to live at the age of five. Two years later he became a choirboy at St. Stephen's Cathedral in Vienna, where he acquired a great deal of practical experience but received no systematic instruction in music theory.

Dismissed when his voice changed, the youth supported himself precariously as a freelance musician and teacher. He mastered counterpoint by studying Fux's *Gradus ad Parnassum.* Meanwhile he made himself known to influential people in Vienna and took lessons in composition from Nicola Porpora, a famous Italian composer and singing teacher, whom he served as accompanist and assistant. In 1758 or 1759, he became music director for a Count Morzin, who lived in Vienna but spent summers in his native Bohemia. Haydn probably wrote his first symphonies for the count's orchestra. The year 1761 was momentous in Haydn's life: he entered the service of Prince Paul Anton Esterházy, head of one of the wealthiest and most powerful Hungarian families, a man devoted to music and a bountiful patron of the art.

Music at Eszterháza

At the court of Paul Anton and his brother Nicholas (the Magnificent), who succeeded to the title in 1762, Haydn passed nearly thirty years under circumstances almost ideal for his development as a composer. Beginning in 1766, Prince Nicholas, whose seat was in Eisenstadt just south of Vienna, lived for most of the year at his remote country estate of Eszterháza. The palace and grounds were designed to rival the splendor of Versailles. There were two theaters, one for opera and one for marionette plays, as well as two large and sumptuously appointed music rooms in the palace itself. Haydn had to compose whatever music the prince demanded, to conduct the performances, to train and supervise all the musical personnel, and to keep the instruments in repair. He built up the orchestra to about twenty-five players. Operas and concerts became weekly events and special operas and concerts were put on for

Eszterháza Palace, built 1762–66 as a summer residence on the Neusiedler Sea by the Hungarian prince Nikolaus Esterházy, whom Haydn served for almost thirty years. The palace opera house opened in 1768 with a performance of Haydn's Lo speziale. *Engraving, 1791, by János Berkeny after Szabó and Karl Schütz.* (BUDAPEST, HUNGARIAN NATIONAL MUSEUM)

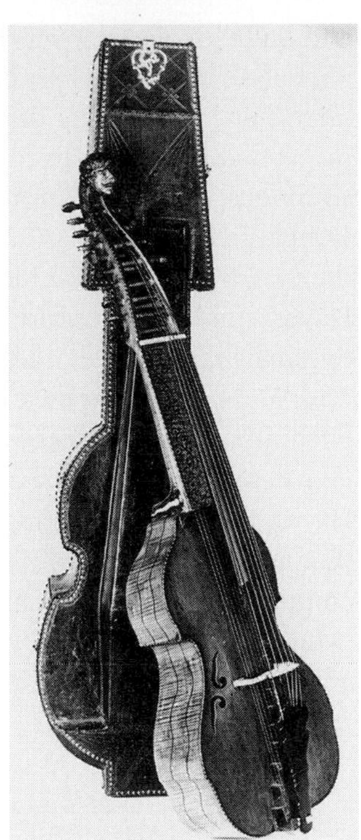

This baryton, shown leaning against its case, was owned by Prince Nikolaus Esterházy; it was made in Vienna by Johann Joseph Stalmann in 1750. The instrument, a favorite of the prince's, resembled a bass viol but had a set of sympathetic strings that could be plucked and that added to its resonance. Haydn created a baryton repertory of some 165 pieces so that the prince could participate in chamber music. (BUDAPEST, HUNGARIAN NATIONAL MUSEUM)

notable visitors. In the almost daily chamber music sessions in the prince's private apartments, the prince himself usually played the baryton, an instrument resembling a large viola da gamba with an extra set of resonating metal strings that could be plucked like a harp. Haydn wrote some 165 pieces for the baryton, mostly trios with viola and cello.

Although Eszterháza was isolated, Haydn kept abreast of current developments in the world of music through the constant stream of distinguished guests and artists and through occasional trips to Vienna. He had the inestimable advantages of having a devoted, highly skilled band of singers and players and an intelligent patron, whose requirements may have been burdensome but whose understanding and enthusiasm were inspiring. As Haydn once said,

> My Prince was satisfied with all my works; I received applause. As head of an orchestra, I could make experiments, observe what created an impression and what weakened it, and thus improve, add, make cuts, take risks. I was isolated from the world; no one in my vicinity could make me lose confidence in myself or bother me, and so I had to become original.[1]

Haydn's contract with Prince Paul Anton Esterházy forbade him to sell or give away his compositions, but this provision was later relaxed. As his fame spread in the 1770s and 1780s, he filled many commissions from publishers

1. Trans. Elaine Sisman, "Haydn, Shakespeare, and the Rules of Originality," in *Haydn and His World*, ed. Sisman (Princeton: Princeton University Press, 1997), p. 3.

and individuals all over Europe. He remained at Eszterháza until Prince Nicholas's death in 1790. Nicholas's son Anton became the next Prince Esterházy and immediately disbanded his father's orchestra. Haydn was given a pension and went to live in his own house in Vienna, but not for long. Two strenuous but highly productive and profitable seasons in London followed (January 1791 to July 1792 and February 1794 to August 1795), mostly under the management of the impresario and violinist Johann Peter Salomon. Here Haydn conducted concerts and wrote a multitude of new works, including the twelve *London* Symphonies.

London visits

Anton Esterházy died while Haydn was in London and was succeeded by Nicholas II, who cared less for Haydn's music than for the glory that accrued to himself for having such a famous person in his employ. He persuaded Haydn to resume directing music for the court, which now resided almost all year in Vienna. Haydn's duties were light, the principal obligation being to compose one Mass a year (which he did between 1796 and 1802) for the princess's name day. He therefore had ample time to compose quartets, trios, and his last two oratorios, *Die Schöpfung* (The Creation, 1798) and *Die Jahreszeiten* (The Seasons, 1801), both performed in Vienna with resounding success.

Last years in Vienna

Although Haydn's music responded to changing tastes and to a variety of genres, certain enduring traits stand out, especially in the symphonies.

HAYDN'S INSTRUMENTAL MUSIC

Symphonic Form

Many of Haydn's earliest symphonies are in the early Classic three-movement form derived from the Italian opera overture (sinfonia). They typically consist of an Allegro, an Andante in the parallel minor or subdominant key, and a Minuet or a rapid gigue-like movement in $\frac{3}{8}$ or $\frac{6}{8}$ (for example, Symphonies Nos. 9 and 19). Other symphonies from the early period (for example, Nos. 21 and 22) are in four movements, all in the same key, usually Andante–Allegro–Minuet–Presto, recalling the slow–fast–slow–fast sequence of the *sonata da chiesa.* Soon after composing these early symphonies, Haydn adopted the standard Classic four movements: I. Allegro; II. Andante moderato; III. Minuet and Trio; IV. Allegro. One symphony, No. 3, dating from 1762 or earlier, had used this sequence.

First-movement form

A typical first-movement Allegro alternates stable and unstable periods. The stable periods are not tension-free, but their tonality and their rhythmic and melodic profiles are consistent. These passages—the statements of the primary, secondary, and closing material—are usually phrased symmetrically, most often in balanced four-measure phrases, and are clearly delimited by cadences, at least in the early symphonies. The ideas are presented through a combination of string and wind ensembles, with some tutti punctuations. The unstable passages in the exposition, mainly transitions, are often tutti or culminate in a tutti. They are characterized by nervous rhythmic energy, sequences, modulatory thrusts, asymmetrical phrasing, powerful harmonic drive, and avoidance of cadences. The development sections are, of course, the least stable; unlike transitions, they may draw material from various sections in any order and may contain episodes that are relaxed and relatively stable. Although the recapitulation is tonally stable, Haydn endowed the transitions with unexpected deviations that add suspense to the anticipated arrival of the familiar thematic sections. Slow introductions, when they occur, are usually unstable from the outset.

Exposition

In a typical Allegro movement, Haydn reiterated the opening statement immediately, but with some destabilizing turns of harmony or rhythm that steer the music in a new direction. A transition or bridge passage, sometimes in several sections, to the dominant or relative major or minor follows. This transition is most often a loud tutti, with dramatic, rushing figures, a perfect foil for the second thematic section, which is more lightly scored, graceful, ornamented, melodically distinctive, and harmonically stable. In most of the symphonies of the 1770s and 1780s, Haydn clearly contrasted the secondary material with the opening idea. But in some, as in the later *London* Symphonies, Haydn built the second thematic section on the opening material. The exposition usually ends with a closing tutti based on a cadential, repetitive, vigorous figure, sometimes harking back to the opening but usually distinct from the primary and secondary subjects. In some of the movements, the section in the secondary key is devoted entirely to the closing subject.

Development

Haydn rarely introduced new thematic ideas after the exposition's closing double bar (an exception is the famous D-major melody at measure 108 in his Symphony No. 45 in F♯ minor, the *Farewell*). The development often begins with a restatement of the opening subject, or sometimes with transition material or with one of the other subjects. Motives from the exposition are combined, superimposed, extended; put through sequences, fugue-like counterpoints and strettos; or made into figurations for rushing passages. Abrupt changes of subject, digressions, and silences are particularly characteristic of Haydn. In the course of his career, Haydn increased the length and weight of the development section until it achieved parity with the other two sections.

Recapitulation

We are usually well prepared for the arrival of the recapitulation, but its actual onset is sometimes disguised or played down and not even recognized until after the fact. All of the material is recapitulated in the tonic, though sometimes a theme originally in the major mode may return in the minor, or vice versa. Only in some early symphonies did Haydn cling to the older technique of recapitulating just the secondary or closing section in the tonic. He almost always began the reprise with the opening subject, sometimes rescoring and extending it in new ways. Rather than curtailing the transitions because he did not need to modulate, he often intensified and animated them with a simulated modulation. He might even alter the comparative weight given to the secondary and closing subjects. Haydn did not usually write a coda but instead amplified the closing section.

This model of a Haydn symphonic sonata-form movement is only an abstract template that matches any specific movement more or less well. This process may be observed in action by studying the first movement of Symphony No. 56 (see NAWM 94, CD 7 [47] / 3 ⟨11⟩, and the accompanying commentary).

Minuet

A Minuet-and-Trio movement appears in most Classic symphonies. The Minuet itself is always in a two-part ‖ : a : ‖ : a′ (a) : ‖ form. The Trio is built along similar lines; it is usually in the same key as the Minuet (possibly with a change of mode), but it is shorter and has lighter orchestration; after the Trio, the Minuet returns da capo, resulting in a three-part ABA form for the movement as a whole. Haydn's Minuets with their Trios contain some of his most charming music, remarkable for their wealth of musical ideas and happy traits of harmonic invention and instrumental color in such a modest medium. He said once that he wished someone would write "a really new minuet," but he himself succeeded admirably in doing so nearly every time he wrote one.

The Classic symphony generally demanded the most attention from its audience in its first movement. The second movement offered an oasis of calm and gentle melody after the complexity and contrasts of the first movement. The Minuet provided relaxation, since it was shorter than either of the two preceding movements; it was written in a more popular style, and its form was easy for the listener to follow. But the Minuet does not make a satisfactory closing movement. It is too short to balance the preceding two, and the spirit of relaxation it induces must be balanced by a further buildup of tension, climax, and release.

Finale

Haydn soon came to realize that the $\frac{3}{8}$ or $\frac{6}{8}$ Presto finales of his earliest symphonies were inadequate to accomplish this, being too light in form and content to produce a satisfying effect in the symphony as a whole. He therefore developed a new type of closing movement, which first appeared in the late 1760s: an Allegro or Presto in $\frac{2}{4}$ or ¢, usually shorter than the first movement, compact, swiftly moving, overflowing with high spirits and nimble gaiety, and abounding in little whimsical tricks of silence and all sorts of impish surprises.

Haydn's first ninety-two symphonies were completed by 1789, most of them for Prince Esterházy's orchestra. He composed Nos. 82–87, now known as the *Paris* Symphonies, on commission in 1785–86 for a concert series in the French capital. Nos. 88–92 were privately commissioned. No. 92, now called the *Oxford* Symphony, was played when Haydn received an honorary Doctor of Music degree from Oxford University in 1791. Many of the other symphonies (as well as many of the quartets) have acquired special names for one reason or another, few of them from the composer himself. The last twelve symphonies (Nos. 93–104) were composed for London.

Early Symphonies

Haydn's earliest contemporary critics and listeners praised the strikingly inventive primary material in his symphonies. For his sonata-form movements, he chose, rather than catchy tunes, themes that were easily broken up and recombined, and he dispensed them frugally. Broken-chord patterns, wide or even wild leaps, combinations of scales and turns, and rushing figures, sometimes with measured tremolos, are common in the main themes of the symphonies of the 1760s.

Symphonies No. 6 to 8

Certain exceptional features appear in three symphonies, Nos. 6 to 8, which Haydn composed soon after entering the service of Prince Esterházy in 1761. He gave them the suggestive titles *Le Matin, Le Midi,* and *Le Soir* (Morning, Noon, Evening), without further explanation. Nos. 6 and 7 have brief Adagio introductions, the one for *Le Matin* undoubtedly meant to depict a sunrise. In the Allegro of *Le Midi,* Haydn chose several orchestra members to play concertante solos between returns of a tutti that acts as a ritornello. This symphony's slow movement is an instrumental recitativo obbligato followed by an aria for solo violin and cello.

Symphony No. 31

Many of the symphonies dating from the 1760s are experimental. No. 31 (*With the Horn Signal*) is divertimento-like in its conspicuous use of winds (four horns instead of the customary two) and in the theme-and-variations form of the finale.

The Symphonies of 1768–74

The symphonies of 1768–74 show Haydn as a composer of mature technique and fertile imagination. No longer viewing it as light entertainment or as a delightful overture to an opera, Haydn now regarded the symphony as a serious work that demanded close listening. The deeply emotional and agitated character of the symphonies, particularly those in minor keys, has been associated with the movement in literature known as *Sturm und Drang* (storm and stress), but some of these symphonies antedate the movement, whose name derives from a 1776 play by Friedrich Maximilian Klinger. Five symphonies in minor keys (Nos. 26, 39, 44, 45, and 49, all from 1768) manifest this intensity of feeling. Haydn was probably responding in them to the challenges of his immediate surroundings and to the talk then in the air about "the sublime" as a goal of music, particularly orchestral music.

Sturm und Drang

Minor keys

Symphonies Nos. 44, 45, 47

Symphonies Nos. 44, 45, and 47 are typical of these years. They are all on a larger scale than the symphonies of the previous decade. Themes are more broadly laid out, those in the fast movements often beginning with a bold unison proclamation followed immediately by a contrasting idea, with the whole theme then restated, as in No. 56 (discussed below). Development sections, limited to motives from the exposition, have become more propulsive and dramatic. The changes from *forte* to *piano* and the crescendos and *sforzati* that entered Haydn's writing at this time are also startling. The harmonic palette is richer than in the early symphonies; modulations range more widely, the harmonic arches are broader, and counterpoint is integral to the musical ideas.

Slow movements

The slow movements have a romantically expressive warmth. Most of the slow movements are in sonata form, but with such leisurely, freely drawn out progression of thought that a listener is hardly conscious of the structure. In Symphony No. 44 in E minor, known as the *Trauersinfonie* (Symphony of

Mourning), we find one of the most beautiful Adagios in all of Haydn's works. The slow movement of No. 47 is a theme with variations, favored for slow movements in Haydn's later works. The first period of the theme is constructed in double counterpoint at the octave, so that the last period of the theme (and of each of the four variations) is the same as the first but with the melody and the bass interchanged. Another contrapuntal device is exhibited in the Minuet of No. 44, which is in a canon at the octave. The Minuet of No. 47 is written *al rovescio*—that is, the second section of the Minuet, and also of the Trio, consists of the first section played backward.

Farewell Symphony

According to a well-known story, Haydn wrote the *Farewell* Symphony (No. 45) as a hint to Prince Esterházy that it was time to move back to Eisenstadt from his summer palace and give the musicians a chance to see their families again. The final Presto breaks off into an Adagio, in the course of which one group of instruments after another concludes its part and the players get up and leave; only two first violins remain to play the closing measures. The *Farewell* Symphony is unusual in several other respects. The first movement introduces a long new theme in the course of the development section—a device that Haydn never used again. The key of this symphony, F♯ minor, is unusual for the eighteenth century, but such remote tonalities are a mark of Haydn's style at this time (see also Symphony No. 46 in B major and No. 49 [*La Passione*, 1768] in F minor). Characteristically, he departed from the minor mode in the Adagio (A major) and Minuet (F♯ major) of the *Farewell* Symphony, and although the Presto is in F♯ minor, the closing Adagio begins in A major and ends in F♯ major. This slow ending, of course, is exceptional, for reasons not purely musical.

The Symphonies of 1774–88

The symphonies of 1774–88 exhibit a striking change, most evident in Nos. 54 and 57, both composed in 1774. The minor keys of the preceding period, the passionate accents and the experiments in form and expression, now give way to a smooth and assured exploitation of orchestral resources.

Symphony No. 56

Symphony No. 56 (1774; see NAWM 94, CD 7 [47] / 3 ⟨11⟩, for first movement) is one of twenty symphonies set in C major. Except for the very earliest, these symphonies constitute a special group, many of them composed for particular celebrations at Eszterháza. Like his five previous C-major symphonies (Nos. 20, 33, 38, 41, and 48), No. 56 is festive and brilliant, with high trumpets (labeled clarino in the score), high French horns, two oboes, a bassoon, and timpani (but no flutes, which Haydn used then only rarely). The work reflects the high regard in which the genre was held in the 1770s. Audiences expected works that were serious, ambitious, stirring, and impressive, yet immediately intelligible and appealing. The principal subject contains three elements: a two-octave descending unison sweep of the major triad (marked *a* in Example 14.1), a soft passage built on a suspension (*b*), and a cadential phrase dominated by a repeated appoggiatura figure (*c*). In a four-measure codetta to this theme group, a martial dotted figure turns the broken-chord unison into a fanfare.

Example 14.1 *Haydn, Symphony No. 56, Allegro di molto*

The six *Paris* Symphonies of 1785–86 (Nos. 82–87) were commissioned for the large orchestra of the *Concerts de la Loge Olympique.* Queen Marie Antoinette, who frequently attended these concerts, is said to have especially loved No. 85, called "La Reine." After the six symphonies were performed again in 1787, this time at the *Concert spirituel,* a reviewer of the *Mercure de France* noted how "this great genius could draw such rich and varied developments from a single subject, so different from the sterile composers who pass continually from one idea to another."

Paris Symphonies

Symphonies Nos. 88 to 92 of 1787–88 foreshadow the *London* Symphonies. Four of these symphonies begin with a slow introduction, whose themes are sometimes related to those of the following Allegro. Contrasting subjects in sonata-form movements now appear more infrequently. Rather, a set of ideas announced at the beginning prevails throughout the movement. Many of the slow movements close with a quiet, introspective coda that features woodwind instruments and employs colorful chromatic harmonies (as in No. 92, NAWM 95; CD 7 [54]). The wind instruments are prominent also in the Trios of the Minuets. In the finales, Haydn made considerable use of contrapuntal devices and texture—for example, he included a canon in the last movement of No. 88. By such means he endowed closing movements with both popular appeal and sufficient weight to balance the rest of the symphony. The finale of No. 88 is a particularly fine example, uniting the tuneful and popular rondo format with deeper sonata procedures.

Symphonies Nos. 88 to 92

The *London* Symphonies

Like other composers of his time, Haydn wrote music mostly for specific occasions and for players and singers he knew. When he accepted a commission from outside Eszterháza, he found out as much as he could about the performers, the concert hall, and related matters so that he could adapt the music to the specific circumstances of the performance. The invitation from Salomon in 1790 to compose and conduct six, and later six more, symphonies for the cosmopolitan and exacting audiences of London spurred him to supreme efforts. Hailed by the British as "the greatest composer in the world," he was determined to live up to what was expected of him, and the *London* Symphonies are indeed his crowning achievements. Everything he had learned in forty years of experience went into them. While there are no radical departures from his previous works, all the elements are brought together on a grander scale, with more brilliant orchestration, more daring harmonic conceptions, intensified rhythmic drive, and, especially, more memorable thematic inventions.

Surprise Symphony

Haydn's shrewd appraisal of London's musical tastes is evident in little things as well as great ones. There is a sudden *fortissimo* crash on a weak beat in the slow movement of Symphony No. 94 that has given this work its nickname *Surprise.* It was put there because, as Haydn later acknowledged, he wanted something novel and startling to take people's minds off the concerts of his pupil and rival Ignaz Pleyel (1757–1831; see vignette). The greater tunefulness may also have been prompted by this competition, since Pleyel's strong suit was melody. Haydn turned to Slovenian, Croatian, and other peasant tunes he remembered from his youth. The first, second, and fourth movements of Symphony No. 103 display characteristic instances of folklike melodies. The finale of No. 104 (NAWM 96; CD 7 [58]), with its imitation of the bagpipe, is particularly suggestive of a peasant dance (Example 14.2). Similar allusions are the "Turkish" band effect (triangle, cymbals, bass drum) and the trumpet fanfare in the Allegretto of the *Military* Symphony (No. 100), and the ticking accompaniment in the Andante of No. 101 (the *Clock*). He always aimed to please both the music lover and the expert, and it is a measure of his greatness that he succeeded.

Pleyel

Orchestration

The orchestra of the *London* Symphonies includes trumpets and timpani, which (contrary to Haydn's earlier practice) are used in most of the slow movements as well as in the others. Clarinets appear in all of the second set of *London* Symphonies except No. 102. Trumpets sometimes have independent

Example 14.2 *Haydn, Symphony No. 104: Finale, Allegro spiritoso*

HAYDN, ON HIS RIVALRY WITH HIS PUPIL PLEYEL

There isn't a day, not a single day, in which I am free from work, and I shall thank the dear Lord when I can leave London—the sooner the better. My labours have been augmented by the arrival of my pupil Pleyel, whom the Professional Concert have brought here. He arrived here with a lot of new compositions, but they had been composed long ago; he therefore promised to present a new work every evening. As soon as I saw this, I realized at once that a lot of people were dead set against me, and so I announced publicly that I would likewise produce 12 different new pieces. In order to keep my word, and to support poor Salomon, I must be the victim and work the whole time. But I really do feel it. My eyes suffer the most, and I have many sleepless nights, though with God's help I shall overcome it all. The people of the Professional Concert wanted to put a spoke in my wheel, because I would not go over to them; but the public is just. I enjoyed a great deal of success last year, but still more this year. Pleyel's presumption is sharply criticized, but I love him just the same. I always go to his concerts and am the first to applaud him.

Haydn in London, writing to Marianne von Genzinger in Vienna, March 2, 1792. Trans. from the German in H. C. Robbins Landon, *The Collected Correspondence and London Notebooks of Joseph Haydn* (London: Barrie & Rockliff, 1959), p. 132.

parts instead of doubling the horns as they had previously, and the cellos are now more often independent of the basses. In several of the symphonies, Haydn featured solo strings against the full orchestra. He treated woodwinds even more independently than before, and the whole sound of the orchestra achieves a new spaciousness and brilliance.

Harmony

Even more striking than the orchestration is the expanded harmonic range of the *London* Symphonies and Haydn's other works of the same period. Between the various movements, or between Minuet and Trio, the mediant relationship is sometimes exploited instead of the conventional dominant or subdominant; examples of this occur in Symphonies Nos. 99 and 104. Within movements there are sudden shifts, with little or no modulation, to remote keys (as in the first movement of Symphony No. 97 at the beginning of the development section) or wide-ranging modulations (as in the recapitulation of the same movement at measures 248–61, where the music passes quickly through E♭, A♭, D♭, and F minor to reach the dominant of the principal key, C major).

Harmonic imagination plays an important part also in the slow introductions of the *London* Symphonies. These opening sections have a portentous quality, a deliberate dramatic suspense that grips the listener awaiting the Allegro. They are set either in the tonic minor of the Allegro (as in Symphonies Nos. 101 and 104) or they gravitate toward the minor mode as a foil for the major mode of the ensuing fast movement (as in No. 94).

Example 14.3 *Haydn, Symphony No. 103, Allegro con spirito*

Sonata form

The movements in sonata form tend to revolve around the primary subject. This subject often pervades the section in the dominant, which in Haydn's earlier work usually presented a light, graceful contrast to the dynamic opening. The slow movements take either the form of a theme with variations (Nos. 94, 95, 97, 103) or a free adaptation of sonata form; one feature common to both is a contrasting minor section. The minuets, no longer courtly dances, are allegro movements in Minuet-and-Trio pattern. Like the corresponding movements of the late quartets, they are already Scherzos in everything but name and tempo.

Finales

Some of the finales are in sonata form, but Haydn's favored pattern is the rondo, a form in which an opening A section returns following each of several contrasting sections—ABACABA is typical for Haydn. Some of his rondos, however, are infused with sonata-form elements. A brilliant example is the finale of the *Drum Roll* Symphony, No. 103 in E♭, in which the A and B sections serve as the first and second themes in the exposition and recapitulation. The first return of A is a tonic interlude in the development section, C is a modulatory passage in the development, and the final return of A acts as a closing section before the coda. The entire movement grows out of two opening ideas, a fanfare for two horns and a sprightly theme heard against it (Example 14.3).

The Quartets up to 1781

Haydn composed his ten early quartets as Opp. 1 and 2 during the late 1750s. The six quartets of "Opus 3," though passed off by a London publisher as Haydn's, were written by someone else. The quartets of Opp. 17 (1771) and 20 (1772) established both Haydn's fame while he was still alive and his historical position as the first great master of the string quartet. All the four movement-types—sonata-allegro, minuet, slow, and fast finale—are treated with assurance and finesse. The four instruments make their individual contributions: the first violin plays the most virtuosic part, but the cello shares increasingly in carrying the melodic line. The texture is free of any dependence on a basso continuo; at the same time, counterpoint contributes tension and excitement. In the quartets of Opp. 9 (ca. 1769–70) and 17 and half of those in Opp. 20 and 33 (1781), the Minuet appears before the slow movement instead of after it, its usual place in the symphonies.

Sonata-form movements

In the sonata-form movements, Haydn adopted strategies peculiar to his quartets. After the exposition of a primary subject, almost always dominated by the first violin, he usually chose a looser texture in which the primary motives pass from one instrument to another. In place of the orchestral tuttis that typically announce the bridge and other transitions in the symphonies, Haydn favored loud unisons or stark modulatory gestures. The arrival of landmark moments, such as the secondary thematic section in the recapitulation, may be marked not by a cadence but by subtler means. For example, in Op. 20, No. 4 in D major, the second theme at measure 83 is preceded by a *fortissimo* broken-chord unison spelling out the dominant seventh of the tonic, D (Example 14.4). The tonality remains ambiguous for several more measures, and the first emphatic cadence does not arrive until measure 99, when a short closing section begins. The development sections of the Op. 20 quartets are nearly equal in length to the exposition and recapitulation. Moreover, motives first presented in the exposition are developed over the entire movement, a procedure that Haydn followed throughout his career.

Fugues

Three of the finales in Op. 20 are labeled "fuga": No. 5 is based on two subjects, No. 6 on three, and No. 2 on four. Several of Haydn's contemporaries, including Richter, Carlos d'Ordoñez (1734–1786), and Gassmann, also

Example 14.4 *Haydn, String Quartet Op. 20, No. 4 (Hob. III:34): Allegro di molto*

Example 14.5 *Haydn, String Quartet Op. 20, No. 6 (Hob. III:36): Fuga con 3 Sogetti, Allegro*

included fugal movements in their quartets. In Haydn's Op. 20, No. 6 (Hob. III:36), the second and third subjects are clearly subordinate and function more like countersubjects to the first (see Example 14.5). They are re-exposed less in the course of the movement, although the third subject does frequent duty in episodes. All three subjects are treated in strettos, and the first and second also in pedal points, and the first appears in inversion.

Opus 33

Nine years after Op. 20, Haydn composed the six quartets of Op. 33 in 1781 and proclaimed to two admirers that they were written in a "quite new and special way." They are lighthearted, witty, and tuneful. Haydn's quartets are very much addressed to the players, who are all invited to share in the fun. Only the first movements are in sonata form; the finales (except that of No. 1) are either rondos or variations. The Minuets, here titled "scherzo" (Italian for jest) or "scherzando" (playful), do literally play tricks on the courtly dance by breaking the normal metrical pattern. For example, it required two three-beat measures of music to complete a pattern of steps, but in measures 2 and 3 of No. 5 (Example 14.6), Haydn deliberately broke into duple meter. Then we hear three proper three-beat measures and a silence in lieu of the fourth. Two chords now intrude to end the period in the tonic, but, for a dance, the phrase is two measures too long.

Humor

Even apart from the scherzos, Op. 33 contains some of Haydn's happiest strokes of humor. Near the opening of Op. 33, No. 4 (Example 14.7), in the

Example 14.6 *Haydn, String Quartet Op. 33, No. 5 (Hob. III:41): Scherzo, Allegro*

Example 14.7 *Haydn, String Quartet Op. 33, No. 4 (Hob. III:40): Allegro moderato*

midst of a serious exposition, Haydn's rhythmic displacements and unexpected rests mock the normal logic of melodic succession. Haydn also indulged in a lot of playfulness in the themes themselves and in the dialogue between players, thereby adding merriment to the amateur quartet evenings that were held in the cities, such as London, Paris, and Vienna, in the country estates of the nobility, and even in the monasteries.

One of three rondo finales in Op. 33 is the Presto of No. 2 (NAWN 97; CD 8 [1] / 3 ⟨18⟩), nicknamed "The Joke" because of enigmatic rests in the coda. But humor pervades the whole movement: The composer deliberately plays with the listener's response throughout. Haydn employs a clever suspense-building strategy of repetitive figures over a pedal point, which lead through a diminished chord to a dominant seventh chord momentarily left unresolved. This occurs four times; after each pause—surprise!—a witty letdown, a simple return of the rondo theme.

The Quartets of 1785–90

Between 1785 and 1790 Haydn composed Op. 42 (one quartet, 1785), Op. 50 (the six *Prussian* Quartets, 1787), Opp. 54 and 55 (three each, 1788), and Op. 64 (six quartets, 1790). Opus 50 stands out because of Haydn's increasingly frequent use of monothematic first movements. In Op. 50, No. 1 (Hob. III:44), the second thematic section is almost a variation on the first. In No. 3 (Hob. III:46), the second theme is a transposition of the first to the dominant, with a new counterpoint in the viola. This unifying technique affects some of the finales also.

Variations

Many of the slow movements are themes and variations, among which we find some special types. The Andante of Op. 50, No. 4 (Hob. III:47), is a set of double variations, alternating an A theme in major with a B theme in minor (ABA′B′A″).

The Last Quartets

The quartets of Haydn's last period include Opp. 71 and 74 (three each, 1793), 76 (six, 1797), 77 (two, 1799, of which the second is probably Haydn's greatest work in this genre), and the two-movement Op. 103 (1803). In these quartets, Haydn frequently based his second thematic section on the first, and used the closing section to inject contrast. Some good examples are the Finale of Op. 74, No. 1 (Hob. III:72), the first movement of Op. 76, No. 2 (Hob. III:76), and the first and final movements of Op. 77, No. 1 (Hob. III:81).

In his last quartets Haydn expanded the harmonic frontiers, foreshadowing Romantic harmony in his chromatic progressions, in his novel uses of the augmented sixth chords, in his enharmonic changes, and in his fanciful tonal shifts. The powerfully emotional outpouring in the Largo assai of Op. 74, No. 3 (Hob. III:74), reaches a climax with double stops in three of the instruments at a "German" sixth (Example 14.8, measure 8) en route to the dominant.

Opus 74

Opus 76, No. 6

The Adagio of the Quartet Op. 76, No. 6 (Hob. III:80; 1797), lives up to the title *Fantasia* that Haydn bestowed on it. It begins in B major and wanders through C♯ minor, E major and minor, G major (Example 14.9, measure 30),

Example 14.8 *Haydn, String Quartet Op. 74, No. 3 (Hob. III:74): Largo assai*

Example 14.9 *Haydn, String Quartet Op. 76, No. 6 (Hob. III:80): Adagio* (Fantasia)

Example 14.10 *Haydn, String Quartet Op. 76, No. 1 (Hob. III:75): Allegro con spirito*

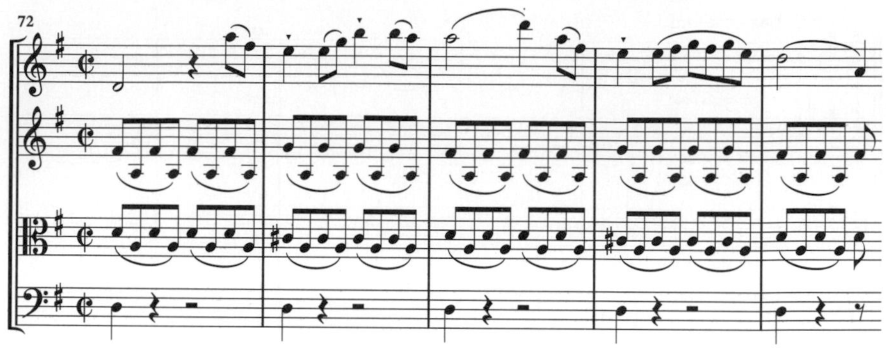

Example 14.11 *Haydn, Hymn,* Gott erhalte Franz den Kaiser

B♭ major and minor, then through an enharmonic change back to B major (measure 40).

Another characteristic of Haydn's late quartets, as in his symphonies of this period, is the juxtaposition of the serious and jocular, the artful and the folksy, the enigmatic and the simpleminded, the sublime and the ridiculous. Opus 76, No. 1 (Hob. III:75), opens with three majestic chords before the cello solemnly unfolds its beautiful main theme. By contrast, the second theme simulates a peasant bagpipe tune with a double drone (*D* and *A*; see Example 14.10). There is a similar bagpipe imitation in Op. 76, No. 3 (Hob. III:77), measures 64–74, in an otherwise sophisticated first movement.

Haydn's use of the slow-movement variations form decreased in the late quartets, but one outstanding example is in Op. 76, No. 3 (NAWM 98; CD 8 [7]). Haydn composed the melody as a birthday hymn for Kaiser Franz (Example 14.11). (It later became the national anthem of the Austro-Hungarian Empire.) The variations, which pass the hymn tune from instrument to instrument, are a study in nonharmonic tones: appoggiaturas, suspensions, and changing notes.

Opus 76 Minuets

The Minuets, though less playful than those of Op. 33, are full of offbeat accents, interpolated measures, exaggerated leaps, and other spoofs of artificial formality. One of the cleverest of Haydn's minuets appears in Op.

Example 14.12 *Haydn, String Quartet Op. 76, No. 2: Menuetto, Allegro, ma non troppo*

76, No. 2, in the form of a canon (Example 14.12), the only complete one in the quartets. Far from being pedantic, it is satirical, as if it represented two drunken courtiers trying vainly to execute this dignified dance with grace to a strain made up of five- and six-bar phrases. The octave doubling of the two voices lays bare the harshness of the dissonances and open fifths. The Trio, as an antidote, is entirely homophonic and is set in the parallel major mode.

Keyboard Sonatas

Haydn's early keyboard sonatas can be performed on a harpsichord, which allows for only certain changes in dynamics. His later sonatas, however, call for the performer to realize dynamic markings such as *sforzando* and *crescendo*, sudden accents, and other variations of touch that require a pianoforte.[2] Haydn used a clavichord in his early years, but by 1780 he had a piano available. The authorized contemporary printed editions of the sonatas after 1780 give "fortepiano" or "pianoforte" as the first option, along with "clavicembalo" (usually meaning harpsichord).

Sonatas of the 1760s and 1770s

Haydn's piano sonatas follow the same lines of development observed in the symphonies and quartets. Notable among the sonatas of the late 1760s and

2. On this question, see A. Peter Brown, *Joseph Haydn's Keyboard Music: Sources and Style* (Bloomington: Indiana University Press, 1986), pp. 134–71.

Example 14.13 *Haydn, Sonata Hob. XVI:49: Allegro*

early 1770s are Nos. 19[3] in D major, 44 in G minor, and 46 in A♭. In the first movement (Moderato) of No. 44, Haydn skillfully exploited the opening ideas in the transitions and in the secondary and closing sections of the exposition. At the same time, the great rhythmic and textural variety and the delicate chromaticism in the movement betray the *empfindsam* approach.[4] Sonata No. 20 in C minor, begun in 1771 but not published until 1780, is a tempestuous work characteristic of this period in the composer's career.

The Piano Sonatas Nos. 21–26, written in 1773 and dedicated to Prince Esterházy, show a general relaxation and lightening of style comparable to what we have noted in the symphonies and quartets of the same period. All are written in major keys, but the first movements often turn to the minor mode during the dominant section.

Late sonatas

Among the late Haydn sonatas, No. 49 in E♭ merits special attention. Haydn composed it in 1789–90 for his friend Marianne von Genzinger, telling her that it "may be given out to no one else." To his great surprise the sonata found its way into print. He later wrote to her, "What a pity that Your Grace does not own a *Fortepiano* by Schanz since everything is expressed better on it."[5] The music is indeed more suited to that instrument: it demands quick changes of dynamics and marked accents, as may be seen in Example 14.13.

3. The sonatas are numbered according to Hoboken's catalogue, category XVI. Reference numbers in other sources may be to the fine edition by Christa Landon (Vienna: Universal Edition, 1963–65).
4. See the extended analysis of the structural and expressive features of this movement in Philip G. Downs, *Classical Music* (New York: Norton, 1992), pp. 219–25, and the score in the accompanying anthology, No. 26.
5. Quoted in Brown, *Haydn's Keyboard Music,* pp. 43–44.

The Adagio cantabile, in B♭ major, has a stormy middle section in B♭ minor, in which the right hand continues its arabesques while the left hand must cross from deep in the bass to the upper reaches of the keyboard, a feature that Frau von Genzinger asked Haydn to change because it exceeded her technical ability.

Another E♭ sonata, No. 52, long a favorite of recitalists, was written in 1794 for the virtuoso Therese Jansen Bartolozzi, one of Clementi's outstanding pupils. This work was published in England around 1800 as a "Grand Sonata for the Piano Forte," and grand it is in every way. It begins in the manner of the French overture, with full chords in dotted rhythm, and thoroughly exploits the power and scope of the new pianos. In the development section of the first movement Haydn lingered for a while in the Neapolitan-related key of E major, which is also the key of the Adagio that follows.

Haydn's last sonatas demonstrate how much in touch he was with the latest musical fashions and developments. Equally important as a contribution to piano writing is the series of brilliant trios Haydn wrote during his second London visit and immediately after.

HAYDN'S VOCAL WORKS

In a modest autobiographical sketch of 1776 written for an Austrian encyclopedia, Haydn named his most successful works: three operas; an Italian oratorio, *Il ritorno di Tobia* (The Return of Tobias, 1774–75); and his setting of the *Stabat Mater* (1767), a work that was famous in Europe in the 1780s. He made no mention of the sixty-odd symphonies he had written by then and referred to his chamber music only to complain that the Berlin critics dealt with it too harshly. Haydn may have been reticent about the symphonies because they were little known outside Eszterháza. Also, he may not have realized their significance and that of the string quartets until their enthusiastic reception in Paris and London showed him how highly regarded they were. Posterity has concurred with this endorsement.

Operas

In contrast, Haydn's operas were very successful in their day, but they were soon dropped from the repertory and are rarely heard even now. Opera occupied a large part of Haydn's time and energy at Eszterháza where, between 1769 and 1790, he arranged, prepared, and conducted some seventy-five operas by other composers; Eszterháza was, despite its remote situation, a center for opera. Besides six little German operas for marionettes, Haydn wrote at least fifteen Italian operas. Most of these were of the *dramma giocoso* variety, with music abounding in the humor and high spirits that came naturally to the composer. Haydn also composed three serious operas; the most famous was the "heroic drama" *Armida* (1784), remarkable for its dramatic accompanied recitatives and arias on a grand scale.

Songs

The songs for solo voice with keyboard accompaniment, especially twelve Haydn set to English words (1794), are unpretentious. In addition to writing

■ *In this hall in the Eszterháza Palace, where the Viennese court spent the summer, Haydn (from around 1768) conducted his symphonies while playing the first violin.* (RAFAEL CSABA/MTI FOTO, BUDAPEST)

original songs, Haydn and his pupils arranged about 450 Scottish and Welsh airs for various English publishers.

Masses

An imperial decree in force from 1783 to 1792 restricted the use of orchestrally accompanied music in the churches. Although Haydn wrote some Masses before the decree—for example, the *Mass of Mariazell* of 1782—his most important Masses were the six composed for Prince Nicholas II Esterházy between 1796 and 1802. They reflect Haydn's earlier preoccupation with the symphony. All are large-scale festive Masses, using orchestra, chorus, and four solo vocalists. Haydn's Masses, like those of Mozart and his other South German contemporaries, have a flamboyance that also characterizes the architecture of the Austrian Baroque churches in which the Masses were performed. These works, which employ a full orchestra, including timpani and trumpets, are written in a musical idiom similar to that of the opera and the symphony. Haydn was occasionally criticized for writing music that was too cheerful. He replied that at the thought of God his heart "leaped for joy" and he did not think God would reproach him for praising the Lord "with a cheerful heart."

True to the Viennese tradition, Haydn interchanged solo voices and chorus in his late Masses. What was new was the prominent position he gave to the orchestra and his pervasive adoption of symphonic style and even symphonic forms. Yet he also retained traditional elements, including contrapuntal writing for solo voices and the customary choral fugues at the conclusion of the Gloria and the Credo.

Lord Nelson Mass

The best known of Haydn's late Masses is the *Missa in angustiis* (Mass for Troubled Times, 1798) in D minor, known as the *Lord Nelson* or *Imperial* Mass. Among many impressive features of this work, the beautiful setting of the Incarnatus and the electrifying close of the Benedictus are moments of particular inspiration. On an equal level with the *Nelson* Mass are the *Missa in tempore belli* (Mass in Time of War; also known as the *Paukenmesse*, or *Kettledrum* Mass) of 1796, the *Theresienmesse* of 1799, and the *Harmoniemesse* (Windband Mass) of 1802.

Oratorios

Creation and *Seasons*

During his stay in London, Haydn became acquainted with Handel's oratorios. At Westminster Abbey in 1791, Haydn was so deeply moved by the Hallelujah Chorus in a performance of *Messiah* that he burst into tears and exclaimed, "He is the master of us all." Haydn's appreciation for Handel is apparent in all the choral parts of his late Masses, above all in his oratorios *Die Schöpfung* (The Creation; completed 1798) and *Die Jahreszeiten* (The Seasons; completed 1801). The text of *Die Schöpfung*, by Baron Gottfried van Swieten, is based on the Book of Genesis and Milton's *Paradise Lost.* That of *Die Jahreszeiten*, also by van Swieten, is distantly related to James Thomson's poem *The Seasons*, which had been published some sixty years earlier. Both oratorios are ostensibly religious, but the God of *Die Schöpfung*, in accordance with eighteenth-century ideas, is more like an artisan than a creator in the biblical sense. *Die*

■ *Performance of Haydn's* The Creation *on March 27, 1808, in the banquet hall of the University of Vienna. Engraving after the watercolor by Balthasar Wigand.* (VIENNA, HISTORISCHES MUSEUM DER STADT WIEN)

Example 14.14 *Haydn,* Die Schöpfung, *Part I: "Und Gott sprach"*

Jahreszeiten, though beginning and ending in expressions of faith, has lighthearted sections concerning hunting and drinking wine.

The charm of both works rests largely in their loving depiction of nature and of innocent joy in the simple life. Haydn's instrumental introductions and interludes are among the finest examples of late eighteenth-century program music. His *Depiction of Chaos* at the beginning of *Die Schöpfung* introduces confusing and disturbingly dissonant harmonies. The transition in the following recitative and chorus, with its awesome choral outburst on the C-major chord at the words "Es werde Licht, und es ward Licht!" (Let there be Light, and there was Light!) was justifiably extolled by contemporary writers as the supreme example of the sublime in music (Example 14.14).

WOLFGANG AMADEUS MOZART

Early Life

Wolfgang Amadeus Mozart (1756–1791) was born in Salzburg, at that time a Bavarian city with a long musical tradition. It was the seat of an archbishop, one of the numerous quasi-independent political units within the German Empire, and a lively provincial center of the arts as well. Mozart's father, Leopold Mozart, served in the archbishop's chapel and later became its assistant director. He was a composer of some ability and reputation and the au-

■ *Three Mozarts making music: Leopold, violin; Amadeus, age 7, piano; and Marianne (Nannerl), age 11, singing from a score. Engraving by Jean Baptiste Delafosse based on a watercolor of about 1764 by Louis Carrogis de Carmonetelle.*

thor of a celebrated treatise on violin playing, published in the year of his son's birth. From earliest childhood Wolfgang showed such a prodigious talent for music that his father dropped all other ambitions and devoted himself to educating the boy and to exhibiting the accomplishments of Wolfgang and his sister Marianne ("Nannerl") in a series of tours that took them to France, England, Holland, and Italy, as well as to Vienna and the principal cities of Germany.

Talent for music

Already a keyboard virtuoso, Mozart soon became an accomplished organist and violinist as well. He spent over half his time from 1762 to 1771 displaying his talents. In these public performances he not only played prepared pieces but also read concertos at sight and improvised variations, fugues, and fantasias. Meanwhile he was composing: he produced his first minuets at the age of five, his first symphony just before his ninth birthday, his first oratorio at eleven, and his first opera at twelve. His more than six hundred compositions are listed and numbered chronologically in a thematic catalogue compiled by Ludwig von Köchel in 1862 and updated by Alfred Einstein and others; the Köchel or "K." numbers are universally used to identify Mozart's compositions.[6]

Thanks to his father's excellent teaching and to the many trips he took during his formative years, young Mozart became familiar with every kind of music that was being written or heard in contemporary western Europe. He absorbed it all with uncanny aptitude, imitating others' works while improving on them. The ideas that influenced him not only echoed in his youthful com-

6. New Köchel numbers that have been assigned to reflect modern research are given in this book in parentheses. A revision of the Köchel catalog by Neal Zaslaw is nearing completion.

positions but also continued to grow in his mind, sometimes bearing fruit many years later. His work became a synthesis of national styles, a mirror that reflected the music of a whole age, illuminated by his own genius.

Early Works

During his apprentice years to around 1773, Mozart was completely under the tutelage of his father in practical affairs and in most musical matters as well. The relationship between father and son was interesting and complex. Leopold Mozart recognized and respected the boy's genius, and he expended major effort in furthering young Wolfgang's career and trying—vainly, as it turned out—to secure for him a worthy permanent position. Leopold was his son's devoted mentor and friend, who saved Wolfgang's every jotting for posterity.

Tours

Mozart's childhood journeys were rich in musical experiences. In June of 1763, the whole family—father, mother, Wolfgang, and his talented elder sister, Nannerl—embarked on a tour that included lengthy stops in Paris and London. They returned to Salzburg three and a half years later. In Paris, young Mozart became interested in the music of Johann Gottfried Eckard (1735–1809) and Johann Schobert (d. 1767), arranging two movements from their piano sonatas as the second movements of his own piano concertos K. 39–40. In his harpsichord writing, Schobert simulated the effect of an orchestra through rapid figuration and thick chordal textures, particularly in the low register, a technique Mozart imitated in some of his sonatas (see Example 14.15b).

J. C. Bach

Johann Christian Bach, whom Mozart met in London, had an important and lasting influence on the boy. Like Bach, Mozart composed for a wide range of genres, from keyboard to symphonic and operatic works. Bach enriched

Example 14.15a *Schobert, Sonata Op. 2, No. 1, Allegro assai*

Example 14.15b *Mozart, Sonata K. 310 (=300d), Allegro maestoso*

these genres with features derived from Italian opera: songful themes, tasteful appoggiaturas and triplets, and harmonic ambiguities. These traits, together with Bach's consistent thematic contrasts, appealed to Mozart and became permanent marks of his writing.[7] In 1772 Mozart arranged three of Bach's sonatas as Piano Concertos K. 107, 1–3. The significant parallels between Mozart's and Bach's formal approaches to the concerto are noted below in connection with NAWM 93 and 99.

Early operas

A visit to Vienna in 1768 led the precocious twelve-year-old to compose an Italian opera buffa, *La finta semplice* (The Pretend Simpleton, performed the following year at Salzburg) and an attractive German Singspiel, *Bastien und Bastienne.* Mozart's extended travels in Italy between 1770 and 1773 left him more thoroughly Italianized than ever and profoundly unhappy with his limited prospects in Salzburg. The highlights of these years were the production in Milan of two *opere serie, Mitridate* (1770) and *Ascanio in Alba* (1772), and his counterpoint studies with Padre Giovanni Battista Martini in Bologna. Mozart's first string quartets also date from this time. The influence of Sammartini and other Italian symphonists may be heard in Mozart's symphonies written between 1770 and 1773, especially K. 81 (=73l), 95 (=73n), 112, 132, 162, and 182 (=173dA); but a new force, the music of Joseph Haydn, manifests itself in other symphonies from this period, particularly K. 133 (composed in July 1772).

Influence of Haydn

During another stay in Vienna, in the summer of 1773, Mozart renewed his contact with Haydn's music, which then became increasingly important in the young composer's creative life. The symphonies K. 183 (=173dB; late 1773) and K. 201 (=186a; early 1774), Mozart's first masterworks in this genre, are striking both in their parallels with Haydn's work and in their independence. Sometimes called the "Little G-minor" Symphony, K. 183 is remarkable not only for its intense, serious quality and its thematic unity but also for the way Mozart expanded the entire symphonic form.

The Salzburg Years

From 1774 to 1781, Mozart lived chiefly in Salzburg, complaining frequently about the narrow provincial life and the lack of opportunities. In a fruitless attempt to improve his situation, he undertook another journey in September

7. Compare, for example, the opening of J. C. Bach's Op. 2, No. 1, illustrated in William Newman, *The Sonata in the Classic Era* (Chapel Hill, 1963), p. 710, with the opening of Mozart's K. 315c.

■ *The cities that were most important in Mozart's career are indicated in color. But his travels, particularly during his younger years, include all those in black as well.*

1777, this time with his mother, to Munich, Augsburg, Mannheim, and Paris. All his hopes for a good position in Germany or France came to nothing. His stay in Paris was further saddened by his mother's death in July 1778. He returned to Salzburg early the following year, more disconsolate than ever. Nevertheless, he was steadily growing in stature as a composer, and he received a commission to compose an opera for Munich. *Idomeneo*, performed there in January 1781, is the best of Mozart's *opere serie*, despite its rather clumsy libretto. The music is dramatic and pictorial; in its numerous accompanied recitatives, its conspicuous use of the chorus, and the inclusion of spectacular scenes, *Idomeneo* shows the influence of Traetta, Gluck, and the French *tragédie lyrique.*

Trip to Vienna

After accompanying the archbishop to Vienna in 1781, Mozart decided to try his luck there as a freelancer. He continued to compose on commission or for particular occasions, but even works not intended for immediate performance he wrote with definite types of performers or audiences in mind, and took their preferences into consideration. Like all of his contemporaries, he was a "commercial composer": he expected his music to be performed, to please his audience, and to make money for him.

Piano and Violin Sonatas

Piano sonatas

Among the important works of this period are thirteen piano sonatas[8] and several sets of variations for piano, including those on the French air *Ah, vous dirais-je maman* (K. 265=300e, Vienna, 1781–82), better known as *Twinkle, twinkle, little star.* The variations and sonatas were probably intended for pupils and house music.

The sonatas K. 279–284 were undoubtedly meant to be published together: there is one in each of the major tonalities in the circle of fifths from D down to E♭, and the six works show a wide variety of form and content. The two Mannheim sonatas (see note 7) have brilliant, showy Allegros and tender, graceful Andantes. Mozart's first minor-key sonata, K. 310 (=300d), betrays the influence of Schobert in its full chordal accompaniments and stringlike

8. Since these sonatas are identified by different authors and editors by either of two sets of numbers, these are listed below.

K. numbers	*Revised*	*Key*	*Place and date of composition*
279	189d	C major	Munich, 1774–75
280	189e	F major	Munich, 1774–75
281	189f	B♭ major	Munich, 1774–75
282	189g	E♭ major	Munich, 1774–75
283	189h	G major	Munich, 1774–75
284	205b	D major	Munich, 1775
309	284b	C major	Mannheim, 1777
311	284c	D major	Mannheim, 1777
310	300d	A minor	Paris, 1778
330	300h	C major	Munich or Vienna, 1781–83
331	300i	A major	Munich or Vienna, 1781–83
332	300k	F major	Munich or Vienna, 1781–83
333	315c	B♭ major	Linz and Vienna, 1783–84

Example 14.16 *Mozart, Piano Sonata in B♭, K. 333 (=315a), Allegro*

tremolos. A first-movement passage in this sonata recalls Schobert's Piano Sonata Op. 2, No. 1, with optional violin part (see Examples 14.15a and b).

The Sonata K. 331 (=300i) is notable among the sonatas from the early 1780s for its first movement in variation form and its finale. The latter, marked *Rondo alla turca*, imitates the Janissary music of the Turkish military bands—then popular in Vienna—with their cymbals and triangles and exaggerated first beats. (Mozart also included "Turkish music" in his comic opera *Die Entführung aus dem Serail.*)

Themes

Mozart's themes, more than Haydn's, have a distinct melodic profile. Although they seem to unfold naturally and spontaneously, often in the fluent manner of the Italian Allegro movements, they give evidence of careful shaping and grooming. The phrases of a statement are usually balanced between antecedent and consequent, but often the second phrase is extended, as in the Sonata in B♭, K. 333 (=315c), shown in Example 14.16. The entire theme grows out of the opening gesture of a stepwise descent to an appoggiatura, which marks the end of every phrase, subphrase, and smaller units in measures 1 to 5.

Violin sonatas

Mozart's piano sonatas are closely related to his sonatas for piano and violin. In his early years these duos were really piano pieces with optional violin accompaniment, like the Schobert sonata illustrated in Example 14.15a. The first of Mozart's works in which the two instruments are treated more equally are K. 296, 301–305 (=293a–d), and 306 (=300l), which were written in Mannheim and Paris in 1777 and 1778. Köchel 304 in E minor (300c) is notable for the exceptional emotional intensity of its first movement, and K. 306 (300i) in D major for its brilliant concerto-like style.

Serenades and Divertimentos

Mozart composed serenades—ever popular in Salzburg—and what are now classed as divertimentos in the 1770s and early 1780s for garden parties or actual outdoor performances, for weddings and birthdays, or for concerts at the homes of friends and patrons. Although usually intended for background music and entertainment, they received serious treatment from Mozart. Some are like chamber music for strings with two or more added wind instruments.

IX. *Jean-Antoine Watteau (1684–1721) painted several versions of this scene, of which* The Shepherds, *from 1716–17, is the most recent. Although the activities and manners are those of peasants, the figures are in courtly dress. At the center is a musette (bagpipe) player, getting ready to accompany the dancers While one couple looks toward the dancers, the woman at the left acquiesces to a rude embrace from the youth with the shepherd's staff. In the background an elegant lady is in mid-swing, not sure how to respond to her courtier; in the foreground a man and his dog wistfully observe the dancers, but no one attends to the sheep. The painting expresses the longing for an idyllic pastoral innocence free of the constraints of middle-class and courtly polite society.* (BERLIN, SCHLOSS CHARLOTTENBURG / ART RESOURCE, NEW YORK)

X. *J. M. W. Turner (1775–1851) painted* Music Party, East Cowes Castle *about 1835. Known mainly for his misty seascapes, the artist depicts here the congenial atmosphere of a country house in Petworth. The women enjoy a quiet moment of music making, to which the red color and the flash of light in the center lend warmth, while the black dress of the pianist hints at a serious performance.* (LONDON, TATE GALLERY, THE CLORE COLLECTION / ART RESOURCE, NEW YORK)

Others, written for six or eight wind instruments in pairs, are meant for the out-of-doors, and still others approach the style of the symphony or concerto. All have in common a certain unaffected simplicity of both material and treatment, a formal charm appropriate to their purpose. The most familiar of Mozart's serenades is *Eine kleine Nachtmusik* (A Little Night-Music, K. 525; 1787), in four movements for string quintet but now usually played by a small string ensemble.

Solo Concertos

Among the notable compositions of Mozart's Salzburg period are the Violin Concertos K. 216, 218, and 219, in G, D, and A, respectively (all 1775), the Piano Concerto in E♭, K. 271 (1777), with its romantic slow movement in C minor, and the hauntingly expressive Symphonie Concertante, K. 364 (=320d) in E♭ for solo violin and viola with orchestra. The three violin concertos are the last of Mozart's compositions in this genre. The Piano Concerto K. 271, on the other hand, is but the first of a long series of great works that reached a climax in the Vienna period.

MOZART'S VIENNA YEARS

In 1781 Mozart decided, against his father's advice, to quit the service of the archbishop of Salzburg and settle in Vienna. He was optimistic about his prospects there. Indeed, his first years in the imperial capital went well: his Singspiel *Die Entführung aus dem Serail* (The Abduction from the Harem, 1782) was performed repeatedly. He had all the distinguished pupils he was willing to take, he was idolized by the Viennese public both as pianist and composer, and he led the bustling life of a successful freelance musician. But after four or five seasons the fickle public deserted him, pupils fell off, commis-

■ *St. Michael's Square, Vienna; in the foreground, the Burgtheater, where Mozart performed most of his piano concertos in the mid-1780s and where the premieres of* Le nozze di Figaro *and* Così fan tutte *(1790) took place.*

sions were few, family expenses mounted, and his health declined. Worst of all, no permanent position with a steady income came his way, except for an appointment in 1787 as chamber music composer to the emperor at less than half the salary that Gluck, his predecessor, had received. The most pathetic pages in Mozart's correspondence are the begging letters written between 1788 and 1791 to his friend and brother Freemason, the merchant Michael Puchberg of Vienna. To Puchberg's honor, he always responded generously to Mozart's appeals.

Most of the works that immortalized Mozart's name were composed in Vienna between the ages of twenty-five and thirty-five, when the promise of his childhood and early youth came to fulfillment. In every kind of composition he achieved a perfect synthesis of form and content, of the *galant* and the learned styles, of polish and charm on the one hand and textural and emotional depth on the other. The principal influences on Mozart during these last ten years of his life came from his continuing study of Haydn and his discovery of J. S. Bach. He was introduced to Bach's music by Baron Gottfried van Swieten, who during his years as Austrian ambassador to Berlin (1771–78) had become an enthusiast for the music of North German composers. Van Swieten was the imperial court librarian and a busy music and literary amateur; he later wrote the librettos of Haydn's last two oratorios. In weekly reading sessions during 1782 at van Swieten's home, Mozart became acquainted with Bach's *Art of Fugue*, *Well-Tempered Keyboard*, and other works. He arranged several of Bach's fugues for string trio or quartet (K. 404a, 405) and composed his own Fugue in C minor for two pianos (K. 426). Bach's influence was deep and lasting; we see it in the increased contrapuntal texture of Mozart's later works (for example, his last piano sonata, K. 576) and in the profoundly serious moods of *The Magic Flute* and the Requiem. It was probably also through van Swieten that Mozart became interested in Handel, whose *Messiah*, *Alexander's Feast*, *Acis and Galatea*, and the *Ode for St. Cecilia's Day* Mozart reorchestrated.

van Swieten

Piano Works

Among the piano solo compositions of the Vienna period, the most important are the Fantasia and the Sonata in C minor (K. 475 and 457). The Fantasia foreshadows Schubert's piano sonatas in its melodies and modulations, while the sonata would serve as the model for Beethoven's *Sonate pathétique*. Other keyboard works of this period are the Sonata in D major for two pianos (K. 448=375a, 1781) and the Sonata in F major (K. 497, 1786) for piano four-hands, the finest of all Mozart's works in this genre.

Chamber Works

The *Haydn* Quartets

In 1785 Mozart published six string quartets dedicated to Joseph Haydn as a token of his gratitude for all that he had learned from the older composer.

Example 14.17 *Mozart, String Quartet K. 421 (=417b): Allegro moderato*

These quartets were, as Mozart said in his dedicatory letter, "the fruit of a long and laborious effort"; indeed, the manuscript shows an unusually large number of corrections and revisions for a Mozart autograph. Mozart had earlier been impressed by Haydn's Quartets Opp. 17 and 20, and had sought to imitate them in his six Quartets K. 168–173, composed in Vienna in 1773. Haydn's later quartets of Op. 33 (1781) fully established the technique of pervasive thematic development with complete equality of the four instruments. Mozart's six *Haydn* Quartets, composed between 1782 and 1785 (K. 387, 421=417b, 428=421b, 458, 464, 465), show his mature capacity to absorb the essence of Haydn's achievement without becoming a mere imitator.

The Quartet K. 421 (=417b) in D minor stands out because of its tragic mood. The old descending tetrachord of the Baroque lament appears in the bass, accompanying a restatement of the opening theme; and although the piece has barely begun, the first violin strains for the highest note heard in the entire movement (Example 14.17). When, following contrasting yet stern secondary and closing groups, the theme returns in E♭ major after the double bar, the same bass line immediately darkens the optimistic reawakening.

The Quartet K. 465 in C major opens with a slow passage that contains striking cross-relations (marked X) occurring simultaneously with appoggia-

Example 14.18 *Mozart, String Quartet K. 465, Adagio*

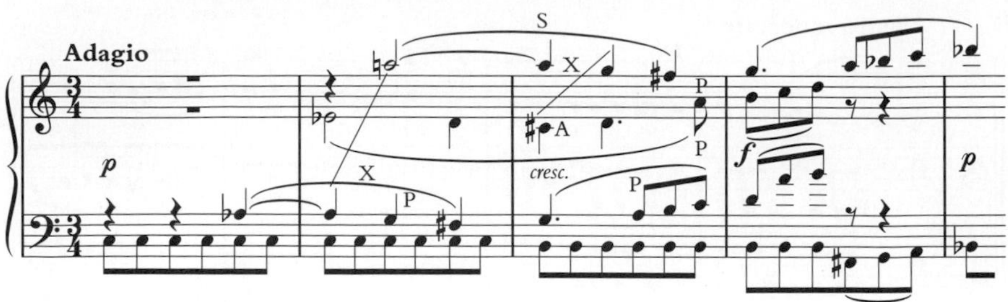

turas (A), suspensions (S), and passing notes (P); the combined effect has earned this work its nickname, *Dissonant* Quartet (Example 14.18).

Quintets

For all the excellence of his quartets, Mozart's genius reveals itself most fully in his quintets for two violins, two violas, and cello. The String Quintets in C major (K. 515) and G minor (K. 516), composed in the spring of 1787, may be compared with the last two symphonies in the same keys. Another masterpiece, the Clarinet Quintet in A (K. 581), was composed at about the same time as the opera buffa *Così fan tutte,* and captured some of the same comic spirit.

The Vienna Symphonies

Like Haydn, Mozart approached the symphony in his mature years with great seriousness. He wrote only six in the last ten years of his life—having earlier produced nearly sixty—and devoted much time and thought to their composition.[9] The symphonies written before 1782 served most often as concert or theatrical curtain raisers; those composed after he settled in Vienna constituted the main feature on concert programs or at least shared billing with concertos and arias. The *Haffner* Symphony, K. 385, written in 1782 for the elevation to nobility of Mozart's childhood friend Sigmund Haffner, and the *Linz* Symphony, K. 425, written in 1783 for a performance in that city, typify the late symphonies in their ambitious dimensions, greater demands on performers (particularly wind players), harmonic and contrapuntal complexity and chromaticism, and final movements that are climatic rather than light. These symphonies are in every way as artful as the *London* symphonies of Haydn, and some may indeed have served as models for the older composer. The others of this group—recognized as his greatest—are the *Prague* Symphony in D major (K. 504) of 1786 and the Symphonies in E♭ (K. 543), G minor (K. 550), and C major (K. 551, named the *Jupiter* by an English publisher). The last three were composed during a space of six weeks in the summer of 1788.

9. In the nineteenth century, the publisher Breitkopf & Härtel numbered forty-one Mozart symphonies. This count, which is still in occasional use, omits some two dozen early symphonic works while including three that are not by Mozart: "No. 2," by Leopold Mozart, "No. 3," by Carl Friedrich Abel, and "No. 37," a symphony by Michael Haydn for which Mozart supplied an introduction.

Each of the six symphonies is a masterpiece with its own special character, in some cases influenced by other music that Mozart was working on at the time. Their opening gestures leave an indelible impression. Both the *Haffner* and the *Jupiter* begin with loud, forceful unison statements followed by delicate ensemble responses (Example 14.19a, c). In both, the disparate elements of the theme are immediately wedded through counterpoint (Example 14.19b, d). The treatment in the *Jupiter* (14.19d) is more ingenious: the flutes and oboes seize upon the segment's soft accompaniment to spin invertible counterpoint against a restatement of the theme.

Opening statements

Another first movement without introduction, K. 550 in G minor, begins with a *piano* marking, a rare opening in symphonies before this one (Example

G-minor Symphony

Example 14.19a-b *Mozart, Symphony K. 385* (Haffner), *Allegro con spirito*

a.

b.

Example 14.19c-d *Mozart, Symphony K. 551* (Jupiter), *Allegro vivace*

c.

d.

Example 14.20 *Mozart, Symphony K. 550, Allegro molto (violin II and viola parts omitted)*

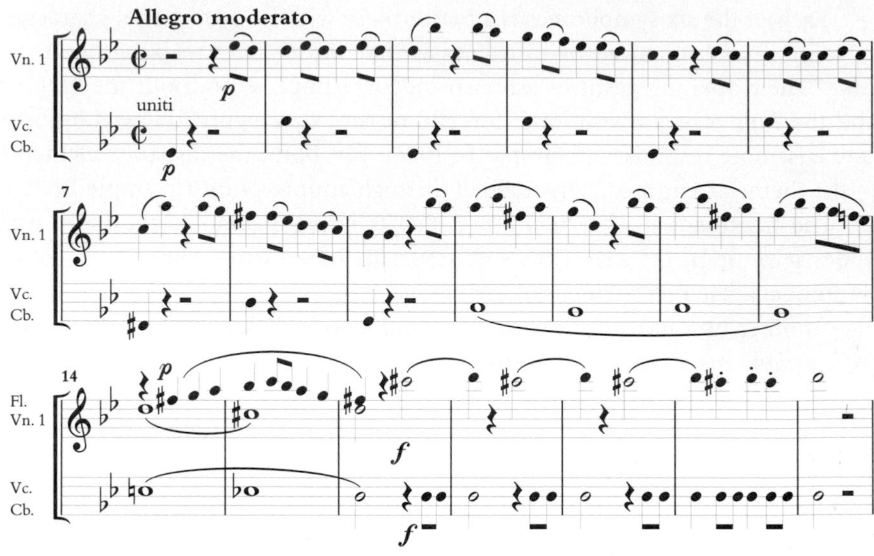

14.20). It bravely ventures forth with a soft, tragicomic melody, lightly accompanied by violas and basses, that alternately descends by step and regains height with leaps of a minor sixth, recalling Cherubino's aria *Non so più cosa son* in *Le nozze di Figaro*, composed two years earlier. Only after an enigmatic augmented sixth chord at measure 15 does a loud tutti respond with a two-chord exclamation over a dominant pedal, repeated four times. Contrapuntal recombinations are deferred to the development section and a short epilogue (measures 279–99).

Jupiter Symphony

There is an element of the comical in the otherwise heroic *Jupiter* Symphony. For the closing section of the first movement, Mozart borrowed the melody of a comic aria that he had written, *Un bacio di mano* (Example 14.21), which was inserted in Anfossi's *Le gelosie fortunate* (The Fortunate Jealousies). In the aria, Monsieur Girò cautions Don Pompeo that he might feel trapped if he marries a pretty young girl. The repeated cadences in the symphony that follow this quotation are also from the world of comic opera.

Example 14.21 *Mozart,* Un bacio di mano, *K. 541*

You are a simpleton, my dear Pompeo/ You'd better go study the ways of the world.

■ *Mozart's violins. His childhood violin, three-quarter size, was made around 1746 by Andres Ferdinard Mayr of Salzburg; the full-size instrument was built by Aegidius Klotz of Mittenwald in 1780. Mozart is most often thought of as a pianist performing his own concertos. But he was also a solo violinist, as discussed in the correspondence with his father about his virtuoso violin playing during concert tours between 1777 and 1778.* (SALZBURG, INTERNATIONALE STIFFUNG MOZARTEUM)

Introductions

The three introductions to Symphonies K. 425, 504, and 543 are animated by the spirit of the French overture, its majestic double-dotted rhythms, intense chordal harmony, and anacrusis figures (see the quotations in Example 14.22). Rather than intimating subtly what is to come, as Haydn sometimes did, Mozart created suspense, tantalizingly wandering away from the key and making its return a major event. The most elaborate of the introductions, to

Example 14.22 *Mozart, Passages from the introductions to Symphonies K. 425, 504, and 543*

a. *K. 425*

b. *K. 504*

c. *K. 543*

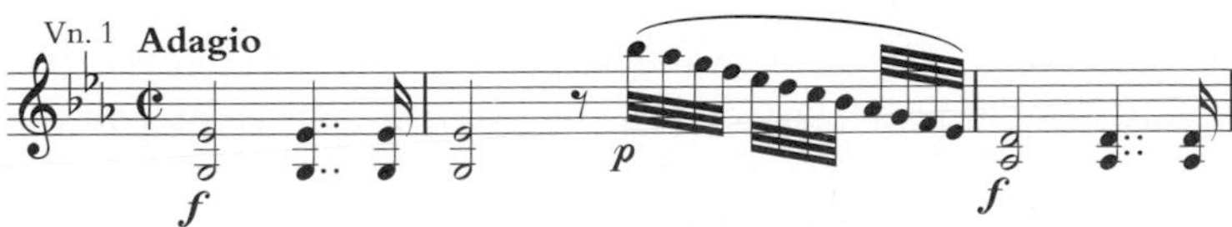

Example 14.23 *Mozart, Symphony K. 550, Allegro assai*

the *Prague* Symphony in D major, dwells mostly on D minor and develops an alternation between syncopated chords and soaring repetitions of a turn motive. The syncopations then link up with the Allegro theme. All three introductions permitted Mozart to begin the fast section with soft chamber-music textures that make the first rousing tutti all the more striking.

Finales

As in Haydn's late symphonies, the finales do more than send an audience away in a cheerful frame of mind. They balance the serious and important opening movement with a highly crafted counterweight fashioned with whimsy and humor. In the development section of the Allegro assai movement of the G-minor Symphony, the acrobatic transformation of the main theme at once startles and pokes fun, with its wild leaps and pregnant silences (Example 14.23).

There is also a touch of whimsy in the finale of the *Jupiter* Symphony, which takes its first theme from a fugue example in Fux's *Gradus ad Parnassum* and combines it in simple and double counterpoint with five other motives: a countersubject, two bridge figures, and both of the two motives that make up the second subject of the sonata scheme. The coda weaves all these together in an unsurpassed triumph of *ars combinatoria*, the art of combination and permutation derived from mathematics that was taught by eighteenth-century music theorists as a means of achieving melodic variety in composition. (See Example 14.24, in which P, S, and T stand respectively for primary theme, secondary theme, and transitional motives.)

Concertos for Piano and Orchestra

Seventeen concertos for piano occupy a central place in Mozart's output during the Vienna years. He wrote many of them as vehicles for his own concerts, and we can gauge the rise and fall of his popularity in Vienna by the number he composed each year: three in 1782–83, four in each of the next two seasons, three again in 1785–86, and only one for each of the next two seasons; after that no more until the last year of his life, when he played a new concerto (K. 595) in an event organized by Joseph Bähr, a local clarinetist. The first three Vienna concertos, K. 414 (=385p), 413 (=387a), and 415 (=387b), as Mozart wrote to his father,

> strike a happy median between too difficult and too easy. . . . Connoisseurs alone can derive satisfaction; the non-connoisseurs cannot fail to be pleased, though without knowing why.[10]

The next concerto, K. 449 in E♭, originally written for a pupil, was later played by Mozart with "unusual success," as he reported. Three magnificent

10. Letter dated December 23, 1782, trans. Elaine Sisman, *The "Jupiter" Symphony* (Cambridge: Cambridge University Press, 1993), p. 69.

works were all completed within a month of one another in the spring of 1784: K. 450 in B♭, K. 451 in D—both, in Mozart's words, "concertos to make the player sweat"—and the more intimate K. 453 in G. Three of the four concertos of 1784–85 are likewise works of first rank: K. 459 in F, K. 466 in D minor—the most dramatic and most frequently played—and the spacious and symphonic K. 467 in C. During the winter of 1785–86, when he was at work on *Le nozze di Figaro,* Mozart turned out three more concertos, of which the first two, K. 482 in E♭ and K. 488 in A (see NAWM 99, first movement), are in a comparatively light mood, while the third, K. 491, in C minor, is one of his great tragic creations. The big C-major concerto of December 1786, K. 503, may be regarded as the triumphal counterpart of K. 491. Of the two remaining concertos, one is the popular *Coronation* Concerto in D, K. 537 (1788), which Mozart played in Frankfurt during the coronation festivities in 1790 for Emperor Leopold II. Mozart's last concerto, K. 595 in B♭, was completed in January of 1791.

Form

Classic piano concertos, such as those by Mozart, preserve certain features of the Baroque concerto. They follow the three-movement sequence fast–slow–fast. The first movement is in a modified concerto-ritornello form: indeed, Koch described the form of the first Allegro as containing "three main periods performed by the soloist, which are enclosed by four subsidiary periods performed by the orchestra as ritornellos."[11] The second movement is a kind of aria, and the finale is generally dancelike or popular in character. A close look at a typical first movement, the Allegro from K. 488 in A major (NAWM 99; CD 8 [12]), will show how the ritornello of the Baroque concerto permeates the sonata form.

K. 488 Allegro

Baroque elements

The opening orchestral section of sixty-six measures displays both the thematic variety of a sonata-form exposition and several elements of the Baroque concerto ritornello: it is in a single key and it contains a transitional tutti (measures 18 to 30) that reappears in various keys in the course of the movement. Maintaining the ritornello results in a version of sonata form that actually has two expositions, one orchestral and one solo with orchestra. (J. C. Bach had employed a similar procedure in his Concerto for Harpsichord or Piano and Strings, Op. 7, No. 5; NAWM 93). In the section that follows the exposition, rather than developing ideas presented earlier, Mozart offers a dialogue between the piano and winds based on new material, with the strings acting as a "ripieno" group. This section makes excursions into several alien keys—E minor, C major, F major—culminating in a twenty-measure pedal point on the dominant.

In the recapitulation, the transitional tutti returns at the beginning of the bridge passage. It is heard yet again—with a dramatic interruption by the new theme of the "development"—as the orchestra reaches the most suspenseful moment of the concerto, a six-four chord, where it pauses. The soloist then is expected to improvise an extended cadenza, and the movement closes with the same tutti that ended the orchestral exposition. The entire movement may be schematized as follows:

Section:	**Exposition**								
Tonal center:	**Tonic**						**Dominant**		
Instruments:	***Orchestra***				***Solo with Orchestra***				
Themes:	P	TT	S	KT	P	TT	S	K	TT
Measure:	1	*18*	*30*	*46*	*67*	*82*	*98*	*114*	*137*

Development		**Recapitulation**						
Modulatory	**Dominant**	**Tonic**						
Solo with Orchestra							***Solo***	***Orchestra***
New material	Short cad.	P	TT	S	K	TT	Cadenza	KT
143	*189*	*198*	*213*	*228*	*244*	*284*	*297*	*298*

Note: P = primary group; S = secondary group; K = closing group; KT = closing tutti; TT = transitional tutti

11. Heinrich Christoph Koch, *Introductory Essay on Composition*, trans. Nancy K. Baker (New Haven: Yale University Press, 1983), p. 210.

Mozart's other first movements do not, of course, conform exactly to the plan of this Allegro. The orchestral expositions and the recapitulations in particular diverge, omitting one or more elements of the soloist's thematic or closing material. In some, Mozart deemphasized the transitional tutti, in others the closing tutti, but the main profile of the scheme remains valid.

Second movements

The second movement of a Mozart concerto is like a lyrical aria, with a tempo of andante, larghetto, or allegretto. It is in the subdominant of the principal key, or, less often, in the dominant or the relative minor. Its form, although greatly variable in details, is most often a kind of modified sonata scheme without development or, like the *Romance* of K. 466, an ABACA rondo. The finale is typically a rondo or sonata-rondo on themes with a popular character; these are treated in scintillating virtuoso style with opportunities for one or more cadenzas. Although the concertos were show pieces intended to dazzle an audience, Mozart never allowed display to get the upper hand. He always maintained a healthy balance of musical interest between the orchestral and solo portions, and his infallible ear is evident in the myriad combinations of colors and textures he draws from the interplay between the piano and orchestral instruments, especially the winds. Moreover, the goal of composing for an immediate public response did not keep him from expressing profound musical ideas.

Finales

Cadenzas

That Mozart put substance before fireworks may be seen in the cadenzas he sketched or fully notated for his own concertos. The cadenza had developed from the trills and runs that singers inserted, particularly before the return of the opening section in the da capo aria. Mozart's early cadenzas were similarly flourishes without thematic links to the movement, but after the 1780s they served to balance the longer modulatory or development sections. These cadenzas, virtually renewed development sections, cast new light on familiar material in daring flights of technical wizardry. In K. 488 Mozart wrote the cadenza into the score, perhaps to make up for the lack of true development earlier. Beethoven and later composers wrote lengthy and demanding cadenzas for their concertos. Audiences in the nineteenth century looked forward to the climactic displays of imagination and digital prowess in the cadenzas improvised by the reigning virtuosos.

Operas

After *Idomeneo* Mozart wrote only one more opera seria, *La clemenza di Tito* (The Mercy of Titus), composed in haste during the summer of 1791 for the coronation in Prague of Leopold II as king of Bohemia. The chief dramatic works of the Vienna period were the Singspiel *Die Entführung aus dem Serail* (The Abduction from the Harem, 1782); three Italian operas, *Le nozze di Figaro* (The Marriage of Figaro, 1786), *Don Giovanni* (Prague, 1787), and *Così fan tutte* (Thus Do All Women, 1790)—all three on librettos by Lorenzo da Ponte (1749–1838); and the German opera *Die Zauberflöte* (The Magic Flute, 1791). Mozart favored librettos that were not ambitiously poetic. Unlike

MOZART ON OPERA LIBRETTOS

In an opera the poetry must be altogether the obedient daughter of the music. Why do Italian comic operas please everywhere—in spite of their miserable libretti—even in Paris, where I myself witnessed their success? Just because there the music reigns supreme and when one listens to it all else is forgotten. Why, an opera is sure of success when the plot is well worked out, the words written solely for the music and not shoved in here and there to suit some miserable rhyme (which God knows never enhances the value of any theatrical performance, be it what it may, but rather detracts from it)—I mean, words or even entire verses which ruin the composer's whole idea. Verses are indeed the most indispensable element for music—but rhymes—solely for the sake of rhyming—the most detrimental. Those high and mighty people who set to work in this pedantic fashion will always come to grief, both they and their music. The best thing of all is when a good composer, who understands the stage and is talented enough to make sound suggestions, meets an able poet, that true phoenix; in that case no fears need be entertained as to the applause even of the ignorant. Poets almost remind me of trumpeters with their professional tricks! If we composers were always to stick so faithfully to our rules (which were very good at a time when no one knew better), we should be concocting music as unpalatable as their libretti.

W. A. Mozart in Vienna, in the midst of composing *Die Entführung*, writing to his father, Leopold, in Salzburg, October 13, 1781. Emily Anderson, ed., *The Letters of Mozart and His Family* (New York: Norton, 1989), p. 773.

Gluck, he believed poetry should serve the music rather than the contrary (see vignette).

Le nozze di Figaro

Figaro followed the conventions of Italian eighteenth-century comic opera (see Chapter 13, pages 440ff). But da Ponte, basing his libretto on a spoken comedy by Beaumarchais, lifted the opera buffa to a higher level, giving greater depth to the characters, intensifying the social tensions between classes, and introducing moral issues. Mozart's psychological penetration and his genius for musical characterization similarly raised the genre's seriousness. Delineation of character occurs not only in solo arias but more especially in duets, trios, and larger ensembles. The ensemble finales allow these characters to clash, combining realism with ongoing dramatic action and superbly unified musical form. Mozart's orchestration, particularly his use of winds, played an important role in defining the characters and situations.

Don Giovanni

Figaro enjoyed only moderate success in Vienna, but its enthusiastic reception in Prague led to the commission for *Don Giovanni*, which was performed there the following year. *Don Giovanni* is a dramma giocoso of a very special sort. The medieval legend on which the plot is based had been treated often in literature and music since the early seventeenth century. But Mozart, for the first time in opera, took the character of Don Juan seriously—not as an

Characterizations

incongruous mixture of farcical figure and horrible blasphemer, but as a romantic hero, a rebel against authority, a scorner of common morality, and a supreme individualist, bold and unrepentant to the last. It was Mozart's music rather than da Ponte's libretto that raised the Don to this stature and at the same time paraded his gluttony and selfishness before all succeeding generations. The Romantic musical imagination of the nineteenth century relished the daemonic quality of the opening measures of the overture, intensified by the sound of the trombones in the cemetery scene and at the apparition of the statue in the finale. Some of the other characters, though they are subtly ridiculed, must also be taken seriously: the tragic Donna Elvira, constantly complaining that the Don jilted her, and Leporello, more than a *commedia dell'arte* servant-buffoon, revealing deep sensitivity and intuition.

The fifth scene of Act I (NAWM 100a; CD 8 [28] / 3 ⟨24⟩) musically sketches three personalities. Elvira's melody, with its angry wide leaps, abetted by the agitated runs and tremolos in the strings, contrasts sharply with the tight-lipped, lighthearted, mocking tone of Don Giovanni and the seemingly idle patter of Leporello, playing down his role as healer of the bruised souls of abandoned women.

The famous *Catalogue* aria that follows (NAWM 100b; CD 8 [31] / 3 ⟨27⟩), in which Leporello enumerates his master's conquests by country and describes the kinds of women he likes, shows another serious side of Mozart's comic art. Awed as we are by the details of his characterization, by his text animation, harmonic shadings, and orchestration, we are compelled to take seriously this most entertaining portion of the opera. The aria is in two discrete parts, an

Don Giovanni about to meet his punishment at the hands of the Commendatore, or stone guest, whom the Don had boldly invited to dinner in the final scene of Don Giovanni. *Title page of an early edition.* (LEIPZIG: BREITKOPF & HÄRTEL, 1801)

Allegro in common time and an Andante con moto in the meter and rhythm of a minuet.

Così fan tutte

Così fan tutte is an opera buffa in the best Italian tradition, with a brilliant libretto glorified by some of Mozart's most melodious music. The fashion of applying neo-Freudian psychology to Mozart's works and reading into them everything from autobiography to romantic irony and crypto-revolutionary sentiments has been extended even to this sparkling opera, where all such ideas seem superfluous.

Die Entführung

Die Entführung is a romantic-comic story of adventure and rescue, set against the popular eighteenth-century "oriental" background, a subject that had been treated earlier by Rameau, Gluck, Haydn, and others. But here, in one stroke, Mozart raised the German Singspiel into the realm of great art without altering any of its established features.

Die Zauberflöte

Die Zauberflöte is a different matter. Though outwardly a Singspiel—with spoken dialogue instead of recitative, and with some characters and scenes appropriate to popular comedy—its action is filled with symbolic meaning and its music is so rich and profound that it ranks as the first great German opera. The largely solemn mood of the score reflects the relationship between the opera and the teachings and ceremonies of Freemasonry. We know that Mozart valued his Masonic affiliation, not only from allusions in his letters but especially from the serious quality of the music he wrote for Masonic ceremonies in 1785 and for a Masonic cantata in 1791 (K. 623), his last completed work. In *Zauberflöte* Mozart wove the threads of many eighteenth-century musical ideas into new designs: the vocal opulence of Italian opera seria; the folk humor of the German Singspiel; the solo aria; the *buffo* ensemble, which is given new musical meaning; a new kind of accompanied recitative applicable to German words; solemn choral scenes; and even (in the duet of the two armed men in Act II) a revival of the Baroque chorale-prelude technique, with contrapuntal accompaniment.

Church Music

Given that Mozart's father worked as a musician for the archbishop of Salzburg and Wolfgang himself held similar appointments—first as concertmaster and later as organist—it was natural for Mozart to compose music for the church from an early age. However, with notable exceptions—his Mass in C minor, Ave verum corpus, and Requiem—his settings of sacred texts are not counted among his major works. The Masses, like those of Haydn, are for the most part written in the current symphonic-operatic idiom, intermingled with fugues at certain customary places, and scored for chorus and soloists in free alternation, with orchestral accompaniment. The Requiem, K. 626, was Mozart's last work. It was commissioned by a wealthy nobleman, Count Walsegg, in July 1791, but Mozart was busy with *La Clemenza di Tito* and *Die Zauberflöte* and made little progress until the fall. Left unfinished at Mozart's death, it was completed by his pupil and collaborator Franz Xaver Süssmayr

Masses

Requiem

(1766–1803), who added some instrumental parts to Mozart's draft and set the Sanctus, Benedictus, and Agnus Dei, in part repeating music that Mozart had composed for an earlier section.

EPILOGUE

This chapter about Haydn and Mozart does not presume to cover the music of the late eighteenth century. These two composers shared the limelight with a host of others. Some of their names are familiar from the pages of this book—the opera composers Gluck, Piccinni, Paisiello, and Salieri. To these may be added Georg Benda (1722–1795), Pasquale Anfossi (1727–1797), Antonio Sacchini (1730–1786), and Domenico Cimarosa (1749–1801). Among the instrumental composers, Ignaz Holzbauer (1711–1783), Luigi Boccherini (1743–1805), Carl Dittersdorf (1739–1799), and Leopold Anton Kozeluch (1747–1818) deserve mention. Some of these composers were also active in opera or Singspiel. Each of them contributed uniquely to the period and merits further attention. But with so much of their music still inaccessible for listening and study, their inclusion would have multiplied the kind of dry, unresonant name-dropping and selective listing that this paragraph regretfully exemplifies. Haydn and Mozart together ranged over all the genres practiced in the late eighteenth century, and their music represents the best that the period produced.

Other composers

BIBLIOGRAPHY

General Reading

Philip G. Downs, *Classical Music: The Era of Haydn, Mozart, and Beethoven* (New York: Norton, 1992) and the coordinated *Anthology of Classical Music*, ed. Downs (New York: Norton, 1992) constitute an excellent introduction to the music and milieu of this period. Daniel Heartz, *Haydn, Mozart, and the Viennese School, 1740–1780* (New York: Norton, 1995) sets their work in the context of eighteenth-century Viennese culture and society. Friedrich Blume, *Classic and Romantic Music* (New York: Norton, 1970), comprehensively surveys all aspects of music in the period *ca.* 1770–1810. Reinhard Pauly, *Music in the Classic Period*, 3rd ed. (Englewood Cliffs, N. J.: Prentice Hall, 1988), is an informative survey. Charles Rosen, *The Classical Style: Haydn, Mozart, Beethoven* (expanded ed., New York: Norton, 1997) is full of insights, as is his most recent book, *Sonata Forms* (New York: Norton, 1980; rev. ed., 1988), a review of the genre's repertory. Leonard Ratner's *Classic Music: Expression, Form, and Style* (New York: Schirmer Books, 1980) draws on original eighteenth-century sources for an enriched discussion of compositional practices. See also Giorgio Pestelli, *The Age of Mozart and Beethoven* (Cambridge: Cambridge University Press, 1984); *Haydn, Mozart, and Beethoven, Studies in the Music of the Classical Period: Essays in Honor of Alan Tyson*, ed. Sieghard Brandenburg (Oxford: Clarendon Press, 1998), and H. C. Robbins Landon, *Essays on the Viennese Classical Style: Gluck, Haydn, Mozart, Beethoven* (New York: Macmillan, 1970).

Haydn

The definitive edition of Haydn's works is being published by the Haydn Institute of Cologne, 59 vols. (Munich-Duisburg: G. Henle, 1958–); thematic catalogue by Anthony van Hoboken, 3 vols. (Mainz: B. Schott's Söhne, 1957–78). See Stephen C. Bryant and Gary W. Chapman, *A Melodic Index to Haydn's Instrumental Music* (New York: Pendragon Press, 1982), to identify the titles of works for which only the melody is known and to locate them in Hoboken's thematic catalogue.

Source material is in H. C. Robbins Landon, ed., *The Collected Correspondence and London Notebooks of Joseph Haydn* (London and New York: Barrie & Rockliff, 1959).

A bibliography listing two centuries of Haydn literature has been compiled by A. Peter Brown and J. T. Berkenstock, "Joseph Haydn in Literature: A Bibliography," in *Haydn-Studien* III/304 (July 1974):173–352; with supplements by Horst Waeter, V/4 (1985):205–306; VI/3 (1992):173–239.

On the life and works of Haydn, see H. C. Robbins Landon's five-volume *Haydn's Chronicle and Works* (Bloomington: Indiana University Press, 1976–80); *The New Grove Haydn*, by J. P. Larsen and G. Feder (New York: Norton, 1983). The best short general biographies are Karl Geiringer, *Haydn, a Creative Life in Music* (Berkeley: University of California Press, 1968; 3rd rev. ed., 1982); Rosemary Hughes, *Haydn*, rev. ed. (London: Dent, 1974). See also H. C. Robbins Landon, *Haydn: A Documentary Study* (New York: Rizzoli, 1981).

Supplemental Reading

On the symphonies, see H. C. Robbins Landon, *The Symphonies of Joseph Haydn* (London: Universal Edition, 1955; with supp., Barrie & Rockliff, 1961); Donald F. Tovey, *Essays in Musical Analysis*, Vol. 1 (London: Oxford University Press, 1935; with subseq. reprints); K. Geiringer, ed., *Haydn, Symphony No. 103 in E-flat*, Norton Critical Scores (New York: Norton, 1974). For a fresh look at Haydn's methods of composition, see James Webster, *Haydn's "Farewell" Symphony and the Idea of Classical Style* (Cambridge: Cambridge University Press, 1991). The central role played by variation is explored in Elaine R. Sisman, *Haydn and the Classical Variation* (Cambridge, Mass.: Harvard University Press, 1993). The social and intellectual background of Haydn's Paris and London symphonies is studied in David P. Schroeder, *Haydn and the Enlightenment* (Oxford: Clarendon Press, 1990). For a serious consideration of Haydn's proverbial humor, see Gretchen A. Wheelock, *Haydn's Ingenious Jesting with Art: Contexts of Musical Wit and Humor* (New York: Schirmer Books, 1992).

On the quartets, see Rosemary Hughes, *Haydn String Quartets* (Seattle: University of Washington Press, 1969; rev. 5th ed., 1975); Hans Keller, *The Great Haydn String Quartets: Their Interpretation* (London: Dent, 1986), for fresh insights; James Webster, "Towards a History of Viennese Chamber Music in the Early Classical Period," JAMS 27 (1974):212–47, which traces the history of terms such as *divertimento* and *quartet.* On the Op. 3 quartets by Hofstetter, see Alan Tyson and H. C. Robbins Landon, "Who Composed Haydn's Opus 3?" *Musical Times* 105 (1964):506–07.

On keyboard works, see A. Peter Brown, *Joseph Haydn's Keyboard Music: Sources and Style* (Bloomington: Indiana University Press, 1986), a detailed study; idem, "The Structure of the Exposition in Haydn's Keyboard Sonatas," *The Music Review* (1975):102–29.

Mozart

The standard collected edition is the *Neue Ausgabe sämtlicher Werke* (Kassel: Bärenreiter, 1955–). An older edition of his works is *W. A. Mozarts sämtliche Werke* (Leipzig: Breitkopf

& Härtel, 1876–1907; repr. Ann Arbor: Edwards, 1951–56), 14 series, including suppl. vols.; repr. in miniature format (New York: Kalmus, 1969). Thematic catalogue: Ludwig Köchel, *Chronologisch-thematisches Verzeichnis*, 6th ed., ed. Alfred Einstein (Wiesbaden: Breitkopf & Härtel, 1964).

Bibliography: Rudolph Angermüller and Otto Schneider, comps., *Mozart-Bibliographie, 1976–1980* (Kassel: Bärenreiter, 1982).

Correspondence: *The Letters of Mozart and His Family*, 2 vols., ed. Emily Anderson (New York: Norton, 1989); *Mozart's Letters, Mozart's Life*, ed. and newly trans. Robert Spaethling (New York: Norton, 2000).

Life and Works: Recommended are Neal Zaslaw, with William Cowdery, *The Compleat Mozart* (New York: Norton, 1990). *The Mozart Companion*, ed. H. C. Robbins Landon and Donald Mitchell (New York: Norton, 1969); and *The Creative World of Mozart*, Paul H. Lang, ed. (New York: Norton, 1963), contain detailed studies on Mozart's life and works; see also *The New Grove Mozart*, by Stanley Sadie (New York: Norton, 1983); and Otto E. Deutsch, *Mozart, a Documentary Biography*, 2nd ed., trans. E. Blom et al. (Stanford: Stanford University Press, 1965); Maynard Solomon, *Mozart* (New York: HarperCollins, 1996).

The standard book about Mozart's life and music is Hermann Abert, *W. A. Mozart*, 2 vols. (Leipzig: Breitkopf & Härtel, 1956; rev. 1975). This is a revision of Otto Jahn's *Mozart*, which was first published in 4 vols. in 1856–59. A. Hyatt King's *Mozart* (London: Bingley, 1970) is a convenient short biography; it includes annotated lists of books about Mozart in English and a bibliography of Mozart editions.

See also by H. C. Robbins Landon: *Mozart's Last Year* (London: Thames & Hudson, 1988), *Mozart and Vienna* (New York: Schirmer Books, 1991), *Mozart, The Golden Years, 1781–1791* (London: Thames & Hudson, 1989), and as ed., *The Mozart Compendium: A Guide to Mozart's Life and Music* (London: Thames & Hudson, 1990).

Wye J. Allanbrook, *Rhythmic Gesture in Mozart* (Chicago: Chicago University Press, 1983); Alfred Einstein, *Mozart: His Character, His Work*, trans. Arthur Mendel and Nathan Broder (New York: Oxford University Press, 1961); David Schroeder, *Mozart in Revolt* (New Haven: Yale University Press, 1999); A. Hyatt King, *Mozart in Retrospect*, 3rd ed. (London: Oxford University Press, 1970); Arthur Hutchings, *Mozart: The Man, the Musician* (London: Thames & Hudson, 1976). Wolfgang Hildesheimer, *Mozart*, trans. Marion Faber (London: Dent; New York: Vintage Books, 1983), has a stimulating psychological portrait of the composer.

On Mozart and Freemasonry, see H. C. Robbins Landon, *Mozart and the Masons: New Light on the Lodge, "Crowned Hope"* (New York: Thames & Hudson, 1983).

Supplemental Reading

On Mozart's symphonies, Georges de Saint-Foix, *The Symphonies of Mozart*, trans. Leslie Orrey (London: Dobson, 1947; repr. New York: Dover, 1968), which contains nontechnical analyses; Robert Dearling, *The Music of W. A. Mozart: The Symphonies* (Rutherford, N. J.: Fairleigh Dickinson University Press, 1982); Nathan Broder, ed., *Mozart, Symphony in G minor, K. 550*, Norton Critical Scores (New York: Norton, 1967).

Chamber Music: A. Hyatt King, *Mozart Chamber Music* (Seattle: University of Washington Press, 1969); Erik Smith, *Mozart Serenades, Divertimenti and Dances* (London: BBC, 1982).

Opera: Edward J. Dent, *Mozart's Operas*, 2nd ed. (London: Oxford University Press, 1960); William Mann, *The Operas of Mozart* (London: Oxford University Press, 1960); Nicholas Till, *Mozart and the Enlightenment* (New York: Norton, 1993); Carolyn Gianturco, *Mozart's Early Operas* (London: Batsford, 1981); Julian Rushton, *W. A. Mozart: "Don Giovanni"* (Cambridge: Cambridge University Press, 1981), a useful handbook; Peter Gammond, *The Magic Flute: A Guide to the Opera* (London: Breslich & Foss, 1979).

Concertos: Neal Zaslaw, *Mozart's Piano Concertos* (Ann Arbor: University of Michigan Press, 1995); A. Hyatt King, *Mozart String and Wind Concertos* (London, 1978); Joseph Kerman, ed., *Mozart, Piano Concerto in C major, K. 503*, Norton Critical Scores (New York: Norton, 1970).

Performance practice: Frederick Neumann, *Ornamentation and Improvisation in Mozart* (Princeton: Princeton University Press, 1985); *Perspectives on Mozart Performance*, ed. R. Larry Todd and Peter Williams (Cambridge: Cambridge University Press, 1991).

Leopold Mozart

Gründliche Violinschule (1756), facs. (Leipzig, 1956), trans. by Editha Knocker as *A Treatise on the Fundamental Principles of Violin Playing*, 2nd ed. (London and New York: Oxford University Press, 1951).

CHAPTER 15

LUDWIG VAN BEETHOVEN

THE COMPOSER AND HIS MUSIC

In 1792 George Washington was president of the United States; Goethe, at Weimar, was directing the ducal theater and publishing studies in the science of optics; Haydn was at the height of his fame; and Mozart had been dead since the previous December. Early in November, an ambitious young composer and pianist named Ludwig van Beethoven, then just under twenty-two years of age, traveled from the city of Bonn on the Rhine to Vienna, a five-hundred-mile journey that took a week by stagecoach. He ran short of money and for a while kept a detailed account of his finances. One of his notebook entries records an expenditure of twenty-five groschen for "coffee for Haidn and me."

Studies with Haydn

Haydn had stopped off at Bonn on his way to London in December 1790. He must have heard some of Beethoven's compositions because he urged the archbishop elector of Cologne to send his young charge to Vienna for further study. Beethoven's lessons with Haydn continued from late 1792 until Haydn left in 1794 on his second visit to London. Meanwhile, Beethoven also received help from Johann Schenk (1753–1836), a popular Viennese composer of Singspiele. After 1794, Beethoven studied counterpoint for a year with Johann Georg Albrechtsberger (1736–1809), the author of a famous treatise on composition and one of the leading teachers of his day. Beethoven also received informal lessons in vocal composition from Antonio Salieri, who had been living in Vienna since 1766. But his earliest music teacher was his father, a singer in the chapel at Bonn, who pushed the boy's progress in the hope of making a second Mozart of him. When he was seventeen, Beethoven actually played for Mozart, who prophesied a bright future for him. Also, before going to Vienna,

Other teachers

SIR JULIUS BENEDICT DESCRIBES HIS FIRST SIGHT OF BEETHOVEN (1823)

If I am not mistaken, on the morning that I saw Beethoven for the first time, Blahetka, the father of the pianist, directed my attention to a stout, short man with a very red face, small, piercing eyes, and bushy eyebrows, dressed in a very long overcoat which reached nearly to his ankles, who entered the shop [the music store of Steiner and Haslinger] about 12 o'clock. Blahetka asked me: "Who do you think that is?" and I at once exclaimed: "It must be Beethoven!" because, notwithstanding the high color of his cheeks and his general untidiness, there was in those small piercing eyes an expression which no painter could render. It was a feeling of sublimity and melancholy combined.

Quoted in *Thayer's Life of Beethoven*, rev. and ed. by Elliot Forbes (Princeton: Princeton University Press, 1967), p. 873.

he had taken lessons in Bonn from the court organist Christian Gottlob Neefe (1748–1798), who was known for his Singspiele and songs.

Impact as composer

Beethoven came on the scene at a time when new and powerful forces were changing society. He witnessed the tremendous upheaval that erupted from the French Revolution. Although he built on the musical conventions, genres, and styles of the Classic period, Beethoven transformed this heritage and created a body of work that became models for composers of the Romantic period.

Output

His compositions include 9 symphonies, 11 overtures, incidental music to plays, a violin concerto, 5 piano concertos, 16 string quartets, 9 piano trios, 10 violin sonatas, 5 cello sonatas, 32 piano sonatas, many sets of piano variations, an oratorio, an opera, and 2 Masses, as well as arias, songs, and numerous lesser compositions.[1] There is an obvious disparity when we compare these figures with the output of Haydn and Mozart: 9 symphonies, for example, to Haydn's 100-plus or Mozart's 60-plus. A partial explanation, of course, is that Beethoven's symphonies are longer and grander, but another reason is that Beethoven wrote music with great deliberation. He kept notebooks in which he jotted down themes and plans for compositions, and thanks to these sketchbooks we can follow the progress of a musical idea or plan through various stages until it reaches the final form (see commentary, NAWM 103). The sketches for the Quartet Op. 131 occupy three times as many pages as the finished work.

1. The traditional count and numbering of Beethoven's symphonies and other genres omit certain compositions, such as his "Battle Symphony" (Op. 91, 1813), several early piano sonatas, and a piano concerto of 1784. Georg Kinsky and Hans Halm in the standard thematic catalogue of Beethoven's music, *Das Werk Beethovens* (Munich, 1955), list his Opp. 1–136 followed by 204 items labeled "WoO" (Werk ohne Opuszahl—work without opus number). A number of additional works are listed in Willy Hess, *Verzeichnis der nicht in der Gesamtausgabe veröffentlichten Werke Ludwig van Beethovens* (Index of Works by L. van Beethoven not in the Collected Edition; Wiesbaden, 1957).

The impression Beethoven gave of being moody and unsociable had much to do with his increasing deafness. He began to lose his hearing around 1796, and by 1820 he could hardly hear at all. In the autumn of 1802 Beethoven wrote a letter, now known as the Heiligenstadt Testament, intended to be read by his brothers after his death. In it he describes in moving terms how he suffered when he realized that his malady was incurable:

Heiligenstadt Testament

> I must live almost alone like one who has been banished, I can mix with society only as much as true necessity demands. If I approach near to people a hot terror seizes upon me and I fear being exposed to the danger that my condition might be noticed. Thus it has been during the last six months which I have spent in the country. . . . What a humiliation for me when someone standing next to me heard a flute in the distance and I heard nothing, or someone heard a shepherd singing and again I heard nothing. Such incidents drove me almost to despair, a little more of that and I would have ended my life—it was only my art that held me back. Ah, it seemed to me impossible to leave the world until I had brought forth all that I felt was within me. . . . Oh Providence—grant me at last but one day of pure joy—it is so long since real joy echoed in my heart. . . .[2]

Yet the same man who issued this cry of despair had, during that very half year in the country, written the exuberantly joyful Second Symphony!

Working methods

It was Beethoven's habit to plan his compositions out-of-doors, often while taking long walks. A young composer he befriended recalled Beethoven saying:

> You will ask me whence I take my ideas? That I cannot say with any degree of certainty: they come to me uninvited, directly or indirectly. I could almost grasp them in my hands, out in Nature's open, in the woods, during my promenades, in the silence of the night, at the earliest dawn. They are roused by moods which in the poet's case are transmuted into words, and in mine into tones, that sound, roar and storm until at last they take shape for me as notes.[3]

Beethoven's "Three Periods"

Scholars have customarily divided Beethoven's works into three periods based on style and chronology. During the first period, to about 1802, Beethoven was assimilating the musical language of his time and finding a personal voice. He composed the six String Quartets Op. 18, the piano sonatas (through Op. 28), the first three piano concertos, and the first two symphonies. The second period, in which his rugged independence took hold, runs to about 1815 and includes the Symphonies Nos. 3 to 8, the incidental music to Goethe's drama *Egmont*, the *Coriolan* Overture, the opera *Fidelio*, the Piano Concertos in G and E♭, the Violin Concerto, the Quartets of Opp. 59 (the *Rasumovsky*

2. *Thayer's Life of Beethoven*, rev. and ed. Elliot Forbes (Princeton: Princeton University Press, 1967), pp. 304–06.
3. *Ibid.*, pp. 851–52.

Quartets), 74, and 95, and the Piano Sonatas through Op. 90. The last period, in which Beethoven's music generally became more reflective and introspective, includes the last five piano sonatas, the *Diabelli* Variations, the *Missa solemnis*, the Ninth Symphony, the Quartets Opp. 127, 130, 131, 132, 135, and the *Grosse Fuge* (Grand Fugue) for string quartet (Op. 133, originally the finale of Op. 130). This division actually occurs at different chronological points in different genres, and there are no hard and fast boundaries between the periods, but it is a convenient way to organize a discussion of his music.

FIRST PERIOD

Patrons

Beethoven established himself in Vienna with the help of contacts he made through his Bonn employer, the elector of Cologne, Maximilian Franz, brother of both the late Habsburg Emperor Joseph II (reigned 1765–80) and Emperor

Beginning of Beethoven's Rondo, Allegro, the third movement of his Sonata, Op. 13, which was published by Eder in Vienna in 1799, a year after the sonata was completed. It is entitled "Grande sonate pathétique pour le clavecin ou piano forte composée et dediée a Son Altesse Monseigneur le Prince Charles de Lichnowsky, Oeuvre 13." The text agrees in most details with modern editions, but the crescendo mark in measure 12 is omitted in most recent editions (compare to NAWM 101). (BEINECKE RARE BOOK AND MANUSCRIPT LIBRARY, YALE UNIVERSITY)

Leopold (reigned 1790–92). Several members of the Austrian, Bohemian, and Hungarian aristocracy encouraged and supported him. For a while, Beethoven had rooms in one of the houses of Prince Karl von Lichnowsky, with whom he traveled to Prague for concerts in 1796 and who sponsored concerts in his palace in Vienna. Prince Lobkowitz kept a private orchestra that played in Vienna and at his Bohemian country estates, and bought rights to first performances of some of Beethoven's works. He, Prince Kinsky, and Beethoven's piano and composition student Archduke Rudolph—Leopold's son and youngest brother of Emperor Franz (reigned 1792–1835)—joined in setting up an annuity for the composer so that he would stay in Austria when he got an attractive offer from Jerome Bonaparte, king of Westphalia. Many of Beethoven's works of this and later periods are dedicated to these patrons, to the German-Bohemian Count Ferdinand von Waldstein, and to Baron van Swieten. He sold a number of important works, including a symphony, a piano concerto, a piano sonata, and the Septet to the Leipzig publisher Hoffmeister. Beethoven played as a pianist in concerts that he or others organized and also taught piano. In this way he managed to make a living as an independent musician and composer.

The Piano Sonatas

Formal elements

The themes and their treatment in the first three piano sonatas are reminiscent of works by Haydn, to whom they are dedicated—see, for example, the Adagio of No. 1, composed in 1787 when Beethoven was fifteen. But these sonatas all have four movements instead of the usual three. Moreover, in the second and third sonatas Beethoven replaced the Minuet with the more dynamic Scherzo, which he did almost consistently from here on. Beethoven's extensive use of the minor mode and the bold modulations in the first three sonatas are highly individual traits. In the first movement of the second sonata, for example, the second theme begins in the dominant minor, E, and immediately modulates, over a rising bass line, through G major and B♭ major before settling down into the "proper" key of E major for the closing part of the exposition.

The Sonata Op. 7 in E♭ (1797) is especially characteristic of Beethoven, with its eloquent pauses in the Largo con gran espressione and the mysterious perpetual arpeggiations that appear in the *minore* trio of the third movement. Opus 10, No. 1 (published in 1798), and the *Sonate pathétique*, Op. 13 (published in 1799), both in C minor, have outer movements of a stormy, passionate character (which Beethoven's predecessors associated with that key), and a calm, profound slow movement in A♭. In the *Pathétique*, the Grave introduction reappears twice in the first movement, and the theme of the Rondo Finale (NAWM 101; CD 8 [33] / 3 ◇29) clearly resembles the second theme (in E♭ minor) of the first movement. These features foreshadow some of the "cyclical" inter-movement connections in Beethoven's later works. (See illustration, page 516.) Some of the harmonic characteristics in these early works, as well as Beethoven's frequent use of octaves and the thick, full texture of the piano writing, may have been inspired by the piano sonatas of Muzio Clementi

Influence of Clementi and Dussek

(1752–1832; see NAWM 102). Other possible influences include the piano sonatas of the Bohemian-born Jan Ladislav Dussek (1760–1812).

Clementi and Dussek deserve to be studied for their own highly original and fine music; a short digression here will call attention to the traits that must have impressed Beethoven. The first movement of Clementi's Op. 34, No. 2 in G minor (1795; NAWM 102; CD 8 [43]), illustrates some of these.

Clementi

The entire movement's thematic material, which is extremely economical, appears in the slow introduction. It has a broad, almost symphonic sweep, in which the individual elements and formal outlines are dramatized through unconventional modulations, audacious harmonies, and abrupt changes of dynamics, texture, and mood. The Largo e sostenuto introduction, for example, begins as a grotesque fugue: the subject is answered at the major seventh below, the subject's descending perfect fifth becoming a diminished fifth, and in the next entry, a major sixth (Example 15.1a). A similar fugato opens the Al-

Example 15.1 *Muzio Clementi, Sonata Op. 34, No. 2*

legro con fuoco; the slightly transformed subject is now escorted by a countersubject, and the second and third entries are compacted into a single simultaneous one. The Largo returns in the development section in C major (Example 15.1b), followed immediately by a section in C minor. It is plain why Beethoven found a kindred spirit in Clementi and was moved at times to imitate him.

Dussek

Jan Dussek's Grande Sonate, Op. 44, *Les adieux*, in E♭ major (published in 1800), may have influenced Beethoven's similarly named sonata in the same key, Op. 81a, written about ten years later. More important, however, we can trace in the Dussek work some of the directions piano-sonata writing was taking about the time of Beethoven's Op. 22. Dussek dedicated this sonata to Clementi, from whom he learned some of the pianistic textures that he applied to his own Op. 44. A few of these textures are illustrated in Example 15.2: (a) broken-chord figures in which certain notes are sustained and reinforced to produce a melodic line, a device particularly well suited to the new pianoforte; (b) broken octaves in the left hand, with chordal and melodic work in the right; (c) figuration charged with appoggiaturas in the right hand against

Example 15.2 *Jan Ladislav Dussek, Sonata Op. 44, Allegro*

chords in the left hand; (d) similar figuration against an Alberti bass. Dussek also took forward strides with his harmonic technique, such as combining pedal points, double suspensions, and single and double appoggiaturas to create a richer palette.

Chamber Music

If Beethoven's piano writing owes stylistic features to Clementi and Dussek, his art of developing motives and animating the texture contrapuntally follows Haydn's example. The Quartets of Op. 18 (composed 1798–1800) demonstrate this indebtedness, yet they are no mere imitations. Beethoven's individuality shows through in the character of his themes, the frequent unexpected turns of phrase, the unconventional modulations, and some subtleties of formal structure. The Adagio of the G-major Quartet (No. 2) has a three-part ABA structure in C major. Its middle section, an Allegro in F, develops a brief motive from the closing cadence of the Adagio. This idea, moreover, is related to the opening themes of the other three movements (Example 15.3).

Among the other chamber works from Beethoven's first period are the three Piano Trios of Op. 1; three Violin Sonatas, Op. 12; two Cello Sonatas, Op. 5; and the Septet in E♭ for strings and winds, Op. 20, which was played for the first time in 1800 and soon became so popular that Beethoven grew to dislike it.

Example 15.3 *Beethoven, Related Motives from Quartet in G major Op. 18, No. 2*

First Symphony

Beethoven's Symphony No. 1 received its first performance at a concert on April 2, 1800. The same program included his Septet and a piano concerto, a Mozart symphony, an aria and a duet from Haydn's *Schöpfung*, and improvisations by Beethoven at the piano. The four movements of the First Symphony

CARL LUDWIG JUNKER DESCRIBES BEETHOVEN'S PLAYING AND IMPROVISING AT THE PIANO, NOVEMBER 23, 1791

The greatness of this amiable, soft-spoken man as a virtuoso may, in my opinion, be safely judged from his nearly inexhaustible wealth of ideas, the highly characteristic expressiveness of his playing, and the skill he displays in performance. I do not know that he lacks anything for the making of a great artist. I have often heard Vogler play by the hour on the pianoforte—of his organ playing I cannot speak, not having heard him on that instrument—and never ceased to wonder at his astonishing ability. But besides skill, Bethofen has greater clarity and profundity of ideas and of expression—in short, he speaks to the heart. He is as good at an adagio as at an allegro. Even the members of this remarkable orchestra [of the elector of Mainz] are, without exception, his admirers and are all ears when he plays. Yet he is exceedingly modest and free from all pretension. . . . His way of handling his instrument is so different from the usual that he gives the impression of having attained his present supremacy through a path that he discovered himself.

From Bossler's *Musikalische Korrespondenz*, adapted from Krehbiel's translation in *Thayer's Life of Beethoven*, rev. and ed. Elliot Forbes (Princeton: Princeton University Press, 1967), p. 105. Junker (1748–97) was a writer on music and art and a composer.

are so regular in form that they could serve as textbook models. Beethoven's originality is evident in the details, in the unusual prominence given to the woodwinds, in the character of the third movement—a scherzo, though labeled Minuet—and especially in the long and important codas of the other movements. The frequent marking *cresc.* < *p* is but one example of the careful attention to dynamic shading that is essential to Beethoven's early style. The Adagio introduction to the first movement of this symphony is especially noteworthy. Beethoven converges on the tonic C from opposite sides, the subdominant and the dominant, avoiding a definitive cadence on the dominant until the first chord of the Allegro itself.

The Second Symphony

The long Adagio introducing the first movement of the Second Symphony in D major (composed in 1802) announces a work conceived on a scale hitherto unknown in symphonic music. The first movement has a long coda that includes extensive new development of the principal material, and the rest of the symphony has correspondingly large dimensions, with a profusion of thematic material held together in perfect formal balance. Especially remarkable is Beethoven's Larghetto with its multiplicity of themes and its rich, singing melody. The Scherzo and finale are, like the first movement, full of energy and fire. In addition, the finale is written in an enlarged sonata form with suggestions of a rondo in extra recurrences of the first theme, one at the end of the exposition and one at the coda.

SECOND PERIOD

Human relations

Within a dozen years after coming to Vienna, Beethoven was acknowledged throughout Europe as the foremost pianist and composer for piano of his time and as a symphonist on a par with Haydn and Mozart. His innovations were recognized, although they were sometimes dismissed as eccentricities. He was befriended by the loftiest noble families of Vienna, and he had devoted and generous patrons. He did not cringe before princes to seek their favor but treated them with independence and even, occasionally, extreme rudeness; still they did not withdraw financial support. As Beethoven once remarked, "It is well to mingle with aristocrats, but one must know how to impress them." He would deliberately keep Prince Lichnowsky, a frequent visitor, waiting in an anteroom, while he concentrated on a composition. He drove hard bargains with his publishers and sometimes offered the same composition to several at once. Although he wrote on commission, he often dodged deadlines. He could afford, as he said, to "think and think," to revise and polish a work until it suited him.

The *Eroica* Symphony

The Third Symphony, which Beethoven eventually named *Sinfonia Eroica* (Heroic Symphony), was immediately recognized as an important work, but its unprecedented length and complexity made it difficult at first for audiences to grasp. It marked, in fact, a departure in Beethoven's symphonic writing. The *Eroica* is not purely absolute or abstract music: it has a subject—the celebration of a hero—and expresses in music the ideal of heroic greatness. The symphony begins, after two introductory chords, with an extremely simple theme on the notes of the E♭-major triad, but an unexpected C♯ gives rise to endless departures and developments. The other movements, aside from the scherzo, are also unusually expansive.

Sketches

The symphony demanded from the composer exceptional efforts in planning, drafting, and redrafting, which happen to be particularly well documented. He sketched first ideas in the summer of 1802, while he was also working on the Variations for Piano, Op. 35, on a theme from his ballet music for *Die Geschöpfe von Prometheus* (The Creatures of Prometheus). He used the bass of this theme and the theme itself as the subjects of the symphony's complex last movement, which is a mixture of variations, fugues, and a march. The principal material of the first movement and the Scherzo may also have been inspired by the music of the ballet. Beethoven left several drafts of the first movement that allow us to follow the progress of his thinking.

Early critiques

Even in Beethoven's own time commentators and analysts pointed out certain seeming peculiarities of that first movement (NAWM 103; CD 8 [52]).

> The development section (245 measures) outweighs the exposition (155 measures) and recapitulation (154 measures), which are about equal. The coda (140 measures) is nearly as long as the exposition.
>
> The bridge from the tonic group to the secondary or dominant thematic group is very short, while the latter has a multiplicity of themes.
>
> A new theme is presented in the development.
>
> There are disconcerting and abrupt changes of key, such as the succession E♭–F–D♭ within fifteen measures (measures 401–416) in the recapitulation and E♭–D♭–C (555–563) within eight measures in the coda.
>
> Certain passages are insistently dissonant.
>
> The French horn states the main theme prematurely just before the recapitulation.

Early drafts

Beethoven's early drafts give us some insight into his grand design and the function of these elements (see excerpts from the drafts in NAWM 103). Although at first glance the exposition, and even the development section, abound in new material, they actually draw much of this substance from the first theme section, in keeping with past symphonic practice. As Beethoven worked on his first draft, the origins of its various components became obscured by imaginative spinoffs. Because Beethoven used many motives in the exposition and avoided obvious cadences, the form of the movement has been debated. Two different interpretations are represented in the diagram below. It may be that Beethoven consciously built ambiguity into the exposition, stimulating these latter-day disagreements about details.

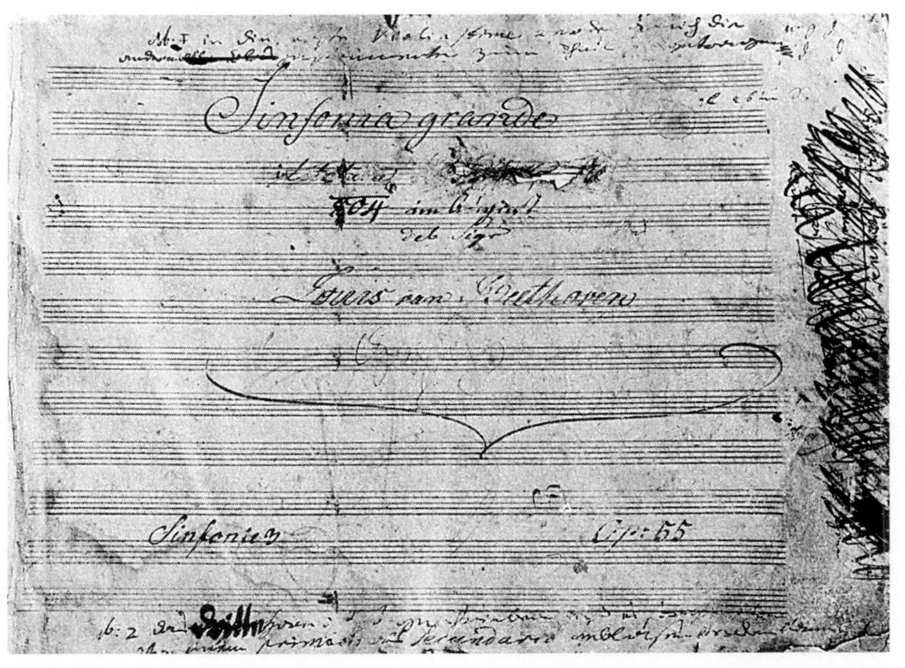

■ *Cover page for Beethoven's own copy of the Eroica Symphony, which reads "Sinfonia grande/intitolata Bonaparte" (Grand Symphony entitled Bonaparte; the last word obliterated), followed by the date "1804 im August/del Sign/Louis van Beethoven." Not visible is Beethoven's hand-penciled correction, "Geschrieben auf Bonaparte" (composed on Bonaparte).*
(VIENNA, GESELLSCHAFT DER MUSIKFREUNDE)

New theme in development

The issue of the "new theme" in the development has occasioned particular comment. Here again the drafts are enlightening. The so-called new theme in E minor played by the oboes at measure 284 does not appear at that point in any of the drafts. Instead we find a variant on the main theme of the movement. Example 15.4a shows a relatively early draft, above the final version, and Example 15.4b shows how this variant derives from the corresponding notes of the main theme, transformed from major to minor. The *sfp* markings (*sforzando* followed by *piano*) on the notes *G* and *B* reinforce the identity of the main theme. At measure 292, where the key of A minor is reached, the draft shows a fragment of the counterpoint that was eventually given to the first oboe to accompany this variant of the main theme. What has been called the new theme is thus a counterpoint to a diminution of the main theme.

Far from crowding the movement with a plethora of themes, Beethoven kept very much to the elemental ideas announced in the first thirty-six measures. He preferred here the unitary motivic concentration of Haydn to the melodic abundance of Mozart.

Example 15.4 *Beethoven, Draft from Landsberg 6, pages 38–39; Symphony No. 3, E♭, Eroica, Allegro con brio*

a.

b.

Dramatization of themes

What is new, however, is that the principal theme is treated like a *dramatis persona*, portrayed as striving, being opposed and subdued but triumphing in the end. The entire symphony, indeed, has the character of a drama. The most dramatic event is the development of the syncopations first heard in measure 25, culminating in the dissonances of measures 276–79, where an *E* suspended from a C-major chord is repercussed repeatedly over an F-chord, the Neapolitan chord of E minor. One of the most suggestive reappearances of the main theme is at measure 394 in the French horn. Here the theme tentatively rears its head against the solitary seventh and ninth of the dominant chord in the violins, just before the full orchestra sounds the complete dominant seventh to mark the arrival of the recapitulation. Early listeners accused the horn of entering too soon; Carl Czerny, Beethoven's pupil, thought this entrance should be eliminated, and even Berlioz thought it was a copyist's mistake, but the sketches show that Beethoven contemplated this clever ploy from the very first drafts.

The main points of arrival are indicated in the diagram below (the spacing is not proportional to time elapsed). Two possible interpretations of the thematic grouping are marked (1) and (2).

Section:	Intro.	Exposition	Development	Recapitulation	Coda
Key:	E♭	→(B♭) B♭	→	E♭	
Themes (1):		P 1T 2T 3T S K		P 1T 2T 3T S K	
Themes (2):		P T 1S 2S 3S K		P T 1S 2S 3S K	
Measure:	*1*	*3 45 57 65 83 109* :‖	*152*	*398 448 460 468 486 512*	*551 691*

Beethoven and Napoleon

Beethoven evidently intended to dedicate the symphony to Napoleon, his admired hero who promised to lead humanity into the new age of liberty, equality, and fraternity. According to the conductor Ferdinand Ries, however, when Beethoven heard that Napoleon had had himself proclaimed emperor (in May 1804), he angrily tore up the title page containing the dedication, disappointed that his idol proved to be an ambitious ruler on the way to becoming a tyrant. The story is an exaggeration; the title page of Beethoven's own score (see illustration, page 523) originally read "Sinfonia grande intitolata Bonaparte" (Grand Symphony entitled Bonaparte), later corrected to read "Geschrieben auf Bonaparte" (composed on Bonaparte). On August 26, 1804, months after this alleged incident, Beethoven wrote to his publisher, Breitkopf & Härtel: "The title of the symphony is really *Bonaparte*. . . . "[4] When the symphony was first published in Vienna two years later, it bore the title "Sinfonia Eroica . . . composta per festeggiare il sovvenire di un grand Uomo" (Heroic Symphony . . . composed to celebrate the memory of a great man). Whatever his feelings toward Napoleon in 1804, Beethoven conducted the symphony in Vienna in 1809 at a concert that Bonaparte was to have attended, and in 1810 he considered dedicating his Mass in C (Op. 86) to the emperor.

4. Emily Anderson, *Letters of Beethoven* (London, 1961), Letter No. 96.

Example 15.5 *Comparison of Passages in Gossec,* Marche lugubre, *and Beethoven,* Marcia funebre

Funeral March

It is the second movement—the Funeral March—more than anything else in the symphony that links the work with France, the republican experiment there, and Napoleon. The customary slow movement is replaced by a march in C minor, full of tragic grandeur and pathos, and a contrasting "trio" in C major, brimming with fanfares and celebratory lyricism, after which the march returns, broken up with sighs at the end. At the opening of the Funeral March, the thirty-second notes of the strings imitate the sound of muffled drums used in the Revolutionary processions that accompanied heroes to their final resting place. The most striking parallel with the French marches is a virtual quotation from François Joseph Gossec's *Marche lugubre* (Example 15.5).

Gossec's *Marche lugubre*

The *Maggiore* section has the character of a hymn punctuated by fanfares and drum rolls and ending in unisons, which in the Revolutionary hymns often brought voices that had been singing parts into a rousing unison chant. It is laid out as follows:

Section:	**Hymn**	**Fanfare**	**Hymn**	**Fanfare**	**Unisons**
Measure:	*69*	*76*	*80*	*96*	*101*

Fidelio

Beethoven began work on his opera *Fidelio* almost immediately after finishing the Third Symphony, and the two works share the Revolutionary atmosphere. Not only was the rescue theme, which is central to the plot, popular at the turn of the century, the libretto itself was borrowed from a French Revolutionary-era opera *Léonore ou L'amour conjugal* (Leonore, or Conjugal Love) in which Leonore, disguised as a man, rescues her husband from prison. Beethoven's music transforms this conventional material, making the chief character Leonore an idealized figure of sublime courage and self-denial. The whole last part of the opera glorifies Leonore's heroism and the great humanitarian ideals of the Revolution. Composing this opera gave Beethoven even more trouble than he had with his other works. The first performances of the original three-act version, *Leonore,* took place in November 1805, just after the French armies

Leonore

had marched into Vienna. A two-act version was brought out the following March but immediately withdrawn. Finally, after still more extensive revisions, in 1814 a third version proved successful. In the course of all these changes, Beethoven wrote no fewer than four different overtures for the opera.

The *Rasumovsky* Quartets

The three quartets of Op. 59 are dedicated to the musical amateur Count Rasumovsky, the Russian ambassador to Vienna, who played second violin in a quartet that was said to be the finest in Europe. As a compliment to the count, Beethoven introduced a Russian melody as the principal theme for the finale of the first quartet and another such tune in the third movement of the second quartet. These two quartets, composed in the summer and autumn of 1806, are the first to show how Beethoven characteristically expressed himself in this medium. The style was so new that musicians were slow to accept them. When Count Rasumovsky's players first read through the Quartet No. 1 in F, they were convinced that Beethoven was playing a joke on them. The first movement is particularly charged with idiosyncrasies: single, double, and triple pedal points, frequent changes of texture—the melody accompanied sometimes by double stops or harmonically tense homorhythmic episodes (measure 19)—horn imitations (measure 34), pointillistic exploitation of the instruments' extreme ranges (measure 85), fugal work (measure 185), and unisons (measures 134, 214). These techniques are represented also in the other movements, but not in such great profusion. Clementi recalled saying to Beethoven, "Surely you do not consider these works to be music?" to which the composer replied, with unusual self-restraint, "Oh, they are not for you, but for a later age." The Allegretto movement in particular gave rise to charges of "crazy music" (Example 15.6). Among the other chamber works of Beethoven's

Opus 59, No. 1

Other chamber music

The Theater an der Wien. Beethoven's famous four-hour concert of December 22, 1808, took place in this bitterly cold hall. The program included the first public performances of the Fifth and Sixth Symphonies, the first Vienna performance of the Fourth Piano Concerto, with the composer as soloist, and following some other pieces, the Choral Fantasy, Op. 80. Anonymous engraving, 1825. (VIENNA, HISTORISCHES MUSEUM DER STADT WIEN)

Example 15.6 *Beethoven, String Quartet Op. 59, No. 1: Allegretto vivace e sempre scherzando*

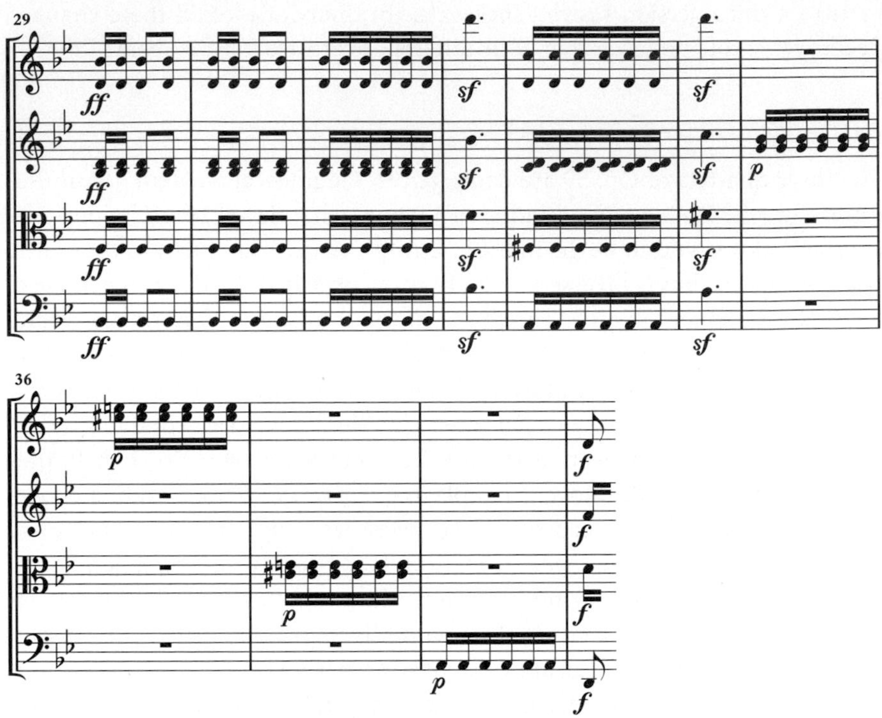

second period, the Violin Sonatas Op. 47 (the *Kreutzer* Sonata) and Op. 96, and the Trio in B♭, Op. 97 (the *Archduke*), abound in similar fresh explorations of their media. Although written in 1815, the two Sonatas for Cello and Piano, Op. 102, belong stylistically to the third period.

The Fourth to Eighth Symphonies

The Fourth, Fifth, and Sixth Symphonies were all composed between 1806 and 1808, a time of exceptional productivity. Beethoven worked on the Fourth and Fifth Symphonies at the same time; the first two movements of the Fifth, in fact, were already done before the Fourth was completed. The two works are very different, as though Beethoven wished to express simultaneously two opposite poles of feeling. Joviality and humor mark the Fourth Symphony, while the Fifth has always been thought of as the musical projection of Beethoven's resolution "I will grapple with Fate; it shall not overcome me." The struggle for victory is symbolized in this symphony by the passing from C minor to C major and by the triumphant finale. The first movement is dominated by the four-note motive emphatically announced in the opening measures, and the same motive recurs in one guise or another in the other three movements as well. The transition from minor to major takes place in an inspired passage that begins with the timpani softly recalling the rhythm of the four-note motive and leading without a break from the scherzo into the finale. Here the en-

Fifth Symphony

Example 15.7 *Beethoven, Symphony No. 6, Scene by the Brook*

trance of the full orchestra with trombones on the C-major chord has an electrifying effect. The finale of the Fifth Symphony adds a piccolo and a contrabassoon as well as trombones to the normal complement of strings, woodwinds, brass, and timpani.

Pastoral Symphony

The Sixth (*Pastoral*) Symphony was composed immediately after the Fifth, and the two first appeared on the same program in December 1808 (see illustration, page 527). Each of the *Pastoral's* five movements bears a descriptive title suggesting a scene from life in the country. Beethoven adapted his descriptive program to the normal sequence of movements, inserting an extra movement (*Storm*) that serves to introduce the finale (*Thankful feelings after the storm*). In the coda of the Andante movement (*Scene by the brook*), flute, oboe, and clarinet join harmoniously in imitating bird calls—the nightingale, the quail, and, of course, the cuckoo (Example 15.7). All this programmatic apparatus is subordinate to the expansive, leisurely form of the symphony as a whole; the composer himself warned against taking the descriptions literally: he called them "expression of feelings rather than depiction."

Seventh Symphony

The Seventh and Eighth Symphonies were both completed in 1812. The Seventh, like the Second and Fourth, opens with a long slow introduction with remote modulations, leading into an Allegro dominated throughout by the rhythmic figure ♩. ♪♩. The second movement, in the parallel minor key of A, received so much applause at the first performance that it had to be repeated. The third movement, in the rather distant key of F major, is a scherzo, although it is not labeled as such. It is unusual because the trio (in D major) recurs a second time as in the Fourth Symphony, thus expanding the movement to a five-part form (ABABA). The finale, a large sonata-allegro with coda, "remains unapproached in music as a triumph of Bacchic fury."[5] By contrast with

5. Donald F. Tovey, *Essays in Musical Analysis* (New York, 1935), 1:60.

HECTOR BERLIOZ ON BEETHOVEN'S SIXTH SYMPHONY, THUNDERSTORM, TEMPEST

Storm, lightning. I despair of trying to give an idea of this prodigious piece. You have to hear it to conceive the degree of truth and sublimity that musical painting can reach at the hands of a man like Beethoven. Listen, listen to these gusts of wind charged with rain, these deaf growlings of the basses, the high whistling of the piccolos that announce a terrible tempest about to unleash. The storm approaches, it spreads; an immense chromatic stroke starting in the higher instruments rummages down to the last depths of the orchestra, hitches on to the basses and drags them with it and climbs up again, shuddering like a whirlwind that overturns everything in its path. Then the trombones burst forth, as the thunder of the tympani redoubles in violence. This is no longer rain and wind; it is an appalling cataclysm, the great flood, the end of the world.

. . . .

Veil your faces, poor great ancient poets, poor immortals. Your conventional language, so pure, so harmonious, cannot compete with the art of sounds. You are glorious in defeat, but vanquished. You did not know what we call today melody, harmony, the association of different timbres, instrumental colors, the modulations, the learned conflicts of inimical sounds that first combat each other, then embrace, our surprises of the ear, our strange accents that make the most unexplored depths of the soul reverberate.

Translated from Hector Berlioz, *A travers chants* (Paris, 1898), pp. 42–43.

Eighth Symphony

the huge scale of the Seventh Symphony, the Eighth reverts to more standard dimensions, aside from the long coda of the first movement and the still longer one of the finale. This is the most mercurial of all the nine symphonies, but its forms are extremely condensed. The second movement is a brisk Allegretto, while the third, by way of compensation, is a deliberately archaic minuet instead of Beethoven's usual scherzo.

Overtures

Beethoven's orchestral overtures are related in style to the symphonies, usually taking the form of a symphonic first movement. The *Leonore* Overtures aside, his most important works in this genre are *Coriolan* (1807), inspired by a tragic drama that was performed occasionally in Vienna, and *Egmont*, composed together with songs and incidental music for an 1810 performance of Goethe's play.

Piano Sonatas and Concertos

Beethoven composed three piano sonatas in 1800–01: Op. 26 in A♭, with the funeral march, and Op. 27, Nos. 1 and 2, each designated as "quasi una fantasia"; the second is popularly known as the *Moonlight* Sonata. The whole opening section of the first movement of the D-minor Sonata Op. 31, No. 2, in its rushing passages and sharp punctuation has the character of a *recitativo obbligato*, anticipating that of the Ninth Symphony. The introductory *largo* arpeggio returns at the start of the development section and again at the beginning of the recapitulation (see Example 15.8a and b), each time in expanded form and with new linkages to the surrounding music; its last appearance leads into an expressive recitative (Example 15.8c). The finale of this sonata is an exciting *moto perpetuo* in rondo form.

Waldstein Sonata

Outstanding among the sonatas of the second period are Op. 53 in C major (1804), called the *Waldstein* Sonata after the patron to whom it was dedicated, and Op. 57 in F minor (1805), usually called the *Appassionata*. In the first movement of the *Waldstein*, Beethoven managed to make the key of C major sound dark and brooding through the obstinate thundering of thick low chords, to which a figure high in the right hand answers like a flash of lightning (Example 15.9a). Then the storm clears, and a bright, chordally accompanied melody in E major gleams where a theme in the dominant is expected (Example 15.9b). The "normal" arrival of the dominant in the second part of the

Example 15.8 *Beethoven, Piano Sonata Op. 31, No. 2*

a. *Opening*

b. *Beginning of development*

c. *Recitative before recapitulation*

Example 15.9 *Beethoven, Piano Sonata in C major Op. 53, Allegro con brio*

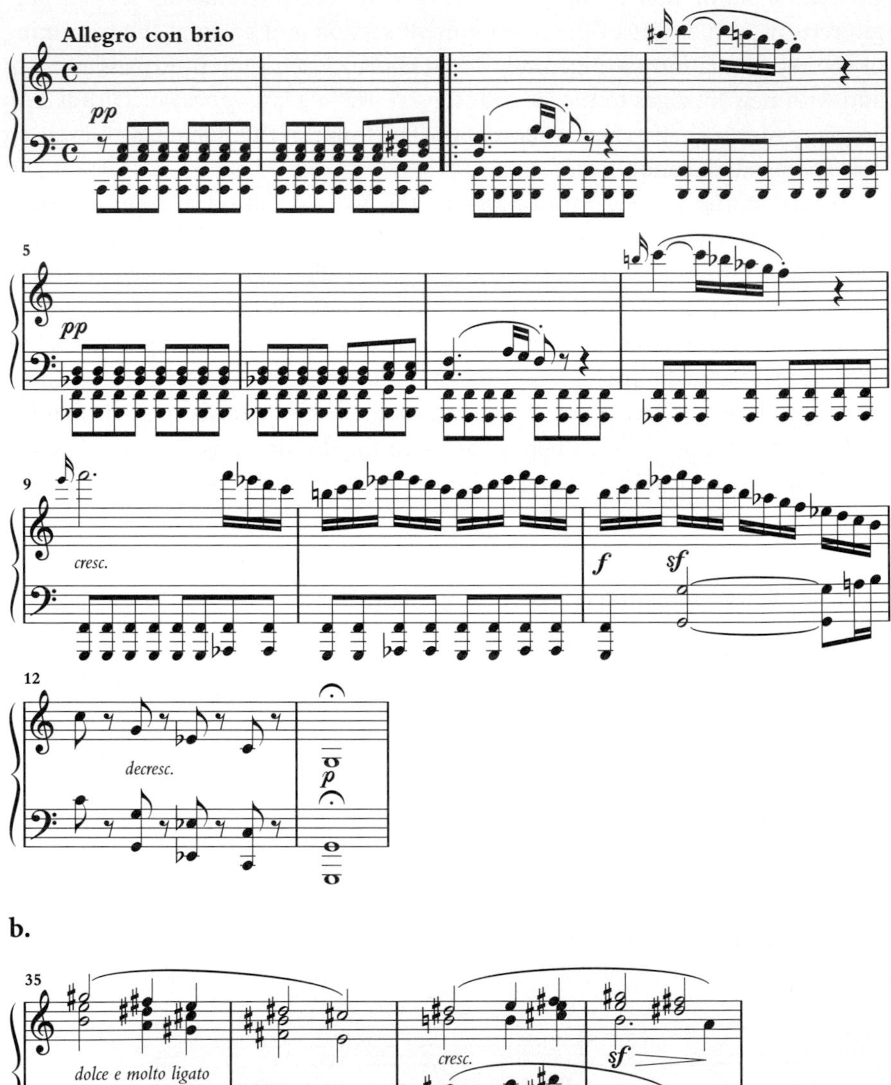

exposition is delayed until near the double bar, just in time to bring back the opening. In the recapitulation, the second theme is first heard in A major, and its restatement in C major is reserved for the coda.

Opus 81a

After the *Waldstein* and the *Appassionata*, there were no more sonatas for four years. The years 1809 and 1810 saw the Sonata in F♯, Op. 78, which Beethoven once declared to be his favorite, and the quasi-programmatic Sonata Op. 81a. The latter was inspired by the departure from and return to Vienna of Archduke Rudolph, one of his patrons and pupils; its three movements are entitled *Lebewohl* (Farewell), *Abwesenheit* (Absence), and *Wiedersehn* (Return). The Sonata Op. 90 (1814) has two movements, an Allegro in E minor in concise sonata form, and a long, leisurely sonata-rondo Andante in E major, which is one of Beethoven's happiest lyric inspirations.

Opus 90

Piano concertos

As a pianist, Beethoven composed concertos to play at his own concerts. His first three piano concertos date from his early years in Vienna (No. 1 in C, No. 2 in B♭, No. 3 in C minor). His two largest works in this genre are the Concerto No. 4 in G major, Op. 58, composed in 1805–06, and the Fifth in E♭, known as the *Emperor* Concerto, composed in 1809 and first performed in Vienna three years later. The soloist, Carl Czerny (1791–1857), had studied piano with Beethoven and subsequently enjoyed a successful teaching career in Vienna, composing many studies and other works for the piano.

Beethoven retained Mozart's division of the concerto into three movements and the general outline of the Classic form, while greatly expanding the music's expressive range and dimensions. Some of Beethoven's most enchanting melodies appear in his piano and violin concertos, and they are all the more haunting because of unexpected harmonic turns. Virtuosity is demanded in the solo parts, which are continuously interwoven with the orchestra yet assert their presence forcefully. For example, in Piano Concertos Nos. 4 and 5, the soloist enters with a cadenza even before the orchestra's exposition begins, a technique Beethoven also applied somewhat differently in his Violin Concerto, Op. 61 in D major (1806).

THIRD PERIOD

Career and life

The years up to 1815 were, on the whole, peaceful and prosperous for Beethoven. His music was played regularly in Vienna, and he was celebrated both at home and abroad. Thanks to the generosity of patrons and the steady demand from publishers for new works, his financial affairs were in good order; but his deafness became a more and more serious trial. As it caused him to lose contact with others, he retreated into himself, becoming morose, irascible, and morbidly suspicious even toward his friends. Family problems, ill health, and unfounded apprehensions of poverty also plagued him, and it was only by a supreme effort of will that Beethoven continued composing amidst all these troubles. He wrote his last five piano sonatas between 1816 and 1821. He completed the *Missa solemnis* in 1822, the *Diabelli* Variations in 1823, and the Ninth Symphony in 1824, each after long years of labor. The final quartets, Beethoven's musical testament, followed in 1825 and 1826. At his death in 1827 he had plans for a tenth symphony and many other new works.

By 1816, Beethoven had resigned himself to living in a soundless world of tones that existed only in his mind. More and more his compositions came to have a meditative character; the urgent sense of communication was replaced by a feeling of assured tranquillity, passionate outpouring by calm affirmation.

The language became more concentrated, more abstract. Extremes meet: the sublime and the grotesque in the Mass and Ninth Symphony, the profound and the apparently naïve in the last quartets. Classic forms remained, like the features of a landscape after a geological upheaval—recognizable here and there under new contours, lying at strange angles beneath the new surface.

Characteristics of Beethoven's Late Style

Variation technique

In his late compositions, Beethoven deliberately worked out themes and motives to their utmost potential. The way he used variation technique epitomizes his late style. Usually composers preserved the essential structure of the entire theme in each statement while introducing new embellishments, figurations, rhythms, even meters and tempos, and disguising the theme itself. Variation differs from development because it treats an entire musical period, not just fragments or motives. In the works of Haydn, Mozart, and Beethoven, variation occurs in three situations: (1) as an independent theme-and-variations composition; (2) as a theme-and-variations movement of a symphony or sonata; and (3) as a technique within a larger formal plan—for example, in a rondo when each recurrence of the principal theme is varied, or in a sonata form when the first theme is varied in the recapitulation.

Variations

Beethoven wrote twenty independent sets of variations for piano. During the last period he composed only one independent set—the *Thirty-three Variations on a Waltz by Diabelli,* Op. 120, completed in 1823—but it is a work that surpasses anything in this genre since Bach's *Goldberg* Variations. Rather than altering the theme in a fairly straightforward manner, Beethoven transformed its very character. Diabelli's commonplace little waltz expands into a world of variegated moods—solemn, brilliant, capricious, mysterious—ordered with due regard for contrast, grouping, and climax. Each variation is built on motives derived from some part of the theme, but altered in rhythm, tempo, dynamics, or context so as to produce a new design. The *Diabelli* Variations became the model for Schumann's *Symphonic études,* Brahms's *Variations on a Theme of Handel,* and many other nineteenth-century works in this genre.

Examples of more concentrated variations are the second (and final) movement of Beethoven's Sonata Op. 111 and the slow movements of the Quartets Opp. 127 and 131. In these we eavesdrop on the composer while he meditates on his theme and finds new depths with each meditation. Variations appear within the slow movements of the Piano Sonatas Op. 106 and Op. 109, the String Quartet Op. 132, and the Ninth Symphony. The finale of the Ninth also begins (after the introduction) as a set of variations.

Continuity

Another feature of Beethoven's late style is a continuity achieved by intentionally blurring the divisions between phrases. A cadence falls on a weak beat, and its closing effect may be further lessened by having the uppermost voice sound the third or fifth scale degrees rather than the tonic. The introduction may be in the same tempo as the Allegro and flow directly into it, as in the first movement of the Ninth Symphony. The wide-spaced harmonic arches and the leisurely march of melodies communicate a feeling of vastness in such movements as the Adagio of the Quartet Op. 127 or the Benedictus of the *Missa solemnis.*

Improvisatory passages

The improvisatory character of some passages may give us an idea of Beethoven's actual improvisations at the piano that so impressed his listeners (see vignette, page 521). This compositional style was forecast in the slow introduction to the Rondo of the *Waldstein* Sonata, Op. 53. At times a phrase is repeatedly and musingly turned over, as in the slow movement of the Sonata Op. 101, or a passage is measured freely, as in the Largo introduction to the finale of the Sonata Op. 106. Sometimes these reflective passages culminate in moments of instrumental recitative, as in the Adagio of the Sonata Op. 110 and in various transitions: to the variations of Op. 131, to the last movement of the Quartet Op. 132, and to the finale of the Ninth Symphony.

Fugal texture

The importance Beethoven placed on fugal textures gives his late style a universal quality. His sympathy for this technique came in part from his lifelong reverence for the music of J. S. Bach but was also a consequence of contemplative habits during his last ten years. There are numerous canonic imitations and learned contrapuntal devices in all the late works, particularly in the fugatos that are incorporated in development sections, as in the finale of Op. 101. Many movements or large sections are predominantly fugal in conception, such as the finales of the Sonatas Opp. 106 and 110, the first movement of the Quartet in C♯ minor, Op. 131, the gigantic *Grosse Fuge* for String Quartet Op. 133, and the two double fugues in the finale of the Ninth Symphony.

New sonorities

Beethoven commanded new sonorities in his last works. The rigorous logic of contrapuntal lines gave rise to unaccustomed sounds and effects. Such new sonorities are apparent in the widely spaced intervals at the end of the Piano Sonata Op. 110, the partition of the theme between the two violins in the fourth movement of the C♯-minor Quartet, and the extraordinary dark coloring of the orchestra and chorus at the first appearance of the words "Ihr stürzt nieder" in the finale of the Ninth Symphony. Early critics deemed some of the experiments unsuccessful, holding that in his late works Beethoven went too far in subordinating euphony and performability to the demands of his musical conceptions, perhaps because of his deafness. There are passages that almost require a miracle to make them "sound" in performance; the ideas seem too big for human capabilities to express. But we have no reason to believe that even a Beethoven with perfect hearing would have altered a single note, either to spare tender ears or to make life easier for performers.

As with texture and sonority, so with form in the instrumental works of Beethoven's third period: two of the last quartets and two of the final sonatas retain the external scheme of four movements, but the rest dispense with even this bow to tradition. The Sonata Op. 111 has only two movements, an Allegro in compact sonata form and an Adagio molto—a long set of variations on an arietta that is so eloquent and so complete that nothing further seems to be

Example 15.10 *Beethoven, String Quartet Op. 131, Allegro molto vivace*

Quartet Opus 131

required. The Quartet Op. 131 has seven movements (the first two are in NAWM 104; CD 8 [67] / 3 ⟨39⟩):

(1) A fugue in C♯ minor, Adagio ma non troppo e molto espressivo, ¢.

(2) Allegretto molto vivace, D major, $\frac{6}{8}$. This movement is in a compact sonata form. It is based on a single theme, a folklike tune first presented against a triple drone that shifts between the tonic and subdominant (Example 15.10).

(3) Eleven measures, Allegro moderato, in the spirit of a *recitativo obbligato*, functioning as an introduction to the following movement and modulating from B minor to E major, the dominant of the next movement.

(4) Andante, A major, $\frac{2}{4}$. A theme made up of two double periods, with six variations and a coda that encloses an incomplete seventh variation.

(5) Presto, E major, ¢. Essentially a scherzo, though in duple rather than triple time, with a trio that returns twice in rondo fashion after the return of the scherzo, as in the Fourth and Seventh Symphonies.

(6) Adagio, G♯ minor, $\frac{3}{4}$. Twenty-eight measures in the form ABB with coda, introducing the next movement.

(7) Allegro, C♯ minor, ¢, in sonata form.

All this could be forcibly equated with the Classic sonata scheme by calling (1) and (2) an introduction and first movement, (3) and (4) an introduction and slow movement, (5) a scherzo, and (6) and (7) an introduction and finale; a similar arbitrary adjustment would also be possible with the Quartet Op. 132, but not with Op. 130, which in the number and order of movements is more like a serenade than anything else.

The *Missa Solemnis*

The most imposing works of the last period are the Mass in D, known as the *Missa solemnis*, and the Ninth Symphony. Beethoven regarded this Mass as his greatest work. It is a deeply personal yet universal confession of faith. The score incorporates far more musical and liturgical symbols in much more de-

Freytag den
K. K. Hoftheater nächst dem Kärnthnerthore.
Große musikalische Akademie
von
Herrn L. van Beethoven,
Ehrenmitglied der königl. Akademie der Künste und Wissenschaften zu Stockholm und Amsterdam, dann Ehrenbürger von Wien.

Die dabey vorkommenden Musikstücke sind die neuesten Werke des Herrn Ludwig van Beethoven.

Erstens. Große Ouverture.
Zweytens. Drey große Hymnen, mit Solo- und Chor-Stimmen.
Drittens. Große Symphonie, mit im Finale eintretenden Solo- und Chor-Stimmen, auf Schillers Lied, an die Freude.

Die Solo-Stimmen werden die Dlles. Sontag und Unger, und die Herren Haizinger und Seipelt vortragen. Herr Schuppanzigh hat die Direction des Orchesters, Herr Kapellmeister Umlauf die Leitung des Ganzen, und der Musik-Verein die Verstärkung des Chors und Orchesters aus Gefälligkeit übernommen.

Herr Ludwig van Beethoven selbst, wird an der Leitung des Ganzen Antheil nehmen.

(Die Eintrittspreise sind wie gewöhnlich.)

Freybillets sind heute ungültig.

Der Anfang ist um 7 Uhr.

■ *Handbill for the concert of May 7, 1824, at the Kärntnerthortheater, advertising a "Great Musical Academy of Herr L. van Beethoven, Honorary Member of the Royal Academy of Arts and Sciences of Stockholm and Amsterdam and later Honorary Citizen of Vienna." The program promises "first, an overture; second, three great hymns for solo and choral voices; third, a great symphony with a finale for solo and choral voices on Schiller's Ode to Joy." The hymns were the Kyrie, Credo, and Agnus Dei of the* Missa solemnis; *the symphony was the Ninth. Beethoven, though deaf, conducted.* (VIENNA, ÖSTERREICHISCHE NATIONALBIBLIOTHEK)

tail than an uninformed listener can grasp.[6] Written to celebrate the elevation of Archduke Rudolph to archbishop of Olmütz, it is, like Bach's B-minor Mass, too long and elaborate for ordinary liturgical use.

The choral treatment owes something to Handel, whose music Beethoven revered. Beethoven adapted the fugal subject of his *Dona nobis pacem* (Agnus Dei, measure 215) from Handel's setting of "And He shall reign forever and ever" in the Hallelujah Chorus, and the lofty style of the whole is in the spirit of Handel. Handel's oratorios, however, were conceived as a series of independent numbers, without interconnecting themes or motives and without any definite plan of musical unity in the work as a whole. Beethoven's Mass by comparison is a planned musical unit—a symphony in five movements, one on each of the five principal divisions of the Ordinary of the Mass: Kyrie in D, Gloria in D, Credo in B♭, Sanctus in D, and Agnus Dei in D. In this respect it resembles the late Masses of Haydn, and like them it freely combines and alternates choruses and solo ensembles in each movement. Beethoven's attention to musical form occasionally led him to take liberties with the liturgical text, such as the repetition of the opening sentence, "Gloria in excelsis Deo," at the end of the second movement, or the rondo-like recurrences of the word "Credo" with its musical motive in the third movement.

Form

6. See the article by Warren Kirkendale, "New Roads to Old Ideas in Beethoven's *Missa solemnis*," MQ 56 (1970):665–701; repr. in Paul Henry Lang, ed., *The Creative World of Beethoven* (New York, 1971), pp. 163–99.

The Ninth Symphony

The Ninth Symphony was first performed on May 7, 1824, on a program with one of Beethoven's overtures and three movements of the Mass (the Kyrie, Credo, and Agnus Dei; see the handbill illustrated opposite). The large and distinguished audience applauded vociferously after the symphony. Beethoven did not turn around to acknowledge the applause because he could not hear it; one of the solo singers "plucked him by the sleeve and directed his attention to the clapping hands and waving hats and handkerchiefs. . . . he turned to the audience and bowed."[7] The receipts at the concert were large, but so little remained after expenses that Beethoven accused his friends who had managed the affair of having cheated him. A repetition two weeks later before a half-full house resulted in a deficit. Thus was the Ninth Symphony launched into the world. The work's most striking innovation is its use of chorus and solo voices in the finale. Beethoven had thought as early as 1792 of setting Schiller's *Ode to Joy*, but more than thirty years went by before he decided to incorporate a choral finale on this text in his Ninth Symphony. Consistent with his ethical ideals and religious faith, he selected stanzas that emphasize universal fellowship through joy, and its basis in the love of an eternal heavenly Father. Beethoven was troubled by the apparent incongruity of introducing voices at the climax of a long instrumental symphony. His solution to this esthetic difficulty determined the unusual form of the last movement:

Form of finale

A brief, tumultuous introduction, inspired by the operatic genre of *recitativo obbligato*, that starts with a sharp dissonant clash of a B♭ appoggiatura in the woodwinds against a D-minor triad in the rest of the orchestra.

A review and rejection (by instrumental recitatives) of the themes of the preceding movements; proposal of the "joy" theme and its joyful acceptance.

Orchestral exposition of the theme in four stanzas, *crescendo*, with coda.

Return of the tumultuous opening measures, starting this time with all the notes of the D melodic-minor scale sounded simultaneously.

Bass recitative: "O Freunde, nicht diese Töne! sondern lasst uns angenehmere anstimmen und freudenvollere" (O friends, not these tones, but let us rather sing more pleasant and joyful ones).

Choral-orchestral exposition of the joy theme, "Freude, schöner Götterfunken" (Beautiful, divine spark of joy), in four stanzas, varied (including a "Turkish March"), and a long orchestral interlude (double fugue) followed by a repetition of the first stanza.

New theme, for orchestra and chorus: "Seid umschlungen, Millionen!" (Join together, O millions!).

Double fugue on the two themes.

A brilliant Prestissimo choral coda, bringing back the Turkish percussion, in which the joy theme is hailed in strains of matchless sublimity.

The first three movements of the symphony are on a comparably grand scale. The scherzo shows Beethoven's uncanny ability to organize an entire movement in sonata form around a single rhythmic motive.

7. Forbes, *Thayer's Life of Beethoven*, p. 909.

Beethoven and the Romantics

Only a few of Beethoven's contemporaries understood his late works, which in any event were so personal that they could hardly be imitated. His influence on later composers resulted mostly from the works of the middle period, especially the *Rasumovsky* Quartets, the Fifth, Sixth, and Seventh Symphonies, and the piano sonatas. Even in these works it was not the Classic element in Beethoven's style but the revolutionary element, the free, impulsive, mysterious, demonic spirit, the underlying conception of music as a mode of self-expression, that fascinated the Romantic generation. As the distinguished writer and musician, E. T. A. Hoffmann (1776–1822), put it, "Beethoven's music sets in motion the lever of fear, of awe, of horror, of suffering, and awakens just that infinite longing which is the essence of romanticism. He is accordingly a completely romantic composer. . . ."[8] Hoffmann realized the importance of structure and control in Beethoven's music and in the works of Haydn and Mozart, whom he also called "romantic." (Perhaps he used the word as a general term of commendation.) Romantic or not, Beethoven was one of the great disruptive forces in the history of music. After him, nothing could ever be the same; he opened the gateway to a new world.

Bibliography

Beethoven

Collected edition: *Ludwig van Beethovens Werke*, 24 series and supp. (Leipzig: Breitkopf & Härtel, 1864–90; repr. Ann Arbor: J. W. Edwards, 1949); also in miniature format (New York: Kalmus, 1971). *Supplemente zur Gesamtausgabe*, ed. Willy Hess (Wiesbaden: Breitkopf & Härtel, 1959–). *Neue Ausgabe sämtlicher Werke*, ed. Joseph Schmidt-Görg and Martin Staehelin (Munich: Henle, 1961–84).

Thematic catalogue: Georg Kinsky and Hans Halm, *Das Werk Beethovens: Thematisch-bibliographisches Verzeichnis seiner sämtlichen vollendeten Kompositionen* (Munich: Henle, 1955); additional material in Kurt Dorfmüller, ed., *Studien und Materialien zum Werkverzeichnis von Kinsky-Halm* (Munich: Henle, 1979); for works not published in the *Gesamtausgabe*, see Willy Hess, *Verzeichnis der nicht in der Gesamtausgabe veröffentlichten Werke Ludwig van Beethovens* (Wiesbaden: Breitkopf & Härtel, 1957).

The Letters of Beethoven, 3 vols., trans. and ed. Emily Anderson (New York: St. Martin's Press, 1961); Donald MacArdle and Ludwig Misch, eds., *New Beethoven Letters* (Norman: University of Oklahoma Press, 1957).

The standard biography is *Thayer's Life of Beethoven*, 2 vols., rev. and ed. Elliot Forbes (Princeton: Princeton University Press, 1967; 1-vol. paperback ed., 1970).

Special insights into Beethoven's life and personality may be gained from Anton Schindler's *Beethoven as I Knew Him* (1840), ed. Donald W. MacArdle, trans. Cynthia S. Jolly (Chapel Hill: University of North Carolina Press; repr. New York: Norton, 1972); and Oscar G. Sonneck, ed., *Beethoven: Impressions by His Contemporaries* (New York: G.

8. From an essay on "Beethoven's Instrumental Music" (1813), trans. O. Strunk in SRrev, p. 1193; 6:153.

Schirmer, 1926; repr. 1967). See also Maynard Solomon, *Beethoven,* 2nd rev. ed. (New York: Schirmer Books, 1998), which has many original interpretations, and his *Beethoven Essays* (Cambridge, Mass.: Harvard University Press, 1988).

General works in English include *Beethoven and His World,* ed. Scott Burnham and Michael P. Steinberg (Princeton: Princeton University Press, 2000); Tia DeNora, *Beethoven and the Construction of Musical Genius* and William Kinderman, *Beethoven* (Berkeley: University of California Press, both 1995); *The Beethoven Companion,* ed. Glenn Stanley (Cambridge: Cambridge University Press, 2000); H. C. Robbins Landon, comp., *Beethoven: A Documentary Study* (London: Macmillan, 1970); Alan Tyson, ed., *Beethoven Studies,* 3 vols. (1, New York: Norton, 1973; 2, London: Oxford University Press, 1977; 3, Cambridge: Cambridge University Press, 1982); Paul H. Lang, ed., *The Creative World of Beethoven* (New York: Norton, 1971); Gerald Abraham, ed., *The Age of Beethoven, 1790–1830* (New York: Oxford University Press, 1982); Martin Cooper, *Beethoven: The Last Decade, 1817–1827* (London: Oxford University Press, 1970); Joseph Kerman and Alan Tyson, *The New Grove Beethoven* (New York: Norton, 1983); Denis Matthews, *Beethoven* (London: Dent, 1985), a readable introduction.

Specialized topics are treated in *Beethoven Forum* (1992–), a specialists' journal with broadly interesting articles; *Beethoven Essays: Studies in Honor of Elliot Forbes,* ed. Lewis Lockwood and Phyllis Benjamin (Cambridge, Mass.: Harvard University Dept. of Music, 1984). The reception of Beethoven's work in his lifetime is considered in Robin Wallace, *Beethoven's Critics* (Cambridge: Cambridge University Press, 1986).

Of the innumerable books about Beethoven's music, only a few can be cited: Donald F. Tovey, *Beethoven* (London: Oxford University Press, 1945), the unfinished last work of a most perceptive critic; see also Tovey's *A Companion to Beethoven's Pianoforte Sonatas* (London: Associated Board of the Royal Schools of Music, 1931; repr. New York: AMS Press, 1976), and his *Essays in Musical Analysis* (London: Oxford University Press, 1935–39), which deal with the symphonies in Vols. 1 and 2, the concertos in 3, and the overtures in 4; Scott G. Burnham, *Beethoven Hero* (Princeton: Princeton University Press, 1995); Leon Plantinga, *Beethoven's Concertos: History, Style, Performance* (New York: Norton, 1999); Joseph Kerman, *The Beethoven Quartets* (New York: Knopf, 1967; repr. Norton, 1979); the classic *Beethoven and His Nine Symphonies,* by Sir George Grove (London: Novello, 1884; repr. New York: Dover, 1962); Elliot Forbes, ed., *Beethoven, Symphony No. 5 in C minor,* Norton Critical Scores (New York: Norton, 1971); Carl Dahlhaus, *Ludwig van Beethoven: Approaches to His Music,* trans. Mary Whittall (Oxford: Clarendon Press, 1991).

On Beethoven's autographs, sketches, and sketchbooks, see NG, s.v. "Beethoven," which includes a list of facsimile editions; Douglas Johnson, Alan Tyson, and Robert Winter, *The Beethoven Sketchbooks: History, Reconstruction, and Inventory* (Berkeley: University of California Press, 1985); Lewis Lockwood, *Beethoven: Studies in the Creative Process* (Cambridge, Mass.: Harvard University Press, 1992). Sketches of a single composition are exhaustively treated in Robert Winter, *Compositional Origins of Beethoven's Opus 131* (Ann Arbor, Mich.: UMI Research Press, 1982). An older study, but important because it contains sketches not published elsewhere, including many for the *Eroica* Symphony, is Gustav Nottebohm, *Two Beethoven Sketchbooks,* trans. Jonathan Katz (London: Gollancz, 1979). Another pioneer work in this area is Paul Mies, *Beethoven's Sketches, An Analysis of His Style Based on a Study of His Sketch-Books,* trans. Doris L. MacKinnon (New York: Dover, 1974).

Clementi and Dussek

Leon Plantinga, *Muzio Clementi: His Life and Music* (London: Oxford University Press, 1977); Alexander Ringer, "Beethoven and the London Pianoforte School," MQ 56 (1970):742–58. Muzio Clementi, *Complete Works* (Leipzig: Breitkopf & Härtel, 1803–19; repr. New York: Da Capo Press, 1973); thematic catalogue by Alan Tyson (Tutzing: Hans Schneider, 1967).

Johann L. Dussek, *Sämtliche Werke für Klavier* (Leipzig: Breitkopf & Härtel, 1813–17; repr. New York: Da Capo Press, 1978).

For facsimiles of first or other authentic editions of works by London pianoforte composers, see *The London Pianoforte School: 1766–1860*, 20 vols., gen. ed. Nicholas Temperley (New York: Garland, 1985). Composers include Clementi, Dussek, Cramer, Field, and others.

CHAPTER 16

ROMANTICISM AND NINETEENTH-CENTURY ORCHESTRAL MUSIC

ROMANTICISM

Classic vs. Romantic

Classic and Romantic are rough and imprecise labels, yet we use them like their counterparts Renaissance and Baroque to define chronological boundaries and to give us starting points for discussing the music of these periods. Contrasting Classic with Romantic has caused confusion in the study of music history because the two are not entirely contradictory: the historical continuity between the two cultural movements is greater than any contrast. The great bulk of music written between 1770 and 1900 lies on a continuum, employing common conventions of harmonic progression, rhythm, and form. E. T. A. Hoffmann considered the instrumental music of Haydn and Mozart "romantic," and Beethoven, as we saw (page 539),"a completely romantic composer."[1]

The term "romantic" enjoyed a vogue at the end of the eighteenth and beginning of the nineteenth century. Novalis (Friedrich von Hardenberg, 1772–1801) borrowed the term from the *Roman* or novel, a genre descended from the medieval *romance*, a tale or poem about heroes or events written in one of the vernacular "Roman" dialects of Latin. The literary critic Friedrich Schlegel (1772–1829) differentiated classic poetry—which was objectively beautiful, self-limited in scope and theme, and had universal validity—from modern romantic poetry, which transgressed rules and limits, and expressed the richness of nature and insatiable longing. (For an example of romantic art, see Plate X, facing page 495.)

"Romantic," however, meant so many things to different people that in 1837 Schumann exclaimed, "I am heartily sick of the term 'romantic', though I

1. E. T. A. Hoffman, "Beethoven's Instrumental Music" (1813), trans. O. Strunk in SRrev, p. 1195; 6:153.

FRANZ LISZT ON MUSIC AS DIRECT EXPRESSION

Music embodies *feeling* without forcing it to contend and combine with *thought*, as it is forced in most arts and especially in the art of words. If music has one advantage over the other media through which a person can represent the impressions of the soul, it owes this to its supreme capacity to make each inner impulse audible without the assistance of reason. Reason, after all, is restricted in the diversity of its means and is capable only of confirming or describing our affections, not of communicating them directly in their full intensity. To accomplish this even approximately, reason must search for images and comparisons. Music, on the other hand, presents at once the intensity and the expression of *feeling*. It is the embodied and intelligible essence of feeling, capable of being apprehended by our senses. It permeates them like a dart, like a ray, like a mist, like a spirit, and fills our soul.

From *Berlioz and His "Harold" Symphony* (1855), by Franz Liszt and Princess Caroline von Wittgenstein, adapted from the translation in SR, 1st ed., p. 849.

have not spoken it ten times in my entire life."[2] Romanticism in music is not so much a collection of style traits as a state of mind that enabled composers to seek individual paths for expressing intense emotions, such as melancholy, yearning, or joy. Composers respected conventions of form and tonal relations up to a point, but their imagination drove them to trespass limits, which had once seemed reasonable, and to explore new realms of sound.

Some nineteenth-century writers considered instrumental music the ideal Romantic art because, being free from the burden of words, it could perfectly communicate pure emotion. An aria is limited by its text and can only express the feelings that develop from a dramatic situation. Although the composer conjures up the emotion, it resides outside the creator in the character represented by the singer. But instrumental music can express the composer's own feelings without limitation to particular emotions. The content, without a name like love or jealousy, may simply be turbulence or indeterminate longing, or even the "vacuum of the passions" (*le vague des passions*)—Chateaubriand's phrase[3]—a full, young heart seeking an object; Berlioz aimed to portray this in the first movement of his *Symphonie fantastique.* The instrumental domain of ordered sound and rhythm does not mirror the concrete world, and this independence allows music to evoke impressions, thoughts, and feelings that are not tied to concepts expressible in words. The philosopher Arthur Schopenhauer (1788–1860) believed that music was the incarnation of the innermost reality, the immediate expression of universal feelings and impulses in concrete, definite form.

2. Quoted in Leon Plantinga, *Schumann as Critic* (New Haven: Yale University Press, 1967), p.104, from *Neue Zeitschrift für Musik* 7 (1837):70.
3. François René de Chateaubriand, *Le génie du Christianisme,* Part 2, Book 3, Chapter 9.

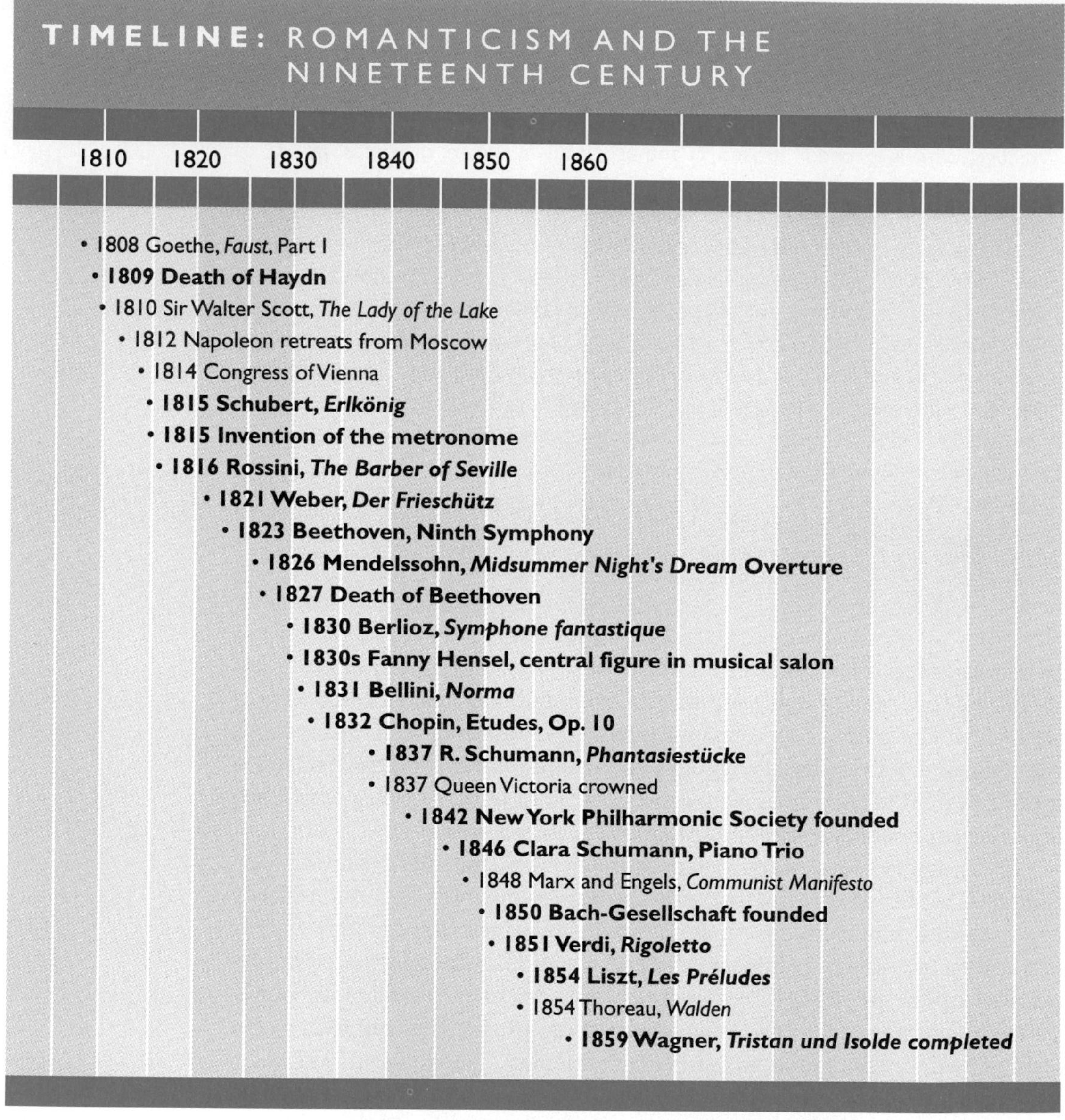

Music and literature

Although composers held instrumental music in the highest regard, poetry and literature occupied a central place in their thoughts and careers. Berlioz, Weber, Schumann, and Liszt, for example, wrote distinguished essays on music, and Wagner wrote his own librettos, essays, and philosophical treatises. Schubert, Schumann, Brahms, and Hugo Wolf attained a new and intimate union between music and poetry in their art songs, and even their instrumental music was dominated by the lyrical spirit of the lied.

Program music

The ideal of instrumental music as the premier mode of expression and the strong literary orientation of nineteenth-century composers converged in the concept of *program music.* As Liszt and others used the term, program

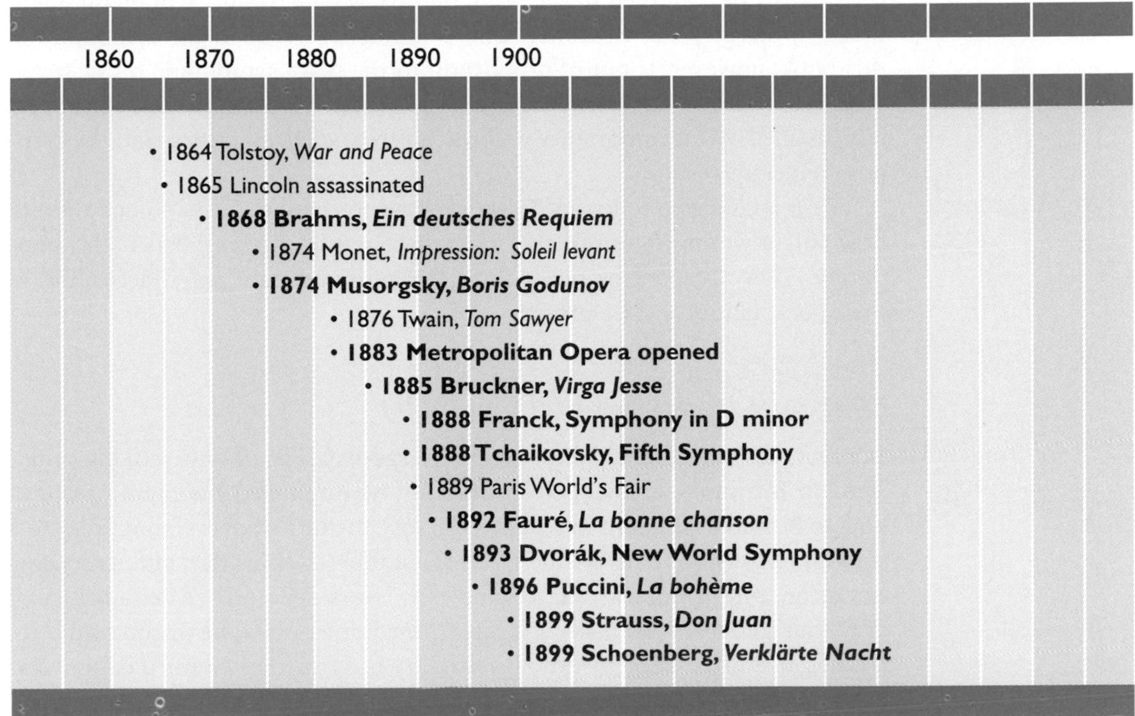

music referred to instrumental music associated with poetic, descriptive, or narrative subject matter. It aimed to absorb and transmute the subject wholly into music, so that the resulting piece included a "program" but transcended it. The program did not necessarily inspire or even precede the music; sometimes it was imposed as an afterthought.

When composers did combine music with words in song, they paid great attention to the instrumental complement, as in Schubert's inventive accompaniments to his lieder or in Wagner's exuberant orchestra enfolding the voices of his music dramas.

ORCHESTRAL MUSIC

The audience for orchestral music in the nineteenth century was increasingly made up of the middle class. The court orchestras of Mannheim, Vienna, Berlin, and other cities in the eighteenth century had played to mixed audiences of nobility and city people, and this continued to be true in the nineteenth. But now public concerts became more popular, such as those organized by choral and other societies, benefit concerts arranged for various causes, and subscription concerts sponsored by individual entrepreneurs. But the experience of hearing a symphony orchestra was still a relatively rare event for a music lover of any class. Among the composers who conducted orchestral concerts, partly of their own music, were Berlioz, Mendelssohn, Schumann, Liszt, Brahms, Mahler, and Bruckner. The prominence given to the symphony in this book, however, is out of proportion to the place symphonic music occupied in the activities of composers, musicians, and the public in this period; yet it is justified by the importance accorded it by audiences, critics, and the composers themselves.

The Beethoven Legacy

Composers who followed Beethoven had to come to terms somehow with how this towering figure of the immediate past had transformed the symphony. They accepted or rejected his legacy in different ways, according to their personalities and talents.

Franz Schubert (1797–1828)

Unfinished Symphony

Schubert, for example, did not attempt a large-scale symphony until his *Unfinished* in B minor—abandoned in 1822—now numbered his Eighth. After a bow to Beethoven's Third in the introductory theme, Schubert launched into a songful melody quite unlike the typical first themes of his day; and its soaring extension, full of anguish and longing, was also a departure. After a bridge of only four measures modulating a major third down to G, he introduced a relaxed, graceful *Ländler* melody, inspired by the Austrian country dance. Another dilution of the Classic tradition was Schubert's bypassing of these two lyrical themes in the development section in favor of treating the introductory subject, which was also the basis of the coda. In this way Schubert met his listeners' expectations without compromising his lyrical nature.

The haunting, colorful instrumental combinations in this movement present a striking new flavor, for example, the quietly stirring figure in the strings that precedes, then combines with, the lyrical melody played *pianissimo* by the oboes and clarinets and later joined by other woodwinds to help build a *fortissimo* climax; the syncopated accompaniment to the cello's G-major second theme for violas and clarinets over the pizzicato of the double basses; and the clarinet solo and the dialogue of clarinet and oboe in the middle section of the slow movement. Schubert had found an orchestral voice that could stand any comparison. Unfortunately, no one heard it until 1865, many years after his death.

Career

Schubert came from a humble family. His father, a pious, strict, but kind and honorable man, was a schoolmaster in Vienna. The boy's formal training in music theory was not systematic, but his environment, both at home and in school, was filled with music making. He was educated to follow his father's profession, but the son's heart lay elsewhere. After teaching school for three years (1814–1817), he devoted himself entirely to writing music. Constantly struggling against illness and poverty, he composed ceaselessly. "I work every morning," he said. "When I have finished one piece I begin another." In the year 1815 alone he wrote 144 songs. He died at the age of thirty-one, and his

SCHUMANN ON SCHUBERT'S SYMPHONY IN C MAJOR*

I must say at once that anyone who is not yet acquainted with this symphony knows very little about Schubert. When we consider all that he has given to art, this praise may strike many as exaggerated, partly, no doubt, because composers have so often been advised, to their chagrin, that it is better for them—after Beethoven—"to abstain from the symphonic form." . . .

On hearing Schubert's symphony and its bright, flowery, romantic life, the city [Vienna] crystallizes before me, and I realize how such works could be born in these very surroundings. . . . Everyone must acknowledge that the outer world—sparkling today, gloomy tomorrow—often deeply stirs the feeling of the poet or the musician; and all must recognize, while listening to this symphony, that it reveals to us something more than mere beautiful song, mere joy and sorrow, such as music has ever expressed in a hundred ways, leading us into regions that, to our best recollection, we had never before explored. To understand this, one must hear this symphony. Here we find, besides the most masterly technicalities of musical composition, life in every vein, coloring down to the finest gradation, meaning everywhere, sharp expression in detail, and in the whole, a suffusing romanticism that other works by Franz Schubert have already made known to us.

And then the heavenly length of the symphony, like that of a thick novel in four volumes (perhaps by Jean Paul, who was also never able to reach a conclusion), and for the best reason—to permit readers to think it out for themselves. How this refreshes, this feeling of abundance, so contrary to our experience with others when we always dread to be disillusioned at the end and are often saddened through disappointment.

**Schumann discovered the unplayed manuscript of Schubert's Symphony in C major when he visited Schubert's brother Ferdinand in 1839. Through his intercession it was performed the same year at the Gewandhaus Concerts in Leipzig under the direction of Mendelssohn.*

From *Neue Zeitschrift für Musik* 12 (1840):82–83, after the translation by Paul Rosenfeld in Robert Schumann, *On Music and Musicians*, ed. Konrad Wolff (New York: Norton, 1946), pp. 108–11.

tombstone was inscribed, "Music has here buried a rich treasure but still fairer hopes."

Given the short span of Schubert's composing career, his enormous output of works is all the more impressive: 9 symphonies, 22 piano sonatas, a multitude of short piano pieces for two and four hands, about 35 chamber compositions, some 200 choral works including 6 Masses, 17 operas and Singspiele, and more than 600 lieder—in all, nearly 1,000 separate works.

Great C-major Symphony

In his "Great" Symphony in C major (No. 9, composed in 1828 and first performed in 1839), Schubert expanded his material almost to the breaking point; the "heavenly length" that Schumann admired (see vignette) would be less heavenly if it were not for the beauty of Schubert's melodies and orchestral effects. Some of these effects are unforgettable: two horns calling softly, as if

Example 16.1 *Franz Schubert, Symphony in C major: Andante con moto*

from a distance, at the start of the slow introduction; the antiphony between strings carrying the first theme, the winds playing quick repeating chords; the *pianissimo* trombones at the end of the exposition (measures 199–217); the repeated *g′* of the horns in the slow movement as the strings vacillate among the dominants of C, F, and D, and finally resolve (by way of the Neapolitan chord) in the dominant of A just before the return of the principal theme (measures 148–59; Example 16.1). This last passage was singled out by Schumann in his review for the *Neue Zeitschrift für Musik* (1840).

Other symphonies

Schubert had earlier written six other symphonies and made a complete sketch for still another. His chief formative influences were Haydn, Mozart, Cherubini, and early Beethoven. Another influence, that of the opera composer Gioachino Rossini, may be detected in some of the symphonies and the orchestral concert overtures, especially the two "in Italian style" (D. 556 and 590) from 1817. All Schubert's symphonies follow regular Classic forms, but the music's lyricism, its adventurous harmonic excursions, and its enchanting colors chart a new path.

Hector Berlioz (1803–1869)

Beethoven's *Pastoral* Symphony gave Berlioz the license to shape a Classic form around a set of feelings or passions. In the *Pastoral,* Beethoven presents a wide array of feelings aroused by a day in the country: contemplative delight in nature, apprehension as a storm approaches, terror at the storm's fury, and joy and gratitude for the fresh, washed calm that follows. In the *Symphonie fantastique* (1830), Berlioz dwells on the passions aroused by his thoughts and fan-

Symphonie fantastique

tasies about a woman whose love he hopes to win. The slow movements of both works evoke an idyllic pastoral atmosphere, with dialogues among piping shepherds or cowherds. On a musical level, the *Eroica*'s monumentality and spacious conception released Berlioz from the earlier confines of the Classic symphony. Beethoven had subjected the main theme in both the Third and Fifth Symphonies to a series of exciting adventures; Berlioz followed this precedent in his device of the *idée fixe*, a melody that he used in several movements to represent the heroine. Instead of a four-note motive inviting development, this melody has the long line of an operatic aria that can be extended and ornamented but resists fragmentation. Berlioz tended to compose from the top down, inventing melody and then harmonizing it, often with unexpected chords and inversions.

Because his imagination tended to run in parallel literary and musical channels, Berlioz subtitled this work "Episode in the Life of an Artist" and provided it with an autobiographical program (see NAWM 105). It is a musical drama without words. As Berlioz wrote, "The program should be regarded in the same way as the spoken words of an opera, serving to introduce the musical numbers by describing the situation that evokes the particular mood and expressive character of each." The literary influences in the program are too numerous to detail—Thomas De Quincey's *Confessions of an English Opium Eater* and Goethe's *Faust* are conspicuous among them—and the supposed situations are depicted in the passionate prose of a young and sensitive artist. The musical influences, besides Beethoven, were from the opera theater—Gluck, Rossini, Meyerbeer, Spontini.

Idée fixe

Berlioz brings back the opening theme of the first Allegro—the *idée fixe*, the obsessive image of the hero's beloved—in all the other movements (Example 16.2). The first movement, *Reveries et passions*, consists of a slow introduction followed by an Allegro that has the outward characteristics of sonata

Example 16.2 *Hector Berlioz,* Symphonie fantastique: *Allegro agitato e appassionato assai*

form, for example, contrasting theme sections and a repeated exposition. But Berlioz interrupts the "development" section with a three-measure grand pause heralding a formal and full statement of the main theme in the dominant, after which he continues reworking it until a triumphant tutti fortissimo statement appears in the tonic that is more a resplendent clarification than a recapitulation. The second movement is a waltz, replacing the Classic scherzo; the third is a pastorale, an Adagio in a large, two-part form (NAWM 105); the fourth movement is a macabre and descriptive orchestral *tour de force* (also in NAWM 105; CD 9 [1] / 3 ⟨43⟩); and the finale, an introduction and Allegro, uses a transformation of the *idée fixe* and two other themes—one of them the chant sequence *Dies irae*—first singly, then in combination.

The *Symphonie fantastique* is original not only in bending the symphony to serve narrative and autobiographical purposes but also in Berlioz's astounding ability to express the many shifting moods, the emotional content of his drama, in music that has great communicative power. His vivid aural imagination and his inventive orchestral sonorities shine through in nearly every measure. Berlioz achieved unity in the symphony as a whole by introducing a recurring theme and by developing the dramatic idea through the five movements; it is the kind of unity Beethoven forged in the Third and Fifth Symphonies.

Harold en Italie

Berlioz's second symphony, *Harold en Italie* (1834; the title was suggested by Lord Byron's *Childe Harold*), is a set of four scenes, suffused with the composer's recollections of an Italian sojourn. The movements are connected by a recurring theme, played by a solo viola. The instrument is featured throughout, though less prominently than in solo concertos—which is why the great violinist Nicolò Paganini (1782–1840), who commissioned the work from Berlioz in lieu of a concerto, refused to play it, since it would not sufficiently display his extraordinary technique. In each movement the viola melody combines contrapuntally with the other themes, and the solo instrument continually blends with different orchestral groups in a ravishing display of sonorities. The finale explicitly sums up the themes of the preceding movements.

Roméo et Juliette

Five years after *Harold en Italie,* Berlioz produced his "dramatic symphony" in seven movements, *Roméo et Juliette* (1839, considerably revised before publication in 1847). Berlioz used Beethoven's Ninth Symphony as a model for his own work, which also combined orchestra, soloists, and chorus in an unstaged concert drama. In adding choral parts to the orchestra, he followed Beethoven's example; but in this work the voices enter in the prologue and are used in three of the symphonic movements as well. Although the Classic order of movements can still be traced, the series of independent scenes approaches an unstaged opera, or what the composer later called a "dramatic legend," a genre he perfected in *La damnation de Faust* (1864). Nonetheless, *Roméo et Juliette* is essentially a symphonic work.

The *Queen Mab* Scherzo from this symphony is another *tour de force* of imagination and deft orchestration. Like Mendelssohn's Scherzo for *A Midsummer Night's Dream,* it characterizes the world of elves and fairies. Berlioz's wondrous and magical Scherzo delicately captures the images of Mercutio's fancies about Mab, the fairies' midwife, "drawn with a team of little atomies over men's noses as they lie asleep," making "traces of the smallest spider web" with her chariot, "an empty hazel-nut." As in the Mendelssohn, the principle of perpetual motion is at work. Berlioz achieves a gossamer texture by muting the violins and dividing them into four parts, often pizzicato. The trio is a spider web of violin harmonics that captures hallucinations of the Scherzo's melodies while muted violas or flute and English horn in octaves drift in.

For the most passionate and tragic parts of the play—the love scene and the tomb scene—Berlioz used the orchestra without voices. "The very sublimity of this love," he wrote in his preface to the score

> made its depiction so dangerous for the musician that he had to give his imagination a latitude that the positive sense of the sung words would not have given him, resorting instead to instrumental language, which is richer, more varied, less precise, and by its very indefiniteness incomparably more powerful in such a case.[4]

Summary

Berlioz's first three symphonies, especially the *Symphonie fantastique*, made him the leader of the Romantic movement's radical wing. All subsequent composers of program music, including Strauss and Debussy, would be indebted to him. His orchestration initiated a new era: he enriched orchestral music with new resources of harmony, color, expression, and form; and his device of having a theme recur in different movements (as in the *Symphonie fantastique* and *Harold en Italie*) gave impetus to the development of the cyclical symphonic forms of the later nineteenth century. By example and precept he was the founder of modern orchestration and conducting.

Felix Mendelssohn (1809–1847)

Felix Mendelssohn's two most important symphonies carry geographical subtitles—the *Italian* (No. 4, 1833) and the *Scottish* (No. 3, 1842). They preserve impressions he gained, both of sounds and landscapes, on trips to Italy and the British Isles. The *Italian* Symphony celebrates the south, sunny and vibrant. The slow movement suggests a procession of chanting pilgrims trudging along the road. In the finale, we can imagine people in the city squares dancing the spirited *saltarello.* The *Scottish* Symphony evokes the north, gray and somber, with the skirling of bagpipes and the sound of old heroic ballads. In both symphonies Mendelssohn skillfully fitted his melodious ideas into the regular Classic forms. Beethoven influenced Mendelssohn's symphonic writing less than did his study of Bach and Handel and the rigorous training in the Classic forms he received under Carl Friedrich Zelter. As Zelter's pupil he wrote thirteen string symphonies that gave him a mastery of form, counterpoint, and fugue and helped determine his personal style.

Unlike Berlioz's essentially vocal unfolding of the *idée fixe* in the *Fantastic* Symphony (Example 16.2), the equally expansive melody that opens the

4. Quoted from the score published in Winterthur [1858] and trans. in D. Kern Holoman, *Berlioz* (Cambridge, Mass.: Harvard University Press, 1989), p. 261.

Example 16.3 *Felix Mendelssohn, Symphony No. 4* (Italian), *Op. 90: Allegro vivace*

Italian Symphony

Italian Symphony (Example 16.3) is thoroughly instrumental. Yet its sighing lurches and sequences and its repeated postponement of closure are inspired, like Berlioz's melody, by Italian opera. The second theme (measures 110–46) is similarly constructed. Assigned first to a clarinet-bassoon choir, then oboes and flutes, it is finally taken up by the strings. Mendelssohn practically forgoes these ideas in the development section, which is dominated by a sprightly Italian-flavored tune that returns at the end of the recapitulation, cleverly combined with the main theme. The trio of the (unlabeled) scherzo, in which a quartet of bassoons and horns holds forth, recalls similar ensembles in the trios of Beethoven's Third and Ninth Symphonies.

Scottish Symphony

The four movements of the *Scottish* Symphony are played without pause. One portion of the slow introduction serves as a bridge to the second movement and to another, fragmentary motive. The Scottish flavor that pervades the entire work comes not only from the trochaic rhythm of the "Scotch snap" in the second movement but also from the pentatonic scales that underlie the themes. In Example 16.4a some of the principal melodic ideas are transposed to A minor/C major for easy comparison. These scales may be reduced to the two most common types of pentatonic found in the folk music of the Hebrides Islands, the anhemitonic (lacking semitones) and hemitonic (with a semitone) (Example 16.4b). The ornamental tones heard in bagpipe performance of Scottish melodies are represented in Mendelssohn's score by grace notes. His use of folk idioms reveals a nostalgia for faraway places and illustrates the Romantics' interest in both native music and local color. It also shows how strongly high-profile tunes determine the character of symphonic music in this period and, at the same time, how easily ethnic flavor can be diluted by lush harmonies and textures.

Violin Concerto

The Violin Concerto (1844), one of Mendelssohn's masterpieces and one of the greatest of all violin concertos, also demonstrates his wish to forge a unity through both thematic content and links between movements. A transition weds the opening Allegro molto appassionato to the lyrical Andante, and an introduction to the last movement alludes to the opening

Example 16.4 *Felix Mendelssohn, Symphony No. 3* (Scottish), *Op. 56*

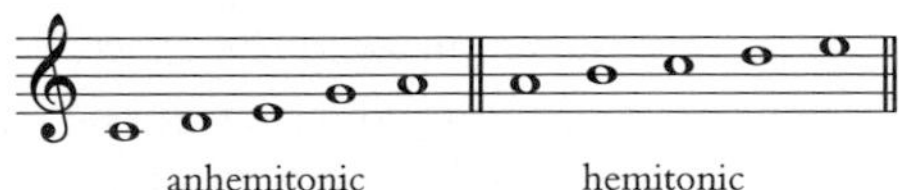

theme. In the first movement Mendelssohn went a step farther than Beethoven by having the soloist state the main theme at the outset, skipping the usual orchestral exposition and placing the cadenza just before rather than after the recapitulation.

Overtures

Mendelssohn's genius for musical landscapes is evident in his overtures *Die Hebriden* (The Hebrides), also called *Fingals Höhle* (Fingal's Cave, 1832), and *Meeresstille und glückliche Fahrt* (Calm Sea and Prosperous Voyage, 1828–32), while *Die schöne Melusine* (The Beautiful Melusine, 1833) is a symphonic incarnation of a fairy tale after a play by Franz Grillparzer. Among his incidental music for plays, the overture for Victor Hugo's *Ruy Blas* (1839) is excelled only by the incomparable *Midsummer Night's Dream* Overture. Written in 1826 when Mendelssohn was seventeen, it set the standard for all subsequent concert overtures of the period. It is a briliant example of self-renewing perpetual motion, of a heavy orchestra tamed to tiptoe like a chamber ensemble. Although the overture is programmatic in the same sense as Beethoven's

Pastoral Symphony, it relies more on orchestral color and appeal to the listener's imagination. The program thinly veils the structure, lending charm to the view but not obscuring the outlines. Seventeen years later Mendelssohn wrote additional incidental music for a production of Shakespeare's play, including the picturesque Scherzo.

Robert Schumann (1810–1856)

Until 1840, Schumann dedicated himself mainly to piano music and lieder. Some critics and historians have maintained that his personality did not lend itself to Classic forms. Liszt wrote in 1855:

> Schumann strove to reconcile his romantic personality, torn between joy and pain, and often driven by a dark urge towards the fantastic and bizarre with the modalities of classical form, whereas the clarity and symmetry of such forms lay beyond his characteristic spirit.[5]

Spring Symphony

After several starts, Schumann completed his First Symphony in B♭ in the spring of 1841 and a second the same year—his "symphony year," as 1840 was the "lieder year" and 1842 the "chamber-music year." The First, known as the *Spring* Symphony, was to have had a descriptive title attached to each movement, such as "Spring's Awakening" and "Spring's Farewell." Appropriately, the music is fresh and spontaneous and is driven by inexhaustible rhythmic energy.

Fourth Symphony

The symphony in D minor, completed at the end of 1841, was revised as Symphony No. 4 ten years later, when Schumann felt the power "to achieve higher things." The prestigious status that Beethoven had conferred on the symphony made it, in Schumann's eyes, a rite of passage to full recognition, although when it came down to writing for orchestra, he followed the examples of Schubert and Mendelssohn. Schumann thought of calling the final version a symphonic fantasia. Whether or not he had a program in mind, the fantasia element is present in the irregular form of the first Allegro and in the fact that each movement contains themes derived from the slow introduction. The four movements, like those of Mendelssohn's *Scottish* Symphony, are played without a break; they are joined by means of skillful harmonic coupling and, like Beethoven's Fifth, by a transitional passage leading to the finale.

Second Symphony

Schumann's Second Symphony in C major (1846) has a first movement dominated by dotted rhythms, like that of Beethoven's Seventh. The Adagio espressivo, in E♭, pits a halting lyrical theme in the woodwinds against nervous syncopations in the strings. At a sublime moment, the violins enlarge on the theme, while the violas play the turbulent accompaniment in double stops and the bass ascends an octave by semitones (Example 16.5). The tension engendered by the chromaticism and the complex single and double appoggiaturas and suspensions make one think ahead to Brahms.

5. Quoted in Ronald Taylor, *Robert Schumann, His Life and Work* (New York: Universe Books, 1982), p. 206.

Example 16.5 *Robert Schumann, Symphony No. 2, Op. 61: Andante espressivo (Violin I and winds omitted)*

Franz Liszt (1811–1886)

Symphonic poem

Liszt, the foremost composer of program music after Berlioz, wrote twelve "symphonic poems"—his term—between 1848 and 1858 and a thirteenth in 1881–82. Liszt did not call these works symphonies, because they were relatively short and not divided into separate movements in a conventional order. Instead, each presents a continuous form with sections in contrasting character and tempo; a few themes are developed, repeated, varied, or transformed. These works are "poems" by analogy to word-poems. Not a drama, narrative, or prose exposition, the symphonic poem is an imaginative structure free of these genres' conventions. The content and form may be suggested by a picture, statue, play, poem, scene, personality, or something else, but the subject is converted into music without specific reference to the details of the original. The title and, usually, a program, which may or may not have been written by the composer, identify the subject. Thus Liszt's *Hunnenschlacht* (The Battle of the Huns) is related to a mural painting, *Mazeppa* to a poem, *Hamlet* to Shakespeare's hero, *Prometheus* to the myth and also to a poem by Herder, and so on. The score of *Die Ideale* is liberally interspersed with quotations from Schiller's poem of that title, although Liszt changed the order of Schiller's passages to make them conform with his own musical plan and to add his own "apotheosis" at the end.

Orpheus

The best of Liszt's symphonic poems, *Orpheus* and *Hamlet*, are concise musical portraits that originated as introductions to theatrical performances. The first, for Gluck's opera, was inspired by an Etruscan vase in the Louvre depicting Orpheus singing to the lyre; the second, an overture for

Shakespeare's play, is a penetrating psychological study. Liszt's programs, like those of Berlioz, do not relate stories told in music but run parallel to them.

Les Préludes

Several of the symphonic poems grew out of concert overtures. Others are single movements that contain lingering vestiges of sonata form and of the contrasts in mood and tempo found in the standard four-movement sequence. Liszt devised a method of unifying a composition by transforming a single motive to reflect the diverse moods needed to portray a programmatic subject. In *Les Préludes* (1854), he applied this method with notable artistic success. A three-note motive that has both a rhythmic and a melodic shape (Example 16.6a) is modified and expanded to take on different characters: amorphous, like a prelude (Example 16.6b), resolute (c), lyrical (d), stormy (e and f), excited (g), and martial (h). A more distant metamorphosis (i) serves as a contrasting theme and is itself subjected to transformations. Liszt used a similar

Example 16.6 *Franz Liszt,* Les Préludes

method in his Piano Concerto in E♭, composed at about the same time (see page 584).

Liszt acknowledged that *Les Préludes* was based on a poem of the same title by Alfonse-Marie de Lamartine (1790–1869). He followed the sectioning of Lamartine's lengthy poem quite faithfully, responding to the sequence of moods: introductory, with pizzicato chords and arpeggios in the strings and harp to suggest a poet summoning his Muse with lyre and song; amorous (measure 47); troubled and pessimistic about human destiny (measure 131); peaceful and pastoral (measure 200); bellicose (measure 344); and a return to the initial mood (measure 405). Liszt did not try to render the images or incidents of the literary text but created a parallel musical poem. In the process he managed to transform the music he borrowed from his unfinished *Ouverture des quatre elemens avec choeurs.*

The genre of symphonic poem was taken up by such composers as Bedřich Smetana (*Má vlast*), César Franck (*Psyché*), Camille Saint-Saëns (*Le Rouet d'Omphale, Danse macabre*), and Piotr Il'yich Tchaikovsky (*Francesca da Rimini*). Liszt's bold chords and chromatic harmonies helped to form Wagner's style after 1854, and his play with cells or small sets of intervals and pitches enjoyed unexpected resonance in the twentieth century.

Faust Symphony

The works that Liszt called symphonies are also programmatic. He dedicated his *Faust Symphony* (1854) to Berlioz. It consists of three movements, labeled *Faust, Gretchen,* and *Mephistopheles,* with a finale (added later) for tenor soloist and men's chorus, setting the *chorus mysticus* that closes Goethe's drama. The three movements correspond to the Classic plan: introduction and Allegro (in sonata form), Andante (three-part form), and Scherzo (three-part form, followed by a long additional development and coda). The first theme of the *Faust* movement uses one of Liszt's favorite chords—the augmented triad, here transposed sequentially downward through four chromatic steps so as to comprise all twelve notes of the chromatic scale (Example 16.7). Themes are interchanged among the movements and transformed in accordance with the program. The *Mephistopheles* movement, for example, is made up largely of sinister caricatures of the *Faust* themes—Berlioz similarly caricatured the *idée fixe* in the *Symphonie fantastique*—and the *Gretchen* melody is used as the principal theme of the finale. In this symphony, Liszt successfully combined a grandiose and momentous program with music of great inspiration, substance, and passion, in a form whose huge dimensions are justified by the scope and power of the generating ideas. The *Dante Symphony* (1856) is a shorter work in two movements—*Inferno* and *Purgatorio*—with a quiet concluding section for women's voices on the text of the Magnificat.

Example 16.7 *Franz Liszt,* Faust Symphony, *First Theme*

Johannes Brahms (1833–1897)

By nature conscientious and severely self-critical, Brahms approached the composition of a symphony with great care and deliberation. His reluctance to put a major symphonic work before the public is notorious: we know, for example, that he worked on his first symphony off and on for over twenty years, beginning in 1855. The conductor Hermann Levi recalled that Brahms exclaimed in 1870, concerning the specter of Beethoven: "I shall never compose a symphony! You have no idea how someone like me feels when he hears such a giant marching behind him all the time." However, far from wanting to write "Beethoven's Tenth"—as the conductor Hans von Bülow dubbed Brahms's First in C minor—the composer deliberately set out to carve a fresh path. In searching for his own way, he probably owed more to the earliest version of Schumann's Fourth—Brahms owned the autograph—than to Beethoven. The portentous slow introductions to the first and final movements envelop the themes of the Allegros that follow in a mist from which they emerge all the more clearly, like mountains when a fog lifts. Gradually unfolding the principal thematic material in the introduction rather than in the Allegro was new, while linking all the movements through references to the slow introduction gave this symphony a strong organic coherence.

First Symphony

The First Symphony in C minor, Op. 68, was finished after some twenty years of work, in 1876. It has the conventional sequence of movements—fast, slow, a light movement, and fast—the first and last having slow introductions. The third movement, like the corresponding movement in the Second and Third Symphonies, retains the lyrical rhythmic grace of an intermezzo rather than the intensity of the Beethoven scherzo. The key scheme of the symphony—C minor; E major; A♭ major and B major; and C minor and major—is characteristic of the late- and post-Beethoven eras in its use of the major-third relation and the shifts between minor and major. As in Bèethoven's Fifth, the initial C minor gives way to a triumphant major at the end of the last movement. The opening theme of the first Allegro (Example 16.8) made up of rising

Example 16.8 *Johannes Brahms, Symphony No. 1, Op. 68: Allegro*

thirds, alternately major and minor, ever reaching for new heights, balances antecedent and consequent phrases in the violins, while the chromatic motive of the introduction is sequentially developed in both the cellos and basses. Symmetry reins in a cry of desperation.

Reminiscences haunt all the movements. Cyclical returns of the introduction's chromatic lines in contrary motion—rising in the violins, descending in the winds and violas—are heard in the second (measures 4–6), third (measures 22–25, 29–32), and fourth movements (measures 4–12). In the introduction to the last movement, we hear a nostalgic, familiar-sounding melody in C major played by horns and flutes against a mysteriously undulating accompaniment of muted violins and divided violas. It breaks out forcefully in the recapitulation (measures 285–95). Brahms identified the melody as an Alpine-horn tune he had heard in Switzerland, but it most resembles the chimes of Great St. Mary's Church at the University of Cambridge, a pattern of bells now known as the Westminster Quarters, which has been copied by many chimes that toll the quarter hours. A solemn four-measure chorale phrase, first played *piano* in this introduction by the trombones and bassoons (measures 47–50), reappears *fortissimo* in the brasses and strings at the climax of the ensuing Allegro (measures 407–13).

Second Symphony

The Second Symphony in D major, Op. 73 (1877), has in contrast to the First a peaceful and pastoral character. Instead of starting with a slow introduction, it begins with a three-note motto in the cellos and double basses, *D–C♯*–D, that pervades the first movement. The second movement, Adagio non troppo, illustrates particularly well Brahms's method, prevalent throughout his work, of continuously building on germinal ideas, which Arnold Schoenberg called "developing variation." The opening cello melody grows out of a stepwise descending diminished fifth, expanded to a perfect fifth in measure 2, with a dotted rhythm stressing the lower boundary (see Example 16.9). The descent is decorated in measure 3, and the eighth-note figuration as well as the descent is varied in measures 6 to 8. Many further subtle variations of this basic material give the movement its remarkable coherence and consistent mood.

Example 16.9 *Johannes Brahms, Symphony No. 2, Op. 73: Adagio non troppo*

Example 16.10 *Johannes Brahms, Symphony No. 3, Op. 70: Allegro con brio, Outline of First Theme*

Third Symphony

The opening measures of the Third Symphony in F major, Op. 90 (1883), illustrate Brahms' characteristic wide melodic spans and the cross-relation between the minor and major forms of the tonic triad (see Example 16.10). The conflict between the two modes and between A-flat and A-natural recurs in the last movement, which begins in F minor and settles in F major only in the coda. At the statement of the second theme, another typical Brahmsian clash occurs, between two diverse simultaneous meters: the accompaniment in four and the melody in six (Example 16.11).

Example 16.11 *Johannes Brahms, Symphony No. 3, Op. 70, IV: Allegro*

Fourth Symphony

Brahms began the Fourth Symphony in E minor, Op. 98 (1885), by setting out a chain of thirds, in which all the notes of the harmonic minor scale are used serially before any is repeated (see Example 16.12). The thematic statement in the first violin continues with a similar series, this time rising from the keynote *E* to *C*, completing an eight-measure phrase. In the subsequent eight-measure phrase, the bass, which has been relatively static, rises chromatically toward the dominant to set up the first cadence on the tonic (measure 19), closing a typically long, broad line that spans two octaves and a fourth. Brahms unfolds the series of thirds in augmentation at the start of the recapitulation (measures 246–55). Such a series accompanies the melodious second subject, illustrating another important device that provides excitement in this symphony: a rhythmic conflict between a melody that squarely emphasizes the first

Example 16.12 *Johannes Brahms, Symphony No. 4, Op. 98: Allegro non troppo*

Example 16.13 *Johannes Brahms, Symphony No. 4, Op. 98: Allegro non troppo*

beat of the measure and an accompaniment that stubbornly throws its weight on the third beat (see Example 16.13).

The modal (Phrygian) tinge of the introduction and principal theme set the mood for the Andante of the Fourth Symphony. The finale of this work is a 32-variation passacaglia/chaconne, a form that reflects Brahms's fascination with Baroque music. It is at once a set of variations on a melody and on a harmonic pattern. The variations are laid out in a broad three-part form, the middle section consisting of four quiet variations in $\frac{3}{2}$ meter (in effect, at half of the surrounding $\frac{3}{4}$). The diversity among the variations of figuration and mood is balanced by a feeling of continuous, controlled movement throughout.

Other orchestral works

Through the age of forty, Brahms completed four orchestral pieces: two Serenades (D major, Op. 11, 1858; A major, Op. 16, 1859), the Piano Concerto No. 1 in D minor (1861), and the masterly *Variations on a Theme of Haydn* (Op. 56a, 1873). Brahms's other late works for orchestra were the *Academic Festival Overture*, Op. 80 (1880) and the *Tragic Overture*, Op. 81 (1881). He also left a second Piano Concerto, Op. 83 in B♭ (1881); the Violin Concerto, Op. 77 in D (1878), which ranks with Beethoven's concerto in the literature of this instrument; and the Double Concerto for violin and violoncello, Op. 102 in A minor (1887).

Anton Bruckner (1824–1896)

Anton Bruckner looked to Beethoven's Ninth as a model for procedure, purpose, grandiose proportions, and religious spirit. Beethoven's first movement, in which the theme emerges from inchoate intervals and rhythms, showed Bruckner how to begin, and Beethoven's final hymn finds a parallel in most of Bruckner's symphonies.

Symphonies

Bruckner composed his First Symphony in 1865–66. It was preceded by one he later called No. 0, or *Die Nullte.* Most of the symphonies exist in two or more of his own versions and, in addition, unauthorized versions made by conductors and editors. All are in the conventional four movements and none is explicitly programmatic, though the composer did at one time furnish a few descriptive tags for the Fourth (*Romantic*) Symphony (1874–80). The symphonies may best be understood as the expression of a profoundly religious spirit, revealed not so much by any quotation of religious themes as by a prevailing weighty mood that is especially evident in the combination of mystic ecstasy and tonal splendor of the chorale-like themes at the climaxes of his finales and sometimes his first movements. Unlike Beethoven, Bruckner exhibited no striking changes in style during his career. His ten symphonies are essentially alike in conception and technique, though the last three undoubtedly represent his highest achievement in this genre.

Style

Certain influences are obvious in Bruckner's musical language. That of his idol Wagner is particularly evident in large-scale structures, the great length of the symphonies, the lush harmonies, the sequential repetition of entire passages, and the huge size of the orchestra. The Wagner tubas, for example, are used in the last three symphonies. Bruckner's experience as an organist is evident from his orchestration. Various instruments or instrumental groups are brought in, opposed, and combined like the contrasting registers or manuals of an organ. Also Bruckner often expanded thematic material by piling up massive blocks of sound in a way that was strongly suggestive of an organist's improvisation.

Fourth Symphony

Bruckner's symphonies typically begin, like Beethoven's Ninth, with a vague agitation in the strings out of which a theme gradually condenses and then builds up in a crescendo. A good example is the Fourth Symphony in E♭ major. It opens with a quiet tremolo in the strings sounding a tonic triad against repeated horn calls that are characterized by falling and rising fifths (sometimes altered to sixths and octaves) and a triple-dotted rhythm (Example 16.14a). After some striking enharmonic modulations, the intervals are filled in by scalar passages in Bruckner's favorite rhythm ($\frac{4}{4}$) ♩ ♩ ♩♩♩ (triplet). Out of this a theme emerges *fortissimo* in measure 51, forcefully proclaiming the rhythm in the tonic key (Example 16.14b). The development of this idea leads to the key of D♭, where a bird call—as Bruckner identified it—is heard against a lyrical melody in the viola (Example 16.14c). Both themes are then reworked until a double bar in measure 193, where a development section seems to begin, but it is really a fantasia, in which previously heard material is combined in a dreamlike sequence resembling Wagner's orchestral interludes. A return to the main key (measure 365) ushers in a "recapitulation" that reviews mate-

Example 16.14 *Anton Bruckner, Symphony No. 4* (Romantic) *in E♭ major: Ruhig bewegt (Allegro molto moderato)*

rial from the exposition in the expected order but with the "bird-call" section now appearing in B major. In a long coda, harmonically static patterns are repeated with an obstinacy that anticipates twentieth-century minimalism. Although we can view this movement in terms of sonata form, the continuous development of musical ideas, already observed in Haydn and more markedly in Beethoven, is here carried to its ultimate stage.

Bruckner had the misfortune of living in Vienna in the shadow of Brahms, whose four symphonies are approximately contemporaneous with Bruckner's last six, and of being continually attacked by critics as a disciple of Wagner. His symphonies received little acclaim during his lifetime. For many years, only two of them—the Fourth and Seventh—were played outside Vienna and in a few other European centers. No doubt their cathedral proportions and monumental character hindered their popular acceptance. Certain movements attained particular notoriety, such as the "Hunter Scherzo," which dates from the 1878 revision of the Fourth (*Romantic*) Symphony. It is strikingly original, with a charming trio that Bruckner labeled "Dance strain during a repast at hunting." The slow movements, which achieve a sublime solemnity with their long-breathed melodies, usually alternate two sections in the form ABABA, often in different tempos (as in the Seventh). Among the finales, the most famous comes from the final pages of the Eighth Symphony in C minor. Starting at measure 679, thematic fragments from all the previous movements pass in review, and in the last twelve measures (697–708) they are heard simultaneously (Example 16.15): in the opening theme of the first movement in the lower winds and brass, the Scherzo theme in the flutes, clarinets, and trumpets; in the Adagio theme in the upper horns, all this against resounding tonic major triads in the tubas. Most of Bruckner's final movements recycle subjects from earlier movements, but none do it so compactly or gloriously.

Eighth Symphony

Piotr Il'yich Tchaikovsky (1840–1893)

Although the Russian Tchaikovsky did not embark on serious musical training until after he had begun a career in law, he did graduate from the St. Petersburg Conservatory and for a while taught harmony at the Moscow Conservatory. He scored his first success with the *Romeo and Juliet* Fantasy (1869; revised 1870 and 1880), in which he adapted sonata form to meet the demands of the Shakespeare play and its characters. Tchaikovsky's best-known symphonies are his last three: No. 4 in F minor, 1877–78; No. 5 in E minor, 1888; and No. 6, the *Pathétique*, in B minor, 1893.

Tchaikovsky acknowledged to his friend and correspondent Nadezhda von Meck that the Fourth Symphony had a program. The idea that fate is inexorable does explain the unexpected intrusion here and there of a ponderous horn call from the introduction, reminiscent of Schumann's First and Schubert's C-major Symphony. The horn motive is recalled after the exposition and before the coda of the final movement. More novel in the first movement is the

Fourth Symphony

Example 16.15 *Anton Bruckner, Symphony No. 8: Finale*

pattern of keys in the exposition and recapitulation. The first thematic section is in F minor, the second in A♭ major, as expected, but the closing section is in B major (equivalent to C♭ major, completing the cycle of minor thirds). The recapitulation begins in D minor, modulates to F major for the second subject, and finally reaches the main key of F minor in the coda.

Fifth Symphony

The Fifth Symphony develops the cyclical method even further. The brooding motto announced in the introduction recurs in all four movements: in the development of the Allegro con anima; before the coda of the otherwise lyrical Andante; as a coda in the Waltz; and, very much recast, as an introduction to the Finale. This symphony shows the composer's mastery of orchestration, particularly in the sweeping effects he achieved setting instrumental choirs against one another: in the *Più mosso* section of the Andante, for example, we hear the wonderful throbbing syncopations in the strings against a soaring melody in the winds. The usual scherzo is replaced by a *Valse* that betrays Tchaikovsky's great affinity for that dance.

Sixth Symphony

He used a waltz again in the second movement of the Sixth Symphony, this time naturalizing the Viennese $\frac{3}{4}$ into a Russian $\frac{5}{4}$. The spirit of dance also pervades the third movement, which has the character of a march, but a *marche macabre.* The deeply pessimistic and brooding character of the work, which also quotes the Russian Orthodox Requiem in the first movement, earned it the sobriquet *Pathétique*, which the composer did not attach to it but did not object to, either.

Other well-known orchestral works of Tchaikovsky are the symphonic poem *Francesca da Rimini* (1876), the First Piano Concerto in B♭ minor (1875), the Violin Concerto in D (1878), and the *1812 Overture* (1880). Thoroughly charming are the ballets, particularly *Swan Lake* (1876), *The Sleeping Beauty* (1889), and *The Nutcracker* (1892).

Antonín Dvořák (1841–1904)

Of the nine symphonies of Dvořák, No. 7 in D minor (1885) is considered the best.[6] The work is rich in thematic ideas; its prevailingly tragic mood is relieved only by the G-major trio of the scherzo. The Symphonies No. 6 in D major (1880) and No. 8 in G major (1889) are more relaxed in spirit, with fresh, folk-like melodies and rhythms and many fine touches of orchestration. No. 9 (*From the New World*), which Dvořák wrote in 1893 during his first sojourn in the United States, is the most familiar. For this symphony, the composer consciously used themes suggested by Native American melodies and, especially, by Negro spirituals that he heard sung in New York by Harry T. Burleigh. Among Dvořák's other orchestral music is a cello concerto that remains a standard in the repertory.

Ninth Symphony

6. References are to the now standard chronological numbering of Dvořák's symphonies. Relation between old and new numbering:

Old	*New*
3	5
1	6
2	7
4	8
5	9

Bibliography

Music Collections

Berlioz *Werke* (Leipzig: Breitkopf & Härtel, 1900–07; repr. New York: Kalmus, 1971), 9 series, incomplete, in 20 vols. *New Berlioz Edition*, ed. Hugh Macdonald et al. (Kassel: Bärenreiter, 1967–), 25 vols. proposed. *Catalogue of the Works of Hector Berlioz*, by D. Kern Holoman (Kassel: Bärenreiter, 1987).

Brahms *Sämtliche Werke*, 26 vols. (Leipzig: Breitkopf & Härtel, 1926–27; repr. Ann Arbor: Edwards, 1949; repr. in miniature format, New York: Kalmus, 1970). Thematic catalogue by Donald and Margit McCorkle (Munich: Henle, 1984).

Bruckner *Sämtliche Werke*, 11 vols., ed. R. Haas et al. (Augsburg: B. Filser, 1930–44). Superseding the Haas edition is the *Sämtliche Werke, kritische Gesamtausgabe*, ed. Leopold Nowak (Vienna: Musikwissenschaftlicher Verlag, 1951–).

Chopin *Werke*, 14 vols. (Leipzig: Breitkopf & Härtel, 1878–80); supplements and reports, 1878–1902. *Complete Works*, ed. Jan Ekier (Cracow: Polskie Wydawn. Muzyczne, 1967–); index of works in chronological order by Maurice J. E. Brown, 2nd ed. (London: Macmillan, 1972); thematic catalogue by K. Kobylańska (Munich: Henle, 1979).

Dvořák Critical edition of the complete works, ed. Otakar Šourek et al. (Prague: Supraphon, 1955–); Jarmil Burghauser and John Clapham, *Thematic Catalogue*, 2nd ed. (Prague: Bärenreiter, Editio Supraphon, 1996).

Liszt *Musikalische Werke*, 34 vols. (Leipzig: Breitkopf & Härtel, 1907–36; repr. 1967), incomplete. *Liszt Society Publications* (London, 1950–), a noncritical collection of works. A new scholarly edition of Liszt's works is in the course of publication, ed. I. Sulyok et al. (Kassel and Budapest: Bärenreiter, 1970–).

Mendelssohn *Kritisch durchgesehene Ausgabe* (Leipzig: Breitkopf & Härtel, 1874–77; repr. Farnborough, Eng.: Gregg International, 1967; miniature format, New York: Kalmus, 1971), 19 series in 35 vols. *Leipziger Ausgabe der Werke*, ed. Internationale Felix-Mendelssohn-Gesellschaft (Leipzig: Deutscher Verlag für Musik, 1960–). Thematic catalogue of works in print (Leipzig: Breitkopf & Härtel, 1882).

Schubert *Kritisch durchgesehene Gesamtausgabe*, ed. Eusebius Mandyczewski et al. (Leipzig: Breitkopf & Härtel, 1888–97; repr. New York: Dover, 1964–69; in miniature format, New York: Kalmus, 1971), 21 series in 41 vols., 10 separate Revisionsberichte. *Neue Ausgabe sämtlicher Werke* (Kassel and New York: Bärenreiter, 1964–). The lieder are also published in a complete edition by Peters, 7 vols. Thematic catalogue by Otto E. Deutsch (London: Dent, 1951; rev. Kassel: Bärenreiter, 1978).

Schumann, Clara Wieck *Ausgewälte Klavierwerke*, ed. Janina Klassen (Munich: Henle, 1987); *Sämtliche Lieder für Singstimme und Klavier*, ed. Joachim Draheim and Brigitte Höft (Wiesbaden: Breitkopf & Härtel, 1990–92).

Schumann, Robert *Werke* (Leipzig: Breitkopf & Härtel, 1881–93; repr. miniature format, New York: Kalmus, 1971). *Thematic Catalogue*, ed. Kurt Hoffman and Siegmar Keil, 5th ed. (Hamburg: Schuberth, 1982).

Tchaikovsky Collected edition (Moscow: State Music Publishers, 1940–; repr. New York: Kalmus, 1974–). Thematic catalogue, comp. B. Jurgenson (New York: Am-Rus Music, n.d.), a reprint of the 1897 edition.

For Further Reading

General

On "romantic," see Arthur Lovejoy, "On the Discrimination of Romanticisms," in *Essays in the History of Ideas* (Baltimore: Johns Hopkins University Press, 1948; repr. Greenwood Press, 1978); Friedrich Blume, *Classic and Romantic Music* (New York: Norton, 1970); René Wellek, "The Concept of Romanticism in Literary History," in *Concepts of Criticism* (New Haven: Yale University Press, 1963); Meyer H. Abrams, *The Mirror and the Lamp: Romantic Theory and the Critical Tradition* (New York: Oxford University Press, 1953).

A comprehensive and up-to-date study of nineteenth-century music, with an accompanying anthology and a good bibliography, is Leon Plantinga, *Romantic Music* (New York: Norton, 1984). A very original approach to the history of the period that considers not only the music but criticism, historiography, and sociological issues is *Nineteenth-Century Music* by Carl Dahlhaus, trans. J. Bradford Robinson (Berkeley and Los Angeles: University of California Press, 1989). Some briefer surveys are Rey M. Longyear, *Nineteenth-Century Romanticism in Music*, 3rd ed. (Englewood Cliffs, N. J.: Prentice Hall, 1988); Gerald Abraham, *A Hundred Years of Music*, 4th ed. (London: Duckworth, 1974). For excellent essays on the political, social, and historical background of music centers in Europe and the Americas, see *The Early Romantic Era*, ed. Alexander Ringer, and *The Late Romantic Era*, ed. Jim Samson (Englewood Cliffs, N.J.: Prentice Hall, 1990, 1991). A source book for the musical vocabulary of the period is Leonard G. Ratner, *Romantic Music: Sound and Syntax* (New York: Schirmer Books, 1992). Specialized topics are treated in the journal *19th-Century Music* (Berkeley: University of California, 1977–). A study of musical forms and styles and the literary background is in Charles Rosen, *The Romantic Generation* (Cambridge, Mass.: Harvard University Press, 1995).

Revised articles of NG relevant to these chapters have been published under *The New Grove Early Romantic Masters*, Vol. 1: *Chopin, Schumann, and Liszt*; and Vol. 2: *Weber, Berlioz, and Mendelssohn* (New York: Norton, 1985).

On the sonata, refer to William S. Newman, *The Sonata since Beethoven*, 3rd ed. (New York: Norton, 1983), and Charles Rosen, *Sonata Forms*, rev. ed. (New York: Norton, 1988), Chapter 14; on the symphony, see Robert Simpson, ed., *The Symphony*, 2 vols. (London: David & Charles, 1967), and Donald F. Tovey, *Essays in Musical Analysis* (London: Oxford University Press, 1935–39).

On the social history of the piano, read Arthur Loesser, *Men, Women, and Pianos* (New York: Simon & Schuster, 1954); on its mechanical history, R. E. M. Harding, *The Pianoforte: Its History to the Great Exhibition of 1851* (Cambridge: Cambridge University Press, 1933); also Edwin M. Good, *Giraffes, Black Dragons, and Other Pianos* (Stanford: Stanford University Press, 1982).

Individual Composers

Berlioz His *Treatise on Instrumentation* (1843), rev. and enl. by Richard Strauss (1905), trans. New York, 1948; his *Memoirs*, trans. and ed. David Cairns (New York: Norton, 1975). The most complete study of the man and his music is D. Kern Holoman, *Berlioz* (Cambridge, Mass.: Harvard University Press, 1989); David Cairns, *Berlioz, 1803–1832: The Making of an Artist* (London: Deutsch, 1989). For a shorter introduction, see Hugh Macdonald, *Berlioz* (London: Dent, 1982). Other books: Peter Bloom, *The Life of Berlioz* (Cambridge: Cambridge University Press, 1998); Jacques Barzun, *Berlioz and the Romantic Century* (New York: Columbia University Press, 1969); Brian Primmer, *The Berlioz Style* (London: Oxford University Press, 1973); Julian Rushton, *The Musical Language of Berlioz* (Cambridge: Cambridge University Press, 1983); D. Kern Holoman, *The Creative Process in the Autograph Musical Documents of Hector Berlioz, ca. 1818–1840* (Ann Arbor: UMI Research Press, 1980); and his "The Present State of Berlioz Research," AM 47 (1975): 31–67; Edward T. Cone, ed., *Berlioz, Fantastic Symphony*, Norton Critical Scores (New York: Norton, 1971). For further references: Michael G. H. Wright, *A Berlioz Bibliography: Critical*

Writing on Hector Berlioz from 1825 to 1986 (Farnborough: Saint Michael's Abbey Press, 1988).

Brahms Recommended are Jan Swafford, *Johannes Brahms: A Biography* (New York: Alfred A. Knopf, 1997); Karl Geiringer, *Brahms, His Life and Work*, rev. ed. (London, 1961); James Burnett, *Brahms: A Critical Study* (New York: Praeger, 1972); and Malcolm MacDonald, *Brahms* (New York: Schirmer Books, 1990). For a more analytical approach, go to Walter Frisch, *Brahms and the Principle of Developing Variation* (Berkeley: University of California Press, 1984), and idem, ed., *Brahms and His World* (Princeton: Princeton University Press, 1990). Other books: *Brahms, Biographical, Documentary, and Analytical Studies*, ed. Robert Pascall (Vol. 1) and Michael Musgrave (Vol. 2) (Cambridge: Cambridge University Press, 1983–87); Leon Botstein, ed., *The Compleat Brahms: A Guide to the Musical Works of Johannes Brahms* (New York: Norton, 1999). Bernard Jacobson, *The Music of Johannes Brahms* (London, 1977); Edwin Evans, *Handbook to the Chamber and Orchestral Music*, 2 vols. (London: 1933–35); John Horton, *Brahms Orchestral Music* (Seattle: University of Washington Press, 1969); Max Harrison, *The Lieder of Brahms* (New York: Praeger, 1972); Arnold Schoenberg, "Brahms the Progressive," in his *Style and Idea* (New York: Philosophical Library, 1950), and in GLHWM 9:132–75. *Johannes Brahms: His Life and Letters*, selected and annotated by Styra Avins; trans. by Josef Eisinger and Styra Avins (New York: Oxford University Press, 1997). For further bibliography, see Thomas Quigley with Mary I. Ingraham, *Johannes Brahms: An Annotated Bibliography of the Literature from 1982 to 1996 with an Appendix on Brahms and the Internet* (Lanham, MD: Scarecrow Press, 1998).

Bruckner A helpful introduction is Robert Simpson's *The Essence of Bruckner*, 2nd ed. (London: Gollancz, 1977); see also Timothy L. Jackson and Paul Hawkshaw, eds., *Bruckner Studies* (New York: Cambridge University Press, 1997); Hans H. Schönzeler, *Bruckner* (London and New York: Grossman, 1970), and Erwin Doernberg, *The Life and Symphonies of Anton Bruckner* (London: Barrie & Rockliff, 1960; repr. 1968).

Chopin The standard study is Jim Samson, *Chopin* (New York: Oxford University Press, 1996). See also Jeffrey Kallberg, *Chopin at the Boundaries: Sex, History, and Musical Genre* (Cambridge, Mass.: Harvard University Press, 1996); Jean-Jacques Eigeldinger, *Chopin: Pianist and Teacher as Seen by His Pupils*, trans. Krysia Osostowics and Naomi Shohet, ed. Roy Howat (Cambridge: Cambridge University Press, 1987); J. Samson, ed., *Chopin Studies*; idem, *The Cambridge Companion to Chopin* (Cambridge: Cambridge University Press, 1988, 1992); Gerald Abraham, *Chopin's Musical Style* (London: Oxford University Press, 1939); Alan Walker, ed., *The Chopin Companion: Profiles of the Man and the Musician*, 2nd ed. (New York, 1973); *Selected Correspondence*, ed. and trans. A. Hedley (London: Heinemann, 1962); Thomas Higgins, ed., *Chopin, Preludes, Op. 28*, Norton Critical Scores (New York: Norton, 1973).

Clementi See Chapter 15.

Dvořák The best book in English is John Clapham's *Antonin Dvořák*, rev. ed. (New York: Norton, 1979). See also *Dvořák and His World*, ed. Michael Beckerman (Princeton: Princeton University Press, 1993). *Letters and Reminiscences*, ed. Otakar Šourek, trans. Roberta Samsour (Prague: Artia, 1958; repr. New York: Da Capo Press, 1983); Robert Layton, *Dvořák's Symphonies and Concertos* (London: BBC, 1978).

Franck Wilhelm Mohr, *César Franck*, 2nd ed. (Tutzing: H. Schneider, 1969), with thematic catalogue; Laurence Davies, *César Franck and His Circle* (London: Barrie & Jenkins, 1970); idem, *Franck* (London: Dent, 1973).

Liszt Alan Walker, *Franz Liszt: The Virtuoso Years, 1811–1847* (Ithaca, N.Y.: Cornell University Press, 1987); Humphrey Searle, *The Music of Liszt*, 2nd ed. (New York: Dover, 1966), a good introductory study but not up-to-date. See also A. Walker, comp., *Franz Liszt: The Man and His Music* (London: Barrie & Jenkins, 1970; 2nd ed., 1976); Michael Saffle and James Deaville, eds., *New Light on Liszt and His Music: Essays in Honor of Alan Walker's 65th Birthday* (Stuyvesant, N.Y.: Pendragon Press, 1997); Derek Watson, *Liszt* (New York: Schirmer Books, 1989); Liszt, *An Artist's Journey: Lettres d'un bachelier ès musique, 1835–1841*, trans. and annotated by Charles Suttoni (Chicago: University of Chicago Press, 1989); *Letters of Franz Liszt*, trans. Constance Bache (New York: C. Scribner, 1894); William R. Tyler, ed. and trans., *The Letters of Franz Liszt to Olga von Meyendorff, 1871–1886* (Cambridge, Mass.: Harvard University Press, 1979); M. Saffle, *Franz Liszt: A Guide to Research* (New York: Garland, 1991).

Mendelssohn Philip Radcliffe, *Mendelssohn*, rev. ed. (London: Dent, 1976), a general study; Wilfred Blunt, *On Wings of Song: A Biography of Felix Mendelssohn* (New York: Scribner's Sons, 1974), documented, with illustrations; *Felix Mendelssohn: A Life in Letters*, ed. Rudolf Elvers, trans. Craig Tomlinson (New York: Fromm International, 1986), originally published as *Felix Mendelssohn Bartholdy Briefe* (Frankfurt am Main, 1984). Specialized studies in *Mendelssohn and Schumann: Essays on Their Music and Its Context*, ed. Jon W. Finson and R. Larry Todd (Durham, N.C.: Duke University Press, 1984). An insightful study on Mendelssohn's musical training is Todd, *Mendelssohn's Musical Education: A Study and Edition of His Exercises in Composition* (Cambridge: Cambridge University Press, 1983).

Paganini G. I. C. de Courcy, *Paganini* (Norman: University of Oklahoma Press, 1957; repr. 1977); Alan Kendall, *Paganini: A Biography* (London: Chappell, 1982).

Schubert On Schubert's life, see Elizabeth Norman McKay, *Franz Schubert: A Biography* (Oxford: Clarendon Press, 1996); John Reed, *Schubert*, 2nd ed. (New York: Oxford University Press, 1997); O. E. Deutsch, *Schubert: A Documentary Biography*, trans. Eric Blom (London: Dent, 1946; repr. New York: Da Capo Press, 1977); O. E. Deutsch, ed., *The Schubert Reader: A Life of Franz Schubert in Letters and Documents*, trans. E. Blom (New York: Norton, 1947); O. E. Deutsch, ed. *Schubert: Memoirs by His Friends* (London: A. and C. Black, 1958); Maurice J. E. Brown, *Schubert: A Critical Biography* (London: Macmillan, 1958; repr. New York: Da Capo Press, 1977). For general studies on the composer's life and works, see Brian Newbould, *Schubert, the Music and the Man* (London: V. Gollancz, 1997); George R. Marek, *Schubert* (New York: Viking, 1985); M. J. E. Brown and Eric Sams, *The New Grove Schubert* (New York: Norton, 1983). Other books: Raymond Erickson, ed., *Schubert's Vienna* (New Haven: Yale University Press, 1997); Charles Osborne, *Schubert and His Vienna* (New York: Knopf, 1985); Walter Frisch, ed., *Schubert: Critical and Analytical Studies* (Lincoln: University of Nebraska Press, 1981); Brian Newbould. ed., *Schubert Studies* (Aldershot, Hants, Eng.: Ashgate, 1998); Eva Badura-Skoda, ed., *Schubert Studies* (Cambridge: Cambridge University Press, 1982); Roger Capell, *Schubert's Songs* (New York: Macmillan, 1957; 3rd ed., London: Duckworth, 1973); Susan Youens, *Schubert's Poets and the Making of Lieder* (Cambridge: Cambridge University Press, 1996); Marjorie Wing Hirsch, *Schubert's Dramatic Lieder* (Cambridge: Cambridge University Press, 1993); Lawrence Kramer, *Franz Schubert: Sexuality, Subjectivity, Song* (Cambridge: Cambridge University Press, 1998); Martin Chusid, ed., *Schubert, Symphony in B minor ("Unfinished")*, Norton Critical Scores (New York: Norton, 1968).

Clara Wieck Schumann Nancy B. Reich, *Clara Schumann: The Artist and the Woman* (Ithaca, N.Y.: Cornell University Press, 1985); Joan Chissell, *Clara Schumann, a Dedicated Spirit: A Study of Her Life and Work* (London: Hamilton, 1983); *The Complete Correspon-*

dence of Clara and Robert Schumann, ed. Eva Weissweiler, trans. Hildegard Fritsch, Ronald L. Crawford (New York: P. Lang, 1994–).

Robert Schumann For an introduction to his life and work, see John Daverio, *Robert Schumann: Herald of a "New Poetic Age"* (New York: Oxford University Press, 1997); Ronald Taylor, *Robert Schumann, His Life and Work* (New York: Universe Books, 1982); Joan Chissell, *Schumann*, rev. ed. (London: Dent, 1977); Alan Walker, ed., *Robert Schumann: The Man and His Music*, 2nd ed. (London: Barrie & Jenkins, 1976); R. Larry Todd. ed., *Schumann and His World* (Princeton: Princeton University Press, 1994); Gerald Abraham, ed., *Schumann: A Symposium* (London: Oxford University Press, 1952). Other books: Schumann, *On Music and Musicians*, trans. Paul Rosenfeld (New York: Pantheon Books, 1964); Leon Plantinga, *Schumann as Critic* (New Haven: Yale University Press, 1967); Eric Sams, *The Songs of Robert Schumann*, 2nd ed. (London: Methuen, 1975); Arthur Komar, ed., *Dichterliebe*, Norton Critical Scores (New York: Norton, 1971); Rufus Hallmark, *The Genesis of Schumann's Dichterliebe: A Source Study* (Ann Arbor, Mich.: UMI Research Press, 1979).

Tchaikovsky The most comprehensive biography is by David Brown in 4 vols.—*Tchaikovsky: The Early Years, 1840–1874* (New York: Norton, 1978); *The Crisis Years, 1874–1878* (New York: Norton, 1982); *The Years of Wandering, 1878–1885* (New York: Norton, 1986); and *The Final Years* (New York: Norton, 1992). A shorter study is Edward Garden's *Tchaikovsky* (London: Dent, 1973). Other books: John Warrack, *Tchaikovsky* (London: Hamilton, 1973); Tchaikovsky, *Letters to His Family: An Autobiography*, trans. Galina von Meck (New York: Stein & Day, 1981); Alexander Poznansky, *Tchaikovsky: The Quest for the Inner Man* (New York: Schirmer Books, 1991). On the music: Gerald Abraham, ed., *The Music of Tchaikovsky* (New York: Norton, 1946); Henry Zajaczkowski, *Tchaikovsky's Musical Style* (Ann Arbor, Mich.: UMI Research Press, 1987).

CHAPTER 17

SOLO, CHAMBER, AND VOCAL MUSIC IN THE NINETEENTH CENTURY

THE PIANO

The piano of the nineteenth century was quite different from the one in Mozart's day. Nor was it the same as our modern piano, with its iron frame, greater string tension, ringing and sustained sound, and big volume. By 1800 the piano had been reshaped, enlarged to seven octaves, provided with felt-covered hammers, and strengthened by metal plates and braces. It was capable of producing a full, firm tone at any dynamic level, of responding in every way to demands for both expressiveness and virtuosity. The piano was the quintessential instrument of the salon or living room and therefore it created a steady demand for music that amateurs and professionals could play in a domestic setting. This was particularly important to freelance composers like Schubert and Chopin.

Performing styles

At the beginning of the century there were two distinct schools of piano playing. One, represented by Mozart's talented pupil Johann Nepomuk Hummel (1778–1837), emphasized clear textures and fluent technique. The other school, to which Beethoven belonged, emphasized full tone, wide dynamic range, orchestral effects, dramatic execution, and an abundance of technical equipment. Both styles are present in the works of Muzio Clementi, influential Italian composer, pianist, teacher, and manufacturer of pianos. Clementi's famous *Gradus ad Parnassum*, published 1817–26, consists of one hundred études "in strict and free style," that is, contrapuntal exercises and virtuoso studies; his many sonatas were highly regarded by Beethoven. (See NAWM 102 and the discussion on pages 517–20.)

Composers and performers

Later in the nineteenth century several more approaches to piano performance and composition emerged. Elegance, sentiment, brightness, and clarity

■ *Grand piano by Anton Walter and Son, Vienna, ca. 1810.* (YALE UNIVERSITY, COLLECTION OF MUSICAL INSTRUMENTS)

were achieved by Clementi's pupil John Field (1782–1837), whose nocturnes served as models for Chopin (see NAWM 108; CD 9 [18]). Hummel's pupil Adolf von Henselt (1814–1899) was noted for his legato playing of fast arpeggios. Chopin's early works show Hummel's influence. Other pianists celebrated for their audacity and showmanship were Friedrich Kalkbrenner (1785–1849), Henri Herz (1803–1888), Sigismund Thalberg (1812–1871), and the globe-trotting American Louis Moreau Gottschalk (1829–1869)—all successful display pianists and composers whose works were published widely in Europe and America. Standing apart from these was Valentin Alkan (1813–1888), friend and admirer of Chopin, who included earlier Classic works in his concert programs and wrote exacting and long pieces that challenged even his own virtuosity. Then there were the "titans of the piano," outstanding for both technical and interpretive gifts: Franz Liszt, Anton Rubinstein (1829–1894), Hans von Bülow (1830–1894), and Karl Tausig (1841–1871). Of these, Liszt and Rubinstein left their mark as composers and von Bülow as a conductor.

MUSIC FOR PIANO

The nineteenth-century cult of expressive, songful melody presented a challenge to composers of piano music. The long lyrical lines so natural to the voice had to be contained within the limits of ten fingers without sacrificing the active accompaniments that had become fashionable in lieder and in piano arrangements of opera arias. One way to accommodate both was by splitting the accompaniment between the two hands; deft fingerings and pedaling enabled the player to bring out a legato melody with some fingers of the right hand while the remaining ones provided harmonic figuration. An inner "alto"

Example 17.1 *Felix Mendelssohn,* Lieder ohne Worte, *Op. 38, No. 6: Duetto, Andante con moto*

or "tenor" voice could also be projected this way. Mendelssohn's *Lieder ohne Worte* abound with examples of this tactic. Example 17.1 shows the last notes of a soprano melody and a tenor response.

By embedding the melody in harmonic figuration spanning an octave, as in Example 17.2, we get an illusion of orchestral doubling at the octave, while a hornlike part provides an inner voice paralleling the melody. The resonance and power of the modern piano invited exploration in loud, full chords with a variety of touch, shadings, and accents (Example 17.3 and NAWM 107a; CD 9 [12] / 3 ⟨49⟩). These are some of the ways that composers adapted their expressive designs to the instrument and took advantage of its potential.

Example 17.2 *Robert Schumann,* Phantasiestücke, *Op. 12: Aufschwung,* Sehr rasch

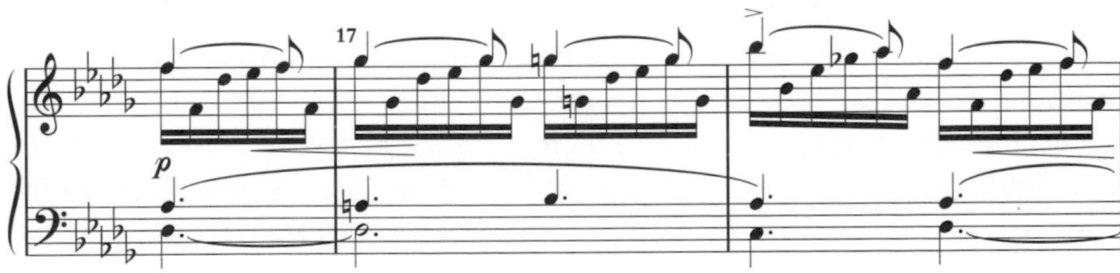

Example 17.3 *Robert Schumann,* Phantasiestücke, *Op. 12:* Grillen

The Early Romantic Composers

Weber

The piano works of Carl Maria von Weber (1786–1826) include four sonatas, two concertos, and the better-known *Konzertstück* in F minor for piano and orchestra (1821), as well as many short pieces. *Aufforderung zum Tanz* (Invitation to the Dance, 1819) has been played by generations of pianists and enjoys a parallel life in its orchestral version. Weber's piano style is rhythmic, picturesque, full of contrast, and technically brilliant.

Bohemians A distinctive school of pianists and composers came out of Bohemia in the early nineteenth century. Jan Ladislav Dussek was known throughout Europe especially for his sonatas, which include some notable examples of early Romantic harmony. Jan Václav Tomášek (1774–1850) and his pupil Jan Hugo Voríšek (1791–1825) wrote short lyrical piano pieces with titles such as *eclogue*, *rhapsodie*, and *impromptu*. Voríšek composed a remarkable piano sonata, Op. 20; he moved to Vienna in 1813 and exerted a strong influence on Schubert.

Schubert

Output In addition to marches, waltzes, and other dances, Franz Schubert wrote fourteen short pieces that became for piano literature what his lieder were to the vocal repertory. Each of his six *Moments musicaux* (D. 789)[1] and eight Impromptus (D. 899, 935) creates a distinctive mood, and the works became models for every subsequent composer of intimate piano pieces. Schubert's most important larger works for the piano are his eleven completed sonatas and a Fantasia in C major (1822) on a theme adapted from his song *Der Wanderer*. The *Wanderer Fantasie* (D. 760), unlike most of his other compositions for piano, makes considerable demands on the player's technique. Its four movements, which are linked together, center around the Adagio and Variations; the theme is the song itself. The remaining movements use motives from the song as well. He composed serious duets for piano four-hands, among them the *Grand Duo* (D. 812), the sublime and haunting Fantasia in F minor (D. 940), and the Rondo in A major (D. 951). He wrote no concertos.

Sonatas In his sonatas Schubert departs in subtle ways from the standard Classic patterns by using "substitute" dominants and introducing three keys in his expositions instead of two. Schubert's expansive melodies in his sonata movements, though not themes that lend themselves to motivic development, recur in different environments that give them new meaning each time. Some of the slow movements might well have been published as impromptus or *moments musicaux*—in particular, those from the sonatas in B major, Op. 147 (D. 575), and A major, Op. 120 (D. 664). The three sonatas of 1825–26, in A minor, D major, and G major (Opp. 42, 53, and 78 = D. 845, 850, 894), are on a larger scale than the earlier ones but not radically different in character. Schumann wrote of them, "We must call all three of these sonatas of Schubert 'masterly,' but the third seems to us his most perfect one, both in form and spirit."

In composing his last three piano sonatas (all 1828) Schubert was obviously aware of Beethoven's works, as witness the stormy first movement of the

1. Schubert's works are best identified by the number assigned to them in Otto Erich Deutsch and Donald R. Wakeling, *Schubert: Thematic Catalogue of All His Works in Chronological Order* (London and New York, 1951); corrections and additions by O. E. Deutsch in *Music and Letters* 34 (1953):25–32; trans., rev., and enl. by Walter Dürr, Arnold Feil, Christa Landon, and others as *Franz Schubert: Thematisches Verzeichnis seiner Werke in chronologischer Folge von Otto Erich Deutsch*, Neue Ausgabe Sämtlicher Werke 8/4 (Kassel: Bärenreiter, 1978).

Example 17.4 *Franz Schubert, Sonata in B♭: Molto moderato*

Sonata in C minor (D. 958) and the finale of the Sonata in B♭ (D. 960), which begins somewhat like the finale of Beethoven's Quartet Op. 130. But these are superficial similarities; Schubert is nowhere more independent, more the lyricist, than in these sonatas. The last of these, in B♭, perhaps his greatest work for the piano, opens with a long singing melody, doubled at the lower octave and sixth below that (Example 17.4). Before the dominant section is reached in the exposition Schubert spins out a long digression in F♯ major, prolonging the upper-neighbor to the dominant heard in the trill on G♭ at the end of Example 17.4. The singing melody returns in various guises in both major and minor, both complete and fragmented, as if set to new words in conflict with those of before. The slow movement is in C♯ minor (the enharmonic lowered mediant key), with a middle section in A major. The delicately varied ostinato rhythm of this movement is typical of Schubert, as are the expressive suspensions and the unexpected shifts between major and minor in the coda.

Mendelssohn

Career

Felix Mendelssohn was himself a virtuoso pianist. Although his piano music requires a fluent technique, the style does not indulge in violence or excess bravura. Mendelssohn's harmony has few of the surprises that one encounters in Schubert, nor do his melodies, rhythms, and forms introduce many unexpected features. His larger compositions for piano comprise two concertos—one of which, the Concerto in G minor (1831), was long a favorite with pianists—three sonatas, preludes and fugues, variations, and fantasias. The preludes and fugues reveal Mendelssohn's interest in the music of J. S. Bach. (The performance he conducted in Leipzig of the *St. Matthew Passion* helped spark a revival of Bach's music, which led eventually to the publication of his complete works in forty-seven monumental volumes.)

A certain elfin lightness and clarity in scherzo-like movements, a quality unique to Mendelssohn's music, is evident in the familiar *Andante and Rondo Capriccioso*, Op. 14, which was probably written when the composer was fifteen. In a similar vein but more brilliant is the *Capriccio* in F♯ minor, Op. 5 (1825). An ambitious large work for piano is the *Variations sérieuses* in D minor, Op. 54 (1841).

Lieder ohne Worte

The eight books of forty-eight short pieces issued at intervals under the collective title *Lieder ohne Worte* (Songs without Words; most of the names attached to the separate pieces were supplied by publishers) contain many distinguished examples of the short piano piece and of Mendelssohn at his best. Among his last works, composed on two days in May 1845, Op. 85, no. 4 (published posthumously; NAWM 106a; CD 9 [7]), and Op. 67, no. 4 (published in 1845; NAWM 106b; [9]), exploit the pianoforte's ability to respond to the player's varying touch, louder for the melody, softer for the accompaniment, even when the two are played by fingers of the same hand. The accompaniment of Op. 85, no. 4, uses a rising arpeggio followed by a descending broken chord pattern in sixteenth notes, relieved only at crucial cadences and turning points. In Op. 67, no. 4, alternating sixteenth notes accompany the melody, and, when the melody is absent in the introduction and interludes, a chromatic figure takes its place. This piece further tests the performer's technique because the melodic notes are frequently embedded in the accompanying pattern. While the first example requires the instrument to sustain a lyrical line, the second demands a playful lightness. The pianos manufactured in the mid-nineteenth century rose to these challenges.

Organ works

Mendelssohn's three organ preludes and fugues and six sonatas are among the century's most distinguished contributions to the literature of that instrument. Most of the sonata movements were first written as separate voluntaries and only later brought into their present state. Notable in the sonatas is the frequent fugal writing, as is Mendelssohn's use of Lutheran chorale melodies, particularly in the first movement of the Third Sonata and the first two movements of the Sixth Sonata.

■ *Felix Mendelssohn performing for the young Queen Victoria and the Prince Consort. In 1842, on one of his numerous visits to England, Mendelssohn was twice received by the Queen. In gratitude he dedicated the Scottish Symphony to her. Engraving by H, Hannal after G. Durand.* (LONDON, MANSELL COLLECTION/TIMEPIX)

Robert Schumann

Career

After university studies in law, Robert Schumann devoted himself with enthusiasm to becoming a concert pianist. An injury to his right hand cut short this career. He then turned his energies wholly to composition and to the Leipzig *Neue Zeitschrift für Musik* (New Journal of Music), which he edited from 1834 to 1844. His essays and reviews became an important force in the Romantic movement; he was one of the first to recognize the genius of Chopin and Brahms as well as Schubert's instrumental music. All of Schumann's published compositions (Opp. 1–23) up to 1840 were for piano, and, except for his one concerto (1845), they include most of his important works for that instrument. The concerto, the Fantasia in C major, Op. 17 (1836), and the set of variations titled *Symphonische Etüden* (1834–37) comprise his most important longer works for piano, though he also wrote several other sets of variations and three sonatas. The rest of his piano compositions are short character pieces, which he often grouped into loosely organized cycles that are colorfully named: *Papillons* (Butterflies), *Carnaval, Phantasiestücke* (Fantasy Pieces; see NAWM 107; CD 9 [12] / 3 ⟨49⟩), *Kinderscenen* (Scenes from Childhood), *Kreisleriana, Novelletten, Nachtstücke* (Night Pieces), and *Faschingsschwank aus Wien* (Carnival Fun from Vienna). Attractive little pieces for children are gathered in the *Album für die Jugend* (Album for the Young).

Output

Extramusical associations

The titles he gave to the collections and to separate pieces suggest that Schumann wanted listeners to associate them with extramusical poetic fancies. This attitude, typical of the period, is significant, considering Schumann's admission that he usually wrote the music before he thought of the title. He instilled in his music the depths, contradictions, and tensions of his own personality. It is by turns ardent and dreamy, vehement and visionary, whimsical and learned. Both in his literary writings and in a piano work entitled *Davidsbündlertänze*, the different facets of his own nature are personified in the figures of Florestan, Eusebius, and Raro, members of an imaginary league called the *Davidsbund*, which took its name from the biblical David and campaigned against the Philistines of music. Florestan was the impulsive revolutionary, Eusebius the youthful dreamer, and Raro the wise, mature master. Musical sketches of the first two characters appear in *Carnaval*. We might also say that Florestan speaks in the fiery finale of the *Symphonische Etüden*, Eusebius in the Aria of the F♯-minor Sonata (based on the melody of an early song), and Raro in the *Studien für den Pedal-Flügel*, Op. 56, a set of canons for piano with a pedal keyboard. Raro is also unmasked in the fugues of Opp. 60, 72, and 126 and the subtly contrapuntal inner voices and fugal passages in many of Schumann's other piano works that pay homage to the music of Bach. He advised students: "Diligently play fugues of good masters, especially those of Johann Sebastian Bach. Let the *Well-Tempered Keyboard* be your daily bread and you will certainly become a fine musician."[2]

2. This is among the maxims first published in *Neue Zeitschrift für Musik*, Vol. 32 (1850), Appendix to no. 36, and in the second edition of the *Album for the Young*, Op. 32, 1851.

Example 17.5 *Robert Schumann*, Phantasiestücke, *Op. 12:* In der Nacht

Phantasiestücke

Schumann gave each of the *Phantasiestücke* (Fantasy Pieces) a whimsical title; what binds them together is their flights of fantasy. *Grillen* (Whims, NAWM 107a; CD 9 [12] / 3 ⟨49⟩) exemplifies Schumann's approach to composition at the time. Four-measure phrases join to form five distinct musical periods, which recur in the rondo-like pattern A B C B A–D E–A B C B A. Although the periods are subtly linked through rhythmic, melodic, and harmonic motives, as well as *Viertaktigkeit* ("four-barredness"), they are essentially independent blocks of music. The periods are repeated intact and can be joined front to back or back to front, that is, A can proceed to B, B to A, C to B, and so forth. Like most of Schumann's short pieces, *Grillen* has a triple-time dance flavor in which the middle section (D E) functions as a trio.

In der Nacht (In the Night, NAWM 107b; CD 9 [15]), marked "Mit Leidenschaft" (with passion), has a persistent sixteenth-note motion in $\frac{2}{4}$, a true *moto perpetuo.* A repeated broken-chord figure serves as a background to a descending-second motive and brief melodic eruptions in triplets (Example 17.5). Unprepared lower neighbors (for example, the G♯ in measure 5, the F♯ in measure 6) disturb the smooth surface of the broken chords.

Fryderyk Chopin (1810–1849)

Chopin wrote almost exclusively for the piano. His principal works are 2 concertos and a few other large pieces for piano with orchestra, 3 sonatas, 27 études, 4 scherzos, 4 ballades, 24 preludes, 4 impromptus, 21 nocturnes, numerous waltzes, mazurkas, and polonaises, a *Barcarolle* in F♯, a *Berceuse* in D♭, a *Fantasia* in F minor, and a cello sonata.

National idiom

Although Chopin lived in Paris from 1831, he never stopped loving his native Poland or grieving because of its political misfortunes. The failure of the Polish revolt against Russian domination in 1830 was not his reason for leaving Warsaw, as it was for many other exiles who settled in Paris. He was in Germany en route to London when he got the news, and continued to France, where he settled. But he shared with other expatriates the dream of Polish independence. Some of his friends and colleagues back home thought he should do more for Polish national music, like write an opera on a patriotic theme, but in his own nonactivist way, he expessed his ardor and faith in a happier Polish future by composing mazurkas suffused with the rhythms, harmonies, forms, and melodic traits of Polish dance music. These pieces are among the earliest and best examples of music inspired by national idioms. He incorporated the "Lydian" raised fourth characteristic of Polish folk music—as well as of some other European folk idioms—in his earliest works. Chopin's polonaises go beyond the conventional character piece of Bach's time to assert a national identity. The knightly and heroic spirit of his native land glows anew in some of them, particularly those in A♭ (Op. 53) and F♯ minor (Op. 44).

Performing style

Most of Chopin's pieces are introspective and, within clearly defined formal outlines, suggest the quality of improvisation. An infrequent public performer, Chopin was not theatrically overwhelming as a pianist, and other virtuosos have emphasized the heroic side of his music more than he himself could or would have. All his works, however, demand of the player not only a flawless technique and delicate touch but also an imaginative use of the pedals and a discreet application of *tempo rubato*, which Chopin described as a slight pushing or holding back of the right-hand part while the left-hand accompaniment continues in strict time (although the composer himself was known to depart from the regular pulse in both hands at once).

Field's Nocturnes

The nocturnes, impromptus, and preludes are Chopin's most intimate works. Chopin's initial conception of the nocturne owed much to the nocturnes by the Irish pianist and composer John Field (1782–1837). Both composers also drew inspiration from the vocal nocturne, a type of vocal music related to the romance but written for two or more voices with piano or harp accompaniment that was popular in the first decade of the nineteenth century. Field's teacher, Clementi, took him to St. Petersburg in 1802 and helped him get established there. His nocturnes, the first of which appeared in 1814, reflect Field's fluent, pearly runs, and lavish pianistic technique, which so impressed Liszt when he heard him in Paris.

Field's Nocturne No. 8 (NAWM 108; CD 9 [18]) exhibits a number of parallels to Chopin's, particularly the rising major sixth, the soulful turn, and the chromatic ornamentation of the melody against a chordal accompaniment (Example 17.6a, page 580). In embellishing this line (Example 17.6b) Field looked to the ornamentation and cadenzas practiced by opera singers and taken over by pianists in their improvised sets of variations on favorite arias (many such sets have come down to us as published pieces). Although Field anticipated some of Chopin's mannerisms, he could not match the rich harmonic imagination that so powerfully supports Chopin's lyrical lines, as in the E♭ Nocturne (NAWM 109; CD 9 [19] / 3 ◇52◇).

Preludes

Chopin composed his preludes at a time when he was deeply immersed in the music of Bach. Like the preludes in *The Well-Tempered Keyboard*, these brief, sharply defined mood pictures utilize all the major and minor keys, though the circle of fifths determine the succession: C major, A minor, G major, E minor, and so on. Bach's are arranged in rising chromatic steps: C major, C minor, C♯ major, C♯ minor, etc. Chopin's rich chromatic harmonies and modulations, which influenced later composers, are evident in many of the preludes, most notably in Nos. 2, 4, 8, and in the middle sections of Nos. 14 and 24.

Ballades

Chopin projected his artistic ideas onto a larger canvas in the ballades and scherzos. He was the first composer known to have used the name *ballade* for

Example 17.6 *John Field, Nocturne No. 8*

an instrumental piece. His works in this genre—especially Op. 23 in G minor and Op. 52 in F minor—capture the charm and fire of the narrative ballads written by the great Polish poet Adam Mickiewicz, combining these qualities with constantly fresh turns in harmony and form. The principal scherzos are his Op. 20 in B minor, Op. 31 in B♭ minor/D♭ major, and Op. 39 in C♯ minor. They are serious, vigorous, and passionate works rather than "joking" or "playful," which the title "scherzo" implies; but they are tricky and quirky, which the term also implies, particularly in their thematic material and rhythm.

Scherzos

The Scherzo Op. 31, which begins in B♭ minor and ends in D♭ major, surely exhibits these qualities, as well as the scherzo—trio—scherzo form. The opening theme (Example 17.7) lays claim to the entire keyboard and takes advantage of both the soft and sustaining pedals to realize an orchestral effect. Although made up of four-measure phrases, the rests and the measures of silence surprise the listener, as a good trick should do. It is not a theme we want to sing; it is strictly instrumental. In the scherzo section—a binary dance-form, expanded in the manner of a sonata—a brief modulation leads from the opening theme section to one in the relative major, D♭, which after some widely spaced tonic-dominant flourishes elaborates for fifty-two bars a long-breathed singing melody accompanied by a rapid broken-chord pattern. After some briliant cadential dominant-tonic broken-chord effects, this entire exposition is repeated with modest embellishment. The trio, in A major, by contrast, is based on motives having a very narrow compass and contains the greatest

Example 17.7 *Fryderyk Chopin, Scherzo, Op. 31*

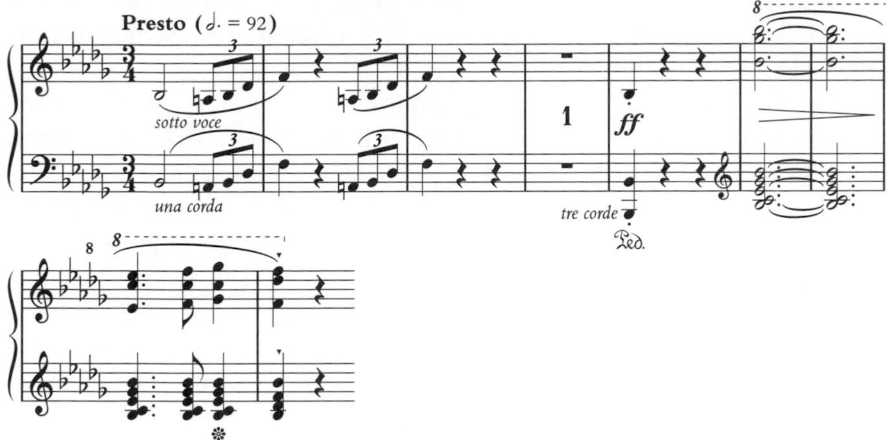

amount of thematic development, mingling the closing material of the scherzo at the end of the trio section. The scherzo is then recapitulated. The coda develops scherzo material, cleverly pitting the opening flourishes against the lyrical melody of the second theme section.

Fantasias

On an equally grand scale but even more varied in content is the great Fantasia in F minor (Op. 49), a worthy companion to the fantasias of Schubert and Schumann. The *Polonaise-Fantaisie*, Op. 61, Chopin's last large work for the piano, and the Cello Sonata, Op. 65, point in directions he probably would have explored had he lived longer than his thirty-nine years.

Études

Chopin's études—twelve in each of Opp. 10 and 25, and three without opus number—are important landmarks in defining the piano idiom. Because études are intended primarily to develop technique, each one as a rule is devoted to a specific technical skill and develops a single figure. Among the formations exercised in Op. 25 are parallel diatonic and chromatic thirds in the right hand (No. 6), parallel sixths in the right hand (No. 8), and chromatic octaves in both hands (No. 10). In No. 11, a brilliant yet highly evocative étude, the right hand spins out a perpetual filigree of sixteenth notes against a vigorous march theme in the left hand (Example 17.8). Through much of the piece the right hand's passage work alternates between chromatic appoggiaturas or passing notes and chord tones. Chopin's études are transcendent studies in

Example 17.8 *Fryderyk Chopin, Étude, Op. 25, No. 11*

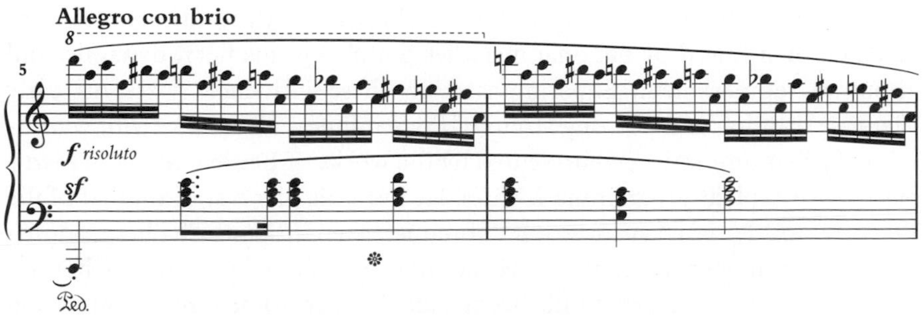

technique and intensely concentrated poetic statements. Unlike thousands of contemporaneous piano études, Chopin's successfully combine the practical goal of developing advanced technique with significant artistic content; Liszt and Brahms followed his lead.

Sonatas

The B♭-minor Sonata, Op. 35, resisted by critics and players at first, eventually entered the repertoires of pianists such as Bülow, Liszt, and Busoni. Opus 35 is in four movements, including the famous funeral march that, orchestrated, was played at Chopin's own funeral. The finale, in spare parallel octaves throughout, made up of twelve eighth-notes to the bar in presto tempo and occupying less than two minutes, shocked listeners. The first movement is unusual because the first subject, built on a brief syncopated motive, is worked over extensively in the development section but overlooked in the recapitulation in favor of an intense, sweeping, lyrical second theme. The B-minor Sonata, Op. 58, with its attractive themes and more conventional set of movements, including an Allegro maestoso, Scherzo, Largo, and a brilliant grand Finale, won adherents more readily.

Concertos

The comparatively early concertos in E minor, Op. 11, and in F minor, Op. 21 (1830 and 1829, respectively), contain some beautiful pianistic writing, especially in the slow movements. Following the fashion in works by pianist-composers, the relationship between piano and orchestra is that of a solo with accompaniment and interludes rather than that of an equal partnership.

Liszt

Franz Liszt (1811–1886) was born in Hungary, son of an official in the service of Prince Nicholas Esterházy. He studied piano with Carl Czerny in Vienna and at the age of eleven began a dazzling career as a concert virtuoso that lasted, with a few interruptions, until 1848. During most of this time he made his home in Paris. From 1848 to 1861 he was court music director at Weimar, where he encouraged new music by conducting performances of many important works, among them the premiere of Wagner's *Lohengrin* in 1850. Several well-publicized love affairs with women of elevated social status, and honors showered upon him all over Europe, added glamor to his fame as pianist, conductor, and composer. From 1861 until about 1870 Liszt resided chiefly in Rome, where he took minor orders in the Catholic Church. The remainder of his life was divided among Rome, Weimar, and Budapest.

Style

Liszt's cosmopolitan career was matched by his eclectic style, the result of many diverse factors. His Hungarian roots show not only in his compositions based on or inspired by national melodies but also in his fiery, dynamic, and impulsive temperament. Superimposed on these influences were his early Viennese training and a strong strain of French literary Romanticism, with its ideal of program music as represented by the works of Berlioz; many of Liszt's pieces have explicit programmatic titles. He built his piano style on that of the Viennese and Parisian virtuosos, Kalkbrenner, Henselt, and Thalberg, adding his own stunning effects to theirs. He adopted as well the lyricism of Chopin's melodic line, his *rubato* rhythmic license, and his harmonic innovations, again amplifying and enhancing them.

Paganini's influence

In Paris Liszt came under the spell of the great Italian violinist Nicolò Paganini (1782–1840), one of the most hypnotic artists of the nineteenth century. Stimulated by Paganini's fabulous technical virtuosity, Liszt resolved to accomplish similar miracles with the piano. He pushed the technique of the instrument to its furthest limits both in his own playing and in his compositions. He directly imitated the master in his six *Études d'exécution transcendante d'après Paganini* (1851), transcribing five of Paganini's Caprices, Op. 1, for solo violin, and *La Campanella* from the Violin Concerto No. 2 in B minor. While Liszt's technical innovations served to display his keyboard skills, they also allowed him to realize a musical rhetoric equal to his expressive designs.

Un sospiro

Liszt aimed his *Trois études de concert* (1849) at particular technical problems. In *Un sospiro* (A Sigh, NAWM 110; CD 9 [20] / 3 ⟨53⟩), for example, it is the projection of a slower moving melody outside or within rapid broken-chord figurations. The pedal makes this possible by sustaining harmonies while the two hands brave treacherous leaps over each other to pick out a cool pentatonic tune and then a tonally anchored answer.

Transcriptions

Much of Liszt's piano music consists of arrangements: transcriptions of Schubert songs, Berlioz and Beethoven symphonies, Bach organ fugues, excerpts from Wagner's music dramas, and fantasies on operatic airs. These pieces were useful in their day for bringing important works to a wide audience either unacquainted with the originals or pleased to hear a familiar work transformed into a brilliant virtuoso vehicle through the creativity of a second composer. By transferring orchestral idioms to the piano Liszt demonstrated new possibilities for that instrument. Liszt also wrote piano music that makes free use of national tunes. Chief among these are nineteen *Hungarian Rhapsodies*, based on Hungarian Romany music and ornamentation.

Études

His piano studies include a set of the twelve formidable *Études d'exécution transcendante*. Originally published as simple exercises in 1826, they were scaled up to a higher level of technique in 1839 and given individual titles in

■ *Hector Berlioz and Carl Czerny (standing), with Liszt at the piano and violinist Heinrich Wilhelm Ernst at his right. The creator of this 1846 lithograph, Joseph Kriehuber (1800–1876), observes from the left.*

the somewhat easier edition of 1852. Five years earlier, Liszt had expanded and orchestrated the frequently played No. 4, *Mazeppa*, to produce a tone poem about the hero of Hugo's poem. An introductory toccata-like Allegro is followed by a series of variations on a melody—really transformations—in which different moods are established: martial, lyrical, playful, and decisive.

Concertos

Liszt's compositions for piano and orchestra include three concertos, two in E♭ major and one in A major, the *Fantasia on Hungarian Folk Melodies* (1853), and *Totentanz* (Dance of Death, 1849), a paraphrase on the plainsong *Dies irae*. The Piano Concerto No. 1 in E♭ was completed in 1849 and revised in 1855. The four movements are linked together by themes that are transformed from movement to movement. Indeed, Liszt's method of thematic transformation is clearly evident in this concerto. Example 17.9 shows how the theme of the Quasi Adagio is transformed in subsequent appearances from mysterious (a) to lyrical (b and c) and to martial (d).

Short pieces

The breadth of Liszt's poetic imagination is displayed in many of his short, separately published piano pieces. It is also seen in several collections of tone pictures, including *Harmonies poétiques et religieuses* (1834), *Consolations* (1850), and *Années de pélerinage* (Years of Pilgrimage; Books 1 and 2 composed before 1850, Book 3, 1867–77). These collections, which contain some of his best compositions, negate the all too common impression of Liszt as concerned only with bravura effects.

Sonata in B minor

In the Sonata in B minor (1853)—one of the outstanding piano compositions of the nineteenth century—four themes are worked out in one extended movement that is subdivided into three sections analogous to the movements of a Classic sonata. The themes are transformed and combined in a free rhapsodic order, but one that is perfectly suited to the thematic

Example 17.9 *Franz Liszt, Piano Concerto No. 1 in E♭: Thematic Transformations*

c.

d.

material. In this work Liszt successfully adapted the cyclic strategy of the symphonic poem.

Late works

In some of his late works, Liszt experimented with harmonies that surprisingly anticipate late nineteenth- and twentieth-century developments. He was one of the first composers to make extensive use of augmented triads (see Example 16.7, page 557), which are prominent in the B-minor Sonata and in the late piano piece *Nuages gris* (Gray Clouds, 1881). In this short composition, originally called *Trübe Wolken* (Gloomy Clouds), Liszt experimented with unconventional harmony, particularly augmented chords (Example 17.10).

Example 17.10 *Franz Liszt,* Nuages gris

Organ works

Liszt wrote about a dozen works for organ, the most important of which are an extended *Fantasia and Fugue* (1850) on a chorale theme from Giacomo Meyerbeer's opera *Le Prophète*, and a Prelude and Fugue on the letters B–A–C–H (the German spelling of the notes *Bb, A, C, B*).

Brahms

Johannes Brahms was the great conservative of the Romantic era. He did without such pianistic luxuries as Chopin's elegant ornamentation and Liszt's brilliance and rhetoric; his models, rather, were Beethoven and Schumann. Technically his piano style is characterized by full sonority; broken-chord figuration; frequent doubling of the melodic line in octaves, thirds, or sixths; multiple chordlike appoggiaturas; and considerable use of cross-rhythms. These words do not begin to describe the imaginative innovations in texture and the excitement generated by his resourceful development of simple ideas.

Works for piano

Brahms's works for the piano include three sonatas, several sets of variations, and some thirty-five shorter pieces with titles such as ballade, rhapsody, capriccio, and intermezzo. Chief among the larger works are two concertos, particularly the magisterial No. 2 in B♭ (1878–81), the Sonata in F minor (1853), the *Variations and Fugue on a Theme of Handel* (1861), and the difficult, étude-like *Variations on a Theme of Paganini* (1863). Brahms favored variations, not only in his piano music but in other media as well—evidence of his inclination toward Classic forms. He avoided the descriptive titles used by Schumann and Liszt; indeed, he was unsympathetic to program music and to the extreme tendencies of Romanticism in general. His eleven chorale preludes for the organ, written during the last years of his life, hark back to those of Bach.

Other Composers

Among the piano music of Brahms's contemporaries, two Russian works stand out: Modest Musorgsky's *Pictures at an Exhibition* (1874), now better known in Maurice Ravel's orchestration, and Mily Balakirev's Sonata in B♭ minor (1855–56) and *Islamey* (1869; second version 1902).

Franck

The Belgian composer and organist César Franck (1822–1890) also produced distinguished piano music, including a Prelude, Chorale, and Fugue (1884), a Prelude, Aria, and Finale (1887), and the *Symphonic Variations* for piano and orchestra (1885). Franck studied in Paris and made his home there after 1844. Like Brahms, he sought to incorporate the achievements of Romanticism within a Classic framework, but with a harmonic idiom influenced somewhat by the chromaticism of Liszt and Wagner. His compositions for organ include several sets of short pieces and three so-called *Chorales* (1890), which actually are richly developed fantasias on original themes. He founded a new school of organ music in France, and inspired a renewed vitality of French musical education and composition that began with the establishment of the Société nationale de musique française (National Society for French Music) in 1871.

Two women made marks in their day as pianist-composers. Fanny Hensel (1805–1847), Felix Mendelssohn's sister, composed more than four hundred works, chiefly piano pieces and songs, although very few were published during her lifetime. She performed them in her Sunday musicales, a flourishing salon, for which she created most of her compositions. Clara Wieck Schumann (1819–1896) had a remarkable career as a pianist, composer, sponsor of other composers' music, wife of Robert Schumann, mother of eight, and close friend of Brahms. From an early age, she was trained to become a concert pianist by her father, Friedrich Wieck (who also taught Hans von Bülow). Recognized as a child prodigy from her first public appearance in Leipzig at the age of nine, she toured throughout Europe and earned the praise of Goethe, Mendelssohn, Chopin, Paganini, and Schumann. Although she curbed her concertizing after marrying Schumann and while raising a large family, she continued to perform, compose, and teach throughout her long life. Her works include two piano concertos, a piano trio, many pieces for piano, and several collections of lieder (see pages 596–97 and NAWM 114).

Fanny Hensel

Clara Schumann

CHAMBER MUSIC

The medium of chamber music was not congenial to many Romantic composers. It lacked the intimate personal communication of the solo piano piece or the lied and the glowing colors and powerful sound of orchestral music. It is therefore not surprising that Berlioz, Liszt, and Wagner contributed nothing to chamber music, nor that the best nineteenth-century chamber works came from those composers who felt closest to the Classic tradition—Schubert, Brahms, and, to a lesser degree, Mendelssohn and Schumann.

Schubert

Schubert modeled his first quartets on works by Mozart and Haydn and wrote them primarily for his friends to enjoy. He consolidated his own style in the E-major Quartet of 1816 (D. 353), combining warmth of sonority with clarity of line. The most popular work from his early period is the *Trout* Quintet for piano, violin, viola, cello, and bass (1819), so called because of the Andantino variations, inserted between the scherzo and the finale, on his own song *Die Forelle* (The Trout). Schubert's mature period in chamber music begins in 1820 with an Allegro in C minor, D. 703, commonly called the *Quartettsatz*, intended as the first movement of a string quartet that he never completed. Three important works followed—the Quartets in A minor, D. 804 (1824), D minor, D. 810 (1824–26, nicknamed "Death and the Maiden"), and G major, D. 887 (1826).

Trout Quintet

The A-minor Quartet begins with a long singing melody that cries out for words, while the lower strings provide harmony and rhythmic ostinatos but no counterpoint for thirty-one measures. Then, out of the first few notes of the melody, Schubert builds animated transitional episodes, the second theme

Quartet in A minor

group, and most of the development section, all with a variety of textures, returning from time to time to the opening texture. He took the theme of the Andante from his own incidental music to *Rosamunde* (the same subject served him later for the piano Impromptu Op. 142, No. 3). The opening of the minuet quotes from his setting of a stanza by Schiller (D. 677), "Schöne Welt, wo bist du?" (Lovely world, where are you?). The finale, a cheerful Allegro in Hungarian style, contrasts sharply with the dark mood of the preceding three movements.

Quartet in D minor

The grimly serious Quartet in D minor distributes its main ideas among the four instruments. Its central movement is a set of variations on Schubert's song *Der Tod und das Mädchen* (D. 531, Death and the Maiden). The G-major Quartet, on a larger scale than the other two, exhibits Schubert's habit of alternating major and minor forms of the triad (Example 17.11), reversed and differently colored at the recapitulation.

String Quintet in C major

Schubert wrote his chamber music masterpiece, the String Quintet in C major, D. 956, during the last year of his life. As in Boccherini's quintets, the added instrument is a second cello, a low tessitura that had particular appeal to nineteenth-century sensibilities. Schubert obtained exquisite effects from this combination. The ideas are set forth and developed in the first movement in a truly symphonic way. The beautiful E♭-major melody of the secondary the-

Example 17.11 *Franz Schubert, Quartet in G major, D. 887: First Movement*

Example 17.12 *Franz Schubert, Quintet in C major, D. 956: Allegretto*

matic section (measure 60) is heard in the cello before it reaches the first violin. Its recapitulation is in A♭, a third down from the tonic C (just as E♭ is a third up), a characteristic tonal scheme in the nineteenth century. The Quintet has the profound lyricism, unobtrusive contrapuntal mastery, long melodic lines (for example, the first fifteen measures of the Adagio), and wealth of harmonic invention that characterize the late piano sonatas. The finale, like that of the Quartet in A minor, is in a lighter mood, relaxing the tension built up by the first three movements. Not only are the themes playful but so are the modulations, such as the rapid shift from E♭ minor to B major to C major by way of enharmonic and chordal common tones (Example 17.12).

Mendelssohn

Mendelssohn wrote with facility in the Classic forms, but his feeling for descriptive tone color did not find an outlet in the medium of chamber music.

An exception is the early Octet for Strings (1825), whose scherzo exemplifies his flair for this genre, as does the scherzo of the Piano Trio in D minor. Of his six string quartets the best are probably the two in E♭, Opp. 12 and 44, and the late Quartet in F minor, Op. 80 (1847). He also wrote a sonata for piano and violin, two for piano and cello, two quintets, a piano sextet, and a few lesser works and arrangements. The D-minor Piano Trio, Op. 49, and its companion in C minor, Op. 66, among the most popular of Mendelssohn's chamber works, display both the strengths and the weaknesses of the composer in this medium—tuneful, attractive themes, vigorous idiomatic writing, but an occasional looseness of form and a redundancy in developing the material.

Brahms

In the chamber-music medium as in orchestral music, Brahms was the true successor of Beethoven. Not only is the quantity of his production impressive—twenty-four works in all—but the quality as well, including at least a half-dozen masterpieces. He issued his first published chamber work, a Piano Trio in B, Op. 8 (1854), in a thoroughly rewritten version in 1891. Two string sextets, Op. 18 in B♭ (1862) and Op. 36 in G (1865), make an interesting contrast. The B♭ Sextet is a hearty work of ample dimensions, combining humor and Classic poise. Its slow movement presents a set of variations in D minor, whose subject is a sixteen-measure harmonic pattern rather than a melody. The finale resembles a Haydn rondo, with an animated accelerating coda. The Sextet in G has widely spaced, transparent sonorities in the opening Allegro and a quietly vivacious finale. The Adagio, an unbridled set of five strict variations on a twelve-measure theme in E minor, epitomizes Brahms's most characteristic harmonic and rhythmic procedures.

Sextets

Piano Quintet

Opus 34 (1864) in F minor, so stunningly successful as a piano quintet, is the third metamorphosis of this work. Brahms originally composed it as a string quintet with two cellos. He later arranged it effectively for two pianos, and then Clara Schumann, herself a successful composer of chamber music with piano, advised him to combine the string and piano sonorities for the final version. The first movement is a powerful, closely knit Allegro in sonata form. Brahms's treatment of the opening idea (Example 17.13a) during the exposition aptly fits Arnold Schoenberg's phrase "developing variation." In diminution, the theme becomes a piano figure against string chords (b); a lyrical melody in the first violin (c); then, with note values doubled and the figure transformed, it is subjected to close imitation in the two violins (d). The key relationships are remote: the second theme group, in C♯ minor, is recapitulated in F♯ minor; the slow movement, in A♭, has a middle section in E major.

The spirit and even the themes of the scherzo recall Beethoven's Fifth Symphony, which is also in C minor. The opening of Beethoven's movement definitively spells out the key; by contrast, Brahms's A♭-major melody over an insistent *C* pedal clouds the tonal feeling. The ambiguity is not cleared up until the broadly spanned, soaring theme has unfolded in the first violin and reached the dominant of C minor. Both composers' trios are in C major, but

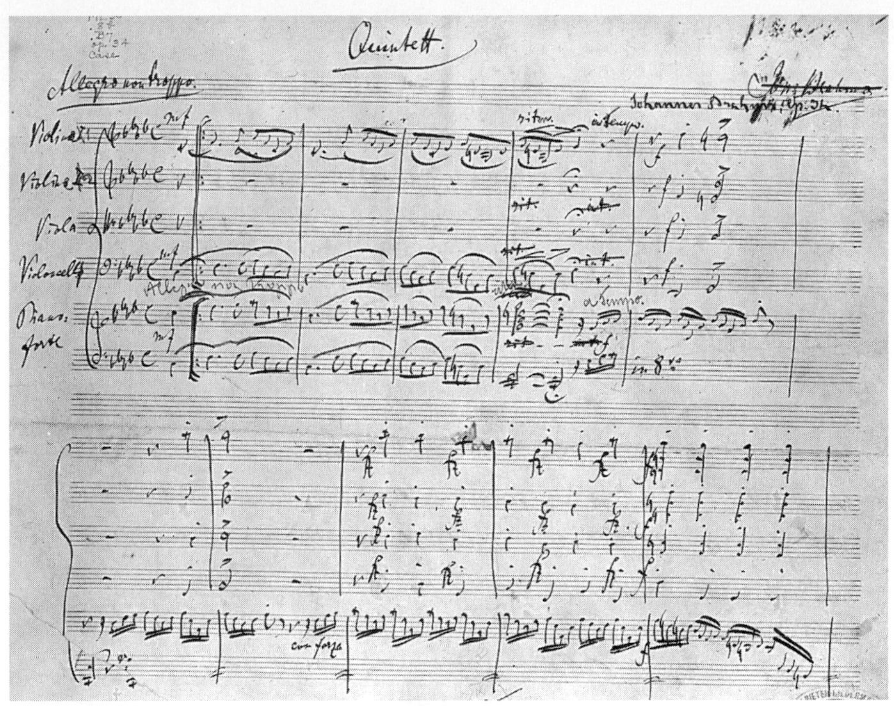

■ *The opening of the Brahms Piano Quintet, Op. 34, in the composer's hand.* (THE GERTRUDE CLARKE WHITTAL FOUNDATION COLLECTION, MUSIC DIVISION, LIBRARY OF CONGRESS, WASHINGTON, D.C.)

Beethoven invented truly contrasting material and textures, whereas Brahms developed the same ideas as in the scherzo. The robust rhythms and the fleeting hints of a hurdy-gurdy in its persistent pedal points give the entire Brahms movement an earthy quality true to the Beethovenian spirit. The rousing finale is preceded by a broad *poco sostenuto.*

Example 17.13 *Johannes Brahms, Piano Quintet in F minor, Op. 34: Allegro non troppo*

Trio Opus 40

In his Trio in E♭, Op. 40, for piano, violin, and Waldhorn (natural horn, without valves), Brahms again united a sonorous, expressive idiom with forms that are well grounded in Classic practice. Composed in 1865, this Trio brings to an end what, by analogy with Beethoven, may be called Brahms's second period. After a pause of eight years came the two String Quartets in C minor and A minor, Op. 51. In the first movement of the A-minor Quartet, Brahms used layered textures in the statement of the second theme, which he pitched in the normal relative major (Example 17.14). The violins proceed in parallel thirds and sixths, while the viola breaks the harmony in triplets, and the cello pizzicato similarly breaks the chords. The first and third beats are gracefully emphasized by double appoggiaturas and dotted figures. Brahms postponed

String quartets

Example 17.14 *Johannes Brahms, String Quartet in A minor, Op. 51, No. 2: Allegro non troppo*

closure until the end of the sixteen-measure period. Suspense mounts when the first violin (measure 58) takes up the viola's triplets and becomes the consonant part, relegating the dissonant suspensions to the lower strings. In 1876 (the year of the First Symphony) Brahms composed his final String Quartet in B♭, Op. 67, and six years later the String Quintet in F major, Op. 88.

Outstanding among Brahms's later works are the two Piano Trios, Op. 87 in C major (1882) and Op. 101 in C minor (1886), the String Quintet in G major, Op. 111 (1890), and the moving Clarinet Quintet in B minor, Op. 115 (1891), one of the glories of the clarinet literature.

Sonatas

The sonatas with piano form a special category of Brahms's chamber music. There are three for violin, two for cello, and two for clarinet. All except the Cello Sonata, Op. 38 (1862–65), are late works. The first two Violin Sonatas, in G major, Op. 78 (1878–79), and A major, Op. 100 (1886), contain some of Brahms's most lyric and melodious writing; the third, in D minor, Op. 108 (1887), is on a more symphonic scale. The two Clarinet Sonatas of Op. 120, written in 1894, are among the most mature achievements of the composer, as are the piano pieces Opp. 116–19, the Clarinet Quintet, and the organ chorale preludes.

Franck

Cyclical method

The founder of modern French chamber music was César Franck. His chief works in this field are a Piano Quintet in F minor (1879), a String Quartet in D major (1889), and the well-known Violin Sonata in A major (1886). All these works employ the *cyclical method*—that is, themes recur identically or become transformed in two or more movements. This constructive practice had attracted Franck as early as 1840, when he used it in his first Piano Trio in F♯ minor. His cyclical use of themes is most effective in his mature chamber works, and in the Symphony in D minor (1888).

THE LIED

The Ballad

Toward the end of the eighteenth century, the German lied admitted a new type of song, the *ballad*. As a poetic genre, it was cultivated in Germany in imitation of the popular ballads of England and Scotland. Most ballads were fairly long poems, alternating narrative and dialogue in a tale filled with romantic adventures and supernatural incidents. At the same time, the poets sought to preserve the forthright quality of the old folk ballads on which they were modeled (as did Samuel Taylor Coleridge later, for example, in his *Rime of the Ancient Mariner*).

Musical settings

Composers eagerly seized on this genre, so well suited to music. Johann Rudolf Zumsteeg (1760–1802) was one of the first to excel in setting this type of poetry. Later Carl Loewe (1796–1869) stood out as a prolific composer of these German ballads. Romantic ballads demanded a musical treatment quite different from the short, idyllic strophic lied of the eighteenth century. Their greater length necessitated a greater variety of themes and textures, which in turn required some means of unifying the whole. Moreover, the contrasts of mood and the movement of the story had to be captured and enhanced by the music. The ballad thus expanded the lied both in form and in range and force of emotional content. The piano part rose in status from the role of accompanist to equal partner with the voice in supporting, illustrating, and intensifying the meaning of the poetry.

Schubert

Schubert's songs reveal his gift for creating beautiful melodies, a talent that few composers have possessed so fully. Many of his melodies have the simple, artless quality of folksong (for example, *Heidenröslein, Der Lindenbaum* [NAWM 112], *Wohin?, Die Forelle*). Others are suffused with sweetness and melancholy (*Am Meer, Der Wanderer, Du bist die Ruh'*). Still others are declamatory, intense, and dramatic (*Aufenthalt, Der Atlas, Die junge Nonne, An Schwager Kronos*). Every mood or nuance of feeling finds spontaneous expression in Schubert's melodic stream, which flows as copiously in the songs as it does in the instrumental works.

Harmonic style

Along with a genius for melody Schubert possessed a feeling for harmonic color. His complex modulations, sometimes embodying long passages in which the tonality is kept in suspense, powerfully underline the dramatic qualities of a song text. Striking examples of harmonic boldness may be found in *Gruppe aus dem Tartarus* and *Das Heimweh*, a song that also illustrates the Schubertian device of hovering between the major and minor forms of the triad (other examples are *Ständchen* and *Auf dem Wasser zu singen*). Masterly use of chromatic coloring within a prevailing diatonic sound is another Schubert characteristic (*Am Meer, Lob der Thränen*). His modulations characteristically move from the tonic toward flat keys, and the mediant or submediant is a favorite relationship. Other modulations may take off from a chord in the mode opposite to the normal one—for example, the sudden introduction of a chord with a minor third where the major third is expected. These are but a few of the hundreds of procedures and instances that demonstrate the harmonic richness of Schubert's music.

Form

Many of Schubert's lieder are in strophic form, in which the music is repeated for each stanza either literally (as, for example, in *Litanei*) or with slight variation (*Du bist die Ruh'*—You are peace). Others, particularly those on longer texts, may alternate between declamatory and arioso style but are always unified by recurring themes and are built on a carefully planned tonal scheme, as *Fahrt zum Hades* (Trip to Hades) and *Der Wanderer* (The Wanderer). The form, however complex, always suits both the poetical and musical requirements of the text.

Accompaniments

Often a piano figuration is suggested by some pictorial image in the text, as in *Wohin?* (Wither) or *Auf dem Wasser zu singen* (Singing on the Water).

Such pictorial features are never merely illustrative but are designed to contribute toward the mood of the song. Thus the accompaniment of *Gretchen am Spinnrade* (Gretchen at the Spinning Wheel, NAWM 111; CD 9 [25] / 3 ⟨58⟩)—one of the earliest (1814) and most famous of the lieder—suggests not only the whir of the spinning wheel by a constant sixteenth-note figure in the right hand and the motion of the treadle by the left hand, but also the agitation of Gretchen's thoughts as she sings of her beloved in Goethe's epic poem *Faust.* Similarly, in *Der Erlkönig* (The Erlking), one of Schubert's relatively few ballads—also on a Goethe text—the pounding octave triplets in the accompaniment depict at once the galloping of the horse and the frantic anxiety of the father as he rides "through night and wind" with his frightened sick child clasped in his arms. The delirious boy imagines that he sees the legendary Erlking, who is enticing him to go with him to his land, where the boy will be comforted by the swaying, dancing, and singing of the Erlking's daughters. Schubert has characterized in an unforgettable manner the three actors in the drama: the concerned father, the wily Erlking, and the terrified child.

Gretchen am Spinnrade

Der Erlkönig

An entirely different style of accompaniment appears in *Der Doppelgänger* (The Double): long, somber chords, with a recurrent sinister melodic motive in low triple octaves, below a declamatory voice part that rises to an awesome climax before sinking in a despairing phrase. With terrifying effectiveness, Schubert depicts the ghostly horror of the scene—in which the poet meets his double staring under the moonlight at the abandoned house where his sweetheart had once lived—using heavy, obsessive dark chords revolving fatally about the tonic of B minor except for one brief, lurid flash of D♯ minor near the end.

Der Doppelgänger

Schubert drew on the works of many poets for his texts. From Goethe alone he took fifty-nine poems, providing five different solo settings for *Nur wer die Sehnsucht kennt* (Only someone who knows longing) from the novel *Wilhelm Meister.* Some of Schubert's finest lieder are found in his two song-cycles on poems by Wilhelm Müller, *Die schöne Müllerin* (The Pretty Miller-Maid, 1823) and *Winterreise* (Winter's Journey, 1827). The *Schwanengesang* (Swan Song, 1828), not intended as a cycle but published as such posthu-

Texts

■ *Schubert at the piano accompanying a singer in the home of Joseph von Spaun. Sepia drawing by Moritz von Schwind, 1868.* (VIENNA, SCHUBERT MUSEUM OF THE CITY OF VIENNA)

mously, includes six songs on poems by Heinrich Heine. Schubert sometimes chose texts of lesser literary quality, but his music could glorify even commonplace poetry.

Winterreise

Winterreise consists of twenty-four poems by Müller that express the nostalgia of a lover revisiting in winter the haunts of a failed summer romance. In *Der Lindenbaum* (The Linden Tree, NAWM 112; CD 9 [30]), the poet dwells on the memory of the tree under which he used to lie dreaming of his love. Now, as he passes it, the chilly wind rustles the branches, which seem to call him back to find rest there once again. The music is in a modified strophic form, each strophe of music setting two stanzas of the poem. The first two stanzas are set to a simple folklike melody made up of four-measure phrases in the form a a b b′ and accompanied by simple chords.

Robert Schumann

Despite their lyrical qualities and harmonic color, Schubert's works nearly always maintained a certain serenity and poise, while Robert Schumann, his first important successor among lied composers, wrote restless and intense melodies and accompaniments. In 1840, the year of his long-delayed marriage to his beloved Clara Wieck, Schumann produced more than one hundred lieder, including two cycles: *Dichterliebe* (A Poet's Love) and *Frauenliebe und -leben* (A Woman's Love and Life). *Dichterliebe* consists of sixteen songs on poems selected from the more than sixty in Heinrich Heine's *Lyrisches Intermezzo* (1823 and later editions). Neither Heine's collection nor Schumann's cycle has an encompassing narrative, but the theme of unrequited love runs through the poems. In the first song of the cycle, *Im wunderschönen Monat Mai* (In the marvelous month of May, NAWM 113a; CD 9 [34]), the poet confesses a springtime love that he fears may not be returned. The tonal ambiguity and tension between voice and piano reflects the ironic spirit of Heine's poem as well as the pessimistic outlook of the cycle as a whole. The appoggiaturas and suspensions that begin almost every other measure underline the bittersweet anxiety expressed in the text. The lover's defiant attitude in *Ich grolle nicht* (I bear no grudge, NAWM 113b; [35]) demands a more declamatory, less tuneful approach. The strong, octave-reinforced bass line and the emphatic chords in the right hand concentrate the expression in the piano part. The harmonic momentum and coloring depend greatly on secondary dominants and on altering minor chords that would normally be major in the key and vice versa. The four-measure piano prelude and postlude are characteristic of the songs of this cycle.

Dichterliebe

Clara Schumann

Six songs that Clara Schumann composed as Op. 23 in 1853 on poems from the cycle *Jucunde* by Hermann Rollett are particularly original. For example, the uniform mood of the three stanzas from No. 3, *Geheimes Flüstern hier und dort* (Secret whispers here and there, NAWM 114; CD 9 [36]), dominated by an

■ *Clara Schumann and Joseph Joachim, who were close friends and gave concerts together. Print after a chalk drawing (1854) by Adolf von Menzel.* (ZWICKAU, ROBERT-SCHUMANN-HAUS)

image of the forest whispering to the poet, permits a strictly strophic setting. A continuous sixteenth-note broken-chord motion in $\frac{3}{8}$ sets up a backdrop of rustling leaves and branches for expressing the poet's reliance on the forest as a refuge and a communicator of life's secrets. The closing lines of the poem refer to unresolved passion that can only be revealed in song.

Brahms

Johannes Brahms too found the lied a congenial medium, for he wrote some 260 songs throughout his life. Many of them, such as the familiar *Wiegenlied* (Lullaby), are in a folksong style. The simplicity of these songs, and Brahms's concern never to detract from the melody by providing complex or harmonically inappropriate accompaniments, is all the more striking in a composer who mastered the most sophisticated musical structures. A similar folklike, popular appeal characterizes the two sets of *Liebeslieder* (Love-Song) Waltzes for a quartet of solo voices with a four-hand piano accompaniment. Brahms made arrangements of many German folksongs, including a set of fourteen (1858) dedicated to the children of Robert and Clara Schumann, sets of twenty-eight (1858) and forty-nine (1894), all for voice and piano, as well as twenty-six for unaccompanied chorus (1854–73).

Folksong arrangements

Brahms considered Schubert as his model in song writing, and he wrote many of his lieder, like Schubert, in a more or less strict strophic form. Among these, *Vergebliches Ständchen* (Vain Serenade) is one of the few Brahms songs that is humorous and outright cheerful, as are also *Tambourliedchen* (Little Drum-Song) and *Der Gang zum Liebchen* (The walk to the sweetheart). For the most part, however, Brahms's tone is serious. His songs do not have the

Serious character of songs

Example 17.15 *Johannes Brahms, Melodic Figures*

a. *Song,* Sapphische Ode

b. *Song,* Der Schmied

c. *Second Symphony, First Movement*

soaring, ardent, impulsive character of Schumann's. Restraint and a certain classic severity—an introspective, resigned, elegiac mood—prevail. This quality is exemplified by one of Brahms's best-known lieder, the *Sapphische Ode,* which also illustrates a frequently recurring mannerism: building a melodic line on or around the notes of a triad, sometimes with the omission of the root (see Example 17.15). Brahms's fundamentally reflective style still leaves room for the expression of passion, which is all the more effective because it is controlled and avoids excess. Brahms's most typical lieder are those that reflect on death, such as *Immer leiser wird mein Schlummer* (Ever lighter is my slumber), *Auf dem Kirchhofe* (At the graveyard), and *Der Tod, das ist die kühle Nacht* (Death, it is a cool night). The *Vier ernste Gesänge* (Four Serious Songs, Op. 121, 1896), on biblical texts, are from the composer's last years.

Brahms's accompaniments are rarely pictorial, and he seldom includes piano preludes and postludes, which are so important in the songs of the Schumanns. Yet the piano parts are greatly varied in texture, frequently using syncopated rhythms or extended arpeggio figuration, as in *O wüsst' ich doch den Weg zurück* (If only I knew the way back).

CHORAL MUSIC

In considering the choral music of the nineteenth century, we must distinguish between works in which the chorus plays a subsidiary role and those in which the choral writing is the principal focus of interest. The first category includes the numerous choruses in operas, choral movements in symphonies, and some of the large choral-orchestral works of Berlioz and Liszt. It is significant that Mendelssohn and Brahms, the two composers who best understood how to write idiomatically for chorus, were also the most knowledgeable about earlier music. Nineteenth-century composers found the chorus less congenial than the orchestra or solo voice for expressing intimate sentiments, and, indeed, many treated the chorus primarily as a division of the orchestra, to supply picturesque touches and supplementary colors.

There were three kinds of choral music in the nineteenth century: (1) part-songs or other short choral pieces, usually on secular texts, in homophonic style with the melody in the upper voice, to be sung either a cappella or with piano or organ accompaniment; (2) music on liturgical texts, intended for home use or in church services; and (3) works for chorus and orchestra, often with one or more solo vocalists, on texts of dramatic or narrative-dramatic character but intended for concert rather than stage performance.

Categories

Part-Songs and Cantatas

Part songs

The composition of part-songs, which had begun before the end of the eighteenth century, received impetus in the nineteenth century from the rise of national sentiments and the awakening interest in folksong. Further stimuli to choral composition were the popular festivals in Revolutionary France and the rapid growth of singing societies in France and Germany during the first half of the nineteenth century. Weber's settings for men's voices (1814) of stanzas from Körner's *Leier und Schwert* (Lyre and Sword) were among the first of thousands of similar patriotic effusions. Schubert, Mendelssohn, Schumann, Gounod, Liszt, and nearly every other composer in Europe produced part-songs and choruses for men's, women's, or mixed voices, accompanied and unaccompanied, on patriotic, sentimental, convivial, and every other kind of verse. This music served its immediate purpose and has for the most part been forgotten.

Cantatas

Of more lasting interest are some of the cantatas, such as Mendelssohn's *Die Erste Walpurgisnacht* (The First Walpurgis Night, 1832; revised 1843), Schumann's *Das Paradies und die Peri* (Paradise and the Peri, 1843), and *Szenen aus Goethes Faust* (Scenes from Goethe's *Faust*, 1844–53). The master in this genre, Johannes Brahms, wrote many short unaccompanied songs for women's, men's, or mixed voices, as well as larger compositions for chorus with orchestra. Among these are the Rhapsody for alto solo and men's chorus (1870), the *Schicksalslied* (Song of Destiny, 1871) and *Nänie* (Song of Lamentation, on verses by Schiller, 1881) for mixed chorus, and the *Gesang der Parzen* (Song of the Fates, 1883), for six-part mixed chorus.

Church Music

Cecilian movement

Toward the middle of the century agitation for musical reform arose within the Roman Catholic Church. The Cecilian movement, named after St. Cecilia, the patron saint of music, was stimulated in part by interest in music of the past. The movement helped bring about both a revival of the sixteenth-century a cappella style and the restoration of Gregorian chant to what was considered its pristine form. The best Catholic church music in the early part of the century came from the pens of Cherubini in Paris and Schubert in Vienna. Schubert's Masses in A♭ and E♭ (D. 678, 950) are considered the period's finest settings of the Ordinary. On the Protestant and Anglican side, the psalms of

Russian church music

Gounod

Mendelssohn and the anthems of Samuel Sebastian Wesley (1810–1876) were acclaimed. In Russia, Dmitri Bortnyansky (1751–1825), Kapellmeister and then director of the imperial chapel choir at St. Petersburg beginning in 1779, was the first in a long line of composers who developed a new style of Russian church music. Inspired by the modal chants of the Orthodox liturgy, it had free rhythm and used unaccompanied voices in single or double choruses with octave doublings in a rich and solemn texture. The Masses and other sacred music of the Parisian Charles Gounod (1818–1893) were highly regarded in their time, but his peculiar blend of piety and sentimentality lost much of its original validity after it was widely copied by later composers. Gounod's most famous Mass, the *St. Cecilia* (1885), was condemned also on liturgical grounds because the composer inserted words in the last movement not normally part of the sung text.

Other Music on Liturgical Texts

Berlioz

Berlioz's Requiem

Berlioz set off a dazzling conflagration in the *Grande Messe des Morts* (Requiem, 1837) and the Te Deum (1855) as explosive musical energy collided with sacred themes. These grandiose religious works were intended for special occasions—the Te Deum for the coronation of Napoleon III. They are dramatic symphonies for orchestra and voices using poetically inspiring texts that happen to be liturgical. They belong not to an ecclesiastical but to a secular and patriotic tradition inspired by the massive music festivals of the French Revolution. Both works are of huge dimensions, not only in length and in the number of performers they require but in grandeur of conception. Much has been written about the Requiem's orchestra of 140 players, the 4 brass choirs, the 4 tam-tams, 10 pairs of cymbals, and 16 kettledrums that accompany the chorus at "Tuba mirum" in the *Dies irae*, yet little is said about the brilliant

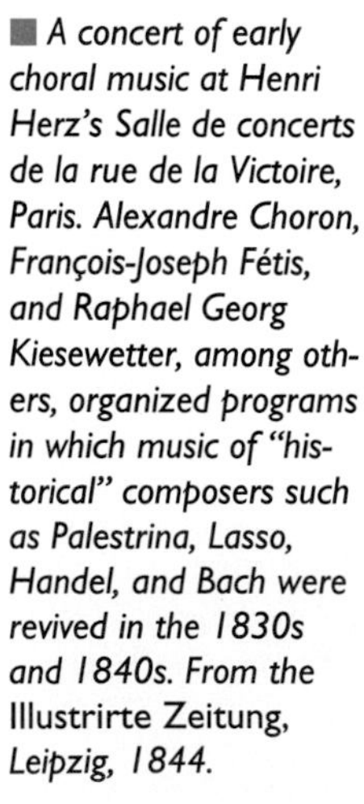

A concert of early choral music at Henri Herz's Salle de concerts de la rue de la Victoire, Paris. Alexandre Choron, François-Joseph Fétis, and Raphael Georg Kiesewetter, among others, organized programs in which music of "historical" composers such as Palestrina, Lasso, Handel, and Bach were revived in the 1830s and 1840s. From the Illustrirte Zeitung, *Leipzig, 1844.*

musical effect Berlioz achieves in the few places where all of them are sounding. Other original orchestral features are the stark lines of the English horns, bassoons, and low strings in combination with unison tenor voices at "Quid sum miser" in the *Dies irae*; the chords for flutes and trombones alternating with men's chorus in the Offertory at "Hostias"; the beginning of the Agnus Dei; and the return of the long tenor melody of the Sanctus, where the five-measure responsive phrases of soloist and chorus are punctuated by *pianissimo* strokes of the bass drum and cymbals. The Te Deum has fewer striking orchestral experiments than the Requiem, but its final number (*Judex crederis*) is one of the thrilling movements for chorus and orchestra.

Liszt

The big sacred scores of Liszt, like those of Berlioz, were created for special occasions: the Festival Mass (1855) for the consecration of the cathedral at Gran (Esztergom), Hungary, and the Mass for the coronation of the king of Hungary in 1867. Their scale and style correspond to Liszt's own ideal of sacred music, which he outlined in 1834:

> For want of a better term we may call the new music "humanitarian." It must be devotional, strong, and drastic, uniting on a colossal scale the theatre and the church, at once dramatic and sacred, splendid and simple, ceremonial and serious, fiery and free, stormy and calm, translucent and emotional.[3]

Liszt never quite welded these dualities into a consistent style in his church music. He came closest in some shorter works, such as his setting of Psalm 13 for tenor solo, chorus, and orchestra (1855) and—in a different way, with many passages of "experimental" harmony—in the *Via Crucis* (Stations of the Cross), a large work for soloists, chorus, and organ, completed in 1879 but not published or performed publicly during Liszt's lifetime.

Two Italian opera composers, Gioachino Rossini (1792–1868) and Giuseppe Verdi (1813–1901), made important contributions to church music.

Rossini

The operatic style of Rossini's *Stabat Mater* (1832, 1841) was expressly forbidden in 1903 by the famous encyclical of Pope Pius X, *Motu proprio*. But the style of the questionable operatic arias was not intended by the composer nor perceived by his public to be flippant or inappropriate.

Verdi

Verdi composed his Requiem (1874) in memory of Alessandro Manzoni (1785–1873), author of *I promessi sposi*, the most famous Italian novel of the century. The Requiem adapts the sacred text—somewhat rearranged—to the vocal and instrumental resources of his operas and adds some powerful choruses.

Bruckner

Anton Bruckner (1824–1896) succeeded as no one before him in uniting the spiritual and technical resources of the nineteenth-century symphony with a reverent and liturgical approach to the sacred texts. His Masses and symphonies have in common many qualities and even some musical themes. A solitary, simple, profoundly religious person, who was thoroughly schooled in counterpoint, Bruckner served as organist of the cathedral at Linz and from 1867 as court organist in Vienna.

3. Reprinted in Liszt, *Gesammelte Schriften* (Leipzig, 1881), pp. 2–57.

Bruckner's Masses

Bruckner composed his D-minor Mass in 1864 and a larger one in F minor in 1867; like all his works, they were subjected to numerous revisions before being published. The influence of the Cecilian movement is apparent in some of Bruckner's motets—for example, the strictly modal Gradual *Os justi* (1879) for unaccompanied chorus, or *Virga Jesse* (NAWM 115; CD 9 [37]), written in a modernized diatonic style.

Bruckner's short Mass in E minor (1866; published 1890) for eight-part chorus and fifteen wind instruments (paired oboes, clarinets, bassoons, and trumpets, four horns, three trombones) is a unique work of neo-medieval complexion. The only comparable church compositions of the period are Brahms's a cappella motets Opp. 74 and 110, which bear much the same relation to the Lutheran chorale that Bruckner's Masses do to plainsong. The last of Bruckner's sacred compositions were his Te Deum in C major (1884) and Psalm 150 (1892), both for soloists, chorus, organ, and full orchestra.

Oratorio

The oratorio flourished chiefly in Protestant England and Germany, developing along lines laid down in the eighteenth century. The main strength of the nineteenth-century oratorio lay in its use of the chorus, and there its descent from Handel is obvious. Some of the themes treated were the last judgment (Ludwig Spohr, 1826), the life of Christ (Liszt, 1856), the Beatitudes, or the kinds of blessedness pronounced by Christ in the Sermon on the Mount (César Franck, 1879), redemption (Gounod, 1882), and the legend of St. Elizabeth (Liszt, 1857–62). Mendelssohn's choice of subjects for his oratorios—the teachings of St. Paul (1836) and the struggles of Elijah (1846)—are significant in view of his parents' conversion from Judaism.

Brahms's *Requiem*

Brahms's *Ein deutsches Requiem* (A German Requiem, 1868), for soprano and baritone soloists, chorus, and orchestra, has for its text not the liturgical words of the Latin Requiem Mass but Old Testament passages of meditation and solace in German, chosen by the composer himself. Brahms's music, like that of Schütz and Bach, is inspired by a deep concern with mortality and by the hope for salvation. In the German Requiem, these solemn thoughts are expressed with intense feeling and clothed with the opulent colors of nineteenth-century harmony, regulated always by spacious formal architecture and guided by Brahms's unerring judgment for choral and orchestral effect.

The fourth movement, "Wie lieblich sind deine Wohnungen" (How lovely are your dwelling places, NAWM 116; CD 9 [38]), is probably the best loved and known. The text expresses a desire to be united with God, and the music's mood of devout reflection and yearning is achieved with simple melodic and harmonic resources. The orchestra dispenses with the trumpets, trombones, tuba, and tympani called for in some of the other movements.

Bibliography

For editions and readings covering this chapter, see the Bibliography for Chapter 16.

CHAPTER 18

OPERA AND MUSIC DRAMA IN THE NINETEENTH CENTURY

ITALY

Although Italian and French serious opera had common roots, they went separate ways until the middle of the eighteenth century, when they began to converge, particularly in the Parisian works of Gluck. Many of the principles that had guided Gluck were already described in Francesco Algarotti's treatise *Saggio sopra l'opera in musica* (1755) and put into practice by Nicolò Jommelli (1714–1774) in his operas written for Parma, Stuttgart, and Mannheim in the 1750s. These three centers of French culture were ripe for a blend of tragédie lyrique and opera seria. A similar combination was also fused by Tommaso Traetta (1727–1779) in his operas for Parma and Mannheim in the late 1750s and early 1760s. His *Ippolito ed Aricia* (1759) for Parma, based on a libretto adapted from Rameau's *Hippolyte et Aricie*, borrows some of Rameau's dance music and deploys nine choruses and a number of non–da capo arias; most of the da capo arias shorten the repeat of the main section. Although Jommelli's and Traetta's reforms were not popular in Italy, they provided models within opera seria for a more continuous dramatic flow and gave the orchestra a more important role, particularly through colorful use of woodwinds and horns.

Nicolò Jommelli

Tommaso Traetta

The distinction between opera seria and opera buffa was maintained throughout the eighteenth century, even while signs of change began to appear in serious opera. The founder of nineteenth-century Italian serious opera was Johann Simon Mayr (1763–1845). Like Hasse before him, he was a German by birth who lived most of his life in Italy. Mayr's works gained general acceptance for many of the changes introduced by Jommelli and Traetta a generation earlier.

Mayr

Rossini

If asked around 1825 who was the most important and most famous living composer, many people in Europe would not have answered Beethoven but rather Gioachino Rossini (1792–1868). By this time Rossini had conquered the opera theaters of Bologna, Rome, Milan, Naples, Paris, and Vienna.

Comic operas

Rossini's witty style is particularly well suited to comic opera. Many of these operas sound as fresh today as they did when he first wrote them. His masterpiece, *Il barbiere di Siviglia* (The Barber of Seville) ranks with Mozart's *Figaro* and Verdi's *Falstaff* among the supreme examples of Italian comic opera. Some of the most amusing and clever moments are the patter arias of *buffo* characters such as Bartolo or Figaro himself in the *Barbiere*, in which clever lines, often repeated, are sometimes mixed with nonsense syllables that must be sung with incredible speed and precision.

Scene structure

Rossini, with the collaboration of his librettists, developed a very specific structure that distributed throughout an act the action previously confined to dry recitative dialogue. A continuous succession of orchestrally accompanied recitatives, solo arias, duets, ensembles, and choruses all contributed to advancing the plot (see diagram below). A typical scene begins with an instrumental introduction followed by a recitative section—either by one character or in dialogue—accompanied by occasional chords in the orchestra mixed with motives from the introduction. This exposition of the situation is usually called the *scena* (see diagram). One of the characters then launches into a formal song, a declamatory yet melodious *cantabile* known as the *primo tempo* or first movement. If it is a duet, another character usually responds with a similar solo; this first section then comes to a formal close. An interlude sometimes follows—a *tempo di mezzo* or middle movement, which may be a declamatory transition, ensemble, or chorus. This section leads us to the final movement, or *cabaletta*, a lively and brilliant solo or duet (in the same key as the first movement) part or all of which is literally repeated, though perhaps with improvised embellishments. The cantabile and cabaletta together constitute an aria, which, when it marks the entrance of a character, is called a *ca-*

Instrumental Intro	I. Aria (so-called double aria)			
	Scena recitative	1. *Primo tempo*: 1st mvmt. slow, cantabile, andante, etc.	2. *Tempo di mezzo*: mid. mvmt. ensemble, chorus, trans.	3. *Cabaletta* often fast

II. Duet				
Scena recitative	1. *Tempo d'attacco* opening mvmt.	2. Slow mvmt.	3. *Tempo di mezzo*	4. *Cabaletta* often fast

III. Finale				
Scena recitative	1. Lyric dialogue	2. *Concertato* concerted slow mvmt.	3. More lyrical dialogue	4. *Stretta* fast

vatina. The act's Finale, which brings together a number of the characters, is organized along similar lines.

Style

Rossini's style combines an inexhaustible flow of melody with snappy rhythms, clear phraseology, and well-shaped though sometimes unconventional structure of the musical period. His spare texture and orchestration respect the quality of the individual instruments, which support rather than compete with the singers; his harmonic schemes are not complex but often original. He shares with other early nineteenth-century composers a fondness for bringing the mediant keys into close juxtaposition with the tonic.

A combination of beautiful melody, wit, and comic description appears in the justly famous "Una voce poco fa" (A voice a short while ago; NAWM 117; CD 9 [43]) from *Il barbiere di Siviglia.* Rossini achieved the illusion of action during this monologue by changing tempo and style. The aria proceeds from a highly embellished recitative-like section to a faster, more flowing, brilliant cabaletta. This particular aria omits the tempo di mezzo, which became more standard in later operas.

In both comic and serious opera, Rossini managed ensemble scenes—those containing duets, trios, and choruses—with ingenious organization and sparkle. In these scenes and elsewhere, he used a simple but effective device, the crescendo: building up excitement by repeating a phrase, often having it sung louder each time and at a higher pitch, for example, the aria "La calunnia" from *Il barbiere.*

In Vienna in 1822, Rossini paid Beethoven a visit. Many years later he told Wagner of the encounter.

> When the door opened, I found myself in a kind of hovel, so dirty as to testify to frightening disorder. . . . When we first entered, he paid no attention to us, but for some moments remained bent over a piece of printed music which he was correcting. Then raising his head, he said to me brusquely in quite comprehensible Italian, "Ah Rossini, you are the composer of *Il Barbiere di Siviglia*? I congratulate you, it is an excellent comic opera. I read it with pleasure, and it delights me. It will be performed as long as Italian opera exists."[1]

Serious operas

Posterity has not been kind to Rossini's serious operas. He is still known today mostly for his comic operas such as *L'Italiana in Algeri* (The Italian Woman in Algiers; Venice, 1813), *Il barbiere di Siviglia* (Rome, 1816), and the "semiserious" opera *La Cenerentola* (Cinderella; Rome, 1817). Yet Rossini's reputation during his lifetime rested as much on his serious operas such as *Tancredi* (1813), *Mosè in Egitto* (Moses in Egypt; Naples, 1818), *Semiramide* (Venice, 1823), and *Guillaume Tell* (William Tell; Paris, 1829), his last. After *Guillaume Tell,* Rossini stopped composing for the stage, having seen thirty-nine of his operas produced. In the remaining forty years of his life, marred by illness and a lengthy lawsuit to regain the pension granted him by Charles X of France, he wrote only sacred music, songs, and albums of piano pieces.

Guillaume Tell

Guillaume Tell, which had five hundred performances at the Paris Opéra

1. Trans. in Charles Osborne, *The Bel Canto Operas* (London: Methuen, 1994), p. 111.

during the composer's lifetime and was the most universally admired of his serious operas, is now remembered for its overture. It is in four sections. The first evokes the pastoral atmosphere of the opening scene; the second is one of the most convincing musical depictions of a storm; the third features a *ranz de vaches*—a Swiss shepherd's call—played by an English horn and repeated throughout the opera; and the last is the famous galloping allegro. The libretto is based on Friedrich von Schiller's *Wilhelm Tell* (1804), a celebration of a folk hero who leads a rebellion on behalf of three Swiss cantons against an Austrian govenor. Captured, the hero is ordered to shoot an apple off his son's head with a bow and arrow. He succeeds and eventually picks off the governor with another shot, liberating the Swiss from the Austrian yoke. The theme was timely—revolution and struggles for national unity were in the air—but it also subjected the work to censorship in Milan, London, Berlin, and St. Petersburg.

Although *Guillaume Tell* generally respects the conventions of Italian opera, many choruses, ensembles, a march, dances, processions, and atmospheric instrumental interludes—foreshadowing the manner of French grand opera—surround the action of the main characters, who, true to the French stage, interact mostly in orchestrally accompanied recitative. But the scenes culminate in tuneful and declamatory arias and duets with little text repetition, only occasionally offering opportunities for virtuosic display. By this time Rossini had abandoned the "dry" keyboard accompaniment of recitative, which he began replacing with the orchestra in *Otello* in 1816.

Vincenzo Bellini (1801–1835)

"The music drama through singing must make one weep, be stricken with horror, to die," Bellini wrote to the librettist of *I Puritani*.[2] He preferred dramas of passion, with fast, gripping action. His favorite librettist, Felice Romani, did not limit action to recitative passages but built it into the arias and provided opportunities for lyrical moments within the recitatives.

Of Bellini's ten operas—all serious—the most important are *La Sonnambula* (The Sleepwalker, 1831), *Norma* (1831), and *I Puritani* (The Puritans, 1835). His style is highly refined; his long, sweeping melodies combine unpredictable form with intense feeling, all qualities exemplified in the scena and cavatina "Casta diva" from *Norma* (NAWM 118; CD 10 [1]). The melody, fourteen measures of a slow $\frac{12}{8}$, continually seeks a resting point but, skirting each opportunity, moves to higher levels of suspense and excitement. Following convention, after a fanfare and transitional declamatory section (the tempo di mezzo), a brilliant cabaletta ensues. Although Bellini alternates recitatives and arias, as in the Baroque opera seria, he creates an illusion of continuous action through the interaction of the principal protagonist with subordinate characters and the chorus.

Opera semiseria

Some influences of Romanticism in general and of French opera in particular appear in the *opera semiseria*, a genre appropriated by both Donizetti and

2. Quoted in Friedrich Lippmann, "Vincenzo Bellini und die italienische Opera Seria seiner Zeit: Studien über Libretto, Arienform und Melodik," *Analecta Musicologica* 6 (1969):33.

Bellini. In this genre, which includes Donizetti's *Linda di Chamounix* and Bellini's *Sonnambula,* a serious plot is leavened with Romantic scenery and sentiment, as in the lyric opera of France. Material for the opera semiseria was drawn increasingly from Romantic sources, such as Victor Hugo (Donizetti's *Lucrezia Borgia*) or Sir Walter Scott (Donizetti's *Lucia di Lammermoor* and Rossini's *La donna del lago)* instead of the ancient classic texts mined by the eighteenth-century opera seria. French grand opera also furnished the model for pseudo-historical subjects treated on a huge scale, as in Bellini's *Puritani* and to a certain extent in *Norma.* The Romantic influence on Italian opera is more marked in the librettos of this period than in the music itself.

Gaetano Donizetti (1797–1848)

One of the most prolific Italian composers during the second quarter of the century, Mayr's pupil Donizetti, composed about one hundred songs, several symphonies, oratorios, cantatas, chamber music, and church music in addition to some seventy operas. His most enduring works were the serious operas *Anna Bolena* (Milan, 1830), *Lucrezia Borgia* (Milan, 1833), *Lucia di Lammermoor* (Naples, 1835), and *Linda di Chamounix* (Vienna, 1842); the opéra comique, *La Fille du regiment* (The Daughter of the Regiment; Paris, 1840); and the buffo operas *L'elisir d'amore* (The Elixir of Love; Milan, 1832) and *Don Pasquale* (1843).

Donizetti, like Rossini, had an instinct for the theater and a talent for melody, and in *Don Pasquale* (Paris, 1843) he created a comic work that is in a class with *Il barbiere.* The farcical action of *L'elisir d'amore* at times borders on chaos, but through all the gaiety a serious romantic relationship grows to maturity and yields several deeply felt arias.

A scene from the second act of Gaetano Donizetti's Don Pasquale *as performed at the Théâtre italien in Paris in 1843. Engraving from the Leipzig* Illustrirte Zeitung.

Serious operas

As a composer of serious opera Donizetti was Verdi's immediate forerunner. He constantly moved the drama forward, averting cadences that would entice applause until a major scene was finished. The beginnings and endings of the formal components of a scene, such as the orchestral introduction, cantabile, tempo di mezzo, and cabaletta, are sometimes disguised by choral or recitative episodes so that the music seems to possess an almost seamless continuity.

The famous mad scene in the last act of *Lucia di Lammermoor*, for example, consists of a scena and aria, but it is really a complex of loosely joined sections that flow one into another through numerous entrances of ensembles and chorus and tempo changes. The scena begins with a short chorus that comments on Lucia's deathly and dishevelled appearance as she enters. We then hear the foreboding music from the opera's prelude, played by the quartet of horns. Against this and a syncopated flute motive Lucia begins her impassioned recitative, calling out to Edgardo, whose voice she imagines hearing. He is the one she loves, but her brother forced her to marry another, whom she has just murdered on their wedding bed. This obbligato recitative leads to a simple recitative that ends with a florid cadenza. The flutes and clarinets then quote the theme of the love-duet between Edgardo and Lucia from Act I, "Verranno a te sull'aure i miei sospir ardenti" (The breeze will carry my burning sighs to you). Lucia now exclaims that a ghost has come between them, while the entire orchestra punctuates her inchoate words.

The recitative continues through several tempo changes, even overlapping the introduction to the famous Larghetto cantabile, "Al fin son tua" (At last I am yours), in which the soprano's coloratura alternately competes with or is doubled at the sixth by the flute. Lucia's tutor, a captain of the guards, and her brother, having learned of the murder, break in to pray for the Lord's mercy. At the tempo di mezzo of the aria, she is joined by her brother and tutor and later the chorus. After a gran pausa and a formal fifteen-bar introduction, Lucia begins the cabaletta, "Spargi d'amaro pianto" (Weep bitter tears). But before she can sing the anticipated repetition, the chorus and the trio break in, joining her again as she brings the repetition to a close and faints. The only lapse in the long frenzied scene is at the gran pausa. At least, this is how the published score reads. In practice, much of the connective tissue is cut out in performance, but the propulsive music still achieves its effect.

FRANCE

The French Revolution, the Napoleonic Empire, and the success of Gluck made Paris the operatic capital of Europe during the first half of the nineteenth century and favored the rise there of a new type of serious opera. In *La Vestale* (The Vestal Virgin, 1807), Gasparo Spontini (1774–1851) united the heroic character typical of the late Gluck operas with the heightened dramatic tension of the then-popular rescue plot, clothing the whole in a grand display of solo,

Spontini

choral, and orchestral magnificence. Spontini, Empress Josephine's favorite musician, was an Italian who had worked in Paris from 1803 to 1820, when he began a second career as court music director in Berlin.

Cherubini

Spontini's principal colleagues at the Paris Opera were Luigi Cherubini—whose *Les deux journées* (The Two Days, 1800; known also by the German title *Der Wasserträger*, The Water Carrier) was a model for Beethoven's *Fidelio*—and Étienne Nicolas Méhul (1763–1817), now chiefly remembered for his biblical opera *Joseph* (1807) and his revolutionary hymns.

Méhul

Spontini became conductor of opera at the Théâtre italien in Paris in 1810. He was succeeded in 1812 by Ferdinando Paër, and in 1824 by Rossini. The house mounted operas by Bellini and Donizetti with casts of international stars. Meanwhile, following Napoleon's defeat at Waterloo, the Bourbon monarchy was restored in 1815 and, as a result, many of those who had fled the city returned. Musical life reawakened and a new theater for French opera was built in 1821. But the Bourbon royal family failed to gain the support of the growing and powerful middle class. The bloodless "July Revolution" of 1830 put Louis-Philippe, of the Orléans line, on the throne as a constitutional monarch. The government continued to subsidize opera and concerts, and the royal family contributed informally to opera and benefit concerts. The opera theater was leased to a businessman, Louis Véron, who found wealthy sponsors. Anyone could purchase tickets, but the boxes were rented at high prices.

Grand Opera

With the decline of royal patronage, a new kind of opera came into being, designed to appeal to the relatively uncultured audiences who thronged the opera theaters looking for excitement and entertainment. *Grand opera*, as this genre came to be called, was as much spectacle as music, consistent with the fashion that had prevailed in France ever since the time of Lully. Writers created librettos that exploited every possible occasion for machinery, ballets, choruses, and crowd scenes. The leaders of this school were the librettist Eugène Scribe (1791–1861), the composer Giacomo Meyerbeer (1791–1864), and Véron, the director of the Paris Opera Theater.

Meyerbeer

Two operas by Giacomo Meyerbeer established the genre: *Robert le diable* (Robert the Devil, 1831) and *Les Huguenots* (1836). Meyerbeer's ability to integrate crowd scenes, public ceremonies, and confrontations on stage is most evident in the closing scenes of Act II of *Les Huguenots*. Here Queen Marguerite de Valois of France tries to reconcile the Protestants and Catholics through a peace-making marriage of the Catholic maiden Valentine to the Protestant Raoul. A timpani solo introduces the oath of peace, sung in unison, unaccompanied and *pianissimo*, by the leaders of the two factions. The chorus, with orchestra, interjects *fortissimo* "Nous jurons" (we swear) three times. In an extended a cappella ensemble in four parts the leaders hail the benefits of harmony among peoples. Only the militant Protestant Marcel defies the others as he vows to make war on Rome and her soldiers. As the orchestra rejoins the singers on a diminished-seventh chord, Marguerite's voice floats above all the

Les Huguenots

others, crowning the scene with coloratura. Later, when Raoul rejects Valentine as a prospective wife, and the truce between the opposing factions breaks down, Marcel in the midst of the fury triumphantly booms a phrase of the Lutheran chorale *Ein' feste Burg ist unser Gott* (A mighty fortress is our God). In this scene Meyerbeer managed the solo, choral, and orchestral forces with broad strokes of extraordinary dramatic effectiveness. Such grand-opera proceedings were admired and emulated by Verdi and others.

Among the most productive composers of grand opera around 1830 were François Auber (*La Muette de Portici*, The Mute Girl of Portici, also known as *Masaniello*, 1828), Rossini (*Guillaume Tell*, 1829), and Jacques Fromental Halévy (1799–1862), whose masterpiece was *La Juive* (The Jewess, 1835). The broad canvas, grand musical structures, and variety of *Guillaume Tell* exemplify the grand operas of this period. The French ideal of grand opera stayed alive to some extent throughout the nineteenth century, influencing the work of Verdi (*Les Vêpres siciliennes*, *Aida*) and Richard Wagner (1813–1883), whose *Rienzi* is grand opera pure and simple. Certain features of the genre are apparent in Wagner's later works, particularly *Tannhäuser*, *Lohengrin*, and even *Götterdämmerung*. The grand-opera tradition survives also in twentieth-century works such as Darius Milhaud's *Christophe Colomb*, Samuel Barber's *Antony and Cleopatra*, and John Corigliano's *The Ghosts of Versailles*.

Opéra Comique

Side by side with grand opera, the *opéra comique* pursued its course in France during the Romantic period. As in the eighteenth century, the technical difference between the two was that opéra comique used spoken dialogue instead of recitative. Apart from this, the differences were primarily those of size and subject matter. The opéra comique was less pretentious than grand opera, required fewer singers and players, and was written in a simpler musical idiom. Its plots, as a rule, presented straightforward comedy or semi-serious drama instead of the historical pageantry of grand opera. Two kinds of opéra comique existed in the early part of the nineteenth century, the romantic and the comic, although many works shared characteristics of both types. The extremely popular *La Dame blanche* (The White Lady), by François Adrien Boieldieu (1775–1834), first performed in Paris in 1825, has a predominantly romantic plot and melodious, graceful, sentimental music. Similar romantic opéras comiques were *Zampa* (1831) and *Le Pré aux clercs* (The Field of Honor, 1832) by Ferdinand Hérold (1791–1833). Daniel François Esprit Auber (1782–1871) displays a more caustic Parisian style in *Fra Diavolo* (Brother Devil, 1830) and his many other comic operas, which mingle humorous and romantic elements in tuneful music of considerable originality.

Romantic and comic operas

The gains of the working-class revolution of 1848 were short-lived: when the elected president Louis Napoleon Bonaparte (Napoleon's nephew) proclaimed himself Emperor Napoleon III in 1851, the Second French Republic became the Second French Empire. While censorship controlled the serious theaters, the *opéra bouffe* could freely satirize the Second Empire society. This new genre (not to be confused with the eighteenth-century Italian *opera buffa*) emphasized the smart, witty, and satirical elements of comic opera. Its founder was Jacques Offenbach (1819–1880), who managed to introduce a can-can for the gods in his opéra bouffe *Orphée aux enfers* (Orpheus in the Underworld, 1858). Offenbach's work influenced developments in comic opera elsewhere, including the operettas of W. S. Gilbert (librettist) and Arthur Sullivan (composer, 1842–1900) in England (for example, *The Mikado*, 1885), and of Johann Strauss the Younger (1825–1899)(for example, *Die Fledermaus* [The Bat], 1874) and many others in Vienna.

Opéra bouffe

The perennial charm of nineteenth-century comic opera owes much to its spontaneous melody and rhythm, simple textures and harmonies, and conventional formal patterns. But the deceptively naïve air should not mislead anyone into underrating this music.

Berlioz

The dramatic works of Hector Berlioz do not belong to any of the categories discussed above, which is one reason that his contribution to French Romantic opera has only recently been recognized. His most important dramatic work, *La Damnation de Faust*, is not an opera because it was not intended for stage performance. The title page calls it a "dramatic legend." It incorporates, with revisions, his earlier *Huit scènes de Faust* (1828–29). In the final version (1846) *La Damnation* consists of twenty scenes and requires three soloists, chorus, and orchestra. Like the *Symphonie fantastique* and *Roméo et Juliette*, it is a symphonic drama whose connecting plot is considered familiar to all, thereby permitting the composer to choose only those scenes most suitable for musical treatment and assuring the maximum variety with the greatest possible compactness.

La Damnation de Faust

The opera *Benvenuto Cellini* (1838), like *La Damnation de Faust*, has a chain of broadly conceived episodes rather than a well-developed plot. The score is notable for the vigor and diversity of its music and for the treatment of the crowd scenes, which foreshadow those of Wagner's *Meistersinger.* The crown of Berlioz's dramatic works is his great five-act opera *Les Troyens*, composed in 1856–58. Its first part, *La Prise de Troie* (The Capture of Troy), was not staged until 1890; the second part, *Les Troyens à Carthage* (The Trojans at Carthage), had a few performances in Paris in 1863. The text, by Berlioz himself, is based on the second and fourth books of Vergil's *Aeneid.* As in *Cellini* and *Faust*, only the essential action is presented, in a series of mighty scene-complexes. Berlioz condensed the narrative and used various appropriate occasions to introduce ballets, processions, and other musical numbers. The drama preserves the antique, epic quality of Vergil's poem, and the music speaks in the same accents. Not a note is there for mere effect; the style is severe, almost ascetic by comparison with Berlioz's earlier works. At the same time, every passion, every scene and incident, is brought to life intensely and on a heroic scale. *Les Troyens* represents the Romantic consummation of the French opera tradition descended from Lully, Rameau, and Gluck.

Benvenuto Cellini

Les Troyens

■ *Poster by J. Chéret announcing the first production of* Mignon *by Ambroise Thomas at the Opéra comique in Paris, 1866.* (PARIS, BIBLIOTHÈQUE DE L'OPÉRA)

French Lyric Opera

The romantic type of opéra comique developed into a genre that might best be termed *lyric opera.* Lyric opera lies somewhere between light opéra comique and grand opera. Like the opéra comique, its main appeal is through melody; its subject matter is romantic drama or fantasy, and its general scale is larger than that of the opéra comique, although still not so huge as that of the typical grand opera.

Gounod's *Faust*

Mignon (1866) by Ambroise Thomas (1811–1896) was a favorite lyric opera, but by far the most famous example of this genre is *Faust* by Charles Gounod (1818–1893). First staged in 1859 as an opéra comique (that is, with spoken dialogue), it was later arranged by the composer in its now familiar form with recitatives. Gounod wisely restricted himself to Part One of Goethe's drama, which deals chiefly with Faust and Gretchen's tragic love affair. The result is a work of just proportions in an elegant lyric style, with attractive melodies that are sufficiently expressive but not overly so. Gounod's other works for the stage include the opera *Roméo et Juliette* (1867) and a number of tuneful opéras comiques. Among Gounod's followers is Camille Saint-Saëns (1835–1921), whose most important dramatic production was the biblical opera *Samson et Dalila* (1877).

Georges Bizet (1838–1875)

Carmen

Bizet's *Carmen,* first performed at Paris in 1875, became a landmark in the history of French opera. Like the original version of *Faust, Carmen* was classified as an opéra comique because it contained spoken dialogue later set in recitative by Bizet's friend Ernest Guiraud. That such a stark, realistic drama ending with a tragic murder could be called "comique" shows that the distinction between opera and opéra comique had become a mere technicality. Bizet's rejection of a sentimental or mythological plot signaled a small but important move toward realism. The borrowed Spanish melodies—the Habanera and the seguidilla, both sung by Carmen in the first act—and the setting in Seville give it an exotic flavor, a vein running through the whole Romantic period and evident in some of Bizet's earlier works, for example, the incidental music to Daudet's play *L'Arlésienne* (The Woman from Arles), as well as in other French operas and ballets of the period. Chromatic harmony, sudden tonal shifts, ninth-chords—the vocabulary of Chopin and Liszt that Bizet surely absorbed as a virtuoso concert pianist in his youth—enrich the score. The famous refrain of Escamillo's second-act Toreador song, accompanied by simple tonic, dominant, and subdominant chords, when heard again in the following act as a disquieting reminiscence, becomes a study in chromatic counterpoint and harmony (Example 18.1). The orchestration, relying a great deal on brass and woodwinds, enhances the dramatic effect.

Example 18.1 *Georges Bizet,* Carmen: *Act 3*

GIUSEPPE VERDI

Career

The career of Giuseppe Verdi (1813–1901) by itself constitutes practically the history of Italian music for the fifty years following Donizetti. Except for the Requiem and a few other pieces, all of Verdi's published works were written for the stage. The first of his twenty-six operas was produced in 1839, the last in 1893. While his approach to dramatic structure evolved during these years, he enjoyed many successes at each stage.

Verdi, like his Italian predecessors Rossini, Donizetti, and Bellini, concentrated on the human drama in his operas, in contrast to the Germans' emphasis on romanticized nature and mythological symbolism. Especially in the earlier stages of his career, his primary medium was simple, direct vocal solo melody, in contrast to the orchestral and choral luxuriance of French grand opera. He had the advantage of strict training in harmony and counterpoint and a wide knowledge of the music of his predecessors. But before accepting anything, Verdi first fully assimilated it and made it part of his own language.

The course of Verdi's creative life reflects some of these influences. Up to *La battaglia di Legnano* (The Battle of Legnano; Rome, 1849) he cultivates a blunt, populist adaptation of the conventions of Rossini, Bellini, and Donizetti. With *Luisa Miller* (Naples, 1849), *Rigoletto* (Venice, 1851), *Il trovatore* (The Troubadour; Rome, 1853) and *La traviata* (The Fallen Woman; Venice, 1853) Verdi reaches new heights of dramatic compression and intensity. His subsequent operas become longer, more expansive. *Les vêpres siciliennes* (Sicilian Vespers; Paris, 1855), *Un ballo in maschera* (Masked Ball; St. Petersburg, 1862), *Don Carlos* (Paris, 1867), and *Aida* (Cairo, 1871) show the increasingly strong influence of the French grand opera. *Otello* (Milan, 1887) and *Falstaff* (Milan, 1893) follow a period of revisions on some earlier works.

Librettos

Verdi's librettists adapted works by Romantic authors, including Schiller (*Giovanna d'Arco*, *I masnadieri* [The Robbers], *Luisa Miller*, and *Don Carlos*), Victor Hugo (*Ernani* and *Rigoletto*), Dumas the Younger (*La traviata*), Byron (*I due Foscari*, *Il corsaro*), and Scribe (*Les vêpres siciliennes*, *Un ballo in maschera*); and by Spanish dramatists (*Il trovatore*, *La forza del destino*, and *Simon Boccanegra*). From Shakespeare, in addition to *Macbeth*, came the librettos of the last two operas, skillfully arranged by Verdi's friend, the poet and composer Arrigo Boito (1842–1918). *Aida* came from a plot sketched by a French Egyptologist, A. F. F. Mariette. Verdi expected from a libretto strong emotional situations, contrasts, and speed of action. As a result, most of his plots are violent blood-and-thunder melodramas, with some improbable characters and coincidences but with plenty of opportunity for exciting, lusty, ferocious themes and rhythms as well as for pretty, flowing melodies.

Early Works

Many of the early operas have notable choruses: *Nabucco* (1842), *I Lombardi* (The Lombards, 1843), *Giovanna d'Arco* (Joan of Arc, 1845), and *La battaglia di Legnano* (1849). *Luisa Miller* (1849) marks a turn toward finer psychological portrayal of character; emotion in the music becomes less raw than in the early operas. Musical characterization, dramatic unity, and melodic invention unite in the masterpiece *Rigoletto* (1851).

La traviata

Many of the features found in his early mature works are summed up in *La traviata* (1853), one of Verdi's most popular. The resources that he now commanded are plainly evident in the scene of the final act in which Violetta, the "fallen woman" of the title, and her lover Alfredo reconcile after she had left him to save his family's reputation (NAWM 119; CD 10 [7] / 3 ⟨63⟩). The scene features a new kind of song—flexible, expressive, semi-declamatory—that Verdi developed still further in *Otello*.

Don Carlos

Two ventures into grand opera, *Les vêpres siciliennes* (1855) and *Don Carlos* (1867), were both premiered in Paris. *Don Carlos* (revised 1884) contains powerful dramatic scenes, and displays orchestral and harmonic effects typical of Verdi's middle and late styles. Throughout the more expansive second period the operas appeared less frequently, as Verdi engaged in a certain amount of musical experimentation. Solo, ensemble, and chorus are more freely combined in the dramatic scheme, harmonies become more daring, and the orchestra is treated with great care and originality. Comic roles are introduced in *Un ballo in maschera* (1859) and *La forza del destino* (The Power of Destiny, 1862; revised 1869). At crucial points in both of these operas, Verdi brought back distinctive themes or motives introduced earlier in the score. Such "reminiscence motives," already common among other composers and used previously in *Ernani*, *Rigoletto*, and *La traviata*, help to unify the work both dramatically and musically. All the advances of the second period are gathered up in *Aida* (1871), which unites the heroic quality of grand opera with sound dramatic structure, vivid character delineation, pathos, and a wealth of melodic, harmonic, and orchestral color.

Reminiscence motives

Late Works

Sixteen years elapsed before the public saw another new opera by Verdi. A number of important works had appeared during this interval, among them Verdi's own Requiem, Bizet's *Carmen*, all four of Brahms's symphonies, Bruckner's Seventh Symphony, Wagner's *Ring* (in its first complete performance), and his *Parsifal*. Wagner's music was heard in Italy: *Lohengrin* and *Tannhäuser* in several major cities, other works as well in Bologna. Weber's *Der Freischütz* was staged in Milan in a translation by Boito, and Meyerbeer's operas were frequently performed. The publisher Giulio Ricordi, eager to see Verdi give Italian opera a boost, proposed *Otello* in a projected new libretto by Boito, who had scored a success in Bologna with his own opera *Mefistofele*. The final libretto presents a powerful human drama that the music penetrates, sustains, and intensifies at every turn. Verdi began *Otello* in 1884, four years after he received the first draft of Boito's libretto; it was produced at Milan in 1887. *Otello* was Verdi's response to the changed musical situation, for, despite his deliberate isolation, he was sensitive to new currents. Like Donizetti before him, Verdi had been striving for greater continuity in the music, and here he

Otello

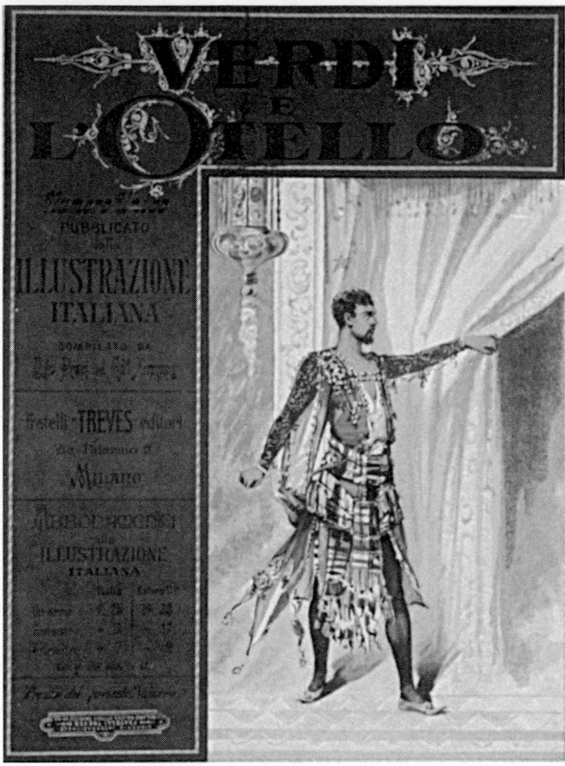

■ *Otello approaching Desdemona's bed in Verdi's* Otello, *Act IV. Special* Otello *issue of* L'Illustrazione italiana, *February 1887.* (MILAN, RICORDI, ARCHIVIO STORICO)

realized it most completely, through unifying motives in the orchestra and in the unbroken flow of the music within each act. Closer inspection reveals that the traditional scheme of declamatory and lyrical solos, duets, ensembles, and choruses is still present. But the units are arranged in larger scene-complexes in which a stretch of recitative-like blank verse is set in a free declamatory style, while rhymed verse is set melodically, sometimes culminating in a short aria, followed by a transition to another such complex.

Act IV, set in Desdemona's bedroom and ending in her murder by Otello, is a good example of this musical continuity. After a brief woodwind prelude, Desdemona and Iago's wife Emilia converse as Desdemona apprehensively gets ready for bed. Passages marked "recitativo," with sparse chords in the orchestra, alternate with fragments of melody that pick up motives previewed in the prelude. Desdemona then sings an incomparably sad song she learned from her mother's maid about a woman, abandoned by her lover, who asks that her funeral garland be cut from a willow tree. The melody of the first line of this *Willow Song,* "Piangea cantando" (She wept singing), was already heard in the first measures of the prelude. Between the strophes, she issues instructions to Emilia and even breaks the strophes with comments. After Desdemona bids Emilia good night, an instrumental epilogue dwells on a motive from the prelude played against an ominous chromatic descending tremolo.

This merges directly into the next scene, in which Desdemona, kneeling before an image of the Virgin, says her nightly *Ave Maria* (Hail Mary), at first reciting on a monotone, then breaking into a hymnlike aria. As she falls asleep, several soft motives are developed in the lower strings. Otello then makes his stealthy entrance, lays a scimitar on the table, looks at Desdemona, extinguishes a candle, opens the bed curtains, and kisses her three times. The most prominent of these motives are a staccato turn-figure in the violas punctuated by a soft bass drum (Example 18.2a) and a reminiscence of the love duet from Act I (Example 18.2b). The vocal lines are declamatory, varying from unmeasured recitation on one note to lyrical moments in which the orchestra doubles the voice.

Falstaff

If *Otello* was the consummation of Italian tragic opera, *Falstaff* (1893) holds a parallel place in comic opera. As *Otello* transformed dramatic lyrical melody, so *Falstaff* transformed that characteristic element of opera buffa, the ensemble. Carried along over a nimble, fine-spun, endlessly varied orchestral background, the comedy speeds to its climaxes in the great finales of the second and third acts. At times Verdi seems to be satirizing the entire Romantic century, himself included. The last scene culminates in a fugue on the words "Tutto nel mondo è burla. L'uom' è nato burlone"—All the world's a joke. We are all born fools.

Nationalism

Verdi maintained a resolute independence in his own musical style and deplored the influence of foreign, especially German, ideas in the work of his younger compatriots. A few of his early operas contain choruses that were politically inflammatory, thinly disguised appeals to his compatriots struggling for national unity and against foreign domination during the stirring years of the *Risorgimento* (national rebirth). By 1859 Verdi's name had become a patriotic symbol and rallying cry: "Viva Verdi!" to Italian patriots stood for "**Viva V**ittorio **E**manuele **R**e **d'I**talia!"—Long live Victor Emanuel, king of Italy.

Example 18.2 *Giuseppe Verdi,* Otello, *Act IV, Scene 3: Motives*

a.

b.

GERMANY

The interaction between music and literature, so typical of nineteenth-century Romanticism, developed most fully in the German-speaking lands, in opera as well as song and instrumental music. At the root of German opera was the Singspiel, which in the early nineteenth century soaked up Romantic elements from French opera while keeping and even intensifying its specific national features. Both trends are illustrated by two operas produced in 1816: *Undine* by E. T. A. Hoffmann and *Faust* by Ludwig Spohr (1784–1859), a famous violinist and a leading German composer of symphonic music. But the work that established German Romantic opera was Weber's *Der Freischütz,* first performed at Berlin in 1821.

Hoffmann and Spohr

Carl Maria von Weber (1786–1826)

From early childhood his principal music teachers were Michael Haydn and Georg Joseph Vogler (1749–1814), generally known as Abbé or Abt Vogler, an organist, organ builder, theorist, and composer of operas and church music. Weber became director of the opera at Prague in 1813 and at Dresden in 1816. Weber was familiar with the theater. His chief dramatic compositions besides *Der Freischütz* were *Euryanthe* (Vienna, 1823) and *Oberon* (London, 1826).

German Romantic opera

The libretto of *Der Freischütz* exemplifies the characteristics of German Romantic opera. Plots are drawn from medieval history, legend, or fairy tale. The story involves supernatural beings and happenings set against a background of wilderness and mystery, but scenes of humble village or country life are frequently introduced. Supernatural incidents and the natural setting are not incidental or decorative but are intertwined with the fate of the human protagonists. Mortal characters act not merely as individuals, but as agents or representatives of superhuman forces, whether good or evil. The triumph of good is a form of salvation or redemption, a vaguely religious concept of deliverance from sin and error through suffering, conversion, or revelation. In giving such importance to the physical and spiritual background, German opera differs sharply from contemporary French and Italian opera. But its musical styles and forms resemble those of other countries, although the use of simple folklike melodies introduces a distinctly German national element. German opera also displays increasingly chromatic harmony, the use of orchestral color for dramatic expression, and an emphasis on the inner voices of the texture in contrast to the Italian stress on melody.

Der Freischütz

Certain details of *Der Freischütz* will serve to illustrate these generalizations. In a story line derived from folklore and immortalized in Goethe's *Faust,* Caspar, Max's unsuccessful rival for the love of Agathe, has sold his soul to the devil (who has taken the form of Samiel, the legendary Black Huntsman) and must procure another victim for him. To this end, Caspar persuades Max to make a pact with Samiel for magic bullets that will allow Max to win a marksmanship contest and thereby Agathe's hand. The bullets work their magic, but the last one is controlled by Samiel, who has destined it to kill Agathe. Max uses up three bullets to impress the Prince before the contest begins and has only one left—that guided by Samiel—for the fateful trial. Although Agathe unexpectedly appears in the line of fire as Max shoots, she is protected by an old hermit's magical wreath. The bullet kills Caspar instead, and all ends well. The somber forest background is depicted idyllically by the horns at the beginning of the overture and diabolically in the eerie midnight scene in the Wolf's Glen (finale of Act II, NAWM 120; CD 10 [11]). Rustic choruses, marches, dances, and airs mingle in the score with full-bodied arias in the Italian style.

Melodrama

Unlike other overtures from the period, Weber's for *Der Freischütz* is not a simple medley of tunes; rather, it introduces several themes from the opera in a complete sonata-form movement with a slow introduction. The Wolf's Glen Scene, during which the bullets are cast, incorporates elements of the *melodrama*, a genre of musical theater that combined spoken dialogue with background music. In speaking his lines over continuous orchestral music, Caspar first evokes Samiel. Then, as he casts each bullet, with Max cowering beside him, Caspar counts *eins*, *zwei*, *drei*, etc., and the mountains echo each count. For each casting Weber paints a different miniature nature-picture of the terrifying setting and wildlife of the dark forest. Throughout, Weber ingeniously exploits the resources of the orchestra: timpani, trombones, clarinets, and horns in the foreground, often against string tremolos. Shocking diminished and augmented intervals and daring chromaticism are prominent in the melody and harmony.

Setting by Carl Wilhelm Holdermann for the Wolf's Glen Scene in Weber's Der Freischütz *(Weimar production of 1822). As Caspar casts the bullets, Max looks around with growing alarm, while "night birds crowd around the fire" and the "cracking of whips and the sound of galloping horses is heard."* (WEIMAR, STAATLICHE KUNST SAMMLUNGEN, SCHLOSS MUSEUM)

Der Freischütz's immense popular success, based both on its appeal to national sentiment and on the beauty of its music, was not matched either by Weber's later works or by those of his immediate followers. *Euryanthe*, Weber's only opera with no spoken dialogue, is on a scale approaching grand opera. *Euryanthe* is unified, even more than *Der Freischütz*, by its continuous musical texture, its contrasting harmonic styles that characterize the opposing dramatic forces, and by the recurrence and transformation of musical themes. This device of recurring themes in opera resembles the cyclical method used in symphonic music by Liszt. It was not altogether new in opera, but it was first used extensively and systematically by the nineteenth-century composer. This approach represents a radical departure from the older convention, in which the various divisions of an opera or a symphony were thematically independent.

Euryanthe

Oberon, Weber's last opera, suffers from an insignificant and rambling libretto. By way of compensation, however, the score contains some of his most sophisticated passages of orchestral color, along with some good examples of tone painting.

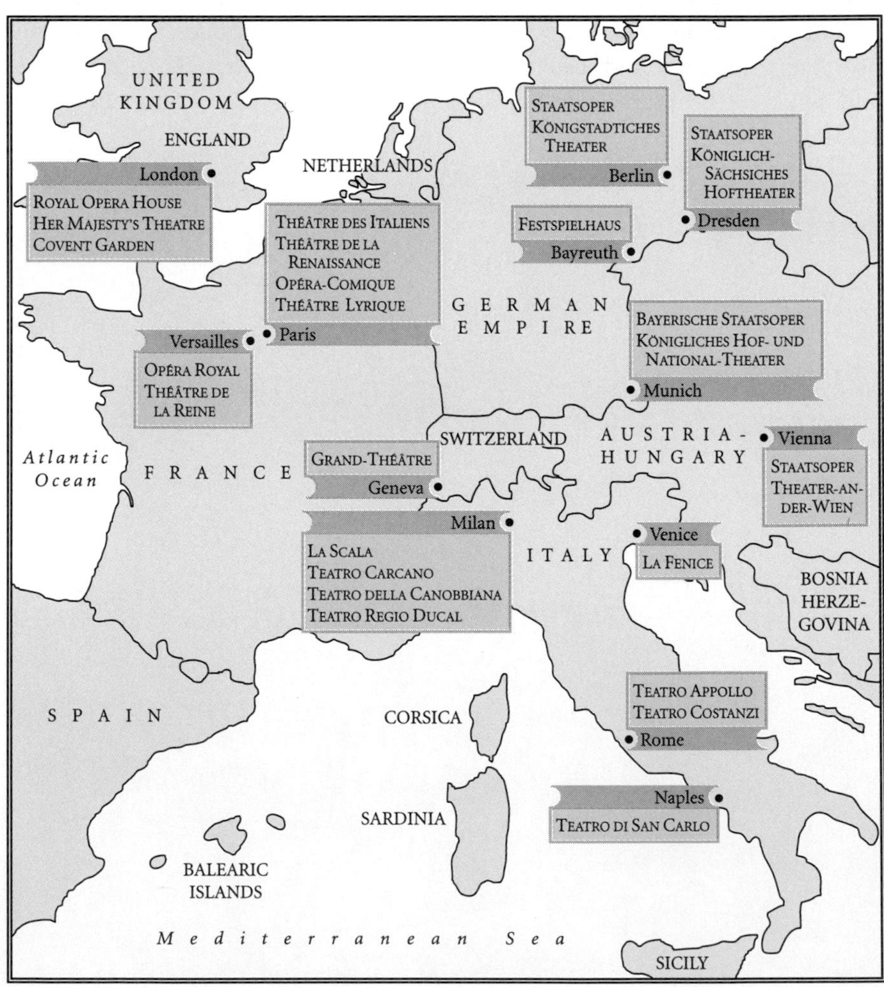

European opera houses in the nineteenth century

Other German Opera Composers

Most of Schubert's thirteen operas—some unfinished—and seven Singspiele never reached the stage during his lifetime and have remained without influence, although they contain a great deal of excellent music. German opera for twenty years after Weber was carried on by a number of worthy composers, including Heinrich Marschner (1795–1861) and Albert Lortzing (1801–51). Marschner specialized in the Romantic Singspiel of a semi-popular sort. His most important work, *Hans Heiling* (1833), derives from Weber and at the same time looks forward to Wagner in both its plot and its musical style. Lortzing's *Zar und Zimmermann* (Czar and Carpenter, 1837) is a good example of the comic genre in which he excelled. Other German composers of comic opera were Otto Nicolai (1810–1849) and Liszt's disciple, Peter Cornelius, whose *Der Barbier von Bagdad* (The Barber of Bagdad, 1858) is witty and original. Schumann's romantic opera *Genoveva* (1850), despite critical praise for the quality of its music, won no success in the theater. In addition to the national opera, the French opéra comique was popular in Germany between 1830 and 1850.

Marschner and Lortzing

Nicolai and Cornelius

RICHARD WAGNER AND THE MUSIC DRAMA

The outstanding composer of German opera, and one of the crucial figures in the history of nineteenth-century music, was Richard Wagner. His significance is threefold: he brought German Romantic opera to its consummation, as Verdi did for Italian opera; he created a new genre, the *music drama*; and he hastened the dissolution of tonality through the harmonic idiom of his late works. As a published writer, Wagner made his views known not only about music but also about literature, drama, and even political and moral topics. The reception of his work in the twentieth century has been affected by political, ethnic, and religious policies and issues. The National Socialist (Nazi) movement in Germany appropriated Wagner's music as a symbol of the best of Aryan and German culture. This and the anti-Semitism expressed in his *Das Judentum in der Musik* (Judaism in Music), which appeared under a pseudonym in 1850 and under Wagner's name in 1869, has alienated some listeners and musicians from his music dramas.

What drove him to write this essay, he explained to Liszt, was his antipathy toward Meyerbeer, whose music he once admired and from whom he had sought help to get his early works performed. But Wagner's feelings turned against the composer when critics wrote how much Meyerbeer influenced his own music. One critic in 1850 asserted that Wagner in *Rienzi* and *Tannhauser* had combined the styles of Weber and Meyerbeer. In his essay Wagner attributed the weakness of Meyerbeer's music to the fact that he was Jewish and therefore lacked national roots, without which a composer could not have an authentic style. Wagner implied that Mendelssohn, whom he had revered in his younger days, also suffered from this deracination, despite his conversion to Christianity. Wagner's essay added strength to an anti-semitic undercurrent in German culture.[3]

For Wagner, the function of music was to serve the ends of dramatic expression, and all his important compositions are for the stage. His first triumph came with *Rienzi*, a five-act grand opera performed at Dresden in 1842. The following year Dresden saw a production of *Der fliegende Holländer* (The Flying Dutchman), a Romantic opera in the tradition of Weber and Marschner. The success of these two works led to Wagner's appointment as director of the Dresden Opera, putting a temporary end to a long period of wandering and struggle in his life.

Der fliegende Holländer

The lines of development that Wagner followed in his later works are established in *Der fliegende Holländer*. The libretto—written, like those of all his operas, by the composer himself—is based on a legend. The action takes place against a background of a stormy sea, and the hero is redeemed through the unselfish love of the heroine, Senta. Wagner's music is most vivid in its depiction of the storm and of the contrasting ideas of curse and salvation, which are clearly set forth in Senta's ballad, the central number of the opera. The themes of the ballad appear in the overture and recur elsewhere throughout the opera.

Tannhäuser

In *Tannhäuser* (Dresden, 1845), Wagner brilliantly adapted medieval legend to the framework of grand opera. The music, like that of *Der fliegende Holländer*, evokes the contrasting worlds of sin and blessedness, but with greater emotional fervor and more luxuriant harmony and color. The display numbers—the Venusberg ballet added for Paris in 1861, the Pilgrims' choruses, and the song contest—are plausibly connected with the course of the drama, and effective use is made of thematic recurrence. Wagner introduced a new kind of flexible, semi-declamatory vocal line in Tannhäuser's narrative in Act III, "Inbrunst im Herzen" (With ardor in my heart). This became his normal method of setting text.

Lohengrin

Lohengrin, first performed under Liszt's direction at Weimar in 1850, embodies several other changes that foreshadow the music dramas that followed. In this work, Wagner's treatment of medieval legend and German folklore is both moralizing and symbolic. Lohengrin may represent divine love descending in human form, and Elsa the weakness of humanity unable to receive with faith the offered blessing. Such a symbolic interpretation is suggested by the Prelude, which depicts the descent of the Holy Grail and its return to Heaven.

The orchestration of *Lohengrin* is at once fuller and more subdued than that of *Tannhäuser*; the music flows more continuously, with fewer traces of separate numbers. The well-written choruses are combined with solo singing and orchestral background into long, unified musical scenes. Wagner's new style of declamatory, arioso melody, as in Act III, Scene 3, Lohengrin's "In fernem Land" (In a distant land) appears more often. The technique of recurring

3. For a well-documented review of this question, see Jacob Katz, *The Darker Side of Genius: Richard Wagner's Antisemitism* (Hanover, N.H.: University Press of New England, 1986).

WAGNER SUMS UP HIS EARLY CAREER IN A LETTER TO A FRIEND

Despite a serious scholarly education, I kept in close touch with the theater in my younger years. These coincided with the last years of Carl Maria von Weber, who periodically performed his operas in the same city of Dresden. I owed my first musical experiences to this master, whose airs filled me with enthusiastic admiration and whose personality greatly fascinated me. His death in a distant land [London, June 5, 1826] filled my child's heart with dread. I became aware of Beethoven just as I learned of his death [March 26, 1827], not long after Weber's. I then came to know his music also, drawn to it first by the puzzling reports concerning his death. Stirred by these deep impressions, a pronounced inclination for music kept growing in me. But it was only after broader studies introduced me to classical antiquity and awoke my urge to write poetry that I began to study music systematically. I wanted to compose music for a tragedy [*Leubald*] that I had written.

Rossini once asked his teacher whether an opera composer needed to learn counterpoint. The teacher, thinking of modern Italian opera, replied that he did not, and the pupil gladly desisted. After my teacher [Christian Theodor Weinlig, cantor of the Thomaskirche in Leipzig] had taught me the most difficult contrapuntal methods, he said to me, "You may never have to write a fugue, but being able to write one will give you technical self-reliance and will make everything else seem easy." Thus trained, I embarked on a career as a music-director in a theater[at Würzburg in 1833] and began to set to music opera librettos I had written [e.g., *Die Feen*].

Richard Wagner, *Zukunftsmusik* (Music of the Future), a letter to a friend, François Villot, as a preface to a prose translation into French of four of Wagner's librettos, Paris, September 15, 1860. Trans. from Wagner, *Gesammelte Schriften*, ed. Julius Rapp (Leipzig: Hesse & Becker, 1914), 1:183. For a translation of the entire essay, see *Richard Wagner's Prose Works*, trans. William Ashton Ellis (London: William Reeves, 1907), 3:295–345.

themes is further developed and refined, particularly with respect to the motives associated with Lohengrin and the Grail and the motive of the forbidden question, heard first in Act I, Scene 3, at Lohengrin's words "Nie sollst du mich befragen" (You must never ask me [my name and origins]; Example 18.3). Like Weber, Wagner used tonality to help organize both the drama and the music: Lohengrin's key is A major, Elsa's A♭, and that of the evil personages F♯

Example 18.3 *Richard Wagner,* Lohengrin: *Act I, Scene 3*

■ *The Bayreuth Festival Theater, designed by Otto Brückwald, incorporated Wagner's ideals for the production of music drama. There he was able to produce the* Ring *in its entirety for the first time in August 1876.* Parsifal *(1882) was written for this theater, which continues to be the stage for the Bayreuth Festival today.*

minor. The style on the whole is diatonic, with modulations usually toward the mediant keys.

Wagner's involvement in the political unrest in Germany during 1848–49 obliged him to emigrate to Switzerland, which became his home for the next ten years. Here he found the leisure to formulate his theories about opera and to publish them in a series of essays, the most important of which is *Oper und Drama* (Opera and Drama, 1851; revised 1868). At the same time he was writing the poems of a cycle of four dramas with the collective title *Der Ring des Nibelungen* (The Ring of the Nibelungs). The music of the first two—*Das Rheingold* (The Rhine Gold) and *Die Walküre* (The Valkyrie)—and part of the third, *Siegfried*, was finished by 1857; the entire cycle was completed with *Götterdämmerung* (The Twilight of the Gods) in 1874, and the first complete performance took place two years later in a theater built in Bayreuth according to Wagner's specifications. The four dramas, woven out of stories from Norse legends, are linked by a common set of characters and musical motives. The "Ring" of the title refers to a ring that the gnome Alberich fashioned out of gold he stole from the Rhine, where it was guarded by the Rhine maidens. Wotan, the ruler of the gods, with the help of the clever Loge, manages to retrieve the ring from Alberich and captures, in addition, a hoard of gold, which he uses to pay the giants Fafner and Fasolt for bulding his new castle, Valhalla.

Essays and Librettos

Der Ring des Nibelungen

But Alberich has put a curse on the ring that will bring its wearer misery and death. In the course of the four dramas the curse is fulfilled and the Rhine maidens get back the ring. During a break from composing *Siegfried*, Wagner wrote *Tristan und Isolde* (1857–59), and during another, *Die Meistersinger von Nürnberg* (The Mastersingers of Nuremberg, 1862–67). His final work was *Parsifal* (1882).

Gesamtkunstwerk

Wagner believed in the absolute oneness of drama and music—that the two are organically connected expressions of a single dramatic idea. Poetry, scenic design, staging, action, and music work together to form what he called a *Gesamtkunstwerk* (total or joint artwork). He considered the action of the drama to have an inner and an outer aspect. The orchestra conveys the inner aspect, while the sung words articulate the outer aspect—the events and situations that further the action. The orchestral web is, then, the chief factor in the music, and the vocal lines are part of the musical texture.

In Wagner's music dramas, the music is continuous throughout each act, not formally divided into recitatives, arias, and other set numbers, thus accelerating a growing tendency toward continuity in nineteenth-century opera. Yet broad scene divisions remain, and we can distinguish between recitative-like passages with orchestral punctuation and others of arioso melody with continuous orchestral scoring. Moreover, the drama is occasionally interrupted or adorned with scenes that are plainly grand opera and not strictly necessary to the plot.

The Leitmotif

Wagner achieved coherence within the continuity of the action and music by means of the *Leitmotif*, a musical theme or motive associated with a particular person, thing, emotion, or idea in the drama. The association is established by sounding the leitmotif (usually in the orchestra) at the first appearance on stage or mention of the subject, and by its repetition at subsequent appearances or citations. Often the significance of a leitmotif can be recognized from the words to which it is first sung. Thus the leitmotif is a sort of musical label, but it is more than that: it accumulates significance as it recurs in new contexts; it may recall an object in situations where the object itself is not present; it may be varied, developed, or transformed as the plot develops; similar motives may suggest a connection between the objects to which they refer; motives may be contrapuntally combined; and, finally, by their repetition, motives may help unify a scene or an opera as recurrent themes unify a symphony. Theoretically there is a complete correspondence between the symphonic web of leitmotifs and the dramatic web of the action; in practice, however, Wagner sometimes introduced certain motives for purely musical reasons, without any obvious connection with the dramatic situation of the moment.

Tristan

Wagner's idea of music drama and the use of leitmotifs may be illustrated through *Tristan und Isolde*. The story comes from a thirteenth-century medieval romance by Gottfried von Strassburg. Example 18.4 shows the leitmotifs of *Tristan* in the order of their appearance in the last section of Act 1, Scene 5, from the entrance of the sailors (NAWM 121; CD 10 [22] / 4 ⟨1⟩). The text sung at the leitmotif's most characteristic appearance is given along with the motive.

Wagner's use of the leitmotif differs from that of reminiscence motives by Weber, Verdi, and others. Wagner's motives themselves are for the most part short, concentrated, and intended to characterize their object at various levels of meaning. The first motive of Example 18.4d, for example, is identified with the longing that Tristan and Isolde feel for each other, now intensified by the love potion. At the same time, the harmonic progression from the dominant seventh of A minor to the chord on the sixth degree—the deceptive-cadence pattern first heard in the prelude—symbolizes the very essence of the drama, a love doomed to remain unfulfilled.

Function of leitmotifs

Another and more important difference is that Wagner's leitmotifs are the basic musical material of the score. He uses them not once in a while but constantly, in intimate alliance with every step of the action. They also serve as ele-

Example 18.4 *Richard Wagner,* Tristan und Isolde: *Leitmotifs*

ments for forming melodies, replacing the four-square phrases set off by caesuras and cadences of earlier composers. The leitmotifs, their development, their restatements and variants, and the connective tissue linking these, form the stuff of "musical prose" with which Wagner wanted to replace the "poetic" rhythms of symmetrical phrases. The impression we have of "endless melody" results from the ongoing continuity of line, unbroken by the stops and restarts of Classic musical syntax.

Act I, Scene 5, of *Tristan*, in which Tristan and Isolde fall in love (NAWM 121), demonstrates the effective intertwining of action, scenery, and musical forces. The shipboard gear, sails, lines, Isolde's private quarters, and the nearby shore objectify Tristan's assigned mission, to deliver the reluctant Isolde to the king as his bride. As the ship's crew drops anchor and hails the king on shore, the two lovers, oblivious of the excitement around them, succumb to a love potion that Brangäne substituted for the poison Isolde had demanded. The chorus, with its realistic shouts, interrupts the declamation of Tristan and Isolde, which is sometimes speechlike, sometimes lyrical and passionate. The large orchestra maintains continuity throughout the action, but within each segment of the text it elaborates motives that back up the content of the speech or the underlying emotions and associations. Thus action, dialogue, musical scene-painting, and lyrical expression are not parceled out to different moments of music, but all constantly mingle and reinforce one another.

Some details of the scene will illustrate how the motives acquire meaning, and how the harmonic progressions come to symbolize the dramatic situation. The motive of Tristan's honor (Example 18.4a), identified by the sung text "Tristans Ehre," will be developed later on. As Isolde begins to drink the potion, she sings "Ich trink' sie dir!" (I drink to you) to a rising major sixth, followed by two descending semitones (Example 18.4b), a motive that from then on is associated with the love potion. The orchestra takes up the motive and provides a new twist through ascending semitones (Example 18.4c), suggesting mutual longing. The climactic moment is reached when the two stare lingeringly at each other (Example 18.4d), and the rising chromatic motive is accompanied by a progression from a dominant-ninth chord to a deceptive F-major harmony instead of the expected A minor, symbolizing perhaps the foiled death wish. Now Isolde and Tristan call to each other, and a new motive (Example 18.4e) is developed. The words "Sehnender Minne" (passionate love), which they pronounce together, identify a still further motive (Example 18.4f), which is churned through a series of rising sequences. The celebratory music hailing the king (Example 18.4g) increasingly competes for attention with the continued rapture of the lovers until the curtain falls at the end of Act I.

Die Meistersinger

In contrast to the tragic gloom and extreme chromaticism of *Tristan* are the sunny human comedy and pronounced diatonic passages of *Die Meistersinger.* Here Wagner succeeded most fully in fusing his ideas about music drama with the conventions of Romantic opera and in combining nationalism with universal appeal. *Parsifal*, by comparison, is less assured, less unified both in content and musical form, but abounds, as does *Die Meistersinger*, in beautiful choral scenes and instrumental episodes.

Wagner's Influence

Few works in the history of Western music have so deeply affected succeeding generations of composers as did *Tristan und Isolde.* In the harmony of his later works, especially in *Tristan* and the prelude to the third act of *Parsifal,* we see the culmination of a personal style that was influenced in the 1850s by the chromatic idiom of Liszt's symphonic poems. The complex chromatic alterations of chords in *Tristan,* together with the constant shifting of key, the telescoping of resolutions, and the blurring of progressions by means of suspensions and other nonharmonic tones, produces a novel, ambiguous kind of tonality that can be explained only partially in terms of the harmonic system of the previous two centuries.

Wagner's peculiar use of mythology and symbolism did not appeal much to subsequent composers, but his ideal of opera as a drama with words, stage setting, visible action, and music all working closely together profoundly influenced later composers. Almost equally influential was his method of minimizing divisions within an act and charging the symphonic orchestra with maintaining continuity by developing pregnant musical motives while the voices sang in free, arioso lines rather than in the balanced phrases of the traditional aria. As a master of orchestral color Wagner had few equals, and here also his example bore fruit.

Bibliography

Music Collections

For collected editions, see below; refer also to the Bibliography for Chapters 16–17.

Most of the operas mentioned in this chapter are available in piano-vocal scores, a few in full or miniature orchestral scores. For facsimiles of operas by early Romantic composers, see Philip Gossett and Charles Rosen, eds., *Early Romantic Opera* (New York: Garland, 1977–). Composers include Bellini, Rossini, Meyerbeer, and others. See also *Italian Opera: 1810–40,* 58 vols., ed. P. Gossett (New York: Garland, 1986–), for facsimiles of printed editions of complete operas and excerpts by the contemporaries of Rossini, Bellini, and Donizetti (e.g., Mercadante, Ricci brothers, Mayr).

Non-operatic works of Rossini appear in the *Quaderni Rossiniani* (Pesaro: Fondazione Rossini, 1954–).

Wagner, *Musikalische Werke,* ed. Michael Balling (Leipzig: Breitkopf & Härtel, 1912–29); this incomplete edition has been reprinted (New York: Da Capo Press, 1971). A new edition, presumably to be complete and authoritative, was begun at Mainz, ed. Carl Dahlhaus et al. (B. Schott's Söhne, 1970–). The catalogue of works is *Richard Wagner Werk-Verzeichnis: Verzeichnis der musikalischen Werke Richard Wagners und ihrer Quellen,* ed. John Deathridge, Martin Geck, and Egon Voss (Mainz: Schott, 1986).

Carl Maria von Weber, *Gesamtausgabe* (Mainz: Schott, 1997–).

For Further Reading

General

A rich source of information, interpretation, and bibliography in the entire field of opera is the *New Grove Dictionary of Opera,* 4 vols. (New York: Grove's Dictionaries of Music,

1992). Key articles from the general *New Grove* are assembled in Stanley Sadie, ed., *History of Opera* (New York: Norton, 1990). More strictly bibliographical is Guy A. Marco, *Opera: A Research and Information Guide* (New York: Garland, 1984). For a chronological survey consult Donald J. Grout, *A Short History of Opera*, 3rd ed. with Hermine Weigel Williams (New York: Columbia University Press, 1988). Particularly pertinent to this chapter are *The New Grove Masters of Italian Opera* (Rossini, Donizetti, Bellini, Verdi, and Puccini), by Philip Gossett et al. (New York: Norton, 1983); Edward J. Dent, *The Rise of Romantic Opera*, ed. Winton Dean (Cambridge: Cambridge University Press, 1976); Joseph Kerman, *Opera as Drama*, new and rev. ed. (Berkeley: University of California Press, 1988). For a history of the libretto, see Patrick Smith, *The Tenth Muse* (New York: Knopf, 1970); see also the Bibliography for Chapters. 16–17. For some provocative new approaches read the essays in *Analyzing Opera: Verdi and Wagner*, ed. Carolyn Abbate and Roger Parker (Berkeley: University of California Press, 1989) and Abbate, *Unsung Voices: Opera and Musical Narrative in the Nineteenth Century* (Princeton: Princeton University Press, 1991).

On French grand opera, consult William L. Crosten, *French Grand Opera: An Art and a Business* (New York: King's Crown Press, 1948; repr. Da Capo Press, 1972); Karin Pendle, *Eugène Scribe and French Opera of the Nineteenth Century* (Ann Arbor, Mich.: University Microfilms International, 1980); and Jane F. Fulcher, *The Nation's Image: French Grand Opera as Politics and Politicized Art* (Cambridge: Cambridge University Press, 1987).

On individual operas, see the Cambridge Opera Handbooks (Cambridge: Cambridge University Press), including Bizet, *Carmen*, ed. Susan McClary (1992); Berlioz, *Les Troyens*, ed. Ian Kemp (1989); Verdi, *Falstaff* and *Otello*, ed. James A. Hepokoski (1983 and 1987); Wagner, *Parsifal*, ed. Lucy Beckett (1981).

Individual Composers

Bellini John Rosselli, *The Life of Bellini* (Cambridge: Cambridge University Press, 1996); Leslie Orrey, *Bellini* (London: Dent, 1969); Simon Maguire, *Vincenzo Bellini and the Aesthetics of Early Nineteenth-Century Italian Opera* (New York: Garland, 1989).

Berlioz See Bibliography for Chapter 16.

Bizet Mina Curtiss, *Bizet and His World* (New York: Knopf, 1958); Winton Dean, *Georges Bizet, His Life and Work*, 3rd ed. (London: Dent, 1975).

Donizetti William Ashbrook, *Donizetti and His Operas* (Cambridge: Cambridge University Press, 1982); Philip Gossett, *Anna Bolena and the Artistic Maturity of Gaetano Donizetti* (Oxford: Clarendon Press, 1985); Herbert Weinstock, *Donizetti and the World of Opera in Italy, Paris and Vienna in the First Half of the Nineteenth Century* (New York: Pantheon Books, 1963); John Allitt, *Donizetti in the Light of Romanticism and the Teaching of Johann Simon Mayr* (Shaftesbury, Dorset: Element, 1991).

Rossini Herbert Weinstock, *Rossini: A Biography* (New York: Knopf, 1968); Richard Osborne, *Rossini* (London: Dent, 1986); Stendhal [Marie Henri Beyle], *Life of Rossini*, 1824, trans. Richard N. Coe (Seattle: University of Washington Press, 1972), a book by a hero-worshiping contemporary, who gives delightful insights though not accurate information. On Rossini's overtures, see Philip Gossett, "The Overtures of Rossini," *19th-Century Music* 3 (July 1979):3–31.

Verdi For biography, see Julian Budden, *Verdi* (London: Dent, 1985) and Frank Walker's *The Man Verdi* (New York: Knopf, 1962); for a treatment of his music, see Budden's *The Operas of Verdi*, 3 vols. (New York: Praeger, 1973–82). Other books: James A. Hepokoski, *Falstaff* and *Otello* (Cambridge: Cambridge University Press, 1983 and 1987); *The Verdi Companion*, ed. William Weaver and Martin Chusid (New York: Norton, 1979); *Verdi's Middle Period: Source Studies, Analysis, and Performance Practice*, ed. Martin Chusid

(Chicago: University of Chicago Press, 1997); David Rosen, *Verdi: Requiem* (Cambridge: Cambridge University Press, 1995); Cecil Hopkinson, *A Bibliography of the Works of Giuseppe Verdi, 1813–1910*, Vol. 2: Operatic Works (New York: Broude Brothers, 1978); William Weaver, *Verdi: A Documentary Study* (London: Thames & Hudson, 1977); David Kimbell, *Verdi in the Age of Italian Romanticism* (Cambridge: Cambridge University Press, 1981).

Wagner Still useful is the monumental biography by Ernest Newman, *Life of Richard Wagner*, 4 vols. (London: Cassell, 1933–47; repr. New York: Cambridge University Press, 1976). An excellent 1-vol. account of his life is Martin Gregor-Dellin, *Richard Wagner*, trans. J. Maxwell Brownjohn (San Diego: Harcourt Brace Jovanovich, 1983). Refer also to *The New Grove Wagner*, by John Deathridge and Carl Dahlhaus (New York: Norton, 1984). Other studies include Herbert Barth et al., eds., *Wagner: A Documentary Study*, trans. P. R. J. Ford and Mary Whittall (New York: Oxford University Press, 1975); Curt von Westernhagen, *Wagner: A Biography*, 2 vols., trans. Mary Whittall (Cambridge: Cambridge University Press, 1978); Peter Burbridge and Richard Sutton, eds., *The Wagner Companion* (Cambridge: Cambridge University Press, 1979); Carl Dahlhaus, *Richard Wagner's Music Dramas*, trans. Mary Whittall (Cambridge: Cambridge University Press, 1979); Ernest Hutcheson, *A Musical Guide to Richard Wagner, Ring of the Nibelung* (New York: Simon & Schuster, 1940; repr. 1972); Robert Bailey, *Prelude and Transfiguration from 'Tristan and Isolde'* (New York: Norton, 1985), Norton Critical Scores, which gives historical background, views and comments, and analytical essays of the work. Some significant new interpretations of Wagner's life and works are in Robert W. Gutman, *Richard Wagner; the Man, His Mind, and His Music* (New York: Harcourt Brace Jovanovich, 1974); Derek Watson, *Richard Wagner: A Biography* (New York: Schirmer Books, 1981); Robert Bailey, "The Structure of the Ring and Its Evolution," *19th-Century Music* 1 (July 1977):48–61.

See also Wagner's *Prose Works*, 8 vols., trans. William Ashton Ellis (London, 1892–99; repr. New York: Broude Brothers, 1966), esp. Vol. 1 ("Art and Revolution" and "The Artwork of the Future") and Vol. 2 ("Opera and Drama"). Commentary on these is in Edward A. Lippman, "The Esthetic Theories of Richard Wagner," MQ 44 (1958):209–20; Dieter Borchmeyer, *Richard Wagner, Theory and Theatre*, trans. Stewart Spencer (Oxford: Clarendon Press, 1991); and Thomas S. Grey, *Wagner's Musical Prose: Text and Contexts* (Cambridge: Cambridge University Press, 1995). Personal documentary material: Wagner, *My Life*, trans. Andrew Grey, ed. Mary Whittall (Cambridge: Cambridge University Press, 1983); also made available are *Cosima Wagner's Diaries*, ed. Martin Gregor-Dellin and Dietrich Mack, trans. Geoffrey Skelton, 2 vols. (New York: Harcourt Brace Jovanovich, 1978–80).

On Wagner's compositional process, see Curt von Westernhagen's *The Forging of the 'Ring': Richard Wagner's Composition Sketches for 'Der Ring des Nibelungen,'* trans. Arnold and Mary Whittall (Cambridge: Cambridge University Press, 1976); and Warren Darcy, *Wagner's Das Rheingold* (New York: Oxford University Press, 1993).

Weber John H. Warrack, *Carl Maria von Weber*, 2nd ed. (Cambridge: Cambridge University Press, 1976), is the best book about this composer, his works, and his position in the history of nineteenth-century music. Weber's biography by his son, Max von Weber, was published in a 2-vol. English translation (London, 1865), and has been reprinted, New York, 1969. Thematic catalogue by Friedrich W. Jähns, comp. (Berlin: Robert Lienau, 1871; repr. 1967). For bibliography, see Donald G. Henderson, *Carl Maria von Weber: A Guide to Research* (New York: Garland, 1990).

CHAPTER 19

EUROPEAN MUSIC FROM THE 1870s TO WORLD WAR I

Europe was relatively peaceful and stable in the late 1800s, but increasing social unrest and international tension marked the first two decades of the twentieth century, culminating in World War I (1914–18). The same period saw radical experiments in the musical realm, which also aroused uneasiness and tension in concert audiences. Composers challenged the conventions of tonality that had ruled in the eighteenth and nineteenth centuries, effectively bringing the Classic-Romantic period to a close.

THE GERMAN TRADITION

Wagner held an enormous fascination for European musicians in the last quarter of the nineteenth century. Many composers came under his spell, even as most of them consciously struggled to find their own solutions while making use of his advances in harmony and orchestration.

Wolf

Hugo Wolf (1860–1903) continued the German tradition of the solo song with piano accompaniment. He also wrote piano pieces, choruses, symphonic works, one completed opera (*Der Corregidor*, 1896), a string quartet, and the *Italian Serenade* for small orchestra (1892; originally composed as a string-quartet movement in 1887).

Songs

Most of Wolf's 250 lieder were produced in short periods of intense creative activity between 1887 and 1897. They were published in five principal collections, each devoted to a single poet, or group of poets: 53 on poems of

Mörike (1889); 20 of Joseph Freiherr von Eichendorff (1889); 51 of Goethe (1890); 44 songs on German translations of Spanish poems—the *Spanisches Liederbuch* (1891); and 46 settings of translations from the Italian—the *Italienisches Liederbuch* (Part I, 1892; Part II, 1896). The composer suffered a mental breakdown in 1897 and was incapacitated for the last years of his life.

In choosing texts Wolf showed greater literary taste than earlier German songwriters had. He concentrated on one poet at a time, and he placed the poet's name above his own in the titles of his collections, indicating a new ideal of equality between words and music derived from Wagner's music dramas. Wolf had no love for the folksong type of melody and little use for the strophic structures that were so characteristic of Brahms. Precedents for his lieder are the five songs that Wagner composed during 1857–58 on poems of Mathilde Wesendonck. But though Wolf arranged some of his piano accompaniments for orchestra, they seldom suggest an orchestral texture or a predominant instrumental sound, as Wagner's do. In short, Wolf adapted Wagner's methods with discrimination; he achieved the fusion of voice and instrument without sacrificing either to the other.

A good illustration of such balance is his setting of *Kennst du das Land?* (NAWM 122; CD 10 [31]). The singer's line, which is not organized into periodic melodic phrases but rather in an arioso, almost recitative style, always preserves a truly vocal, speechlike character. As in Wagner's work, continuity is sustained by the instrumental part rather than the voice. The chromatic voice-leading, appoggiaturas, anticipations, and the wandering tonality are clearly inspired by the idiom of *Tristan.*

Wolf obtains equally beautiful effects in a sensitive diatonic style—for example, in *Nun wand're Maria,* one of the Spanish songs. His treatment of pictorial images is always restrained but at the same time highly poetic and original; one instance among many is the suggestion of distant bells in the piano part of *Nepomuks Vorabend* (Goethe). Only close study reveals the remarkable variety of psychological and musical details found in Wolf's songs.

Mahler

Career

Gustav Mahler (1860–1911), another admirer of Wagner, made a few unsuccessful attempts at composing opera. After that he built a successful career writing symphonies and orchestral lieder. An eminent interpreter as well, Mahler conducted at numerous opera houses, among them Prague, Leipzig, Budapest, Hamburg, and the Metropolitan in New York. He served as director of the Vienna Opera from 1897 to 1907 and led the New York Philharmonic Society from 1909 to 1911. Composing mainly in the summers between busy seasons of conducting, he completed nine symphonies and left a tenth unfinished (it has since been completed by others). He repeatedly revised his first six symphonies and would probably have reworked the later ones had he lived longer. Of his five song-cycles for solo voices with orchestra, the best known is *Das Lied von der Erde* (The Song of the Earth; composed in 1908).

Works

■ *Caricature of Gustav Mahler as conductor by Hans Schliessmann in the* Fliegende Blätter *of March 1901. The German captions (not shown) read (top) "A hypermodern conductor" and (bottom) "Kapellmeister Kappelmann conducts his Diabolical Symphony." Between 1907 and 1911 Mahler conducted at the Metropolitan Opera and led the New York Philharmonic Society.* (VIENNA, GESELLSCHAFT DER MUSIKFREUNDE)

Mahler's Symphonies

Instrumentation

Like those of Bruckner, Mahler's symphonies are long, formally complex, and programmatic. They require an enormous number of performers. The Second Symphony, first performed in 1895, calls for a huge string section, 17 woodwinds, 25 brasses, 6 kettledrums and other percussion instruments, 4 or more harps, and an organ, in addition to soprano and alto soloists and a large chorus. The Eighth, composed in 1906–7 and popularly known as the "Symphony of a Thousand," demands an even larger array of players and singers. But the size of the orchestra tells only part of the story. Mahler showed great imagination and daring in combining instruments, comparable in this respect only to Berlioz. Practical experience as a conductor allowed him to perfect details of scoring. Instances of his keen ear for orchestral effects, ranging from the most delicate to the most overwhelmingly gigantic, abound in all the symphonies. Mahler's instrumentation is an intrinsic part of the composer's musical language, as are his extremely detailed indications of phrasing, tempo, and dynamics, and his occasional use of unusual instruments—mandolins in *Das Lied von der Erde* and the Seventh and Eighth Symphonies, sleigh bells in the Fourth.

Programmatic content

Mahler's symphonies usually have a program, even if it is not explicit. For the first four, he wrote out detailed programs in the manner of Berlioz and Liszt but later suppressed them. No such clues exist for the Fifth, Sixth, and Seventh Symphonies (composed between 1901 and 1905). Yet, quotations from and references to some of his own songs, the presence of obviously pictorial details, and the overall plan of each work combine to suggest that the composer had extramusical ideas in mind like those ascribed to Beethoven's Third and Fifth Symphonies. Thus, Mahler's Fifth moves steadily from the funereal gloom of the opening march to the triumph of the scherzo and the joy of the finale. The Sixth, by contrast, is his "tragic" symphony, culminating in a colossal finale in which heroic struggle, hedged in by a persistent A-minor tonality, seems to end in defeat and death. In the Seventh, two slow movements of "night music" frame a scherzo that is a ghost of a waltz. The polyphonic textures of the Eighth Symphony pay tribute to Bach, in whose music Mahler immersed himself from the 1890s on. It ends in a grand chorale, the *Chorus mysticus*, based on the closing scene of Part II of Goethe's *Faust*. The Ninth, Mahler's last completed symphony (1909–10), conjures up a mood of resignation mixed with bitter satire, a strange and sad farewell to life, symbolized by deliberate reference to the *Lebewohl* (farewell) theme of Beethoven's Piano Sonata Op. 81a.

Songs in the symphonies

Mahler the symphonist cannot be separated from Mahler the song composer. Themes from his early *Lieder eines fahrenden Gesellen* (Songs of a Wayfarer, 1883–84) appear in the opening and closing movements of the First Symphony; the Second, Third, and Fourth Symphonies incorporate melodies from his cycle of twelve songs on folk poems from the early nineteenth-century collection *Des Knaben Wunderhorn* (The Boy's Magic Horn, 1892–98) and introduce texts of some of the songs in the vocal movements. Following the examples of Beethoven, Berlioz, and Liszt, Mahler used voices as well as instruments in four of his symphonies. The Second and Eighth Symphonies make the most extensive use of sung text.

Second Symphony

The Second is known as the *Resurrection* Symphony. Like Beethoven's Ninth, it brings in voices for the work's climax. A long, agitated, and highly developed first movement gives way to an Andante in the easy, swinging folk rhythm of an Austrian *Ländler*, or slow waltz. The third movement is a symphonic adaptation of one of the *Wunderhorn* songs; the brief fourth movement, a new setting for contralto solo of another poem from that collection, serves to introduce the finale. A vivid and dramatic orchestral section depicting the day of Resurrection leads to a monumental setting for soloists and chorus of a Resurrection ode by the eighteenth-century German poet Friedrich Gottlieb Klopstock.

Third Symphony

The Third Symphony also requires vocal participation: a contralto solo on a text from Nietzsche's *Also sprach Zarathustra* and a soprano solo with boys'

Example 19.1 *Gustav Mahler, Symphony No. 4: First Movement, a) first theme; b) second theme; c) closing theme*

a.

b.

c.

and women's chorus on a merry song from *Des Knaben Wunderhorn.* The diversity of styles and of material in this work corroborates Mahler's remark while working on it that to write a symphony was to "construct a world." Preceding the vocal movements are a full-blown first movement, a minuet, and a scherzando that is based on another of Mahler's *Wunderhorn* songs, *Ablösung im Sommer* (Summer Relaxation), and that ends, Bruckner-like, with a broadly expressive Adagio.

Fourth Symphony

The Fourth Symphony likewise mirrors a variegated "world." It is shorter than the Third, more lightly orchestrated, almost conventional in form, and altogether more accessible. This symphony and the Second have always been among the most popular of Mahler's works, along with *Das Lied von der Erde.* Its first movement observes many of the Classic constraints. The exposition, in G major, has clearly articulated theme sections: a squarely phrased principal theme (measure 3, Example 19.1a), a lyrical second theme on the dominant (measure 38, Example 19.1b), and a playful closing theme (measure 58, Example 19.1c), also on the dominant. Unexpected, though, is the repeat of the opening (measure 72) before the development (measure 101) and its failure to

Example 19.2 *Gustav Mahler, Symphony No. 4: First Movement*

appear with the return of the tonic in the recapitulation (measure 240). Mahler's precise use of instruments is displayed well in his orchestration of this opening material. After a three-measure introduction by an ensemble of flutes, clarinets, and sleigh bells, phrases of the long winding melody are assigned to the first violins, cellos paired with double basses, French horns, and oboes paired with clarinets (Example 19.1a). When motives are later reassigned to different instruments they sound ironic and self-parodying. For example, in an intricately contrapuntal passage in the development section (Example 19.2), fragments of bass motives are given to the trumpet and upper woodwinds, and the three marked repeated notes of the lyrical second theme first heard in the cellos become ghostly apparitions in the soft woodwinds, harp harmonics, and *pianissimo* cymbal claps (measures 202, 204). Though the original ideas are dismembered and recombined as in a Classic development, the listener experiences something more like a feverish dream in which remembered images pop up from the subconscious in strange and distorted guises. The recapitulation then has the effect of restoring sanity, lucidity, and logic.

The second movement, in $\frac{3}{8}$, is a musical representation of the Dance of Death, a favorite subject in old German paintings. A solo violin, played with *scordatura*—the strings retuned a whole tone higher than normal—suggests the medieval *Fiedel* (fiddle) of the grisly Freund Hain, a folklore demon.

After this grim scherzo, the slow movement is down-to-earth in its mournful and at times impassioned lyricism. Two sections are each restated with variations, followed by a coda in which an unexpected outburst momentarily shatters the calm. The second of the melodic themes illustrates Mahler's technique of intensification, not through Wagnerian sequences, but, like Brahms, through seeking ever higher pitch levels with wider strides, returning each time to base camp (Example 19.3).

The last movement, composed years before the others, is a song on a text from *Des Knaben Wunderhorn* that presents a child's vision of heaven. Here the jingling open fifths and running figures of the first-movement introduction, where this music sounded out of place, find their true habitat and disclose their inspiration in the lines "Wir tanzen und springen, Wir hüpfen und singen" (We dance and leap, we skip and sing). This music serves as an interlude between the strophes of the song.

Tonal organization

The Fourth Symphony begins in one key (G major) and ends in another (E major), in keeping with Mahler's feeling for the significance of the various tonalities. Other symphonies shaped this way are the Fifth (C♯ minor to D major), Seventh (B minor to E to C major), and Ninth (D major to D♭ major). The strong linear trajectories of individual voices, which create chords rather than succumb to them, also contributed to a weakening sense of traditional tonal harmony.

Eighth Symphony

The Eighth Symphony consists of two huge choral movements. For the first, Mahler used the texts of the plainsong hymn *Veni creator spiritus.* The second movement, which sets the entire closing scene of Part 2 of Goethe's *Faust,* is practically a complete secular oratorio, resembling Liszt's *Faust Symphony* and *St. Elisabeth.*

Summary

In nearly all his symphonies Mahler freely transferred motives from one movement to another as he did in the Fourth, though never to the extent of suggesting a cyclical scheme. Bruckner's influence is evident in Mahler's "chorale" themes, his fondness for motives based on fourths and fifths, his introductions, and the adagio movements of the Third and Ninth Symphonies. The three middle symphonies (Nos. 5, 6, and 7) approach the Classic forms, but on a colossal scale and in an impassioned idiom, with prominent pictorial features and sharp contrasts of mood and style. Even the device, by then

Example 19.3 *Gustav Mahler, Symphony No. 4: Third Movement, Leidenschaftlich-Appassionato*

common, of shifting from the major to the minor triad is used with symbolic intent to portray the change from optimism to despair (Symphony No. 6). The Eighth Symphony, the climax of Mahler's second period, also represents the extreme point of expanding the performing forces.

Mahler's Lieder with Orchestra

Kindertotenlieder

With the *Kindertotenlieder* of 1901–04, a song cycle for solo voice and orchestra on poems of Friedrich Rückert, Mahler began the change in style that would characterize his last two symphonies and *Das Lied von der Erde.* The typically full, crowded textures of the earlier works are replaced by a more austere idiom. For example, the first song of the cycle, *Nun will die Sonn' so hell aufgehen* (Now the sun will rise again, NAWM 123; CD 10 [39] / 4 ⟨10⟩), achieves a chamber-music transparency through its spare use of instruments, allowing the delicate counterpoint to shine through. The post-Wagnerian chromatic harmony, here stripped to its bare essentials, acquires unaccustomed freshness and clarity.

Das Lied von der Erde

Das Lied von der Erde is based on a cycle of six poems translated from the Chinese by Hans Bethge under the title *The Chinese Flute.* The texts alternate between frenzied grasping at the dreamlike whirl of life and sad resignation at having to part from all its joys and beauties. Just as Mahler called on the human voice in his symphonies to complete his musical thought with words, here he called on the orchestra to sustain and supplement the tenor and contralto solos, both in accompaniment and in extensive connecting interludes. The exotic atmosphere of the words is lightly suggested by details of instrumental color and the use of the pentatonic scale. *Das Lied von der Erde* epitomizes hallmarks of Mahler's genius. Nowhere else did he so perfectly define and balance the two sides of his personality—ecstatic pleasure and deadly foreboding—a dualism that also characterizes the autumnal mood of the late nineteenth century.

Mahler inherited all the Romantic traditions of Berlioz, Liszt, Wagner, and, of course, the Viennese branch of Beethoven, Schubert, Brahms, and above all Bruckner. A restless experimenter with wide-ranging interests, Mahler expanded the symphony, the symphony-oratorio, and the orchestral lied while clearing the path for a new age that became a prime influence on Schoenberg, Berg, Webern, and other Viennese composers.

Richard Strauss

Career

Richard Strauss (1864–1949), the most famous German composer around 1900, played a historical role considerably different from Mahler's. Mahler used many programmatic and even operatic elements but held essentially to the traditional symphony made up of several distinct movements whose form was determined by principles of musical architecture. He was, in fact, the last in the line of German symphonists that extended from Haydn through Mozart, Beethoven, Schubert, Schumann, Brahms, and Bruckner. Strauss, on the contrary, soon attached himself to the more radical Romantic genre of the symphonic poem. His chief models were Berlioz and Liszt.

Strauss, like Mahler, was a celebrated conductor. Trained under Hans von Bülow, he held positions in the opera houses of Munich, Weimar, Berlin, and Vienna, and in the course of numerous tours conducted most of the great orchestras of the world. He received many official honors both at home and abroad and was universally recognized as the dominant figure in German musical life during the first part of the century.

Strauss is remembered today for his symphonic poems, which date mainly before 1900, and his operas, all but one of which came later. He also wrote some 150 lieder, but only a dozen or so mostly early ones are commonly known outside Germany and Austria. Nevertheless, songs such as *Allerseelen* (All Souls, 1883), *Ständchen* (Serenade, 1887), and the evocative *Traum durch die Dämmerung* (Dream through the Twilight, 1895) prove that Strauss was a master of the nineteenth-century lied.

Strauss's Symphonic Poems

Types of symphonic programs

There are two kinds of program for a symphonic poem. One, which we may call the philosophical, lies in the realm of general ideas and emotions; Liszt's *Les Préludes* and most of his other symphonic poems have such programs. In the other, which we may call descriptive, the composer represents in music specific nonmusical events; Berlioz wrote programs of this kind. The two types cannot be strictly differentiated, since philosophical programs often include descriptive elements, and descriptive programs usually convey a more general message as well. If the descriptive details are obvious, we call the program descriptive.

Music lends itself quite well to the philosophical type of program, which probably lies behind many compositions that are not acknowledged as program music: Beethoven's Fifth Symphony, for example, Schumann's Third, the symphonies of Bruckner generally, and the purely instrumental symphonies of Mahler. By contrast, the descriptive type of program is more difficult to reconcile with the essentially abstract nature of music. The danger of producing a work that is a mere curiosity is greatest when the event being described is definite and specific or when natural sounds are concerned. The skillful composer must absorb the imitated events and sounds into a musical whole using normal procedures. Successful examples are the birdsongs of Beethoven's *Pastoral* Symphony, the distant thunder in Berlioz's *Symphonie fantastique*, and the depiction of Resurrection Day in Mahler's Second Symphony.

Strauss wrote symphonic poems with both philosophical and descriptive programs. His best works of the first type are *Tod und Verklärung* (Death and Transfiguration, 1889) and *Also sprach Zarathustra* (So Spoke Zoroaster, 1896). *Till Eulenspiegels lustige Streiche* (Till Eulenspiegel's Merry Pranks, 1895) and *Don Quixote* (1897) are highly descriptive early works. The symphonic fantasia *Aus Italien* (From Italy, 1886) presents travel sketches like those of Mendelssohn's *Italian* Symphony. *Don Juan* (1889), after a poem by Nikolaus Lenau, is Strauss's first completely mature work; vividly descriptive, it is music of prodigious verve, with brilliant orchestration. *Macbeth* (1886; revised version 1891) is Strauss's one venture into Shakespeare. *Ein Heldenleben* (A Hero's Life, 1898) is openly autobiographical, a mocking and defiant challenge to Strauss's critics, whom he caricatures in cacophonous passages while glorifying his own deeds and triumphs with citations from his early works. The *Sinfonia domestica* (1903) paints the family life of the composer on a broad canvas. The picturesque *Alpensymphonie* (Alpine Symphony, 1915) is simpler and less chromatic in style than the previous works.

Tod und Verklärung

Tod und Verklärung embraces a program and approach similar to that of many nineteenth-century symphonies and operas: the progress of the soul through suffering to self-fulfillment. This is the work's general, philosophical program, though Strauss later admitted that he had had certain descriptive details in mind. After the music was written, Alexander Ritter specified them in a poem now prefixed to the score. The musical form can best be understood as a free sonata Allegro with a slow introduction and a hymnlike epilogue. The principal themes pervade all three parts in cyclical fashion. Here as in his other works, Strauss used the dissonances, which so shocked some of his contemporaries, to express violent feelings freely.

Also sprach Zarathustra

Zarathustra is a musical commentary on the celebrated prose-poem by the philosopher-poet Friedrich Nietzsche. In choosing a subject from this author, whose ideas on the *Übermensch* (superman) were agitating all of Europe at the end of the century, Strauss revealed a good nose for publicity. Nietzsche's original four-part poem proclaimed that the Christian ethic of exalting the humble and poor should be replaced by the ideal of an aristocratic and moral superman who is above good and evil. Strauss had the prologue to Nietzsche's poem printed before the score, and he placed titles from the book at the head of musical sections: "Of the inhabitants of the unseen world," "Of the great longing," "Of joys and passions," "Dirge," "Of knowledge," "The convalescent," "The dance song." Without a close reading of the poem itself, a listener could hardly make sense of this. Nietzsche's ideas served chiefly to stimulate Strauss's musical imagination.

Zoroaster's (Zarathustra's) opening address to the sun in the prologue—"Great star, how happy would you be if you did not have those whom you light up?"—must have inspired the splendid opening, with a deep *C* in the organ pedal and contrabassoon, accompanied by soft tremolos in the double basses. This passage is followed by a trumpet fanfare and a tutti C-minor chord that turns to major when the passage is immediately repeated. (The passage became a commonplace after it was quoted in the soundtrack of the film *2001.*) Another obvious illustration is the fugue theme, which uses all twelve notes of the chromatic scale (see Example 19.4) to symbolize the all-embracing dark realm

Example 19.4 *Richard Strauss,* Also sprach Zarathustra: *Fugue Subject*

of *Wissenschaft* (science, learning, knowledge). The symbolism is reinforced by the low-lying thick sound of the fugal exposition given to the double basses and cellos, each divided into four parts.

Till Eulenspiegel

In *Till Eulenspiegel*, the popular favorite among his symphonic poems, Strauss developed a comic program in music of unfading freshness and melodic attractiveness. The realistic details of Till's adventures (specified by a few marginal notes that the composer added to the printed score) are so thoroughly blended into the musical flow that the work could easily be heard simply as a character sketch of a particularly appealing rascal, or even more simply as a piece of musical humor, reminiscent of Haydn. A further suggestion of Haydn lies in Strauss's indication that *Till* is "in rondo form." It is not a rondo in the Classic sense, but rondo-like because the two *Till* themes keep recurring in a variety of guises, enlivened by shrewd touches of instrumentation. In no other work does Strauss seem so unrestrained, so spontaneous, as in this merry musical tale.

Don Quixote

If *Till* is a children's tale that Strauss turned into a sophisticated but sentimental mock-heroic epic, *Don Quixote* is very much an adult comedy, an instrumental dramatization of Cervantes's picaresque novel. As the rondo was appropriate to Till, who remains the same fool after each successful prank, so the variation fits the adventures of the knight Don Quixote and his squire Sancho Panza (see excerpt in NAWM 124; CD 10 [41]/ 4 ⟨12⟩), whose personalities are shaped by their frustrating experiences. We are no longer in a world of merry pranks but in one of split personalities and double meanings. The wry humor and cleverness in *Don Quixote* lie not so much in the apt depiction of real things as in the play with musical ideas. Much of this work has a chamber-music sound, because it is conceived in contrapuntal lines, and its themes attach to particular solo instruments. "Variations" here does not mean preserving a melody or harmonic progression and its form through a number of statements. Rather, the themes of the two main characters are transformed so that the beginnings of the themes sprout new melodic characters.

Operas

Strauss leaped into fame as an opera composer in 1905 with *Salome*. He had previously written an unsuccessful opera, *Guntram* (1893), and in 1901 enjoyed a moderate success with *Feuersnot* (The Fire Famine). But after *Salome*, the powers of depiction and characterization that he had put into symphonic poems went almost exclusively into opera. Like Beethoven, Berlioz, Liszt, Wagner, and Mahler, Strauss came to feel that he needed words to supplement the language of music. In his operas he dealt with subjects, actions, and emotions stranger than any attempted in opera before. These stimulated him to create harmonically complex and dissonant musical idioms that greatly influenced the later growth of expressionism and the dissolution of tonality in German music.

Salome

Salome is a setting of Oscar Wilde's one-act play in German translation. In this decadent version of the biblical story, Salome entices Herod, with her

Example 19.5 *Richard Strauss,* Elektra: *Harmony*

a. The germinal chord of *Elektra*

b. *Elektra* motive

famous dance of the seven veils, to deliver the head of John the Baptist so that she can kiss his cold lips. With orchestral splendor, novel rhythms, and keenly descriptive harmonies, Strauss captured the macabre tone and atmosphere of the drama with such expressive force as to lift it to a plane where artistry outweighs perversion.

Elektra

With *Elektra* (1908), Strauss began his long and fruitful collaboration with the Viennese playwright Hugo von Hofmannsthal (1874–1929) that would result in seven operas. For Hofmannsthal's version of Sophocles' play, which dwells throughout its long single act on the emotions of insane hatred and revenge, Strauss conceived music with sharp dissonance and apparent harmonic anarchy that outdid anything previously experienced in an opera house. The anarchy is only apparent, however. In spite of *Tristan*, audiences in 1909 still expected chords sounding like dominants to resolve to a tonic, which Strauss's seldom do. The prevailing chromatic harmony is offset by some dissonant polytonal passages and tonal sections that are purely diatonic. The sound of the harmony emanates from a single germinal chord (Example 19.5a), thereby anticipating a technique used by later twentieth-century composers. The score is further unified by leitmotifs and by the association of certain keys with particular characters or situations: B♭ with Agamemnon, E♭ with Chrysothemis, and a C–E complex with Elektra's triumph. Strauss frequently set up chord relationships at the interval of a tritone as in the Elektra motive (Example 19.5b). Dissonances most often occur in the meeting of contrapuntal lines but are sometimes chosen deliberately for their shock value.

Der Rosenkavalier

Der Rosenkavalier (The Cavalier of the Rose, 1911), on a libretto in three acts by Hofmannsthal, takes us into a sunnier world of elegant, stylized eroticism and tender feeling in the aristocratic powdered-wig milieu of eighteenth-century Vienna. *Der Rosenkavalier* is Strauss's operatic masterpiece. The sultry harmonies of *Salome* and the cacophonies of *Elektra* are softened. The mock-Romantic, sensuous melodic curves, the novel harmonic twists (see Example 19.6), the magical orchestral colors, and a lively sense of comedy are couched in a deceptively simple diatonic style derived from South German dances and folksongs. The human voice is once again prominent. Woven into the orchestral background and alternating with much cleverly wrought *parlando* dialogue are melodious arias, duets, and trios. These ensembles are not really separate numbers as in the Classic opera but still depart significantly from the Wagnerian (and earlier Straussian) singing that was purely declamatory, or, at

Setting for Act III of Richard Strauss's Der Rosenkavalier, *designed by Alfred Roller for the original 1911 Vienna production. The legend below reads "Private room in a small inn."*
(BY PERMISSION OF BOOSEY & HAWKES, INC.)

most, arioso and that was dominated by the orchestra. The whole score, with its mingling of sentiment and comedy, overflows with the lighthearted rhythms and melodies of Viennese waltzes.

Ariadne auf Naxos

Ariadne auf Naxos (Ariadne at Naxos, 1912) originated as incidental music to Hofmannsthal's adaptation of Molière's play *Le bourgeois gentilhomme.* It has survived in revised form (1916) as an independent work, half opera buffa and half mythological drama. Set in a modernized Mozartean idiom and using a small orchestra, it includes recitatives, ensembles, and arias in Classic forms; it is, in short, a model of neo-Classic chamber opera. The comic opera *Intermezzo* (1924) treats nearly all the dialogue in realistic speech-recitative above the bustling accompaniment of a chamber orchestra that also plays lyrical interludes.

Example 19.6 *Richard Strauss,* Der Rosenkavalier: *Introduction*

Humperdinck, Reger, and Pfitzner

Renewed interest in the fairy-tale opera (*Märchenoper*) became a feature of this period in Germany. The principal work in this style was *Hänsel und Gretel* (1893) by Engelbert Humperdinck (1854–1921), which incongruously but successfully combines Wagnerian orchestral polyphony and the use of leitmotifs with simple and charming folklike melodic material. Brief mention must suffice for two other German composers. Max Reger (1873–1916), a spiritual descendant of Brahms, possessed a prodigious contrapuntal technique and a copious imagination. Reger's harmony is for the most part a complex post-Wagnerian mixture of extreme chromaticism and restless modulation, which he kept within bounds of strict forms, such as the fugue, the chorale prelude, or the theme and variations. Typical are the orchestral *Variations and Fugue on a Theme of J. A. Hiller* (1907) and a similar work (1914) on the theme of the first movement of Mozart's Piano Sonata K. 331. Hans Pfitzner (1869–1949), the leading conservative German composer of his generation, is remembered chiefly for his operas, especially *Palestrina* (1917), though he also composed songs, chamber music, and a notable Violin Concerto in B minor (1925).

NATIONAL TRENDS

Nationalism had already emerged in the eighteenth century in both cultural affairs and music. For example, scholars stopped writing treatises in Latin in favor of the vernaculars, despite the vernaculars' poverty of technical vocabulary. When their own language was not adequate to the task, German music critics such as Johann Mattheson, Friedrich Marpurg, or Johann Adolph Scheibe would toss in French, Italian, and Latin terms. Whatever their regional political allegiance, they boasted of the superiority of German music over their neighbors'.

In Hamburg, Dresden, London, Prague, and elsewhere, resistance to Italian opera led native composers to mount operas in their own language. In London, Handel abandoned Italian opera to compose oratorios on English texts, turning some of the oratorios into virtual sacred operas. In Germany and Austria the Singspiel challenged the Italian opera seria. And in France, the *Querelle des bouffons* (see pages 442–43) was a reaction to visits by an Italian troupe producing Italian comic and serious operas.

Napoleonic wars

Napoleon's campaigns (1796–1809) at first encouraged national movements and the search for independence from tyrants and monarchs. But the French administration was soon resented and it too became the target of liberation movements. In German-speaking territories, hundreds of tiny states were eliminated, reducing the number to around forty and thereby making the idea of unification easier though still impractical. In Italy Napoleon drove the Austrians out of the north. Although people commonly spoke of Italy or of the Italians, an Italian nation did not actually exist. Most of what is now Italy was ruled by Spanish kings, the papacy, the Habsburg Empire, and France until unification in 1870.

Bohemia (the present-day Czech and Slovak Republics), Poland, and Hungary remained under Habsburg rule and were continually in political and religious turmoil. Chopin and Liszt felt the tug of Polish and Hungarian patriotic feelings, respectively, one writing mazurkas and polonaises, the other Hungarian rhapsodies, in addition to their largely cosmopolitan oeuvre. Wagner, whether he was in Germany, Switzerland, or France, championed things German in his writings. A sense of pride in a language and its literature formed part of the national consciousness that ultimately led to German and Italian unification.

Germany

During the eighteenth century composers aspired to styles fashionable in other countries as well as in their own. The situation in German-speaking areas is perhaps the most complex. J. S. Bach wrote much of his music in an Italian or French style, doing so with such technical mastery that he outshone the native composers. At the same time, his church music was strongly Lutheran and German in its poetic texts and its reliance on chorale melodies, many of which were originally German secular and sacred songs. Handel wrote in a mixture of Italian, French, English, and German styles, depending on the genre and destination of the music. Hasse wrote Italian opera in the Italian style then fashionable. In Charles Burney's opinion, Germans lacked a national music; he rather cynically characterized their compositions as full of "patience," "profundity," "prolixity," and "pedantry." The Viennese composers of the Classic period reflected the tastes of the Habsburg rulers and the society around the imperial court. Both were fond of Italian opera, French theater and ballet, Italian and German orchestral music, and the dance and popular music of Hungary, Poland, Bohemia, and Croatia.

Bach revival

All this began to change in the nineteenth century. In 1802 Johann Nikolaus Forkel's biography and study of the music of J. S. Bach began a movement to revive his music, a movement which gathered force in 1829 when Mendelssohn directed Bach's *St. Matthew Passion* in Berlin and which culminated in the edition of his complete works by the Bach-Gesellschaft (Bach Society), established in 1850. The compilation of works by other composers such as Handel, Beethoven, Schumann, Schubert, Haydn, as well as the establishment of the *Denkmäler der Tonkunst* (Monuments of Musical Art) started in 1869, bear witness to the recognition of these composers as national jewels.

How much national consciousness affected what, and how composers wrote is difficult to say. If we attach German or Italian traits to the musical styles of Wagner and Verdi, it is partly because their music defines these national styles. Up to a point, Wagner and Verdi chose subject matter that reflected their patriotic feelings, but neither composer was particularly national in this respect. Verdi's libretti were more often based on French, Spanish, English, and German literary works than on Italian subjects. Some of his libretti dealt with political oppression and aspiration for independence, but Verdi became a symbol for national unity as much because lovers of his music throughout the Italian peninsula could take pride in his fame and could identify themselves with his position of leadership in the world. Wagner, who allowed his opera texts to be sung in languages other than German, was also seen by a divided population as a leader of the German spirit.

Folklore

Interest in folklore and the use of traditional and popular songs in art music is usually associated with nationalism. It was not, however, exclusively a nineteenth-century tendency, nor did it always involve the folklore of the composer's national allegiance. Haydn arranged Scottish songs and appropriated Croatian melodies in his symphonies, just as Dvořák borrowed African-American spirituals and Indian themes or imitated their styles in the "New World" Symphony.

Dvořák and Smetana

Haydn recognized the special character of the songs without intending to make a statement about nationalism. Dvořák's borrowings, on the other hand, were taken as a spur to American nationalism and to the possible development of a native American music. In works such as the Slavonic Dances, the Bohemian Dvořák deliberately used traditional music of his own people to achieve a national idiom. His compatriot Bedřich Smetana, although he could neither speak nor write Czech at the time (he spoke German, the official language of Bohemia), participated in the failed Prague Revolution of 1848. Later (ca. 1872–79) he decided to create a national music in his cycle of symphonic poems *Má vlast* (My Country), the best known of which is *The Moldau.* When Brahms arranged German folksongs and wrote folklike melodies, he also identified himself with his own ethnic tradition. However, there is a difference in motivation and effect, because German music was dominant, while Bohemian composers were asserting their independence and distinctiveness.

Such a search for an independent, native voice was keenest in England, France, the United States, Russia, and the countries of Eastern Europe, where the dominance of German music was felt as a threat to homegrown musical creativity. In addition, composers from these countries wanted to be recognized as equals to those in the Austro-German orbit. By employing native folksongs and dances or imitating their musical character, composers could develop a style that had ethnic identity. Although individual composers in these countries differed in their enthusiasm for a nationalist agenda or the exploitation of their traditional music, it is convenient to deal with both nationalists and non-nationalists in this section.

Russia

Until the nineteenth century, secular art music in Russia was largely in the hands of imported Italian, French, or German composers. The first composer recognized by both Europeans and Russians as an authentic native voice and an equal of his Western contemporaries was Mikhail Glinka (1804–1857). He established his reputation in 1836 with the patriotic opera *Zhizn za tsarya* (A Life for the Czar). Some of the recitative and melodic writing has a Russian character, attributable to modal scales, quotation of folksongs, and folklike idiom. Glinka's second opera, *Ruslan and Lyudmila* (1842), contains many

Glinka

CÉSAR CUI ON THE RUSSIAN MIGHTY HANDFUL

We formed a close-knit circle of young composers. And since there was nowhere to study (the Conservatory didn't exist) our *self-education* began. It consisted of playing through everything that had been written by all the greatest composers, and all works were subjected to criticism and analysis in all their technical and creative aspects. We were young and our judgments were harsh. We were very disrespectful in our attitude toward Mozart and Mendelssohn; to the latter we opposed Schumann, who was then ignored by everyone. We were very enthusiastic about Liszt and Berlioz. We worshipped Chopin and Glinka. We carried on heated debates (in the course of which we would down as many as four or five glasses of tea with jam), we discussed musical form, program music, vocal music and especially operatic form.

Trans. from Cui, *Izbrannye stat'i*, by Richard Taruskin in "Some Thoughts on the History and Historiography of Russian Music," JM 3 (1984):335.

imaginative uses of the whole-tone scale, chromaticism, dissonance, and variation technique applied to folksongs. Alexander Dargomïzhsky (1813–1869), in his opera *Rusalka* (1856), continued the quest for a characteristic intonation of Russian speech, partly by imitating patterns found in folk music. His most successful opera, set to Aleksander Pushkin's *The Stone Guest* (1872), influenced Musorgsky in its expressive melodic declamation.

Dargomïzhsky

Meanwhile, Tchaikovsky, trained in Germany and writing in a cosmopolitan style, was not particularly interested in furthering the nationalist cause, although he chose Russian subject matter. He wrote a great deal of music for the stage, including background music, ballet music, and operas. *Eugene Onegin* (1879) is notable for penetrating the passions of its characters and for the way numerous themes are generated from a germ motive first announced in the orchestral prelude. In *The Queen of Spades* (1890) Tchaikovsky matched the ghoulish atmosphere of Pushkin's story and also recreated the spirit of the eighteenth-century Russia of Catherine the Great by borrowing musical ideas from that period.

Tchaikovsky

In the second half of the nineteenth century five leading Russian composers banded together in a group known as *moguchaya kuchka* or the Mighty Handful—that is, the Mighty Five: Alexander Borodin (1833–1887), Modest Musorgsky (1839–1881), Mily Balakirev (1837–1910), César Cui (1835–1918), and Nikolay Rimsky-Korsakov (1844–1908). Only Balakirev had conventional training in music, but it would be wrong to call the others amateurs. They admired Western music but felt alienated from the St. Petersburg Conservatory, founded in 1862 by Anton Rubinstein (1829–1894), a Germanic dogmatist. They were disillusioned with the academic musical establishment and found little worthwhile in the exercises and prizes that it fostered. Seeking a fresh

The Mighty Handful

approach, they called on the materials nearest at hand, namely folksong, modal and exotic scales, and folk polyphony. Balakirev, the most professional of the Mighty Handful, made particularly effective use of folksong melodies in his symphonic poem *Russia* (1887) and his piano fantasia *Islamey* (1869), clothing them in modern harmony.

Balakirev

Borodin

Borodin, a chemist by profession, at first fell under the spell of Mendelssohn's music but shifted his interests to Russian music and became an ardent nationalist. Like Mendelssohn's, his talent lay in lyrical and descriptive writing. His principal instrumental works are his Second Symphony in B minor (1876), the Second String Quartet in D major (1885), and a symphonic sketch, *In Central Asia* (1880). Borodin seldom quoted folk tunes, but his melodies are filled with their spirit. Borodin succeeded by reason of the individuality of his themes, his transparent orchestral texture—modeled on Glinka's—his delicate, modally tinged harmonies, and his original method of spinning out an entire movement from a single pregnant thematic idea, for example, the first movement of the Second Symphony. The key schemes of both his symphonies typify the Russian fondness for unusual tonal relationships: the First Symphony, in E♭, has its third, slow, movement in D, with a middle section in D♭; the four movements of the Second Symphony are, respectively, in B minor, F major, D♭ major, and B major.

Prince Igor

Borodin's four-act opera *Prince Igor* was completed after his death by Rimsky-Korsakov and Glazunov and premiered in 1890. It is less a drama than a series of picturesque tableaux. The familiar *Polovetsian Dances* in Act II illustrate the iridescent harmonies, bright colors, graceful melodic lines, and refined, exotic, oriental flavor that characterize much Russian music after Glinka's *Ruslan.*

Musorgsky

The greatest of the Mighty Handful, Modest Musorgsky earned a living as a clerk in the civil service and received most of his musical training from Balakirev. His principal works are a symphonic fantasy, *Night on Bald Mountain* (1867); the set of piano pieces *Pictures at an Exhibition* (1874; later orchestrated by Ravel); the song cycles *The Nursery* (1872), *Sunless* (1874), and *Songs and Dances of Death* (1875); and the operas *Boris Godunov* (first performed in 1874) and *Khovanshchina,* which was completed by Rimsky-Korsakov and privately performed in 1886 but not produced publicly until 1892.

Influence of Russian folk tunes

Musorgsky's individuality shines through every aspect of his music. He treated texts as Dargomïzhsky had, following the accents of Russian speech as closely as possible, so his vocal music generally lacks lyrical melodic lines and symmetrical phrasing. Although Musorgsky quoted actual folk tunes only occasionally, as in the Coronation Scene of *Boris,* Russian folksong was rooted in his musical nature even more deeply than in Borodin's. Russian folk tunes (see Example 19.7) tend to move within a narrow range and to be made up either of obsessive repetition of one or two rhythmic motives or of phrases in mixed meters constantly sinking to a cadence, often by the interval of a descending

Example 19.7

a. *Folksong from the collection of* 30 Chants populaires russes, *ed. Mily Balakirev*

Oh, my little meadow duck!

b. *Folksong, idem*

**Oĭli* is a stock folksong refrain, like fa-la-la or tra-la-la. *Liushenki* is a diminutive of another stock refrain, *livli.*

How near the wood, near the wood, silky grass.

c. *Modest Musorgsky, melody from the Prologue of* Boris Godunov

To whom do you abandon us, our father! to whom do you leave us, our own [father]!
We orphans beg you, we implore you with tears, with scalding tears.

fourth. Another prominent feature of Russian folksongs, and of Musorgsky's melodies, is their modal character, which affected Musorgsky's harmonic style. Brahms had used modal chords and progressions, but it was the Russians who introduced modality into the general musical language, an important influence on Western music of the early twentieth century. Musorgsky's use of nonfunctional harmonic progressions in *Okonchen prazdnyi, shumnyi den'* (The idle, noisy day is over, NAWM 125; CD 11 [1]), from the cycle *Sunless,* attracted the attention of Debussy, who borrowed an accompaniment pattern from it for his *Nuages* (NAWM 128; see Example 19.15, page 665). Musorgsky's songs are among the finest of the nineteenth century.

Musorgsky's harmony was highly original, indeed revolutionary. Unfettered by traditional procedures and unpracticed in manipulating standard formulas, he labored at the piano to work out his innovative progressions; these, along with his rhythms, may have been culled from his memories of polyphonic folk singing. His harmonic vocabulary is limited, but his apparently simple progressions convey precisely the effect he wanted and resist any attempt to explain them (see Example 19.8).

Boris Godunov

The realism so prominent in nineteenth-century Russian literature found an echo in Musorgsky's *Boris Godunov,* not only in the way he imitated the

Example 19.8 *Modest Musorgsky,* Boris Godunov: *End of Act II*

Lord! You do not wish the death of a sinner. Forgive the soul of guilty Czar Boris!

spoken word but in the lifelike musical depiction of gestures and, in the choral scenes, the sound and stir of the crowds. The psychological insight displayed in the songs on a miniature scale is applied in the operas with equal mastery in depicting the character of the Czar Boris. Like other Russian composers, Musorgsky built his effects by the repetition and accumulation of single impressions, not by thematic development to a climax. Rather than continuously developed action, *Boris* is a series of episodes held together by an epic thread and the central figure of the Czar.

Rimsky-Korsakov and Others

Nikolay Rimsky-Korsakov forms a link between the first generation of Russian composers—Glinka and the Mighty Handful—and those of the early twentieth century. In the 1880s he led some Russian musicians away from the insular Balakirev circle toward a style that was based on broader, more eclectic methods and resources but was still strongly impregnated with national idioms. He proved his abiding interest in national music not only by arranging and editing folksongs but by incorporating them and their characteristic turns and harmonies into his own compositions. Particularly in his late works, he experimented with whole-tone and octatonic scales (alternating half and whole steps) and with parallel chord progressions such as those used in improvised polyphony.

Abandoning an early career in the navy, Rimsky-Korsakov served from 1871 as professor of composition at the St. Petersburg Conservatory and was also active in Russia as a conductor. To supplement his rather sketchy musical training under Balakirev, he studied counterpoint on his own. Rimsky-Korsakov's compositions include symphonies, chamber music, choruses, and songs, but his principal works are symphonic poems and operas. His music, in contrast to the intense dramatic realism of Musorgsky's, is distinguished by lively fantasy and bright orchestral colors. The *Capriccio espagnol* (1887), the symphonic suite *Sheherazade* (1888), and the *Russian Easter Overture* (1888) manifest his genius for orchestration; he systematized his teachings on this subject in a treatise published in 1913. In the two most important of his fifteen operas—*Sadko* (1897) and *The Golden Cockerel* (first performed in 1909)—he alternated a diatonic, often modal style with one that was lightly chromatic, fanciful, and most apt at suggesting their fairy-tale world.

Style

Rimsky-Korsakov's leading pupils were Alexander Glazunov (1865–1936), the last of the Russian nationalists and a minor master of the symphony, and Igor Stravinsky (see pages 702ff), whose early works, especially *The Firebird* (1910), are descendants of Rimsky-Korsakov's style and orchestral technique.

Glazunov

Sergei Rakhmaninov (1873–1943), like Tchaikovsky, cultivated a sweepingly passionate, melodious idiom. He was not interested in the national movement, and, indeed, left Russia in 1917 and never returned. Apart from numerous songs and piano pieces his most notable works are the Second Piano Concerto (1901), the Third Piano Concerto (1909), the Second Symphony (1906–1907), the symphonic poem *The Isle of the Dead* (1907), and *Rhapsody on a Theme of Paganini* for piano and orchestra (1934).

Rakhmaninov

Second Piano Concerto

The Second Piano Concerto demands superior agility, rhythmic control, power, and endurance from the soloist, since the piano is almost never silent and its part always technically difficult. When Rakhmaninov gives the piano one of several irresistible lyrical melodies, he demands that the pianist accompany them as well with ever varied arpeggiated figures, while the orchestra sustains the notes of the melody and harmony, occasionally adding rhythmic background. For example, in the recapitulation of the primary theme in the first movement (Example 19.9), the first clarinet doubles the piano's melody, while the other winds and strings sustain the chords broken in the piano figuration. When the piano does not have thematic material, it plays arabesques against the orchestra's melody—heavily doubled at as much as three octaves in the manner of Tchaikovsky—or the soloist accents the melodic notes sustained in the orchestra within rapid and inventive filigree. The complex harmonies in Example 19.9 result from contrapuntal motion but strike the listener as successions of augmented, seventh-, and ninth-chords that resolve by half-step while making an excursion within the key of the movement, C minor.

Example 19.9 *Sergei Rakhmanivov, Second Piano Concerto: First Movement*

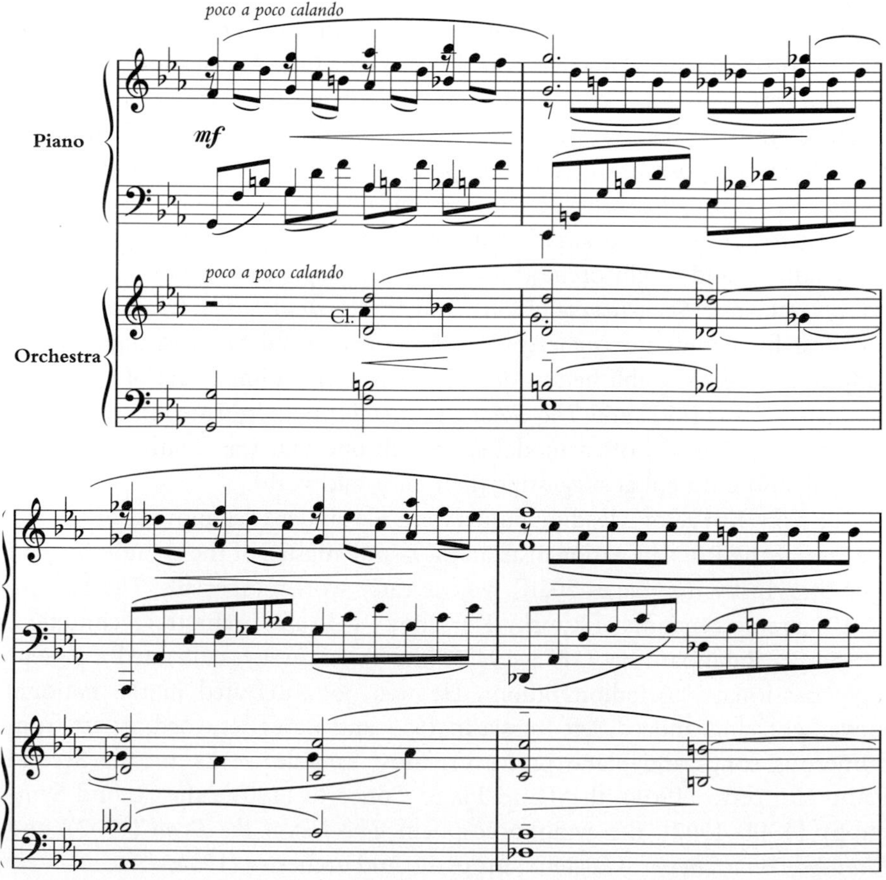

Third Piano Concerto

The Third Piano Concerto is even more dominated by the piano, the orchestra's role reduced to accompaniment and a few transitional passages. Its subtle, less singable thematic material is ingeniously interlinked and rhythmically diverse throughout. This concerto remains one of the foremost challenges in the piano literature.

Skryabin

Alexander Skryabin (1872–1915), influenced by the chromaticism of Liszt and Wagner, and to some extent also by the mood-evoking methods of impressionism, gradually evolved a complex harmonic vocabulary all his own. A concert pianist, he began by writing nocturnes, preludes, études, and mazurkas in the manner of Chopin. The growth of this language can be followed step by step in his ten piano sonatas, of which the last five, composed 1912–13, dispense with key signatures and drift toward atonality. He replaced the common tonal hierarchy with a complex chord chosen to serve as the root of a work's melodic and harmonic material. These chords contain one or more tritones, and some, like the "mystic" chord of *Prometheus*, have whole-tone properties (see Example 19.10). The last chord in Example 19.10 is heard in several transpositions and finally, with an added third, in the introductory section of a piano work, *Vers la flamme*, Op. 72 (1914; NAWM 126; CD 11 [3]). Traditional formal articulations dissolve in a stream of strange, colorful, and sometimes magnificent sound effects.

Two of Skryabin's most original compositions are orchestral works, the *Poem of Ecstasy* (1908) and *Prometheus* (1910). During the playing of the latter,

Example 19.10 *Alexander Skryabin, Chord Forms*

Prometheus Sonata No. 7 Sonata No. 8 Sonata No. 8 *Vers la flamme*

the composer wished the concert hall to be flooded with changing light. Skryabin aspired to a synthesis of all the arts with the aim of inducing states of mystic rapture. He had no important disciples, though his radical antitonal tendencies doubtless encouraged others to take this path.

Central Europe

Smetana and Dvořák

Bedřich Smetana (1824–1884) and Antonín Dvořák were the two principal Czech (Bohemian) composers of the nineteenth century. (Both have already been mentioned earlier in this chapter in connection with folklore, see page 646.) Bohemia had for centuries been an Austrian crown land, and so, unlike Russia, had always been in the mainstream of European music. Besides, its folksongs resemble those of Western nations more than the Russian folksongs do. The musical language of these two composers was basically European: Smetana's derived from Liszt's, Dvořák's leaning more toward Brahms. The nationalism of Smetana and Dvořák is chiefly apparent in their choice of national subjects for program music and operas, and in their generous use of folklike tunes and popular dance rhythms. For example, the slow movements of Dvořák's String Quartet in E♭, Op. 51, and his Piano Quintet Op. 81, are based on the melancholic folk ballad, the *dumka.* The shifting accents of the fiery Bohemian dance the *furiant* dominate the scherzo of the Sixth Symphony. National traits stand out most in some of their operas—Smetana's *Bartered Bride* (1866) above all, but also in his later *The Kiss* (1876)—and in some works in small forms, such as Dvořák's *Slavonic Dances.*

Janáček

Leoš Janáček (1854–1928) consciously renounced the styles of western Europe in his works after 1890. He anticipated Bartók in deliberately collecting and editing folk music, and his own mature style grew out of the rhythms and inflections of Moravian peasant speech and song. Public recognition came late, beginning only with the staging of his opera *Jenůfa,* first performed in Brno in 1904, at Prague in 1916, and Vienna in 1918. Based on the play *Her Foster Daughter* by Gabriela Preissová, it is set in Slovakia and dramatizes the conflicts that arise when Jenůfa is expecting a child by a playboy and draft-dodger who refuses to marry her. Jenůfa ends up with his long enamored half-brother, after her foster mother—who has the biggest part—secretly kills the new-born child; the discovery of the infant's body breaks up the wedding ceremony. Now in the repertory of many theaters, *Jenůfa* ranks with Puccini's *Tosca* and Strauss's *Salome* as an outstanding "realist" opera (see *verismo,* page 670). The setting of the unrhymed text, in a declamatory style that rises in moments of emotional intensity to a melodious lyricism, rarely approaches the structure of an aria. Janáček often repeats a line to realize pairs of balanced phrases and has instruments and voice exchange motives in a continuous stream of dramatically fitting invention. Much of the orchestral accompaniment uses a proto-minimalist technique of long stretches of ostinato figures repeating the same or slightly varied pitches and rhythms in a static harmonic medium, at times building up to powerful climaxes. The succession of chords is for the most part not functionally determined, and both melody and harmony are sometimes

XI. *Claude Monet (1840–1926) entered* Impression: Soleil levant *(Sunrise) along with eight other works in an exhibition he helped to organize for the* Société Anonyme des Artistes Peintres, Sculpteurs, Graveurs, Etc. *(Association of artist-painters, sculptors, engravers, etc.) in 1874. A critic headlined his mocking review "Exhibition of the Impressionists," and thus the term was launched. Instead of mixing his colors on a palette, Monet juxtaposed them on the canvas to capture a fleeting moment of the early light of day. Apart from the rowboats in the foreground, the tall ships, smokestacks, and cranes blend into the misty blue-gray background against a reddish sky.* (PARIS, MUSÉE MARMOTTAN / ART RESOURCE, NEW YORK)

XII. *The* Angel Concert *from the Isenheim altarpiece by Matthias Grünewald (d. 1528). This painting inspired the first movement of Hindemith's* Mathis der Maler *Symphony and the* Sechstes Bild *of the opera, which is based on incidents in the life of the painter.* (© COLMAR, MUSÉE D'UNTERLINDEN. PHOTOGRAPHY BY O. ZIMMERMAN)

built on the whole-note scale. The sonorities vary according to the character and content of the speech, lush and sweet for some, sharply dissonant for others. A few peasant choruses and dance songs, probably imitations rather than authentic folk material, inject a Moravian flavor.

Janáček's creative power continued unabated to the end of his life. Later operas were *Kát'a Kabanová* (1921), *The Cunning Little Vixen* (1924), *The Makropulos Affair* (1925), and *From the House of the Dead* (1928). He composed much choral music, among which the *Glagolitic Mass* of 1926, on a text in Old Slavonic, is outstanding. His chamber music includes two quartets and a violin sonata; his works for orchestra are the symphonic rhapsody *Taras Bulba* (1918) and a *Sinfonietta* (1926).

Norway

Grieg

Nationalism in Norway is represented by Edvard Hagerup Grieg (1843–1907), whose best works are his short piano pieces, songs, and orchestral incidental music to plays. The two suites that Grieg arranged from his music for Ibsen's *Peer Gynt* (1875; reorchestrated 1886) include only eight of the original twenty-three numbers. Among his larger compositions are the well-known Piano Concerto in A minor (1868; revised 1907), a piano sonata, three violin sonatas, a cello sonata, and a string quartet (1878) that apparently provided Debussy with a model for his own fifteen years later.

Grieg superimposed national characteristics on an orthodox style that he learned in his youthful studies at the Leipzig Conservatory. An ethnic character emerges most clearly in the songs on Norwegian texts, the choruses for men's voices Op. 30, the four Psalms for mixed chorus Op. 74, many of his *Lyric Pieces* for piano (ten collections), the four sets of piano arrangements of folksongs, and especially the *Slåtter*, Norwegian peasant dances that Grieg arranged for the piano from transcripts of country fiddle playing. His piano style, with its delicate grace notes and mordents, owes something to Chopin, but the all-pervading influence in his music is that of Norwegian folksongs and dances, reflected in his modal turns of melody and harmony—Lydian raised fourth, Aeolian lowered seventh, alternative major-minor third—frequent drone basses (suggested by old Norwegian stringed instruments), and the fascinating combination of $\frac{3}{4}$ and $\frac{6}{8}$ rhythm in the *Slåtter*. These national characteristics blend with Grieg's sensitive feeling for harmony in a personal, poetic music that has not lost its freshness.

Other Countries

Poland

Denmark

Composers elsewhere in Europe can be mentioned only briefly. Stanisław Moniuszko (1819–1872), creator of a Polish national opera with *Halka* (1848; expanded to four acts in 1858), was notable also for his songs, which display marked national qualities in both texts and music. In Denmark, Carl August Nielsen (1865–1931) composed songs, operas, piano and chamber music, concertos, and symphonies. His best-known work, the Fifth Symphony (1922), is unconventional in form and orchestration and original in its adaptation of tonality to a sometimes very dissonant harmonic idiom. Contemporary with Nielsen was the outstanding nineteenth-century Netherlands composer Alfons Diepenbrock (1862–1921), whose music, influenced first by Palestrina and Wagner and later by Debussy, includes sacred works for chorus and orchestra, songs, and incidental music for stage plays.

Netherlands

Finland

Sibelius

The great Finnish composer Jean Sibelius (1865–1957) was devoted to the literature of his country, particularly the *Kalevala*, the Finnish national epic, which he mined for texts to use in his vocal works and for subjects to treat in his symphonic poems. It is easy to imagine that much of his music—"somber," "bleak," and "elemental" are favorite adjectives—was inspired by his profound love of nature, and particularly aspects typical of northern countries. Surprisingly, he does not quote or imitate folksongs in his works, the best of which contain nothing that can be concretely defined as national. For a long time his music was extremely popular in England and the United States but hardly known in continental western Europe. Unlike Grieg, who was essentially a miniaturist, the genius of Sibelius is best revealed in his symphonies, symphonic poems, and the Violin Concerto (1903).

Although Sibelius lived until 1957, he published no important works after 1925. The first of his seven symphonies appeared in 1899, the last in 1924. Three symphonic poems—*En Saga, The Swan of Tuonela,* and the familiar *Finlandia*—were works of the 1890s (all revised about 1900); the principal later symphonic poems were *Pohjola's Daughter* (1906) and *Tapiola* (1925). The programs of these poems, except for *Pohjola's Daughter*, are very general; the symphonies have no expressed programs.

Themes

Most original in Sibelius's music are his themes, his technique of thematic development, and his treatment of form. Instead of full periodic melodies, a theme may be built on short motives that first sound separately, then gradually coalesce into a complete entity, as happens in the third movement of the Fourth Symphony (Example 19.11, second excerpt under III). Motives from one theme may be transferred to another, or themes may be dissolved and their motives recombined in such a way that the original theme is gradually transformed, its motivic units replaced one by one until a new structure results, as in the first movement of the Third Symphony. One or two basic motives may recur throughout an entire movement or even an entire symphony. The structure, which may vaguely suggest formal schemes like exposition, development, and recapitulation, really grows out of the unifying ideas.

Fourth Symphony

The Fourth Symphony is a model of concision, intensity, and thematic unity, exploiting in every movement the tritone interval *C–F♯* of the opening phrase (Example 19.11). It is also ascetic and astringent in its use of orchestral resources. It preserves, however, the traditional variety of movements—adagio, scherzo with trio, largo, and allegro. At the other end of the spectrum is the Seventh, in one continuous movement.

Example 19.11 *Jean Sibelius, Fourth Symphony: Some Thematic Transformations*

Fifth Symphony

The Fifth Symphony, finished in 1915, revised in 1916, put in its final form in 1919, and published in 1921, was Sibelius's response to the new music of Strauss, Schoenberg, and Stravinsky, whose innovations fascinated him. But he decided not to follow in their footsteps and instead to take his own path guided by tonality. The entire symphony is built around the sonority of the E♭-major triad. Two subsidiary sonorities color the first movement: B-major—a major-third below; and G-major—a major third above. E♭ = D♯ is the common tone in the first shift, *G* in the second. The E♭-major sonority is most often heard in its first or second inversion; its dominant is suppressed except at climactic points, when it usually occurs over a tonic pedal. Example 19.12 (page 658) illustrates the skirting around the dominant, the play with fragmentary motives that will later be combined into thematic statements, and the gradual shift to the B-major sonority, in which a contrasting idea is forcefully introduced by the winds in triple octaves.

A climactic point in the last movement of the symphony is the full flowering of a theme that Sibelius acknowledged in his diary for April 21, 1915, was suggested to him by the call of sixteen swans circling over him. It sounded like a sarrusophone or trumpet, he remarked. Preceded by an unusually lengthy dominant-chord preparation, the theme marks the return of the E♭ harmony

Example 19.12 *Sibelius, Fifth Symphony: First Movement*

Source: James A. Hepokoski, *Sibelius, Symphony No. 5* (New York: Cambridge University Press, 1993), p. 61. Reprinted with the permission of Cambridge University Press.

Example 19.13 *Sibelius, Fifth Symphony: Last Movement*

as two trumpets play it *mezzo piano e nobile* very broadly (*largamente assai*), near the end of the movement (Example 19.13)

England

Elgar

Edward Elgar (1857–1934) was the first English composer in more than two hundred years to enjoy wide international recognition. His music is not touched by folksong in the least, nor do its technical characteristics derive from the national musical tradition. The oratorio *The Dream of Gerontius* (1900), on a Catholic poem by John Henry Newman, influenced by Wagner's *Parsifal*, gives the orchestra an expressive role as important as the chorus. Elgar also composed a number of notable orchestral scores, including two symphonies, the *Enigma Variations* (1899), the overture *Cockaigne* (1901), and the "symphonic study" *Falstaff* (1913). From Brahms and Wagner he derived his harmonic style, from Wagner the system of leitmotifs in his oratorios and perhaps also his persistent sequential repetitions.

The English musical renaissance signaled by Elgar took a nationalist turn in the twentieth century. Folksong collections by Cecil Sharp (1859–1924), Ralph Vaughan Williams (1872–1958), and others led to the use of these melodies in compositions such as Vaughan Williams's *Norfolk Rhapsodies* for orchestra (1907) and the *Somerset Rhapsody* by Gustav Holst (1874–1934). These two composers became the leaders of a new English school, which will be discussed in the following chapter.

Spain

Pedrell

Felipe Pedrell (1841–1922) sparked a comparable nationalist revival in Spain with his editions of sixteenth-century Spanish composers and his operas, chief of which was *Los Pirineos* (The Pyrenees; composed 1891). Further nationalist impetus came from the works of Isaac Albéniz (1860–1909), whose piano suite *Iberia* (1909) used Spanish dance rhythms in a colorful virtuoso style. The principal Spanish composer of the early twentieth century, Manuel de Falla (1876–1946), collected and arranged national folksongs, and his earlier works—the opera *La vida breve* (Life Is Short; composed 1905), for example, and the ballet *El amor brujo* (Love, the Sorcerer; 1915)—are imbued with the melodic and rhythmic qualities of Spanish popular music. *Nights in the Gar-*

Albéniz

Falla

dens of Spain, three "symphonic impressions" for piano and orchestra (1916), testify both to national sources and the influence of Debussy. Falla's finest mature works are the concerto for harpsichord with five solo instruments (1926) and the little stage piece *El retablo de maese Pedro* (Master Peter's Puppet Show, 1923), based on an episode from *Don Quixote*. Here the specific national elements are transformed into a delicately colored musical fabric.

NEW CURRENTS IN FRANCE

France, too, showed concern for the recovery of its national musical heritage and the encouragement of its native composers. The National Society for French Music was founded at the end of the Franco-Prussian War in 1871. Its purpose was to give performances of works by French composers, and the society can be credited with a marked rise, both in quantity and quality, of symphonic and chamber music. The society also sought to revive the great French music of the past through editions and performances of Rameau, Gluck, and sixteenth-century composers. The Schola Cantorum, founded in Paris in 1894, introduced broad historical studies in music, in contrast to the narrow technical training (emphasizing opera) that had prevailed at the century-old Conservatoire. These and similar activities allowed France to regain a leading position in music in the first half of the twentieth century. Thus the French revival, begun as elsewhere with nationalistic aims, produced results of prime importance for Western music.

Three traditions

Three interdependent lines of development may be traced in French music from 1871 to the early 1900s: (1) the cosmopolitan tradition, transmitted through César Franck and carried on by his pupils, especially Vincent d'Indy; (2) the specifically French tradition, transmitted through Camille Saint-Saëns and continued by his pupils, especially Gabriel Fauré; and (3) a later tradition, rooted in the French one, led by Debussy in directions that could hardly have been predicted.

The Cosmopolitan Tradition

Franck

César Franck (1822–1890) worked mainly in the conventional instrumental genres—symphony, symphonic poem, sonata, variations, chamber music—and oratorio. He shaped and developed his themes in traditional ways, but he enriched his essentially homophonic texture by contrapuntal means. Underlying all his work was his warm religious idealism and his belief in the serious social mission of the artist. He worked out his ideas logically, and pointedly avoided extremes of expression. Franck introduced some mildly chromatic innovations in harmony and systematically applied the cyclical method.

D'Indy

Vincent d'Indy (1851–1931), Franck's leading pupil, held faithfully to his master's ideals and methods. D'Indy's First Symphony, "On a French Mountain Air" (1886), is exceptional for a French work because it uses a folksong as its principal subject. Both that symphony and his Second exhibit the cyclical

■ *Paris, Théâtre de l'Opéra. Inaugurated on January 5, 1875, and known also as the Palais Garnier (after its architect Charles Garnier), it remained the main opera house in Paris until the Opéra Bastille took its place in 1989.* Thaïs *(1894) and a number of other operas by Massenet were first performed there, and, starting in 1891, Wagner's operas were sung in French. But the Opéra-Comique produced most premières of French works: among them Bizet's* Carmen *(1875), Offenbach's* Les contes d'Hoffmann *(1881), Delibes'* Lakmé *(1883), and Debussy's* Pelléas et Mélisande *(1902).* (ARCHIVO ICONOGRAFICO, S.A./CORBIS)

transformation of themes, a process that d'Indy learned from Franck. The quasi-programmatic *Istar* variations (1896) stands the usual plan on its head: the set begins with the most complex variation and progresses to the simple statement of the theme at the end. *Istar* and the First Symphony are the most spontaneous and attractive of d'Indy's compositions. His opera *Fervaal* (1897) reflects the French fascination for Wagner, especially in the poem, which d'Indy wrote himself. The beautiful closing choral scene, which incorporates the melody of the plainsong hymn *Pange lingua*, testifies to his poetic power and profound religious faith.

Chausson

Ernest Chausson (1855–99), also an admirer of Wagner in his youth, carried on Franck's exploration of cyclical form and adventurous harmonies. His symphonic poems are no longer heard, but his songs and chamber music, thanks to recordings, are again attracting attention, particularly the piano sextet, *Concert*, Op. 21 for piano, violin, and string quartet (1892).

The French Tradition

The French tradition is essentially Classic, regarding music as a sonorous form rather than as an expression. Order and restraint are fundamental. Instead of emotional displays and musical depiction we get subtle patterns of tones, rhythms, and colors. The music sounds more lyric or dancelike than epic or dramatic. It is economical, simple, and reserved rather than profuse, complex, and grandiloquent. It delivers no message about the fate of the cosmos or the state of the composer's soul. To comprehend such music, listeners must be sensitive to quiet statement, nuance, and exquisite detail, able to distinguish calmness from dullness, wit from jollity, gravity from portentousness, lucidity from emptiness. This kind of music was written by French composers as far apart in time and temperament as Couperin and Gounod. (Berlioz did not write such music, and he was not a success in France.)

Saint-Saëns

In Camille Saint-Saëns this French inheritance was coupled with high craftsmanship, facility in managing Classic forms, and the ability to adopt at will any fashionable devices. A similar eclectic approach runs through the many successful operas of Jules Massenet (1842–1912), chief of which were *Manon* (1884), *Werther* (1892), *Thaïs* (1894), and *Le Jongleur de Notre Dame* (The Juggler of Notre Dame, 1902). His operas also exhibit a talent for suave, sensuous, charming, and often sentimental melody, qualities always appreciated in France.

Massenet

Fauré

Gabriel Fauré (1845–1924) was a founder of the National Society for French Music and the first president of the Independent Musical Society, which branched off from the parent association in 1909. After studying composition with Saint-Saëns from 1861 to 1865, Fauré held various posts as an organist. He became professor of composition at the Paris Conservatoire in 1896 and its director from 1905 to 1920, when he was forced to resign because of a hearing loss.

Fauré's refined, highly civilized music embodies the aristocratic qualities of the French tradition. Primarily a composer of lyric pieces and chamber music, he wrote a few works in larger forms, including the Requiem (1887), incidental music to Maurice Maeterlinck's *Pelléas et Mélisande* (1898), and the operas *Promethée* (1900) and *Pénélope* (1913). His characteristics are most fully revealed in nearly one hundred songs, of which we may note particularly *Lydia, Après un rêve* (both 1865), *Claire de lune* (1887), *Au cimetière* (1889), the *Cinq mélodies* (1890) to poems of Verlaine, and especially the cycles *La bonne chanson* (Verlaine; 1892; see NAWM 127; CD 11 [6]), *La chanson d'ève* (Charles van Lerberghe; 1907-10), and *L'Horizon chimérique* (Jean de la Ville de Mirmont; 1922). Fauré's piano pieces, like the songs, were written during all periods of his creative life; they include impromptus, preludes, thirteen barcarolles, thirteen nocturnes, and a few larger works. His principal chamber compositions are three late works: the Second Violin Sonata (1917), the Second Piano Quintet (1921), and the String Quartet (1924).

Songs

Fauré began by composing songs in the manner of Gounod, followed by piano salon pieces derived from Mendelssohn and Chopin. In some respects he never changed: lyrical melody, with no display of virtuosity, remained the basis of his style, and small dimensions were always congenial to him. But in his maturity, from about 1885, he began to fill these small forms with a new language. Fauré added innovations in harmony to his flowing, pliant melodies. *Avant que tu ne t'en ailles* (Before you depart, NAWM 127; CD 11 [6]) from *La bonne chanson* illustrates some of his melodic and harmonic idiosyncrasies.

Example 19.14 *Gabriel Fauré,* Avant que tu ne t'en ailles

What joy in the fields of ripe wheat.

The fragmentary phrases of melody, one for each verse, pay no allegiance to any major or minor scale. Fauré's ambiguous tonality, with its lowered leading tone, results perhaps from the modal idiom of plainchant he studied in school. His harmony thus lacks the usual pull of the tonic and neutralizes the chords' tendency to resolution through the introduction of foreign notes. These factors combine to give his music certain equilibrium and repose that is the opposite of the emotional unrest in Wagner's music. In Example 19.14 the chords consist mainly of dominant sevenths and ninths, as in Wagner, but the tension melts as one chord fades into another and the unresolved seventh or ninth becomes a wayward member of another chord.

Fauré's music has often been described as Hellenic, its clarity, balance, and serenity recalling the spirit of ancient Greek art. Such qualities are evident not only in the more intimate works but also in *Pénélope* (where, of course, they are particularly appropriate) and in the Requiem. After 1910 Fauré's style became even more concentrated, his textures more austere (*L'Horizon chimérique*, the Tenth Barcarolle), and his lines more contrapuntal (Second Quintet, Thirteenth Nocturne). Through his pupil Ravel and through the famous teacher Nadia Boulanger (1887–1979), who was also his student, Fauré influenced countless later composers.

Debussy

Impressionism

Claude Debussy (1862–1918) was one of the most potent influences on the course of twentieth-century music. One aspect of his style—too often overemphasized—is summed up in the term *impressionism*. The word was first applied to a school of French painting that flourished from about 1880 to the end of the century. Its chief representative was Claude Monet (1840–1926; see Plate XI, facing page 654). His musical counterparts aimed to evoke moods and sensuous impressions mainly through harmony and tone color. Unlike earlier program music, impressionism did not seek to express deeply felt emotion or tell a story but to evoke a mood, a fleeting sentiment, an atmosphere. It used enigmatic titles, reminiscences of natural sounds, dance rhythms, characteristic bits of melody, and the like to suggest the subject. Impressionism relied on allusion and understatement, the antithesis of the forthright, energetic, deep expressions of the Romantics.

Various early influences contributed to the formation of Debussy's style. The immediate background included Franck, Saint-Saëns, and the witty and original Emmanuel Chabrier (1841–1894), but contemporary French painters and poets had at least as much impact on his thinking. Debussy's admiration for Wagner was coupled with revulsion against his bombastic rhetoric and his attempts to expound philosophy in music. Debussy found potential new directions, for example, in Russian music, especially Musorgsky's *Boris* and his songs. The influence of Grieg has been mentioned, and after 1900 that of Ravel stands out, especially in the piano music. Spanish local color, inspired in part by Chabrier's *España* and Ravel's *Habanera*, is evident in the *Soirée dans Grenade* (No. 2 of *Estampes*) and the *Ibéria* movement of the orchestral *Images* (1912).

Some technical features of the impressionist style already existed in Chopin's works (end of the D♭-major Nocturne) and in Liszt's *Les jeux d'eau à la Villa d'Este* (in the third set of *Années de pèlerinage*) and some of the late piano works. From the French tradition Debussy inherited his fine sensibilities, his aristocratic taste, and his anti-Romantic conception of music's function. In his last works he turned with renewed conviction to the heritage of Couperin and Rameau.

Debussy's most celebrated orchestral work, *Prélude à l'après-midi d'un faune* (1894), is based on a symbolist poem by Mallarmé. Debussy treats the subject the same way that French symbolist poets did—by evoking a mood through suggestion, connotation, and indirection rather than through intense emotional expression.

Like the impressionist painters, Debussy was fascinated with atmosphere, color, and light. This is evident in the symphonic sketches *La Mer* (1905) and in the orchestral *Nocturnes* (1899). *Nuages* (Clouds, NAWM 128; CD 11 [11] / 4 ⟨18⟩), the first of the *Nocturnes*, reveals some of the sources of Debussy's style. The piece begins with a chordal pattern borrowed from Musorgsky's song *Okonchen prazdnyi, shumnyi den'* (The idle, noisy day is over, NAWM 125), but Musorgsky's alternating sixths and thirds are replaced by the starker sounding fifths and thirds (see Example 19.15a). As in the Musorgsky, we feel an impression of movement but no harmonic direction, a perfect analogy for slowly moving clouds. To articulate disparate segments of the piece, Debussy used descending parallel seventh and ninth chords (Example 19.15b). Like Musorgsky and Fauré, Debussy did not use chords to shape a phrase by ten-

Nocturnes

Example 19.15 *Chord progressions in* Nuages *(Debussy) and* The idle, noisy day is over *(Musorgsky)*

a.

b.

sion and release; instead he conceived each chord as a sonorous unit in a phrase whose structure was determined more by melodic shape or color value than by harmonic motion. Debussy usually maintained a tonal focus—a kind of key center—but he defied the common tonal relationships between chords to empower them as independent structures with distinctive properties.

The middle section of *Nuages*, which is in the ABA form Debussy favored, had a more exotic source: the Javanese *gamelan*, an orchestra made up mainly of gongs and percussion that Debussy heard at the 1889 Paris Exposition. Simulating the *gamelan* texture, Debussy gave the flute and harp a simple pentatonic tune, while the other instruments were assigned a static background.

Orchestration

Debussy's orchestration admirably suits his musical ideas. His works require a large orchestra, but it is seldom used to make a loud sound. Strings are frequently divided and muted, and harps add a distinctive touch. Among the woodwinds, the flute (especially in the low register), oboe, and English horn are featured in solos. Horns and trumpets, also often muted, are heard in short *pianissimo* phrases. Percussion instruments of many types—kettledrums, large and small drums, large and small cymbals, tamtams, celesta, glockenspiel, xylophone—provide still another source of color. Debussy's orchestral technique is well illustrated in the *Nocturnes*: the brilliance of the full ensemble in *Fêtes*; and the magic of rich, subdued instrumentation in *Nuages* (see NAWM 128) and *Sirènes*, supplemented in *Sirènes* by a wordless chorus of women's voices.

Piano music

Pianistic counterparts of all these devices are found in Debussy's piano music, which, along with Ravel's, contributed importantly to early twentieth-century literature for that instrument. The chord structure is often veiled by figuration and by the blending effect of the damper pedal. No mere listing of technical features can suggest the sparkling play of color, the ravishing

■ *The opening page of Debussy's autograph manuscript for* Prélude à l'après-midi d'un faune, *with a dedication by the composer to Gaby Dupont dated 1899. This short score shows the intended instrumentation. The tempo is given as* Assez lent, *but the edition based on Debussy's conducting score of 1908–13 reads* Très modéré. (ROBERT LEHMAN COLLECTION)

pianistic effects, the subtle poetic fancy these pieces display. Debussy's principal impressionistic piano works occur in collections published between 1903 and 1913: *Estampes*, two books of *Images*, and two books of *Préludes*.

Impressionism, of course, is only one aspect of Debussy's style; a Hellenistic detachment, as in Fauré, distinguishes many of his compositions. Examples may be heard in the piano music: the early *Suite Bergamasque* (1893), the suite *Pour le piano* (1901), and the delightful *Children's Corner* (1908). In the latter, halfway through the *Golliwog's Cake Walk*, we hear a satirical quotation from Wagner's *Tristan*, while *Dr. Gradus ad Parnassum* takes a sly poke at Czerny. The String Quartet (1893) fuses Debussy's harmonic and coloristic traits with Classic forms and cyclic treatment of themes.

Pelléas et Mélisande

In his only completed opera, *Pelléas et Mélisande* (1902), Debussy set a symbolist play by Maurice Maeterlinck (1862–1949). The veiled allusions and images of the text are matched by the strange, often modal harmonies, subdued colors, and restrained expressiveness of the music. The voices, in fluent recitative, are supported but never dominated by a continuous orchestral background, while the instrumental interludes connecting the scenes carry on the mysterious inner drama.

Songs

Notable among Debussy's songs are two sets of *Fêtes galantes* to poems by Paul Verlaine (1892, 1904), the *Chansons de Bilitis* of Pierre Louys (1897), and *Trois ballades* (1910) of the fifteenth-century poet François Villon. He also wrote incidental music (1911), both choral and orchestral, to the mystery play *Le Martyre de Saint-Sébastien* by Gabriele d'Annunzio.

Influence

The changes that Debussy introduced in harmonic and orchestral usage made him one of the seminal forces in the history of music. To name the composers who at one time or another came under his influence would be to name nearly every distinguished composer of the early and middle twentieth century. Such a list, in addition to Ravel, Messiaen, Boulez, and all others of French nationality, would include Skryabin, Reger, Strauss, Falla, Puccini, Janáček, Stravinsky, Bartók, Berg, Webern, Hindemith, and Orff, all of whom developed their personal languages. Composers for whom impressionism had a more conspicuous or lasting effect were the Alsatian-born American Charles Martin Loeffler (1861–1935), the Swiss-American Ernest Bloch (1880–1959), the American Charles Griffes (1884–1920), the Pole Karol Szymanowski (1882–1937), the Englishman Arnold Bax (1883–1935), and the Italian Ottorino Respighi (1879–1936). The Austrian Franz Schreker (1878–1934) revealed a strong influence from Debussy in his first opera, *Der ferne Klang* (1910), before turning in an expressionist direction, assimilating Wagnerian and Straussian harmonic idioms, ultimately rejecting these too for a sparer, more formalistic approach.

Satie

Erik Satie (1866–1925) spearheaded a movement that was anti-impressionist, though not altogether anti-Debussy. It paralleled a similar position taken

Piano pieces

by Jean Cocteau in the literary and theatrical domains. Some of Satie's early piano pieces, for example, the three *Gymnopédies* of 1888, anticipated Debussy's unresolved chords and quasi-modal harmonies in an ostentatiously plain texture. By 1891 he was writing chords in parallel motion built on perfect fourths. Surrealistic titles headed his piano caricatures written between 1900 and 1915: *Trois morceaux en forme de poire* (Three Pieces in the Form of a Pear), *Embryons desséchés* (Dehydrated Embryos), and the like. The scores contain running commentary and tongue-in-cheek directions to the player: *pp en un pauvre souffle* (*pianissimo*, short of breath), *avec beaucoup de mal* (with much difficulty). Some of these satirized the titles and directions of Debussy. But the comic spirit lives also in the music itself—spare, dry, capricious, brief, repetitive, parodistic, and witty in the highest degree.

Works for media

Among Satie's works for media other than the piano are the stylized "realistic ballet" *Parade* (1917) on a scenario by Cocteau, with scenery and costumes by Picasso, and the "symphonic drama" *Socrate* (1920), for soloists and chamber orchestra on texts translated from Plato. The last scene, *The Death of Socrates*, attains a poignancy that is intensified by the stylistic monotony and the studied avoidance of a direct emotional appeal. Satie's biting, antisentimental spirit, economical textures, and severe harmony and melody influenced the music of his compatriots Milhaud, Honegger, and Poulenc, among others.

Costume for a ballet on Erik Satie's Trois morceaux en forme de poire *(Three Pieces in the Form of a Pear, 1890–1903) for piano four hands.* (PARIS, ARCHIVES DE LA FONDATION ERIK SATIE)

Ravel

Maurice Ravel (1875–1937) gives a hint of his move away from Debussy in the titles of his first two piano compositions—*Menuet antique* (1895), *Pavane pour une infante défunte* (Pavane for a Deceased Infanta, 1899)—and in his last, *Le Tombeau de Couperin* (Memorial for Couperin, 1917). Although Ravel adopted some impressionist techniques, he was more attracted to clean melodic contours, distinct rhythms, and firm structures; his harmonies, while complex and sophisticated, are functional.

Le Tombeau de Couperin

In the Menuet from *Le Tombeau de Couperin* (NAWM 129; CD 11 [17]), originally written for piano, Ravel achieves a classic simplicity of musical form, using conventional cadences to demarcate the short phrases and sections of the binary dance form. The orchestration is finely detailed: strings constantly changing from *arco* (bow) to pizzicato or from unison to divisi, not to mention special effects such as harmonics and muted passages. Mutes also mask the color of the horns and trumpets. Rather than the shifting veils of impressionism, we hear blocked-out phrases, contrapuntal lines, and a transparency that recalls Mozart more than Couperin.

Impressionistic works

Ravel's partiality for Classic forms is clearest in works such as the *Sonatine* for piano (1905) and the chamber music, which includes a quartet (1903), a piano trio (1914), a sonata for violin and violoncello (1922), and one for violin and piano (1927). His most markedly impressionistic works for piano are the *Jeux d'eau* (1901), the five pieces titled *Miroirs* (1905), and the three titled *Gaspard de la nuit* (1908). Others are the orchestral suite *Rapsodie espagnole* (1907) and the ballet *Daphnis et Chloé* (1909–1911).

Like Debussy, Ravel was a brilliant colorist who orchestrated several of his piano pieces (see NAWM 129). He also absorbed ideas from elsewhere, adapting them to his own use with as much assurance as he adapted impressionism. He used Viennese waltz rhythms in the "choreographic poem" *La Valse* (1920), jazz elements in the *Concerto for the Left Hand* (1930), and Spanish idioms in the *Rapsodie*, the comic opera *L'Heure espagnole* (1910), and the haunting *Bolero* (1928), which became the musical equivalent of a best-seller. One of his most charming works is *Ma Mère l'Oye* (Mother Goose), a set of five little piano duets written in 1908, children's music comparable to Musorgsky's *Nursery Songs* and Debussy's *Children's Corner*. Equally perceptive and compassionate, although different in technique and intent, is the "lyrical fantasy" *L'Enfant et les sortilèges* (The Child and the Sorceries, 1925).

Songs

Ravel's songs include many settings of folk melodies from various countries. His important original songs are the five humorous and realistic characterizations of animal life in the *Histoires naturelles* (1906), and the *Chansons madécasses* (Songs of Madagascar, 1926) for voice, flute, cello, and piano. The chamber ensemble for the three Mallarmé poems (1913)—voice, piano, string quartet, two flutes, and two clarinets—was suggested to Ravel by Schoenberg's *Pierrot lunaire*.

Other French Composers

Dukas

Three other French composers of the early twentieth century deserve brief commentary. Paul Dukas (1865–1935) belongs in the Franck-d'Indy line. His most popular work, *The Sorcerer's Apprentice* (1897), is a symphonic poem that was later visually realized in Walt Disney's animated film *Fantasia* (1940). His one opera, *Ariane et Barbe-bleue* (Ariadne and Bluebeard, 1907), was a serious attempt to combine the symphonic drama of Wagner and d'Indy with some features suggested by the music of Debussy. Florent Schmitt (1870–1958), the one French composer of this period who shows some kinship with the German late Romantics, is notable for a symphonic poem, *La Tragédie de Salomé* (1910; originally written as a ballet in 1907).

Schmitt

Roussel

A composer whose significance extends beyond the first decade of the century is Albert Roussel (1869–1937). He studied at the Schola Cantorum under d'Indy. In his three symphonic *évocations* (1911) and the opera-ballet *Padmâvatî* (composed 1914; first performed 1923) he carried the musical treatment of exotic subjects to new heights. Both of these works depict scenes and impressions of India and make use of scales derived from Indian music. Roussel's later works show the then-current trend toward neo-Classicism, evident particularly in the orchestral Suite in F (1926), the Third Symphony in G minor (1930), and the *Sinfonietta* for string orchestra (1934).

ITALIAN OPERA

Verismo

One of the most characteristic musical "isms" of the late nineteenth century was verism (*verismo*) in Italian opera. Literally "truthism," it is sometimes translated as "realism" or "naturalism." The librettos present everyday people in familiar situations acting violently under the impulse of primitive emotions. Veristic opera is the innocent grandparent of the television and movie thriller. Among the best examples of this genre are two works usually paired in performance, *Cavalleria rusticana* (Rustic Chivalry, 1890) by Pietro Mascagni (1863–1945) and *I Pagliacci* (The Clowns, 1892) by Ruggero Leoncavallo (1858–1919). Though short-lived, verism had some parallels or repercussions in France and Germany, and its progeny still live in the repertory around the world.

Mascagni and Leoncavallo

Puccini

Only some of the operas of Giacomo Puccini (1858–1924) fall in this category. In works such as *Tosca* (1900) and *Il tabarro* (1918), Puccini achieved a musical style appropriate to the realistic libretto. Musical ideas grow out of the action, as if recitative suddenly sprouted melody. From a large harmonic palette—parallel chords, augmented triads, added sixths, whole-tone scales, chromatic alterations, all within a base of functional and even Wagnerian harmony—he applied the most suitable devices in a fluid succession that is some-

■ *Theatrical poster (1899) by Adolfo Hohenstein for Giacomo Puccini's* Tosca, *premiered in Rome in 1900. Illustrated is the highly dramatic scene at the end of Act II, in which Tosca, having killed the chief of police Scarpia, places lighted candles beside his head and a crucifix on his chest.* (MILAN, MUSEO TEATRALE ALLA SCALA)

times seamless and sometimes abrupt. Puccini had a flair for representing swift action and also for the lyrical pause. He paid great attention to mood, both psychological and external—the Japanese local color in *Madama Butterfly* (1904), for example, the Chinese flavor in *Turandot* (1926), and the aura of the Parisian Latin Quarter in *La bohème* (1896). Like Massenet a successful eclectic, Puccini combined a late-Romantic taste for intense emotion with realism and exoticism.

BIBLIOGRAPHY

For editions of music by composers discussed in this chapter, see under the composer's name.

For Further Reading

LATE ROMANTICISM

General studies on composers in this chapter can be found in *The New Grove Turn of the Century Masters* (Janáček, Mahler, Strauss, and Sibelius), by John Tyrrell et al. (New York: Norton, 1985); see also Chapters 16–17.

Mahler Donald Mitchell, *Gustav Mahler: The Early Years* (London: Rockliff, 1958), revised by Paul Banks and David Matthews (Berkeley: University of California Press, 1980), and idem, *Gustav Mahler: The Wunderhorn Years* (Boulder, Col.: Westview Press, 1976), are very good studies; Peter Franklin, *The Life of Mahler* (Cambridge: Cambridge University Press, 1997); Henry-Louis de La Grange, *Mahler* (Vol. 1, New York: Doubleday, 1973; Vols. 2 and 3, Oxford University Press, 1984 and 1995); Kurt Blaukopf, *Mahler: A Documentary Study* (New York: Oxford University Press, 1976); Deryck Cooke, *Gustav Mahler: An Introduction to His Music* (London: Faber & Faber, 1980). Interesting insights into Mahler's life are in Alma Mahler-Werfel, *Diaries, 1898-1902*, transcribed and ed. Antony Beaumont and Susanne Rode-Breymann, selected and trans. A. Beaumont (Ithaca, N.Y.: Cornell University Press, 1999); Mahler: *Memories and Letters*, 3rd rev. ed., by Donald Mitchell and Knud Martner, trans. B. Creighton (Seattle: University of Washington Press, 1975). A critical edition of Mahler's works is in progress, ed. Internationale Gustav Mahler Gesellschaft (Vienna, 1960–).

Reger Max Reger's works are issued in a collected edition by the Max Reger Institute (Wiesbaden: Breitkopf & Härtel, 1954–70). Thematic catalogue by Fritz Stein, *Thematisches Verzeichnis der im Druck erschienenen Werke von Max Reger* (Leipzig: Breitkopf & Härtel, 1953). Bibliography published by the Max Reger Institute (Bonn: F. Dümmler Verlag, 1983). See also Mitchell, "Max Reger," *The Music Review* 12 (1951):279–88.

Strauss Norman Del Mar, *Richard Strauss: A Critical Commentary on His Life and Work*, 3 vols. (Philadelphia: Chilton Books, 1969–73; repr. with corr., 1978), is the best general study; Michael Kennedy, *Richard Strauss: Man, Musician, Enigma* (Cambridge: Cambridge University Press, 1999); Bryan Gilliam, *The Life of Richard Strauss* (Cambridge: Cambridge University Press, 1999); idem, ed., *Richard Strauss: New Perspectives on the Composer and His Work* (Durham: Duke University Press, 1997); idem, *Richard Strauss and His World* (Princeton: Princeton University Press, 1992); William Mann, *Richard Strauss: A Critical Study of His Operas* (London: Cassell, 1964); Thomas Armstrong, *Strauss' Tone Poems* (London: Oxford University Press, 1931); Alan Jefferson, *The Lieder of Richard Strauss* (New York: Praeger, 1972); Richard Strauss, *Recollections and Reflections*, ed. Willi Schuh (London: Boosey & Hawkes, 1953). Collected songs, 4 vols., ed. Franz Trenner (Fürstner: Boosey & Hawkes, 1964–65); thematic catalogue by E. H. Mueller von Asow (Vienna: Doblinger, 1955–66).

Russia On Russian music in general, see Gerald Abraham, *Studies in Russian Music* (London: William Reeves, 1935; rev. 1969); idem, *Slavonic and Romantic Music* (New York: St. Martin's Press, 1968); Gerald R. Seaman, *History of Russian Music*, Vol. 1 (New York: Praeger, 1967); Robert C. Ridenour, *Nationalism, Modernism, and Personal Rivalry in 19th-Century Russian Music* (Ann Arbor: UMI Research Press, 1981); *The New Grove Russian Masters*, 2 vols. (New York: Norton, 1986); Richard Taruskin, *Opera and Drama in Russia as Preached and Practiced in the 1860s* (Ann Arbor: UMI Research Press, 1981).

There are collected editions of the works of Glinka (Moscow, 1955–57), Borodin (Moscow, 1938–), Musorgsky (Moscow and Vienna, 1928–34; repr. New York, 1969; Russian State Edition, 1939–), Rimsky-Korsakov (Moscow, 1948–), and Skryabin (1950–).

Balakirev Edward Garden, *Balakirev: A Critical Study of His Life and Music* (London: Faber & Faber, 1967).

Glinka Alexandra Orlova, *Glinka's Life in Music: A Chronicle*, trans. Richard Hoops (Ann Arbor: UMI Research Press, 1988); *Memoirs*, trans. R. B. Mudge (Norman: University of Oklahoma Press, 1963); David Brown, *Mikhail Glinka: A Biographical and Critical Study* (London: Oxford University Press, 1974); Richard Taruskin, "Glinka's Ambiguous Legacy and the Birth Pangs of Russian Opera," *19th-Century* Music 1 (1977):142–62.

Musorgsky Jay Leyda and Sergei Bertensson, eds., *The Musorgsky Reader: A Life of M. P. Musorgsky in Letters and Documents* (New York: Norton, 1947; repr. 1970); Michel-Dimitri Calvocoressi, *Mussorgsky*, rev. Gerald Abraham (London: Dent, 1974); Richard Taruskin, *Musorgsky: Eight Essays and an Epilogue* (Princeton: Princeton University Press, 1993); Caryl Emerson and Robert William Oldani, *Modest Musorgsky and Boris Godunov: Myths, Realities, Reconsiderations* (Cambridge: Cambridge University Press, 1994); David Lloyd-Jones, *Boris Godunov: Critical Commentary* (London: Oxford University Press, 1975); Alexandra Orlova, *Musorgsky's Works and Days*, trans. Roy E. Guenther (Ann Arbor: UMI Research Press, 1983); *Musorgsky Remembered*, comp. and ed. A. Orlova, trans. Véronique Zaytzeff and Frederick Morrison (Bloomington: Indiana University Press, 1991).

Rimsky-Korsakov His *My Musical Life*, trans. Judah A. Joffe (New York: Knopf, 1923; repr. 1974). *Reminiscences of Rimsky-Korsakov*, ed. V. V. Yastrebtsev; ed. and trans. Florence Jonas (New York: Columbia University Press, 1985). His *Principles of Orchestration* has music examples from his own works (New York: Dover, 1964). Gerald Abraham, *Rimsky-Korsakov: A Short Biography* (London: Duckworth, 1945); Gerald R. Seaman, *Nikolai Andreevich Rimsky-Korsakov: A Guide to Research* (New York: Garland, 1988).

Skryabin Hugh Macdonald, *Skryabin* (London: Oxford University Press, 1978); Faubion Bowers, *Scriabin: A Biography of the Russian Composer*, 2 vols. (Tokyo and Palo Alto: Kodansha International, 1969); idem, *The New Scriabin: Enigma and Answers* (New York: St. Martin's Press, 1973); Boris de Schloezer, *Scriabin: Artist and Mystic*, trans. N. Slonimsky (Berkeley: University of California Press, 1987), an account by a friend and relative; James M. Baker, *The Music of Alexander Scriabin* (New Haven: Yale University Press, 1986).

Eastern Europe and Scandinavia

Janáček Jaroslav Vogel, *Leoš Janáček: His Life and Works*, rev. ed. by Karl Janovicky (New York: Norton, 1981); Zdenka Janáček, ed. and trans. John Tyrell, *My Life with Janáček* (London: Faber, 1998); Michael Ewans, *Janáček's Tragic Operas* (London: Faber & Faber, 1977). Nigel Simeone et al., *Janacek's Works: A Catalogue of the Music and Writings of Leos Janáček* (Oxford: Clarendon Press, 1997). The complete works are published (Prague/Kassel: Supraphon/Bärenreiter, 1979–).

Grieg Finn Benestad and Dag Schjelderup-Ebbe, *Edvard Grieg: The Man and the Artist*, trans. William H. Halverson and Leland B. Sateren (Lincoln: University of Nebraska Press, 1988); another biography by David M. Johansen, trans. Madge Robertson (Princeton: Princeton University Press, 1938); Gerald Abraham, ed., *Grieg: A Symposium* (London: Lindsay Drummond, 1948; repr. Greenwood Press, 1972).

Nielsen His *Living Music* and *My Childhood* (Copenhagen: W. Hansen, 1968 and 1953); Jack Lawson, *Carl Nielsen* (London: Phaidon, 1997); Mina Miller, ed., *The Nielsen Companion* (Portland, Ore.: Amadeus Press, 1995); Robert Simpson, *Carl Nielsen, Symphonist* (London: Dent, 1964); *Centenary Essays*, ed. J. Balzer (London: D. Dobson, 1966); Mina F. Miller, *Carl Nielsen: A Guide to Research* (New York: Garland, 1987).

Sibelius Recommended biographies are Erik Tawastjerna, *Sibelius*, trans. and rev. Robert Layton (London: Faber & Faber, 1976); R. Layton, *Sibelius* (New York: Schirmer Books, 1993); Guy Rickards, *Jean Sibelius* (London: Phaidon Press, 1997); Glenda Dawn Goss, ed., *The Sibelius Companion* (Westport, Conn: Greenwood Press, 1996). On Sibelius's music, see G. Abraham, ed., *The Music of Sibelius* (New York: Norton, 1947); James Burnett, *The Music of Jean Sibelius* (Rutherford, N. J.: Fairleigh Dickinson Press, 1983); Fabian Dahlström, *The Works of Jean Sibelius* (Helsinki: Sibelius-Seura, 1987); James A. Hepokoski, *Sibelius, Symphony No. 5* (New York: Cambridge University Press, 1993). See also

Jean Sibelius: An International Bibliography on the Occasion of the Centennial Celebrations, 1965 (Detroit Information Service). Antony Hodgson, *Scandinavian Music: Finland and Sweden* (Rutherford, N. J.: Fairleigh Dickinson University Press, 1984).

England and Spain

On English musical nationalism in the early twentieth century, see Chapter 13 of Ernest Walker, *History of Music in England,* 3rd rev. ed., by J. A. Westrup (Oxford: Clarendon Press, 1952), and *The New Grove Twentieth-Century English Masters,* by Diana McVeagh et al. (New York: Norton, 1986).

Elgar Percy Young, ed., *Letters of Elgar and Other Writings* (London: Geoffrey Bles, 1956). On Elgar's life and works, see D. McVeagh, *Edward Elgar: His Life and Music* (London: Dent, 1955); Michael Kennedy, *Portrait of Elgar,* 2nd rev. ed. (London: Oxford University Press, 1982); Jerrold N. Moore, *Edward Elgar: A Creative Life* (London: Oxford University Press, 1984); *Elgar Studies,* ed. Raymond Monk (Aldershot, Hants, Eng. and Brookfield, Vt.: Scholar Press, 1990). Complete collected edition of his works, ed. J. N. Moore (Sevenoaks, Kent: Novello, 1981–).

Falla Jorge de Persia, ed., *Manuel de Falla: His Life & Works* (Spain: Ministerio de Cultura, 1996); Jaime Pahissa, *Manuel de Falla: His Life and Works,* trans. Jean Wagstaff (London: Museum Press, 1954); James Burnett, *Manuel de Falla and the Spanish Musical Renaissance* (London: Gollancz, 1979); Nancy Lee Harper, *Manuel de Falla: A Bio-bibliography* (Westport, Conn.: Greenwood Press, 1998); Gilbert Chase and Andrew Budwig, *Manuel de Falla: A Bibliography and Research Guide* (New York: Garland, 1985); Antonio Ruiz-Pipó, *Catalogue de l'oeuvre de Manuel de Falla* (Paris: M. Eschig, 1993).

New Currents in France

General Martin Cooper, *French Music from the Death of Berlioz to the Death of Fauré* (London: Oxford University Press, 1951); Rollo Myers, *Modern French Music from Fauré to Boulez* (New York: Praeger, 1971); Roger Shattuck, *The Banquet Years: The Arts in France, 1885–1918* (London, 1959; rev. 1968); Paul Collaer, *A History of Modern Music,* trans. S. Abeles (Cleveland: World Publishing, 1961), Chapters 4–7; *The New Grove Twentieth-Century French Masters,* by Jean M. Nectoux et al. (New York: Norton, 1986).

Debussy Debussy's essays were published in Paris, 1923, under the title, *Monsieur Croche, anti-dilettante*; in translation, *Debussy on Music,* ed. François Lesure and R. L. Smith (New York: Knopf, 1977). The best biography is Edward Lockspeiser, *Debussy: His Life and Mind,* 2 vols. (New York: Macmillan, 1962–65); a shorter version is *Debussy,* 5th ed. (London: Dent, 1980). See also Roger Nichols, *The Life of Debussy* (Cambridge: Cambridge University Press, 1998); Arthur B. Wenk, *Claude Debussy and Twentieth-Century Music* (Boston: Twayner, 1983); Richard S. Parks, *The Music of Claude Debussy* (New Haven: Yale University Press, 1989); Claude Abravanel, *Claude Debussy: A Bibliography* (Detroit Information Service, 1974); William Austin, ed., *Debussy, Prelude to "The Afternoon of a Faun,"* Norton Critical Scores (New York: Norton, 1970).

Fauré Robert Orledge, *Gabriel Fauré* (London: Eulenburg, 1979); *Gabriel Fauré: A Life in Letters,* trans. and ed. J. Barrie Jones (London: B. T. Batsford, 1989); Jean M. Nectoux, *Gabriel Fauré: A Musical Life,* trans. Roger Nichols (New York: Cambridge University Press, 1991).

D'Indy Andrew Thomson, *Vincent d'Indy and His World* (New York: Clarendon Press, 1996).

Ravel Norman Demuth, *Ravel* (London: Dent, 1947); A. Orenstein, *Ravel, Man and Musician* (New York: Columbia University Press, 1975); Rollo Myers, *Ravel: His Life and Works* (London, 1960; repr. 1973); Gerald Larner, *Maurice Ravel* (London: Phaidon, 1996); Roger Nichols, *Ravel Remembered* (New York: Norton, 1988).

Books about other French composers: Rollo Myers, *Emmanuel Chabrier and His Circle* (London: Dent, 1969); Laurence Davies, *César Franck and His Circle* (London: Barrie & Jenkins, 1970); Basil Deane, *Albert Roussel* (London: Barrie & Rockliff, 1961); Pierre-Daniel Templier, *Erik Satie* (New York: Da Capo Press, 1980).

Italian Opera

Puccini Mosco Carner, *Puccini: A Critical Biography*, 2nd ed. (London: Duckworth, 1974); Conrad Wilson, *Giacomo Puccini* (London: Phaidon, 1997); Timothy Ramsden, *Puccini* (Staplehurst: Spellmount, 1996); Howard Greenfield, *Puccini* (New York: Putnam, 1980), which contains an extensive bibliography; William Ashbrook, *The Operas of Puccini* (New York: Oxford University Press, 1968); for programmatic notes on all the operas, with musical examples, see William Weaver and Simonetta Puccini, eds. *The Puccini Companion* (New York: Norton, 1994).

On verismo, see Carl Dahlhaus, *Realism in Nineteenth-Century Music*, trans. Mary Whittall (Cambridge: Cambridge University Press, 1985).

CHAPTER 20

THE EUROPEAN MAINSTREAM IN THE TWENTIETH CENTURY

INTRODUCTION

Of the allied victors of World War I, Britain and France sustained enormous losses in human and material resources. Only the United States, which suffered many fewer casualties, experienced a financial boom after the war. In 1929, however, the stock market crashed, and a worldwide Depression followed.

Europe between the wars

Europe between the two world wars (1918–39) enjoyed a peace made uneasy by increasing international tension. The Austro-Hungarian Empire was split into independent states—Austria, Czechoslovakia, Hungary, Yugoslavia, and Romania—where democracy mostly gave way to authoritarian rule. In Russia the Bolsheviks—radical Marxist revolutionaries—had seized power by 1917 and set up a dictatorship. Fearing a similar "proletarian" revolution, Benito Mussolini and the Fascists took over the Italian government in 1922. In Germany, Adolf Hitler and the National Socialists (Nazis) took advantage of the weakened Weimar Republic (1918–33) to turn the chancellorship, which Hitler had won in a legitimate election, into a dictatorship. The Nazis, in a fierce arousal of latent anti-Semitism, passed laws to deprive people of Jewish origin of their citizenship and all other rights, driving many intellectuals, writers, artists, composers, and scholars into exile. The Spanish Civil War (1936–39) and its aftermath, the totalitarian rule of Francisco Franco, practically closed that country off from the rest of the world until the mid-1970s.

These movements and events tended to isolate even neighboring areas from each other: Germany from Austria, Hungary from Austria and its Slavic neighbors, and these from Russia. England and France distanced themselves from Italy and the German-speaking countries, and the Western hemisphere from Europe. As we shall see, the course of music history followed suit, inevitably branching into divergent paths.

1914–30, Musical innovatum

Although the period 1914–30 was marked by bold innovation in musical composition, the seeds for many of the changes were sown earlier. By 1908 Arnold Schoenberg had given up the major-minor system of relationships around a single keytone that we call tonality. This was a significant break, to be sure, but equally important was a tendency to suppress the goal-directed harmonic progressions that had provided both continuity and formal organization for more than two centuries. Musorgsky and Debussy had cultivated a harmony of static blocks that eliminated the tension and relaxation of dominant and tonic, dissonance and resolution. Others had questioned the validity of themes and development and explored different ways to focus compositions, such as unifying chords or pitch collections, or contrasts of tone color.

Non-Western and folk music

Non-Western musics and the traditional (folk) music of Eastern Europe offered composers resources free of such familiar constraints as fixed meters and the conventional tonal relationships. "Exotic" scales, such as the pentatonic and whole-tone, lacked the leading tones that demanded particular melodic and chordal successions. The traditional music of Eastern Europe and Russia offered modal melodies and polyphonic practices that did not fit western conventions. Complex meters, alternating duple and triple, introduced novel rhythmic irregularities. The open form of performance-oriented music that had no clear beginning or end, such as Indonesian and of other traditional musics, also offered models for some composers.

Music for the people

As the gap widened between the "new music" and the responsiveness of listeners, special efforts were made throughout the interwar period to bring contemporary music closer to the general public. Leading composers were invited to provide background music for films, theater, and dance. Germany cultivated *Gebrauchsmusik* (workaday or utility music) for use by school groups or other amateurs. Similar movements arose elsewhere, such as "proletarian" music in the Soviet republics. Hungary, under the leadership of the composer Zoltán Kodály, sought to make music serve the people, and he set up an educational program based on folksong, a method that later spread to other countries, especially the United States.

1930–50

Beginning in the early 1930s government censorship in Russia and Germany attempted to "protect" the public from the new music, condemned in the one country as bourgeois decadence, in the other as cultural Bolshevism. In Poland, the Nazi occupation drove artistic activity underground between 1939 and 1945, when a musical renaissance began, only to be bent in ideological directions during the Stalinist period from 1949 to 1956.

1950s and 1960s

After 1950 the gulf widened further between what the concert-going public would tolerate and the output of avant-garde composers. Aleatoric music, in which composers left much of the pitch and rhythm content to chance or to performers' options, confounded most listeners. Serial music, which was highly organized on an intellectual level but seemingly chaotic on the audible surface, reached only a small circle of connoisseurs.

1970s and 1980s

From about 1970 some of the very composers who had written serial or avant-garde music began to use musical languages intended to reach a much wider audience. Some reintroduced tonality, resurrected styles of the past, or adopted a neo-Romantic idiom. Minimalism, in which a small amount of material is repeated many times and undergoes slow processes of change, evolved from a branch of avant-garde experimentation into a broad and increasingly popular stream that incorporated African drumming, Asian music, and other influences. Younger composers combined elements of popular music with the classical tradition to create new idioms that won a relatively large following. By the 1990s, most composers sought to communicate directly with audiences through the use of familiar musical idioms and gestures, drawn from the entire range of music history, musics of the world, and popular styles, often juxtaposed, mixed, or blended in unprecedented ways.

Technology

Technological factors played a significant role in the changes in twentieth-century musical culture. Recordings, radio, and television spawned an unparalleled growth in the size of the audience for many kinds of music. These technologies brought about widespread dissemination of the standard repertory from Vivaldi to Stravinsky, as well as other "serious" music from the more remote past to the present. They also furthered the growth of a huge body of "popular" music—blues, jazz, rock, soul, country, and various strains of newer urban music—much of it originating in the United States.

Summary of trends

In sum, disparate trends may be observed in the music of twentieth-century Europe. Musical styles that employed national folk idioms continued to emerge. Various movements, including neo-Classicism, combined the innovations of the early part of the century with the principles, forms, and techniques of the past, especially the Baroque and Classic eras. The German idiom of Wagner and others evolved into the serial or twelve-tone approaches of Arnold Schoenberg, Alban Berg, and Anton Webern, sometimes manifesting an extreme expressionism in its disjointed melody, dissonant clashes, sudden turns, and dynamic contrasts. Partly in reaction to the cerebral, systematic side of serial composition, some composers returned to audience-pleasing, eclectic, simpler idioms. Other composers, most notably Igor Stravinsky and Olivier Messiaen, cut across these tendencies, participating to some extent in one or more of them. Still other composers explored new paths altogether. One compositional philosophy, under the leadership of John Cage, gave control over to chance, allowing performers to take a greater role in determining the final form and even the pitches and rhythms of a work, while at the same time extending the range of sounds admitted into the musical palette.

It is not practical to deal with this complex century of European music chronologically. Partly because of the wars and political movements, different regions and individual nations experienced widely divergent trends and styles. However, certain movements—such as expressionism, neo-Classicism, twelve-tone composition, and the basing of art music on folk materials—crossed geographical boundaries. In this discussion national movements, particularly those exploiting traditional musics, are considered first. Next we take up neo-Classic, essentially anti-Romantic, trends in France. Then we consider Stravin-

TIMELINE: EARLY TWENTIETH CENTURY

1910 1920 1930 1940

- **1900 Debussy, *Nocturnes***
- 1900 Freud, *The Interpretation of Dreams*
- **1901–04 Mahler, *Kindertotenlieder***
- 1903 Wright brothers' successful airplane flight
- **1904 Puccini, *Madama Butterfly***
- **1905 Strauss, *Salome***
- **1907 Skryabin, *Poem of Ecstasy***
- **1908 Bartók, *First String Quartet***
- **1911 Mahler, *Das Lied von der Erde***
- **1912 Schoenberg, *Pierrot lunaire***
- 1913 Proust, *Remembrance of Things Past*
- **1913 Stravinsky, *Le Sacre du printemps***
- 1914–1918 World War I
- **1915 Ives, *Concord Sonata***
- 1916 Einstein, general theory of relativity
- **1918 Prokofiev, *Classical* Symphony**
- 1920 Sinclair Lewis, *Main Street*
- 1922 T. S. Eliot, *The Waste Land*
- **1924 Gershwin, *Rhapsody in Blue***
- **1925 Berg, *Wozzeck***
- **1926 Crawford Seeger, Violin Sonata**
- 1927 International Musicological Society founded
- 1927 Charles Lindbergh flies solo across the Atlantic
- **1928 Webern, Symphony, Op. 21**
- 1929 New York stock market crash
- 1933 Hitler, chancellor of Germany
- 1933–1945 F. D. Roosevelt, president of the United States
- 1934 American Musicological Society founded
- **1934 Hindemith, *Mathis der Maler* (symphony)**
- 1937 Picasso, *Guernica*
- **1937 Shostakovich, Fifth Symphony**

sky, whose influence pervaded Europe and America into the 1950s, followed by Schoenberg and his adherents. Though Schoenberg embarked on his radical path early in the century, its impact on music outside his own group was not much evident until after World War II. For a while, Webern became a model for many composers, but soon the avant-garde pressed in other directions, including electronic music.

ETHNIC CONTEXTS

The distinctive character of the ethnic musics of central and Eastern Europe became an important resource for composers in the first half of the twentieth century. Recording technology and speedier communication made the differences among traditional cultures evident to a wider public. Recording also led to more complete documentation of ethnic music than had been possible previously. Researchers in the field no longer collected folk music by clumsily transcribing it into conventional notation but instead recorded it on disks and tapes, then analyzed the collected specimens using techniques developed in the new discipline of ethnomusicology. Rather than trying to absorb folk idioms into more or less conventional styles by smoothing out their "irregularities" and making them fit the rules of art music, composers came to respect their uniqueness and drew inspiration from these idioms to create new styles, to expand the tonal and rhythmic vocabulary.

Central Europe saw some of the earliest efforts toward a scientific study of folk music. Janáček's pioneer work in the Czecho-Slovak region was soon followed by that of two Hungarian scholar-composers, Béla Bartók (1881–1945) and Zoltán Kodály (1882–1967).

Bartók

Béla Bartók made important contributions as a musical ethnologist, performer, and composer. He published nearly two thousand traditional tunes, chiefly from Hungary, Romania, Croatia, Slovakia, Serbia, and Bulgaria—only a small part of what he had collected in expeditions ranging over central Europe, Turkey, and North Africa. He wrote books and articles on this music and arranged and created original works based on traditional tunes. He developed a style that, more intimately than ever before, fused folk elements with highly developed techniques of art music. A virtuoso pianist, he taught piano at the Budapest Academy of Music from 1907 to 1934. His *Mikrokosmos* (1926–37)—153 piano pieces in six books of graded difficulty—is a work of great pedagogical value that also summarizes Bartók's own style and presents in microcosm the development of European music in the first third of the twentieth century.

Early works

Bartók first manifested a personal style about 1908, shortly after he had become interested in Hungarian, Romanian, Serbian, Croatian, Slovak, and other traditional songs. Compositions from this period include the First Quartet (1908), the one-act opera *Duke Bluebeard's Castle* (1911), and the *Allegro barbaro* for piano. Like many other twentieth-century composers, Bartók often treated the piano more as an instrument of percussion than as a spinnner of cantabile melodies and arpeggiated chords, as the Romantics had done. By 1917, the year he wrote the Second Quartet, he had thoroughly absorbed the influences from late Romanticism and impressionism into a combination of characteristic rhythmic vigor, exuberant imagination, and elemental folk qualities. His compositions over the next ten years show him pushing toward the limits of dissonance and tonal ambiguity, reaching the furthest point with his two Violin

■ *Béla Bartók in 1907, recording Slovakian folksongs on an acoustic cylinder machine in the Hungarian village of Zobordarázs.* (COLLECTION OF FERENC BÓNIS)

Sonatas (1922, 1923). Other works of this decade were the pantomime *The Miraculous Mandarin* (1919), the *Dance Suite* for orchestra (1923), the Piano Sonata (1926), the first Piano Concerto (1926), and the Third Quartet (1927).

Late works

The later works of Bartók are the most widely known. The Second Violin Concerto (1938) and the Concerto for Orchestra (1943) represent masterpieces in large form. Other works of the late period include the Fifth and Sixth Quartets (1934, 1939), the *Mikrokosmos*, the *Music for Strings, Percussion, and Celesta* (1936), the Sonata for Two Pianos and Percussion (1937), the Divertimento for string orchestra (1939), and the Third Piano Concerto (his last completed composition, 1945).

Style

Bartók combined contrapuntal textures, thematic development, and sensitivity to the purely sonorous value of chords in a way that is true to the Western musical heritage. With these he blended melodic lines derived or inspired from Eastern European traditional music. Powerful motoric rhythms are characteristically inflected by irregular meters and offbeat accents. Strong formal design controls an intense expressionistic drive. His polyphony of contrapuntal lines, carried on with secondary regard for vertical sonorities, includes free use of imitative, fugal, and canonic techniques (No. 145 of the *Mikrokosmos*, the first movement of the *Music for Strings, Percussion, and Celesta*, and the two outer movements of the Concerto for Orchestra). Frequently, parallel-moving voices in chord streams enrich one or more of the lines.

Harmony

Bartók's harmony is in part an incidental result of contrapuntal movement. It develops from the character of the melodies, which may be based on pentatonic, whole-tone, modal, or irregular scales (including those found in traditional music) as well as on the regular diatonic and chromatic scales. All kinds of chords appear, from triads to combinations built on fourths and other more complex constructions. Bartók often gave pungency to a chord by adding dissonant major or minor seconds (see Example 20.1a). Sometimes

Example 20.1 *Examples of Bartók's Chords with Seconds and Tone Clusters*

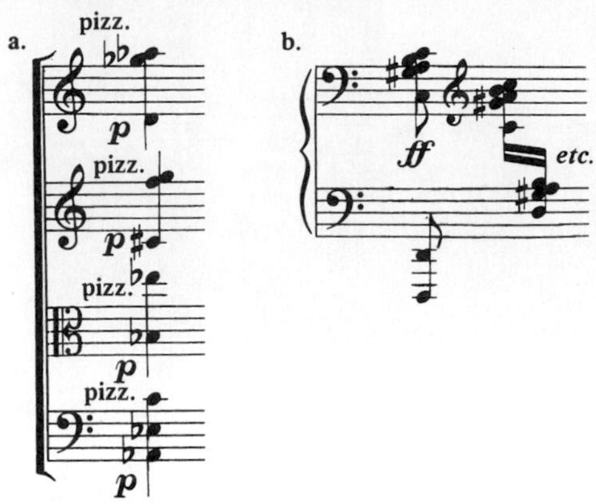

seconds pile up in tone clusters, as in the Piano Sonata, the first Piano Concerto (Example 20.1b), and the slow movement of the Second Concerto.

Tonal organization

In most of Bartók's music a primary tonal center recurs, though it may be obscured for long stretches by modal or chromatic means, or both. Sometimes, especially in the works from the 1920s, Bartók wrote simultaneously on two or more harmonic planes—a procedure that resulted in so-called *polytonality*—but he did not aim to negate tonality. Moreover, though he sometimes composed a theme that included up to twelve different tones in a row (as in the first movement of the Second Violin Concerto, measures 73–75, and the finale, 129–34), or otherwise used all the notes of the chromatic scale in a single phrase (as in the opening of the Third and Fourth Quartets), he never systematically used Schoenberg's serial technique. In some of Bartók's late works (the Third Piano Concerto, the Concerto for Orchestra, and the Second Violin Concerto) tonality is defined by more familiar procedures. More commonly, however, the tonal field is less definite and the relations within it are harder to grasp. The quartets, for example, are built around keynotes as points of departure and return.

Music for Strings, Percussion, and Celesta illustrates several aspects of Bartók's approach to composition. The main tonality of the first and last movements is A, with an important secondary center at the augmented fourth D♯ (rather than the conventional dominant E). The second movement is in C, with a similar tritonic subcenter on F♯. The Adagio (NAWM 130; CD 11 [23] / 4 ⟨24⟩), the third movement, is ambiguous, fluctuating in the region F♯–C (the two keys equidistant on either side from the main tonality of the work). Some of the principal themes of the four movements and all of the final cadences clearly bring out this tritone relationship (Example 20.2), which is common in works by Bartók, Schoenberg, and many other twentieth-century composers.

Mirror form

In the Adagio, Bartók experimented with mirror form on both a minute and a large scale. In microcosm, this mirror form is seen in the xylophone solo, which, from the midpoint at the beginning of measure 3, is identical going in either direction (Example 20.3). On a larger scale at the middle of the piece, measures 49–50 are essentially a retrograde of measures 47–48, and this is also

Example 20.2 *Béla Bartók,* Music for Strings, Percussion, and Celesta

Example 20.3 *Béla Bartók,* Music for Strings, Percussion, and Celesta: *Adagio, Xylophone Solo*

the midpoint of the formal scheme of the movement: Prologue, ABCDCBA, Epilogue.

Folk styles

The Adagio also exhibits the use of traditional ethnic styles. The *parlando-rubato* idiom of Serbo-Croatian song is heard immediately after the xylophone solo (compare the song of Example 20.4a with the first measures of the Adagio molto in 4b). Later in the movement (measures 20–34) instruments play in octaves against drones and a chordal tapestry of sound produced by plucked

Example 20.4 *Relationships between Folk and Art Styles in Bartók,* Music for Strings, Percussion, and Celesta

instruments, as found in the textures of Bulgarian dance orchestras. The Bulgarian dance rhythm of 2 + 3 + 3 is also adopted here.

Kodály

The music of Zoltán Kodály, more narrowly national, is less thoroughgoing than Bartók's in integrating folk and art styles. His most famous compositions, the *Psalmus hungaricus* for tenor soloist, chorus, and orchestra (1923) and the Singspiel *Háry János* (1926), are rich in allusions to plainchant, Renaissance and Baroque polyphony, and ethnic Hungarian music. Kodály's most pervasive influence has been in music education. His method of teaching children through a movable-*do* solfège system, songs, musical games, and graded exercises has been adopted in many primary schools throughout Europe and North America.

Music education

THE SOVIET ORBIT

Much of the music of the former Soviet republics betrays national influences. But, despite official encouragement of this line of development, several leading composers cultivated international styles. Thus the *Scythian Suite* for orchestra (1916), the cantata *Alexander Nevsky* (originally a film score, 1938), both by Sergey Prokofiev (1891–1953), and his opera *War and Peace* (1941), as well as the opera *Lady Macbeth* (1934) by Dmitri Shostakovich draw on Russian material, but neither Prokofiev nor Shostakovich was a nationalist in the narrow meaning of the word.

Prokofiev

Style

Prokofiev lived outside Russia from 1918 to 1934. The *Classical* Symphony (1918) inventively mixes styles and formal plans of earlier historical periods in fresh contexts—melodies that are essentially tonal with wide skips and sweeping long lines, and triadic harmony full of strange inversions, unusual spacings, and jarring juxtapositions. The Third Piano Concerto (1921); the symphonic suite *Lieutenant Kijé* (arranged from music for a film, 1934), the "symphonic fairy tale" *Peter and the Wolf*, for narrator and orchestra (1936), and the ballet *Romeo and Juliet* (1935–36) have entered the standard repertory.

Years abroad

During the many years abroad, Prokofiev toured in Europe and America as a pianist and fulfilled a variety of commissions as a composer, among them an opera for Chicago, *The Love for Three Oranges* (1921), and ballets for the choreographer and impresario Serge Diaghilev in Paris. His style did not change radically once he settled permanently in the Soviet Union, but he took to heart the charge of "formalism" that was directed at him, at Shostakovich, and at others by the Soviet critics and party leaders in 1948. By "formalism" critics meant music that did not celebrate the revolutionary ideology and its heroes nor reflect the working-class experience through an accessible "socialist realism." Prokofiev in his own defense said that he sincerely strove for a language that was clear and appealing (see vignette).

Late Symphonies

Prokofiev's Symphonies No. 5 (1944) and No. 7 (1951–52) bear witness to his successful search for clear melody; they are triumphs of lyricism, without being saccharine or commonplace. Although he was fond of building excite-

PROKOFIEV ON THE IMPORTANCE OF MELODY

I have never questioned the importance of melody. I love melody, and I regard it as the most important element in music. I have worked on the improvement of its quality in my compositions for many years. To find a melody instantly understandable even to the uninitiated listener, and at the same time an original one, is the most difficult task for a composer. He is beset by a great multitude of dangers: he may fall into the trivial or the banal, or into the rehashing of something already written by him. In this respect, composition of complex melodies is much easier. It may also happen that a composer, fussing over his melody for a long time, and revising it, unwittingly makes it over-refined and complicated, and departs from simplicity. I fell into this trap, too, in the process of my work.

Prokofiev, Letter to Tikhon Khrennikov, Secretary of the Union of Composers, 1948, trans. William W. Austin, *Music in the 20th Century* (New York: Norton, 1966), pp. 459–60.

ment by repetition, the richness of his novel subordinate ideas played against his main themes invite repeated hearings to savor the exquisitely fashioned details. He never ceased to pursue structural clarity and refinement, despite his admission that he had been infected by "formalism" in the West.

Shostakovich

Dmitri Shostakovich (1906–1975) broke upon the international musical scene at the age of nineteen with his First Symphony (1926), and although every one of his subsequent symphonies (he wrote fifteen altogether) was enthusiastically received (the Fourth of 1935–36 was not heard until 1961), only the Fifth (1937) and Tenth (1953) have won a prominent place in the repertory. He received his education and spent his entire career within the Soviet system, which treated him generously, though he was not immune to official criticism.

Lady Macbeth of Mtsensk

His opera *Lady Macbeth of Mtsensk*, which enjoyed success in St. Petersburg (1934, then called Leningrad), New York, and elsewhere, was withdrawn after being condemned in the Moscow newspaper *Pravda* in 1936. In Act IV, Scene 9 (NAWM 131; CD 11 [29]), Katerina ("Lady Macbeth") and Sergey, who have murdered her husband, are being marched to Siberia with other prisoners; the passage displays the realistic and often satirical musical portrayal of violence and sex that offended the Soviet leaders.

Fifth Symphony

Some considered the Fifth Symphony, because of its optimistic outlook, easy communicativeness, and boisterous finale, a concession to the "socialist realism" required by the Communist Party. Widely acepted as a masterpiece of symphonic composition, it holds to the traditional architecture of the genre. Endowed with sweep and grandeur, the work opens majestically with a two-measure canon in the strings on a theme with double-dotted rhythm, but the bold leaps and chromaticism remove it from the courtly atmosphere of the French overture that this rhythm might otherwise evoke. (See Example 20.5.) As the dotted rhythms continue in the lower strings, a soaring melody resembling those of Prokofiev takes the foreground in the violins. The second theme is subtly related to the opening by the expansion of both intervals and durations. A formal closing theme, when taken up by the piano (an instrument not heard until then), marks the beginning of a classic development section. This includes a march episode, which is very characteristic of Shostakovich. The remaining movements are a Scherzo (not so marked), a Largo for reduced orchestra, and an Allegro non troppo that fully utilizes the big orchestra.

Seventh Symphony

The Seventh (*Leningrad*) Symphony (1941) programmatically deals with the heroic defense of St. Petersburg against Hitler's armies, and its movements originally had the titles "War," "Evocation," "Native Expanse," and "Victory."

Tenth Symphony

The composer musically signed the third movement of the Tenth Symphony with a theme drawn, German-style, from his name, D-E♭-C-B (that is, D-Es-C-H, or D-S-C-H, from Dmitri SCHostakovich). He also used this motto in the Fifth and Eighth String Quartets and the concertos for violin and for cello. The merits of the Tenth Symphony were debated for three days in a public forum at the Union of Composers (the agency that subsidized composers and looked

Example 20.5 *Dmitri Shostakovich, Fifth Symphony: Moderato, measures 1–4*

after their interests), some declaring that it was too pessimistic, not "realistic," and not at all representative of Soviet life; others praised its assertion of creative freedom.

Post-Soviet Music

Although the Union of Soviet Socialist Republics did not break up until 1991, the state began to relax its control over culture well before that, in the 1970s and 1980s. Scores and recordings from western Europe and America were difficult to get, but a number of young composers managed to become familiar with specimens of serial, aleatoric, and electronic music. The policy of *glasnost*, or openness, intensified the interest in foreign developments and permitted both Russian and Western audiences to become acquainted with composers who had been working quietly for decades without much official recognition. Although these creative efforts were not "post-Soviet" in the chronological sense, they were so in spirit. Among the most notable of the composers who thus became known to the West are Alfred Schnittke and Sofia Gubaidulina.

Relaxation of Soviet control

Alfred Schnittke (1934–98), whose father was a German Jew of Russian extraction and mother a German from the Volga region, spent almost all of his

Schnittke

career in the Soviet Union, where he was known to the public chiefly for his film music, before taking up residence in Hamburg. His approach, which he called polystylistic, incorporated music from the Baroque to the present, including his own earlier creations, as well as popular music. The Concerto Grosso No. 1 (1976–77) for two violins, harpsichord, prepared piano, and string orchestra recalls several Baroque genres in the first four of its six movements: Prelude, Toccata, Recitative, and Cadenza. The concertino is accompanied by a continuo group and exploits in its figurative solos the technical virtuosity of two outstanding violinists for whom it was written. The harmonic idiom, however, is entirely modern. The fifth movement, Rondo, surrealistically juxtaposes gypsy-tango episodes against distortions of a main subject inspired by Corelli.

In the third (1981) of Schnittke's eight symphonies, the first movement tested the acoustical properties of the new Gewandhaus Hall in Leipzig with a canonic subject based on the harmonic series that is taken up in turn by each individual instrument. The second movement passes in review the monograms (such as B-A-C-H) and some of the styles of thirty German composers, a scheme analogous to engraving famous names in the proscenium arch of a theater.

Among his solo concertos (four for violin, one for viola, and two for cello), that for cello of 1986 is free of quotations and represents Schnittke at his most personally intense, aggressive, and blustery. The soloist's part is extremely chromatic and even microtonal. Among the chamber works, Hymn No. 4 for cello, double bass, bassoon, harpsichord, harp, timpani, and tubular bells (1980), an essay in minimalism, escapes from Schnittke's usual rhythmic predictability and also hits upon some striking combinations of instrumental color in which the ensemble serves as a continuo accompaniment to the melody in the bells.

Gubaidulina

Sofia Gubaidulina (b. 1931), who was not well known in her own country and was not permitted to travel to the West before 1986, attained international stature shortly thereafter. Born and trained in the Tatar Republic, she moved to Moscow in 1954, when she began eight years of study at the national conservatory. Almost all of her works have a spiritual dimension, and even the titles of her instrumental pieces reveal a Christian inspiration (*Introitus, In croce, Offertorium, Jubilatio, De profundis*).

Her spiritual dimension

The spiritual element is deeply rooted in Gubaidulina's sonata for violin and cello, *Rejoice!*, written in 1981 but not performed until 1988 in Finland. Its five movements are inspired by eighteenth-century devotional texts. The sonata, according to the composer, expresses the transcendence from ordinary reality to a state of joy, and relies particularly on the passage from a fundamental note to its harmonics to embody this transition. The fifth movement (NAWM 132; CD 11 [34] / 4 ◇30◇), inscribed with the text "Listen to the still small voice within," is a study in chromatics, tremolos, and harmonics, particularly glissandos from low fundamental notes in the cello to their higher harmonics.

Offertorium

Offertorium (1981; revised 1982–86), is a violin concerto written for Gidon Kremer, who performed it throughout the world. It is an offertory in a very special sense. Its subtext is the royal theme from Bach's *Musikalisches Opfer* (see Example 12.5, page 396), which is stated at the outset. The twenty notes of this subject before the final tonic, which is postponed to the end of the work, are distributed among five wind instruments that take turns articulating the melody. Then the soloist begins to play upon the intervals of these notes in reverse order, while the orchestra answers with mysterious ensemble passages and violent solo exclamations. The theme thus *offers* itself as a sacrifice, as Gubaidulina has explained, note by note. No trace of Bach's counterpoint or style is evident in the work. Nor is there any system or model, which is typical in Gubaidulina's compositions, but rather a composite of intuitive choices made by a creative personality of great originality and resourcefulness.

ENGLAND

Vaughan Williams

Career

The foremost English composer in the first half of the twentieth century was Ralph Vaughan Williams (1872–1958), whose works include nine symphonies and other orchestral pieces, songs, operas, and a great many choral pieces. Amid all the variety of dimensions and forms, Vaughan Williams's music drew inspiration from national sources—English literature and traditional song, hymnody, and earlier English composers such as Purcell and Tallis—as well as from the European traditions of Bach and Handel, Debussy and Ravel. From 1904 to 1906 Vaughan Williams served as musical editor of the new *English Hymnal.* Concerning this experience he wrote long afterward in his *Musical Autobiography*: "Two years of close association with some of the best (as well as some of the worst) tunes in the world was a better musical education than any amount of sonatas and fugues." He modestly neglected to add that he himself composed a half-dozen new tunes, one of which was the well-known *Sine nomine* for the hymn *For all the Saints* (Example 20.6a).

Choral works

Throughout his long career, he conducted local amateur singers and players for whom he wrote a number of choral works, including the *Benedicite* (1930). Among his other compositions for amateurs are his

Example 20.6 *Examples of Themes by Ralph Vaughan Williams*

a. Hymn tune, *Sine nomine*

b. *Pastoral* Symphony, fourth movement

c. *Pastoral* Symphony, third movement

d. *Pastoral* Symphony, first movement

Fantasia on a Theme of Thomas Tallis

Household Music (1941) for string quartet or "almost any combination of instruments," a Concerto Grosso for triple string orchestra (1950) in which the third section may consist of "those players who prefer to use only open strings," and many choral settings of traditional songs, including the cycle *Folk-Songs of the Four Seasons* written for a 1950 choir festival. The profoundly national quality of Vaughan Williams's compositions, large or small, owes something to his quoting or imitating British folk tunes, but even more to his assimilation of the "modal harmony" of the Elizabethans. His *Fantasia on a Theme of Thomas Tallis* (1909) for double string orchestra and string quartet, in which the antiphonal sonorities and the rich texture of unadorned triads in parallel motion are heard within a modal framework, illustrates this aspect of his style.

London Symphony

The *London* Symphony (1914; revised 1920) is a loving evocation of the sounds and atmosphere of the city, a program symphony in the same sense as Mendelssohn's *Italian* and Schumann's *Rhenish.* It has the usual four movements—the third is called *Scherzo (Nocturne)*—and dies away at the end in an Epilogue on the theme of the Lento introduction to the first movement.

Pastoral Symphony

In the *Pastoral* Symphony (1922) a wordless melisma in unbarred free rhythm for solo soprano appears at the beginning and in shortened form at the close of the last movement (Example 20.6b). It exemplifies a type of melody with gapped scales—here of pentatonic character—that often occurs in Vaughan Williams's music. Equally characteristic and folklike is the trumpet tune in the trio of the third movement (Example 20.6c). His contrapuntal treatment of parallel chords is especially effective (Example 20.6d).

Fourth Symphony

The Fourth Symphony in F minor (1934) and its two successors in D major (1943) and E minor (1947) have been said to reflect Vaughan Williams's concern with world events, although the composer himself offered no such interpretation. On the other hand, he supplied each movement of the *Sinfonia antartica* with a few words that suggest its underlying reference. The symphony celebrates the heroism of Captain Scott and his crew, and, by extension, all human struggles against overwhelming forces of nature.

Holst and Walton

Holst

The music of Vaughan Williams's close friend Gustav Holst (1874–1934) was influenced not only by English traditional song but also by Hindu mysticism. The latter is evident in his choice of texts (*Choral Hymns from the Rig-Veda*, 1912), occasional peculiarly static passages of harmony (*The Hymn of Jesus*, for double chorus and orchestra, 1917), and details of exotic harmony and color, as in the last movement (*Neptune*) of the orchestral suite *The Planets* (1916), Holst's best-known work. He shares with Vaughan Williams a practical, direct musical expression and imaginative sensitivity to texts, exemplified in two settings of Walt Whitman poems—*Ode to Death* (1919) and, on a smaller scale, the *Dirge for Two Veterans* (1914), for men's voices, brass, and drums.

Walton

William Walton (1902–1982) also occupied a prominent position in mid-twentieth-century English music. His works include symphonic and chamber music; a viola concerto; *Façade* (1921–22; revised 1942), an amusing entertainment for reciter and chamber ensemble on surreal poems by Edith Sitwell; a large oratorio, *Belshazzar's Feast* (1931); and the opera *Troilus and Cressida* (1954).

Britten

Benjamin Britten (1913–1976), the most prolific and best-known English composer of the mid-twentieth century, is distinguished especially for his choral compositions, songs, and operas. Among the choral works are *A Boy Was Born* (1935), *A Ceremony of Carols* (1942), and *Spring Symphony* (1947). His most celebrated operas are *Peter Grimes* (1945) and *The Turn of the Screw* (1954).

Peter Grimes

The tragic last scene of *Peter Grimes* (NAWM 133; CD 11 [38]) eloquently displays the remarkable dramatic effects that Britten creates out of simple means, orchestrally dressed up. In a most successful application of bitonality, arpeggiated thirds that encompass all the notes of the C-major scale form a haunting background to the solo and choral lines in A major (Rehearsal No.

54). More typical of Britten, however, is his adherence to tonal and diatonic techniques colored with modal and chromatic elements.

War Requiem

Britten's *War Requiem* (1962) received worldwide acclaim following its first performance at Coventry Cathedral. It is an impressive, large work for soloists, chorus, boys' choir, and orchestra on the Latin text of the Requiem Mass alternating with verses by Wilfred Owen, a young English soldier who was killed in France in 1918. The music incorporates many modern features in a very individual way.

Tippett

Although he was not recognized until the 1940s, Michael Tippett (1905–1998) has a large number of significant works to his credit. His many vocal compositions, including the oratorio *A Child of Our Time* (1939–41) and a large-scale composition for baritone, chorus, and orchestra, *The Vision of St. Augustine* (1963–65), reflect his long career as a choral conductor. As a composer, Tippett was remarkably open to historical, traditional ethnic, and non-Western styles and materials. The rhythmic and metrical independence he assigns to instrumental parts derives partly from English Renaissance music. Most of his early sonatas, quartets, and symphonies apply Classic forms. One of the central themes of *A Child of Our Time* is the African-American spiritual *Nobody knows the trouble I've seen.* His Piano Sonata No. 1 (1938; revised 1942) uses both jazz and folksong.

Style

Both the Piano Concerto (1953–55) and the Triple Concerto for violin, viola, and cello (1979) reveal Tippett's admiration for Javanese music, the first in its textures and instrumental combinations, the second in its use of a Javanese melody with rippling figuration and sounds such as gongs in the accompaniment of the slow movement. The opening of the Piano Concerto (Example 20.7) exemplifies several aspects of Tippett's compositional approach: the pervading diatonic environment, the suggestion of a gamelan in the piano's arpeggiating fourths in the left hand, the harmonization of the melody in parallel fourths sounding like bells high in the right hand, the layered scoring, and the gonglike drone note in the bass. The modal feeling in the melody, reinforced by the absence of dominant-tonic relationships and set against a carpet of slowly changing blocks of static harmony gives this movement an oriental serenity that is rare in twentieth-century Western music.

More Recent Composers

Of the fellow students in Manchester who formed the New Music Manchester Group—Alexander Goehr (b. 1932), Peter Maxwell Davies (b. 1934), and Harrison Birtwistle (b. 1934)—the last has received the greatest international attention. Fiercely dissonant and inscrutable in his more abstract works, Birtwistle shows a flair for the dramatic in his theatrical and virtually theatrical works. *Punch and Judy* (1966) turns a puppet comedy into a murderous

Example 20.7 *Michael Tippett, Concerto for Piano and Orchestra: Allegro non troppo*

tragedy with a jaunty, sardonic accompaniment for fifteen players that matches every mood. *Secret Theatre* (1984) endows instruments with personalities that play roles in a voiceless music drama. Each instrument—flute, oboe, horn, bassoon, and so on performs only its own kind of music, holding forth by turn and drawing reactions, supporting or contrary, from the other instruments. At more anarchic moments they sound like musicians rehearsing their parts on the concert stage before the conductor arrives. In another work, *Ritual Fragment* (1990)—a memorial to the artistic director of the London Sinfonietta—Birtwistle subdues the individual instrumental characters while they deliver their eulogies with the ensemble's sympathetic contrapuntal and harmonic underpinning.

GERMANY

Germany, the country that harbored the most aggressive nationalism in the years between the two wars, had been at the center of music developments for so long that it hardly needed to assert itself as a musical culture. Yet the Nazis did try to enforce an abhorrent kind of national purity. This policy led, in the end, to the dissolution of its creative forces, as some of its most talented musicians, whether Jewish or not, took refuge abroad.

Hindemith

Career as teacher

Paul Hindemith (1895–1963) excelled not only as a composer but also as a teacher and theorist. His book, *The Craft of Musical Composition,*[1] presents both a general system of composition and an analytical method. As a teacher—at the Berlin School of Music (1927–37), the Yale University School of Music (1940–53), and the University of Zurich (after 1953)—he influenced generations of musicians and composers.

Hindemith thought of himself first of all as a practicing musician. An experienced solo, orchestral, and ensemble player of the violin and viola, he learned to play many other instruments as well. Younger than Schoenberg, Bartók, and Stravinsky, he soon freed himself from the late-Romantic and impressionist influences evidenced in his compositions before 1918, plunging with remarkable creative energy and facility into the confused world of the new music of the 1920s. Some twenty-five years later, in the light of his changed conceptions of tonality and chordal harmony, he revised his three principal large works of this decade: a song cycle for soprano voice and piano on poems of R. M. Rilke, *Das Marienleben* (The Life of Mary, 1923; revised 1948); the tragic expressionist opera *Cardillac* (1926); and the comic opera *Neues vom Tage* (News of the Day, 1929). Four string quartets and a large quantity of other chamber music also date from this period. But, disturbed by the widening gulf between composers and an increasingly passive public in the late 1920s and early 1930s, Hindemith began composing *Gebrauchsmusik*—music for use, as distinguished from music for its own sake.

Works from the 1920s

The 1930s

His works from the 1930s display a new quality of almost Romantic warmth, along with less dissonant linear counterpoint and more systematic tonal organization. Representative is the opera *Mathis der Maler* (Matthias the Painter, 1934–35; first performed in Zurich, 1938), and the symphony *Mathis der Maler* (1934), probably his best-known work, composed while he was working on the libretto of the opera. Also dating from this time are the three piano sonatas (1936), a sonata for piano four-hands (1938), the ballets *Nobilissima visione* (1938, on St. Francis of Assisi) and *The Four Temperaments* (1940), and the Symphony in E♭ (1940).

Mathis der Maler

Hindemith's libretto for *Mathis der Maler* is based on the life of Matthias Grünewald, painter of the famous Isenheim altarpiece (see Plate XII, facing page 655; the altarpiece is now at the Musée d'Unterlinden in Colmar, France). Composed in Germany in the 1930s when Hindemith was under attack from the Nazi government, the opera examines the role of an artist in times of stress. In the libretto, Mathis leaves his studio to join the peasants in their rebellion

1. Hindemith, *Unterweisung im Tonsatz,* 2 vols., 1937, 1939, trans. Arthur Mendel as *The Craft of Musical Composition* (New York: Associated Music Publishers, 1942; rev. ed. 1945), 3rd vol., 1970, ed. Andres Briner, P. Daniel Meier, and Alfred Rubeli (Mainz: Schott, 1970).

against the nobles during the Peasants' War of 1525. In despair over the defeat of the peasants, Mathis is tormented by visions resembling the demons in one of the scenes from his altarpiece, *The Temptation of Saint Anthony* (Scene 6). The restless, tortured chromatic line of the melody reflects these troubling images (Example 20.8a). Here, as elsewhere in the score, Hindemith followed a new harmonic method which he called "harmonic fluctuation." Fairly consonant chords progress toward combinations containing greater tension and dissonance, which are then resolved either suddenly or by slowly moderating the tension until consonance is reached again. Another good example of this technique appears at the beginning of the seventh scene (Example 20.8b), which represents Mathis painting Christ's entombment.

Hindemith wrote much music for teaching purposes. The title *Klaviermusik: Übung in drei Stücken* (Piano Music: Three Practice Pieces, 1925) resembles Bach's *Clavier-Übung,* and *The Well-Tempered Keyboard* served as a model for Hindemith's *Ludus tonalis* (Tonal Play, 1942) for piano. Subtitled "Studies in Counterpoint, Tonal Organization, and Piano Playing," it consists of twelve fugues, one in each key, with modulating interludes, a Prelude (C–F♯), and Postlude (F♯–C).

Late works

Hindemith's compositions after 1940 include the Fifth and Sixth Quartets (1943, 1945), the *Symphonic Metamorphosis on Themes of Weber* (1943), a "requiem" on words of Walt Whitman (*When lilacs last in the dooryard bloom'd*) and other choral works, and the new version of the *Marienleben* (1948). The opera *Die Harmonie der Welt* (The Harmony of the World), begun in the 1930s, was laid aside when the composer came to the United States because he saw no chance of getting it performed. In 1952 he made a three-movement orchestral symphony out of his drafts, then continued work on the opera, which was finally presented in Munich in 1957.

Hindemith perpetuated the German cosmopolitan line of Beethoven, Schumann, Brahms, and Reger; additional influences in his work came from Bach, Handel, Schütz, and the German sixteenth-century lied composers.

Orff

Carmina burana

In his best-known work, *Carmina burana* (1936), Carl Orff (1895–1982) arrived at an attractive, deceptively simple idiom, indebted in spirit and rhythm to folksong and in sonority to Stravinsky's *Les Noces.* He carefully graded the collection *Music for Children* (1950–54, in revised form) for use in schools. Along with Kodály's method and materials, Orff's have won a following among educators in many countries. His method calls for movement, singing, and playing on suitable instruments (mostly percussive in the early stages), and leads children in a natural way to experience a great variety of scales and rhythms and to arrive at a broadly based understanding of music.

Weill

Kurt Weill (1900–1950) had two careers, first as opera composer in Berlin, then later as a Broadway composer in New York. In Berlin he embraced *Gebrauchsmusik* in the sense that he did not aim to produce masterpieces but rather to promote social programs and ideologies, entertaining common people rather than intellectual elites. He collaborated with a number of playwrights, most notably Bertolt Brecht. Weill was first drawn to Brecht through a collection of verse, *Die Hauspostille,* from which he selected texts for the *Mahagonny-Songspiel* (1927). He called it a "Songspiel," a pun on the operatic "Singspiel," because it was a set of six extended songs, sophisticated imitations of American popular songs. It turned out to be a testing ground for an opera, *Aufstieg und Fall der Stadt Mahagonny* (Rise and Fall of the City of Mahagonny, first performed in 1930). The Songspiel's occasional atonal accompaniments and instrumental interludes were dropped in the operatic version in favor of a simpler triadic harmony, often spiced with augmented fifths and triads superimposed on single and double drones, as in the famous *Alabama Song.*

Songspiel

Mahagonny

Berlin found the opera version of *Mahagonny* too shocking, so its first performance went to Leipzig in 1930. Its form is that of a number opera: lyrical

■ *Lotte Lenya in a scene from Kurt Weill's* The Threepenny Opera, *New York production mid-1950s.* (PHOTO BY NEIL FUJITA, 1956. THE PAPERS OF KURT WEILL AND LOTTE LENYA, YALE MUSIC LIBRARY)

scenes for individual characters, with some choruses and ensembles. The pit orchestra includes two saxophones, piano, banjo, and bass guitar as well as winds and timpani, while three saxophones, zither, a bandoneon (a kind of accordion), strings, and brass play in the stage orchestra. The intent is satirical. Fugitives from justice build a town dedicated to pleasure, free of legal or moral taboos, but they soon find that they have created a hell rather than a paradise on earth. Many of the theater people in Weill's circle were on the political left and were bent on exposing the failures of capitalism, which the city of Mahagonny exemplified.

Die Dreigroschenoper

The most famous product of the Brecht-Weill collaboration, *Die Dreigroschenoper* (The Threepenny Opera), is based on the text of Gay's *Beggar's Opera* (see NAWM 87), although the composer borrowed only one air from Pepusch's score. At the premiere in Berlin in 1928, the orchestra consisted of seven musicians who played twenty-three instruments. The cast included an unknown actress, Lotte Lenya, whom Weill had married in 1926 and who became his favorite interpreter and after his death a champion of his work. The music parodied rather than imitated American hit songs, then the rage in Europe. In the surrealistic juxtaposition of the eighteenth-century ballad texts, European dance music, and American jazz, at once provocative as well as appealing, the composer intended to explore "new expressive possibilities for simple human actions and relationships."[2]

The original production ran for over two years, and within five years of the premiere *Dreigroschenoper* enjoyed more than ten thousand performances in nineteen languages. The Nazis banned it as decadent in 1933, when Weill

2. Kurt Weill, "Korrespondenz über *Dreigroschenoper*," *Anbruch* 11 (January 1929):24, trans. in Stephen Hinton, "*Neue Sachlichkeit*, Surrealism, *Gebrauchsmusik*," in *A New Orpheus: Essays on Kurt Weill*, ed. Kim H. Kowalke (New Haven: Yale University Press, 1986), p. 74.

left for Paris; soon after he emigrated to the United States and devoted himself mostly to musical comedies and operettas. The most successful were *Knickerbocker Holiday* (1938), *Lady in the Dark* (1940), *One Touch of Venus* (1943), *Street Scene* (1946), the college opera *Down in the Valley*, and the musical tragedy *Lost in the Stars* (about apartheid in South Africa, 1948). He wrote occasional "art music," such as his *Four Songs of Walt Whitman* (1942). The first of the songs, *O Captain! My Captain!*, slips with ease from the tuneful contours of measures 9–17 (Example 20.9a), with their honey-glazed jazzy sevenths and augmented chords in the piano, to the dark poignant clashes of measures 59–62 (Example 20.9b). Like his work for Broadway, this music was addressed to a broad musical public and meant to be immediately grasped by mind and heart.

Broadway works

Four Songs of Walt Whitman

Example 20.9 *Kurt Weill,* Four Songs of Walt Whitman: O Captain! My Captain!

LATIN AMERICA

The principal representatives of nationalism in Latin American music were the Brazilian Heitor Villa-Lobos (1887–1959) and the Mexicans Silvestre Revueltas (1898–1940) and Carlos Chávez (1899–1978). Villa-Lobos's best-known works, for various vocal and instrumental combinations under the general designation *choros*, make use of Brazilian rhythms and sonorities. Chávez is particularly notable for his *Sinfonia India* (1936) and his Piano Concerto (1940). Among more recent Latin American composers, the Argentinian Alberto Ginastera (1916–1983) made a strong impression with the opera *Bomarzo* when first heard in 1967. After a series of works dependent on traditional songs and dances, he adopted the twelve-tone technique. For his opera *Don Rodrigo* he devised a formal plan inspired by Berg's *Wozzeck* in which Classic instrumental forms shape the music of the scenes, while the scenes themselves are joined by instrumental interludes.

Villa-Lobos
Chávez

Ginastera

NEO-CLASSICISM IN FRANCE

The term *Neo-Classicism* has had many shades of meaning since its introduction to music in the late nineteenth century. It represented a broad movement from the 1910s to the 1950s in which composers revived, imitated, or evoked the styles, genres, and forms of pre-Romantic music, especially of what we now call the Baroque and Classic periods. Prokofiev's *Classical* Symphony (1918) was truly neo-Classic, a parody of the Haydn symphony, and like most parodies, was partly humorous, partly nostalgic. Stravinsky's *Dumbarton Oaks* Concerto (1938) was actually neo-Baroque beause it took as its model the Vivaldi-Bach concerto grosso. Stravinsky's Symphony in C (1939–40) and Symphony in Three Movements (1942–45) followed Classic models. Schoenberg's Piano Suite, Op. 25, although based strictly on twelve-tone rows, uses the procedures and dance rhythms of the keyboard suites of the 1720s. Works such as these are manneristic in their return to earlier approaches. A great many other mid-twentieth-century works hark back to earlier procedures in less obvious ways. Beethoven often lurks behind Hindemith's instrumental works, for example. Many composers tried to absorb the more experimental elements from the previous decades while maintaining continuity with tradition. They held to some recognizably familiar features of the past—such as tonal centers (defined or alluded to, often in quite new ways), melodic shape, and goal-oriented movement of musical ideas—while incorporating fresh and unfamiliar elements. Arthur Honegger, Darius Milhaud, and Francis Poulenc illustrate these trends in France. Igor Stravinsky will be dealt with separately.

Honegger

Arthur Honegger (1892–1955) excelled in music of dynamic action and graphic gesture, expressed in short-breathed melodies, strong ostinato rhythms, bold colors, and dissonant harmonies. Born in France of Swiss parentage, he resided in Paris after 1913. Honegger's "symphonic movement" *Pacific 231*, in which he aimed not to imitate the sound but to translate into music the visual and physical impression of a speeding locomotive, was hailed as a sensational piece of modernistic program music in 1923.

King David

Honegger became an instant celebrity with the concert performance in 1923 of his oratorio *King David*, which had appeared two years earlier in an original stage version. This work signals the rise of an important new genre, a compound of oratorio and opera. *King David* may be popular because the choruses, written for amateurs, are easy to sing, the rhythmic and formal patterns conventional; few harmonic audacities mar the familiar consonant diatonic writing; and the action is illustrated graphically by vivid music that captures some of the aura of the Bach Passions.

On a grander scale, *Jeanne d'Arc au Bûcher* (Joan of Arc at the Stake, 1938), has five speaking parts, five soloists, mixed chorus (which both sings and speaks), children's chorus, and large orchestra. Based on an elaborate oratorio-drama by Paul Claudel, it mixes Gregorian chant, dance tunes, and modern and medieval folksongs with Honegger's highly colored idiom.

Milhaud

Output

Darius Milhaud (1892–1974), a native of Aix-en-Provence in southern France, created a gracious memorial to his native region in the *Suite Provençale* for orchestra (1937), which incorporates melodies from works by the early eighteenth-century composer André Campra. Milhaud produced an immense quantity of music, composing with a facility rare in the twentieth century. His works include piano pieces, chamber music (his eighteen string quartets are especially notable), suites, sonatas, symphonies, film music, ballets, songs, cantatas, and operas. The frivolity, mockery and satire of the ballets—*Le Boeuf sur le toit* (The Ox on the Roof, 1919) and *Le Train bleu* (The Blue Train, 1924)—contrast with the cosmic earnestness of the opera-oratorio *Christophe Colomb* (1928) and the religious devotion of the (Jewish) *Sacred Service* (1947). Milhaud did not subscribe to theories or systems; rather, he was receptive to many

Example 20.10 *Polytonality in Works of Darius Milhaud*

Saudades do Brasil, *I:* No. 4, Copacabaña

kinds of stimuli—Brazilian folk melodies and rhythms, for example, in the orchestral dances (later arranged for piano) *Saudades do Brasil* (Souvenirs of Brazil, 1920–21). Saxophones, ragtime syncopations, and the blues find their way into the ballet *La Création du monde* (The Creation of the World, 1924). Milhaud blends ingenuousness and ingenuity with clear and logical form, offering objective statements, not personal confessions.

Polytonality

Like many composers of his time, Milhaud often employed *polytonality*, as in Example 20.10, where two lines of melody and planes of harmony, each in a distinct and different key, sound simultaneously.

Operas

Milhaud's operas span the gamut of his style. Three of them set translations by Paul Claudel of plays from Aeschylus (composed between 1913 and 1924). Others are *Les Malheurs d'Orphée* (The Misfortunes of Orpheus, 1924); *Le pauvre matelot* (The Poor Sailor, 1926) on a libretto by Jean Cocteau; three *opéras minutes*, running about ten minutes each, on parodies of classical myths (1927); the huge oratorio-opera *Christophe Colomb* (1928, text by Claudel); the formally more conventional *Maximilien* (1930), *Médée* (1938), and *Bolivar* (1943); and the biblical opera *David*, commissioned to celebrate the three-thousandth anniversary of Jerusalem as the capital of David's kingdom and first performed in a concert version there in 1954. All Milhaud's operas are organized in distinct scene complexes with arias and choruses, the singing voices rather than the orchestra serving as the focus.

Poulenc

The compositions of Francis Poulenc (1899–1963), many in small forms, revel in an ingratiating harmonic idiom; they wear the grace and wit of the Parisian popular *chansons*, and wed satirical mimicry to fluent melody. His comic opera *Les Mamelles de Tiresias* (The Breasts of Tiresias, 1940) offers good examples. The *Concert champêtre* (Pastoral Concerto) for harpsichord or piano and small orchestra (1928) evokes the spirit of Rameau and Domenico Scarlatti. Among his other compositions are a Mass in G for chorus a cappella (1937), several motets, other choral works, and numerous songs. His three-act opera *Dialogues des Carmelites* (Dialogues of the Carmelites, 1956), a serious, effective setting of an unusually fine libretto by Georges Bernanos, has entered the repertory of many opera houses.

STRAVINSKY

Career

In the course of a long career, Igor Stravinsky (1882–1971) participated in the most significant musical developments of the first half of the twentieth century. Indeed, he gave impetus to some of these developments, and his influence on three generations of composers has been enormous. Born in Russia in 1882, he went to Paris in 1911, moved to Switzerland in 1914, to Paris again in 1920, to California in 1940, and lived in New York after 1969 until his death in 1971. Stravinsky's principal early compositions include three ballets commissioned by Sergei Diaghilev (1872–1929), the founder and director of the Ballets Russes, which reigned in Paris from 1909 to 1929 as a European institution that attracted many leading artists. For Diaghilev and Paris, Stravinsky wrote *The Firebird* (1910), *Petrushka* (1911), and *Le Sacre du printemps* (The Rite of Spring, subtitled Pictures of Pagan Russia, 1913).

Early Works

The Firebird stems from the Russian nationalist tradition, and has the exotic orientalism and rich sensuous orchestration of Stravinsky's teacher, Rimsky-Korsakov. *Petrushka*, rich in Russian traditional songs and polyphonic textures, brings a touch of *verismo* to its carnival scenes and characters, while the alert rhythms, bright orchestral colors, and lean counterpoint tested paths that Stravinsky would later explore further. *Le Sacre*, the most famous composition of the early twentieth century, provoked a notorious riot at its first premiere in Paris (see vignette, page 704), though in the long run the three ballets for Diaghilev were to enjoy more public favor as concert works than Stravinsky's later compositions.

Petrushka

Petrushka contains many stylistic ingredients that remain identified with Stravinsky. The opening scene of the ballet, a fair in St. Petersburg during the climactic week of carnival, presents blocks of static harmony against which repetitive melodic and rhythmic patterns shift abruptly as the spotlight turns from the general scene to particular groups of dancers, each given its characteristic music: a band of tipsy revelers, an organ grinder with a dancer, a music-box player with another dancer, the puppet theater. Seemingly unconnected musical events succeed each other without transition, and only the frequent return of the opening music (Example 20.11) makes the scene a unit.

Example 20.11 *Igor Stravinsky,* Petrushka, *First Scene*

Example 20.12 *Igor Stravinsky,* Petrushka, *Second Part: Easter Song (from Russian Edition)*

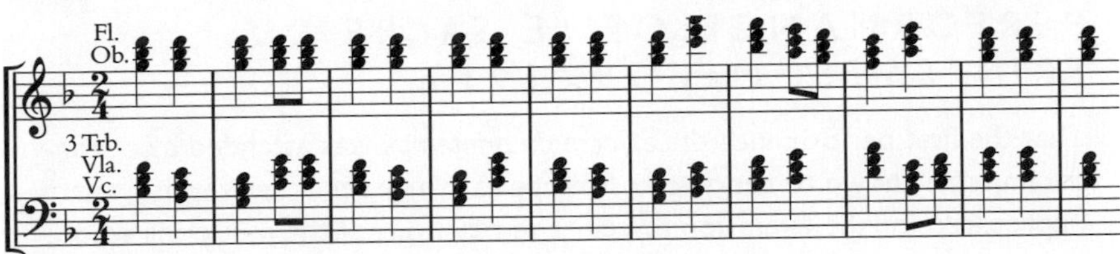

The abrupt juxtaposition of diverse sections has been compared to the cubism of Pablo Picasso (see Plate XIII, facing page 718).

The Russian and popular carnival atmosphere is enhanced throughout the ballet by the quotation and elaboration of several folk tunes (as well as a popular French song and Viennese waltzes by Joseph Lanner). Rather than working these quotations into artful arrangements, as previous Russian composers had done, Stravinsky restores them to their ethnic environment. For example, the Easter song from the Smolensk region that accompanies the drunken merry-makers, taken from Rimsky-Korsakov's 1877 collection of traditional songs, avoids the dominant-tonic harmony of Rimsky's version and simulates instead folk heterophony, in which voices sing in parallel fifths and octaves (Example 20.12), often against drones. Similarly, the Russian dance and *Song of St. John's Eve* in the duet between the Moor and the Ballerina recall a Balkan improvising orchestra, the winds and strings playing rapid repetitive figurations, while the harps imitate the plucked and strumming sounds of a balalaika ensemble.

Petrushka chord

The notorious *Petrushka* chord (Example 20.13) near the opening of the second scene (Petrushka's room) can be explained as a juxtaposition of two tonalities, an interpretation Stravinsky himself once offered.[3] More recently scholars have recognized the passage as one of the many uses by Stravinsky of the octatonic scale that alternates whole tones and semitones—*C–C♯–D♯–E–F♯–G–A–A♯*—with the *D♯* and *A* omitted.[4] The two-key effect remains, however, on the audible surface. *Petrushka* also hints at the rhythmic innovations that will be so striking in *Le Sacre*—for example, at the end of the third scene, where the meter changes from $\frac{4}{8}$ to $\frac{5}{8}$ to $\frac{6}{8}$ to $\frac{5}{8}$ and so on, and silences take the place of expected downbeats.

Le Sacre du printemps

Example 20.13 *Igor Stravinsky,* Petrushka, *Opening of Second Scene*

3. Stravinsky and Robert Craft, *Expositions and Developments* (London: Faber & Faber, 1959), p. 136.
4. See the analysis in Pieter C. van den Toorn, *The Music of Igor Stravinsky* (New Haven: Yale University Press, 1983), pp. 31ff.

STRAVINSKY RECALLS THE FIRST PERFORMANCE OF *LE SACRE DU PRINTEMPS*, May 29, 1913

That the first performance of *Le Sacre du printemps* was attended by a scandal must be known to everybody. Strange as it may seem, however, I was unprepared for the explosion myself. The reactions of the musicians who came to the orchestra rehearsals were without intimation of it and the stage spectacle did not appear likely to precipitate a riot. . . .

Mild protest against the music could be heard from the very beginning of the performance. Then, when the curtain opened on the group of knock-kneed and long-braided Lolitas jumping up and down [*Danses des adolescentes*], the storm broke. Cries of "*Ta guele*" ["Shut up!"] came from behind me. I heard Florent Schmitt shout "*Taisez-vous garces du seizième*" ["Be quiet, you bitches of the sixteenth"]; the *garces* of the sixteenth arrondissement [the most fashionable residential district of Paris] were, of course, the most elegant ladies in Paris. The uproar continued, however, and a few minutes later I left the hall in a rage. . . . I arrived in a fury backstage, where I saw Diaghilev flicking the house lights in a last effort to quiet the hall. For the rest of the performance I stood in the wings behind Nijinsky holding the tails of his *frac*, while he stood on a chair shouting numbers to the dancers, like a coxswain.

Stravinsky, in *Expositions and Developments* (New York: Doubleday, 1962), pp. 159–64.

Le Sacre struck listeners as the culmination of primitivism; Cocteau called it "a pastorale of the prehistoric world." Its novelty consists not only in the rhythms but even more in the previously unheard orchestral effects and chordal combinations, and in the ruthless logic and elemental power with which all these are combined.

Despite a large number of folksong quotations, which should have made the music of *Le Sacre* palatable to the audience, there were disturbing features in both the music and the scenario, which calls for an adolescent girl who has been chosen for sacrifice to dance herself to death. One of the most striking passages (Example 20.14) is in the second scene, the *Danse des adolescentes* (Dance of the Adolescent Girls; NAWM 134; CD 11 [41] / 4 ⟨34⟩). The lower strings, divisi, play the F♭-major triad, while the upper strings, also divisi, sound a first-inversion seventh chord on *E*♭.

The barring is regular but marked with an extraordinary pattern of syncopations and accents. Eight horns doubling the notes of the strings reinforce the accented chords, which group the eighth notes as follows: 9 + 2 + 6 + 3 + 4 + 5 + 3, destroying any feeling of metrical regularity. Yet while the spectator-listener is utterly disoriented metrically and rhythmically, the music is cleverly conceived for ballet: the passage makes an eight-measure period, and the dancers can continue to count four-measure phrases.

Example 20.14 Igor Stravinsky, Le Sacre du printemps: Dance of the Adolescent Girls: Augurs of Spring

1913–1923

Economy of instrumentation

Wartime economy during the years 1913 to 1923 forced Stravinsky to turn away from the large orchestra toward small combinations of instruments to accompany stage works. In *L'Histoire du soldat* (The Soldier's Tale, 1918) he called for solo instruments in pairs (violin and double bass, clarinet and bassoon, cornet and trombone) and a battery of percussion played by one person. He scored *Les Noces* (The Wedding, 1917–23) for four pianos and percussion. *Pulcinella* (1919–20) requires a small orchestra with strings divided into concertino and ripieno groups. The Octet for Wind Instruments (1922–23) was also part of this trend. *Ragtime* (see illustration, page 707) and *Piano Rag Music* betray the composer's fascination with jazz (followed up in the *Ebony Concerto* of 1945), an interest reflected also in the instrumentation and rhythms of *L'Histoire.*

Interest in jazz

Stravinsky's Neo-Classicism

In the works between the octet and the opera *The Rake's Progress* (1951), Stravinsky adopted an approach called neo-Classic, a term that refers here to his preference for balance, coolness, objectivity, and absolute (as opposed to program) music. At the same time, he turned away from Russian folk music and back to earlier Western art music as a source for imitation, quotation, or allusion. The work that symbolized the transformation of his style around 1920 was *Pulcinella,* a ballet for which Diaghilev asked Stravinsky to arrange some eighteenth-century music to accompany a *commedia dell'arte* scenario. Stravinsky threw himself into music of Pergolesi (and music erroneously attributed to him), eventually reworking a number of sonata movements and arias in a manner at once faithful to the older models and true to his own sensibilities. He later spoke of this experience as his "discovery of the past, the epiphany through which the whole of my late work became possible."[5] Other

Pulcinella

5. Stravinsky and Craft, *Expositions and Developments,* pp. 128–29.

excursions into the past led to borrowings and allusions in numerous works: to Bach-style counterpoint in the Octet, to Bach's keyboard concertos in the Concerto for Piano and Winds (1924), to Tchaikovsky in the ballet *Le baiser de la fée* (The Fairy's Kiss, 1928), to Weber in the Capriccio for piano and orchestra (1929), to Bach's Brandenburg Concertos in the *Dumbarton Oaks* Concerto (1938), and to Machaut's Mass in his Mass (1948).

But his most significant debt was to the eighteenth-century Classic tradition. Period genres, forms, and styles served as prototypes for the Piano Sonata (1924), the Serenade in A (1925), the Symphony in C (1940), and the Symphony in Three Movements (1945). These basically diatonic works adhere to tonal centers and areas, if not to major and minor keys or dominant-tonic polarities.

Symphony in C

The exposition of the first theme in the Symphony in C (after a Haydn-like introduction) exemplifies Stravinsky's approach to diatonic melody and harmony (Example 20.15). While the melodic and harmonic material is drawn from the C-major scale, the bass and static harmony strongly point to E minor. The frequency of the pitch C, though not emphasized rhythmically, pulls the melody in that direction, and the closing measure of the oboe solo suggests a

Example 20.15 *Igor Stravinsky, Symphony in C, Moderato alla breve.*

■ *Title page designed by Picasso for Stravinsky's piano arrangement of* Ragtime, *published by J. & W. Chester, London, 1919.* (© 1995 ESTATE OF PABLO PICASSO/ ARTISTS RIGHTS SOCIETY [ARS], NEW YORK)

dominant function for G. This tonal ambiguity is typical of Stravinsky's diatonic writing. Although Russian folk music has been left behind, the constant reference to the motive *B–C–G* (first heard in the introduction) in different metrical contexts resembles the play with folk motives in his earlier music. The way the eighth-note pulses are organized asymmetrically is also consistent with his earlier practices. If we let the longer notes guide our grouping, we get in quarter notes 2 + 6(= 3 + 3) + 7 + 3 + 2 + 4. The form of the movement, however, is clearly Classic, with a transition starting two bars before Rehearsal No. 15, a second theme at Rehearsal No. 19, a closing section at three bars after 24, a development section plainly announced by a measure's rest two bars after 29, and a clear recapitulation at 45.

The Andante of the Symphony in Three Movements shows another side of Stravinsky's flirtation with eighteenth-century practices: a diatonic melody, decorated with turns and trills, is accompanied by parallel sixths. The long line of the melody and its elaborations through triplets, however, reminds us more of Bellini (whose melodic gift Stravinsky very much admired) and looks forward to the style Stravinsky adopted in the arias and duets of *The Rake's Progress* (1951). The subject of this opera was suggested by Hogarth's engravings; the libretto is by W. H. Auden and Chester Kallman.

The Rake's Progress

In keeping with this eighteenth-century subject, Stravinsky adopted the convention of recitatives, arias, and ensembles. For example, in the card-game scene that will decide the fate of the hero, Tom Rakewell, the duet between Tom and Nick Shadow (the Devil in disguise) is introduced by a five-measure, Baroque-style ritornello in which two flutes play in thirds throughout, over clarinet arpeggios and a pseudo-basso continuo. The duet itself is accompanied mostly by harpsichord, but interludes resembling recitativo obbligato involve either the wind or string choir of the orchestra (Example 20.16). Broken chords in strict rhythm accompany Rakewell's vocal line, which is full of Mozart-like turns and appoggiaturas. Shadow admits defeat in a short strophic aria, "I burn."

Stravinsky's two major contributions to the choral literature reveal an affinity for Baroque genres: the oratorio-opera *Oedipus rex* (Oedipus the King, 1927) on a Latin translation of Cocteau's adaptation of Sophocles, for soloists, narrator, men's chorus, and orchestra; and the *Symphony of Psalms* (1930) for mixed chorus and orchestra on Latin texts from the Vulgate Bible. Stravinsky

Example 20.16 *Igor Stravinsky,* The Rake's Progress: *Act III, Scene 2, Duet,* My heart is wild with fear

Example 20.17 *Igor Stravinsky,* Symphony of Psalms: "Laudate Dominum" *(winds and strings omitted)*

used Latin because the ritualistic language left him free to concentrate on its "phonetic" qualities.

The *Symphony of Psalms* is one of the great works of the twentieth century, a masterpiece of invention, musical architecture, and religious devotion. Baroque features include the ubiquitous ostinato constructions and the fully developed fugue of the second movement ("Expectans expectavi Dominum"), complete with tonic-dominant statements and answers and strettos. By applying ostinato toward the end of the third movement, "Laudate Dominum in sanctis Ejus," Stravinsky achieves considerable harmonic richness (Example 20.17). Here an ostinato bass of four half-notes is heard against a choral setting made up of three-measure phrases in $\frac{3}{2}$. One particular melodic pattern, three half-notes long, plays six times against the ostinato bass. As a result the beginnings and endings of the ostinato and the choral phrases rarely coincide and the many possible vertical combinations of the pitches of the E♭-major scale form a diatonic kaleidoscope that has been dubbed "pandiatonicism."

Symphony of Psalms

In parts of the *Canticum sacrum* and other compositions of the 1950s, Stravinsky very gradually and idiosyncratically adapted some of the techniques from the Schoenberg school. These works include the Septet (1953), the song *In memoriam Dylan Thomas* (1954), the ballet *Agon* (1954–57), and *Threni* (1958), for voices and orchestra on texts from the Lamentations of Jeremiah. He further explored this technique in *Movements* (1959) and the *Orchestra Variations* (1964).

Other works

Bibliography

For Further Reading

General

The most authoritative critical book on twentieth-century music is Robert P. Morgan's *Twentieth-Century Music: A History of Musical Style in Modern Europe and America* (New York: Norton, 1991). It is accompanied by an *Anthology of Twentieth-Century Music*, ed. with analytical comments by Morgan (New York: Norton, 1992). Other recommended readings: William W. Austin, *Music in the Twentieth Century from Debussy through Stravinsky* (New York: Norton, 1966); Elliott Antokoletz, *Twentieth-Century Music* (Englewood Cliffs, N.J.: Prentice-Hall, 1992); Paul Griffiths, *Modern Music and After* (Oxford: Oxford University Press, 1995); Eric Salzman, *Twentieth-Century Music: An Introduction*, 3rd ed. (Englewood Cliffs, N.J.: Prentice Hall, 1988); Bryan Simms, *Music of the 20th Century: Style and Structure* and the accompanying anthology (New York: Schirmer, 1986); Glenn Watkins, *Soundings: Music in the Twentieth Century* (New York: Schirmer, 1988) and his *Pyramids at the Louvre: Music, Culture, and Collage from Stravinsky to the Postmodernists* (Cambridge, Mass.: Harvard University Press, 1994); Arnold Whittall, *Music since the First World War* (London: St. Martin's Press, 1995); Joseph N. Straus, *Remaking the Past: Music Modernism and the Influence of the Tonal Tradition* (Cambridge, Mass.: Harvard University Press, 1990); Elliott Schwartz and Daniel Godfrey, *Music since 1945* (New York: Schirmer, 1993); Elliott Schwartz and Barney Childs, eds., *Contemporary Composers on Contemporary Music* (New York: Holt, Rinehart & Winston, 1967). An excellent technical guide is Joel Lester, *Analytic Approaches to Twentieth-Century Music* (New York: Norton, 1989).

On Soviet composers, see Gerald Abraham, *Eight Soviet Composers* (New York: Oxford University Press, 1943); Dmitri Shostakovich, *The Power of Music* (New York: Music Journal, 1968); Boris Schwarz, *Music and Musical Life in Soviet Russia, Enlarged Edition, 1917–1981* (Bloomington: Indiana University Press, 1983); Malcolm H. Brown, ed., *Russian and Soviet Music: Essays for Boris Schwarz* (Ann Arbor: UMI Research Press, 1984).

The New Grove Modern Masters: Bartók, Stravinsky, Hindemith (New York: Norton, 1984); *The New Grove Twentieth-Century English Masters: Elgar, Delius, Vaughan Williams, Holst, Walton, Tippett, Britten* (New York: Norton, 1986); *The New Grove Twentieth-Century French Masters: Fauré, Debussy, Satie, Ravel, Poulenc, Messiaen, Boulez* (New York: Norton, 1986).

Individual Composers

Bartók Halsey Stevens, *The Life and Music of Béla Bartók*, 3rd rev. ed., ed. Malcolm Gillies (New York: Oxford University Press, 1993); Paul Griffiths, *Bartók* (London: Dent, 1984); Elliott Antokoletz, *The Music of Béla Bartók: A Study of Tonality and Progression in 20th-Century Music* (Berkeley: University of California Press, 1984) and *Béla Bartók: A Guide to Research* (New York: Garland, 1988); Kenneth Chalmers, *Béla Bartók* (London: Phaidon, 1995); László Somfai, *Béla Bartók: Composition, Concepts, and Autograph Sources* (Berkeley: University of California Press, 1996); *Bartók and His World*, ed. Peter Laki (Princeton: Princeton University Press, 1995); Ernö Lendvai, *The Workshop of Bartók and Kodály* (Budapest: Editio Musica, 1983) and *Béla Bartók: An Analysis of His Music* (Atlantic Highlands, New Jersey: Humanities, 1971).

Britten *Cambridge Companion to Benjamin Britten*, ed. Mervyn Cooke (Cambridge: Cambridge University Press, 1999); Arnold Whittall, *The Music of Britten and Tippett: Studies on Themes and Techniques*, 2nd ed. (Cambridge: Cambridge University Press, 1990); Peter

Evans, *The Music of Benjamin Britten* (Minneapolis: University of Minnesota Press, 1979); Eric W. White, *Benjamin Britten, His Life and Operas*, 2nd ed. (Berkeley: University of California Press, 1983); Michael Oliver, *Benjamin Britten* (London: Phaidon, 1996); Philip Brett, ed., *Benjamin Britten, Peter Grimes* (Cambridge: Cambridge University Press, 1983); Peter J. Hodgson, *Benjamin Britten: A Guide to Research* (New York: Garland, 1996).

Hindemith His *The Craft of Musical Composition* (New York: Associated Music Publishers, 1954) and *A Composer's World; Horizons and Limitations* (Cambridge, Mass.: Harvard University Press, 1952). David Neumeyer, *The Music of Paul Hindemith* (New Haven: Yale University Press, 1986); *Selected Letters of Paul Hindemith*, ed. and trans. Geoffrey Skelton (New Haven: Yale University Press, 1995).

Hindemith's complete works have been published in *Sämtliche Werke*, ed. Kurt von Fischer and Ludwig Finscher (Mainz: B. Schott, 1975–86).

Holst Imogen Holst, *The Music of Gustav Holst, and Holst's Music Reconsidered* (Oxford: Oxford University Press, 1984); idem, *A Thematic Catalogue of Gustav Holst's Music* (London: Faber & Faber, 1974).

Honegger His *I Am a Composer*, trans. Wilson O. Clough (London: Faber & Faber, 1966). Harry Halbreich, *Arthur Honegger*, trans. Roger Nichols (Portland: Amadeus, 1999).

Kodály His *Folk Music of Hungary*, trans. Ronald Tempest and Cynthia Jolly (London: Barrie & Jenkins, 1971). László Eösze, *Zoltán Kodály*, trans. Istvan Farkas and Gyula Gulyas (London: Collet's, 1962); Ernö Lendvai, *The Workshop of Bartók and Kodály* (Budapest: Editio Musica, 1983).

Milhaud His *My Happy Life*, trans. Donald Evans and Christopher Palmer, intro. by Christopher Palmer (London and New York: Marion Boyars, 1995). Paul Collaer, *Darius Milhaud* (San Francisco: San Francisco Press, 1988).

Poulenc His *My Friends and Myself*, trans. James Harding (London: Dobson, 1978) and *Diary of My Songs*, trans. Winifred Radford (London: Gollancz, 1985). Pierre Bernac, *Francis Poulenc: The Man and His Songs*, trans. Winifred Radford (New York: Norton, 1977); Benjamin Ivry, *Francis Poulenc* (London: Phaidon, 1996); Keith W. Daniel, *Francis Poulenc: His Artistic Development and His Musical Style* (Ann Arbor: UMI Research Press, 1982).

Prokofiev His *Prokofiev by Prokofiev: A Composer's Memoir*, ed. David H. Appel, trans. Guy Daniels (New York: Doubleday, 1979). Neil Minturn, *The Music of Sergei Prokofiev* (New Haven: Yale University Press, 1997); Israel V. Nestyev, *Prokofiev*, trans. Florence Jonas (Stanford: Stanford University Press, 1960); Harlow Robinson, *Prokofiev, A Biography* (New York: Viking, 1987).

Shostakovich Laurel Fay, *Shostakovich: A Life* (New York: Oxford University Press, 1999); Roy Blokker and Robert Dearling, *The Music of Dimitri Shostakovich: The Symphonies* (London: Tantivy Press, 1979); Christopher Norris, ed., *Shostakovich: The Man and His Music* (Boston and London: Marion Boyars, 1982); *Shostakovich Studies*, ed. David Fanning (Cambridge: Cambridge University Press, 1995); Elizabeth Wilson, *Shostakovich: A Life Remembered* (London: Faber & Faber, 1994); Solomon Volkov, ed., *Testimony: The Memoirs of Dmitry Shostakovich*, trans. Antonina W. Bouis (New York: Harper & Row, 1979)—to be used with caution; see the review by Laurel Fay, "Shostakovich versus Volkov: Whose Testimony?" *The Russian Review* 39 (1980):484–93; defense of Volkov's book by Allan B. Ho and Dmitry Feofanov, *Shostakovich Reconsidered* (London: Toccata Press, 1998).

Stravinsky His *An Autobiography* (New York: Norton, 1962), *Poetics of Music* (New York: Knopf, 1960), and *Selected Correspondence*, ed. Robert Craft, 3 vols. (London: Faber & Faber, 1982–85). Stravinsky's numerous books in collaboration with Craft contain many wise and penetrating observations on music and musicians in the twentieth century. Richard Taruskin, *Stravinsky and the Russian Traditions: A Biography of the Works through* Mavra (Berkeley: University of California Press, 1996); Mikhail S. Druskin, *Igor Stravinsky: His Life, Works, and Views*, trans. Martin Cooper (Cambridge: Cambridge University Press, 1983); Benjamin Boretz and Edward T. Cone, eds., *Perspectives on Schoenberg and Stravinsky* (Princeton: Princeton University Press, 1968) has articles from the periodical *Perspectives of New Music*; Allen Forte, *The Harmonic Organization of "The Rite of Spring"* (New Haven: Yale University Press, 1978); Pieter van den Toorn, *The Music of Igor Stravinsky* (New Haven: Yale University Press, 1983) and *Stravinsky and "The Rite of Spring": The Beginnings of a Musical Language* (Berkeley and Los Angeles: University of California Press, 1987). See also *Confronting Stravinsky*, ed. Jann Pasler (Berkeley: University of California Press, 1986); Ethan Haimo and Paul Johnson, eds., *Stravinsky Retrospectives* (Lincoln: University of Nebraska Press, 1987); Paul Griffiths, *Igor Stravinsky, The Rake's Progress* (New York: Cambridge University Press, 1982).

Tippett His *Moving into Aquarius*, 2nd ed. (London: Palladin, 1974) and *Music of the Angels* (London: Eulenburg, 1980). Ian Kemp, *Tippett: The Composer and His Music* (London: Eulenburg, 1984); David Clarke, *Language, Form, and Structure in the Music of Michael Tippett* (New York: Garland, 1989); David Matthews, *Michael Tippett: An Introductory Study* (London: Faber & Faber, 1980). See also under Britten.

Vaughan Williams His *National Music* (New York: Oxford University Press, 1964). Michael Kennedy, *The Works of Ralph Vaughan Williams*, rev. ed. (London: Oxford University Press, 1982); Elliott S. Schwartz, *The Symphonies of R. Vaughan Williams* (Amherst: University of Massachusetts Press, 1964, 1982); James Day, *Vaughan Williams* (Oxford: Oxford University Press, 1998); Michael Kennedy, *A Catalogue of the Works of Ralph Vaughan Williams*, 2nd ed. (Oxford: Oxford University Press, 1996).

Walton Frank S. Howes, *The Music of William Walton*, 2nd ed. (London: Oxford University Press, 1974); Neil Tierney, *William Walton, His Life and Music* (London: Hale, 1984); Stewart R. Craggs, ed., *William Walton: A Source Book* (Aldershot, Hants, England, 1993).

Weill David Drew, *Kurt Weill: A Handbook* (London: Faber & Faber, 1987); David Farneth et al., *A Life in Pictures and Documents* (New York; Overlook Press, 1999); Kim Kowalke, *Kurt Weill in Europe* (Ann Arbor: UMI Research Press, 1979); idem, ed., *A New Orpheus: Essays on Kurt Weill* (New Haven: Yale University Press, 1986); *Speak Low (When You Speak Love): The Letters of Kurt Weill and Lotte Lenya*, ed. and trans. Lys Symonette and Kim H. Kowalke (Berkeley: University of California Press, 1996).

CHAPTER 21

ATONALITY, SERIALISM, AND RECENT DEVELOPMENTS IN TWENTIETH-CENTURY EUROPE

SCHOENBERG AND HIS FOLLOWERS

Romantic origins

The twelve-tone system devised by Arnold Schoenberg (1874–1951) springs from late German Romanticism. The chromatic idiom of Schoenberg's earliest important work, the string sextet *Verklärte Nacht* (Transfigured Night, 1899), evolves from *Tristan*, while the symphonic poem *Pelleas und Melisande* (1903) draws on Gustav Mahler and Richard Strauss. The huge symphonic cantata *Gurrelieder* (Songs of Gurre) for five soloists, narrator, four choruses, and large orchestra (1901; orchestration completed 1911) outdoes Wagner in emotional fervor and Mahler and Strauss in complexity of scoring.

Schoenberg's second period

We hear new direction in Schoenberg's second-period works, which include the first two Quartets (D minor and F♯ minor, 1905 and 1908), the first *Kammersymphonie* (Chamber Symphony, 1906) for fifteen instruments, the *Five Orchestral Pieces*, Op. 16 (1909), two sets of short piano pieces (Op. 11, 1908, and Op. 19, 1911), a cycle of songs with piano accompaniment, *Das Buch der hängenden Gärten* (Book of the Hanging Gardens, 1908), for soloist and orchestra, *Erwartung* (Expectation, 1909), and a dramatic pantomime, *Die glückliche Hand* (The Lucky Hand, 1911–13). Turning away from post-Romantic gigantism, Schoenberg chose small instrumental combinations or, in large orchestral works, a soloistic treatment of instruments or swift alternation of colors (as in the *Five Orchestral Pieces* and *Erwartung*). Concurrently, rhythm and counterpoint became more complex, the melodic line fragmented, and the composition as a whole more concentrated and compact. For example, in the First Quartet, all the themes of its one-movement cyclical form, even the material of subsidiary voices, evolve from a few germinal motives through variation and combination. Around 1908 Schoenberg moved from a chromatic style centered on a keynote to something that is commonly called *atonality.*

Atonality

Atonal as currently used refers to music not based on the harmonic and melodic relationships revolving around a key center. The term is no longer applied to music built on *serial* principles, such as on a twelve-tone row (see pages 716-18). From 1908 to 1923 Schoenberg composed "atonal" music, that is, music not bound by traditional tonalities. He referred to his compositional method during this period as "composing with the tones of a motive"; each motive had three or more pitches. Theorists later developed the concept of "pitch-class set" to describe this collection of notes from which melodies or harmonies were formed by arranging the notes in normal order, inverted order, reverse order, or in transposition. Holding to the set gave the music a consistent sound. Schoenberg tended to integrate a composition even more by using all twelve notes of the chromatic scale within a phrase or segment. After 1923 he wrote music based on twelve-tone rows only. Twelve-tone music, however, need not be atonal; it may observe a tonal center.

Late-Romantic origins

Much late-Romantic music, especially in Germany, had been tending toward atonality. Chromatic melody lines and chord progressions—in the music of Wagner, for example—had resulted in passages lacking a perceived tonal center.

Schoenberg explored the extreme possibilities of chromaticism within the limits of tonality in the *Gurrelieder* and *Pelleas.* After that, it was an easy step to cut loose altogether from a key center and treat all twelve notes of the octave as equal instead of regarding some of them as chromatically altered tones of a diatonic scale. Without a key tone, harmonies ceased to have their own conventional functions—something foreshadowed in the free chord successions of Debussy—and any combination of tones could constitute a chord not requiring resolution, a situation Schoenberg called "the emancipation of the dissonance." He proceeded gradually from tonality clouded by extreme chromaticism to atonality with free dissonance. The song cycle *Das Buch der hängenden Gärten* and the last movement of the Second Quartet (apart from the final cadence in F♯), mark the transition to atonality.

Pierrot lunaire

Pierrot lunaire (Moonstruck Pierrot, 1912; see Nos. 8 and 13 in NAWM 135; CD 11 [45]), Schoenberg's best-known composition of the prewar era, is a cycle of twenty-one songs drawn from a larger poetic cycle published in 1884 by the Belgian symbolist poet Albert Giraud and later translated into German. It is scored for a woman's voice with a chamber ensemble of five players and eight instruments: flute (doubling piccolo), clarinet (bass clarinet), violin (viola), cello, and piano. The poet imagines himself as the clown Pierrot; he expresses all aspects of himself through the symbol of a moonbeam, which is capable of taking many shapes and colors. Instead of the comic adventures of Pierrot the clown, however, the poet invents a gruesome fantasy. The voice

■ *Schoenberg conducting a performance of* Pierrot lunaire *with soprano Erica Stiedry-Wagner at Town Hall, New York, on November 17, 1940. A sketch by Benedict Fred Dolbin (1883–1971).* (USED BY PERMISSION OF LAWRENCE SCHOENBERG)

Sprechstimme

throughout the cycle declaims the text in a so-called *Sprechstimme* (speech-voice; also called *Sprechgesang,* or speech-song), only approximating the written pitches but keeping closely to the notated rhythm. To achieve this effect Schoenberg used the sign ♩. Some of the pieces rely on constructive devices such as canons to assure unity, since they cannot depend on chord relationships within a tonality for this purpose.

Schoenberg called No. 8, *Nacht* (Night), a passacaglia, but it is an unusual one because the unifying motive—a rising minor third followed by a descending major third—reappears in various note values throughout the parts. The constant ostinato fittingly illustrates Pierrot's obsession with the giant moths that enclose him in a frightening trap and shut out the sun. No. 13, *Enthauptung* (Beheading), shows another side of Schoenberg's music at the time: thematic development is abandoned for what appears to the listener as anarchic improvisation, subject only to the changing message of the text. Here Pierrot imagines that he is beheaded by the moonbeam for his crimes.

Expressionism

Certain painters belonging to a movement called *expressionism* depicted real objects in distorted representations, to reflect their feelings about their surroundings and themselves (see, for example, Plate XIV, facing page 719). Similarly Schoenberg used exaggerated graphic images and speech inflections to express the poet's inner feelings.

Schoenberg and his pupil Alban Berg were the chief exponents of expressionism in music. Where impressionism (another term first used in connection with painting) aimed to represent objects of the external world as perceived at a given moment, expressionism, proceeding in the opposite direction, sought to represent *inner* experience. Expressionism grew out of the subjectivity of Romanticism; it differed from Romanticism in the kind of inner experience it aimed to portray and in the means chosen to portray it. Expressionism dealt with the emotional life of the modern person, isolated, helpless in the grip of poorly understood forces, prey to inner conflict, tension, anxiety, fear, and all the elemental irrational drives of the subconscious (as Schoenberg's fellow-Viennese Sigmund Freud conceived the deepest level of memory and emotional activity), and in angry rebellion against the established order and accepted forms (see vignette).

Portrayal of emotional life

Because of such subject matter, expressionistic art is characterized by desperate and revolutionary modes of utterance. Both are illustrated in Schoenberg's *Erwartung*, a work of tremendous emotional force written in a dissonant, rhythmically and melodically fragmentary, nonthematic musical idiom. *Erwartung*, *Die glückliche Hand*, and *Pierrot lunaire* are all expressionist works. In none of them did the composer aspire to make music that was either pretty or realistic. Instead, he deployed the most forceful and direct means, no matter how unusual—whether in music, subject matter, text, scenic design, or lighting—to communicate the particular compelling thought and emotion that he wanted. At this period of his development, Schoenberg was depending mostly on the text to establish a thread in his extended works. The early atonal piano pieces of Op. 19 (1911) were so short—models of concise, epigrammatic style—that the composer did not have to face the problem of integrating a long instrumental composition into a formal unity.

Twelve-Tone Method

The method

By 1923, after six years during which he published no music, Schoenberg had formulated a "method of composing with twelve tones that are related only to one another." The essential points of the theory of this twelve-tone ("dodecaphonic") technique may be summarized as follows: the basis of each composition is a *row* or *series* consisting of the twelve tones or pitch classes of the octave arranged in an order the composer chooses. The tones of the series may be used both successively (as melody) and simultaneously (as harmony or counterpoint), in any octave and with any desired rhythm. The row may be used not only in its original or "prime" form but also in intervalically inverted form, in retrograde order (backward) or retrograde inverted form, and in transpositions of any of the four forms. In practice, the twelve-tone series is often broken into segments of three to six pitches, which are then used to create melodic motives and chords. As a rule, the composer exhausts all twelve pitches of the series before going on to use the series in any of its forms again. Ultimately it is intervals, not pitches, that count. The common denominator between the various form and transpositions of the row—that which unites them and hence the composition—is a basic set of intervals and the motives created out of them.

Schoenberg's twelve-tone works

The first works in which Schoenberg deliberately applied tone rows were the five piano pieces Op. 23 (1923), of which, however, only the last has a complete row of twelve tones. Over the next few years he perfected his method in the Serenade, Op. 24; Suite for Piano, Op. 25; the Wind Quintet, Op. 26; the Third Quartet (1926), and the *Variations for Orchestra* (1928). Most of the works Schoenberg wrote after coming to America in 1933, particularly the Violin Concerto (1936) and the Fourth Quartet (1937), also employ tone rows. "In olden [and tonal] style" is his Suite for String Orchestra (1934). In the *Ode to Napoleon* and the Piano Concerto (both 1942), he approached a synthesis of his own system with some elements of orthodox tonality; but these works are less characteristic than other late works, such as the String Trio (1946) and the *Fantasy for Violin and Piano* (1949), both of which employ serialism.

Variations for Orchestra

Generally acknowledged to be among Schoenberg's finest works, the *Variations for Orchestra* (1926–28; see NAWM 136; CD 11 [51] / 4 ⟨38⟩) illustrates the blending of traditional procedures with the twelve-tone method. Following an introduction, in which the row is surrounded in a veil of mystery and mood of expectation, we hear a twenty-four-measure theme. Four forms of the twelve-note row (Example 21.1) determine the pitch successions of the melodic subject in the cello, while the same four forms in reverse order supply the harmonic accompaniment to this melody. The subject is clearly laid out in motives employing groups of three to six notes of the row, and these are given distinct rhythmic shape, so that their rhythms, when heard with different pitches in the course of the theme, contribute to the overall cohesion. Example 21.1 shows the first half of the theme, with numbers to indicate the pitch order in the four forms of the row shown below the theme. The first three motives use up the row in its original state (P-0 stands for the Prime [P] form at the original pitch, that is, at zero half-steps of transposition). The harmony for each of the motives is drawn from the same numbers of the row but in the Inversion (I) transposed up a major sixth to the ninth half-step (I-9). As the first group of motives had 5, 4, and 3 different pitches, respectively, the second

ARNOLD SCHOENBERG ON ARTISTIC EXPRESSION

Art is a cry of distress from those who live out within themselves the destiny of humanity, who are not content with it but measure themselves against it, who do not obtusely serve the engine to which the label "unseen forces" is applied, but throw themselves into the moving gears to understand how it works. They are those who do not turn their eyes away to protect themselves from emotions but open them wide to oppose what must be attacked. They do, however, often close their eyes to perceive what the senses do not convey, to look inside of what seems to be happening on the surface. Inside them turns the movement of the world; only an echo of it leaks out—the work of art.

From "Aphorismen," in *Die Musik*, Berlin, 9. Jahrgang, Vol. 36 (1909–10):159.

Example 21.1 *Arnold Schoenberg,* Variations for Orchestra, *Op. 31: Forms of the Twelve Tone Row, First Half of Theme (measures 34–35)*

group has the reverse, 3, 4, and 5 pitches. Melody is now drawn from the Retrograde (R) of the Inversion at the ninth half-step (RI-9), which had previously furnished the accompaniment. The method may strike one as mechanical, but the sensivity and taste of the composer governs every choice from the many possibilities.

Moses und Aron

Libretto In 1930–32 Schoenberg composed the first two acts of a three-act opera, *Moses und Aron*, on his own libretto. Although the score remains uncompleted, the opera has entered the repertory. Against the Old Testament background, Schoenberg presents the tragic conflict between Moses, the philosopher-mystic, as mediator of the word of God, and Aron, the statesman-educator, who acts as Moses' interpreter to the people. Moses is unable to communicate his vision, while Aron, who can communicate, does not rightly understand it.

XIII. *Pablo Ruiz y Picasso (1881–1973),* The Treble Clef *(1912). This painting is done in a style known as "cubism," which was developed by Georges Braque and Picasso between 1907 and 1911. In cubism, real objects are broken down into geometric shapes, such as cubes and cones, and juxtaposed or overlapped in a lively, colorful design. During 1912 Picasso painted a series of canvases that used the violin as a subject. In this example he also includes a clarinet, stylized as a brown bar with three holes; the instrument's bell is represented by concentric circles and a cone. The sheet of paper with a staff and treble clef gives the work its name. Stravinsky's abrupt juxtaposition of disparate blocks of music has been compared to cubism, as, for example, in his* Petrushka *(1911) for Diaghilev's Ballet Russes. Picasso later created set designs for that company.* (OIL ON CANVAS. PRIVATE COLLECTION. © 2000 ESTATE OF PABLO PICASSO / ARTISTS RIGHTS SOCIETY [ARS], NEW YORK. PHOTO: © EDIMÉDIA / CORBIS)

XIV. *Vassily Kandinsky,* Der blaue Reiter *(The Blue Rider, 1903), oil on canvas. From an early age Kandinsky loved horses and their riders and frequently depicted them in his works. This ghostly image of a horseman in a blue cloak projects the artist's sense of mystery and adventure about his subject. The direction of the rider is particularly significant to Kandinsky, who once said: "Movement to the right gives the impression of heading home, to the left going out into the world." We can see precursors of the artist's later turn toward abstraction here—for example, his use of color, as in the blue of the distant hills, for expressionist purposes. Between 1911 and 1912, Kandinsky and Franz Marc founded the annual periodical* Der blaue Reiter, *an organ of the expressionist movement that published art, essays, and music, including songs by Schoenberg and Berg. (E. G. BÜHRLE COLLECTION. ZURICH, SWITZERLAND. © 2000 ARTISTS RIGHTS SOCIETY [ARS], NEW YORK / ADAGP. PARIS. PHOTO BY ERICH LESSING / ART RESOURCE, NEW YORK)*

■ *Autograph short score of the opening measures of Schoenberg's* Moses und Aron. *"Hz" stands for woodwinds, "Bl" for brass, "Str" for strings, and "Schlg" for percussion.* (LOS ANGELES, ARNOLD SCHOENBERG INSTITUTE ARCHIVES. COPYRIGHT 1957 BY B. SCHOTT'S SÖHNE. USED BY PERMISSION OF BELMONT MUSIC PUBLISHERS, PACIFIC PALISADES, CA 90272, AND EUROPEAN AMERICAN MUSIC DISTRIBUTORS CORP.)

Example 21.2 *Arnold Schoenberg,* Moses und Aron: *Act I, Scene 2*

Aron says to Moses (Act III, Scene 1), "I was to discourse in images, you in concepts; I to the heart, you to the mind." Symbolically, Moses speaks—in *Sprechstimme*—but does not sing; his speech turns to music at only one moment, when Moses warns Aron, "Purify your thought: set it free from earthly things, dedicate it to Truth" (Act I, Scene 2). The solemn alliteration of the German text is reminiscent of Wagner (see Example 21.2). Throughout, Schoenberg employs vowel and consonant sounds in symbolic connection with the music and the dramatic ideas.

The music

Moses und Aron is as much oratorio as opera. The choruses of the people of Israel play a large part. A group of six solo voices (in the orchestra pit, not on the stage) represents the Voice of God, in *Sprechstimme* like Moses. In the most picturesque part of the score—the complex of solos, choruses, and dances in the big scene depicting the worship of the Golden Calf (Act II)—rhythm, instrumental color, and sudden contrasts combine in a spectacle of oriental splendor and dramatic effect. The entire opera is based on a single tone row, one form of which is represented in Example 21.2. *Moses und Aron* embodies a profound philosophical conception in appropriate dramatic form and powerfully expressive music.

Alban Berg

Alban Berg (1885–1935), Schoenberg's famous pupil, adopted most of his master's methods of construction. But he used them with freedom, and in his twelve-tone works he often chose tone rows that allowed for tonal-sounding chords and chord progressions. Moreover, Berg invested the technique with a warmth of feeling that gives it more immediate impact than it had in the hands of other twelve-tone composers. His chief works are the *Lyric Suite* for string quartet (1926); a Violin Concerto (1935); and two operas, *Wozzeck* (composed 1917–21; first performed 1925) and *Lulu* (composed 1928–35; the orchestration not quite completed at Berg's death).

Wozzeck

Wozzeck is the outstanding example of expressionist opera. The libretto, arranged by Berg from fragments of a drama by Georg Büchner (1813–1837), presents the soldier Wozzeck as a symbol of "wir arme Leut" (we poor people), a hapless victim of his environment, despised by his fellow men, betrayed in love, driven finally to murder and suicide. The music is atonal, not twelve-tone, and is continuous throughout each of the three acts, the changing scenes (five in each act) being connected by orchestral interludes as in Debussy's *Pelléas.* Berg's music is unified by several leitmotifs, by pitch-class sets identified with the main characters, and by adaptations of traditional closed forms. The first act contains a Baroque suite, a rhapsody, a march and lullaby, a passacaglia, and a rondo. The second act is a symphony in five movements, in-

Leitmotifs and form

Example 21.3 *Alban Berg, Wozzeck: Act III, Scene 3*

cluding a sonata form, a fantasia and fugue, a ternary slow movement, a scherzo, and a rondo. The third act consists of six so-called inventions: on a theme (seven variations and fugue); on a note (the pitch *B*); on a rhythm; on a chord; on a key (D minor); and on a duration (the eighth note).

A wild polka, played on a barroom piano, announces the rhythmic theme and the six-pitch set (Example 21.3) for Act III, Scene 3 (NAWM 137; CD 11 [53] / 4 ⟨40⟩). Wozzeck sits in a tavern singing and drinking. He asks Margret, the barmaid, to dance with him. After they dance, she sits on his lap and sings a song, in the midst of which she notices blood on his hand. He becomes agitated and obsessed with his blood, for just before entering the tavern he murdered his unfaithful mistress, Marie. The set, nearly a whole-tone scale, recurs frequently throughout the opera. Somewhat as in a medieval isorhythmic motet, the set of eight durations is continually reiterated, sometimes in diminution, sometimes in augmentation.

Berg's vocal parts move fluidly among ordinary speech, *Sprechstimme*, and conventional singing. Passages of stylized realism—snoring chorus, gurgling water, a tavern orchestra with an out-of-tune piano caricaturing a waltz motive from Strauss's *Rosenkavalier*—aptly serve expressionistic ends. The grim, ironic, symbolical action is supported by a wealth of musical invention and ever varied, ingenious, and appropriate orchestration. The music's formal clarity and concentration intensify the impact of the graphic descriptions and dramatic confrontations, and the almost constant use of references to tonality and to familiar musical styles helps to keep listeners engaged.

Other works

The *Lyric Suite* and the Violin Concerto typify Berg's constant effort to connect the new style with the past. Both the suite and the concerto are partially written according to the twelve-tone method. The basic row of the concerto is designed so that tonal combinations become almost inevitable (Example 21.4). In the finale, the last four pitches of the tone row introduce a statement of the chorale *Es ist genug* (It is enough), which ends Bach's Cantata No. 60—an allusion to the death of Manon Gropius, to whose memory the concerto is dedicated. She was the daughter of Berg's close friend Alma Mahler and died at eighteen of polio.

Example 21.4 *Alban Berg, Violin Concerto: Tone Row*

Anton Webern

If Berg's music represents the warm, lyrical side of Schoenberg's compositional approach, the music of his other celebrated pupil, Anton Webern (1883–1945), personifies the cool, constructive side. Webern wrote no opera and never used *Sprechstimme.* Economy and extreme concentration reign. His mature compositions unfold by imitative counterpoint, often strictly canonic. He used inversion and rhythmic shifts, but avoided sequences and, for the most part, repetitions. The melodic outline of the generating "cells" usually involves intervals, such as major sevenths and minor ninths, that exclude tonal implications. Textures are stripped to bare essentials. Complex rhythmic patterns result from simultaneous duple and triple divisions of all or part of a measure. The dynamics, specified down to the finest gradations, seldom rise above the level of *forte.*

Instrumentation

Most remarkable is Webern's instrumentation. A melodic line may be distributed among different instruments somewhat in the manner of a medieval hocket, so that only one or two—seldom more than four or five—successive tones are heard in the same timbre. In Example 21.5, the leading voice of one canon begins in horn 2 (measures 1–4), stating tones 1 to 4 of the row; it continues in the clarinet (measures 6–8), with tones 5 to 8; and concludes in the cello (measures 9–12), with tones 9 to 12. Sparks and flashes of color leap from a texture dotted with special effects—pizzicato, harmonics, tremolo, muting, and the like. Webern's striving for color and clarity often led him to choose unusual combinations, as in the Quartet Op. 22 for violin, clarinet, tenor saxophone, and piano, or the three songs Op. 18 for soprano, E♭ clarinet, and guitar.

Brevity of works

Intense concentration resulted in short compositions. Not all are so brief as the *Six Bagatelles* for string quartet, Op. 9, or the Five Pieces for Orchestra, Op. 10 (both 1913), which average respectively about 36 and 49 seconds for each movement (No. 5 of Op. 10 runs only 19 seconds). But even "larger" works like the Symphony Op. 21 (1928) and the String Quartet, Op. 28 (1938), take only eight or nine minutes' playing time.

Webern, like Schoenberg, passed through the stages of late Romantic chromaticism, free atonality, and organization by tone rows, the last beginning with the three songs of Op. 17 (1925). With few exceptions, his works, about equally divided between instrumental and vocal, are in chamber style. His chief instrumental compositions are the Symphony; the String Quartet; the Concerto for nine instruments, Op. 24 (1934); and the Piano Variations, Op. 27 (1936). For voices he wrote numerous collections of solo songs—some with piano, others with small ensembles—and a few choral pieces, notably *Das Augenlicht* (Light of the Eyes, 1935) and two cantatas (1939, 1943) for soloists, chorus, and orchestra. These cantatas, and also the Variations for Orchestra, Op. 30 (1940), are written in a more relaxed and expressive style than Webern's previous works. They employ the serial technique but include homophonic as well as contrapuntal texture.

Serial technique

We may observe Webern's use of the serial technique in the first move-

Example 21.5 *Anton Webern, Symphony Op. 21: First Movement*

■ *Europe during the Cold War (1945–1991)*

ment of the Symphony Op. 21 (NAWM 138; CD 11 56). Example 21.5 shows the beginning of the first movement. The "original" tone row is designated by the numbers 1, 2, etc. (some analysts start the numbering with 0). Note that the second half of the row is the retrograde of the first half transposed by a tritone, so that the retrograde form of the entire row transposed up a tritone or six half-steps (R–6) is a duplicate of its original form (P–0). The numbers 1′, 2′, and so forth, designate an inversion of the original form, beginning a major third lower. The numbers 1″, 2″, and so forth, designate an inversion beginning at the original pitch. The harp's *C*♮ in measure 4 begins a statement of the original form of the row transposed a major third upward. This example also illustrates the characteristically spare, open texture, with numerous rests in all the parts, making every single note count. The music emerges as a succession of tiny points or wisps of sound, in a technique described as "pointillism."

Canonic writing

What meets the ear is a rather static mosaic of instrumental colors, but close study reveals many constructive strategies. For example, the two horns begin in canon by contrary motion, then the same canonic voices are continued in the clarinet and bass clarinet. Meanwhile the harp begins another canon by contrary motion, using the same intervallic sequences (disregarding octave register) as the first canon but with a new scheme of durations and rests. A complete analysis would show that the movement is very tightly organized, that it consists of an exposition, development, and recapitulation, and that entire sections are mirror images of other sections.[1] The movement as a whole forms a palindrome, with the point of retrograde return occurring at the beginning of measure 35.

Webern's output was small. Although he received little acclaim during his lifetime, recognition of his work grew steadily in the years after World War II, and his music launched important new developments in Italy, Germany, France, and the United States.

AFTER WEBERN

The first half of the twentieth century witnessed a progressive breakup of the tonal harmonic system that had prevailed for the preceding two hundred years, roughly from Bach to Richard Strauss. Schoenberg, at first intuitively and later methodically with his twelve-tone rows, introduced a new conception of musical structure and, with his "emancipation of the dissonance," in effect abolished the traditional distinction between consonance and dissonance. Stravinsky participated, in turn, in all the movements of the time, arriving in the 1950s at his own accommodation to the twelve-tone system. Many other composers had by 1950 accepted the system in principle, modifying and adapting it to their own purposes. It was Webern, however, more than anyone else, who anticipated and stimulated a movement that engaged a group of young composers centered about the "holiday courses for new music" at Darmstadt. These courses began immediately after the end of the war, in 1946. At a memorial concert of his works at Darmstadt in 1953, Webern was hailed as the father of the new movement.

Darmstadt

Many of the ideas fostered at Darmstadt inspired experiments by composers in other countries, including, eventually, Eastern Europe. But every composer worked independently, striking out in new directions, cultivating a personal language and style. There was no allegiance to one consistent body of principles, no well-defined "common practice," as there had been in the eighteenth and nineteenth centuries. Pierre Boulez (b. 1925) of Paris and Karlheinz Stockhausen (b. 1928) of Cologne, both pupils of Messiaen, became the two principal composers of the Darmstadt group.

Serialism

Even before 1950, composers applied the principle of Schoenberg's tone rows to musical elements or parameters other than pitch. Thus arose "total serial-

1. See the analysis in William W. Austin, *Music in the 20th Century* (New York: Norton, 1966), pp. 357–65, where the entire movement is printed in reduced score.

ism": if the twelve tones of the chromatic scale could be serialized, so also could duration, intensity, timbre, and texture. In the eighteenth and nineteenth centuries, all these elements had been interdependent, combined in certain accepted melodic, harmonic, rhythmic, dynamic, and instrumental patterns. Now a series of pitches could be combined with a series of one or more of the other factors. Milton Babbitt (b. 1916) combined series of pitches and of durations and manipulated them by the usual operations of inversion and retrograde in his Three Compositions for Piano (1947). By similar means, a composer could achieve serial control over every detail of a composition. Naturally, the relationships among the parameters had to be worked out in a way that made sense musically, not merely mathematically.

The listener

A totally serial composition could easily give a listener an impression of randomness, because music based on these principles lacks themes in the classic sense of readily perceived melodic-rhythmic-harmonic entities and their recognizable extensions, derivations, and developments. Besides, it lacks a distinct rhythmic pulse and—even more important—a sense of progression toward points of climax or culmination. Instead, the listener hears only successive, unrepeated, and unpredictable musical "events." Such events may take the form of minute "points" of sound—color, melody, rhythm—intertwining, dissolving into one another. To be sure, the totality of these events in a well-constructed work does form a logical pattern.

Boulez

The rigidity of total serialism soon relaxed. In *Le Marteau sans maître* (The Hammer without a Master, 1954; revised 1957), Pierre Boulez fused the pointillist style and serial method with sensitive musical realization of the text. This work in nine short movements is a setting of verses from a cycle of surrealist poems by René Char, interspersed with instrumental "commentaries." The ensemble—a different combination in each movement—comprises alto flute, xylorimba, vibraphone, guitar, viola, and a variety of soft percussion instruments. The ensemble produces a translucent scrim of sound, all in the middle and high registers, with effects often suggestive of Balinese music. The contralto vocal line, characterized by wide melodic intervals, glissandos, and occasional *Sprechstimme*, often the lowest voice in the texture, relates in a deliberate way to particular instruments in the ensemble.

Messiaen

Olivier Messiaen (1908–1992) was an influential, unique, and unclassifiable figure. Born in Avignon, Messiaen studied organ and composition in Paris and remained there to become professor of harmony at the Conservatoire in 1942. His many distinguished pupils, besides Boulez and Stockhausen, included the Italian Luigi Nono (b. 1924), the Netherlander Ton de Leeuw (b. 1926), and many other important composers of their generation. It is a tribute to the quality of Messiaen's teaching that each pupil went his own way. Messiaen was not the founder of a school of composition in the ordinary sense of the word. In *Mode de valeurs et d'intensités* (the third of *Quatre études du rythme* for piano, 1949), Messiaen experimented with assigning each pitch a duration, dynamic level, and articulation, to be used each time that pitch occurred. This inspired his former pupil, Boulez, to make the first attempt at total serialism in *Structures* (1952).

Méditations

An intricate system of verbal and grammatical allusions pervades the *Méditations sur la mystère de la Sainte Trinité* (Meditations on the Mystery of the Holy Trinity) for organ, composed in 1969 (NAWM 139; CD 12 [1] / 4 ⟨43⟩). A motive represents the auxiliary verb "to be," which initiates in the part of the Father a dialogue among the persons of the Trinity. The motive emphasizes the "being," the existence, of God. The themes of the dialogue are mixed in extremely subjective and rhythmically free sections utilizing several combinations of organ registrations. In the fourth section marked *Vif*, the recurrent thematic material consists partly of bird calls that are identified in the score: the syncopated raucous sound of the black woodpecker, the call of the ring ouzel (*merle à plastron*), the bell-like sounds of Tengmalm's owl (*chouette de Tengmalm*), and the song thrush's melodious voice (*grive musicienne*).

Réveil des oiseaux

Messiaen wrote down birdsongs in musical notation. He used these transcriptions as material in his compositions, most extensively in *Réveil des oiseaux* for orchestra (1953), where each birdsong is identified. In a note to the published score he stated: "There is nothing in this score but birdsongs. All were heard in the forest and are perfectly authentic."[2]

Quatuor pour la fin du temps

Besides numerous works for piano and for his own instrument, the organ, Messiaen's principal compositions include the *Quatuor pour la fin du temps* (Quartet for the End of Time) for violin, clarinet, cello, and piano, written at a German military prison camp in 1941 for performance by the composer and three fellow-prisoners; *Trois petites liturgies pour la Présence Divine* (Three Short Liturgies of the Divine Presence) for unison chorus of women's voices and small orchestra (1944); a symphony *Turangalîla* in ten movements for large orchestra (1948); *Cinq rechants* (Five Refrains) for unaccompanied chorus of mixed voices (1949); and *Chronochromie* (literally, "Timecolor") for orchestra (1960).

In the opening movement, *Liturgie de cristal* (Crystal Liturgy), of the *Quatuor pour la fin du temps*, Messiaen used several characteristic devices. A serious student of both Western music history and the music of India, he was evidently inspired by fourteenth-century isorhythm as well as Indian music and based this piece on the repetition of extended rhythmic patterns. This "rhythmic pedal," as Messiaen called it, resembling a medieval *talea*, is complemented by an overlapping pitch pattern analogous to the medieval *color*. The two together constitute a melodic-harmonic ostinato. The isorhythmic pattern as notated in the piano part is shown in Example 21.6a, its resolution into integral note values in 21.6b.

Rhythmic schemes

The notation varies according to where the pattern falls in the metric scheme. When the pattern is resolved into untied note values, as in Example 21.6b, it becomes evident that its measures are of unequal length. Messiaen

2. The accuracy and validity of Messiaen's transcriptions have been challenged. See T. Hold, "Messiaen's Birds," *Music and Letters* 52 (1971):113.

Example 21.6 *Oliver Messiaen,* Quatuor pour la fin du temps: *I*

a. *Rhythmic pattern in the piano*

b. *Resolution in integral values*

c. *Rhythmic pattern in the cello*

d. *Resolution in integral values*

called the additional three sixteenths in the first measure and one sixteenth in the last, *valeurs ajoutées* or added note values. Messiaen also uses what he called a "non-retrogradable rhythm," a pattern whose second half is a retrograde of the first half, so that the retrograde of the whole pattern is identical to the original form. An example occurs in the cello (Example 21.6c, the notation in the cello part, and 21.6d, its resolution into integral note values).

Style

Messiaen's music is highly personal. At the same time a certain mystical detachment calls our attention to its unusual technical features. He worked mainly within a rich homophonic texture or with sweeping gestures, sometimes in counterpoint against one another. He drew melodic and harmonic material from a variety of sources, among them the plainchant modes, conventional tonality, octatonic scales, and pitch-sets. He often used contrasts of timbre to serve a structural function. His complex vertical sound aggregations sometimes incorporate the upper partials of a fundamental, as in the organ stops called mixtures. Rhythmic pedals akin to isorhythm, mirror-patterns of note values, and added notes in measures create an impression of a fluid, nonmetrical stream of ideas.[3]

RECENT DEVELOPMENTS

New Timbres

Post-Webern music introduced a large number of unaccustomed sounds. Earlier, the most revolutionary new sounds were the piano "tone clusters," employed by the American Henry Cowell (1897–1965) in the 1920s and the "prepared piano" of John Cage (1912–1993) in the 1940s (see Chapter 22). Now, other unfamiliar sounds were produced by new uses of conventional instruments, such as the flutter-tongue technique on wind instruments, as well as glissandos, harmonics, and *col legno* (playing with the wood part of the bow) on strings. Dense chromatic clusters or "bands" of sound for strings or voices were often employed by the Greek composer Iannis Xenakis (b. 1922), the Polish Krzysztof Penderecki, and the Italian Luigi Nono (1924–1990). Composers sometimes demanded spoken and whispered sounds of vocalists and even instrumentalists. New instruments, such as the vibraphone and the *Ondes Martenot*, appeared in the orchestra. The percussion group enjoyed a major expansion, often including instruments drawn from Asian or African musics.

Varèse

Edgard Varèse (1883–1965) wrote music in which timbre played a most important role. For Varèse, sounds as such were the essential structural components of music, more basic than melody, harmony, or rhythm. In his *Ionisation* (1933), written for a huge battery of percussion instruments (including piano and bells) along with chains, anvils, and sirens, Varèse created a form defined by contrasting blocks and masses of sound. Some of his late works (*Déserts*, 1954; *Poème électronique*, 1958) utilized new sound resources that became available soon after the middle of the twentieth century. (For more on Varèse, see Chapter 22.)

Electronic Resources

Musique concrète

No development after 1950 attracted more public attention or held greater potential for far-reaching changes in the world of music than electronically produced or manipulated sounds. In the so-called *musique concrète* of the late 1940s, the raw material consisted of recorded musical tones or other natural sounds that were transformed in various ways by mechanical and electronic means and then assembled on tape to be played back. The next step was to replace or supplement sounds of natural origin by sounds generated electronically in a studio. One of the most prominent early electronic compositions,

3. These means are described in detail in Messiaen's *The Technique of My Musical Language* (Paris, 1944), trans. John Satterfield (Paris: Leduc, 1956).

Stockhausen's *Gesang der Jünglinge* (Song of the Youths, 1956),[4] as well as many of his later works in this medium, used sounds from both sources. *Musique concrète* and electronic music encouraged listeners to accept sounds not produced by voices or musical instruments.

Role of performers

The new medium freed composers from all dependence on performers and empowered them to exercise complete, unmediated control over the sound of their compositions. Much of the new music already demanded minute shadings of pitch, intensity, and timbre that could be notated only approximately in a score, as well as complexities of "irrational" rhythms that could barely be realized by performers. Besides, the specially qualified personnel and lengthy rehearsal time required to perform this music were scarce. But in the electronic studio, every detail could be accurately calculated and recorded. Moreover, a whole new realm of possible sounds became available, including sounds not producible by any "natural" means. Different acoustical effects could be attained by placing loudspeakers in various positions relative to the audience. Composers in Europe, America, and Japan industriously exploited all these advantages. Further possibilities (and problems) arose when tape recordings were combined with live performers.

New Technology

Synthesizers

Electronic music was at first produced by combining, modifying, and controlling in various ways the output of oscillators, then recording these sounds on tape. The composer had to splice the tapes and mix their output, sometimes in combination with recorded sounds of physical objects in motion or of musicians, speakers, singers, and so forth. Electronic sound synthesizers were developed to make the process much easier. The composer could call on pitches from a music keyboard and with switches and knobs control harmonics, waveform, resonance, and location of sound sources. By the 1980s, electronic keyboards combined with computers made synthesized music accessible to composers outside the large electronic studios that had been set up in the 1950s and 1960s. Through computers, composers could define and control all the parameters of pitch, timbre, dynamics, and rhythm, and the characteristics thus digitally encoded could be translated directly into music through MIDI (Musical Instrument Digital Interface), a standard interface developed for this purpose.

Experimentation with live performers improvising against synthesized or computer-generated music is now commonplace. Equipment and software programs permit the computer to respond to music—played either on a synthesizer or on an instrument—according to formulas devised by the composer. Imitative polyphony, nonimitative polyphony, music on one or more rhythmic or melodic ostinatos, heterophony, and a variety of other textures can be generated by the composer at a synthesizer keyboard in "real time"—that is, as actually played and listened to, rather than laboriously prepared in advance and tape-recorded.

4. The reference is to Daniel 3:12 and the apocryphal insertion after 5:23.

Influence of Electronic Music

Electronic and synthesized music has not superseded live music and is not likely to do so. A good many composers have not worked at all, or to any important extent, with electronic media. Nonetheless, electronic sounds stimulated the invention of new sound effects obtainable from voices and conventional instruments, a development that is especially noticeable in the music of Krzysztof Penderecki and the Hungarian composer György Ligeti.

Spatial effects

In both electronic and live music, many composers worked with the idea of dispersing the various sound sources throughout a concert hall in order to manipulate space as an additional dimension of music. This effect, of course, was not altogether a new discovery. Antiphonal singing of plainchant, the *cori spezzati* and the choral-instrumental canzone and sinfonie of sixteenth-century Venetians, and the Requiem of Berlioz had exemplified the same fascination with spatial relationships. A more recent example was Bartók's *Music for Strings, Percussion, and Celesta* of 1936, which required a particular placement of players and instruments. In the second half of the twentieth century, composers began to use space with more calculation and inventiveness than ever before. They might place two or more groups of instruments on different parts of the stage, or locate loudspeakers or performers at the sides or back of the hall, above or below the level of the audience, or even in the midst of the audience. Varèse's *Poème électronique* at the Brussels Exposition in 1958 was projected by 425 loudspeakers ranged all about the interior space of Le Corbusier's pavilion (see illustration), while moving colored lights and projected images accompanied the music. Direction and location in space thus became a factor in the overall form of a work.

■ *Philips Pavilion, Brussels World's Fair, 1958. Edgard Varèse collaborated with the architect Le Corbusier to fill this building with the sound of* Poème électronique, *composed at the Philips laboratories in Eindhoven.* (NEW YORK, MUSEUM OF MODERN ART)

The Pitch Continuum

From at least the end of the seventeenth century, Western music generally utilized a set of twelve more-or-less equidistant semitones systematically dividing the space of an octave. Proposals at one time or another for including more tones in the octave came to no practical end. In practice, however, shifting pitches have always been used, such as glissandos in singing and on stringed instruments. Sounds outside the twelve semitones of the tempered scale were common in minute adjustments by string players, but more recently quarter tones or other microtones were sometimes required, as in Berg's *Chamber Concerto* (1925). Fuzzy pitch characterized the *Sprechstimme* of Schoenberg and Berg. By the mid-twentieth century, however, distinct pitches and intervals (including the octave itself) could be supplemented by a *continuum*, an unbroken range of sound from the lowest to the highest audible frequencies, without distinguishing separate tones of fixed pitch. The sirens in Varèse's *Ionisation* and similar electronic sounds in his later works provide striking examples of a composer's use of the pitch continuum. Other examples are the glissandos of the *Ondes Martenot*, used in Messiaen's *Turangalîla* symphony, and the frequent glissando effects on traditional instruments in the music of Penderecki and others. Related to this is the use of complex or unpitched nonmusical sounds, from whatever source, as elements in composition.

Penderecki, *Threnody*

The *Threnody for the Victims of Hiroshima* (1960) for fifty-two string instruments by Krzysztof Penderecki (b. 1933) expands the conventional resources of the orchestra in numerous ways. Players may choose pitches relative to the instrument's range, such as the "highest note," rather than specific notes. When particular pitches are called for, they may progress by quarter tones or multiples of these. Stringed instruments may bow between the bridge and the tailpiece or arpeggiate on four strings behind the bridge (that is, where the pitch is not controlled by the left hand), or bow on the bridge or tailpiece, or strike the soundboard. Different groups of instruments are assigned narrow pitchbands that may gradually become narrower or wider or move by glissando to a different level. The score gives few definite pulses or note values, the intervals of time measured by units of clock time. The beginning and ending sections give the players the greatest latitude, while the middle section is the most precisely notated and has the most intense variety of sound. Despite the individual freedom, the composer carefully controlled the outcome. The entire pitched and unpitched world, animate and inanimate, wailing and weeping at once, often in polychoral and antiphonal calls and responses, seems to mourn in this dirge.

Canticum canticorum

A similar technique is applied to all the voices in Penderecki's *Canticum canticorum Salomonis* (Solomon's Song of Songs, 1970–73) for eight men's and eight women's solo voices, accompanied by an orchestra of specially selected and proportioned ensembles and individual instruments. The Latin text is fragmented and distorted so as to be rendered incomprehensible. As in *Threnody*, bands of pitches fluctuate in narrowness and breadth, in dynamics, and sound production; voices sing, whisper, shout, hiss. Each voice goes its own way, but haunting and emotionally moving patterns shape the aggregate of the voices. In more recent works, such as the Viola Concerto (1983), Penderecki still relied on special instrumental effects, particularly of the soloist, but wrote conventional notation and developed easily grasped ideas in a highly charged, almost Romantic, rhetorical idiom.

Ligeti

The music of György Ligeti (b. 1923) achieved world renown through Stanley Kubrick's science-fiction film *2001*, which uses excerpts from three of his works, *Atmosphères* (1961), the Requiem (1963–65), and *Lux aeterna* (1966). Listeners were impressed that this music was in constant motion, yet static both harmonically and melodically. *Atmosphères* begins with fifty-six muted strings, together with a selection of woodwinds and horns playing simultaneously all the notes of the chromatic scale through a range of five octaves. Instruments imperceptibly drop out until only the violas and cellos remain. An orchestral tutti follows with a similar panchromatic layout, but out of it emerge two clusters: one, in the strings, made up of the diatonic "natural" notes of the chromatic scale, contrasts with the other, a pentatonic cluster of the "flat" notes in the woodwinds and horns. Similar textures, peppered with vibratos, sudden changes of dynamics, and string harmonics, and saturated with churning, dense canonic imitations, continue throughout the piece.

Atmosphères

Lontano

In Ligeti's *Lontano* for orchestra (1967) and *Continuum* for harpsichord (1968), individual pitches and intervals, though still in clusters, play a more prominent part. *Lontano* begins with a unison *A*♭, other pitches enter into a relationship with it, but neither serially nor in terms of tonal harmony. A second section focuses on the tritone *E–B*♭, and a third section on the fourth *D–G*. Ligeti has called the process of change in the intervallic relationships "harmonic crystallization." He defines this as

> a gradual metamorphosis of intervallic constellations, that is to say, certain harmonic formations merge and develop into others, as it were. Within one harmonic formation the precognition of the next harmonic constellation appears and then prevails, gradually clouding the first until only traces of it remain and the new formation has completely evolved. This is achieved technically by polyphonic means. The imaginary harmonies are the result of the complex canonic interweaving of the parts, whereas the gradual clouding and renewed crystallization are the result of the discrete changes in the separate parts.[5]

When we compare a work such as Penderecki's *Threnody* with Ligeti's *Atmosphères* or *Lontano*, we are struck by the similarity of effect achieved through different strategies of control: Penderecki often left the choice of pitches or durations to the individual players, while Ligeti carefully notated both, forming a mosaic of precisely chiseled pieces.

5. György Ligeti, Notes in "Konzert für Violoncello und Orchester, Lontano, etc." (Wergo CD WER 60163-50; 1988), liner notes.

Indeterminacy

Throughout the history of Western music, there has been continual interaction between composer and performer, between those factors (such as pitch and relative duration) that the composer could specify by notation and those left to the performer, either by convention or because adequate notational signs were lacking. In most secular polyphonic music before about 1600, performers could choose whether to sing or play the parts. Throughout the seventeenth century, instrumentation was mostly optional. The harpsichordist or organist supplied a harmonic filling over the bass line, the written basso continuo. Trumpets and drums played undesignated parts in the orchestras of the eighteenth century. Both vocalists and players added unspecified ornaments to a melodic line well into the nineteenth century.

Dynamics

The parameter least subject to a composer's determination has traditionally been dynamics. Despite the increased number of signs for different levels and gradations of loudness in the nineteenth century, indications were still only approximate and relative. Instrumentation by this time had come to be strictly specified. But slight fluctuations of tempo (rubato), use of the damper pedal of the piano, the relative prominence of different parts of the texture, and many other details were matters about which performers for the most part had to use their own judgment.

Control by composer

In the twentieth century some composers tried to exercise near-total control over performance by including a plethora of detailed indications for dynamics, manner of attack, tempo—through frequent metronome marks—pauses, and rhythms. But total control became possible, or nearly possible, only in all-electronic works, where the performer was eliminated. In fact, the range of gradations and fluctuations of control (exercised by the composer) and freedom (exercised by the performer) widened in the twentieth century.

The indeterminate features in twentieth-century music did not originate, as they had in the sixteenth century, from deliberately giving performers a conventional choice, such as to play or sing the notated music, or by leaving certain things to performers by purposely or inevitably using imprecise notation, as in the nineteenth century. Rather, the degree of control, or *determinacy*, and freedom, or *indeterminacy*[6] may be programmed for each composition. This may take the form of indeterminate sections, somewhat like the Baroque or Classic cadenza, within a composition otherwise fixed by the score. Or the composer may specify more or less exactly a series of distinct musical events, leaving their succession partly or wholly unspecified. In such an "open" form,

6. "Indeterminacy" (John Cage's term) covers a wide range of options that allows the composer to leave certain aspects of the music unspecified—from improvisation within a fixed framework to situations where the composer gives only the minimum of directions to the performer. It should not be confused with "chance" or "aleatory" (from the Latin *aleae*, "dice") music, in which the composer (or in some cases the performer) uses chance operations, such as rolling dice or flipping coins, to determine certain aspects of the music, since something determined by chance is not indeterminate.

the performer (soloist, member of a group, or conductor) may either determine the order of the events by choice or be led by means of certain devices into an apparently chance or random order. The performer may also, both within an event and in choosing the order of events, be guided by reactions to what others in the group, or even members of the audience, are doing. In short, the possibilities of indeterminacy, of modes of interaction between freedom and authority, are limitless.

Stockhausen

The European composer who worked most consistently with indeterminacy is Karlheinz Stockhausen (b. 1928). (He was indebted to the American John Cage for stimulating his interest in this medium; see Chapter 22.) A look at two of his compositions may help clarify some of the procedures. The score of *Klavierstück XI* (Piano Piece No. 11; 1956) consists of nineteen short segments of notation displayed on a large sheet (about 37 by 21 inches). These segments can be put together in various ways as the player's eye happens to light on one after another. Certain directions are given for choosing and linking the segments played: not all need be played, and any may be repeated. When in the course of a performance the pianist plays any one segment a third time, the piece ends.

The setup in Stockhausen's *Opus 1970* is a little more complicated. This piece is performed by four players—piano, electric viola, electronium, and tam-tam—and four loudspeakers.

> Material is obtained from a regulating system (radio short waves), selected freely by the player and immediately developed . . . spread, condensed, extended, shortened, differently colored, more or less articulated, transposed, modulated, multiplied, synchronized. . . . The players imitate and vary, adhering to the sequence of development specified by the score. . . . As a regulating system each of the four players has a magnetophone [tape recorder] on which, for the whole of the recording period, a tape, prepared differently for each of the players, continuously reproduces fragments of music by Beethoven. The player opens and shuts the loudspeaker control whenever he wishes.[7]

A new element here is the incorporation of fragments (transformed but immediately recognizable) from Beethoven. Stockhausen had already used borrowed material in similar ways in some of his earlier works, notably the *Gesang der Jünglinge, Telemusik* (1966), and *Hymnen* (1967). *Hymnen* incorporates words and melodies of many different national anthems in a performance combining electronic sounds with voices and instruments. The intention in every instance is, in Stockhausen's words, "not to interpret, but to hear familiar, old, preformed musical material with new ears, to penetrate and transform it with a musical consciousness of today." This aim represents a new way of relating music of the present to that of the past. "Quotation" music is also exemplified in works by George Rochberg, Lukas Foss, and Ellen Taaffe

7. Wilfried Daenicke: from liner notes, DGG 139-461 SLPM.

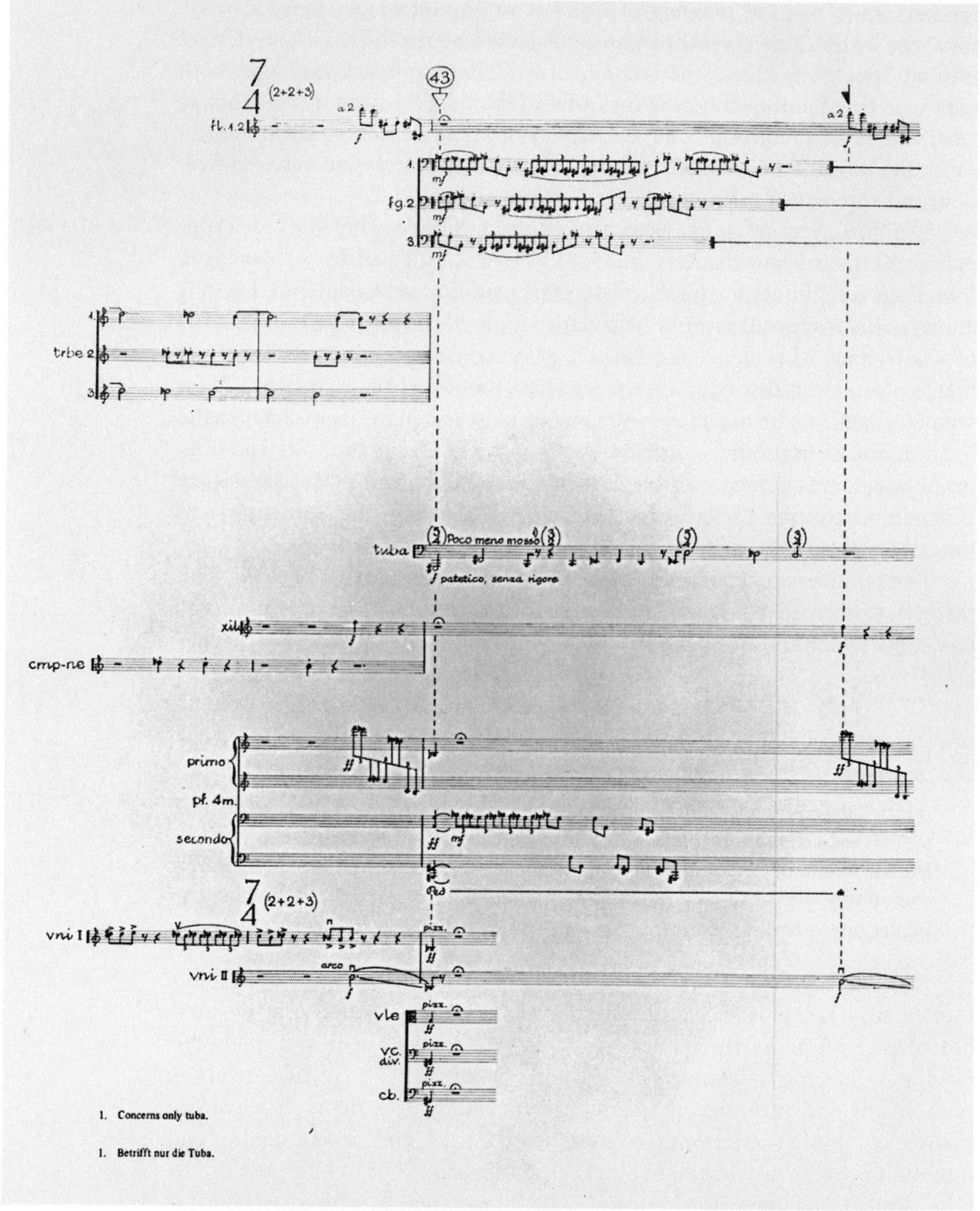

■ *Witold Lutosławski, Symphony No. 3 (1983), p. 46. The composer employed a full arrowhead to indicate when the conductor should signal the entire orchestra to play together. The half-arrowhead marks a signal to selected* ad libitum *players. The music written in regular measures, such as that for the three trumpets, is governed by the conventional correspondence of parts; the music written without bars is played freely with respect to durations but accurately with respect to pitches.*

Zwilich (see NAWM 150) in America (see Chapter 22), Peter Maxwell Davies in England, and Hans Werner Henze (b. 1926) in Germany.

Lutosławski

The Polish composer Witold Lutosławski (1913–1994) made selective use of indeterminacy. A graduate in composition and piano of the Warsaw Conservatory, he was deeply influenced by Bartók in his own early folkloristic works. Later he briefly adopted a personal version of the twelve-tone serial method. With *Venetian Games* (1961), he began to give some leeway to performers, while insisting very much on his own authorship of the entire composition. In his String Quartet (1964), for example, the players begin a section together, but each plays a pitch-determined part in the notated rhythm independently, without a coordinated tempo or meter, introducing ritards, and accelerations as individual expressive interpretations, until the next checkpoint is reached. Then, at a signal from one of the players, they begin again together. Performances of such a short section may differ hardly at all.

In Symphony No. 2 (1966–67) a similar procedure is used, except that the conductor signals the beginning of each section. The result is a series of harmonically static blocks, since the composer limits the players to a small set of pitches for each section. Symphony No. 3 (1983) applies this method with great subtlety and art. *Ad libitum* sections permit the individual orchestral player to dwell upon a figure or develop a motive in the manner of a soloist playing a cadenza (see the facsimile on facing page). At times, eight stands of violins, guided by the prescribed pitches but only approximate durations, go their own way like tendrils of a vine, each scaling its own adventurous peak. These passages achieve a freedom and eloquence hardly possible through precise notation. The symphony consists of two movements, the first of which is preceded by an introduction, the second followed by an epilogue and coda. The first movement consists of three episodes, each slower than the previous one. The work begins and ends with a motto of four rapid hammer strokes on the pitch *E* in the clarinets, brass, and percussion, and this motto recurs to demarcate some of the key points in the form, such as the end of the introduction, the beginning of the second and third episodes, and the beginning of the second movement, where the motto is immediately repeated eight times.

One by-product of indeterminacy is the variety of new kinds of notation. Scores range all the way from fragments of conventional staff notes through purely graphic suggestions of melodic curves, dynamic ranges, rhythms, and the like to even more slippery and meager directives. One main consequence of indeterminacy is that no two performances of a piece are identical. The difference, whether small or great, between one performance and another is not merely a matter of interpretation but a substantive difference in musical content and order of presentation. A recording of such a work captures only one particular performance. "A composition" comes to mean something unlike the traditional notated work. In effect, a composition does not exist as such, but only as a performance, or as the sum of possible performances.

BIBLIOGRAPHY

For Further Reading

GENERAL

See the Bibliography for Chapter 20.

INDIVIDUAL COMPOSERS

Berg John D. Headlam, *The Music of Alban Berg* (New Haven: Yale University Press, 1996); Douglas Jarman, *The Music of Alban Berg* (Berkeley: University of California Press, 1979); Mosco Carner, *Alban Berg: The Man and the Work*, 2nd ed. (New York: Holmes & Meier, 1983); David Gable and Robert P. Morgan, eds., *Alban Berg: Historical and Analytical Perspectives* (Oxford: Clarendon Press, 1991); George Perle, *The Operas of Alban Berg*, 2 vols. (Berkeley: University of California Press, 1980–85); Janet Schmalfeldt, *Berg's Wozzeck: Harmonic Language and Dramatic Design* (New Haven: Yale University Press, 1983); *The Berg-Schoenberg Correspondence*, ed. and trans. Juliane Brand, Christopher Hailey, and Donald Harris (New York: Norton, 1986); Douglas Jarman, ed., *The Berg Companion* (Boston: Northeastern University Press, 1990); Bryan R. Simms, *Alban Berg: A Guide to Research* (New York: Garland, 1996); idem, ed., *Schoenberg, Berg, and Webern: A Companion to the Second Viennese School*, (Westport, Conn: Greenwood Press, 1999).

Boulez His writings include *Notes of an Apprenticeship*, trans. Herbert Weinstock (New York: Knopf, 1968), two passages of which are in GLHWM 10; *Boulez on Music Today*, trans. Susan Bradshaw and Richard Rodney Bennett (Cambridge, Mass.: Harvard University Press, 1971); *Orientations: Collected Writings*, ed. Jean-Jacques Nattiez, trans. Martin Cooper (Cambridge, Mass.: Harvard University Press, 1986); and *The Boulez-Cage Correspondence*, ed. J. J. Nattiez, trans. Robert Samuels (Cambridge: Cambridge University Press, 1993). Paul Griffiths, *Boulez*, Oxford Studies of Composers (London: Oxford University Press, 1979); Dominique Jameux, *Pierre Boulez*, trans. S. Bradshaw (London: Faber & Faber, 1991); *Pierre Boulez: A Symposium*, ed. William Glock (London: Eulenburg, 1986).

Ligeti Paul Griffiths, *György Ligeti* (London: Robson Books, 1983); Robert W. Richart, *György Ligeti: A Bio-bibliography* (New York: Greenwood, 1990).

Lutosławski Steven Stucky, *Lutosławski and His Music* (Cambridge: Cambridge University Press, 1981); Charles B. Rae, *Music of Lutosławski*, exp. 3rd ed. (London: Omnibus Press, 1999); Tadeusz Kaczynski, *Conversations with Witold Lutosławski* (London: J. & W. Chester, 1984).

Messiaen His *The Technique of My Musical Language* (Paris: A. Leduc, 1956). Roger Nichols, *Messiaen* (Oxford: Oxford University Press, 1985); Claude Samuel, *Oliver Messiaen: Music and Color*, trans. E. Thomas Glasow (Portland: Amadeus, 1994); Madeleine Forte, *Oliver Messiaen, the Musical Mediator* (Madison, N.J.: Farleigh Dickinson University Press, 1996); Carla Huston Bell, *Olivier Messiaen* (Boston: Twayne, 1984); Robert S. Johnson, *Messiaen* (Berkeley: University of California Press, 1980); Paul Griffiths, *Olivier Messiaen and the Music of Time* (Ithaca, N.Y.: Cornell University Press, 1985); Peter Hill, ed., *The Messiaen Companion* (Portland: Amadeus, 1995).

Penderecki Wolfram Schwinger, *Krzysztof Penderecki: His Life and Works*, trans. William Mann (London: Schott, 1989); Ray Robinson, *Krzysztof Penderecki: A Guide to His Works* (Princeton: Prestige, 1983).

Schoenberg His essays, *Style and Idea: Selected Writings*, exp. edition, ed. Leonard Stein, trans. Leo Black (Berkeley and Los Angeles: University of California Press, 1984), and his *Letters*, ed. Erwin Stein (London: Faber & Faber, 1964). Carl Dahlhaus, *Schoenberg and the New Music*, trans. Derrick Puffett and Alfred Clayton (Cambridge: Cambridge University Press, 1987); Walter Frisch, ed., *Schoenberg and His World* (Princeton: Princeton University Press, 1999); *Constructive Dissonance: Arnold Schoenberg and the Transformations of Twentieth-Century Culture*, ed. Juliane Brand and Christopher Hailey (Berkeley: University of California Press, 1997); Willi Reich, *Schoenberg, a Critical Biography*, trans. Leo Black (New York: Praeger, 1971); René Leibowitz, *Schoenberg and His School*, trans. Dika Newlin (New York: Philosophical Library, 1949; rep., 1975); Ethan Haimo, *Schoenberg's Serial Odyssey: The Evolution of His Twelve-Tone Method, 1914–1928* (Oxford: Clarendon Press, 1990); Charles Rosen, *Arnold Schoenberg* (Chicago: University of Chicago Press, 1996); Joan A. Smith, *Schoenberg and His Circle: A Viennese Portrait* (New York: Schirmer, 1986); Benjamin Boretz and Edward Cone, eds., *Perspectives on Schoenberg and Stravinsky* (New York: Norton, 1972) has articles from the periodical *Perspectives of New Music.* The complete works appear in *Sämtliche Werke*, ed. Josef Rufer and Carl Dahlhaus (Mainz: B. Schott; Vienna: Universal, 1966–85); see also Rufer, *The Works of Arnold Schoenberg: A Catalogue of His Compositions, Writings, and Paintings*, trans. Dika Newlin (London: Faber & Faber, 1962).

Stockhausen His *Stockhausen on Music: Lectures and Interviews*, ed. Robin Maconie (London: Marion Boyars, 1989). Jonathan Cott, *Stockhausen: Conversations with the Composer* (New York: Simon & Schuster, 1973); Robin Maconie, *The Works of Karlheinz Stockhausen* (London: Oxford University Press, 1990); Jonathan Harvey, *The Music of Stockhausen* (Berkeley and Los Angeles: University of California Press, 1975); Karl H. Wörner, *Stockhausen*, trans. Bill Hopkins (Berkeley: University of California Press, 1973).

Webern His *The Path to New Music*, trans. Leo Black (Bryn Mawr, Pa.: Presser, 1963), and *Letters*, ed. Josef Polnauer, trans. Cornelius Cardew (Bryn Mawr, Pa.: Presser, 1967). Allen Forte, *The Atonal Music of Anton Webern* (New Haven: Yale University Press 1998); Kathryn Bailey, *The Life of Webern* (Cambridge: Cambridge University Press, 1998); Malcolm Hayes. *Anton von Webern* (London: Phaidon, 1995); Hans and Rosaleen Moldenhauer, *Anton von Webern* (New York: Knopf, 1979); Zoltan Roman, *Anton von Webern: An Annotated Bibliography* (Detroit: Information Coordinators, 1983).

CHAPTER 22

THE AMERICAN TWENTIETH CENTURY

The United States led the production of new music in the second half of the twentieth century. The number of art music composers—Americans by birth or choice—the volume, strength, and originality of their creative output, and the important fresh directions nurtured made America the center for new musical developments in this period.

Twentieth-century American art music was in large measure an extension of European music, and in the second half of the century many of Europe's leading composers for political, professional, or personal reasons spent a significant proportion of their creative years in the United States. The most prominent were Bartók, Hindemith, Stravinsky, Schoenberg, Varèse, Weill, Stefan Wolpe (1902–1972), Bohuslav Martinů (1890–1959), Krenek, and Milhaud; others, including Dallapiccola, Berio, Penderecki, and Boulez, paid shorter visits. Hindemith, Schoenberg, Milhaud, Dallapiccola, Wolpe, and Berio had a host of American pupils, though it would be wrong to say that they founded "schools" of composition. One of the forums where American and European composers interacted was the Berkshire (now Tanglewood) Music Center in western Massachusetts. Each summer since 1940, the Center awarded scholarships to promising young composers and brought to the Berkshires eminent figures from inside and outside the country to teach.

Starting in the 1920s a steady stream of Americans went to Europe to study composition, many with Nadia Boulanger, who continued her classes in Paris and Fontainebleau until her death in 1979 at the age of ninety-two. Among those who studied with her were Aaron Copland, Virgil Thomson, Roy Harris, Walter Piston, Ross Lee Finney, Elliott Carter, and Philip Glass. These exchanges contributed to the Europeanization of American music.

In other ways American music in the twentieth century remained true to the traditions of its colonial and indigenous past and to the multicultural ethnic mix that was only partly European. Protestant psalmody and hymnody; British folk and popular songs; African and African-American spiritual songs, rhythms, and textures; ragtime, blues, jazz, swing, wind-band music, country music, cowboy songs, rock, musical comedy songs, and sentimental ballads—these are some of the strains that have made America's music recognizably different from that of other continents. A brief review of these traditions will shed light on the art music we will be studying.

THE HISTORICAL BACKGROUND

Music in the Colonies

The earliest documented music-making in the North American colonies is the singing of psalms. The very first book printed in North America was the

Virgil Thomson, Walter Piston, Herbert Elwell, and Aaron Copland at the home of Nadia Boulanger (inset), June 1926, before a concert of works by young American composers. Elwell, less famous than the other three, was head of composition and theory at the Cleveland Institute of Music and music critic of the Cleveland Plain Dealer *(1932–64).* (PHOTO BY THERÈSE BONNEY. VIRGIL THOMSON PAPERS, YALE UNIVERSITY MUSIC LIBRARY. BOULANGER PORTRAIT COURTESY OF LOUISE TALMA)

Bay Psalm Book

Bay Psalm Book (*The Whole Booke of Psalmes Faithfully Translated into English Metre*), published in Boston in 1640. Although it contained no music, the book directed that the 150 psalms, translated by a committee of New England Puritans, were to be sung. In fact, the ninth edition of 1698 furnished thirteen melodies for this purpose. Congregations were taught and encouraged to read notes and not to depend simply on rote learning. The singing schools established in the eighteenth century, often by itinerant masters, trained a core of amateurs to sing psalm settings and anthems in parts. The availability of such singers became an invitation for composers to write new music.

Billings

William Billings (1746–1800), the most prominent of these composers, left a significant body of music and writings. His *The New-England Psalm-Singer* (1770) contains 108 psalm and hymn settings and 15 anthems and canons for chorus. He issued several more collections, including *The Continental Harmony* in 1794. Most of Billings's settings were "plain tunes," that is, homophonic four-part harmonizations of his newly invented melodies, such as the famous *Chester*, a patriotic song for which he also wrote the text. But his later collections showed a preference for "fuging tunes." These usually open with a syllabic and homophonic section, then one voice begins a florid melody and the others follow in free imitation; the piece closes with voices joined once again in homophony. Billings defended the form in his introduction to *The Continental Harmony* (see vignette, page 744).

Billings declared his independence from the normal rules of counterpoint, claiming that he had devised a set of rules better suited to his aims and method. Indeed, his settings, as exemplified in the fuging tune *Washington Street* (see facsimile), exhibit numerous parallel fifths and octaves (for exam-

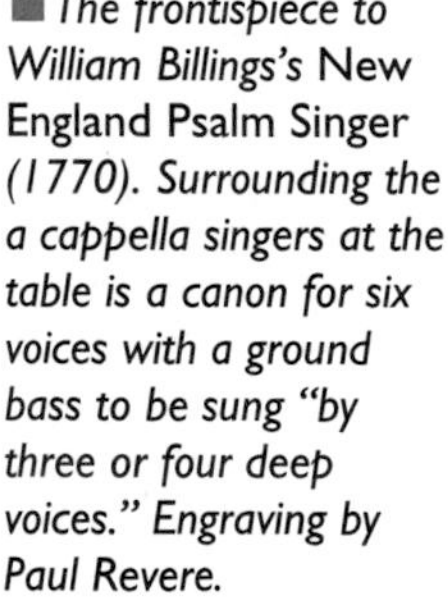

■ *The frontispiece to William Billings's* New England Psalm Singer *(1770). Surrounding the a cappella singers at the table is a canon for six voices with a ground bass to be sung "by three or four deep voices." Engraving by Paul Revere.*

■ Washington-Street, *arranged by William Billings in* The Continental Harmony *(Boston: Isaiah Thomas and Ebenezer T. Andrews, 1794). After a mainly note-against-note opening, a single voice begins a series of entrances in free imitation, or "fuging style."* (YALE UNIVERSITY MUSIC LIBRARY)

ple, measures 1–2, 3, 3–4, 5, 6, 7, and 10), as well as chords without thirds (measures 5, 8, and 11). Other hymns are spiced with unconventional dissonances. The rugged character of the music matches the colorful and eccentric personality revealed in Billings's writings (see vignette). Other composers who contributed to the Yankee tunebooks—for example, Daniel Read (1757–1836), Andrew Law (1748–1821), and Supply Belcher (1752–1836)—either followed his lead or were similarly inclined.

Read, Law, and Belcher

Immigration and Its Influences

Outside New England, diverse immigrant groups brought with them or later imported elements of their religious and secular music. Most notable were the Moravians, German-speaking Protestants from Moravia and Bohemia, the regions of Austria-Hungary that eventually became the Czech and Slovak Republics. They settled in Bethlehem (Pennsylvania), Salem (North Carolina), and surrounding areas. Embellishing their church services with concerted arias and motets, Moravians also collected substantial libraries of imported music, which fostered chamber-music making. Johannes Herbst (1735–1812), who came to Pennsylvania in 1786 and served as a pastor in Lancaster, Lititz, and Salem, wrote hundreds of sacred songs and anthems. Anthony Philip Heinrich (1781–1861), a German-Bohemian active in secular rather than church music, led the first known American performance of a Beethoven symphony and became widely known for his idiosyncratic programmatic works, some of them utilizing Native American themes or quoting popular and patriotic tunes.

Moravians

Herbst

Heinrich

Immigration from Germany intensified after the 1848 Revolution, and crop failures there caused many musicians and music teachers to leave. Germans and Americans who had studied in Germany dominated the teaching of composition and music theory in conservatories and universities. Hermann Kotzschmar, a refugee from Germany who settled in Portland, Maine,

WILLIAM BILLINGS ON THE VIRTUES OF THE FUGING TUNE

It is well known that there is more variety in one piece of fuging music, than in twenty pieces of plain song, for while the tones do most sweetly coincide and agree, the words are seemingly engaged in a musical warfare; and excuse the paradox if I further add, that each part seems determined by dint of harmony and strength of accent, to drown his competitor in an ocean of harmony, and while each part is thus mutually striving for mastery, and sweetly contending for victory, the audience are most luxuriously entertained, and exceedingly delighted; in the mean time, their minds are surprizingly agitated, and extremely fluctuated; sometimes declaring in favour of one part, and sometimes another.

From William Billings, Introduction to *The Continental Harmony* (Boston: I. Thomas and E. T. Andrews, 1794; facsimile reprint, ed. Hans Nathan, Cambridge, Mass.: Belknap Press of Harvard University Press, 1961), p. 28n.

Paine

Damrosch

in 1848, taught organ and composition to John Knowles Paine (1839–1906), who became a prominent composer and organist and Harvard's first professor of music. Paine also spent four years in Berlin, one of almost forty American organ pupils of Karl August Haupt. Leopold Damrosch, conductor of the Breslau (Wrocław) Philharmonic, came to New York in 1871 and within a few years founded the Oratorio Society and the Symphony Society. His son Walter Damrosch succeeded him as the conductor of both groups and became a leader in radio broadcasting of orchestral music and in music education.

Mason

Lowell Mason (1792–1872), one of the most influential of the German-educated musicians, was born of a musical family in Medfield, Massachusetts. He was a partner in a dry-goods firm in Savannah, Georgia, when he began studying music with Frederick Abel, who had just come from Germany. Mason became president of the Boston Handel and Haydn Society in 1827 and led the founding in 1833 of the Boston Academy of Music, dedicated to the musical instruction of children. He deplored the crude music of the Yankee tunesmiths, leaning rather toward a correct and modest European style, in which he composed some 1,200 original hymn tunes as well as arrangements of others. Even today, many Protestant hymnals contain more than a dozen of his melodies and arrangements. As superintendent of music for the public schools of Boston, he introduced music into the regular curriculum, prompting other cities to follow suit.

Shape-note publications

While Mason was reforming New England hymnody, the Yankee tunes were kept alive in the south, transcribed into various shape-note notations (for example, *fa*, △; *sol*, ○; *la*, □; *mi*, ◇) in collections such as *Kentucky Harmony* (1816), *The Southern Harmony* (1835), and *The Sacred Harp* (1844). The last included some spiritual songs and others used in Southern revival meetings.

The thirteen colonies, 1789

So-called Negro spirituals, although they had a pre–Civil War history, were not published until after the war, when *Slave Songs of the United States* (1867) appeared. The Fisk Jubilee Singers of the all-black Fisk University in Nashville, Tennessee, popularized these songs in the 1870s through their polished and enthusiastic performances in concert tours on both sides of the Atlantic.

New England continued to be a center of creative music in the generation after John Knowles Paine, partly through his Harvard composition students, among them John Alden Carpenter (1876–1951), Frederick S. Converse (1871–1940), Arthur Foote (1853–1937), and Daniel Gregory Mason (1873–1953). A piano prodigy of her time, Amy Marcy Cheney turned her focus to compositon after her marriage to another Harvard professor. Signing her works from then on "Mrs. H. H. A. Beach," Amy Cheney Beach cut out most concertizing. She had little formal training in composition but taught herself by studying both the standard texts and the music of leading eighteenth- and nineteenth-century composers. Her songs, which number about 120, were widely performed, as was her Quintet for Piano and Strings. The Boston Symphony premiered both her piano concerto and her symphony.

Beach's Quintet for Piano and Strings received its first performance—Beach at the piano with the Hoffmann Quartet—in Boston on February 27, 1908; it was published the following year. She based the themes of the first and third movements on the second theme of the last movement of Brahms's Piano Quintet, Op. 34, which she had played with the Kneisel Quartet in 1900. Beach's individual voice emerges forcefully in the third (last) movement (NAWM 140; CD 12 [6]), breaking from the Brahmsian influence evident in the first movement. Its rich harmony, rooted in late nineteenth-century chromatic progressions, ventures into unusual inversions, augmented triads, and

The original Fisk Jubilee Singers, photographed in London, 1873, during their European tour. Founded at Fisk University in Nashville, Tennessee, the group consisted of black student musicians who performed spirituals and other songs in four-part harmony. Their example inspired other "jubilee" groups to form. (SCHOMBURG CENTER, THE NEW YORK PUBLIC LIBRARY, ASTOR, LENOX AND TILDEN FOUNDATIONS)

Example 22.1 *Amy Beach,* Quintet for Piano and Strings: *Allegro agitato*

colorful non-chord tones. The most characteristic element in the movement is the upward leap of the minor ninth and the augmented second of the main theme (Example 22.1).

Brass and Wind Bands

The instrumental counterparts of the singing schools were the town, village, and school bands. The earliest of these became attached to military units, but in the nineteenth century local bands cropped up everywhere, and no parade was complete without one or more. Among the most important were the Repasz Band of Williamsport, Pennsylvania, founded in 1831, the Salem (North Carolina) Brass Band, and the Boston Brass Band. In 1869 the Boston conductor Patrick S. Gilmore (1829–1892) led 486 wind and percussion players during a colossal five-day National Peace Jubilee in that city; a hundred choral organizations totaling 10,296 singers took part. The wind band became one of the fixtures of American life; every high school and college had one. By the 1960s there were fifty thousand wind bands in schools throughout the country.

Gilmore

The repertory of early nineteenth-century bands consisted of marches, quicksteps (fast marches), dances including the two-step (in march time), waltzes, polkas, arrangements of songs, such as those by Stephen Foster (1826–1864), and display pieces often scored for special soloists. The most famous of the bandmaster-composers was John Philip Sousa (1854–1932), who in 1880 became leader of the U.S. Marine Band. In 1892 he organized his own band, which toured throughout the world. A highly skilled composer of marches himself, he wrote more than a hundred, including the famous *The Stars and Stripes Forever* (1897). Edwin Franko Goldman (1878–1956), a pupil of Dvořák, also composed many marches and pioneered the training of bandmasters. He and his son, Richard Franko Goldman (1910–1980), acquainted the American public with this repertory and promoted the idea of the summer town-band concert through the nationally broadcast Goldman Band summer series from New York's Central Park.

Sousa

Black musicians

Brass bands, dance orchestras, and black churches were the main training ground for African-American musicians. Black bands occupied an important place in both the black and the white social life in New Orleans, Baltimore, Memphis, Newark, Richmond, Philadelphia, New York, Detroit, Chicago, and other cities early in the twentieth century and even before. Among the leaders

J. R. Europe

who attracted national and international attention were James Reese Europe (1881–1919), Tim Brymn (1881–1946), William H. Tyers (1876–1924), and Ford Dabney (1883–1958). These bands performed from notation and did relatively little improvisation, although they played with a swinging and syncopated style that distinguished them from white bands. Europe's band created a sensation in Paris, and the French Garde Républicaine tried in vain to imitate its sound.

VERNACULAR MUSIC

Ragtime

Syncopation

Joplin

Among the dances played by both the brass and concert bands were pieces in ragtime, sometimes in march-and-trio form. Ragtime apparently originated in the cakewalk, a couples dance marked by strutting and acrobatic movements that was popular in minstrel-show finales. Ragtime prominently featured syncopation against a regular bass rhythm. This syncopation, often involving silence on a downbeat, derived from the "clapping" or "patting" *Juba* of American blacks, a survival of African drumming and hand clapping. The emphasis on off-beats reflects the complex cross-rhythms common in African music. Piano and band pieces identified as cakewalks, "rags," or "ragtime" were first published in the 1890s. The success of *Maple Leaf Rag* (Example 22.2) by Scott Joplin (1868–1917), son of an ex-slave musician, added momentum to the ragtime craze. Soon the syncopated rhythms found their way into the music for ballroom dancing, reflected in new steps such as the turkey trot and the chicken glide, evolving eventually into the most enduring of them, the foxtrot.

Example 22.2 *Scott Joplin,* Maple Leaf Rag

Blues

The dance rhythms derived from ragtime and the syncopated style of the black brass bands were major components of jazz; another was blues. The origin of the blues is obscure. Black singers around 1900 in the rural south—especially in Georgia, Mississippi, and Tennessee—sang laments in a style that later became known as blues. The subject might be the loss of a lover or a job, or simply general depression. The text usually consisted of two-line stanzas, with the first line repeated and the last rhyming with the first. The music used "blue" notes, a slight lowering of the third, seventh, and sometimes the fifth degrees of the major scale. However, the chordal accompaniment, by a guitar, piano, or band, adapted European triadic harmony. Early blues used a variety of period lengths and successions of chords. Eventually the preferred form distributed the tonic, subdominant, and dominant chords over a period of twelve measures, as shown in Example 22.3. The accompanist or instrumental soloist,

Subject

Form

Example 22.3 *W. C. Handy,* St. Louis Blues

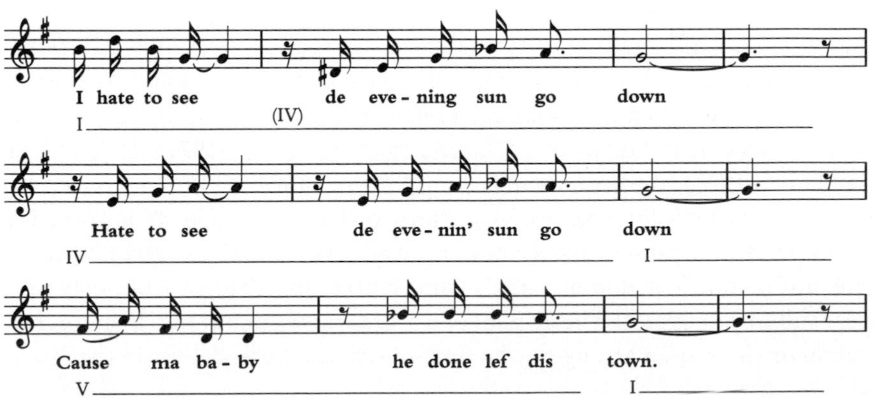

such as a cornet player, usually improvised "breaks" at the ends of lines, and this has been likened to the choral responses of African music. Bessie Smith's rendering of *St. Louis Blues* by W. C. Handy (1873–1958), recorded in 1925 with Louis Armstrong on cornet, exemplifies this style of music and performance.

Jazz

The recognition of jazz as a distinct phenomenon occurred outside the culture in which it grew up. Black musicians in their own circles had been improvising *choruses*, that is, variations on blues tunes. When white orchestras—such as Tom Brown's "Dixieland Jass Band, Direct from New Orleans," which played in Chicago in 1915—began imitating this music, it was evident that a new kind of music had emerged, different from ragtime and blues particularly in the way it was performed. Instead of playing the music "straight," observing the rhythms and textures of the model, players extemporized arrangements that distinguished one musician from another and one performance from another. Listening to famous pianist Ferdinand Joseph (Jelly Roll) Morton (1890–1941) play Joplin's *Maple Leaf Rag*, recorded admittedly late in 1938, we recognize that this is unmistakably jazz and not ragtime because of the anticipations of beats, the swinging, uneven rendering of successions of equal note values (like the *inégales* of French Baroque music), the grace notes, the enriched harmony, and the tiding over of ragtime's choppy motivic units into a more continuous line.

Characteristics

The essence of jazz is improvisation on an existing tune or scheme—it is very much a player's art. Group improvisation, practiced especially in New Orleans, resulted in a counterpoint of improvised melodic lines alternating with improvised solo episodes in which the rest of the ensemble supplied a rhythmic and harmonic background. A typical New Orleans ensemble, such as Joseph (King) Oliver's Creole Jazz Band of the 1920s, consisted of cornet(s), clarinet, trombone, piano, banjo, and drums. In later combos trumpets substituted for the cornets, and saxophones replaced or doubled the clarinet.

Improvisation

Big Bands

The fashion for larger bands that began in the 1920s was propelled partly by the availability of larger performance spaces for jazz: supper clubs, ballrooms, auditoriums, and theaters. White musicians, such as Paul Whiteman (1890–1967) and Benny Goodman (1909–1986), as well as blacks, such as Fletcher Henderson (1898–1952), Louis Armstrong (1901–1971), Duke Ellington (1899–1974), and William (Count) Basie (1904–1984), organized *big bands*, which typically comprised sections of trumpets, one or more trombones, reeds, including saxophones and clarinets, sometimes a violin, and a "rhythm section" of double bass, piano, guitar, and drums. Although solos were still improvised, the basic plan of a piece was written down as an orchestration or *chart* by an arranger, who was sometimes the leader (as in the case of

Band leaders

Chart

■ *King Oliver's Creole Jazz Band, 1923. Left to right: Honoré Dutrey, trombone; Baby Dodds, drums; King Oliver, cornet; Louis Armstrong, slide trumpet; Lil Hardin (later Armstrong), piano; Bill Johnson, banjo; Johnny Dodds, clarinet.* (WM. RANSOM HOGAN JAZZ ARCHIVES, TULANE UNIVERSITY)

Ellington) but more often a member of the band or a skilled orchestrator. For example, Henderson arranged for Goodman both before and after his own band broke up. In addition to instrumental pieces, which were jazz-oriented, more and more of the big-band repertory was taken over by popular songs in which the band both accompanied a singer and elaborated on the song through clever, harmonically adventurous arrangements that featured one or another of the band's sections. The arrangers and leaders, modeling their style on the black bands, developed a swinging manner that led to their music being called *swing*. It was intended for dancing as well as casual listening, but some ambitious compositions commanded an attentive audience, such as Ellington's *Mood Indigo* (1930) or his *Concerto for Cootie* (1940).

Modern Jazz

Bebop

While the big-band arrangements and the thoroughly scored jazz compositions downplayed one of the most essential elements of jazz, improvisation, the *bebop* or *bop* style of the 1940s and 1950s and the freer idioms of jazz that followed it inspired a kind of music that was planned in advance but realized in largely improvised performance. Bebop and post-bop styles often were not based on standard songs but on newly created music. Bebop admitted techniques that were outside the common vocabulary of popular music; some of these techniques were borrowed from classical music—non-chordal dissonance, chromaticism, complicated and conflicting rhythms that were not danceable, irregular phrase structures, modality, atonality, and unaccustomed instrumental effects. Performances in which one of the players was essentially the composer are preserved on recordings that have become classics, listened to over and over again, analyzed, and reviewed in critical essays. Some of the composer-performers were

Composer-performers

trumpeters John Birks (Dizzy) Gillespie (1917–1993) and Miles Davis (1926–1991), saxophonists Charlie (Bird) Parker (1920–1955), John Coltrane (1926–1967), and Ornette Coleman (b. 1930), and pianists Thelonious Monk (1917–1982), Bill Evans (1929–1980), and Cecil Taylor (b. 1933). They and many others created music that demands attentive listeners.

Country Music

While jazz got its start in cities, rural areas nurtured other kinds of music. One of these, the hillbilly-country music of the southeast, was at first based on traditional narrative and lyrical Anglo-American ballads and fiddle tunes. Partly through commercial sponsorship of the recording and broadcast industry, hillbilly combined with the western cowboy themes and manners popularized by the Texan Gene Autry, to produce *country-and-western*, often called *country* music. Typically the singer strummed the accompaniment on the guitar. Bands were later formed to support the singers, but, unlike the big bands that inspired them, these groups were dominated by violins and guitars (eventually electric and pedal steel-guitars) rather than trumpets and saxophones. The band also adapted some of the practices of jazz, notably its driving and syncopated rhythms and virtuoso improvisations. A different approach was taken by Roy Acuff, whose weekly radio show from Nashville in the 1940s, *Grand Ole Opry*, promoted conservative religious sentiments. Out of this background emerged two country-and-western stars of the 1960s, Hank Williams and Johnny Cash.

Rhythm-and-Blues

The urban black counterpart to this music was called by the music trade *rhythm-and-blues*, a term that embraces a variety of genres common in the post–World War II years. The most characteristic of these is performed by small groups consisting of a vocalist or vocal quartet, a piano, organ, or electric guitar, string or electric bass, and drums. It is distinguished from traditional blues by an insistent rhythm, with emphasis on the second and fourth beats—the backbeats—whining treble guitar, mannered articulation of the lyrics, and repetitive amplified bass line. *Hound Dog* (1952) by Willie Mae (Big Mama) Thornton (1926–1984) received wide recognition through the version recorded by Elvis Presley (1935–1977) in 1956.

Rock-and-Roll

The two guitar-dominated genres just described merged during the 1950s into the popular interracial movement originally called *rock-and-roll* and later shortened to *rock*. This music was launched in the 1955 film *Blackboard Jungle* with the hit song *Rock around the Clock* by Bill Haley (1925–1981). It had the unrelenting beat of rhythm-and-blues and the milder guitar background of

Haley

country-and-western. Elvis Presley enjoyed phenomenal success in the late 1950s and early 1960s with a southern, insinuating version of this amalgamation. The instrumentation of rock-and-roll consisted of amplified or electric guitars for both rhythm and melody, with saxophone inserting jazzlike rejoinders. Additional harmony, rhythmic effects, and ostinatos were supplied by an organ or synthesizer. The texts, most often concerned with sex, were delivered in an explosive, raucous, sometimes wailing, shrieking, or shouting voice, though there were also gentle ballads, often about teenage love, sung in a deliberately subdued mode. An eclectic version of the idiom developed by the British quartet The Beatles achieved unprecedented success starting in 1964, when they first toured the United States. The group included two creative songwriters, John Lennon (1940–1980) and Paul McCartney (b. 1942), who continued on their own after The Beatles broke up in 1970.

Musical Comedy

The Broadway musical or *musical comedy* reflected the fashions popular at any given time and supplied new songs for adaptation. The genre differed in important ways from other plays with songs, such as the ballad opera, opéra comique, Singspiel, or operetta. The production and the plot were built around the songs, vocal ensembles, and dances, all of which determined the success or failure of the enterprise. Although George M. Cohan (1878–1942) wrote the music for his own lyrics and plays, and Cole Porter (1891–1964) wrote his own witty lyrics, most shows were *ad hoc* collaborations or products of long-standing teams. For example, Richard Rodgers (1902–1979) collaborated with the lyricist Lorenz Hart (1895–1943) and later with Oscar Hammerstein II (1895–1960); Frederick Loewe (1904–1988) wrote music for the books and lyrics of Alan Jay Lerner (1918–1986). In 1944 a young assistant conductor—who became an overnight celebrity after brilliantly directing the New York Philharmonic during Bruno Walter's illness—saw his Broadway musical *On the Town* open the same year for a run of 463 performances. This was Leonard Bernstein (1910–1990), who was to enjoy one of his greatest popular successes and creative achievements in *West Side Story* (1957), with lyrics by Stephen Sondheim (b. 1930).

Cohan

Rodgers, Loewe

Bernstein

Although these successful shows consisted of many components, including stage sets, choreography, costumes, and lighting designs, in most cases the music and the lyrics are all that have survived (apart from cinematic versions of a few shows like *Oklahoma, My Fair Lady*, and *West Side Story*). It is easy to forget that *Smoke Gets in Your Eyes* and *All the Things You Are* by Jerome Kern (1885–1945), two "standards" for jazz improvisation, are taken from theater pieces, the first from *Roberta* (1933), the second from *Very Warm for May* (1939), among the thousand or so creations that he left. Similarly, an even larger number by Irving Berlin (1888–1989), including *A Pretty Girl Is Like a Melody*, from *Ziegfeld Follies of 1919*, are from Broadway shows. George Gershwin (1898–1937), who began as a songwriter rather than a theater person, by 1924 had three hits on lyrics by his brother Ira in the show *Lady, Be*

Kern

Berlin

Gershwin

■ *A year after its premiere at the Winter Garden Theater in New York in 1957,* West Side Story *was produced in London. This scene, from that production, shows the battle between the two gangs, the white Jets and the Puerto Rican Sharks. Tony, a former leader of the Jets, is in love with the Puerto Rican Maria. The music by Leonard Bernstein, with lyrics by Stephen Sondheim, is often heard in concerts.* (LONDON, MANDER AND MITCHESON THEATRE COLLECTION)

Good: the title song, *Fascinating Rhythm*, and *The Man I Love*. Gershwin's *Porgy and Bess* (1935), which he called a folk opera, has been produced both as a musical and as an opera, erasing the boundary between so-called popular or vernacular on the one hand, and classical or cultivated traditions on the other. In the same way, his *Rhapsody in Blue* (1924) bridged the gulf between popular music and the concert hall by combining the languages of jazz and Lisztian Romanticism.

FOUNDATIONS FOR AN AMERICAN ART MUSIC

Charles Ives

Career

Charles Ives (1874–1954) was the first distinctively American art-music composer to gain eminence. He studied with his father, a bandmaster and church musician, and at Yale with Horatio Parker (1863–1919). Thus his musical training was solid, both before Yale and during his time there, when he also served as organist at Centre Church in New Haven. But his esthetic aims failed to coincide with those of the musical establishment, so, he went to work in a relative's insurance business, later starting his own firm. Public recognition of

TIMELINE: WORLD WAR II AND AFTER

1940 1950 1960 1970 1980 1990 2000

- 1939–1945 World War II
- **1944 Copland, *Appalachian Spring***
- **1945 Britten, *Peter Grimes***
- 1949 Arthur Miller, *Death of a Salesman*
- 1950–53 Korean War
- **1951 Cage, *Music of Changes***
- **1955 Boulez, *Le Marteau sans maître***
- **1956 Stockhausen, *Gesang der Jünglinge***
- **1957 Bernstein, *West Side Story***
- 1957 Orbit of first Sputnik
- **1959 Carter, *Second String Quartet***
- **1959 Schuller, *Seven Studies on Themes of Paul Klee***
- **1960 Penderecki, *Threnody for the Victims of Hiroshima***
- **1961 Earle Brown, *Available Forms I***
- 1962 Vatican Council II
- 1963 U.S. president John F. Kennedy assassinated
- **1964 Babbitt, *Philomel***
- 1967 The Beatles, *Sergeant Pepper's Lonely Hearts Club Band*
- 1968 Martin Luther King, Jr., assassinated
- 1968 U.S.S.R. invades Czechoslovakia
- 1969 Astronauts walk on the moon
- **1969 Messiaen, *Méditations sur la mystère de la Sainte Trinté***
- 1969 Woodstock rock festival
- **1970 Crumb, *Black Angels***
- 1973 End of U.S. involvement in Vietnam
- 1974 U.S. president Richard Nixon resigns
- **1976 Glass, *Einstein on the Beach***
- 1977 *Star Wars*
- 1979 Premiere of completed *Lulu* by Berg
- ***1980 The New Grove Dictionary of Music and Musicians***
- **1981 Gubaidulina, *Rejoice!***
- 1981 Sandra Day O'Connor appointed first woman justice, U.S. Supreme Court
- **1983 Zwilich, first woman to receive Pulitzer Prize in Music**
- 1985 Compact disc becomes favored format
- **1987 John Adams, *Nixon in China***
- 1990 East and West Germany reunited
- 1991 Dissolution of the U.S.S.R.
- **1991 Corigliano, *The Ghosts of Versailles***
- **1999 Harbison, *The Great Gatsby***

Ives's musical achievements came only in the 1930s, many years after he had created, in isolation and apparently without models, a body of highly original works. Mostly unperformed and unpublished during his lifetime, his pieces anticipated some of the radical developments of twentieth-century music: free dissonance, polytonality, polyrhythm, and experimental form. Almost all were written between 1890 and 1922, and they include some two hundred songs, five violin sonatas and other chamber music, two piano sonatas, five symphonies, and other orchestral music.

Concord, Mass., 1840–60

His most famous work was the second piano sonata, *Concord, Mass., 1840–60* (1916–19), which he published privately with a book of essays in 1920. There he described its musical content succinctly:

> The whole is an attempt to present (one person's) impression of the spirit of transcendentalism that is associated in the minds of many with Concord, Massachusetts, of over a half century ago. This is undertaken in impressionistic pictures of Emerson and Thoreau, a sketch of the Alcotts, and a *scherzo* supposed to reflect a lighter quality which is often found in the fantastic side of Hawthorne. The first and last movements do not aim to give any programs of the life or of any particular work of either Emerson or Thoreau, but, rather, composite pictures or impressions.[1]

Use of existing music

Conventional and unconventional elements stand side by side in Ives's works or are mingled—in John Kirkpatrick's phrase—"with a transcendentalist's faith in the unity behind all diversity." Fragments of folksongs, dance tunes, gospel hymns as well as motives from Beethoven and Bach emerge from a complex, uniquely ordered flow of sound.

The borrowed material was not simply quotation in an allusive sense but most often the very starting point and basis of a composition.[2] Ives sometimes modeled a work or movement on an existing piece, such as a song or hymn, identifying the model by quoting some part of it but then following its structure in a subtler way. Or he paraphrased and transformed a borrowed melody into a new personal version. Often he first quoted fragments of a tune, then gradually pieced together a full statement. Two or more familiar tunes were sometimes strung together or sounded simultaneously in a humorous, surprising, or shocking way. Ives also quoted tunes in the ordinary way, to allude to or support a text he was using or to illustrate an extramusical program.

They Are There!

They Are There! (NAWM 141; CD 12 [11] / 4 ⟨48⟩) illustrates several of these techniques. Ives composed the song *He Is There* for unison chorus and orchestra in 1917 to mark the entrance of the United States in World War I, when it joined the Allies (Belgium, Britain, France, Italy, Japan, Montenegro, Russia, and Serbia) in fighting the Central Powers (Austria-Hungary, Germany, and the Ottoman Empire). In 1942, he revised the words to fit the new circumstances of World War II. Rhymed lines paraphrased from patriotic songs occa-

1. C. Ives, Author's Preface, *Essays Before a Sonata and Other Writings*, ed. Howard Boatwright (New York: Norton, 1961), p. xxv.
2. See J. Peter Burkholder, *All Made of Tunes: Charles Ives and the Uses of Musical Borrowing* (New Haven: Yale University Press, 1995), on which this paragraph is based.

CHARLES IVES ON AMERICANISM IN MUSIC

If a man finds that the cadences of an Apache war-dance come nearest to his soul—provided he has taken pains to know enough other cadences, for eclecticism is part of his duty; sorting potatoes means a better crop next year—let him assimilate whatever he finds highest of the Indian ideal so that he can use it with the cadences, fervently, transcendentally, inevitably, furiously, in his symphonies, in his operas, in his whistlings on the way to work, so that he can paint his house with them, make them a part of his prayer-book—this is all possible and necessary, if he is confident that they have a part in his spiritual consciousness. With this assurance, his music will have everything it should of sincerity, nobility, strength, and beauty, no matter how it sounds; and if, with this, he is true to none but the highest of American ideals (that is, the ideals only that coincide with his spiritual consciousness), his music will be true to itself and incidentally American, and it will be so even after it is proved that all our Indians came from Asia.

From "Epilogue," in Charles Ives, *Essays Before a Sonata and Other Writings*, ed. Howard Boatwright (New York: Norton, 1961), pp. 79–80.

sionally ring out, sometimes with the pertinent tune but mostly not. An example is "Tenting in a new camp ground" (misquoting "Tenting on the old camp ground" paired with new music). Similarly, the tunes of patriotic songs leap out of a melodic continuity that has its own logic apart from them. The quotations and misquotations seem less like semi-conscious borrowings than deliberate invocations of familiar songs for their power to add punch to the message, the way vivid images or rhetorical figures do in poetry. The most obvious of such allusions are the opening fragment of *O Columbia, the Gem of the Ocean* in the chorus, immediately followed by the incipit of *Dixie's Land* in the higher woodwinds; and, just before the end, a bit of the *Star-Spangled Banner* in the brass, followed by *Reveille* in the trumpets and flutes.

Influence

Ives's technical procedures were dictated by an uncompromising idealism in the pursuit of his artistic aims, coupled with an extraordinary musical imagination and a biting sense of humor. His work has been of incalculable importance to younger generations of American musicians. He questioned the value of the traditional forms and of thematic unity, setting meter and tonality adrift. He indulged in apparently irrational tone clusters, allowing several independent layers of sound to coexist without a harmonic relationship. He admitted melodies from the sacred and secular, popular and artistic realms as equally valid material for his compositions. He gave performers a chance in certain compositions to choose among several options. In all these departures from the conventional, Ives set an example for later composers, tempting them to cast constraints overboard and to experiment.

Carl Ruggles

Carl Ruggles (1876–1971; see Plate XV, facing page 782), both a friend of Ives and a kindred spirit, was fiercely independent of all influences, including those of the American past. Although conscious of the methods of Schoenberg and Berg, he struck out on an atonal path of his own. His best-known composition, *Sun-Treader* (1926–31) for a large orchestra, is dominated by the tritone and semitone, the latter most often in octave displacements, which makes the music strident, always reaching for new goals.

Henry Cowell

That Henry Cowell (1897–1965) was a Californian is significant, because it shows that the musical frontier had reached the West Coast. He balanced the northeastern composers' European orientation with one that looked inward to the American midwest and outward to Asia. In the 1920s Cowell embarked on a search to obtain new effects from the grand piano. In *The Aeolian Harp* (1923) the strings of the piano are strummed by the player while holding down three- and four-note chords on the keyboard. Soft harplike broken chords emerge, resembling but not as elusive or mysterious as those of the wind-driven Aeolian harp, which was popular in Asia and the United States. In *The Banshee* (1925), an assistant holds the damper pedal down while the pianist plays glissandos with both hands, sometimes in opposite directions, at other times rubbing along the length of the lower, wound string to create an eerie, almost voice-like howl similar to that of a banshee, a spirit in Irish legend.

The Aeolian Harp

Tone clusters

Cowell is remembered most for his tone clusters, which he used in *The Tides of Manaunaun* (1912; Manaunaun was the legendary Irish sea-god), written when he was fifteen, *Advertisements* (1914), and *Piano Piece* (1924). The tone clusters are obtained by striking the keys with the fist or forearm, thereby creating harmonies based on the interval of the second. He later applied them to orchestral music, as in *Some More Music* (1917) and the Piano Concerto (1929).

In his later compositions, Cowell made use of Irish folk music, rural hymns and fuging tunes, non-Western music, and even non-Western instruments such as the Indian tabla and the Japanese koto. Cowell promoted music by his contemporaries as well as his own through the periodical *New Music*, in which he published scores by Ruggles and Ives, among others.

Ruth Crawford Seeger

Cowell also published the works of Ruth Crawford (1901–1953). She was introduced to the circle around Ruggles by the pioneering musicologist Charles Seeger, with whom she studied composition and whom she married in 1931. She was most productive as a composer in Chicago between 1924 and 1929 and in New York between 1930 and 1933. One of her most successful works from the Chicago period was the Violin Sonata (1926; see second movement,

Buoyant, in NAWM 142; CD 12 [14]). In the New York period she experimented with serial techniques, including their application to parameters other than pitch. Her best-known work is the String Quartet of 1931. Later she collaborated with writer Carl Sandburg and folklorists John and Alan Lomax, editing American folksongs from field recordings; she also published many transcriptions and arrangements in which she was faithful to the songs' native contexts.

Edgard Varèse

The French-born Edgard Varèse (1883–1965) moved to New York in 1915 after a short career as a composer as well as a conductor of early and contemporary music in Paris and Prague. Apart from brief sojourns in Europe, he remained in New York for the rest of his life. Varèse celebrated his adopted country in his first major work, *Amériques* (1918–21). Its fragmentary melodies and loose structure betray links to Debussy, whom he knew and who approved of his independent spirit. Even more, *Amériques* points in the direction of Varèse's future work: his concerns with the manipulation of sound masses more than with themes and their development. Next came a series of works that laid down a new agenda: *Offrandes* (1921), *Hyperprism* (1923), *Octandre* (1923), *Intégrales* (1925), *Ionisation* (for percussion only, 1931), and *Ecuatorial* (1934). In these works, Varèse aimed to liberate composition from conventional melody, harmony, meter, regular pulse, recurrent beat, and traditional orchestration. In their place, he envisioned individual and massed instrumental ensembles as the raw material of organized sound. In the compositions of the 1920s, non-pitched percussion sounds and pitches, played mostly by winds, collide, balance, intersect, attract, repel, speed up, slow down, combine, split up, crystallize, diffuse, and expand and contract in range, volume, and timbre. A great variety of percussion instruments, some drawn from non-Western cultures, others, such as the siren, from city life, get key roles in these works, acting independently as equals to the winds and strings.

Intégrales

Two measures from *Intégrales* demonstrate how pitch, duration, register, dynamics, and instrumental color interact (Example 22.4, page 760). The *B♭* has been sounding in the E♭-clarinet from the very first measure of the piece. Now the pitch-classes on either side, *A* and *B*, collide with it in the piccolos, while the *B♭*-clarinet adds an *E♭*. A moment later these sustained tones are simultaneously joined by more semitone intervals in the muted trombones—*C* against the *B*, *E* against the *E♭*—while the ninth *B♭*–B in the woodwinds is confronted and counterpoised by the ninth *C*–*C♯* in the trombones. The E♭-clarinet's *B♭* remains the focus, but relinquishes it soon (in measure 10) to the trumpet, which proceeds to decorate it. Meanwhile, rolls on the tenor drum (*caisse roulante*), strokes on the rim and membrane of the muffled snare drum, and thumb-beats on the tambourine offer their own characteristic versions of the passage of time. Later, a fanfare rudely intrudes, Ives-like, into the athematic surroundings. In this almost constantly explosive, expletive, and exclamatory medium there are few relaxing moments; it is the music of urban

Example 22.4 *Edgard Varèse, Intégrales: Andantino*

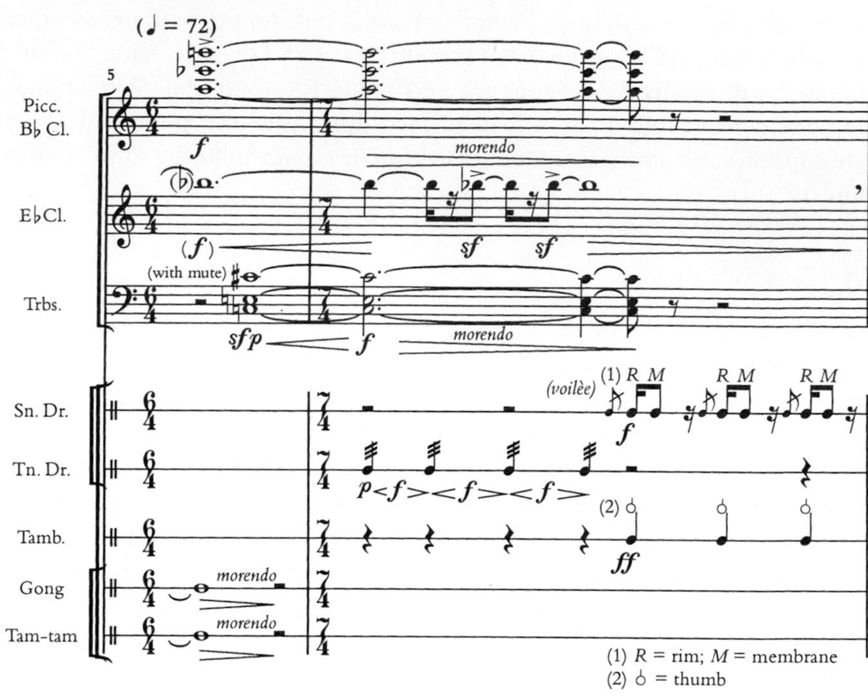

noise and clashes, reflecting the midtown New York scene that Varèse heard and saw from his apartment.

Aaron Copland

Aaron Copland (1900–1990) integrated national American idioms into his music with technical polish. He was the first of many American composers to study with Nadia Boulanger in Paris (see illustration, page 741). Jazz idioms and dissonance figure prominently in some of his earlier works, such as the *Music for the Theater* (1925) and the Piano Concerto (1927). These were followed by compositions of a more reserved and harmonically complex style, including the Piano Variations of 1930. In a desire to appeal to a larger audience, Copland turned toward simplicity, diatonic harmonies, and the use of traditional song—Mexican folksongs in the brilliant orchestral suite *El Salón México* (1936), cowboy songs in the ballets *Billy the Kid* (1938) and *Rodeo* (1942). The school opera *The Second Hurricane* (1937) and scores for a number of films (including *Our Town*, 1940) represent music in this period composed specifically "for use."

Appalachian Spring

The apex of this trend toward simpler music was reached in *Appalachian Spring* (1944), first written as a ballet with an ensemble of thirteen instruments but better known in the arrangement as an orchestral suite (see excerpt in NAWM 143; CD 12 [17] / 4 ⟨51⟩). The work incorporates variations on the Shaker hymn *'Tis the Gift to Be Simple.* The song (NAWM 143a) is subtly transfigured and its essence is absorbed in music that sincerely and simply expresses the pastoral spirit in authentically American terms. The wide spacing of chords and the empty octaves and fifths suggest country fiddling.

Copland's later works encompassed numerous styles. On the one hand, new large-scale synthesis appeared with the Third Symphony (1946), which has no overt program, though some of its tunes are suggestive of folksongs. On the other, the finely wrought chamber-music idiom of the Piano Sonata (1941) evolved from the style of the Piano Variations. In the songs on *Twelve Poems of Emily Dickinson* (1950), and more markedly in the Piano Quartet (1950), the Piano Fantasy (1957), and the orchestral *Inscape* (1967), Copland adopted some features of twelve-tone technique. After 1970 he was more active as a conductor and lecturer than as a composer. Despite the various influences reflected in the range of styles he employed, Copland retained an unmistakable artistic identity. His music preserves a sense of tonality, though not always by traditional means. His rhythms are live and flexible, and he was adept at obtaining new sounds from simple chords by exploiting instrumental color and spacing. Through encouragement, counsel, and by example, he influenced many younger American composers, among them Leonard Bernstein, Lukas Foss, Marc Blitzstein, David Diamond, and David Del Tredici.

Other National Idioms

Harris

A more self-conscious nationalist, Roy Harris (1898–1979) wrote music that suggests at its best (as in the Third Symphony, 1939) something of the rugged simplicity of Walt Whitman's poetry. Some of his works embody actual folk themes—for example, in the choral *Folk Song Symphony*, his fourth of fourteen symphonies (1940). His sweeping modal melodies and transparent counterpoint impart a sense of the expansiveness reminiscent of the American West. His orchestral music sounds American also because of its wind-band scoring. A student of early music, Harris was fond of fugue and ostinato.

Virgil Thomson

Virgil Thomson (1896–1989), a witty and caustic critic as well as a composer, returned to the simplicity of the colonial past and its hymnody in his *Variations and Fugue on Sunday School Tunes* (1926) and the *Symphony on a Hymn Tune* (1928). He spent many years in Paris, and although he studied with Nadia Boulanger, his model became Satie, whom he met in 1922 and whose playfulness, directness, and striving for simplicity he imitated. He found a kindred soul in another American expatriate, Gertrude Stein, whose opera libretto, *Four Saints in Three Acts*, he set in 1928. Its music is a sophisticated tongue-in-cheek mix of Protestant hymns, patriotic tunes, tangos, waltzes, and marches. *The Mother of Us All* (1947), also a collaboration with Stein, is based on the life of the suffragist Susan B. Anthony. The repetitive, stripped-down, triadic accompaniments anticipate the minimalists of the 1970s and 1980s, while the vocal parts reveal an uncanny facility for turning speech into music (see Example 22.5 and vignette on facing page).

Still

William Grant Still (1895–1978) likewise incorporated specifically American idioms in his *Afro-American Symphony* (1931). The opening movement, in sonata form, has a first theme in twelve-bar blues structure. The third movement (NAWM 144; CD 12 25 / 4 56) is a colorful, syncopated, cleverly orchestrated dancelike scherzo. The lowered third and seventh "blue notes" are prominent melodically and harmonically, particularly in the transformations of the opening motive (Example 22.6a), which evolves into a sixteen-bar tune

Example 22.5 *Virgil Thomson,* The Mother of Us All: *Act I, Scene 2,* Susan B. Anthony is my name

VIRGIL THOMSON ON SETTING WORDS TO MUSIC

My hope in putting Gertrude Stein to music had been to break, crack open, and solve for all time anything still waiting to be solved, which was almost everything, about English musical declamation. My theory was that if a text is set correctly for the sound of it, the meaning will take care of itself. And the Stein texts, for prosodizing in this way, were manna. With meanings already abstracted, or absent, or so multiplied that choice among them was impossible, there was no temptation toward tonal illustration, say, of birdie babbling by brook or heavy heavy hangs my heart. You could make a setting for sound and syntax only, then add, if needed, an accompaniment equally functional. I had no sooner put to music after this recipe one short Stein text than I knew I had opened a door.

From "Langlois, Butts, and Stein," in *Virgil Thomson* by Virgil Thomson (New York: Alfred A. Knopf, 1966), p. 90.

(Example 22.6b) accompanied by off-beat banjo chords that punctuate the orchestral texture.

Price

Florence Price (1888–1953) adapted the antebellum *Juba* folk dance as well as melodic and harmonic elements reflecting her black musical heritage—particularly the pentatonic scale of many spirituals—in several of her large works, outstanding among which are the Piano Concerto in One Movement (1934) and the First Symphony (1931).

In the music of most American composers of this period the genuinely national element is not easily isolated or defined, because it is blended with cosmopolitan style features of European music. One obvious sign, of course, is the

Example 22.6 *William Grant Still,* Afro-American Symphony: *Animato*

a. *Opening motive*

b. *Tune*

■ *Virgil Thomson looking over Gertrude Stein's shoulder at the score of their* Four Saints in Three Acts. *(VIRGIL THOMSON PAPERS, YALE UNIVERSITY MUSIC LIBRARY)*

choice of American subjects for operas, cantatas, or symphonic poems, as in the *American Festival Overture* (1939) of William Schuman (1910–1992), and his *William Billings Overture* (1943), which borrowed some tunes from Billings. But most often nationalism is injected more subtly. It may show itself in a certain forthrightness and optimism or in the flowing, unconstrained color and melody of the *Serenade for Orchestra* (1954) and *Umbrian Scene* (1964) by Ulysses Kay (b. 1917). Some eminent American composers wrote habitually in a language that cannot be called national in any narrow sense of the word. Howard Hanson (1896–1981) was an avowed neo-Romantic with a style influenced by Sibelius. Walter Piston (1894–1976) composed chamber music and symphonies in a sturdy and sophisticated, craftily wrought, and lucid neo-Classic idiom, of which his Third Symphony (1948) is a beautiful example.

Schuman

Kay

Hanson and Piston

SINCE 1945

Abstract Idioms

Sessions

Roger Sessions (1896–1985) employed the serial method freely in his Sonata for Unaccompanied Violin (1953) and later works. However, it hardly affected

ROGER SESSIONS ON THE LIMITATIONS OF THE SERIAL METHOD

Once the initial choice has been made, the series will determine the composer's vocabulary; but once the vocabulary has been so determined, the larger questions of tonal organization remain. My own strong feeling is that, while these questions must certainly be answered in terms not alien to the nature of the series, it is not serialism as such that can ever be made to account for them. I do not mean at all that I am opposed in principle to the idea of basing the structure entirely on the series itself, as Webern and others have tried to do. What I am saying is that even in structures so based, the acoustical effect seems to me to derive in the last analysis not from the manipulation of the series as such, but from the relationships between notes, as the composer has by these means set them up. . . . The series governs the composer's choice of materials, only the composer's ear and his conception determine the manner or the effect of their usage.

Quoted in Andrew Imbrie, "Roger Sessions, In Honor of His Sixty-fifth Birthday," in *Perspectives on American Composers*, ed. Benjamin Boretz and Edward T. Cone (New York: Norton, 1971), p. 64.

his consistent method of continuous motivic development. His music, stoutly individual, intense, and complex, is dissonant and chromatic. His nine symphonies, rarely performed, are among the best of the post–World War II years. The Second Symphony (1946) is particularly powerful, almost stridently expressionistic. The first movement begins as though in sonata form, with distinct first- and second-theme sections and development, but there is no formal recapitulation; indeed, the avoidance of literal repetition is characteristic of the work. A vigorous and distinctive theme announced in a trumpet solo (brasses are prominent throughout the movement), continually mutates into new forms (Example 22.7). The densely contrapuntal scoring keeps the large orchestra almost constantly busy.

The compositions of Elliott Carter (b. 1908) demonstrate an equally personal style, with notable innovations in the treatment of rhythm and form. Beginning with his Cello Sonata (1948), Carter experimented with what he

Carter

Example 22.7 *Roger Sessions,* Symphony No. 2: *Molto agitato*

Example 22.8 *Elliott Carter, String Quartet No. 1: I. Fantasia*

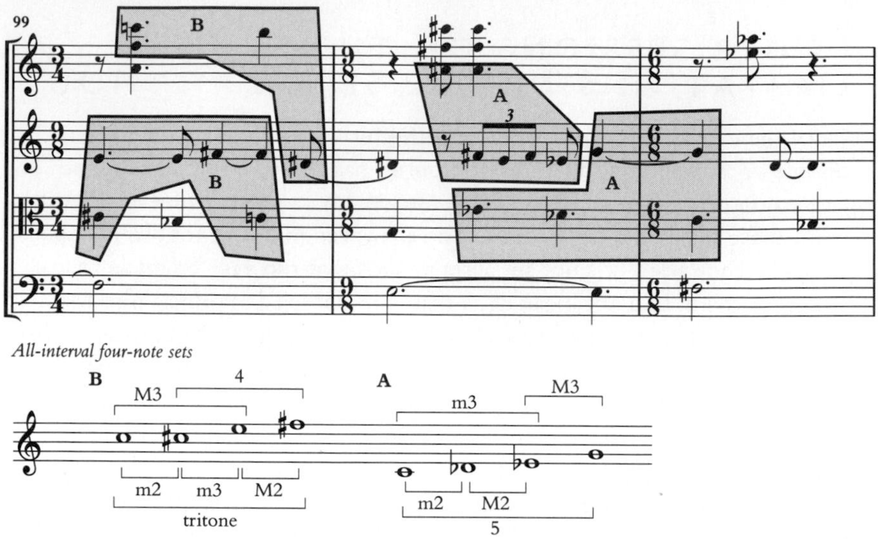

Metric modulation

called *metric modulation*, in which the tempo changes proportionally as in some fifteenth-century music. A transition is made in a performer's part from one tempo and meter to another through an intermediary stage that shares aspects of the previous and subsequent rhythmic organization. It realizes a precise proportional change in the value of a durational unit. Carter further developed this device in the First String Quartet (1950–51). While one player continues in the previous tempo, another speeds up, which imparts to each a sharp individual profile. This counterpoint of sharply differentiated lines was inspired in part by Ives's collages quoting familiar hymns and popular music and by the cross accents heard in English madrigals. The continuous pulse and rhythmic variety invest each part with remarkable fluency and consistency as well as independence.

In the First Quartet, this interaction results partly from two four-note sets and their transpositions. They are two forms of the *all-interval tetrachord*, a set of four pitch-classes that can be paired to produce every possible interval. The two all-interval four-note sets (the only two possible) may be seen in Example 22.8, each in two transpositions.

In the Quartet No. 2 (1959; Introduction and Allegro fantastico in NAWM 145; CD 12 [28]), each instrumental part takes on a personality that interacts with others in the ensemble as if in a dramatic work, realizing a virtual counterpoint of musical *dramatis personae.* The tempo modulations are still present but less frequent. A trend toward expressionistic writing is evident here and even more in the Variations for Orchestra (1955), a piece rich in motivic contrasts and interplay of what Carter called "musical behaviors," referring to the character both of particular instruments and of episodes in a larger work. The Piano Concerto (1964–65), written in Berlin in the shadow of the newly built Wall dividing the city, continued the dynamic confrontation. This tragic work pits the piano with a supporting concertino of seven instruments against the full orchestra in an irreconcilable bout in which each of the two groups is assigned different pitch-trichords and metronomic speeds.

Piano Concerto

The University as Patron

A peculiarity of contemporary composition in North America is its close association with universities. In Europe composers have been partly supported by the state through radio networks, composers' unions (in socialist countries), research centers, festivals, annual subsidies, and grants. But in the United States and Canada, steady employment in universities and colleges has given them time to compose, a ready audience, and, often, access to nearby or campus performing organizations. Of the composers just considered, most had university positions. In the 1990s commissions by symphony orchestras, opera companies, individual performers (aided by the National Endowment for the Arts), and foundations have freed some composers from teaching institutions.

Contrary to fears, university composers have generated notable avant-garde experiments, not staid "academic" music. The universities did, however, tend to isolate composers from the public and make them independent of its support. This isolation allowed certain elitist vogues to spread through symposia and lectures in which composers presented and explained their works.

Boston area

Around Boston, the presence of Nadia Boulanger during the war years (1940–46) and her promotion of Stravinsky's music combined to give much of the local music a specific regional character. She taught at Wellesley and Radcliffe Colleges and the Longy School of Music in Cambridge. Walter Piston, a Boulanger pupil who taught at Harvard, also encouraged a neo-Classic approach; among the composers affected were Arthur Berger (b. 1912), Elliott Carter, and Irving Fine (1914–1962).

Yale

The presence of Paul Hindemith at Yale between 1940 and 1953 turned its School of Music for a time, even after he left for Zurich, into a nest of his disciples. Among them, Mel Powell (1923–98), once a jazz pianist with Benny Goodman, became the first dean of the California Institute of the Arts, and

Paul Hindemith teaching a composition class at the Yale University School of Music, 1953. In the foreground Sam di Bonaventura (b. 1920), at right Yehudi Wyner (b. 1929). Wyner directed the music program at the State University of New York in Purchase and has taught at Yale, Brandeis, Harvard, and Tufts Universities. Di Bonaventura was professor of music at George Mason University in Virginia. (THE PAUL HINDEMITH COLLECTION, YALE UNIVERSITY MUSIC LIBRARY)

Norman Dello Joio (b. 1913) was influential nationally as the head of the Contemporary Music Project, which placed young composers in high schools to write for school ensembles.

Berkeley, Oakland

The University of California at Berkeley, which had links to Harvard, also felt the Stravinsky wave, though Sessions injected a different point of view when he taught there between 1944 and 1952. Nearby Mills College in Oakland was the base for Darius Milhaud between 1940 and 1970; among his pupils were Dave Brubeck (b. 1920), Pauline Oliveros (b. 1932), Steve Reich (b. 1936), Leland Smith (b. 1925), Morton Subotnick (b. 1933), and William Bolcom (b. 1938).

UCLA

The University of California at Los Angeles became the hub of Schoenberg's influence from 1936, when he was appointed professor, until his death in 1951. Princeton was also dominated by the teachings of the Schoenberg school, particularly through the influence of Roger Sessions, who was appointed professor in 1953, and his student Milton Babbitt (b. 1916), who became the principal theorist of the twelve-tone method. Among Sessions's other pupils were Conlon Nancarrow (1912–1997), Hugo Weisgall (1912–1997), Andrew Imbrie (b. 1921), and Leon Kirchner (b. 1919), who taught at Harvard from 1961 to 1989. At Princeton, Sessions and Babbitt taught Donald Martino (b. 1931), Peter Westergaard (b. 1931), Benjamin Boretz (b. 1934), and James K. Randall (b. 1929). Through a grant from the Rockefeller Foundation, Columbia and Princeton Universities established a pioneering center for electronic music in 1959 to which many composers from the United States and abroad were invited. From this studio issued the electronic works of Otto Luening (1900–1996), Mario Davidovsky (b. 1934) of Argentina, and Jacob Druckman (1928–1996), and it was there that Varése put the finishing touches on his *Déserts*, composed years before in Paris.

Princeton

Illinois

The Universities of Illinois and Michigan were also important centers, where the annual festivals of contemporary music served as forums for both avant-garde and traditional approaches. Illinois cultivated talents among students and faculty as varied as Subotnick, Gordon Binkerd (b. 1916; a pupil of Piston), Kenneth Gaburo (1926–1993), Lejaren Hiller (1924–1994), Ben Johnston (b. 1926), and Michael Colgrass (b. 1932). Subotnick later founded the San Francisco Tape Music Center, in which Pauline Oliveros and Larry Austin (b. 1930) collaborated.

Michigan

At the University of Michigan at Ann Arbor, Ross Lee Finney (1906–1997), who had studied with Boulanger and Alban Berg, was a mentor to talents as different as Leslie Bassett (b. 1923), William Albright (b. 1944; later a pupil of Messiaen), George Crumb (b. 1929), and Roger Reynolds (b. 1934). Robert Ashley (b. 1930), a native of Ann Arbor and a graduate of Michigan, returned in the late 1950s to manage the Cooperative Studio for Electronic Music with Gordon Mumma (b. 1935). In 1963 he founded the ONCE group, dedicated to multimedia experiments and free-form operas. Ashley moved to Mills College in 1969 to direct the college's Center for Contemporary Music. At the University of California at San Diego, Reynolds became the first director of its Center for Music Experiment, a magnet for multimedia and electronic innovation.

Stanford University took the lead in computer-assisted composition under the guidance of John Chowning (b. 1934), who established the Center of Computer Research in Music and Acoustics (CCRMA). His success inspired Boulez to inaugurate a similar program in Paris. Stanford

At the Eastman School of the University of Rochester, Howard Hanson and Bernard Rogers (1893–1968) hatched an "Eastman Group," which included David Diamond (b. 1915), Robert Palmer (b. 1915), Robert Ward (b. 1917), William Bergsma (b. 1921), Peter Mennin (1923–1983), who became president of The Juilliard School of Music, and Salvatore Martirano (1927–1995), later a professor at Illinois. Eastman

The Post-Webern Vogue

Although Schoenberg had a small following after settling in California, the twelve-tone method acquired its most ardent devotees not through any personal contact with its European practitioners but through fascination with the works of Schoenberg's pupil Anton Webern. Without the university network, Webern's advancement as the model for the 1950s would surely not have gained such strength and diffusion among young North American composers. These artists embraced Webern's lean, transparent, objective, formally clear, concentrated approach in which harmony and melody annihilated each other, partly as a rebellion against the Americanists, partly as a new phase of the neo-Classic movement. The reflexive, symmetrical structures and the systematic handling of little cells or units held particular appeal for those who wanted to insulate their art music from their own involvement in jazz, musical comedy, arranging, or film.

Milton Babbitt was one such composer. He studied with Sessions and received all his education in the United States (mathematics and music, both of which he taught at Princeton). Babbitt furthered serial composition in the United States through his analysis of the characteristics of twelve-tone rows as mathematical sets. He described the principles of this method in a number of fundamental articles and through his teaching. In his Three Compositions for Piano (1947), Babbitt subjected both pitch and duration to serial control for the first time, preceding similar experiments by Boulez and Stockhausen. Babbit

Babbitt went beyond the practices of Schoenberg and his circle to realize new potentials of the twelve-tone system. In his Second String Quartet (1954) he used the basic row as a source for derived rows. For example, he opened the quartet by developing a row with pairs of pitches a minor third apart (the first interval in the source row), proceeding then to exploit other intervals of the source row. In the Third String Quartet (1970), the twelve pitches of the source row are distributed among eight layers or voices (each instrument having two voices, arco and pizzicato). Each voice traverses the row over several segments of the piece, while each segment, as short as a measure or two, contains in the sum of the parts the entire content of the row or *aggregate*—the unordered set of pitch-classes of the chromatic scale (Example 22.9). On the audible level, many intervallic and rhythmic relationships occur within the voices that enrich the tangled strands. This way of achieving maximum inter- Aggregate

Example 22.9 *Milton Babbit, Quartet No. 3*

relatedness of material has been called *maximalism,* as an ironic and deprecatory jab at an opposing school of composition, discussed below.

New Sounds and Textures

Nancarrow

The exploration of new sounds begun by Cowell and Varèse was taken up by several composers. Conlon Nancarrow, born in Texarkana, Arkansas, eventually settled in Mexico, but kept in touch with developments in American jazz and the music of Africa and India. These interests merged in his experiments with complex rhythms that could not be adequately expressed in notation. The player piano of his day used perforated paper rolls to activate the keys. By punching out the holes himself, Nancarrow was able to control precisely the keys of a player piano, producing time- and pitch-intervals between notes that were beyond the capability of human hands either because of their speed or their rhythmic quirkiness. He wrote more than thirty studies for the Ampico player piano, which could respond to the roll's instructions with respect to dynamics as well as pitch and duration. Some of these pieces are obviously influenced by jazz; others employ canons and ostinato figures. Before electronic

MILTON BABBITT ON COMPOSERS AND THEIR AUDIENCE

Why refuse to recognize the possibility that contemporary music has reached a stage long since attained by other forms of activity? The time has passed when the normally well-educated man without special preparation can understand the most advanced work in, for example, mathematics, philosophy, and physics. Advanced music, to the extent that it reflects the knowledge and originality of the informed composer, scarcely can be expected to appear more intelligible than these arts and sciences to the person whose musical education usually has been even less extensive than his background in other fields.

I dare suggest that the composer would do himself and his music immediate and eventual service by total, resolute, and voluntary withdrawal from his public world to one of private performance and electronic media, with its very real possibility of complete elimination of the public and social aspects of musical composition. By so doing, the separation between the domains would be defined beyond any possibility of confusion of categories, and the composer would be free to pursue a private life of professional achievement, as opposed to a public life of unprofessional compromise and exhibitionism.

From Milton Babbitt, "Who Cares if You Listen?," *High Fidelity* 8/2 (February 1958), pp. 39–40, repr. in Elliott Schwartz and Barney Childs, *Contemporary Composers on Contemporary Music* (New York: Holt, Rinehart & Winston, 1967), pp. 243–50. Babbitt's title for the article was "The Composer as Specialist." An editor invented the published title. See Babbitt's Haskins lecture (1991) in *The Life of Learning*, ed. Douglas Greenberg and Stanley N. Katz (New York: Oxford University Press, 1994), p. 134.

and computer means could accomplish similar feats, Nancarrow offered the ear exciting new experiences.

Partch

Harry Partch (1901–1974) undertook a ruggedly individualistic, single-minded search for new sonic media. He repudiated equal temperament and the Western harmonic and contrapuntal practices in the 1920s to seek a wholly new system inspired partly by various traditional and non-Western musics—Chinese, Native American, Jewish, Christian, African, and rural American. He designed and built new instruments that could play his octave-scale of forty-three notes based on just intonation. Among his instruments were cast-off cloud-chamber bowls used in early particle physics, a large kithara-like string instrument, and marimbas. In his multimedia works of the 1950s, these instruments accompany speaking and chanting voices and dancing by singer-actor-dancers. *Oedipus—A Music-Dance Drama* (1951) and *Revelation in the Courthouse Park* (1962), based on Euripides' *The Bacchae,* aspired to the elusive ideal of the Greek tragedy.

Johnston

Ben Johnston, who worked with Partch and performed on his instruments, continued Partch's pursuit of just intonation and microtones, that is, intervals smaller than the semitone. But unlike the just-intonation idealists of

■ *Harry Partch playing the gourd tree, one of the instruments he invented to realize his music, mostly monophonic, based on the just (untempered) scale. Beside him are two cone gongs. Among his other novel instruments were cloud-chamber bowls, originally used to trace particles in nuclear-physics experiments, and a variety of marimbas and modified guitars.*

the Renaissance, who wanted all the consonances to sound pure (as in the simple ratios of string lengths, such as 3:2 for the fifth), Johnston targeted the odd-numbered intervals: thirds, fifths, sevenths, and so forth. His *Sonata for Microtonal Piano* (1965) permits the hearer to savor in melody, arpeggios, and chords the justly tuned thirds, fifths, and their compounds, while seconds, fourths, sixths, octaves, tenths, twelfths, and fourteenths sound out of tune. The slow movement, which has a Middle Eastern flavor because of the melodic microtones against the purely consonant double-drones, is particularly moving and fresh. In his String Quartets Nos. 1 and 2 (1959, 1964), Johnston combined this approach with serial procedures.

Crumb

George Crumb has been most imaginative in coaxing new sounds out of ordinary instruments and objects. In *Ancient Voices of Children* (1970), a cycle of four songs (based on texts by Federico Garcia Lorca) and two instrumental interludes, unusual sound sources include a toy piano, a musical saw, and a number of instruments rarely heard in concerts—namely, harmonica, mandolin, Tibetan prayer stones, Japanese temple bells, and electric piano. He obtained special effects also from conventional instruments: for example, players must bend the pitch of the piano by applying a chisel to the strings, thread paper in the harp strings, tune the mandolin a quarter tone flat, vocalize into an amplified piano, and shout and whisper as well as sing. *Black Angels* (1970; NAWM 146; CD 12 [31]) derives special sound effects from everyday concert instruments. In this work, a string quartet is electronically amplified to produce surrealistic dreamlike juxtapositions. The composer also explored unusual means of bowing, such as striking the strings near the pegs with the bow, holding the bow in the manner of viol players, and bowing between the left-hand fingers and the pegs; he also used glissandos, *sul ponticello*, and percussive pizzicato.

Electronic Music

The absence of a performer in purely electronic music has hindered its acceptance, since the public responds more warmly to performers than to composers. When composers no longer depend on performers to realize their music, they also lose promoters and communicators. Electronic pieces occasionally figure on concert programs of contemporary music, but unless they require more than two channels of sound and elaborate equipment, they are best listened to in the comfort of one's home. Even so, a significant body of purely electronic music is being created, particularly now that a personal computer or work station combined with a synthesizer can achieve what once required a big studio. Still, in the field of classical music, synthesizers are being used more to compose music in notation for performers to realize than in direct communication with listeners.

Babbitt *Philomel*

Nevertheless, the combination of prerecorded tape and live performers is a familiar phenomenon in concerts and continues to evolve technologically. One of the most moving early examples was Milton Babbitt's *Philomel* (1964; the first section is in NAWM 147; CD 12 [37] / 4 ⟨59⟩), for soprano soloist with a tape that incorporates an altered recording or echo of the voice together with various electronic sounds. The poem, written expressly for this setting by John Hollander, is based on a fable by Ovid (*Metamorphoses* 6:412–674). Procne, wife of Tereus, king of Thrace, is eager to see her sister Philomela, after an absence of many years, and sends Tereus to fetch her. On the return trip Tereus rapes Philomela in a Thracian wood and cuts out her tongue to prevent disclosure, but his guilt is eventually discovered. In a rage, he pursues the two sisters, but before he can catch them, all three are transformed: Tereus into a hoopoe bird, Procne into a swallow, and Philomela into a nightingale. In the metamorphosis Philomela regains her voice. The vocal sections are answered by the tape voice, and both are accompanied by synthesized sounds; the score gives evidence that every detail was worked out in serial terms. The vocal sections alternate with unnotated synthesized interludes that are more freely composed. The tape voice often answers by distorting the soloist's line or, speaking, comments like a Greek chorus. In a poignant moment, Philomel discovers that she can sing like a bird and asks a thrush, "Do you, too, talk with the forest's tongue?" (Example 22.10). The counterpoint of three voices exchanges three four-note pitch-sets that make up the tone row: *C♯–F♯–A–D*, first heard in the lowest part, migrates to the soloist's part; *E♭–A♭–G–C*, sounded in the upper tape part, passes next to the lower tape part; and *E–F–A♯–B*, the soloist's first notes, are taken up by the tape's upper part. The first set is then used to imitate birdsong. This orderly counterpoint contrasts with the opening of the composition, when Philomel cried out in pain, and all twelve notes of a row were heard at once.

Example 22.10 *Milton Babbitt,* Philomel: *Section 2*

Druckman

Jacob Druckman, working in the Columbia-Princeton Electronic Music Studio, produced a series of dramatic dialogues between live performers and recorded electronic music: *Animus I* (1966) for trombone, *Animus II* (1968) for female voice and percussion, and *Animus III* (1969) for clarinet. (Since the 1970s Druckman's major compositions have been for conventional ensembles such as the string quartet and symphony orchestra.) In *From Behind the Unreasoning Mask* (1975) by Roger Reynolds, a four-channel tape (the "mask" of the title) provokes three live performers whose parts are mostly written out to emulate, yet rebel, against the tape.

Reynolds

Recent explorations of the live-performer-cum-synthesizer medium seize on the capability of high-speed computers to analyze a performer's improvisation and to respond immediately according to a programmed scheme and range of possibilities. The strange aptness of the unpredictable (though far from random) participation of the computer-driven synthesizer produces an exciting tension between the human imagination and the mechanical partner, each reacting to the other.

Digital player piano

Another new medium available to the creative musician is the digital player piano. The piano hammers, instead of being controlled by a paper roll, are depressed according to digitally coded instructions. The composer uses a computer keyboard to enter the precise pitches, durations, and dynamics in any conceivable combination and at any speed that the instrument can support.

Third Stream

Many composers, both European and American, introduced aspects of jazz into their concert music. Debussy, Ravel, Stravinsky, Hindemith, and Milhaud at one time or another imitated the rhythms of jazz, its typical harmonies, or its improvisational manners of playing the trumpet, saxophone, or percussion. But they did not write whole pieces or even parts of works that insiders would recognize as jazz and that also fit into the concert repertory. George Gershwin's *Rhapsody in Blue* (1924) accomplished this feat unselfconsciously. Similarly, Duke Ellington's more ambitious compositions, such as *Black, Brown and Beige*, used symphonic means as a natural extension of his jazz ideas.

Gershwin, Ellington

In the 1950s there was a deliberate quest by certain composers who were conversant with both kinds of music to merge the two. One of the most successful of these, Gunther Schuller (b. 1925), called this combination "third stream." In his *Transformation* (1957), a pointillistic twelve-tone context is transformed into a full-blown modern jazz piece that also preserves elements of tone-color-melody (inspired by Schoenberg's *Klangfarbenmelodie*) heard at the work's beginning. In Schuller's *Seven Studies on Themes of Paul Klee* (1959), the third, *Kleiner Blauteufel* (Little Blue Devil, NAWM 148a; CD 12 [42]), is unmistakably in jazz style, though the blues pattern is reduced from twelve bars to nine and there are unexpected asymmetries of rhythm. It is a genre picture in the same way that another of the studies, *Arabische Stadt* (Arab Village, NAWM 148b; CD 12 [44]), captures with flair and sensibility the slightly off-tune nasal woodwinds playing in unison with bowed and plucked strings.

Schuller

Composers not associated in the public mind with the third-stream movement or with popular music have also used jazz as a model. One of the most unusual examples is Milton Babbitt's *All Set* (1957), written for a seven-piece jazz ensemble and dedicated to Gunther Schuller. Its title is a pun on the jazz term "set" (a performing session on stage) and on the concept of Babbitt's all-combinatorial pitch-class set, a hexachord that can be combined with any one of its possible transformations (retrograde, inversion, retrograde-inversion) or with one of its transpositions to produce a twelve-tone row. Although highly disjunct and totally controlled through set-manipulations, the music has the improvisatory character of jazz, with saxophone, trumpet, and trombone riffs, a rhythmic background of cymbals, hi-hat, vibraphone, and drum-set, and even drum solos.

Babbitt, *All Set*

William Bolcom, a participant in the ragtime revival of the 1960s, injected a Viennese Kaffee-Konzert sentimentalism in his own rag, *Graceful Ghost*. This feeling is even more pronounced in the concert version for violin and piano, in which the violin plays a subsidiary role but adds the spice of jazz-violin mannerisms. The result captures the spirit of Schumann's character pieces more than that of a true rag. Vernacular idioms also find their way into Bolcom's more ambitious works, such as the Second Sonata for Violin and Piano (1978), in which blues are worked into the opening movement, and "slurs and smears" jazz up the final ragtime movement in memory of the great jazz violinist Joe Venuti.

Bolcom

Davis

Joining the third stream from the direction of jazz is the pianist Anthony Davis (b. 1951), leader of a free jazz ensemble, Episteme. This improvising group became the orchestral nucleus for his opera *X: The Life and Times of Malcolm X* (1984), which enjoyed a successful New York premiere at the City Opera in 1986. The opera does not so much merge jazz and classical styles as juxtapose them. The solo roles are declaimed syllabically against a lightly orchestrated background, which develops motives in an idiom that is sometimes expressionistic and at other times agitated and Stravinskyesque. The many choruses elaborate on text-driven rhythmic figures, stylizing the obsessive chanting of street demonstrators. Improvised jazz breaks out only occasionally, as in a Harlem scene at the end of Act I, when the gambler Street delivers a rap song in which he tries to sell the neighborhood youths on a life of play and drug dealing. The music of *X* is a cosmopolitan product of a university-trained composer whose roots are in modern jazz.

John Cage and Indeterminacy

Random techniques of all kinds, which Cage summed up in the term *indeterminacy*, raised questions about the nature and purposes of music. A work of total serialism or its offshoots can be heard as a succession of discrete musical events that are unconnected to what had just been heard or what is to follow. The complex interrelationships overwhelm the innocent listener, and the music seems random, although the composer exercised complete control. With partly indeterminate music, both composer and performer make choices, resulting in a musical form that may differ every time the work is performed.

When a composer extends spontaneity to a point where all control is voluntarily abandoned, the listener simply hears sounds as sounds, enjoying (or not) each as it comes along, not trying to connect one sound with preceding or following ones, not expecting the music to communicate feelings or meanings of any kind. The sounds may not even be limited to intentional ones; any mistake or accidental noise from anywhere that occurs in the course of a performance is perfectly acceptable. Value judgments become irrelevant and musical time becomes simply duration, something that can be measured by a clock.

However strange such an esthetic may seem and however much its practice encourages sheer dilettantism, it has a tenable basis in the philosophies of East Asia. The enigmatic John Cage, the chief proponent of these principles of indeterminacy, has stood in the forefront of new musical developments in both America and Europe since the late 1930s. Indeed, his influence in Europe was greater than that of any other American composer.

4′33″

Cage's most extreme work along these lines was *4′33″* (Four Minutes and Thirty-three Seconds, 1952), in which the performer or performers sit silently for a period of time while noises in the concert hall or from outside constitute the music. The piece implies that musical silence is not true silence, that there are always environmental sounds worth contemplating, and that nature is the greatest creator of music. In other works, Cage also abdicated the composer's decision-making to chance operations such as the Chinese *I Ching* (Book of

Changes), which determines the arrangement of pitches in *Music of Changes* (1951). Beginning about 1956, he moved more and more toward complete openness in every aspect of composition and performance, by offering performers such options, as in his *Variations IV* (1963): "for any number of players, any sounds or combinations of sounds produced by any means, with or without other activities." The "other activities" might well include dance and theater. All this coincided with Cage's growing interest in Zen Buddhism; more important, it is consonant with what is probably a tendency for Western artists—and for Western civilization generally—to become more open to the ideas and beliefs of other great world cultures.

Music of Changes

Variations IV

Among Cage's protégés were Morton Feldman (1926–1987) and Earle Brown (b. 1926). Brown's approach was partly inspired by the mobiles of Alexander Calder, in which the material was always the same but a spectator's perception of it constantly changed. His *Available Forms I* (1961) for eighteen players and *Available Forms II* (1962) for large orchestra divided into two groups realize a musical parallel by giving the musicians completely scored fragments—with some leeway in the choice of pitches—that are played in the order and tempos (including accelerations and decelerations) determined by the conductor(s). This procedure permits a spontaneity and multiplicity of perceptions that could not be achieved through normal notation.

Feldman, Brown

The term *entropy*, from thermodynamics and information science, is sometimes used to describe the total randomness that is one extreme of indeterminate music. *Redundancy* is its opposite, the reduction of information to the minimum by excessive repetition. This is the direction taken in a trend called *minimalism*.

Minimalism

The musics of Asia, frequently heard in North America since 1960, stimulated composers to cultivate a simpler style in which subtleties of melody, intonation, and rhythm could be brought to the fore. The controlled improvisation on Indian ragas, with their alternating patterns of rhythmic units, microtonal intervals, drones, and rhapsodic figurations, was one source of inspiration. The cool, entrancing, repetitive, contemplative music of the Javanese and Balinese gamelans presented a model of complex structures that depend on reiteration of simple rhythmic and melodic patterns. Synthesizers provided an easy means to improvise over prerecorded rhythms and melodic motives. Rock music, which itself absorbed elements of jazz, blues, folk, electronic music, and Asian idioms, was the common experience of most composers born after the 1930s. They were enticed by rock's directness, hypnotic rhythms, consonant harmonies, repeated phrases, and ostinatos.

Whether pursuing simplicity or reacting to the complexity of serial music, a number of composers took up what is now known as *minimalism*. The term was apt, because their vocabulary, whether rhythmic, melodic, harmonic, or instrumental, was intentionally limited. The term as well as the direction may owe something to the New York group of visual artists who designed cyclic and repetitive structures consisting of simple elements such as lines and dots (see, for example, Plate XVI, facing page 783). The lengths, however, of many of these musical compositions or improvisations and the durations of particular gestures—in contrast to the compression and constant change of most serial music—were anything but minimal.

Young

One of the pioneers in this movement was La Monte Young (b. 1935), whose *The Tortoise: His Dreams and Journeys* (1964) was an improvisation in which instrumentalists and singers come in and out on various harmonics over a fundamental played as a drone by a synthesizer.

Riley

Terry Riley (b. 1935), who once performed in Young's ensemble, experimented at an electronic studio in the 1960s with tape loops containing many repetitions of short phrases against a continuous regular pulse and piling these up on one another. The tape piece *Mescalin Mix* (1962–63) used this procedure. His *A Rainbow in Curved Air* (1970) for keyboard depends on improvisation on modal scales and rhythmic cycles similar to those of Indian music.

Reich

Steve Reich (b. 1936) developed a quasi-canonic procedure in which musicians play the same material slightly out of phase with each other. He was led to this methodology by superimposing tape loops of the same spoken phrase in such a way that one loop was slightly shorter and thus gradually moved ahead of the other. He applied the idea to two pianos in *Piano Phase* (1967), and in *Violin Phase* (1967) he juxtaposed a live violinist with a second one on tape. The piece evolved into a published version (1979) for four violinists or for a single violinist with three synchronous recording tracks. In the version for a single violinist and three-track tape, the performer first records the music reproduced in Example 22.11a over and over again for one to five minutes. Then, after rewinding the tape, the violinist superimposes repetitions of the same pattern of notes, but now four eighth-notes ahead of the first track (see Example 22.11b). The performer then rewinds the tape again and records the pattern four eighth-notes ahead of track 2. The best three to seven repetitions are made into a tape loop, resulting in the ostinato shown in Example 22.11c and d, which serves as a background for further improvisation.

Piano Phase, Violin Phase

Glass

Philip Glass (b. 1937), who had published twenty works by the time he completed degrees at the University of Chicago and The Juilliard School and finished his studies with Nadia Boulanger, withdrew all of them after working with the Indian sitarist Ravi Shankar in Paris. Even earlier he had reacted negatively to the contemporary music he heard in Paris at Pierre Boulez's series, Domaine Musical. Glass's works since the mid-1960s were deeply influenced by the rhythmic organization of Indian music; they emphasized melodiousness, consonance, and the simple harmonic progressions and abundant amplification of rock music. His one-act, four-and-a-half-hour opera *Einstein on the Beach*, a collaboration with Robert Wilson (scenario and staging), received its premiere at the Metropolitan Opera House in 1976. Other operas followed, including *Satyagraha* (1980), about Gandhi's nonviolent struggle, and *Akhnaten* (1984), about an Egyptian pharaoh martyred for his monotheistic worship of the sun god. Otherwise he wrote mainly for his own ensemble. *Einstein* is non-narrative and has no sung text other than solfège syllables. The orchestra consists of elec-

Example 22.11 *Steve Reich,* Violin Phase

a. Measure 1

b at measure 7

c. at measure 18

d. at measure 18

tronic keyboard instruments, woodwinds, and a solo violinist. Glass has won the admiration of a large and diversified audience that includes concert-goers, frequenters of art galleries (where the music is sometimes played), rock enthusiasts, and the record-buying public. His *The Voyage* (1992), commissioned by the Metropolitan Opera to commemorate the five hundredth anniversary of Columbus's trip to the New World, uses a full orchestra. Its recitatives and arias and its multilayered rhythms and ostinatos came closer to meeting the expectations of opera-goers than his other previous stage works.

Adams

Leading up to his successful opera, *Nixon in China* (1987), John Adams (b. 1947) experimented with many minimalist designs. His *Phrygian Gates* for piano (1977–78; NAWM 149; CD 12 [47] / 4 ⟨64⟩) is representative of the early phase of this movement. Except for a middle section entitled "A System of

Weights and Measures," which consists of shifting sustained chords, this twenty-four minute piece relies almost entirely on rapid repetitive figuration or alternating chords. The pitch-range gradually expands from a single note to six octaves, while the number of notes per bar goes from eight to twenty-four, and the pitches in the perpetual-motion figuration go from one to eleven, almost entirely confined to the pertinent major scale. Because of the constant use of the pedal—though sometimes half or even quarter pedal—the notes of each figuration pattern blend into a single chord, so that the listener experiences a kaleidoscope of pandiatonic harmonies. The music goes through what Adams calls "gates," changing from one set of notes to another: from the Lydian scale on A to the Phrygian scale on A (at measure 114), then the Lydian and Phrygian scales on E (at measures 137 and 236, respectively), and so on. These changes give the work its title.

In the light, provocative *Grand Pianola Music* (1982), Adams recalled from his youth the gospel music and band marches he played in New Hampshire, and he bent the Beethoven piano style to sound like a pianola. *Fearful Symmetries* (first performed in 1988) was written for the same ensemble that would ultimately be used in *Nixon in China*, dominated by saxophones, brass, and winds, with strings, synthesizer, and relentless percussion in the background. As in the opera, short, driving, pulsating ideas, insistently repeated, constantly evolve and modulate, particularly by semitone. Adams avoided monotony by continually shuffling instrumental colors and pitting conflicting rhythmic patterns, beats, and syncopations against one another. His later music returned to more traditional harmonic and contrapuntal means.

The Mainstream

To speak only of the newest, most prominent, or most novel trends does not do justice to the large proportion of "mainstream" composers. This term does not mean that they share a set of beliefs about music or esthetics; rather, they compose in a great diversity of styles within a generally conservative and somewhat retrospective posture. Tonality or at least the maintenance of a tonal center often, though not necessarily, characterizes their music. Because they want to communicate with a large public, these composers offer listeners a thread that can be followed through identifiable musical themes, musical designs that are on the surface rather than hidden, and programmatic subjects or titles, and they strike a balance between lyricism and liveliness, expression and logic, caution and risk. The successful middle-of-the-roaders have also discovered the secret of inspiring performers to champion their music, creating works that musicians are eager to play more than once.

Among these are three composers noted particularly for their vocal music: Samuel Barber (1910–1981), Ned Rorem (b. 1923), and Gian Carlo Menotti (b. 1911). Barber's *Dover Beach* (1931) for baritone and string quartet is marked by the intense lyrical flow that characterizes his later music, such as the cycle *Hermit Songs* (1952–53), his opera *Antony and Cleopatra* (which opened the new Metropolitan Opera House in 1966), and his ever-popular *Adagio for*

Barber

Strings (1936). Rorem's songs, which number in the hundreds, have become favorites in vocal recitals because of their sensitive setting of English poetry. Menotti's operas descended from the Italian tradition of Puccini and Mascagni familiar to opera-goers. But in his own librettos he put aside the old Romantic and veristic plots in favor of dramatic situations that modern audiences could identify with. *The Medium* (1946), *The Telephone* (1947), *The Consul* (1950), and *The Saint of Bleecker Street* (1954) all enjoyed popular success.

Rorem

Menotti

Among the younger generation, two may be singled out for hewing to their own middle paths, thereby avoiding the extremes. Joan Tower (b. 1938), regarded by some as eclectic because of the variety of approaches she chooses, can more judiciously be termed "inclusive," since she plucks expressive resources out of a rich bouquet gathered as a performer in her contemporary-music ensemble, the Da Capo Chamber Players. *Amazon* (for orchestra, 1977–82) traverses several seemingly incompatible idioms as we hear impressions of the great river of South America, where the composer grew up, but these diverse sources present a unified whole thanks to the force of the personality and purpose.

Tower

Ellen Taaffe Zwilich (b. 1939) sometimes found her idiom in the innate character and capability of an instrument, as she did in her Concerto for Trumpet and Five Players (1984) and in the Sonata in Three Movements for Violin and Piano (1973–74). Alternatively, her approach may be born of the occasion, as in *Symbolon,* written for the New York Philharmonic's tour of the Soviet Union in 1988. *Symbolon* in Greek meant a "sign" or "token," and more specifically, in the plural, the halves of a bone or coin that two persons broke between them as a symbol of friendship. The composer handed her hosts their half of the token in the form of subtle stylistic allusions to Shostakovich. Her Symphony No. 1 (1982) earned her the first Pulitzer Prize in Music awarded to a woman. She wrote her Concerto Grosso 1985 (fourth and fifth movements in NAWM 150; CD 12 [53]) in commemoration of the three hundredth anniversary of George Frideric Handel's birth, basing the first and fifth (last) movements on the first and second halves respectively of the first movement of Handel's Violin Sonata No. 4 in D. The three middle movements, including the fourth, are freely composed. Although none of the movements is in ritornello form, there are obvious tutti and soli sections. The harpsichord has a dual function, realizing a figured bass during the quotations from the Handel sonata, otherwise acting as a member of the orchestra. Zwilich assimilates the Baroque elements into a spirited personal style.

Zwilich

Post-Modern Styles

A number of architects, such as Robert Venturi, Philip Johnson, and Cesar Pelli, turned away from the faceless glass façades of the mid-twentieth century by incorporating elements of earlier styles into essentially modern designs, a mixture that became known as "post-modern." This term may fit better than "collage" to describe the technique used by Zwilich in her concerto and in recent music by others. A central aspect of "post-modernism" is a turning away from the belief that history progresses in an irreversibly linear fashion. In

Example 22.12

a. *Johann Sebastian Bach, Partita No. 6, BWV 830: Toccata*

b. *George Rochberg,* Nach Bach

music this amounts to an abandonment of the related notion of the continuous development of musical language. To the post-modernist, history has ceased to place such demands; the styles of all epochs and cultures are equally available as musical material, to be utilized as the composer sees fit.

Rochberg George Rochberg (b. 1918), who had earlier depended on serial methods, constructed a quilt from the music of Mozart, Beethoven, Mahler, Webern, Varèse, Stockhausen, and from previously composed works of his own in his *Music for a Magic Theater* (1965). In the Fantasy for harpsichord or piano *Nach Bach* (1966), he adopted the style of a Baroque toccata and quoted short passages from J. S. Bach's Partita No. 6 for keyboard, BWV 830. Like Bach, Rochberg begins with an arpeggio followed by a typical double-dotted effect and a descending appoggiatura (Example 22.12). But where Bach's arpeggio contains only the notes of the E-minor triad, Rochberg's contains all twelve notes of the chromatic scale. Similarly, the arpeggio that resolves the appoggiatura includes all of the notes of Bach's chord but in addition *B*♭, *E*♭, and *B*.

Foss In *Baroque Variations* (1967) Lukas Foss (b. 1922) reworked a Larghetto of Handel, a sonata of Domenico Scarlatti (Kirkpatrick 380), and a prelude of J. S. Bach (Partita for Violin, BWV 1006). One of the richest pieces of this kind, dedicated to Leonard Bernstein and the New York Philharmonic, is *Sinfonia*

Berio *for Eight Voices and Orchestra* (1968) by the Italian composer Luciano Berio (b. 1925). The third movement incorporates most of the scherzo (third) movement of Mahler's Second Symphony; on it Berio superimposed an amplified verbal commentary by a vocal ensemble (originally the Swingle Singers) and a musical commentary by a large orchestra, including alto and tenor saxophones, piano, electric organ and harpsichord, divisi violins, and a solo violin. The bar-to-bar continuity of the Mahler is mostly maintained, although sometimes only sketchy fragments are heard, and quotations from dozens of other

XV. The Sun-Treader, *a portrait of Carl Ruggles by Thomas Hart Benton (1889–1938).* Sun-Treader *was the title of an important one-movement orchestral work that Ruggles wrote between 1926 and 1931.* (KANSAS CITY, THE NELSON-ATKINS MUSEUM OF ART. GIFT OF THE FRIENDS OF ART)

XVI. *Frank Stella (b. 1936),* Le Neveu de Rameau *(Rameau's Nephew, 1974) acrylic on canvas. This painting is a sequel to Stella's* Les Indes galantes, *a series of five prints alluding to the prologue and four entrées (or acts) of Jean-Philippe Rameau's opera-ballet, which had several runs between 1735 and 1743.* Rameau's Nephew *was the title of a satirical dialogue by the encyclopedist and* philosophe *Denis Diderot. In that work, the fictional nephew and the author exchange views about the music, literature, mores, and personalities of mid-eighteenth-century France. The multicolored concentric squares in Stella's mitered maze are representative of the repetitive geometric patterns and shapes that became favorite subjects for works of art associated with minimalism, a trend that partly inspired a parallel movement in music.* (LOWE ART MUSEUM, UNIVERSITY OF MIAMI, GIFT OF MARTIN Z. MARGULIES.

Example 22.13 *David Del Tredici,* In Memory of a Summer Day: *Allegretto*

works leap to the foreground. The most obvious of these are a waltz from Richard Strauss's *Der Rosenkavalier,* a fragment from Ravel's *La Valse,* and moments from Berg's *Wozzeck* and Debussy's *La Mer.* It ends, as did the "parody" or imitation Masses of the sixteenth century, with a literal quotation of the last measures of its model. Yet the piece creates a strongly individual impression, akin to a stream of consciousness—in this case Berio's musical consciousness—which he appears to be placing on display, with different styles and epochs occupying the same musical space.

Del Tredici

One of the most remarkable re-creations of an earlier musical world is David Del Tredici's *In Memory of a Summer Day* (*Child Alice,* Part One, 1980). In a soaring, passionate transformation of the work's principal melody (Example 22.13), Del Tredici (b. 1937) translated Wagner's *Liebestod* into modern—but not too modern—terms without borrowing any of Wagner's motives, only his manner of developing them, his harmony, and his sumptuous orchestration. The resemblance of the theme to the "kiss" motive in Verdi's *Otello* may be accidental. The aim of the backward look seems in this case to be communication rather than parody or irony (see vignette, page 784). Del Tredici, a student of Earl Kim and Roger Sessions at Princeton, established his

■ *Philip Johnson, the architect of Tycon Towers (1983–88) in Vienna, Virginia, blends elements from the past in his design—for example, columns and arches, with patterns of glass and concrete. This approach, sometimes called "post-modern," rejects the stark glass walls and undecorated façades of many mid-twentieth-century buildings.* PHOTOGRAPH BY RICHARD PAYNE, © 1987)

DAVID DEL TREDICI ON COMPOSING *FINAL ALICE*

About halfway through the piece, I thought, "Oh my God, if I just leave it like this, my colleagues will think I'm crazy." But then I thought, "What else can I do? If nothing else occurs to me I can't go against my instincts." But I was *terrified* my colleagues would think I was an idiot. . . . People think now that I wanted to be tonal and have a big audience. But that was just not true. I *didn't* want to be tonal. My world was my colleagues—my composing friends. . . . The success of *Final Alice* was very defining as to who my real friends were. I think many composers regard success as a kind of threat. It's really better, they think, if *nobody* has any success, to be all in one boat. Composers now are beginning to realize that if a piece excites an audience, *that doesn't mean it's terrible*. For my generation, it is considered vulgar to have an audience really, *really* like a piece on a first hearing. But why are we writing music except to move people and to be expressive? To have what has moved us move somebody else?

Right now, audiences just reject contemporary music. But if they start to like *one* thing, then they begin to have perspective. That will make a difference, it always has in the past. The sleeping giant is the audience.

From an interview with John Rockwell, in *The New York Times*, Sunday, October 26, 1980, Section D, pp. 23, 28.

contemporary credentials by composing atonal music before beginning his extended series of works (1968–86) on Lewis Carroll's *Alice's Adventures in Wonderland* and *Through the Looking Glass. Final Alice* (1975) is brilliantly scored for soprano, orchestra, and a "folk group" of two soprano saxophones, mandolin, banjo, and accordion. Here the manner owes more to Richard Strauss than to Wagner, but in the midst of this determinedly Romantic tonal writing there are also folklike episodes as well as others that are atonal, all fused into a compound of irresistible charm.

CONCLUSIONS

Of the four basic components of Western music that began taking shape as far back as the eleventh century—composition, notation, principles of order, and polyphony and harmony—some have been altered and others restored by twentieth-century developments. Composition, in the sense that a work of music exists apart from any particular performance, has in some quarters given way to controlled improvisation, which was the practice in antiquity and the early Middle Ages. As to notation, the score in many cases is now less than ever a definitive set of directions. The performer, instead of being only a

Composition

Notation

mediator between composer and audience, is sharing in the creation of a work with the composer, as was true until the eighteenth century. Principles of order have been challenged by indeterminacy and by chance, allowing an outside force to impose the succession of musical events, as liturgy and ritual did in earlier times and still do in many situations. Polyphony and to a lesser extent harmony, though transformed, remain. What the twentieth century has witnessed has been a realignment of values and means, rather than a revolution.

Principles of order

Polyphony and harmony

The radical changes that have come and gone affected only a small number of listeners. The audience for "serious" music—art music of a certain complexity that requires some effort to understand—has never been more than a small fraction of the population. That audience is still relatively small, and within it the audience for the new and experimental is even smaller. Composers who write in a difficult, unfamiliar idiom cannot expect a large popular following.

Most composers have always cared about their audience, and in the last quarter of the twentieth century more and more composers addressed their works to the public rather than to other composers, connoisseurs, and analysts. A concern with the gap between composer and listener has led to simplification and even minimalization of content. Hybrid styles have sprung from marriages between art music and popular, ethnic, non-Western, and traditional musics. Composers are once again letting the organization of music be heard instead of concealing it. Finally, they have built bridges between the familiar music of the past and the music of the present.

Bibliography

For Further Reading

General

The best short introduction to twentieth-century American music, both "vernacular" and "cultivated," is in Parts 2, 3, and 4 of H. Wiley Hitchcock's *Music in the United States*, 3rd ed. (Englewood Cliffs, N.J.: Prentice-Hall, 1988). A more studious approach is Robert P. Morgan, *Twentieth-Century Music* (New York: Norton, 1991) and the accompanying anthology with analytical notes. Other recommended books are Charles Hamm, *Music in the New World* (New York: Norton, 1983); Gilbert Chase, *America's Music: From the Pilgrims to the Present*, 3rd ed. (Urbana: University of Illinois Press, 1987); John Rockwell, *All American Music: Composition in the Late Twentieth Century* (New York: Knopf, 1983), a survey of American music with chapters on Krenek, Babbitt, Carter, Cage, and others; William Duckworth, *Talking Music: Conversations with John Cage, Philip Glass, Laurie Anderson, and Five Generations of American Experimental Composers* (New York: Schirmer Books, 1995). Barbara L. Tischler, *An American Music: The Search for an American Musical Identity* (New York: Oxford University Press, 1986); Otto Karolyi, *Modern American Music: From Charles Ives to the Minimalists* (Madison, N.J.: Fairleigh Dickinson University Press, 1996). See also the Bibliographies for Chapters 20 and 21; Frank Tirro, *Jazz, A History*, 2nd ed. (New York: Norton, 1993); Gunther Schuller, *Early Jazz: Its Roots and Musical Development* and *The Swing Era: The Development of Jazz, 1930–1945* (New York: Oxford University Press, 1968,

1989); Scott DeVeaux, *The Birth of Bebop: A Social and Musical History* (Berkeley: University of California Press, 1997).

Individual Composers

Babbitt His *Words about Music*, ed. Stephen Dembski and Joseph N. Strauss (Madison: University of Wisconsin Press, 1987); *Perspectives of New Music*, 14/2–15/1 (1976), special issue with articles on the composer, and his response. Andrew Mead, *An Introduction to the Music of Milton Babbitt* (Princeton: Princeton University Press, 1994).

Cage His own writings, particularly *Silence: Lectures and Writings* (Middletown, Conn.: Wesleyan University Press, 1973), which gives the best idea of his work and theories; *A Year from Monday* (London: Calder & Boyars, 1968); *M: Writings, 1967–73* and *X: Writings, 1979–82* (Middletown, Conn.: Wesleyan University Press, 1973, 1979); *Composition in Retrospect* (Cambridge, Mass.: Exact Change, 1993). Richard Kostelanetz, *John Cage (ex)plain(ed)* (New York: Schirmer Books, 1996); Paul Griffiths, *Cage* (London: Oxford University Press, 1981); James Pritchett, *The Music of John Cage* (Cambridge: Cambridge University Press, 1993); Christopher Shultis, *Silencing the Sounded Self: John Cage and the American Experimental Tradition* (Boston: Northeastern University Press, 1998).

Carter David Schiff, *The Music of Elliott Carter*, 2nd ed. (Ithaca, N.Y.: Cornell University Press, 1998); Allen Edwards, ed., *Flawed Words and Stubborn Sounds: A Conversation with Elliott Carter* (New York: Norton, 1971); *Elliott Carter: Collected Essays and Lectures, 1937–1995*, ed. Jonathan W. Bernard (Rochester, N.Y.: University of Rochester Press, 1997); William T. Doering, *Elliott Carter: A Bio-Bibliography* (Westport, Conn.: Greenwood Press, 1993).

Copland His own writings include *Music and Imagination* (Cambridge, Mass.: Harvard University Press, 1952); *The New Music 1900–1960*, rev. ed. (New York: Norton, 1968); *Copland on Music* (Garden City, N.Y.: Doubleday, 1960). JoAnn Skowronski, *Aaron Copland: A Bio-bibliography* (Westport, Conn.: Greenwood Press, 1985); Neil Butterworth, *The Music of Aaron Copland* (New York: Universe Books, 1986); Aaron Copland and Vivian Perlis, *Copland: 1900 through 1942* and *Copland: Since 1943* (New York: St. Martin's Press, 1984, 1989); Howard Pollack, *Aaron Copland: The Life and Work of an Uncommon Man* (New York: Henry Holt, 1999).

Cowell His *New Musical Resources*, ed. David Nicholls (Cambridge: Cambridge University Press, 1996) and *The Writings of Henry Cowell*, ed. Bruce Saylor and William Lichtenwanger (Brooklyn: Institute for Studies in American Music, 1977). Lichtenwanger, *The Music of Henry Cowell: A Descriptive Catalog* (Brooklyn: Institute for Studies in American Music, 1986); Hugo Weisgall, "The Music of Henry Cowell," *Musical Quarterly* 45 (1959):484–507.

Crumb Don Gillespie, ed., *George Crumb: Profile of a Composer* (New York: Peters, 1985).

Glass Robert T. Jones, ed. *Music by Philip Glass* (New York: Harper & Row, 1987); *Writings on Glass: Essays, Interviews, Criticism*, ed. Richard Kostelanetz and Robert Flemming (Berkeley: University of California Press, 1999).

Gershwin Steven E. Gilbert, *The Music of Gershwin* (New Haven: Yale University Press, 1995); Isaac Goldberg, *George Gershwin: A Study in American Music*, rev. ed. (New York: Simon & Schuster, 1958). *The Gershwin Style: New Looks at the Music of George Gershwin*, ed. Wayne Schneider (New York: Oxford University Press, 1999); Joan Peyser, *The Mem-*

ory of All That: The Life of George Gershwin (New York: Simon & Schuster, 1993); Rodney Greenberg, *George Gershwin* (London: Phaidon, 1998).

Ives His *Essays Before a Sonata, The Majority, and Other Writings* (New York: Norton, 1970) and *Memos*, ed. John Kirkpatrick (New York: Norton, 1972). Philip Lambert, *The Music of Charles Ives* (New Haven, Conn.: Yale University Press, 1997); J. Peter Burkholder, *Charles Ives: The Ideas behind the Music* (New Haven: Yale University Press, 1985); H. Wiley Hitchcock, *Ives* (London: Oxford University Press, 1977); Hitchcock and Vivian Perlis, eds., *An Ives Celebration* (Urbana: University of Illinois Press, 1977); Perlis, *Charles Ives Remembered: An Oral History* (New York: Norton, 1976); *Ives Studies*, ed. Philip Lambert (Cambridge: Cambridge University Press, 1997); Jan Swafford, *Charles Ives: A Life with Music* (New York: Norton, 1996). J. Peter Burkholder, *All Made of Tunes: Charles Ives and the Uses of Musical Borrowing* (New Haven: Yale University Press, 1995); *Charles Ives and His World*, ed. J. Peter Burkholder (Princeton: Princeton University Press, 1996); *Charles Ives and the Classical Tradition*, ed. Geoffrey Block and J. Peter Burkholder (New Haven, Conn.: Yale University Press, 1996).

Rochberg His *The Aesthetics of Survival: A Composer's View of Twentieth-Century Music*, ed. William Bolcom (Ann Arbor: University of Michigan Press, 1984). Joan DeVee Dixon, *George Rochberg, A Bio-bibliographic Guide to His Life and Works* (Stuyvesant, N.Y.: Pendragon, 1992).

Sessions His writings in *The Musical Experience of Composer, Performer, Listener* (Princeton: Princeton University Press, 1962) and *Questions about Music* (New York: Norton, 1971); *Roger Sessions on Music: Collected Essays*, ed. Edward T. Cone (Princeton: Princeton University Press, 1979). Andrea Olmstead, *Roger Sessions and His Music* (Ann Arbor: UMI Research Press, 1985); Olmstead, ed., *Conversations with Roger Sessions* (Boston: Northeastern University Press, 1987) and *The Correspondence of Roger Sessions* (Boston: Northeastern University Press, 1992).

Thomson His own writings in *Music with Words: A Composer's View* (New Haven: Yale University Press, 1989), his *American Music since 1910* (London: Weidenfeld & Nicolson, 1967), and *The Art of Judging Music* (New York: Knopf, 1948). Anthony Tommasini, *Virgil Thomson: Composer on the Aisle* (New York: Norton, 1997); Michael Meckna, *Virgil Thomson, A Bio-bibliography* (New York: Greenwood Press, 1986). Kathleen Hoover and John Cage, *Virgil Thomson, His Life and Music* (New York: T. Yoseloff, 1959).

Varèse Louise Varèse, *Varèse: A Looking-Glass Diary* (New York: Norton, 1972); Sherman Van Solkema, ed., *The New Worlds of Edgard Varèse* (Brooklyn: Institute for Studies in American Music, 1979); Jonathan Bernard, *The Music of Edgar Varèse* (New Haven: Yale University Press, 1987); Fernand Ouellette, *A Biography of Edgard Varèse* (New York: Orion Press, 1966, 1981).

See also the bibliographies in *The New Grove Twentieth-Century American Masters: Barber, Bernstein, Cage, Carter, Copland, Cowell, Gershwin, Ives, Sessions, Thomson* (New York: Norton, 1988).

GLOSSARY

Within a definition, terms that are themselves defined in this glossary are printed in SMALL CAPITALS. Terms that are special to a narrow topic are explained in the text and are not included here, nor are terms that are defined in general dictionaries. Page numbers following the definitions refer to discussions in the text that concern the defined term.

Language abbreviations: Fr. = French; Ger. = German; Gr. = Greek; It. = Italian; Lat. = Latin; Port. = Portuguese; Sp. = Spanish. *Also:* sing. = singular; pl. = plural.

Abgesang See **Bar form**.

Accidental Sign that calls for altering the pitch of a note: raising it by a sharp, ♯; lowering it by a flat, ♭; or canceling a previous such sign by a "natural," ♮ (pp. 53, 113).

Ad libitum (Lat. "at pleasure") Details of execution left to the discretion of the performer (p. 737).

Affection Fixed state of mind, such as rage, fear, or wonder, not unlike a persistent emotion (pp. 257, 431–32).

Aggregate Unordered set of the PITCH-CLASSES of the CHROMATIC SCALE (p. 769).

Agrément (Fr. "charm") ORNAMENT in French music, usually indicated by a sign (pp. 303, 354–55).

Air (1) Tune. (2) Tuneful song in a French stage work, usually in a dance METER (pp. 318, 385). (3) English or French art song with lute or viol accompaniment (pp. 202–4, 218).

Air de cour French MONODIC song (pp. 197, 285).

Alberti bass Broken-CHORD accompaniment named after Domenico Alberti, a composer who used it frequently (pp. 429, 520).

Aleatory (Lat. *alea* "dice") Deliberately leaving the choice of pitches, rhythmic values, or the order of events to chance (pp. 677, 687).

Allemande, alman Dance in moderate duple METER, often the first dance of a SUITE (pp. 216, 352).

Ambitus Pitch range of a MODE or PLAINCHANT.

Anthem MOTET-like composition on an English text; a *verse anthem* is for solo voice and chorus with instrumental accompaniment, a *full anthem* for chorus without soloist (pp. 231–33, 333–34).

Antiphonal Pertaining to a method of performance in which one group answers another (pp. 44, 286–88).

Archlute Lute with an extra pegbox for long bass strings tuned DIATONICALLY to play bass notes in a CONTINUO; also called *theorbo.*

Aria (It. "air") (1) Tune or formula for singing poetry (p. 301). (2) Strophic song. (3) Songful monologue or duet in an OPERA or other vocal work (pp. 274, 276–78, 281–82).

Arioso (It. "airy") (1) Short for *recitativo arioso,* "tuneful RECITATIVE" (p. 313). (2) Free lyric passage not formally organized as an aria.

Arpeggio (from It. *arpa* "harp") Broken-CHORD FIGURE.

Atonal (atonality) Pertaining to music that avoids a TONAL center but is not built on SERIAL principles (pp. 714–15).

Authentic A mode's primary form, in which the final is the lowest note of the octave range. See also **Plagal** (pp. 52–54).

Ballad opera Eighteenth-century English comic play with songs in which new texts are set to familiar tunes (pp. 444–45).

Ballade (1) One of the French FORMES FIXES of the fourteenth and fifteenth centuries, each stanza having an overall AAB form (pp. 102–3, 135). (2) Instrumental piece inspired by the genre of narrative poetry (pp. 578, 580). (3) Composed setting of a narrative poem (pp. 593–94).

Ballet Entertainment in which both professionals and guests danced; later, a stage work danced by professionals (pp. 214–15, 273–74).

Bar form Song form in which the first melodic component is sung twice with different texts (the two *Stollen*); the remainder (the *Abgesang*) is sung once (p. 63).

Baroque (from Port. *barroco* "misshapen," as in a bulbous pearl) (1) Bizarre, extravagant (pp. 251–52, 373). (2) Period of music history from ca. 1580 to ca. 1730.

Basse danse Family of dances, some duple, some triple, or a mixture of the two, whose music was often IMPROVISED over a TENOR CANTUS FIRMUS (p. 216).

Basso continuo A foundation for IMPROVISED CHORDS that filled in the HARMONY in the BAROQUE period (pp. 257–58). See also FIGURED BASS.

Bel canto (It. "beautiful singing") Smooth, fluent, vocal line that shows off the singer's voice (pp. 278, 282).

Binary (Lat. "made up of two") A two-part form (pp. 354, 359–60, 450, 452).

Blue notes Lowered third, seventh, and sometimes fifth degrees of the MAJOR SCALE, used especially in African-American music (p. 749–50).

Blues (1) Standard 12-bar chord progression: I-I-I-I-IV-IV-I-I-V-IV-I-I (p. 749). (2) African-American vocal genre (pp. 749–50).

Bridge See **Transition**

Cadence Melodic or harmonic succession that closes a musical phrase, section, or composition (pp. 109–10, 114–18, 134). A cadence may be evaded by preparing the close but then moving on (pp. 170–71).

Cadenza (It. "cadence") IMPROVISED passage usually placed just before the end of a piece or section (pp. 362, 505).

Camerata Circle of intellectuals and amateurs of the arts that met in Florence at the home of Giovanni Bardi in the 1570s and 1580s (p. 263).

Canon (Gr. *kanōn* "rule") (1) Rule for performing music, particularly for deriving more than one voice from a single line of notated music, as when several voices sing the same MELODY, entering at certain intervals of time or singing at different speeds simultaneously (pp. 158–160). (2) Composition in which the voices enter successively at determined pitch and time intervals, all performing the same melody.

Cantata (It. "sung") (1) Composition for solo voice containing RECITATIVES and ARIAS (pp. 284–85, 324–26). (2) SACRED CONCERTO.

Cantus firmus (Lat. "plain chant"; pl. *cantus firmi*) PLAINCHANT or other MELODY used as a basis for a POLYPHONIC composition (pp. 126–27, 137–41).

Canzona In the sixteenth century an instrumental chanson; later, a piece for ensemble in several sections or tempos (pp. 182–83, 209–11, 297, 358).

Chaconne (Fr; Sp. **chacona**; It. **ciaccona**) (1) Dance song in triple time, originating in Latin America. (2) A composition having an extended pattern of CHORDS. (3) French dance with REFRAINS (pp. 279, 354).

Chanson (Fr. "song") Secular French song, either of popular origin or composed anew, usually arranged POLYPHONICALLY (pp. 194–97).

Chant See **Plainchant**.

Chitarrone See **Archlute**.

Choirbook Large-format manuscript or printed book of music NOTATION large enough to be read by the choir standing around it (pp. 90, 152, 195).

Chorale STROPHIC hymn used in the German Lutheran Church (pp. 225–28, 334–35).

Chorale prelude Organ arrangement of a CHORALE played before the congregation sings it (pp. 350, 390–91).

Chord Three or more simultaneous pitches heard as a single entity.

Chromatic (chromaticism) (1) One of the GENERA of Greek music (p. 8). (2) Pertaining to a MELODY or SCALE that uses successive half steps (pp. 188, 259–60). (3) In mid-sixteenth-century MADRIGALS, writing many black notes in the TIME SIGNATURE **C** (pp. 188, 109).

Classic, classical (1) Art music as opposed to VERNACULAR or entertainment music. (2) Period or style from ca. 1730 to ca. 1820 (pp. 425–26, 542).

Clausula (Lat. "end, concluding sentence or verse") (1) CADENCE. (2) Phrase of PLAINCHANT. (3) Measured ORGANUM set to MELISMATIC fragment of PLAINCHANT (pp. 80–81).

Clavecin French term for harpsichord (p. 302).

Coda (It. "tail") A supplementary ending to a composition (p. 453).

Collegium musicum Ensemble or orchestra made up mostly of amateurs such as university students (pp. 365, 397).

Color (From Lat. rhetoric "ornament," particularly repetition) In an ISORHYTHMIC composition, a repeated melodic, as opposed to rhythmic, pattern (pp. 100–101, 104).

Commedia dell'arte Professional, IMPROVISED Italian comedy of the sixteenth and seventeenth centuries using standard characters (pp. 316, 432, 708).

Concertato (adj. from It. *concertare* "to agree upon or act together") (1) Concerted, that is, joining instruments and voices. (2) Performing as a soloist, as in *violino concertato* (pp. 280–82, 335).

Concertino (It. "little concerto") Ensemble of few solo instruments, as opposed to CONCERTO GROSSO, large ensemble with numerous players to part (p. 328).

Concerto (Fr. **concert**; Eng. **consort**) (1) Ensemble of instruments or voices. (2) Composition for instruments or voices. (3) Composition in which one or more solo performers join an orchestral ensemble (pp. 280, 287–89, 292, 366–69, 502–5). See also SACRED CONCERTO.

Concerto for few voices See **Sacred concerto.**

Concerto grosso (It. "large concerto") (1) TUTTI or RIPIENO—the full orchestra in a CONCERTO. (2) Composition for a full orchestra or for such an orchestra alternating with a small group of soloists, the CONCERTINO (pp. 367–68, 409–10).

Concitato (It. "excited") Style in which a single note or CHORD is rapidly repeated, mixed with fanfares, to suggest belligerence and battle (p. 281).

Conductus (pl. *conductus*) (1) Medieval MONOPHONIC song, usually sacred, on rhythmical Latin verse (pp. 57–58, 92). (2) Measured POLYPHONIC setting of an original MELODY (pp. 84, 90, 92, 124).

Consonance (consonant) INTERVAL or CHORD that has a stable, agreeable sound. In early times only octaves, fifths, and fourths were considered consonant; later, thirds and sixths were included (pp. 72–73, 147, 186–87, 237, 239).

Consort See **Concerto.**

Continuo See **Basso continuo.**

Contrafactum (pl. *contrafacta*) Composition in which a new text is substituted for the original one—for example, a sacred text for a secular one (pp. 165, 224–26).

Counterpoint (contrapuntal) Artful combination of two or more simultaneous melodic lines (pp. 105–6, 153–54, 163, 236–37, 258–59).

Courante, corrente Fluent dance in moderate triple METER (pp. 216, 352).

Da capo aria Two-section ARIA form. The first section is repeated after the second section's close, which carries the instruction *da capo* (It. "from the head") (pp. 313–14, 436–38).

Development Process or section in which a subject is taken apart, combined with other ideas, and reworked (p. 452).

Diatonic (1) One of the GENERA of Greek music (p. 8). (2) Pertaining to a MELODY or SCALE that mixes whole tones and semitones without consecutive half steps.

Diminution (1) Uniform reduction of note values in a MELODY or phrase. (2) Replacing a long note with a run or other FIGURE composed of short notes, also called "division" (pp. 254, 350, 362).

Discant (Lat. "singing apart") (1) TREBLE part. (2) IMPROVISED or written POLYPHONY in which voices move at same speed, particularly when all are measured (p. 74).

Dissonance (dissonant) (1) INTERVAL or CHORD that is disagreeable or that requires RESOLUTION. Seconds, TRITONES, and sevenths, and chords containing them are considered dissonant (pp. 147, 237, 239). (2) A note not belonging in a chord, a nonharmonic tone (p. 259).

Ditone INTERVAL spanning two whole tones.

Divertissement (Fr. "entertainment, diversion") Entertaining episodes of BALLET, tuneful AIRS, and spectacle within serious French OPERAS (pp. 316, 320, 384).

Division See **Diminution.**

Dodecaphonic Pertaining to composition with TWELVE-TONE ROWS (p. 716).

Dominant Fifth degree of a MAJOR or MINOR scale.

Double (Fr. "double") Immediate embellished repetition of a piece, such as a SUITE movement (pp. 352, 394).

Drone Note or notes, usually in the bass, sustained throughout an entire piece or section (p. 74).

Duplum (Lat. *duplus* "double") Voice part in early POLYPHONY set against a TENOR (p. 85).

Dynamics Variation of loudness and intensity (pp. 211, 456).

Empfindsamkeit (Ger. "sentimentality, sensitivity"; adj. *empfindsam*) Quality of refined passion and melancholy in eighteenth-century music (pp. 330, 425–26, 428, 454–56).

Enharmonic (1) One of the GENERA of Greek music (p. 8). (2) Pertains to a MELODY or SCALE that uses steps smaller than a semitone. (3) Pertains to a change in the NOTATION and function of a single pitch, as from *E*♭ to *D*♯.

Episode Passage, especially in a FUGUE, that does not state the principal subject (p. 348).

Ethos (Gr. "custom") Character, mood, or emotional effect of a certain TONOS, MODE, meter, style, or composition (pp. 6-7, 12–13, 146).

Étude Exercise to develop instrumental technique (p. 581).

Exposition Section of a FUGUE, SONATA, or CONCERTO in which the main subject or subjects are announced (p. 452).

Expressionism Exaggerated and extreme subjectivity in artistic expression (pp. 715–16, 720–21).

Fancy Fantasy for a solo instrument or ensemble (pp. 217, 297).

Fantasia (It. "fantasy") Instrumental composition lacking a strict form, often IMPROVISATORY (pp. 212, 214). (2) Instrumental piece developing an abstract subject, often invented by the composer (p. 577). See also FANCY.

Fauxbourdon (Fr. "false bass") Scheme for IMPROVISING a third part between a PLAINCHANT in the TREBLE and a lower voice. The outer voices form parallel sixths, while the middle voice is a fourth below the PLAINCHANT, though they start and end phrases with an octave mediated by a fifth (pp. 125–26).

Figure, figuration Melodic pattern, usually ORNAMENTAL, made of commonplace material such as SCALES, ARPEGGIOS, and turns, not distinctive enough to be considered a MOTIVE or THEME (pp. 217–18, 346, 362).

Figured bass THOROUGHBASS with numbers to indicate the intervals above it that form the required CHORDS (p. 258).

Final Step of a mode that is the normal closing note of a PLAINCHANT or TENOR part (pp. 52–54).

Finale Last movement of a work or the closing scene of an act in an OPERA (p. 470).

Folk music See **Traditional music**.

Formes fixes (Fr. "fixed forms") Schemes of poetic and musical repetition used in the late Middle Ages, such as VIRELAI, RONDEAU and BALLADE (pp. 102, 120).

French overture See **Ouverture**.

Fret Raised strip of material, such as leather, guiding and aiding the stopping of strings on a fingerboard (p. 208).

Fugato Short FUGUE, usually in the midst of nonfugal music.

Fuging tune Arrangement of hymn using free IMITATION (pp. 742–43).

Fugue, fuga (fugal) (Lat. and It. "flight") (1) Composition or section of a composition in which a subject is answered or repeated successively by several parts (pp. 346, 392–93). (2) Before 1550 one type of *fuga* was a strict CANON (p. 158).

Galant (Fr. "elegant") (1) Smart, chic, sophisticated. (2) Light, HOMOPHONIC early eighteenth-century style of music that treats CONTRAPUNTAL rules freely (pp. 427–28).

Galliard Lively dance in triple meter that usually followed a PAVANE (p. 215).

Gamut (Contraction of *gamma*—Greek Γ (*G*)—and the first solmization syllable, *ut*, of the hard hexachord) Entire range of pitches (p. 55).

Gebrauchsmusik (Ger. "utilitarian music") Music for amateurs, children, and workers to play and sing (p. 677).

Genera (Lat. "classes"; sing. *genus*) In Greek music, three classes of MELODY or ways of tuning the TETRACHORD: DIATONIC, CHROMATIC, and ENHARMONIC (pp. 8, 149).

Gesamtkunstwerk (Ger. "joint or integrated artwork") Theatrical work envisioned by Richard Wagner that unites poetry, scenery, staging, action, and music, all working toward a dramatic goal (p. 625).

Gigue (Eng. **jig**) Quick dance usually in triple METER (p. 352).

Grand concerto See **Sacred concerto.**

Grand motet (Fr. "large motet") Seventeenth- and eighteenth-century French SACRED CONCERTO for soloists, double choruses, and orchestra (p. 332).

Ground bass Pattern of bass notes repeated as a foundation for HARMONY (p. 279). See also OSTINATO, CHACONNE, and PASSACAGLIA.

Gruppo Early Italian word for trill (p. 266).

Harmonia (Gr.; pl. *harmoniai*) Greek SCALE or MODE having a certain OCTAVE SPECIES or configuration of INTERVALS, not unlike a PLAINCHANT mode. Harmoniae were sometimes given ethnic names, such as Dorian and Lydian (pp. 13, 53). See also TONOS.

Harmonic (1) High thin tone produced by lightly touching the string, such as of a violin, at $\frac{1}{2}$, $\frac{1}{3}$, $\frac{1}{4}$, etc., of its length. (2) Overtone, or partial, of a vibrating string or air column (p. 729).

Harmony Aspect of music that pertains to simultaneous combinations of sounds, particularly CONSONANT ones.

Hemiola (from Gr. *hemiolios* "one and a half") Three beats against two in an equivalent amount of time, whether between voices or successive MEASURES, as in one measure of $\frac{3}{2}$ against two measure of $\frac{3}{4}$ (pp. 134, 352).

Heterophony Same MELODY performed simultaneously in more than one way, for example, simply and ORNAMENTED (pp. 4, 71).

Hexachord (1) Set of six pitches. (2) In medieval theory and practice, three types of hexachord were distinguished: according to whether the *B* was absent ("natural" hexachord, as in *C–A*); *B* was natural ("hard hexachord," as in *G–E*); or *B* was flat ("soft" hexachord, as in *F–D* with *B*♭) (pp. 55, 217–18). See also SOLMIZATION.

Hocket (Lat. *hoquetus;* Fr. *hoquet* "hiccup") Device of splitting a melodic line between two voices, or a composition based on this device (pp. 89, 100–1).

Homophony (homophonic) Music in which the HARMONY is chordal and not made up of distinctive lines (pp. 123, 182).

Homorhythmic Having the same RHYTHM, as when several voices sing the same syllables with the same durations (p. 84).

Humanism Movement in the RENAISSANCE to revive ancient Greek and Roman culture (pp. 144–47).

Imitation Device of repeating a MOTIVE or MELODY announced in one part in a second or more parts, often at a different pitch level and not always accurately (p. 168).

Imitation Mass Mass in which movements are based on a single POLYPHONIC model, such as a MOTET or MADRIGAL, all of whose voices may be borrowed or reworked; also called "parody Mass" (p. 166).

Impressionism Style that evokes moods and sensuous impressions through HARMONY and tone color (pp. 663–65).

Improvisation (improvised) Spontaneous invention of music, embellishment, or accompaniment while performing (pp. 32, 71, 105, 123, 214, 361–62, 750–51).

In nomine CANTUS FIRMUS, derived from the Benedictus of Taverner's *Western Wynde* Mass, used in sets of instrumental VARIATIONS by English composers (pp. 209, 231).

Indeterminacy Freedom from a composer's NOTATIONAL prescription (pp. 734–37, 776–77).

Intermedio Pastoral, allegorical, or mythological interlude of vocal and instrumental music performed before and between the acts of a spoken comedy or tragedy (p. 261).

Intermezzo A brief comic operatic work performed between the acts of a serious OPERA (pp. 434–35).

Interval Distance in pitch between two notes.

Interval class If the half-steps or PITCH CLASSES of the chromatic octave are numbered from 0 to 11, the differences between the integers yield seven interval classes, namely the intervals possible in an octave if inversions are not counted. For example, the major third and the minor sixth belong to the same interval class 4, the pitch classes being four half-steps apart in the nearest direction.

Intonation The first notes of a plainchant, sung by a soloist to establish the pitch for the choir, which joins the soloist to continue the chant (pp. 42–43).

Inversion (1) Shifting the position of the notes in a CHORD so that a different one is the lowest. (2) Reversing the upward or downward direction of melodic INTERVALS while maintaining their size. (3) In COUNTERPOINT, placing a part above a given part that had been below it.

Isorhythm (Gr. "equal rhythm") Repetition in a voice part (usually the TENOR) of an extended pattern of durations throughout a section or an entire composition (pp. 99–101, 104, 727).

Jig See **Gigue**

Just intonation Method of tuning that affords both perfect and imperfect CONSONANCES in their purest form as demonstrated by the simple ratios of their frequencies, such as 3:2 for the perfect fifth and 5:4 for the major third (p. 149).

Key See **Tonality**.

Key signature Sharp(s) or flat(s) placed on line(s) or space(s) at the beginning of each staff.

Kitharode Singer or poet who accompanies self on the kithara (p. 4).

Petit motet (Fr. "little motet") French version of the SACRED CONCERTO for a few voices (p. 333).
Phrygian cadence CADENCE in which the lowest voice descends by a semitone and the highest ascends by a whole tone (pp. 114–15).
Pitch-class One of twelve pitches of the CHROMATIC SCALE without reference to register, such as *C* when it refers to all *C*s in the GAMUT.
Plagal (Gr. **plagios**, "placed sideways") Refers to the collateral MODE that shares a FINAL with an AUTHENTIC mode and has a range approximately a fourth lower (pp. 52–54).
Plainchant, plainsong (Lat. *cantus planus*) Monophonic sacred chant or song of the Christian church, performed in free rhythm (pp. 31, 137).
Polychoral TEXTURE in which two or more choruses alternate and join together (pp. 282–88).
Polyphony (polyphonic) Musical TEXTURE consisting of two or more lines of MELODY (pp. 33, 70–73). See also COUNTERPOINT.
Polytonality Combination of two or more lines of melody that are in different TONALITIES (pp. 682, 701).
Prelude Introductory piece in an OPERA, SUITE, or instrumental composition (pp. 212, 214, 388).
Prima pratica See **Seconda pratica.**
Program music Music that is descriptive, narrative, or that develops a nonmusical subject (pp. 379, 544–45, 639–41).
Prologue Dramatic scene or speech before the beginning of a spoken or musical stage work (p. 269).
Proper (Lat., *proprium de tempore* "proper of the time") Texts and PLAINCHANTS of the Mass that are assigned to particular days in the church calendar (pp. 36, 44–45).
Psalm tone Formula for chanting psalms on a reciting tone, which varies with the MODE, including patterns for beginning (*initium*), continuing (TENOR), temporarily resting (*flex*), resuming (*mediatio*), and closing (*terminatio*) (pp. 42–43).
Pythagorean tuning Having perfect CONSONANCES in ratios of 2 : 1 (octave), 3 : 2 (fifth), and 4 : 3 (fourth), unlike other INTERVALS, which have irrational ratios, such as 81 : 64 (DITONE, or major third) (pp. 148–49, 349).

Quodlibet (Lat. "whatever you please") Composition juxtaposing several borrowed melodies (p. 394).

Recapitulation Section of a movement in which the subjects announced in the EXPOSITION are reviewed (p. 453).
Récitatif mesuré (Fr. "measured recitative") Songful RECITATIVE in French seventeenth- and eighteenth-century OPERA that maintained a uniform METER (pp. 317–18).
Récitatif simple (Fr. "simple recitative") Speechlike RECITATIVE in French seventeenth- and eighteenth-century OPERA that frequently shifted between duple and triple METERS (p. 317).

Ländler Austrian and South German dance in triple METER (pp. 546, 634).
Lauda (Lat. *laudare* "to praise") Italian devotional song (pp. 64, 183).
Leitmotif (Ger. "leading motive") Musical THEME or MOTIVE associated with a person, thing, emotion, or idea in a drama (pp. 625–27).
Libretto Literary text for a musical stage work (pp. 274, 410, 436).
Lied (Ger. "song"; pl. lieder) German song, such as a POLYPHONIC partsong or an accompanied art song (pp. 197–98, 447–49, 593–98).
Ligature NEUME-like shape used to indicate a short rhythmic pattern in the NOTATION of the twelfth to the sixteenth centuries (p. 77, 89–90).

Madrigal (It. *madrigale* "song in the mother tongue") (1) Fourteenth-century Italian VERSE form and its musical setting having two or three stanzas followed by a RITORNELLO (pp. 106–7). (2) Sixteenth-century Italian poem having any number of lines, each of seven or eleven syllables (p. 183). (3) POLYPHONIC or CONCERTATO setting of such a poem or of a canzona, sonnet, etc. (4) English part-song imitating the Italian models (pp. 200–2).
Major scale DIATONIC succession of notes with a major third as the third step.
March Piece in duple METER to accompany military stepping (p. 747).
Masque English entertainment in which guests and professionals joined in a dance performance, sometimes including RECITATIVES, songs, and choruses (pp. 273, 320–21).
Measure Metrical unit set off by barlines.
Meistersinger (Ger. "master singer") German singer and composer of song (*Meistergesang*) practiced by fourteenth- to sixteenth-century burgher-musicians' guilds (pp. 63–64).
Melisma (melismatic) Flowing passage of many notes sung to a single syllable, particularly of PLAINCHANT (pp. 20, 40, 44–45).
Melodrama Theatrical genre that combined spoken dialogue with background music (p. 619).
Melody (1) Succession of tones perceived as a coherent line. (2) Tune. (3) Principal part accompanied by other parts or CHORDS.
Meter Pattern of beats in a MEASURE, such as $\frac{3}{4}$.
Minimalism Type of music deliberately limiting musical material and vocabulary, often marked by continual repetition of a short MELODY, FIGURE, or CHORD with only slight variation (pp. 777–80).
Minnesinger (Ger. "singer of love") Composer or singer of medieval German song (*Minnesang*), particularly about love (pp. 62–63).
Minor scale DIATONIC succession of notes with a minor third as the third step and optional lowered sixth and seventh steps.
Minuet Dance in triple METER usually followed by a second minuet, called "Trio," after which the first minuet returns (p. 470).
Mode (1) MELODY type characterized by a certain FINAL or ending pitch, a particular arrangement of tones and semitones, and an approximate AMBITUS (pp. 7, 20–21, 52–54). (2) Rhythmic pattern of two or three short and longer durations—for example, Mode 1, long-short (pp. 76–77).

Modulation Change from one TONALITY to another in the course of a composition.

Monochord Instrument used to locate INTERVALS through dividing and measuring lengths of its single string (pp. 51, 148).

Monody Accompanied solo song (p. 265).

Monophony (monophonic) Unaccompanied MELODY (pp. 4, 57, 101).

Motet (from Fr. *mot* "word") POLYPHONIC vocal composition, most often on a sacred text (pp. 84–90, 98–101, 134, 292, 402).

Motetus DUPLUM or TRIPLUM voice part in early POLYPHONY to which words are set.

Motive Short melodic or rhythmic idea.

Motto (1) Musical idea that recurs (p. 138). (2) Introduction of the main idea in the voice, prior to the completion of the instrumental RITORNELLO, in what is called a "motto ARIA" (p. 312).

Musica ficta (Lat. "feigned music") (1) Practice of raising or lowering by a semitone the pitch of a written note in a POLYPHONIC TEXTURE, particularly at a CADENCE, for the sake of smoother HARMONY or stronger part movement. (2) In early music, notes outside the standard GAMUT (*musica vera*), which excluded all flatted and sharped notes except *B*♭ (pp. 113–15, 118, 149).

Musique concrète (Fr. "concrete music") Natural sounds that are stored, combined, modified, and arranged (pp. 729–30).

Musique mesurée (Fr. "measured music") Style of sixteenth-century French music in which poetry simulating the ancient Greek and Latin syllable quantities (*vers mesurés à l'antique*) is set to combinations of long and short notes that do not fit a regular METER (p. 197).

Neo-Classicism Movement in the twentieth century to revive forms, genres, and styles of the eighteenth century (pp. 699–701).

Neume Sign placed above a syllable to indicate the pitch height of one or more PLAINCHANT notes (pp. 36–37, 56–57).

Notation Writing down of music, usually on a staff of lines, using signs that define the pitch, duration, and other qualities of sound (pp. 13, 36–38, 56–57, 90, 100, 116–17, 188).

Octave species (sing. and pl.) Arrangement of INTERVALS, such as whole tones and semitones, in an octave (p. 11).

Office Monastic ritual celebrated at certain hours of the day and night (pp. 32–33, 42–44).

Opera (operatic) (It. "work") (1) Dramatic stage composition, ordinarily in two or more acts (p. 260). (2) Work.

Opera buffa (It. "comical opera") Italian full-length comic OPERA sung throughout (pp. 432–35, 508).

Opéra comique (Fr. "comic opera") French full-length comic OPERA with spoken dialogue instead of RECITATIVE (pp. 442–44, 610–11).

Opera seria (It. "serious opera") Serious Italian OPERA of the eighteenth century, purged of comic scenes and characters (pp. 436–40).

Opus (Lat. "work"; pl. *opera*) A composition or set of compositions.

Oratorio Composition for solo singers, chorus, and instruments, usually dramatic and on a biblical or religious subject (pp. 289–90, 332, 412–16).

Oratorio volgare ORATORIO on a vernacular (Italian) text (p. 332).

Orchestration (1) Art of assigning musical material to individual instruments. (2) The product of this process (pp. 474–75, 606–8, 665).

Ordinary (Lat. *ordinarium missae* "the ordinary of the Mass") Texts and PLAINCHANTS of a Mass that remain the same throughout the church calendar, such as the Kyrie and Gloria (pp. 36, 45–46).

Ordre (Fr. "order") French collection of pieces that are mostly in dance rhythms, such as a SUITE (pp. 352–354).

Organum (pronounced or'-ga-num) IMPROVISED or written voice part sung against a PLAINCHANT, or the work resulting from this procedure (pp. 71–83).

Ornament, ornamentation, ornamented Decorative element, such as a TRILL or turn, written or IMPROVISED, that adds expression or charm to a melodic line (pp. 110, 193, 361–62).

Ostinato Short melodic FIGURE persistently repeated, most often in the bass (p. 216).

Ottava rima (It. "eighth rhyme") Poem of eight eleven-syllable lines in which the eighth line rhymes with the seventh (p. 183).

Ouverture (Fr. "opening") (1) French OVERTURE in two-part form, the first slow and majestic with dotted rhythms, the second quick, fluent, and FUGAL, after which the first section is often recalled (p. 320). (2) A SUITE having such an introduction (p. 366).

Overture Introduction to a stage work, ORATORIO, or instrumental SUITE; later also a brief orchestral work in one movement.

Parody Mass See **Imitation Mass.**

Partbook Volume, particularly printed, containing the music for a single vocal or instrumental part of a POLYPHONIC ensemble (p. 152).

Partita Single VARIATION of a THEME or a set of such variation (pp. 299–300, 352, 393–94).

Passacaglia (It.; Sp. *passecalle*; Fr. *passecaille*) (1) Pattern of guitar CHORDS played before and between strophes of a song. (2) Pattern of pitches usually serving as a foundation for HARMONY (pp. 279, 354).

Passion Setting of a New Testament account of the crucifixion of Jesus (pp. 340–41, 402–3).

Pastoral Poetic genre to which the early OPERA LIBRETTOS, such as *Euridice* of 1600, belonged (p. 262).

Pavane, pavana, paduana Slow, stately dance in duple METER, often followed by a GALLIARD (pp. 204, 215, 303).

Periodicity Quality of being organized in discrete phrases and periods (p. 428).

Recitative (from It. *stile recitativo* "recitative style") A manner of singing approaching speech (pp. 266–70, 274). See also RECITATIVO SEMPLICE and RECITATIVO OBBLIGATO.

Recitativo obbligato Orchestrally accompanied RECITATIVE, later called *recitativo accompagnato* or *recitativo stromentato* (pp. 313, 411, 436).

Recitativo semplice RECITATIVE accompanied by BASSO CONTINUO only, later called *recitativo secco* (It. "dry recitative") (p. 313).

Refrain In a song, a recurring line (or lines) of text, usually set to a recurring MELODY (pp. 60, 62, 86).

Renaissance (Fr. "rebirth") (1) Period in art and cultural history, ca. 1350–1600. (2) Period of music history, ca. 1450–1600, dominated by the rebirth of secular musical activity and the ideals of antiquity (p. 144).

Requiem Mass for the dead (pp. 35, 600).

Resolution (resolve) Relief of DISSONANCE through CONSONANCE, as in a SUSPENSION or in a dissonant seventh followed by a consonant sixth (p. 237).

Responsorial Pertaining to chanting in which a chorus answers a soloist (p. 24).

Rhythm Pattern of short and long durations.

Ricercare At first an IMPROVISED PRELUDE, later, a sedate FUGAL piece on one or more subjects (pp. 216, 295).

Ripieno (It. "full") (1) TUTTI as opposed to solo. (2) The chordal filling in a THOROUGHBASS texture (p. 367).

Ritornello (It. "refrain") (1) Instrumental interlude between sung strophes. (2) Instrumental introduction or interlude in an ARIA, CONCERTO movement, or similar piece (pp. 279, 369, 503–4).

Rococo (from Fr. *rocaille* "rockwork") Delicate architectural arabesques and similar features in music, as in the highly ORNAMENTED clavecin music composed around 1700 (p. 427).

Romanesca Formula for singing OTTAVE RIME (p. 279).

Romantic (1) Quality of free, imaginative storytelling characteristic of the nineteenth-century French *roman* (romance). (2) Period in music covering all but the first and last decades of the nineteenth century (pp. 542–45).

Root Lowest note of a CHORD built up by successive thirds.

Rondeau (Fr.; pl. *rondeaux*) One of the FORMES FIXES usually in the form A B a A a b A B (capital letters indicating a REFRAIN) (pp. 60, 103–4, 111–13).

Rubato (It. *tempo rubato* "stolen time") Advancing or delaying a beat, or slowing down and speeding up, usually for expressive effect, before restoring the regular beat or TEMPO (pp. 266, 579).

Sacred concerto Composition on a sacred text for one or more soloists and instrumental accompaniment, with chorus (*grand concerto*) or without (*concerto for few voices*) (pp. 280, 287–89, 334–35). See also GRAND MOTET and PETIT MOTET.

Sarabande Slow dance in triple METER often emphasizing second beat (p. 352).

Scale Series of pitches in ascending or descending order.

Scherzo (It. "joke") Jesting type of movement that evolved from the MINUET (pp. 478, 538, 580).

Scordatura Unusual tuning of strings to facilitate playing certain notes or CHORDS (pp. 364, 637).

Seconda pratica Monteverdi's term for a practice of COUNTERPOINT that permits license to express the feelings of a text, also called STILE MODERNO; Monteverdi called the stricter counterpoint *prima pratica* (p. 255). See also STILE GRAVE.

Sequence (Lat. **sequentia** "something that follows") (1) A category of PLAINCHANT deriving from the MELISMA or **jubilus** that followed the alleluia to which poetic verses were set (pp. 47–49). (2) Immediate repetition of a pattern of MELODY or HARMONY on successive levels of pitch (p. 359).

Serenata (It. "serenade") Semi-dramatic piece, usually for a special occasion (p. 326).

Serial (1) Pertaining to method of composition, either with rows or with series of twelve tones or PITCH-CLASSES (pp. 716, 724). (2) Also applied to other parameters, such as duration, DYNAMICS, TIMBRE, TEXTURE (pp. 725–26).

Shape-note SOLMIZATION syllables *mi, fa, sol, la,* notated respectively by means of diamond, triangle, circle, and square shapes (p. 744).

Sinfonia (It. "symphony"; pronounced sin-fo-nee'-ah) Italian ensemble piece, OVERTURE, orchestral PRELUDE, or SYMPHONY (pp. 320, 335, 356, 365).

Singspiel (Ger. "sing-play") Spoken play interspersed with songs, choruses, instrumental music (pp. 323–24, 445).

Sketch General term for compositional ideas jotted down in a notebook, or early draft of a work (p. 522).

Solmization Pedagogic scheme for learning to sing melodies at sight by assigning the syllables *ut, re, mi, fa, sol, la* to a SCALE of six notes in which *mi-fa* is the only semitone (pp. 54–56).

Sonata (from It. *sonare* "to play") (1) Literally, a piece to be played on one or more instruments. (2) After ca. 1650, a work in several movements for church use (*sonata da chiesa*) or a SUITE of dances for secular use (*sonata da camera*) (pp. 211, 357). (3) After ca. 1750, an ambitious work in several movements for one or two solo instruments (pp. 298–99, 354, 356, 450).

Sonata form Form used mostly in first movements, usually consisting of an EXPOSITION, DEVELOPMENT, and RECAPITULATION of a limited number of themes (pp. 452–53, 476–77).

Sprechstimme (Ger. "speech-voice") Approximate speechlike intonation of written pitches according to the notated rhythm (p. 715).

Stile grave, stile antico (It. "severe style" or "old style") CONTRAPUNTALLY correct, serious, POLYPHONIC style of sacred music practiced by Palestrina and his school (pp. 240, 255).

Stile moderno (It. "modern style") Early seventeenth-century manner of composition with BASSO CONTINUO that applied COUNTERPOINT rules freely (pp. 255, 285). See also SECONDA PRATICA.

Stimmtausch (Ger. "voice exchange") Swapping of musical phrases between parts (p. 124).

Stollen See **Bar form**.

Stop Mechanism on an organ or harpsichord to turn on or off the sounding of certain sets of pipes or strings (p. 207).

Stopping Pressing a string down to the fingerboard or FRET to shorten the length of the vibrating portion (p. 208).

Stretto IMITATION of a subject at a close time-interval, even before the complete subject has been stated, as in a FUGUE (p. 348).

Strophic Poetry in which stanzas (strophes) are in equivalent form, permitting them to be sung with a single MELODY; setting such a poem to music in this way (pp. 277, 309).

Style brisé (Fr. "broken style") Technique in lute and keyboard of splitting a CHORD into a succession of individual notes (p. 303).

Suite Set of pieces, usually dances (pp. 302, 352–54, 365, 393–94).

Suspension DISSONANCE caused by a voice that moves from a CONSONANT to a dissonant relationship with a sustained note, which then descends a step to RESOLVE the dissonance (p. 237).

Syllabic One note sung to each syllable of text (p. 232).

Symphonia (Latinized Gr. "sounding together"; pronounced sim-fo'-nee-ah) (1) Ensemble piece for chorus and instruments. (2) SINFONIA (p. 292).

Symphonic poem One-movement orchestral work based on a program or nonmusical subject (pp. 555–57).

Symphony Work for orchestra in several movements (pp. 452–53).

Syncopation Displacing the normal recurrence of a strong beat by placing a long duration after a short one so that the long note seems to be accented (pp. 105, 117, 748).

Synthesizer Electronic instrument that generates musical sounds (p. 730).

Tablature NOTATION showing graphically the location of the FRETS on a lute, viol, or similar instrument that must be STOPPED to produce the music (pp. 200, 215, 301–2).

Talea An extended rhythmic pattern repeated several times in an ISORHYTHMIC composition, usually in the TENOR part (pp. 100–101).

Temperament Instrumental tuning that reduces or increases the INTERVAL size of some CONSONANCES to make others more pleasing. *Equal temperament* has equal tones and semitones (pp. 218, 349). *Meantone temperament* compromises the tuning of fifths and fourths to achieve better-sounding thirds and sixths (p. 349). See also JUST INTONATION, PYTHAGOREAN TUNING.

Tempo (It. "time") Slowness or quickness of performance.

Tenor (Lat. *tenere* "to hold") (1) Voice part that holds a long note, or the music for that part (pp. 74, 79–82, 86–88, 99–100). (2) Voice whose compass is approximately from *c'* to *g''*. (3) Reciting tone, or repercussio, in a MODE or PLAINCHANT (pp. 42, 52–53).

Ternary (Lat. **ternarius**, "made up of three") A three-part form, most often A B A (p. 650).

Tetrachord (1) In Greek and medieval theory, SCALE of four notes spanning a fourth (pp. 8–10). (2) In modern theory, set of four pitches.

Texture Interweaving, spacing, and contrasting of vocal and instrumental parts or groups of them—for example, HOMOPHONIC, POLYPHONIC, POLYCHORAL textures (pp. 84, 257–59).

Theme Musical subject of a composition or section, or of a set of VARIATIONS (pp. 216–18, 299–302, 352, 494).

Theorbo See **Archlute.**

Thoroughbass See **Basso continuo.**

Through-composed Translation of German **durchkomponiert**, meaning composed "throughout," as when each stanza or other unit of a poem is set to new music rather than in a STROPHIC manner to a single melody (p. 183).

Timbre Characteristic color or sound of an instrument or voice (p. 729).

Time signature Sign or numerical proportion, such as $\frac{3}{4}$, placed at the beginning or in the course of a composition to indicate the METER or MEASURE (pp. 116–17).

Toccata Introductory instrumental piece in IMPROVISATORY style; later, such a piece containing FUGAL sections or serving as a prelude to an independent fugue (pp. 212–14, 304, 346–48, 392).

Tombeau (Fr. "tomb") Musical tribute to a dead composer or musician (pp. 304, 669).

Tonality (tonal) (1) Means by which music is organized around a central pitch to which the other pitches of a major or minor scale are related (p. 260). (2) The central pitch of a composition.

Tone cluster Collection of notes obtained by striking piano keys with the hand or forearm (p. 758).

Tonic The first and central note of a MAJOR or MINOR SCALE.

Tonos (Gr.; pl. *tonoi*) In Greek music, a DIATONIC, CHROMATIC, or ENHARMONIC system or SCALE at a certain pitch level, similar to a modern TONALITY. Tonoi were given ethnic names, such as Dorian, Phrygian, and Lydian; some writers recognized seven, others thirteen or fifteen (pp. 10–13).

Traditional music Music indigenous to an ethnic or national group; folk music, consisting mainly of anonymous songs, dances, and patriotic music (pp. 61, 217, 646, 654–55, 680, 683–84).

Tragédie lyrique (Fr. "lyrical tragedy") French seventeenth- and eighteenth-century music drama, often modeled on contemporaneous spoken tragedies (pp. 315–317).

Transcription Arrangement of a piece for an instrumental medium different from the original, such as a reduction of an orchestral score for piano (p. 583).

Transition Section having no subject of its own serving as a bridge between thematic statements (p. 452).

Treble (1) Pertaining to highest part. (2) Highest voice or part.

Trecento (It., short for **mille trecento** "one thousand three hundred") The fourteenth century, particularly with reference to Italian art, literature, or music (p. 106).

Triad CHORD consisting of three CONSONANT notes.

Trill Rapid alternation between a tone and its neighbor (p. 361).

Trillo Vocal ORNAMENT consisting of a rapid repetition of the same pitch (p. 266).

Triplum (Lat. *triplus* "triple") Second part in early POLYPHONY set against a TENOR and DUPLUM (p. 85).

Tritone INTERVAL spanning three whole tones, such as *F* to *B* (p. 653).

Trobairitz A female poet-composer of southern France who employed the Old Occitan (**langue d'oc**, or Old Provençal) language. See also **troubadour** (p. 58).

Trope (noun and verb) (1) Passage of text added to the original words of a PLAINCHANT, particularly to furnish words for singing a MELISMA. (2) Interpolation of both new text and new MELODY in an existing composition (pp. 47, 92).

Troubadour Poet-composer of MONÓPHONIC song in Old Occitan (*langue d'oc*) in twelfth- and thirteenth-century southern France (pp. 58–62).

Trouvère Poet-composer of MONOPHONIC song in Old French (*langue d' oïl*) in twelfth- and thirteenth-century northern France (pp. 58–62).

Tutti (It. "all") (1) Instruction to an ensemble that all should play. (2) In a CONCERTO, denotes the orchestra, as opposed to the soloist(s) (p. 367).

Twelve-tone row Ordered series of twelve different PITCH-CLASSES (p. 716).

Variation Reworking of an existing tune, song, AIR, ARIA, or THEME, often in a series of movements called "variations" (pp. 216–18, 299–302, 349–50, 352, 394, 534).

Verismo (It. "realism") Type of OPERA in which ordinary people are portrayed in passionate and violent situations (p. 670).

Vernacular music Popular, entertainment, and show music not intended for the concert hall (p. 748).

Verse (1) Line of poetry. (2) Strophe or stanza of a hymn. (3) Sentence of a Psalm, which consists of two parallel statements or versicles.

Verset Organ piece that replaces a VERSE of a PLAINCHANT, such as of a hymn (p. 209).

Vibrato Slight fluctuation of pitch in performing a single note.

Virelai French FORME FIXE in which each stanza has the form A b b a A (capital letters indicating the REFRAIN) (p. 102).

Virtuoso (It. "virtuous") Musician who excels in technical ability (p. 3).

CREDITS

Chapter 1
Ex. 1.4 *Seikilos Song.* Reprinted from *Apollo's Lyre: Greek Music and Music Theory in Antiquity and the Middle Ages* by Thomas Mathieson. By Permission of the University of Nebraska Press. Copyright © 1999 by the University of Nebraska Press.

Chapter 2
Ex. 2.2 Tract *Deus, Deus meus.* Reprinted from MQ 60 (1974): 361. Used by permission of Oxford University Press.

Chapter 5
Ex. 5.1 *Rondellus.* © by Hänssler-Verlag/American Institute of Musicology. Used by permission. All rights reserved.

Chapter 9
Ex. 9.11 Viadana, *Sacred Concerto: O Domine, Jesu Christe.* Reprinted by permission of Bärenreiter-Verlag, Kassel, Basel, Tours, and London, from: *Cento concerti ecclesiastici opera duodecima* (Venice, 1602), ed. Claudio Gallico (Kassel, etc., 1964), pp. 64–65.

Chapter 12
Ex. 12.1 Vivaldi, *Concerto Grosso Op. 3, No. 2.* By kind permission of Casa Ricordi, Milan.

Chapter 16
Ex. 16.14 Bruckner, *Symphony No. 8: Finale.* © 1955. Reprint permission granted by C. F. Peters Corporation on behalf of Musikwissenschaftlicher Verlag, Wien.

Chapter 19
Ex. 19.5 Strauss, *Elektra: Harmony.* © Copyright 1908, 1909 by Adolph Furstner. Copyright Renewed. Copyright assigned 1943 to Hawkes & Son (London) Ltd. (a Boosey and Hawkes company) for the World excluding Germany, Italy, Portugal and the Former Territories of the USSR (excluding Estonia, Latvia, and Lithuania). Reprinted by permission of Boosey and Hawkes, Inc.

Ex. 19.6 Strauss, *Der Rosenkavalier: Introduction.* © Copyright 1910, 1911 by Adolph Furstner. Copyright Renewed. Copyright assigned 1943 to Hawkes & Son (London) Ltd. (a Boosey and Hawkes company) for the World excluding Germany, Italy, Portugal and the Former Territories of the USSR (excluding Estonia, Latvia, and Lithuania). Reprinted by permission of Boosey and Hawkes, Inc.

Chapter 20

Ex. 20.2 Bartók, *Music for Strings, Percussion, and Celesta.* © Copyright 1937 in the USA by Boosey & Hawkes, Inc. Copyright Renewed. Reprinted by permission.

Ex. 20.3 Bartók, *Music for Strings, Percussion, and Celesta.* © Copyright 1937 in the USA by Boosey & Hawkes, Inc. Copyright Renewed. Reprinted by permission.

Ex. 20.4 Bartók, *Music for Strings, Percussion, and Celesta (Relationships between Folk and Art Styles in Bartók).* © Copyright 1937 in the USA by Boosey & Hawkes, Inc. Copyright Renewed. Reprinted by permission.

Ex. 20.5 Shostakovich, *Fifth Symphony: Moderato, Measures 1–4.* Copyright © 1939 (Renewed) by G. Schirmer, Inc. (ASCAP) International Copyright Secured. All Rights Reserved. Reprinted by Permission.

Ex. 20.6 *Examples of Themes by Ralph Vaughan Williams.* Copyright © 1924 (Renewed) by J. Curwen & Sons. International Copyright Secured. All Rights Reserved. Reprinted by Permission. Territory: World (excluding the UK, Republic of Ireland, Canada, Australia, New Zealand, Israel, Jamaica and South Africa).

Ex. 20.7 Tippett, *Concerto for Piano and Orchestra: Allegro non troppo.* © Copyright 1957. Schott & Co. Ltd., London. © renewed. All Rights Reserved. Used by permission of European American Music Distributors Corporation, sole U. S. and Canadian agent for Schott & Co. Ltd., London.

Ex. 20.8 Hindemith, *Mathis der Mahler.* Copyright B. Schott's Söhne, Mainz, 1935. Copyright renewed. All Rights Reserved. Used by permission of European American Music Distributors Corp. Sole U.S. and Canadian agent for B. Schott's Söhne.

Ex. 20.9 Weill, *Four Songs of Walt Whitman: O Captain! My Captain!* Copyright 1942, Renewed 1970 by Hampshire House Publishing Corp. and Chappell & Co., Inc., New York.

Ex. 20.10 Milhaud, *Saudades do Brasil, I: No. 4, Copacabaña.* © 1922, renewed 1950 by Editions Max Eschig. Used by permission of the publisher. Sole representative USA, Theodore Presser Company.

Ex. 20.11 Stravinsky, *Petrushka, First Scene.* © Copyright 1947, 1948 by Hawkes & Son (London) Ltd. Copyright Renewed. Reprinted by permission of Boosey & Hawkes, Inc.

Ex. 20.12 Stravinsky, *Petrushka, Second Part: Easter Song.* © Copyright 1947, 1948 by Hawkes & Son (London) Ltd. Copyright Renewed. Reprinted by permission of Boosey & Hawkes, Inc.

Ex. 20.13 Stravinsky, *Petrushka, Opening of Second Scene.* © Copyright 1947, 1948 by Hawkes & Son (London) Ltd. Copyright Renewed. Reprinted by permission of Boosey & Hawkes, Inc.

Ex. 20.14 Stravinsky, *Le Sacre du printemps: Dance of the Adolescent Girls: Augurs of Spring.* © Copyright 1912, 1921 by Hawkes & Son (London) Ltd. Copyright Renewed. Reprinted by permission of Boosey & Hawkes, Inc.

Ex. 20.15 Stravinsky, *Symphony in C, Moderato alla breve.* Copyright 1948 by Schott & Co., Ltd., London. Reprinted by permission of European American Music Distributors Corp.

Ex. 20.16 Stravinsky, *The Rake's Progress: Act III, Scene 2, Duet, My heart is wild with fear.* Copyright 1949, 1950, 1951 by Boosey & Hawkes, Inc. Copyright Renewed. Reprinted by permission.

Ex. 20.17 Stravinsky, *Symphony of Psalms.* © Copyright 1951 by Hawkes & Son (London) Ltd. Copyright Renewed. Reprinted by permission of Boosey & Hawkes, Inc.

Chapter 21

Ex. 21.1 Schoenberg, *Variations for Orchestra, Op. 31.* Used by permission of Belmont Music Publishers, Pacific Palisades, CA 90272.

Ex. 21.2 Schoenberg, *Moses und Aron: Act I, Scene 2.* Used by permission of Belmont Music Publishers, Pacific Palisades, CA 90272.

Ex. 21.5 Webern, *Symphony Op. 21: First Movement.* Copyright 1929 by Universal Edition. Copyright renewed. All Rights Reserved. Used by permission of European American Music Distributors Corporation, sole U.S. and Canadian agent for Universal Edition.

Ex. 21.6 Messiaen, *Quatuor pour la fin du temps: I.* © 1942 Durand S. A. Used by permission of the publisher. Sole representative U. S. A. Theodore Presser Company.

Chapter 22

Ex. 22.4 Varèse, *Intégrales: Andantino.* Copyright Casa Ricordi–BMG/Ricordi. Reprinted by permission of Hendon Music, Inc., agent.

Ex. 22.5 Thomson, *The Mother of Us All.* Copyright © 1947 (Renewed) by G. Schirmer, Inc. (ASCAP) International Copyright Secured. All Rights Reserved. Reprinted by Permission.

Ex. 22.6 Still, *Afro-American Symphony: Animato.* Copyright © 1931 (Renewed) Novello & Co., Ltd. All rights for the USA & Canada controlled by G. Schirmer, Inc. (BMI) International Copyright Secured. All Rights Reserved. Reprinted by Permission.

Ex. 22.7 Sessions, *Symphony No. 2: Molto agitato.* Copyright © 1949 (Renewed) by G. Schirmer, Inc. (ASCAP) International Copyright Secured. All Rights Reserved. Reprinted by Permission.

Ex. 22.8 Carter, *String Quartet No. 1: I. Fantasia.* Copyright © 1956 (Renewed) by Associated Music Publishers, Inc. (BMI) International Copyright Secured. All Rights Reserved. Reprinted by Permission.

Ex. 22.9 Babbitt, *Quartet No. 3.* Used by permission of C. F. Peters Corporation.

Ex. 22.10 Babbitt, *Philomel: Section 2.* Copyright © 1964 (Renewed) by Associated Music Publishers, Inc. (BMI) International Copyright Secured. All Rights Reserved. Reprinted by Permission.

Ex. 22.11 Reich, *Violin Phase.* © Copyright 1979 by Universal Edition (London) Ltd., London. All Rights Reserved. Used by permission of European American Music Distributors Corporation, sole U.S. and Canadian agent for Universal Edition (London) Ltd., London.

Ex. 22.12 Bach, *Partita No. 6, BWV 830: Toccata.* © 1967 by Theodore Presser Co. Used by permission of the publisher.

Ex. 22.13 del Tredici, *In Memory of a Summer Day: Allegretto.* Copyright 1980 by Boosey & Hawkes, Inc. Reprinted by permission.

INDEX

A **boldface** page number indicates the primary discussion or definition of the entry word. *Italics* refer to illustrations or music examples. An italicized *v* following a page number indicates a vignette; an italicized *n* refers to a footnote.

Ländler Austrian and South German dance in triple METER (pp. 546, 634).

Lauda (Lat. *laudare* "to praise") Italian devotional song (pp. 64, 183).

Leitmotif (Ger. "leading motive") Musical THEME or MOTIVE associated with a person, thing, emotion, or idea in a drama (pp. 625–27).

Libretto Literary text for a musical stage work (pp. 274, 410, 436).

Lied (Ger. "song"; pl. lieder) German song, such as a POLYPHONIC partsong or an accompanied art song (pp. 197–98, 447–49, 593–98).

Ligature NEUME-like shape used to indicate a short rhythmic pattern in the NOTATION of the twelfth to the sixteenth centuries (p. 77, 89–90).

Madrigal (It. *madrigale* "song in the mother tongue") (1) Fourteenth-century Italian VERSE form and its musical setting having two or three stanzas followed by a RITORNELLO (pp. 106–7). (2) Sixteenth-century Italian poem having any number of lines, each of seven or eleven syllables (p. 183). (3) POLYPHONIC or CONCERTATO setting of such a poem or of a canzona, sonnet, etc. (4) English part-song imitating the Italian models (pp. 200–2).

Major scale DIATONIC succession of notes with a major third as the third step.

March Piece in duple METER to accompany military stepping (p. 747).

Masque English entertainment in which guests and professionals joined in a dance performance, sometimes including RECITATIVES, songs, and choruses (pp. 273, 320–21).

Measure Metrical unit set off by barlines.

Meistersinger (Ger. "master singer") German singer and composer of song (*Meistergesang*) practiced by fourteenth- to sixteenth-century burgher-musicians' guilds (pp. 63–64).

Melisma (melismatic) Flowing passage of many notes sung to a single syllable, particularly of PLAINCHANT (pp. 20, 40, 44–45).

Melodrama Theatrical genre that combined spoken dialogue with background music (p. 619).

Melody (1) Succession of tones perceived as a coherent line. (2) Tune. (3) Principal part accompanied by other parts or CHORDS.

Meter Pattern of beats in a MEASURE, such as $\frac{3}{4}$.

Minimalism Type of music deliberately limiting musical material and vocabulary, often marked by continual repetition of a short MELODY, FIGURE, or CHORD with only slight variation (pp. 777–80).

Minnesinger (Ger. "singer of love") Composer or singer of medieval German song (*Minnesang*), particularly about love (pp. 62–63).

Minor scale DIATONIC succession of notes with a minor third as the third step and optional lowered sixth and seventh steps.

Minuet Dance in triple METER usually followed by a second minuet, called "Trio," after which the first minuet returns (p. 470).

Mode (1) MELODY type characterized by a certain FINAL or ending pitch, a particular arrangement of tones and semitones, and an approximate AMBITUS (pp. 7, 20–21, 52–54). (2) Rhythmic pattern of two or three short and longer durations—for example, Mode 1, long-short (pp. 76–77).

Modulation Change from one TONALITY to another in the course of a composition.

Monochord Instrument used to locate INTERVALS through dividing and measuring lengths of its single string (pp. 51, 148).

Monody Accompanied solo song (p. 265).

Monophony (monophonic) Unaccompanied MELODY (pp. 4, 57, 101).

Motet (from Fr. *mot* "word") POLYPHONIC vocal composition, most often on a sacred text (pp. 84–90, 98–101, 134, 292, 402).

Motetus DUPLUM or TRIPLUM voice part in early POLYPHONY to which words are set.

Motive Short melodic or rhythmic idea.

Motto (1) Musical idea that recurs (p. 138). (2) Introduction of the main idea in the voice, prior to the completion of the instrumental RITORNELLO, in what is called a "motto ARIA" (p. 312).

Musica ficta (Lat. "feigned music") (1) Practice of raising or lowering by a semitone the pitch of a written note in a POLYPHONIC TEXTURE, particularly at a CADENCE, for the sake of smoother HARMONY or stronger part movement. (2) In early music, notes outside the standard GAMUT (*musica vera*), which excluded all flatted and sharped notes except *B*♭ (pp. 113–15, 118, 149).

Musique concrète (Fr. "concrete music") Natural sounds that are stored, combined, modified, and arranged (pp. 729–30).

Musique mesurée (Fr. "measured music") Style of sixteenth-century French music in which poetry simulating the ancient Greek and Latin syllable quantities (*vers mesurés à l'antique*) is set to combinations of long and short notes that do not fit a regular METER (p. 197).

Neo-Classicism Movement in the twentieth century to revive forms, genres, and styles of the eighteenth century (pp. 699–701).

Neume Sign placed above a syllable to indicate the pitch height of one or more PLAINCHANT notes (pp. 36–37, 56–57).

Notation Writing down of music, usually on a staff of lines, using signs that define the pitch, duration, and other qualities of sound (pp. 13, 36–38, 56–57, 90, 100, 116–17, 188).

Octave species (sing. and pl.) Arrangement of INTERVALS, such as whole tones and semitones, in an octave (p. 11).

Office Monastic ritual celebrated at certain hours of the day and night (pp. 32–33, 42–44).

Opera (operatic) (It. "work") (1) Dramatic stage composition, ordinarily in two or more acts (p. 260). (2) Work.

Opera buffa (It. "comical opera") Italian full-length comic OPERA sung throughout (pp. 432–35, 508).

Opéra comique (Fr. "comic opera") French full-length comic OPERA with spoken dialogue instead of RECITATIVE (pp. 442–44, 610–11).

Opera seria (It. "serious opera") Serious Italian OPERA of the eighteenth century, purged of comic scenes and characters (pp. 436–40).

Opus (Lat. "work"; pl. *opera*) A composition or set of compositions.

Oratorio Composition for solo singers, chorus, and instruments, usually dramatic and on a biblical or religious subject (pp. 289–90, 332, 412–16).

Oratorio volgare ORATORIO on a vernacular (Italian) text (p. 332).

Orchestration (1) Art of assigning musical material to individual instruments. (2) The product of this process (pp. 474–75, 606–8, 665).

Ordinary (Lat. *ordinarium missae* "the ordinary of the Mass") Texts and PLAINCHANTS of a Mass that remain the same throughout the church calendar, such as the Kyrie and Gloria (pp. 36, 45–46).

Ordre (Fr. "order") French collection of pieces that are mostly in dance rhythms, such as a SUITE (pp. 352–354).

Organum (pronounced or'-ga-num) IMPROVISED or written voice part sung against a PLAINCHANT, or the work resulting from this procedure (pp. 71–83).

Ornament, ornamentation, ornamented Decorative element, such as a TRILL or turn, written or IMPROVISED, that adds expression or charm to a melodic line (pp. 110, 193, 361–62).

Ostinato Short melodic FIGURE persistently repeated, most often in the bass (p. 216).

Ottava rima (It. "eighth rhyme") Poem of eight eleven-syllable lines in which the eighth line rhymes with the seventh (p. 183).

Ouverture (Fr. "opening") (1) French OVERTURE in two-part form, the first slow and majestic with dotted rhythms, the second quick, fluent, and FUGAL, after which the first section is often recalled (p. 320). (2) A SUITE having such an introduction (p. 366).

Overture Introduction to a stage work, ORATORIO, or instrumental SUITE; later also a brief orchestral work in one movement.

Parody Mass See **Imitation Mass.**

Partbook Volume, particularly printed, containing the music for a single vocal or instrumental part of a POLYPHONIC ensemble (p. 152).

Partita Single VARIATION of a THEME or a set of such variation (pp. 299–300, 352, 393–94).

Passacaglia (It.; Sp. *passecalle*; Fr. *passecaille*) (1) Pattern of guitar CHORDS played before and between strophes of a song. (2) Pattern of pitches usually serving as a foundation for HARMONY (pp. 279, 354).

Passion Setting of a New Testament account of the crucifixion of Jesus (pp. 340–41, 402–3).

Pastoral Poetic genre to which the early OPERA LIBRETTOS, such as *Euridice* of 1600, belonged (p. 262).

Pavane, pavana, paduana Slow, stately dance in duple METER, often followed by a GALLIARD (pp. 204, 215, 303).

Periodicity Quality of being organized in discrete phrases and periods (p. 428).

Petit motet (Fr. "little motet") French version of the SACRED CONCERTO for a few voices (p. 333).

Phrygian cadence CADENCE in which the lowest voice descends by a semitone and the highest ascends by a whole tone (pp. 114–15).

Pitch-class One of twelve pitches of the CHROMATIC SCALE without reference to register, such as *C* when it refers to all *C*s in the GAMUT.

Plagal (Gr. **plagios**, "placed sideways") Refers to the collateral MODE that shares a FINAL with an AUTHENTIC mode and has a range approximately a fourth lower (pp. 52–54).

Plainchant, plainsong (Lat. *cantus planus*) Monophonic sacred chant or song of the Christian church, performed in free rhythm (pp. 31, 137).

Polychoral TEXTURE in which two or more choruses alternate and join together (pp. 282–88).

Polyphony (polyphonic) Musical TEXTURE consisting of two or more lines of MELODY (pp. 33, 70–73). See also COUNTERPOINT.

Polytonality Combination of two or more lines of melody that are in different TONALITIES (pp. 682, 701).

Prelude Introductory piece in an OPERA, SUITE, or instrumental composition (pp. 212, 214, 388).

Prima pratica See **Seconda pratica.**

Program music Music that is descriptive, narrative, or that develops a nonmusical subject (pp. 379, 544–45, 639–41).

Prologue Dramatic scene or speech before the beginning of a spoken or musical stage work (p. 269).

Proper (Lat., *proprium de tempore* "proper of the time") Texts and PLAINCHANTS of the Mass that are assigned to particular days in the church calendar (pp. 36, 44–45).

Psalm tone Formula for chanting psalms on a reciting tone, which varies with the MODE, including patterns for beginning (*initium*), continuing (TENOR), temporarily resting (*flex*), resuming (*mediatio*), and closing (*terminatio*) (pp. 42–43).

Pythagorean tuning Having perfect CONSONANCES in ratios of 2:1 (octave), 3:2 (fifth), and 4:3 (fourth), unlike other INTERVALS, which have irrational ratios, such as 81:64 (DITONE, or major third) (pp. 148–49, 349).

Quodlibet (Lat. "whatever you please") Composition juxtaposing several borrowed melodies (p. 394).

Recapitulation Section of a movement in which the subjects announced in the EXPOSITION are reviewed (p. 453).

Récitatif mesuré (Fr. "measured recitative") Songful RECITATIVE in French seventeenth- and eighteenth-century OPERA that maintained a uniform METER (pp. 317–18).

Récitatif simple (Fr. "simple recitative") Speechlike RECITATIVE in French seventeenth- and eighteenth-century OPERA that frequently shifted between duple and triple METERS (p. 317).